Abnormal Child Psychology

Eric J. Mash
University of Calgary

David A. Wolfe
University of Western Ontario

Brooks/Cole • Wadsworth

I(T)P® an International Thomson Publishing Company

Belmont, CA • Albany, NY • Bonn • Boston • Cincinnati • Johannesburg • London
Madrid • Melbourne • Mexico City • New York • Pacific Grove, CA • Scottsdale, AZ
Singapore • Tokyo • Toronto

Sponsoring Editor: *Marianne Taflinger*
Marketing Team: *Lauren Harp, Christine Davis*
Editorial Assistant: *Rachael Bruckman*
Production Coordinator: *Keith Faivre*
Production Service: *Graphic World Publishing Services*
Manuscript Editor: *Alice Jaggard*
Permissions Editor: *Linda Rill*
Interior Design: *Jeannie Wolfgeher*

Interior Illustration: *Jeannie Wolfgeher*
Cover Design: *Vernon T. Boes*
Cover Photo: *Ken Wightman, London Free Press*
Photo Research: *Linda Rill*
Typesetting: *Graphic World, Inc.*
Cover Printing: *Phoenix Color Corporation*
Printing and Binding: *R. R. Donnelley & Sons, Willard*

For more information, contact WADSWORTH PUBLISHING COMPANY, 10 Davis Drive, Belmont, CA 94002, or
electronically at http://www.wadsworth.com

International Thomson Publishing Europe
Berkshire House 168–173
High Holborn
London WC1V 7AA
England

Thomas Nelson Australia
102 Dodds Street
South Melbourne, 3205
Victoria, Australia

Nelson Canada
1120 Birchmount Road
Scarborough, Ontario
Canada M1K 5G4

International Thomson Editores
Seneca 53
Col. Polanco
11560 México, D. F., México

International Thomson Publishing GmbH
Königswinterer Strasse 418
53227 Bonn
Germany

International Thomson Publishing Asia
60 Albert Street
#15-01 Albert Complex
Singapore 189969

International Thomson Publishing Japan
Hirakawacho Kyowa Building, 3F
2-2-1 Hirakawacho
Chiyoda-ku, Tokyo 102
Japan

International Thomson Publishing Southern Africa
Building 18, Constantia Square
138 Sixteenth Road, P.O. Box 2459
Halfway House, 1685 South Africa

Printed in the United States of America.

10 9 8 7 6 5 4 3 2

Library of Congress Cataloging-in-Publication Data

Mash, Eric J.
    Abnormal child psychology / Eric J. Mash, David A. Wolfe.
      p.   cm.
    Includes bibliographical references and index.
    ISBN 0-534-34290-6
    1. Child psychopathology. 2. Child psychiatry. 3. Psychology,
Pathological.   I. Wolfe, David A. II. Title.
RJ499.M296 1999
  618.92′89—dc21   98-33318
                                CIP

About the Authors

ERIC J. MASH completed his undergraduate studies at City University of New York, and his graduate work in Philadelphia and Florida. He earned his Ph.D. in clinical psychology at Florida State University in 1970. After completing his residency in clinical child psychology at the Oregon Health Sciences University in Portland, Oregon, he joined the faculty at the University of Calgary where he is currently a Professor in the Department of Psychology. He is a Fellow of the American and Canadian Psychological Associations and has served as an editorial board member and consultant for numerous scientific and professional journals and grant agencies at the local and federal levels. Eric's research interests are in abnormal child psychology, child and family assessment, child psychotherapy, and child development, and he has published many books and journal articles on these topics. He has studied interaction patterns in families with children with attention-deficit disorder and conduct problems, and in families in which children have been physically abused. Eric enjoys teaching undergraduate courses in abnormal child psychology, behavior modification, and child development, and graduate courses in clinical psychology including child psychopathology, child assessment, and child psychotherapy. When he is not working, Eric enjoys exploring the Canadian Rockies and walking on the beaches of Oregon with his wife Heather and dog Sadie.

DAVID A. WOLFE completed his undergraduate degree at the University of Rochester in New York, and his graduate work at the University of South Florida in Tampa, Florida. After completing his residency in clinical psychology at the University of Mississippi Medical Center in 1980, he joined the faculty at the University of Western Ontario in London, Canada, where he is currently Professor of Psychology and Psychiatry. He is a founding member of the Center for Research on Violence Against Women and Children, and a fellow of the American Psychological Association (APA). He served as President of Division 37 (Child, Youth, and Family Services) of the APA and is an editorial board member of several scientific and professional journals and funding agencies.

David has broad research and clinical interests in abnormal child psychology, with a special focus on child abuse, domestic violence, and developmental psychopathology. He has authored numerous articles on these topics, especially in relation to the impact of early childhood trauma on later development in childhood, adolescence, and early adulthood. He is currently studying ways to prevent violence in relationships with adolescents. He enjoys teaching undergraduate courses in abnormal child psychology, child assessment and psychotherapy, and community psychology.

For joy and recreation, David spends his time with his wife and three children at their cottage on Georgian Bay, where they enjoy skiing, hiking, and sailing.

Contents in Brief

PART I   Understanding Abnormal Child Psychology

Chapter 1   Introduction to Abnormal Child Psychology   1
Chapter 2   Theories and Causes of Abnormal Development   28
Chapter 3   Research Strategies in Abnormal Child Psychology   58
Chapter 4   Clinical Issues: Assessment, Diagnosis, and Treatment   98

PART II   Behavioral Disorders

Chapter 5   Attention-Deficit/Hyperactivity Disorder   143
Chapter 6   Conduct Problems   185

PART III   Emotional Disorders

Chapter 7   Anxiety Disorders   233
Chapter 8   Mood Disorders   284

PART IV   Developmental and Learning Disorders

Chapter 9   Mental Retardation   337
Chapter 10 Autism and Childhood-Onset Schizophrenia   372
Chapter 11 Communication and Learning Disorders   419

PART V   Problems Related to Physical and Mental Health

Chapter 12 Health-Related Disorders   455
Chapter 13 Eating Disorders and Related Conditions   491
Chapter 14 Child Abuse and Neglect   524

Contents

PART I
Understanding Abnormal Child Psychology

CHAPTER 1
Introduction to Abnormal Child Psychology   1

A Portrait of Children's and Adolescents' Health Issues   1
Terminology and Features of Abnormal Child Psychology   3

■ *Georgina: Let Me Count the Ways*   3

What Is Abnormal Child Behavior?   4
    Establishing Boundaries   5
    Risk and Resilience   8

■ *Raoul and Jesse: Why the Difference?*

Describing Psychological Disorders of Childhood and
   Adolescence   11
    Clinical Description   12
    Causes   16
    Assessment, Diagnosis, and Treatment   16
The Significance of Children's Mental Health Problems   17
Historical Views and Breakthroughs   20
    The Emergence of a Social Conscience   20
    Distinguishing Psychiatric Disorder from Mental
      Retardation   21
    Early Biological Influences   22
    Early Psychological Influences   23
    Evolving Treatment Applications   26
Summary   26
Key Terms   27

CHAPTER 2
Theories and Causes of Abnormal Development   28

■ *Jake: Not Keeping Up*   28

What Caused Jake's Problems?   29
The Role of Theory   30
    Developmental Considerations   31
    Developmental Psychopathology Framework   31
Theoretical Foundations   33
    Underlying Assumptions about Abnormal
      Development   34
    An Integrative Approach   38

Biological Perspectives   39
    The Developing Brain: A Work in Progress   39
    Genetic Contributions   40
    Neurobiological Contributions   42
Psychological Perspectives   45
    Emotional Influences   46
    Behavioral and Cognitive Influences   49
    Evolution and Infant-Care-giver Attachment   51
Family and Social Influences   52
    The Family and Peer Context   54
    The Social and Cultural Context   55
Summary   56
Key Terms   57

CHAPTER 3
Research Strategies in Abnormal Child Psychology   58

■ *Shelley and Mike Dumas: Research Participants*   58

A Scientific Approach   60
    Facilitated Communication: A Case Example   62
The Research Process   63
    Research Ideas and Questions   64
Methods Used to Study Abnormal Child Behavior   70
    Standardization, Reliability, and Validity   70
    Methods of Measurement   71
Research Strategies   78
    Identifying the Research Sample   78
    General Research Approaches   80
    Research Designs   83
    Designs for Studying Developmental Change   87
    Qualitative Research   90
Ethical and Pragmatic Issues   93
    Informed Consent and Assent   93
    Voluntary Participation   93
    Confidentiality and Anonymity   93
    Nonharmful Procedures   95
    Other Ethical and Pragmatic Concerns   95
Summary   96
Key Terms   97

CHAPTER 4
Clinical Issues: Assessment, Diagnosis, and Treatment   98

■ *Felicia: Multiple Problems*   98

Clinical Issues   98
   The Decision-Making Process   99
   Developmental Considerations   100
   Purpose of Assessment   101
Assessing Children's Psychological Disorders   103
   Clinical Interviews   104

■ *Felicia: Developmental and Family History*   106

■ *Felicia: Mental Status Exam*   107

   Behavioral Assessment   109
   Psychological Testing   115
Classification and Diagnosis   124
   Categories, Dimensions, or Both?   124
   Evolution of Current Systems   126
Treatment of Childhood Disorders   130
   What Is Intervention?   131
   Special Considerations   132
   General Approaches to Treatment   136

■ *Felicia: Multiple Solutions*   138

   Treatment Effectiveness   139
Summary   140
Key Terms   142

PART II
Behavioral Disorders

CHAPTER 5
Attention-Deficit/Hyperactivity Disorder   143

Description   143

■ *John: Inattentive, Overactive, and Impulsive*   143

Historical Background of ADHD   145
DSM-IV: Defining Features of ADHD   146
Core Characteristics   146
   Inattention   146

■ *Lisa: Predominantly Inattentive*   146

   Hyperactivity-Impulsivity   148

■ *Mark: Predominantly Hyperactive-Impulsive*   148

   Additional Criteria   150
ADHD Subtypes   151
Differential Diagnosis   152
DSM-IV Criteria: What They Don't Tell Us   152
Associated Characteristics of ADHD   152
   Cognitive Deficits   153

■ *Ian: Failing School*   153

   Speech and Language Impairments   154
   Medical and Physical Characteristics   155
   Interpersonal Difficulties   155

■ *Dennis: Yesterday's Rules Are Long Forgotten*   155

   Problems in the Family   156

■ *Ian: Sibling Conflict*   156

   Problems with Peers   156
Accompanying Disorders and Symptoms   157
   Oppositional Defiant Disorder and Conduct
   Disorder   157

■ *Shawn: Defiant and Breaking Rules*   157

   Anxiety Disorders   158

■ *T. J.: Overactive and Anxious*   158

   Depression   159
   Tourette's Disorder   159
Task and Situational Factors   159
Prevalence and Course   160
   Prevalence   160
   Course and Outcome   161

■ *Ian: Off and Running*   162

■ *Alan: Singled Out in Kindergarten*   162

■ *Alan: I Couldn't Do Anything Right*   162

■ *A Parent's Viewpoint*   163

■ *Jeremy: Still Not Organized After 10 Years*   163

Theories of ADHD   164
   Deficits in Motivation   164
   Deficits in Arousal Level   164
   Deficits in Self-Regulation   165
   Deficits in Behavioral Inhibition   165
Causes of ADHD   166
   Genetic Contributions   167
   Neurobiological Factors   168
   Pregnancy, Birth, and Early Development   171
   Environmental Toxins, Allergy, and Diet   172
   Family Influences   172
Treatment   173

■ *Mark: Hyperactive and Impulsive*   173

■ *Lisa: Inattentive and Depressed*   173

Medication   174
The Great Debate   175
Parent Management Training   177
Educational Intervention   178

■ *Alan: Boxed In at School and Hating It*   178

   Additional Interventions   179

■ *Ian (4th Grade)*   179

   Intensive Interventions   180
   Controversial Treatments   182
   Keeping Things in Perspective   182

■ *Alan, age 15: Learning to Survive*   182

Summary   183
Key Terms   183

CHAPTER 6
Conduct Problems   185

Description   185

■ *Andy (4 years old): Rage at a Young Age*   185

■ *Marvelle (6 years old): Impossible to Manage*   185

■ *Nick (10 years old): Not Like Other Kids*   186

■ *Names Withheld: Child Killers*   186

■ *Steve: A Tough Life*   186

　　The Significance and Cost of Conduct Problems   187
　　Antisocial Behavior and Normal Development   187
Perspectives on Conduct Problems   188
　　Legal Perspective   190
　　Psychological Perspective   190
　　Psychiatric Perspective   194
DSM-IV: Defining Features of Conduct Problems   194
　　Oppositional Defiant Disorder   195

■ *Not an Easy-Going Bone in His Body*   195

　　Conduct Disorder   195

■ *Greg: Conduct Disorder and Other Problems*   195

　　Antisocial Personality Disorder   198

■ *Jason: No Conscience*   198

Associated Characteristics of Conduct Problems   199
　　Impairments in Cognition and Learning   199
　　Self-Esteem Deficits   200
　　Interpersonal Difficulties with Peers   200

■ *In the Company of "Friends"*   201

　　Social-Cognitive Deficits   201
　　Family Disturbances   201

■ *Sam: Nothing Ever Gets Resolved*   201

　　Health-Related Problems   202
　　Accompanying Disorders and Symptoms   203
Prevalence, Gender, and Developmental Pathways   204
　　Prevalence   204
　　Gender Differences   205

■ *Ann: Runaway*   205

　　Developmental Pathways for Antisocial Behavior   206

■ *Marcus: Adolescent Rule Breaker*   208

　　Course and Adult Outcomes   208
Causes of Conduct Problems   209

■ *Mike and Brian: Bad Twin, Good Twin*   210

　　Biological Factors   211
　　Social-Cognitive Factors   215
　　Family Factors   216

■ *Multiple Sources of Family Disturbance*   219

　　Societal Factors   220
　　Cultural and Ethical Factors   223
　　Summary of Causal Influences   224

Treatment   224
　　Parent Management Training   225
　　Cognitive Problem-Solving Skills Training   226
　　Multisystemic Treatment   227
　　Medications   228
　　Preventive Interventions   229
Summary   230
Key Terms   231

PART III
Emotional Disorders

CHAPTER 7
Anxiety Disorders   233

Description   233
　　The Experience of Anxiety   234

■ *Chantelle: Home Alone*   237

　　Anxiety versus Fear and Panic   237
　　Normal Fears, Anxieties, Worries, and Rituals   238
　　The Anatomy of Anxiety: From Symptoms to
　　　Disorders   240
An Overview of DSM-IV Anxiety Disorders   240
Separation Anxiety Disorder   241

■ *Brad: Separation Anxiety*   241

　　Prevalence and Comorbidity   243
　　Age of Onset, Developmental Course, and
　　　Outcome   243
School Reluctance and Refusal   244

■ *Eric: Won't Go to School*   244

　　Test Anxiety   245
　　Generalized Anxiety Disorder   246

■ *Alesha: Perpetual Worrywart*   246

　　Prevalence and Comorbidity   247
　　Age of Onset, Developmental Course, and
　　　Outcome   248
　　Specific Phobia   248

■ *Charlotte: Arachnophobia*   248

　　Prevalence and Comorbidity   251
　　Age of Onset, Developmental Course, and
　　　Outcome   251
Social Phobia   251
　　Prevalence, Comorbidity, and Course   254
　　Selective Mutism   254

■ *Keisha: Mum's the Word*   254

Obsessive-Compulsive Disorder   255

■. *Paul: Stuck in a Doorway*   255

■ *Charlie: A Different Kind of Check Stop*   258

　　Prevalence and Comorbidity   259
　　Age of Onset, Developmental Course, and
　　　Outcome   259

Panic Attacks and Panic Disorder   260
   Panic Attacks   260
   Panic Disorder   261

■ *Claudia: Panic*   261

   Prevalence and Comorbidity   262
   Age of Onset, Developmental Course, and
     Outcome   262
Posttraumatic Stress Disorder   263

■ *Marcie: Trauma*   263

   Prevalence and Comorbidity   265
   Age of Onset, Developmental Course, and
     Outcome   265
Acute Stress Disorder   266
Associated Characteristics of Anxiety Disorders   266
   Cognitive Disturbances   266
   Physical Symptoms   268
   Social Deficits   268
   Accompanying Disorders and Symptoms   268
Gender, Ethnicity, and Culture   269
Theories and Causes   270
   Early Theories   270
   Temperament   271
   Genetic and Family Risk   273
   Neurobiological Factors   273
   Family Influences   274
   Developmental Pathway   275
Treatment   275

■ *Candy: Dehydrated*   275

Overview of Treatments   277
Primary Treatments for Children with Anxiety
  Disorders   278
Combined Cognitive-Behavioral Treatments for Specific
  Disorders   280
Summary   282
Key Terms   283

CHAPTER 8
Mood Disorders   284

■ *David: Depressed*   284

■ *Beth: Sad Since Childhood*   284

■ *Mick: Sad and Manic*   284

An Overview of DSM-IV Mood Disorders   285
   Mood Episodes   285
   Mood Disorders   285
Depression   286
   Description of the Disorder   286
   Historical Background   288
   The Significance of Depression in Young People   289
   Depression at Different Developmental Periods   289
   The Anatomy of Depression: Symptom, Syndrome, and
     Disorder   290
Major Depressive Disorder   292

■ *Nine-year-old Joey: "I Feel Worthless"*   292

■ *Seventeen-year-old Alison: "I Couldn't Take It
Anymore"*   292

   Differential Diagnosis   294
   Prevalence   294
   Comorbidity   295

■ *Raymond: Sad and Aggressive*   295

   Age of Onset, Course, and Outcome   296
   Gender and Ethnicity   297
Dysthymic Disorder   298

■ *Deborah: A Childhood without Laughter*   298

   Prevalence and Comorbidity   300
   Age of Onset, Course, and Outcome   300
Associated Characteristics of Depressive Disorders   301
   Intellectual and Academic Functioning   301
   Cognitive Disturbances   301

■ *Fifteen-year-old Ellie: Feels Worthless*   302

   Self-Esteem and Self-Perceived Personal
     Competence   303

■ *Farah: Never Quite Good Enough*   303

   Interpersonal Difficulties   304
Theories and Causes of Depression   306
   Theories of Depression   306
   Causes of Depression   310
Bipolar Disorder   316

■ *Ben: Highs and Lows*   316

Prevalence   319
Comorbidity and Differential Diagnosis   320
Age of Onset, Course, and Outcome   320
Gender and Ethnicity   321
Associated Characteristics of Bipolar Disorder   321
Causes of Bipolar Disorder   322

■ *Gabrielle: A Family Disorder*   322

Suicide and Depression   322

■ *Carla: "It Became Too Much"*   322

■ *Jenna: "I Wish I Could Sleep Forever. . ."*   323

Prevalence and Comorbidity   325
Age of Onset, Developmental Course, and
  Outcome   326
Gender and Ethnicity   326
Risk Factors   327
Treatment of Mood Disorders   327
   Treatment of Depression   327

■ *Leeta: Feeling Better*   327

   Overview of Treatments   328
   Psychosocial Interventions   329
   Medications   332
   Prevention   333
   Treatment of Bipolar Disorder   333

Summary 334
Key Terms 335

PART IV
Developmental and Learning Disorders

CHAPTER 9
Mental Retardation 337

Perspectives on Intelligence and Mental Retardation 337
  The Eugenics Scare 338
  Defining and Measuring Children's Intelligence and
    Adaptive Behavior 340
  The Controversial IQ 341
Features of Mental Retardation 343

■ *Matthew: Gaining at His Own Pace 343*

■ *Vanessa: Gaining at Home 344*

Clinical Description 344
Levels of Functioning 346
Prevalence 349
Developmental Course and Adult Outcomes 350

■ *Dan: With His Brother's Help 350*

Motivation 351
Changes in Developmental Progress 352
Related Developmental Disabilities 352
Language and Social Behavior 353
Emotional and Behavioral Problems 355

■ *Pattie: Disturbed or Disturbing? 355*

Causes 356
  Heritability and the Role of the Environment 358
  Genetic and Constitutional Factors 359
  Neurobiological Influences 361
  Social and Psychological Dimensions 362
Prevention, Education, and Treatment 363
  Prenatal Education and Screening 364
  Psychosocial Treatments 365
Summary 370
Key Terms 370

CHAPTER 10
Autism and Childhood-Onset Schizophrenia 372

Autism 372
  Historical Background of Autism 372
  Description 373

■ *Jay: Not Normal 373*

■ *Jerry: Fear and Order 374*

  DSM-IV: Defining Features of Autism 374
  Autism across the Spectrum 374

■ *Lucy: Autism with Mental Retardation 375*

■ *John: Autism with Average Intelligence 376*

Core Characteristics 378
  Social Impairments 378
  Communication Impairments 379
  Repetitive Behaviors and Interests 383

Associated Characteristics of Autism 384
  Intellectual Deficits and Strengths 384

■ *Trevor: Autistic Savant 385*

  Sensory and Perceptual Impairments 385
  Cognitive Deficits 386
  Physical Characteristics 390
  Characteristics of Family Members 391

■ *Emilie: Hard on the Family 391*

  Subtypes 392
  Accompanying Disorders and Symptoms 392
  Differential Diagnosis and Other Pervasive
    Developmental Disorders 392
Prevalence and Course 394
  Prevalence 394
  Age of Onset 394

■ *Ann-Marie: First Birthday 394*

  Course and Outcome 395
Causes of Autism 396
  Problems during Pregnancy and Birth 396
  Genetic Contributions 396
  Neuropsychological Findings 398
  Neurobiological Factors 398
  Autism as a Disorder of Brain Development 401
Treatment 401
  Different Children, Different Treatments 402
  Overview of Treatments 403

■ *Emilie: A Full-Time Job 403*

■ *Nile: Learning to Communicate Nondisruptively 405*

Childhood-Onset Schizophrenia 411

■ *Mary: Depressed, Disorderly, Doomed 412*

DSM-IV: Defining Features of Schizophrenia 412
Psychotic Symptoms 413
Related Symptoms and Comorbidities 413
Prevalence 413
Causes 413
  Biological Factors 414
  Environmental Factors 415
Treatment 416
Summary 417
Key Terms 418

CHAPTER 11
Communication and Learning Disorders 419

■ *James: Fear and Frustration 419*

■ *Francine: Alone and Withdrawn 419*

Description 420
Historical Background 422
Language Development and Disorders 423
  Phonological Awareness 424
Communication Disorders 425

■ *Jackie: Screaming, not Talking   425*

Expressive Language Disorder   426
Stuttering   430

■ *Sayad: Family Legacy   430*

Learning Disorders   431

■ *James: Strong Points Shine   432*

■ *Tim: Warning with Interest   432*

Clinical Description   433

■ *Carlos: Slowly Taking Shape   436*

Prevalence and Developmental Course   437
Causes   441
Treatment and Prevention   448

■ *Francine: Slowly but Surely   449*

The Regular Education Initiative   450
Instructional Methods   450

■ *Carlos's PLANS   451*

Summary   453
Key Terms   454

PART V
Problems Related to Physical and Mental Health

CHAPTER 12
Health-Related Disorders   455

■ *Jeremiah: Breath Is Life   455*

■ *Anita: Too Worried to Sleep   455*

Historical Developments   456
Sleep Disorders   457
    Normal Stages of Sleep   458
    Features of Sleep Disorders   461

■ *Mario: Troubled by Sleep Attacks   463*

    Treatment   467

■ *Anita's Bedtime Routine   468*

Elimination Disorders   469
    Enuresis   469
    Encopresis   473
Chronic Childhood Illness   474
    Normal Variations in Children's Expression of Health Concerns   476
    Representative Chronic Childhood Illnesses   477

■ *Amanda: Daily Struggle with Diabetes   478*

■ *Chen: A Determined Boy Fighting Leukemia   479*

    Development and Course   480
    A Biopsychosocial Model of Children's Adaptation to Chronic Illness   483
    Intervention   486
Summary   498
Key Terms   489

CHAPTER 13
Eating Disorders and Related Conditions   491

Development of Eating Patterns   492
    Normal Development   492
    Developmental Risk Factors   493
    Biological Regulators   496
Feeding and Eating Disorders of Infancy and Early Childhood   497
    Pica   497
    Rumination Disorder   499
    Feeding Disorder of Infancy or Early Childhood   500
    Associated Disorders   501
    Obesity   502

■ *Ellen: Changes in Self-Image   502*

Eating Disorders of Adolescence   505
    Anorexia Nervosa   506

■ *Martha: Obsessed with Food and Weight   506*

    Bulimia Nervosa   508

■ *Phillipa: A Well-Kept Secret   508*

Prevalence and Development of Anorexia and Bulimia   511
    Cross-Cultural Considerations   511
    Development and Course   512
Causes of Anorexia and Bulimia   513
    Biological Dimension   513
    Social Dimension   515
    Psychological Dimension   517
Treatments for Anorexia and Bulimia   520
    Pharmacological   520
    Psychosocial   520
Summary   522
Key Terms   523

CHAPTER 14
Child Abuse and Neglect   524

■ *Mary Ellen's Legacy   524*

■ *Nadine: What Went Wrong?   524*

Perspectives on Child-Rearing and Maltreatment   526
    Family Context   527
    Categories of Care   528
Description   529
    Physical Abuse   530

■ *Milton: Abused and Abusive   530*

    Neglect   530

■ *Jane and Matt: Used to Neglect   530*

    Sexual Abuse   532

■ *Rosita: No Haven at Home   532*

    Emotional Abuse   533

■ *Evan: If This Is Love...   533*

Prevalence and Context   533
    Incidence of Abuse and Neglect   534

The Increasing Rate of Child Maltreatment 535
Characteristics of Victimized Children 535
Characteristics of Family and Perpetrator 535
Cross-Cultural Comparisons 536
Developmental Course and Psychopathology 536

■ *Rosita: Feeling Trapped* 536

Resilience and Adaptation 537
Developmental Consequences 538
Psychopathology and Adult Outcomes 543

■ *Celia: Walled Away* 545

Causes 548
Physical Abuse and Neglect 549

■ *Brenda: Unhappy Childhood, Unhappy Motherhood* 549

Sexual Abuse 554
Social and Cultural Dimensions 556
Prevention and Treatment 557
Physical Abuse and Neglect 558

■ *Milton's Treatment—Session 1* 558

■ *Milton's Treatment—Session 4* 558

Sexual Abuse 560
Summary 561
Key Terms 562

Epilogue 563

Glossary

References

Subject Index

Name Index

Credits

Preface

The past decade has produced extraordinary advances in understanding the special issues pertaining to abnormal child psychology. Today we have a much better ability to distinguish among different disorders, which has given rise to increased recognition of poorly understood or undetected problems like learning disorders, depression, teen suicide, eating disorders, conduct disorders, problems stemming from chronic health problems, abuse and neglect, and many others. Similarly, the field is more aware of the ways in which children's and adolescents' psychological disorders are distinguishable from those of adults, and how important it is to maintain a strong developmental perspective.

In a relatively short time, the study of abnormal child psychology has moved well beyond the individual child and family to consider the roles of community, social, and cultural influences in an integrative, developmentally sensitive manner. Similarly, those of us working in this field are more attuned to the many struggles faced by children with psychological disorders and their families, as well as the demands and costs such problems place on the mental health, education, medical, and juvenile justice systems.

These rapid advances and demands have helped the field of abnormal child psychology to become clearly distinctive, yet vitally important to related disciplines and mental health issues. Such growth and maturity, of course, deserve comprehensive, up-to-date, and interesting coverage. In designing this textbook, we began with a firm commitment to empirical findings and scientific methods, wishing to highlight current advances and identify questions that are in need of further research study. We also sought to present such information in a stimulating, engaging fashion that cultivates student interest.

This textbook was written to the same standard for disorders of childhood that is typically reached in general abnormal psychology textbooks on adult disorders. We emphasize the multidimensional, reciprocal nature of children's and youths' expression of problem behavior, within a developmental framework. A guiding principle is to provide a balance among developmental, clinical/ diagnostic, and experimental approaches to child and adolescent psychopathology, with a clear and visible emphasis on the special issues pertaining to children and youth.

EASY-TO-UNDERSTAND ORGANIZATION

The textbook is organized into a logical, five-part framework to facilitate an understanding of the disorders and mastery of the material. Following the introductory chapters, the contents can be readily assigned in any order that suits the goals and preferences of the instructor:

I. Understanding Abnormal Child Psychology (definitions, theories, clinical description, research, assessment and treatment issues);
II. Behavioral Disorders (ADHD and conduct problems);
III. Emotional Disorders (anxiety and mood disorders);
IV. Developmental and Learning Disorders (mental retardation, autism, childhood-onset schizophrenia, and communication and learning disorders);
V. Problems Related to Physical and Mental Health (health-related disorders, eating disorders, and child abuse and neglect).

Key terms introduced in each chapter are listed at the chapter's end and defined in a separate Glossary to help students grasp important terminology.

A FOCUS ON THE CHILD, NOT JUST THE DISORDERS

We believe that one of the best ways to introduce students to a particular problem of childhood or adolescence is to describe a real child. Clinical descriptions, written in an accessible, engaging fashion, help students understand a child's problem in context and provide a framework from which to explore the complete nature of the disorder. We introduce case examples of children with disorders in each chapter, from our own clinical files and from those of colleagues. We then refer to these children when describing the course of the disorder, which provides the student with a well-rounded picture of the child in the context of his or her family, peers, and community. For example, in Chapter 1 we discuss the case of Georgina, a 10-year-old girl suffering from obsessive-compulsive disorder, to highlight important features of child and adolescent disorders and how we go about finding the multiple causes of such problems.

In addition to clinical case material, we use extracts, quotes, and photos throughout each chapter so that the student never loses focus on the real challenges faced by children with disorders and their families. First-person accounts and case descriptions enrich the reader's understanding of the daily lives of children with problems, and allow for a more realistic portrayal of individual strengths and limitations.

A COMPREHENSIVE AND INTEGRATIVE APPROACH

To reflect the expansion of this field, causes and effects of various childhood disorders are explained from an integrative perspective that acknowledges biological, psychological, and social influences and their interdependence. This strategy was further guided by a consideration of developmental processes that shape the expression of each disorder. The broader family, cultural, and social settings affecting development are also important considerations for understanding child disorders, and one that is a critical feature of this text.

We use both categorical and dimensional approaches in describing disorders, for each method offers unique and important definitions and viewpoints. Each topic area is defined using DSM-IV criteria, accompanied by clinical descriptions, examples, and empirically derived dimensions. The clinical features of each disorder are described in a manner that allows students to gain a firm grasp of the basic dimensions and expression of the disorder across the lifespan. We use DSM-IV criteria as the core working definition for each major disorder because these criteria are widely used in research and clinical practices. DSM-IV criteria have become increasingly sensitive to child and adolescent disorders and are more operationally defined and empirically supported than in previous editions. Since children referred for psychological services often show symptoms that overlap into more than one diagnostic category, each chapter discusses comorbidities and developmental norms that help inform diagnostic decisions.

DEVELOPMENTAL PATHWAYS AND ADULT OUTCOMES

Abnormal child psychology has traditionally been taught with an emphasis on children's deficits and specific disorders, with less attention given to their strengths and weaknesses across different dimensions of development and behavior. To redress this oversight and to provide greater balance to the particular problems associated with the disorder, we approach each disorder from the perspective of the whole child. DSM-IV criteria, therefore, are accompanied by an added emphasis on the strengths of the individual and environmental circumstances that influence the developmental course. Moreover, the developmental course of each disorder is followed through adolescence into adulthood, highlighting the special issues pertaining to younger and older age groups and the risk and protective factors affecting developmental pathways. In this regard we examine developmental continuities and discontinuities, and attempt to understand why some children with problems continue to experience difficulties as adolescents and adults, whereas others do not.

CHILD MALTREATMENT AND RELATIONSHIP-BASED DISORDERS

A distinguishing feature of this textbook is its expansion and emphasis on several of the more recent and important areas of child psychopathology that do not easily fit into a deficits model or categorical approach. These problems are sometimes referred to as relationship-based disorders, because they illustrate the transactional nature of children's behavior in the context of significant relationships. Along with a recognition of the importance of biological dispositions in guiding development and behavior, we discuss the strong connection between children's behavior patterns and the availability of a suitable childrearing environment. Students are made aware of how children's overt symptoms can be adaptive in particular settings or with caregiving relationships that are atypical or abusive, and how traditional diagnostic labels may thus be unhelpful.

INTEGRATION OF TREATMENT AND PREVENTION

Treatment and prevention approaches are integral parts of understanding a particular disorder. Applying knowledge of the clinical features and developmental courses of childhood disorders to benefit children with these problems and their families always intrigues students and helps them make greater sense of the material. Therefore, we emphasize current approaches to treatment and prevention in each chapter, where such information can be tailored to the particular childhood problem. Consistent with current health system demands for accountability, we emphasize interventions for which there is some empirical support.

ACKNOWLEDGMENTS

One of the most rewarding aspects of this project has been the willingness and commitment on the part of many to share their knowledge and abilities. With great pleasure and appreciation we wish to acknowledge individuals who have in one way or another contributed to its completion.

In Calgary, Alison and Megan Wiigs, as creative and talented a mother and daughter team as there is, contributed enormously to every phase of this project. For their devotion to the project, they have our special gratitude. Caroline Schnitzler and Christy Bryceland also provided generous help in locating resource material. In London, Annalee Pittman deserves rich praise for her skilled efforts at locating resource material, no matter how hopeless (no matter how far). Nadine Church, Katie Hildyard, and Kira Legate were our sounding board, offering advice and feedback not only about clarity of content, but also harmony of wit and humor.

Our colleague, Susan Graham, provided invaluable feedback for many of the chapters as well as technical assistance and ongoing support throughout this project. Generous feedback and suggestions for individual chapters were also provided by other valued colleagues and friends, including Sharon Foster, Charlotte Johnston, James Mosley, and Greg Fouts. We are also grateful to colleagues who generously provided us with case materials and other information, including William Pelham, Ann Marie Albano, Alan Kazdin, John Piacentini, Russell Barkley, Thomas Achenbach, Philip Kendall, Gerald Patterson, David Shaffer, Ivar Lovaas, David Kolko,

Jerry Sattler, Margaret McKim, Douglas Murdoch, Rosemary Tannock, John Weisz, Don Kline, John Pearce, David Dozois, and Phyl and Rachel Prout.

The production of a textbook involves many behind-the-scenes individuals who deserve special thanks. Marianne Taflinger, our Senior Editor at Wadsworth, contributed creative ideas, valuable assistance, and friendly reality checks from start to finish. The devoted and talented staff at Wadsworth, including Keith Faivre, Penelope Sky, Margaret Parks, Laura Harp, Jennifer Wilkinson, and Rachael Bruckman; the editing of Alice Jaggard and Mike Ederer, and the skilled composition of Graphic World, Inc.; and the talents of Linda Rill, Permissions Editor, all deserve our thankful recognition for their contribution toward making this textbook top quality.

Last but not least, we wish to thank our families, whose steadfast support and tolerance for the demands and excesses that go into a project such as this were critically important and exceedingly strong. The preparation of this textbook placed a heavy burden on our time away from them, and we are grateful for their unyielding support and encouragement. Eric Mash thanks his wife and soul mate of 30 years for her tolerance of the time that a project like this takes away from family life, and her wise advice on many matters relating to this book. David Wolfe thanks his three children (Amy, Anne, and Alex) and wife (Barbara Legate), who were incredible sources of inspiration, information, and humor (each in his or her own unique way!).

Eric J. Mash   David A. Wolfe

REVIEWERS

A critical part of writing this textbook involved feedback from teachers and experts. We would like to thank several dedicated reviewers and scholars who read most of the chapters for this book and provided us with detailed comments and suggestions that were enormously helpful in shaping the final manuscript.

Debora Bell-Dolan
University of Missouri–Columbia

June Madsen Clausen
University of San Francisco

Richard Clements
Indiana University Northwest

Nancy Eldred
San Jose State University

Gary Harper
DePaul University

Christopher Kearney
University of Nevada–Las Vegas

Janet Kistner
Florida State University

Marvin Kumler
Bowling Green State University

Patrick McGrath
Dalhousie's University

Kay McIntyre
University of Missouri–St. Louis

Robert McMahon
University of Washington

Richard Milich
University of Kentucky

Martin Murphy
University of Akron

Michael Roberts
University of Kansas

Michael Vasey
Ohio State University

Introduction to Abnormal Child Psychology

> When I was a boy of fourteen, my father
> was so ignorant I could hardly stand to have the
> old man around. But when I got to be twenty-one,
> I was astonished at how much he had
> learned in seven years.
>
> —Mark Twain (1835–1910)

After centuries of silence, misunderstanding, and outright abuse, children's mental health problems and needs are receiving greater attention, corresponding to society's more recent concern about children's well-being. Fortunately, today more people like yourself are interested in understanding and addressing the needs of children and adolescents. Perhaps you've begun to recognize that children's mental health problems differ in many ways from those of adults, so you've chosen to have a closer look. Maybe you're thinking of a career in teaching, counseling, medicine, law, rehabilitation, or psychology—all of which rely to some extent on knowledge of children's special needs to shape their focus and practice. Whatever your reason, we are pleased to welcome you to an exciting and very active field of study that we believe will expose you to concepts and issues that will have a profound and lasting influence. Children's mental health issues are becoming very relevant to many of us in our current and future roles as professionals, community members, and parents.

To gain an immediate sense of the magnitude of children's mental health needs, consider that each year nearly 3 million children and adolescents in North America receive some type of mental health service, at an estimated cost of $1.5 billion or more (Weisz & Weiss, 1993). These numbers represent only the tip of the iceberg, however, because compared with the number of children needing mental health–related services, very few actually receive them. Surveys conducted in New Zealand, England, the United States, and elsewhere find that about one child in five has a mental health problem that significantly impairs functioning, and about one in ten meets criteria for a specific psychological disorder (Costello & Angold, 1995). Some children have difficulties adapting to school or to family circumstances, so they behave in ways that are developmentally or situationally inappropriate. Others, however, show more pronounced patterns of development and adjustment that suggest one or more specific disorders of childhood or adolescence. The process of deciding which problems merit professional attention and which ones might be outgrown involves a good understanding of both normal and abnormal child development and behavior.

A PORTRAIT OF CHILDREN'S AND ADOLESCENTS' HEALTH ISSUES

If all children and adolescents with known psychological disorders could be captured in a photograph, the current picture would be much clearer than that of only a generation or so ago. The improved focus and detail are the result of efforts to increase recognition and assessment of children's psychological disorders. In the past, children with various mental health and educational needs were too often described in global terms, such as "maladjusted," because assessment devices were not sensitive to different syndromes and diagnostic clusters of symptoms (Achenbach, 1995). Today, we have a better ability to distinguish among the various disorders, which has given rise to increased recognition of previously poorly understood or undetected problems such as learning disorders, depression, teen suicide, eating disorders, conduct disorders, and problems stemming from chronic health conditions and from abuse and neglect.

Another difference in today's portrait would be the group's composition: Younger children and teens would appear more often in the photo, reflecting greater awareness of their unique mental health issues. Specific communication and learning disorders, for example, have only recently been recognized as significant concerns among preschoolers and young school-age children. Similarly, emotional problems such as anxiety and depression, which increase dramatically during adolescence (Velez, Johnson, & Cohen, 1989), were previously overlooked because the symptoms are often less visible or disturbing to others than are the symptoms of behavior or learning problems.

Unfortunately, what would *not* have changed in our photo is the proportion of children who are receiving proper services—fewer than 10% of children with mental health problems today receive proper services to address impairments related to personal, family, or situational factors, a figure that has remained unchanged for over 30 years (Costello & Angold, 1995).

The children and teens in the picture would not reflect a random cross section of all children, because mental health problems are unevenly distributed. Children from disadvantaged families and neighborhoods (McLoyd, 1998); children from abusive or neglectful families (Emery & Laumann-Billings, 1998); those receiving inadequate child care (Scarr, 1998); those born with very low birth weight due to maternal smoking, diet, or abuse of alcohol and drugs (McCormick, Gortmaker, & Sobol, 1990); and those born to parents with criminal histories (Gabel & Schindledecker, 1993) or severe mental illness (Resnick, Harris, & Blum, 1993) are disproportionately afflicted with mental health problems. Nor could the children in the picture easily be grouped according to these categories, because children often face combinations of environmental stressors and psychosocial deprivations. These children are especially at risk of having their healthy development compromised to such a degree that they are said to show abnormal behavior or to suffer from a mental disorder (Steinhauer, 1998).

If you looked beyond the faces, you would note that in many cases the background and circumstances of children and youth with mental health problems provided obvious clues to their problems. One of the most telling clues would be the experiences of poverty, disadvantage, and violence faced by many, which can have a cumulative effect on their mental health over time (Garmezy, 1991). The impact of childhood poverty provides a case in point: Children from poor and disad-

Surveys estimate that about 1 child in 5 has a mental health problem that interferes with his or her development, and 1 in 10 has a specific psychological disorder.

vantaged families show almost 3½ times the conduct disorders, almost twice the chronic illness, and more than twice the rate of school problems, hyperactivity, and emotional disorders than do those who are not poor (Ross, Shillington, & Lochhead, 1994). Moreover, the deeper the level of poverty, the higher the incidence of children's violence: 3 times greater in girls, 5 times greater in boys (Tremblay, Pihl, Vitaro, & Dobkin, 1994). Economic deprivation alone is not responsible for these higher rates, however, for many children do succeed even under harsh circumstances. Nevertheless, the greater the degree of inequity, powerlessness, and lack of control over their lives, the more children's physical and mental health are undermined (Canadian Institute of Advanced Research, 1991; Davey Smith, Bartley, & Blane, 1990).

The photograph captures only a moment in time; over the long term the impact of children's mental health problems is most severe when the problems continue untreated for months or years. The developmental tasks of childhood are challenging enough without the added burden of emotional or behavioral disturbances that interfere with the progress and course of development in many different ways. About 20% of the children in the photograph—those with the most chronic and serious disorders—face sizable difficulties throughout their lives (Costello & Angold, 1995). They are less likely to finish school and more likely to have social problems or psychiatric disorders that affect many aspects of their lives throughout adulthood.

In this text we look at current research on the nature and course of psychological disorders among children and adolescents. To continue with the photographic metaphor, we examine which children appear in the photograph and why, how long they stay, and whether they will appear as adults with mental health problems in later photographs.

TERMINOLOGY AND FEATURES OF ABNORMAL CHILD PSYCHOLOGY

We begin our discussion of children's mental health problems by clarifying current terminology and concepts. **Child psychopathology,** derived from the Greek words for psyche (mind) and pathos (suffering), refers to the field concerned with the scientific study of children's psychological and behavioral disorders. **Abnormal child psychology** and **developmental psychopathology** are two major and related approaches to describing and studying disorders of childhood and adolescence in a manner that recognizes the importance of developmental processes and tasks. How children develop and how normal development goes awry are fundamental issues for the study of abnormal child psychology, because normal and abnormal development inform one another. Within the field of child psychopathology are a number of disciplines and specially trained professionals who evaluate and treat disturbed children and their families—for example, pediatricians, psychiatrists, nurses, social workers, educators, and psychologists, as well as speech, music, art, and recreational therapists. Given this expansive list of disciplines, it is not surprising that a tremendous number (over 200) of diverse psychosocial treatments exist for children and families (Kazdin, 1988).

Let's first consider Georgina's problems, which raise several fundamental questions that guide our current understanding of children's psychological disorders. Ask yourself, "Does Georgina's behavior seem abnormal, or are aspects of her behavior normal under certain circumstances?"

Georgina: Let Me Count the Ways

At age 10, Georgina's strange symptoms had reached the point where her mother needed answers—and fast. Her behavior first became a concern about two years ago, when she started talking about harm befalling herself or her family. Her mother recalled how Georgina would come home from the third grade and complain that "I need to finish stuff but I can't seem to," and "I know I'm gonna forget something so I have to keep thinking about it." Her mother expressed her frustration

and worry: "As early as age five, I remember Georgina would touch and arrange things a certain way, such as brushing her teeth in a certain sequence and rearranging folders in her backpack for several minutes. Sometimes I'd notice that she would walk through doorways over and over, and she seemed to need to check and arrange things her way before she could leave a room." Georgina's mother had spoken to their family doctor about it back then and was told "it's probably a phase she's going through, like stepping on cracks will break your mother's back. Ignore it and it'll stop."

But it didn't stop. She developed more elaborate rituals related to counting words and objects, primarily in groups of four. Georgina told her mom that "I need to count things out and group them a certain way—only I know the rules how to do it." When she came to my office, Georgina told me that "when someone says something to me or I read something I have to count the words in groups of four and then organize these groups into larger and larger groups of four." She looked at the pile of magazines in my office and the books on my shelf and explained, matter-of-factly, that she was counting and grouping these things while we talked! Georgina was constantly terrified of forgetting a passage or objects or being interrupted, because she felt if she was not able to complete her counting some horrible tragedy would befall her parents or herself. Nighttime was the worst, she explained, because "I can't go to sleep until my counting is complete, and this can take a long time" (in fact, up to several hours, her mother acknowledged). Understandably, her daytime counting rituals had led to decline in her schoolwork and friendships. Her mother showed me her report cards: Georgina had gone from above average to near failing in several subjects. (Based on Piacentini & Grace, 1997; removed by permission)

How would you describe Georgina's problem? Does she have a learning problem? an emotional problem? Does she suffer from a developmental disability? Could something in her environment be causing these strange rituals, or is it more likely that she is responding to some internal cues that we are not aware of? What's her course of development, and what might we do to help?

How you choose to describe the impairments children show and what harm such impairments may lead to is often the first step toward understanding the nature of

Calvin and Hobbes

by Bill Watterson

Calvin and Hobbes © Watterson. Reprinted with permission of Universal Press Syndicate. All rights reserved.

their problems. As we will see in Chapter 7, Georgina fits the diagnostic criteria for obsessive-compulsive disorder. This diagnostic label, although far from perfect, tells a great deal about the nature of her disorder, what course it may follow, and what treatments may be useful. When seeking assistance or advice, parents often ask questions similar to these about their child's behavior, and understandably need to know what the likely course and outcome might be. These questions also exemplify the issues that research studies in child psychopathology seek to address: defining what constitutes normal and abnormal behavior for children of different ages and sexes, identifying the causes and correlates of abnormal child behavior, making predictions about long-term outcomes for varying childhood problems, and developing and evaluating methods for the treatment and/or prevention of abnormal child behavior.

Georgina's problems illustrate some important features that distinguish most child and adolescent disorders from adult disorders. First, when services are sought for children, it is not often clear whose "problem" it is. Children usually enter the mental health system as a result of concerns raised by adults—parents, pediatricians, teachers, or school counselors and—the children themselves may have little choice in the matter. This has important implications for how children's problems are detected and how we respond to them. Second, many child and adolescent problems involve failure to show expected developmental progress in areas such as speech, toileting, friendships, academic achievement, adaptation to school, relations with family members, and preparation for adulthood. The problem may be transitory, or it may be an initial indication of more severe problems ahead. Determining which it is requires familiarity with

normal as well as abnormal development (Achenbach, 1995). Furthermore, many problem behaviors shown by children and youth are not intrinsically abnormal; rather, they are shown to some extent by most children and youth. For instance, worrying from time to time about forgetting things or losing track of thoughts is not uncommon; Georgina's behavior, however, seems much different from these normal concerns. Thus, decisions about what to do also require familiarity with known psychological disorders and troublesome problem behaviors. Finally, unlike interventions for most adult disorders, those for children and adolescents are often intended to promote further development rather than merely to restore a previous level of functioning.

WHAT IS ABNORMAL CHILD BEHAVIOR?

The study of abnormal behavior often makes us more sensitive to and wary of the ways used to describe the behavior of others. Whose standard of "normal" do we adopt, and who decides when this arbitrary standard has been breached? Does abnormal behavior or performance in one area, such as mood or behavior, have implications for the whole person?

Although there are no easy answers to these questions, Georgina's real-life problems require that we come to some agreement as to how we define a **psychological disorder.** Regardless of whether we are considering children, adolescents, or adults, a psychological or mental disorder traditionally has been defined as a pattern of behavioral, cognitive, emotional, or physical symptoms shown by an individual. Such a pattern is associated with one or more of the following three prominent features: First, the person shows some degree of *distress,* such as fear or sadness; second, his or her behavior indicates some degree of *disability,* such as impairment in one or more important areas of functioning, including physical, emotional, cognitive, and behavioral; third, the person may have an *increased risk* of suffering death, pain, disability, or an important loss of freedom (American Psychiatric Association [APA], 1994). To account for the fact that we sometimes show transitory signs of distress, disability, or risk under unusual circumstances (such as the loss of a loved one), this definition of a syndrome or pattern excludes circumstances where such reactions are expected and appropriate as defined by our culture.

Although abnormality is often defined as a pattern displayed by *individuals,* children's dependency on other people means that many childhood problems are better depicted in terms of *relationships,* rather than as problems contained in the individual. Many of these relationships, such as those with family members, involve critical aspects of dependency, caring, and trust. Other relationships involve the larger social network of peers and other adults who help shape a child's behavior. Children of all ages are active, vibrant beings who act on and are acted upon by their environment, so their psychological profile is almost always a reflection of such interactions. Even in cases of pervasive developmental disorders like autism, children's responses to their environment emerge from the interplay of their inherent learning abilities and available environmental opportunities.

It is very important to keep in mind that terms used to describe abnormal behavior do not describe people; they only describe patterns of behavior that may or may not occur in certain circumstances. We must be careful to avoid the common mistake of identifying the person with the disorder, as reflected in such expressions as "retarded child" or "autistic child." Accordingly, throughout this text we separate the child from the disorder by using language such as "Ramon is a child with mental retardation," rather than "Ramon is mentally retarded." Children like Ramon have many other attributes that should not be overshadowed by global descriptives or negative labels.

Similarly, the problems shown by some children may be the result of their attempts to adapt to abnormal or unusual circumstances. Children with chronic health problems must adapt to their medical regimens and to negative reactions from peers; children who are raised in abusive or neglectful environments must learn how to relate to others adaptively and to regulate emotions that may, at times, be overwhelming. Therefore, the primary purpose of using terms such as *disorder* and *abnormal behavior* for describing the psychological status of children and adolescents is to aid clinicians and researchers in describing, organizing, and expressing the complex features often associated with various patterns of behavior. By no means do the terms imply a common cause, since the causes of abnormal behavior are almost always multifaceted and interactive. We return to this topic of diagnosis, classification, and labeling often throughout the text, and deal with it in specific detail in Chapter 4.

Another important consideration is arriving at a definition of what is abnormal behavior for a child or adolescent. Traditionally, psychological disorders in children have been defined by concepts such as symptoms, diagnosis, illness, and treatment, which have strongly influenced the way we think about abnormal child psychology (Richters & Cicchetti, 1993). Childhood disorders, like adult disorders, have commonly been viewed in terms of deviancies from normal, yet disagreement remains as to what constitutes normal and abnormal. In the discussion to follow, keep in mind that attempting to establish boundaries between abnormal versus normal functioning is an arbitrary process at best, and current guidelines are constantly being reviewed for their accuracy and completeness.

Establishing Boundaries

I felt sorry for him. I asked him why he didn't go to school: "Oh," he said, "school is just a waste of time. I'm not learning anything there. I got other things to do. Besides, the kids all make fun of me. I wear jeans and they laugh at me. I talk with a Southern drawl and they laugh at me. They don't like me. I don't like them." Although he had hobbies, "most of all, I like to be by myself and do things by myself." And that's what he did a good part of those 18 months in New York. He'd get up at 9 AM, watch television till 2 or 3 in the afternoon. There was no one else at home. His mother was out working. I asked him what he thought about his mother. He answered: "Well, I've got to live with her, so I guess I love her." But he showed no real relationship to her nor did she to him. (Sites, 1967)

These comments were made by a probation officer, reflecting on his involvement with a 13-year-old boy named Lee Harvey Oswald, who was under probation for chronic truancy. Notice that the presenting complaint—truancy—was linked to dislike of school, embarrassment by peers, social isolation and alienation, and even his lack of emotional closeness to his mother. This illustration reveals how a relatively discrete problem can be difficult to classify into its causes, expression, and contributing factors. It also raises several key questions: First, how do we judge what is normal? A lot of kids skip school at one time or another during adolescence. Second, when does an issue become a problem? In this instance, did anyone sense that Oswald's truancy might lead to or be due to social problems that were potentially serious? Finally, why are some children's abnormal patterns of behavior relatively continuous from early childhood through adolescence and into adulthood, whereas other children show more variable (discontinuous) patterns of development and adaptation? Was there anything about Oswald's behavior in childhood that could have possibly predicted that he would assassinate President John F. Kennedy years later?

Although these questions are central to defining and understanding abnormal child behavior, and warrant thoughtful consideration, no simple, straightforward answers exist. (This should be familiar ground to those of you who are psychology majors.) More often than not, childhood disorders are accompanied by various layers of abnormal behavior or development, ranging from the more visible and alarming (such as truancy and conduct problems), to the more subtle yet critical (such as peer rejection), to the more hidden and systemic (such as family problems or parental rejection). Moreover, mental health professionals, in attempting to understand children's weaknesses, too often unintentionally overlook their strengths. Yet, many children cope effectively in other areas of their lives despite the limitations posed by specific psychological disorders. An understanding of children's unique strengths and abilities can lead to ways to assist them in healthy adaptation. Similarly, some children may show less extreme forms of difficulty or only the early signs of an emerging problem, rather than a full-blown disorder. Therefore, to judge what is abnormal, we need to be sensitive to each child's stage of development and consider each child's unique methods of coping and ways of compensating for difficulties (Adelman, 1995).

Impairment in Functioning. One way to determine whether or not a child's behavior may be abnormal is to consider the degree to which his or her behavior is *impaired,* meaning maladaptive or harmful to self or others. For example, the behavior of many children who are considered disruptive or shy is not necessarily abnormal. But if such children are so disruptive that they cannot participate in normal classroom activities, then their social functioning is impaired and their academic progress is likely to suffer as well. Likewise, if the children are so shy that they find it very difficult to talk in class and make every attempt to avoid being around other kids their age, some impairment is present. The difference between Georgina's obsessive-compulsive behavior and the behavior of someone who simply worries or fusses a lot underscores an important point about

determining what is abnormal child behavior: Most psychological disorders are closely tied to otherwise normal emotions, behaviors, and cognitive processes; they are merely more extreme expressions or exaggerations of these human qualities.

Related to the concept of impairment is the important notion of *dysfunction,* which means harmful disruption or deficiency in cognitive, emotional, or behavioral functioning (Wakefield, 1992). To be considered dysfunctional, a child's behavior or emotional expression must be an unusual or unexpected pattern, not simply a reaction to an event, such as grief or anger in response to the death of a close family member. Consider a boy who avoids playing with or even being around a group of popular children at school. If you were aware that he had been told by his parents to avoid certain kids at school because they were bad influences, you would not consider his behavior unusual or inappropriate. On the other hand, if this boy wanted to make friends but could not find the courage to approach others, his behavior would be considered unusual and could become maladaptive if it persists. In the latter case, we might suspect that he has not achieved normal abilities in some areas of cognitive, emotional, and behavioral development. At the same time, however, we must avoid blaming the child by implying that his problem of shyness is due to some inherent fault or weakness. We need to consider situational and environmental factors that might be affecting his behavior around peers. Perhaps his parents recently separated, and he is upset and worried about what other children might say or do. Maybe his family immigrated to this country very recently from Asia or Europe, and he has not been exposed to the nuances of North American culture that are often required before children "fit in" to their peer group?

In short, three primary considerations are useful in defining abnormal child behavior and psychological disorders. First, the child is experiencing psychological dysfunction or disability; that is, some internal mechanism is failing to perform its natural function, such as thinking, feeling, or behaving. Second, the individual shows signs of severe distress or impairment; that is, he or she is behaving in a manner that is extreme and maladaptive. Third, such distress and disability increase the risk of further suffering or harm. Such dysfunction and impairment would not normally be expected or culturally appropriate. Also, this definition only *describes* what a person does or does not do in certain circumstances; it does not assume that the causes or reasons for abnormal behavior can be attributed to the individual alone. To the contrary, considering the whole child in any deliberations of maladaptive dysfunction balances the understanding of particular impairments with a recognition of developmental strengths and weaknesses. A person's behavior, thinking, and physical status are all important considerations in determining his or her degree of success or failure in adapting to the demands of the environment.

The above approach to defining abnormal behavior is similar to the one most often used to classify and diagnose mental disorders, according to the guidelines in the *Diagnostic and Statistical Manual* (DSM-IV) (American Psychiatric Association, 1994). We use this approach in guiding the thinking and structure of this book because of its clinical and descriptive utility. Yet, despite advances in defining abnormality and vast improvements in the diagnostic and classification systems, ambiguity still remains, especially in terms of how decisions are made regarding a particular child's maladaptive dysfunction (Richters & Cicchetti, 1993). A certain degree of ambiguity may be inevitable, since categories of mental disorder stem from linguistic distinctions and abstractions, rather than from scientific findings alone. Boundaries between what constitutes normal and abnormal conditions, or distinctions among different abnormal conditions, are not easily drawn. At present, the DSM-IV approach has achieved some consensus supporting its value in facilitating greater communication and increased standardization of research and clinical knowledge concerning abnormal child psychology. We will consider the DSM-IV and current alternatives to classification of childhood disorders in Chapter 4.

Competence.

Definitions of abnormal child behavior must take children's **competence**—that is, their ability to adapt in the environment—into account. Judgments of deviancy require knowledge of children's performance relative to that of their same-age peers as well as to their individual course of development. In effect, the study of abnormal child psychology considers not only the degree of maladaptive behavior children show, but also the extent to which they achieve normal developmental milestones. As with deviancy, the criteria for defining competence can be very specific and narrow in focus, or as plentiful and broad as we wish (Masten & Coatsworth, 1998).

How do we know whether or not a particular child is doing well, and how do we, as parents, teachers, or professionals, guide our expectations? Knowledge of major psychosocial tasks of childhood and adolescence, referred to as **developmental tasks,** provides an important backdrop for considering a child's developmental progress and impairments. These tasks reflect several broad domains of competence, such as conduct and academic achievement, and tell how children typically progress within each domain as they grow. Examples of developmental tasks are shown in Table 1.1. Conduct, one of the fundamental domains, indicates how well a

Table 1.1   Examples of Developmental Tasks

Age Period	Task
Infancy to preschool	Attachment to caregiver(s)
	Language
	Differentiation of self from environment
	Self-control and compliance
Middle childhood	School adjustment (attendance, appropriate conduct)
	Academic achievement (e.g., learning to read, do arithmetic)
	Getting along with peers (acceptance, making friends)
	Rule-governed conduct (following rules of society for moral behavior and prosocial conduct)
Adolescence	Successful transition to secondary schooling
	Academic achievement (learning skills needed for higher education or work)
	Involvement in extracurricular activities (e.g., athletics, clubs)
	Forming close friendships within and across gender
	Forming a cohesive sense of self-identity

Source: Masten & Coatsworth, 1998.

person follows the rules. From a young age, children are expected to begin controlling their behavior and to comply with their parents' requests. (This doesn't mean they always *do so,* but that's another matter!) By the time children enter school, they are expected to follow the rules for classroom conduct and restrain from harming others. Then, by adolescence, they are expected to follow the rules set by the school, home, and society without direct supervision (Masten & Coatsworth, 1998). Similar developmental progression occurs in the self domain, where children initially learn to differentiate themselves from the environment and gradually develop self-identity and autonomy. In the discussion of disorders in the chapters to follow, we attempt whenever possible to balance the information on abnormal behavior with the growing awareness of children's competencies and strengths.

Developmental Pathways.

Another aspect of judging deviancy involves deciding when a concern or issue about a child's behavior starts to turn into a more recognizable pattern, especially since children's behavior fluctuates and changes considerably as they develop. Therefore, in addition to distinguishing between normal and abnormal adaptation, for each disorder we must consider the temporal relationship between emerging concerns, say, in early childhood, and later disorders.

The concept of **developmental pathways** is useful in understanding the course and nature of normal and abnormal development. Such pathways are not directly observable, but are inferred from repeated assessments of individual children over time (Loeber, 1991). A pathway refers to the sequence and timing of particular behaviors, and highlights the known and suspected relationships between behaviors over time (Loeber, 1991). The concept allows us to visualize development as an active, dynamic process that can account for very different beginnings and outcomes.

Some children, for example, may start out on very similar "paths," such as learning and behavior problems at school, but end up with very different outcomes, including anxiety disorder, eating disorder, normal adjustment, and so on, as depicted in Figure 1.1 (a). This example illustrates the concept of **multifinality,** in which various outcomes may stem from similar beginnings. Child abuse and similar experiences of maltreatment (discussed in Chapter 14) provide another example of how a child's initial course of development can be altered significantly, with very diverse and often unpredictable outcomes later on. In contrast, other children might set out on their developmental journeys with varied strengths and weaknesses based on genetic, familial, and psychological influences, but end up with similar expressions of psychopathology later on. This illustrates the concept of **equifinality,** depicted in Figure 1.1 (b), in which similar outcomes stem from different early experiences (Loeber, 1991; Sroufe & Jacobvitz, 1989). Mood disorders and conduct disorders in adolescence are separate illustrations of equifinality; children with one or the other of these disorders may have very diverse early experiences and risk factors, but show similar patterns of behavior later on. By looking at possible developmental pathways, we gain a better understanding of the ways in which children's problems may change or remain the same over time.

In summary, diversity in how children acquire psychological strengths and weaknesses is a hallmark of abnormal child psychology. Because no clear cause-and-effect relationship exists for each child and adolescent disorder, the following assumptions need to be kept firmly in mind (Cicchetti & Cohen, 1995):

❖ There are many contributors to disordered outcomes in each individual.

❖ Contributors vary among individuals who have the disorder.

❖ Even individuals who have the same specific disorder express the features of their disturbance in different ways (for example, some children with a conduct disorder are aggressive, whereas others may be destructive to property or engage in theft or deceit).

❖ The pathways leading to any particular disorder are numerous and interactive, as opposed to unidimensional and static.

Risk and Resilience

I am convinced that, except in a few extraordinary cases, one form or another of an unhappy childhood is essential to the formation of exceptional gifts.
—Thornton Wilder (1897–1975)

Raoul's and Jesse's life circumstances put the concepts of risk and resilience into focus:

Raoul and Jesse: Why the differences?

Raoul and Jesse were childhood friends who grew up in the same rundown housing project, within a neighborhood plagued by drugs and crime. By the time they were 10 years old they were both familiar with domestic and community violence, and each lived with his mother and an older sibling after his parents divorced. The boys rarely saw their fathers, and if they did it usually wasn't a pleasant experience. By the time they reached grade 6 they were falling behind at school and started to get into trouble with the police for staying out too late, hassling kids at school, and breaking into cars. Despite these problems and a struggle to keep up, though, Raoul finished high school and received two years of training in a local trade school. He is now 30 years old, works at a local factory, and lives with his wife and two children. Raoul sums up his life thus far as "dodging bullets to reach where I want to go," but he's happy to be living in a safe neighborhood and to have hopes of sending his children to college.

His friend Jesse, however, never graduated from high school. He dropped out for good after being expelled for bringing a weapon to school, and he has been in and out of prison several times. At age 30, Jesse drinks too much and has a poor record of finding and keeping a job. He had several short-term relationships that produced two children, but he rarely visits them and never married either mother. Jesse has lived in several locations over the years, mostly in his old, unchanged neighborhood. (Based on Zimmerman & Arunkumar, 1994)

(a) Multifinality: Similar early experiences lead to different outcomes.

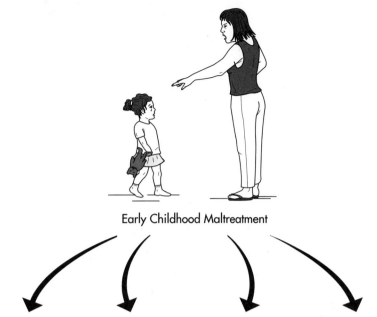

Early Childhood Maltreatment

Possible Outcomes: Eating disorder   Mood disorder   Conduct disorder   Normal adjustment

(b) Equifinality: Different factors lead to a similar outcome.

Possible Beginnings: Genetic pattern   Familial characteristics   Environmental features

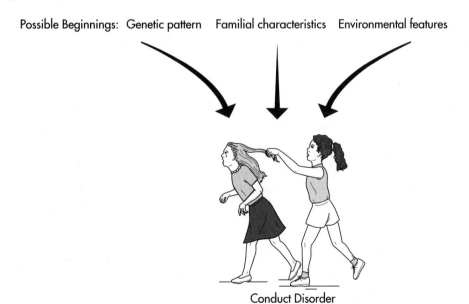

Conduct Disorder

FIGURE 1.1   Developmental pathways: multifinality and equifinality.

These brief life histories illustrate two very different developmental paths that started out at the same place. Jesse's troubles might have been predicted on the basis of what is presently known of abnormal development, but it is more difficult to explain how some children, like Raoul, seem to escape harm despite stress and adversity (Cicchetti & Garmezy, 1993). Perhaps you are familiar with someone—from a novel, movie, or personal friendships—who seems to come out on top, despite adversity and limited resources (see Box 1.1). How do you suppose such individuals escape the odds and achieve their life goals?

The answer to this complicated question is coming into focus, thanks to studies that look at **risk** as well as

Box 1.1

Who's That Girl?

Sometimes we can learn a lot by the personal stories of individuals who are famous or well known for their talent or achievements. And in some cases, like that of Madonna, the popular singer and actress, these personal stories reveal early experiences of adversity or loss that they remember as being instrumental in setting them on a life course.

Madonna grew up in a low income family of six children. She often talks about the death of her mother from cancer (when Madonna was five) as a pivotal event of her life: "I knew I could be either sad and weak and not in control or I could just take control and say it's going to get better." Part of Madonna's desire for control arises from loss, which she turned into a wish to have the largest possible audience love her to negate that loss. She explains, "I know if I'd had a mother I would be very different. It gave me a lot of what are traditionally masculine traits in terms of my ambitiousness and my aggressiveness.... When my mother died, all of a sudden I was going to become the best singer, the best dancer, the most famous person in the world; everybody was going to love me." Whether or not you agree with her achievement of such a magnitude, her manner of adapting to unfavorable life circumstances illustrates the diversity and impact of resiliency.

Source: Layton, 1994.

Chronic poverty is one of several factors that can put children at higher risk for the development of psychopathology.

resilience factors affecting children's courses of development. As you might suspect, children like Raoul and Jesse, who face a multitude of known risk factors like community violence and parental divorce, are vulnerable to abnormal development. Acute, stressful situations as well as chronic adversity put children's successful development at risk. Chronic poverty, serious care-giving deficits, parental psychopathology, death of a parent, community disasters, homelessness, family breakup, and perinatal stress are known risk factors that increase children's vulnerability to psychopathology, especially in the absence of compensatory strengths and resources (Brooks-Gunn & Duncan, 1997; Steinhauer, 1998).

Yet, like Raoul, some vulnerable children do not develop later problems. Instead, they seem resilient to their stress-filled environments, managing to achieve positive outcomes despite being at significant risk for psychopathology (Luthar, 1993). Resilient children survive risky environments because of their strong self-confidence, coping skills, and abilities to avoid risk situations, and they are able to fight off or recover from their misfortune (Zimmerman & Arunkumar, 1994). They are also more likely to show sustained competence when under stress, or to rebound to a previously healthy level of competence following traumatic or stressful

experiences (Werner, 1995). Resilience is not a universal, categorical, or fixed attribute of the child, however; it varies according to the type of stress, its context, and similar factors. Individual children may be resilient to some specific stressors but not to others, and resilience may vary over time and across contexts (Zimmerman & Arunkumar, 1994).

Resilience does not suggest the existence of a direct causal pathway leading to a particular outcome; instead, it involves ongoing interactions between protective and vulnerability factors within the child, between the child and his or her surroundings, and among the particular risk factors. Protective and vulnerability factors should be thought of as processes rather than absolutes, since the same event or condition can function as either a protective or a vulnerability factor depending on the overall context in which it occurs (Rutter, 1987). For example, placing young children with another family may serve to protect them if they were being severely mistreated, but for some children out-of-home placement could increase their vulnerability if it creates added stress due to being removed from their primary attachment figure. Throughout each chapter, we offer similar examples of children's vulnerability and resilience in relation to particular circumstances and disorders.

Figure 1.2 illustrates some of the better-known characteristics of resilient children and adolescents. Together, these characteristics constitute a *protective triad* of resources and health-promoting events, involving individual opportunities, close family ties, and opportunities for individual and family support from resources available in the school and community (Garmezy, 1991). Protective factors vary tremendously in magnitude and scope, however, and not all three sources are necessary (Werner & Smith, 1992). For some children, merely the availability of a supportive adult, such as a grandparent or teacher, can effectively change the course and direc-

Source	Characteristics
Individual 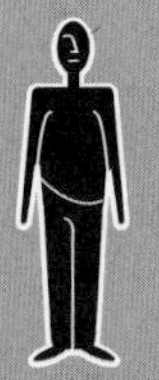	Good intellectual functioning
	Appealing, sociable, easygoing disposition
	Self-efficacy, self-confidence, high self-esteem
	Talents
	Faith
Family 	Close relationship to caring parent figure
	Authoritative parenting, warmth, structure, high expectations
	Socioeconomic advantages
	Connections to extended supportive family networks
Extrafamilial context 	Adults outside the family who take an interest in promoting the child's welfare
	Connections to prosocial organizations
	Attendance at effective schools

FIGURE 1.2 Characteristics of resilient children and adolescents. (Based on Masten & Coatsworth, 1998)

tion of their development; for others, additional or different protective factors may be necessary, such as a better learning environment, community safety, or sufficient family resources.

The characteristics of resilient children and their environments, such as those in Figure 1.2, are sometimes forgotten in attempts to explain abnormal development. Individual protective factors—those related to the child's inherent abilities—are probably the most familiar and straightforward: a temperament that easily engages others, as exhibited by a child who is energetic, affectionate, cuddly, good-natured, and easy to manage; early coping strategies that combine autonomy with help-seeking when needed; high intelligence and scholastic competence; effective communication and problem-solving skills; positive self-esteem and high self-efficacy (Werner, 1995). One or any combination of these individual characteristics can have a major, positive influence on how children adapt to their circumstances. At the family level, resilience is associated with healthy relationships with at least one person who is attuned to the child's needs. It is associated as well with positive parenting, availability of resources such as safe and stimulating child care, a talent or hobby that is valued by adults or

peers, and spiritual guidance and support that provide greater stability and meaning during times of hardship or adversity (Werner & Smith, 1992). In addition, the extrafamilial context often plays a role in the protective triad through relationships with caring neighbors, community elders, or peers; an effective school environment with teachers who serve as positive role models and sources of support; and new opportunities attached to major life transitions, such as adult education, voluntary military service, church or community participation, or a supportive friend or marital partner.

Rather than operating in only one direction, children's individual, family, and community circumstances shape their development in a reciprocal, interactive manner. Some factors cause stress and adversity, leading to problems in adaptation and, in some cases, mental disorders. Other circumstances, however, provide building blocks for strong character and healthy adaptational ability. Although adverse circumstances can impair a young child's ability to accomplish important developmental milestones, they do not inevitably or directly lead to psychological maladjustment. Rather, many different factors, including chance events and encounters, can provide turning points whereby success in a particular developmental task, such as educational advances and peer relationships, alters a child's course toward more adaptive outcomes (Rutter, 1987).

DESCRIBING PSYCHOLOGICAL DISORDERS OF CHILDHOOD AND ADOLESCENCE

I would there were no age between ten and three-and-twenty, or that youth would sleep out the rest; for there is nothing in the between but . . . wronging the ancientry, stealing, fighting.
—William Shakespeare (1564–1616)

Like Shepherd laments in Shakespeare's *The Winter's Tale*, childhood and adolescence have long been considered periods of development that try adults' patience. For centuries, many considered children and youth to be uncivilized beings, so their disturbing behaviors were easily blamed on their intrinsic, disturbed nature. Profound ignorance of children's development and special needs led to a form of societal discrimination, based on the popular opinion that disturbed or annoying behaviors were due to evil forces and sinful acts. Throughout much of Western culture well into the 19th century, this discrimination resulted in children having fewer rights, and being treated as second-class citizens.

Fortunately, clinical and empirical knowledge of children's psychological disorders has evolved considerably within the last half-century, as have the definitions of abnormal behavior and how this knowledge is applied to clinical situations. Helping children with psychological disorders requires a firm understanding of how other children with similar presenting problems respond to certain interventions, or what the course of the disorder may be if left untreated. Childhood problems, like children themselves, do not come in neat packages, and most forms of child psychopathology are known to overlap or coexist with other disorders. Many behavioral and emotional disturbances in children are also associated with specific physical symptoms, medical conditions, and learning problems. Distinct boundaries are not easily drawn between many commonly occurring childhood difficulties, such as noncompliance and defiance, and those childhood problems that come to be labeled "disorders," such as oppositional defiant disorder. Wishing youth to mature in advance of their age, as Shakespeare's character desired, suggests an unwillingness to face these challenging but important concerns.

Understanding children's and adolescents' psychological disorders involves an ongoing process of information gathering, aided by an **assessment,** to identify the distinguishing features of each case, and by knowledge of **taxonomy,** a system for grouping cases according to their distinguishing features (Achenbach, 1995). These simple concepts are central to research, theory, and development of services for children, yet you can imagine how difficult the task of gathering information can become because of the amount of information that has to be collected, weighed, and combined. To accomplish this task, mental health professionals follow scientific methods that allow a careful reduction of possible causes into the more major and significant ones, and test their hypotheses about causal connections and treatment outcomes one step at a time. Findings from psychological research, coupled with clinical experience, guide scientist-practitioners in forming their choices of assessment and intervention strategies for children.

In brief, current study of children's and adolescents' disorders involves three primary steps: attempts to describe the presenting problems and abilities, attempts to understand contributing causes, and attempts to treat or prevent them. These three steps provide an organizational structure that we use throughout the book when discussing different disorders. They are described briefly here to introduce you to this perspective on our efforts to understand abnormality.

Clinical Description

The first step in understanding a child's particular problem is to provide a **clinical description,** which summarizes the individual's unique behaviors, thoughts, and feelings that together make up the features of a given psychological disorder. A clinical description attempts to establish basic information about children's (and usually the parents') presenting complaints, especially how their behavior or emotions differ from or are similar to those of others of their same age and sex.

Diagnosing disorders of children and adolescents is almost always a social judgment, reflecting characteristics and behavior not only of the child but also of significant adults and professionals. This judgment is guided by current standards and scientific knowledge, but it is not always uniform or simple. Throughout the text you will read excerpts of clinical descriptions from various cases, some of them from our own clinical files, to provide you with a sense of how a child with a particular type of disorder might present at a clinic or be described by a parent or teacher.

If you were to conduct an evaluation of Georgina, what would be most important to include in your clinical description? You would start by describing how her behavior differs from normal behavior of girls her age. Considering three important parameters of her presenting behavior would help you in this task (Garber, 1984). First, assessing and describing the *intensity, frequency,* and *severity* of her problem would communicate a sense of how excessive or deficient her behavior is, under what circumstances it may be a problem, how often it does or does not occur, and how severe the occurrences are. Second, you would need to describe the *duration* of her difficulties. Some problems are transient and spontaneously remit, while others persist over time. Like frequency and intensity, duration of the problem behavior must be appraised with respect to what is considered normative for a given age. Finally, you would want to convey a full picture of her *different symptoms and their configuration.* Although Georgina may have been referred for help because of a particularly troublesome problem, you need to know the full range, or profile, of her strengths and weaknesses in order to make informed choices about the likely course, outcome, and treatment of the disorder.

After establishing an initial picture of Georgina's presenting complaints, you would next determine whether or not this description meets criteria for **diagnosis** of one or more psychological disorders. (This issue is covered in some detail in Chapter 4.) A description and diagnosis are also aided by statistical information concerning *prevalence;* that is, how many other girls like Georgina show these problems or fit the criteria for this disorder? Are such problems relatively common or rare, and do they vary in relation to certain demographic features, such as age or gender? These data are derived from *epidemiological studies,* which determine the prevalence and distribution of psychological disorders and their correlates among representative populations of children (Costello, 1989). As we will see when discussing childhood disorders in Chapters 5–14, prevalence rates vary considerably according to the nature of the disorder; the age, sex, social class, and ethnicity of the child; the criteria used to define the problem; sampling considerations; and other factors.

Certain disorders among children and adolescents are likely to co-occur within the same individual, especially disorders that share many common symptoms. Awareness of one disorder (say, depression) alerts us to the increased possibility of another disorder (say, anxiety). These co-occurrences are known as **comorbidity**: two or more disorders overlap at a rate that is greater than what would be expected by chance alone. Some of the more common comorbid disorders are conduct disorder (CD) and attention-deficit/hyperactivity disorder (ADHD), autistic disorder and mental retardation, and childhood depression and anxiety.

Clearly, any clinical description of childhood symptoms and disorders will vary in relation to demographic variables, so these, too, should be carefully noted. The child's age and sex; the parents' socioeconomic status (usually shortened to SES)—an aggregated measure of family income, level of education, and occupational status; ethnicity; geographical region; family size and constellation; and parents' marital and/or mental health status are some of the most prominent demographic factors associated with various child and adolescent disorders. In addition, different disorders follow different patterns or developmental courses, so information about what to expect in the short and long run is extremely important for understanding and treating these problems.

Far greater attention has been devoted to the description and classification of psychopathology in children than to healthy child functioning and how children adapt to the challenges of growing up. In light of this imbalance, throughout this text we introduce each disorder with a discussion of normal developmental processes, such as children's normal intellectual development (in relation to mental retardation) and the normal range of misbehavior and acting-out (in reference to ADHD and CD). We also consider children's strengths and adaptive abilities, regardless of the presence of a particular disorder, and factors that are believed to encourage healthy adaptation regardless of other impairments. We then present the core features of each disorder (such as hyperactivity-impulsivity, sad mood, or conduct problems), followed by significant associated features, such as problems in self-esteem, peer relations, or substance abuse.

Gender and Age Considerations. You may have noticed that behavior problems such as aggression, noncompliance, and rule breaking seem more common among boys than girls, whereas emotional problems, such as sadness, anxiety, and withdrawal, seem more common among girls than boys. This pattern has been well-documented by research (Achenbach, Howell, Quay, & Conners, 1991; Anderson, Williams, McGee, & Silva, 1987; Bird et al., 1989; Offord et al., 1987; Verhulst, Akkerhuis, & Altaus, 1985). Even cross-culturally, boys have been found to display more fighting, impulsivity, and other undercontrolled behaviors than girls (Olweus, 1979). Why might these gender differences be important to the study of abnormal child psychology?

The relationship of gender and age to childhood disorders is critical to understanding the expression and course of these disorders (Kavanagh & Hops, 1994). Gender differences are evident in normal as well as abnormal development, and have relevance to how we identify and interpret behaviors, keeping in mind, however, that individual children may present very differently from the average.

Longitudinal studies (in which the same children are followed over time) and cross-sectional studies (in which different age groups are compared at the same point in time) reveal how specific problem behaviors change among boys and among girls as they grow older. The studies also tell us how children's behaviors normally change across development, and whether certain child characteristics are more or less connected to these changes. Armed with such important information, the clinician is more prepared to determine how unusual or atypical a particular child's presenting problems may be, which provides a fundamental backdrop to our clinical portrait.

Gender differences also interact with age, meaning that boys show a pattern of behavior different from that of girls as they grow older. As shown in Figure 1.3, boys typically have more difficulties than girls during early or middle childhood, particularly with respect to disruptive behavior disorders, such as conduct disorder and ADHD (Boyle et al., 1987; Offord, Boyle, Fleming, Munroe Blum, & Rae Grant, 1989). This may be a function of their greater cognitive immaturity and higher incidence of genetically based learning disabilities relative to that of girls (Steinhauser, 1998). Girls' problems are more likely to increase during adolescence, with higher prevalence rates for depression and dysphoric mood from mid-adolescence through adulthood.

Different patterns of continuity and change in behavior are also found between girls and boys over the course of their development from late childhood to mid-adolescence. For girls, emotional problems such as anxiety or depression are more likely to persist over time, whereas boys with *either* behavior problems *or* emotional problems as children are more likely to end up with behavior disorders in adolescence (McGee et al., 1992). These findings underscore how important it is to

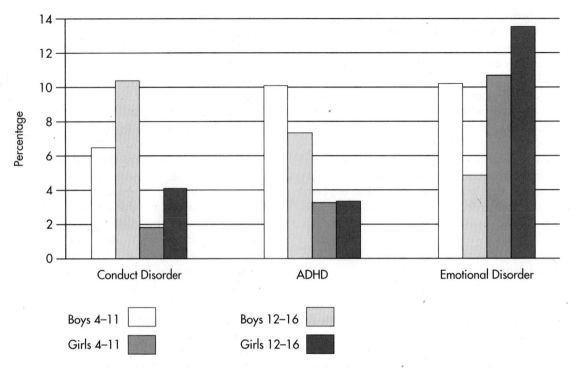

FIGURE 1.3 Prevalence of individual psychiatric disorders by age and sex. (Adapted from Offord et al., 1989)

identify and assist children and youth as early as possible, to prevent or reduce the long-term consequences of such disorders (Newman et al., 1996).

Despite their appeal, these findings must be interpreted with caution. Global comparisons based on gender and age can disguise important psychological processes that account for unique outcomes, such as qualitative differences in how psychopathology is expressed in boys versus girls, the long-term consequences of certain behaviors for boys versus girls, and the impact of certain environmental events and socialization experiences on boys versus girls (Zahn-Waxler, 1993). For instance, boys' problems may be recognized more easily because the behaviors are more troublesome and disruptive, resulting in higher rates of reporting by parents and teachers. (As we discuss in Chapter 4, some assessment instruments adjust for gender differences by having separate norms.) Girls may be more inclined to show emotional as opposed to behavioral problems because of their greater abilities in interpersonal sensitivity, caring, and empathy. These abilities may serve to protect them from heading in an antisocial direction, but at the same time, their overreceptivity to the plight of others and their reluctance to assert their own needs in situations involving conflict and distress may elevate their risk for emotional problems (Zahn-Waxler, Cole, Welsh, & Fox, 1995).

Finally, the types of child-rearing environments predicting *resilience* to adversity may also differ for boys and girls. Resilience in boys is associated with households in which there is a male role model such as a father, a grandfather, or an older sibling; structure; rules; and some encouragement of emotional expressiveness. In contrast, resilient girls come from households that combine risk taking and independence with support from a female care-giver, such as a mother, a grandmother, or an older sister (Werner, 1995).

To recap, gender and age considerations do not cause abnormal behavior. Rather, they influence how children's symptoms and behavior may be expressed and recognized. Although pathways from childhood to adolescent and adult disorders are clearly age- and gender-specific, these differences are probably due to interactions between biology and different social experiences that shape the development of boys and girls in unique ways (Hops, 1995). Regardless of the differences in development, the psychological difficulties of girls and boys merit the same level of concern.

Cultural Considerations. The meaning of children's social behavior is also influenced by cultural and societal values; what is considered abnormal may vary from one culture to the next (Lambert & Weisz, 1992). For example, children's shyness and oversensitivity are likely to lead to peer rejection and social maladjustment in Western cultures, but are associated with leadership, school competence, and academic achievement in Chinese children in Shanghai (Chen, Rubin, & Li, 1995).

Biological influences and socialization practices likely interact to create different interests and behavioral profiles of girls and boys.

Similarly, Jamaican children report more internalizing problems than do American children, which is consistent with Afro-British Jamaican cultural attitudes and practices that discourage child aggression and other under-controlled behavior, and foster inhibition and other overcontrolled behavior (Lambert & Weisz, 1989).

Because the expression of and tolerance for many child behavioral and emotional disturbances are related to social and cultural values, it is important not to generalize the findings from one culture to another unless there is support for doing so. The rates of expression of some disorders, particularly those with a strong neuro-biological basis, such as ADHD and autistic disorder, may be less susceptible to cultural influences than others. Even so, social and cultural beliefs and values are likely to influence the meaning given to these behaviors, the way in which they are responded to, their form of expression, and their outcomes. As with gender-related problems, cultural attitudes can influence patterns of referral for treatment, which in turn affect who partici-pates in research studies. Thus, in making cross-cultural comparisons we need to consider whether or not real differences exist in the rates of the disorder, or differ-ences in the criteria used to make judgments about these problems (Weisz & Suwanlert, 1989).

Developmental Course. Most childhood disor-ders follow a particular pattern, or **developmental course.** This course may be *episodic*, like that of depres-sion, whereby the child or adolescent tends to recover within a few months but often suffers a recurrence of the disorder at a later time. Other childhood disorders are *time-limited*, meaning that the disorder improves on its own, usually in a relatively short period of time as the child develops. Enuresis and encopresis are good ex-amples of time-limited disorders, since they occur during early childhood and, except in rare cases, disappear by late childhood or mid-adolescence (Walker, Kenning, & Faust-Campanile, 1989). Finally, some childhood disor-ders follow a *chronic* course in which the condition persists throughout childhood and into adulthood. Men-tal retardation, autistic disorder, and early-onset conduct disorder are examples of chronic disorders affecting children and youth.

When describing the course of a psychological disor-der, we also need to consider whether the symptoms or behavior patterns are relatively new or if they have been apparent in one form or another for some time. Some disorders, such as certain types of sleep and anxiety problems, have an acute onset; that is, they typically begin suddenly. Others, such as conduct disorders, most

SPEED BUMP   Dave Coverly

WRONG ANSWER

By permission of Dave Coverly and Creators Syndicate.

anxiety disorders, and childhood-onset schizophrenia, tend to have an *insidious* onset; that is, they develop gradually over time. An insidious onset often reflects the fact that particular symptoms change over the child's development (for example, grabbing another child's toy turns to pushing and, later on, to punching and hitting), but the pattern (in this case, one of aggression) remains fairly evident.

In addition to onset and expected course, we need to describe how a psychological disorder may change with the individual's development and how it might be expressed, in a similar or modified way, across various stages of childhood, adolescence, and adulthood. We go into detail describing the specific developmental course of each disorder in the chapters to follow, because many problems of childhood and adolescence, much more so than those of adulthood, are subject to change or may even disappear across the course of development.

Causes

A major goal of this textbook is to organize and make sense of the various possible causes of abnormal child behavior. These causes must be considered from an **interdisciplinary perspective,** which acknowledges the considerable investment in children on the part of many disciplines and professions. Causes and treatments of abnormal child behavior remain prominent subject matter for study in the fields of psychology, education, psychiatry, social work, medicine, and other disciplines, with each field formulating child psychopathology in terms of its own unique perspective.

The study of **etiology,** or causation, of childhood disorders considers how biological, psychological, and environmental processes interact to produce the outcomes that are observed over time. Research into biological determinants has focused on such possible causes as structural brain damage or dysfunction, neurotransmitter imbalances, and genetic influences, whereas psychological and environmental models emphasize the role of environmental toxins, sociocultural contexts, disciplinary practices, early experiences, learning opportunities, and family systems. Although these factors are often described as possible "causes," they are in fact mostly risk factors and correlates that are *associated* with certain disorders—their causal role is not always clear. We return to this important distinction between correlates, risk factors, and causes in our discussion of research methods in Chapter 3.

Unlike a particular medical outcome that can be attributed to a specific injury, most forms of child psychopathology cannot be attributed to a single cause. At the risk of sounding vague, we must acknowledge that child and family disturbances result from multiple, frequently co-occurring, reciprocal, and interacting risk factors, causal events, and processes (Ge, Conger, Lorenz, Shanahan, & Elder, 1995). As we noted in the discussion of risk and resilience, contextual events, such as the family or school environment, exert considerable influence over an individual's course of development. For this reason, a given child's problems are often considered in relation to all three levels of influence—individual, family, and community—rather than being attributed to any one factor alone. Since etiology of psychological disorders is of considerable importance, we devote Chapter 2 to a description of the primary contributions derived from biological, cognitive, and environmental influences.

Assessment, Diagnosis, and Treatment

Assessment is usually an ongoing, progressively more narrow, process that helps focus attention on behaviors, patterns, and contextual factors that relate to known psychological disorders and developmental conditions. Along with a clinical description of a child's presenting problem, a careful assessment of strengths and weaknesses helps determine a diagnosis and a treatment plan. As we discuss in Chapter 4, child assessment can take many forms, but its overall purpose is to pinpoint the child's problem areas and strengths, to reduce the number of alternative explanations, and to use this information to formulate a plan for treatment. Assessment may lead to a formal diagnosis based on a classification system of mental disorders. As noted earlier, the DSM-IV diagnostic system (APA, 1994) is one of the most comprehensive systems for classifying symptoms and behavior patterns into various types of mental disorders.

Finally, we usually need to consider which treatments and prevention strategies will best match our understanding of a child's disorder. Sometimes specialized psychological treatment is unnecessary because of the likelihood that a child will outgrow the problem or the situation will change for the better. Assistance from family members or community, school, and health care services may adequately address the personal and social adjustment difficulties the child is experiencing. For other children, however, specific psychological, educational, or pharmacological interventions are critical to their developmental progress or recovery.

We will be describing general treatment issues in Chapter 4 to introduce the various approaches and considerations that apply to interventions for children and adolescents. Because psychological interventions vary considerably in relation to each disorder, however, we will describe the most recent and effective treatments for specific disorders in the context of the chapters to which they apply. This allows information on treatments and their effectiveness to be woven into our knowledge about the description and causes of the disorder. In addition to the major psychological interventions involving behavioral, educational, cognitive and affective approaches, each chapter considers biological interventions, such as medications, if they have been shown to be an effective adjunct or alternative to psychological interventions. Moreover, we describe intervention plans for each disorder, taking into account children's different individual and family situations that have a bearing on the course of their disorder.

THE SIGNIFICANCE OF CHILDREN'S MENTAL HEALTH PROBLEMS

Mankind owes to the child the best it has to give.
—United Nations Convention on
the Rights of the Child (1989)

Until very recently, children's mental health problems were the domain of folklore and unsubstantiated theories in both the popular and scientific literatures. Consider that it was only a few generations ago, in the mid-19th century, that overstimulation in the schools was seen as a cause of insanity (Makari, 1993), and only one generation ago, in the mid-20th century, that autism was believed to be caused by inadequate, uncaring parents (Bettelheim, 1967). We now recognize that mental health problems of children and adolescents are a frequently occurring and significant societal concern (Institute of Medicine, 1989). We highlight the significance of children's mental health issues by presenting our short-list of *CONCERNs*. These issues resurface throughout the text, and are intended to orient you to these major themes and our state of knowledge.

C: *Common occurrence*
Child psychopathology is a relatively common occurrence. About one in five children suffer significant developmental, emotional, and behavioral problems that affect their daily lives (Brandenburg, Friedman, & Silver, 1990; Offord, 1995). About 1 in 10 has a specific mental disorder fitting DSM-IV criteria (Boyle et al., 1987; Rutter, 1989). Many others have emerging problems that place them at risk for the later development of a psychological disorder (McDermott & Weiss, 1995).

O: *Ongoing difficulties*
Many childhood adjustment problems and disorders are ongoing. The chapters that follow make clear that a significant proportion of children do not grow out of their childhood difficulties, although the ways in which these difficulties are expressed are likely to change in both form and severity over time. Moreover, a child's developmental impairments may have a lasting negative impact on later family, occupational, and social adjustment.

N: *New pressures*
New pressures and social changes may place children at increasingly greater risk for the development of disorders at younger ages (Duncan, Brooks-Gunn, & Klebanov, 1994). Many of the stressors today are quite different from those faced by our parents and grandparents. Some have been around for generations—chronic poverty, inequality, family breakup, single parenting, and so on. Others are more recent or more visible than before, such as homelessness, adjustment problems of children in immigrant families, inadequate childcare for working parents, and conditions associated with the impact of prematurity, HIV, cocaine, and alcohol on children's growth and development (National Commission on Children, 1991). Even welcome medical advances can have a negative side. Higher rates of fetal survival have contributed to a greater number of children with behavior and learning difficulties who require specialized services at a younger age.

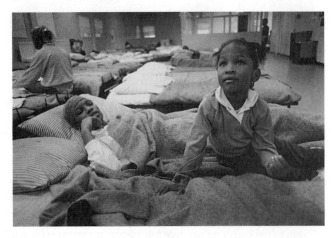

Mother and child at a shelter in Brooklyn, New York; 88% of homeless families in the United States are headed by women.

Cultural changes and pressures may be contributing to increases in childhood depression, eating disorders, child maltreatment, and other conditions that have gained considerable recognition over the last two decades. Although social changes are not necessarily bad, and in fact some have been extremely beneficial (such as greater support for preschool and head start programs), changes in family and social situations place added pressure on children to adapt to circumstances that are often outside their control.

C: *Costly outcomes*
The lifelong consequences associated with child psychopathology are exceedingly costly in terms of economic impact and human suffering. The costs are enormous with respect to demands on community resources, such as health, education, mental health, and criminal justice systems; loss in productivity; the need for repeated and long-term interventions; and the human suffering of both the afflicted children and the family and community members with whom they come into contact. Fortunately, children and youth can overcome major impediments when circumstances and opportunities promote healthy adaptation and competence (Rutter, 1987).

E: *Emergence into adolescence*
Early- to mid-adolescence is a particularly important transitional period for healthy versus problematic adjustment. Substance use, sexual behavior, violence, accidental injuries, and mental health problems are just a few of the major issues that make adolescence a particularly vulnerable period (U.S. Department of Health and Human Services, 1991). Disturbingly, mortality rates more than double between early (ages 10 to 14) and later (15 to 19) adolescence, confirming how serious these issues are (Millstein, Petersen, & Nightingale, 1993). Despite these figures, adolescents'

problems have received even less attention than those of children (Kazdin, 1993).

R: *Resources and priorities*
Lack of resources and the low priority given to children's mental health issues mean that children do not receive appropriate mental health services at the appropriate time. Societal neglect of children's mental health needs is shown by the lack of empirically supported prevention and treatment programs for many childhood disorders (Jensen et al., 1993). As a result, current services are often limited to treating only the most visible symptoms, usually in response to major crises or situations like suicide attempts or academic failure. Regrettably, this approach results in too little, too late for children and youth whose problems are not easily recognized.

N: *Neglect and abuse*
Children and adolescents are being neglected and abused at an epidemic rate worldwide (U.S. Advisory Board on Child Abuse and Neglect, 1990; World Health Organization, 1997). There are over 1 million verified reports of child abuse and neglect in the United States each year (Sedlak & Broadhurst, 1996), and many reports of "accidental" injuries to children may be the result of unreported mistreatment by parents or siblings (Peterson & Brown, 1994). In addition, phone surveys of children and youth between 10 and 16 years old estimate that over one-third (6 million) experience physical and/or sexual assaults during these ages, not only by family members but also by persons they may know from their communities and school (Boney-McCoy & Finkelhor, 1995). To no one's surprise, the staggering number of children who are adversely affected by the impact of maltreatment has psychological significance regarding their long-term adjustment at school, with peers, and in future relationships (Wekerle & Wolfe, 1996). We acknowledge this concern by devoting an entire chapter (Chapter 14) to this issue.

These concerns emerge over and over again throughout this text, as we consider the many different individual, family, social, and cultural influences that define abnormal child psychology. Because children cannot advocate on their own behalf, and their mental health needs and developmental issues differ markedly from those of adults, it is important that we keep these concerns in mind.

The remaining section of this chapter is an overview of early attempts to recognize and understand children's abnormal behavior and special needs. Familiarity with the history of attempts to understand abnormal behavior will provide a more grounded perspective on current approaches. The following three chapters discuss theo-

Table 1.2	DSM-IV Categories That Apply to Children

I. Disorders Usually First Diagnosed in Infancy, Childhood, or Adolescence

Mental Retardation (mild, moderate, severe, profound)

Learning Disorders (in reading, mathematics, and written expression)

Communication Disorders (expressive, mixed receptive-expressive, phonological, and stuttering)

Pervasive Developmental Disorders (autistic disorder, Childhood-onset schizophrenia, Rett's disorder, Asperger's disorder)

Attention Deficit and Disruptive Behavior Disorders (attention-deficit/hyperactivity, conduct, oppositional defiant)

Feeding and Eating Disorders of Infancy or Early Childhood (pica, rumination, feeding disorder of infancy or early childhood)

Elimination Disorders (encopresis, enuresis)

Other Disorders of Infancy, Childhood, or Adolescence (separation anxiety, selective mutism, reactive attachment disorder of infancy or early childhood, stereotypic movement disorder)

II. Selected Categories for Disorders of Childhood or Adolescence That Are Not Listed Separately for Children in DSM-IV

Mood Disorders (depressive disorders, bipolar disorders)

Anxiety Disorders (specific phobia, social phobia, obsessive-compulsive disorder, posttraumatic stress disorder, acute stress disorder, generalized anxiety disorder, anxiety disorder due to a general medical condition)

Eating Disorders (anorexia nervosa, bulimia nervosa)

Sleep Disorders (dyssomnias, parasomnias)

Source: Based on DSM-IV Copyright © 1994 by APA.

---

ries, causes, research, and clinical issues. Chapter 2 looks at current ways of viewing child and adolescent disorders. It includes the exciting advances made possible by new discoveries about the brain, and notes how these discoveries have become more integrated with knowledge of the biological and psychological processes affecting children's development and disorders. Chapter 3 reviews research methods with children, youth, and families that help us understand features, causes, course, and treatment methods; then Chapter 4 discusses clinical issues pertaining to children's mental health, especially current approaches to assessment, diagnosis, and treatment. Chapters 5 through 13 examine specific disorders and conditions affecting children and adolescents. Four general types of disorders are examined:

❖ *Behavioral disorders.* Chapters 5 and 6 deal with attention-deficit/hyperactivity disorder and oppositional and conduct problems, which are sometimes referred to as externalizing problems because they tend to involve conflicts with the environment.

❖ *Emotional disorders.* Chapters 7 and 8 discuss anxiety and mood disorders, which are sometimes referred to as internalizing problems because they involve internal conflicts, which are less visible to others.

❖ *Developmental and learning disorders.* Chapters 9 through 11 examine a broad range of disorders affecting children's ability to learn or perform normally, including mental retardation, pervasive devel-

opmental disorders such as autistic disorder, specific problems related to reading and mathematics, and communication difficulties. Many of these disorders constitute chronic conditions that often reflect deficits in capacity rather than performance difficulties.

❖ *Problems related to physical and mental health.* Chapters 12 and 13 discuss child and adolescent disorders that stem from medical or physical conditions that may affect children's overall psychological functioning, and vice versa. Included are such health-related problems as enuresis, sleep disorders, and chronic illness, as well as eating disorders and related conditions.

Chapter 14 is unique because it considers conditions that may be a focus of clinical attention during childhood but which are not mental disorders. This chapter, with its particular focus on children at risk, deals with the significance of child abuse and neglect on children's developmental progress and course.

The DSM-IV also groups mental disorders into categories for convenience. As shown in Table 1.2, most of the disorders addressed in this text fall under the DSM-IV section "Disorders Usually First Diagnosed in Infancy, Childhood, or Adolescence." These disorders traditionally have been thought of as first occurring in childhood, or as exclusive to childhood, so they require operational criteria that differ from those used to define disorders in adults. The second section in Table 1.2 lists several disorders that are not listed separately for children in DSM-IV. Under the current DSM-IV guidelines, diagnostic criteria for mood, anxiety, eating, and sleep disorders can apply to children as well as adults, with minor modifications. You should not try to remember all of these terms right now, but simply get a feel for the organization and coverage to follow.

HISTORICAL VIEWS AND BREAKTHROUGHS

> These were feverish, melancholy times; I cannot remember to have raised my head or seen the moon or any of the heavenly bodies; my eyes were turned downward to the broad lamplit streets and to where the trees of the garden rustled together all night in undecipherable blackness; yet the sight of the outer world refreshed and cheered me; and the whole sorrow and burden of the night was at an end with the arrival of the first of that long string of country carts that, in the dark hours of the morning, with the neighing of horses, the cracking of whips, the shouts of drivers and a hundred other wholesome noises, creaked, rolled, and pounded past my window. (Robert Louis Stevenson, describing memories of childhood illness and depression [quoted in Calder, 1980, p. 36])

In this section you will discover how society's interest in, and approaches to, problems of children and youth across recent generations have created a strong upswing in their quality of life and mental health, even though a long road still remains. Many children, especially those with special needs, fared poorly in previous societies, as they were forced to work as coal miners, field hands, or beggars. Concern about children's needs, rights, and care requires a social sensitivity and awareness that simply did not exist in a prominent, consistent manner prior to the 20th century (Aries, 1962). As you read the following historical synopsis, notice how abnormal child psychology's relatively short history has been strongly influenced by philosophical and societal changes in how children in general have been viewed and treated by adults (Borstelmann, 1983; French, 1977).

The ability of a society to help children develop normal lives and competencies requires not only medical, educational, and psychological resources, but also a social philosophy that recognizes children as persons who have a value independent of any other purpose. Although this view of children should seem self-evident to us today, valuing children as persons in their own right has not been a priority of most societies. Early writings suggest that children were considered servants of the state in the city-states of early Greece, and ancient Greek and Roman societies believed any person—young or old—with a physical or mental handicap, disability, or deformity was an economic burden and a social embar-

rassment, and thus was to be scorned, abandoned, or put to death (French, 1977).

Children's mental health problems, unlike the documented references to adult disorders, were seldom even mentioned in either professional or other forms of communication prior to the 18th century (Barlow & Durand, 1995). Some of the earliest historical interest in abnormal child behavior surfaced toward the end of the 18th century. Through the strong influence of the church, children's unusual or disturbing behaviors were attributed largely to their inherently uncivilized and provocative nature (Kanner, 1962). In fact, during this period nonsecular explanations for disordered behavior in children were rarely given serious consideration, because possession by the devil and similar forces of evil was the only explanation anyone needed (Rie, 1971). No one was too eager to challenge this view, given that they too could be seen as possessed and dealt with accordingly.

Sadly, during the 17th and 18th centuries as many as two-thirds of children died before their fifth birthday, often because there were no antibiotics or similar medications to treat deadly diseases (Zelizer, 1985). Unfortunately, many children were also subjected to harsh treatment or indifference by their parents. Acts ranging from extreme parental indifference and neglect to physical and sexual abuse of children simply went unnoticed or were considered an adult's right for educating or disciplining a child (Radbill, 1968). For many generations, the implicit societal viewpoint that children are the exclusive property and responsibility of their parents was unchallenged by any countermovement to seek more humane treatment for children who suffered from improper care. A parent's prerogative to enforce child obedience, for example, was formalized by Massachusetts' Stubborn Child Act of 1654, which permitted a parent to put "stubborn" children to death for noncompliance (fortunately, no one met this ultimate fate), and into the mid-1800s allowed children with severe developmental disabilities to be kept in cages and cellars (Donohue, Hersen, & Ammerman, 1995).

The Emergence of a Social Conscience

> If the children and youth of a nation are afforded the opportunity to develop their capacities to the fullest, if they are given the knowledge to understand the world and the wisdom to change it, then the prospects for the future are bright. In contrast, a society which neglects its children, however well it may function in other respects, risks eventual disorganization and demise. (Urie Bronfenbrenner, 1973)

Fortunately, the situation gradually improved for children and youth throughout the 19th century, and the improvement picked up speed during the latter part of

This drawing, from an 1884 *Harper's Weekly*, expresses the plight of women and children. It was decades later, however, before fundamental rights and opportunities were recognized.

the 20th century. But, until very recent changes in laws and attitudes, children (along with women, members of minority groups, and persons with special needs) were often the last to benefit from society's prosperity and the primary victims of its shortcomings. With the acuity of hindsight, we know that a philosophy of humane understanding is required before any real change occurs in how society recognizes and addresses the special needs of some of its members. In addition to humane beliefs, each society has to develop ways and means to recognize and protect the rights of individuals, especially children, in the broadest sense (U.N. Convention on the Rights of Children, 1989). An overview of some of these major developments provides important background for understanding today's approaches to children's mental health issues.

An inkling of such necessary prerequisites of a social conscience first occurred in the 17th century, when both a philosophy of humane care and institutions of social protection began to take root in Western society. One individual at the forefront of these changes was John Locke (1632–1704), a noted English philosopher and physician who influenced the beginnings of present-day attitudes and practices of childbirth and child-rearing.

Locke was a believer in individual rights, and he expressed the novel opinion that children should be raised with thought and care, instead of indifference and harsh treatment. Rather than uncivilized tyrants, he saw children as emotionally sensitive beings who should be treated with kindness and understanding, and who should be given proper educational opportunities (Illick, 1974). In his words, "the only fence [archaic use, meaning "defense"] against the world is a thorough knowledge of it."

Then, at the turn of the 19th century, one of the first documented efforts to work with a special child was undertaken by Jean-Marc Itard (1775–1838). Victor, discovered living in the woods outside Paris, was treated for his severe developmental delays by Itard, rather than being sent to an asylum (see Box 1.2). Symbolically, this undertaking launched a new era of a helping orientation toward special children, which initially focused on the care, treatment, and training of what were then termed "mental defectives."

Distinguishing Psychiatric Disorder from Mental Retardation

As the influence of Locke and others fostered the expansion of universal education throughout Europe and North America during the latter half of the 19th century, children who could not handle the demands of school became a visible and troubling group. This situation led to an important and basic distinction between persons with mental retardation ("imbeciles") and those with psychiatric, or mental, disorders ("lunatics"), although this distinction was far from clear at the time (Costello & Angold, 1995). Essentially, local governments needed to know whose responsibility it was to help children whose cognitive development appeared normal but who showed serious emotional or behavioral problems. The only previous guidance they had in distinguishing children with intellectual deficits from those with behavioral and emotional problems was derived from religious views of immoral behavior: Children who had normal cognitive abilities but who were disturbing were thought to suffer from *moral insanity*, which implied a disturbance in personality or character (Pritchard, 1837). Benjamin Rush (1745?–1813), a pioneer in psychiatry, argued that children were incapable of true adultlike insanity, because the immaturity of their developing brains prevented them from retaining the mental events that caused insanity (Rie, 1971). Consequently, the term *moral insanity* grew in acceptance as a means of accounting for nonintellectual forms of abnormal child behavior.

The implications of this basic distinction created a brief, yet significant, burst of optimism among profes-

Box 1.2

Victor of Aveyron

Victor, often referred to as the "wild boy of Aveyron," was discovered in France by hunters when he was about 11 or 12 years old, having lived alone in the woods presumably all his life. Jean-Marc Itard, a young physician at the time, believed the boy to be "mentally arrested" because of social and educational neglect, and set about to demonstrate if such retardation could be reversed. Victor—who initially was mute, walked on all fours, drank water while lying flat on the ground, and bit and scratched—became the object of popular attention as rumors spread that he had been raised by animals. He was dirty, nonverbal, incapable of attention, and insensitive to even basic sensations of hot and cold. Despite the child's appearance and behavior, Itard believed that environmental stimulation could humanize him. Itard's account of his efforts poignantly reveals the optimism, frustration, anger, hope, and despair that he experienced in working with this special child. His experiences are familiar to those of us who have undertaken a similar responsibility.

Itard used a variety of methods to bring Victor to an awareness of his sensory experiences: hot baths, massages, tickling, emotional excitement, even electric shocks. After 5 years of training by Dr. Itard, Victor had learned to identify objects, identify letters of the alphabet, comprehend many words, and apply names to objects and parts of objects. Victor also showed a preference for social life over the isolation of the wild. Despite his achievements, Itard felt his efforts had failed, because his goals of socializing the boy to make him normal were never reached. Nevertheless, the case of Victor was a landmark in the effort to assist children with special needs. For the first time, an adult had tried to really understand—feel and know—the mind and emotions of a special child, and had proved that a child with severe impairments could improve through appropriate training. This deep investment on the part of an individual in the needs and feelings of another person's child remains a key aspect of the helping orientation to this day. *Source:* Kanner, 1964.

FRONTISPIECE.

*The Wild Boy,
found in the Woods
in Aveyron.*

Printed for R.Phillips, N°71 S.ᵗ Pauls Church Yard, March.1.1802.

---

sionals (Achenbach, 1982). Concern for the plight and welfare of children with mental and behavioral disturbances began to rise in conjunction with two important sources of influence. First, advances in general medicine, physiology, and neurology led to a replacement of the moral insanity view of psychological disorders by the *organic disease model,* which placed greater emphasis on more humane forms of treatment. Second, the growing influence of the philosophies of Locke and others led to the view that children needed *moral guidance and support.* With these changing views came an increased concern for moral education, compulsory education, and improved health practices. These early efforts to assist children provided the foundation for evolving views of abnormal child behavior as resulting from combinations of biological, environmental, and psychological influences.

Early Biological Influences

The successful treatment of infectious diseases during the latter part of the 19th century strengthened the emerging belief that illness and disease, including mental illness, were biological problems. However, early attempts at biological explanations for deviant or abnormal behavior were highly biased in favor of locating the cause of the problem within the individual child or adult. The public generally distrusted and scorned persons who

Masturbatory Insanity

Today, most parents hardly balk at discovering their child engaging in some form of self-stimulation—it is considered a normal part of self-discovery and pleasant sensations. Such tolerance, however, was not always the case. In fact, children's masturbation is historically significant because it was the first "disorder" unique to children and adolescents (Rie, 1971). One hundred years ago, masturbatory insanity was a form of mental illness and, in keeping with the contemporaneous view that such problems resided within the individual, it was believed to be a very worrisome problem (Cattell, 1938; Rees, 1939; Rie, 1971; Szasz, 1970).

Society's objections to masturbation originated from religious views, which by the 18th century were augmented by the growing influence of science (Rie, 1971; Szasz, 1970). Moral convictions regarding the wrongfulness of masturbation led to a physiological explanation with severe medical ramifications, based on pseudoscientific papers such as *Onania, or the Heinous Sin of Self-Pollution* (circa 1710) (Szasz, 1970). The medical view of masturbation focused initially on adverse effects on physical health, but by the middle of the 19th century the dominant thought shifted to a focus on the presumed negative effects on mental health and nervous system functioning. With amazing speed, masturbation became the most frequently mentioned "cause" of psychopathology in children.

Interest in masturbatory insanity gradually waned toward the end of the 19th century, but the argument still remained tenable as psychoanalytic theory gained acceptance. Eventually, the notion of masturbatory insanity gave way to the concept of neurosis. Not until much later in the 20th century, however, was the misguided and illusory belief in a relationship between masturbation and mental illness dispelled. Let this example remind us of the importance of scientific skepticism in confirming or disconfirming new theories and explanations for abnormal behavior.

appeared "mad" or "possessed by the devil" and similar evil forces. The notion of masturbatory insanity (see Box 1.3) provides a good illustration of how such thinking, in the absence of objective scientific findings and without consideration of the base rate of masturbation in the general population, can lead to an explanation for abnormal behavior. It also illustrates how the prevailing political and social climate influences definitions of child psychopathology. The impact of religious thought was clearly reflected in the transformation from the moral judgment against the sins of the flesh, to the medical opinion that masturbation was harmful to one's physical health, to the psychiatric assertion that sexual overindulgence caused insanity.

In contrast to the public's general ignorance and avoidance of issues concerning persons with mental disorders that remained during the late 19th century was the Mental Hygiene Movement, which provides a benchmark of changing attitudes toward children and adults with mental disorders. In 1909 Clifford Beers, a layperson who had recovered from a severe psychosis, spearheaded efforts to change the plight of children and adults so afflicted. Believing that mental disorders were a form of disease, he criticized society's ignorance and indifference and sought to prevent mental disease by raising the standards of care and disseminating reliable information (M. Levine & A. Levine, 1992). As a result, detection and intervention methods began to flourish, based on a more tempered, yet still quite frightened and ill-informed, view of afflicted individuals.

Unfortunately, because this paradigm was based largely on a biological disease model, intervention was limited to those with the most visible and prominent disorders, such as persons with psychoses or severe mental retardation. Although developmental explanations were a part of this early view of psychopathology, they were quite narrow: The development of the disease was progressive and irreversible, tied to the development of the child only in that it manifested itself differently as the child grew, but impervious to other influences such as treatment or learning. All one could do was to prevent the most extreme manifestations by strict punishment, and to protect those not affected.

Sadly, this early educational and humane model for assisting persons with mental disorders soon returned to a custodial model during the early part of the 20th century. Once again, attitudes toward children and adults with mental or intellectual disabilities turned from cautious optimism to dire pessimism, hostility, and disdain. Children, youth, and adults with mental retardation, in particular, were blamed for crimes and social ills during the ensuing alarmist period (Achenbach, 1982). Rather than viewing knowledge as a form of protection, as Locke had argued, society returned to the view that mental illness and retardation were diseases that could spread if left unchecked. For the next two decades, many communities chose to prevent the procreation of the insane through eugenics (sterilization) and segregation (institutionalization). We return to these important developments in our discussion of the history of mental retardation in Chapter 9.

Early Psychological Influences

Today, many of us take for granted the idea that biological influences must be balanced with important developmental and environmental factors, including the family, peer group, school, and other sources of influence, in the attempt to conceptualize and understand abnormal child psychology (Fauber & Long, 1991; Kazdin, 1993; Mash & Dozois, 1996). Of course, this perception was not always the case. The long-standing, medically based view that abnormal behavior is a disorder or disease residing within the person led unfortunately to neglect of the essential role of a person's surroundings, context, and relations, and of the interactions among these variables.

The roots of psychological influences emerged early in the 20th century, when attention was drawn to the importance of recognizing major psychological disorders and formulating a taxonomy of illnesses. Such recognition allowed researchers to organize and categorize ways to identify various problems of children and adults, which gave some semblance of understanding and control. At the same time, there was concern that attempts to recognize the wide range of mental health needs of children and adults could easily backfire and lead to the neglect of persons who had more severe disorders. This shift in perspective and increase in knowledge also prompted the development of diagnostic categories, new criminal offenses, and expanded descriptions of deviant behavior, and added more comprehensive monitoring procedures for identified individuals (Costello & Angold, 1995). Two major theoretical paradigms helped shape these emerging psychological and environmental influences: psychoanalytic theory and behaviorism. We'll limit our discussion here to their historical importance, but additional content concerning their contemporary influences appears in Chapter 2's discussion of theories and causes.

Psychoanalytic Theory. In Sigmund Freud's day, near the turn of the 20th century, many child psychiatrists and psychologists had grown pessimistic about their ability to treat children's mental disorders in a fashion other than custodial or palliative. To his credit, Freud was one of the first to reject such pessimism and raise new possibilities for treatment as the roots of these disorders were traced further and further back into childhood (M. Levine & A. Levine, 1992). Although he believed that individuals have innate drives and predispositions that strongly affect their development, he also believed that experiences play a necessary role in psychopathology. For perhaps the first time, the course of mental disorders was not viewed as inevitable; children and adults could be helped if provided with the proper environment, therapy, or both.

Psychoanalytic theory significantly influenced advances in our ways of thinking about causes and treatment of mental disorders. Perhaps most important from the perspective of abnormal child psychology was that Freud was the first to give meaning to mental disorder by linking it to childhood experiences (Fonagy, Target, Steele, & Gerber, 1995). His radical theory incorporated developmental concepts into an understanding of psychopathology at a time when early childhood development was virtually ignored by mainstream child psychiatry and psychology. Rather than focusing on singular, specific causes (a hallmark of the disease model in vogue at the time), psychoanalytic theory emphasized that personality and mental health outcomes had multiple roots, and that outcomes depended to a large degree on the interaction of developmental and situational processes that change over time in unique ways (Costello & Angold, 1995). In effect, Freud's writings shifted the view of children from one of innocence or insignificance to that of human beings in turmoil, struggling to achieve control over biological needs and to make themselves acceptable to society at large through the microcosm of the family (Freud, 1930/1991).

Contributions based on Freud's theory continued to expand throughout the early part of the 20th century, as clinicians and theorists broke from some of his earlier teachings and brought new insights into the field. In recent years, however, psychoanalytic theory's approach to abnormal child psychology has had less influence on clinical practice and teaching, largely because of the popularity of the phenomenological (descriptive) approach to psychopathology, as reflected in the DSM and similar systems (Costello & Angold, 1995). Nevertheless, it is important to remember that current **nosologies** (efforts to classify psychiatric disorders into descriptive categories) are essentially nondevelopmental in their approaches. Rather than attempting, as the Freudian approach does, to describe the development of the disease in the context of the development of the individual, nosologies, such as that of the DSM-IV, attempt to find common denominators that describe the manifestations of a disorder at every age (Achenbach, 1995). Despite valid criticism and a lack of empirical validation of the content of psychoanalytic theory and its many derivatives (such as object relations theory), the idea of emphasizing the interconnection between children's normal and abnormal development retains considerable attraction as a model for abnormal child psychology (Costello & Angold, 1995).

Behaviorism. The words of John Watson, the "Father of Behaviorism," exemplify the faith some early researchers—and the public—placed in laboratory-based research on learning and behavior:

> Give me a dozen healthy infants, well-formed, and my own specified world to bring them up in and I'll guarantee to take any one at random and train him to become any type of specialist I might select—doctor, lawyer, artist, merchant-chief and, yes, even beggar-man and thief, re-

Box 1.4
Little Albert, Big Fears, and Sex in Advertising

Most of us are familiar with the story of little Albert and his fear of white rats and other white furry objects, thanks to the work of John Watson and his graduate assistant (soon to become wife) Rosalie Rayner. However, understanding the times and background of John Watson helps put these pioneering efforts in a broader historical perspective, and highlights the limited awareness and concern for values and ethics in research that existed in his day.

Watson's fascination and life dedication to the study of fears may have stemmed from his own acknowledged fear of the dark, which afflicted him throughout his adult life. His career break arrived when he was given an opportunity to create a research laboratory at Johns Hopkins University for the study of child development. Instead of conditioning rats, he could now use humans to test his emerging theories of fear conditioning. However, the only source of human subjects in his day was persons whose rights were considered insignificant or who had less than adequate powers to protect themselves, such as orphans, mental patients, and prisoners. Just as he had studied rats in their cages, Watson now studied babies in their cribs.

Clearly, his method of obtaining research subjects and experimenting with them would be highly unethical today. To demonstrate how fear might be conditioned in a baby, Watson and Rayner set out to condition fear in an 11-month-old orphan baby they named Albert B. Albert B. was given a small white rat to touch, to which he showed no fear. After this warm-up, every time the infant would reach to touch the rat, Watson would strike a steel bar with a hammer. After repeated attempts to touch the rat brought on the same shocking sounds, "the infant jumped violently, fell forward and began to whimper." The process was repeated intermittently, enough times so that eventually Albert B. would break down and cry, desperately trying to crawl away, whenever he saw the rat. Watson and Rayner had successfully conditioned the child to fear rats. They then conditioned him to fear rabbits, dogs, fur coats and—believe it or not—Santa Claus masks.

It is disconcerting that Albert B. was adopted and moved away before any deconditioning was attempted, destined to go through life with a strange set of fears he would never understand. It is ironic, moreover, that Watson went on to develop a career in advertising after he was ousted from the university as a result of concerns over his extramarital relationship with his graduate student. His brand of behaviorism, with its emphasis on the prediction and control of human behavior, met with unqualified success on Madison Avenue. As he explained, "No matter what it is, like the good naturalist you are, you must never lose sight of your experimental animal—the consumer." We can thank John B. Watson for advertising's dramatic shift in the 1930s toward creating images around any given product that exploited the sexual desires of both men and women whenever possible.

Source: Based on Karier, 1986.

---

gardless of his talents, penchants, tendencies, abilities, vocations, and race of his ancestors. (Watson, 1925, p. 82)

The development of research-based treatments for children, youth, and families can be traced to the rise of behaviorism in the early 1900s, as reflected in Pavlov's experimental research, which established the foundations for classical conditioning, and the classic studies on the conditioning and elimination of children's fears (Jones, 1924; Watson & Rayner, 1920) (see Box 1.4).

Beyond the work in their lab, the Watson household must have been an interesting place from time to time. Consider the following contrasting views and advice on raising children from one of America's first "child experts" and his wife:

From John Watson:

Never hug and kiss them, never let them sit in your lap. If you must, kiss them once on the forehead when they say goodnight. Shake hands with them in the morning (J. Watson, 1925).

From Rosalie Rayner Watson:

I cannot restrain my affection for the children completely. The respect by which I am the very worst behaviorist is because I too want to break all the rules once in a while. I love to help the children tie up their father's pajamas in knots and put hair brushes in people's bed. I like being merry and gay and having the giggles. The behaviorists think giggling is a sign of maladjustment, so when the children want to giggle I have to keep a straight face or rush them off to their rooms (R. Watson, 1930/1996).

This example and the study of Little Albert illustrate the importance of keeping a perspective on any "new" advancements and insights that at first may seem like panaceas for age-old problems. As any soiled veteran of parenting would attest, no child-rearing shortcuts or uniform solutions guide us in dealing with children's problems—raising children is part skill, part wisdom, and part luck. Nonetheless, families, communities, and societal values play a strong role in determining how successful current child-rearing philosophies are at benefiting children.

Evolving Treatment Applications

Compared with the times that followed, the period from 1930 to 1950 was a quiet time for research and treatment in abnormal child psychology, with a few reports in the 1930s describing the treatment of isolated problems such as bed-wetting (O. H. Mowrer & W. M. Mowrer, 1938), stuttering (Dunlap, 1932), and fears (Holmes, 1936; Weber, 1936). As a carryover from the 1800s, most children with intellectual or mental disorders were still institutionalized. This practice came under mounting criticism by the late 1940s, however, when studies by Renè Spitz raised serious questions about the harmful impact of institutional life on the children's growth and development (Spitz, 1945). He discovered that infants raised in institutions without adult physical contact and stimulation developed severe physical and emotional problems. Efforts were undertaken to close institutions and place dependent and difficult children in foster family homes or group homes. Within a 20-year period, from 1945 to 1965, there was a rapid decline in the number of children in institutions, while the number of children in foster family homes and group homes increased.

During the 1950s and early 1960s, behavior therapy emerged as a systematic approach to the treatment of child and family disorders. The therapy was based on operant and classical conditioning principles established through laboratory work with animals (see Chapter 2). In their early form, these laboratory-based techniques to modify undesirable behaviors and shape adaptive abilities stood in stark contrast to the dominant psychoanalytic approaches, which stressed resolution of internal conflicts and unconscious motives. Behavior therapy focussed initially on children with mental retardation or severe disturbances, for whom psychoanalytic practices were perceived as being ineffective or inappropriate. Much of this work took place in institutions or classroom settings that were thought to provide the kind of environmental control needed to change behavior effectively.

Over the last two decades, treatment approaches based on expanding research and clinical knowledge of children's behavioral, cognitive, and emotional development have grown tremendously in terms of both their sophistication and their breadth. Interventions today are often planned by combining the most effective approaches to particular problems in an ongoing, developmentally sensitive manner (Kazdin, 1993). Behavioral methods, for example, may be very useful for teaching parents of a young, difficult child ways to encourage desirable behavior. Once the child is a bit older, however, he or she may profit from cognitive-behavioral methods that address the child's manner of processing social information, such as making friends and avoiding conflicts. Throughout this text, treatment approaches are presented as an integral part of understanding the nature and course of child and adolescent disorders.

As you begin your journey into the field of abnormal child psychology, keep in mind that the threats facing children today—child poverty, chronic illness, maltreatment, and indifference—are no less significant than those of the past, although they sometimes fail to arouse the indignation of society to the extent that major changes are implemented and maintained. Even in a world that has outlawed child labor, child abuse, and many other forms of actual and potential harm, we have only recently begun to recognize the profound importance of the quality of the early childhood environment on children's health, well-being, and competence. Fortunately, it is unlikely that children and youth will ever again be seen as insignificant, costly burdens on society in the mainstream of North American culture. As each chapter in this text indicates, efforts aimed at change in policies and programs directed toward children and youth are gaining momentum.

SUMMARY

Introduction to Abnormal Child Psychology

1. The field of abnormal child psychology has grown considerably in the past two decades, leading to a better understanding of childhood disorders and to more effective intervention and prevention programs.

2. Many childhood problems have lifelong consequences for the child and for society.

3. Abnormal child psychology involves the study of both normal and abnormal development because they inform one another.

What Is Abnormal Child Behavior?

4. Defining a psychological disorder involves agreement as to particular patterns of behavioral, cognitive, and physical symptoms shown by an individual.

5. Because of children's dependency on others, a child's psychological problems need to be considered in terms of relationships, rather than as problems contained solely within the child.

6. Terms used to describe abnormal behavior are not meant to be used as labels to describe people.

7. Defining abnormal behavior requires judgment concerning the degree to which a person's behavior

is maladaptive or harmful, as well as dysfunctional or impaired.

8. Diversity in how children acquire psychological strengths and weaknesses is a hallmark of abnormal child psychology. The many contributors to abnormal behavior may vary within and between individuals with similar disorders.

9. Studies of risk and resilience in children indicate that children's individual, family, and community circumstances shape their development in a reciprocal, interactive manner.

Describing Psychological Disorders of Childhood and Adolescence

10. The study of psychological disorders involves attempts to describe the presenting problems and abilities, to understand contributing causes, and to treat or prevent them.

11. Girls and boys and younger and older children express psychological adjustment problems differently. Such differences are primarily due to an interaction between biological differences, maturation, and socialization practices.

The Significance of Children's Mental Health Problems

12. Mental health problems of children and adolescents have become recognized as significant societal concerns. We summed these CONCERNs in terms of their: Common occurrence, Ongoing difficulties, New pressures, Costly outcomes, Emergence into adolescence, Resources, and Neglect and abuse.

Historical Views and Breakthroughs

13. Greater attention to the problems of children and youth in recent years has created a strong upswing in their quality of life and mental health. This resulted from greater societal recognition and sensitivity to children's special status and needs since the turn of the 20th century.

14. Early biological explanations for abnormal child behavior favored locating the cause of the problem within the individual, which sometimes led to overly simplistic or inaccurate beliefs about causes of such behavior.

15. Early psychological approaches attempted to integrate basic knowledge of innate processes with environmental conditions that shape behavior, emotions, and cognitions.

KEY TERMS

child psychopathology, 3
abnormal child psychology, 3
developmental psychopathology, 3
psychological disorder, 4
competence, 7
developmental tasks, 7
developmental pathways, 8
multifinality, 8
equifinality, 8
risk, 9
resilience, 10
assessment, 12
taxonomy, 12
clinical description, 12
diagnosis, 12
comorbidity, 13
developmental course, 15
interdisciplinary perspective, 16
etiology, 16
nosologies, 24

Theories and Causes of Abnormal Development

Canst thou not minister to a mind diseased,
Pluck from the memory a rooted sorrow,
Raze out the written troubles of the brain,
And with some sweet oblivious antidote
Cleanse the fraught bosom of that perilous stuff
Which weighs upon the heart?

—William Shakespeare (1564–1616)

As Macbeth laments, desire to understand the "troubles of the brain" is perhaps as old as humankind. It was not until the 20th century, however, that considerable theoretical development led to advances in knowledge of the causes of abnormal behavior. In this chapter we consider theories and findings on genetic and neurobiological factors; psychological influences, such as the role of cognitive and emotional processes; and environmental influences, such as family patterns and cultural norms, that shape the child's ongoing development in many different ways. Some of these influences (such as biological factors) are contained within the child, whereas many others lie at various distances from the child's immediate surroundings. We will see how these various causal influences contribute to a better understanding of abnormal child development and how they are conceptually related to one another. Let's begin by considering Jake's situation:

Jake: Not Keeping Up

Jake was almost 12 years old when he was referred to me because of academic problems. Since the fourth grade he had been performing well below average in his academic work, had difficulty concentrating, and was considered to be "too quiet and nervous" in class. For the last four summers he took summer classes to improve his reading, which was currently at about the third-grade level. Nonetheless, his parents received a letter from the school saying he likely would not progress to the next grade if things didn't improve. Everyone seemed angry at Jake for not keeping up.

When I met with Jake, his version of his school problems was short and to the point: "It's the teachers," he said, as he looked at the floor and squirmed in his seat. "How am I expected to learn anything when they yell at you? When I told my English teacher that I hadn't finished reading my book for class, he said I take too long 'cuz my mind wanders too much. How am I expected to learn when they think I'm dumb?" After further discussion, Jake summed up his view of the problem in a quiet, sullen voice: "I know I'll never get anywhere with the brain I've got. I can't figure stuff out very fast, and the teachers aren't much help. Just thinking about school makes me jittery."

Jake's mother and father met with me separately and were quick to add their own opinion about why their son didn't do well in school. His mother admitted that she becomes aggravated and starts to yell when Jake says he doesn't want to go to school or can't do his schoolwork, but she didn't think this was an issue. She quickly added, "I've read about learning disabilities and I think he's got one. He can't control his mind enough to center on anything. He's scared to go to school, and avoids homework as if his life depended on it." By the end of the interview it was evident that Jake's parents were angry at him. They felt Jake blamed his teachers for his own lack of effort, and that he should be in a special classroom and maybe given medications to calm him down so he wouldn't worry so much about school.

Jake's situation and his parents' complaints raise important issues. Could Jake have mild mental retardation that impairs his learning? Is Jake's mother right about his having a learning disability? Does Jake have a specific communication or learning problem unrelated to mental retardation that affects his schoolwork? Perhaps his school and family environment have contributed to his learning difficulties and fear of school. Have his parents and teachers expected him to fail? Has he been given much assistance? Has he been abused or neglected at home?

WHAT CAUSED JAKE'S PROBLEMS?

Suppose you were asked to interview Jake, his teachers, and his parents to find out what was going on with his schoolwork. How would you go about this task? What information do you feel would be essential to know, and what plan might you follow to organize and explore the many possible reasons for his problem? Most likely, you would form a theory in your mind that would assist you in determining what to ask and why. At first, your theory might be very basic and unrefined, such as, "Jake's problem in school might be connected to the negative comments and pressure he is getting from his parents and teacher." As you proceed, your theory about Jake's problem would likely expand and become more detailed, allowing you to probe particular questions with greater precision.

Let's briefly consider possible causes of Jake's behavior:

1. *Biological influences.* Because we know little about Jake's early development, we might conduct an assessment, and ask his mother about her prenatal history, including major illnesses, injuries, or such circumstances as marital problems or undue stress that might have affected her pregnancy. Jake's problems also reflect a tendency toward *behavioral inhibition,* meaning that he may approach new or challenging situations with greater apprehension and fear than other children. Behavioral inhibition, as well as other early temperament styles, is often noticeable from birth and is sometimes associated with problems like Jake's later on (Biederman et al., 1993).

Children with fears and anxiety, which are affected by levels of stress hormones circulating in the body, are more likely to have parents who had similar problems when they were children. Jake may have inherited a tendency to respond to his environment with heightened arousal or sensitivity. Alternatively, his early neurological development and the patterns of connections established within his brain may have been influenced by the child-rearing styles used by his parents when he was an infant (Dawson, Hessl, & Frey, 1994). These early patterns, in turn, can influence how Jake approaches new tasks, reacts to criticism, or relates to others. One further possibility is that Jake may have inherited a gene or genes that influence his phonological awareness—that is, his ability to recognize and process all the phonemes (the individual sounds) of his native language (discussed in Chapter 11).

2. *Behavioral and cognitive influences.* Jake had been performing below level in reading for some time. Using our knowledge of learning principles, we might investigate Jake's current situation from the perspective of events that elicit fear or avoidance and events that maintain such avoidance by reducing unpleasant reactions. Jake's lack of progress may be a function of punitive events at school or home—for example, being criticized by his parents or singled out by his teacher.

Without undue concern about how his early failure experiences might have led to his initial fear of school, we might take a behavioral approach to Jake's problem and try to manipulate aspects of his environment, such as teacher or parental attention for his gradual efforts to do his schoolwork, to see what effect this approach has on his school performance and avoidance. We might also consider other aspects of his school environment that may make him fearful, such as teasing or rejection by peers. By observing Jake at school, and narrowing down the list of possible events that may contribute to his fears, we can begin to develop hypotheses about Jake's learning history and, most importantly, possible ways to remediate the problem. One way might be to change the *contingencies* between his behavior and its consequences, such as increasing the likelihood of reinforcement contingent on Jake's efforts to complete his schoolwork.

Cognitive influences, such as a person's interpretation of events, are also important to consider. How does Jake view the situation, and does his view reflect the situation accurately? Children with fears and worries sometimes develop a belief system that can be self-defeating, leading them to believe that they will fail no matter what they try (Kendall &

MacDonald, 1993). Jake has experienced failure in relation to reading and other school-related events, and it is plausible that he anticipates further struggles with schoolwork and other children's attitudes toward him. His own words are quite clear in this respect: "How am I expected to learn when they think I'm dumb?" "I know I'll never get anywhere with the brain I've got." "Just thinking about school makes me jittery." Such thoughts, of course, only tend to make him more anxious and more likely to want to avoid school as much as possible. In short, his expectations about his performance at school could be heavily laden with fear of failure or ridicule, issues that certainly warrant attention. Children's self-expressions and other cognitions offer a unique window on their inner world, which may provide clues that we missed when observing their actions.

3. *Emotional and relationship influences.* Children like Jake not only think and behave in ways that provide clues to their distress, but also show various emotional signals, which at first are not all that easy to recognize. Emotional expression offers another unique window for viewing Jake's inner world, especially his emotional reactions to challenging situations like reading. Consider this possibility: As Jake approaches his reading assignment or thinks about returning to school the next morning, he is overwhelmed by a sense of fear, bordering on panic. His heart races, his breathing quickens, and his thoughts turn to ways to escape from this dreaded situation as quickly as possible. Preoccupied by such feelings and worry, his concentration further declines.

Jake's inability to regulate his emotions, such as the feelings of arousal, distress, or agitation that may surface without warning, is a key element in describing his problem, but we still have not determined how this might have originated. Emotional reactivity and expression, such as distress or comfort, are the ways infants and young children first communicate with the world around them, and their ability to regulate these emotions in an adaptive fashion is a critical aspect of their early relationships with caregivers (Cicchetti, Ackerman, & Izard, 1995). Emotions can be powerful events, demanding that the child find ways to reduce their force. The most adaptive way, of course, is to seek comfort from a care-giver, which gradually helps the child learn his or her own ways of self-regulation. By extension, Jake's school refusal or phobia could have emerged from his anxiety about his mother's availability (probably at a younger age), which has grown into a more pronounced and generalized insecurity (Bowlby, 1973).

4. *Family and social influences.* An understanding of the possible causes of Jake's difficulties would be incomplete without consideration of his larger social network, family and peer relationships, and community context. Although his early relationship with his parents may have contributed to a lessened ability to regulate his emotions adaptively, his current relationships with his teachers, peers, and family members offer further clues. At the family level, how sensitive are his parents to recognizing his special limitations, and how willing are they to teach him alternative strategies? His mother has high hopes and expectations for her child, as well as a life and problems of her own (including a job). Even though she wants only what's best for Jake, her behavior, understandable as it is, may still be a problem. Her pointed statement, "I've read about learning disabilities and I think he's got one," suggests that she dismisses the problem by labeling it as "his" problem. Neither parent gave the impression that they were open to considering other possible explanations. Furthermore, his mother admitted to becoming exasperated and yelling at Jake. What effect might this have on his tenuous self-concept and his attempts to regulate his fear and arousal?

All children, not just those with problems, require a parenting style that is sensitive to their unique needs and abilities, and that places appropriate limits on them to help them develop self-control (Maccoby & Martin, 1983). Significant adults both within Jake's family and at school were not responding to him in a very sensitive manner, so it's not surprising that Jake's behavior grew worse over time. Finally, for proper development, children require a basic quality of life that includes a safe community, good schools, proper health and nutrition, access to friends their own age, and opportunities to develop close relationships with extended family and members of their community. These opportunities and necessities, which are in the background of every child's developmental profile, can emerge as very significant issues for some children, such as those undergoing parental divorce or living in poverty.

THE ROLE OF THEORY

Defining what is abnormal within the context of children's ongoing adaptation and development, and sorting out the most likely causes of identified problems, is a complicated process. To a much greater extent than the study of abnormal adult behavior, the study of abnormal *child* behavior requires an appreciation of developmental processes as well as individual and situational events that can have a major bearing on the course and direction a particular child follows. Studying abnormal development informs our theories of normal development, and vice versa. Additionally, very few simple or unidimensional cause-and-effect relationships exist.

Most clinical as well as research activity begins with a theoretical formulation for guidance and information. Theory is essentially a language of science that allows us to assemble and communicate existing knowledge more comprehensively. A theory permits us to make educated guesses and predictions about behavior based on samples of knowledge, moving us forward to explore these possible explanations. Like a treasure map that provides clues and signposts, a theory offers some basic guidance for our pursuit of causal explanations. Knowledge, skill, and experience must be added to bring these theoretical clues to life.

Three central issues (raised in Chapter 1) help focus our definition and understanding of abnormal behavior. First is the importance of studying both normal and abnormal development, since they are highly related to one another. Second is the need to consider *context* in determining the expression and outcome of childhood disorders. In Jake's case, hearing his perspective on his reading problem and learning that he was feeling pressure from both his parents and teachers was informative. Third is the realization that behavior is multiply determined. Seldom in abnormal child psychology does a single event or factor directly cause a particular outcome; instead, behavior is a function of multiple and interacting events and processes that influence development. Likewise, children's ongoing development has a reciprocal influence on their environment. This chapter builds on these three fundamental issues by considering different theoretical perspectives that help explain the complex connections between possible causes and outcomes.

Developmental Considerations

As we have stated, relationships lie at the interface between biological predispositions and environmental influences. Children's successful adaptation, and perhaps their very survival, depend on relationships. Infants and children are keenly attuned to the cues they receive from care-givers, and they are especially sensitive to signs of indifference. Responsive, sensitive parents inspire trust in their children, giving rise to secure attachment. Insensitive or withdrawn parents, on the other hand, can foster insecure attachments that affect future relationship formation and regulation in significant ways. Thus, a relationship, or attachment, with a parent or other care-giver is as essential to normal child development as learning to walk and talk. If the relationship with the attachment figure has been consistent and reliable, children are able to regulate their emotions and cope with

stress more effectively. Conversely, lack of such a relationship creates the breeding ground for a number of stress-related disorders.

Even though children's psychological disorders have very different symptoms and causes, they share a common ground: They are an indication of **adaptational failure** in one or more areas of development (Sroufe & Rutter, 1984). In other words, at the broadest level, children with psychological disorders deviate from others their own age on some aspect of normal development, or they fail to master or progress in accomplishing developmental milestones (Loeber, 1991). Again, such failure or deviation is rarely due to a single cause, but more typically results from an ongoing interaction between individual development and environmental conditions.

The causes and outcomes of abnormal child behavior operate in dynamic and interactive ways over time, making them a challenge to disentangle. Designating a specific factor, like Jake's reading problem, as a cause or an outcome of a particular disorder usually reflects the point at which we take notice of the problem. His reading problem, for example, may be viewed as a disorder in its own right (such as a learning disorder in reading), the cause of his other difficulties (such as poor study habits and oppositional behavior), or the outcome of some other condition or disorder, such as a communication disorder.

Developmental Psychopathology Framework

The **developmental psychopathology** perspective provides a useful framework for organizing the study of abnormal child psychology around milestones and sequences in physical, cognitive, social-emotional, and educational development. We adopt this perspective as an organizing framework to describe this dynamic, multidimensional process leading to abnormal outcomes in development (Mash & Dozois, 1996). This framework emphasizes the role of developmental processes, the importance of context, and the influence of multiple and interacting events in shaping adaptive and maladaptive development.

Essentially, this perspective is a way of integrating different approaches around a common core of phenomena and questions. For this reason, it is viewed as a **macroparadigm** (*macro,* "broad or global"; *paradigm,* "philosophical approach or framework for studying phenomena"), meaning that it serves to coordinate other paradigms that deal with particular subsets of variables, methods, and explanations (Lewis, 1990; Sroufe & Rutter, 1984). Figure 2.1 illustrates relations between developmental psychopathology viewed as a macroparadigm and relevant microparadigms and theories. A developmental psychopathology perspective does not

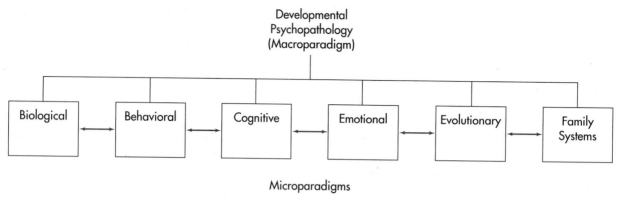

FIGURE 2.1 Developmental psychopathology as a macroparadigm. (Based on Achenbach, 1990)

replace particular theories, but rather is intended to sharpen our awareness of connections among phenomena that might otherwise seem unrelated (Achenbach, 1990).

A central tenet of developmental psychopathology states that to understand maladaptive behavior adequately, one needs to view it in relation to what may be considered normative for a given period of development (Edelbrock, 1984). Its main focus is to highlight developmental processes and how they function by looking at extremes and variations in developmental outcome (Cicchetti & Richters, 1993). In so doing, it emphasizes the importance and complexity of family, social, and cultural factors in predicting and understanding developmental changes (Lewis, 1990). It draws on knowledge from several disciplines, including psychology, psychiatry, sociology, and neuroscience, and integrates this knowledge within a developmental framework. Throughout each chapter it adds developmental relevance and richness to categorically based DSM-IV disorders.

Organization of Development. Developmental psychopathology assumes that change and reorganization are fundamental aspects of biological and behavioral systems (Sroufe & Rutter, 1984). This viewpoint looks closely at the psychological processes that may explain how these various systems influence each other. In attempting to understand abnormal development, we may choose to focus on any or all aspects of this organizational process. **Organization of development** means that early patterns of adaptation, such as infant eye contact and speech sounds, evolve over time and transform into higher-order functions, like speech and language (Carlson & Sroufe, 1995), in a structured fashion. That is, prior patterns of adaptation are incorporated into successive reorganizations at subsequent periods of development, much like toddlers learn to

make certain speech sounds before they develop the ability to use language.

An organizational view of development implies an active, dynamic process of continual change and transformation. As the child's biological abilities unfold during each new stage of development, they interact with environmental factors to direct and redirect the course of development (Cicchetti, 1993). Because development is organized, **sensitive periods** play a meaningful role in any discussion of normal and abnormal behavior. Sensitive periods are windows of time during which environmental influences on development are enhanced (Bornstein, 1989). Infants, for example, are highly sensitive to emotional cues and proximity to their care-givers, which assists them in developing secure attachments. Toddlers are sensitive to the basic sounds of language, which helps them distinguish these sounds and combine them to form words. Sensitive periods imply enhanced opportunities to learn, but not the only opportunities; change can take place at other times. Human development is a process of increasing differentiation and integration, more like a network of interconnecting pathways than a straight line.

Typical and Atypical Changes. Guidelines for the typical sequence of development across several important dimensions are helpful, but we must keep in mind that age in years is an arbitrary way to segment sequences of development that are basically continuous. Figure 2.2 presents an overview of developmental periods by age. It gives examples of normal achievements for each period, as well as behavior problems most often reported in general population samples and the clinical disorders that typically become evident at each period. You may find yourself turning back to this table to reorient yourself to children's normal and abnormal development during subsequent chapters.

Because we can seldom pinpoint a singular or an initial cause for a particular disorder, we seek to clarify

Approximate Age	Normal Achievements	Areas of Common Behavior Problems	Clinical Disorders
0–2	Eating, sleeping, attachment	Stubbornness, temper, toileting	Mental retardation, feeding disorders, autistic disorder
2–5	Language, toileting, self-care skills, self-control, peer relationships	Arguing, demanding attention, disobedience, fears, overactivity, resisting bedtime	Speech and language disorders, problems stemming from child abuse and neglect, some anxiety disorders, such as phobias
6–11	Academic skills and rules, rule-governed games, simple responsibilities	Arguing, inability to concentrate, self-consciousness, showing off	ADHD, learning disorders, school phobia, conduct problems
12–20	Relations with opposite sex, personal identity, separation from family, increased responsibilities	Arguing, bragging	Anorexia, bulimia, delinquency, suicide attempts, drug and alcohol abuse, schizophrenia, depression

FIGURE 2.2 A developmental overview. (Based on Achenbach, 1982)

the role of different biological and environmental factors as they interact with one another and form new behaviors. This task requires sensitivity to developmental continuities and discontinuities, developmental pathways, coexisting conditions, and the larger context in which the behavior occurs. The attempt to understand the seemingly endless possible causes that influence children's abnormal development is made easier by the fact that children's development, both normal and abnormal, generally proceeds in an *organized, hierarchical* manner (Carlson & Sroufe, 1995; Cicchetti & Tucker, 1994). Simply stated, this means that a child's current abilities or limitations are influenced by his or her prior accomplishments, in much the same way as your progress through trigonometry or calculus depends upon the command of arithmetic you acquired in grade school. As children develop greater abilities or show signs of adaptational failure, these changes in turn influence their further developmental success or failure. Studying abnormal child behavior within a developmental framework, such as developmental psychopathology, fosters an understanding of the interactive, progressive nature of children's abilities and difficulties.

THEORETICAL FOUNDATIONS

> To be a real philosopher all that is necessary is to hate someone else's type of thinking.
> —William James (1842–1910)

Ever since Freud's prominent influence during the early part of the 20th century, we have suspected that some children may be prone to develop psychological disorders or adjustment problems as a result of the powerful influence of negative early experiences. However, determining whether one's life course is set from early childhood or whether adaptation continues over time involves more than a simple answer. We have to formulate theoretical models and painstakingly test their assumptions over the course of development, involving children both with and without specific disorders.

Numerous theoretical models have been proposed

to explain and treat children's psychological disorders, although most of the theories have not been substantiated or even tested (Kazdin, 1988). Until recently, most models focused on single explanations that failed to consider other influences and their interactions. Such one-dimensional models do not capture the complexities of child psychopathology that are increasingly evident from research (Kazdin & Kagan, 1994). The alternative to single-factor explanations, of course, is more complex. It involves consideration of multiple causes that can interact in various ways to affect normal and abnormal development. Keeping in mind this central theme of *multiple, interactive causes* will help you grasp the complexity of each disorder discussed throughout this text.

Even models that consider more than one primary cause are sometimes limited by the boundaries of their own discipline or orientation. Biological explanations, for instance, emphasize genetic mutations, neuroanatomy, and neurobiological mechanisms as factors contributing to psychopathology; similarly, psychological explanations emphasize such causal factors as excessive, inadequate, or maladaptive reinforcement and/or learning histories. Both of these models are multicausal and distinctive in terms of the relative importance each attaches to certain events and processes, yet each is restricted in its ability to explain abnormal behavior to the extent that it fails to incorporate important components of other models. Fortunately, such disciplinary boundaries are gradually diminishing, as different perspectives take into account important variables derived from other models. For example, biological influences are often taken into account when explaining how psychological factors, like behavior or cognition, interact over time and result in a psychological disorder.

Underlying Assumptions about Abnormal Development

Every step in the process of understanding children's disorders is influenced by the clinician's or researcher's theory and preconceptions (Maxwell & Delaney, 1990). While overrelying on a grand theory or explanatory model can lead to inaccurate conclusions, gathering data without theoretical guidance and hypotheses can be meaningless (Rutter & Garmezy, 1983). The value of theory lies not just in providing answers, but also in raising new questions and looking at familiar problems in different ways.

Theory, research, and practice in abnormal child psychology all require an understanding of the assumptions underlying work in this area. Let's look at three prominent assumptions and how they have shaped our approach to abnormal child psychology.

Abnormal Development Is Multiply Determined. Our first underlying assumption is that abnormal child behavior is *multiply determined*. This means that we have to look beyond the child's current symptoms and consider developmental pathways and interacting events that, over time, contribute to the expression of a particular disorder.

Let's return to Jake's problems to illustrate this assumption. One way to look at Jake's problems is to say that he lacks motivation. Although it is a reasonable explanation, this one-dimensional causal model, which attempts to trace the origins of Jake's reading difficulty to a single underlying cause, is probably too simplistic. On the one hand, such a simplification is understandable, because scientific goals emphasize the need to simplify variables and control for factors other than those of interest to our theory (Kazdin & Kagan, 1994). On the other hand, focusing on one primary explanation, such as lack of motivation, rather than identifying and allowing for several possible explanations for Jake's reading problem (such as genetic factors, his reinforcement history, and peer problems) fails to consider the concept of developmental pathways (discussed in Chapter 1). That is, a particular problem or disorder may stem from a variety of causes, and similar risk factors may lead to very different outcomes.

Another way to view Jake's difficulties, and the one we emphasize here, takes into account *multiple dimensions,* including his developmental profile and abilities, his home and school environment, and the ongoing, dynamic interactions between these factors. Addressing Jake's reading problem from such a multidimensional perspective, we would first assess his current abilities, using multiple sources of data on his functioning in different settings. Even if we were interested only in his reading ability, we would consider a wide range of characteristics besides those that we initially believe to be signs of reading problems. Otherwise, our assumptions about the nature of reading problems might prevent us from considering other explanations. Could Jake's mother's criticism and yelling affect his concentration or self-esteem? Is Jake different from other children in terms of his ability to recognize language sounds from written words? These are some of the questions we would want to answer through careful observation and assessment, using a theoretically guided decision-making strategy.

The Child and Environment Are Interdependent. Our second assumption extends the influence of multiple causes by stressing how the child and environment are **interdependent**. Rather than separating environmental and child influences into discrete categories, this concept appreciates how nature and nurture work together and are, in fact, interconnected. Departing

Table 2.1 Passive and Active Roles of the Child and the Environment

	Passive Child	Active Child
Passive environment	**I. Passive child, passive environment** Children passively receive information from their world. Much of behavior is innately programmed.	**II. Constructivist** Child's reality is socially and cognitively constructed, and follows predictable stages of development.
Active environment	**III. Behavioral** Behavior is a function of environmental contingencies that shape and direct development.	**IV. Transactional** Normal and abnormal development emerges from the dynamic interaction of child and environmental factors. Child and environment are interdependent.

from the tradition of viewing the environment as acting upon the child to cause changes in development, this notion argues that children also influence their own environment. In effect, different children elicit different reactions from the same environment. Likewise, different environments, such as home or school, elicit different reactions from the same child. This *dynamic* interaction, a process referred to as **transaction** (Sameroff, 1995), means that the child and the environment both contribute to the expression of a disorder, and one cannot be readily separated from the other.

This assumption of interdependence takes on more significance when we consider how it emerged from other alternatives. Theoretical models of abnormal child psychology have varied according to whether the roles of the child and the environment are viewed as passive or active (Lewis, 1990; Sameroff, 1993). The four possible combinations of these roles are shown in Table 2.1. The first quadrant—the passive-child/passive-environment view—originated from the philosophical ideas of John Locke (1632–1704), who argued that the environment does not actively influence children's behavior; rather, children receive information from their world in a passive, absorbent manner. Although this view currently receives little attention, it earned its place in history as an early attempt to consider how children adapt to their environment.

A second view is that children may be active and the environment more or less passive. Constructivist theories, such as Piaget's, are based on this view, since they regard the child's reality as socially and cognitively constructed. The third, behavioral, view emphasizes an active environment, with children being more passive recipients of external influences. In their initial enthusiasm, early behaviorists argued that behavior is strictly a function of the contingencies of reinforcement (Lewis, 1990). The Watsonian assertion that, given enough time and control over the environment, one could turn a child into a thief, a doctor, or any other outcome illustrates this position.

The fourth view, the one emphasized in this text, regards both children and the environment as *active contributors* to adaptive and maladaptive behavior. This view is the one that most persons who know children best—parents, teachers, child care workers, and others—would probably agree makes the most sense: Children act upon their environment, and their environment acts upon them. According to this transactional perspective, children's psychological disorders do not reside within the child, nor are they due solely to environmental causes. They most often emerge from a combination of both factors, which interact in ways that follow general laws of organized development.

A basic example of this transactional process as applied to infants and toddlers is the goodness-of-fit model, shown in Figure 2.3 (Thomas & Chess, 1977). Consider the case of an infant girl who is born with a difficult temperament, which involves fussiness and crying. How well does this infant's temperament match her environment, and vice versa? Figure 2.3(a) illustrates a good match between infant and parent, in which her initial fussiness is met with maternal soothing and proper

Children's comfort with their environment is shown by their actions.

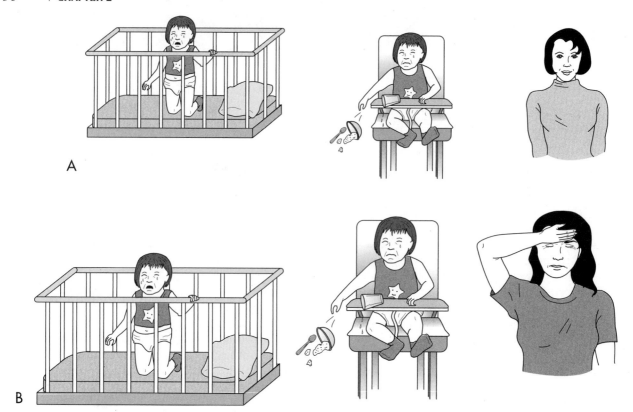

FIGURE 2.3 (A) The child's actions or behavior fit within the mother's (or father's) tolerance and coping levels. (B) The child's behaviors and actions exceed the parent's coping levels and get blown out of proportion.

care. Such care-giving, in turn, helps the infant regulate her emotions more easily. As she becomes more calm and pleasant to be around, her mother and others will likely respond with even more attention and nurturance. A transaction has occurred, which has led to a positive outcome. Now consider this same fussy infant with a different parent, illustrated in Figure 2.3(b) as a poor fit. This mother feels tense whenever her daughter is fussy and thinks her infant is being fussy purposefully rather than, say, because of some discomfort. Can you see how this transaction can lead to deviant child outcomes, if the mother responds with angry retaliation rather than loving care (Brazelton & Cramer, 1990)? Box 2.1 offers another example of a transactional process, which contributes to a child's psychological disorder over time.

Over the past two decades or so, theories of abnormal child psychology have shifted more toward the integration of divergent theoretical foundations under the active-child/active-environment position. This trend is reflected in the emergence of integrative theoretical paradigms such as developmental psychopathology, and the increased use of research designs incorporating a larger number of variables that influence one another.

Although a transactional view considers general principles of development that apply to all children, it is also sensitive to unique individual circumstances, say, in the child's family or in her biological makeup, that influence or alter typical outcomes. Learning about such deviations from the norm, of course, is what this textbook is all about.

Abnormal Development Involves Continuities and Discontinuities. Think for a moment about how Jake's various problems might have begun and how they might change or even disappear over time. Might his current problems be connected to his earlier difficulties, say, in reading? Are his current problems qualitatively different from those he had when younger, since today his problems include avoiding school and homework?

In the real world few psychological disorders or impairments suddenly emerge without at least some warning signs or connections to earlier developmental issues. This connection is readily apparent, for example, in early-onset conduct disorder, where parents and other adults often see troublesome behaviors early on that

Box 2.1

Explaining Causation: It's Not That Simple

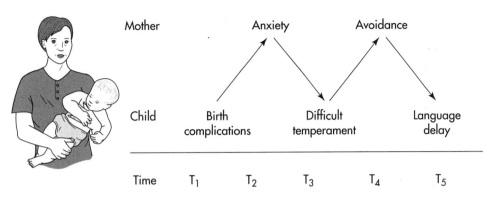

Transactional process leading from birth complications to language delays. (Sameroff, 1995)

Consider how a child's language delay may result from the interplay of child and environment over time, as shown in the accompanying figure. Complicated childbirth may have made an otherwise calm mother worried about her new role and her child's health. The mother's anxiety during the child's first few months of life may cause her to be less sensitive and nurturant toward her infant. In response to such inconsistent or insensitive child care, the infant may develop some irregularities in sleeping and feeding patterns, which give the appearance of a difficult temperament. This difficult temperament decreases the mother's pleasure and enjoyment of her infant, so she tends to spend less time with her child. If care-givers do not actively interact with their child and, especially, if they don't speak clearly and appropriately,

the youngster falls behind in language development, resulting in a diagnosis of language delay.

What caused the child's language delay? A complicated childbirth, the mother's anxiety, the child's difficult temperament, or the mother's avoidance of social interaction? Too often we select the cause that is closest in time to when the disorder was discovered (which, in this case, would be the mother's avoidance of her child), but this clearly oversimplifies a complex developmental sequence. From a prevention and early-intervention standpoint, efforts to assist this mother and child can be applied at any of the points along this sequence, with some degree of benefit. However, to be of most benefit, intervention must be sensitive not only to the presenting problems but to their developmental history as well.

---

continue in some form or another into childhood and adolescence (McGee, Freehan, Williams, & Anderson, 1992). However, whether some forms of abnormal child development are continuous or discontinuous across childhood, adolescence, and adulthood, in either a consistent or transformed manner, is a critical issue (M. Rutter & M. Rutter, 1993). **Continuity** implies that normal and abnormal developmental changes are gradual and *quantitative,* whereas **discontinuity** implies that such changes are more abrupt and *qualitative* (see Figure 2.4). The theoretical position that children pass through developmental stages, such as those described in Piaget's and Erickson's models, is illustrative of discontinuity in explaining normal development. Each stage is considered a distinct phase of life marked by a particular set of abilities, emotions, motives, or behaviors that form a coherent pattern. The underlying assumption is that each stage is qualitatively different from the stage pre-

ceding or following it. In contrast, continuity theorists argue that development is an additive, ongoing process.

The concepts of continuity and discontinuity apply to the understanding of abnormal as well as normal development. For example, continuity is well supported for early-onset conduct disorders in boys (McGee et al., 1992). However, continuity does not mean that identical symptoms remain over time; continuity over time for *patterns of behavior,* rather than for specific symptoms, is the norm. Although behavior problems in boys are stable over time, the ways in which they are expressed are likely to change dramatically over the course of development (Olweus, 1979). Even with wide fluctuations in the expression of behavior over time, children show some degree of consistency in how they organize their experiences and interact with their environment, whether it be adaptive or maladaptive (Garber, 1984).

Like many problems in abnormal child psychology,

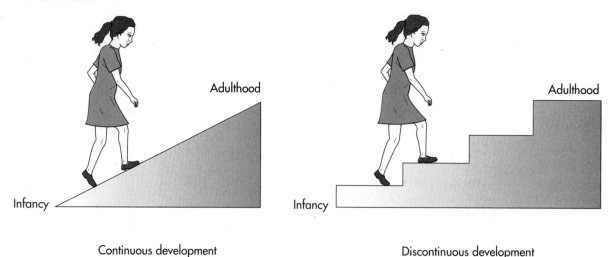

FIGURE 2.4 Continuity and discontinuity. (Based on Shaffer, 1977)

Jake's current behavior pattern involves *both* continuities and discontinuities. Some of his troubles, like school and homework avoidance, may represent qualitatively different problems from his earlier reading disorder, whereas other behaviors, like slow reading and comprehension, may show quantitative changes only. The degree of continuity or discontinuity will vary as a function of changing environmental circumstances and transactions between the child and environment. These continual changes in turn will affect the child's developmental course and direction.

In sum, a central theme of our basic assumptions is that the study of abnormal child psychology needs to consider abnormality in relation to multiple, interdependent causes and major developmental changes that typically occur across the life cycle. Until recently, developmental aspects of abnormal child behavior were often overlooked in relation to children's behavioral and emotional problems (Achenbach, 1990). To redress this imbalance, we discuss developmental issues pertaining to the nature, symptoms, and course of each disorder throughout this text.

An Integrative Approach

Get your facts first, and then you can distort them as much as you please.
—Mark Twain (1835–1910)

Because abnormal child behavior is influenced by complex interactions between individual and environmental variables, we need to have some structure that unifies the vast number of possible influences into meaningful relationships. These relationships, of course, need to be testable, so that we can rule out some possibilities and narrow our focus more precisely when considering particular disorders. Since no single theoretical orientation can be used to explain various behaviors or disorders, we need to be familiar with many different theories and conceptual models, each of which contributes important insights into normal and abnormal human behavior.

The major theories of abnormal child psychology have become quite compatible with one another. Rather than offering contradictory views, each theory contributes one or more pieces of the puzzle of human behavior. As all the available pieces are assembled, the picture of a particular child or adolescent disorder becomes more and more distinct. Psychological theories are merely tools to study human behavior; the more you learn what these tools can and can't do and which tool to use for which purpose, the more knowledgeable and skilled you will become.

Remember, there is no single integrative theory that fully captures the diversity of perspectives and findings represented by current research in abnormal child psychology. Initial theoretical perspectives that have guided the study of child development and psychopathology during its formative stage, such as psychoanalytic and learning theories (described in Chapter 1), are insufficient to account for the dynamic and interacting contextual, developmental, and system influences that have been identified as important in recent research. To explain the complexity of abnormal child behavior, we must take into account the full range of biological, psychological, and ecological factors that influence children's development.

We turn now to three major influences on abnormal child development: (1) biological contributions, which include both genetic and neurobiological factors that are often established at birth or soon thereafter; (2) psychological influences, such as emotions, relationships, and thought processes; and (3) family and social influences, which set additional parameters on normal and abnormal development.

BIOLOGICAL PERSPECTIVES

Broadly speaking, a **neurobiological perspective** considers brain and nervous system functions as underlying causes of psychological disorders in children and adults. Biological influences on the very young child's brain development include genetic and constitutional factors, neuroanatomy, and rates of maturation. Different regions of the brain are highly influenced by the availability of various biochemicals and neurohormones, which interact in different ways to affect an individual's psychological experiences (Kaplan & Sadock, 1991). This process depends on environmental factors that serve to direct or reroute ongoing brain processes. Thus a neurobiological perspective acknowledges the importance of environmental influences.

The Developing Brain: A Work in Progress

The developing brain has long been a mystery, but its secrets are gradually being revealed. Clarifying the roles of nature (the biological determinants) and nurture (the social determinants) has traditionally been at the forefront of research on medical and psychological illnesses. Nature is now being revealed in considerable detail, allowing scientists to search new avenues for understanding the vulnerability of the brain as a basis for the development of psychopathology.

To appreciate the amazing process of neuronal growth and differentiation, we'll start at the beginning. Throughout pregnancy the fetal brain develops from a few all-purpose cells into a complex organ made up of billions of specialized, interconnected neurons (Thatcher, 1994). The speed and distance that these emerging neurons travel are astonishing, as they multiply to form various brain structures and functions, such as the brain stem, to command heartbeat and breathing; the cerebellum, to control posture and movement; and the cortex, where thought and perception originate.

Embryonic development generates an initial overabundance of neurons, with a diverse state of synaptic connectivity (Innocenti, 1982). At first these cells are largely undifferentiated, but as they reach their destinations, they become neurons with axons that carry electrical signals to other parts of the brain. These axonal connections, or **synapses,** form the brain's circuits, and lay the foundation for further growth and differentiation. Notably, genes determine the main highways along which axons travel to make their connection, but to reach particular target cells, axons follow chemical cues strewn along their path that tell them the direction to various destinations.

By the fifth month of gestation most axons have reached their general destination, although there are far more axons than the target cells can accommodate. Thus, during early childhood synapses multiply; then selective **pruning** reduces the number of connections in a way that gradually shapes and differentiates important brain functions (Derryberry & Reed, 1994). It's as if the nervous system prepares itself for new growth and demands by sending in reinforcements and then cutting back once the environment has signaled what it needs. Throughout our life course we undergo cycles that narrow the gap between structure and function. At the level of the nervous system, the microanatomy of the brain is constantly redefined to meet the demands and requirements of an adult world (Nelson & Bloom, 1997). Like the pruning of a tree, this process fosters healthy growth of different areas of the brain according to individual needs and environmental demands, and eliminates connections that serve to restrict healthy growth.

How permanent are the early connections formed as brain development proceeds along its way in an organized, predictable fashion? This question has provoked different theories and agonized many parents who are concerned about the significance of children's early development. For instance, if early brain functions are unlikely to change, this would imply that early experiences set the course for lifetime development, a theory similar to Freud's contention that an individual's core personality is formed from an early age, which sets the pace and boundaries for further personality formation. To the contrary, scientists now believe that brain functions undergo continual changes as they adapt to environmental demands.

Neural Plasticity. Many early neural connections are not stable; some are strengthened and become more established due to use, while many others regress or disappear. Thus, the answer to the question about the permanence of early connections is that the brain shows **neural plasticity,** or malleability, throughout the course of development (Fox, Calkins, & Bell, 1994). Neural plasticity means the brain's anatomical differentiation is *use-dependent:* Nature provides the basic processes, whereas nurture provides the experiences needed to select the most adaptive network of connections, based on their use and function (Cicchetti & Tucker, 1994). It is truly fascinating how nature and nurture work together to create such highly specific, extremely adaptive central nervous system functions.

The Role of Experience. Instead of viewing neural connections as being prespecified, think of the developing brain as a work in progress, one in which the environment plays an essential role as supervisor of this dynamic rewiring project (Thatcher, 1994). In fact, environmental experience is now recognized to be critical to the differentiation of brain tissue itself. Although nature has a plan for creating the human brain and central nervous system, environmental opportunities and limitations influence this plan in significant ways right from the beginning. Thus a transactional model is needed to explain normal and abnormal development. Because the structure of a child's brain remains surprisingly malleable for months and even years after birth, transaction occurs between ongoing brain development and environmental experiences; neither nature nor nurture is sufficient to explain the complexity of the developing brain.

Experience, of course, comes in all shapes and sizes. Childhood illness and diet count as experience, as do maltreatment and inadequate stimulation. Children's early care-giving experiences play an especially important role in designing the parts of the brain involved in emotion, personality, and behavior (Sameroff, 1993). Children's attachment with their care-givers, for instance, may increase their ability to learn and cope with stress (Carlson & Sroufe, 1995), whereas abuse and neglect can prime the brain for a lifetime of struggle forming healthy relationships (Wolfe, Wekerle, Reitzel-Jaffe, & Lefbevre, 1998).

Even though brain development is dependent on environment, we might expect brain functions to become highly stable and enduring by a certain age, say, early adolescence. On the contrary, evidence points to continued restructuring and growth of brain structures throughout the life span (Thatcher, 1994). This does not imply that all brain structures undergo major reconnections or serve new functions (we don't expect, for example, to write our next textbook on organic chemistry); rather, brain maturity is viewed as an organized, hierarchical process that builds on earlier function.

The primitive areas of the brain mature first, during the first 3 years of life; thus, these brain regions, which govern basic sensory and motor skills, undergo the most dramatic restructuring early on. Moreover, these perceptual centers, along with instinctive ones, such as the limbic system, are strongly affected by early childhood experiences and set the foundation for further development (Thatcher, 1994). The frontal cortex, which governs planning and decision making, and the cerebellum,

a center for motor skills, don't get rewired until a person is 5 to 7 years old. Another major restructuring of the brain occurs between ages 9 and 11. So the brain certainly does not stop changing after 3 years. For some functions the windows of influence are only beginning to close at that age, while for others they are only beginning to open (Fox et al., 1994). Our brain functions undergo lifelong renovation, with restructuring being a natural by-product of maturity.

Understandably, during this evolution of brain growth and differentiation many things can go wrong, thereby altering how neurons form or interconnect. Critical brain stem development, which controls basic life functions such as breathing and pulse, occurs in the early stages of pregnancy, so proper prenatal care is essential. The right and left hemispheres of the brain then begin to differentiate, followed by localized areas that process sensory information and cognitive functions, such as attention, thinking, and emotion (Davidson, 1994). Neurons rapidly develop networks with other parts of the brain, thereby allowing information to be shared among various regions of the brain. Brain development is vulnerable to disruptions at any time, and earlier disruptions are generally associated with more severe organic disorders and central nervous system complications. Safeguards such as proper prenatal care, proper nutrition, and avoidance of harmful substances can go a long way in reducing the risk of complications and lifelong disabilities.

Genetic Contributions

Genetics explains why you look like your father, and if you don't, why you should.
— Tammy, age 8

To address the important role of genetic influences, we first need to understand the nature of genes, bearing in mind that virtually any trait a child possesses results from the *interaction* of environmental and genetic factors (Rende & Plomin, 1995). A review of genetics terminology and function may assist our understanding of some causes of abnormal child behavior. Genes reside within chromosomes, and we each have 22 matched pairs of chromosomes and a single pair of sex chromosomes. In males, the sex chromosome pair consists of an X and a Y chromosome (XY), and in females the sex chromosome pair consists of two X chromosomes (XX). Each chromosome contains thousands of genes, which are essentially segments of DNA that contain genetic information from each parent. Chromosome analysis was first introduced as a diagnostic procedure for persons with mental retardation in the 1960s, and is still widely used today. Such analysis permits the determination of

Calvin and Hobbes   by Bill Watterson

Calvin and Hobbes © Watterson. Reprinted with permission of Universal Press Syndicate. All rights reserved.

abnormalities in the structure or location of the 23 pairs of human chromosomes. The abnormalities may involve loss (**monosomy**) or duplication (**trisomy**) of an entire chromosome or chromosomal band. More rarely, complex disruptions involving transfer of a piece of one chromosome onto another (**translocation**) may occur. In addition, fragile sites or breaks on the chromosome can occur, leading to abnormalities in development (Scott, 1990).

Genetic factors have been implicated in a number of childhood disorders, such as autistic disorder, ADHD, conduct disorder, mood disorders, and schizophrenia (Lombroso, Pauls, & Leckman, 1994; Torgersen, 1993). Genetic influences play a role in forming children's basic temperaments as well, influencing, for example, the degree of behavioral inhibition and emotion regulation children may show (Baum, Grunberg, & Singer, 1992). Despite support and enthusiasm for the role of genetic influences in childhood disorders, however, very few specific genetic causes have been isolated or identified as the underlying cause of child psychopathology (Lombroso et al., 1994). Therefore, rather than asking whether a specific disorder is due to genetic makeup or environmental influences, we should be concerned with a different question: To what extent are given behaviors due to variations in genetic endowment, variations within the environment, or the interaction between these two factors? An understanding of the nature of genes sheds light on this question.

The Nature of Genes. A common misconception is that genes and the DNA they contain represent the fundamental code that explains just about all human behavior (Sapolsky, 1997). This misconception about the

importance of genetic influence is derived from two false assumptions. First, we mistakenly assume that genes have a great deal of autonomy or authority over behavior. In reality, genes must obey other factors that regulate when and how they function. Very often, those factors are environmental (Nelson & Bloom, 1997; Rende & Plomin, 1995).

The second false assumption is that genes tell cells how to construct their structure and function. If those cells happen to be neurons, the functions include thought, feelings, and behavior. In the extreme, this view of the role of genes would reinforce the notion that genes are the biological roots of all behavior. To correct this second false assumption, we must consider exactly what genes do. A gene is basically a stretch of DNA, and by itself, it does not produce a behavior, an emotion, or even a passing thought. Rather, it produces a protein. Each gene is a specific DNA sequence that codes for a specific protein. Some of these proteins certainly have lots to do with behavior and feelings and thoughts, such as **hormones** (which carry messages to various cells throughout the body) and **neurotransmitters** (which carry messages between nerve cells). Although these proteins are vital for the brain to function, very rarely do hormones, neurotransmitters, or other proteins cause a behavior to happen. Instead, they produce *tendencies to respond* to the environment in certain ways (Sapolsky, 1997).

So, biological factors in the nervous system, produced by genetic codes, rarely *determine* behavior. Instead, they affect how we respond to very subtle influences in the environment. Each of us may have different genetic vulnerabilities, tendencies, and predispositions, but rarely are the outcomes inevitable (Fox et al., 1994). The lesson to remember in all of this is simple, yet important: The false notion that genes determine behavior should be replaced with the more accurate statement that genes influence how we respond to the environment.

Behavioral Genetics. Discoveries in behavioral genetics are appearing at a phenomenal rate—an obesity gene that affects weight regulation, an enuretic gene that affects the production of a hormone related to bladder control, among many others. Where are the discoveries taking the study of abnormal child psychology? Sorting out these interactive influences is the not-so-easy task of **behavioral genetics,** a branch of genetics that investigates possible connections between a genetic predisposition and observed behavior. Behavioral genetics researchers often begin their investigation by conducting **familial aggregation** studies. They look for nonrandom clustering of disorders or characteristics within a given family and compare these results with the random distribution of the disorders or characteristics in the general population (Szatmari, Boyle, & Offord, 1993). For example, parents of children with overanxious disorder or separation anxiety disorder tend to have higher rates of anxiety in their own childhood histories relative to normative prevalence rates (Last, Hersen, Kazdin, Francis, & Grubb, 1987).

Genetics researchers examine both genotypes and phenotypes in linking genes to abnormal behavior. The **genotype** refers to the individual's specific genetic makeup, and the **phenotype** refers to his or her observable characteristics or behavior. Essentially, this approach assumes that if there is a specific genotype for a given disorder, the frequency of the disorder will be higher among biological relatives of the family member whose trait has been singled out for study (this person is called the **proband**) (Deutsch & Kinsbourne, 1990; Lombroso et al., 1994).

Although family aggregation studies are certainly valuable, they do not control for environmental variables that may also contribute to a particular outcome. For example, a child may be anxious because of his parents' child-rearing methods, rather than their genetic contributions. To increase scientific rigor following suggestive familial aggregation studies, researchers may conduct twin studies to control for the contribution of genetic factors (Lombroso et al., 1994). Twin studies may involve identical, or *monozygotic* (MZ), twins, who have the same set of genes, as well as fraternal, or *dizygotic* (DZ), twins, who share about half of each other's genes (the same as all first-degree relatives). The crucial scientific question is whether identical twins share the same trait—say, reading difficulties—more than fraternal twins (Gillis, Gilger, Pennington, & DeFries, 1992).

Twin studies provide a powerful research strategy for examining the role of genetic influences in both psychiatric and nonpsychiatric disorders, but they are not perfect. Even though we can assume that monozygotic twins have the same genetic makeup and dizygotic twins do not, we still cannot say for certain whether MZ twins have the same experiences or environment as do DZ twins. Identical twins may affect each other more than fraternal twins (Carey, 1992), among other things. Consider this finding: In a twin study Willerman (1973) found a concordance rate for ADHD of approximately 70%, meaning that if one twin had ADHD, there was a 70% chance that the other one would as well. However, this result does not necessarily mean that genetics account for 70% of the variance in ADHD. This high concordance could be due to the fact that MZ twins spend more time together, frequently engage in similar activities, and have many of the same friends in common (Torgersen, 1993). Thus, the common or shared environment presents a potential confound in any twin study; unless twins are reared apart, it becomes impossible to separate the effects of genetic and environmental influences (Deutsch & Kinsbourne, 1990).

In summary, a very complex reciprocal interaction between genes and the environment seems to exist, and in each childhood disorder this interaction plays an important role. Genetic endowment influences behavior, emotions, and thoughts, and environmental events are necessary for this influence to be expressed. Much of our development and most of our behavior, personality, and even intelligence are influenced by many genes, each contributing only a tiny effect. Most important, no individual genes have been proved to account for the major psychological disorders presented in this text. Although specific genes are sometimes associated with certain psychological disorders, the conclusions of behavioral geneticists are that genetic contributions to psychological disorders come from many genes, each of which makes a relatively small contribution (Rende & Plomin, 1995).

Neurobiological Contributions

The study of abnormal child psychology requires a working familiarity with brain structures. This section provides an overview of major structures that are mentioned later in the context of specific disorders (see Figure 2.5). Once you are familiar with the different areas and functions of the brain, you will have the basic vocabulary needed to understand the remarkable discoveries being made.

Brain Structure and Function. The brain is often divided into the *brain stem* and the *forebrain* (telencephalon) because of their unique functions. The brain stem, located at the base of the brain, handles most

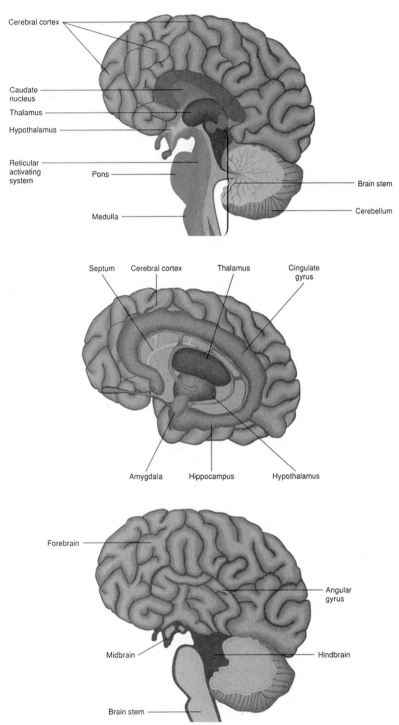

FIGURE 2.5   Structures of the brain. (Barlow and Durand, 1995)

of the autonomic functions necessary to stay alive. The lowest part of the brain stem, called the *hindbrain*, contains the *medulla*, the *pons*, and the *cerebellum*. The hindbrain provides essential regulation of autonomic activities such as breathing, heartbeat, and digestion, and the cerebellum controls motor coordination. The brain stem also contains the *midbrain*, which coordinates movement with sensory input. The midbrain houses the reticular activating system (RAS), which contributes to processes of arousal and tension.

At the very top of the brain stem is the *diencephalon*, located just below the forebrain. The diencephalon

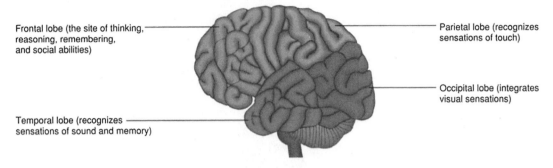

Frontal lobe (the site of thinking, reasoning, remembering, and social abilities)

Parietal lobe (recognizes sensations of touch)

Occipital lobe (integrates visual sensations)

Temporal lobe (recognizes sensations of sound and memory)

FIGURE 2.6 The four lobes of the human cerebral cortex. (Barlow and Durand, 1995)

contains the thalamus and hypothalamus, both of which are essential to the regulation of behavior and emotion. The diencephalon functions primarily as a relay between the forebrain and the remaining lower areas of the brain stem.

Next is the forebrain, which has evolved in humans into highly specialized functions. At the base of the forebrain is an area known as the *limbic,* or border, *system.* It contains a number of structures that are suspected causes of psychopathology, such as the *hippocampus, cingulate gyrus, septum,* and *amygdala.* These important structures regulate emotional experiences and expressions, and play a significant role in learning and impulse control. The limbic system also regulates the basic drives of sex, aggression, hunger, and thirst.

Also at the base of the forebrain lies the *basal ganglia,* which includes the *caudate nucleus.* Researchers are discovering that this area controls motor behavior, which is why it is implicated in ADHD (discussed in Chapter 5) and other disorders affecting motor behavior, such as tics and tremors. The basal ganglia has also been implicated in relation to obsessive-compulsive disorder (discussed in Chapter 7).

The cerebral cortex, the largest part of the forebrain, gives us our distinctly human qualities and allows us to look to the future and plan, to reason, and to create. The cerebral cortex is divided into two hemispheres that look very much alike, but which have unique specialities, or functions. The left hemisphere (which is usually dominant in right-handed persons) plays a chief role in verbal and other cognitive processes. The right hemisphere (which is usually dominant in left-handed persons) is better at social perception and creativity. (This is why we left-handed persons are considered the only ones in our right minds.) Researchers believe that each hemisphere may play a different role in certain psychological disorders, such as communication and learning disorders.

Each hemisphere is divided into four separate areas, or lobes: *temporal, parietal, occipital,* and *frontal* (see Figure 2.6). Each lobe is associated with different processes. Briefly, the temporal lobe is associated with

recognition of various sights and sounds, as well as long-term memory storage. The parietal lobe helps us recognize various sensations of touch. The occipital lobe processes and interprets visual information. These three lobes also communicate to one another in such a manner that they process various sensations of sight, touch, and hearing, as well as other signals from our senses, in an integrated, meaningful fashion.

The **frontal lobe** contains the functions underlying much of our thinking and reasoning abilities, including memory. The frontal lobe enables us to make sense of social relationships and customs and to relate to the world and the people around us, which is why it has considerable relevance to the study of abnormal child psychology. This brain area has been implicated in ADHD, conduct disorders, autism, and several other psychological disorders.

Remarkably, these critical brain areas perform their functions in an integrated, harmonious fashion, which permits the whole to be much larger than the sum of its parts. The brain's integrated operation requires the assistance of important regulatory systems and neurotransmitters.

The Endocrine System. The **endocrine system** is an important regulatory system that has been linked to specific psychological disorders in both children and adults, such as anxiety and mood disorders. There are several endocrine glands, each of which produces a particular hormone that it releases into the bloodstream. The *adrenal* glands (located on top of the kidneys) are most familiar because they produce **epinephrine** (also known as adrenalin) in response to stress. Epinephrine energizes us and gets our bodies ready for possible threat or challenge. The *thyroid* gland produces a hormone, thyroxine, that is needed for proper energy metabolism and growth, and is implicated in certain eating disorders of children and youth (discussed in Chapter 13). Finally, the *pituitary* gland, located deep within the brain, orchestrates the body's regulatory functions by producing a variety of regulatory hormones, including estrogen and testosterone. Because the endocrine system is closely related to the immune system, which protects us from disease and many other biological threats, it is not surprising that it is implicated in a variety of disorders, particularly health- and stress-related disorders (discussed in Chapter 12).

As discussed earlier, the brain develops in an interconnected, use-dependent fashion, beginning well before birth and carrying on throughout our lives. One brain connection that is implicated in some psychological

---

Box 2.2
The HPA Axis and Stress Regulation

Hypothalamus

Pituitary Gland

ACTH

CORTISOL

Brainstem

Adrenal Gland

To Immune System

The hypothalamic-pituitary-adrenal (HPA) axis.

The HPA axis is a central component of the brain's neuroendocrine response to stress. The hypothalamus, when stimulated, secretes corticotropin-releasing hormone (CRH), which stimulates the pituitary gland to secrete andrenocorticotropic hormone (ACTH) into the bloodstream. ACTH then causes the adrenal glands to release cortisol, the familiar stress hormone that arouses the body to meet a challenging situation. This system, like many others, works on a feedback loop: Cortisol modulates the stress response by acting on the hypothalamus to inhibit the continued release of CRH (Sternberg & Gold, 1997). Researchers are discovering that this important feedback loop that regulates our level of arousal and apprehension can be seriously disrupted or damaged by various traumatic and uncontrollable events, such as physical and sexual abuse, that cause a child or adolescent to maintain a state of fear or alertness that becomes toxic over prolonged periods of time (DeBellis, Burke, Trickett, & Putnam, 1996; Van der Kolk & Fisler, 1994).

---

disorders involves the hypothalamus and the endocrine system. The hypothalamus carries out the commands it receives from the adjacent pituitary gland and from other hormones, such as those regulating hunger and thirst. The pituitary gland in turn stimulates the adrenal glands to produce epinephrine to arouse us. The adrenal glands also produce the stress hormone known as **cortisol.** The hypothalamus control center, coupled with the pituitary and adrenal glands, which produce cortisol, make up a regulatory system in the brain known as the **hypothalamic-pituitary-adrenal (HPA) axis** (see Box 2.2). This axis has been implicated in several psychological disorders, especially those that are connected to a person's response to stress and ability to regulate emotions, such as anxiety disorders (Chapter 7) and mood disorders and depression (Chapter 8).

Neurotransmitters. Neurotransmitters are much like biochemical currents in the brain. These currents develop in an organized fashion, so that they make meaningful connections that serve a larger function, like thinking and feeling. Neurons that are more sensitive to one type of neurotransmitter, such as serotonin, tend to cluster together and form paths, known as **brain circuits,** from one part of the brain to the other (Dean, Kelsey, Heller, & Ciaranello, 1993). Tens of thousands of these currents operate in our brains. Their connective pathways and function have been revealed in recent years in ways that were inconceivable over a decade ago.

Brain circuits and neurotransmitters have been tied to particular psychological disorders. They also offer possible avenues for treatment, since psychoactive drugs work by either increasing or decreasing the flow of various neurotransmitters. However, like the influence of genetics, noted above, changes in neurotransmitter activity may make people *more* or *less likely* to exhibit certain kinds of behavior in certain situations, but they do not cause the behavior directly. Table 2.2 summarizes the four neurotransmitter systems most often mentioned in connection with psychological disorders.

PSYCHOLOGICAL PERSPECTIVES

In addition to a need for an integrative framework such as developmental psychopathology, we also need theories that apply to specific problems or disorders, and which offer testable hypotheses and explanations for certain outcomes. The major theoretical viewpoints described below each have value in explaining the development of psychopathology. At the same time, however, each has certain limitations and may be more or less applicable to particular disorders or situations. Again, bear in mind that abnormal behavior results from

Table 2.2 Major Neurotransmitters and Their Implicated Roles in Psychopathology

Neurotransmitter	Normal Functions	Implicated Role In
Serotonin	Plays a role in information processing and motor coordination (Spoont, 1992)	Regulatory problems, such as eating and sleep disorders
	Inhibits children's tendency to explore their surroundings	Obsessive-compulsive disorder
	Moderates and regulates a number of critical behaviors, such as eating, sleeping, and expressing anger	Schizophrenia and mood disorders
Benzodiazepine-GABA	Reduces arousal and moderates emotional responses, such as anger, hostility, and aggression	Anxiety disorder
	Is linked to feelings of anxiety and discomfort	
Norepinephrine	Facilitates or controls emergency reactions and alarm responses (Gray, 1985)	Not *directly* involved in specific disorders (acts generally to regulate or modulate behavioral tendencies)
	Plays a role in emotional and behavioral regulation	
Dopamine	May act as a *switch* that turns on various brain circuits, allowing other neurotransmitters to inhibit or facilitate emotions or behavior (Spoont, 1992)	Schizophrenia Mood disorders
	Is involved in exploratory, extroverted, and pleasure-seeking activity (Depue, Luciana, Arbisi, Collins, & Leon, 1994)	

transactions between environmental and individual influences. Children's inherited characteristics coupled with the experiences and influences in their environment make them the way they are today. Also, some seemingly maladaptive behaviors, like fearfulness or watchfulness, may in fact be understandable when considered in the context of the child's environment, such as those involving parental abuse or school violence.

Emotional and cognitive functions have provided the backbone for many theories of human behavior, perhaps because they define so many of our qualities and thus serve as primary signals of psychological distress. Psychoanalytic theory, with its concept of defense mechanisms like anger, embraces emotional experiences, as does social-cognitive theory, which stresses the role of thought patterns and behavior as determinants of emotion. Similarly, attachment theory maintains that an internal working model, formed on the basis of early relationships, continues to regulate emotion in subsequent relationships (Cassidy, 1994). As we have just seen, biological theories also emphasize the structural and hormonal aspects of emotion regulation and cognitive processes (Pennington & Ozonoff, 1991).

Our interest in psychological bases for abnormal behavior begins with a focus on the role of emotions in establishing an infant's ability to adapt to her new surroundings. To an infant, who has very limited means of expression and interpretation of the many new things going on around her, emotions provide the initial filter for organizing massive amounts of new information and avoiding potential harm. Similarly, early relationships with one or more care-givers provide structure and regulation to these emotional responses. As the child develops, cognitive processes, like self-efficacy and subjective values, play a larger role in assisting the young child to make sense of her world, and to reorganize earlier functions that may be unnecessary or even maladaptive as she faces new challenges involving language development, peer interactions, and similar skills. As with brain development, things can go wrong at any point along this continuum of emotional and cognitive development as a function of the child's interaction with her environment.

Emotional Influences

Emotions and affective expression are core elements of human psychological experience. From birth, they are a central feature of infant activity and regulation (Emde, 1989). Throughout our lives, emotional reactions assist us in our fight-or-flight response—to alert us to danger and to ensure our safety. From an evolutionary perspective, emotions give special value to events and make particular actions likely to occur. In effect, emotions

The ability to infer another person's emotional state by reading facial, gestural, postural, and vocal cues has an important adaptive function, especially for infants and toddlers. If they are faced with something unfamiliar, they can look to the reactions and guidance of a familiar adult to help them interpret the new situation.

tell us what to pay attention to and what to ignore, what to approach and what to avoid (Breger, 1974). Not surprisingly, given their important job, backed up by powerful stress-regulating hormones like cortisol, emotions are critical to healthy adaptation.

Interest in emotional processes and their relation to abnormal child behavior has grown considerably in recent years (Fox, 1994). Children's emotional experiences, expressions, and regulation affect the quality of their social interactions and relationships, and thus are at the foundation of early personality development. Researchers are discovering a wealth of information relating to the influential role of emotion in children's lives. One important discovery relates to how children learn, from a very young age, through the emotional expressions of others (Bretherton, 1995). Emotions serve an important role in adaptation, such as an infant's fear of heights or strangers. They not only serve as important internal monitoring and guidance systems that are designed to appraise events as being beneficial or dangerous, but also provide motivation for action (Cassidy, 1994).

Children have a natural proclivity toward attending to emotional cues from others, which helps them learn to interpret and regulate their own emotions. Within their first year of life, they learn the importance of emotions for communication and regulation, and by their second year, they have some ability to attribute cause to emotional expression. Of particular interest to abnormal child psychology is the finding that children look to the emotional expression and cues of their care-givers to provide them with the information needed to formulate a basic understanding of what's going on. To a young child, emotions are a primary form of communication

that permits them to explore their world with increasing independence.

Emotion Reactivity and Regulation.

We can divide emotional processes into two dimensions: **emotion reactivity** and **emotion regulation**. Reactivity refers to individual differences in the threshold and intensity of emotional experience, which provide clues to an individual's level of distress and sensitivity to the environment. Emotion regulation, on the other hand, involves enhancing, maintaining, or inhibiting emotional arousal, which is usually done for a particular purpose or goal (Rubin, Coplan, Fox, & Calkins, 1995). A young child with ADHD, for example, may be emotionally reactive to unfamiliar tasks or unwanted demands and become upset. This emotional reaction, in turn, may lead to poor regulation, resulting in the child's becoming very distraught and unmanageable. Once again, a transactional process is at work, whereby emotional reactions prompt the need for regulation, and this in turn influences further emotional expression.

A further distinction can be made between problems in *regulation* and problems in *dysregulation*. Regulation problems involve weak or absent control structures, such as those of the boy with ADHD who could not control his temper; dysregulation means that existing control structures operate maladaptively (Cicchetti et al., 1995). An example of dysregulation is when a child is fearful even when there is no reason in the environment to be fearful or anxious.

Children's emotion regulation abilities, as often shown by their emotion reactivity and expression, are important signals of normal as well as abnormal development. Emotions also help young children learn more about themselves and their surroundings, as part of the process of learning to identify and monitor their feelings and behavior. The child–care-giver relationship plays a critical role in this process, for it provides the basic setting for children to express emotions and to have caring guidance and limits placed on them. Authoritative parents are those who establish limits for the child that are both sensitive to the child's individual development and needs, and at the same time, demanding of the child to foster self-control and healthy regulation (Maccoby & Martin, 1983). Because of its vital role in emotional development, the child–care-giver relationship surfaces again and again in discussing various childhood disorders.

Some forms of emotion dysregulation may be adaptive in one environment or at one time, but maladaptive in other situations. Children who have been emotionally and sexually abused, for example, may show shallow emotions, known as numbing, which is a symptom of a post-traumatic stress reaction that serves to protect the child from overwhelming pain and trauma (described in Chapter 14). If numbing becomes a characteristic way of coping with stressors later in life, however, it may interfere with adaptive functioning and with long-term goals. Similarly, in response to attachment figures who are rejecting or inconsistent, infants may develop an insecure/avoidant attachment, in which emotional expression is minimized. The infant's reduced emotional expression, while serving the strategic function within the attachment relationship of minimizing loss by reducing investment in the relationship, may establish a pattern of emotional responding that is maladaptive for the development of subsequent relationships (Cassidy, 1994).

Temperament.   You hear it all the time: "She was an easy baby, right from the first day I brought her home from the hospital," or "Sleep? What's that? Since little Freddy was born, we are up all hours of the night, feeding, changing, and trying to soothe him." Unmistakably, some infants are more placid than others, some are more active, and some are more high-strung, and these differences are often recognizable in the first few days or weeks of life (Thomas & Chess, 1977). What relevance does this have to abnormal development?

The development of emotion regulation or dysregulation is thought to derive from both socialization and innate predispositions, or **temperament**. Temperament refers to the child's constitutionally based reactivity and self-regulation, usually in reference to the domains of emotions, activity level, and attention (Rothbart, Posner, & Hershey, 1995). Temperament is a subset of the broader domain of personality, so it is often considered one of the early building blocks of personality. Such biological predispositions do not imply a certain destiny leading to a psychological disorder; rather, a particular outcome appears to be based on a series of reciprocal interactions, like those described in Box 2.1, between innate predispositions (debilitative or protective) and situational circumstances, such as a supportive or stressful environment.

Much of the research in the field of infant temperament emerged from Thomas and Chess's pioneering work from the New York Longitudinal Study (Thomas & Chess, 1977), in which they identified nine basic temperament characteristics, or dimensions: (1) activity level, (2) rhythmicity, (3) approach to or withdrawal from new situations, (4) adaptability, (5) threshold or responsiveness, (6) intensity of reaction, (7) quality of mood, (8) distractibility, and (9) attention span and persistence. These nine characteristics have been further collapsed into three primary dimensions of temperament, which have relevance to risk conditions for psychopathology:

1. *Positive affect and approach*. This dimension describes the "easy child," like the infant girl noted above. Such children are generally approachable and adaptive to their environment, possessing the ability to regulate their basic functions, such as eating, sleeping, and elimination, relatively smoothly.
2. *Fearful or inhibited*. This dimension describes the "slow-to-warm-up child," who is cautious in his or her approach to novel or challenging situations. These children are more variable in self-regulation and adaptability, and may show distress or negativity toward some situations.
3. *Negative affect or irritability*. This dimension describes the "difficult child," who is predominantly negative or intense in mood, not very adaptable, and arrhythmic. Some children with this temperament show distress when faced with novel or challenging situations, and others have a general distress proneness or irritability, including when limitations are placed on them (Rothbart & Mauro, 1990).

These temperament dimensions, or early self-regulatory styles, may be linked to the development of psychopathology or risk conditions in several ways. In some instances, a temperamental style may be very highly related to a particular disorder, like a social phobia or fearfulness. In other instances, however, the condition may develop from the features closely related to temperament, but the condition itself may appear unrelated (Rothbart et al., 1990). For example, an infant's extreme sensitivity to emotional stimuli may contribute to a tendency to withdraw from others as a toddler or preschooler; over time, this tendency may transform into an interpersonal style characterized by a self-reported lack of feeling toward others and, consequently, peer rejection or other risk conditions. Also, infant negative affect can contribute to maternal withdrawal or indifference, leading to insecure attachment and its associated risk conditions.

To recap, emotion regulation involves a variety of increasingly complex developmental tasks, all of which are aided by the formation of healthy relationships and by other environmental resources. The degree of interference with these tasks depends on the fit between the child, her or his environment, and the interaction between the child and the environment. Emotion dysregulation is believed to be the consequence of interference in the associated developmental processes.

Behavioral and Cognitive Influences

As we mentioned in Chapter 1, early approaches to behaviorism arose partially in response to the difficulty of scientifically evaluating the active components of psychoanalytic theory, such as conflicts, instincts, and unconscious motivations. Through laboratory-based procedures, greater control over the antecedents and consequences of behavior was possible, so scientists could more readily study how well-defined behaviors, such as Little Albert's fear, were acquired. A basic assumption of classical and operant conditioning models is that behavior is a function of associations between environmental stimuli (classical conditioning), or a function of environmental contingencies between a behavioral response and its consequences (operant conditioning).

There are three major approaches to abnormal behavior based on principles of learning. Although each approach is different for reasons described below, they are usually considered to fall within a behavioral or cognitive-behavioral model: (1) applied behavior analysis (also known as operant or instrumental learning), (2) principles of classical, or respondent, conditioning, and (3) social learning and social cognition theories. These approaches differ essentially in the extent to which they apply cognitive concepts and procedures to the understanding of behavior (Wilson, 1995). Applied behavior analysis, at one end of this continuum, focuses exclusively on observable behavior and rejects the notion that cognitive mediation is a necessary consideration for explaining behavior. At the other end is social learning theory, which relies more broadly on cognitive processes and explanations.

Although conceptually different, behavioral and cognitive approaches to abnormal child psychology are committed to the scientific method, with the intention of testing assumptions and modifying cause-and-effect relationships on the basis of empirical findings. Most behavioral explanations assume that the child is best understood and described by what he or she does in a particular situation, rather than in terms of stable personality traits. Although a child's particular learning history is of interest, behavioral methods focus on the most pragmatic, parsimonious explanation for a particular problem behavior. By the same reasoning, this approach recognizes that success in changing a problem behavior does not imply knowledge about its origin or causes. Cognitive theorists, on the other hand, are interested in how certain thought patterns develop over time, and how they relate to particular behavioral strategies, such as problem solving.

Applied Behavior Analysis (ABA). Based on B. F. Skinner's classical studies, ABA takes a functional approach to behavior, especially the relationships between behavior and its antecedents and consequences. No implicit assumptions are made about underlying needs or motives that contribute to abnormal behavior; rather, ABA describes and tests functional relationships between stimuli, responses, and consequences. Four primary learning principles explain how behaviors are acquired or changed as a result of particular consequences. Positive and negative reinforcement are defined as any action that *increases* the target response, which is why they are both considered reinforcement processes. In positive reinforcement, something is provided, such as praise, that increases the response; in negative reinforcement, something is withdrawn (such as an unpleasant event or threat) contingent upon target behavior, which increases that behavior. To grasp this latter principle, consider a child whose tantrums increase over time because they successfully remove his parent's resistance to purchasing a toy or getting his way.

Extinction and punishment, in contrast, have the effect of *decreasing* a response. Extinction means some consequence has been removed, as when you take away positive attention by ignoring a child who's acting inappropriately, which has the effect of decreasing the inappropriate behavior. Punishment means some consequence has been added, which also decreases behavior. Although we usually think of a "punisher" as being some aversive or unpleasant event, remember that an action is considered punitive on the basis of its consequence, not its intention. Lots of intended punishers ("Go to your room"; "Stay away from your little brother") in practice may have little effect on the intended outcome. Children are quite accomplished at learning contingencies, and have an uncanny ability to apply some of their own.

Classical Conditioning. Based on extension of Pavlov's famous learning trials and Watson's experiments with Little Albert (described in Chapter 1), classical, or respondent, conditioning explains the acquisition of deviant behavior on the basis of paired associations between previously neutral stimuli (like a bell) and unconditioned stimuli, like food or noise. Any neutral event can become a *conditioned stimulus* if it is paired enough times with an event that already elicits a certain response. This was the fundamental learning paradigm for Little Albert; the rat was initially a neutral stimulus (no fear) and the loud noise was an unconditioned stimulus (fear). As Little Albert reached for the rat and the loud noise occurred, he learned to associate the rat with the noise, and over seven trials the rat became the conditioned stimulus.

Similar paired associations can help explain a number of different types of adjustment problems in children and adolescents, although we do not typically know what the original association may have been. Additionally, more than one learning paradigm may be going on at the same time. For this reason, dual learning explanations for undesirable behavior are common (that is, combinations of features of both operant and classical conditioning). Returning to Jake's problem, imagine if he associated reading (a neutral event) with humiliation or anxiety (unconditioned stimuli), prompting him to escape or avoid such activity. His avoidance, in turn, is negatively reinforced by its consequences: His anxiety reduces and he avoids feelings of humiliation. This analysis considers both instrumental and respondent conditioning as part of his learning history. Can you think of possible environmental changes or contingencies that might modify his behavior in a desirable fashion?

Social Learning and Cognition. Like individual differences in temperament and emotion regulation, crucial differences exist in how children process information and make sense of their worlds. Like adults, children have a natural desire to evaluate their behavior or performance in various circumstances, especially those involving some element of possible failure, harm, or personal risk (Seligman et al., 1984). For some children, teens, and adults, these self-appraisals of performance may be based on faulty beliefs or distortions; for others, an *attributional bias* about their ability or the intention of others leads them to reinterpret the event in a way that fits their preexisting belief about themselves or others ("I got a good grade in math because the exam was too easy"; "He's a jerk, so who cares if I tease him"). Let's look at how some children learn a style of appraisal of themselves and others that can be self-defeating or distorted, and how such a style relates to behavior disorders.

Social learning theory is interested not only in overt behaviors, like Jake's school phobia, but also in the role of possible *cognitive mediators* that may influence such behaviors directly or indirectly. According to Albert Bandura's (1977, 1986) social learning explanation,

behavior may be learned not only by operant and classical conditioning, but also indirectly through *observational* (vicarious) learning. Children can learn a new behavior by merely watching another person model the behavior, without apparent reinforcement or practice (incidentally, such vicarious learning need not require the model's awareness that his or her actions are being observed).

Bandura's social learning model is sensitive to the role of **social cognition** in the acquisition of both desirable and undesirable behavior. Social cognition relates to how children think about themselves and others, resulting in the formation of *mental representations* of themselves, their relationships, and their social world. These representations are not fixed, but are continuously updated on the basis of maturation and social interaction (Noam, Chandler, & LaLonde, 1995). Children's ongoing cognitive development, in such areas as reasoning, problem solving, and making attributions, helps them make sense of who they are and how they relate to their surroundings. Moreover, social learning and social-cognitive viewpoints also consider the role of affect and the importance of contextual variables, such as family and peers, in both the etiology and maintenance of problem behaviors (Kendall, 1991).

Although children's cognitive development follows general rules, similar events and situations may be interpreted very differently by individual children. Children make meaning out of *their* reality, which may differ slightly or dramatically from the meanings chosen by others, such as teachers, parents, and siblings. However, their interpretations are not entirely idiosyncratic, which is why social-cognitive theorists are able to generate developmental typologies of meaning-making that have come to be known as stages. Children continually attempt to bring some organization to varied and often fragmented social experiences. Although the concept of stages still has utility, today social cognition theory and its various applications (e.g., cognitive-behavioral interventions, discussed in Chapter 4) are less attached to the notion that children form a sense of themselves and their surroundings in a stepwise (discontinuous) progression. More and more, children's development of meaning-making is seen as being fundamentally interactive, similar to their other developmental processes (Noam et al., 1995).

Cognitive structures and content. *Cognitive structures* and *cognitive content* (Beck et al., 1979; Dobson & Kendall, 1993) are important elements of cognition that are useful in understanding possible connections between children's thought processes and particular disorders or abnormal outcomes. Cognitive structures represent the way in which information is organized and stored in memory; they serve the function of filtering or screening ongoing experiences. Cognitive content (or propositions) refers to the information that is stored in memory—that is, the substance of the cognitive structures.

Together, cognitive structures and content make up what is termed the schema. The schema stems from a child's processing of life experiences and acts as a guideline or core philosophy influencing expectations and filtering information in a fashion consistent with the child's core philosophy. This is why cognitive schemata are sometimes referred to as filters or templates (Kendall & MacDonald, 1993), and why a child's thoughts and behavior tend to have some consistency and pattern (Stark, Rouse, & Livingston, 1991). According to Beck et al.'s model (1979), maladaptive schemata develop in early childhood and remain dormant until some event triggers the latent schemata and the individual begins to encode, process, and interpret information consistent with his or her schema. Individuals with depressive schemata, for instance, might process and interpret information about themselves, the world, and the future in a negatively biased fashion, known as the cognitive triad (Beck et al., 1979). Similarly, children with anxiety schemata interpret environmental stimuli with a cognitive focus on future threat (Kendall et al., 1988).

Deficits and distortions. Another important cognitive influence is the distinction between cognitive *deficits* and cognitive *distortions* (Kendall, 1993). *Deficits* refer to an absence of thinking where it would be beneficial. Aggressive youths, for example, frequently lack the ability to adequately solve social problems (Crick & Dodge, 1994), and impulsive children often fail to think before they respond (Moore & Hughes, 1988). In contrast, children who display cognitive *distortions* typically do not lack the ability to organize or process information; rather, their thinking is biased, dysfunctional, or misguided (Kendall & MacDonald, 1993). The depressed individual's negative view of him- or herself, the world, and the future is an example of distorted thinking. The distinction between deficient and distorted thinking may be related to the common distinction between externalizing and internalizing disorders (Kendall, 1993). In general, externalizing disorders are commonly associated with cognitive deficits, whereas internalizing disorders are often related to distortions in thinking.

Social information processing. Why is it that some children seem to interpret social situations inappropriately, leading to poor solutions and outcomes? For example, children who are aggressive more often interpret ambiguous social situations as entailing hostile intent ("You bumped into me *on purpose!*").

According to the social information processing model (Dodge, 1986), children approach unfamiliar social situations and try to resolve them in a three-step process. First, the child encodes and interprets social cues shown by others. In cases of peer conflict, this involves making an attribution regarding the other party's intent ("I think he *meant* to trip me"). Second, the child thinks about how to respond and decides which choice to pursue. To do this requires generating possible solutions to the situation, evaluating their potential effectiveness, and deciding on an initial solution (all of which are often done in a split second). The third and final step involves action or carrying through a selected problem-solving method, followed by monitoring of the outcome and possible return to an earlier step in the process. Children with conduct disorders, especially disorders involving aggression (discussed in Chapter 6), are most likely to attribute hostile intent when exposed to an ambiguous provocation by a peer. Moreover, these children have more deficits in problem-solving ability, which means they generate fewer or lower-quality solutions to unfamiliar situations (Dodge, 1980).

Since the discovery of observational learning in the early 1960s, cognitive models have grown both in richness and in complexity, and their constructs appear quite often throughout the text. Several of these key concepts are described in Table 2.3. The role of cognitive distortions, insufficient cognitive mediation, and attributional styles and expectations are important determinants in the development of behavioral and emotional problems (Kendall, Howard, & Epps, 1988).

Evolution and Infant–Care-Giver Attachment

The study of abnormal development has profited from extensive work with nonhuman species, which has painted a dramatic picture of how important early care-giver attachment is to a child's emotional health. In their pioneering work in the late 1950s and early 1960s, H. K. and M. K. Harlow found that monkeys reared in total isolation developed strange feeding, mating, parenting, and socializing behaviors. When stressed, infant monkeys reared without their biological mothers chose to seek comfort from the surrogate mother that allowed them to cling when frightened (a wire monkey covered with cloth, as opposed to just wire). The importance of placing human relationships within a biological-evolutionary context grew from these beginnings (Kraemer, 1992).

Bowlby (1973, 1988) integrated aspects of evolutionary biology with existing psychodynamic conceptions of early experiences to derive his theory of **attachment**. He conceptualized attachment as a set of behaviors that promote interaction, and which have likely evolved in social species, like humans and primates, because of the role they play in promoting survival (Carlson & Sroufe, 1995). Within attachment theory, instinctive behaviors are not rigidly predetermined but rather

Table 2.3 Social-Cognitive Terms and Concepts

Competencies: Ability to construct or generate certain cognitions and behaviors in an adaptive fashion. A child's competencies refer to what the child knows and is able to do.

Attributions: One's typical explanations about the causes of events. Attributions vary along three or more dimensions: *internal-external,* or the degree to which a person views a cause as due to something about him- or herself or the environment; *stable-unstable,* or the degree to which a person sees the cause as being permanent or temporary; and *global-specific,* meaning the extent to which a person sees the cause as being specific to a particular situation or occurring in all situations.

Cognitive appraisal and distortion: One's interpretation or evaluation of an event, which can be subjectively distorted. We evaluate our performance and that of others every day. Such cognitive evaluations, or appraisals, can be marked by faulty logic or reasoning (distortions), which can have an impact on our behavior. Consider Jake's appraisals of his difficulty at school: "It's the teachers," and "they think I'm dumb." Although there may be some grain of truth to his appraisal, from a more objective standpoint he has overstated, or distorted, the situation.

Encoding strategies and schemata: Methods the child uses to categorize events, people, and the self. Schemata represent guidelines or core philosophies that influence a child's expectations and filter information in a fashion consistent with the child's core philosophy.

Expectancies: Relative likelihood of certain outcomes in particular situations, usually derived from previous experiences and appraisals. *Self-efficacy* refers to the confidence one has in performing the behavior necessary to achieve the desired outcome. A low self-efficacy is reflected in Jake's comment, "I know I'll never get anywhere with the brain I've got."

Subjective values: One's personal set of values. These subjective values motivate children as well as adults and arouse them to action. They also provide them with incentives or disincentives: "How important is it for me to do this?" "Will I get something out of it that I want?"

Self-regulatory systems and plans: A set of rules and reactions that can be applied to new or unfamiliar situations. These systems and plans help both children and adults form their personal methods of regulating stressful situations by developing coping strategies used to approach unfamiliar situations. One's self-regulatory system is the culmination of previous learning experiences and self-efficacy: "How likely is it that I can do this?"

become organized into flexible, goal-oriented systems through learning and goal-corrected feedback. Infants, he reasoned, are preadapted to engage in relationship-enhancing behaviors, such as orienting, smiling, crying, clinging, signaling, and, as they learn to move about,

proximity seeking. In order to survive, however, infants must become attached to a specific person who is available and responsive to their needs. Adults are similarly equipped with attachment-promoting behaviors to respond to an infant's needs, which are complementary to those of the infant—smiling, touching, holding, and rocking.

The evolving infant–care-giver relationship helps the infant regulate her or his behavior and emotions, especially under conditions of threat or stress. Accordingly, attachment serves an important stress-reduction function. The infant is motivated to maintain a balance between the desire to preserve the familiar and the desire to seek and explore new information. Self-reliance develops when the attachment figure provides a secure base for such exploration (Bretherton, 1995). Moreover, a child's *internal working model* of relationships—what he or she expects from others and how he or she relates to others—emerges from this first crucial relationship. A description of the three major, organized patterns of attachment is summarized in Table 2.4, along with their theoretical and empirical links to various forms of psychopathology.

FAMILY AND SOCIAL INFLUENCES

In addition to biological and psychological influences, children's normal and abnormal development depends on its social and environmental contexts. Understanding context requires a consideration of both *proximal* (close-by) and *distal* (further-removed) events, as well as those that impinge directly on the child in a particular situation at a particular time. We consider these wide-ranging environmental conditions and learning experiences in relation to the family and peer context and the social and cultural context.

What exactly do we mean when we refer to a child's environment? Family? Peer groups? Clean air? To appreciate the complex network that constitutes a child's world and contributes to maladjustment, we need to go beyond the traditional view of the environment as being unidimensional or narrowly defined. A child's environment is constantly changing in relation to its many components, much like a lake or stream is affected by proximal events, such as a rainstorm, as well as more distal events, such as the seasons.

Bronfenbrenner's (1977) **ecological model** shows the richness and depth of the various layers of a child's environment by portraying it as a series of nested and interconnected structures (see Figure 2.7). Notice that the child is at the nucleus of this sphere of influence, which contains various levels that are interconnected in

Table 2.4 Types of Organized Attachment and Their Relation to Psychopathology

Type of Attachment	Description During Strange Situation[1]	Influence on Relationships	Possible Disordered Outcomes
Secure	Infant readily separates from care-giver and likes to explore. When wary of a stranger or distressed by separation, infant seeks contact with and proximity to care-giver. Infant returns to exploration and play after contact.	Individuals with secure attachment histories tend to seek out and make effective use of supportive relationships.	Although individuals with secure attachments may suffer psychological distress, their relationship strategy serves a protective function against disordered outcomes.
Insecure: anxious, avoidant type	Infant engages in exploration, but with little affective interaction with care-giver. Infant shows little wariness of strangers and generally is upset only if left alone. Avoidant infants do not show a preference for a care-giver over a stranger. As stress increases, avoidance increases.	Individuals with *insecure, avoidant* patterns of early attachment tend to mask emotional expression. They often believe they are invulnerable to hurt and others are not to be trusted. Underlying resentments may be present, derived from unmet emotional needs and from relationship experiences that include exploitation and victimization.	Conduct disorders, aggressive behavior, depressive symptoms (usually resulting from lack of self-reliant image).
Insecure: anxious, resistant type	Infant shows disinterest or resistance to exploration and play, and is wary of novel situations or strangers. Infant has difficulty settling down when reunited with care-giver and may mix active contact seeking with crying and fussiness.	Individuals with *insecure, resistant* patterns of early attachment have difficulties managing anxiety. They tend to exaggerate emotions and maintain negative beliefs about the self.	Phobias, anxiety, psychosomatic symptoms, depression.

[1]The Strange Situation is a method of assessing infant–care-giver attachment. It involves a series of increasingly stressful separations and reunions that resemble typical daily occurrences, such as meeting strangers and being left alone (Ainsworth, Blehar, Waters, & Wall, 1978).

Note: A fourth attachment style, labeled "disorganized, disoriented type," has also been identified, but is not considered an *organized* strategy. An infant showing a disorganized style lacks a coherent strategy of attachment. The infant appears disorganized when faced with a novel situation and has no consistent pattern of regulating emotions. It is believed that the care-giver has served both as a source of fear as well as a biologically based source of reassurance, leading to the infant's conflict and disorganized approach. This style may be connected to child abuse and neglect.

The relationships between attachment styles and abnormal development are based on both theoretical and empirical findings, summarized in Carlson & Sroufe (1995).

meaningful ways. The *microsystem,* at the center of the model, refers to relations between the child and the immediate environment. For young children this consists primarily of family members and their home surroundings, but it quickly grows more complex as children enter preschool, visit neighborhood parks, and make friends. The next level, the *mesosystem,* describes the links or interrelationships among the child's various microsystems, such as visits to the doctor, relations among family members, and day care experiences.

The third level, the *exosystem,* represents social settings that affect the child, but which the child does not experience directly. Parents' friends and jobs, the availability of family support services such as health and welfare programs, and similar community resources and activities (positive as well as negative) make up the child's larger social framework and should not be overlooked when considering possible reasons for a particular child's maladaptive behavior. Finally, the *macrosystem* refers to the cultural or subcultural context in

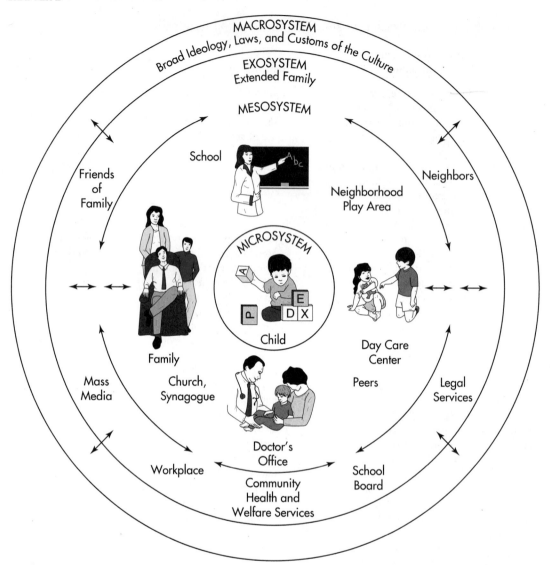

FIGURE 2.7 An ecological model of environmental influences. (Based on Bronfenbrenner as presented in Shaffer, 1996)

which all the other systems are embedded. The macrosystem, though far removed from the child's day-to-day activities, represents a cultural ideology or identity, which governs how children should be treated (e.g., the sanctioning of corporal punishment), what they should be taught, and what goals are important to achieve. These levels of environmental influences and their reciprocal connections (they affect the child, and the child affects them) are key elements in understanding the nature of particular disorders—child abuse and neglect, eating disorders, and many others.

The Family and Peer Context

The ecological model shows the multiple contexts that can influence development. It visually portrays the importance of moving beyond the traditional mother-child relationship, to include the effects of other relationships the child participates in without the parent, and vice versa. A child's family and peer relationships constitute perhaps the most influential context influencing development.

Child psychopathology research has increasingly focused on the role of the family system, the complex relationships within families, and the reciprocal influences among various family subsystems. There is a need to consider the processes occurring within disturbed families and the common and unique ways in which these processes affect both individual family members and subsystems. Within the family, the roles of the mother-child and marital subsystems have received the most research attention to date, with less attention given to the role of siblings (Hetherington, Reiss, & Plomin, 1994) or fathers (Phares & Compas, 1992).

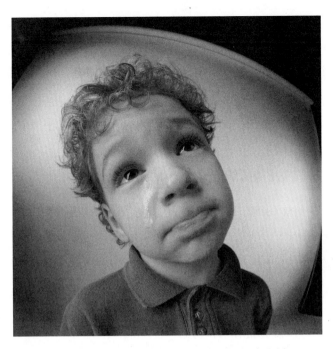

Who can explain the mysteries and fascination of children's thoughts, feelings, and behaviors?

Family systems theorists argue that it is difficult to understand or predict the behavior of a particular family member, such as a child, in isolation from other family members (Wagner & Reiss, 1995). This view is in line with our earlier discussion of underlying assumptions about children's abnormal development: *Relationships*, not individual children or teens, are very often the crucial focus. This view, however, is often at odds with mainstream psychological and psychiatric approaches to psychopathology, yet it is compatible with developmental processes, such as transaction. More and more, the study of individual factors and the study of the child's context, such as family and peer relationships, are being seen as mutually compatible and beneficial to both theory and intervention. Furthermore, the manner in which the family, as a unit, deals with typical and atypical stresses, such as conflict and unemployment, plays an instrumental role in children's adjustment and adaptation. Stress brings about change, growth, and reorganization of families (C. P. Cowan, P. A. Cowan, Heming, & Miller, 1991), and the outcome of such events depends in part on the nature and severity of the stress, the level of family functioning prior to the stress, and the family's coping skills and resources (Wagner & Reiss, 1995).

Some of the more influential family-related issues that are involved in discussions of childhood disorders are parental depression, child abuse, parental alcoholism, parental divorce, marital violence, and parental criminality. Parental alcoholism, for example, is associated with a pattern of inconsistent and unpredictable child care, which interferes with normal child-rearing and the development of a healthy parent-child relationship. Not surprisingly, alcoholism is associated with adjustment problems in children, especially males (West & Prinz, 1987). Although quite distinct, these major family and individual issues share a common thread in terms of their impact on child development: They disrupt, disturb, or interfere with consistent and predictable child care and basic necessities. Such disruption or impairment, in turn, affects the child's ability to form satisfactory relationships with peers, teachers, and other adults (Sameroff, 1995).

The Social and Cultural Context

Cultural and ethnic variations and situational opportunities and circumstances can all influence the course and expression of children's development and psychological disorders, either singly or in combination. Once again, however, caution is necessary in interpreting these connections. They rarely affect children's development *directly*, but instead, interact with individual and situational factors.

Childhood poverty is a disturbing reality for about one in five children in both the United States (Corcoran & Chaudry, 1997) and Canada (Statistics Canada, 1997), and unfortunately, has been steadily increasing in both countries over the past quarter century. Growing up with poverty has a substantial effect on the well-being of children and adolescents, especially in terms of impairments in learning ability and school achievement (Brooks-Gunn & Duncan, 1997; Institute of Medicine, 1989; Schteingart, Molnar, Klein, Lowe, & Hartmann, 1995). Moreover, low income is tied to many other forms of disadvantage, such as less education, poor-paying jobs, inadequate health care, single-parent status, limited resources, poor nutrition, and greater exposure to violence, any of which can impair children's developmental progress significantly (Brooks-Gunn & Duncan, 1997). Poverty has a significant, yet indirect, effect on children's adjustment, most likely because of its association with such negative influences, particularly harsh, inconsistent parenting and elevated exposure to acute and chronic stressors, that define the day-to-day experiences of children in poverty (McLoyd, 1998).

Minority children are often overrepresented in rates of some disorders, such as substance abuse, delinquency, and teen suicide (McLoyd, 1998). However, once the effects of SES, sex, age, and referral status are controlled (that is, the unique contributions of these factors are removed or accounted for), very few differences in children's psychological disorders emerge in relation to race or ethnicity (Achenbach, Howell, Quay, & Conners, 1991; Lahey et al., 1995). What might these results indicate? Consider how minority children and youth face multiple disadvantages, such as exclusion from society's benefits (often referred to as *marginalization*), as well as poverty. Marginalization can result in a sense of alienation, loss of social cohesion, and rejection of the norms of the larger society (Steinhauer, 1996). Resisting the combined effects of poverty and marginalization takes unusual personal strength and familial support. Since there is an overrepresentation of minority-status children in low SES groups in North America, we must interpret with caution the relationships among SES, ethnicity, and behavior problems that often emerge in discussing childhood disorders (Guerra et al., 1995; Lahey et al., 1995).

Recently, society's understanding of children's healthy, normal development has been gradually evolving toward a more holistic, health-promoting orientation, which is having an impact on definitions and services related to children's mental health (Millstein et al., 1993). This emerging dynamic, interactive view of health recognizes the importance of both individual and environmental factors in achieving positive development. The ecological and system perspectives on human health and behavior noted above add momentum to this growing view, because they consider human adaptation within its normal context.

Children's health and successful adaptation are today seen as worthy and appropriate aspects of the study of abnormal child psychology. Along with an increased emphasis on **health promotion**—encouraging changes, opportunities, and competence to achieve one's health potential (Millstein et al., 1993)—today's research and thinking accepts the notion that childhood disorders share many clinical features and causes. This view recognizes the multicausal and interactive nature of many child and adult psychological disorders and the importance of contextual factors, and speaks to the importance of balancing the abilities of individuals with the challenges and risks of their environments. Throughout the text we return to the many ways that abnormal child psychology can be studied in a developmentally sensitive, systems-oriented manner.

These conceptual shifts are gradually changing the face of mental health and educational services for children and youth, with important implications for fields such as pediatrics, psychology, psychiatry, social work, nursing, education, and child development. How individuals think about health, how daily life is organized and experienced, how social policy is developed, how social resources are allocated, and how people are trained to implement these policies have reached their greatest potential in the history of humankind for achieving a major impact on improved services to assist younger populations that cannot speak for themselves. Although this tremendous impact on the field of mental health, and on children and youth in particular, has not yet become reality (Takanishi, 1993), we are encouraged by how society has progressed throughout this century in addressing the needs of children.

SUMMARY

What Caused Jake's Problems?

1. The study of causes of abnormal child behavior involves theory and findings on genetic and neurobiological factors; psychological influences, such as the role of cognitive and emotional processes; and environmental influences, such as family patterns and cultural norms.

The Role of Theory

2. A theory allows us to make educated guesses and predictions about behavior based on existing knowledge, and to explore these possible explanations empirically.

3. Developmental psychopathology provides a useful framework for organizing the study of abnormal child psychology around milestones and sequences in physical, cognitive, social-emotional, and educational development.

Theoretical Foundations

4. A central theme of the text is the importance of considering multiple, interactive causes for abnormal behavior, in conjunction with major developmental changes that typically occur.

5. Three underlying assumptions about abnormal development are stressed: It is multiply determined, the child and the environment are interdependent, and it involves continuities and discontinuities.

Biological Perspectives

6. Brain functions undergo continual changes, described as neural plasticity, as they adapt to environmental demands.

7. Genetic influences depend on the environment. Genetic endowment influences behavior, emotions, and thoughts; environmental events are necessary for this influence to be expressed.

8. Neurobiological contributions to abnormal child behavior include knowledge of brain structures, the endocrine system, and neurotransmitters, which perform their functions in an integrated, harmonious fashion.

Psychological Perspectives

9. Emotion reactivity and regulation are critical aspects of early and subsequent development, affecting the quality of children's social interactions and relationships throughout the life span.

10. Three major approaches to abnormal behavior, based on principles of learning, are applied behavior analysis, principles of classical conditioning, and social learning and social cognition theories. The latter theories place more significance on cognitive processes, in addition to overt behavior.

11. Evolutionary approaches to abnormal child behavior emphasize the evolving infant–care-giver relationship, which helps the infant regulate behavior and emotions, especially under conditions of threat or stress.

Family and Social Influences

12. Children's normal and abnormal development depends on a variety of social and environmental settings, including the child's family and peer system as well as the larger social and cultural context.

KEY TERMS

adaptational failure, 31
developmental psychopathology, 31
macroparadigm, 31
organization of development, 32
sensitive periods, 32
interdependent, 34
transaction, 35
continuity, 37
discontinuity, 37
neurobiological perspective, 39
synapses, 39
pruning, 39
neural plasticity, 39
monosomy, 41
trisomy, 41
translocation, 41
hormones, 41
neurotransmitters, 41
behavioral genetics, 42
familial aggregation, 42
genotype, 42
phenotype, 42
proband, 42
frontal lobe, 44
endocrine system, 44
epinephrine, 44
cortisol, 45
hypothalamic-pituitary-adrenal (HPA) axis, 45
brain circuits, 45
emotion reactivity, 47
emotion regulation, 47
temperament, 48
social learning theory, 50
social cognition, 50
schema, 51
attachment, 51
ecological model, 52
family systems, 55
health promotion, 56

Research Strategies in Abnormal Child Psychology

Shelly and Mike Dumas: Research Participants

"What have I forgotten?" says Shelly Dumas as she rushes about the house getting her 7-year-old son Mike and herself ready for their 3 o'clock session at the hospital. Mike has attention-deficit/hyperactivity disorder (ADHD), and she and Mike have agreed to participate in a study being carried out by researchers at the clinic where Mike was first evaluated for his ADHD a year ago and was put on medication. Mrs. Dumas has a slight headache and thinks, "I'm really not in the mood to do this—maybe I'll call and cancel." She decides, however, that she'd better not cancel because the appointment is only a half hour away and people are waiting for them. "Hurry up, Mike. Put your coat on," she shouts into the other room where Mike is watching TV. Mike's been off his medication for about a day now because the researchers want to study him when he's not taking his pills. "He's getting really 'hyper,'" she thinks. The doorbell rings—it's the baby-sitter who will be looking after her 4-year-old daughter, Maggie, while Mrs. Dumas and Mike are at the clinic. "Let's see, have I got everything? Directions to the clinic? The parking pass they sent me? The questionnaires my husband and I completed? Mike's medication for after the study?" Mrs. Dumas rushes into the other room. "Let's go," she says to Mike. "But I want to watch TV!" he protests. She takes Mike by the hand, wrestles him into his coat, and drags him out of the house. "Do I really need this aggravation?" she wonders as they get into the car. "Well, this is important. This research could find something to help children with ADHD and parents like me. We could sure use the help."

As Mrs. Dumas and Mike turn the corner to pull into the hospital parking lot, Dr. Ellen Johnson and her research assistant, Maria Perez, are meeting to review the research procedures and to make sure the interview forms, test materials, and video equipment are ready. It took months of planning to develop the research protocol for this study, to get approval from the institutional ethics committee, and to obtain a grant for the thousands of dollars needed to carry out a project like this. Everything must go exactly as specified. Dr. Johnson is a clinical psychologist and a postdoctoral research fellow who is part of a research team working on this study with Dr. Charles Barker, a world-renowned expert on ADHD who developed the idea for the project. Dr. Johnson has been interested in children with ADHD for years, and working on this project is exactly what she wants to give her more research experience. It's a lot of work, but it's also very rewarding. Maria Perez has an undergraduate degree in psychology and has been working on the project for about a year. It's been a wonderful experience for her as she's learned how to administer tests, to code observations of parent-child interactions, and to train others how to do this. Maria hopes to go on to graduate school in psychology herself one day. She wants to work with children who have problems. The research grant pays both Dr. Johnson's and Maria's salaries, as well as the many other costs of the project.

The research procedures today will take about 2 hours. Dr. Johnson will be explaining the procedures to Mrs. Dumas and interviewing her about her son and her family, while Maria administers several tests and other tasks to Mike. After these procedures are completed, Mike and his mother will be observed through a one-way mirror while they interact in the clinic observation-playroom. These interactions will be videotaped and later coded by two observers who don't know anything about the project or Mrs. Dumas and Mike. Maria checks the video equipment to make sure that everything is working. If it isn't, hours of time will be lost at considerable expense. Dr. Johnson checks to make sure that she has all the necessary consent forms. Everything is ready to go. There is a sense of anticipation about the first appointment with this family. There will be three sessions altogether. In the next session Mr. Dumas, Mike's father, will be coming in to interact with Mike, and in the final session Mike will be observed while interacting with his sister, Maggie. If today's session doesn't go well, the family might not return for their other scheduled appointments. Just then the phone rings. It's the receptionist calling to say that Mrs. Dumas and Mike have arrived. Dr. Johnson and Maria make their way to the waiting room to see a somewhat nervous-looking young woman and her very active 7-year-old son. Mike is climbing on the waiting room furniture as Mrs. Dumas tries unsuccessfully to coax him back to his chair. Dr. Johnson says, "Good afternoon Mrs. Dumas, I'm Dr. Johnson." Maria approaches Mike, and says, "Hi, I'm Maria. You must be Mike." The research session begins.

As this brief, behind-the-scenes look at the events immediately preceding the research session with Mike and his mother indicates, a considerable amount of thought, time, energy, and money goes into most research projects—on the part of both the researchers and the study participants. Therefore, it is critical that any research project be carefully planned and executed in a way that will yield meaningful and interpretable results. In this chapter we take a close look at the process of research and the numerous challenges faced by investigators who study disturbed children and their families. Many different ideas exist about what constitutes research. In fact, if you were to ask ten different people what research is, you just might get ten different answers! Although people may differ on the specifics, research is generally viewed as a systematic way of asking questions—a method of inquiry that follows certain general rules.

Planning and implementing a research study in abnormal child psychology includes several important steps. First, the researcher needs to develop an idea based on theory and prior research findings about childhood disorders. For example, Dr. Barker was interested in learning more about the impact of attention-deficit/hyperactivity disorder (ADHD) on parent-child interactions and family relationships. As you will discover in Chapter 5, ADHD is a severe disorder involving developmentally inappropriate levels of inattention, hyperactivity, and impulsivity, behaviors that place considerable demands and stress on the child and his or her family (Anastopoulos, Guevremont, Shelton, & DuPaul, 1992). On the basis of social learning theories of parent-child interaction and findings from previous studies, Dr. Barker made several predictions. One was that there would be fewer positive and more negative exchanges between children with ADHD and their parents as compared with exchanges between children without ADHD and their parents. Another prediction, based on the fact that mothers typically have more responsibility for the day-to-day demands of child care than do fathers, was that children with ADHD would display more negative behavior when interacting with mothers than with fathers. This first stage of research, developing a meaningful research question, is often the most challenging part of the research process.

Second, the researcher must decide on an appropriate research method—a way to carefully observe and systematically evaluate children with problems under varying conditions. This step involves choosing from among a large number of research methods and deciding exactly what the participants will do—be interviewed, complete questionnaires, take tests, be observed. For Mike and his mother, all these methods were used. Research methods provide the investigators with a reliable way of assessing the variables of interest.

Third, the researcher must select a **research design,** an overall strategy for testing the idea. Mike and his mother are part of a group made up of families with children with ADHD who will be compared with a control group consisting of families with children who have no disorder. Finally, all the procedures must be carefully examined from an ethical standpoint for any possible harm they might cause the children and families who agree to participate in the research. For example, will taking Mike off his medication for a day, as required in this study, have any lasting adverse effects on his real-life behavior? Will being in a study like this make Mike feel that something is wrong with him—that he is different from other children? Before discussing the steps in the research process in more detail, we consider the

Reaching for answers in abnormal child psychology involves the careful planning and implementation of a research strategy.

overall importance of a scientific approach to the study of abnormal child psychology.

A SCIENTIFIC APPROACH

All who drink this remedy recover in a short time except those whom it does not help, who all die. Therefore, it is obvious that it only fails in incurable cases.
—*Attributed to Galen (second century A.D.)*

What's wrong with Galen's conclusion? How might you go about testing Galen's claims? Scientific research strategies provide systematic ways of investigating claims in ways that improve on casual observations. Science requires that claims such as the one attributed to Galen be based on logic and systematically constructed theories that are backed up by empirical evidence from controlled studies, and that observations be checked and repeated before conclusions are drawn. A scientific approach is especially important in abnormal child psychology. Although relations between variables of interest may seem obvious when observed casually—such as the one between a child's consuming too much sugar and hyperactivity—these relations are often obscured by complex interactions and combinations of variables. For example, on days when children consume too much sugar—Halloween, birthdays, or outings—they may also be tired or excited. Or mothers who know their children have consumed a lot of sugar may see them as more active, even when they are not, because of expectations the mothers have about the relation between sugar and activity (Hoover & Milich, 1994). The task of recogniz-

ing relations is complicated by our own shortcomings as observers as well as those of our informants, particularly with regard to children, who may not be reliable informants for their own behavior, thus often making it necessary to rely on information provided by others. Parents and professionals who work with children have a tendency to associate variables that they observe and to integrate them with their own belief systems. These relations can become firmly established, independent of the extent to which these variables are really connected or whether the relationship is supported by facts (Kazdin, 1998).

Many opinions about children and childhood disorders are characterized by casual observations or common-sense explanations between variables involving references to metaphysical influences, such as "hard work builds a child's moral character," or "spare the rod and spoil the child." These explanations do not fit easily into an observable, empirically testable framework. The field of abnormal child psychology is also characterized by considerable folklore and numerous home remedies and fad treatments. Simple explanations, such as "sugar causes hyperactivity," or simple solutions, such as "a parent should never give in to a child's demands" or "children with ADHD should be placed in isolated cubicles in the classroom in order to reduce distractions" are appealing because they promise parents or teachers an easy answer or quick remedy for a complex problem. Folklore and fad treatments, unintentionally or otherwise, play to the vulnerabilities of parents of children with problems, parents who desperately want the best for their children. More often than not, these answers or remedies don't work, and they sometimes bring unfortunate consequences and costs for disturbed children and their families.

As noted in Chapter 1, many things that psychologists once believed were true about childhood disorders (e.g., masturbation leads to insanity) have turned out to be false when subjected to scientific analysis. Moreover, even though childhood disorders have been recognized for some time, their scientific study is relatively recent. Thus, the knowledge base is growing and changing rapidly, almost daily in some areas of research. Consequently, some of the things you learn about abnormal child psychology in this text will likely turn out to be untrue (hopefully this will not happen until after you've written your next exam!). For this reason, maintaining a healthy degree of skepticism about research findings presented here and elsewhere and challenging them at every turn are vital. To be a knowledgeable consumer who can separate reliable information from dubious claims, you must know the strengths and weaknesses of the various research methods and strategies for studying childhood disorders.

A scientific approach to the study of abnormal child psychology is a way of thinking about how to best understand and answer questions of interest, not an accumulation of specific methods, practices, or procedures. Placing too much emphasis on concrete research practices can lead to a rigid adherence to specific methods, such as the use of large sample sizes, random assignment of subjects to groups, the use of arbitrary levels of statistical significance, an overreliance on certain data sources, and an obsession with data rather than what the data mean (a disorder facetiously dubbed "quantiphrenia"), when these practices may not be necessary to reach valid inferences (Kazdin, 1998).

People have always shown some skepticism about scientific research leading to new knowledge. Mark Twain (1883) had a healthy suspicion of both science and statistics: "There is something fascinating about science," he said. "One gets such wholesale returns of conjecture out of such a trifling investment of fact" (p. 141). Also consider the following comments:

> After a few more flashes in the pan, we shall hear very little more of Edison and his electric lamp. Every claim he makes has been tested and proved impracticable.
> —*New York Times,* January 16, 1880

> Louis Pasteur's theory of germs is ridiculous fiction.
> —Pachet, Professor of Physiology, Toulouse, 1872

Fortunately, the lightbulb, pasteurization, and many other ideas that were once viewed with skepticism seem to have caught on. Some good reasons exist for skepticism of research in abnormal child psychology (Kazdin, 1998). First, experts on childhood disorders frequently disagree—newspapers, magazines, and TV talk shows provide a steady diet of conflicting opinions. The answers we get to questions—Does watching violence on TV make children more aggressive? Does day care have a harmful effect on children's emotional adjustment? Do we need more discipline in our schools?—often depend on whom we ask. Second, research findings in abnormal child psychology are often in conflict with one another. For example, most studies find that girls are more prone to depression than boys, but some report higher rates of depression in boys than in girls, and others report no differences. Even studies that ask a seemingly simple question such as "How common is ADHD?" produce widely discrepant estimates, some indicating that ADHD is a relatively rare disorder and others, that it runs rampant among school-age children. How do we make sense out of these inconsistent and often contradictory findings?

A third reason for skepticism is that research has led to different recommendations regarding the ways in which children with problems should be helped. In some cases, the same treatment has been shown to be helpful, to have no effects, or to be harmful. As one practitioner put it after hearing about an effective new treatment method at a conference, "I'd better hurry home and use it quickly before a study is published to show that it doesn't work!" Fourth, many conclusions from research with children are qualified—rarely are there black-and-white answers: A moderate amount of discipline is good; too little or too much discipline is bad. Certain treatments may work for some children but not for others, for boys but not for girls, for younger but not for older children, and in some situations but not in others. Fifth, even when scientific evidence is relatively clear and produces a consensus, many parents and professionals may dismiss the findings because they have encountered an exception, usually one drawn from personal experience. For example, despite the voluminous research showing that the habitual use of harsh physical punishment by parents can have extremely negative effects on children's development (see Chapter 14), a parent may still say, "My father used his belt on me when I was a kid and it sure taught me how to behave properly!" Finally, many people are skeptical of research with children and families because they believe research is intrusive and can have potentially harmful effects on the participants.

As a student of abnormal child psychology, you will find that interpreting and making sense out of the morass of conflicting opinions, theories, and findings that surround children with problems and their families is not always easy. Practitioners, parents, teachers, and public policymakers who must take action based upon these conflicting research findings often experience a similar sense of frustration. In view of this state of affairs, keep in mind that inconsistent and contradictory research findings are not necessarily a problem with scientific research, but rather, may reflect the complexities of empirical relationships in the study of child psychopathology. One shouldn't criticize the method because the same variable is found to be associated with one outcome in some children and a different outcome in others (Kazdin, 1998).

Many studies in abnormal child psychology have produced inconclusive findings, and trying to draw conclusions from knowledge that is not convincing presents certain complexities and challenges. Because no single study is perfect, it's important to be an informed consumer and to keep in mind that it's the accumulation of findings—not a single study—that advances the field. Recent research in abnormal child psychology has led to enormous and exciting advances in understanding children with problems and how they can best be helped. The next section provides an example of some of the lessons to be learned when scientific methods and evidence are ignored or dismissed.

Facilitated Communication: A Case Example

The story of facilitated communication provides an interesting illustration of a fad treatment, and an example of how the general public and, unfortunately, some professionals, may fail to recognize the need for a scientific approach and evidence in assessing the value of a treatment (Jacobson, Mulick, & Schwartz, 1995). *Facilitated communication (FC)* is a seemingly well-meant but highly controversial and misused procedure for teaching communication skills to children with autism and other impairments. With this method a "facilitator" provides manual assistance by lightly holding a child's hand, wrist, or arm, while the child supposedly communicates by typing on a keyboard or by pointing to letters on an alphabet board. The alleged purpose of the manual support by the facilitator is to help the child press the keys that she or he wants to press—*not* to influence key selection. However, because manual assistance by the facilitator is continued indefinitely, the possibility of direct influence by the facilitator exists.

FC was widely publicized when it was reported that children who received FC showed feats of literacy and intellectual competence far in excess of their presumed abilities (Biklen, 1990). The results were seen as especially remarkable because the typical youngster using FC had a lifelong history of autism or profound mental retardation, or both, and had never talked (Jacobson et al., 1995). In one report, for example, a mute young girl with no apparent awareness of the meaning of money or the importance of holidays or gifts, allegedly typed out that she didn't like Christmas because she didn't have money to buy her mother a present (Dillon, 1993). Proponents of FC claim that with this method, children with autism can generate phrases and sentences describing complex memories and feelings, and demonstrate other advanced language skills (Biklen & Cardinal, 1997). FC has received widespread and relatively uncritical exposure in the popular media, and is used with thousands of handicapped youngsters each day at a likely cost of millions of dollars per month (Mulick, Jacobson, & Kobe, 1993). However, critics of FC view the procedure as quackery—no different from using a Ouija board. Are the extraordinary outcomes attributed to FC fact, or are they fiction? Scientific research would indicate fiction—objective demonstrations and controlled studies have consistently found that the child's supposed communication is being controlled by the facilitator (see Box 3.1). It is the facilitator, not the child, who is doing the communicating (Jacobson et al., 1995).

FC is of special interest to our discussion of a scientific approach because it meets many of the criteria of pseudoscience: Demonstrations of benefit are based

---

Box 3.1

Facilitated Communication: Who's Doing the Communicating?

The controversy surrounding facilitated communication (FC) heated up and led to disastrous consequences for some families when their facilitators believed they had uncovered reports of child molestation by family members. In one such case of alleged child abuse by a family member, FC was tested by an independent evaluator under three conditions. In the first condition, the girl and her facilitator both could hear the questions. In this condition, the girl answered eight or nine of ten questions correctly. In the second condition, the facilitator heard music through headphones while the girl heard the questions. In this condition, the girl answered none of the questions correctly. In the third condition, both the facilitator and the girl wore headphones and sometimes heard the same questions and sometimes heard different questions. In this condition, the girl answered four of ten questions correctly when she heard the same questions as the facilitator, but answered none correctly when she heard different questions. Interestingly, four of the girl's incorrect answers were correct answers to the questions heard by the facilitator. What conclusions would you draw from this demonstration? Who's doing the communicating?

Source: Autism Research Review, 6(1), 1992; cited in Dillon, 1993, p. 287.

---

on anecdotes or testimonials; the child's baseline abilities and the possibility of spontaneous improvement are ignored; and related scientific procedures are disavowed (Jacobson et al., 1995). FC also illustrates the potentially damaging effects of using practices that are not based on scientific evidence. Parents who want the best for their children and overburdened staff are particularly vulnerable to the false promise of questionable interventions, especially when recognized authorities misrepresent or misinterpret treatment effects in introducing the approach to parents. The negative impact of FC on families is apparent in the following comments by the father of a young boy with autism:

> Professionals are very quick to dismiss the abilities of autistics. . . . So when Facilitated Communication (FC) proponents say they have found a way around the wall, parents are quick to believe. FC confirms our faith in our children. But . . . the workshops can cost $250. The equipment $800 more. And what do we get for our money? Parents themselves "can't facilitate," they tell us. Our children will require FC for life, they say, and will never communicate on their own. . . . In short, the price we are asked to pay in an effort to communicate with our children is to allow strangers into our families to mediate our

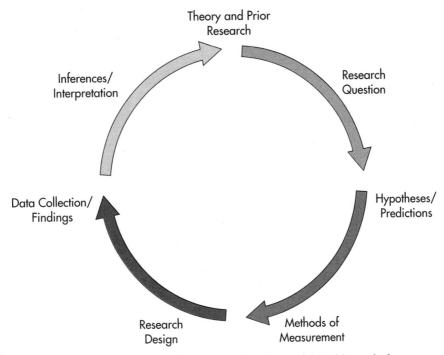

FIGURE 3.1 The research process in abnormal child psychology.

relationships with our own kids and to accept everything the stranger tells us on blind faith. Mark S. Painter, Sr. (Dillon, 1993, p. 286)

In the sections that follow, we consider the research process in abnormal child psychology. We first discuss the kinds of ideas and questions that researchers who study childhood disorders typically seek to address. Next, we consider the methods, general approaches, and research designs used to study developmental psychopathology. Lastly, we discuss important ethical and pragmatic issues related to research with disturbed children and adolescents.

THE RESEARCH PROCESS

Research activities in abnormal child psychology are best characterized as a multistage process involving a series of key decisions at various points. Like Dr. Barker's research in the opening case, the process typically begins with developing hypotheses on the basis of theory and previous findings, and deciding on a general approach to research. Next is selecting or developing data-collection measures, identifying the population to be studied, and developing a plan for sampling from that population. The research design and procedures must balance the practicalities of implementation with the adequacy of the research to address the hypotheses under investigation. The final stage consists of gathering and analyzing the

data, and interpreting the results in relation to theory and previous findings. In an ongoing process, findings and interpretations from the study can then be used to generate future research questions and stimulate further research. The main stages of the research process are summarized in Figure 3.1. Keep in mind that ethical considerations in conducting research with children and families must be taken into account at every stage of this process.

The research process guides how the events surrounding normal and atypical development are examined and interpreted. Since answers to most questions in abnormal child psychology depend on the nature of the child's problem and other child and family characteristics, using research methods and strategies that are appropriate to the types of questions being asked is crucial. A research method that is effective for answering one type of question may prove ineffective for others. A microscope can be a useful instrument for observing germs, but won't do the job if we wish to study the social behavior of baboons in the wild. Similarly, in abnormal child psychology, direct observation may be appropriate for answering questions about disturbed parent-child interactions—but questionnaires and interviews will likely tell more if we are interested in what parents and children think about the difficulties they are experiencing.

In practice, most problems in abnormal child psychology are best studied through the use of multiple research methods and strategies. Since there is no one correct approach to research in abnormal child psychology, research activities are best conceptualized within a decision-making framework. Such a framework requires an understanding of the theoretical, methodological, and practical considerations that permit the researcher to make informed decisions about when certain research methods and strategies are appropriate, and when they are not. As indicated in Chapters 1 and 2, developmental psychopathology involves multiple correlates, risk factors, and causes; direct and indirect effects; and reciprocal influences among variables. Consequently, to study developmental psychopathology, researchers need to include research designs and methods of data analysis that can distinguish direct and indirect effects, and that can identify, compare, and evaluate alternative pathways for different disorders. We next consider some of the specific issues encountered at various stages of the research process.

Research Ideas and Questions

Charles: Still Wets the Bed

My 6-year-old son Charles still wets the bed one or two nights a week. It's become much worse since my husband and I separated 3 months ago. Is this behavior normal for a boy his age?

Whitney: Always Sad

I just don't understand why my 11-year-old daughter Whitney is so sad all the time. She's constantly arguing with her brother, hates school, and has no friends. She's always been a moody child, but became much worse after my husband and I divorced. Is her sadness due to her personality, the divorce, or is something at home or at school making her feel this way?

Tito: Constantly Fighting

My 9-year-old son Tito is constantly fighting with other kids at school. He never does what we ask him to do. When things don't go his way, he has a full-blown tantrum and throws and breaks things. My husband thinks Tito's just a tough kid, and that all he needs is firm discipline. He uses his belt a lot with Tito, but it doesn't seem to make a difference. I'm really worried. Will Tito outgrow his behavior? Is my husband being too strict? What can I do about it?

These questions are typical of ones that parents ask about their children's behavior and development—they are also the kinds of questions that spawn research into abnormal child behavior (Achenbach, 1978; Kazdin, 1998). Research typically begins with a *hypothesis*, which is a prediction about behavior that follows from a theory. Hypotheses for research are often based on the theories of atypical development and behavior that we discussed in Chapter 2. Some research studies attempt to compare hypotheses based on one theory versus another. For example, theories that attribute aggressive behavior in children to a neurobiological deficit may predict that parenting practices will not play much of a role in the development of aggressive behavior, in contrast to those theories that view aggressive behavior as due to faulty parenting practices, such as the use of inconsistent discipline or harsh punishment. Other research studies attempt to test predictions drawn from one theory. For example, attachment theory would predict that children who have a secure early attachment with their parents will develop better peer relationships than those with an insecure attachment. Alternatively, learning theory might predict that parents who give their children lots of attention when they have tantrums will have children who display tantrums more frequently than children whose parents ignore their tantrums. When little or no theory is available, investigators may also develop a research question without making an explicit prediction. For example, what impact does growing up in a single-parent family have for children's psychological adjustment? What is the effect of day care on children? Are more children depressed these days than a generation ago? Is suicide among adolescents increasing? Is child abuse more prevalent in our society than in other parts of the world?

Theory and Research. As discussed in Chapter 2, the knowledge base of psychology has traditionally developed through the dynamic interplay of theory and empiricism, leading to new information. Theory, often developed from observations, leads to predictions that are empirically supported or refuted. These empirical findings, in turn, lead to refinement, alteration, or abandonment of the theory. Through theoretical formulations researchers can integrate related research results and develop meanings that extend beyond the immediate findings. Theory also provides the context for the formulation of new hypotheses and generalizations. The theoretical model of normal and abnormal child development and behavior that the researcher adopts will dictate the variables deemed important to study, the choice of research methods, and the interpretation of research findings.

Levels of theories for conceptualizing child psychopathology vary (Overton & Horowitz, 1991). Theory at more general levels can provide an overarching conceptualization of maladaptive behaviors, which can then be examined from a more focused perspective. For example, general theories of development may conceptualize atypical development in terms of the child's failure to adapt to age-related developmental tasks. More focused theories are then needed to determine the specific adaptations and tasks that are important to study within this general framework. Attachment theory, for example, emphasizes the importance of forming a secure bond with a care-giver as a critical age-related task during the first 2 years of life (Bowlby, 1988). As we discussed in Chapter 2, developmental psychopathology provides a broad perspective that integrates different approaches around common phenomena and questions (Achenbach, 1990; Cicchetti & Cohen, 1995). In addition, the more focused theories we discussed, such as social learning theory, cognitive theory, and emotion regulation theory, attempt to make immediate empirical reference to the specific domains that they seek to explain, for example, antisocial behavior, social cognition, or emotion dysregulation, respectively.

Recognizing that broad theories rarely yield testable hypotheses, researchers must also develop minitheories that are amenable to empirical testing (Kazdin, 1989). After these minitheories are confirmed, their focus can be expanded and generalized, forming the building blocks for a broader conceptualization of childhood disorders. For example, Gerald Patterson's (1982) coercion model, which we consider in Chapter 6, proposes a number of family interaction processes to account for the development of antisocial behavior in children. In a series of empirical studies spanning more than 3 decades, Patterson identified specific characteristics and processes that are important in the learning of antisocial behavior (e.g., parental failure to follow through on demands, inadequate monitoring of child behavior, use of harsh discipline) and has used these findings to formulate a broader developmental model of how these events unfold over time in the larger social context to produce a variety of antisocial outcomes (Patterson, Reid, & Dishion, 1992).

Although research that is driven by theory is an essential part of a scientific approach, a rigid insistence that *all* research be based on formal hypothesis testing is limiting in a field of study as young as abnormal child psychology. Research directed at establishing the existence of a clinical phenomenon or a rare disorder, exploring the conditions under which certain events occur, and trying out a new diagnostic method or treatment technique also has value (Sidman, 1960). Sometimes it is important to describe what is happening before we can explore why or how something happens. We next turn to a discussion of the types of research questions that are typically asked in studies of atypical development in children and adolescents.

Common Research Questions. Research hypotheses and questions guide the researcher's choice of methods and the research designs most appropriate for answering particular kinds of questions. Common

research questions in abnormal child psychology include questions about

- ❖ the nature and distribution of childhood disorders
- ❖ correlates, risk and protective factors, and causes of childhood disorders
- ❖ moderating and mediating variables
- ❖ outcomes for children with disorders
- ❖ interventions for childhood disorders

These types of questions are discussed in the sections that follow. Can you see how these questions resemble the ones raised by Charles's, Whitney's, and Tito's parents?

Questions about the nature and distribution of childhood disorders. These questions are concerned with the ways in which disorders are defined and diagnosed, the ways disorders are expressed at different ages and in different settings, patterns of symptoms, base rates for various problems and competencies, and natural progressions of problems and competencies over time. For example: How common are certain child behaviors? What's normal and what's not normal for children of different ages, gender, family backgrounds, and cultures? Does Charles's mother need to be concerned that her 6-year-son wets the bed one or two nights a week?

These and similar questions are frequently addressed through **epidemiological research,** or studies of the incidence, prevalence, and co-occurrence of childhood disorders and competencies in clinic-referred and community samples (Costello, 1990). **Incidence rates** refer to the extent to which *new* cases of a disorder appear over a specified period of time. **Prevalence rates** refer to *all* cases, whether new or previously existing, that are observed during a specified period of time. Estimates of incidence and prevalence can be obtained over a limited period of time, such as 6 months, or over a longer period. *Lifetime prevalence* refers to whether or not children in the sample have ever had the disorder. Knowledge about the risk for, and expression of, individual disorders over the life course helps us understand the nature of the disorder and use this understanding as the basis for prevention and treatment (Costello & Angold, 1995). For example, longitudinal studies of teens have found depression to be a recurrent disorder with poor long-term outcomes for many youngsters. This knowledge about the course of depression has resulted in promising new approaches to treating and preventing depression in young people, which we present in Chapter 8 on mood disorders.

As noted in Chapter 1, about 10% of children have a clinically diagnosable disorder, and many more exhibit specific symptoms or subclinical problems. However, these overall rates obscure the enormous variability in reported rates from study to study. It can be very confusing when one study reports a prevalence rate of 1% and another reports a rate of 20% for the same disorder. Similarly, rates of reported problems in children have been found to vary from 6% to 20% when reported by teachers, and from 10% to 40% when reported by parents (Costello & Angold, 1995). Some studies would lead you to conclude that almost every child you come into contact with has a particular problem; others, that the problem is so rare you wonder if it even exists. Which conclusion is accurate? To answer this question we need to know something about epidemiological research and how estimates are obtained.

An important question in epidemiological research is, "What constitutes a case?" Cases may be defined in terms of single symptoms, multiple symptoms, or patterns of symptoms with known etiologies and associated characteristics. Estimates of the prevalence of a problem vary widely depending on which definition we use. Case definition in abnormal child psychology is complex because children don't refer themselves for treatment. Therefore, equating illness with seeking treatment can be misleading. The factors that lead to referral sometimes have much more to do with the characteristics of a child's parents, teachers, or doctor than with the child's behavior. For these reasons it is important that we study developmental psychopathology in groups of children who are *not* referred to clinics for treatment as well as in groups who are. Throughout this book you will see many examples of striking differences in research findings depending on whether children from clinic versus community samples are the focus of study.

In one illustrative epidemiological study, Achenbach, Howell, Quay, and Conners (1991) conducted a national survey in the United States with parents of over 5000 four- to sixteen-year-old children. Parents of nonreferred and clinic-referred children completed checklists and were interviewed concerning problem child behaviors (e.g., arguing, cheating, being lonely) and competencies (e.g., number of friends, social activities, school performance). Important differences in problem patterns were found for children of different ages and gender. Regional and ethnic differences were minimal, but lower-SES children were reported to have more problems and fewer competencies than upper-SES children.

As these and other epidemiological findings that we present throughout the book indicate, the rate and expression of childhood symptoms and disorders often vary in relation to such variables as the child's age and gender, the parents' SES, ethnicity, geographical region, family size and constellation, parents' marital and/or mental health status, and culture. Consequently, these variables must be assessed and/or controlled for in most studies of child psychopathology. Many inconsistent findings in abnormal child psychology are the direct result of research designs and/or interpretations of findings that fail to take these important variables into account.

Physically abused children, for example, display more parent-rated problem symptoms than nonabused children. However, this difference may not be found when groups of abused and nonabused children are well matched with respect to SES (Wolfe & Mosk, 1983). Similarly, although behavior disorders are reported to be more frequent in African-American than Caucasian youngsters, this finding is likely an artifact related to SES; that is, behavior disorders are more prevalent in low-SES families, and since African-American children are overrepresented in such families in North America, it is likely that the link between race and behavior disorders is accounted for by the conditions associated with growing up in a poor family (Lahey et al., 1995). An example of an epidemiological research study into the types of behavior problems reported by parents of children in 7 cultures is presented in Box 3.2.

Questions about correlates, risk and protective factors, and causes of childhood disorders. Whitney, described at the beginning of this section, displays persistent sadness, which seems to be related to several variables—her history of being a moody child, her parents' divorce, her problems at school, and her lack of friends. Do any of these variables, alone or in combination, account for her sadness? If so, in what ways? Variables of interest in abnormal child psychology can be correlates, risk or protective factors, or causes of other variables. Much of the research in abnormal child psychology is designed to answer questions about the relation between these three general types of variables and childhood disorders. Because most childhood disorders are the result of multiple variables of different types interacting with one another over time, answers to these questions are rarely straightforward.

Correlated variables are associated at a particular point in time with no clear proof that one precedes the other. For example, Whitney's having no friends is associated with her sadness. Is she sad because she has no friends, or has her sadness prevented her from making friends? Since we don't know which of these variables came first, her lack of friends and sadness are correlated variables.

As discussed in Chapter 1, a **risk factor** is a variable that precedes an outcome of interest and increases the chances that the outcome will occur. For example, Whitney's mood got worse following her parents' divorce. Do you think parental divorce constitutes a risk factor for the development of depression or other problems in children? Remember, a risk factor increases the chances that a certain outcome may occur—it does not mean that it *will* occur, which will depend on other

Box 3.2

Cross-Cultural Epidemiological Research: Behavior Problems Reported by Parents of Children in Seven Cultures

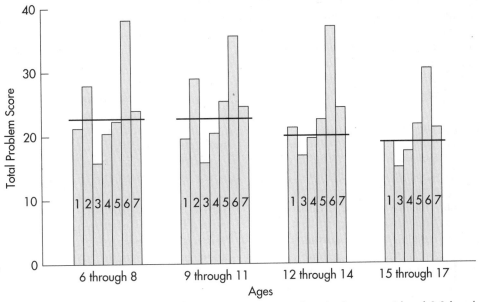

Overall mean Child Behavior Checklist (CBCL) problem scores and mean CBCL problem scores for each culture at ages 6 through 8, 9 through 11, 12 through 14, and 15 through 17. Overall mean scores at different ages are indicated by *solid lines*. China did not provide enough 12- through 17-year-olds. Key to cultures: 1. Australia; 2. China; 3. Germany; 4. Israel; 5. Jamaica; 6. Puerto Rico; 7. United States.

Total problem scores for children in seven different cultures.

Widespread movements of refugees and immigrants are placing millions of children into new and unfamiliar environments. Evaluating the mental health of these children can be difficult because of cultural variations in what constitutes abnormal behavior, how to identify such behavior, and what to do about it. Crijnen, Achenbach, and Verhulst (1997) examined the 6-month prevalence rates of child problems as reported by parents or parent surrogates in studies carried out in 7 cultures, using the same measurement instrument—the Child Behavior Checklist (CBCL) (Achenbach, 1991). The CBCL includes more than 100 items describing a wide array of problem child behaviors. **Informants,** or persons in contact with the child who provide information, such as parents, teachers, or peers, indicate the extent to which an item is or is not true of their child during the previous 6 months on a 3-point scale (0 = not true,

1 = somewhat or sometimes true, and 2 = very true or often true). The total score is the sum of scores on all but two items (allergies, asthma). Across studies, nearly 10,000 children and adolescents ranging in age from 6 to 17 years were assessed. As shown in the accompanying figure, the total problem scores of children in Puerto Rico and China were above the overall cultural mean. In contrast, the total problem scores of children in Israel, Germany, and Australia were below the overall mean. These epidemiological studies indicate that parents in different cultures report different rates of problem behavior in their children. However, they do not indicate why these differences occur. Other kinds of studies are needed to answer that question.

Source: Crijnen et al., 1997. Note: Original report included data from 12 cultures.

factors. Obviously, most children of parents who divorce do not become depressed. Divorce is not a cause of depression and low self-esteem—but it can be a risk factor (Hetherington, Bridges, & Insabella, 1998). A **protective factor** is a variable that precedes an outcome of interest and decreases the chances that the outcome will occur. The close relationship enjoyed by Whitney

and her mother may serve as a protective factor against future episodes of depression.

Research into risk and protective factors often requires that large samples of children be studied, and that multiple areas of child functioning (i.e., physical, intellectual, psychosocial) be evaluated over long periods of time. This is necessary because (1) only a small proportion of children who are at risk for a problem will actually develop the disorder; (2) the areas of child functioning that will be affected, and how they will be affected, are not known in advance; and (3) the points in development at which a disorder may occur or reoccur are also not known in advance. Sometimes the effects of exposure to a risk factor during infancy or early childhood may not be visible until adolescence or adulthood. The possibility that delayed, or sleeper, effects will occur complicates the study of risk and protective factors, since children must be studied for many years if delayed effects are to be detected.

In an illustrative study of risk and protective factors for child maltreatment (Egeland, 1991), 267 first-time expectant mothers who were assessed to be at risk for poor-quality care-giving were recruited during the last trimester of their pregnancy. The mothers' high-risk status was based on their young age, low education, unplanned pregnancy, and single-parent status. Mothers and children were evaluated at regular intervals from the last trimester of pregnancy through the time that the children were in the sixth grade. Evaluations included information about the children, mothers, mother-child interactions, life circumstances, and stresses. When the children were 2 years of age, approximately 16% of these high-risk mothers exhibited one or more forms of maltreatment (e.g., physical abuse, verbal abuse, psychological unavailability, neglect), a proportion that is considerably higher than the base rate of 3% to 5% that would be expected in a community sample of mothers who had not been preselected to be at risk for maltreatment of their children. The at-risk approach in this investigation also enabled the researchers to identify a comparison group of mothers who were at high risk for poor care-giving but who did not later maltreat their children. Through a comparison of high-risk families showing positive child-rearing outcomes with those showing negative outcomes, possible protective factors can then be identified and used as the basis for designing prevention programs for child maltreatment.

Finally, other variables are *causes,* which means that they influence, either directly or through other variables, the occurrence of an outcome of interest. Tito's father uses severe punishment when his son misbehaves. Is this punishment the cause of Tito's aggressive behavior? Is Tito learning how to be aggressive from his father? Questions about causes are complicated because what qualifies as a cause will vary according to the variables of interest and how far back in time a causal chain can be traced. Imagine pushing over the first domino in a long line of dominoes, which then results in all the others' falling over. What caused the last domino to fall? Where in this chain of events does the cause begin? As we discussed in Chapter 2, in most cases, *original* causes for

childhood disorders cannot be identified. Further, the determinants of childhood disorders rarely involve simple one-to-one cause-and-effect relations (Kazdin & Kagan, 1994). Because child disorders are almost always the result of multiple causes, a challenge for researchers is to identify the relative contributions of each of these factors and determine how they combine and interact over time to produce specific outcomes.

Questions about moderating and mediating variables. Factors that influence the direction or strength of the relationship of variables of interest are called **moderator variables.** The association between two variables depends on or is different as a function of moderating variables, such as the child's sex, age, SES, ethnicity, or family characteristics. For example, in one study of a predominantly African-American sample of adolescents, Farrell and White (1998) found that peer pressure was significantly related to adolescents' reported frequency of drug use. However, this relationship was found to be stronger among girls than boys, among adolescents in families without fathers or stepfathers, and in families experiencing greater mother-adolescent distress. Thus, gender, family structure, and the quality of the mother-adolescent relationship were significant moderating variables for the relationship between peer pressure and drug use.

In another study, examining the relation between adolescents' self-reported history of physical abuse and their self-reports of internalizing problems (e.g., anxiety and depression), McGee, Wolfe, and Wilson (1997) found that the correlation between the severity of abuse history and internalizing problems was greater for females than males (see Figure 3.2)—gender was a moderating variable. That is, the relationship between two of the variables (in this case, abuse and internalizing problems) differed, depending on the third (i.e., whether the participant was a boy or a girl).

The process, mechanism, or means through which a variable produces a particular outcome is known as a **mediator variable.** Beyond the knowledge that one variable may cause another, mediating variables describe precisely what happens at the psychological or neurobiological level to explain how one variable results from another. For example, have you ever noticed that when a mother is having a particularly bad day (e.g., the washing machine breaks down, she has an argument with her mother-in-law, the baby-sitter doesn't show up), her child may be more difficult to manage than usual? Why do you think this happens? In one study, Snyder (1991) found that on days on which mothers of 4- to 5-year-old children experienced negative moods and frequent hassles, they were more likely to respond negatively to their children's misbehavior and to reinforce their children's coercive tactics during mother-child

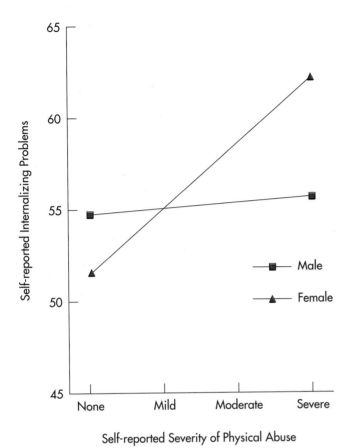

FIGURE 3.2 Self-reported internalizing problems.
(McGee et al., 1997)

conflicts. In turn, the use of this type of maternal discipline was related to an increase in same-day child behavior problems. These findings indicate that the relation between maternal distress and child conduct problems is partly mediated by the disciplinary strategies used by mothers on days when they are feeling distressed (see Figure 3.3). The disciplinary strategies help explain the relationship between maternal distress and child conduct problems.

Questions about outcomes for children with disorders. What are the long-term outcomes for children who experience problems? Many childhood problems decrease or go away as children mature. It's almost certain that Charles will stop wetting the bed—but at what age, and will this problem lead to other

difficulties? For example, will Charles begin to develop a low opinion of himself because he wets the bed? Will he fail to develop friendships because his bed-wetting prevents him from going to sleepovers at other children's houses or from going on overnight trips? Will Tito's oppositional and aggressive behaviors decrease or go away as he gets older, or do they forecast continued conflict with peers, future school problems, and later difficulties in social adjustment? Is Tito on the road to an adult life of crime?

Questions about interventions for childhood disorders. Can children like Charles, Whitney, and Tito and their families be helped to overcome their difficulties? How effective are our methods for treating or preventing these and other child problems? Are some types of intervention more effective than others? Questions about treatment and prevention are concerned with evaluating the immediate and long-term effects of psychological, environmental, and biological treatments; comparing the relative effectiveness of differing forms and combinations of treatment; and identifying the reasons that a particular treatment works. They are also concerned with identifying factors that influence the referral and treatment process; understanding how intermediate therapy processes, such as the therapist-client relationship, contribute to treatment outcomes; and assessing the acceptability of equivalent forms of treatment for children and significant adults (Conduct Problems Prevention Research Group, 1997).

Unfortunately, the great majority of treatments used with children and adolescents have not even been evaluated (Kazdin, 1988). As we discuss in Chapter 4, although integrative reviews suggest that children who receive treatment are generally better off than children who do not, a pressing need currently exists for research to evaluate and compare the efficacy and effectiveness of specific types and combinations of child intervention and prevention programs as carried out in real-world clinical settings (Weisz, 1998; Kazdin & Weisz, 1998).

An important distinction needs to be made between treatment efficacy and treatment effectiveness. **Treatment efficacy** refers to whether or not a treatment can produce changes under well-controlled conditions. In efficacy research, careful control is exercised over the selection of cases, therapists, and delivery and monitoring of treatment. In contrast, **treatment effectiveness** refers to

FIGURE 3.3 Mediating variables: The type of discipline used by mothers on days they are feeling distressed mediates the relation between maternal distress and child behavior problems.

whether the treatment can be shown to work in actual clinical practice rather than in well-controlled laboratory conditions. In research on effectiveness, treatment is evaluated in clinical settings, clients are usually referred rather than selected, and therapists provide services without many of the rigorous controls used in research (American Psychological Association Task Force on Psychological Intervention Guidelines, 1995). The benefits of treatment for children with problems have generally been found to be greater in controlled research settings (efficacy trials) than in clinical practice (effectiveness trials) (Weisz, Donenberg, Han, & Weiss, 1995).

Now that we've looked at the kinds of questions that researchers in abnormal child psychology commonly seek to address, we turn to the methods used to answer these questions.

METHODS USED TO STUDY ABNORMAL CHILD BEHAVIOR

The methods that we use to study abnormal child behavior contribute to our research findings and the conclusions that we can draw from those findings. The study of emotional and behavioral problems of children requires that we measure these problems in ways that are reliable, valid, and statistically analyzable. This is no easy task. Children's problems must be evaluated on the basis of samples of behavior in particular situations that often reflect differing perspectives of adults. Judgments of behavior are also likely to be affected by the child's age, gender, and cultural background, as well as the assessors' personal norms for reporting the behavior. As a result, no single measurement can provide an entirely adequate picture of children's problems, and multiple measures and sources of information are needed.

Standardization, Reliability, and Validity

The measures and methods that we use to study child and family behavior have to undergo careful study to determine how well they measure certain constructs, such as depression, anxiety, or mental retardation. The use of well-standardized, reliable, and valid measures and procedures is essential to scientifically sound research (see Figure 3.4). **Standardization** refers to a process by which a set of standards or norms is specified for a measurement procedure so that it can be used consistently across different assessments of the construct. These standards and norms relate to the procedures that need to be followed during administration, scoring, and evaluation of findings. In some cases, the measure may be given to large numbers of children who vary on

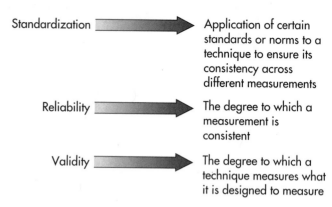

FIGURE 3.4 Concepts that determine the value of our methods of measurement and assessment.

certain characteristics, such as age, gender, race, SES, or diagnosis. These scores can then be used for comparison purposes. For example, the test scores of an 8-year-old boy from a low-SES background should be compared with the scores of other children like him—not with the scores of a 16-year-old girl from an upper-SES background. What is average for 8-year-old boys may not be average for teenage girls. Existing standardized measures of child and family behaviors include tests of intelligence and achievement, parent-completed checklists of child behavior, scales of children's depression or anxiety, and parent reports of their marital satisfaction, mental health, and family environment.

Reliability refers to the consistency, or repeatability, of measures. To be reliable, measures must not depend on a single observer or clinician; various people must agree on what they see. This is known as *interrater agreement*. Imagine how you might react if you took your child to see three different psychologists and received three different diagnoses and three different treatment recommendations. How would you know which one was correct? In this case, the diagnoses would not be reliable because two or more of the psychologists did not agree. If parents take their child to three psychologists, they should rightly expect these professionals to reach the same conclusion. Similarly, different measures, such as tests or interviews, when repeated within a short time interval need to yield similar results on both occasions. In other words, the results need to be stable over time, referred to as *test-retest reliability*. If your child is tested on Monday and you are told that he or she is of normal intelligence, you should expect a similar result if your child is tested again with the same test on Friday.

The reliability of the data obtained using different measures is arrived at in different ways. With observational data, observers record the same behavioral sequences, and the extent to which they agree is assessed.

Similarly, with diagnostic interviews, reliability is evaluated in terms of the extent to which different interviewers agree on their diagnosis of the same child or adolescent. The reliability of self-report or psychophysiological data can be determined by assessing the similarity of children's responses when the measures are readministered on a later occasion. Reliability may also be assessed by comparing children's scores on different forms of the same questionnaire or test, or on different halves of these measures, or by examining the degree to which a person's answers to items measuring the same construct on a questionnaire or test are consistent with one another (e.g., if you had a high need for achievement, you might respond "true" to the statements "I want to get a good job" and "I want to make a million dollars").

Measures that produce undependable and inconsistent information cannot provide believable results. How can we draw a dependable conclusion about the relationship between depression and self-esteem, for example, if our measures of these constructs in the same child or assessed by different people vary from occasion to occasion or from observer to observer? However, reliability alone isn't sufficient to determine whether a method reflects the investigator's goals—validity must also be demonstrated. The **validity** of a method is reflected in the extent to which it actually measures the dimension or construct that the researcher sets out to measure.

Validity can be assessed in a number of ways. First, the measure can be examined for its *face validity,* or the extent to which it appears to assess the construct of interest. This is not part of the formal evaluation of the measure, but rather, an attempt to see if the measure seems to include the content or behaviors of interest—a measure of ADHD that includes symptoms of inattention, hyperactivity, or impulsivity has high face validity. *Construct validity* refers to whether scores on a measure behave as predicted by theory or past research—the meaning ascribed to scores. *Convergent validity* reflects the correlation between measures that are expected to be related—an indication of the extent to which the two measures assess similar or related constructs. This is in contrast to *discriminant validity,* which refers to the degree of correlation between measures that are not expected to be related to one another. The discriminant validity of a measure is supported if the measure does not correlate significantly with measures that it is not expected to correlate with, because the measures are presumed to assess different constructs.

Criterion-related validity refers to how well a measure predicts behavior in settings where we would expect it to do so, either at the same time (concurrent validity), or in the future (predictive validity). For example, a child's high scores on a measure of social anxiety should predict that the child will display anxiety or avoidance in current social situations, and perhaps have difficulties making friends in the future. Criterion-related validity tells whether scores on a measure can be used for their intended purpose—whether or not the measure has utility.

Methods of Measurement

A variety of measurement methods are available to assess important dimensions of children's cognitive, behavioral, and emotional functioning (Mash & Terdal, 1997a). These methods are explicit plans to observe and assess children and their surroundings in ways that will reveal relatively unambiguous relations among variables of interest. An important question regarding methods of measurement relates to who will make inferences about behaviors—the participants through self-report methods, or the researcher using observational methods?

Among the numerous methods used in research and practice in abnormal child psychology are unstructured and structured interviews, questionnaires, behavioral checklists and rating scales, psychophysiological recordings, and direct observations of behavior. (Bellack & Hersen, 1998; Kamphaus & Frick, 1996; Mash & Terdal, 1997b; Messick, 1983). A wide range of intellectual, academic, and neuropsychological tests are also used. This chapter focuses primarily on how these methods are used in research. We will talk more about their use in clinical practice, and about tests and testing in general, in Chapter 4.

As presented in Table 3.1, a comparison of three of the most commonly used methods of gathering data—interviews, questionnaires, and observations—shows how they differ on important dimensions. We will present specific examples of each of these methods here and in Chapter 4. Because the information we obtain from children and families often varies as a function of the methods used, researchers frequently rely on a multimethod approach to define and assess the constructs of interest.

An investigator's choice of the measures used in any research study is the result of a decision process based on a number of factors, a process for which there are no hard-and-fast rules. In addition to the characteristics of the measure itself (e.g., norms, reliability, validity, training requirements), other factors that influence a researcher's choice of measures include the research question being asked (e.g., epidemiological, treatment evaluation); the nature of the construct being evaluated (e.g., frequent or rare, observable or unobservable); child characteristics (e.g., age, cognitive level, language skills); family characteristics (e.g., education, SES); characteristics of the

Table 3.1 Interview, Questionnaire, and Observation: A Comparison of Three Commonly Used Data-Gathering Methods

	Interview	Questionnaire	Observation
Structure of situation	Semistructured or structured.	Highly structured.	Structured or naturalistic.
Structure of responses	Opportunity for probes, expansion, and clarification.	Highly structured; no opportunity for probes or clarification.	Data to be recorded can vary from very inclusive to highly selective.
Resource requirements	Considerable time needed for interviewing and coding responses.	Little experimenter time needed.	Extensive time needed for observing and coding observations.
Sources of bias	Relies on participants' perception and willingness to report. Responses may be influenced by interviewer characteristics and mannerisms.	Relies on participants' perception and willingness to report.	Does not rely on participants' disclosure, but may be influenced by reactivity.
Data reduction	Requires analysis of narrative responses or recoding into categories.	Little data reduction needed.	What is observed is highly influenced by the observational coding system.

research setting (e.g., home, clinic); desired comparability with other research (e.g., use of a new measure versus an existing one); and characteristics and resources of the researcher (e.g., theoretical preferences, time, and personnel).

Reporting Methods: Self-Report and Reports by Others.

Reporting methods assess the perceptions, thoughts, abilities, attitudes, beliefs, feelings, and past experiences of the child, parents, and teachers. These instruments include relatively unstructured clinical interviews, highly structured interviews, and questionnaires. A concern with all reporting methods is how accurately children and parents report their own thoughts, feelings, and behaviors. Inaccuracies may occur because of a failure to recall important events, selective recall or bias, and, in some cases, intentional distortions. For example, some informants may try to make themselves or another person look better or worse than they are. Furthermore, reporting methods require a certain level of verbal ability and may not accurately assess individuals who have difficulties expressing themselves. Obviously, young children would fall into this category—children under the age of 7 or 8 are usually not very reliable informants.

Interviews. Interviews can vary widely in structure, both in the nature and phrasing of questions to be asked and in the manner in which responses are recorded (word for word—e.g., "I like you," or according to predetermined categories—e.g., "Positive Verbal"). Depending on the degree of structure, interviews allow the

researcher to listen and adapt to additional insights or directions that the participants' responses may suggest (Sattler & Mash, 1998). At the less structured end of the interview spectrum are clinical interviews, which we discuss in Chapter 4. At the opposite end of the spectrum, structured interviews use a format in which each individual is asked the same questions in the same way. Most research uses structured interviews because of the need to quantify responses and obtain reliable results. Using a standardized interview procedure removes some of the error associated with unstructured (and unstandardized) clinical interviews and is more efficient and economical. However, these procedures may not provide the same depth of information as an unstructured interview and may still be affected by inaccurate or biased reporting. A sequence of questions drawn from a structured interview for parents of children with behavior problems is presented in Table 3.2.

One type of structured interview that is frequently used in research studies in abnormal child psychology is the structured diagnostic interview, of which there are several different versions. All versions, however, are based on the diagnostic criteria provided in the DSM-IV (APA, 1994), and are designed to assess children to obtain a DSM-IV diagnosis. Diagnostic interview schedules consist of particular questions and specific procedures for administration and scoring. Similar to the parent interview in Table 3.2, structured diagnostic interviews usually begin with a stem question, such as, "Have you ever been anxious when speaking in front of a class?" If the youngster or parent answers, "Yes,"

Table 3.2 Structured Parental Interview Format

1. Is getting your child dressed in the morning a problem area?
   (If parent answers yes, then the interviewer proceeds to ask the following questions.)
2. What does your child do in this situation that bothers you?
3. What is your response?
4. What does your child do next?
5. If the problem continues, what will you do next?
6. What is usually the outcome of this interaction?
7. How often do these problems occur in this situation?
8. How do you feel about these problems?
9. On a scale of 0 to 9 (0 = no problem; 9 = severe problem), how severe is the problem to you?

Source: Adapted from Barkley, 1990.

follow-up questions relating to other relevant factors, such as the frequency, severity, and degree of impairment, are asked. An example of a stem and follow-up question for assessing a social phobia using the *Diagnostic Interview Schedule for Children* (NIMH-DISC-IV; Shaffer, Fisher, & Lucas, 1997) is shown in Box 3.3.

Diagnostic interview schedules have a number of strengths. These schedules often elicit information about the duration and developmental history of the problem, the order in which certain behaviors appeared, and the degree of associated impairment. Since the item content corresponds with commonly accepted diagnostic practices, these schedules can be used to obtain a formal diagnosis. Most diagnostic interview schedules have versions that can be used with children and parents, permitting comparisons of findings across informants. They also have high reliability in comparison with unstructured interviews.

Nevertheless, a number of weaknesses are associated with diagnostic interview schedules. First, they are quite time-consuming relative to questionnaires. Second, their dependence on DSM-IV criteria may limit their usefulness for those DSM-IV disorders that are not well established. Third, they are susceptible to the same biases in reporting that can occur with any other self-report measure. Finally, they tend to be less reliable when used with children than with parents (Kamphaus & Frick, 1996; Shaffer et al., 1996).

Questionnaires. Questionnaires are extremely popular as a relatively efficient and economical way of gathering a defined set of information about one or more dimensions of interest. Some of the more frequently used questionnaires in research in abnormal child psychology include child behavior checklists (completed by the parent, teacher, or child) and measures of personality, cognition, and affect. We will present specific examples

Box 3.3

Example of Question Format from a Structured Diagnostic Interview Schedule

I'm going to start by asking you some questions about how you feel when you're with other people.
1. Do you have any friends?

   IF NO, ask: Have you had any friends in the past year?
2. Do you have any relatives your own age who you like being with?
3. In the last year—that is, since ([name event]/[name current month]) of last year—have you often felt very nervous or uncomfortable when you were with people you don't know well?

   IF YES, ask: Have you felt nervous or uncomfortable like this even with people your own age?
4. In the last year, have you often felt very nervous or uncomfortable when you have been with a group of (children/young people)—say, like (in the lunchroom at school or) at a party?
5. In the last year, have you often felt nervous when you had to do things in front of other people?

IF A + RESPONSE WAS CODED IN Q 3–5, CONTINUE. ALL OTHERS GO TO SAD, P. 9. *(Note: These are instructions for the interviewer.)*

6. You said that in the last year you felt nervous or uncomfortable when you (were with people you didn't know well/were with a group of people/had to do things in front of other people).

   Now I'd like to ask some more questions about being nervous like that around other people.

   Have you been nervous around other people because you thought you might embarrass yourself or make a fool of yourself in front of them?
7. In the last year—that is, since (name current month) of last year—have you been afraid that other people would notice that you were nervous when you were with them?

Source: Shaffer, Fisher, and Lucas, 1997.

of these measures in Chapter 4 when we discuss the use of questionnaires in the context of clinical assessment. The information provided by questionnaires is typically precise but narrow in content. Thus, questionnaires are often used in conjunction with interviews or other measures of the related variables of interest.

When used as self-report measures, questionnaires provide a window on children's internal thoughts and feelings—provided, of course, children have developed sufficient verbal abilities. However, any self-rating is susceptible to distortion or bias. As with interviews, sometimes the distortion may be intentional, for example, when a child underreports the amount of antisocial activity or conflict with others. Other types of distortion may be more subtle, perhaps even a part of the child's disorder. For example, a study that examined children's self-perceptions in areas related to cognitive competence, physical competence, peer acceptance, and maternal acceptance found that aggressive children rated themselves as more competent than did nonaggressive children with respect to both physical competence and acceptance by mothers (Hughes, Cavell, & Grossman, 1997). In addition, aggressive children tended to idealize; they provided a higher proportion of "everything is perfect" scores than did nonaggressive children, suggesting an unrealistic appraisal of self and others.

Another example of how information from self-report measures may be misleading comes from the behavior of mothers who scored zero on the Beck Depression Inventory (BDI), a self-report measure of their own depression, when their behavior was compared with that of depressed and nondepressed mothers during face-to-face interactions with their 3- to 6-month-old infants (Field et al., 1991). A BDI score of zero indicates that the mothers reported no symptoms of depression. However, like depressed mothers, mothers with zero scores on the BDI displayed lower activity levels, less expressivity, and less frequent vocalizing when interacting with their infants than did nondepressed mothers—a pattern suggestive of depressive behavior. In fact, mothers with zero BDI scores received even worse ratings on these dimensions than depressed mothers, and their infants were rated as even less responsive (e.g., less active, fewer vocalizations, more gaze aversion) than infants of depressed mothers. Mothers with zero BDI scores may be denying their depressive symptoms, and may constitute a particularly disturbed group. If we relied solely on these mothers' self-reports to assess their depression, we might well draw some erroneous conclusions about their emotional state and behavior.

Psychophysiological and Neuroimaging Methods.

In an effort to uncover the biological bases of abnormal perceptual, cognitive, and emotional behavior in children, researchers have used *psychophysiological methods,* which assess the relationship between physiological processes and behavior. These methods attempt to identify which central nervous system structures and processes contribute to children's atypical development and behavior. Among the most common physiological responses recorded are measures of autonomic nervous system activity, such as heart rate, blood pressure, respiration, pupil dilation, and electrical

conductance of the skin. Changes in heart rate, for example, may be related to emotional states such as interest, anger, or sadness. In addition, specific patterns of autonomic arousal may be associated with differences in children's temperament, for example, their degree of shyness with people or responses to novel events (discussed in Chapter 7).

Psychophysiological methods may also provide information about biological reactions of infants and young children, who are unable to report their psychological experiences directly. For example, changes in an infant's or young child's heart rate can be used to infer whether the child is reacting neutrally to a stimulus (heart rate is stable) or attending to or processing information (heart rate slows during concentration).

A number of limitations are associated with the use of psychophysiological measures, especially with young children. As you will see in the chapters that follow, findings for many physiological measures are inconsistent from one study to the next. Even when a consistent pattern of responding is found, how that pattern should be interpreted is not always clear. Sometimes a high level of inference is needed, with assumptions about how the child may have processed a particular event or stimulus. Further, numerous factors may influence the child's physiological response. Changes in heart rate, breathing, or brain activity may sometimes reflect a child's reaction to the recording equipment or to other states, such as hunger, fatigue, or boredom. These extraneous influences need to be minimized if conclusions are to be based on psychophysiological measures.

Many studies have used *electrophysiological measures* of brain functioning, such as the electroencephalogram and event-related potentials, which reflect the by-product of synaptic activity. The goal of such studies is to link this electrical activity with ongoing thinking, emotion, or states of arousal. The **electroencephalogram (EEG)** records electrical activity of the brain, using electrodes that are taped to the surface of the child's scalp. Because different EEG waves are related to different states of arousal, EEGs allow a determination of how these states may be associated with underlying sleep disorders.

Differential patterns of EEG activation may also suggest different experiences and expressions of emotion. For example, fearful or inhibited children have been found to show more electrical activity in the right frontal lobe of the brain relative to the left frontal lobe, when compared with nonfearful children (Fox, 1991). Similarly, 1-month-old infants of depressed mothers have been found to show greater relative right frontal lobe EEG activation (Jones et al., 1997). This *asymmetrical* pattern of right frontal EEG activity was related to more frequent negative facial expressions by these infants during an examination, suggesting its association with negative mood. In the future, recordings of such asymmetrical patterns of EEG activation may prove useful in identifying infants who may be at risk for developing depression.

EEG recordings are physically noninvasive and relatively inexpensive. Their sensitivity to changes in state and emotionality makes them useful for studying social and emotional processes in children. However, because the EEG cannot easily be time-locked to discretely presented events, it is not well suited to studying cognitive processes. A close relative of the EEG, **event-related potentials (ERPs)**, are better suited for this purpose. ERPs are EEG waves that are time-locked to specific events in the environment such as a brief visual stimulus (Nelson & Bloom, 1997). A number of recent ERP studies have measured the P300 wave (P3b), which is generated when the subject is attending to and discriminating visual, auditory, and other events. ERP studies attempt to link cognitive processing of these events and neurophysiologic disturbances for various childhood disorders. For example, P3b abnormalities, such as smaller amplitude or longer latency, have been found in children with ADHD, schizophrenia, and autism. Such a pattern of underreactivity to stimulation or other patterns identified in ERP studies may provide support for one or more theories about these disorders (Tannock, 1998).

Finally, new ways of studying the brain using neuroimaging procedures make it possible to test neurobiologic theories for many childhood disorders (Thatcher, Lyon, Rumsey, & Krasnegor, 1996; Zametkin, Ernst, & Silver, 1998). The term **neuroimaging** refers to the ability to examine the structure and/or function of the brain (Nelson & Bloom, 1997). Structural brain imaging procedures include *magnetic resonance imaging* (MRI) and *coaxial tomographic* (CT) scan. MRI uses radio signals generated in a strong magnetic field and passed through brain tissue to produce fine-grained analyses of brain structures. CT scans reveal the gross structure of the brain. As we will see, findings from CT and MRI studies have led to the formulation of pathophysiological models, such as the cerebellar model in autism (Chapter 10) and the hypothesis of abnormal neural maturation in ADHD (Chapter 5).

A variety of functional-imaging techniques have also been used. Two of the more commonly used techniques are *positron emission tomography* (PET) and *functional magnetic resonance imaging* (fMRI). PET scans assess cerebral glucose metabolism. Glucose is the brain's main source of energy, so measuring how much is used is a good way to determine the brain's activity level. Changes in blood flow within brain tissue in response to specific stimulus events are detected magnetically, with extremely clear computerized pictures of the areas of the brain that

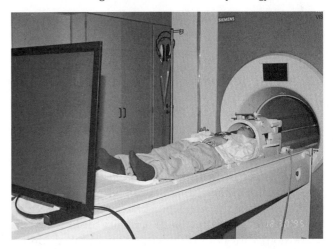

A normal, healthy 10-year-old child about to be tested using functional magnetic resonance imaging (fMRI).

are activated. Functional imaging procedures provide three-dimensional images of brain activity, and supply the most precise information regarding which regions of the brain are specialized for certain functions or are functioning abnormally in cases of certain disorders.

As you will see, neuroimaging procedures have been used to study brain structure and function for most of the disorders that we will discuss. However, although neuroimaging studies tell us that in children with a particular disorder there are structural differences or less activity in certain areas of the brain, they do not tell us why. To date, most neuroimaging studies with children and adolescents have used small samples, have produced variable results, and have been difficult to replicate. Although promising, the use of brain imaging procedures in studying developmental psychopathology is still in its early stages. Since these methods can be scary and difficult for children, the development of procedures for use specifically with children, such as imaging at nighttime, permitting the child to bring stuffed animals or a favorite blanket into the scanner, and having the child's parents present during the procedures, may serve to reduce their invasiveness and increase their use in research with children (Tannock, 1998).

Observational Methods

You can see a lot by observing.

—Yogi Berra

Using systematic *observational methods*, a researcher can directly observe the child's and other people's behavior under conditions that range from unstructured observations in the child's natural environment, referred to as **naturalistic observation,** to highly structured situations involving specific tasks or instructions that are usually carried out in the clinic or laboratory, referred to as **structured observation** (Mash, 1991). When using naturalistic observation, the researcher goes into the child's home, classroom, or day care center, and observes and records the behaviors of interest of the child, and often of other people with whom the child interacts, such as parents, teachers, siblings, and peers. Alternatively, the researcher may videotape behavior in the natural environment, which can be coded at a later time.

In an illustrative naturalistic observation study, Dadds, Sanders, Morrison, and Rebgetz (1992) videotaped families in their homes during a "typical" evening meal to examine the interaction patterns in families of 7- to 14-year-old children with conduct disorder, with depression, with both disorders, and with no disorder. These videotaped interactions were then independently coded by trained observers. Observational measures of positive behaviors (e.g., praise, social attention), negative behaviors (e.g., noncompliance, negative contact), and emotional expression were coded for both parents, the referred children, and their siblings. Children with conduct disorder displayed more negative behavior and anger than the other groups, and their families exhibited more conflict and aggression. In contrast, although children with depression and those with both depression and conduct disorder were exposed to negative behavior from their mothers, they did not display higher levels of anger or negative behavior than control children. High levels of depression were associated with low levels of conflict and anger in family members. Interestingly, the siblings of referred children showed very similar patterns of behavior and were exposed to similar patterns of parental behaviors.

Direct observation of behavior in naturalistic settings is relatively rare in research on child psychopathology. The use of interviews, rating scales, questionnaires, and tests is much more common. The strength of naturalistic observations is that investigators can directly observe the behaviors they hope to explain in the settings in which these behaviors typically occur. However, there are weaknesses as well. Although the real-world validity of observations made in the child's natural environment should be greater than in the clinic or laboratory, this may not be so when the observer's presence has a strong influence on the behavior of interest. **Reactivity** refers to the extent to which performance is altered as a function of the subject's awareness of being observed, the measurement procedures, or participation in a study. How would you react to the presence of an observer who instructs you to "act naturally" while he or she (or a video camera) sits in the background and observes and records everything you do during an evening meal? Young children under the age of 7 or 8 may get used to the presence of an observer after a few sessions. Older children and adults, however, may try to engage in more socially desirable behaviors than usual—to be on their best behavior. In addition, children and parents with severe problems may have difficulty engaging in appropriate behavior even when they are aware that they are being observed (Johnson & Lobitz, 1974). Naturalistic studies may also require that constraints be placed on behavior by asking parents and children to remain in certain rooms of the house, or to restrict incoming phone calls or the use of TV. Additionally, because it takes a long time to observe behaviors that don't occur very often in the natural environment, this form of data collection can become extremely expensive.

A researcher who uses structured observations in the laboratory or clinic sets up a situation or provides instructions to elicit behaviors of particular interest. For example, numerous studies of attachment have assessed young children's reactions to increasingly stressful episodes of separation from and reunion with their caregivers in the laboratory, using a task known as the Ainsworth Strange Situation (Ainsworth, Blehar, Waters, & Wall, 1978). By structuring the situation to elicit specific attachment behaviors, the strange situation permits researchers to assess the security of children's attachment by noting how effectively they can use their care-givers as a source of comfort during times of distress.

Studies of noncompliant behavior in children with oppositional disorder frequently employ tasks in which increasing demands are placed on the child by the parent, such as having the child pick up the toys he or she is playing with and put them away. The use of such tasks elicits multiple instances of the parent's issuing commands and the child's having the opportunity to demonstrate compliance or noncompliance. Another commonly used structured observation task involves family problem-solving discussions, in which family members are given or identify a relevant problem of concern (e.g., chores, curfew, smoking) and then are asked to discuss this problem while observations are made of the interactions.

Structured laboratory or clinic-based observations are cost-effective and offer the advantage of focusing observations on the phenomena of interest. The method is especially useful for studying child behaviors that occur infrequently in everyday life. Structured observations give the researcher greater control over the situation than do naturalistic observations, and also permit the use of other assessment procedures. For example, when a problem-solving discussion is videotaped, replays of the interaction can be used to ask family members what they were thinking during the discussion (Sanders & Dadds, 1992). On the negative side, questions arise as to whether observations made in the laboratory or clinic provide a representative sample of the behaviors of

The Ainsworth Strange Situation: Cassandra, a securely attached 18-month-old girl [top left] shows concern as her mother leaves the laboratory playroom (shown in split screen in the upper right-hand corner of the photo), and becomes distressed [top right] during the separation. However, she soon calms down [bottom right] and greets her mother enthusiastically when she returns (shown in split screen in upper right-hand corner).

interest (Dadds & Sanders, 1992). Being videotaped or observed through a one-way mirror is a bit like being in a fishbowl—children and parents may not behave in the laboratory as they do in real-life settings. In general, samples of behavior that are obtained using observational methods, whether obtained in the laboratory or in real-world settings, should be regarded as "behavior in the presence of an observer."

Numerous other issues are associated with the use of observational methods in research in abnormal child psychology. Among these are the design of the code system, the coding procedures, the training of observers, possible biases, the reliability of observations, and the summary and interpretation of findings (Foster & Cone, 1986; Hops, Davis, & Longoria, 1995; Reid, Patterson, Baldwin, & Dishion, 1988). The decisions we make regarding these issues will influence the quality of data obtained in any observational study. One issue that deserves special mention is **observer bias,** which refers to the fact that observers who are aware of the purpose of a

A 7-year-old child with a behavior disorder is observed while playing in a structured laboratory situation.

study may see and record what is expected rather than the actual behavior. We usually guard against observer bias by using observers who are well trained and who are unaware of and have little investment in the hypothesis of the study. Although systematic observation provides the researcher with valuable information about how children and adults behave, it tells us little about the thinking, reasoning, and emotions that underlie their behavior.

RESEARCH STRATEGIES

The research strategies used to study children with problems ultimately contribute to the overall accuracy of research findings and conclusions. If a researcher selects subjects in a biased fashion or chooses a research task that is unrepresentative of the problem of interest, then the validity of the results may be on shaky grounds—the study may not be a fair test of the research question. Research studies may be examined with respect to their internal and external validity. **Internal validity** reflects the extent to which a particular variable, rather than extraneous influences, accounts for the results, changes, or group differences. Threats to internal validity include maturation, the effects of testing, and subject selection biases. For example, let's suppose you found that providing relaxation training over several months to a group of 5-year-old children decreased their nighttime fears. It's possible that the observed decrease may be due to the extraneous influences of maturation or testing—the children's fears decrease because they are getting older or are being assessed repeatedly, rather than as a result of the relaxation training procedures. Or the reduction in fears may be due to *subject selection biases*, which are factors

that operate in selecting subjects or in the selective loss or retention of subjects during the study. For example, if only children with mild fears are selected for our study, a high likelihood exists that their fears will decrease over time, even in the absence of treatment, relative to children with more severe fears. Also, if children with more severe fears or those who were not benefiting from relaxation training dropped out of the study prematurely, the observed decrease in fears may be the result of this selective loss of subjects rather than our treatment. These and other threats to internal validity need to be addressed in our research design and interpretation of findings.

External validity refers to the degree to which findings can be generalized, or extended to people, settings, times, measures, and characteristics other than the ones in a particular study. Threats to external validity may include the reactivity of subjects to participating in the research, the setting in which the research is carried out, or the time at which measurements are made (Kazdin, 1998). For example, children or parents may not behave very naturally in an unfamiliar laboratory setting. If findings from a study in the laboratory are quite different from what is found in real-life settings, our study would have low external validity.

Identifying the Research Sample

Random number generation is too important to be left to chance.
—Robert Coveyou (1915–1996)

Careful thought needs to be given to how samples of children to be studied are identified and selected. A number of sampling issues are important. First, the validity of any research study in abnormal child psychology is ultimately dependent on the classification systems that are used to identify the samples of children who participate in the research. A careful definition of the sample is critical for comparability of findings across studies and clear communication among researchers. Without such uniform standards, wide differences may result in estimated base rates for various childhood disorders. As noted, estimates of the incidence of ADHD vary widely because studies have differed in their definitions of ADHD, their use or nonuse of exclusionary criteria (e.g., excluding children with low IQ), the sample studied (clinic versus community), the informant (e.g., parent, teacher, physician), and the geographical locale of the survey (Barkley, 1996).

In the past, a lack of consensus on how childhood disorders should be defined led to many research studies' being carried out on poorly defined groups of children who were given such nonstandardized labels as "emotionally disturbed" or "clinically maladjusted," labels that tell little more than that the children being studied have a problem. Although this situation has improved considerably over the last decade, samples are still defined in very different ways from study to study. Even when standard diagnostic practices are used, children may differ widely in their pattern and severity of symptoms and associated characteristics. For example, two children with the same DSM-IV diagnosis may have qualified for this diagnosis in hundreds or thousands of different ways, depending on their specific constellation of symptoms.

In addition to our sample definition, a second issue is the need to consider possible *comorbidities* among our sample. Recall that comorbidity is the simultaneous occurrence of two or more childhood disorders that is far more common than would be predicted from the general population base rates of the individual disorders. Such comorbidity has direct implications for the selection of research participants and for the interpretation of results. Research samples that are drawn from clinic populations will have a disproportionately high rate of comorbidity because referral for treatment is likely to be based on the combined symptomatology of all disorders. To deal with comorbidity in research samples, some researchers may adopt exclusionary criteria in order to select only participants with single, or pure, disorders. This strategy may yield small, atypical samples whose findings do not generalize to other populations. Alternatively, a failure to consider comorbidity may result in an interpretation of findings in relation to one disorder, when these findings are more validly attributed to a second disorder or to some combination of disorders. Research strategies that compare children showing single disorders with those showing comorbid disorders are needed to help disentangle the effects of comorbidity.

Third, we need to be sensitive to the setting and source of referral of children for research. *Random selection,* which means that subjects are drawn from a population in such a way that each individual in that population has an equal chance of being selected for the study, is rare in studies of child psychopathology. At the other end of the spectrum are studies that use *samples of convenience,* in which subjects are selected for a study merely because of their availability, regardless of whether or not they provide a suitable test of the questions or conditions of interest. Research samples in abnormal child psychology have been selected from numerous settings, including outpatient psychology and psychiatry clinics; public and private schools; pediatric, developmental, and learning disorder clinics; hospitals; day care centers; social welfare agencies; youth or church groups; and the general community. Effects related to different settings are often confounded with those related to different referral sources, since across settings, referral sources also differ. Keep in mind that samples of children drawn from different settings and referral sources can be quite different from one another with respect to the nature and severity of the children's problems, and with respect to the children's associated behavioral, learning, and developmental characteristics. Samples from different settings may also show systematic differences with respect to important family characteristics and demographics.

The following example illustrates the effects that referral setting and source can have on research findings: In school-identified samples of children with ADHD and in samples of children with ADHD drawn from learning disorder clinics, girls with ADHD have been found to exhibit fewer behavioral and conduct problems and more cognitive and developmental difficulties than boys. However, in psychology and psychiatry clinic samples, where referral is often based on problem severity, differences between boys and girls with ADHD have not been found (Barkley, 1996). These and other findings reinforce the importance of carefully examining the ways in which the characteristics of specific settings and referral sources may influence research results, and the need to take this into account when attempting to generalize one study's findings to other groups of children.

The question of how large a *sample size* is needed is an important one in any study of child psychopathology. Too often, sample size is based on subject availability rather than on logical or statistical criteria. Since many childhood disorders occur infrequently (e.g., autistic disorder) or are difficult to study, it is not uncommon for studies to use very small samples of children. Small sample sizes tend to reduce the likelihood that significant effects will be found, preclude multifactorial analysis of the results, and limit the generalizability of findings. The concept of *statistical power* is relevant to any discussion of sample size. The statistical power of a test refers to the probability of detecting a true difference between groups when in fact such a difference exists (Cohen, 1988). Small samples reduce the statistical power of a study by making it more likely that a researcher will erroneously conclude that there is no difference between groups when in fact such a difference may exist.

Sample **attrition,** or dropout, is a major problem in research in abnormal child psychology, particularly in longitudinal studies of high-risk populations. Attrition is not a randomly distributed event, since children and families who drop out of a research study are more likely to have certain characteristics (e.g., multiple problems, low SES, single-parent status) when compared with those who remain. Sample attrition results in a reduced sample size, unequal group sizes, and difficulties in generalizing to other samples because of a lack of sample representativeness. For example, a study of high-risk mothers may produce misleading findings if during the course of the study, the most severely impaired mothers drop out, and interpretations are based on those mothers who remain. Researchers who conduct studies with high-risk populations have devised a number of methods for keeping families involved in the investigation, including subject payment, flexible research schedules, and provision of information and services. Although these procedures are necessary if high-risk samples are to be studied, the researcher needs to be cognizant of the possibility that such procedures can influence and distort the data that are obtained.

General Research Approaches

Research in abnormal child psychology varies in the extent to which a study uses a nonexperimental versus an experimental approach, employs a longitudinal versus cross-sectional strategy, collects data prospectively or retrospectively, or uses an analogue versus a natural context to study behavior. These alternative, but complementary, approaches offer various advantages and disadvantages. The choice of approach frequently depends on the research questions being addressed, the nature of the disorder under investigation, and the availability of resources.

Nonexperimental versus Experimental Research.
Scientific research tries to simplify and isolate variables in order to study them more closely. This goal is met by varying or manipulating values of the variable(s) of interest while trying to control or hold constant other factors that could influence the results. Doing this makes it possible to study the association between the particular variables of interest (Kazdin, 1998). The basic distinction between nonexperimental versus experimental research reflects the degree to which the investigator can manipulate the experimental variable or, alternatively, must rely on examining the natural covariation of several variables of interest. The *independent variable* is the one that the researcher manipulates—on the basis of a research hypothesis, the independent variable is anticipated to cause a change in another variable. The variable that is expected to be influenced by the independent variable is called the *dependent variable*. The greater the degree of control that the researcher has over the independent variable(s), the more the study approximates a true experiment.

A **true experiment** is one in which the researcher has maximum control over the independent variable or conditions of interest and can use random assignment of subjects to groups, include needed control conditions, and control possible sources of bias. Conversely, the less control the researcher has in determining which participants will and will not be exposed to the independent variable(s), the more nonexperimental the research will be. Most variables of interest in child psychopathology cannot be manipulated directly (e.g., the nature or severity of the child's disorder, parenting practices, genetic influences). As a result, much of the research conducted with disturbed children and their families relies extensively on nonexperimental, correlational approaches.

In *correlational studies* researchers often examine relationships among variables by using a **correlation coefficient,** a number that describes the degree of association between two variables. (Although many different measures can be used to examine relationships, we will present numerous correlation coefficients throughout this text, so it's important to know what these coefficients are and how they are to be interpreted.) A correlation coefficient can range from +1.00 to −1.00. The size of the correlation indicates the strength of the association between two variables. A zero correlation indicates no relationship; the closer the value gets to +1.00 or −1.00, the stronger the relationship. A correlation of −.70 indicates a stronger relationship than one of −.30, but correlations of +.70 and −.70 indicate relationships of equal strength. The sign of the correlation coefficient (+ or −) indicates the direction of the relationship. A positive sign (+) indicates that as one variable increases in value, so does the other, whereas a negative sign (−) indicates that as one variable increases, the other decreases.

For example, a positive correlation of +.60 between symptoms of anxiety and depression indicates that those children who show many symptoms of anxiety are also likely to display many symptoms of depression. Alternatively, children who show few symptoms of anxiety are likely to display few symptoms of depression. However, a negative correlation of −.70 between symptoms of depression and social skills, for example, indicates that children who show many symptoms of depression have fewer social skills. As you will see, the correlation between two variables often depends on how these variables are measured in particular research samples, as well as on many other factors. Thus, correlations between the same two variables may vary quite a bit from study to study. In view of this, a range of correlations (e.g., +.40 to +.70) is often presented in describing the relationship between variables. Although a correlation does indicate an association between variables, it does not answer the more important questions of whether the relationship is of interest, and if so, why.

The primary limitation of correlational studies is that, for various reasons, interpretations of causality are difficult to make. A correlation between two variables

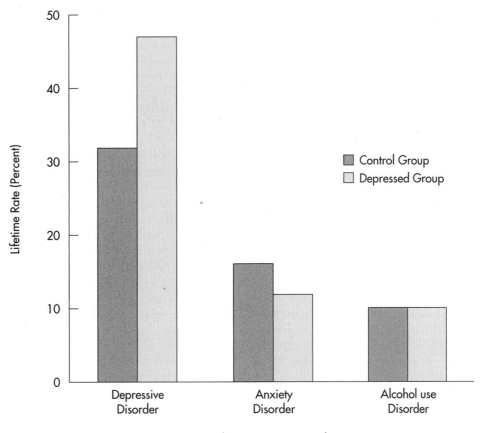

FIGURE 3.5 Lifetime risk of disorder among first-degree relatives of depressed children and nondepressed child psychiatric controls. (Harrington et al., 1993)

does not imply that one variable causes the other. In an examination of the relation between depression in children and their first-degree relatives, for example, being around a child who is depressed may lead to depression in other family members, or alternatively, depression in other family members may lead to depression in the child. Or the correlation may occur because the two variables are both measures of some other more fundamental variable. Depression in children and their first-degree relatives may both be caused by a common genetic disposition to become depressed. We will consider these different hypotheses in Chapter 8.

Correlations among variables of interest in abnormal child psychology can be difficult to interpret for other reasons. For example, in a comparison of the lifetime risk of depressive disorder among the first-degree relatives of children with depression versus the first-degree relatives of nondepressed psychiatric control children, it was found that first-degree relatives of children with depression had a higher lifetime risk for depression (Harrington et al., 1993). However, the correlation does not indicate whether this association

between depression in children and their first-degree relatives is specific to depression, or if depression in the child is related to a higher likelihood of other forms of psychopathology in family members as well. As shown in Figure 3.5, the association seems to be specific to depression, since first-degree relatives of children with depression do not display significantly elevated rates of anxiety disorder or alcohol use disorder when compared with first-degree relatives of psychiatric control children who are not depressed.

Another example of the limitations of correlational research is research that has identified a correlation between ADHD in children and high levels of maternal directiveness (Danforth, Barkley, & Stokes, 1991). Because the variables of ADHD and parenting behavior cannot be randomly assigned, these findings are necessarily correlational in nature and do not lend themselves to making a clear causal interpretation. For example, common symptoms of ADHD, such as inattention, impulsivity, and noncompliance, may result in a greater use of directiveness by mothers in order to control their children's difficult behavior. Alternatively, the use of high levels of directiveness by mothers could provoke inattentive, impulsive, and noncompliant child behaviors. Or symptoms of ADHD and maternal directiveness may both be the result of some other more fundamental variable, such as shared genetic dispositions or environmental stressors.

Having demonstrated a significant relationship between ADHD and maternal directiveness, a researcher then tries to clarify these correlational findings using an experimental approach. One approach is to alter the child's behavior using stimulant medication and to examine the subsequent impact on maternal behavior. In this instance, the administration of stimulant medication that reduces the child's ADHD symptoms would be the independent variable because it is hypothesized to cause a change in another variable. The dependent variable, maternal directiveness, is expected to be influenced by the independent variable. Because the researcher directly controls or manipulates the independent variable, inferences about cause and effect relationships are possible. In one such study, children with ADHD who were given stimulant medication showed a reduction in their ADHD symptoms, which led to a corresponding reduction in maternal directiveness (Humphries, Kinsbourne, & Swanson, 1978). These experimental findings support the causal interpretation that higher levels of maternal directiveness are at least partly the result of the difficult-to-manage behaviors of the child with ADHD.

In experimental investigations, researchers need to take steps to control for the characteristics of participants that could decrease the accuracy of the findings. For example, if two groups of children differ with respect to education, intellectual functioning, socioeconomic status, or the presence of related disorders, it would be impossible to determine whether the independent variable or these other characteristics led to the results. **Random assignment** of participants to treatment conditions protects against this problem, because the probability of a subject's appearing in any of the groups is equal. By assigning subjects to groups on the basis of the flip of a coin, numbers drawn from a hat, or a table of random numbers, the chance that characteristics other than the independent variable will be equally distributed across treatment groups is increased.

As we have noted, many hypotheses in abnormal child psychology cannot be tested by randomly assigning participants to conditions and manipulating conditions in the real world. Obviously, if we wished to study the effects of physical abuse on children's development, randomly assigning children to two groups—one consisting of children who will be abused and the other, of children who will not—would be highly unethical, even criminal. A compromise involves the use of **natural experiments**, also called *quasiexperimental designs* or *known-group comparisons*. In these experiments, comparisons are made between conditions or treatments that already exist; experiments may involve children with different disorders, parents with different problems, or different family environments—for example, a group of children who have, unfortunately, been abused versus another group, who have not. These studies are essentially correlational, but subjects are selected to ensure that their characteristics are as comparable as possible with the exception of the independent variable. For example, in comparing a group of mothers with depression versus those who are not depressed, we want to be sure that the mothers in the depressed group are as similar to one another as possible and as similar as possible to mothers in the control group, with the exception of the characteristic of depression. Despite the extreme care exercised by researchers to equate existing groups, natural experiments cannot achieve the same level of precision and rigor as true experimental research. Nevertheless, for many important questions in abnormal child psychology, natural experiments may be the only option.

Prospective versus Retrospective Research.

Research designs that address questions about the causes of childhood disorders and long-term outcomes may differ with respect to when the sample is identified and when data are collected (Verhulst & Koot, 1991). In a **retrospective design,** a sample is identified at the current time and asked for information relating to an earlier time period. Cases are identified who already show the outcome of interest, and they are compared with controls who do not show the outcome. Assessments focus on other characteristics in the past, and inferences are made about past characteristics and the current outcome. For example, a sample of young adults with a substance use disorder might be asked to provide retrospective ratings and descriptions of their early family experiences. Although data are immediately available in retrospective studies, they are also highly susceptible to bias and distortion in recall. For example, parents of teenagers diagnosed with schizophrenia may reinterpret their views of the teen's childhood, distorting their recollection of the teen's prior behavior or friendships. Moreover, retrospective designs fail to identify individuals who were exposed to certain earlier experiences but do not develop the problem. For example, young adults with a substance use disorder may report more negative early experiences. However, this finding could *not* serve as the basis for a conclusion that negative early experiences were specific precursors of adult substance abuse, since the retrospective study fails to identify those children whose early experiences were negative, but who did not develop substance use disorders as young adults.

In **real-time prospective designs,** the research sample is identified and then followed longitudinally over time, with data collected at specified time intervals. A design in which the researcher studies an intact group or groups over time is also referred to as a *prospective longitudinal study* or *cohort design.* The same youngsters are followed or assessed over time in order to understand the course of change or differences over time. For example, infants who are fearful in response to novel events may be followed over time to see if they develop later anxiety disorders or other problems when compared with infants who are not fearful. Prospective designs correct for several of the problems associated with retrospective research. By following a sample over time we can identify children who develop a disorder as well as those who do not. Since information is collected at the time it occurs, problems relating to bias and distortion in recall are minimized. Disadvantages of prospective designs include sample attrition over time and the length of time needed to collect data that reflect changes over time. In *catch-up prospective designs,* a sample of children is identified from records from an earlier time and then located at a second, later time. This design provides for faster data collection, but the results can be seriously compromised by the unrepresentativeness of individuals who can be located at the later time. In addition, this design is only as good as the original records used to identify the sample, which may often be of poor quality.

Analogue Research. Analogue research evaluates a specific variable of interest under conditions that only resemble or approximate the situation to which one wishes to generalize. Analogue studies focus on a circumscribed research question under well-controlled conditions. Often, the purpose of the research is to illuminate a specific process that would otherwise be difficult to study. A study by Lang, Pelham, Johnston, and Gelernter (1989) provides an example. These investigators were interested in whether the higher-than-normal rates of alcohol consumption observed in fathers of boys with attention-deficit disorder (ADD)/conduct disorder (CD) might be partly due to the distress associated with interacting with their difficult children. Male and female single college students who were social drinkers were randomly assigned to interact with boys who were trained to perform behaviors characteristic of either normal children (e.g., friendly and cooperative) or children with ADD/CD (e.g., overactive, disruptive). Participants also rated their own mood before and after interactions with the child. Following the interaction, participants were given a 20-minute-break while they anticipated another interaction with the same child. During the break, beer was freely available for their consumption. Both male and female participants reported comparable levels of elevated distressed mood after interacting with children enacting the ADD/CD role. However, only men who had interacted with these children drank enough to increase blood alcohol levels.

The findings suggest that interacting with a child with ADD/CD may increase alcohol consumption in fathers. However, because an analogue study only resembles the conditions of interest—the study participants were single college students, not parents of children with ADD/CD; the children did not really have ADD/CD; drinking was confined to an artificial laboratory setting; only beer was available—it is difficult to know whether similar effects would occur in real-life circumstances (despite anecdotal reports by some parents that their kids drive them to drink)! These conditions raise the question of external validity, or the generalizability of research findings. A later study using similar procedures reported similar or stronger effects when subjects were parents of normal boys and were given their alcoholic beverage of choice (Pelham et al., 1997). In this case both fathers *and* mothers consumed more alcohol following interactions with a deviant child confederate; they also rated the child as more of a problem and the interactions as less pleasant and more distressing (see Figure 3.6).

Research Designs

Case Study. The **case study,** which involves an intensive, usually anecdotal, observation and analysis of an individual child, has a long tradition in the study of abnormal development and behavior. Itard's description of Victor, the Wild Boy of Aveyron; Freud's treatment of a phobia in Little Hans; John Watson's conditioning of a phobic reaction in Albert B (Chapter 1); and many other similar case studies have played an influential role in shaping the way we think about children's problems. The case study, especially as used in the clinical context, brings together a wide range of information about an individual child from various sources, including interviews, observations, and test results. The goal is to get as complete a picture as possible of the child's psychological functioning, current environment, and developmental history. Sometimes the goal is to describe the effects of treatment on the child.

Case studies yield narratives that are rich in detail and provide valuable insights into factors associated with a child's disorder. Nevertheless, they also have drawbacks. They are typically viewed as unscientific and flawed because of the uncontrolled methods and selective biases that characterize them, as well as the inherent difficulties associated with integrating diverse observations, drawing valid inferences among the variables of interest, and generalizing from the particular child of

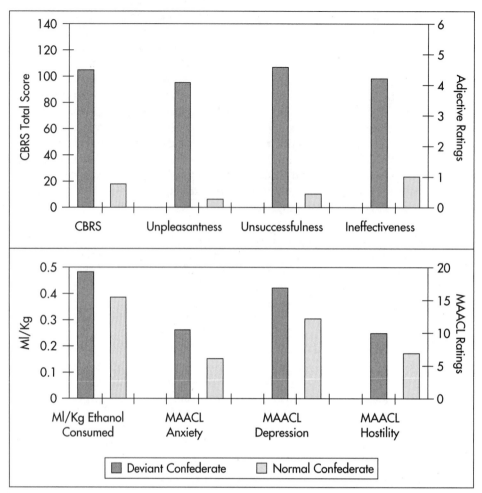

The top panel shows the Child Behavior Rating Scale (CBRS) total score (range = 0 to 140) and single-item adjective ratings (unpleasantness, unsuccessfulness, and ineffectiveness: range from 0. positive to 6. negative) of parents as a function of confederate role. The bottom panel shows the amount of ethanol [in milliliters per kilogram (Ml/Kg) body weight] consumed and subjective self-reports of distress [using the Multiple Affect Adjective Checklist (MAACL), on which higher scores indicate more distress] by parents as a function of confederate role.

FIGURE 3.6   Analogue research: deviant child behavior and parent drinking. (Pelham et al., 1997)

interest to other children. Hence, case studies have been viewed mostly as rich sources of descriptive information that provide a basis for subsequent testing of hypotheses in research with larger samples and using more controlled methods. They also have served as a source for developing and trying out treatment techniques (Kazdin, 1981).

Despite their unscientific nature, systematically conducted case studies are likely to continue to play a useful role in research on childhood disorders. First, many childhood disorders (e.g., autism and childhood-onset schizophrenia) are rare, making it difficult to generate large samples of children for research. Second, the analyses of individual cases may contribute to the understanding of many striking symptoms of childhood disorders that either occur infrequently (e.g., acts of extreme cruelty) or that are hidden and therefore difficult

to observe directly (e.g., stealing, fire setting). Third, significant childhood disturbances such as post-traumatic stress disorder (Chapter 7) often develop as the result of naturally occurring extreme events and circumstances, such as natural disasters, severe trauma, or abuse. These events and circumstances are not easily studied using controlled methods. Nevertheless, generalization remains a problem with case studies, as does the time-consuming nature of the intensive analyses of single cases.

The case study highlights the gap that frequently exists between clinical practice and research. The study of the individual child is typically the clinician's most convenient and feasible investigative tool, but limitations exist in the inferences that can be drawn because of the inherent research limitations of a case study. In contrast, the rigorous demands of controlled research

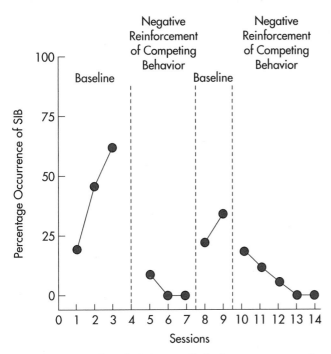

FIGURE 3.7 A-B-A-B (reversal) design: treatment of Ann's self-injurious behavior. (Adapted from Steege et al., 1990)

may obscure important aspects of the clinical phenomenon of interest. Single-case experimental designs have been suggested as a way of bridging this gap, although their special requirements, such as introducing and withholding treatment at particular times, may limit their feasibility of use in the clinical context.

Single-Case Experimental Designs. Single-case experimental designs

have most frequently been used to evaluate the impact of a clinical treatment, such as reinforcement or stimulant medication, on a child's problem. The central features of single-case experimental designs that distinguish these from uncontrolled case studies include systematic repeated assessment of behavior over time, the replication of treatment effects within the same subject over time, and the participant's serving as his or her own control by experiencing all treatment conditions (Barlow & Hersen, 1984; Kazdin, 1982). Many types of single-subject designs exist, the most common being the A-B-A-B (reversal) design and the multiple-baseline design carried out across behaviors, situations, or individuals.

In an **A-B-A-B (reversal) design,** the behavior of a participant is evaluated on some measure over time across four successive phases: (1) a *baseline phase* (A) prior to the intervention, in which no treatment occurs; (2) an *intervention phase* (B), in which treatment is introduced and behavior is typically observed to change

in the desired direction; (3) a *reversal phase* (A), or return-to-baseline phase, in which the baseline condition is reintroduced (treatment is withdrawn) to see whether performance returns to the level of the original baseline; and (4) a *final phase* (B), in which treatment is reinstituted. If the treatment was responsible for the observed change during the intervention phase, the behavior should revert to its baseline level during the reversal phase, and should again change in the desired direction when the treatment is reinstituted during the final phase.

Findings from a study using a reversal design are presented in Figure 3.7. In this example, a behavioral intervention was used to reduce self-injurious behavior (SIB) in Ann, a 5-year-old girl with profound mental retardation and multiple handicaps. Ann's SIB consisted of biting her hand and wrists during grooming activities, such as brushing her teeth. These behaviors were getting progressively worse and causing open wounds. During the initial baseline phase, the percentage of intervals in which Ann engaged in SIB during three brief sessions of tooth brushing ranged from 20% to 60%. Intervention consisted of a negative reinforcement procedure in which Ann was permitted to escape from the grooming activity when she performed an appropriate competing behavior. She was also physically guided by a trainer to brush her teeth whenever she engaged in SIB (guided compliance). When these procedures were implemented during the intervention phase, an immediate reduction of SIB to 10% resulted, with no SIB occurring in the next two sessions. During the reversal, or return-to-baseline, phase, Ann's SIB increased to previous baseline levels. When treatment was reinstituted, SIB decreased again, with no biting observed during the final two sessions. The data that indicate that Ann's levels of SIB decreased only during the intervention phases, and not during the baseline or return-to-baseline phases, provide evidence to suggest that the reductions in Ann's SIB resulted from the intervention procedures.

The reversal design is applicable for use with a wide range of behaviors; however, there are limitations. One limitation is that if a treatment really works, the behavior may not reverse. Do you see any other limitations of this design? Once Ann stopped engaging in SIB following intervention, do you think there is sufficient justification for reinstituting her harmful behavior for experimental purposes? We intentionally selected this example to illustrate a major limitation of the A-B-A-B design—the ethical concerns surrounding the return-to-baseline condition following effective treatment for dangerous or even undesirable behaviors. The multiple-baseline design that we describe next gets around this concern, because no reversal is needed once intervention is introduced.

In a **multiple-baseline design** across *behaviors,* different responses of the same individual are identified and

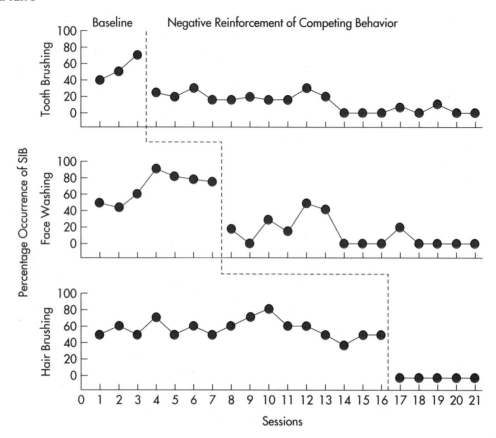

FIGURE 3.8 Multiple-baseline design across situations: treatment of Dennis's self-injurious behavior. (Adapted from Steege et al., 1990)

measured over time to provide a baseline against which changes may be evaluated. Each behavior is then successively modified in turn. If each behavior changes *only* when it is specifically treated, the inference of a cause-and-effect relationship between the treatment and the behavior change is made. Other common varieties of multiple-baseline designs involve successive introductions of treatment for the same behavior in the same individual across different *situations,* or for the same behavior across several *individuals* in the same situation. The critical feature of the multiple-baseline approach is that change must occur only when treatment is instituted, and only for the behavior, situation, or individual that is the target of treatment. Accompanying changes must not occur for untreated behaviors, situations, or individuals until the time that each of these is, in turn, targeted for treatment.

Findings from a study using a multiple-baseline design across *situations* are presented in Figure 3.8. In this example, the same types of intervention procedures that were used with Ann were used to reduce self-injurious behavior (SIB) in Dennis, a 6-year-old boy, also with profound mental retardation and multiple handicaps. Dennis's SIB consisted of biting his hands, wrists,

or arms during such grooming activities as tooth brushing, face washing, and hair brushing. His SIB was getting worse and causing open wounds. During the initial baseline phase, the percentage of intervals in which Dennis engaged in SIB averaged 54% during tooth brushing, 70% during face washing, and 58% during hair brushing. When intervention was implemented during tooth brushing, an immediate decrease in Dennis's SIB resulted, with consistently low rates of SIB maintained throughout treatment. Moreover, no changes in Dennis's SIB were observed during face washing or hair brushing until the intervention was introduced during those situations. When intervention was introduced during face washing, an immediate reduction in SIB occurred, with SIB occurring only one time during the final eight sessions. During the hair-brushing situation, no SIB occurred after intervention was introduced. Because changes in Dennis's SIB occurred *only* when intervention was introduced during each of the specific situations, there is support for the hypothesis that intervention led to those changes. A multiple-baseline design avoids the problem associated with the reversal design of having to return to baseline when treating dangerous or unwanted behaviors.

Several advantages and limitations are associated with the use of single-case designs. These designs preserve the personal quality of the case study and offer some degree of control for potential alternative explanations of the findings, such as the effects of maturation and reactivity to observation. They also provide an objective evaluation of treatment for individual cases, permit the study of rare disorders, and facilitate the development and evaluation of alternative and combined forms of treatment. On the negative side are the possibility that specific treatments will interact with unique characteristics of a particular child, the limited generality of findings to other cases, and the subjectivity involved when visual inspection is used as the primary means for evaluating the data. The findings in the two examples we presented were fairly clear-cut. Difficulties in interpretation arise when baseline data or observed changes are highly variable, which is not atypical.

Between-Group Comparison Designs.
Rather than comparing an individual with his or her own performance under different conditions, many research designs are based on comparisons between a group of individuals assigned to one or more conditions and other groups of individuals assigned to one or more different conditions. When subjects are randomly assigned to groups, and groups are presumed to be equivalent in all other respects, one group typically serves as the *experimental group* and the other as the *control group*. Any differences observed between groups are then attributed to the experimental condition. More commonly, as we have indicated, the nature of the event (e.g., marital discord) or the disorder of interest (e.g., childhood depression) in studies of child psychopathology precludes random assignment to groups. A *comparison group* is then selected to provide contrasting information, but with the recognition that the experimental and comparison groups may vary on dimensions other than those of interest to the researcher.

The selection of a comparison group requires careful attention to specific characteristics of the disorder and the inferences the researcher desires to make. The choice of comparison groups is particularly important if inferences are to be made as to the *specificity* of findings to the particular disorder under consideration. One strategy to help address this issue is the use of multiple comparison groups. Each group can provide comparative data on a relevant dimension. For example, in a study of the parent-adolescent interactions of families with a father with alcoholism, Jacob, Krahn, and Leonard (1991) used families with fathers who were depressed and families with fathers who were nondistressed as comparison groups. Both alcoholic father- and depressed father- adolescent dyads showed lower rates of congeniality and problem solving than nondistressed father–adolescent dyads, but the two clinical groups did not differ from one another. Thus, there was a nonspecific effect of parental disturbance on father-adolescent relationships. Had the study used only fathers with alcoholism and a nondistressed comparison sample, the researchers might have erroneously concluded that family disturbances were specific to alcoholism rather than to general parental disturbance.

The choice of an appropriate control or comparison group often depends on what we know prior to the study and the questions we wish to answer. For example, if an established and effective treatment for depression exists, testing a new approach against a no-treatment control group will likely answer the wrong question. We don't want to know if the new approach is better than nothing, but rather, if it is better than the best available alternative treatment. An example from the literature on social interactions illustrates the importance of careful selection of a comparison group. When compared with children of normal intelligence, children with mental retardation of various etiologies have long been known to show dampened affect, or a lack of emotional expressiveness, during social interactions with their parents and others (e.g., Cicchetti & Serafica, 1981; Yoder & Feagans, 1988). These differences have led to the interpretation that dampened affect is a specific feature of mental retardation. However, it has also been found that children with physical but not mental delays exhibit dampened affect during social interactions (Wasserman, Shilansky, & Hahn, 1986). These findings with children who are not mentally retarded call into question previous interpretations regarding the specificity and possible causes of this symptom and illustrate the importance of careful selection of comparison groups.

Designs for Studying Developmental Change

Researchers interested in developmental psychopathology need information about the ways in which children and adolescents change over time. To obtain this information, researchers extend correlational and experimental approaches to include measurements taken at different ages. Both cross-sectional and longitudinal designs are research strategies in which a comparison of children of different ages serves as the basis for research. In **cross-sectional research,** different individuals at different ages or stages of development are studied at the same point in time, whereas in **longitudinal research,** the same individuals are studied at different ages or stages of development. Most cross-sectional and longitudinal studies provide only correlational information, making it difficult to draw strong causal inferences about developmental psychopathology. But we may note a relation between earlier and later events, which can then be manipulated in a later study. For example, if we find that poor child-rearing skills are related to increases in child psychopathology over time, we can introduce a parent education program to see what impact it has on child behavior. If increasing parents' child-rearing skills results in a later reduction in child psychopathology, a strong causal inference about the relationship between these two variables can be drawn.

Cross-Sectional Designs. The length of time required for many behaviors to change has led researchers to use cross-sectional designs, in which groups of children differing in age are studied at the same point in time. These groups need to be comparable in all ways except for age. In an illustrative cross-sectional study, McKeough, Yates, and Marini (1994) studied different groups of behaviorally aggressive and nonaggressive boys, ages 6, 8, and 10 years, in order to assess group- and age-related differences in children's reasoning about conflict resolution. Behaviorally aggressive children used more developmentally naive reasoning relative to nonaggressive children and showed more socially maladaptive thought. McKeough et al. (1994) also found that the complexity of reasoning for both behaviorally aggressive and normal children increased across age levels, but less so for the aggressive children.

In cross-sectional studies researchers don't have to worry about the many problems associated with studying the same group of children over a long period of time. When participants are measured only once, researchers need not be concerned about selective attrition, practice effects, or general changes in the field that would make the findings obsolete by the time the study is complete. Although cross-sectional approaches are efficient, they are limited in the kind of information they generate regarding developmental change. Evidence about change in the individual is not available. Rather, comparisons are limited to age-group averages. In the study just described, we can't tell if important individual differences exist in the development of social reasoning with age. It is possible that some children develop more complex forms of social reasoning with age, while others remain the same, or even deteriorate.

Cross-sectional studies, especially ones that cover a wide age range, have another disadvantage. Comparisons of 8-year-olds and 16-year-olds—groups of children born at different times and reared in different ways—may not really represent age-related changes. Rather, they might just reflect the unique experiences associated with the different time periods in which the age groups were growing up. Although cross-sectional research can provide suggestive information concerning developmental changes, more definitive answers to questions about continuities and discontinuities in child psychopathology can best be obtained through the use of longitudinal designs.

Longitudinal Designs. Longitudinal designs are conducted prospectively, with data collection occurring at specified points in time from the same individuals who were initially selected because of their membership in one or more populations of interest. In studies of child psychopathology the populations of interest often consist of children who are at risk for developmental problems due to exposure to any one of a number of factors—for example, having a mother who uses drugs or alcohol during pregnancy or who has a mental disorder, or living in an abusive family situation.

The prospective longitudinal design allows the researcher to identify patterns that are common to all individuals, as well as to track individual differences in developmental paths that children follow. For example, a longitudinal study can tell that certain kinds of fears may decrease with age for all children, but that some children, for example, those with an anxious disposition, may show less of a reduction in specific fears with age. Because data are collected on the same individuals at Time 1 and Time 2, *causal inferences* between earlier events and later events and behavior based on temporal ordering can be made. Such inferences of causality cannot be made in cross-sectional designs, where different individuals are assessed at the two time points. Longitudinal designs also allow for identification of individual developmental trends that would be masked by aggregating over individuals. The prepubertal growth spurt exemplifies this, where rapid accelerations in growth occurring at different ages across the population are not reflected in growth measures aggregated across adolescents.

In an illustrative longitudinal study, Dodge, Pettit, and Bates (1994) were interested in the effect of physical maltreatment on the development of peer relationships. A representative sample of 585 boys and girls were assessed for physical maltreatment in the first 5 years of life and then followed for 5 consecutive years from kindergarten through the fourth grade. Twelve percent of the sample was identified as having experienced maltreatment. The children's peers, teachers, and mothers independently rated the maltreated children as being more disliked, less popular, and more socially withdrawn than the nonmaltreated children in every year of evaluation—and the magnitude of the difference increased over time. As shown in Figure 3.9, by grade four more than twice as many maltreated as nonmaltreated children were rejected by their peer group. The results suggest that early maltreatment may disrupt relationships with adults, which in turn impairs a child's ability to form effective relationships with other children.

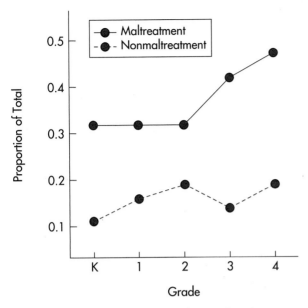

These children are in the same cohort and will be followed over time.

FIGURE 3.9 Proportions of maltreated and nonmaltreated children rejected by their peer group. (Adapted from Dodge et al., 1994)

Despite their advantages, longitudinal designs have a number of pragmatic and design difficulties. Practical concerns include obtaining and maintaining research funding and resources over many years and the long wait for meaningful data. Design difficulties relate to aging effects, cohort effects, and period effects. *Aging effects* refer to general changes that occur because of aging of the participants, such as increases in physical prowess, impulse control, or social opportunity.

Cohort effects refer to influences related to being a member of a specific **cohort**—that is, a group of individuals who are followed over time, who experience the same cultural or historical events during the same time period. An example is children who are born in the same year. Findings based on one cohort might not apply to a different cohort, children growing up at other times. For example, children's performance on intelligence tests might be affected by the quality of public education from one decade to another, by generational changes in parental values regarding the importance of stimulating children's cognitive development, or by increased exposure to computer technology at a younger age. *Period effects* refer to influences occurring at particular times historically, such as the economic recession or the increased awareness of child abuse in the 1980s.

Other disadvantages of longitudinal designs include biased sampling and selective attrition. *Biased sampling* often occurs in longitudinal research because people who willingly participate in research over many years are likely to have unique features—at a minimum, an appreciation of the value of scientific research. Because of this bias, we may not be able to generalize the results from this sample to the rest of the population of interest. In addition, as a result of selective attrition, longitudinal samples become increasingly biased with time. Participants may move away or drop out of the study for other reasons, and those who remain may differ in important ways from those who do not continue.

The experience of being repeatedly studied, observed, interviewed, and tested may also threaten the validity of a longitudinal research study. Children and adults may become more sensitized to the thoughts, feelings, and behaviors under investigation, thus thinking about them and revising them in ways that have nothing to do with age-related change. Furthermore, with repeated testing, participants may improve as the result of practice effects—greater familiarity with test items and better test-taking skills. Finally, changes within the field of abnormal child psychology may create problems for longitudinal studies that cover an extended period of time. Theories and methods are constantly changing, and those that first led to the longitudinal study may become outdated. One common example that has plagued research in child psychopathology is changes in diagnostic definitions or measurement instruments. For these and other reasons, many longitudinal studies are short-term, spanning only a few months or years of a child's life, thereby avoiding some of the problems encountered in long-term longitudinal investigations.

Accelerated Longitudinal Design. Some of the difficulties associated with longitudinal research can be reduced by combining a cross-sectional and a longitudinal approach—referred to as an **accelerated longitudinal design** (Farrington, 1991). With this approach, multiple groups are followed, each at different but overlapping ages or stages of development. The groups

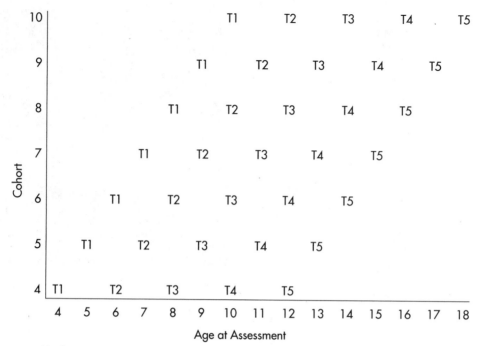

Cohorts are named by their age at Time 1. For example, Cohort 4 was first assessed at age 4. *T* refers to time of measurement 1 through 5.

FIGURE 3.10 An accelerated longitudinal design. (Stanger et al., 1994)

are selected so that the ages span the total time frame of interest, but no one group is followed for the entire duration. The overlap allows the researcher to connect short-term longitudinal studies into a single longitudinal study that spans a period of development that is longer than the period required for the data to be collected. In one accelerated longitudinal study, Stanger, Achenbach, and Verhulst (1997) were interested in the developmental trajectories for aggressive versus delinquent syndromes in children and adolescents. The aggressive syndrome is characterized by overtly aggressive behaviors, such as attacking others, bullying, and fighting. In contrast, the delinquent syndrome is characterized by covert behaviors, such as lying, stealing, and substance abuse. Stanger et al. studied a large community sample of seven different groups of Dutch children who were initially assessed at ages 4 through 10 years using standardized parent reports of behavioral problems. Each cohort was then reassessed at 2-year intervals spanning a period of 8 years. The overall design for this study is shown in Figure 3.10.

The accelerated longitudinal design has three advantages. First, it permits researchers to examine cohort effects by comparing children of the same age who were born in different years. We can compare, for example, the behaviors of the different groups at ages 8 and 10 years, and if the groups don't differ, we can rule out cohort effects. Second, we can make both longitudinal and cross-sectional comparisons. If outcomes are similar

for both, we can have greater confidence in our findings. Third, the design is efficient; in this instance, we can find out about changes from ages 4 to 18 years by following each cohort for 8 years. As shown in Figure 3.11, Stanger et al. found that scores for both the aggressive and delinquent syndromes declined from ages 4 to 10. However, after about age 10 years, scores for the aggressive syndrome continued to decline, whereas those for the delinquent syndrome increased until about age 17 years. Although males showed higher mean scores than females, the developmental trajectories for both the aggressive and delinquent syndromes were similar for boys and girls. In addition, changes were found for the aggressive syndrome over time, indicating that the normative level of aggressive behavior increased in the Dutch population over the course of the investigation. The accelerated longitudinal design, although not used frequently, gives researchers in developmental psychopathology a convenient way to benefit from the strengths of both longitudinal and cross-sectional approaches.

Qualitative Research

Qualitative research focuses on narrative accounts, description, interpretation, context, and meaning (Berg, 1998; Fiese & Bickham, 1998). This approach can be contrasted with a quantitative approach, which emphasizes operational definitions, careful control of the subject matter, attempts to isolate variables of interest,

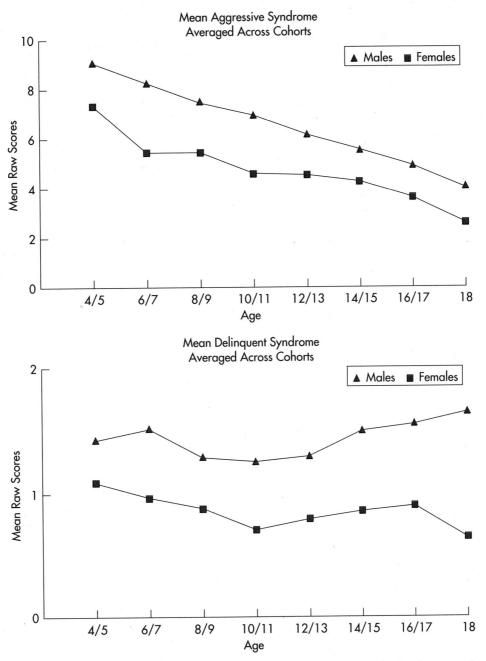

FIGURE 3.11 By using an accelerated longitudinal design, it was possible to study developmental trajectories for the aggressive and delinquent syndromes from ages 4 to 18 years in only 8 years. (Stanger et al., 1994)

quantification of dimensions of interest, and statistical analysis. The purpose of qualitative research is to describe, interpret, and understand the phenomenon of interest in the context in which it is experienced (Patton, 1990). Rather than beginning with already developed observational systems or assessment tools, qualitative researchers strive to understand the phenomenon from the participant's perspective. Qualitative data are typi-

cally collected through observations or open-ended interviewing and are recorded narratively, as case study notes, for example. The observations and narrative accounts obtained are examined to build general categories and patterns. Table 3.3 describes the key characteristics of qualitative research.

To give you a feel for what qualitative methods are like, consider the qualitative study described in Box 3.4,

Table 3.3 Key Characteristics of Qualitative Research

❖ Qualitative research is conducted through an intense and/or prolonged contact with a "field," or life, situation. These situations are typically "banal," or normal, ones, reflective of the everyday life of individuals, groups, societies, and organizations.

❖ The researcher's role is to gain a holistic (systemic, encompassing, integrated) overview of the context under study: its logic, its arrangements, its explicit and implicit rules.

❖ The researcher attempts to capture data on the perceptions of local actors from the inside, through a process of deep attentiveness, empathic understanding, and suspension of preconceptions about the topics under discussion.

❖ Using the information obtained the researcher may isolate certain themes and expressions that can be reviewed with informants, but that should be maintained in their original forms throughout the study.

❖ A main task is to explicate the ways people in particular settings come to understand, account for, take action on, and otherwise manage their day-to-day situations.

❖ Many interpretations of this data are possible, but some are more compelling for theoretical reasons or on grounds of internal consistency.

❖ Relatively little standardized instrumentation is used at the outset. The researcher is essentially the main measurement device in the study.

❖ Most analysis is done with words. The words can be assembled, subclustered, and broken into segments. They can be organized to permit the researcher to contrast, compare, analyze, and bestow patterns on them.

Source: Miles and Huberman, 1994.

which looks at ways in which parents of children with mental retardation and professionals may arrive at a consensus during a diagnostic feedback session.

Proponents of qualitative research believe that it provides an intensive and intimate understanding of a situation that is rarely achieved in quantitative research (e.g., Denzin & Lincoln, 1994; Murphy, 1992). On the other hand, qualitative methods may be biased by the researcher's values and preferences, and the findings cannot easily be generalized to individuals and situations other than the ones studied. However, quantitative and qualitative research methods can be used in complementary ways. Common combinations of these methods are to use a qualitative approach to identify important dimensions, which are then developed into a theoretical model that can be tested quantitatively, or to use qualitative case studies to illuminate the meaning of quantitatively derived findings. Additionally, if qualitative data have been reduced to numbers (e.g., through word

Box 3.4

Professionals and Parents Negotiate Bad News

In a study using qualitative research methods, Abrams and Goodman (1998) were interested in what transpires between parents of children with developmental delays and professionals during a diagnostic feedback session. In particular, they wanted to learn more about the process of negotiation—a process that describes the socially constructed nature of encounters in which participants come to a mutual understanding through the natural use of language. Parents were told that the purpose of the study was to examine how professionals communicate information to parents, and signed a release form so that the feedback sessions could be audiotaped. Tapes from ten feedback sessions with different parents were then transcribed in complete detail, resulting in over 700 pages of transcription. Analysis of the discourse identified negotiation over the diagnostic label in eight of the ten cases. As a form of negotiation, some parents engaged in "bargaining," in which they tried to circumscribe the label and limit its impact. Here's an example of bargaining in the case of a child who received a diagnosis of mental retardation:

Professional: This degree of delay means that he's mentally retarded.

Father: Is there anything that can be done for him?

Professional: There are always things that can be done. [Mother weeps]

Mother: But he's not severely retarded?

Professional: No.

Father: More moderate.

Psychologist: Our best guess is that he will continue to be slow and probably in the mildly retarded range—which would mean that he would be—let's call him "educable."

At first, the mother found the diagnosis of mental retardation emotionally difficult to accept. However, after regaining her composure, she actively engaged in a cognitive adjustment of the diagnostic label to make it less overwhelming. By doing this, she was able to locate her son's label in the mildly retarded range and in so doing, limited her sense of loss. In reality, her son had an IQ score of 54, which placed him on the borderline between moderate and mild retardation. On the basis of their analysis of this and many other samples of discourse, the researchers concluded that interpretations made during a diagnostic feedback session are arrived at through a process of negotiation and are not simply "given" by professionals.

Source: Abrams and Goodman, 1998, p. 94.

counts or frequency counts of themes), the data can be analyzed using quantitative methods.

ETHICAL AND PRAGMATIC ISSUES

The image of overzealous scientists using children as guinea pigs for their experiments is a far cry from current research practices in abnormal child psychology. Researchers have become increasingly sensitive to the possible ethical misuses of research procedures and correspondingly more aware of the need for standards to regulate research practices (Hoagwood, Jensen, & Fisher, 1996; Vitiello & Jensen, 1997). Research in abnormal child psychology needs to meet certain standards that protect children and families from stressful procedures. Any study must undergo careful ethical review before it can be conducted. Current ethical guidelines for research with children are provided through institutional review boards, federal funding agencies, and professional organizations, such as the American Psychological Association (1992) and the Society for Research in Child Development (1996).

Ethical standards for research with children are presented in Box 3.5. These standards attempt to strike a balance between supporting freedom of scientific inquiry and protecting the rights of privacy and the overall welfare of the research participants. Finding such a balance is not always easy, especially with children. For example, although researchers are obligated to use non-harmful procedures, exposing the child to stressful conditions may be necessary in some instances if therapeutic benefits associated with the research are to be realized. Children are more vulnerable than adults to physical and psychological harm, and their immaturity may make it difficult or impossible for them to evaluate exactly what research participation means. In view of these realities, precautions need to be taken to protect children's rights during the course of a study.

Informed Consent and Assent

The individual's fully **informed consent** to participate, obtained without coercion, serves as the single most protective regulation for research participants. Informed consent requires that all participants be fully informed of the nature of the research, as well as the risks, benefits, expected outcomes, and alternatives, before they agree to participate. Informed consent includes informing participants of the option to withdraw from the study at any time and of the fact that participation or nonparticipation in the research does not affect eligibility for other services. Regarding research with children, protection is extended to obtaining the informed consent of the parents acting for the child, as well as the assent of the child. **Assent** means that the child shows some form of agreement to participate without necessarily understanding the full significance of the research, which may be beyond younger children's cognitive capabilities. Guidelines for obtaining assent of the child call for doing so when the child is around the age of 7 or older. Researchers need to provide school-age children with a complete explanation of the research activities in language they can understand. In addition to parents and children, consent must be obtained from other individuals who act on behalf of children—for example, from institutional officials when research is carried out in schools, day care centers, or medical settings.

Voluntary Participation

Participation in research is to be voluntary; yet some individuals may be more susceptible to subtle pressure and coercion than others. Protection for vulnerable populations, including children, has received considerable attention. Fisher (1991) identifies families of high-risk infants and children as potentially more vulnerable, related in part to the families' distress over their children's high-risk status. Although instructed otherwise, parents recruited from social service agencies or medical settings may still feel that their treatment or quality of care will be threatened if they do not participate in the research. Maltreating parents may feel that their failure to participate in research could result in the loss of their child, a jail sentence, or failure to receive services. The role of the researcher requires balancing successful recruiting and avoiding placing pressure on potential participants (Grisso et al., 1991). Volunteerism is itself a biasing factor in research. Individuals agreeing to participate in research obviously differ from those who are approached but refuse, and the question of whether volunteerism significantly biases findings on the variables of interest remains unanswered.

Confidentiality and Anonymity

Information revealed by individuals through participation in research is to be safeguarded. Most institutions require that individuals be informed that any information they disclose will be kept confidential and that they be advised regarding any exceptions to confidentiality. Adult informants need to be told about the limits of confidentiality prior to their participation in research. In research with children, one of the most frequently encountered challenges to confidentiality occurs when the child or parent reveals past abuse or information that would suggest the possibility of future abuse of the child.

Box 3.5
Ethical Standards for Research with Children

Principle 1. Non-harmful procedures: The investigator should use no research operation that may harm the child either physically or psychologically. The investigator is also obligated at all times to use the least stressful research operation whenever possible.

Principle 2. Informed consent: Before seeking consent or assent from the child, the investigator should inform the child of all features of the research that may affect his or her willingness to participate and should answer the child's questions in terms appropriate to the child's comprehension. The investigator should respect the child's freedom to choose to participate in the research or not by giving the child the opportunity to give or not give assent to participation as well as to choose to discontinue participation at any time.

Principle 3. Parental consent: The informed consent of parents, legal guardians or those who act *in loco parentis* (e.g., teachers, superintendents of institutions) similarly should be obtained, preferably in writing. Informed consent requires that parents or other responsible adults be informed of all the features of the research that may affect their willingness to allow the child to participate. This information should include the profession and institution affiliation of the investigator. Not only should the right of the responsible adults to refuse consent be respected, but they should be informed that they may refuse to participate without incurring any penalty to them or to the child.

Principle 4. Additional consent: The informed consent of any persons, such as school teachers, for example, whose interaction with the child is the subject of the study should also be obtained. As with the child and parents or guardians, informed consent requires that the persons interacting with the child during the study be informed of all features of the research which may affect their willingness to participate. All questions posed by such persons should be answered and the persons should be free to choose to participate or not, and to discontinue participation at any time.

Principle 5. Incentives: Incentives to participate in a research project must be fair and must not unduly exceed the range of incentives that the child normally experiences. Whatever incentives are used, the investigator should always keep in mind that the greater the possible effects of the investigation on the child, the greater is the obligation to protect the child's welfare and freedom.

Principle 6. Deception: Although full disclosure of information during the procedure of obtaining consent is the ethical ideal, a particular study may necessitate withholding certain information or deception. Whenever withholding information or deception is judged to be essential to the conduct of the study, the investigator should satisfy research colleagues that such judgment is correct. If withholding information or deception is practiced, and there is reason to believe that the research participants will be negatively affected by it, adequate measures should be taken after the study to ensure the participant's understanding of the reasons for the deception. Investigators whose research is dependent upon deception should make an effort to employ deception methods that have no known negative effects on the child or the child's family.

Principle 7. Anonymity: To gain access to institutional records, the investigator should obtain permission from responsible authorities in charge of records. Anonymity of the information should be preserved and no information used other than that for which permission was obtained. It is the investigator's responsibility to ensure that responsible authorities do, in fact, have the confidence of the participant and that they bear some degree of responsibility in giving such permission.

Principle 8. Mutual responsibilities: From the beginning of each research investigation, there should be clear agreement between the investigator and the parents, guardians or those who act *in loco parentis,* and the child, when appropriate, that defines the responsibilities of each. The investigator has the obligation to honor all promises and commitments of the agreement.

Principle 9. Jeopardy: When, in the course of research, information comes to the investigator's attention that may jeopardize the child's well-being, the investigator has a responsibility to discuss the information with the parents or guardians and with those expert in the field in order that they may arrange the necessary assistance for the child.

Principle 10. Unforeseen consequences: When research procedures result in undesirable consequences for the participant that were previously unforeseen, the investigator should immediately employ appropriate measures to correct these consequences, and should redesign the procedures if they are to be included in subsequent studies.

Principle 11. Confidentiality: The investigator should keep in confidence all information obtained about research participants. The participants' identity should be concealed in written and verbal reports of the results, as well as in informal discussion with students and colleagues. When a possibility exists that others may gain access to such information, this possibility, together with the plans for protecting confidentiality, should be explained to the participants as part of the procedure of obtaining informed consent.

Principle 12. Informing participants: Immediately after the data are collected, the investigator should clarify for the research participant any misconceptions that may have arisen. The investigator also recognizes a

---

Box 3.5

Ethical Standards for Research with Children—cont'd

duty to report general findings to participants in terms appropriate to their understanding. Where scientific or humane values justify withholding information, every effort should be made so that withholding the information has no damaging consequences for the participant.

Principle 13. Reporting results: Because the investigator's words may carry unintended weight with parents and children, caution should be exercised in reporting results, making evaluative statements, or giving advice.

Principle 14. Implications of findings: Investigators should be mindful of the social, political and human implications of their research and should be especially careful in the presentation of findings from the research. This principle, however, in no way denies investigators the right to pursue any area of research or the right to observe proper standards of scientific reporting.

Source: Society for Research in Child Development, 1996, pp. 337–338.

Procedures for handling this situation vary across studies and across states, depending upon the circumstances of the disclosure (e.g., by an adult within the context of therapy) and the reporting requirements of the state. The quality of research data that is collected may vary with the degree to which the confidentiality of information is emphasized (Blanck, Bellack, Rosnow, Rotheram-Borus, & Schooler, 1992).

Information that is videotaped is regarded as particularly sensitive because it stores data that ordinarily would not be permanently recorded (Grisso et al., 1991) and because identities are difficult to mask. Most institutional review boards have policies about the storing and eventual erasing of videotaped information. Particular sensitivity must be exercised in handling videotaped data and in sharing it with other researchers.

Nonharmful Procedures

No research operations should be used that may harm the child either physically or psychologically. Whenever possible, the researcher is also obligated to use procedures that are the least stressful to the child and family. In some instances, psychological harm may be difficult to define, but when doubt is present, the researcher has the responsibility to seek consultation from others. If harm seems inevitable, alternative methods must be found or the research must be abandoned. In cases where exposure of the child to stressful conditions may be necessary if therapeutic benefits associated with the research are to be realized, careful deliberation and analysis of the risks and benefits by an institutional review board are needed.

Other Ethical and Pragmatic Concerns

Sensitivity to ethical concerns is especially important when the research involves potentially invasive procedures, deception, the use of punishment procedures, the use of subject payment or other incentives, or possible coercion. Investigators must be particularly sensitive, especially in longitudinal research, to the occurrence of unexpected crises, unforeseen consequences of research, and issues surrounding the continuation of the research when findings suggest that some other course of action is required to ensure the child's well-being.

Many research problems that are typically addressed through standardized instructions and procedures, and through a reliance on the prior experiences and expectations of the participants, are compounded by children's generally limited experience and understanding of novel research tasks, and by the particular characteristics of disturbed children and families. Children with ADHD, children with oppositional and conduct disorders, or children with limited intellectual functioning, learning difficulties, or language and sensory impairments may present special research challenges associated with establishing rapport, motivating the children, keeping within time limitations, ensuring that instructions are well understood, maintaining attention, and coping with possible boredom, distraction, and fatigue. Similarly, the families of children with problems often exhibit characteristics that may compromise their research participation and involvement. These include high levels of stress, marital discord, parental psychiatric disorders (e.g., anxiety and depression), substance use disorders, restricted resources and/or time for research, and limited verbal abilities.

The final responsibility for the ethical integrity of any research project is with the investigator. Researchers are advised, or in the case of research funded by the federal government, required, to seek advice from colleagues. Special committees exist in hospitals, universities, school systems, and other institutions to evaluate research studies on the basis of risks and benefits. This evaluation involves weighing the costs of the research to the participants in terms of inconvenience and possible psychological or physical harm against the value of the study for advancing knowledge and improving the child's life situation. If there are any risks to the safety and welfare of the child or family that the research does not warrant, priority is always given to the participants.

SUMMARY

A Scientific Approach

1. Science requires that theories be backed up by empirical evidence from controlled studies, and that observations be checked and repeated before conclusions are drawn.
2. A scientific approach to the study of abnormal child psychology is a way of thinking about how to best understand and answer questions of interest—not an accumulation of specific methods, practices, or procedures.

The Research Process

3. Research is a multistage process that involves generating hypotheses, devising an overall plan, selecting measures, developing a research design and procedures, gathering and analyzing the data, and interpreting the results.
4. A researcher's theory of abnormal child behavior will determine the variables studied, the choice of research methods, and the interpretation of research findings.
5. Common questions in abnormal child psychology focus on correlates, risk and protective factors, causes, moderating and mediating variables, outcomes, and interventions for childhood disorders.

Methods Used to Study Abnormal Child Behavior

6. The measures and methods used to study child and family behavior need to be standardized, reliable, and valid.
7. Self-report methods include unstructured clinical interviews, structured interviews, questionnaires, and formal tests.
8. Psychophysiological methods are used to assess the relationship between physiological processes and behavior, and include measures of heart rate, blood pressure, respiration, pupil dilation, and electrical conductance of the skin.
9. Electrophysiological measures, such as the EEG, link electrical activity of the brain with ongoing thinking, emotion, or states of arousal.
10. Neuroimaging procedures are used to examine the structure and/or function of the brain.
11. Observational methods are used to directly observe the child's and other people's behavior in unstructured situations such as the home or classroom,

and in structured task situations in the laboratory or clinic.

Research Strategies

12. Careful attention needs to be given to the way in which samples are identified for research in abnormal child psychology, including such issues as how the disorder of interest is defined, criteria for inclusion in the study, comorbidity, the setting from which subjects are drawn, and sample size.
13. We can distinguish between nonexperimental versus experimental research strategies on the basis of the degree to which the investigator can manipulate the experimental variable or, alternatively, must rely on examining the covariation of variables of interest.
14. In prospective research a sample is followed over time, with data collected at specified intervals. In retrospective research a sample is identified at the current time and asked for information relating to an earlier time period.
15. Analogue research evaluates a specific variable under conditions that only resemble the situation to which the researcher wishes to generalize.
16. The case study involves an intensive, usually anecdotal, observation and analysis of an individual child.
17. Single-case designs involve repeated assessments of the same subject over time, the replication of treatment effects within the same subject, and the subject's serving as his or her own control. The A-B-A-B (reversal) design and multiple-baseline design across behaviors, situations, or individuals are two common examples.
18. Between-group designs compare the behavior of groups of individuals assigned to different conditions, such as an experimental group or a comparison group and a control group.
19. In cross-sectional research, different individuals at different ages or stages of development are studied at the same point in time. In longitudinal research, the same individuals are studied at different ages or stages of development.
20. Qualitative research focuses on narrative accounts, description, interpretation, context, and meaning, and strives to understand the phenomenon from the participant's perspective and in the context in which is it experienced.

Ethical and Pragmatic Issues

21. Research in abnormal child psychology needs to meet certain standards that protect children and families from stressful procedures, including informed consent and assent, voluntary participa-

tion, confidentiality and anonymity, and nonharmful procedures.

22. To ensure that research meets ethical standards, researchers seek advice from colleagues and have their research evaluated by institutional ethics review committees. The final responsibility for the ethical integrity of any research project is with the investigator.

KEY TERMS

research design, 59
epidemiological research, 65
incidence rates, 65
prevalence rates, 65
risk factor, 66
informants, 67
protective factor, 67
moderator variables, 68
mediator variable, 68
treatment efficacy, 69
treatment effectiveness, 69
standardization, 70
reliability, 70
validity, 71
electroencephalogram (EEG), 74

event-related potentials (ERPs), 75
neuroimaging, 75
naturalistic observation, 75
structured observation, 76
reactivity, 76
observer bias, 77
internal validity, 78
external validity, 78
attrition, 79
true experiment, 80
correlation coefficient, 80
random assignment, 82
natural experiments, 82
retrospective design, 82
real-time prospective designs, 83
analogue research, 83
case study, 83
single-case experimental designs, 85
A-B-A-B (reversal) design, 85
multiple-baseline design, 85
cross-sectional research, 87
longitudinal research, 87
cohort, 89
accelerated longitudinal design, 89
qualitative research, 90
informed consent, 93
assent, 93

Clinical Issues: Assessment, Diagnosis, and Treatment

The problem child is invariably trying to solve a problem rather than be one. His methods are crude and his conceptions of his problem may be faulty, but until the physician has patiently sought, and in a sympathetic fashion found, what the child was trying to do . . . he is in no position to offer advice.

—George Senn

Felicia: Multiple Problems

Thirteen-year-old Felicia was referred by her parents because of her severe depression, school refusal, social withdrawal at home and school, and sleep disturbance. Her parents first noticed her current difficulties about a year previously, just after her mother was hospitalized for pneumonia. Felicia, who was in a regular sixth-grade class, began to refuse to attend school. She complained of frequent stomach pains before school as a reason not to attend. Her social behavior also got worse at this time. She wanted to be close to her mother at all times and frequently requested her mother's help with her homework or chores. Felicia became extremely quiet, appeared sad and unhappy, and withdrew from social activities at home and school. Not long after, she began to complain of sleep problems and a loss of appetite. At about this time her grades in school dropped from mostly Bs to Cs and Ds. Felicia reported that no one liked her, that she couldn't do anything well, and that her life was hopeless. (Adapted from Kolko, 1987, p. 159)

CLINICAL ISSUES

Like Felicia, most youngsters who are referred for assessment and treatment have multiple problems. More often than not, the accumulation of these problems over time results in a referral. We have emphasized that most childhood disorders involve breakdowns in normal adaptations associated with different periods of development. Felicia, for example, is having difficulty coping with the normal developmental demands associated with adolescence—gaining autonomy from her parents, getting along with other children, performing well in school, establishing her self-identity, and regulating her emotions. Felicia also experienced the added stress of her mother's hospitalization for pneumonia. The clinician who sees Felicia will need to evaluate how well she is able to cope with these and other events in her life in relation to numerous influences—the nature of the events; Felicia's appraisal of the events; her physical status, cognitive abilities, and personality; and support from her parents or teachers. To sort out the relative importance of these complex and interacting forces, we need to have a well-devised plan of assessment that leads to diagnostic and treatment decisions.

In this chapter we emphasize the clinical strategies and methods used to assess children with psychological and behavioral problems, as well as different approaches to the classification and diagnosis of childhood disorders. In addition, we provide a brief introduction to the treatment of childhood disorders, a topic that we will discuss in detail for the individual disorders in the chapters that follow. We begin this important overview of clinical issues with children, youth, and families with a look at the decision-making process that surrounds assessment, diagnosis, and treatment.

The Decision-Making Process

How do we determine whether Felicia has a psychological disorder that requires professional attention, or whether her problems will simply be outgrown or overcome on their own? Mental health clinicians have to consider a number of important questions in a systematic way in order to understand the child's basic problem(s) and to make diagnoses and devise treatment plans. In many ways this process is like good detective work. It requires sorting through the many factors that bring a youngster to the attention of professionals and checking out alternative hypotheses and plans. This ongoing decision-making or problem-solving process is aimed at finding answers to both immediate and long-term questions about the nature and course of the child's disorder and its optimum treatment (Mash, 1998; Schroeder & Gordon, 1991).

The decision-making process typically begins with a **clinical assessment,** which is directed at differentiating, defining, and measuring the behaviors, cognitions, and emotions that are of concern, as well as the environmental circumstances that may be contributing to these problems. Clinical assessments involve the use of a range of deliberate problem-solving strategies to understand children with disturbances and their family, school, and peer relationships (Mash & Terdal, 1997a). These strategies form the basis of a flexible and ongoing process of *hypothesis testing* regarding the nature of the problem, its causes, and the likely outcomes if treated or left untreated. Clinical assessment is a much broader process than either testing or interviewing, although tests and other methods play a crucial role in the overall process. The ultimate goal of this decision-making process is to achieve effective solutions to the problems being faced by children and their families, and to promote and enhance their well-being. *Assessments are meaningful to the extent that they result in practical and effective interventions.* In other words, a close and continuing partnership between assessment and intervention is vital—they should not be viewed as separate processes (Meyer et al., 1998).

Because of the complexities of human nature, hypothesis testing is often a blend of scientific knowledge and clinical experience and skills. Clinicians are faced with a variety of decisions, including the determination of whether or not to treat, problem identification and monitoring, case conceptualization, and development of a treatment plan. These decisions usually begin with what we already know about specific childhood disorders. For example, you will learn in Chapter 8 that children like Felicia, who suffer from depression, are likely to stop feeling depressed after several months, but more than likely will experience future episodes of depression and other impairments. This knowledge suggests that early intervention is needed to reduce the likelihood that Felicia will experience a recurrent pattern of mood-related problems and adjustment difficulties.

Although general knowledge about specific disorders can provide guidelines regarding which variables are important to assess in all children referred for a certain kind of problem, clinical assessment must focus on these variables in relation to the individual child and family. Detailed understanding of the individual child or family as a unique entity is referred to as an **idiographic** case formulation. This is in contrast to a **nomothetic** formulation, which emphasizes more general laws that apply to broad groups of individuals. A clinician's knowledge about general principles of psychological assessment, normal and abnormal child and family development, and specific childhood disorders is likely to result in the generation of better hypotheses to test at the idiographic level.

As you can imagine, the process of decision making is similar to studying for several exams at the same time—you have to be familiar with fundamental information (such as childhood depression or learning disorders), and then be able to integrate this knowledge in new ways to make it applicable to a particular problem that you are being asked to solve. Like studying for exams, this process at first seems like you are trying to cram everything into a funnel so that you can distill what is most important. Unlike studying for exams, however, working with children and families and applying your training and experience to new situations is often very enjoyable!

Clinicians begin their decision-making steps with an assessment, which can range from a clinical interview with the child and parents, to more structured behavioral assessments and psychological testing. Keep in mind that assessment is not something that is done *to* a child or family, but rather, is a collaborative process in which the child, family, and teacher all play an active role. Because adults play such a critical role in defining the child's problem and in providing information, the establishment of rapport and active collaboration are particularly important when assessing children and families.

As you will see, many of the specific methods used in clinical assessment are the same as, or similar to, those used in research studies, methods introduced in Chapter 3. As with research, the methods of assessment used in clinical practice need to be reliable and valid, and based on strong scientific evidence. However, the realities of clinical practice may prevent the routine use of some research methods that are particularly time-consuming or costly—for example, systematic observation and coding of behavior or psychophysiological recordings. Typically, clinical observations are carried out informally by

Clinical assessment is like good detective work.

Developmental Considerations

Age, Gender, and Culture. A recognition of differences in the growing array of children's developmental functions and capacities at different ages is a crucial building block for assessment and treatment (Achenbach, 1997). Does Felicia's age, gender, or cultural background have a bearing on our approach to assessment, diagnosis, and treatment? School refusal in a 13-year-old girl like Felicia is significant because it results in missed academic and social opportunities. In contrast, a 13-year-old youngster's refusal to travel by airplane may be inconvenient or distressing, but in most cases would not have the same serious consequences as school refusal. A child's age has implications not only for judgments about deviancy, but also for selecting the assessment and treatment methods that are most appropriate. For example, how old does a child need to be before he or she can provide reliable information in an interview? With respect to treatment, how might the use of a time-out procedure for misbehavior differ for a 3-year-old versus a school-age child?

Like age, the child's gender also has implications for assessment and treatment. Numerous studies have reported sex differences in the rates and expression of childhood disorders (Kavanagh & Hops, 1994; Zahn-Waxler, 1993). As shown in Table 4.1, males outnumber females for most disorders of childhood (Hartung & Widiger, 1998). This imbalance does not occur for adult disorders, suggesting that there may be something about the way in which behaviors or symptoms are recognized in children that leads to this imbalance. As we have emphasized, most childhood disorders are defined by adults, usually because they find the child's symptoms particularly salient or troublesome. In general, outward displays of overactivity and aggression are more common in boys and girls tend to express their problems in less overt ways (Keenan & Shaw, 1997), which may result in an excess of referrals of boys and an underrecognition of less visible forms of suffering in girls. Our assessments and interventions need to be sensitive to these possible referral biases related to gender and to gender differences in the development and expression of childhood disorders in general.

One other gender-related difference is noteworthy. Girls are more likely to be emotionally upset by aggressive social exchanges than are boys (Crick, 1995) and,

Table 4.1 Sex Ratios for Selected Disorders of Childhood and Adolescence

Disorder	Sex Ratio
More Common in Males	
Mental retardation	1.5M:1F
Reading disorder	1.5–4M:1F
Language disorder	M > F
Stuttering	3M:1F
Autistic disorder	4–5M:1F
Attention-deficit/hyperactivity disorder	3–6M:1F
Conduct disorder	M > F
Oppositional defiant disorder	M > F
Tourette's disorder	1.5–3M:1F
Encopresis	M > F
Enuresis	M > F
More Common in Females	
Eating disorders	9F:1M
Adolescent depression	2–3F:1M
Anxiety disorders	2F:1M
Selective mutism	F > M
Equally Common in Males and Females	
Childhood depression	M = F
Feeding disorder	M = F

Note: M = male; F = female
Source: Adapted from Hartung & Widiger, 1998, p. 261.

when angry, are more likely than boys to use indirect and relational forms of aggression, such as verbal insults, gossip, tattling, ostracism, threats to withdraw friendship, getting even, or third-party retaliation (Crick, Bigbee, & Howes, 1996). As girls move into adolescence, the function of their aggressive behavior increasingly centers on group acceptance and affiliation, whereas for boys, aggression remains confrontational in nature. Thus, the targets for change in treatments for aggressive girls versus aggressive boys may be quite different. In addition, children who engage in gender-nonnormative forms of aggression (overtly aggressive girls and relationally aggressive boys) are significantly more maladjusted than those who engage in gender-normative forms of aggression (Crick, 1997).

Lastly, cultural factors need to be carefully considered during assessment and treatment, especially when working with ethnic minority children and their families. Cultural information is needed to establish a relationship with the child and family, obtain valid information, arrive at an accurate diagnosis, and develop meaningful recommendations for treatment. A clinician must recognize the wide diversity that exists across and within ethnic groups and in patterns of acculturation and lifestyle. Generalizations about cultural practices frequently fail to capture the regional, generational, SES, and lifestyle differences that exist within and across ethnic groups. Nevertheless, an awareness of the cultural customs and values that can affect the child's and family's behaviors, perceptions, and reactions to assessment and treatment puts the clinician in a better position to develop a meaningful strategy for assessment and treatment (Sattler, 1998).

Normative Information. Felicia's school refusal and sad mood began to occur following her mother's hospitalization. Is Felicia showing a normal reaction to this kind of stressful event in her life? How common are these symptoms in youngsters of this age after a brief period of separation from a parent? Felicia also withdrew from social contact and was experiencing sleep disturbances. Since adolescence is a time of biological and social upheaval for many youngsters, how do we know if Felicia is different from other girls her age with respect to these problems, and if so, when do we become concerned and take action? Knowledge, experience, and basic information about norms of child development and behavior problems are the crucial beginning to understanding how children's problems or needs come to the attention of professionals. As many parents discover, figuring out what to expect of their children at different ages can be very challenging. Parents are faced with determining what difficulties are likely to be chronic versus common and transient, deciding when to seek

Table 4.2	**Individual Parent-Rated Problems that Best Discriminate Between Referred and Nonreferred Children**
❖ Poor schoolwork	❖ Sad or depressed
❖ Can't concentrate; can't pay attention for long	❖ Uncooperative
❖ Lacks self-confidence	❖ Nervous, high-strung, or tense
❖ Punishment doesn't change his or her behavior	❖ Feels worthless or inferior
❖ Disobedient at home	❖ Disobedient at school
❖ Has trouble following directions	❖ Looks unhappy without good reason

Source: Achenbach, 1991, pp. 107–115.

advice of others, and determining what type of treatment is best for their child.

Isolated symptoms of behavioral and emotional problems generally show little correspondence with children's overall adjustment. This is so even for symptoms once thought to be significant indicators of psychological disturbances in children, such as thumb sucking after 4 years of age (Friman, Larzelere, & Finney, 1994). Usually, the age inappropriateness and pattern of symptoms, rather than individual symptoms, define childhood disorders. Nevertheless, certain symptoms do occur more frequently in children who are referred for assessment and treatment than in those who are not.

Examples of parent-reported symptoms that best distinguish between referred and nonreferred children aged 4 to 16 are shown in Table 4.2. As you can see, these problems are relatively common behaviors that occur to some extent in all children—poor schoolwork and a lack of concentration top the list—behaviors that are not particularly strange or unusual. In fact, most individual problem behaviors (approximately 90% of those on standard behavior problem checklists) do not, by themselves, discriminate between referred and nonreferred children (Achenbach, Howell, Quay, & Conners, 1991). For the most part, the individual behavior problems displayed by children who are referred for treatment are similar to those that occur in less extreme forms in the general population or in children of younger ages.

Purposes of Assessment

To understand the different ways clinicians assess children's psychological problems, we first need to consider three common purposes of assessment:

❖ **Diagnosis:** analyzing information and drawing conclusions about the nature or cause of the problem, or assigning a formal diagnosis. Does Felicia meet standard diagnostic criteria for a depressive disorder, and if so, what might be causing it?

❖ **Prognosis:** generating predictions concerning future behavior under specified conditions. If Felicia does not receive help for her problem, what is likely to happen to her in the future? Will her problems diminish as she gets older?

❖ **Treatment planning and evaluation:** using assessment information to generate a treatment plan and to evaluate its effectiveness. Felicia's mother keeps her daughter home from school when Felicia complains of stomach pains. She also does Felicia's homework. Does this information suggest a possible course of action? Felicia thinks she can't do *anything* well. Will helping her change this and other irrational beliefs make a difference in her depression? When action is taken, how can we evaluate whether or not it is having the desired effect?

The word *diagnosis* literally means "to distinguish" or "to know apart." However, the term has acquired two separate meanings, which can be confusing. The first, *taxonomic diagnosis,* focuses on the formal assignment of cases to specific categories drawn from either a system of disease classification such as the DSM-IV (APA, 1994) or from empirically derived categories (discussed later in this chapter) (Achenbach, 1993). The second, much broader meaning of diagnosis, *problem-solving analysis,* views diagnosis as a process of gathering information, which is used to understand the nature of an individual's problem, its possible causes, treatment options, and outcomes. This broader view of diagnosis is almost synonymous with the term *assessment.* Thus, Felicia's assessment will involve a complete diagnostic workup (problem-solving analysis) that includes gathering information and formulating conclusions about her developmental history, possible causes, strengths, vulnerabilities, treatment options, and prognosis in order to get as comprehensive a picture as possible (Achenbach, 1985). In addition, Felicia may also receive a formal diagnosis of major depressive disorder (discussed in Chapter 8), which means that she possesses characteristics that link her to similar youngsters presumed to have the same disorder (taxonomic diagnosis). A **differential diagnosis** may also be needed, which means that in making a diagnosis, the clinician may need to rule out certain other possible disorders.

Diagnosis. Initial diagnostic assessments are often undertaken to assist with general screening and administrative decision making, such as whether or not a child can be appropriately served by a particular agency, clinic,

therapist, or educational program, or whether the child's behavior is actually any different from the norm for children of a similar age and sex. In some cases, the child's behavior may not be unusual when considered in relation to his or her age and situation. However, parents or teachers may *label* the child's behavior as a problem because of their own norms and expectations for behavior, their emotional state, or possible misconceptions they hold about child development and behavior (Mash, Johnston, & Kovitz, 1983). For example, a young and inexperienced mother might expect that her 3-year-old son can look after her 1-year-old daughter, and she labels him as stubborn, difficult, or noncompliant when he fails to do so. Or a mother's depressed mood may cause her to see her child's behavior as being more negative than it actually is. In these instances it may be the parents' views that become the focus of intervention—not the child's behavior (Chilcoat & Breslau, 1997).

Common questions addressed during the diagnostic phase of assessment include: "What is the child doing, thinking, or feeling that causes her distress or that brings her into conflict with others?" or "What are the possible events or circumstances that may be contributing to the child's behavior?" Such initial diagnostic screening focuses on the nature and extent of the problem by addressing the fundamental reasons for referral. Assessment methods used during the early diagnostic phase tend to be general and extensive and include unstructured interviews, self-report measures, and observational narratives. The diagnostic phase of assessment then continues to narrow down the nature of the problem through a process of elimination and determination, involving more specific measures and observations chosen on the basis of initial findings, feedback from the child and family, and clinical judgment. Along the way, certain plausible alternative hypotheses about the child's problem must be explored and either accepted or discarded. For example, is Felicia's school refusal related to her anxiety about separation from her mother, or is it due to her desire to avoid social interactions with other children at school? In the former case Felicia might receive a diagnosis of separation anxiety disorder; in the latter, one of social phobia (Chapter 7). Is the decline in Felicia's school performance related to her inability to focus her attention on academic material, or is it due to a lack of knowledge from having missed classes? Exploring these and other explanations are part and parcel of the assessment process.

Prognosis. Naturally, parents and others want to know, as soon as possible, what the possible short- and long-term outcomes for their child might be, and what events might alter such projections. Remember, many childhood concerns, such as fears, worries, and bed-wetting, are common at various ages, so any decision regarding whether or not to treat a child's particular problem has to be based on an informed prognosis. Clinicians have to weigh the probability that things will remain the same, improve, or deteriorate with or without treatment, as well as what course of treatment should be followed.

Unlike many treatments for adults, treatments for children and adolescents often also focus on enhancing social, cognitive, or emotional development rather than just removing symptoms or restoring a previous level of functioning. In Felicia's case, for example, an assessment might reveal that she has poor social skills, so intervention plans might revolve around efforts to teach her these skills in a concerted fashion in order to reduce the chances of continuing social relationship difficulties. In addition to treatment decisions and predictions, a prognosis based on careful assessment can also serve to inform parents and others about the importance of doing something now that may reduce the likelihood of major problems later on.

Treatment Planning and Evaluation.
This final phase of assessment seeks to obtain information that is directly relevant to developing an effective treatment plan and evaluating the effects of treatment. Treatment planning may involve further specification and measurement of possible contributors to the problem, determination of the child's and family's resources and motivation for change (that is, their strengths and psychological assets), and recommendations for the types of treatments that are likely to be most acceptable and effective for the child and family. For example, are Felicia's parents unintentionally rewarding her physical complaints and school refusal by giving her a lot of attention when she doesn't go to school? Is Felicia willing to discuss her refusal to go to school with a therapist? Are her parents willing to set limits on her behavior despite a history of struggle and failure when they have previously attempted to do so?

Hypothesis testing remains a priority, so the assessment procedures that characterize this phase are more problem-focused than during the diagnostic phase (for example, problem-focused checklists and observations of the child in specific settings). Similarly, the evaluation phase of assessment commonly involves the ongoing use of methods that help determine whether treatment objectives are being met, whether the changes are long-lasting and generalize to other behaviors and situations, and whether the child and family are pleased with the process and results.

ASSESSING CHILDREN'S PSYCHOLOGICAL DISORDERS

If something exists, it exists in some amount. If it exists in some amount, then it is capable of being measured.

—René Descartes

Not everything important can be measured, and not everything that can be measured is important.

—Albert Einstein

If you were planning to assess Felicia's problems, where would you begin and what might you include in your assessment? Should you interview both parents, Felicia, and her teacher? Do you need to observe Felicia at home? At school? Are there psychological tests or questionnaires that can help you pinpoint Felicia's strengths and weaknesses, such as intelligence, emotion, concentration, social skills, and learning ability? You'll soon recognize how quickly the decision-making process can seem massive. In view of this complexity, many clinical settings use a multidisciplinary team approach to assessment. Individuals with specific expertise in, say, psychological test administration and interpretation work together with others to generate the most complete picture of a child's mental health needs. Multidisciplinary teams may include a psychologist, a physician, an educational specialist, a speech pathologist, and a social worker.

Some children may need to be referred for a medical exam as part of a comprehensive assessment, in order to investigate whether a physical problem might be related to their disorder. For example, a physiological problem might be related to a particular child's bed-wetting or sleep disorder. A thorough medical assessment by a physician may be required to evaluate Felicia's stomach pains, sleep disturbances, and weight loss. The medical assessment could also be used to determine whether Felicia's depression was related to drug use or to a general medical condition such as hypothyroidism (low levels of thyroid hormone).

The clinical assessment of children who are experiencing difficulties relies on a multimethod approach, which emphasizes the importance of obtaining information from different informants, in a variety of settings, using a variety of procedures, including interviews, observations, questionnaires, and tests. Decisions regarding which of the many available assessment methods will be useful in a specific case are based on the purpose of a particular assessment (such as whether it is for diagnosis or treatment evaluation), the nature of the problem (e.g., is it overt, like aggression, or more covert, like anxiety?), nd the child's and family's characteristics and abilities. n addition, the use of methods that have high reliability and validity is critical. As discussed in Chapter 3, psychological measures need to meet certain strict requirements, especially research evidence that they provide consistent results and do what they are supposed to do.

Clinical assessment consists of a number of strategies and procedures designed with the intention of understanding the child's thoughts, feelings, and behaviors as they occur in specific situations. Clinical interviews, usually conducted with the parents and child separately, or in a family interview, help establish rapport with the child and family. They are also extremely useful in obtaining basic information about existing concerns as viewed by the child and family members and in pinpointing directions for further inquiry. Behavioral assessments, checklists and rating scales, and psychological tests are then used in accordance with a decision-making approach. Information is also obtained from teachers and other significant individuals who interact with the child across a range of settings. The hope is to obtain as complete a picture as necessary to develop and implement an appropriate treatment plan.

A comprehensive assessment requires that some consideration be given to evaluating the child's strengths and weaknesses in numerous specific areas. These areas are listed in Table 4.3. This imposing slate of potential areas to assess is not exhaustive, and obviously, not all children who are referred will be evaluated in all areas. This is where clinical decision making comes into play. If our detective work suggests that a particular area of functioning deserves closer scrutiny, then a more in-depth assessment of this area is warranted. However, if initial assessments indicate that certain areas of functioning are not a problem, then assessment of these areas may not be

necessary. For example, for a child who is performing poorly in school, an assessment of intellectual functioning and academic performance is essential. On the other hand, for a child who is experiencing difficulties at home but is doing fine at school, further assessment of intellectual and academic functioning may be unnecessary.

We now turn to descriptions of some of the different methods used to assess children and adolescents, with discussions of the settings and related social environments that are critical for understanding the nature of a given child's problem. The general methods considered are much the same as those used in research (discussed in Chapter 3). However, in this chapter we focus specifically on the application of these methods with individual children and their families in the context of clinical assessment.

Clinical Interviews

Unlike adults, who most often seek psychological help on their own or following someone's advice, children and adolescents don't usually refer themselves for treatment. Typically, they are referred for assessment because of the impact of their behavior on others. This often means that they do not understand why they are seeing someone, and in fact they may not even experience any distress or recognize any cause for concern (to be fair, some adults are like this too!). Despite concerted efforts to combat myths about mental illness, children's initial reactions to seeing a mental health professional are often ones of fear or resistance. (How do you think an 8-year-old child might respond if you asked her what it would mean if she was sent to see a psychologist?) Thus, the initial clinical interview can be very important not only in obtaining information, but also in setting the stage for collaboration and cooperation between the child, family members, and other concerned parties, such as teachers, guidance counselors, and probation officers.

The clinical interview continues to be the most universally used assessment procedure with parents and children (Sattler, 1998). In practice, based on interviewers' theoretical orientations, styles, expectations, and purposes, interviews may vary considerably in terms of the kinds of information obtained and the meaning assigned to that information (Sattler & Mash, 1998). Interviews allow professionals to gather information in a flexible manner over a number of sessions, and the findings can then be easily integrated with other, more time-consuming types of assessment, such as family observations or psychological testing.

Clinical interviews, which are typically less structured than research interviews, use a flexible, conversational style that encourages the child or parent to expand

Table 4.3   Possible Areas to Evaluate in Child and Family Assessments

Physical status	Motor coordination
Adaptive behavior	Social maturity
Self-care	Leadership
Communication	Interpersonal skills
Speech and language	Emotional stability
Thinking and intelligence	Psychological well-being
Academic performance and study skills	Reactions to stress
Class participation and behavior	Coping skills
Attention	Developmental history
Motivation	Family child-rearing practices
Task persistence	Social support and resources

on or develop his or her ideas to present as complete a picture as possible. Interviewees will be encouraged to tell their stories with minimal guidance. Clinical interviews permit children and parents to convey their thoughts and feelings in ways that approximate how they think in everyday life. During the clinical interview, the interviewer may observe nonverbal communications by the child and parent, such as facial expressions, body posture, vocal behaviors, gestures, mannerisms, and motor behavior. Clinical interviews also provide a large amount of information in a brief period of time. For example, in an hour-long interview with a parent, much detail about the child's developmental history, likes and dislikes, behavioral strengths and deficits, response to discipline, relationships with others, and school performance can be obtained—far more than would be learned by observing the parent and child interacting for the same amount of time (Sattler, 1998). The following dialogue illustrates an unstructured interview with Martha, a 14-year-old girl referred because of her social anxiety:

Dr. M.: In what situations do you feel most anxious?

Martha: When I have to talk in class, eat in the school cafeteria, or go to gym class. Almost any situation where other kids are around makes me anxious.

Dr. M.: When you have to talk in class, when do you first start to feel anxious?

Martha: Even thinking about it the day before makes me anxious. It gets worse the following morning. By class time I'm a wreck.

Dr. M.: Tell me how you feel when you get anxious.

Martha: I get this empty feeling in the pit of my stomach. My heart starts to race and my hands sweat. My mind fogs up and I can't think of anything to say. It's terrible. Sometimes I just skip class.

Dr. M.: What's going through your mind that makes you want to skip class?

Martha: I worry that the teacher will ask me to speak. I wouldn't know what to say. If I did say something it would be real dumb. My teacher and other kids would think I'm stupid—a real jerk.

Dr. M.: How are your grades in school?

Martha: Pretty good. I'm a B student. But I'd probably do a lot better if I didn't miss so many classes.

Dr. M.: So you get good grades. Why do you think other kids would think you're stupid if you spoke up in class?

Martha: I don't know. They just would.

Many clinicians develop their own style for engaging school-age children and adolescents in discussing what they know of their situation (we often use video games, crafts, and similar enticements to help the child feel more comfortable). When younger children are referred, it may be more appropriate to involve one of the parents in a joint game or activity initially, since younger children are more likely to "be themselves" around their parents than with a stranger (for this age group, drawing, coloring, and similar fun activities are almost always successful at initiating a new relationship). Also, because of their developmental level, younger children or children with mental retardation may be capable of providing only general impressions of their internal states, behavior, and circumstances.

Depending on the child's age, you may want to interview the child, adopting a child-friendly approach that fits with the child's developmental status, the nature of the problem, and the interview purpose (Greenspan, 1981). Interviews with children typically attempt to elicit information about the child's self-perceptions and perceptions of others, and to obtain samples of how the child responds in a social situation with an adult. Children's views of the circumstances that brought them to the clinic, their expectations for improvement, and their understanding of the assessment situation are all important to consider, along with the manner in which they interpret significant events in their lives, such as divorce or family violence. Remember, children's perceptions of their parents, siblings, teachers, and peers will likely influence their reactions to them, and are therefore especially important for understanding the child's problem, designing interventions, and assessing the suitability of involving such individuals in intervention programs. Additionally, some childhood disorders, such as depression and anxiety, require assessment of the child's self-reported feelings, so the interview may serve an important purpose in this regard.

Typically, the initial clinical interview, especially in the case of young children, is conducted with one or both parents, who provide information about the child, themselves, their relationship with each other and with their children, and their family circumstances and other characteristics. In most instances, the interview leads to a discussion of the specific problem and surrounding circumstances rather than attempting to cover all possible difficulties. For instance, interviews with parents who are concerned about their child's anxiety focus on anxiety-related symptoms and the situations in which they occur; those with parents of children with autism focus on commonly identified problems, situations, and controlling variables known to be associated with autism, such as language and social interaction.

In some cases, however, it is necessary to begin more broadly because the problem may seem to cut across a number of dimensions and settings or the child may have multiple problems. This process gives the clinician a first glimpse at the relationship between the referral problem (usually something the child is doing too much or not doing enough) and the various systems and subsystems that make up the child's world—for example, family, school, peers, and culture. In addition, the clinical interview with parents serves the dual purpose of gathering information about their concerns, expectations, and goals, and assessing their perceptions and feelings about the child's problems. Initial hypotheses are formed from this information, such as possible factors that may be contributing to the child's problem behaviors.

Considering Felicia's case, what questions would you want to ask her parents? Perhaps you would want to know how long Felicia's reluctance to separate from her parents has been a concern, and whether prior help has been sought. You might also want to discuss with Felicia's parents the exact nature of the problems they are concerned about, and to provide them with some indication of the next steps in the assessment and treatment process.

Developmental and Family History. Initial assessments often include a **developmental history** or **family history,** in which information about potentially significant historical milestones and events that might have a bearing on the child's current difficulties is obtained from the parents. This information can be gained using a background questionnaire or an initial interview that typically covers the following areas (Nay, 1979):

❖ the child's *birth and related events,* such as pregnancy and birth complications or a mother's use of drugs, alcohol, or cigarettes during pregnancy

❖ the child's *developmental milestones,* such as age of walking, use of language, bladder and bowel control, and self-help skills

❖ the child's *medical history,* including injuries, accidents, operations, illnesses, and prescribed medications

❖ *family characteristics and family history,* including age, occupation, and marital status of family members, and medical, educational, and mental health history of parents and siblings

❖ the child's *interpersonal skills,* including relations with adults and other children, and play and social activities

❖ the child's *educational history,* including schools attended, academic performance, attitudes toward school, relations with teachers and peers, and special services

❖ for adolescents, *occupational information and relationships* with others of the same and opposite sex

❖ a *description of the presenting problem,* including a detailed description of the problem and surrounding events, and how parents have attempted to deal with the problem in the past

❖ the *parents' expectations* for assessment and treatment of their child and themselves

Here is part of the developmental and family history that was obtained from Felicia's parents:

Felicia: Developmental and Family History

Her parents reported that Felicia was the result of an unplanned pregnancy following an initial miscarriage, the adoption of a son, and birth of a sister. The pregnancy and Felicia's early life were described as uncomplicated and generally happy. Felicia reached developmental milestones late, required extra assistance with tasks, was quite reserved and uncommunicative, and experienced speech articulation problems. Her parents said they tended to "baby" Felicia since she was seen as "slow." She was similarly described as developmentally immature by her teachers, although her attendance and academic performance were consistently good ever since she repeated the first grade.

Felicia's adopted brother, age 23, attended a local college and lived at home. Her sister, age 16, also lived at home and attended high school. Felicia's mother had trained to become a registered nurse; her father held a Ph.D. in chemistry and was a manager in the research department of a large company. No significant problems were reported for the other children, with the exception of some difficulty in establishing independence by the brother.

Felicia's mother described experiencing a significant depression after each of her pregnancies and following her father's death 1 year previously, a loss that was reported to have been a very painful one to both Felicia and her mother. The father reported no difficulties and was considered a stable and dependable person. Family history was significant for heart disease, migraine headaches, and high blood pressure. (Adapted from Kolko, 1987, pp. 159–160)

A number of events presented in this developmental and family history may be relevant to the assessment of Felicia's current problems and will need to be explored as assessment proceeds. For example, the babying

Box 4.1
Mental Status Exam

APPEARANCE AND BEHAVIOR

The clinician observes the child's dress, physical appearance, posture, facial expression, gestures, mannerisms, and motor behavior. For example, a sad facial expression and very slow and effortful movements (psychomotor retardation) could be signs of severe depression; abnormal staring or gaze avoidance may suggest social disturbances.

THOUGHT PROCESSES

The clinician listens to the rate, flow, continuity, and content of the child's speech. Does the child make sense when she speaks, or are ideas presented in an unconnected manner? Does the child's speech reflect a distorted view of reality (delusion)? For example, does the child think that people are out to get him or that he is all-powerful? Does the child see or hear things that aren't there (hallucinations)? Does the child have unrealistic expectations, such as being convinced that she will become a famous musician even though she knows nothing about music? As you will learn in Chapters 8 and 10, disturbances in thought processes are common in youngsters with bipolar disorder or schizophrenia.

MOOD AND AFFECT

Mood refers to the child's dominant feeling state. Does he or she feel continually sad or elated? Does she speak in a depressed and hopeless fashion about most things? Affect refers to the feeling state associated with what a child says at a specific point in time. Affect is inappropriate when the child's feeling state doesn't match what is going on at the time—for example, if the child laughs upon hearing that a classmate is seriously ill or cries when he hears that he's going on a trip to Disney World.

Some children may display little emotion whether talking about sad or about happy things, referred to as flat or blunted affect. You will learn in Chapters 7 and 8 that observations of mood and affect are important in assessing many emotional disorders in children and adolescents.

INTELLECTUAL FUNCTIONING

A clinician can make an estimate of the child's intellectual functioning just by talking to him or her. What is the child's vocabulary like? Can she speak in abstract terms? How well does he understand instructions? What's her memory like? These are some of the areas that are assessed more precisely with intelligence tests. Nevertheless, clinicians usually make a rough estimate of intellectual functioning during the mental status exam, especially if it is noticeable that the child's intelligence is above or below that of children of a similar age and background.

SENSORIUM

Sensorium refers to the entire sensory apparatus of the body—how the child's brain receives and coordinates information from the environment. Does the child have a general awareness of his or her surroundings? The following questions can be asked to assess the child's general orientation to person, time, and place: "What is your name? How old are you? What is today's date? What is the season? Where are you? What is the name of this city?" Children with lasting brain injury or dysfunction, or those experiencing temporary brain injury or impairment as a result of drugs or other toxic states, may have difficulty answering these kinds of questions.

described by Felicia's parents may reflect a more general pattern of overdependency on her parents that is contributing to Felicia's school refusal. The significant depression experienced by Felicia's mother following her pregnancies may suggest a family risk for depression. The death of Felicia's grandfather a year earlier may have been a triggering event, leading to a mood disturbance in both Felicia and her mother. During the early stages of assessment, these are hypotheses; as evidence accumulates as a result of ongoing detective work, hypotheses can be supported or rejected as indicated by new data.

Mental Status Exam. As part of an initial interview, a clinician may wish to conduct a **mental status exam** to assess the child's general mental functioning. In a mental status exam, which is usually carried out during the course of an interview, the clinician asks questions

and observes the child in five general areas: appearance and behavior, thought processes, mood and affect, intellectual functioning, and sensorium (Barlow & Durand, 1995). A description of each of these areas is presented in Box 4.1.

Here are the findings from a brief mental status exam that was carried out during an initial interview with Felicia:

Felicia: Mental Status Exam

A mental status exam indicated that Felicia presented herself as a quiet, uncommunicative, and resistant girl who used only a few basic social skills. She rarely made eye contact, spoke in an inaudible tone of voice, used few words, infrequently initiated a conversation, and was unable to report anything positive about herself. She admitted to feeling depressed and denied any positive attributes, giving few details regarding her experiences. She also acknowledged sleep difficulties. Felicia denied any anxiety or panic attacks. She denied suicidal or homicidal thoughts, intent, or plan; gave no evidence for perceptual or thought disturbance; and was oriented to person, time, and place (i.e., she knows who she is, the time and day, and where she is). (Kolko, 1987, p. 160)

How are these informal observations from a mental status exam used? Essentially, they allow the clinician to zoom in on aspects of the child's behavior and condition that need to be assessed in greater depth through the use of more focused behavioral assessments or formal psychological tests. What can we learn from Felicia's mental status exam? The flow of her speech was slow and the content limited. She made little eye contact, did not initiate any social interaction, and reported sleep difficulties. These observations are consistent with Felicia's report of depression and suggest a depressive disorder. However, additional information, obtained perhaps via structured interviews or questionnaires, will be needed to confirm or disconfirm this possibility, and other areas related to her social anxiety and social skills deficits will need to be assessed. Additionally, the exam indicated that Felicia's intelligence was well within the normal range, and her sensorium was "clear," meaning working normally. As with any other assessment, the findings from a mental status exam must be interpreted using age-appropriate norms and expectations.

Semistructured Interviews. Most interviews with children and parents are unstructured, which means that clinicians use their preferred interview style and format as well as their knowledge of the disorder to pursue various questions in an informal and flexible manner. Unstructured clinical interviews provide a rich source of clinical hypotheses. However, their lack of standardization may result in low reliability and selective or biased gathering of information. To address this problem, clinicians sometimes use semistructured clinical interviews to obtain certain concrete information and provide comprehensive coverage of particular problems. Semistructured interviews include specific questions designed to elicit information in a relatively consistent manner regardless of who is doing the interview. In addition, the format of the interview usually ensures that the most important aspects of a particular disorder are covered. Semistructured interviews also permit the clinician to follow up on issues of importance that may emerge during the interview. The consistency and coverage of semistructured interviews may be offset by a loss of spontaneity between the child and clinician, especially when the interview is applied in a rigid fashion. Under such circumstances, children and adolescents may be reluctant to volunteer important information that is not directly relevant to the interviewer's questions. Semistructured interviews are less reliable with children under the age of ten than with older children, especially in regard to reporting on their internal mood states (Edelbrock, Costello, Dulcan, Kalas, & Conover, 1985). Further, these interviews are generally less reliable when used with children than with parents (Shaffer et al., 1996).

Many semistructured and structured interviews have been developed (Sattler, 1998). Some are quite specialized, probing for certain problems in great depth—for example, depression, anxiety, or eating disorders. Sample questions from a semistructured interview for youngsters with an eating problem are presented in Table 4.4. The areas of questioning in this interview cover all the important aspects of eating problems (discussed in Chapter 13), including the child's current eating patterns and difficulties, attitudes toward eating and food, body image, weight, binge eating and purging, methods used to control weight, exercise and activity patterns, and health status.

Other semistructured interviews, for example, the diagnostic interview schedules discussed in Chapter 3, are more general and cover a wide range of disorders. One of the attractions of these interviews for the clinician is the opportunity to rule out certain diagnoses in a comprehensive fashion, and establish whether or not a child fits the diagnostic criteria for one or more DSM-IV categories. For example, consistent with a diagnosis of depression, a structured interview with Felicia revealed symptoms of depression as primary concerns—sadness, isolation, disinterest in previously enjoyed activities, low self-image, somatic complaints, low energy level, reduced concentration, and chronic sleep problems. An appealing feature of semistructured interviews, especially for older children and youth, is that they can be administered by computer, something that many children find both entertaining and, oftentimes, less threatening at first than a face-to-face interview.

The clinical interviews that we have described are valuable in eliciting information from parents and school-age children. They provide an initial look at how the child

Table 4.4 Semistructured Interview Questions for a Child or Adolescent with an Eating Problem

Current Eating Patterns
- ❖ Do your eating habits vary from day to day?
- ❖ Do you feel that the way you eat is different from the way others eat?

Specific Eating Problems
- ❖ Do you avoid eating foods you like?
- ❖ Do you ever eat in secret?

Attitudes toward Eating and Food
- ❖ Do you ever feel guilty after eating?
- ❖ Do you think you can control your eating?

Body Image
- ❖ Do you always think about wanting to be thinner?
- ❖ Are you scared of being overweight?

Weight
- ❖ Has your weight changed in the last 3 months? [If yes] By how much?
- ❖ Are you now trying to lose weight or are you on a diet to lose weight?

Binge Eating
- ❖ Have you ever been unable to control the amount or type of food you ate?
- ❖ How do you feel after you eat lots of food quickly?

Purging Behavior
- ❖ Do you deliberately try to vomit after you eat?
- ❖ [If yes] How do you go about getting yourself to vomit?

Other Methods Used to Control Weight
- ❖ Do you take laxatives, diet pills, or anything else to control your weight?
- ❖ How often do you take [cite substance]?

Exercise and Activity Patterns
- ❖ What kind of exercise do you do?
- ❖ Is your exercising connected with your eating in any way?

Health Status
- ❖ How are your teeth? (Tooth decay can accompany purging because regurgitated stomach acid erodes the enamel that protects teeth.)
- ❖ Tell me about your menstrual periods [for female adolescents].

Source: Adapted from Sattler, 1998.

and family think, feel, and behave, and the factors that might be contributing to the child's problems. However, it is often necessary to obtain a firsthand look at the child's behavior in everyday life situations at home or at school, or to ask someone who sees the child on a regular basis to rate his or her behavior.

Behavioral Assessment

Behavioral assessment is a strategy for evaluating the child's thoughts, feelings, and behaviors in *specific settings,* and then using this information to formulate hypotheses about the nature of the problem and what can be done about it (Bellack & Hersen, 1998; Mash & Terdal, 1997a). In general, behavioral assessment emphasizes observing the child's behavior directly, rather than inferring how children think, behave, or feel on the basis of their descriptions of inkblots or the pictures they draw. Using behavioral assessment, the clinician or another person who sees the child regularly identifies **target behaviors,** or the primary problems of concern, with the goal of then determining what specific factors may be controlling or influencing these behaviors. Sometimes this is a straightforward task, as with a child who complains of illness every Monday morning and, as a result, is kept out of school for the day (sound familiar?). In other cases, the child displays multiple problems at home or school. Felicia's school refusal, for example, appears to be part of a larger pattern of difficulties that includes social withdrawal, depression, and possible separation anxiety.

Even the seemingly simple task of identifying what is bothering a child can be a challenge. Remember, an adult usually decides that the child has a problem and whether or not the child is referred for an assessment. Adults frequently disagree about the nature of the problem,

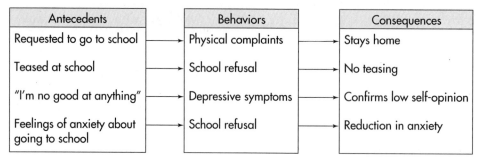

FIGURE 4.1 Functional analysis: antecedents, behaviors, consequences.

especially when they observe children in different settings (Achenbach, McConaughy, & Howell, 1987). Further, a child's presenting problem can often be very different from the one eventually identified as the target for intervention.

A commonly used and simple framework for organizing findings in behavioral assessment has been dubbed the "ABCs of assessment":

A = antecedents, or events that immediately precede a behavior

B = behavior(s) of interest

C = consequences, or the events that follow a behavior

In Felicia's case we might observe the following sequence: (A) whenever Felicia's mother asks her to go to school (antecedent), (B) Felicia complains that she has stomach pains and refuses to go (behaviors), and (C) her mother lets Felicia stay home (consequence). This antecedent-behavior-consequence sequence might suggest that Felicia is being reinforced for her physical complaints and school refusal by not having to go to school. In addition, because there are no positive consequences for going to school, and no negative ones for staying at home, Felicia might act this way again on future school days. The ABCs of assessment can be used to organize information in specific contexts, as just described, or as a more general framework for assessment (e.g., DuPaul & Ervin, 1996).

The more general approach to organizing and using assessment information in terms of antecedents, behaviors, and consequences across many different levels is called **behavior analysis** or **functional analysis of behavior** (Scotti, Morris, McNeil, & Hawkins, 1996). As shown in Figure 4.1, functional analysis can be used to identify a wide range of antecedents and consequences that might be contributing to Felicia's school refusal and depression. The antecedents and consequences for Felicia's behavior include events in the immediate situation (a reduction in anxiety), more remote occurrences (being teased at school), events in the external environment,

and Felicia's inner thoughts and feelings. The goal of functional analysis is to identify as many factors as possible that could be contributing to a child's problem behavior, thoughts, and feelings, and to develop hypotheses about which ones are the most important and/or most easily changed. In some cases hypotheses can be confirmed or rejected by changing the antecedents and consequences to see if the behavior changes. For example, we might teach Felicia to relax when thinking about going to school (changing an antecedent) to see if this decreases her school refusal. Or she could be instructed to substitute more positive self-statements ("I can succeed in school") for her negative ones ("I'm no good at anything") to see if this decreases her depressive symptoms and raises her self-esteem. In these examples, you can see how there is a close interplay between assessment and intervention when carrying out a functional analysis.

Functional analysis is not without its difficulties. First, the boundaries between antecedents, behaviors, and consequences are not nearly as distinct as the above discussion would suggest. The same event (e.g., school refusal) could be an antecedent, a behavior, or a consequence, depending on where we decide to "slice off" an ongoing stream of behavior. Second, because there are no standard guidelines for carrying out a functional analysis, the reliability and validity of these procedures are difficult to evaluate. Usually, the validity of a functional analysis is assessed in terms of whether or not it leads to strategies that produce meaningful changes in the child's problem behavior, sometimes referred to as *treatment validity*. In general, functional analysis can be viewed as an approach to organizing assessment information for an individual child, and for developing hypotheses for treatment.

The process of gathering information about the child's behavior in specific settings takes many different forms. Often it involves either (a) asking the parent, teacher, or child about what goes on in specific situations (e.g., asking a mother what she does when her child doesn't listen) or (b) observing the child (e.g., watching how the child and parent interact with one another during play). Clinicians develop their initial hypotheses on the basis of information provided by the parents and the child during the interview, and pursue them further through the use of behavioral assessments, such as behavior checklists and rating scales, and observations of behavior in real life or in role-play simulations.

Checklists and Rating Scales. Reports concerning child behavior and adjustment can be obtained using global checklists and problem-focused rating scales. Global behavior checklists ask parents, teachers, and, sometimes, youngsters themselves to rate the presence or absence of a wide variety of child behaviors or, in some cases, the frequency and intensity of these behaviors. Unlike a clinical interview, the use of a well-developed checklist is strengthened by its known degree of standardization and by the opportunities to compare an individual child's score with a known reference group of children of a similar age and the same gender. Checklists are also economical to administer and score, and provide a rich source of information about parents' or teachers' perceptions of children's behavior, including possible differences in the perceptions of parents in the same family, and differences between parent perceptions and those of teachers (e.g., McDermott, 1993). Keep in mind, however, that informants may differ in their views of the child's strengths and weaknesses, since they interact with the child in different surroundings and circumstances. These discrepancies are not necessarily bad, however, because they inform the clinician of the possible range of behavior the child engages in, possible circumstances that increase or decrease target behaviors (like being asked to read aloud at school), and possible demands or expectations placed on the child that may be unrealistic.

The Child Behavior Checklist/4–18 (CBCL) developed by Thomas Achenbach (1991a) and his colleagues is a leading checklist for assessing behavioral problems in children and adolescents. The reliability and validity of the CBCL has been documented in a number of research studies. The study of children's behavior problems in various cultures, described in Chapter 3 (Box 3.2), is one of many published reports that have used the CBCL to measure children's behavior. The clinical use of the CBCL in treatment settings and schools is even more frequent. The parent-completed form of the CBCL is part of a set of scales for children ages 4 to 18 years that also includes a teacher and youth self-report, a classroom observation measure, and an interview.

The CBCL covers a wide range of presenting complaints and, to a lesser extent, the child's competencies related to participation in activities, social involvement, and school performance. In addition to an overall

problem score, the CBCL provides scores for eight syndromes: withdrawn, somatic complaints, anxious/ depressed, social problems, thought problems, attention problems, delinquent behavior, and aggressive behavior (examples of items for each of these syndromes are presented in a later section on classification and diagnosis in Table 4.6). The CBCL also provides an *internalizing* score (a composite of the withdrawn, somatic complaints, and anxious/depressed syndromes) and an *externalizing* score (a composite of the delinquent behavior and aggressive behavior syndromes).

The eight scales of the CBCL can be used to form a *profile* that gives the clinician an overall picture of the variety and degree of the child's behavioral problems. A CBCL profile derived from a checklist completed by Felicia's mother is shown in Figure 4.2. The profile shows that the major areas of concern for Felicia's mother about her daughter were with respect to symptoms of social withdrawal, somatic complaints, anxiety/ depression, and other social problems. Felicia's scores on the first three of these dimensions are extreme, and place her in the upper 5% or higher when compared with girls of a similar age.

In addition to behavior checklists, such as the CBCL, that cover a wide range of child problems, numerous rating scales are available that focus on the symptoms of specific childhood disorders, such as depression, anxiety, autism, ADHD, and antisocial behavior, or on particular areas of child functioning, such as social competence, adaptive behavior, or school performance (Kamphaus & Frick, 1996; Mash & Terdal, 1997b). Ratings of the child are usually provided by parents and teachers, and by older children and adolescents themselves. Many of these scales provide the clinician with a more focused look at specific problems than is provided by a global behavior checklist. You will see many examples of rating scales used to assess specific problems in the chapters to follow. In Chapter 6, we present a rating scale for child psychopathy that includes items such as "acts without regard for consequences," "shallow and ingenuine," and "no feelings of remorse." In Chapter 10, we describe a rating scale for young children with autism that includes items related to "pretend play," "gaze monitoring," and "social interest." You can see how these measures are used by clinicians to zoom in on a focal problem that has been identified through interviews and global behavior checklists as being important.

In Felicia's case, because the initial interview and checklist assessments pointed to symptoms of depression, she and her mother were asked to complete the Children's Depression Inventory (CDI) (Kovacs, 1991). The CDI is a frequently used 27-item self-report scale that assesses a wide range of depressive symptoms,

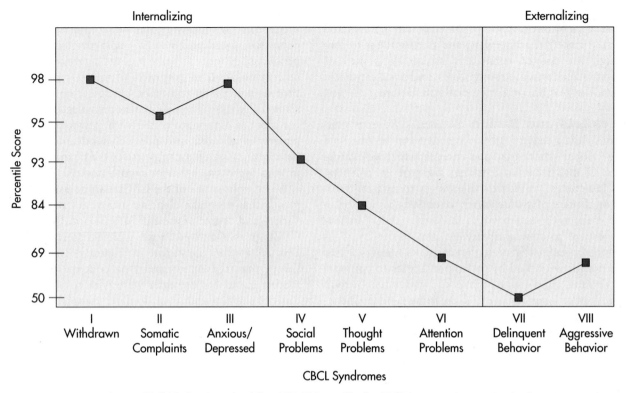

FIGURE 4.2 Child behavior checklist (CBCL) profile for Felicia. (Based on Achenbach, 1993)

including sadness, such cognitive symptoms as hopelessness, social problems, and acting-out behaviors. The scale provides *cutoff scores* to be used as guidelines for suggesting when a child is experiencing significant depressive symptomatology. Children who score above a cutoff are thought to be experiencing significant depression, those below are not. Felicia's mother rated her daughter as depressed as compared with children in the general population: Her ratings described a child with moderate depression of average duration. In contrast, Felicia's self-report on the CDI indicated a low severity and duration of depression. How do we reconcile these discrepant findings? Is Felicia depressed, as her mother's ratings would indicate? Or is she not depressed, as indicated by Felicia's self-ratings?

As we have noted, a lack of agreement between informants is often the rule rather than the exception and, in itself, provides important information for further hypothesis testing. Felicia's low scores on the CDI could indicate her denial of her problems and her lack of motivation to receive help. Or perhaps Felicia's mother's ratings are colored by her own bouts with depression and a history of unpleasant interactions with her daughter. Rather than looking for a "true" score, as if one informant's rating is correct and the other's incorrect, a clinician, during assessment, tries to make sense of both

discrepant and consistent findings in the context of other assessment information, and to use this information to formulate a useful treatment plan.

The main advantage of the CDI and similar rating scales is their low cost. These measures are easy to administer and score, taking only minutes to complete by a competent reader. However, cutoff scores from these measures should never be used rigidly or by themselves in making a diagnosis. Children just above a cutoff may not be all that different from those just below a cutoff, and, over time, the same child may move above or below a cutoff as a result of ongoing changes in the child or the environment.

Using checklists and rating scales, parents are often asked to describe not only their child, but also their own behavior, thoughts, and feelings; their style of parenting; and their family environment. Like Felicia's mother, many parents of children referred for assessment and treatment have problems of their own, including depression, anxiety, marital discord, and substance abuse. The assessment of these problems in the parent is critical in understanding the child's disorder and in formulating treatment plans. In some cases a parent's depression is a long-standing problem that contributes directly to the child's difficulties. In other cases, a parent's depression may be the result of a history of stressful and unsuccessful interactions with a difficult child. These different patterns of depression in parents might suggest different interventions for the child and family.

Child-completed checklists and rating scales also serve an important assessment function (Reynolds, 1993). Child self-report measures are used mostly with older children (typically, age 8 or older) who have rudimentary reading and comprehension skills, unless the wording and content are specifically geared to a younger level. Clinicians may opt to administer self-report checklists in an engaging, child-friendly manner that increases the child's interest in the material. For example, as noted earlier, we like to administer questionnaires to adolescents by computer, simply because they find this approach more interesting. With younger children, we like to hand them a card showing the range of responses they can give, using happy or sad faces and similar icons that appeal to that age group.

Behavioral Observation and Recording.

Because of the large amount of training, time, and costs that are involved, and the difficulties in determining reliability and validity, observations and recordings of behavior that are made by most clinicians are usually less formal than those used in research studies. Since some children are not old enough or skilled enough to report on their own behavior (and since it is usually the parent who sees the problem), parents, teachers, or clinicians may keep careful records of specific target behaviors. Parents or other observers typically record *baseline* (prior to intervention) data on one or two problems that they wish to change, such as how often their child complies with their requests, or how often he or she throws a temper tantrum.

A baseline recording that was made by the mother of Eric, a 10-year-old boy who displayed high rates of noncompliance, is shown in the top portion of Figure 4.3. Eric's mother was asked to note the specific forms of noncompliance that she was concerned about, such as arguing or not doing as asked, and to record each instance of noncompliance that occurred between 3:30 and 4:30 in the afternoon. This time period was selected because Eric's mother viewed it as especially problematic. After 5 days of baseline data were recorded, it was clear that Eric engaged in some form of noncompliance about once every 10 minutes. Following this baseline period, a treatment program that used a combination of rewards for compliance and time-out for noncompliance (5 minutes alone in the bathroom) was initiated by his parents. Eric's mother continued to keep records of his noncompliance following the start of treatment, and within a month his noncompliance showed a dramatic reduction (see Figure 4.4, bottom portion).

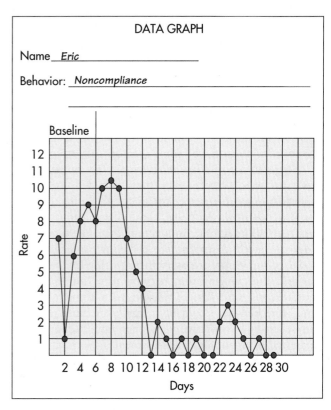

FIGURE 4.3 Parent's recording of child behavior. (Patterson, 1975)

In some cases, following the ABC format presented earlier, parents may also collect systematic information about antecedent and consequent events in order to identify potentially important contributing factors that may serve as a focus of treatment. Having parents keep records is particularly beneficial if the behaviors of concern occur at times that they are unlikely to be seen by others, such as late at night or during the early morning hours. For example, the parents of a child who was referred to us because of nightmares were asked to keep a record of what she did before bedtime, when she went to bed, when she awoke with a nightmare, and how they and she reacted to the disruption. The parents recorded this information for 2 weeks before coming into the clinic, so that precise details were available right from the beginning.

Recordings by parents have the advantage of providing ongoing information about behaviors of interest in life settings that might not otherwise be accessible to observation by the clinician. Parental monitoring may also provide secondary benefits that are not directly related to assessment, such as teaching parents better observation, tracking, and monitoring skills; assessing parental motivation; and providing parents with more realistic estimates of their children's rate of responding and feedback regarding the effects of treatment. However, many practical problems arise in getting parents to keep accurate records, and children often know when they are being watched and may react differently as a result. Of course, this can have benefits too—when we started monitoring our children's TV viewing to eliminate some of the more questionable shows, this had the positive side effect of teaching our children which shows are appropriate and why some are not.

Sometimes observing behavior directly can lead to a more accurate picture than that provided by verbal reports of what life is like for the child (and others) at home and school. At times, these observations can be extremely illuminating. In a recent case, the mother of a 4-year-old child with severe behavior problems came to one of our clinics for assistance. During the interview she told the clinician that her son was "impossible to get dressed," and "doesn't listen to a thing I say to him." She had been told by a family member that her son seemed "hyperactive," and her family doctor had requested a psychological assessment as a result of her insistence on this diagnosis. A note from his preschool teacher painted a very different picture of this young boy, however. His teacher spoke frankly of his undeveloped skills at following directions or concentrating on a task for any length of time, but pointed out how he settled down much like the other children once he found something to do that he enjoyed. This boy seemed calm during our visit with him at the clinic, so we decided to get a clearer picture of the situation by visiting his home and school.

Once we entered the home, the problem stood out within minutes. His home was littered with his toys and games, which his mother let him rummage through and toss around the room freely. Attempts to get her to provide some structure to his play and other activities resulted in an immediate confrontation between the two—he simply turned away and grabbed the toys he wanted, and she became upset and started to chase after him, yelling at him to put his toys away. "See," she said, turning to the observer, "he doesn't do a thing I ask him to do." The boy clutched his toys and quieted down at this point, turned on the TV, and plunked himself in front of it. Similar attempts on the boy's part to avoid doing what his teacher asked were observed during our school visit, although his teacher was more successful at getting him back to the activity at hand by using praise and other positive rewards.

Obviously, the description this mother gave us of her son's behavior lacked a few of the details that make an accurate diagnosis possible. Her description also failed to mention how upset she got when he "didn't listen," and that the home environment was rather chaotic and unstructured for a child his age. Without this home observation visit, our assessment of the problem and recommendations for treatment might have been quite different if, say, we attributed his misbehavior primarily to hyperactivity, as the mother had led us initially to assume. We developed strategies to teach the mother how to structure her home in a child-friendly manner, how to spend time playing with her son, and how to encourage his compliance by starting with simple requests and using positive rewards, such as praise, attention, and activities he enjoyed.

The clinician may also set up a *role-play simulation* in the clinic to see how the child and family might behave in daily situations encountered at home or school, such as problems at mealtime or cleanup time, or problem-solving situations, such as figuring out how to play a game together. When observing families who have physically abused their preschool-age child, for example, we choose activities that are likely to elicit both parent-child cooperation and conflict: We first ask parents to play with their child so that we can observe their teaching style, and then ask them to have the child put away her or his favorite toys, which often results in noncompliance and conflict (Wolfe, 1991). In Felicia's case, role-play simulations were used to assess her social skills. The clinician first described the situation to Felicia as follows: "You're sitting in the school cafeteria eating lunch by yourself when Janet, a girl from your math class, comes over to your table and sits across from you." Next, the clinician takes the role of Janet and says, "Hi Felicia. How's your lunch?" Felicia then responds, and the interaction continues, giving the clinician a chance to directly observe Felicia's social skills in a situation that might come up in everyday life (Kolko, 1987).

Sometimes, when time and resources permit, structured observations of behavior may be carried out in clinics, inpatient settings, and schools. For example, observations of Felicia's behavior during the interview

Table 4.5 Target Behaviors and Behavioral Definitions

GAZE

2 = Maintains gaze in direction of speaker; breaks in eye contact only fleeting (less than 3 seconds)
1 = Brief, occasional glances at speaker; covers eyes only briefly
0 = No gaze or covers eyes with hands; fleeting eye contacts of 1 second or less

FACIAL EXPRESSION

2 = Very expressive, animated; appropriate use of smile
1 = Appropriate expression and facial movement; occasional smiles
0 = Head pulled in toward body and held rigidly; no, or inappropriate use of, smile

VOICE VOLUME

2 = Appropriate expression, clear diction; easy to understand
1 = Some difficulty in understanding all spoken words
0 = Much difficulty in understanding spoken words; mumbling or whispering

SPEECH CONTENT

2 = Complete sentences; use of descriptive phrases revealing personal thoughts and feelings or requesting information
1 = Brief affirmations or responses to questions with minimal elaboration; two-word phrases
0 = Single-word or extremely vague or irrelevant responses, or no response

Source: Adapted from Kolko, 1987, p. 162.

suggested a number of deficits in her social skills, including minimal eye contact, lack of facial expressiveness, mumbling, and lack of elaboration in her speech. Specific target behaviors in these areas were identified and defined along a 3-point scale, as shown in Table 4.5. Portions of interactions between Felicia and her therapist were then videotaped before, during, and following intervention, and later coded by trained assistants. The clinician used this procedure to monitor changes in Felicia's social skills over the course of treatment.

Remember, however, that direct observation is not foolproof. Clinicians have to take into account the informant, the child, the nature of the problem, and the family context, because any of these issues can distort the findings. As noted in Chapter 3, parents can sometimes make their children look better or worse, depending on how they structure the situation (Johnson & Lobitz, 1974). On the other hand, some problem families find it difficult to make themselves look good, even when they know they are being observed. Abusive parents, for example, continue to be harsh and inappropriate toward their children even when they are aware that they are being observed (Mash et al., 1983). Despite its limitations, direct observation is a valid and beneficial step in the decision-making process for most families who voluntarily seek assistance and understand what may be required to conduct a thorough assessment and treatment plan, and can be quite helpful to less motivated families as well.

Psychological Testing

A **test** is usually defined as a task or set of tasks given under standard conditions with the purpose of assessing some aspect of the child's knowledge, skill, or personality. Most tests are standardized on a clearly defined reference group—for example, children of a certain age, sex, or SES—referred to as a *norm group*. An individual child's scores can then be compared with the scores of a comparable group of children to determine the extent to which that child's scores deviate from the norm. The prevalence and visibility of test use in our culture have led some people to adopt the mistaken view that testing and psychological assessment are one and the same. Although tests play an important role in a child's assessment, they represent just one part of the overall decision-making process.

People have been using tests to evaluate other people for a long time. Over 2000 years ago, the Chinese used tests to select civil servants. Socrates advocated combining teaching and testing, and his student Plato recommended selecting future leaders by identifying children who could detect deceit, learn quickly, and separate truth from superstition (French & Hale, 1990). The tradition of testing children with special needs has continued unabated since Alfred Binet invented the first intelligence test in Paris in 1905. Despite the many controversies surrounding the interpretation and use of psychological tests with children, clinicians commonly use developmental

Table 4.6 Domains Assessed by Developmental Screening Tests

Personal-Social Domain	Adaptive Domain	Motor Domain	Communication Domain	Cognitive Domain
Adult interaction	Attention	Muscle control	Receptive communication	Perceptual discrimination
Expression of feelings/affect	Eating	Body coordination	Nonverbal communication	Memory
Self-concept	Dressing	Locomotion	Verbal communication	Reasoning and academic skills
Peer interaction	Toileting	Fine motor skills		Conceptual development

scales, intelligence and educational tests, projective tests, personality tests, and neuropsychological tests to assess children's disorders of development, learning, and behavior (Halperin & McKay, 1998; Reynolds & Kamphaus, 1990a, 1990b; Sattler, 1992). In fact, tests (particularly intelligence tests) are among the most frequently used assessment methods with children (Mooney & Harrison, 1987). In this section we will introduce you to some of the more commonly used tests for assessing children. Remember, test scores should always be interpreted in the context of other assessment information. Often, observations of a child's behavior in the test situation can tell us as much or more about the child as his or her scores on a test.

Developmental Tests. Developmental tests are used to assess infants and young children, and are generally carried out for the purposes of screening, diagnosis, and evaluation of early development. **Screening** refers to the identification of children who are at risk, who are then referred for a more thorough evaluation. The assessment of risk in infants and young children has increased in frequency as new laws direct public attention and action to the importance of early assessment in developing effective strategies for early intervention and prevention (Osofsky, 1998).

A child's at-risk status may reflect delays or disruptions in motor, cognitive, language, emotional, or behavioral development. The Battelle Developmental Inventory (Newborg, Stock, Wnek, Guidubaldi, & Svinicki, 1984) is one example of a developmental screening instrument that can be used to assess personal-social, motor, adaptive, communication, and cognitive functioning in infants and children from birth through 8 years. Some of the specific aspects of development assessed by this inventory, which are representative of the content of developmental tests in general, are shown in Table 4.6. Screening instruments are intended to be brief so that they can be administered to large numbers of children in a wide range of settings, ranging from newborn clinics to preschools.

Because screening tests are brief, a more thorough assessment of a young child's development is needed.

Perhaps the most popular and well-standardized test of developmental status in infants ages 1 to 42 months is the second edition of the Bayley Scales of Infant Development (Bayley, 1993). The Bayley includes three scales: the Mental scale and Motor scale, which assess the child's current level of cognitive, language, personal-social, and fine and gross motor development; and the Behavior Rating scale, which assesses the child's behavior during testing. Normative data are available for normal children and children with high-incidence clinical diagnoses, such as Down syndrome, prematurity, and prenatal exposure to drugs. Developmental tests such as the Bayley scales can be used by clinicians to identify children with developmental delays, to monitor a child's progress following the initiation of an intervention program, or as a tool for teaching parents about their infant's development.

Intelligence and Educational Testing

We must guard against defining intelligence solely in terms of the ability to pass the tests of a given intelligence scale. It should go without saying that no existing scale is capable of adequately measuring the ability to deal with all possible kinds of material on all intelligence levels.
—Lewis M. Terman

Evaluating a child's intellectual and educational functioning is a key ingredient in clinical assessments for a wide range of childhood disorders, making it essential that these areas be carefully assessed prior to making any recommendations for treatment. For some children, impairments in thinking and learning may result from their behavioral or emotional problems. For example, the drop in Felicia's grades from Bs to Cs and Ds was likely a function of the impact of her school refusal and depression on school performance. For other children, particularly those with mental retardation or learning and language disorders, problems in thinking and learning may be part of the disorder itself. In many other cases the nature of the relationship between the child's disorder and disturbances in thinking and learning is less clear. For example, children with ADHD score lower on

Table 4.7   Subscales of the WISC-III

Verbal Subscale	Area Assessed
Information	Broad range of general knowledge
Similarities	Perception of common elements and bringing them together to form a concept
Arithmetic	Mental computation and concentration
Vocabulary	Word knowledge
Comprehension	Understanding situations and providing answers to specific problems
Digit span*	Short-term auditory memory and attention

Performance Subscale	Area Assessed
Picture completion	Visual recognition and identification of familiar objects
Picture arrangement	Comprehending and evaluating a total situation
Block design	Analysis and synthesis of forms; perceptual organization
Object assembly	Synthesis, or putting things together to form familiar objects
Coding	Discrimination and memory of visual pattern stimuli
Mazes*	Planning ability and perceptual organization
Symbol search*	Mental processing speed; visual search

*Supplementary subtest

standard tests of intelligence and do more poorly in school than other children. Is this lowered performance related to their inattentiveness in the test situation or classroom, or to some other more basic deficit in the way in which they process information? These are some of the questions that intellectual and educational assessments can help answer.

How would you define intelligence? Most people think of intelligence as involving problem-solving ability, verbal ability, and social intelligence. This definition is consistent with theories on which commonly used intelligence tests are based. David Wechsler, whose test has come to be the one most frequently used to assess intelligence in children, defined intelligence as "the overall capacity of an individual to understand and cope with the world around him" (Wechsler, 1974, p. 5). However, debate continues about how intelligence should be defined. Numerous theories of intelligence and numerous tests based on these different theories have been proposed (Kamphaus, 1993; Sattler, 1992). Keep in mind that Binet's original scale in 1905 was developed to answer a practical question rather than a theoretical one—to identify children who would not succeed in a regular classroom. Although intelligence tests have come to be used in many other ways, for example, in describing possible learning disabilities, they still work best when used to the answer the question for which they were originally designed.

Numerous tests for assessing intelligence in children exist, each with unique strengths and weaknesses. The most popular intelligence scale in use today with children is the Wechsler Intelligence Scale for Children (WISC-III) (Wechsler, 1991), which is the most recent version of a test that was introduced about 50 years ago. The WISC-III is made up of ten mandatory and three supplementary subtests, all of which span the age range of 6 to 16 years. According to Wechsler, these subtests assess the child's global capacity in different ways, but do not represent different types of intelligence. Other tests assess intelligence in younger children, including the Wechsler Preschool and Primary Scale of Intelligence-Revised (WPPSI-R) (Wechsler, 1989), Binet-4 (Thorndike, Hagen, & Sattler, 1986), and Kaufman Assessment Battery for Children (K-ABC) (A. S. Kaufman & N. L. Kaufman, 1983).

The subtests making up the Verbal and Performance scales of the WISC-III are presented in Table 4.7, along with a brief description of what each subtest assesses. In actuality, each subtest assesses multiple and overlapping abilities. Examples of the kinds of questions and items that are included on each WISC-III subtest are shown in Box 4.2. The WISC-III is individually administered to the child by a highly trained examiner who follows specific procedures.

The WISC-III yields a Verbal IQ score, a Performance IQ score, and a combined Full Scale IQ score. Felicia obtained a Verbal IQ score of 107, a Performance IQ score of 105, and Full Scale IQ score of 106 on the WISC-III, which means that her intelligence is in the average range. The WISC-III is well standardized and possesses excellent reliability and validity. True to tradition, IQ scores on the WISC-III are good predictors of academic achievement. As a clinical tool, the WISC-III can be used to diagnose mental retardation (in combination with measures of the child's adaptive ability), and, because of the verbal/performance distinction, may be

Box 4.2

Items Similar to Those Included in WISC-III

Information (30 questions)

How many legs do you have?
What must you do to make water freeze?
Who discovered the North Pole?
What is the capital of France?

Similarities (19 questions)

In what way are pencil and crayon alike?
In what way are tea and coffee alike?
In what way are inch and mile alike?
In what way are binoculars and microscope alike?

Arithmetic (24 questions)

If I have one piece of candy and get another one, how many pieces will I have?
At 12 cents each, how much will 4 bars of soap cost?
If a suit sells for ½ of the regular price, what is the cost of a $120 suit?

Vocabulary (30 words)

ball   summer   poem   obstreperous

Comprehension (18 questions)

Why do we wear shoes?
What is the thing to do if you see someone dropping his packages?
In what two ways is a lamp better than a candle?

Digit Span (15 items; 8 in Digits Forward, 7 in Digits Backward)

The task is to repeat digits presented by the examiner in a forward direction in one part (2 to 9 digits in length; example: 1–8) and in a backward direction in the other part (2 to 8 digits in length; example: 3–9–1).

Picture Completion (30 items)

The task is to identify the essential missing part of the picture, such as (a) a car without a wheel, (b) a dog without a leg, and (c) a telephone without numbers on the dial (see below).

Courtesy of The Psychological Corporation.

Coding (59 items in Coding A and 119 items in Coding B)

The task is to copy symbols from a key (see below).

Courtesy of The Psychological Corporation.

Picture Arrangement (14 items)

The task is to arrange a series of pictures into a meaningful sequence (see below).

Courtesy of The Psychological Corporation.

Block Design (12 items)

The task is to reproduce stimulus designs using four or nine blocks (see below).

Object Assembly (5 items)

The task is to arrange pieces into a meaningful object (see below).

Courtesy of The Psychological Corporation.

continued

Box 4.2

Items Similar to Those Included in WISC-III—cont'd

Symbol Search (45 items in Part A and 45 items in Part B)

The task is to decide whether a stimulus figure (a symbol) appears in an array (see below).

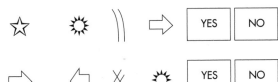

Courtesy of The Psychological Corporation.

Mazes (10 items)

The task is to complete a series of mazes (see below).

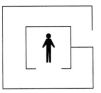

Courtesy of The Psychological Corporation.

Note. The questions resemble those that appear on the WISC-III but are not actually from the test, except for the sample items shown for Symbol Search and Mazes.

---

useful in assessing children who are blind, deaf, or handicapped.

Several important questions need to be asked when using the WISC-III and other IQ tests in the clinical decision-making process: How are the test scores interrelated? What patterns are detected? Why might the child have received these scores? What circumstances in the testing situation might have affected the child's performance—for example, anxiety, personality factors, motivation, medication? How do the child's test scores compare with those of other children of comparable age, gender, grade, class, ethnic group, and/or disability? How do the child's test scores compare with the scores he or she received on similar tests given at an earlier time? Finally, and most important, how will the test scores be used in treatment and educational planning?

Evaluation of educational achievement also plays an important role in psychoeducational assessments carried out for mental retardation, learning disorders, or behavior disorders. Many available tests assess a child's reading, arithmetic, spelling, language processing, receptive vocabulary, comprehension, and numerous other skills. A popular screening test of academic achievement is the Wide Range-Achievement Test (WRAT-3) (Wilkinson, 1993), which consists of Reading, Spelling, and Arithmetic subtests. The Reading subtest measures the child's ability to recognize and name letters and pronounce words. The Spelling subtest measures the ability to write one's name and to write words from dictation. The Arithmetic subtest measures skills such as counting, reading number symbols, and solving oral and written computations. Felicia's academic achievement scores on the WRAT-3 were at grade 8.2 for reading, grade 8.0 for spelling, and grade 9.5 for arithmetic—all above her

current grade level. The findings that Felicia is of average intelligence and has academic achievement at or above grade level suggest that her poor school performance may be due to her social withdrawal and depression.

The WRAT-3 and similar measures are useful as screening measures of academic achievement. However, because such measures provide norm-referenced information for global areas of achievement, their usefulness in planning specific educational interventions is limited (Kamphaus, Slotkin, & DeVincentis, 1990). More thorough assessment of academic achievement and performance is needed in cases where decisions about diagnosis, academic placement, or educational planning are required. Numerous measures of academic achievement and performance are available to meet these purposes (Reynolds & Kamphaus, 1990a; Sattler, 1992).

Projective Testing

Sometimes a cigar is just a cigar.
—Sigmund Freud

Psychoanalytic theories focus our attention on the existence and influence of unconscious processes in children's psychological disorders. However, if children aren't aware of their thoughts and feelings, how do we assess them? Psychoanalytically oriented clinicians try to address this problem by using **projective tests.** These tests present the child with ambiguous stimuli, such as inkblots or pictures of people. The child is then asked to describe what she or he sees. The hypothesis is that the child will project his or her own personality—unconscious fears, needs, and inner conflicts—on the ambiguous stimuli of other people and things. By doing this, and without realization, the child discloses his or her unconscious thoughts and feelings to the clinician, thus revealing information that would not be shared in response to direct questioning (Chandler, 1990). Many "junior-sized" versions of projective tests have been developed for younger children, in which the ambiguous stimuli have been made child-friendly by incorporating family scenes or pictures of animals (Levitt & French, 1992).

Projective testing has generated more controversy over the past 50 years than any other type of clinical assessment method. Most clinicians have strong views about projective testing—either pro or con. You may very well have some strong opinions about the Rorschach inkblot and similar methods yourself. Some clinicians believe that projective tests provide a rich source of information about the child's coping styles, affect, self-concept, interpersonal functioning, and ways of processing information (Rabin, 1986; Weiner, 1986). Other clinicians view projectives as woefully inadequate with respect to meeting even minimum standards for reliability and validity, so much so that they damage the credibility of psychological testing with the general public and other professionals (Anastasi & Urbina, 1997; Gittelman-Klein, 1986). Despite the controversy surrounding their use, projective tests continue as one of the most frequently used clinical assessment methods with children and adults (Levitt & French, 1992; Mooney & Harrison, 1987; Watkins, Campbell, Nieberding, & Hallmark, 1995).

Representative of the many projective techniques for use with children and adolescents are the Rorschach inkblot test, thematic picture tests such as the Roberts Apperception Test for Children (RATC), and human figure drawings. The Rorschach hardly needs an introduction. The test consists of ten inkblot pictures (ambiguous stimuli) that are presented one by one, and the child tells the examiner what he or she sees. According to proponents of the test, the child's responses can be used to provide information about coping operations, affect, self-concept, and interpersonal functioning, as well as how the child processes information. Standardized versions of the Rorschach, most notably the Comprehensive System of John Exner (1993), have been developed to combat criticisms related to the rampant unstandardized use of the Rorschach (remember, if a test is administered differently by each clinician who uses it, the results won't be very reliable). The Exner system specifies how the cards should be presented, what the examiner should say, and how the child's responses should be recorded. It also provides norms for children and adolescents, and evidence for reliability. This test, when used in a standardized way, may have the potential for identifying certain forms of child psychopathology. However, research support with children is sparse and validity remains a concern. In addition, despite efforts to standardize the administration of the Rorschach, many clinicians continue to use and interpret Rorschach test results in their own idiosyncratic way, thus reducing reliability and validity. This is a problem for all projective tests.

The Roberts Apperception Test for Children (RATC) (McArthur & Roberts, 1982) is a thematic picture test for children aged 6 to 15 that depicts common situations, conflicts, and stresses in children's lives. The drawings are intended to represent important personal themes, such as parental affection, peer conflicts, and sibling rivalry. Although the pictures in this and other thematic apperception tests aren't as obscure as inkblots, they are ambiguous with respect to the relations portrayed, previous and future circumstances of the relationships, and what the characters are thinking or feeling. Drawings are shown to the child, and he or she is asked to make up a story about them. It is presumed that in telling a story about the character in the picture, the child says things that apply to her- or himself that would not be revealed in response to direct questions. A unique aspect of the RATC is its emphasis on standardization, reliability, and validity. Versions are available for both white and African-American children. The RATC has a comprehensive scoring system with adequate reliability and is one of the more objective and popular projective tests. However, as with the Exner system for the Rorschach, evidence for its validity is limited (Sines, 1985).

Human figure drawings or other types of art production are another form of projective testing, in which the child is asked to draw a picture of a person or people or objects, with the assumption that the child's thoughts and feelings will be revealed in his or her drawings. Traditionally, the content of the child's drawings, such as the size of the person depicted, placement of the drawing on the page, erasures, or missing body parts, was interpreted as an indication of the child's personality. For example, a drawing of an unelaborated stick figure might be interpreted as an indication of defensiveness, or heavy shading as a sign of anxiety. However, these kinds of interpretations of content have proved extremely unreliable and research is generally lacking (Knoff, 1990; Swensen, 1968). Thus, it is not advisable to generate interpretations based on the characteristics, positions, or actions of figures in projective drawings. Interpretation based on the overall quality of the child's drawings presents a possible alternative for making judgments about the child's mental health; however, reliability and validity data for such judgments are also lacking. Consider the drawings made by three different children aged 4 to 5 years that are shown in Figure 4.4. Do you think it's possible to make reliable and valid interpretations of these children's personalities based on these drawings?

"You must be Mary's parents. I recognized you from her drawings!"

Psychoanalytic clinicians also attempt to assess children's inner life through play—for example, through the use of puppets, storytelling, or other material (Chethik, 1989). Although not a formal projective test, for psychoanalytic clinicians, play is presumed to function in much the same way as projectives; in an unstructured or ambiguous play situation, free play is believed to represent fantasy production and a window into the child's unconscious processes.

The reliability and validity of figure drawings and play as formal assessment procedures are questionable, especially when interpretations based on specific content are made. However, figure drawings and play are commonly used by clinicians across a wide range of theoretical persuasions as a way to help children relax during assessment and to make it easier for them to provide information or talk about events that they may have difficulty expressing verbally (Malchiodi, 1998). For

FIGURE 4.4 Examples of human figure drawings. (Left figure: Pearce and Pezzot-Pearce, 1997; middle and right figures: Selfe, 1983)

Table 4.8 Self-Report of Personality: Scale Definitions

Construct	Definition
Anxiety	Feelings of nervousness, worry, and fear; the tendency to be overwhelmed by problems
Attitude toward school	Feelings of alienation, hostility, and dissatisfaction regarding school
Attitude toward teachers	Feelings of resentment and dislike of teachers; belief that teachers are unfair, uncaring, or overly demanding
Atypicality	The tendency toward gross mood swings, bizarre thoughts, subjective experiences, or obsessive-compulsive thoughts and behaviors
Depression	Feelings of unhappiness, sadness, and dejection; belief that nothing goes right
Interpersonal relations	The perception of having good social relationships and friendships with peers
Locus of control	The belief that rewards and punishments are controlled by external events or other people
Relations with parents	A positive regard for parents and a feeling of being esteemed by them
Self-esteem	Feelings of self-esteem, self-respect, and self-acceptance

Source: Kamphaus and Frick, 1996, p. 89.

example, the drawing on the left in Figure 4.4 was made by a 4-year-old girl who had been sexually abused and was asked by a clinician to draw how she felt when it happened (Pearce & Pezzot-Pearce, 1997). This drawing allowed the child and therapist to label her feelings so that they could be addressed in therapy. (The other two drawings in Figure 4.4 were done by children without problems who were asked to draw a picture of a human figure.)

Personality Testing. The informal assessment of *personality* in children begins almost at the time of birth, when parents begin to label their child as active, cheerful, or cranky. Personality is usually thought of as an enduring trait or pattern of traits that characterize the individual and determine the ways in which he or she interacts with the environment. For example, children who withdraw from social contact may be characterized by their parents as shy; others, who are socially busy, as outgoing. A concept that is related to personality is *temperament,* although temperament is usually thought of as a more biologically based characteristic that is present early in life. In a sense, a child's early temperament provides the foundation on which personality is built.

Several dimensions have been identified that seem to capture the essence of personality, including whether a child or adolescent is timid or bold, agreeable or disagreeable, dependable or undependable, tense or relaxed, or reflective or unreflective (Goldberg, 1992). These central dimensions of personality have been dubbed the "Big 5" factors. Many of the methods already discussed, such as interviews, projective techniques, and behavioral measures, provide some information about the child's personality. However, a number of objective inventories focus specifically on personality, using either the child or parent as informants. Two of the more

frequently used personality inventories with children are the Minnesota Multiphasic Personality Inventory—Adolescent (MMPI-A) (Butcher et al., 1992) and the Personality Inventory for Children (PIC) (Wirt, Lachar, Klinedinst, & Seat, 1990).

A recently developed measure of personality is the Behavior Assessment System for Children—Self-Report of Personality (BASC-SRP) (Reynolds & Kamphaus, 1992). This measure, which can be used with children aged 8 through 18, assesses the child's perceptions and feelings about parents, peers, school, and his or her own behavior problems. To give you a feel for the kind of content that may be included in personality inventories, definitions for each of the scales of the BASC-SRP are presented in Table 4.8. Four composite scales can also be constructed: Clinical Maladjustment, School Maladjustment, Personal Maladjustment, and an Emotional Symptoms Index. The BASC-SRP has good reliability and validity, and the scales seem to tap settings that are relevant to children, such as attitudes toward teachers and parents.

Neuropsychological Testing. In the clinical context, **neuropsychological assessment** attempts to link brain functioning with objective measures of behavior that are known to depend on an intact central nervous system. For example, try closing your eyes and then touching the tip of your nose with your ring finger—first with your right hand and then with your left. How do you think you'd do on this task if you were sleep-deprived? Even a simple task like this one is dependent on a number of psychological functions and an intact nervous system. For children with certain types of brain injury or dysfunction, carrying out this or other tasks may prove difficult. The premise underlying neuropsychological assessments is that behavioral measures can be used to make inferences about central nervous system dysfunction and, more importantly, the consequences of this dysfunction for the child. Neuropsychological assessments use this information clinically for determining a diagnosis, planning treatment, documenting the course of recovery, measuring subtle but significant improvements, and following up on children with neurological impairments or learning disorders (Dean & Gray, 1990).

Although neuropsychological assessments were originally used to identify an underlying brain injury or process, this is no longer their primary purpose. The routine use of neuroimaging procedures (Chapter 3), combined with mixed or inconsistent neuropsychological findings, has led to a change in focus away from diagnosis to obtaining information about deficits in functioning that will lead to effective treatment and rehabilitation for children with neurological disorders and learning problems. The kinds of neurological disorders in children for which neuropsychological assessments have been conducted include traumatic brain injury (e.g., head injury due to a fall); brain malformations (e.g., spina bifida, hydrocephalus); genetic, metabolic, or degenerative disorders; tumors; infectious disorders; cerebrovascular disease; and epilepsy (Fletcher & Taylor, 1997).

Neuropsychological assessments frequently consist of comprehensive batteries that assess a full range of psychological functions (e.g., Halstad-Reitan Neuropsychological Test Battery; Reitan & Wolfson, 1992; Rourke, Fiske, & Strang, 1986). In practice, the specific batteries used vary widely across clinicians (Fletcher & Taylor, 1997). Among the functions assessed are verbal and nonverbal *cognitive functions,* such as language, abstract reasoning, memory, learning, problem solving, numerical ability, perceptual organization, and spatial concept formation; *perceptual functions,* including visual, auditory, and tactile-kinesthetic; *motor functions* relating to strength, speed of performance, coordination, and dexterity; and *emotional/executive control* functions, such as attention, concentration, frustration tolerance, flexibility, and emotional functioning.

The clinician must consider all these functions in relation to one another since neurological dysfunction is rarely isolated to one specific function, and because higher-order functions rely on lower-order functions. For example, to remember the material you are now reading for your next exam you need to be able to attend to it, take in the main elements, and register the features to be recalled. In other words, the higher-order function of memory is related to the lower-order functions of attending to, receiving, and registering information; thus these functions need to be assessed in relation to one another (Boll & LaMarche, 1992; Dean & Gray, 1992).

Recent approaches to neuropsychological assessment in children have taken an integrative multilevel

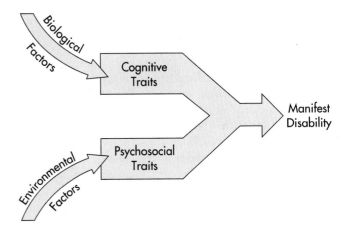

FIGURE 4.5   A comprehensive approach to neuropsychological assessment. (Taylor & Fletcher, 1990)

approach that considers the child's manifest or visible disability in relation to both child characteristics and biological and environmental factors (Taylor & Fletcher, 1990). The different levels of this model for the neuropsychological assessment of children are shown in Figure 4.5. At the first level, manifest disability reflects the inability of the child to meet family, cultural, or school expectations—in other words, the presenting problem that led to referral. At the second level—child traits—basic cognitive functions are assessed using psychometric tests (this level has traditionally been the focus of neuropsychological assessments), as are psychosocial factors—the child's behavioral adjustment, personality, self-esteem, and other aspects of development. The child's cognitive and psychosocial traits interact with one another to directly influence the manifest disability. At the third level, both biological and environmental factors are presumed to have an indirect impact on the child's manifest disability. Biological factors at this level include central nervous system lesions and neuroimaging findings; characteristics of the disorder that led to the brain injury; and how the brain injury was treated. Environmental factors at this level include family and cultural background, parenting practices, the school environment, and the child's past learning (Fletcher & Taylor, 1997).

This approach to neuropsychological assessment is different in that it integrates the more traditional methods of assessing basic psychological and cognitive functions using neuropsychological assessments, with a broader systems perspective that views central nervous system disturbances as just one of many influences on learning and behavior. This comprehensive approach can then be used to develop a detailed treatment or rehabilitation plan based on the assessment findings.

CLASSIFICATION AND DIAGNOSIS

Over the past two decades, major changes have occurred in the way childhood disorders are classified (Adelman, 1995). By *classification,* we mean a system for representing the major categories or dimensions of child psychopathology, and the boundaries and relations among them. As you may recall, diagnosis refers to the assignment of cases to categories of the classification system. We begin our discussion of this important topic by discussing some of the reasons for classification and diagnosis with children and adolescents, and go into some detail on the current strategies available. Because diagnosis is not without criticism, we also raise awareness of the impact of labeling children.

Until now, we have looked at Felicia's problems on a very individual basis. We looked at her depression, school refusal, and social skills deficits, and assessed her mental status, general intellectual functioning, and behavior. This information tells us what is *unique* about Felicia and how she differs from others her age. Isn't this enough, you might ask? Why do we need to pigeonhole Felicia by tagging her with a diagnostic label such as "major depressive disorder"? Can't we just find a way to help her with her problems based on what we have learned about her unique characteristics?

The problem with this approach is that if we treated every child as totally unique, research into the causes and treatment of childhood disorders would be impossible to conduct, and we would have little direction in how to proceed in treating an individual case (Waldman & Lilienfeld, 1995). For this reason, we also need to consider what Felicia has in *common* with others who present with similar problems or symptoms, and whether there are general principles that apply across many children. In effect, this is what is done throughout this text, as we learn about the core symptoms of current child and adolescent disorders, their prevalence and course, their prognosis, and their treatment. Without such information to use for comparison, making the best decisions concerning Felicia's problem and course of action would be difficult.

As you may recall from our earlier discussion, clinical assessment and diagnosis involve two related strategies for determining the best plan for a given individual. We use an idiographic strategy when we want to highlight a child's unique circumstances, personality, cultural background, and similar features that pertain mostly to his or her particular situation. Without question, each child who comes in for an assessment has unique strengths as well as challenges that make his or her problem seem a little different than the "textbook" case description. In addition, we use a nomothetic strategy as part of our assessment, to benefit from all the information accumulated on a given problem or disorder and to attempt to determine the general class or grouping of problems to which the presenting problem belongs. That is, we attempt to name or classify the problem using an existing system of diagnosis, such as DSM-IV (APA, 1994). Classifying the problem leads to the existing body of knowledge from which we can draw to understand the child and family, and to choose an intervention, preferably one shown through treatment-outcome studies to be effective for children with similar difficulties.

Although most of us recognize the advantages of a system of classification for medical and psychological problems, developing a classification system that is simple and concise enough to be of practical benefit is not an easy task. In fact, despite years of effort, there is no single, agreed-upon, reliable and valid, worldwide classification system for childhood disorders. Although the DSM-IV has become the standard in North America (Garber, 1984; Mash & Terdal, 1997a), concerns continue to be raised that current classification systems are inadequate in their coverage of childhood disorders and insensitive to the developmental complexities that characterize these problems (Scotti et al., 1996).

Categories, Dimensions, or Both?

How do we make sense of the various symptoms expressed by children and classify their behavior in ways that lead to practical forms of communication? One method would be to make distinct categories of disorders that had little or nothing in common with one another. Alternatively, we could quantify the various attributes of a psychological disorder along several dimensions and generate scores that indicate the degree to which a person experiences particular symptoms or symptom combinations.

The first approach for diagnosis and classification of child psychopathology mentioned above involves the use of **categorical classification** systems. Categorical systems are based primarily on informed professional consensus, an approach that has dominated and continues to dominate the field of both child and adult psychopathology (APA, 1994). A *classical* (or pure) categorical approach assumes that every diagnosis has a clear underlying cause, such as an infection or a malfunction of the nervous system, and that each disorder is fundamentally different from every other disorder. Therefore, cases can be placed into distinctive categories. We might say, for example, that Felicia meets criteria for a major depressive disorder, but not for separation anxiety disorder. The disadvantage to this approach, of course, is that children's behavior seldom falls neatly into established categories, so a certain degree of confusion remains.

Table 4.9 Commonly Identified Dimensions of Child Psychopathology and Examples of Items that Reflect Each of the Dimensions

Withdrawn	Social Problems	Anxious/Depressed
Would rather be alone	Acts too young	Unhappy, sad, depressed
Refuses to talk	Too dependent	Worries
Secretive	Doesn't get along with peers	Feels worthless
Shy, timid	Gets teased	Nervous, tense
Somatic Complaints	**Thought Problems**	**Aggressive Behavior**
Feels dizzy	Hears things	Argues
Overtired	Sees things	Mean to others
Aches, pains	Strange behavior	Attacks people
Headaches	Strange ideas	Destroys others' things
Attention Problems	**Delinquent Behavior**	
Inattentive	Lacks guilt	
Can't concentrate	Bad companions	
Can't sit still	Lies	
Confused	Runs away from home	

Source: Adapted from Achenbach, 1993.

Moreover, categories of behavior, as opposed to some medical diseases, for example, do not typically share the same underlying causes; thus the mental health field has had to modify the classical categorical approach to accommodate the current state of knowledge.

The second approach to describing abnormal child behavior involves empirically based **dimensional classification.** Dimensional approaches to classification assume that a number of independent dimensions or traits of behavior exist and that all children possess these to varying degrees. For example, rather than saying that Felicia's symptoms fit the category of major depressive disorder, we might say that she is significantly above average (often referred to as being within the *clinical range*) on the dimension of depression, and that she is somewhat above average on the dimension of anxiety. These and other traits or dimensions are typically derived using statistical methods, from samples drawn from both clinically referred and nonreferred child populations to establish ranges along each dimension (Achenbach, 1993).

Although empirically derived schemes are more objective and potentially more reliable than clinically derived classification systems, they too have limitations. First and foremost, the derived dimensions are dependent on sampling, method, and informant characteristics, as well as the age and sex of the child (Mash & Terdal, 1997a). Consequently, integrating information obtained from different methods and various informants, over time or across situations, can be difficult. Dimensional approaches are also insensitive to contextual influences. For example, if you were a parent and you were asked to describe whether your child "acts too young" using the scale "never, sometimes, a lot," you may want to clarify the circumstances or context under which he sometimes acts too young ("whenever I take him grocery shopping" or "when he is playing with other children"). Dimensions provide a useful estimate of the degree to which a child displays certain traits and not others, yet they often have to be tailored to the child's unique circumstances and developmental opportunities.

A number of general as well as more specific dimensions of child psychopathology have been identified through research. These include the externalizing and internalizing dimensions and the subdimensions or syndromes that we talked about earlier in our discussion of behavior rating scales. Some of the most common syndromes in children and adolescents are presented in Table 4.9, along with selected examples of specific problem behaviors.

Although the debate has not been resolved as to which approach is "best"—categories, dimensions, or some combination—there is agreement that each approach has value in classifying childhood disorders. Some disorders, such as autistic disorder, may be best conceptualized as qualitatively distinct conditions (categories), whereas others, such as depression or anxiety, may be best described as extreme points on one or more continuous dimensions. Also, depending on the purpose—clinical diagnosis or research—one approach may be more useful than the other (Kazdin & Kagan, 1994). For example, a dimensional approach to conceptualizing

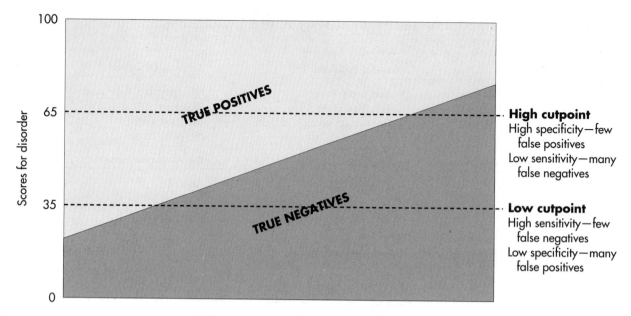

FIGURE 4.6 Effects of using low versus high cutpoints in classification.

psychological factors, such as behavior, affect, and cognitive abilities, among children is compatible with research methods that determine the degree of association among two or more variables, and thus is often preferred by those conducting psychological research. A categorical approach, on the other hand, is often more compatible for clinical purposes, where the objective is to incorporate the whole pattern of the child's behavior into a meaningful diagnosis and treatment plan. In addition, categorical diagnoses are often required to determine a child's eligibility for services.

An additional point to consider in any system of classification relates to the number of required symptoms, or the degree of the disorder needed, before a child meets the criteria for a diagnosis. If the number or degree is very low, then most children who have the disorder will be correctly classified (true positives). The downside in this instance is that many children who are normal will also receive the diagnosis (false positives). On the other hand, if the cutoff is too high, most normal children will be correctly classified as normal (true negatives), but many children who have the disorder will be misclassified as normal (false negatives). The term **sensitivity** refers to the percent of children with the disorder who are rightly classified as having the disorder. **Specificity** refers to the percent of true normals rightly classified as normal. Where the cutpoints for a diagnosis are set influences sensitivity and specificity. If cutpoints are too high, sensitivity is low and specificity is high. If cutpoints are too low, however, the reverse occurs. These relationships are depicted in Figure 4.6.

Evolution of Current Systems

The following synopsis of the evolution of current systems provides a perspective on how far we have come in recognizing mental disorders in children and adolescents. The terminology and focus of prior systems reflected the major theoretical views of mental illness at the time; a shift to a more objective, informed approach occurred by the 1980s.

Etienne Esquirol was likely the first individual to classify mental diseases in children. In 1838, he classified insanity by age group using a rather crude system—childhood was the period of "imbecility" and youth, of "mania and monomania" (Rie, 1971). The U.S. census of 1840 was the first systematic effort to collect data on mental illness. It recorded the frequency of a single category, called "idiocy/insanity," since nothing else was known at the time. By 1880 the number of categories of mental illness had grown to seven: dementia, dipsomania, mania, melancholia, monomania, and paresis (APA, 1994), terms that have all but disappeared from use today. But it was not until 1948 that mental disorders were included in the same manual as other major illnesses—when the sixth edition of the World Health Organization's *International Classification of Diseases* (ICD) added, for the first time, a section on mental disorders (APA, 1994; Clementz & Iacono, 1993). Thus began the slow process of formal recognition of the prevalence and significance of mental disorders.

Because this early attempt of the ICD system for classifying mental disorders was felt to be inadequate, the American Psychiatric Association (APA) Committee on Nomenclature and Statistics developed its own *Diagnostic and Statistical Manual* (DSM-I) in 1952 (APA, 1952) and revised it in 1968 (DSM-II) (APA, 1968). These first attempts by the APA were not a huge success, but they launched a sustained effort to improve the classification of mental disorders, an effort that continues today. Unfortunately, children and adolescents were virtually neglected in the early versions of DSM; most childhood disorders were relegated to the adult categories, with the exception of mental retardation and schizophrenia—childhood type (Cass & Thomas, 1979).

As a formal classification system, the DSM-III (APA, 1980) was a significant advance over the earlier editions. The first and second editions contained only narrative descriptions of symptoms, and clinicians had to decide their own definitions for making a diagnosis. In the DSM-III, these descriptions were replaced by explicit criteria which, in turn, enhanced diagnostic reliability (Achenbach, 1985; APA, 1980). Moreover, unsubstantiated inferences which were heavily embedded in psychoanalytic theory were dropped, and the system became more descriptive and less tied to a particular theoretical framework. In addition, DSM-III included more child categories, adopted a multiaxial system (described below), and placed a greater emphasis on empirical data (Achenbach, 1985). These changes reflected the beginnings of a conceptual shift in both diagnostic systems and etiological models away from an isolated focus on a disorder as existing within the child alone, toward an increased emphasis on also considering the surrounding context in which the problem occurred.

The DSM-III was revised in 1987 (DSM-III-R) to help clarify the numerous inconsistencies and ambiguities that were noted in its use. For example, empirical data at that time did not support the category of attention-deficit disorder *without* hyperactivity as a unique disorder (Routh, 1990), so this category, present in DSM-III, was not included in DSM-III-R (as you will learn in Chapter 5, ADD without hyperactivity has reemerged in DSM-IV, another indication that our knowledge of childhood disorders and our efforts to classify them are still very much in a state of flux). The DSM-III-R was also developed to be a *prototypical* classification system, whereby a child could be diagnosed with a certain subset of symptoms without having to meet all criteria. This was an important change, especially in view of the heterogeneity associated with most childhood disorders (Mash & Terdal, 1997a). On the other hand, it also means that individuals with the same diagnosis can and often do show very different patterns of symptoms. To make this point stick, consider that there are nearly 150 million *different* ways for an individual to meet the DSM-III-R criteria for an antisocial personality disorder (Widiger, 1993).

DSM-IV. The DSM-IV is a **multiaxial system** consisting of five axes (APA, 1994). Each axis refers to a particular domain of information that may assist the clinician in treatment planning. In other words, the axes serve to add further context and detail to the description of an individual's particular circumstances, by organizing and communicating clinical information, capturing the complexity of clinical situations, and describing the heterogeneity of individuals presenting with the same diagnosis. The five axes are as follows (APA, 1994):

Axis I   Clinical disorders
          Other conditions that may be a focus of clinical attention
Axis II   Personality disorders
          Mental retardation
Axis III General medical conditions
Axis IV   Psychosocial and environmental problems
Axis V   Global assessment of functioning

Axis I is where the various clinical disorders or conditions are reported, except for mental retardation and personality disorders (which are reported on Axis II because they are presumed to be stable). (Axis I diagnostic categories that apply to infants, children, and adolescents were listed in Chapter 1 and will be discussed in detail in the chapters to follow.) A child can receive more than one Axis I diagnosis, with the principal diagnosis listed first (e.g., attention-deficit/hyperactivity disorder; reading disorder).

Axis II is for reporting personality disorders and mental retardation. The purpose of using a separate axis for these two types of disorders is to ensure that consideration is given to them, especially when a more visible or acute Axis I disorder is present. Axis II is often used for diagnosing children with mental retardation. However, personality disorders are rarely diagnosed until late adolescence. This is because **personality disorders** represent enduring patterns of inner experience and behavior that deviate markedly from cultural expectations and that are inflexible and pervasive across situations. For example, an individual with a *borderline personality disorder* displays a pervasive pattern of unstable interpersonal relationships, self-image, and affects, and marked impulsivity. Personality disorder categories may be applied to children or adolescents in unusual circumstances. However, these categories are rarely used with children because the rapid developmental changes that are occurring during childhood and adolescence make it difficult to determine how enduring or inflexible a child's personality traits are going to be

(APA, 1994). No doubt there are links between early personality traits and later personality disorders, but these are just beginning to be explored (e.g., Lynam, 1996).

Axis III is for reporting current general medical conditions that may be relevant to the understanding or management of the individual's mental disorder. Because the DSM-IV assumes that mental disorders are closely related to physical and biological factors, the purpose of distinguishing general medical conditions is to encourage thoroughness in evaluation and to enhance communication among health care providers. General medical conditions can be related to mental disorders in a variety of ways. In some cases, the medical condition may play a direct causal role in the development of behavioral or psychological problems, such as a disruption in the sleep cycle due to depression. Most commonly with children, however, an Axis I disorder, such as anxiety, may be a psychological reaction to a medical condition, such as being diagnosed with childhood cancer or diabetes. Clearly, it is important to document the co-occurrence of problems—cancer and anxiety, for example—to gain an overall understanding and to develop an appropriate treatment plan for an individual.

Axis IV describes any psychosocial and environmental problems that may affect the diagnosis, treatment, and prognosis of disorders listed on Axes I and II. Such problems include negative life events, environmental disruptions or deficiencies, family or other interpersonal stress, and lack of social support or personal resources (APA, 1994). Typically, clinicians note only those problems that have been present over the past year, unless prior events—say, an automobile accident—have likely contributed to the mental disorder. The following list of psychosocial and environmental problems, grouped according to categories (adapted from DSM-IV 1994 by permission of APA) gives examples of these contextual factors—and reemphasizes the importance of context in determining a complete diagnosis:

❖ *Problems with the primary support group.* Death of family member; health problems in family; disruption of family by separation, divorce, or estrangement; removal from the home; remarriage of parent; sexual or physical abuse; parental overprotection; neglect of child; inadequate discipline; discord with siblings; birth of a sibling

❖ *Problems related to the social environment.* Death or loss of friend; inadequate social support; living alone; difficulty with acculturation; discrimination; adjustment to life cycle transition (e.g., beginning school)

❖ *Educational problems.* Illiteracy, academic problems; discord with teachers or classmates; inadequate school environment

❖ *Housing problems.* Homelessness; inadequate housing; unsafe neighborhood; discord with neighbors or landlord

❖ *Economic problems.* Extreme poverty; inadequate finances; insufficient welfare support

❖ *Occupational problems* (for older adolescents). Unemployment; threat of job loss; stressful work schedule; difficult work conditions; job dissatisfaction; job change; discord with boss or co-workers

❖ *Problems with access to health care services.* Inadequate health care services; transportation to health care facilities unavailable; inadequate health insurance

❖ *Problems related to interaction with the legal system.* Arrest; incarceration; litigation; victim of crime

❖ *Other psychological and environmental problems.* Exposure to disasters, war, other hostilities; discord with nonfamily care-givers, such as counselor, social worker, or physician; unavailability of social service agencies

As you can see, the list of contextual factors that are potentially important for understanding an individual's behavior and emotions is quite extensive. We remind you of this important consideration throughout our discussion of different disorders of childhood and adolescence, because a child's presenting problem is often better understood if we can see the whole picture.

Finally, Axis V is for reporting the clinician's ratings of the individual's overall level of functioning, primarily for planning treatment and monitoring its impact. A Global Assessment of Functioning (GAF) rating scale, ranging from 1 to 100, provides a hypothetical continuum of mental health and mental illness with respect to psychological, social, and occupational functioning. A low score indicates greater impairment in social functioning or personal care, such as suicidal ideation or avoiding friends, whereas a higher score reflects mild or transient symptoms or the absence of symptoms. For example, a high rating of overall functioning would indicate that a child has minimal symptoms or an absence of symptoms, good functioning in all areas, interest and involvement in a wide range of activities, social effectiveness, general life satisfaction, and no more than everyday problems. At the mid-range, a child may display moderate symptoms or moderate difficulty in social or school functioning. At the low end, a child may be in danger of hurting self or others, fail to maintain minimal personal hygiene, and be largely incoherent or mute.

On the basis of our clinical assessment, Felicia was given the following DSM-IV diagnosis and multiaxial evaluation:

Axis I   Major Depressive Disorder, single episode
Axis II   No diagnosis
Axis III   None
Axis IV   Death of a family member; disruption of family by separation; academic problems
Axis V   GAF = 60 (this score indicates moderate symptoms and moderate difficulties in social and school functioning as the *highest* level of functioning in the past year)

A diagnosis of Major Depressive Disorder (MDD), which you will learn much more about in Chapter 8 on mood disorders, was made because Felicia showed symptoms of depressed mood, loss of interest in almost all activities, significant weight loss, insomnia nearly every day, and feelings of worthlessness that persisted for more than 2 weeks and represented a change from her previous functioning. These symptoms were causing significant distress and impairment in Felicia's social and school functioning. Although the loss of her grandfather may have been a factor in Felicia's depression, it did not seem to be the major factor accounting for her symptoms.

Criticisms of DSM-IV. Although DSM-IV includes numerous improvements over the previous versions, with its greater emphasis on empirical research and more explicit diagnostic criteria sets, it is not faultless. Because DSM-IV focuses on superficial descriptions of symptoms as the basis for generating categories, it has been criticized for failing to capture the complex adaptations, transactions, and setting influences that we have identified as crucial to understanding and treating psychopathology in children (Jensen & Hoagwood, 1997; Mash & Terdal, 1997a; Routh, 1990). DSM-IV also gives relatively less attention to disorders of infancy and childhood than to those of adulthood, and fails to capture the interrelationships and overlap known to exist among many childhood disorders.

A further difficulty with DSM-IV diagnostic criteria for children is the relative lack of emphasis on the situational and contextual factors surrounding and contributing to various disorders in making a clinical diagnosis (Scotti et al., 1996). This is a reflection of the fact that DSM-IV views mental disorder as individual psychopathology or risk for psychopathology, rather than in terms of problems in psychosocial adjustment or adaptation. However, DSM-IV does consider factors such as

culture, age, and gender associated with the expression of each disorder, and has increased its recognition of the importance of family problems and extrafamilial relational difficulties from previous versions. In all likelihood, this awareness of the context for childhood disorders will increase in sophistication and depth with future revisions.

A final criticism deals with how DSM-IV is used rather than with the classification system itself. In some cases, DSM-IV categorical diagnoses can be an impediment to gaining proper services to address children's needs. For example, to qualify for a special education class, a child may be required to meet specific diagnostic criteria for a learning disorder. In the "typical" case such requirements are usually met. However, some children may not have developed problems to the degree that they meet specific diagnostic criteria or their problems may relate to more than one DSM category. These children may not qualify for services that otherwise could prove beneficial.

Diagnostic Classification:0–3. An alternative diagnostic system has been proposed to provide greater coverage of the mental health and developmental problems of infants and young children than does DSM-IV. The Diagnostic Classification (DC:0–3) was developed by the Diagnostic Classification Task Force of the Zero to Three/National Center for Clinical Infant Programs (Zero to Three/National Center for Clinical Infant Programs, 1994). DC:0–3 is intended to provide a comprehensive system for classifying problems during the first 3 to 4 years of life (Greenspan & Wieder, 1994). Unlike DSM-IV, DC:0–3 is based on the explicit premise that diagnosis must be guided by the principle that all infants and young children are active participants in relationships within the family. Hence, a description of infant–care-giver interaction patterns and the links between these interaction patterns and adaptive and maladaptive patterns of infant and child development constitute an essential part of the diagnostic process.

Like DSM-IV, DC:0–3 utilizes a multiaxial approach to classification. In explicitly recognizing the significance of relational problems, DC:0–3 includes a Relationship Disorder classification as a separate axis (Axis II). Clinicians diagnose relationship disturbances or disorders based on observations of parent-child interaction, in addition to the parents' verbal report regarding their subjective experience of the child. Relational difficulties are rated in terms of severity, taking into account such factors as the behavioral quality, affective tone, and degree of psychological involvement in the interaction. In this regard, a parents' sensitivity or insensitivity in responding to the child's cues, a parent's or an infant's tenseness or anger, and a parent's perceptions of the child and what can be expected in a relationship are all considered.

A separate axis of DC:0–3 assesses the infant or young child's functional level of emotional development as reflected in the way he or she organizes affective, interactive, and communicative experiences in the context of parent-child interaction. Social processes such as mutual attention, mutual engagement, or joint emotional involvement; reciprocal interaction; and affective/symbolic communication are all assessed. Problems in any one of these areas are considered in relation to possible constrictions in the child's range of affect under normal or stressful circumstances, or the child's failure to reach expected levels of emotional development. The remaining three axes of DC:0–3 are similar to those in DSM-IV and include the primary diagnosis, medical conditions and developmental disorders, and psychosocial stressors.

Although only a beginning, DC:0–3 has made some inroads in recognizing the significance of early relational difficulties, the need to integrate diagnostic and relational approaches in classifying child psychopathology, and the need to apply both quantitative and qualitative criteria in describing relational problems (Lyons-Ruth, 1995; Mash & Johnston, 1996). In addition, the dimensions and specific processes that are used for classification—negative affect, insensitivity, uninvolvement, lack of mutual engagement, lack of reciprocity in interaction, and similar observable behaviors—are based on processes deemed important in developmental and clinical research studies on early relationships. For these reasons, the DC:0–3 system is decidedly more sensitive to developmental and contextual parameters than is DSM-IV. But, like the early versions of DSM, DC:0–3 is still new and untested, having been generated on the basis of uncontrolled clinical observations. The descriptive categories have unknown reliability and validity, and at this time many of the criticisms that have been noted for DSM-IV can be made of DC:0–3 as well. Nevertheless, the scheme provides a rich descriptive base for further exploration of the ways in which psychopathology is expressed during the first few years of life, and calls attention to the need to examine potential continuities between such early problems and later individual and/or family disorders.

Pros and Cons of Diagnostic Labels

Despite every attempt to the contrary, the history of classification of mental disorders has been fraught with negative connotations that become attached to whatever terms are used to describe them. The word *moron*, for instance, was originally chosen as a neutral term to describe a lower range of intellectual functioning, but quickly became an insult when it began to be used in common language. Much has been written about the positive and negative aspects of assigning diagnostic labels to children.

On the positive side, labels help clinicians summarize and order observations, which can facilitate communication among professionals and sometimes aid parents by providing more recognition and understanding of their child's problem (Fernald & Gettys, 1978). Moreover, descriptive labels are consistent with the natural tendency to think in terms of categories. That is, we tend to talk about ourselves, our friends, and our children as being happy, angry, depressed, or fearful, rather than using a number on a scale that signifies a range of emotion, even if a number might give a more accurate account. Finally, the use of descriptive terms or labels assists clinicians in locating a relevant body of detailed research and clinical data, and facilitates research on the causes, epidemiology, and treatment of specific disorders (Rains, Kitsuse, Duster, & Friedson, 1975).

On the negative side are criticisms as to whether current diagnostic labels are effective in achieving any of the aforementioned purposes, as well as concerns about negative effects associated with the assignment of labels to children. Once labeled, children may be perceived by and reacted to differently by others ("he's a hyperactive boy—you'll never get him to listen") (Bromfield, Weisz, & Messer, 1986). Even classmates pick up on the use of labels, especially when those labels are associated with visible treatment requirements such as taking medication. A note sent by a classmate to a boy with ADHD reflects this fact: "Jack was ill, he took his pill, let's hope it makes him sit still." Equally disturbing is the finding that labels can influence children's views of themselves and their behavior (Guskin, Bartel, & MacMillan, 1975). In general, others' reactions to persons who seem different or who have been diagnosed with a mental illness reveal a tendency to generalize inappropriately from the labels.

TREATMENT OF CHILDHOOD DISORDERS

If there is anything that we wish to change in the child, we should first examine it and see whether it is not something that could better be changed in ourselves.

—C. G. Jung

A thorough clinical assessment and diagnosis constitute a critical first step in helping Felicia and other children who have psychological problems and their families. However, assessment and diagnosis are just the beginning of an ongoing helping process. We next need to ask: "How can we help Felicia reduce her feelings of depression and hopelessness, eliminate her sleep disturbances and other somatic complaints, increase her school attendance and performance, and improve her social skills and relationships with other children and her parents?" This is where intervention comes into play.

How do we determine the best type of intervention for children like Felicia and for those with other problems? We will consider this question in some detail for each disorder discussed in the chapters that follow; thus the coverage of treatment and prevention in this introductory section is intended to be brief. Our discussion of intervention in the context of specific disorders follows from our general conviction that the most useful treatments are likely to be ones that are based on what we know about the nature, course, associated characteristics, and causes of a particular childhood disorder. However, this is not enough. We also need to have empirical support for the effectiveness and efficacy of our interventions (Hibbs & Jensen, 1996; Kazdin & Weisz, 1998; Lonigan & Elbert, 1998). Interventions that zoom in on a specific problem in a focused way with clear guidelines for treatment appear to be the most effective (Weisz & Weiss, 1993). Thus, our chapter-by-chapter coverage of intervention strategies will be selective, focusing primarily on those interventions that are tailored to what we know about individual disorders and that have shown promising results in controlled outcome studies.

In this section, we present an overview of what we mean by intervention, discuss special considerations in intervention such as different models of treatment, highlight some of the major approaches and strategies used to help children with problems and their families, and take stock of what we know about the general effectiveness of interventions for children. The overall goal is to introduce the important general issues associated with interventions for children. This introduction is intended as an appetizer that we hope will whet your appetite for the main course to follow.

What Is Intervention?

The term *intervention* means different things to different people. What do you think of when we use this term in the context of helping children and families with problems? Depending on whom you ask and the nature of the problem, intervention may be described as playing with a child in a clinic playroom (Chethik, 1989), setting up a program of rewards and punishment in the home or classroom (Forehand & McMahon, 1981; Sanders & Dadds, 1993), changing the child's maladaptive thoughts (Kendall, 1991), participating in therapy for the entire family (Gurman & Kniskern, 1991), or prescribing stimulant or antidepressant medications (DuPaul & Kyle, 1995). Descriptions may involve multilevel interventions in the home, school, and community (Henggeler et al., 1998), combinations of one or more approaches (Kazdin, 1996a), or literally hundreds of other possibilities (Kazdin, 1988). Intervention is a broad concept that encompasses many different theories and methods. There is no single approach to working with children and families—multiple problems require multiple solutions.

Clinical assessment and diagnosis are usually followed by efforts to select and implement the most promising approach to intervention (Mash, 1998). Since psychological disorders represent failures in adaptation on the part of the child and/or his or her social environment, **intervention** includes a range of problem-solving strategies directed at helping the child and family adapt more effectively to their current and future circumstances. These strategies are part of a spectrum of activities for treatment, maintenance, and prevention (Adelman, 1995). An illustration of one such intervention spectrum is shown in Figure 4.7.

Treatment refers to corrective actions that will permit successful adaptation by eliminating or reducing the impact of an undesired outcome that has already occurred. Felicia was already experiencing depression and social withdrawal when first referred, and efforts are directed at reducing her distress and enhancing her functioning at school, with other children, and at home. Typically, this approach is what most people think of when hearing the terms *treatment* and *therapy*.

Maintenance refers to efforts to increase adherence with treatment over time in order to prevent relapse or recurrence of a problem. Not only do we want to increase Felicia's social skills, but we also want her to continue to use the skills that she has learned during treatment so that her problems don't return. Many treatments for children and families produce short-term benefits, but their effects may not be long-lasting.

Finally, **prevention** refers to activities directed at decreasing the chances that undesired future outcomes will occur. Felicia's depression may very well predict later negative outcomes, such as recurrent mood disturbances or social maladjustment, during adulthood. Is there anything we can do now that will reduce the chances that these undesired outcomes will occur at a later time? An even more fundamental question is whether we could have done something when Felicia was younger to prevent her from developing depression and social withdrawal in the first place. The basic assumption underlying prevention follows the adage that "it's better to build a fence at the edge of a cliff than to have an ambulance waiting at the bottom."

Given the wide variety of circumstances leading up to and surrounding the identification, referral, evalua-

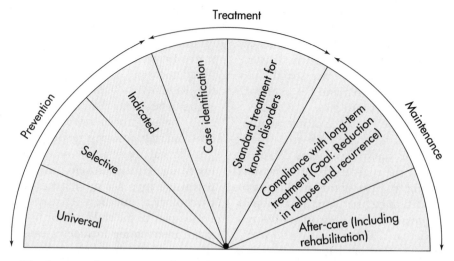

FIGURE 4.7 The intervention spectrum for childhood disorders. (Adapted from Mrazek & Haggerty, 1994)

tion, and treatment of children with problems, interventions are best depicted as part of the ongoing decision-making approach that we have been discussing throughout this chapter (e.g., Evans & Meyer, 1985; Herbert, 1991; Mash, 1998; Schroeder & Gordon, 1991). Our assessments should help us answer a number of questions that are extremely important for intervention. In Felicia's case, our answers to the following questions will guide us in determining which, if any, of the numerous treatment options that are available will be used:

❖ Should Felicia's difficulties be treated? If so, which ones? Depression? School refusal? Social skills deficits? Relations with family members? All of them?

❖ What are the projected outcomes for Felicia in the absence of treatment?

❖ What types of treatment are likely to be most effective, efficient, and cost-effective for Felicia's depression, school refusal, and social skills deficits?

❖ Who are the best persons to provide treatment? Where should treatment be carried out (e.g., clinic, home, school)?

❖ Which interventions are likely to be the most acceptable to Felicia, her parents, and other family and community members?

❖ When should treatment for Felicia begin? Are adjustments needed? When should treatment be terminated?

❖ Is the intervention having the desired impact on Felicia's behavior? Are the effects maintained over time? Are the changes meaningful for Felicia and her family?

The ultimate goal of addressing these kinds of questions should be to achieve effective solutions to the problems being faced by Felicia, her family, and other children like her, and to promote and enhance long-term adjustments.

Enormous advances have been made in the treatment of children's psychological disorders during this century. The age at which children are assessed and treated has steadily decreased, and the search for the determinants of childhood disorders has become increasingly thorough, detailed, and systematic. In addition, as you will see, countless variants of child psychotherapy, educational strategies, residential treatment, family therapy, and psychopharmacological interventions have appeared. Today, the child, family members, teachers, peers and other significant individuals are often actively involved in all phases of treatment. Accordingly, increased attention is being given to intervention models that are sensitive to changing societal demographics and needs (American Psychological Association, 1996), the realities and constraints of present-day health care delivery systems (Norcross, Karg, & Prochaska, 1997; Roberts & Hurley, 1997), and the everyday demands of clinical practice (Kazdin, 1997). Despite these advances, progress has been slow, as evidenced by the large number of children who continue to have psychological problems and the relatively small number of these children who actually receive help. In addition, as you may recall, many treatments for children have not been evaluated, particularly as they are applied in real-world clinical settings (Kazdin, 1988).

Special Considerations

As interventions have developed, a growing awareness has arisen of the need to give greater attention to the cultural context of children and families receiving

Table 4.10   Cultural Values and Parenting Practices and Beliefs

	African-American	Asian-American	Latino	Native American
Cultural values	Independence Respect for authority Obedience Racial identity	Self-control Social courtesy Emotional maturity Respect for elders	Family loyalty Interpersonal connectedness Mutual respect Self-respect	Centrality of family Sharing Harmony Humility
Common parenting practices and beliefs	Strict discipline Communal parenting	Parental control Strict discipline Negotiation of conflict Parent as teacher	Permissive discipline Communal parenting Freedom	Permissive discipline Communal parenting Shame as discipline

Source: Forehand and Kotchick, 1996, p. 197.

psychological interventions. Parenting values and child-rearing methods vary among different ethnic minority groups, such as African, Asian, Latino, and Native Americans, and more interventions involving parent education and training are becoming sensitive to these cultural variations (Forehand & Kotchick, 1996; Neal-Barnett & Smith, 1996). Treatment services for children, therefore, must not only attend to the presenting symptoms, but also consider the specific values, norms, and expectations held by different social classes and within different cultures; the different religious beliefs and practices of each family; and other circumstances that might make a successful treatment for one family a failure for another. Cultural values and common parenting practices and beliefs in four ethnic minority groups are shown in Table 4.10. Because, as we emphasized earlier, generalizations about cultural practices and beliefs may fail to capture the diversity that exists within and across ethnic groups, we must be extremely careful not to stereotype individuals of any cultural group.

Treatment Goals. What are the typical goals of treatment—reducing symptoms (problems), producing more substantial changes that will enhance the child's long-term functioning, or both? Because children's symptoms are often an expression of their unsuccessful attempts to adapt to their circumstances, more emphasis today is placed on the child's family and peers, not just on the child (Howard & Kendall, 1996). Accordingly, treatment goals often focus on building children's skills for adapting to their social environment, skills that will facilitate long-term adjustment, not just on eliminating problem behaviors or reducing subjective distress in the short term. Although symptom reduction is one important goal of therapy, other treatment goals and outcomes are also of crucial importance to the child, family, and society at large (Jensen, Hoagwood, & Petti, 1996). These treatment goals and outcomes are summarized here (Kazdin, 1997):

❖ **Outcomes Related to Child Functioning:** Reduction or elimination of symptoms, reduced degree of impairment in functioning, enhanced social competence, improved academic performance

❖ **Outcomes Related to Family Functioning:** Reduction in level of family dysfunction, improved marital and sibling relationships, reduction in stress, improvement in quality of life, reduction in burden of care, enhanced family support

❖ **Outcomes of Societal Importance:** Improvement in child's participation in school-related activities (increased attendance, reduced truancy, reduction in school dropout), decreased involvement in the juvenile justice system, reduced need for special services, reduction in accidental injuries or substance abuse, enhancement of physical and mental health

The interlocking network of physical, behavioral, social, and learning difficulties that characterizes most childhood disorders necessitates a multidisciplinary approach to attain these treatment and prevention goals. In many instances, children require medication or medical intervention that must be coordinated with psychosocial interventions, such as we discuss in connection with ADHD, autism, anxiety disorders, eating disorders, depression, and chronic medical conditions. Thus, combined interventions are becoming increasingly more common (Kazdin, 1996a). In addition, psychological interventions for children and adolescents often require integration with effective teaching strategies, as illustrated in later chapters on learning disorders, communication disorders, and mental retardation. Finally, some children require the integration of community and social services that aid in their protection and basic needs, which we discuss in Chapter 14 on child abuse and neglect.

Models of Treatment Delivery.

When we think of psychological treatment, most of us picture someone going to see a therapist whenever he or she has "symptoms" or is struggling with situational problems at home or school. This is the *conventional* model of treatment, in which a child is seen individually by a therapist for a limited number of treatment sessions in the clinic. However, as we have seen, many other options are in use today for helping children with problems, involving various treatment agents, such as parents and teachers, and settings where the problems are most likely to emerge. The growing emphasis on a systems perspective toward abnormal child behavior translates into the need for a variety of intervention activities and treatment delivery models that range from universal (primary) prevention programs available to all, to selective preschool and early school interventions aimed at children with particular risk signs, to standard treatments that focus on the current needs of children with known disorders, to follow-up, and maintenance (Adelman, 1995; Offord, Kraemer, Kazdin, Jensen, & Harrington, 1998).

The conventional model of delivering treatment services for children, youth, and families is driven primarily by symptoms or problems that prompt a referral. Although this method is still widely used and is well matched to some types of childhood problems (such as bed-wetting, certain fears, and problems adjusting to new circumstances), two types of *continuing care* models have emerged as alternatives to the conventional care model of treatment in some cases (Kazdin, 1997). The first is a *chronic care model,* in which treatment is maintained and adjusted in the same way that it would be for a child with a chronic illness such as diabetes mellitus or asthma. Ongoing treatment is provided to ensure that the benefits of treatment are maintained. ADHD and early-onset conduct disorder are two long-term and persistent problems in which a chronic care model of treatment may be the best strategy in order to establish basic competencies at each developmental level. The second approach to continuing care is a *dental care model,* in which ongoing follow-ups are carried out on a regular basis following initial treatment, in much the same way that regular dental checkups are recommended at 6-month intervals. Follow-ups may be conducted on a periodic basis at prescribed intervals or on an as-needed basis related to emergent issues in development and adjustment. Several childhood disorders described in this text would be well served by such ongoing checkups, such as child abuse and neglect, eating disorders, and mood disorders.

Ethical and Legal Considerations. Research and treatment have come a long way since the days of John Watson, when researchers or clinicians could use orphans or other disadvantaged persons in conducting research or trying out new treatments. As we have seen, most children who are referred for assessment and treatment experience multiple disadvantages and are arguably in need of special protection. Both ethically and legally, clinicians who work with children are required to think not only about the impact that their actions will have on the children they see, but also on the responsibilities, rights, and relationships that connect children and parents (DeKraai & Sales, 1991; Melton & Ehrenreich, 1992; Sandoval & Irvin, 1990).

Minimum ethical standards for practice include selecting treatment goals and procedures that are in the best interests of the client, making sure that client participation is active and voluntary, keeping records that document the effectiveness of treatment in achieving its objectives, protecting the confidentiality of the therapeutic relationship, and ensuring the qualifications and competencies of the therapist (MacDonald, 1986; Melton & Ehrenreich, 1992; Weithorn & McCabe, 1988). There is also a growing emphasis on involving children, depending on their developmental level, as active partners in decision making regarding their own psychological or medical treatment (McCabe, 1996).

Ethical issues are complex with children because of ongoing changes in the legal status of children and a trend toward recognition of minors' constitutional rights, including self-determination and privacy. However, an even more basic issue is determining when a minor is *competent* to make his or her own decisions, not just whether he or she has the legal right to do so. Some of the challenging issues faced by clinicians working with children involve deciding when a minor can provide informed consent or refuse treatment and balancing the rights of the child to confidentiality against those of the parents and the integrity of the family.

In addition to these ethical and legal concerns, much larger ethical questions concern the provision of services for children and families. Many interventions that are currently used to treat children with complex problems are known to be limited in scope—for example, 1 hour a week of therapy—and cannot realistically be expected to have a meaningful or lasting impact on children who are experiencing severe problems. Further, many current interventions are intrusive, expensive, and not supported by data. Thus, a more fundamental ethical question in some cases is whether we should provide any treatment at all when we know that the treatment may not make a difference, or even worse, may have harmful effects. In a sense, in maintaining the integrity of their helping role, clinicians may be forced into implementing treatment plans that may not serve anyone's interests (Melton & Ehrenreich, 1992). What are the alternatives? Does the clinician have a responsibility to become a political advocate for alternative treatments or for prevention programs that might have a greater impact? There are no simple answers to these questions.

Box 4.3

Protecting the Rights of Children with Disabilities and Their Parents: It's the Law

The Education for All Handicapped Children Act and the Individuals with Disabilities Education Act (IDEA-97) guarantee a free, appropriate education for all children with disabilities. They require state and local education agencies to actively seek out and identify children who have special education needs, and to prepare and execute a plan to deliver that special education. In addition, these laws protect the rights of children with disabilities and their parents.

CHILD'S RIGHTS

Evaluation: A child may be referred for evaluation by a parent or by school personnel. The evaluation must be comprehensive, nondiscriminatory, and in the child's own language. The evaluation may be conducted by a team consisting of a school psychologist, a specialist in special education, teachers, a physician and/or school nurse, a social worker or counselor, and other specialists.

Individualized Education Program (IEP): Each child is entitled to an *individualized education program (IEP)* based on this evaluation. The IEP must indicate the child's present levels of educational performance, specify yearly goals, and provide a statement of specific educational services, including the extent to which the child will participate in regular education with nondisabled children, and the date and duration of services. Related services have to be provided on an individualized basis to assist the child to benefit from special education. Each child must be educated to the maximum extent appropriate with students who are not disabled. Removal of children with disabilities from the regular educational environment occurs only when the nature or severity of the disability of a child is such that education in regular classes with the use of supplementary aids and services cannot be achieved satisfactorily. In other words, the child is to be educated in the *least restrictive environment (LRE).*

PARENTS' RIGHTS

Notice: Before a child is tested or placed in a special education program, parents have the right to be notified of what the school plans to do.

Consent: Parents must give their consent before special tests are conducted and before their child is initially placed in a special education program. In addition, parents have a right to consent to periodic reevaluations of their child's program.

Involvement: Parents have a right to be included in groups making eligibility and placement decisions about their child.

Evaluation: Parents have a right to have a full evaluation of their child's individual educational needs. Parents may request an independent evaluation if they do not feel the school evaluation is accurate or complete. Parents have a right to receive regular reports on their child's progress.

Records: Parents have a right to know what records are kept on their child, and they have the right to see them and to request that they be amended.

Confidentiality: Other than certain school officials, no one may see a child's records unless written permission is provided by the parent.

Least Restrictive Environment: Parents have a right to have their child educated with nonhandicapped children to the maximum extent appropriate. The child also has a right not to be grouped with children who have much different special education needs.

Due Process: Parents and children have a right to due process, which includes notice, the right to a hearing, and appeal procedures. If parents can't come to an agreement with the school, they have the right to a due process review.

Clinicians who work with children and their parents need to be aware of federal, state, and local laws that affect both the assessment and treatment of children with special needs. Many of these laws apply to children with mental and physical disabilities and handicaps, and are based on the recognition that disability is a natural part of the human experience and that all citizens (children included) are entitled to equal treatment and education. One law that has had a profound influence on services for children with disabilities is the Education for All Handicapped Children Act (Public Law 94-142, 1975) and the recent amendment, the Individuals with Disabilities Education Act (Public Law 105-17, 1997). Following are two of the many purposes of these laws:

❖ to ensure that all children with disabilities have available to them a free, appropriate public education that emphasizes special education and related services designed to meet their unique needs and prepare them for employment and independent living

❖ to ensure that the rights of children with disabilities and parents of such children are protected

Some of the rights of children and parents that are protected under these acts are presented in Box 4.3.

Clinicians who offer services to children with disabilities and their families must be aware of these and other laws.

General Approaches to Treatment

*J have found the best way to give advice
to your children is to find out what
they want and then advise them to do it.*
—Harry S Truman

The first systematic treatment of a child took place nearly 100 years ago in the now celebrated case of Little Hans, a 5-year-old boy with a phobia of horses who was treated by Sigmund Freud (or more accurately, by the boy's father under the direction of Professor Freud) using psychoanalysis (Freud, 1909/1955). Following one of his therapy sessions, in referring to Freud, Little Hans said: "Does the Professor talk to God?" In some ways Little Hans's innocent comment about his therapist proved to be prophetic—psychoanalysis and its many derivatives reigned supreme and dominated the field of child treatment for the next 50 years. Although disagreements concerning Freud's methods existed, no serious challengers to psychoanalysis appeared during that time period. Not until the 1950s did serious challenges to psychoanalysis emerge. At that point, behavior therapy became a contender, offering a more testable and efficient alternative (Ullmann & Krasner, 1965). Other approaches have since proliferated, including client-centered therapy, family therapy, cognitive-behavioral therapy, and psychopharmacotherapy.

The rapid growth of treatments for children over the past 50 years has not been without problems. Approaches to treatment have been beset by rivalries, splinter groups, enthusiasms, and rapid disillusionments (Rosenblatt, 1971). Many controversies reflect differences in the tacit underlying assumptions of different treatment approaches, since the way in which children's problems are conceptualized will determine how a particular clinician will go about changing them. For example, depending on the theory, a child's bed-wetting, or *enuresis,* has been viewed as a sexual disturbance, a developmental disturbance, a result of faulty conditioning, a physical ailment, or a reaction to a stressful family environment. These different views lead to very different avenues of intervention, ranging from play therapy to bladder conditioning, to antidepressant medication, to family therapy.

Currently, a tremendous number and diversity of treatments for children and families exist (Kratochwill & Morris, 1993; Mash & Barkley, 1998; Walker & Roberts, 1992). In the following sections we provide a brief overview of several of these approaches. We present them in their most elementary form to give you a beginning picture of the main treatment approaches for children. However, many different approaches exist within each of the categories discussed, and many other treatment approaches exist that do not fit neatly into any single category. A recent emphasis is on the use of integrative or combined approaches for treating children and families (Fauber & Kendall, 1992; Russ, 1998).

More than 70% of practicing clinicians who work with children and families identify their approach as **eclectic** (Kazdin, Siegel, & Bass, 1990), which means that they use different approaches for children with different problems and circumstances, and they see most of these approaches as having value. At its best, eclecticism reflects a thorough assessment of the problem, leading to the careful selection of specific treatment methods based on their known or presumed effectiveness for particular problems. At its worse, eclecticism reflects the haphazard combination of elements of different approaches by a clinician in his or her unique way, with little rationale in terms of effectiveness or what is known about the problem being treated. Let's now turn to a description of some of the general approaches to treatment and see how they might apply to Felicia.

Psychodynamic Treatments. Psychodynamic approaches view child psychopathology as determined by underlying unconscious and conscious conflicts (Lesser, 1972). Therefore, the focus is on helping the child develop an awareness of unconscious factors that may be contributing to his or her problems (Chethik, 1989; Scharfman, 1978). With younger children, this awareness can occur through play therapy; with older children, through verbal interactions with the therapist. As underlying conflicts are brought to light, the therapist helps the child resolve the conflicts and develop more adaptive ways of coping. In Felicia's case, a therapist would help her gain insight into her problem through a long and intensive process of psychotherapy. The assumption is that once the underlying problems have been resolved, Felicia's overt symptoms of depression, social withdrawal, school refusal, and physical complaints will disappear.

Behavioral Treatments. Behavioral approaches assume that most abnormal child behaviors are learned via operant and classical conditioning. Therefore, the focus of behavior therapy is on reeducating the child, using procedures derived from theories of learning or from research (Krasner, 1991). Such procedures include operant conditioning procedures such as positive reinforcement or time-out, modeling and systematic desensitization (Morris & Kratochwill, 1998). Behavioral treatments often focus on changing the child's environment by working with parents and teachers. In Felicia's case, a therapist might try to decrease her school refusal by instructing her parent to not let her stay at home when she protests, and by rewarding her for going to school with praise or a preferred activity. In addition, the therapist might use modeling and practice to help Felicia learn more effective social skills.

Cognitive Treatments.

Cognitive approaches view abnormal child behavior as the result of deficits and distortions in the child's thinking, including perceptual biases, irrational beliefs, and faulty interpretations (Kendall, 1991). For example, a beautiful girl who gets A grades thinks she is ugly and is going to fail in school. The emphasis in treatment is on changing these faulty cognitions. As cognitions change, the child's behaviors and feelings are also expected to change. In Felicia's case, she may be convinced beyond belief that she can't do well in school, or that if she goes to school, harm will befall her mother, or that children at school will think she's stupid. Changing these negative views by challenging them, and by helping Felicia develop more rational and more adaptive forms of thinking, should lead to changes in her behavior.

Cognitive-Behavioral Treatments.

Cognitive-behavioral approaches view psychological disturbances as partly the result of faulty thought patterns, and partly the result of faulty learning and environmental experiences. These approaches begin with the basic premise that the way in which children and parents think about their environment determines how they will react to it (Meichenbaum, 1977). Combining elements of both the behavioral and cognitive models, the cognitive-behavioral approach grew rapidly as behavior therapists began to focus increasingly on the important role of cognition in treatment for both the child (Harris, Wong, & Keogh, 1985; Kendall, 1991) and the family (Foster & Robin, 1998; Schwebel & Fine, 1994).

Faulty thought patterns that are the targets of change include deficiencies in cognitive mediators and distortions in both cognitive content (e.g., erroneous beliefs) and cognitive process (e.g., irrational thinking and faulty problem solving). As you will learn, cognitive distortions and attributional biases have been identified in children with a variety of problems, including depression, conduct disorder, and anxiety disorders. Major goals of cognitive-behavioral treatment are to identify maladaptive cognitions and to replace them with more adaptive ones, to teach the child to use both cognitive and behavioral coping strategies in specific situations, and to help the child learn to regulate his or her own behavior. Treatment may also involve the ways in which others respond to the child's maladaptive behavior. Using a cognitive-behavioral approach, a therapist would help

Felicia learn to think more positively and to use more effective social skills and coping strategies.

Client-Centered Treatments.

Client-centered approaches view child psychopathology as the result of social or environmental circumstances that are imposed on the child and interfere with his or her basic capacity for personal growth and adaptive functioning. Because of this interference, the child experiences a loss or impairment in self-esteem and emotional well-being, resulting in even further problems. The therapist relates to the child in an empathic way, providing unconditional, nonjudgmental, and genuine acceptance of the child as an individual. This often occurs through the use of play activities with younger children and through verbal interaction with older youngsters (Axline, 1947; Ellinwood & Raskin, 1993). The therapist respects the child's capacity to achieve his or her goals without the therapist's serving as a major adviser, analyst, coach, or provocateur—the therapist respects the child's self-directing abilities. In Felicia's case, being babied by her parents who viewed her as slow may have led to interference in her adaptive functioning and to low self-esteem. In treatment, a therapist would comment on what Felicia is saying and feeling to help her understand her feelings and to increase the congruence between her feelings and behavior. In therapy, Felicia would lead the way as the clinician follows.

Family Treatments.

Family models challenge the view of psychopathology as residing only within the individual child and, instead, view child psychopathology as determined by variables operating in the larger family system of which the child is a part (Gurman & Kniskern, 1991). Like the other approaches, many varieties of family therapy differ widely in their underlying assumptions and approach to treatment (Stroh Becvar & Becvar, 1988). However, all of them view individual child disorders as manifestations of disturbances in family relations.

Treatment involves a therapist and sometimes a co-therapist, who interact with the entire family or a select subset of family members, such as the parents and child or the husband and wife. Therapy typically focuses on the family issues underlying problem behaviors. Depending on the approach, the therapist may focus on family interaction, communication, dynamics, contingencies, boundaries, or alliances. In Felicia's case, her overall helplessness and physical symptoms may be serving to maintain her role as the baby in the family or may be serving as the parents' way of avoiding their own marital difficulties by focusing the problem on Felicia. A therapist would assist Felicia and her family in identifying and changing this and other dysfunctional ways in which family members related to one another.

Biological Treatments. Medical models view child psychopathology as resulting from biological impairment or dysfunction and rely primarily on pharmacological and other biological approaches to treatment. Examples include the use of stimulant medications for the treatment of ADHD, antipsychotic medications for the treatment of schizophrenia or serious aggressive and destructive behavior, tricyclic antidepressants for enuresis, and selective serotonin reuptake inhibitors (SSRIs) such as fluoxetine (Prozac) for depression and other disorders (Gadow & Pomeroy, 1993). In Felicia's case, a psychiatrist might consider using tricyclic antidepressants or other medications to treat her depressive symptoms. Other much more controversial forms of biological intervention include electroconvulsive therapy (ECT) for severe depression, the administration of large doses of vitamins or minerals to children with ADHD or autism, and the scrupulous elimination of food additives and preservatives from the diets of children with ADHD.

Combined Treatments. *Combined treatments* refers to the use of two or more interventions, each of which can stand on its own as a treatment strategy (Kazdin, 1996a). In some instances, combinations of stand-alone interventions may cross conceptual approaches—for example, using cognitive-behavioral and pharmacological treatments for children with ADHD (Arnold, Abikoff, & Wells, 1997; Barkley, 1990) or children with obsessive-compulsive disorder (Piacentini & Graae, 1997), or using cognitive-behavioral treatment and family therapy in combination (Fauber & Kendall, 1992). In other instances, combined treatments may be derived from the same overall conceptual approach—for example, using social skills training and cognitive restructuring in a group treatment program for adolescents with a social phobia (Marten, Albano, & Holt, 1991) or using individual behavior management and family behavior therapy in the treatment of children with oppositional disorders (Fauber & Long, 1991).

In Felicia's case, we used a combined treatment approach that included cognitive-behavioral treatment for depression, behavioral treatment for school refusal, and social skills training.

Felicia: Multiple Solutions

Our clinical assessment of Felicia suggested the need to treat three significant problems: school refusal, depression, and social difficulties. A combined treatment approach was used in which several strategies were used to combat these problems.

To treat Felicia's school refusal a behavioral program was implemented in which she was required to attend class on a daily basis. Felicia earned points for her attendance, class participation, and completion of class assignments, that could later be traded in for the opportunity to engage in preferred activities such as a movie, or for money that could be used to purchase CDs and other things that Felicia had previously selected. When Felicia refused to go to school she lost points and was given a brief period of time-out from positive reinforcement where she had to sit in the kitchen by herself and was not permitted to read or watch TV. This program resulted in consistent school attendance and much improved academic performance.

To treat Felicia's depressive symptoms we used a cognitive-behavioral approach. Felicia learned that depression can occur for many reasons, for example, stressful situations such as the loss of her grandfather, thinking lots of negative thoughts such as "I can't do anything right," and not having any friends. We next taught Felicia how to relax to give her some immediate relief and to provide her with a successful experience. Felicia then learned to monitor and rate her mood on a daily basis, and to identify thoughts and events that accompanied both her positive and negative moods. Felicia increased her positive thinking by learning to identify, challenge, and change her negative cognitions. After several weeks of treatment Felicia began to feel less depressed, as reflected in her more positive daily mood ratings and reports by her parents.

Both Felicia's teacher and parents felt that her feelings of depression might be the result of her social interaction difficulties at home and school and thought that she might become less depressed if these problems could be decreased. Therefore, a social-cognitive skills training program was also implemented to address both her depressive symptoms and interpersonal difficulties simultaneously. This program consisted of three parts. First, Felicia was given behavioral social skills training which consisted of instruction, modeling of appropriate and inappropriate social behaviors by her therapist, role playing and rehearsal, coaching, feedback, and a final role play. This training focused on the social skills that our initial assessment identified as lacking, such as making eye contact and speaking clearly [see Table 4.5]. Training was conducted in the situations that Felicia and her therapist identified as being problematic, for example, the role-play simulation we described earlier in which another youngster sits at Felicia's table in the school cafeteria.

The second part of the treatment focused on cognitive skills including general problem-solving skills, self-evaluation, and self-reinforcement. Felicia was taught to use certain cues that would prompt the correct use of her individual social skills in different situations. For example, "What do I want to accomplish?" or "How do I do this now?" She also learned to evaluate the adequacy of her social behavior and whether she had improved on each social skill. To support Felicia's use of these strategies, a third behavioral component was included whereby Felicia could earn points for the accuracy of her judgments and the effectiveness of her social skills during the role plays.

The results of the behavioral role-playing assessment for Felicia are shown in Figure 4.8. Significant improvements were observed in all of the targeted behaviors following intervention.

Following treatment Felicia began to show increased emotional expressiveness and social responsiveness at home. She smiled more and argued less with her parents. She also began to assert herself more appropriately. Attempts by her teacher to have her speak up in class were met with considerable success. Gradually, she began to engage in more interactions with other youngsters and to participate in activities. Her mood also began to brighten as she made efforts to initiate conversations and engaged in more reciprocal interactions with other children, her teacher, and parents. At the end of the treatment program Felicia was more interactive and assertive, and had learned to be more socially appropriate during interactions. She was less depressed and more animated. One year following her treatment Felicia reported no symptoms of depression and few feelings of hopelessness. She was attending school on a regular basis, showed improved academic performance, and was participating in activities and interacting more with other children. In this example, a combined approach of cognitive-behavioral therapy, behavioral social skills training and cognitive problem-solving training was successful in helping Felicia and her family. (Adapted from Kolko, 1987, pp. 163–166)

Treatment Effectiveness

It is becoming increasingly apparent that as health care practices change, attention to improved care is likely to depend on evidence for the efficacy of treatment

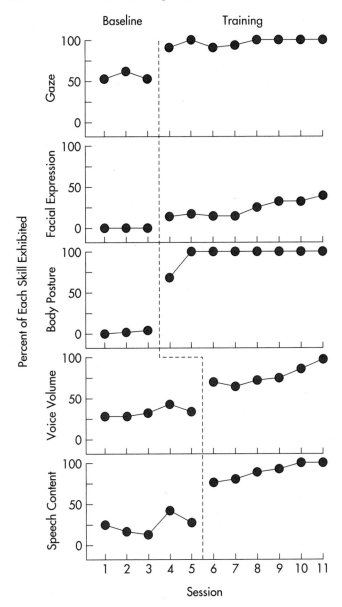

FIGURE 4.8 Results of behavioral role-play assessment. (Kolko, 1987)

(Hoagwood, Jensen, Petti, & Burns, 1996; Strosahl, 1994). Several broad-based reviews of treatment outcome studies with children have been conducted (Casey & Berman, 1985; Kazdin, Bass, Ayers, & Rodgers, 1990; Weisz, Weiss, Alicke, & Klotz, 1987; Weisz, Donenberg, Han, & Weiss, 1995), as well as more focused reviews of cognitive-behavioral therapy (Durlak, Fuhrman, & Lampman, 1991) and other interventions. What do these reviews tell us about the effectiveness of treatment approaches?

Let's begin with the good news. First, the changes achieved by children receiving psychotherapy are consistently greater than those for children not receiving therapy. Second, the average child who is treated is better off at the end of therapy than at least 75% of those children who did not receive treatment. Third, treatments have been shown to be equally effective for children with internalizing and externalizing disorders. Fourth, treatment effects tend to be lasting, with the effects at follow-up (usually around 6 months after treatment) being similar to those found immediately following treatment. Finally, effects are about twice as large for problems that are specifically targeted in treatment than they are for changes in nonspecific areas of functioning. This result suggests that treatments are producing focused changes in targeted areas such as anxiety, rather than producing nonspecific or global effects such as changes in how the child feels (Kazdin, 1996b; Weisz, 1998; Weisz & Weiss, 1993).

So what's the bad news? Although research findings present a generally positive picture of psychotherapy with children, and of behavioral and cognitive-behavioral approaches in particular, there are a number of important caveats. First, we need to be aware of the difference between research therapy that is carried out in laboratory outcome studies and therapy as it is carried out in clinics. Most of the treatment outcome studies for specific disorders that we will discuss in this text fall into the category of research therapy. However, compared with research therapy, clinic therapy is typically conducted with more severe cases, is directed at a heterogeneous set of problems and children, focuses on multiple problems and goals, and is carried out in clinic or hospital settings by professional career therapists with large caseloads (Weisz & Weiss, 1993). In general, clinic therapy is less structured and more flexible than research therapy and uses proportionately more nonbehavioral methods, such as psychodynamic and eclectic approaches. In stark contrast to the findings for research therapy, similar analyses for studies of clinic therapy have resulted in minimal or no effects (Weisz et al., 1995).

Similarly, other community-based mental health delivery systems for children have not found incremental improvement in outcomes related to the availability of comprehensive services. For example, in one large-scale study, the Fort Bragg Project, an integrated range of services was successfully implemented that provided good access, greater continuity of care, and more client satisfaction, and treated children in less restrictive environments. However, costs were higher and clinical outcomes were no better than those at a comparison site that provided services in a conventional manner (Bickman, 1996, 1997). These and other findings present a discouraging picture and suggest that conventional services for children may be of limited effectiveness, and that integrating these commonly used interventions into more coordinated systems of care also shows minimal support for the beneficial effects of treatment (Weisz, 1998). However, few studies exist of child therapy outcomes in settings where it is typically conducted; thus it is premature to draw any conclusions from the findings from clinic and community studies until more empirical data about therapy in practice are available (Shadish et al., 1997).

A clear need exists for additional information about the effectiveness of conventional forms of treatment for children. Not only is more research needed, but also a different kind of research—research that focuses on the conditions under which therapy for children is normally provided and on the therapies used most often in clinic settings (Kazdin, 1997; Weisz, 1998). If systematic investigations of conventional treatments continue to provide weak results, further attention to the *reasons* for the large discrepancy between research therapy and clinic therapy will be needed. Since research therapy generally includes more behavioral and cognitive-behavioral treatments, and since these approaches are often not the first choice of treatment for many practitioners, one possible conclusion is that clinic therapy with children may be enhanced if cognitive-behavioral therapies are used more often. However, the exportability of these therapies may be premature, because the conditions under which cognitive-behavioral therapies have been evaluated are quite different from those in which therapy is typically conducted in clinics. Empirically supported treatments need to be taken out of the laboratory and evaluated in clinic practice before their generalizability can be assessed (Weisz, 1998).

SUMMARY

Clinical Issues

1. Clinical assessment is directed at differentiating, defining, and measuring the child's behaviors, cognitions, and emotions that are of concern, as well as the environmental circumstances that may be contributing to these problems.

2. Assessments are meaningful to the extent that they result in effective interventions; a close and continuing partnership must exist between assessment and intervention.

3. Idiographic case formulation involves the detailed representation of the child as a unique entity, whereas nomothetic formulation emphasizes general laws that apply to many children.

4. Age, gender, and culture have implications for making judgments about deviancy, as well as for selecting the most appropriate methods of assessment and treatment.

5. The age inappropriateness and pattern of symptoms, rather than individual symptoms, usually define childhood disorders.

Assessing Children's Psychological Disorders

6. Three purposes of assessment are diagnosis (determining the nature and causes of the child's problem, formal diagnosis), prognosis (predictions about future behavior under specified conditions), and treatment planning and evaluation (obtaining information directly relevant to treatment and its evaluation).

7. Clinical assessment relies on a multimethod assessment strategy, which emphasizes obtaining information from different informants, in a variety of settings, using a variety of procedures.

8. The clinical interview continues to be the most universally used assessment procedure with parents and children.

9. A developmental history or family history is used to obtain information about potentially significant historical milestones and events that might have a bearing on the child's current difficulties.

10. A mental status exam is often used to assess the five general areas of appearance and behavior, thought processes, mood and affect, intellectual functioning, and sensorium.

11. In unstructured interviews, interviewers use their preferred style and format to pursue various questions in an informal and flexible manner. In contrast, semistructured interviews include specific questions designed to elicit information in a relatively consistent manner regardless of who is doing the interview.

12. Behavioral assessment evaluates the child's thoughts, feelings, and behaviors in specific settings, and uses this information to formulate hypotheses about the nature of the problem and what can be done about it.

13. Reports concerning child behavior and adjustment can be obtained using global checklists and problem-focused rating scales. Checklists are standardized so that an individual child's score can be compared with a known reference group of children of similar age and same gender.

14. In many cases, observing behavior directly can lead to a more accurate picture than verbal reports of what life is like for the child (and others) at home and school.

15. Tests are tasks given under standard conditions with the purpose of assessing some aspect of the child's knowledge, skill, or personality.

16. Developmental tests are used to assess infants and young children, and are generally carried out for the purposes of screening, diagnosis, and evaluation of early development.

17. Evaluating a child's intellectual and educational functioning is a key ingredient in clinical assessments for a wide range of childhood disorders.

18. Although projective tests are controversial with respect to reliability and validity, they continue to be used frequently in clinical practice.

19. Objective personality tests assess such traits as whether a child is timid or bold, agreeable or disagreeable, dependable or undependable, tense or relaxed, reflective or unreflective.

20. Neuropsychological assessment attempts to link brain functioning with objective measures of behavior that are known to depend on central nervous system functioning, and to use this information for treatment planning and follow-up of children with neurological impairments or learning disorders.

Classification and Diagnosis

21. Classification refers to a system for representing the major categories of child psychopathology and the relations among them, whereas diagnosis refers to the assignment of cases to categories of the classification system.

22. Childhood disorders have been classified using categories and dimensions.

23. The DSM-IV is a multiaxial system consisting of five axes: clinical disorders, personality disorders and mental retardation, general medical conditions, psychosocial and environmental problems, and global assessment of functioning.

Treatment of Childhood Disorders

24. Interventions for childhood disorders cover a range of strategies related to prevention, treatment, and maintenance.

25. Treatment goals now include outcomes related to child and family functioning as well as those of societal importance.

26. Both ethically and legally, clinicians who work with children are required to think not only about the impact that their actions will have on the children they see, but also on the responsibilities, rights, and relationships that connect children to their parents.

27. A tremendous number and diversity of treatments for children and families now exist, including psychodynamic, behavioral, cognitive, cognitive-

behavioral, client-centered, family, medical, and combined approaches.

28. Integrative reviews of controlled treatment outcome studies have found that the changes achieved by children receiving therapy are consistently greater than those for children not receiving therapy. However, these differences are not found in studies of clinic therapy.

KEY TERMS

clinical assessment, 99
idiographic, 99
nomothetic, 99
diagnosis, 101
prognosis, 102
treatment planning and evaluation, 102
differential diagnosis, 102
developmental history, 106

family history, 106
mental status exam, 107
behavioral assessment, 109
target behaviors, 109
behavior analysis, 109
functional analysis of behavior, 110
test, 115
screening, 116
projective tests, 119
neuropsychological assessment, 122
categorical classification, 124
dimensional classification, 125
sensitivity, 126
specificity, 126
multiaxial system, 127
personality disorders, 127
intervention, 131
treatment, 131
maintenance, 131
prevention, 131
eclectic, 136

Attention-Deficit/ Hyperactivity Disorder

Attention-deficit/hyperactivity disorder, or ADHD, describes children who consistently and repeatedly show age-inappropriate behaviors in the two general categories of inattention and hyperactivity-impulsivity (American Psychiatric Association [APA], 1994). Interest in ADHD has skyrocketed over the past decade. Witness just a few recent newspaper and magazine headlines:

❖ BEWARE LABELS FOR KIDS DOING BADLY IN SCHOOL, DOCTOR WARNS
❖ IMPATIENT JERKS MAY HAVE ATTENTION DEFICIT DISORDER
❖ NOT ALL CHILDREN GROW OUT OF ATTENTION DEFICIT DISORDER
❖ ATTENTION DEFICIT DISORDER LINKED TO GENE
❖ ESTABLISHMENT EDUCATORS PUSH DRUGS ON DISRUPTIVE FUSSY KIDS

These headlines not only reflect the enormous scientific and media attention that ADHD has generated in recent years, but they also preview the many controversies, confusions, hopes, and disappointments that have surrounded efforts to find answers to such questions as: What is ADHD? What causes it? How can we best help children with this problem? Consider the case of John, a 7-year-old boy with ADHD.

DESCRIPTION

John: Inattentive, Overactive, and Impulsive

John's mother came to her pediatrician's office desperate to get help for her son. "He's always in motion, impulsive, and never follows directions," she says. "When I ask him to pick up his shirt and place it in the hamper, I find him playing in his room with the shirt still on the floor." His mother recalls that John was "active in the womb." John never has a routine and seldom sleeps. Discipline doesn't work, nor do the parenting techniques that work for her other two boys. John seems totally oblivious to his behavior: he could be eating a piece of forbidden cake and with the cake in his hand, deny any knowledge of taking it. He never finishes anything he starts and, except for sitting down long enough to play a video game, rarely watches TV except on the run.

John's teacher says his major problems in school are staying on task and keeping track of what is happening in the classroom. "He blurts things out in class and is constantly fidgeting or out of his chair," she says. Although John can complete his assignments, he forgets to take home the book he needs for his homework. When he completes his homework, he forgets to put it in his backpack or forgets to hand it in. John has great difficulty waiting his turn or following rules when playing with other children. The kids in his class think John is "weird" and don't want to play with him. John's mother brought him to the doctor after he gave his two-year-old brother a book of matches to play with and showed him how to strike them. Both parents are demoralized and don't know what to do. (Adapted from Kennedy, Terdal, & Fusetti, 1993)

John displays many of the inattentive and hyperactive-impulsive behaviors of children with ADHD—he doesn't follow instructions, is in constant motion, and can't wait his turn. Do you think John's behavior is normal for a 7-year-old boy? Why does he behave this way? Will he outgrow his problem? What can be done to change his behavior now? These are some of the challenging questions that we will explore in this chapter.

ADHD is a severe disorder with suspected biological underpinnings, not simply an overused label to excuse bad behavior in children. Although the term *ADHD* may be relatively new, descriptions of children with ADHD's patterns of overactive and unrestrained behavior have been around for more than a hundred years. In 1845, a German neurologist named Heinrich Hoffmann wrote in a children's storybook one of the first known accounts of hyperactive behavior in a child. The poem describes the unruly mealtime behavior of a child aptly named "Fidgety Phil," who "won't sit still; / He wriggles, / And jiggles," and "Swings backwards and forwards, / And tilts up his chair." When his chair falls, Philip screams and grabs the tablecloth, and "Down upon the ground they fall, / Glasses, plates, knives, forks, and all" (Hoffman, 1845).

In 1994, a compelling article about ADHD titled "Life in Overdrive" appeared in *Time* magazine. It describes the inattentive and hyperactive-impulsive mealtime behaviors of Dusty N., a child of our own time:

> *Seven-year-old Dusty awoke at 5:00 one recent morning in his Chicago home. Every muscle in his 50-pound body flew in furious motion as he headed downstairs for breakfast. After pulling a box of cereal from the cupboard, Dusty started grabbing cereal with his hands and kicking the box, scattering the cereal across the room. Next he began peeling the decorative paper covering off the TV table. Then he started stomping the spilled cereal to bits. After dismantling the plastic dustpan he had gotten to clean up the cereal, he moved on to his next project: grabbing three rolls of toilet paper from the bathroom and unraveling them around the house (Wallis, 1994).*

Although the descriptions of Phil and Dusty are separated by almost 150 years, the behaviors of both children typify the primary features of ADHD. Phil and Dusty are **inattentive,** not focusing on mealtime demands and behaving carelessly, as if they are not listening. And both are **hyperactive** and **impulsive,** constantly in motion and acting without thinking.

ADHD does not have any distinct physical signs that can be seen in an X ray or a lab test. At present, the disorder can be identified only by characteristic patterns of behavior, which can vary quite a bit from child to

Fidgety Phil, 1845

Dusty N., 1994

Then and now: Mealtimes are an especially trying time for children with ADHD and their parents.

child. No single cause for the many behavior patterns of children with ADHD has been identified—and it is doubtful that we will ever find just one cause. More likely, ADHD has become a blanket term used to describe several different patterns of behavior that differ slightly.

Almost everyone finds the behavior of children with ADHD puzzling and full of contradictions. The child's disorganized and rash behavior is a constant source of stress and frustration for the child and for his or her parents, siblings, teachers, and classmates. Why can't he sit still? Why can't she ever get anything done? Why does he make so many careless mistakes? Why can't he plan ahead? Why does she do her homework and then forget to hand it in? Why does she insist on playing games by her own rules? However, at certain times of the day and in some situations, the child with ADHD seems fine.

These profound inconsistencies may lead others to think that the child could control the seemingly bratty behavior if only he tried harder or if her parents or teachers would set firmer limits on behavior. Increased effort and stricter rules may help some children, but most children with ADHD already *are* trying hard. They want to do well but are constantly thwarted by their limited capacity for self-control. As a result, they frequently experience the hurt, confusion, and sadness of being blamed for not paying attention; of being called names like "space cadet"; of being scolded, put down, or even spanked for failing to complete their homework or chores; and of not understanding why things went wrong or what they could have done differently.

The feelings of frustration and hopelessness that may overwhelm a child with this disorder are apparent in this moving comment by David, a 9-year-old boy with ADHD: "I got no friends cos I don't play good and when they call me Dope Freak and David Dopey I cry, I just can't help it" (D. Ross & S. Ross, 1982). Comments like David's leave little doubt that ADHD can severely disrupt the child's daily life, consume vast amounts of energy, produce emotional pain, lower self-esteem, and seriously damage the child's relationships at home and at school.

HISTORICAL BACKGROUND OF ADHD

Compulsory education, with its demands for self-controlled behavior in group settings, focused attention on children with the symptoms of ADHD (Hinshaw, 1994). These symptoms were first described as constituting a disorder at the beginning of this century by the English physician George Still (1902), who believed they arose out of poor "inhibitory volition" and "defective moral control" (see Figure 5.1). Another view of the disorder and its causes arose from the encephalitis (brain infection) epidemic of 1917 to 1918, which left many child survivors with multiple behavior problems, including irritability, obstinacy, impaired attention, poor motor control, and hyperactivity. These children and others who had suffered brain infection, birth trauma, head injury, or exposure to toxins displayed behavior problems that were labeled brain injured child syndrome, which was associated with mental retardation. This label was then applied to children with similar behaviors but who showed no evidence of brain damage or retardation. The brain injury hypothesis led to the frequent use of the terms *minimal brain damage* and *minimal brain dysfunction* (MBD) during the 1940s and 1950s (Kessler, 1980; Strauss & Lehtinen, 1947). The concepts of minimal brain damage and dysfunction provided a convenient

THE LANCET, APRIL 19, 1902.

The Goulstonian Lectures

ON

SOME ABNORMAL PSYCHICAL CONDITIONS IN CHILDREN.

Delivered before the Royal College of Physicians of London on March 4th, 6th, and 11th, 1902,

BY GEORGE F. STILL, M.A., M.D. CANTAB., F.R.C.P. LOND.,

ASSISTANT PHYSICIAN FOR DISEASES OF CHILDREN, KING'S COLLEGE HOSPITAL; ASSISTANT PHYSICIAN TO THE HOSPITAL FOR SICK CHILDREN, GREAT ORMOND-STREET.

———

LECTURE II.

Delivered on March 6th.

MR. PRESIDENT AND GENTLEMEN, — In my first lecture I drew your attention to some points in the psychology and development of moral control in the normal child and then considered the occurrence of defective moral control in association with general impairment of intellect; before going further it may be well to review briefly the points which have been raised. Moral control, we saw, is dependent upon three psychical factors, a cognitive relation to environment, moral consciousness, and volition, which in this connexion might be regarded as inhibitory volition. Moral control, therefore, is not present at birth, but under normal psychical conditions is gradually developed as the child grows older. The variation in the degree of moral control which is shown by different children at the same age and under apparently similar conditions of training and environment suggested that the innate capacity for the development of such control might also vary in different individuals.

FIGURE 5.1 The symptoms of ADHD were first described at the beginning of this century by the English physician George Still. (*Lancet*, April 19, 1902)

vehicle for attributing behavior problems to a physical cause (Schachar, 1986). Although certain types of head injury can explain some cases of ADHD, the brain damage theory was eventually rejected because it could explain only a very small number of cases (Rie, 1980).

In the late 1950s, ADHD was referred to as hyperkinetic impulse disorder or hyperkinesis, attributed by some to the poor filtering of stimuli entering the brain (Laufer, Denhoff, & Solomons, 1957). This view was followed by hyperactive child syndrome or hyperactivity, in which problems with motor overactivity were seen as the major feature of ADHD (Chess, 1960). However, it was soon realized that hyperactivity was not the only problem: More important was the child's failure to regulate motor activity in relation to the demands of the situation.

In the 1970s, Virginia Douglas made the persuasive argument that in addition to hyperactivity, deficits in attention and impulse control were the primary symptoms of ADHD (Douglas, 1972; Douglas & Peters, 1978), a theory that became widely accepted. This acceptance is reflected in the current diagnostic criteria for ADHD, which include symptoms of inattention, impulsivity, and hyperactivity. More recently, a greater emphasis has been given to poor self-regulation and the child's difficulty in inhibiting behavior as a central impairment of ADHD (Barkley, 1997d; Schachar, Tannock, & Logan, 1993; Quay, 1988).

DSM-IV: DEFINING FEATURES OF ADHD

The DSM-IV criteria for diagnosing ADHD, presented in Table 5.1, were developed by a committee of experts who reviewed past research and items on rating scales used to assess ADHD. In addition, field trials were conducted with children from different clinics in North America to identify the best items for defining ADHD (APA, 1994; Lahey et al., 1994). The experts came up with two lists of symptoms for defining ADHD, and distinguishing it from conduct disorder and oppositional defiant disorder (see Chapter 6). The first list includes symptoms of inattention, poor concentration, and disorganization; the second includes symptoms of hyperactivity and behavioral impulsivity.

CORE CHARACTERISTICS

To say that the two main features of ADHD are inattention and hyperactivity-impulsivity is to oversimplify. In each of these dimensions are numerous distinct processes that have been defined and measured in different ways. Only recently have we come to understand the specific deficits that characterize children with ADHD.

Inattention

Lisa: Predominantly Inattentive

At age 17, Lisa still struggles to pay attention and act appropriately. But this has always been hard for her. She still gets embarrassed thinking about the night her parents took her to a restaurant to celebrate her 10th birthday. She had gotten so distracted by the waitress's bright red hair that her father called her name three times before she remembered to order. Then, before she could stop herself, she blurted, "Your hair dye looks awful!"

In elementary and junior high school, she was quiet and cooperative but often seemed to be daydreaming. She was smart, yet couldn't improve her grades no matter how hard she tried. Several times, she failed exams. Even though she knew most of the answers, she couldn't keep her mind on the test. Her parents responded to her low grades by taking away privileges and scolding, "You're just lazy. You could get better grades if you only tried." Lisa found it agonizing to do homework. Often, she forgot to plan ahead by writing down the assignment or bringing home the right books. And when trying to work, every few minutes she found her mind drifting to something else. As a result, she rarely finished and her work was full of errors. One day, after Lisa had failed yet another exam, the teacher found her sobbing, "What's wrong with me?" (Adapted from NIMH, 1994)

Children who are inattentive find it difficult to sustain mental effort during work or play activities. They have a hard time keeping their minds on any one thing or following through on requests or instructions. For example, while playing a game of soccer, as the rest of the team heads downfield with the ball, the child with ADHD may get sidetracked playing in a mud puddle at the side of the field. Children with ADHD may attend automatically to things they enjoy, but have far greater difficulty than other children focusing their attention when asked to complete a less enjoyable task or to learn something new. Common complaints about inattention by parents and teachers are that the child doesn't or won't listen; can't concentrate; doesn't follow instructions; is disorganized; is easily distracted; is forgetful; daydreams; doesn't finish tasks, chores, or assignments; and is quick to lose interest in boring activities (Barkley, 1996; Hinshaw, 1994; Milich & Lorch, 1994).

Because there are many different types of attention (Taylor, 1995), to say that a child has an attention deficit isn't sufficient. The child could have a deficit in one or more of the following types of attention (Bjorklund, 1995):

**Selective attention** is the ability to concentrate only on relevant stimuli and not to be distracted by "noise" in the environment. When you're studying for a test (relevant stimuli), how easily are you distracted by the sounds from a TV in another

Table 5.1   Diagnostic Criteria for Attention-Deficit/Hyperactivity Disorder

A. Either (1) or (2):

(1) six (or more) of the following symptoms of **inattention** have persisted for at least 6 months to a degree that is maladaptive and inconsistent with developmental level:

Inattention

(a) often fails to give close attention to details or makes careless mistakes in schoolwork, work, or other activities
(b) often has difficulty sustaining attention in tasks or play activities
(c) often does not seem to listen when spoken to directly
(d) often does not follow through on instructions and fails to finish schoolwork, chores, or duties in the workplace (not due to oppositional behavior or failure to understand instructions)
(e) often has difficulty organizing tasks and activities
(f) often avoids, dislikes, or is reluctant to engage in tasks that require sustained mental effort (such as schoolwork or homework)
(g) often loses things necessary for tasks or activities (e.g., toys, school assignments, pencils, books, or tools)
(h) is often easily distracted by extraneous stimuli
(i) is often forgetful in daily activities

(2) six (or more) of the following symptoms of **hyperactivity-impulsivity** have persisted for at least 6 months to a degree that is maladaptive and inconsistent with developmental level:

Hyperactivity

(a) often fidgets with hands or feet or squirms in seat
(b) often leaves seat in classroom or in other situations in which remaining seated is expected
(c) often runs about or climbs excessively in situations in which it is inappropriate (in adolescents or adults, may be limited to subjective feelings of restlessness)
(d) often has difficulty playing or engaging in leisure activities quietly
(e) is often "on the go" or often acts as if "driven by a motor"
(f) often talks excessively

Impulsivity

(g) often blurts out answers before questions have been completed
(h) often has difficulty awaiting turn
(i) often interrupts or intrudes on others (e.g., butts into conversations or games)

B. Some hyperactive-impulsive or inattentive symptoms that caused impairment were present before age 7 years.

C. Some impairment from the symptoms is present in two or more settings (e.g., at school [or work] and at home).

D. There must be clear evidence of clinically significant impairment in social, academic, or occupational functioning.

E. The symptoms do not occur exclusively during the course of a Pervasive Developmental Disorder, Schizophrenia, or other Psychotic Disorder and are not better accounted for by another mental disorder (e.g., Mood Disorder, Anxiety Disorder, Dissociative Disorder, or a Personality Disorder).

Code based on type:

Attention-Deficit/Hyperactivity Disorder, Combined Type: if both Criteria A1 and A2 are met for the past 6 months

Attention-Deficit/Hyperactivity Disorder, Predominantly Inattentive Type: if Criterion A1 is met but Criterion A2 is not met for the past 6 months

Attention-Deficit/Hyperactivity Disorder, Predominantly Hyperactive-Impulsive Type: if Criterion A2 is met but Criterion A1 is not met for the past 6 months

Coding note: For individuals (especially adolescents and adults) who currently have symptoms that no longer meet full criteria, "In Partial Remission" should be specified.

Source: DSM-IV Copyright © 1994 by APA.

room? A term commonly used to describe deficits in selective attention is **distractibility.**

Attentional capacity is the amount of information in short-term memory to which we can attend. When someone gives you directions or a phone number, how much information can you attend to and remember briefly?

Sustained attention is the ability to maintain a persistent focus of attention over time or when fatigued. When you're tired and don't really feel like studying for an exam, are you still able to pay attention to the task at hand until you've reviewed all the required material? Another term for sustained attention is **vigilance.**

Placing children with ADHD in barren or unstimulating cubicles to work so that they won't be distracted, as some have recommended, does not solve their real problem. Children with ADHD may be more distractible in a behavioral sense, jumping from one activity to another, but most types of irrelevant stimuli are no more disruptive for them than they are for comparison children (Sergeant & Sholten, 1985), with two possible exceptions: First, children with ADHD may be distracted by stimuli that are highly salient and appealing (Milich & Lorch, 1994). Second, children with ADHD may be more distracted than other children by irrelevant material that is *embedded in the task* they are working on. For example, playing with the keys on a computer keyboard may be more interesting than the information on a computer screen needed to solve a problem. Although distractions can be disruptive to all children, the primary attention deficit in ADHD is not predominantly one of selective attention. Nor does it appear to be in the child's overall attentional capacity. Children with ADHD can remember the same amount of information for a short time as other children can (Taylor, 1995).

Ever since the groundbreaking work of Douglas (1972), the prevalent view has been that sustained attention, or vigilance, is the core attention deficit in ADHD. When a child with ADHD is presented with an uninteresting or repetitive task, his or her performance deteriorates over time in comparison with the performances of other children. Although no one likes to work on uninteresting tasks, most of us can do so when we have to. Children with ADHD, in contrast, may not be able to persist at a task even when they want to. They are at their best working on self-paced tasks that they have chosen—playing a computer game or building a model airplane—and on tasks that they find especially interesting and that do not require them to sustain their attention over time. Unfortunately, most situations necessarily require sustained attention for successful performance, and many situations may not be particularly interesting. A common way to assess sustained attention (and impulsivity) is with a **continuous performance test (CPT)**, as illustrated in Box 5.1.

Although support for a core deficit in sustained attention in ADHD continues to accumulate (Seidel & Joschko, 1990), findings related to sustained attention remain inconsistent and are highly dependent on the definitions, stimuli, and laboratory tasks used to assess this construct (Hinshaw, 1994). Some investigators have found that the performance of children with ADHD does

---

Box 5.1

Assessing Sustained Attention and Impulsivity: A Continuous Performance Test

In a continuous performance test (CPT), the child is presented with a series of stimuli, such as letters, that appear one at a time on a computer screen. The child is seated in front of the computer screen and instructed to press a button only when a certain letter follows another. In the sequence below, the child is instructed to press the button only when the letter Z follows the letter A and not at any other time. If the child fails to press the button when Z follows A, this is an **error of omission (O)**, and a sign of inattention. If the child presses the button when Z does not follow A, this is an **error of commission (C)**, and a sign of impulsivity.

A A C Z A A A Z A A A B Z A A A Z A B Z A A A Z
            O   O   O
    C   C   C

Children with ADHD typically make more errors of omission and commission than other children make when performing on continuous performance tests.

---

not deteriorate over time any more than that of other children; the relative deficits of children with ADHD are present in tasks lasting just a few seconds as much as in tasks lasting 10 minutes or an hour. These investigators have concluded that the unique deficit in ADHD is not one of attention at all, but one of regulating motor output or inhibiting a response (Taylor, 1995; van der Meere, van Baal, & Sergeant, 1989; van der Meere, 1996; Voeller, 1991). Although the discussion has recently shifted to the role of motor response systems in ADHD, it is still far too early to close the door on attention deficit as a key factor in the disorder (Douglas, in press).

Hyperactivity-Impulsivity

Mark: Predominantly Hyperactive-Impulsive

Mark, age 14, has more energy than most boys his age. But then, he's always been overly active. At age 3 he was a human tornado, dashing around and disrupting everything in his path. At home, he darted from one activity to the next, leaving a trail of toys behind him. At meals, he upset dishes and chattered nonstop. He was reckless and impulsive, running into the street despite oncoming cars, no matter how often his mother explained the danger or scolded him. On the playground, he seemed no wilder than the other kids. But his tendency to overreact—like socking playmates simply for bumping into him—had already gotten him into trouble several times. His parents didn't know what to do. Mark's doting grandparents reassured them, "Boys will be boys. Don't worry, he'll grow out of it." But he didn't. (Adapted from NIMH, 1994)

Although symptoms of impulsivity and hyperactivity are listed separately in DSM-IV, when children display one of these types of behaviors they usually display the other. Therefore, hyperactivity and impulsivity are best viewed as a single dimension of behavior, referred to as hyperactivity-impulsivity or behavioral disinhibition (Barkley, 1996; Lahey et al., 1988).

Impulsivity. Children who are impulsive seem unable to bridle their immediate reactions or to think before they act. They may run into the street without looking or take an expensive clock apart with little thought about how to put it back together again. It's very hard for them to stop an ongoing behavior or to regulate their behavior in accordance with situational demands or the wishes of others. As a result, they may blurt out inappropriate comments or give incorrect answers to questions that are not yet completed. Children who are impulsive find it difficult to wait or take turns, usually responding too quickly or too often. They often interrupt conversations, intrude on others' activities, and lash out in frustration when they're upset (Malone & Swanson, 1993). They also have difficulty resisting immediate temptations or delaying gratification (Anderson, Hinshaw, & Simmel, 1994). Minor mishaps such as spilling drinks or knocking things over are common. So too are more serious accidents and injuries that result from reckless behavior such as running into the street without looking.

Impulsivity, like attention, takes different forms (Milich & Kramer, 1984). One distinction is between cognitive and behavioral impulsivity:

Cognitive impulsivity: These symptoms reflect disorganization, hurried thinking, and the need for supervision. Remember John not handing in his homework even though it was done? The randomly distributed stacks of papers, books, pencils, unopened mail, and unanswered telephone messages that litter the desk of one of your textbook authors may be a sign of cognitive impulsivity.

Behavioral impulsivity: These symptoms include calling out in class or acting without considering the consequences of one's actions. Remember the case of

John teaching his two-year-old brother how to strike matches? A child who touches a stove to see if it is hot, when she is old enough to know better, is also showing behavioral impulsivity. Children who are behaviorally impulsive have difficulty inhibiting their response when the situation calls for them to do so.

Cognitive and behavioral impulsivity appear to be separate dimensions of behavior, the former related to inattentiveness and the latter to motor hyperactivity, and both predict problems with academic achievement. However, only behavioral impulsivity predicts antisocial behavior (White et al., 1994) and thus may be a specific sign of increased risk for oppositional and conduct problems (Hinshaw, 1994).

Some tasks that have been used to assess impulsivity, such as the Matching Familiar Figures Test (MFFT) (see Box 5.2), do not correlate highly with impulsive responding in real-life situations. Results are often dependent on the context and outcome of the testing situation, for example, the length of a test session or the consequence of a fast response.

More recently, methods that permit a more precise assessment of the cognitive processes underlying ADHD have been developed. One such method, the Stop Task (see Box 5.3), has been used to assess children's deficiencies in response inhibition. Further research will be needed to clarify whether performance decrements on this task are specific to children with ADHD, or whether they reflect a general deficit in speed of information processing or a specific deficit in behavioral impulsivity (Tannock, 1998).

Hyperactivity. Hyperactivity, or overactive behavior, also takes many forms. Children with ADHD are in constant motion. Sitting still through a class lesson can be impossible for them. The child may fidget, squirm, climb, run about the room aimlessly, touch everything in sight, noisily tap a pencil, or jostle other children. Parents and teachers describe children with ADHD as "driven by a motor," always on the go, and talking incessantly. The child's activity is excessively energetic, intense, inappropriate, and not goal-directed. These children are extremely active, but unlike other children with a high energy level, they don't accomplish very much.

Although hyperactivity (motor overactivity) and impulsivity together make up one behavioral dimension, a few separate comments about hyperactivity are warranted. After all, the popular image of a child with ADHD as a motor-driven hyperkinetic speedball is the stereotype of this disorder. Interestingly, for a brief period in the early 1980s there was a decline in the belief that hyperactivity was a core feature of ADHD, because of a growing interest in attention deficits and in findings

Box 5.2
Matching Familiar Figures Test

The Matching Familiar Figures Test (MFFT) is a match-to-sample task in which the child is asked to look at the sample stimulus and to pick the one below that is exactly like it.

Cognitively impulsive children respond more quickly and make more errors than do other children.

Source: Kagan, Rossman, Day, Albert, & Philips, 1964.

that children with ADHD were not hyperactive at all times or in all situations. Hyperactivity was found to occur primarily when the child was required to inhibit his or her motor responding (for example, in the classroom).

As it turned out, the conclusion that hyperactivity is not a central feature of ADHD was premature. It was based on relatively unsophisticated ways of measuring motor activity, such as placing a "wiggle cushion" on a child's chair or soliciting global ratings of activity from observers. Sophisticated computerized recordings of body movements prove that children with ADHD do in fact display more motor activity than other children throughout the entire day (Porrino et al., 1983)—even when they are asleep. However, the greatest differences are still found when the child is required to inhibit motor activity.

The current view is that motor overactivity is an essential feature of ADHD. In contrast to inattention, motor overactivity distinguishes children with ADHD from those with other disorders and from normal children (Halperin, Matier, Bedi, Sharma, & Newcorn, 1992; Roberts, 1990). In other words, hyperactivity appears to be a *specific* marker for ADHD whereas attention deficit is not. Inattention is a core symptom of ADHD, but it may not be unique to this disorder. Although symptoms of inattention and hyperactivity-

impulsivity receive equal status in DSM-IV, their relative importance in defining ADHD continues to be a matter of some debate. The strong link between hyperactivity and behavioral impulsivity has led to recent proposals that both are part of a more fundamental deficit in behavioral inhibition (Barkley, 1997a; Quay, 1997).

The core features of ADHD—inattention, impulsivity, and overactivity—are complex processes. Children with ADHD display a unique constellation and severity of symptoms but don't necessarily differ from comparison children on *all* types and measures of inattention, impulsivity, and hyperactivity (Barkley, 1996). Deficits in behavioral inhibition and motor control are the symptoms that provide the sharpest contrast between children with and without ADHD.

Additional Criteria

Not every child who displays inattentive, impulsive, or hyperactive behavior has ADHD. At times, most children (and adults too) blurt out things they didn't mean to say, jump from one thing to another, make careless mistakes, or become forgetful and disorganized. This doesn't mean they will have a lifelong problem controlling their impulses. So, in order to define and diagnose ADHD, we must ask these important questions:

Children with ADHD display more motor activity than other children throughout the entire day—even when they sleep.

The Stop Task is a laboratory measure designed to simulate real-life activities that call for quick and precise decision-making processes regarding the execution or inhibition of selected actions. The Stop Task consists of two components: a *go response* and a *stop response*.

Go trials: The subject is asked to focus on a computer-generated letter stimulus. Each letter is paired with a response button located on a response box which the subject holds. When either an *X* or *O* appears on the screen, the subject is asked to push the corresponding button on the response box.

Stop trials: At given times during the presentation of the letters, a tone, known as a "stop-signal" will sound. The subject is instructed to withhold responding when the tone sounds.

Stop-signals are presented on one-quarter of all trials. Relative to children without ADHD, children with ADHD have difficulty inhibiting their responses on the Stop trials. The task thus gives an accurate measure of the time required for a child to inhibit responses.

Youngster performing on a Stop Task.

Source: Schachar, Tannock, & Logan, 1993.

❖ Are the child's behaviors excessive, long-term, and pervasive?
❖ Do they occur more often than in other children of the same age and gender?
❖ Are they a persistent problem and not just a reaction to a temporary situation?
❖ Do they occur across several settings and not just in one location?
❖ Do they produce significant impairments in the child's social or academic performance?
❖ Are they better accounted for by some other disorder, such as mental retardation, epilepsy, or autism?

DSM-IV provides specific guidelines for answering these questions. The child's behaviors must appear before the age of 7 and continue for at least 6 months; they must be more frequent or severe than in other children of the same age; they must produce a significant impairment in at least two areas of the child's life, such as school, home, or friendships; and they must not be due to another disorder.

ADHD SUBTYPES

Because children with ADHD differ in many ways, investigators have tried to identify subtypes. A **subtype** is a group of individuals who have something in common—symptoms, etiology, problem severity, or likely outcome—that makes them distinct from other subtypes. One important distinction is between children who display symptoms primarily of inattention and those who show primarily hyperactive-impulsive behavior, either by itself or in combination with inattention. DSM-IV specifies three subtypes of ADHD: (1) predominantly inattentive type; (2) predominantly hyperactive-impulsive type; and (3) combined type.

The **predominantly inattentive type** (**ADHD-PI**), or pure attention deficit, is found in 1 out of every 100 elementary school children (Szatmari, Offord, & Boyle, 1989). These children are described by their teachers and parents as inattentive and drowsy, daydreamy, spacey, in a fog, or easily confused, and commonly experience a learning disability. They process information slowly and find it hard to retrieve information from memory. Their primary deficits seem to be in their speed of information processing and in focused or selective attention. Children with predominantly inattentive symptoms are often rated as anxious and apprehensive and may display mood disorders. Socially, they may be withdrawn, shy, or neglected. They are also responsive to lower dosages of stimulant medication than are children with hyperactive-impulsive symptoms (Barkley, 1996). Growing (though not yet conclusive) evidence suggests that predominantly inattentive children with ADHD constitute a distinct subgroup, or perhaps have a completely different disorder than do the hyperactive-impulsive or combined subtypes (Goodyear & Hynd, 1992). These children appear to display different symptoms, associated conditions, family histories, outcomes, and responses to treatment (Barkley, 1996).

In contrast to children who are predominantly inattentive, children with ADHD of the **predominantly hyperactive-impulsive (ADHD-HI)** type *and* those with the **combined (ADHD-C)** type are more likely to display problems in inhibiting behavior and in behavioral persistence. They are also more likely to be aggressive, defiant, and oppositional, and to be rejected by their peers (Lahey & Carlson, 1992). They show higher rates of school suspension and placement in special education classes, and are more likely to show antisocial outcomes than children who are predominantly inattentive. Since children who are predominantly hyperactive-impulsive are usually younger than those with the combined type, it is not yet known whether there are actually two distinct subtypes or the same type at different ages (Barkley, 1996).

Although the DSM-IV subtypes of ADHD have received some support in preliminary studies (Eiraldi, Power, & Nezu, 1997; Gaub & Carlson, 1997a; Lahey et al., 1994; Paternite, Loney, & Roberts, 1996), the validity of these subtypes awaits further research.

DIFFERENTIAL DIAGNOSIS

Illness, accidents, stressful life events such as a major move or the loss of a parent, chronic abuse, mild seizures, or a middle ear infection can produce symptoms similar to those of ADHD. For example, a normally agreeable 9-year-old boy who becomes hyperactive, distractible, or argumentative immediately following the separation of his parents probably is having an adjustment reaction, not exhibiting ADHD. The disruptive behaviors of children with mild mental retardation, learning disabilities, or conduct problems may also be mistaken for ADHD. Before a diagnosis of ADHD is made, it is essential that a thorough assessment that includes developmental history, parent and teacher reports, and behavioral observations is carried out and that other possible reasons for the child's symptoms are investigated (Barkley, 1997b).

DSM-IV CRITERIA: WHAT THEY DON'T TELL US

The DSM-IV criteria are not without flaws. First, although clinical judgment may be used to assess whether symptoms are "inconsistent with developmental level," in general, the criteria are not developmentally sensitive. The same symptoms are applied to individuals of all ages, even though some symptoms, such as running and climbing, are more applicable to younger children than to older children and adolescents. In addition, DSM-IV symptom cutoffs are not adjusted for children of different ages or levels of maturity, even though many of these symptoms show a general decline with age.

Second, DSM-IV views ADHD categorically—a disorder that the child either has or doesn't have. However, because the number and severity of symptoms of ADHD are also a matter of degree, children who are just below the cutoff for ADHD are not necessarily qualitatively different from those who are just above it. In fact, over time, some children may move in and out of the category as a result of fluctuations in their behavior. Nevertheless, it can still be useful to talk about extremes even when a disorder is of a continuous or changing nature. For example, there is no "magic" cutoff for high blood pressure, but most of us would agree that people with high blood pressure are at greater risk for certain negative outcomes than those without.

Third, the DSM-IV requirement of age of onset before 7 years is questionable. There seems to be little difference between children with ADHD with onset before or after age 7 (Barkley & Biederman, 1997), and nearly half of children with ADHD who are predominantly inattentive do not manifest the disorder until *after* age 7 (Applegate et al., 1997). Finally, the requirement of persistence for 6 months may be too brief a time for preschool children, because these kinds of symptoms may be displayed by many preschoolers for 6 months and then go away (Barkley, 1996).

These limitations highlight the fact that DSM criteria are designed for a specific purpose—classification and diagnosis. They help shape our understanding of ADHD, but they are also shaped by, and in some instances lag behind, new research findings.

ASSOCIATED CHARACTERISTICS OF ADHD

In addition to their primary difficulties of inattention and hyperactivity-impulsivity, many children with ADHD display a number of related problems. For example, Mark got into fights with playmates. Lisa was failing in school and felt completely helpless about her situation. The associated problems of children with ADHD are of three general types: (1) Some are the *direct result* of the child's ADHD symptoms—for example, when a child's inattentiveness interferes with school performance; (2) some are an *indirect outcome* of ADHD—for example, when a child becomes depressed following rejection by other children; and (3) some are an *independent disorder* that occurs along with ADHD—for example, when children with ADHD also have an anxiety disorder. Since all three types of associated problems are usually present in the same child, it is seldom possible to fit a problem neatly into one of the preceding categories.

Cognitive Deficits

Metacognition and Executive Functions.

Children with ADHD often have deficits in metacognition and executive functions (Pennington & Ozonoff, 1996). These are higher-order mental processes that underlie the child's capacity for self-regulation, such as self-awareness, planning, self-monitoring, and self-evaluation).

Metacognition refers to the child's awareness of his or her own thought processes, or "knowing about knowing." The following comments by an 11-year-old girl suggest that she is keenly aware of the way in which she thinks, an awareness that is often lacking in children with ADHD:

> If I had to teach a plan to someone who grew up in the jungle—like a plan to work on a project at 10 A.M. tomorrow—I'd tell her what to say to herself to make it easier at the start for her. Like "if I do this plan on time I'll get a reward and the teacher will like me and I'll be proud." But for myself, I know all that already, so I don't have to say it to myself—besides, it would take too long to say, and my mind doesn't have time for all that, so I just remember that stuff about why I should do it real quick without saying it—it's like a method that I know already in math; once you have the method you don't have to say every little step. (Adapted from Mischel, 1979)

Executive functions typically refer to the child's ability to maintain a problem-solving set in order to attain a future goal (Welsh & Pennington, 1988). Although precise definitions remain elusive (Eslinger, 1996), executive functions include:

- ❖ *cognitive* processes, such as working memory and mental computation, planning and anticipation, flexibility of thinking, and the use of organizational strategies;
- ❖ *language* processes, such as verbal fluency, communication, and the use of self-directed speech;
- ❖ *motor* processes, such as allocation of effort, following prohibitive instructions, response inhibition, and motor coordination and sequencing; and
- ❖ *emotional* processes, such as self-regulation of arousal level and mature moral reasoning.

Children with ADHD consistently show deficits in executive functions related to motor inhibition (Pennington & Ozonoff, 1996).

Intellectual Deficits and Strengths. One of the puzzling questions about ADHD is why these children never quite live up to potential. Most children with ADHD are of at least normal intelligence, and many are quite bright. Their difficulty is not in a lack of intelligence but rather in applying their intelligence to everyday life situations (Barkley, 1996). There is, however, a small but significant negative relationship between intelligence and hyperactive-impulsive behavior: Brighter children tend to show fewer symptoms (Sonuga-Barke, Lamparelli, Stevenson, Thompson, & Henry, 1994).

Children with ADHD score about 10 points lower on IQ tests than both control children and their own siblings (remember, their IQ scores are still within the average or above-average range). Since popular IQ tests, like the WISC-III, include subtests related to working memory (doing mental arithmetic), the lower scores of children with ADHD are not surprising. Children with ADHD also do especially poorly on tests that require sustained attention (Anastopoulos, Spisto, & Maher, 1994). The lower IQ scores of children with ADHD may also be due to the direct effect of their symptoms on test-taking behavior. A child who scores lower on an IQ test because she or he is not paying attention to instructions is not necessarily less intelligent.

Academic Functioning. Most children with ADHD experience severe difficulties throughout their school years, regardless of whether or not they have a specific learning disability. These difficulties are reflected in the following comments by 14-year-old Ian:

Ian: Failing in School

The days are overcast, cold, steel gray. I don't seem to know what's going on at school. I'm failing everything. . . . Throughout grade school some teachers made sincere efforts to help, others opted to pass me over, demanding little, expecting even less, and hoping for my eventual classroom conformity which would not undermine the rights of others. Rote phrases I hear throughout my childhood are

The structured demands of the classroom can be painful for children with ADHD.

> "Slow down Ian," or "Now remember Ian, you are fooling nobody but yourself." They were wrong. I never wanted to fool myself and I did not know how to slow down. Often I am sent out of the class for disruptive behavior. . . . I knew that I had fallen so far behind the others that no amount of catching up would change the perceptions or expectations that others had of me. (Murray, 1993)

School performance difficulties for children with ADHD like Ian include lower productivity, grades, and scores on achievement tests; failure to advance in grade; and more frequent placements in special education classes. About 40% of children with ADHD receive some form of special education by adolescence. Between 25% and 35% or more of children with ADHD have been retained in grade at least once; 10% to 25% have been expelled; and 10% to 35% never finish high school (Barkley, 1996; Fischer, Barkley, Edelbrock, & Smallish, 1990; G. Weiss & Hechtman, 1993). Particularly disturbing are recent findings that the academic skills of children with ADHD are impaired even before they enter the first grade (Mariani & Barkley, 1997).

Learning Disabilities. Many children with ADHD also have a specific learning disability. This means they have trouble with language or certain academic skills, typically reading and math (see Chapter 11). Problems with handwriting and poor motor coordination also occur, but these difficulties are not as well documented as those in reading and math. Estimates of the number of children with both ADHD and a learning disability depend on how learning disabilities are de-

fined. When *learning disability* is defined broadly as performance below expected grade level, then as many as 80% of children with ADHD may have a learning disability by late childhood (Cantwell & Baker, 1992). However, when it is defined more narrowly as a significant delay in reading, arithmetic, or spelling relative to the child's general intellectual functioning or achievement in one of the other areas, between 10% and 25% of children with ADHD have at least one type of specific learning disability (Barkley, 1990; Semrud-Clikeman et al., 1992).

Why do ADHD and learning disabilities occur together? There are several possibilities: (1) ADHD symptoms may lead to learning difficulties; (2) learning problems may lead to inattention in the classroom and other ADHD-related symptoms; and (3) both disorders may be the result of a common underlying biological or environmental factor. One study found that early ADHD symptoms result in later reading problems but that early reading problems do not usually give rise to later symptoms of ADHD (Wood & Felton, 1992). Some evidence supports common genetic factors for ADHD and spelling disorders, but not for ADHD and reading disorders (Stevenson, Pennington, Gilger, Pennington, DeFries, & Gilies, 1993).

Speech and Language Impairments

As many as 30% to 64% of children with ADHD have impairments in their speech and language (Baker & Cantwell, 1992; Beitchman, Hood, Rochon, & Peterson, 1989; Gross-Tsur, Shalev, & Amir, 1991). In addition to having a higher than expected prevalence of formal speech and language disorders, children with ADHD frequently have difficulties using language in everyday situations at home and school. Excessive and loud talking, frequent shifts in conversation, not listening, interrupting others, and initiating conversation inappropriately are just a few common examples.

Children with ADHD not only ramble on but also use fewer pronouns and conjunctions, which makes it difficult for the listener to understand who and what the child is talking about (Tannock, Purvis, & Schachar, 1993). Children with ADHD may also use *unclear links* in their conversation, so that information from another part of the conversation or from the surrounding context must be used to understand what the child is saying. Can you understand the following statement by an 8-year-old boy with ADHD? (Words in capital letters indicate unclear links.)

> And all of a sudden the soldiers—and all of a sudden HE, gets faint and you know when HE says "Good doctors, I want to talk with you" and all of a sudden HE goes in

THE DOOR and inside they come off IT from THE THING. So HE puts—I think THIS SOMETHING on THE DOORKNOB. (Tannock, Fine, Heintz, & Schachar, 1995)

How did you do? When links are unclear, as they are in this example, the listener must either make an inference about what the child means or be left with an inadequate understanding. Unfortunately, miscommunication is all too common for children with ADHD.

Medical and Physical Characteristics

Health-Related Problems.
Children with ADHD are susceptible to health difficulties, such as recurring upper respiratory infections, asthma, and allergies in the later preschool and childhood years (Szatmari et al., 1989). Bed-wetting, other problems of elimination, and sleep disturbances are also common (Prince et al., 1996; Safer & Allen, 1976). Some children with ADHD sleep very little, often from birth, playing or reading in their room at night while their parents sleep. However, the precise nature of the sleep disturbance in ADHD is unclear (Corkum, Tannock, & Moldofsky, 1998). Some studies have found that it takes the child with ADHD a long time to fall asleep, others that the child is tired on waking, and still others that the child wakes up frequently during the night (Trommer, Hoeppner, Rosenberg, Armstrong, & Rothstein, 1988).

Accident-Proneness and Risk Taking.
Up to half of all children with ADHD are described as *accident-prone*, with 15% having had at least four or more serious injuries (Barkley, 1996). In one study, nearly half of children who were hospitalized with minor head injuries by age 10 had been rated as hyperactive at age 5 (Bijur, Haslum, & Golding, 1990). Children with ADHD are nearly 3 times more likely than other children to experience accidental poisonings (Stewart, Thach, & Friedin, 1970). Many children injured as pedestrians or bike riders in traffic accidents perform poorly on tests of attention and impulse control and are rated as hyperactive/aggressive by their teachers (Pless, Taylor, & Arsenault, 1995). As young adult drivers, individuals with ADHD are at higher risk than others for traffic accidents and offenses (Barkley, Guevremont, Anastopoulos, DuPaul, & Shelton, 1993; Barkley, Murphy, & Kwasnik, 1996; Nada-Raja et al., 1997; Weiss & Hechtman, 1993). The impulsivity and dangerous behaviors of children with ADHD may also place them at higher risk than others for experiencing trauma and subsequent post-traumatic stress disorder (Cuffe, McCullough, & Pumariega, 1994).

A recent follow-up study of young men with ADHD found that 16% of them had fathered a total of 41 children compared with only 1 child (1%) for the controls. More than half of the offspring were not in their fathers' custody. The young men with ADHD also reported having 3 times as many sexual partners and far more unprotected sex than controls (Barkley, Fisher, & Fletcher, 1997). These findings suggest a progression of hyperactive-impulsive behaviors into a pattern of irresponsible and risky adult behavior. However, some of these excesses may be related to co-occurring conduct disorders rather than to ADHD alone.

Do accident-prone and risk-taking individuals with ADHD live as long as other people? One study found that the most significant childhood characteristic that predicted reduced life expectancy by all causes was impulsive, undercontrolled behavior (Friedman et al., 1995). A lifelong pattern of accident proneness, auto accidents, and risk taking, combined with a reduced concern for health-promoting behaviors, such as exercise, proper diet, safe sex, and moderate use of tobacco, alcohol, and caffeine, may very well be predictive of a reduced life expectancy for individuals with ADHD (Barkley, 1996). For example, ADHD is a significant and independent risk factor for the early initiation of cigarette smoking (Milberger, Biederman, Faraone, Chen, & Jones, 1997) and the early onset of substance use disorders (Biederman et al., 1997; Wilens, Biederman, Mick, Faraone, & Spencer, 1997).

Interpersonal Difficulties

Dennis: Yesterday's Rules Are Long Forgotten

With my other children, I could tell them one time, "Don't do that," and they would stop. But Dennis, my child with ADHD, I could tell him a hundred times, "Dennis, don't carve soap with my potato peeler," "Don't paint the house with used motor oil," or "Don't walk on Grandma's white sofa in your muddy shoes," but he still does it. It's like every day is a brand new day and yesterday's rules are long forgotten . . . I just cannot stay one step ahead of him. He does things my other kids never thought of. (Kennedy et al., 1993)

Impairments in social functioning in family life, peer relations, school, and spare-time activities are common in children with ADHD. Those who experience the most severe social disability are at greatest risk for poor adolescent outcomes, other psychiatric disorders such as depression and conduct disorder, and high levels of family conflict (Greene et al., 1996; Greene, Biederman, Faraone, Sienna, & Garcia-Jetton, 1997). Like Dennis, children with ADHD don't listen and are often hostile and defiant, argumentative, short-tempered, unpredictable, and explosive. As a result, they are in frequent conflict with adults and other children—to get along with others, you need to follow social rules and respect conventions. Unfortunately, children with ADHD do not play by the same rules as others and, like Dennis, don't seem to learn from past mistakes. This is so despite their awareness of expected social behaviors and a desire to conform to them. Many of the social blunders of children with ADHD appear more thoughtless than intentional. Nevertheless, the behaviors of children with ADHD have an annoying quality and are a source of great distress for their parents, siblings, teachers, and classmates.

Problems in the Family

Ian: Sibling Conflict

I see Andrea and David talking seriously to each other. I feel left out and cheated when they share secrets or activities. Suddenly, Andrea bellows out that someone has been in her room because things are not as she left them. "Look, even my drawers have been gone through. Ian, it's you. Who else could it be? Stay out of my goddam room, do you understand? I can't keep anything without you getting your grubby little fingers on it." I refuse to admit my culpability and adamantly swear up and down I wasn't in her room. Besides, it could have been someone else. Better see what's on TV. (Murray, 1993)

A poor family environment is not the primary cause of ADHD, but families of children with ADHD experience many difficulties. Their interactions are characterized by negativity, child noncompliance, high parental control, and sibling conflict (Mash & Johnston, 1982). In addition, parents may experience high levels of distress and related problems, the most common ones being depression in mothers and antisocial behavior (for example, substance abuse) in fathers. Further stress on family life stems from the fact that parents of children with ADHD may themselves have ADHD and other associated conditions.

Conflict between mothers and their children with ADHD is known to be severe during the preschool years and to continue throughout childhood and into adolescence (Mash & Johnston, 1982). Conflict with fathers occurs less frequently, but still more often than between other children and their fathers (Tallmadge & Barkley, 1983). Mother-child conflict during early childhood is a significant predictor of parent-adolescent conflict 8 to 10 years later (Barkley, Fischer, Edelbrock, & Smallish, 1991). It is also not a self-contained problem, because it predicts child noncompliance in play settings, stealing outside of the home, and disobedience in the classroom (Anderson et al., 1994; Whalen, Henker, & Dotemoto, 1980).

Interestingly, mothers tend to interact similarly with their children without ADHD as they do with their child with ADHD (Tarver-Behring, Barkley, & Karlsson, 1985). These findings suggest that problems in the family are not restricted just to situations in which the child with ADHD is directly involved, but may spill over into interactions between parents and other children in the family.

The families of children with ADHD also display greater parenting stress and a lower sense of parenting competence (Anastopoulos, Guevremont, Shelton, & DuPaul, 1992; Mash & Johnston, 1983), greater maternal depression, fewer contacts with extended family members, and higher rates of marital conflict, separation, and divorce (Barkley, 1996). Parents of children with ADHD also show increased alcohol consumption that may, in some cases, be a direct result of the stressful interactions they have with their children (Pelham & Lang, 1993; Pelham, Lang et al., 1997).

It is extremely important to note that conflict between children with ADHD and their parents, and the links between ADHD and parental psychopathology, marital discord, and divorce, seem to be related to the co-occurrence of oppositional and conduct disorder symptoms, rather than to ADHD alone (Barkley, Anastopoulos, Guevremont, & Fletcher, 1992).

Problems with Peers

Children with ADHD display little of the give-and-take, cooperation, and sharing that characterize the social interactions of other children (Milich & Landau, 1982; Pelham & Bender, 1982; Whalen & Henker, 1985, 1992). Instead, when interacting with peers they are often intrusive, inappropriate, intense, disorganized, impulsive, aggressive, emotional, bossy, and uncooperative (Cunningham & Siegel, 1987). Hardly a winning combination for making friends! Although there is much variation in how difficulties with peers are expressed, we also find some common themes (Whalen & Henker, 1985):

❖ Children with ADHD can be bothersome, stubborn, socially awkward, and socially insensitive.

❖ They are noncompliant and disruptive in group settings such as the classroom.

❖ They are socially conspicuous, loud, intense, and quick to react.

❖ Many children with ADHD are socially aggressive.

❖ Children with ADHD may be puzzled by the negative reactions of others to their behavior.

❖ Children with ADHD seem to get into trouble even when they are trying to be helpful.

❖ They are socially active, but "off the mark" with respect to the style, content, or timing of their behavior.

❖ Their behavior has an annoying and inappropriate quality.

❖ Their behavior seems thoughtless, but unintentional.

❖ Children with ADHD often bring out the worst in other children.

In light of the above, it is not surprising that children with ADHD are disliked and uniformly rejected by their peers, have few friends, and are often unhappy (Flicek & Landau, 1985; Johnston & Pelham, 1985; Whalen & Henker, 1992). The aggressiveness that often accompanies ADHD leads to peer conflict and negative reputation (Bickett & Milich, 1990; Erhardt & Hinshaw, 1994). However, even nonaggressive children with ADHD experience disapproval by peers (Milich & Landau, 1989). Stimulant medications that decrease the negative and disruptive behaviors of children with ADHD often do not result in improved prosocial behavior or social acceptance, probably because medication alone does not increase the child's social competence or change a bad reputation.

> We've tried to keep her from finding out about these things, but kids can be cruel. What do you say to your daughter when she comes to you with tears in her eyes and wants to know why she's the only one in her kindergarten class who wasn't invited to the birthday party—again? (Adapted from Barkley, 1995)

Interestingly, children with ADHD are not deficient in their social reasoning or ability to interpret social situations accurately (Whalen & Henker, 1992). They simply can't readily apply their knowledge during the ebb and flow of social exchange, continuing to be dominant or assertive even after the situation has changed to one that calls for accommodation, negotiation, or submission (Landau & Milich, 1988). Their social agenda may also differ from their peers', especially when ADHD is accompanied by aggression. Children with ADHD who are aggressive may actually value and prefer troublemaking, sensation seeking, and fun at the expense of following rules and getting along with other children (Melnick & Hinshaw, 1996).

ACCOMPANYING DISORDERS AND SYMPTOMS

In addition to their cognitive, learning, health-related, and social deficits, children with ADHD have much higher than expected rates of other psychiatric disorders. Between 50% and 80% of children with ADHD also meet criteria for another disorder (Jensen, Martin, & Cantwell, 1997). The most common of these are oppositional defiant disorder and conduct disorder, emotional disorders such as anxiety and depression, and developmental learning disorders. The combination of ADHD and another problem seriously complicates the situation for the child and family.

Oppositional Defiant Disorder and Conduct Disorder

Shawn: Defiant and Breaking Rules

Shawn is an energetic and talkative 29-year-old who recalls his childhood as being a total disaster: "I did really bad in school. My parents and teachers were always on my back. They bugged me about being a bully—too aggressive, too explosive, too loud, too defiant. I had no friends. Then I began to use drugs: marijuana, and later, cocaine. I barely managed to squeak through high school. I couldn't concentrate at all. I'd study for hours and then forget everything I'd read. I had to cheat my way through high school."

Nearly half of all children with ADHD—mostly boys—have another condition called oppositional defiant disorder (ODD). Like Shawn, such children overreact, lashing out at adults and other kids; for example, shoving a child who accidentally bumps into them. Children with ODD are stubborn, short-tempered, defiant, and combative. Between 35% and 60% of clinic-referred children with ADHD also meet criteria for a diagnosis of ODD by 7 years of age or later (Barkley, 1990; Biederman, Faraone, & Lapey, 1992).

Sometimes, as with Shawn, ODD progresses to conduct disorder (CD), a more serious condition. Children with CD violate societal rules and are at high risk of getting into serious trouble at school or with the police. They may fight, cheat, steal, set fires, destroy property, or use illegal drugs. About 30% to 50% of children with ADHD eventually develop CD (Barkley, 1990; Biederman et al., 1992). ADHD is thus one of the most reliable

"Sam, neither your father nor I consider your response appropriate."

predictors of both ODD and CD (Loeber, 1990; Mannuzza & Klein, 1992; Taylor, 1995).

ADHD, ODD, and CD tend to run in families, which suggests a common causal mechanism (Biederman et al., 1992). On this basis, some have argued that ADHD symptoms and conduct problems are different expressions of the same disorder. However, ADHD is usually associated with cognitive impairments and neurodevelopmental difficulties, whereas conduct problems are more often related to family adversity, parental psychopathology, and social disadvantage (Schachar & Tannock, 1995).

The frequent co-occurrence of ADHD and CD has led some to suggest an "aggressive subtype" of ADHD (Jensen et al., 1997). The rationale is that the presence of an accompanying CD may fundamentally alter the clinical expression, course, outcome, and response to treatment of ADHD. Children with ADHD and comorbid CD have been found to display more severe neuropsychological deficits in the areas of verbal ability and memory and worse outcomes in terms of substance abuse and driving-related accidents; they also seem to respond more poorly to stimulant medication than do children with either ADHD or conduct disorder alone.

Anxiety Disorders

T. J.: Overactive and Anxious

T. J. was first referred for help at age 6. He had been very active and impulsive since he was a toddler. His parents reported that he had a lot of trouble sleeping and would wake up several times each night. They also said that he showed great anxiety during even brief separations from them and seemed to be worrying about something the whole time. T. J. confirmed that he had "terrible bad dreams," worried about the fighting and arguing at home, and felt that no one liked him. (Adapted from Tannock, in press)

Like T. J., about 25% of children with ADHD—usually younger boys—experience excessive anxiety (Biederman, Newcorn, & Sprich, 1991; Tannock, in press). Children with ADHD and an anxiety disorder are worriers. They may worry about being separated from their parents, trying something new, taking tests, making social contacts, or visiting the doctor. They may feel tense or uneasy and constantly seek reassurance that they are all right. Because their anxieties are unrealistic, more frequent, and more intense than normal, they have a negative impact on the child's thinking and behavior. In adolescence, the overall relationship between ADHD and anxiety disorders is reduced or eliminated. Possibly, the co-occurrence of an anxiety disorder inhibits the child from engaging in the impulsive behaviors that characterize other children with ADHD of this age (Pliszka, 1992).

Depression

About 15% to 20% of children and adolescents with ADHD experience depression (Jensen et al., 1997), feeling so hopeless and overwhelmed that they are unable to deal with everyday life. Depression may also make them irritable and disrupt their sleep, appetite, or ability to think. The lowered self-esteem and "learned helplessness" that characterize many children with ADHD (Dulcan, 1989; Milich & Okazaki, 1991) are often associated with depression. As many as 40% to 50% of youngsters with ADHD may eventually develop depression or another mood disorder (see Chapter 8), usually in late adolescence or early adulthood. This may be a function of the fact that a family risk for one disorder increases the risk for the other (Biederman, Faraone, Keenan, & Tsuang, 1991; Biederman et al., 1995; Carlson, 1990). Such a family link means that depression in a child with ADHD should not be viewed solely as the result of the child's demoralization related to his or her symptoms, and that depression in mothers of children with ADHD may not be entirely due to the cumulative stresses of living with a child with ADHD (Faraone & Biederman, 1997).

Tourette's Disorder

A very small proportion of children with ADHD have a rare disorder called **Tourette's disorder**. Children with Tourette's exhibit uncontrollable movements, such as tics, eye blinks, and facial twitches. They may grimace, shrug, sniff, or bark out words. ADHD does not appear to elevate the child's risk for Tourette's disorder. However, about 50% of individuals with Tourette's also have ADHD (Comings & Comings, 1988). In cases where Tourette's and ADHD co-occur, ADHD usually precedes the onset of Tourette's disorder. A child with Tourette's disorder is also more likely to be referred for help if ADHD is also present.

Most children with ADHD have an accompanying disruptive behavior disorder, and many also experience anxiety or depression. This reality complicates the search for possible causes, outcomes, and treatments for ADHD. In many cases it is hard to know whether a specific outcome, such as rule violations during adolescence, is due to the child's ADHD or to a co-occurring CD. And children with ADHD and an anxiety disorder do not seem to respond as well to stimulant medication as do those with ADHD alone (Pliszka, 1989).

TASK AND SITUATIONAL FACTORS

In many situations, the *average* performance of a child with ADHD is only slightly below that of other children. However, children with ADHD show enormous *variability* in their performance over time, across tasks, and in different situations. These sharp peaks and valleys are what usually make children with ADHD stand out from their peers. For example, a child with ADHD may watch a favorite video attentively but be unable to focus on pictures in a magazine when asked to do so, or may come to dinner when called one day and the next day seem not even to hear the call that it's ready.

The child with ADHD is especially challenged in settings where certain behaviors are expected. As we saw with Fidgety Phil and with Dusty N., mealtime is a good example, with its behavioral expectations of coming to the table when called, using utensils not hands, asking for things to be passed, keeping elbows off the table, not leaning back in the chair, not throwing food, participating in a family discussion, and so on. This is a challenging task for any child. Not surprisingly, children with ADHD often have difficulty meeting most of these requirements.

Many situational factors make it difficult for children with ADHD to attend to tasks, regulate their activity levels, control their impulsive behaviors, and work consistently (Gomez & Sanson, 1994). Some of the more common factors are (Barkley, 1997b):

❖ the time of day and whether the child is tired
❖ whether the task is a complex one that requires organizational strategies
❖ the amount of behavioral restraint required by the task
❖ the amount and level of stimulation within the situation
❖ the immediacy of feedback and consequences associated with the task
❖ whether the task is performed without adult supervision

It is very difficult for the child with ADHD to perform tasks that are boring, distasteful, or complex, or that contain highly salient or novel distractions. Additionally, ADHD symptoms are more likely to occur in public places such as a restaurant, church, or synagogue; in frustrating situations at home such as when a parent is on the phone; and at school when projects require task-directed persistence, such as working on a series of math problems. In contrast, ADHD symptoms occur less frequently during unstructured play, in novel or unfamiliar circumstances such as a medical exam, and during school periods that do not require task-directed persistence, such as recess, lunch, special events, and field trips (Barkley, 1996).

PREVALENCE AND COURSE
Prevalence

ADHD is one of the most common referral problems to child guidance clinics in the United States, with as many as one-third to one-half of all clinic-referred children displaying ADHD symptoms either alone or in combination with other disorders (Barkley, 1990). It is difficult to determine precisely how many children are affected by ADHD. Estimates vary widely—from as low as 1% to as high as 20% of all school-age children. The best current estimate is that ADHD affects about 3% to 5% of all school-age children: as many as 2 million or more children in North America. An average of one child in every classroom requires help for this problem (APA, 1994; Szatmari, 1992). However, estimates of the prevalence of ADHD are a function of a number of factors: how the disorder is defined, who is consulted, the child's gender, and cultural and ethnic factors.

How the Disorder Is Defined.

Almost all children display symptoms of inattention and hyperactivity-impulsivity at certain times and in some situations. If children who display only one or two ADHD symptoms were considered hyperactive, the label would apply to nearly two-thirds of all children (Barkley, 1996). However, when DSM-IV criteria are used and ADHD is defined as a persistent and impairing disorder, then prevalence estimates usually fall in the 3% to 5% range.

Whom You Ask. The reports of parents, teachers, and physicians are all used to identify children with ADHD. But these adults don't always agree because the child's behavior may differ according to setting. Also, different adults may emphasize different symptoms when making a judgment. Teachers, for example, are especially likely to rate a child as inattentive when oppositional symptoms are also present (Abikoff, Courtney, Pelham, & Koplewicz, 1993). Since adults are likely to disagree, prevalence estimates are much higher when they are based on just one person's opinion than when they reflect a consensus (Lambert, Sandoval, & Sassone, 1978).

Gender. ADHD occurs much more frequently in boys than in girls. Estimates range from 2% to 3% for girls and from 6% to 9% for boys in the 6- to 12-year age range. In adolescence, the overall estimates of ADHD drop for both boys and girls, but boys still outnumber girls by a ratio of about 2:1 or 3:1.

In community samples, boys are 3 times more likely to be diagnosed as having ADHD than are girls. This discrepancy is even greater in clinic populations, where boys outnumber girls by a ratio of 6:1 or higher. Boys with ADHD are probably referred more frequently than girls because of their related symptoms of defiance and aggression. In fact, one study found that once these antisocial symptoms are controlled for statistically, the frequency of ADHD in boys and girls is about the same (Szatmari, 1992).

It is also possible that ADHD in girls may go unrecognized and is underreported. Teachers usually fail to recognize and report inattentive patterns of behavior unless they are also accompanied by the disruptive symptoms normally associated with boys (McGee & Feehan, 1991). Interestingly, when ADHD girls do display oppositional symptoms, they may be referred at a younger age than boys, a finding that implies lower adult tolerance or greater concern for these behaviors when they occur in girls than in boys (Silverthorn, Frick, Kuper, & Ott, 1996). These findings suggest that sampling and referral biases may contribute to ADHD's being reported to occur more often in boys than in girls. However, the extent to which these biases can explain gender differences in the prevalence of ADHD is not known at this time.

The kinds of symptoms used to make a diagnosis of ADHD may also contribute to the apparent higher incidence among boys. DSM-IV checklists were devel-

Girls with ADHD may be described by their teachers as "spacey" or "in a fog." Without hyperactivity and disruptive behavior, ADHD in girls may go unrecognized or be ignored.

oped and tested mostly with boys with ADHD, and many symptoms, such as excessive running around, climbing, and blurting out answers in class, are more common in boys than in girls. Thus, girls with ADHD may need to behave in ways that are not only more extreme but also uncharacteristic of their same-sex peers, making it less likely that they will be referred and diagnosed as having ADHD (Barkley, 1996).

Girls with ADHD are a highly understudied group, although the way in which the disorder is expressed and the severity of most symptoms are similar for boys and girls (Silverthorn et al., 1996). Boys and girls with ADHD do not differ in impulsivity, academic performance, social functioning, or fine motor skills, and they display comparable patterns of parent-child interaction, have similar family histories of psychopathology and similar rates of ADHD in relatives, and show the same response to stimulant medications (Befera & Barkley, 1984; Faraone, Biederman, Keenen, & Tsuang, 1991; Hinshaw, 1994). When gender differences are found, boys show more hyperactivity, more accompanying aggression and antisocial behavior, and greater impairment in executive functions; girls show greater verbal and nonverbal intellectual impairment (Gaub & Carlson, 1997b; Seidman, Biederman, Faraone, & Weber, 1997). The potential confounding effects of referral bias and comorbidity make findings related to gender differences in ADHD uncertain. Controlled studies of girls with ADHD are needed to resolve issues related to gender differences and to better understand the expression and developmental course of ADHD in girls (Arnold, 1996).

Culture and Ethnicity. Although ADHD affects members of all social classes, there are slightly more children with ADHD in lower SES groups than in higher ones. Such differences in prevalence, however, are best accounted for by the co-occurrence of ADHD with antisocial disorders, which are known to be related to both family adversity and SES (Szatmari et al., 1989).

ADHD has been identified in every country around the world in which it has been studied (Barkley, 1996). Estimates of the prevalence of ADHD across cultures vary widely, ranging from 2% for girls in Japan (Kanbayashi, Nakata, Fujii, Kita, & Wada, 1994), to 20% for boys in Italy (O'Leary, Vivian, and Nisi, 1985), to a high of over 29% for boys in India (Bhatia, Nigam, Bohra, & Malik, 1991). These variations undoubtedly reflect differences in the ages and gender of the children studied and the way in which ADHD is defined. For example, the prevalence of ADHD is extremely low in England because the label is used narrowly to describe children who display excessive motor overactivity that is pervasive across situations (Pendergrast et al., 1988).

Differences across cultures may also relate to cultural norms and differences in tolerance for symptoms of ADHD. In cultures that value reserved and inhibited patterns of child behavior, such as Thailand, symptoms of ADHD are less common than in the United States. Moreover, when ADHD symptoms do occur, teachers in Thailand view them as more problematic, perhaps as a reflection of their culture-linked values and expectations (Weisz, Chayaisit, Weiss, Eastman, & Jackson, 1995). Even within the United States, where ADHD is diagnosed in children of all races and ethnic groups, rates of hyperactivity may be related to cultural differences (Ross & Ross, 1982). It is safe to conclude that ADHD is a universal phenomenon that is reported to occur more frequently in boys than girls in every culture in which it has been studied.

Course and Outcome

The behaviors of children with ADHD of different ages are naturally very different in frequency, severity, and type. Although most children with ADHD will have problems throughout their lives, their symptoms tend to decline in prevalence and intensity as they grow older, because inattention and hyperactivity-impulsivity decline with age in *all* children. As many as 25% to 50% of children with ADHD *do* outgrow their problem or learn to cope with it effectively. As you might guess, these are children whose symptoms are less severe than others, who show fewer hyperactive-impulsive symptoms, and who do not experience accompanying disorders, particularly oppositional and conduct disorders (Hart, Lahey, Loeber, Applegate, & Frick, 1996).

The extent to which the observed decline in the diagnosis of ADHD with age is real and how much reflects the unsuitability of DSM-IV symptoms for diagnosing ADHD in older individuals is unclear (Barkley, 1996). For example, some symptoms, such as running, climbing, and leaving one's seat, seem especially unsuitable for assessing the behavior of adolescents and adults with ADHD. As we noted earlier, the DSM-IV symptom lists are unadjusted for age and thus do not take into account changes related to an increasing level of maturity. The prevalence of ADHD at different ages might prove to be more stable if the number and/or type of symptoms required for the diagnosis were adjusted for age (Barkley, 1996).

In the usual development of ADHD, the child's hyperactive-impulsive symptoms appear first, usually at 3 to 4 years of age, and continue throughout early and middle childhood (Hart et al., 1996). By the time children with ADHD are in grade school, at 5 to 7 years of age, they begin to encounter difficulties with sustained attention. The symptoms of hyperactivity-impulsivity decline with age during the elementary school years, but inattention remains relatively stable. All symptoms are likely to show some decline by adolescence (Hart et al., 1996).

Infancy

Ian: Off and Running

I was born on Labor Day several days earlier than expected. Mom says that during my first six months I was a good, happy baby, waiting quietly in my crib for her to come to me. Our baby-sitter swears I was sitting up watching TV by 4 months. Then from a crawling position I ran, and we were off. . . . I was all over the house, into everything, and Mom soon realized I could not be left alone. Darting here, there, and anywhere, I didn't like playing with my toys, preferring to explore on my own. (Adapted from Murray, 1993)

It is likely that ADHD is present at birth (some mothers have even reported that their children were so overactive in the womb that the kicking nearly knocked them over!). However, we do not know precisely what form ADHD takes during infancy because reliable and valid methods for identifying the disorder prior to 3 years of age are simply not available. When parents of an older child with ADHD are asked to describe what their child was like as a baby, they often say that their infant had a **difficult temperament**—extremely active, unpredictable, over- or undersensitive to stimulation, and irritable, with erratic sleep patterns or feeding difficulties. Such statements by parents indicate the presence of ADHD very early in the child's development. However, there are two problems with interpreting these reports. First, parents'

recollections of early development may be colored by the child's current difficulties. Second, and perhaps more critical, is that most infants who display these patterns *do not* go on to develop ADHD. Although difficult infant temperament may indicate something amiss in development, it cannot by itself be taken as an early sign of ADHD.

Preschool

Alan: Singled Out in Kindergarten

I often wondered why I wasn't in group time in kindergarten. The teacher sent me in the corner to play with a toy by myself. Because of being singled out I didn't have many friends. I was different, but I didn't know why or what it was. (Barkley, 1995)

ADHD is increasingly visible at 3 to 4 years of age. Preschool children with ADHD usually display a negative temperament, acting suddenly without thinking, dashing from activity to activity, grabbing at immediate rewards; they are easily bored and react strongly and negatively to routine events (Barkley, DuPaul, & McMurray, 1990; Campbell, 1990). Parents find it very hard to manage the activity and noncompliance of their children, who may also be defiant and aggressive. During the preschool years, the interactions of parents and children with ADHD are especially likely to be characterized by conflict, negativity, and struggles for control (Mash & Johnston, 1982).

The preschool child with ADHD often roams about the classroom, talking excessively and disrupting other children's activities. Even at this early age, deficits in the child's academic skills and adaptive functioning are apparent (Mariani & Barkley, 1997). Preschoolers who show significant amounts of hyperactive-impulsive behavior, who are difficult to manage and oppositional, and who *persist in this pattern for at least a year or more* are likely to have ADHD. More often than not, their difficulties will continue into the elementary school years (Barkley, 1996; Campbell, 1990).

Elementary School

Alan: I Couldn't Do Anything Right

Toward the middle half of the first grade the teacher called my Mom in for a conference. She was telling my Mom, "I'm always having to call on Alan. 'Alan, be still. Please. Yes, you can sharpen your pencil for the third time. You have to go to the bathroom again?'" By the time I got to third grade things were getting off track. I felt like nothing I did was right. I would try to do good work. My teacher would write on my papers, "Needs to concentrate more on answers," "Needs to turn in all work," "Needs to follow directions." I really didn't think my teacher liked me. She was very stern, never seemed to smile, and was always watching me. (Barkley, 1995)

Symptoms of ADHD become especially evident when the child starts school. Classroom demands for focused attention and goal-directed persistence are formidable challenges for children with ADHD. Not surprisingly, this is when children are usually identified as having ADHD and are referred for special assistance. The hyperactive-impulsive behaviors that were present in preschool continue, with some decline, during the years from 6 to 12. The symptoms of inattention that emerge at 5 to 7 years of age continue through grade school, manifesting in low academic productivity, distractibility, poor organization, trouble meeting deadlines, and an inability to follow through on social promises or commitments to peers (Barkley, 1996).

During elementary school, oppositional defiant behaviors may develop in as many as 40% to 70% of children with ADHD (Barkley, 1990). By 8 to 12 years of age, defiant and hostile behavior may take the form of serious problems, such as lying or aggression, in as many as half of children with ADHD. Through the school years, ADHD increasingly takes its toll on children's overall adjustment and functioning as they experience problems with self-care, personal responsibility, chores, trustworthiness, independence, social relationships, and academic performance (Barkley, 1996; Hinshaw, Herbsman, Melnick, Nigg, & Simmel, 1993; Koplowicz & Barkley, 1995; Stein, Szumoski, Blondis, & Roizen, 1995).

Adolescence. Most children with ADHD do not outgrow their problems when they reach adolescence, and sometimes problems can get much worse. The following comments by a mother of a teenage boy with ADHD illustrate this point:

A Parent's Viewpoint

It wasn't until my son was thirteen that I understood that ADHD was a lifelong condition. My son's inability to block out the high level of activity

in junior high caused him to become a frequent visitor to the principal's office. And he began to do poorly in math, the subject he had always done well at, because he couldn't concentrate on all the steps involved. I had him thoroughly evaluated for ADHD and discovered he wasn't outgrowing it. In fact, it was causing him more trouble, not less. And during the course of my son's evaluation, his father, by then my ex-husband, was evaluated as having it too. It was then that I realized how ADHD shapes personality, torments the victims, and fragments relationships. (Adapted from L. Weiss, 1992)

Although hyperactive-impulsive behaviors decline significantly by the time the child with ADHD reaches adolescence, these behaviors still occur at a level higher than in 95% of same-age peers (Barkley, 1996). The disorder continues into adolescence for as many as 50% to 80% of clinic-referred elementary school children (Barkley, Fisher, Edelbrock & Smallish, 1990; Gittelman, Mannuzza, Shenker, & Bonagura, 1985; Klein & Mannuzza, 1991; Weiss & Hechtman, 1993). About three out of four boys diagnosed with ADHD at ages 7 to 12 meet diagnostic criteria at ages 10 to 15 (Barkley et al., 1990; Hart et al., 1996). Childhood symptoms of hyperactivity-impulsivity (more so than those of inattention) are generally related to adolescent outcomes (Barkley, 1996).

Adulthood.   Some youngsters with clinically diagnosed ADHD either outgrow their disorder or learn to cope effectively with it. Although difficult to confirm, many well-known and highly successful adults, ranging from Thomas Edison to Robin Williams, have been suspected of having had ADHD as children. However, for most children and adolescents, ADHD will continue to cause significant social, psychological, and adjustment problems that can lead to a lifelong pattern of suffering and disappointment. Jeremy's case is a good example:

Jeremy: Still Not Organized After 10 Years

My file cabinet symbolizes my inadequacy for me. Ten years ago I was going to straighten it out. Now, ten years later, the file cabinet still isn't straightened out. . . . It makes me feel ashamed and inadequate. It makes me feel frustrated and helpless. How big a deal is it to organize a file cabinet? We're not talking about brain surgery . . . I feel like I'm not a grownup yet. (L. Weiss, 1992)

Until recently ADHD was thought of as a children's disorder. However, as many as 30% to 50% or more of children with ADHD continue to have the disorder as adults, and rates are even higher in clinic-referred samples (Barkley, 1996; Mannuzza & Klein, 1992). In addition, as many as 25% of clinic-referred children with ADHD will also meet diagnosis for antisocial personality disorder (see Chapter 6) in adulthood (Biederman et al., 1992; Mannuzza & Klein, 1992).

Although this situation may be changing, many adults with ADHD have never been diagnosed, particularly those without accompanying behavior problems. As a result they may feel that something is wrong with them, but they don't know what it is. Since many are bright and creative individuals, they often feel frustrated about not living up to their potential. Many adults with ADHD are restless and easily bored, constantly seeking novelty and excitement; they may experience impaired social relations and suffer from major depression, low self-concept, and substance abuse (Weiss & Hechtman, 1993).

THEORIES OF ADHD

Numerous explanations for ADHD have been advanced, some of them highly controversial. For example, it has been argued (without much support) that ADHD is a trait left over from our evolutionary past as hunters (Hartmann, 1993; see Box 5.4). Others have argued that ADHD is a myth, a disorder that has been fabricated because as a society we *need* it (Armstrong, 1995).

Despite much attention to questions about the nature and causes of ADHD, clear answers have been elusive, because diagnostic practices are not standardized and research strategies have been inadequate. Recent, better-controlled research has shed new light on the basic nature of ADHD and led to fascinating theories about possible underlying mechanisms and possible causes.

Theories of ADHD emphasize one or more underlying processes to account for core symptoms, performance variability, and associated academic and social difficulties. The most intriguing theories focus on deficits in motivation, arousal level, self-regulation, and behavioral inhibition. An overview of these interrelated theories is provided in Box 5.5.

Deficits in Motivation

Some investigators argue that ADHD is best viewed as a motivational deficit (Glow & Glow, 1979). Theories of motivation deficit are varied: ADHD may arise from poor stimulus control, deficient rule-governed behavior, a diminished sensitivity to rewards, or, most commonly, a heightened sensitivity to rewards (Barkley, 1989;

Box 5.4

Hail to the Hyperactive Hunter?

ADHD may have evolved in the first place because, like the sickle-cell trait, which can help thwart malaria, attention deficit confers an advantage in certain circumstances. In *Attention Deficit Disorder: A Different Perception,* Thom Hartmann has laid out a controversial but appealing theory that the characteristics known today as ADHD were vitally important in early hunting societies and became a mixed blessing only when culture turned agrarian. "If you are walking in the night and see a little flash, distractibility would be a tremendous asset. Snap decision making, which we call impulsiveness, is a survival skill if you are a hunter." For a farmer, however, the trait would be disastrous. 'If this is the perfect day to plant the crops, you can't suddenly decide to wander off into the woods.'

Modern society, Hartmann contends, generally favors the farmer mentality, rewarding those who develop plans, plod through schedules, and meet deadlines. But there's still a place for hunters, says the author, who counts himself as one: they can be found in large numbers among entrepreneurs, police detectives, emergency-room personnel, race-car drivers and, of course, those who stalk the high-stakes jungle known as Wall Street.

Source: Wallis, 1994.
Comment: Hartmann's analysis is based on a view of the traits of hunters that is not shared by all. While such theories may sound plausible, Shelley-Tremblay and Rosen (1996) point out that primitive hunters may have needed stealth, concentration, silence, and a keen sense of the environment—not snap decision making! (While we're speculating, any thoughts about hyperactive gatherers?)

Haenlein & Caul, 1987). Children with ADHD have been shown to perform well when rewards are frequent but otherwise become frustrated and do poorly (Douglas & Parry, 1983, 1994). However, not all studies have replicated these findings (Barber, Milich, & Welsh, 1996; Pelham, Milich, & Walker, 1987). Results are highly dependent on the types of procedures and rewards used to investigate this issue.

General explanations of ADHD as based on motivational deficits may unintentionally attribute laziness or disinterest as reasons for the child's unmotivated behavior. The current consensus is that to explain ADHD in terms of a motivational deficit is not very satisfying, has not met wide acceptance, and has not led to much new research (Barkley, 1997d; Hinshaw, 1994).

Deficits in Arousal Level

The **optimal stimulation theory** of ADHD contends that hyperactivity arises from a low level of arousal. From this perspective, hyperactivity is seen as an underaroused

Box 5.5

An Overview of Theories of Attention-Deficit/Hyperactivity Disorder

❖ **Deficits in Motivation** Children with ADHD display a deficit in their sensitivity to rewards and punishments, most typically, a heightened sensitivity to rewards. As a result, the child's performance deteriorates when rewards are infrequent.

❖ **Deficits in Arousal Level** Children with ADHD have an abnormal level of arousal, either too high or, more commonly, too low. Hyperactivity reflects an underaroused child's effort to maintain an optimal level of arousal by excessive self-stimulation.

❖ **Deficits in Self-Regulation** Children with ADHD have a higher-order deficit in their ability to self-regulate: to use thought and language to direct behavior. Deficient self-regulation leads to impulsivity, poor maintenance of effort, deficient modulation of arousal level, and attraction to immediate rewards.

❖ **Deficits in Behavioral Inhibition** Children with ADHD have a fundamental deficit in their ability to inhibit a likely response or an ongoing behavior. This core deficit in behavioral inhibition is the basis for the many cognitive, language, and motor difficulties of children with ADHD.

child's effort to maintain an optimal level of arousal by self-stimulation (Zentall, 1985). This theory has received some support. However, it has not yet been presented as a comprehensive model to account for the full range of problems found in children with ADHD.

Deficits in Self-Regulation

Some theories emphasize higher-order difficulties in self-regulation as the basis for such characteristics of ADHD as hyperactivity-impulsivity, a lack of consistent and sustained allocation of effort and attention, deficient modulation of arousal to meet changing situational demands, a lack of preparation to process and respond to task stimuli, and a strong inclination to seek immediate rewards (Douglas, 1988, in press). Self-regulation is mediated by the frontal lobes of the brain, particularly the prefrontal areas of the cortex. Neuropsychological evidence suggests decreased frontal lobe functioning for some children with ADHD, although findings are not always consistent (Barkley, Grodzinsky, & DuPaul, 1992; Zametkin et al., 1990).

One self-regulatory deficit that has received attention is seen in children who fail to use internalized or private speech to regulate their behavior. During the preschool and early school years, the following develop-

mental sequence in the acquisition of self-regulation occurs (Luria, 1961; Vygotsky, 1962). First, the child's behavior is regulated by adults who provide verbal directions and prohibitions—adults tell the child what to do and what not to do. Second, adults' commands and prohibitions are learned by the child, who begins to regulate her own behavior using overt speech—she talks to herself out loud. Finally, verbal control becomes internal or private—it goes underground. The child exerts control over her own behavior by talking silently to herself—that is, by thinking. Such internalized or private self-speech becomes increasingly automatic as a mechanism for self-regulation.

Delays in children's use of private speech may be associated with impulsivity and a lack of inhibition. The fact that children with ADHD show early delays in both receptive and expressive language provides indirect support for this view (Beitchman, Hood, & Inglis, 1990). Grade-school children with ADHD display private speech less often than other children, especially during tasks that require effortful responding (Berk, 1994; Berk & Potts, 1991).

Some therapists have attempted to increase self-regulation by systematically teaching impulsive children how to talk to themselves during effortful tasks. In the following example the therapist performed the task, which required copying line patterns, while modeling the following self-instructions for the child:

> Okay, what is it I have to do? You want me to copy the picture with the different lines. I have to go slowly and carefully. Okay, draw the line down, down, good; then to the right, that's it; now down some more and to the left. Good, I'm doing fine so far. Remember, go slowly. Now back up again. No, I was supposed to go down. That's okay. Just erase the line carefully. . . . Good. Even if I make an error I can go on slowly and carefully. I have to go down now. Finished. I did it! (Meichenbaum & Goodman, 1971)

Although children with ADHD may underuse internalized speech, or thought, to regulate their behavior, we cannot draw a clear causal sequence from poor internalization of speech and language delay to the symptoms of ADHD. Age-inappropriate levels of hyperactive-impulsive behaviors are often present early in development, sometimes before internalized speech occurs. Early ADHD symptoms might easily disrupt the parent-child interactions that, hypothetically, lead to private speech.

Deficits in Behavioral Inhibition

Theories of deficits in **behavioral inhibition** propose that the difficulties of children with ADHD (excluding those who are predominantly inattentive) stem from a fundamental inability to delay their initial reactions to events

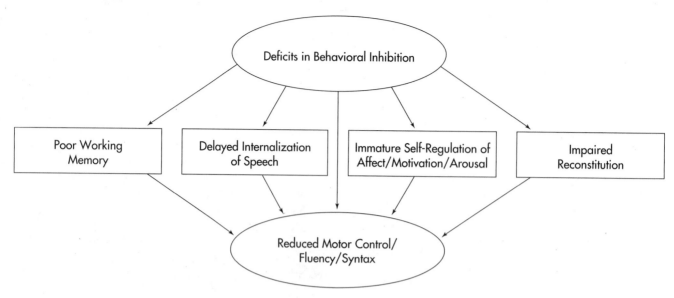

FIGURE 5.2 A model of the impairments in cognitive functioning predicted to be associated with the deficits in behavioral inhibition that characterize children with ADHD. (Barkley, 1997a)

or to stop their behavior once it gets going. Such behavior has been likened to a ballistic missile—once fired, there's no turning back (Logan, 1994). Barkley (1997a, 1997d) has recently proposed that the cognitive, emotional, language, analytic, and motor control difficulties of children with ADHD reflect a primary deficit in behavioral inhibition (see Figure 5.2). He contends that the child with ADHD's basic inability to wait before responding interferes very early in life with the development of five important executive functions (Barkley, 1997d):

❖ *working memory/prolongation:* the ability to hold events and ideas in memory and to use them to organize future behavior in relation to past experience; sense of time

❖ *internalization of speech:* using private speech in the service of rule-governed behavior

❖ *self-regulation of affect/motivation/arousal:* the ability to regulate emotions and arousal level in support of goal-directed behavior

❖ *reconstitution:* analysis and synthesis of information, generating ideas, creativity

❖ *motor control/fluency/syntax:* motor fluency, goal-directed performance, and persistence

Although theories of deficits in behavioral inhibition differ somewhat in how they view the basic nature of the inhibitory dysfunction in children with ADHD, evidence continues to accumulate concerning the importance of inhibitory problems for these children (Schachar, Tannock, & Logan, 1993; Tannock, 1998). Since the ability

to inhibit behavior seems to be controlled by areas in the front part of the brain, and injuries to this area are associated with deficits in the ability to inhibit and control behavior (Fuster, 1989), ADHD would appear to stem from a fundamental neurobiological deficit. Although many of the specific predictions of models of deficits in behavioral inhibition have yet to be tested, there is a substantial and growing body of research findings in support of this general theory (Barkley, 1997a, 1997d; Gray, 1982; McBurnett, 1992; Quay, 1988, 1997).

CAUSES OF ADHD

Understandably, one of the first questions that comes to mind when you learn that a child has ADHD is "Why?" or "What went wrong?" Numerous causes for ADHD have been proposed. However, many of them have not been adequately tested or have fallen by the wayside in the face of weak, inconsistent, or nonexistent support, including theories that ADHD is caused by too much sugar, food allergies, yeast, fluorescent lighting, motion sickness, bad parenting, poor school environment, urban living, or too much TV (would you believe tight underwear?).

If by *cause* we mean the direct, necessary, and sufficient conditions that lead to the disorder, then no one knows exactly what causes ADHD. There are likely to be numerous causes and in the vast majority of cases it is not possible to identify a primary one with any degree of certainty. However, several factors have been

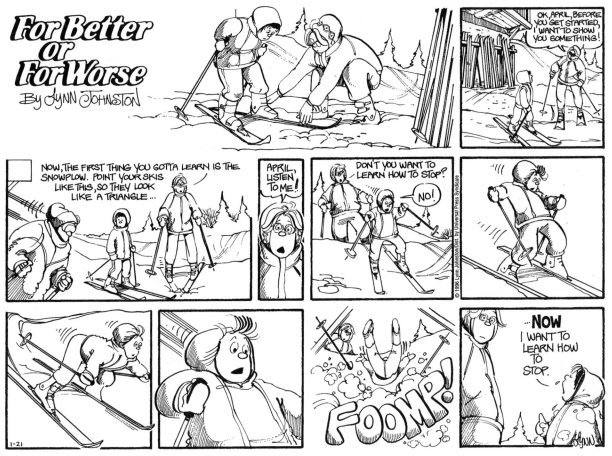

© Lynn Johnston, Inc./Dist. by United Features Syndicate, Inc.

identified that are *related to* an increased risk of the disorder (Hinshaw, 1994). Recent research into causes has emphasized biological factors that have a direct effect on brain development and functioning, with a rapidly growing literature on genetics and neuroimaging (Tannock, 1998). However, the precise causal pathways by which biological factors result in ADHD are still not known. Even if biological causal pathways are identified, it is crucial to remember that biological and environmental risk factors, family functioning, as well as school, community, and cultural influences *together* shape the expression of ADHD symptoms over time. Therefore, any explanation of ADHD that focuses on a single cause is likely to provide an incomplete picture of the disorder. Transactional models that emphasize complex causal pathways of interacting biological and environmental risk factors, precipitating events, and maintaining conditions in determining the expression and outcome for the disorder are needed (Hinshaw, 1994; Tannock, 1998). However, available data do not yet permit an integration of these many factors into a comprehensive model of ADHD.

Genetic Contributions

Although specific genetic abnormalities are rare in children with ADHD, other lines of evidence point to heredity as an important causal factor. First, ADHD runs in families (Hechtman, 1994). In fact, a child with ADHD may be described by his parents as "a chip off the old block" or "just like his dad." Some parents of children with ADHD may not initially see their child's behavior as a problem, because it so closely resembles their own. As many as 35% of the immediate and extended family members of children with ADHD are also likely to have ADHD, including 32% of siblings (Faraone & Biederman, 1994; Faraone, Biederman, & Milberger, 1996). Of fathers who had ADHD as children, one-third of their offspring have ADHD (Biederman et al., 1992; Pauls, 1991; Welner, Welner, Stewart, Palkes, & Wish, 1977).

Recent studies of biologically related and unrelated pairs of adoptees have found a strong genetic influence that accounts for nearly half of the variance in attention-problem scores on commonly used child behavior rating scales (van den Oord, Boomsma, & Verhulst, 1994). Findings from twin studies provide further evidence for genetic influences on ADHD (Sherman, Iacono, & McGue, 1997; Sherman, McGue, & Iacono, 1997). Both the symptoms and diagnosis of ADHD have a much higher concordance rate for monozygotic (MZ) than for dizygotic twins (O'Connor, Foch, Sherry, & Plomin, 1980). On average, identical twins have concordance rates for ADHD of about 65%, in comparison with rates of 29% for fraternal twins (Gilger, Pennington, & DeFries, 1992). Estimates of the heritability of ADHD are very high, averaging .80 or higher (Tannock, 1998). Twin studies also suggest that the greater the severity of ADHD symptoms, the greater the genetic contributions (Stevenson, 1992). Twin studies add considerable weight to findings from family and adoption studies in support of a strong genetic basis for ADHD (Barkley, 1996; Edelbrock, Rende, Plomin & Thompson, 1995; Levy & Hay, 1992; Tannock, 1998).

Although the evidence for genetic transmission of ADHD is convincing, the mode of inheritance is unclear. Quantitative genetic analyses of a large sample of families of children with ADHD suggest that a single gene may account for the expression of ADHD in *some* children (Faraone et al., 1992). However, general support for a single gene locus for ADHD is lacking at this time. A rare autosomal disorder that results in a generalized resistance to thyroid hormone (GRTH) has been related to a diagnosis of ADHD in the affected families (Hauser et al., 1993), although this genetic linkage has not been supported in recent studies (e.g., Valentine et al., 1997). Moreover, this genetic condition is extremely rare and would not account for most cases in which ADHD occurs. Nevertheless, the importance of thyroid hormone for the normal development of those brain structures in which abnormalities have been identified in children with ADHD, as well as the relationships between thyroid hormone levels and symptoms of hyperactivity (but not inattention), suggest that the possible link between ADHD and thyroid dysfunction warrants further study (Hauser, Soler, Brucker-Davis, & Weintraub, 1997; Tannock, 1998).

Studies that have looked for specific genes associated with ADHD have focused on those within the dopamine system, for two primary reasons. First, medications that reduce ADHD symptoms act primarily on the dopaminergic and noradrenergic systems. Second, brain structures implicated in ADHD are rich with dopamine innervation. Early research implicated the dopamine type 2 gene and its increased association with alcoholism, Tourette's disorder, and ADHD (Comings et al., 1991). However, findings related to this gene have not been replicated (Barkley, 1996). Preliminary studies have found a relation between the *dopamine transporter gene*

(DAT) and ADHD (Cook et al., 1995; Gill et al., 1997), although these findings are based on small samples of children with high levels of comorbidity and need to be interpreted cautiously. However, the dopamine transporter gene is of particular interest because many drugs used to treat ADHD inhibit the dopamine transporter.

Recent studies have also focused on the gene that codes for the dopamine receptor gene (DRD4), which has been linked to the personality trait of novelty, or sensation seeking (high levels of thrill-seeking, impulsive, exploratory, and excitable behavior) (Benjamin et al., 1996; Ebstein et al., 1996). Some children with ADHD tested for this gene show a genetic pattern of extra replications of trinucleotides (LaHoste et al., 1996). This finding is of interest because more replications are associated with a blunted response to dopamine signals and less inhibited behavior.

Despite their preliminary nature, the findings that implicate genes within the dopamine system in ADHD are intriguing and consistent with a model suggesting that hypo-dopaminergic activity may be related to the behavioral symptoms of ADHD. In the vast majority of cases, the heritable components of ADHD are likely to be polygenic, the result of multiple interacting genes on several different chromosomes. However, the connection of even a single gene and ADHD in a small minority of individuals is of interest in linking the behavioral deficits to a single protein.

Neurobiological Factors

Several indirect and direct lines of support exist for the possible role of neurobiological factors as a primary cause of ADHD (Barkley, 1996). *Indirect* evidence for the role of neurobiological factors includes (1) the early onset and the persistence of ADHD symptoms over time, (2) the relationship between ADHD symptoms and peri- and postnatal events and diseases that are known to negatively affect brain development, (3) the finding that exposure to certain environmental toxins known to affect neurological status (such as lead) may produce symptoms of ADHD, (4) the association between ADHD and other developmental disorders thought to be related to neurological impairment (e.g., learning disabilities and language disorders), and (5) the possible relation between symptoms of ADHD and certain signs of neurological immaturity such as clumsiness, poor balance and coordination, and abnormal reflexes. Further indirect support for the role of neurobiological factors is derived from (1) the dramatic improvement in ADHD symptoms produced by stimulant medications known to directly affect the central nervous system; (2) the similarity between the symptoms of ADHD and the symptoms associated with lesions to the prefrontal cortex, including deficits in sustained attention, inhibition, regulation of emotion and motivation, and organization of behavior over time (Fuster, 1989; Grattan & Eslinger, 1991); and (3) the deficient performances of children with ADHD on neuropsychological tests associated with prefrontal lobe functions, such as inhibition, persistence, working memory, motor control and fluency, and verbal fluency (Barkley, Grodzinsky, & DuPaul, 1992). Any one of these indirect observations or findings is far from conclusive. However, their cumulative weight gives strong support to neurobiological factors as possible causes for ADHD.

More *direct* evidence for the connection between ADHD and brain function comes from three sources (Barkley, 1996, 1997a). First, studies that have obtained psychophysiological measures of nervous system activity, including electroencephalographic, galvanic skin response, and heart rate deceleration, have consistently found differences between children with ADHD and controls. These findings support the idea that children with ADHD show diminished arousal or arousability. Second, studies using evoked response potential (ERP) measures of brain activity during children's performances on vigilance tests have found that children with ADHD have smaller amplitudes in the late components of their responses than other children (Frank, Lazar, & Seiden, 1992; Klorman, Salzman, & Borgstedt, 1988). These late components are believed to be a function of the prefrontal areas of the brain and are corrected by stimulant medication. ERP findings suggest that children with ADHD are underresponsive to stimulus events (Barkley, 1996). Third, studies of cerebral blood flow in children with and without ADHD have found decreased blood flow to the prefrontal regions and the pathways connecting these regions to the limbic system via the caudate and specifically its anterior region, known as the striatum (Lou, Henriksen, Bruhn, Borner, & Nielson, 1989).

Brain Abnormalities.

Neuroimaging studies make it possible to test neurobiological theories about the causes of ADHD. CT scan studies have not found differences between ADHD and normal children in overall brain structure (Shaywitz, Shaywitz, Byrne, Cohen, & Rothman, 1983). However, recent MRI studies suggest structural abnormalities in two primary brain regions: the corpus callosum and the frontostriatal circuitry. These regions of the brain and the specific structures implicated are shown in Figure 5.3. Most studies have found that individuals with ADHD have a smaller **corpus callosum**—the area of the brain that assists with the transfer of information between hemispheres—although findings are inconsistent with respect to the specific regions involved (Baumgard-

ner et al., 1996; Castellanos et al., 1996a; Giedd et al., 1994; Hynd et al., 1991: Semrud-Clikeman et al., 1994).

Other MRI studies have focused on the structure of the **frontostriatal circuitry** (prefrontal cortex and basal ganglia). These areas of the brain are associated with attention, executive functions, delayed responding, and response organization (Castellanos et al., 1996a). Lesions in this region are associated with symptoms similar to ADHD. Children with ADHD have been found to have a smaller right prefrontal cortex than those without ADHD (Castellanos et al., 1994; Filipek et al., 1997; Hynd, Semrud-Clikeman, Lorys, Novey, & Eliopulos, 1990). Most studies of the basal ganglia have reported differences in caudate volumes in children with ADHD and a corresponding loss or reversal of symmetry compared with normal controls (Castellanos et al., 1994; Filipek et al., 1997; Hynd et al., 1993). However, the specific patterns of differences in caudate volume and assymetries have varied from study to study. Other findings of interest are that boys with ADHD do not show the age-related decreases in caudate volume usually found in males, have a smaller globus pallidus than normal controls, and show no differences in volume or symmetry of the putamen (Castellanos et al., 1996a, 1996b).

Although simple direct relationships cannot be assumed between brain size and abnormal function, significant correlations have been reported between localized irregularities in brain structure and behavioral functioning in children with ADHD. For example, recent work has found performance on response inhibition tasks to be correlated with anatomic measures of the frontostriatal circuitry that we have just described as abnormal in children with ADHD (prefrontal cortex, caudate, and globus pallidus, but not the putamen), mainly in the right hemisphere of the brain (Casey et al., 1997). In general, these findings suggest that the right prefrontal cortex plays a role in suppressing responses to salient, but otherwise irrelevant, events, while the basal ganglia appear to be involved in executing these behavioral responses.

Studies of brain structure in children with ADHD using structural MRI are especially intriguing in that the specific abnormalities that have been identified are consistent with the theories (e.g., deficits in behavioral inhibition) and deficits (e.g., working memory, planning, rule-based learning) of ADHD that we have described. The fact that abnormalities in frontostriatal circuitry consistently turn up, despite many differences in samples and methods used, suggests the importance of this region of the brain in understanding ADHD.

PET scan studies that have measured the level of glucose used by the areas of the brain that inhibit impulses and control attention have found diminished

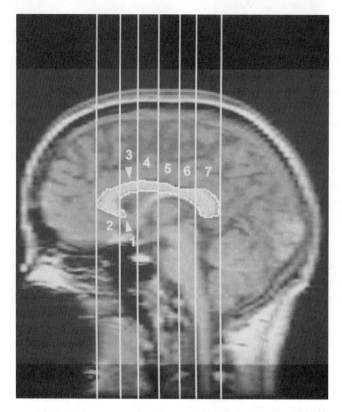

Corpus callosum

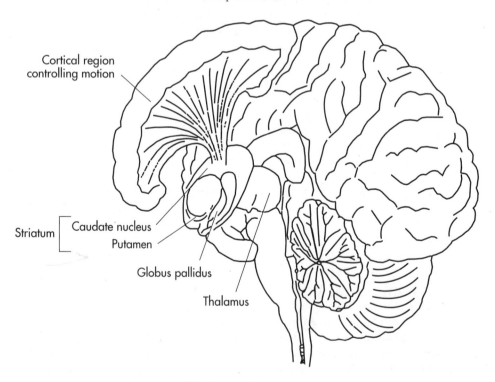

Right fronto-striatal circuitry

Diagram of the human brain showing the right hemisphere, and particularly the location of the striatum, globus pallidus, and thalamus. Most of the left hemisphere has been cut away up to the prefrontal lobes to reveal the striatum and other midbrain structures. (Adapted from an illustration by Carol Donner in Youdin and Riederer 1997.) Copyright 1997 by *Scientific American*. Adapted with permission.

FIGURE 5.3 Regions of the brain implicated in ADHD: (top) Corpus callosum: Semrud-Clikeman et al., 1994; (bottom) right frontostriatal circuitry: Youdin & Riederer, 1997.

glucose metabolism in adults with ADHD and in adolescent girls with ADHD (Ernst et al., 1994). Diminished metabolism has not been found, however, in adolescent boys with ADHD. The reasons that girls with ADHD seem to show greater brain metabolism abnormalities than boys is not known at this time. Significant correlations have also been noted between diminished metabolic activity in the left anterior frontal region and the *severity* of ADHD symptoms in adolescents with ADHD (Zametkin et al., 1993). Such findings are critical in establishing a link between specific brain regions and the hyperactive-impulsive behavior of children with ADHD, even though the nature of this evidence is correlational.

Most neuroimaging studies of individuals with ADHD to date have used small samples, produced variable findings, and been difficult to replicate. None has found evidence of brain damage in any of the structures studied. Where differences in brain activity or structure have been found between children with ADHD and controls, they are likely to be the result of abnormalities in brain development, the causes of which are unknown. In other words, neuroimaging studies tell us that in children with ADHD there is less activity or structural difference in certain regions of the brain, but they don't tell us why.

Neurophysiological and Neurochemical Findings. Consistent differences have not been found in the biochemistry of urine, plasma, blood, platelets, and cerebrospinal fluid of children with ADHD and comparison children (Zametkin & Rapoport, 1987). At a neurochemical level, the known action of effective medications for ADHD suggests that mediating neurotransmitters include the monoamines dopamine, norepinephrine, and epinephrine, and the indoleamine serotonin (McCracken, 1991; Shaywitz, Cohen, & Shaywitz, 1978; Zametkin & Rapoport, 1987). However, we must be cautious in drawing conclusions about causes from the effects of medications alone. Effective chemical treatment of ADHD symptoms does not prove that deficits in the drug or its action were the cause of the symptoms any more than the elimination of a headache by aspirin implies that the headache was caused by an aspirin deficiency. Medications may operate at levels of neurochemistry and neuroanatomy that are far removed from primary causal influences (Hinshaw, 1994).

Pregnancy, Birth, and Early Development

A number of occurrences before, near, and during birth may interfere with nervous system development. Retrospective studies have suggested numerous factors in early development that may be related to variations in the expression of ADHD symptoms. These include pre-, peri-, and postnatal complications; low birth weight; diseases of infancy; maternal smoking during pregnancy; early neurological insult or trauma; malnutrition; and other events that may compromise the development of the nervous system before and after birth (Cantwell & Hanna, 1989; Chandola, Robling, Peters, Melville-Thomas, & McGuffin, 1992; Milberger, Biederman, Faraone, Chen, & Jones, 1996). Although these early factors may predict later symptoms of ADHD, there is little evidence that they are specific to ADHD. These factors may elevate the child's risk of developing many forms of later psychopathology, not just ADHD.

Problems in early neural development are also noted in reports of an increased number of **minor physical anomalies** in children with ADHD (Rapoport, Quinn & Lamprecht, 1974; Waldrop, Bell, McLaughlin, & Halverson, 1978). Minor physical anomalies may be reflected in a head circumference out of the normal range, wide-spaced eyes, asymmetrical or low-set ears, or a wide gap between the first and second toes. These anomalies develop during the first few months prenatally, which indicates prenatal or genetic influences. Although an increased number of minor physical anomalies may constitute an elevated risk for many forms of child psychopathology, they have not been found to be a specific risk factor for ADHD.

A mother's use of cigarettes, alcohol, or other drugs during pregnancy can have damaging effects on her unborn child. Fetal alcohol syndrome (FAS) is a condition associated with low birth weight, mental retardation, and physical defects (see Chapter 9). Many children born with FAS display symptoms of hyperactivity, inattention, and impulsivity (Streissguth et al., 1984). It has been hypothesized that low or moderate levels of drinking by a mother during pregnancy, although not resulting in FAS, may lead to the behavioral impulsivity and associated impairments in learning and behavior that characterize children with ADHD (Brown, Coles, Platzman, & Hill, 1993). Other substances used during pregnancy, such as nicotine or cocaine (including the smokable form known as crack) can adversely affect the normal development of the brain (Nichols & Chen, 1981).

Mothers of children with ADHD use more alcohol and smoke more tobacco than control parents, even when they are not pregnant (Barkley, 1996). Since substance abuse is often associated with a chaotic home environment both before and after birth, it is difficult to disentangle the influence of this and other factors before birth that may affect early nervous system development, from the cumulative impact of a negative family environment during later development.

Environmental Toxins, Allergy, and Diet

Environmental toxins can interfere with brain development and function, which in turn may lead to ADHD. Exposure to low levels of lead is associated with small but significant deficits in intellectual performance and with ADHD symptoms in the classroom (Fergusson, Horwood, & Lynskey, 1993). Lead is found in dust, soil, and flaking paint in areas where leaded gasoline and paint were once used, and in some water pipes. However, most children with ADHD do not have significantly elevated body lead burdens, even though they may show levels higher than those of control children (Gittelman & Eskinazi, 1983). The correlation between body lead (in teeth or blood) and symptoms of ADHD is low, with body lead accounting for no more than 4% of the variance in ADHD symptoms (Barkley, 1996). Thus, the relationship between elevated body lead burden and ADHD is, although significant, at best a very weak one.

There has been widespread controversy about the possibility that allergic reactions and diet are causes of ADHD. This connection has not received much support to date (McGee, Stanton, & Sears, 1993). A popular view in the 1970s and 1980s was that food additives or refined sugar makes children hyperactive and inattentive. Parents were encouraged to withhold foods containing artificial flavorings, preservatives, and sugars. However, research findings do not support the role of food additives as a primary cause of ADHD (Conners, 1980; Kavale & Forness, 1983). Restricted diets help only about 5% of children with ADHD, mostly the very young and those with food allergies.

The relation of sugar to hyperactivity achieved epic significance when "What is sugar?" was the correct response to "The major cause of hyperactivity in North America" on the popular TV show *Jeopardy* (Barkley, 1995). However, study after study has conclusively shown that *sugar is not the cause of hyperactivity* (Milich, Wolraich, & Lindgren, 1986). So why do nearly half the parents and teachers who are asked think that children are sugar-sensitive? It may be the power of suggestion. In one study, mothers who believed their children were sugar-sensitive were told that their children would be given a drink of Kool-Aid containing either sugar or, as a placebo, the sugar-substitute aspartame. After the children drank their Kool-Aid, they and their mothers spent time playing and working together. In fact, none of the children was given sugar—all received Kool-Aid with aspartame. But the mothers who thought their children had received sugar rated them as more hyperactive than those who believed their children had received aspartame. Perhaps even more telling was that during play and work interactions, mothers who thought their children had received sugar were more

critical of them, hovered more, and talked to them more frequently (Hoover & Milich, 1994). These findings suggest that what parents believe about the causes of their children's ADHD can affect both their views of their children *and* the way in which they treat them.

Family Influences

There is no clear relationship between family life and ADHD. We know that not all children from unstable or dysfunctional families have ADHD, and not all children with ADHD come from dysfunctional homes. Genetic studies have found that family and environmental factors account for only a very small amount of the variance in ADHD symptoms, around 10% to 15% (Barkley, 1996). Explanations of ADHD that refer solely to negative family influences have been few and have received little support (Silverman & Ragusa, 1992; Willis & Lovaas, 1977). However, this doesn't mean that family influences are not important.

First, there is some evidence for a relationship between interfering and insensitive early care-giving by mothers and later symptoms of ADHD for a subgroup of children raised in impoverished homes (Bauermeister, Alegria, Bird, Rubio-Stipec, & Canino, 1992; Jacobvitz & Sroufe, 1987). It is possible that some types of ADHD behaviors among lower SES children may be rooted in poor care-giving practices.

Second, family conflict may shape the severity of the child's initial biological vulnerability to hyperactivity-impulsivity to such an extent that it rises to a clinical level (Barkley, 1996). Especially important is the match, or **goodness of fit,** between the child's early temperament and the parent's style of interaction (Chess & Thomas, 1984). An overactive child with an overstimulating parent is a seemingly poor fit. Remember from our discussion of genetic influences that many parents of children with ADHD themselves have the disorder? Family risk may be more than just genetic: The parent's own ADHD symptoms may disrupt early parent-child interactions.

Third, family problems can be the *result* of interacting with a child who is impulsive and difficult to manage, rather than the *cause* of these behaviors (Mash & Johnston, 1990). The clearest support for this child-to-parent direction of effect comes from double-blind placebo control drug studies in which children's ADHD symptoms were decreased using stimulant medications. Decreases in children's ADHD symptoms produced a corresponding decline in the negative and controlling behaviors that parents had previously displayed when their children were not on medication (Barkley, 1988; Humphries, Kinsbourne, & Swanson, 1978).

Finally, family conflict is probably related to the presence, maintenance, and later emergence of associated oppositional and conduct disorder symptoms (Anderson et al., 1994; Campbell, March, Pierce, Ewing, & Szumowski, 1991). Many interventions for ADHD try to change faulty patterns of family interaction to head off an escalating cycle of oppositional behavior and conflict. Family influences may play a major role in determining the outcome of ADHD and its associated problems, even if they are not the primary cause of ADHD.

For most children ADHD is the result of a complex pattern of interacting factors. Few theories have described the complex causal pathways through which various biological risk factors, family relationships, and broader system influences interact to shape the development and outcome of ADHD over time (Hinshaw, 1994). Longitudinal studies are needed if these developmental pathways are to be illuminated.

TREATMENT

Mark: Hyperactive and Disruptive

In third grade, Mark's teacher threw up her hands and said, "Enough!" In one morning, Mark had jumped out of his seat six times to sharpen his pencil, each time accidentally charging into other children's desks and toppling books and papers. He was finally sent to the principal's office when he began kicking a desk he had overturned. In sheer frustration, his teacher called a meeting with his parents and the school psychologist.

But even after they developed a plan for managing his behavior in class, Mark showed little improvement. Finally, after an extensive assessment, they found that he had an attention deficit that included hyperactivity. He was put on Ritalin, a medication to control the hyperactivity during school hours. Although Ritalin failed to help, another drug, Dexedrine, did. With a psychologist's help, his parents learned to reward desirable behaviors, and to have Mark take time out when he became too disruptive. Soon Mark was able to sit still and focus on learning. (Adapted from NIMH, 1994)

Lisa: Inattentive and Depressed

Because Lisa wasn't disruptive in class, it took a long time for teachers to notice her problem. Lisa was first referred to the school evaluation team when her teacher realized that she was a bright girl with failing grades. The team ruled out a learning disability but determined that she had an attention deficit, ADHD without hyperactivity. The school psychologist recognized that Lisa was also dealing with depression.

Lisa's teachers and the school psychologist developed a treatment plan that included a program to increase her attention span and develop her social skills. They also recommended that Lisa receive counseling to help her recognize her strengths and overcome her depression. (Adapted from NIMH, 1994)

How can children like Mark and Lisa and their families be helped? Despite decades of research and practice, opinions differ strongly about the best treatment for ADHD. No one approach works for all children. Although there is no cure for ADHD, a variety of treatments can be used to help children cope with their symptoms and deal with any secondary problems that may arise over the years. The standard primary approach (recommended in a 1997 issue of *Consumer Reports*!) combines stimulant medication, parent management training, and educational intervention. But the specific combination of treatments and the way they are implemented must be tailored to the individual child and family. A central theme in the treatment of children with ADHD is to provide them with external structure that will compensate for their lack of internal structuring and organizational skills. To the primary treatments may be added family counseling and support groups, and such child-focused treatments as social skills training, cognitive-behavioral self-control training, and individual counseling. However, findings regarding the effects of these additional treatments for ADHD are modest, and long-term effects have received little study to date (Barkley, 1998). Recently, intensive treatments that use elements of all approaches have been provided in summer treatment programs. An overview of commonly used treatments is presented in Table 5.2.

Several key considerations underlie any treatment program for a child with ADHD:

❖ There is currently no known cure for ADHD.
❖ A variety of medications, behavior-changing therapies, and educational interventions can help children with ADHD and their families better manage the primary symptoms and cope more effectively with the disorder.
❖ The most effective interventions for ADHD are intensive and ongoing, and use a combination of treatments.
❖ Since ADHD is a disorder of performance, treatment needs to be directed at the point of performance in

Table 5.2   Commonly Used Treatments for Children with ADHD

Primary Treatments	Focus of Treatment
Stimulant medication	Managing ADHD symptoms at school and home
Parent management training	Managing disruptive child behavior at home, reducing parent-child conflict, and promoting prosocial and self-regulating behaviors
Educational intervention	Managing disruptive classroom behavior, improving academic performance, teaching prosocial and self-regulating behaviors

Additional Treatments	Focus of Treatment
Family counseling	Coping with individual and family stresses associated with ADHD, including mood disturbance and marital strain
Support groups	Connecting adults with other parents of children with ADHD, sharing information and experiences about common concerns and providing emotional support
Social skills training	Teaching strategies for reducing conflict in relationships and promoting positive peer and adult interactions
Cognitive-behavioral self-control training	Learning to identify problem situations and cognitive and behavioral reactions to these situations, strategies for coping with ADHD symptoms, and self-reinforcement
Individual counseling	Providing a supportive relationship in which the child can discuss personal concerns and feelings

Intensive Treatment	Focus of Treatment
Summer treatment programs	Enhancing present adjustment at home and future success at school by combining many of the primary and additional treatments in an intensive program

the child's natural environment (e.g., classroom, home) (Barkley, 1998).

❖ To be effective, an intervention must be sensitive to the child's level of development and the child's and family's individual strengths and needs.

Medication

Pete (age 6) says: It makes us not 'hyperphrenalicky.' (sic) (Henker & Whelan, 1980)

Following the chance discovery of their effectiveness in the 1930s (see Box 5.6), **stimulant medications** have been used for decades to treat the symptoms of ADHD in children. Other medications, such as tricyclic antidepressants (imipramine, desiprimine) and antihypertensives (clonidine), have been used less frequently. The use of antidepressants, however, has increased in frequency for the treatment of ADHD, especially in cases where stimulants are ineffective or contraindicated, or where the child has a comorbid mood disorder.

Two medications in the class of drugs known as stimulants are most effective in treating children with ADHD. These are **dextroamphetamine** (Dexedrine or Dextrostat) and, the most commonly used drug, **methylphenidate** (Ritalin). Another stimulant, pemoline (Cylert), has also been used to treat children with ADHD, but is no longer considered to be a primary treatment

because of possible risk for problems in liver functioning (Barkley, 1998). Stimulants have been described by doctors as "working like an antenna adjuster for children whose brains crackle with static interference, as if a dozen stations are coming in on one channel" (Hancock, 1996). Stimulants appear to have their effects by altering activity in the frontostriatal region of the brain through their impact on at least three or more neurotransmitters important to the functioning of this region—dopamine, norepinephrine, and epinephrine, and possibly serotonin (Pliszka, McCracken, & Maas, 1996; Volkow et al., 1997). As we have discussed, the frontostriatal region of the brain is important for the regulation of attention, behavioral inhibition, and self-regulation. For about 80% of children with ADHD, stimulants produce dramatic increases in sustained attention, impulse control, and persistence of work effort, and decreases in task-irrelevant activity and noisy and disruptive behavior (Swanson, McBurnett, Christian, & Wigal, 1995).

Medications may also improve the child's social interactions and cooperativeness with parents, teachers, and peers (Danforth, Barkley, & Stokes, 1991), and sometimes their physical coordination, such as handwriting or sports ability (Lerer, Lerer, & Artner, 1977). Stimulants can also help children with ADHD who have oppositional or conduct problems to control their noncompliant, aggressive, or destructive behaviors (Murphy, Pelham, & Lang, 1992). Academic productivity, defined

Box 5.6

The Discovery of Math Pills: Stimulant Medication and ADHD

The use of stimulant medication for children with learning and behavior problems was first reported in 1937, in a now classic paper by Charles Bradley, the medical director of a small hospital for children with major difficulties in learning or behavior. Dr. Bradley described dramatic improvements in some of the children he treated with Benzedrine. But why did Dr. Bradley decide to use stimulants to treat these problems in the first place? . . .

Dr. Bradley was a very conscientious physician, and all patients were given careful work-ups. These work-ups included a spinal tap, which naturally led to headaches afterward that frequently were lasting or severe or both and were presumed to be due to the loss of spinal fluid. Dr. Bradley speculated that if he could stimulate the choroid plexus to secrete spinal fluid at a faster rate, the headaches would be relieved more quickly. He decided to proceed along these lines and chose the most potent stimulant available at the time, Benzedrine (Note: this type of powerful stimulant is no longer used). The effect on the headaches was negligible, but to his astonishment, the teachers reported major improvements in learning and behavior in a number of the children that lasted until the Benzedrine regimen was withdrawn. The children themselves noted the greater ease of learning and called the medication "math pills," presumably because mathematics was the hardest subject for them, and the improved ability to learn was most noticeable in that subject.

Source: Adapted from Gross, 1995.

---

as the number and accuracy of problems completed, increases with medication (Rapport & Kelly, 1993). However, it is not clear that these gains translate into greater long-term achievement for children with ADHD. Unfortunately, the beneficial effects of stimulants in all of the aforementioned areas are temporary, occurring only while the child is taking medication. In this sense, the use of stimulants is similar to other treatments for chronic conditions, like insulin for diabetes.

Since stimulants do not work for all children, a thorough evaluation is necessary (Barkley, 1997b). Some of the considerations in the decision to use medications for the management of ADHD include the age of the child (more effective for children over age 5 years), the duration and severity of symptoms and the extent to which they disrupt the child's functioning, the success of previous treatments, an absence of stimulant abuse in the family, and the likelihood that parents will use the medication responsibly and in accordance with the

doctor's recommendations (Barkley, 1998). Children who are on medications should be evaluated on a regular basis.

Stimulant medications, when used appropriately and with proper supervision, are usually quite safe. Although stimulants can be addictive if misused (one recreational name for Ritalin is Vitamin R!), they are not addictive for most children who take them. Medications seldom make children "high," nervous, or jumpy, or turn them into non-feeling zombies. Some children may report feeling "funny" or "different" on medication, or experience a bland mood or slight sadness, but these feelings are minor and usually associated with too high a dosage of medication. Most children who receive medication, particularly methylphenidate, view their treatment as useful and may even report improvements in their self-esteem (DuPaul, Anastopoulos, Kwasnik, Barkley, & McMurray, 1996). But children may also report negative feelings about having to take medication, sometimes related to side effects but more commonly related to embarrassment and to feeling different from other children (Weiss & Hechtman, 1993).

The Great Debate

As useful as stimulants have been in treating the symptoms of ADHD, they have also generated much public controversy and debate (Jacobvitz, Sroufe, Stewart, & Leffert, 1990). Ritalin use by children and adolescents has more than doubled since 1990; it is estimated that about 1.3 million children take the drug on a regular basis (Hancock, 1996), with approximately 2.8% of school-age children possibly being treated for symptoms of ADHD (Safer, Zito, & Fine, 1996). Moreover, the use of Ritalin is at least 5 times higher in North America than in the rest of the world. Such massive consumption has inspired accusations of a societal quick fix to make active or noncompliant children more docile and obedient and to increase the profits of drug companies. However, there may be other reasons for increased drug use. First, more children with ADD without hyperactivity are being diagnosed, and these children respond positively to medication. Second, with the growing recognition that stimulant medications may be just as useful for adolescents with ADHD as for children, the frequency of prescriptions for adolescents and young adults has likely increased. Third, as changes in public policy/laws increase eligibility for benefits for individuals with ADHD, more individuals may receive this diagnosis and subsequently be placed on medication. Children with this disorder may qualify for special education and related services under the *Individuals with Disabilities Education Act Amendments of 1997* (Public Law 105-17) solely on the basis of their ADHD, when it impairs educational performance or

Box 5.7

Myths about the Use of Stimulant Medication for Children with ADHD

Myth 1: *Stimulants are dangerous and should not be taken by any child.*

Fact: Some children on medication may experience side effects, such as weight loss, reduced appetite, temporary growth suppression, or problems falling asleep. If symptoms of anxiety or tic disorders are present, some stimulants may make them worse. However, the benefits of medication far outweigh their potential side effects. Side effects can be carefully monitored and can often be eliminated by reducing the dosage.

Myth 2: *Stimulant use leads to drug addiction later in life.*

Fact: Children who take stimulants do not become addicted to them, nor are they more likely to abuse drugs later. Stimulants help children focus and thus be more successful. Avoiding negative experiences at a younger age may actually help prevent addictions and other emotional problems later on.

Myth 3: *Responding well to a stimulant drug proves a child has ADHD.*

Fact: Stimulants allow children to focus and pay better attention, whether or not they have ADHD. The improvement is just more noticeable in children with ADHD.

Myth 4: *Stimulants have the paradoxical effect of slowing hyperactive kids down.*

Fact: Stimulants have the same effect on children with ADHD as they do on other children. Children with ADHD may be underaroused, and stimulants serve to increase their arousal level, which helps them be more attentive.

Myth 5: *Medication should be stopped when the child reaches adolescence.*

Fact: About 80% of those who needed medication as children may still need it as teenagers, and 50% may need medication as adults.

Source: Adapted from NIMH, 1994.

had extremely negative reactions to the medication (such reactions are very rare). The debate on stimulant medication has also been fueled by several myths (see Box 5.7). At the center of the storm surrounding the use of stimulants is a critical question: Is prescribing medication in the child's best interests? In this regard several additional questions need to be raised (NIMH, 1994).

Should medication be used to raise the functioning of children with ADHD to its highest possible level? Although some children with ADHD may not absolutely need medication to function, it is the view of some physicians that medication will enable children with ADHD to function at their highest possible level. This could be one reason that medication use has increased as much as it has over the past few years. This rationale for medicating the child with ADHD, although defensible, is also quite controversial. Since the beneficial effects of stimulant medications are not limited to children with ADHD, the same rationale might be used to medicate any child.

Do medications contribute to the child's feelings of helplessness? Rapid improvements in schoolwork and behavior after a child starts medication can be attributed by the child, parent, or teacher to the drug. Sometimes this minimizes the child's role in bringing about change. Despite concerns that giving too much credit for behavior change to medication can make the child feel helpless or incompetent, improvements still result from the child's own efforts, strengths, and abilities. In fact, children with ADHD have been found to attribute their successes to their own efforts rather than to medication and to report feeling better about themselves when taking medication (Pelham et al., 1992). Although they can occur in some cases, reports that medication leads to dysfunctional attributions, feelings of helplessness, and adverse effects have not been confirmed in controlled studies (Pelham, Hoza, Kipp, & Gnagy, 1997).

Do medications make the child feel different from other children? Medication may make some children feel that they are different or that something is wrong with them. The public labeling by others is evident in these comments by a 12-year-old boy with ADHD:

> I'll go in and take 'em and then during the afternoon she [the teacher] thinks I'm gettin "off," you know, hyperactive, and she'll say, "Bradley, did you forget to take your little trip to the office this morning?" And I'll say, "No!" (Meichenbaum, 1977)

Children need to be helped to feel comfortable about taking medication daily. Comparing the pills to eyeglasses, braces, or allergy medications used by other kids can help. Children can be encouraged to view the medication as a tool to help them attend better.

learning. Since eligibility for services for children with ADHD is under the "other health impaired" category of disabilities in this law, a medical diagnosis is needed, which further increases the likelihood of medication use.

Some of the debate about stimulant use stems from sensationalized accounts of children reported to have

Do medications contribute to better long-term outcomes? The short-term benefits of medication are well documented. Unfortunately, follow-up studies suggest little *long-term* impact of stimulants on school achievement, peer relationships, behavior problems in adolescence, or adult adjustment (Pelham, 1993).

Stimulants are the most studied and most effective treatment for the management of symptoms of ADHD and its associated impairments. Nevertheless, since stimulants are often not used across the entire day and do not address all the associated problems of children with ADHD, psychosocial management strategies and educational interventions are also needed.

Parent Management Training (PMT)

It is difficult and exhausting to be the parent of a child who is overactive, disorganized, and irritable, and who doesn't listen or follow directions. Usual methods of discipline, like reasoning, warning, or scolding, often do not work with children with ADHD. Thus, parents often feel powerless and at a loss as to what to do next. Out of frustration, they may spank, ridicule, or yell at their child, even though they know that it doesn't do any good. These reactions leave everyone in the family feeling more upset than ever. Parents often feel bad and blame themselves.

Parent management training (PMT) helps parents cope effectively with their child's difficult behavior and their own reactions to it. Although there are many versions of PMT, they all have certain elements in common. If the child is young, most of the treatment is carried out with the parents. Parents are first taught about ADHD so that they understand the nature of the disorder. Understanding the biological basis for ADHD can help remove the burden of guilt from parents who might otherwise blame themselves for their child's behavior. Parents are also given a set of general principles for child-rearing that are appropriate for children with ADHD:

Ten Guiding Principles for Raising a Child with ADHD

❖ Give your child more immediate feedback and consequences.
❖ Give your child more frequent feedback.
❖ Use larger and more powerful consequences.
❖ Use incentives before punishment.
❖ Strive for consistency.
❖ Act, don't yak!
❖ Plan ahead for problem situations.
❖ Keep a disability perspective.
❖ Don't personalize your child's problems or disorder.
❖ Practice forgiveness.
(Barkley, 1995, p. 136)

Using these general principles as a framework, parents are taught a number of specific behavior modification techniques. They learn to identify behaviors they wish to encourage or discourage; to use rewards and sanctions to achieve specified goals and to establish a home token program; to find opportunities to notice what their child does well; to find effective ways to attend to their child's behavior; and to praise their child's strengths and accomplishments. Parents also learn to use penalties when their child is disruptive, such as the loss of privileges or the use of a brief time-out for noncompliance, and how to manage noncompliance in public places. Parents may also learn to use a home-based reward program in which the child is evaluated on a daily school behavior report card by his or her teachers. This card serves as a means by which rewards or punishments (usually tokens) will be administered at home for classroom conduct. Parents also learn to manage future misconduct and are given booster sessions in which earlier approaches are reviewed and problems that have arisen are discussed and corrected (Barkley, 1998).

Parents are encouraged to provide a period of time each day in which they share an enjoyable activity with their child. They learn to structure situations in ways that will maximize the child's success and minimize failures. For example, if the child has difficulty completing tasks, it may be necessary to first help the child break the task into smaller steps, and then to praise the completion of each individual step. In PMT, parents also learn to reduce their own levels of arousal through relaxation, meditation, or exercise. Reduced arousal or anger allows parents to respond more calmly to their child's behavior.

Numerous studies support the effectiveness of PMT in decreasing oppositional and defiant child behaviors (Kazdin, 1993), although few controlled studies have evaluated the effectiveness of PMT for children selected specifically for their ADHD. Thus, the relative advantages and long-term benefits of PMT in reducing the primary symptoms of ADHD have yet to be demonstrated. Most studies find the effects of stimulants to be as strong or stronger than those for PMT; combined approaches usually produce the strongest effects (Barkley, 1998).

The primary benefits of PMT appear to be that it (1) reduces oppositional and noncompliant behaviors; (2) provides parents with ways to manage their child's difficult behavior effectively; (3) helps parents cope with the emotional difficulties of raising a child with ADHD; (4) contains the problem so that it does not worsen over time; and (5) keeps the problem from adversely affecting other family members.

Educational Intervention

Alan: Boxed In at School and Hating It

My teacher wanted to make me concentrate better, so one day she put my desk in the far corner, separated from the rest of the class. A few days had passed. I still wasn't finishing my work on time, but I was trying to do the work correctly. The teacher didn't care; it wasn't finished. She then put a refrigerator box around my desk so I couldn't see anyone in class. I could hear as other kids in class would make fun of me. It really hurt; I was ashamed of myself and mad at my teacher. I couldn't tell my Mom because I might get into trouble. I hated school, didn't like my teacher, and started not liking myself. Imagine a nine-year-old going through this day after day. It was hard to face the next day. A week had passed, and I poked holes in the cardboard so I could see who was making fun of me. I started peeping through the holes, making the other kids laugh. The teacher would get so annoyed. So I became the class clown. I was expelled for two days. When my Mom found out what was going on, boy, did she get angry. She was mad that the teacher would do this and mad that the principal allowed it, and no one could see what this was doing to me. (Barkley, 1995)

Classroom requirements to sit still, pay attention, listen to instructions, wait your turn, complete assignments, and get along with classmates are not easily met by children with ADHD such as Alan; their inattention and hyperactivity-impulsivity make learning very difficult, at times even painful. Although some children with ADHD are placed in a special education class for all or part of the day, most are able to remain in the regular classroom. Whenever possible, it is preferable to keep children with ADHD with their peers. However, it is important to recognize that special educational programs may be available for children with ADHD as mandated under the Individuals with Disabilities Act Amendments of 1997 and other legislation (DuPaul & Stoner, 1994; P. Latham & R. Latham, 1992). Since the child's eligibility for such programs is frequently a major concern of teachers and parents, it is important that current federal, state, and local regulations be taken into account when developing a comprehensive and effective educational intervention for a child with ADHD.

Educational interventions should be individualized. Normally, such interventions focus on (1) managing inattentive and hyperactive-impulsive behaviors that interfere with learning, and (2) providing a classroom structure and instructional materials and methods that capitalize on the child's strengths and increase the likelihood of successful learning. Techniques for managing the child's classroom behavior are similar to those recommended to parents. The teacher and child set realistic goals and objectives, set up a mutually agreed upon reward system, carefully monitor the child's performance, and reward the child for meeting goals. Disruptive or off-task classroom behaviors may be punished with predetermined consequences, such as a loss of privileges, removal of tokens, mild sanctions, or brief periods of time-out.

Response-cost procedures, which involve the loss of reinforcers such as privileges, activities, points, or tokens contingent upon inappropriate behavior, are frequently used to manage the disruptive classroom behavior of children with ADHD. One innovative application of a response-cost procedure in the classroom involves placing a small display counter with a light on top on the child's desk during individual work periods (Rapport, Murphy, & Bailey, 1982). Once the box is activated, it is assumed that the child is on-task and following rules, and a point (which the child can later trade in for desired rewards) is added to the display counter at regular intervals. The teacher carries a small transmitter during this class time and if the child is off-task, not working, or disruptive, the teacher presses a button on the remote control, which triggers the light and at the same time subtracts a point from the display. This application, and a variety of other response-cost procedures, have proved to be especially effective in managing both the disruptive behavior and the academic productivity of children with ADHD in the classroom (DuPaul, Guevremont, & Barkley, 1992; Pfiffner & Barkley, 1990).

Many strategies for instructing children with ADHD are simply good teaching methods. Letting children know what is expected of them, using visual aids, providing prompts and cues for expected behavior, and giving written as well as oral instructions all help children focus their attention and remember important points. In addition, children with ADHD may require other accommodations to help them learn. For example, the teacher may seat the child near his or her own desk, provide a designated area in which the child can move about, establish a clearly posted system of rules, and give the child frequent cues for expected behaviors. A card or a picture on the child's desk can serve as a visual reminder for acceptable classroom behavior such as raising a hand instead of shouting out. Repeating instructions, providing extra time, writing assignments on the board, and listing the books and materials needed for a task may increase the likelihood that children with

ADHD will be able to complete their work (DuPaul & Stoner, 1994; Pfiffner & Barkley, 1990).

School-based interventions for managing the symptoms of children with ADHD have received considerable support in a large number of research studies. A recent integrative review of 70 school-based intervention studies with children with ADHD found that contingency management procedures aimed at improving behavior, and interventions directed at increasing academic performance both had substantial positive effects (DuPaul & Eckert, 1997). These findings are promising. However, few studies have examined the maintenance of treatment gains over time or their generalization to other classroom settings in which the treatments were not used. It is possible that behavior and academic improvements that result from classroom management methods may be situation-specific or short-lasting once treatments are removed.

Additional Interventions

Family Counseling. Many families of children with ADHD experience frustration, blame, and anger for some time. Siblings may feel neglected or resent the time their parents spend coping with the child with ADHD. Family members may require special assistance not only in managing behavior but also in dealing with their own thoughts and feelings. Counseling the whole family helps everyone develop new skills, attitudes, and ways of relating more effectively.

Support Groups. Groups of people who are dealing with ADHD in various ways can be very helpful to members. There are many local and national support groups of parents of children with ADHD. Members share information, emotional support, personal frustrations and successes, referrals to qualified professionals, discoveries about what works, and their aspirations for their children and themselves. There are also on-line bulletin boards and discussion groups. Sharing experiences with others who have similar concerns helps parents feel that they are not alone.

Social Skills Training. In light of their many interpersonal difficulties, a special treatment focus on teaching children with ADHD effective social skills may be necessary, especially for those with comorbid conduct problems. As we have seen, children with ADHD do not seem to be lacking in their social knowledge (knowing how to behave) but rather have difficulties in using what they know in real-life social situations. **Social skills training** is often conducted in a group of children. The therapist discusses and demonstrates appropriate social behaviors, such as sharing, asking for assistance, waiting for a turn, or responding to teasing. The children practice these behaviors and receive feedback. For example, a child might learn how to accurately interpret another child's facial expression, tone of voice, or behavior, and how to react appropriately. Children are taught to recognize how their behavior affects others, to develop appropriate ways of responding to things that they may not like, and to discover new ways of achieving desired outcomes. Unfortunately, social skills training programs have had limited success to date (Hinshaw, 1992), possibly because existing programs have not focused on the specific types of social difficulties that characterize children with ADHD, such as performance deficits related to the timing and quality of social behavior.

Cognitive-Behavioral Self-Control Training. Children with ADHD can learn special techniques for monitoring and regulating their own attention and behavior. The purpose of **cognitive-behavioral self-control training** is to teach children to keep track of their own behavior; assess what is required of them in specific situations; examine their thoughts and feelings in these situations; identify their usual reactions; generate more effective alternative responses; manage when things do not go as planned; and reward themselves for a job well done. For example, children may be taught several options for coping when they lose track of what they're supposed to do: "look for instructions on the blackboard"; "raise your hand"; "wait to see if you remember"; or "quietly ask another child." Children may be asked to notice and to record whether they are paying attention to what they are supposed to be doing or whether they are thinking about something else. Although self-control treatments have intuitive appeal and are frequently used with children with ADHD, evidence for their effectiveness is limited (Barkley, 1998). Controlled evaluations and integrative reviews of cognitive-behavioral treatments for children with ADHD have generally found either few or small treatment effects of limited clinical importance (Baer & Nietzel, 1991; Bloomquist, August, & Ostrander, 1991).

Individual Counseling. Life can be very hard for children with ADHD. The disorder can have widespread psychological and emotional effects as the following comments by Ian attest:

Ian (4th grade)

So if that's it, if I am just plain stupid, there was no way that I would let on to anyone that this was the case. I promised myself never to cry in front of others again. If only I could just make a couple of friends, I'd be alright. I know that none of the kids would dare tease me about my stupidness for fear of being punched . . . My dignity and self-esteem rested on my ability to conceal from anyone that there was something wrong with me. This strange dishonesty had stuck with me since my early years . . . (Murray, 1993)

Many children with ADHD have few successes on which to build their sense of self-worth and competence. Being scolded, punished, or told that they are stupid or bad is often the primary form of attention that children with ADHD receive. They have few friends and are constantly in trouble. The cumulative impact of such frustration can leave children with ADHD feeling isolated and believing that they are abnormal, stupid, and doomed to failure. In individual counseling, children learn to accept and like themselves despite their disorder. Children with ADHD usually come into counseling with many questions about their condition and treatment, which are addressed both at the outset and in later sessions. Examples of questions asked by children and adolescents with ADHD are shown in Box 5.8.

With counseling, children learn to identify and build on their strengths. They come to understand that having ADHD does not mean they are bad people. Children discuss upsetting thoughts and feelings, explore self-defeating patterns of behavior, and learn adaptive ways

---

Box 5.8

Questions Asked by Children and Adolescents with Attention-Deficit/Hyperactivity Disorder

CHILDREN (AGES 4 TO 10)

I just found out I have ADD. How can I keep this secret from my brother?

I heard ADD means you're weird. Is that right?

Is it true that if you have ADD you can think faster than other people?

Will the medicine make me smarter?

ADOLESCENTS (AGES 11 TO 17)

How do you know the medicine isn't dangerous?

Any advice on how to deal with the fact that I feel like a reject because I have ADD?

How long am I going to have ADD?

How can I convince [my teacher] that ADD exists and that it affects my performance?

Source: Adapted from Hallowell & Ratey, 1994.

---

of handling their emotions. Strategies for controlling hyperactive-impulsive behavior and for coping with daily problems at school and at home are also developed. A few examples of such coping strategies include asking others to repeat instructions, breaking tasks into small steps, making lists, keeping a daily calendar, or posting visible reminders of things that need doing. Through discussion and practice in individual counseling, children come to understand that they can change and lead happier, more productive lives.

Intensive Interventions

The intermediate and long-term effects of combining medication, PMT, and classroom interventions have not yet been systematically evaluated. A landmark multisite evaluation study sponsored by the U.S. National Institute of Mental Health (NIMH) and Department of Education is currently investigating this issue (Arnold et al., 1997; Richters et al., 1995). NIMH began its study of the multimodal treatment of ADHD to answer questions relating to the relative long-term effectiveness of medication and behavioral treatment alone and in combination with one another, and relative to standard community treatments. Major questions are concerned with what treatments work best for which children (e.g., boys versus girls, children with or without comorbid conditions), and for which areas of functioning (home, school, peers). This test of state-of-the-art treatments for ADHD should go a long way toward answering real-world questions of clinical importance for children with ADHD and their families.

Research to date has told us that there are no quick cures for ADHD. Professionals are beginning to agree that much more intensive treatments than previously used will be required to produce meaningful changes in long-term outcomes for children with ADHD. An exemplary intensive summer program has been developed by William Pelham and his colleagues (Pelham et al., 1996; Pelham & Hoza, 1996). Although this program has yet to be independently evaluated in a controlled investigation, the early findings are promising. Treatment is provided to children with ADHD between the ages of 5 and 15 in a camplike setting where they engage in recreational, classroom, and other activities with other children. Summer treatment has two major advantages over other interventions: It maximizes opportunities to build effective peer relations in normal settings, and it provides continuity of academic work so that gains made during the school year are not lost. These programs are coordinated with stimulant medication trials and PMT in an all-out effort to have a long-term impact on the adjustment of children with ADHD. A description of Matthew, a child with ADHD who participated in the Summer Treatment Program, is presented in Box 5.9,

Box 5.9

An Intensive Summer Treatment Program for a Child with ADHD

Matthew

Matthew is a 10-year-old boy who was referred to the Summer Treatment Program by his parents. Matthew's presenting problems included inattention, arguing and noncompliance with parents, and difficulties in school. Throughout the Summer Treatment Program, Matthew received intensive behavioral treatment including a reward and response-cost system, daily report cards, time out, and skill training in social, athletic, and academic areas.

Matthew also received a concurrent medication assessment of 10 mg methylphenidate (.3 mg/kg) compared with placebo during the last six weeks of the eight-week program (beginning on day 13). As shown in the graphs below, Matthew showed an immediate positive response to medication, with rates of following rules during activities increasing from an average of approximately 50% during the first two weeks to 90% on the first med-ication day. Medication also decreased the frequency of Matthew's noncompliance to near zero levels. The success of the behavioral intervention can also be observed in the graphs below. By the end of the summer, Matthew's rule following was high and his noncompliance was low even on days when he did not receive medication. Thus, by the end of the summer medication effects were considerably smaller than when they were first introduced, because there was less room for improvement.

The behavioral program was also effective in improving other aspects of Matthew's behavior over time. For example, Matthew's rates of good sportsmanship increased by the end of the summer. This was an important accomplishment for Matthew, who possessed advanced sports skills but often displayed frustration, arguing with staff, and "bossy" behavior toward peers in games.

Source: Pelham, Jr. et al., 1996.

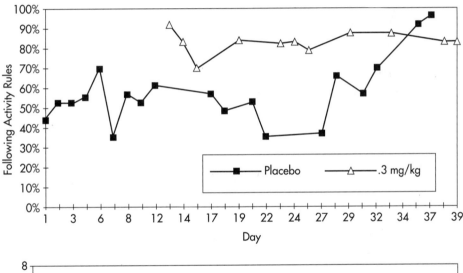

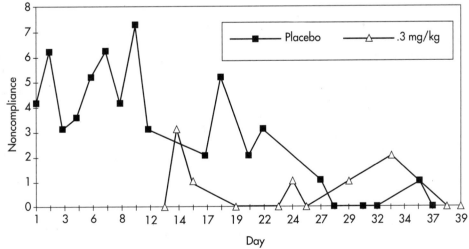

Medication was helpful in increasing Matthew's rule following and decreasing his noncompliance. (Pelham, Jr. et al., 1996)

Children with ADHD participating in the Summer Treatment Program.

and some of the many different elements of this program are listed below.

* a token reinforcement program wherein children earn points for appropriate behavior and lose points for inappropriate behavior throughout the day
* frequent social reinforcement and use of appropriate commands
* prudent discipline, taking the form of loss of privileges or time-out from ongoing activities
* training in social skills and the development of positive dyadic relationships
* sports skills enhancement training in a positive environment
* daily report cards for which parents provide home-based rewards
* behavior modification programs in a classroom context
* parent training designed to facilitate transfer of the gains children make to the home setting
* intensive, individualized evaluations of the effectiveness of stimulant medication
* follow-up treatment consisting of a Saturday Treatment Program, school interventions, and booster parent training

(Pelham et al., 1996)

The Summer Treatment Program packs 360 hours of treatment into a period of 8 weeks, the equivalent of 7 years of weekly therapy. Does it make a difference? According to ratings by parents and counselors, children with ADHD who participate in the Summer Treatment Program show overall improvements in their behavior, decreases in problem severity, and improvements in specific domains such as social skills and academic performance. The children also rate themselves as doing better, and their parents report higher levels of their own personal efficacy. There are low dropout rates from the program and a high degree of consumer satisfaction. The program is also cost-effective in comparison with more traditional forms of treatment. Since long-term studies of outcomes have not yet been conducted, it's still too early to tell whether this kind of intensive program will make a long-term difference for these children.

Controversial Treatments

Understandably, parents want to explore all possible ways of helping their children with ADHD. Over the years, many treatments that sound plausible have been proposed. Some are enthusiastically endorsed by professionals, and individual patient reports claim dramatic success. Others are pure charlatanism. Treatments that have been proposed for children with ADHD that have not been scientifically substantiated include restricted diets, treatments for allergies, medication to correct inner ear problems, treatment for yeast infection, megavitamins, chiropractic adjustment and bone realignment, eye training, special colored glasses, and biofeedback. Fad treatments may prove to be expensive, provide false hope for a quick cure, and delay the use of treatments that are known to be of some benefit.

Keeping Things in Perspective

Alan, Age 15: Learning to Survive

Through my years in school so far, I've been through a lot. My Mom says I have a good heart; I care about those in need. I'm not dumb. You can't always measure smartness by tests. I feel I'm doing better in school. The school psychologist has become an important tool for me. I can talk to him when I get a teacher who doesn't understand, if I disagree with something, or if I'm just having problems. It helps to talk to someone who understands. What I'm trying to say is: no matter what comes my way, I can survive. I have those who really care, and from that I draw my strength. (Barkley, 1995)

Children with ADHD have numerous behavioral, social, educational, and emotional difficulties. These problems should not be minimized, especially if doing so prevents children with ADHD and their families from receiving help. However, as the comments by Alan illustrate, in the attempt to understand and help children and adolescents with ADHD and their families, it is important not to lose sight of the fact that these children also have many strengths and resources that need to be recognized and supported.

SUMMARY

Attention-Deficit Hyperactivity Disorder

1. Attention-deficit/hyperactivity disorder, or ADHD, describes children who consistently and repeatedly show age-inappropriate behaviors in the two general categories of inattention and hyperactivity-impulsivity.

2. As views of the disorder and its causes evolved over the past 100 years, ADHD has had many different names.

Defining Features

3. DSM-IV defines ADHD using two lists of symptoms. The first includes symptoms of inattention, poor concentration, and disorganization. The second includes symptoms of hyperactivity and behavioral impulsivity.

4. Sustained attention, or vigilance, is the core attention deficit in children with ADHD.

5. Hyperactivity and impulsivity are best viewed as a single dimension of behavior.

Associated Characteristics

6. Most children with ADHD are of normal intelligence. Their difficulty is in applying their intelligence to everyday life situations.

7. Children with ADHD experience school performance difficulties that include lower productivity, grades, and scores on achievement tests; failure to advance in grade; and more frequent placements in special education classes.

8. Many children with ADHD have a specific learning disability or speech and language disorder.

9. Children with ADHD experience health-related problems, are accident-prone, and experience numerous interpersonal problems with family members, teachers, and peers.

10. Children with ADHD have much higher than expected rates of other psychiatric disorders, the most common ones being oppositional defiant and conduct disorders, and emotional disorders, such as anxiety and depression.

Prevalence and Developmental Course

11. The best current estimate is that ADHD affects about 3% to 5% of all school-age children, with boys more likely to be diagnosed than girls.

12. Although the symptoms of ADHD tend to decline in prevalence and intensity as children grow older, for many individuals ADHD is a lifelong disorder.

Theories and Causes

13. The most intriguing theories of ADHD focus on deficits in motivation, arousal level, self-regulation, and response inhibition.

14. Although the specific cause of ADHD is unknown, genetic and neurobiological influences are related to an increased risk of the disorder.

15. Direct and indirect sources of evidence indicate that ADHD is likely related to abnormalities in the frontal areas of the cortex associated with behavioral inhibition.

Treatment

16. There is no cure for ADHD, but a variety of treatments can be used to help children cope with their symptoms and deal with any secondary problems that may arise over the years.

17. The primary approach to treatment combines stimulant medication, parent management training, and educational intervention. To the primary approaches can be added family counseling and support groups, and such child-focused treatments as social skills training, cognitive-behavioral self-control training, and individual counseling.

last question on review sheet

KEY TERMS

attention-deficit/hyperactivity disorder (ADHD), 143
inattentive, 144
hyperactive, 144
impulsive, 144
selective attention, 146
distractibility, 147
attentional capacity, 147
sustained attention, 147
vigilance, 148
continuous performance test (CPT), 148
subtype, 151
ADHD: predominantly inattentive type (ADHD-PI), 151
ADHD: predominantly hyperactive-impulsive type (ADHD-HI), 152
ADHD: combined type (ADHD-C), 152
metacognition, 153
executive functions, 153
Tourette's disorder, 159
difficult temperament, 162

optimal stimulation theory, 164
behavioral inhibition, 165
corpus callosum, 169
frontostriatal circuitry, 169
minor physical anomalies, 171
goodness of fit, 172
stimulant medications, 174

dextroamphetamine, 174
methylphenidate, 174
parent management training (PMT), 177
response-cost procedures, 178
social skills training, 179
cognitive-behavioral self-control training, 179

Conduct Problems

Our youth now love luxury. They have bad manners, contempt for authority and disrespect for their elders. Children nowadays are tyrants.

—Socrates, 470–399 B.C.

Few human problems have attracted as much attention as antisocial, violent, and destructive behavior in young people. Such behavior rattles the foundation on which harmonious relationships are built. Despite enormous professional attention and public concern, substantial numbers of children and teens are committing aggression, assault, and murder (Fingerhut & Kleinman, 1990). There are more gun dealers than teachers in California, and bulletproof vests now come in children's sizes (Toch, 1993). Growing rates of antisocial acts by young people fuel popular beliefs that some children are just born bad, that aggression is part of human nature, or that increasing violence is symptomatic of a decaying society with its changing family structure, abuse of drugs and alcohol, and easy access to weapons. The high prevalence and social visibility of youth with conduct problems and the harm done to their victims create an urgent need to describe, understand, and treat such antisocial behavior.

DESCRIPTION

The terms **conduct problems** and **antisocial behavior** refer to age-inappropriate actions and attitudes that violate family expectations, societal norms, and the personal or property rights of others (McMahon & Estes, 1997). Children with conduct problems display a wide range of rule-violating behaviors, from whining, swearing, and temper tantrums to severe vandalism, theft, and assault. Just as wide-ranging are the causes and long-term outcomes of these problems. Because of this diversity, we will consider several different types and pathways of antisocial behavior. The following examples

preview the diversity, range of severity, and impact on others of conduct problems in children and adolescents.

Andy (4 years old): Rage at a Young Age

Andy's mother says: "Just a few weeks ago, Andy threw his booster seat in my face and hit my jaw. And he thought it was funny . . . . He was acting up, and I think he had already had one time-out for yelling and screaming and interrupting us at the table. And I said, 'Fine, you are going upstairs now. You are not having dessert.' And he just flew into a rage. He picked up a metal fork and threw it at me with all his force, and hit me—barely missed my eye. There was blood on my forehead. I was screaming, I was hysterical. And I was terrified, I mean, to see that type of behavior, that type of rage, in a 4-year-old." (Adapted from Webster-Stratton & Herbert, 1994, pp. 44–45)

Marvelle (6 years old): Impossible to Manage

Marvelle's mother says: "She just drives me up the wall. Over the past 8 months she's become impossible to manage. She's irritable all the time and never does anything I ask her to do. She throws a full-blown tantrum at the drop of a hat when she doesn't get her way. Her negative attitude is also becoming a real problem at school. Marvelle's teacher recently complained that it was difficult to get her to do schoolwork—she simply refuses to do assignments. Not only that but she's defiant, won't stay in her seat, and talks constantly. Her behavior is becoming disruptive to the entire class. I'm really worried that she's headed for some serious problems if she doesn't shape up soon."

Bulletproof vests now come in children's sizes.

Nick (10 years old): Not Like Other Kids

To all outward appearances, Nick is a normal healthy boy. . . . he loves sports, especially football, swimming, and fishing. He has a talent for drawing cartoon figures and an aptitude for math. . . . but Nick isn't like other kids. When Nick was just two years old he walked out of his room, put two cans of cat food on the stove, and lit the burner—one of the cans exploded. Over the past eight years, Nick has killed family pets, set fires, beaten classmates, vandalized property, stolen money, and terrorized his younger sister. . . . In one five-day period last March, he threw a rock at a girl at the YMCA, hitting her in the head and drawing blood; set fire to his room; pushed his sister down the stairs; whipped the family dog with a chain; and stole $20 from his mother's wallet. (Adapted from Colapinto, 1993, p. 122)

Names Withheld: Child Killers

On October 13, 1994, 5-year-old Eric Morse and his 8-year-old brother, Derrick, ran into two of the toughest bullies their South Side Chicago neighborhood had to offer. The intimidating boys lured the brothers to a vacant 14th-floor apartment. Twice, they dangled a terrified and wailing Eric—who had refused to steal candy for them—out the window. When Derrick tried to pull in his brother, the older bully hit his hand so hard he let go. Eric plunged to his death. Derrick ran downstairs, thinking he might catch his brother in time. It was a blood-curdling crime at any age. But the killers, whose names have not been released by officials, were all of 10 and 11. (Annin, 1996, p. 5)

The disturbing actions of these youngsters vary widely in type and severity, from temper outbursts, to defiance, to animal abuse, to fire setting, to murder. Yet in each instance the child's behavior meets the definition of conduct problems by clearly violating societal rules and the personal or property rights of others.

Although we are shocked by such actions, we may also be aware that many children with conduct problems grow up in extremely negative family and neighborhood circumstances. Many experience physical abuse, neglect, poverty, or exposure to criminal activity. Consider the case of Steve, a 12-year-old boy who was referred for treatment because he stabbed his father in the leg and stole a car:

Steve: A Tough Life

Steve had a history of lying, fighting at school, and theft, and he was in constant trouble with school personnel and police. During an initial interview, Steve readily admitted that he stabbed his father in the leg. But his story included some interesting details that had not come up previously. He and his two brothers were in their parents' bedroom while the mother was being raped by the father. She was screaming for help and panicked. Steve went and got a knife from the kitchen; his brothers tried to restrain him but could do so only partially. Steve stabbed his father in the calf, deeply and with a long cut. After the stabbing, Steve felt he was going to get beaten, because his father had a long history of physically abusing the boys. He fled to his grandfather's house, took the keys of the car without permission, drove off, and crashed the car in a field. Steve was brought to us by the police. By all accounts, Steve had stabbed his father. And indeed he stole a car. (Adapted from Kazdin, 1995, pp. 17–18)

Steve's tragic family situation may inspire sympathy and concern for him, and for other youngsters in similar circumstances. Many children with conduct problems are distressed, seriously disturbed, and in need of help. On the other hand, the callousness of their actions evokes outrage, great concern for innocent victims, such as 5-year-old Eric Morse, and a desire to severely punish or confine such children (Kazdin, 1995). Not surprisingly, as they grow older, children with conduct problems increasingly walk a fine line between the pleas of the mental health and juvenile justice systems for understanding and rehabilitation, and the tough demands by the criminal justice system and the general public for punishment and protection of victims.

The Significance and Cost of Conduct Problems

James Darby, age 9, wrote a letter to President Clinton, asking for his help:

> Dear Mr. Clinton,
>   I want you to stop the killing in the city. People is dead and I think that somebody might kill me. Would you please stop the people from deading. I'm asking you nicely to stop it. I know you can do it. Do it now. I know you can.
>   Your friend,
>   James
>   (Osofsky, 1996, p. 35)

Just 9 days after writing to President Clinton, James was killed unintentionally in a drive-by revenge shooting, while he was walking home from a picnic with his family. James's senseless death highlights the personal tragedy that results from antisocial behaviors such as arson, drunk driving, rape, and murder. You may be surprised to learn that antisocial behavior is the most costly mental health problem in North America. The emotional, physical, and economic costs of conduct problems for children and for society are staggering (Cohen, Miller, & Rossman, 1994).

In addition, conduct problems result in significant costs to the educational, health, criminal justice, and mental health systems that deal with these children. Aggressive, antisocial, and disruptive patterns of behavior are among the most "referable" for mental health services, accounting for one-third to one-half of all clinic referrals (Achenbach & Howell, 1993; Weisz & Weiss, 1991).

The costs of violent behavior involving youths can be understood not only in terms of lives but also in terms of dollars. More than 3,000 juveniles were arrested for murder in 1994 (see Figure 6.1), and more than 100,000 for other violent crimes (Federal Bureau of Investigation [FBI], 1994). More teenagers die from firearm injuries in the United States than from all diseases combined, and teenagers are more than twice as likely as adults to be the victims of violent crimes, mostly at the hands of other teens (APA Commission on Youth Violence, 1993). Each schoolday, well over 100,000 students stay home—not because of illness, but because they are afraid of being stabbed, shot, or beaten. About 10% to 20% of mental health expenditures in the United States are attributable to crime (National Institute of Justice, 1996).

Antisocial Behavior and Normal Development

As a normal part of growing up, almost all young people break the rules from time to time—Did you ever defy authority, lie, fight, skip school, run away, break curfew, shoplift, destroy property, steal from friends or relatives, drive a car under the influence of alcohol, or smoke a joint? If you answered yes to any of these, welcome to the club! The prevalence of self-reported antisocial acts by young people is surprisingly high, with approximately one-third to one-half admitting to theft, property destruction, assault, or other antisocial acts such as substance abuse, arson, and vandalism (Kazdin, 1995). The close link between normal rule-breaking during adolescence and prevailing social norms is evident when we consider that in 1946 two of the most frequently self-reported offenses by teens were stealing melons and fruit (69%) and loafing in a pool hall (48%)! Drug use was not even mentioned (Tappan, 1949). Only about 6% of adolescents abstain from antisocial behavior *entirely,* and these teens tend to be excessively conventional, overly trusting, anxious, shy, and socially incompetent, not at all what we would think of as models of healthy adjustment (Moffitt, Caspi, Dickson, Silva, & Stanton, 1996).

Antisocial behavior in nonproblem children and youth appears and then declines during the course of normal development (Achenbach, Howell, Quay, & Conners, 1991). In studies of normal children, as many as 50% of parents of 4- to 6-year-olds report that their children steal, lie, disobey, or destroy property, whereas only 10% of parents of young adolescents report these behaviors in their children (Achenbach, 1991a). In part, this decline may reflect parents' lack of awareness about the trouble their adolescents are getting into. However, although the amount of self-reported antisocial behavior by teens is higher than that reported by parents, their self-reports also show an age-related decline in antisocial behavior (Achenbach, 1991b). Parent-reported frequencies for several common antisocial behaviors for normal boys and girls ages 4 to 18 and for comparison groups of clinic-referred children are presented in Figure 6.2. These graphs illustrate several important features of antisocial behavior during normal development:

❖ Significant numbers of children display antisocial behavior at certain points in their development.
❖ Some antisocial behaviors decrease with age for normal children and, in some instances, for clinic-

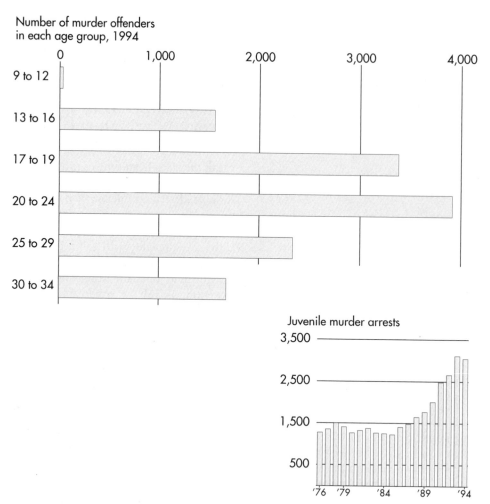

Number of murder offenders
in each age group, 1994

Juvenile murder arrests

FIGURE 6.1 Teenagers are the most crime-prone group. (*Time*, January 15, 1996)

referred children. However, clinic-referred children continue to display relatively higher rates of antisocial behavior at all ages.

❖ Other antisocial behaviors increase with age and opportunity (e.g., skipping school).

❖ As typically defined, antisocial behaviors (e.g., fighting, destructiveness) are more common in boys than girls during childhood (particularly among clinic-referred children), but this difference decreases or disappears by adolescence.

❖ The prevalence of antisocial behavior varies across settings—for example, home versus school.

❖ Antisocial behaviors in children vary in severity, from minor disobedience to attacks on other people.

Children who are the most physically aggressive in comparison with their peers maintain their relative standing over time, even though aggression decreases with age for most children. Longitudinal studies have found aggressive behavior to be highly stable for periods as long as 20, 30, or 40 years, with an average correla-

tion of about .70 for measures of aggressive behavior taken at different times (Farrington, 1991, 1992; Olweus, 1979; Sholevar & Sholevar, 1995). This makes aggressive behavior about as stable as children's IQ scores!

PERSPECTIVES ON CONDUCT PROBLEMS

Isolated antisocial activities are universal in children and adolescents, but an early, persistent, and extreme pattern of antisocial conduct, such as the one displayed by Nick, is much less common, occurring in only about 5% of children (Hinshaw & Anderson, 1996). Although such children are relatively few in number, they cause considerable and disproportionate amounts of physical and psychological harm to others and to themselves. More than half of all crime in the United States is committed by just 6% of youth between the ages of 10 and 20 years, and about one-third of clinic referrals are for the 5% of

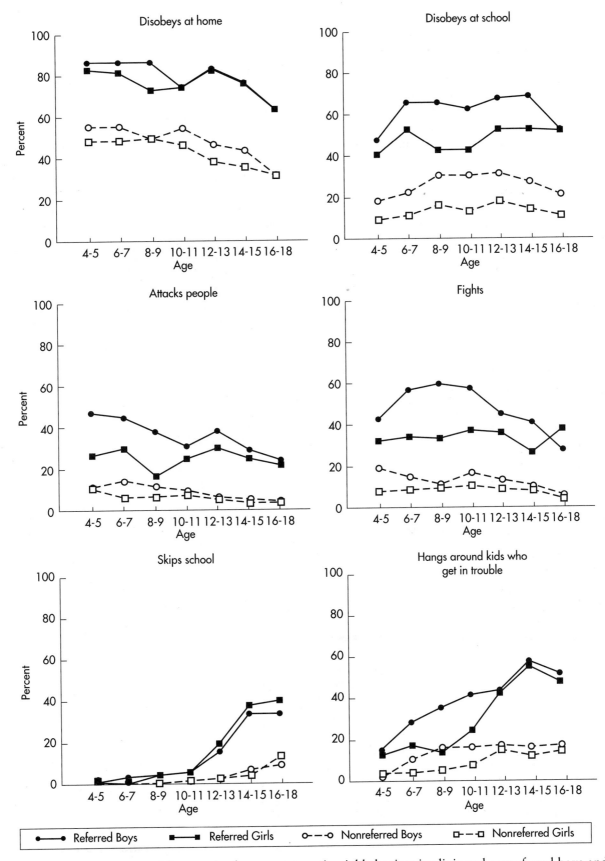

FIGURE 6.2 Parent-reported frequencies for common antisocial behaviors in clinic and nonreferred boys and girls ages 4–18. (Adapted from Achenbach, 1991a)

youths who display the most severe and dangerous antisocial behaviors (APA Commission on Youth Violence, 1993; Capaldi & Patterson, 1994). These children are viewed as unmanageable by their parents and teachers, and show significant impairment in their everyday personal, social, and academic functioning.

Over the years many different terms have been used to describe children with conduct problems, such as *oppositional, aggressive, antisocial, delinquent,* and *psychopathic.* These terms are often used interchangeably, which is inappropriate because they reflect widespread differences, which range from noncompliance in a preschooler to assault or murder by an adolescent (Hinshaw & Anderson, 1996). Most commonly, conduct problems in children are defined from legal, psychological, and psychiatric perspectives.

Legal Perspective

Legally, conduct problems are defined as **delinquent** or criminal acts. Legal definitions of delinquency depend on laws that change over time or that differ from locale to locale within a country, and from country to country. Since legal definitions result from apprehension and court contact, they exclude the antisocial activities of very young children. It is also important to distinguish "official" delinquency from "self-reported" delinquency, since there are likely to be differences between youth who display antisocial patterns and are officially apprehended, and those who display the same patterns but are not apprehended because of their intelligence or resourcefulness. There is an ongoing debate about the age at which children should be held responsible for their delinquent acts. The minimum age of responsibility is 12 in most states and provinces, but legal definitions of delinquent conduct have fluctuated over the years in relation to society's tolerance or intolerance for antisocial behavior.

There are two general types of delinquent acts: status offenses and index offenses. **Status offenses** are acts committed by youth that would not be considered offenses if committed by adults—for example, using alcohol, skipping school, driving a car, and violating curfew. In contrast, **index offenses** are acts that are considered criminal whether committed by a child or an adult—for example, murder, theft, and arson. Firesetting has a higher percentage of juvenile involvement than any other index offense, with about half of all arsons in the United States in 1994 committed by youngsters under the age of 18 (Federal Bureau of Investigation, 1994).

Significant numbers of children and teens are involved in serious criminal activities, creating climates of fear, threat, and intimidation in many communities (Richters & Martinez, 1993). In this general atmosphere we need to ask: Are antisocial criminal acts by young people caused by mental disorders, or are they understandable (albeit objectionable) adaptations to environments that foster such behavior? For example, many youths believe that carrying a weapon is necessary to avoid being bullied or beaten up by others. Unfortunately, there are no clear boundaries between delinquent acts that are a reaction to conditions in the environment, such as a high-crime neighborhood, and antisocial acts that result from factors within the child, such as impulsivity. Some criminal behaviors, such as arson and truancy, are arbitrarily included in current mental health definitions, whereas others, such as selling drugs, underage driving, and prostitution, are not. Legal definitions of delinquency may result from one or two isolated acts, whereas mental health definitions usually require the child to display a persistent pattern of antisocial behavior. Many individuals with conduct problems, particularly very young children, may or may not have contact with the law. Thus, only a subgroup of children who meet legal definitions for delinquency will also display patterns that fit the definition for a mental disorder (Cicchetti & Richters, 1993; Hinshaw & Anderson, 1996).

Psychological Perspective

The psychological perspective views conduct problems as falling along a statistically derived dimension called an **externalizing** pattern of behavior. This dimension is sometimes referred to as **undercontrolled,** a label that is somewhat misleading because only some antisocial children are lacking in control; others are highly calculating (Hinshaw & Anderson, 1996). Children who display extreme scores on the externalizing dimension, usually one or more standard deviations above the mean, are considered to have conduct problems. The externalizing dimension includes a mix of impulsive, overactive, aggressive, and delinquent actions, and itself consists of two independent but related subdimensions commonly labeled "delinquent" and "aggressive" (Achenbach, 1991a). Characteristic behaviors of the delinquent subdimension include running away from home, setting fires, stealing at home and elsewhere, skipping school, using alcohol and drugs, and committing acts of vandalism. Behaviors characteristic of the aggressive subdimension include destroying one's own or others' possessions, disobeying at school and at home, fighting, showing off, being defiant, threatening others, and being disruptive at school (Achenbach, 1993a).

Studies of the externalizing dimension have also identified two other independent dimensions of antisocial behavior, referred to as **overt–covert** and **destructive–nondestructive** (Frick et al., 1993). Overt forms of antisocial behavior correspond roughly to those on the

Two sides of the externalizing dimension: overt and covert.

aggressive dimension, whereas covert behaviors include hidden or sneaky acts, such as lying, stealing, and abusing drugs, which conform roughly to those on the delinquent dimension. Children higher in overt forms of antisocial behavior tend to be more negative, irritable, and resentful in their reactions to hostile situations, and to experience higher levels of family conflict (Kazdin, 1992). Those higher in covert antisocial behavior are less social, more anxious, and more suspicious of others, and come from homes that provide little family support. However, there is much overlap between these categories, and most children with conduct problems display both overt and covert antisocial behaviors. These mixed or diverse types of children are in frequent conflict with authority and show the most severe family dysfunction and the poorest long-term outcomes (Loeber, Lahey, & Thomas, 1991).

The destructive–nondestructive continuum ranges from acts such as cruelty to animals or destruction of property at one end, to nondestructive behaviors such as arguing or irritability at the other. As shown in Figure 6.3, crossing the destructive-nondestructive and overt-covert dimensions results in four quadrants of antisocial behavior: (A) covert–destructive, or prop-erty violations; (B) overt–destructive, or aggression; (C) covert–nondestructive, or status violations; and (D) overt–nondestructive, or oppositional behavior.

Types of Antisocial Behavior. Children display many different types of antisocial behavior, making it difficult to fit a behavior or child into just one category. Nevertheless, the distinctions that follow, which contrast types of aggression, are useful in that the prevalence, causes, course, outcomes, and recommended treatment for a given behavior or child often depend on the type of antisocial behaviors they display. **Aggression** is generally defined as behavior that threatens, attempts, or inflicts intentional physical or psychological harm (APA Commission on Violence and Youth, 1993). Assessing intentionality is never easy, but these criteria help to exclude from the definition any unintended acts that cause injury such as accidentally bumping into another child and causing her to fall down and hurt herself.

Verbal versus physical aggression. **Verbal aggression** includes threats, name-calling, taunts, and swearing, whereas **physical aggression** involves hitting, bullying, assaulting, and fighting. For most nonproblem children, physical aggression appears early in development and

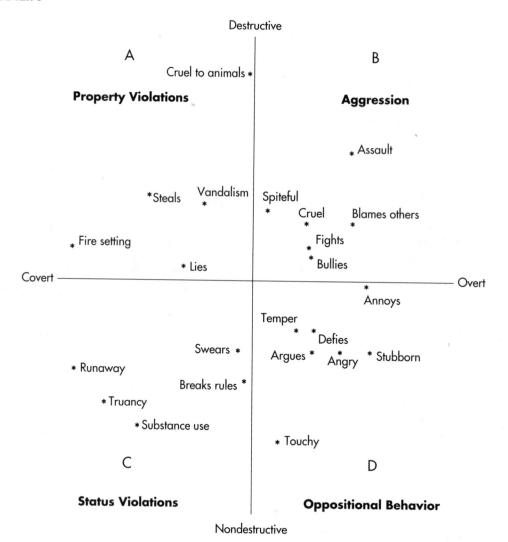

FIGURE 6.3 Two dimensions of conduct problems: overt-covert and destructive-nondestructive. (Adapted from Frick et al., 1993)

peaks during the preschool years, with verbal aggression beginning later and continuing through adolescence (Parke & Slaby, 1983).

Instrumental versus hostile aggression. Instrumental aggression is directed at achieving a specific goal (other than inflicting pain), whereas hostile aggression is directed at inflicting pain on others. Some forms of instrumental aggression in young children, such as pushing another child out of the way to obtain an attractive toy, may represent an age-appropriate expression of the child's effort to establish independence and a sense of self. In contrast, **hostile aggression**, such as beating up another child for no reason other than to inflict pain, is inappropriate at all ages.

Direct versus indirect aggression. Direct aggression involves verbal and physical displays toward others, whereas **indirect aggression** involves getting even by third-party retaliation, or by spreading rumors. The use of indirect aggression may be more common in girls than in boys (Crick, Bigbee, & Howes, 1996).

Reactive versus proactive aggression. Reactive aggression occurs in response to actions by others, whereas proactive aggression involves taking the offensive without provocation through domination, bullying, or threats. Reactive aggression in children is associated with deficits and distortions in taking in and interpreting information in social situations, including a limited use of social information in reaching interpersonal decisions and a tendency to think that others have bad intentions. In contrast, proactive aggression is associated with a restricted and mostly aggressive behavioral repertoire (Crick & Dodge, 1996). Children who display reactive aggression may have histories of physical abuse, early onset of problems, and difficulties in peer relations. By

Box 6.1
Bullies and Their Victims

For two years, Johnny, a quiet 13-year-old, was a human plaything for some of his classmates. The teenagers badgered Johnny for money, forced him to swallow weeds and drink milk mixed with detergent, beat him up in the rest room and tied a string around his neck, leading him around as a "pet." (Olweus, 1995, p. 196)

Bullying among school children is a very old, familiar, and particularly offensive form of antisocial behavior. Bullying occurs when one or more children expose another child, repeatedly and over time, to negative actions. Such actions may take the form of physical contact, words, making faces or dirty gestures, and intentional exclusion from a group. Bullying usually involves an imbalance of power so that the victim has difficulty defending herself or himself (Olweus, 1995). The scope of this problem is large, with 7% or more of school-age children bullying other kids. Boys are much more likely than girls to bully other children, and are also somewhat more likely to be the victims of bullying.

A child's status as a victim or a bully is likely to be stable over time, and victims and bullies display certain typical characteristics. Typical victims are characterized by anxious and submissive patterns of behavior and, in the case of boys, by physical weakness. These children send a signal to others that if they are attacked or insulted, they won't retaliate. Typical bullies are distinguished by their aggressiveness toward both peers and adults. They are often impulsive, have a need to dominate other people, are stronger than other boys, show little empathy for their victims, and derive satisfaction, and often, material gain from inflicting injury and suffering on their victims. One study found that nearly 40% of boys who were bullies in school were later convicted of three or more criminal offenses by the time they were 24 years old (Olweus, 1995). Thus, bullying in the school appears to be part of a more general pattern of antisocial behavior.

1995). Violent youth do not differ from their non-violent peers in age-of-onset or rate or seriousness of their non-violent offenses. Rather, the main difference between these groups seems to be in family support and disciplinary practices, although even these differences are not large (Gorman-Smith, Tolan, Zelli, & Huesmann, 1996). Thus, violent behaviors appear to fall along a continuum, with youths who commit violent offenses displaying a more extreme form of antisocial behavior rather than constituting a group that is qualitatively distinct from other antisocial children.

Four types of youth violence can be distinguished by their presumed causes, the segment of the population most at risk, and the types of intervention they suggest (Tolan & Guerra, 1994):

❖ **Situational violence** is related to specific situational factors, such as times of social stress, weekends, heat waves, availability of a weapon, or drugs.
❖ **Relationship violence** arises from interpersonal disputes between people within ongoing relationships, especially friends and family members.
❖ **Predatory violence** is committed intentionally to obtain some gain or as a pattern of criminal behavior, such as robbery or gang assaults.
❖ **Psychopathological violence** is a by-product of severe pathology related to neurological dysfunction or psychological trauma.

The percentages of adolescents affected, primary determinants, numbers of risk factors, and ages of onset for each of these four patterns of violence are shown in Figure 6.4.

An important conclusion to be drawn from our discussion of different types of antisocial behavior and subgroups of antisocial children is that antisocial behaviors and the children who display them come in many different varieties. The prevalence, developmental course, outcome, and causes may vary for different types of behavior and different subgroups of children. Thus, to understand aggressive and antisocial behavior we need to be sensitive to their many different forms of expression.

Do antisocial behaviors fall along a continuous dimension, or does exceeding some threshold result in a qualitatively different form of behavior, in the way that water turns to ice when the temperature drops below 32 degrees? One way to answer this question is to see whether there is a continuous relation between the number of aggressive/antisocial symptoms that a child displays and an outcome, or whether this relationship changes abruptly once a critical threshold of antisocial behavior is crossed. For example, the extent of adult substance abuse increases gradually as a function of the number of aggressive/antisocial symptoms during childhood. There is no evidence for a sharp increase in

contrast, those who display proactive aggression anticipate positive outcomes for their aggression (Dodge, Lochman, Harnish, Bates, & Pettit, 1997). Reactive aggression may be driven by anger whereas proactive aggression often reflects a child's preference for aggressive solutions as seen in the case of children who are bullies (see Box 6.1).

Violent versus nonviolent acts. In general, violent offenders do not engage in violent behavior to the exclusion of other antisocial activities, but can be distinguished from other antisocial adolescents because they are violent (Tolan & Loeber, 1993; Tolan & Thomas,

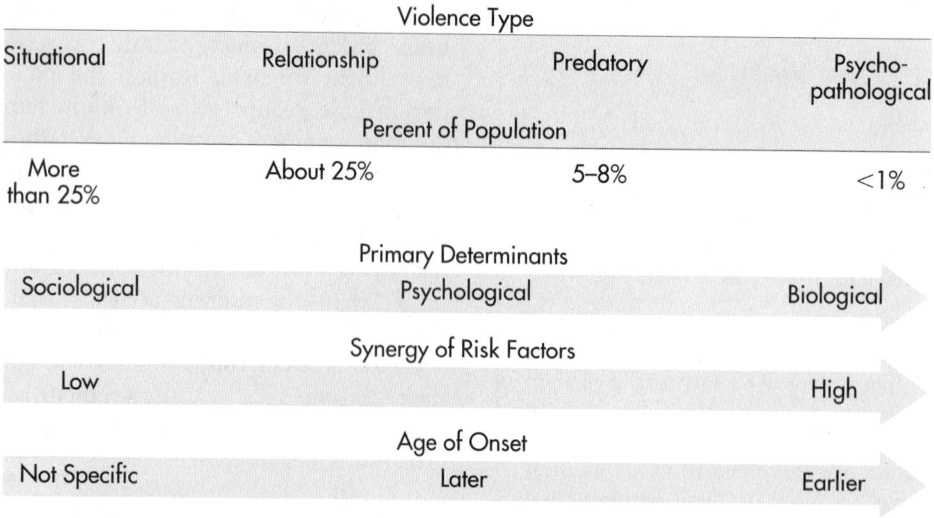

Violence Type			
Situational	Relationship	Predatory	Psycho-pathological
Percent of Population			
More than 25%	About 25%	5–8%	<1%

Primary Determinants		
Sociological	Psychological	Biological →

Synergy of Risk Factors	
Low	High →

Age of Onset		
Not Specific	Later	Earlier →

FIGURE 6.4   Four types of youth violence. (Tolan & Guerra, 1994)

substance abuse at any cut-off of antisocial symptoms (Robins & McEvoy, 1990). These and other findings indicate that most antisocial behaviors fall along a continuous dimension of severity.

Psychiatric Perspective

Conduct problems are identified psychiatrically as discrete mental disorders based on DSM-IV symptom lists (APA, 1994). In DSM-IV, persistent patterns of antisocial behavior are included under the category **disruptive behavior disorders,** which includes oppositional defiant disorder and conduct disorder (as well as the predominantly hyperactive-impulsive type of ADHD, discussed in Chapter 5). Also relevant to understanding conduct problems in children and their adult outcomes is the adult diagnostic category of antisocial personality disorder.

Oppositional defiant disorder (ODD) is the least severe form of disruptive behavior disorder, and is diagnosed in children who show an age-inappropriate and persistent pattern of irritable, hostile, oppositional, and defiant behavior. In contrast, children with **conduct disorder (CD)** display more severe aggressive and antisocial acts involving inflicting pain on others or interfering with others' rights through physical and verbal aggression, stealing, or committing acts of vandalism. Many children diagnosed with CD will be apprehended for delinquent behavior. However, only a small number of adolescents who commit delinquent acts display the persistent pattern of behavior that would qualify for a diagnosis of CD (Hinshaw, Lahey, & Hart, 1993; Moffitt, 1993a).

The diagnosis of **antisocial personality disorder (APD)** applies to about 5% of adults who, beginning in childhood or early adolescence, show a pervasive pattern of disregard for, and violation of, the rights of others, engaging in multiple illegal behaviors (APA, 1994). In addition to displaying early CD, adults with APD may also display a pattern of deceitful, callous, manipulative, and remorseless behavior labeled **psychopathy** (Sutker, 1994). Although the terms *psychopathy* and *antisocial personality* are often used interchangeably, the interpersonal and emotional styles characteristic of psychopathy, which include lack of guilt, lack of empathy, superficial charm, and absence of anxiety, are at least partially independent of the antisocial criminal behavior of adults (Hare, Hart, & Harpur, 1991). For example, mob boss John Gotti grew up and operated in an environment that supported extreme acts of aggression and violence, but he reportedly displayed a pattern of brutal psychopathic behavior that far exceeded the norms for his own criminal environment (Richters & Cicchetti, 1993).

DSM-IV: DEFINING FEATURES OF CONDUCT PROBLEMS

In this section we consider the specific child characteristics used to diagnose ODD and CD. We also consider three related questions: First, is there any special significance associated with the age at which conduct problems begin? Second, what is the relationship between ODD and CD? Third, is there a link between disruptive behavior disorders in childhood and antisocial personality disorder in adults?

Table 6.1	Diagnostic Criteria for Oppositional Defiant Disorder

A. A pattern of negativistic, hostile, and defiant behavior lasting at least 6 months, during which four (or more) of the following are present:

(1) often loses temper
(2) often argues with adults
(3) often actively defies or refuses to comply with adults' requests or rules
(4) often deliberately annoys people
(5) often blames others for his or her mistakes or misbehavior
(6) is often touchy or easily annoyed by others
(7) is often angry and resentful
(8) is often spiteful or vindictive

Note: Consider a criterion met only if the behavior occurs more frequently than is typically observed in individuals of comparable age and developmental level.

B. The disturbance in behavior causes clinically significant impairment in social, academic, or occupational functioning.

C. The behaviors do not occur exclusively during the course of a Psychotic or Mood Disorder.

D. Criteria are not met for Conduct Disorder, and, if the individual is age 18 years or older, criteria are not met for Antisocial Personality Disorder.

Source: DSM-IV, Copyright © 1994 by APA.

Oppositional Defiant Disorder

Not an Easy-Going Bone in His Body

He just digs his heels in, "That's it, I am not wearing these socks! Forget it, I'm not going!" And he is right. He's gone to school in his pajamas, without lunch, in the pouring rain without any coat. . . . He will explain to me, "Mom, we are done with this discussion." . . . He doesn't have an easy-going bone in his body. He is not ever going to say, "Okay, I'll put that turtleneck on." It's going to be, "I will do something but only on my terms. . . . I will do nothing that you want me to do and furthermore I'll throw such a tantrum and throw this cereal bowl all over the wall, so you will be late, and mad at me when you clean it up." . . . He enjoys that power. (Webster-Stratton & Herbert, 1994, p. 47)

Children with oppositional defiant disorder display age-inappropriate amounts of stubborn, irritable, and defiant behaviors. DSM-IV criteria for ODD are presented in Table 6.1.

ODD was included for the first time in the DSM-III (1980) to capture the early displays of antisocial and aggressive behavior by preschool- and school-age children. Because many of these behaviors, such as arguing, displaying anger, or expressing annoyance, are extremely common in young children, doubts have been raised about the viability of this category in both professional and popular circles (Angold & Costello, 1996; Kirk & Hutchins, 1994; Rey et al., 1988). However, an independent ODD cluster of nondestructive-overt behaviors (e.g., defying, arguing) is apparent from factor analytic studies (see Figure 6.2, quadrant D), which offers support for ODD as a distinct disorder.

Conduct Disorder

Greg: Conduct Disorder and Other Problems

Ten-year-old Greg lives at home with his mother, father, younger brothers, and a baby sister. He was referred because of his excessive fighting, hyperactivity, temper tantrums, and disruptive behavior at home and at school. At home, Greg argued with his mother, initiated fights with his siblings, took money from his parents, and constantly threatened to set fires when disciplined by his parents. On three separate occasions, he actually had set fires to rugs, bedspreads, and trash in his home. One of these fires led to major damage, costing several thousand dollars. Greg also lied frequently; at school his lying got others into trouble, precipitating frequent fights with peers and denials of any wrongdoing.

Greg was brought to the clinic because his parents felt that he was becoming totally unmanageable. A few incidents in particular were mentioned as unusually dangerous—for example, Greg's attempt to suffocate his 2-year-old brother by holding a pillow over his face. Also Greg had recently wandered the streets at night and had broken windows of parked cars. Greg's parents occasionally resorted to severe punishment by using paddles and belts or by locking Greg in his room for 2- to 3-day periods. These punishments appear to have been in response to setting fires in the home.

Several characteristics of Greg's family life are noteworthy. Because Greg's mother and father had worked all of Greg's life, his grandmother had primary care responsibility of the children. For 2 years before Greg was brought for treatment, his father had been employed only sporadically. Greg's father spent much of his time at home sleeping or watching TV, and the loss of income led to increased stress at home. Greg said that he could not stand to be with his dad because his dad got mad all the time over little things. Greg's mother worked full-time and was not at home very much. She had a history of depression with two suicide attempts in the last 3 years. She was hospitalized on each occasion for approximately 2 months. Greg's behavior at home and school became worse than usual during these periods.

Greg was in the fourth grade. Although his intelligence was within the normal range, his academic performance was behind grade level, and he was in a special class because of his overactive and disruptive behavior. His parents were told that unless they sought help, Greg could not return to the school the next year. Greg's parents did not know where to turn. They talked about giving Greg up or putting him in a special boarding school where more discipline might make him "shape up." (Adapted from Kazdin, 1995, pp. 2–3)

Table 6.2 Diagnostic Criteria for Conduct Disorder

A. A repetitive and persistent pattern of behavior in which the basic rights of others or major age-appropriate societal norms or rules are violated, as manifested by the presence of three (or more) of the following criteria in the past 12 months, with at least one criterion present in the past 6 months:

Aggression to people and animals
  (1) often bullies, threatens, or intimidates others
  (2) often initiates physical fights
  (3) has used a weapon that can cause serious physical harm to others (e.g., a bat, brick, broken bottle, knife, gun)
  (4) has been physically cruel to people
  (5) has been physically cruel to animals
  (6) has stolen while confronting a victim (e.g., mugging, purse snatching, extortion, armed robbery)
  (7) has forced someone into sexual activity

Destruction of property
  (8) has deliberately engaged in fire setting, with the intention of causing serious damage
  (9) has deliberately destroyed others' property (other than by fire setting)

Deceitfulness or theft
  (10) has broken into someone else's house, building, or car
  (11) often lies to obtain goods or favors or to avoid obligations (i.e., "cons" others)
  (12) has stolen items of nontrivial value without confronting a victim (e.g., shoplifting, but without breaking and entering; forgery)

Serious violations of rules
  (13) often stays out at night despite parental prohibitions, beginning before age 13 years
  (14) has run away from home overnight at least twice while living in parental or parental surrogate home (or once without returning for a lengthy period)
  (15) is often truant from school, beginning before age 13 years

B. The disturbance in behavior causes clinically significant impairment in social, academic, or occupational functioning.

C. If the individual is age 18 years or older, criteria are not met for Antisocial Personality Disorder.

Source: DSM IV, Copyright © 1994 by APA.

Greg's case illustrates several common features of children with CD (Kazdin, 1995):

❖ Children with CD engage in severe behaviors. Greg set fires and tried to suffocate his 2-year-old brother. He also displayed less severe problems, such as noncompliance and temper tantrums, but these weren't the primary reasons for referral.
❖ Children with CD often experience accompanying problems such as ADHD and poor school adjustment.
❖ Parents feel their children with CD are out of control and report feeling helpless to do anything about it. Greg's parents were ready to give him up or to place him in boarding school.
❖ Parents of children with CD often have their own problems and stresses—for example, marital discord, psychiatric problems, and unemployment. Greg's mother had a history of depression.
❖ Children with CD are in contact with multiple social services and agencies, including the school, the courts, and mental health facilities.

Greg's chronic and unmanageable pattern of antisocial behavior, which includes fighting, firesetting, lying, stealing, and breaking windows of parked cars, qualifies for a diagnosis of CD. The DSM-IV criteria for CD are presented in Table 6.2.

Since conduct disorder occurs with varying degrees of severity and impact, DSM-IV also specifies whether a child displays CD that is "mild," "moderate," or "severe," based on the number of conduct problems and the extent of harmful effects on others.

Does Age of Onset Make a Difference?

DSM-IV also makes the crucial distinction between the **childhood-onset** and **adolescent-onset** types of CD. Children with childhood-onset CD display at least one characteristic of CD prior to 10 years of age, whereas those with adolescent-onset CD do not. Increasing evidence points to the importance of age of onset in diagnosing and treating children with CD (Waldman, Lilienfeld, & Lahey, 1995). Children with childhood-onset CD are more likely to be boys, show a greater number of aggressive symptoms, account for a disproportionate amount of illegal activity, and persist in their antisocial behavior over time. For example, conduct problems at age 8 are a strong predictor of offending at age 16, with a correlation between the two of about .50 (Fergusson & Horwood, 1996). In contrast, children who show adolescent-onset CD are as likely to be girls as boys, and do not display the severity or psychopathology that characterizes the early-onset group. Adolescent-onset CD children are also less likely to commit violent offenses or to persist in their antisocial behavior as they get older. Age of onset *does* make a difference.

Are ODD and CD Different Disorders?

An issue currently being hotly debated is whether ODD is a separate disorder from CD, or a milder, earlier version of CD (Achenbach, 1993b; Loeber, Lahey, & Thomas, 1991). Symptoms of ODD typically emerge 2 to 3 years before those of CD, with an average age of onset of 6 years for ODD versus 9 years for CD (Loeber, Green, Lahey, Christ, & Frick, 1992). It is possible that the lower rate of CD in younger children is due to the nature of the DSM-IV criteria. DSM uses the same symptoms for diagnosing CD for children of all ages, even though many of these symptoms are not applicable for very young children (e.g., breaking into houses, skipping school). Thus, the lower rates of CD in young children could reflect the use of an insensitive diagnostic system that is unadjusted for the child's age.

Since ODD symptoms precede those for CD, it is possible that ODD symptoms are precursors of CD for some children. However, most children who display ODD do not progress to more severe CD—50% maintain their ODD diagnosis without progressing, and 25% cease to display ODD problems (Hinshaw et al., 1993). So for most children, ODD is an extreme developmental variation, but not one that necessarily signals further escalation to more serious conduct problems. In contrast, new cases of CD are almost always preceded by ODD, and 90% of children with CD continue to display their ODD symptoms (Biederman, Faraone, & Russell, 1996; Lahey, Loeber, Quay, Frick, & Grimm, 1992).

Box 6.2
Bart Simpson: ODD, CD, or Both?

Sharpen your knowledge of DSM-IV criteria for oppositional defiant disorder and conduct disorder by considering whether or not TV cartoon personality Bart Simpson qualifies for a diagnosis of one or both of these disorders? Here is a list of antisocial acts displayed by Bart:
❖ Flushes a cherry bomb down the toilet
❖ Rearranges party snacks to say "Boy our party sucks"
❖ Loosens the top on Milhouse's salt shaker
❖ Lights Homer's tie on fire
❖ Tricks Flanders kids into giving cookies away
❖ Pretends to be Timmy (trapped in well)
❖ Pulls carpet up, writes "Bart" on carpet
❖ Plays with and later breaks grandpa Abe's false teeth
❖ Flushes Homer's wallet and keys down toilet
❖ Cuts all of baby Maggie's hair off
❖ Paints extra lines on parking lot
❖ Leaves box factory tour
❖ Pops heads off Mr. Burns' statues/floods his car
❖ Smashes Mr. Burns' windows
❖ Recounts throwing mail in sewer with Milhouse
❖ Phones 911 to get babysitter into trouble

Antisocial Personality Disorder

Current DSM-IV criteria for **antisocial personality disorder (APD)** in adults include signs of psychopathy, such as a lack of remorse and deceitfulness, as well as behavioral acts such as repeated fighting, impulsivity, and aggressiveness. Definitions that rely exclusively on behavioral acts run the risk of labeling recurrent criminality as a personality disorder. Nevertheless, persistent aggressive and antisocial patterns of behavior in childhood may be a precursor of adult psychopathy, with as many as 25% to 40% of children with CD developing antisocial personality disorder as adults (Hinshaw, 1994). As this chilling description shows, some children display clear signs of psychopathy at a very young age.

Jason: No Conscience

Thirteen-year-old Jason had been involved in serious crime—including breaking and entering, thefts, and assaults on younger children—by age 6. Listening to Jason talk was frightening. Asked why he committed crimes, this product of a stable, professional family replied, "I like it. My f___ parents really freak out when I get in trouble, but I don't give a sh __ as long as I'm having a good time. Yeah, I've always been wild." About other people, including his victims, he had this to say: "You want the truth? They'd screw me if they could, only I get my shots in first." He liked to rob homeless people, especially "faggots," "bag ladies," and street kids, because, "They're used to it. They don't whine to the police. . . . One guy I got into a fight with pulled a knife and I took it and rammed it in his eye. He ran around screaming like a baby. What a jerk!" (Adapted from Hare, 1993, p. 162)

Far less is known about psychopathy in children than in adults. However, signs of a lack of conscience are found in children as young as 3 to 5 years (Kochanska & DeVet, 1994), and some youths, like Jason, commit brutal acts of violence with little remorse. Adolescents with CD are less likely to show embarrassment than their peers, suggesting a failure to inhibit emotions and actions in accordance with social conventions (Keltner, Moffitt, & Stouthamer-Loeber, 1995). Using the Screening Device for Psychopathy (see Table 6.3), recent research has identified a distinct cluster of school-age children with conduct problems who display a **callous-unemotional interpersonal style** characterized by such traits as lacking in guilt, not showing empathy, and not showing emotions. These children display a greater number and variety of conduct problems, a history of more frequent contacts with police, and a stronger parental history of antisocial personality disorder, despite having higher intelligence than other children with conduct problems (Christian, Frick, Hill, Tyler, & Frazer, 1997; Frick, O'Brien, Wootton, & McBurnett, 1994).

Some children who display hyperactivity, impulsivity, noncompliance, and aggressive behavior at an extremely young age might be showing early signs of a "fledgling psychopathy" (Lynam, 1996). However, since child antisocial behaviors, such as impulsivity and conduct problems (e.g., explosive temper, fighting), and child psychopathy, as reflected in callous, cruel, or unemotional behavior (e.g., torturing a family pet with little remorse), represent two distinct dimensions (Frick et al., 1994), this link is likely to be present in only a very small proportion of children who display antisocial behavior at an early age.

Table 6.3   **Screening Device for Psychopathy**

Blames others	Brags excessively	Reacts to correction with anger
Engages in illegal activities	Is easily bored	Believes him- or herself better than others
Is unconcerned about school	Uses or cons others	Fails to plan
Acts without regard for consequences	Teases or makes fun of others	Is unconcerned about others
Is shallow and ingenuine	Displays no feelings of remorse	Doesn't show feelings
Lies with skill and ease	Engages in risky and dangerous activities	Has unstable friendships
Breaks promises	Is charming but ingenuine	

Source: Frick & Hare, 1997.

ASSOCIATED CHARACTERISTICS OF CONDUCT PROBLEMS

Numerous individual, family, peer, school, and community factors are associated with conduct problems in children. Some of these co-occur with conduct problems, others increase the likelihood of conduct problems, and still others are the result of conduct problems. For example, ADHD or cognitive deficits may co-occur with conduct problems and share a common cause, such as a neuropsychological deficit; substance abuse may increase the likelihood of future conduct problems, such as stealing to obtain money for drugs; and depression may be the result of conduct-related school failure. Often, the same factor can operate in multiple ways, such as when cognitive deficits lead to poor schoolwork, which in turn leads to further cognitive deficits. Part of the challenge in understanding conduct problems in children is in unraveling the ways in which these many factors interact with one another over time to influence antisocial behavior.

Impairments in Cognition and Learning

Cognitive and Verbal Deficits. Although most children with conduct problems are of normal intelligence, on average they score about 8 points lower on IQ tests than their peers. This IQ deficit may be even larger (more than 15 points) for children with early-onset conduct disorder, and cannot be accounted for solely by factors such as low social class, race, or detection by the police (Lynam, Moffitt, & Stouthamer-Loeber, 1993; Moffitt & Silva, 1988). However, lower IQ scores in children with conduct problems may be due to the presence of co-occurring ADHD (Sonuga-Barke, Lamparelli, Stevenson, Thompson, & Henry, 1994).

How might lower IQ scores and antisocial behavior be related? Since children with similar IQ scores have different cognitive strengths and weaknesses, to answer this question we need to identify the specific cognitive impairments underlying the antisocial child's general deficit in IQ. The fact that verbal IQ is consistently lower than performance IQ in children with conduct problems suggests a specific and pervasive deficit in language that may affect the child's receptive listening and reading, problem solving, expressive speech and writing, and memory for verbal material (Caspi & Moffitt, 1995).

How might these verbal and language deficits contribute to antisocial behavior? Several related mechanisms have been proposed, all of which may play a role (Caspi & Moffitt, 1995):

❖ Verbal deficits may interfere with the development of self-control.

❖ Low verbal intelligence is associated with a here-and-now cognitive style that fosters irresponsible and exploitative behavior.

❖ Verbal deficits may interfere with delaying gratification, anticipating consequences, and associating delayed punishment with transgressions.

❖ Verbal deficits may interfere with learning to label behaviors as bad, naughty, or wicked, requiring that the meaning of these terms be learned via more costly trial-and-error methods.

❖ Verbal deficits may lead to difficulties in labeling emotions in others, which may lead to a lack of empathy.

❖ Verbal limitations may narrow response options, leading to physical actions, such as hitting, rather than verbal options, such as negotiation and discussion.

Lower IQ and verbal intelligence are present early in development, well before the emergence of conduct problems and delinquent behavior. However, the presence of these deficits alone does not predict future aggression (Patterson, 1996). Rather, verbal impairments are likely to interact with family factors in predicting antisocial outcomes. Children with low verbal functioning and family adversity combined display 4 times as much aggressive behavior as children with just one or the other factor (Moffitt, 1990). Thus, poor verbal functioning may increase the vulnerability of children to the effects of an adverse family environment. How this occurs is not known, but one possibility is that the child's limited verbal ability may make it more difficult for parents to understand their child's needs, leading to frustration, less positive interactions, more punishment, and greater difficulties in teaching prosocial skills (Hinshaw, Lahey, & Hart, 1993; Patterson, 1996).

Children with conduct problems rarely consider the future implications of their behavior or its impact on others. They fail to inhibit their impulsive behavior, keep social values or future rewards in mind, or adapt their actions to changing circumstances. Such patterns reflect deficits in executive functions similar to those described for children with ADHD (Seguin, Pihl, Harden, Tremblay, & Boulerice, 1995). Although impairments in executive functions are related to lower IQ scores, they cannot be accounted for *solely* by lower IQs (Caspi & Moffitt, 1995). Because conduct problems and ADHD frequently co-occur, some researchers contend that the observed deficits in executive functions in children with conduct problems are due strictly to the presence of ADHD. There is some support for this contention, since children with CD without ADHD do not display deficits in executive functions, and the presence of CD in children with ADHD is not related to a worsening of their executive functions (Pennington & Ozonoff, 1996).

School and Learning Problems

> *Every time you stop a school, you will have to build a jail.*
> —Mark Twain, 1900

Not too long ago such behaviors as talking out of turn, chewing gum, or running in the halls were the top disciplinary problems in schools. Now, the top problems are drug abuse, robbery, and assault. In addition to their disciplinary problems, youngsters with conduct problems display high rates of academic underachievement, grade retention, special education placement, school dropout, detention, suspension, and expulsion (Hinshaw & Anderson, 1996).

The link between school difficulties and antisocial behavior has led to the suggestion that reading-related school failure is a cause of antisocial behavior. However, findings are mixed with respect to whether or not reading difficulties predict later conduct problems (Maughan, Pickles, Hagell, Rutter, & Yule, 1996; Williams & McGee, 1994). Increased risks of juvenile offending among boys referred for reading difficulties appear to be related to poor school attendance, rather than to reading difficulties alone (Maughan et al., 1996). Although the frustration and demoralization associated with school failure may lead to antisocial behavior in some children (Maughan, Gray, & Rutter, 1985), there is little evidence to support academic failure as the primary explanation for antisocial behavior, particularly during childhood. Since many children display antisocial behavior patterns long before they even enter school, it is more likely that a common underlying factor, such as neuropsychological deficits, deficits in verbal functions, or socioeconomic disadvantage, underlies both school difficulties and conduct problems (Farrington, 1991; Hinshaw, 1992).

Children with conduct problems are especially likely to show academic underachievement in language and reading (Moffitt 1993b). As with deficits in verbal and executive functions, the relationship between conduct problems and academic underachievement is best accounted for by the presence of ADHD. When ADHD is not present, children with conduct problems are no more likely to display academic underachievement than other children (Frick et al., 1991; Hinshaw, 1992; Loeber, 1990). So, although school and learning difficulties and conduct problems are related, the nature of this relationship is complex, with the presence of ADHD being a crucial mediating factor. In addition, underachievement and conduct problems are likely to influence one another over time. Subtle early language deficits may lead to reading and communication difficulties, which in turn may heighten antisocial behavior in elementary school (McGee et al., 1986). Children and adolescents with poor academic skills are increasingly likely to lose interest in school and to associate with delinquent peers. By adolescence, the relationship between underachievement and antisocial behavior is firmly established.

Self-Esteem Deficits

A widely publicized report in California titled *Toward a State of Self-Esteem* (1990) focused public attention on the idea that children with conduct problems have low self-esteem, that low self-concept may lead to violent behavior, and that violence in youth can be reduced through interventions designed to raise children's self-esteem. Although some children with conduct problems may have low self-esteem, there is little support for the view that low self-esteem is the primary cause of antisocial behavior. A closer look at the evidence suggests that aggression, crime, and violence may result from a perceived threat to an inflated, unstable, and/or tentative view of self. Any perceived threat to the child's view of self may lead to violence, which provides a mechanism for avoiding a downward revision of self-concept (Baumeister, Smart, & Boden, 1996). Consistent with this view, self-esteem among youth gang members seems to conform to a zero sum pattern, where any increment in status, respect, or prestige in self-esteem for one group member takes away from what is available for others (Anderson, 1994). Thus, although low self-esteem is not the major cause of conduct problems, children with conduct problems may experience a variety of disturbances in self-concept that contribute to their antisocial behavior.

Interpersonal Difficulties with Peers

The mother of a 6-year-old boy describes her son's behavior:

> He is so aggressive around other children. We can't really trust him not to walk up and wallop the smaller ones. He pokes them in the eyes or pushes them down. . . . It's almost like he seeks out other children to hurt them. (Webster-Stratton & Herbert, 1994, p. 46)

Young children with conduct problems display physical aggression, inappropriate play, hostile talk, and poor social skills. Not surprisingly, they are likely to be rejected by many of their peers. As children with conduct problems grow older, they do make friends; unfortunately, their friendships are often based on a mutual attraction between like-minded antisocial individuals (Cairns & Cairns, 1991). The combination of early antisocial behavior and associating with deviant peers is the single most powerful predictor of conduct problems during adolescence, with correlations of .40 to .50 between involvement with deviant peers and antisocial behavior (Moffitt, 1993a; Patterson & Dishion, 1985). Involvement with antisocial peers becomes increasingly stable from ages 9 to 12, and this involvement supports the transition from coercive behavior during childhood, to adolescent criminal acts such as stealing, substance abuse, or truancy (Dishion et al., 1995; Patterson, 1996). About two-thirds of all recorded youth offenses are committed in the company of two to three peers (Aultman, 1980), with peer involvement being greater for property offenses than for violent offenses, and for girls than for boys (Dishion et al., 1995). Involvement with deviant peers also predicts accelerated autonomy in adolescence and early sexual activity (Dishion, Haas, & Poulin, 1997).

The "friendships" between antisocial boys are likely to consist of interactions that are abrasive, unstable, of short duration, and not very satisfying (Dishion, Andrews, & Crosby, 1995). Positive exchanges, when they do occur, are compromised by the bossy and coercive behaviors that accompany them. Antisocial children may selectively reward one another for discussions of rule breaking, but have little to say about prosocial or normative behavior, thus engaging in a "deviancy training" process (Dishion, Spracklen, Andrews, & Patterson, 1996). As a result of this differential reinforcement, individual group members may become more alike in their antisocial tendencies over time, leading to a further escalation in the frequency and variety of their antisocial activities. This insidious phenomenon is called **trait confluence.**

In the Company of "Friends"

On February 16, 1995, in the small Minnesota town of Delano, a 14-year-old boy and his best friend ambushed and killed [the 14-year-old's] mother as she returned home. . . . These two boys spent much time together. The boys have admitted to planning the ambush (one saying they had planned it for weeks; the other, for a few hours). They arrived armed and waiting when the mother arrived home from work. One conclusion seems relatively certain: this murder was an unlikely event until these two antisocial friends reached consensus about doing it. (Adapted from Hartup, 1996, p. 1)

Social-Cognitive Deficits

Children with conduct problems display deficits in how they process information in social situations. Aggressive children seek less information than others before reaching a decision about another child's intentions and fail to attend to relevant social cues. They are overly sensitive to hostile social cues, underestimate their own aggressiveness and its negative consequences, overestimate the amount of aggression that is directed toward them, display a lack of empathy, and are more likely to attribute negative intent to others, especially when the intentions of another child are unclear (e.g., when another child accidentally bumps into them). Aggressive children tend to value social goals of dominance and revenge rather than affiliation. They display limited and mostly aggressive solutions to social problems. Even when their problem solving produces a successful outcome, their solutions are usually aggressive and inappropriate (Dodge, 1989; Crick & Dodge, 1994).

Many of these children live in highly aggressive and threatening circumstances. In some cases, their so-called bias toward seeing threat and aggression in others may be an accurate reflection of the realities of living in a hostile social world, and their aggressive style of responding, an adaptive reaction to that world.

Family Disturbances

Sam: Nothing Ever Gets Resolved

Fifteen-year-old Sam and his mother have bitter arguments over curfew, dating, homework, and household chores. These arguments begin when his mother sets down rules and Sam defies them. During the arguments, Sam curses his mother, puts her down, and accuses her of being unfair and strict. In turn, Sam's mother recites a laundry list of Sam's past misbehaviors and accuses him of disrespect. Sam's mother feels that her son is purposely rebelling against her to hurt her, and that if he doesn't straighten up, he will wind up in jail. Sam feels that his mother's rules will ruin his life and that she does not understand his generation. Sam's father feels that it is his wife's job to raise the children, and that if they misbehave, a "competent" mother would know how to handle the problem. When Sam's mother is fed up with her son, she threatens to divorce her husband and leave him with Sam unless he intervenes to discipline Sam. Sam's father then tells him to "humor mom" and

> avoid these unpleasant conflicts. Sam listens for a short time before he starts his defiant behavior to new rules set by his mother. Nothing ever seems to get resolved. (Adapted from Foster & Robin, 1988, p. 725)

Difficulties with parents, siblings, and members of the extended family are among the strongest and most consistent correlates of antisocial behavior and violent offenses (Patterson et al., 1992). Family disturbances are of two types:

❖ *Specific* disturbances in parenting practices and family functioning, such as the excessive use of harsh discipline, lack of supervision, lack of emotional support, and parental disagreement about discipline
❖ *General* family disruptions, such as parental psychopathology, antisocial family values, a family history of antisocial behavior, family instability, and limited resources

These two types of family disturbances are highly interrelated since a general family disruption such as maternal depression often results in poor parenting practices, which can lead to antisocial child behavior and feelings of parental incompetence, which in turn may lead to increased maternal depression—completing the circle. This section describes a number of specific family disturbances associated with conduct problems in children. Later sections on theories and causes consider how these family difficulties might combine with individual and societal factors to contribute to the development of antisocial behavior.

Families of children with conduct problems show high rates of conflict among family members relative to rates in nonproblem families. These families are more likely to display a lack of family cohesion as reflected in emotional detachment, poor communication patterns, low support among family members, and family disorganization (Henggeler, Melton, & Smith, 1992). Parents may display social-cognitive deficits similar to those of their children, suggesting that the tendency of antisocial children to infer hostile intent may reflect similar social perceptions of their parents (Bickett, Milich, & Brown, 1996). Parents may display one or more poor parenting practices, including the use of ineffective discipline, inappropriate or ineffective use of punishment and rewards, failure to follow through on commands, and a lack of parental supervision and involvement in child rearing (Patterson et al., 1992). Additionally, poor family problem solving, characterized by difficulties in reaching a consensus in defining a problem and getting easily sidetracked, is common.

From the time of Cain and Abel to TV's Bart and Lisa Simpson, conflict between siblings has commanded a great deal of attention (Johnston & Freeman, 1998). Not surprisingly, conflict between siblings is especially high in families of children with conduct problems, as indicated in this parent's comment:

> He is so violent with his sister. He split her lip a couple of times. And he almost knocked her out once when he hit her over the head with a five-pound brass pitcher. He's put plastic bags over her head. Even things you wouldn't think could be dangerous, you have to make sure and keep out of his reach. (Webster-Stratton & Herbert, 1994, p. 45)

In fact, rates of negative behavior are often as high in nonreferred siblings of children with conduct problems as they are for the referred child (Patterson, 1984; Patterson et al., 1992). Nonreferred siblings of children with conduct problems also display antisocial behavior outside the home when their sibling is not present, suggesting that their difficulties are not simply situational reactions to the annoying behaviors of their antisocial brother or sister. Similarities between siblings have been found for teacher ratings of aggression, likability, and behavior adjustment, and for observed positive exchanges with peers in the classroom, negative peer nominations, and teacher disapproval (Lewin, Hops, Davis, & Dishion, 1993). Possible reasons for the similarities in antisocial behavior for children with conduct problems and their siblings include poor parenting practices, the effects of modeling and direct influence, general disturbances in the family such as marital discord or parent psychopathology, and shared hereditary influences.

Health-Related Problems

Young people with conduct problems engage in patterns of behavior that place them at high risk for certain types of health-related problems, such as personal injuries, diseases contracted as a result of risky sexual behaviors, and illnesses or overdoses from drug abuse, necessitating emergency room admissions. Not surprisingly, rates of premature death (before age 30) due to a range of causes (e.g., homicide, suicide, accidental poisoning, traffic accident, drug overdose) are 3 to 4 times higher in boys with conduct problems than in those without (contrary to popular belief, it's not the good that die young!) (Kratzer & Hodgins, 1997). Antisocial behavior, substance abuse, early physical maturity, lax parental supervision, and parental transitions are all associated with an early onset and persistence of sexual intercourse (Capaldi, Crosby, & Stoolmiller, 1996), and being above the average on antisocial behavior is predictive of twice the rate of initiation of sexual intercourse through grade 11 in boys (Tubman, Windle, & Windle, 1996). Early onset of sexual behavior exposes young people to more years at risk for pregnancy or the contraction of sexually transmitted diseases, for which they are already at greater risk than adults because of the immaturity of their reproductive organs and immune systems. Heightened risk for teen pregnancy, AIDS, and other sexually transmitted diseases is also present because aggressive and delinquent behaviors are associated with high-risk sexual behavior such as multiple partners and a failure to use contraceptives (Biglan et al., 1990).

After declining in the 1970s, drug use among young people has increased sharply in the last few years (U.S. Department of Health and Human Services, 1996; Weinberg, Rahdert, Colliver, & Glantz, 1998). Drug use among 12- to 17-year-olds more than doubled from 1992 to 1995, with substantial increases in the use of LSD and other hallucinogens, marijuana, cocaine, crack cocaine, amphetamines, cigarettes, and alcohol. However, after several years of increase, the proportion of 12- to 15-year-old youth using drugs decreased by 2% from 1995 to 1996 (U.S. Department of Health and Human Services, 1997). Levels of drug use in young people are similar for whites, African-Americans, and Hispanics, and for youth from different socioeconomic backgrounds (U.S. Department of Health and Human Services, 1997).

Are conduct problems during childhood a risk factor for later substance use? As early as the preschool years, personality characteristics such as overactivity and an inability to delay gratification have been found to predict later drug use in adolescence (Block, Block, & Keyes, 1988). Early antisocial behavior has been found to be a risk factor for adolescent substance use in many countries including the United States, England, Finland, and elsewhere (Dishion et al., 1995). The prevalence of delinquent behavior has been found to vary with substance use severity, with about 10% of polydrug users between the ages of 15 and 21 committing more than half of all felony assaults, felony thefts, and index offenses (Elliott, Huizinga, & Menard, 1989). One distinguishing feature of adult criminal offenders is their use of tobacco, alcohol, and marijuana prior to age 15 (Farrington, 1991). Thus, the evidence indicates that conduct problems during childhood are a risk factor for adult substance abuse, and that this relationship is mediated by adolescent drug use and delinquency during early and late adolescence (Brook, Whiteman, Finch, & Cohen, 1996).

Accompanying Disorders and Symptoms

Most children with conduct problems have one or more other disorders (Loeber & Keenan, 1994). In community samples, about 60% of children with CD also have ODD, and 47% of those with ODD also have CD. Rates of comorbidity in clinic-referred children, particularly boys, are even higher, with approximately 90% of children with CD also having ODD (Hinshaw, Lahey, & Hart, 1993; Nottelman & Jensen, 1995). The notion that ODD represents an earlier form of or a precursor to CD would explain why the overlap between these disorders is so high. Also associated with conduct problems are ADHD, depression, and anxiety.

Attention-Deficit/Hyperactivity Disorder.
Reported rates of ADHD among children with CD range from 35% to 48% (Nottelman & Jensen, 1995). This high degree of overlap suggests that ADHD and CD may share a common dysfunction, such as impulsivity, poor self-regulation, or impaired executive functions, that leads to the development of aggressive behavior. Alternatively, ADHD may serve as a catalyst for CD by contributing to its persistence and escalation to more serious conduct problems (Loeber, Stouthamer-Loeber, & Green, 1991). The presence of ADHD may also lead to an earlier age of onset of CD, which is a strong predictor of continuing problems (Robins, 1991).

In spite of their large overlap, ADHD and CD are different disorders. Support for their independence comes from factor analytic studies of parent and teacher ratings of hyperactivity, attention deficits, and conduct problems, which have consistently identified separate aggression and hyperactivity factors (Hinshaw, 1987). A two-factor model that includes ADHD and antisocial behavior provides a better fit to the data than one based on just a single disruptive behavior disorder (Fergusson, Horwood, & Lloyd, 1991). In addition, ADHD is more likely than CD to be associated with cognitive impairments, neurodevelopmental abnormalities, social rejection by peers, inattentiveness in the classroom, and higher rates of accidental injuries. Although two lines of evidence indicate that ADHD and CD are distinct problems, because these two disorders are so highly correlated (in the order of .50 to .70), it is difficult to say for certain that they are totally separate problems (Hinshaw, 1987).

Youngsters with comorbid ADHD and conduct problems usually display more severe impairments than those with just one of these diagnoses, including more physical aggression, a wider range and persistence of antisocial behavior, greater academic underachievement, more inattentive behavior in the classroom, greater rejection by peers, and greater long-term impairments (Hinshaw et al., 1993; Moffitt, 1990; Roberts, 1990; Walker, Lahey, Hynd, & Frame, 1987). Parental characteristics also differ for the two groups. CD by itself and CD with ADHD are associated with high rates of parental antisocial personality disorder and a parental history of aggressive behavior, whereas ADHD by itself is not. Although the family histories of children with conduct problems and ADHD differ, independent causes for the two disorders have not been identified nor is there evidence for a differential response to treatment (Hinshaw, 1987).

Depression and Anxiety. Depression and anxiety occur much more frequently than expected in youngsters with conduct problems (Offord et al., 1986; Zoccolillo, 1992; Zoccolillo, Pickles, Quinton, & Rutter, 1992). Most women with a history of CD and an antisocial adult outcome also develop a depressive or anxiety disorder by early adulthood, and for both sexes, increasing severity of antisocial behavior is associated with increasing severity of depression and anxiety (Zoccolillo et al., 1992; Zoccolillo & Rogers, 1991, 1992). The strong connection between disorders of conduct and disorders of mood is evident when we consider that young adolescents diagnosed with externalizing disorders are about equally likely to have internalizing as externalizing problems later in adolescence (Nottelman & Jensen, 1995). This is especially true of adolescent girls, in whom antisocial symptoms are a better predictor of later anxiety, mood, and somatic disturbances than of externalizing problems (Lewis et al., 1991; Robins, 1986; Robins & Rutter, 1990).

Conduct problems and depression are clearly associated (Kovacs, Paulauskas, Gatsonis, & Richards, 1988; Nottelman & Jensen, 1995). However, the degree of association varies with the child's age and gender, with diagnostic criteria, and with the use of clinical versus community samples (Dishion et al., 1995). Comorbidity for conduct problems and depression is highest in boys during preadolescence and then diminishes in adulthood, whereas comorbidity for girls occurs at a consistent rate from adolescence into adulthood (Zoccolillo, 1992). Correlations between conduct problems and depressed mood range from .37 to .51 in community samples of adolescents (Hops, Lewinsohn, Andrews, & Roberts, 1990). In clinical samples, about 33% of children and adolescents with CD are also diagnosed with depression, and boys are disproportionately represented (Dishion et al., 1995):

Do children with mixed disorders of conduct and mood constitute a distinct group from those with conduct problems alone? Apparently not. These youngsters display many of the same characteristics as those with conduct problems alone (e.g., age of onset, gender ratio), suggesting that they are a subgroup of the latter rather than a separate group with a separate disorder (Steinhausen & Reitzle, 1996). In addition, antisocial boys with and without depression show similar correlates, including poor parenting, association with deviant peers, and poor school performance. Findings from twin studies indicate that about 45% of the observed covariation between antisocial behavior and depressive symptoms in adolescence can be explained by a common genetic liability (O'Conner, McGuire, Reiss, Hetherington, & Plomin, 1998).

Estimates of the comorbidity of conduct problems and anxiety disorders have varied widely, from 19% to 53% (Nottelman & Jensen, 1995). Boys with CD and anxiety disorders are less aggressive and less assaultive than those with CD alone, but they do not differ with respect to covert symptoms such as lying and stealing (Walker et al., 1991). It has been suggested that the presence of anxiety in children with CD may serve to inhibit aggressive behavior. Boys with comorbid conduct and anxiety disorder show a higher level of salivary cortisol, which is known to be associated with a greater degree of behavioral inhibition, than do boys with conduct disorder only (McBurnett et al., 1991). Interestingly, although children with conduct problems generally display more anxiety-related symptoms, those children with conduct problems who also have a callous-unemotional interpersonal style experience *less* anxiety and emotional distress (Frick, in press). To date, our understanding of the relationship between conduct problems and anxiety disorders is limited by a failure to consider subgroups of children with conduct problems and the full range of anxiety disorders that occur during childhood.

PREVALENCE, GENDER, AND DEVELOPMENTAL PATHWAYS

Prevalence

Youth crime and violence seem to be everywhere. Still, it is difficult to come up with a precise estimate of the number of children with conduct problems, since prevalence rates vary with the type of conduct problem (e.g., CD versus ODD), the way in which conduct problems are defined (e.g., legal versus psychiatric definitions), and the child's age and gender. Estimates of the frequency of conduct problems in the general population have ranged from 6% to 16% for boys, and from 2% to 9% for girls. Prevalence estimates of clinically diagnosed conduct problems such as CD are lower, but still substantial, ranging from 2% to 6% of all children or about 1 to 4 million children in North America (Hinshaw & Anderson, 1996; Zoccolillo, 1993). Reported rates of ODD range from 10% to 22%, vary across countries, and are consistently higher than rates for CD (Nottelman & Jensen, 1995).

Gender Differences

Ann: Runaway

Ann is a 13-year-old girl who, until recently, lived with her mother, stepfather, and 9-year-old brother. For the last 6 months, she has been living in a youth shelter under the custody of the courts because of repeatedly running away from home. Ann was reported by her parents to be oppositional [and] argumentative, and to lie and steal often. She often stole clothes and jewelry from the homes of relatives and friends, as well as from her parents. . . .

Running away had been a major problem as well. Over the past 3 years, Ann had run away from home on four occasions. Each time, the police had to be called. Running away was precipitated by being grounded for stealing or smoking cigarettes at home. . . . One time when she escaped and ran away, Ann was gone for 3 nights. The police found her wandering the streets late at night on the other side of town (about 10 miles from her home). Ann would not tell them who she was or where she lived; consequently, several hours elapsed before she was returned home. (Adapted from Kazdin, 1995, pp. 3–5)

There are few differences in the rate or severity of problem behaviors in boys and girls in the first few years of life, but clear differences are apparent by about 4 years of age (Keenan & Shaw, 1997). During childhood, rates of CD are about 3 or 4 times higher for boys than for girls, with boys showing an earlier age of onset and greater persistence than girls (Anderson, Williams, McGee, & Silva, 1987; McGee, Feehan, Williams, & Anderson, 1992; Zoccolillo, 1993). Although rates of CD, delinquent behavior, and adult criminality are higher in boys than in girls, many girls also display severe conduct problems, with estimates ranging from about 1% to 6% of all girls (Eme & Kavanagh, 1995; Webster-Stratton, 1996). The higher prevalence of conduct problems in boys versus girls is not found in all studies, however, and although the gender disparity increases during middle childhood, it decreases or disap-

Girls will be girls.

pears completely by about age 15 (McDermott, 1996; McGee, Feehan, Williams, & Anderson, 1992). The increasing prevalence of conduct problems in girls during adolescence is related primarily to a rise in covert nonaggressive antisocial behaviors (Zoccolillo, 1993). For example, Ann steals, lies, and runs away from home, but she is not physically aggressive. For boys, the early symptoms of conduct disorder are aggression and theft, whereas for girls, early symptoms are usually sexual misbehavior (Offord, Alder, & Boyle, 1986). Antisocial girls are more likely than others to develop relationships with antisocial boys (Caspi, Elder, & Bem, 1987), become pregnant at an early age, and display a wide spectrum of later disorders, including anxiety, depression, and poor parenting (Lewis et al., 1991; Serbin, Moskowitz, Schwartzman, & Ledingham, 1991).

Although the differences between boys and girls in their overall amounts of antisocial behavior decrease in adolescence, boys remain more violence-prone than girls throughout their life spans, and are much more likely than girls to engage in repeated acts of violence (Chesney-Lind & Shelden, 1992; McGee et al., 1992; Robins, 1991). However, this does not mean that girls are nonviolent. About 45% of females commit at least one violent act (compared with 65% of males). Unfortunately, violence is becoming an equal opportunity affliction.

The higher rates of antisocial behavior in boys may be the result of definitions that place a strong emphasis on overt forms of antisocial conduct, such as physical aggression, and minimal emphasis on the less physical forms of aggressive behavior that characterize girls. Girls are more likely to be emotionally upset by aggressive social exchanges than are boys (Crick, 1995) and, when angry, are more likely than boys to use indirect and relational forms of aggression, such as verbal insults, gossip, tattling, ostracism, threatening to withdraw one's friendship, getting even, or third-party retaliation (Bjorkqvist & Niemela, 1992; Crick et al., 1996). As girls move into adolescence, the function of their aggressive behavior increasingly revolves around group acceptance and affiliation, whereas for boys aggression remains confrontational in nature.

Fewer differences in antisocial behavior exist between boys and girls referred for treatment than for children in community samples. Although clinically referred boys and girls with conduct problems display comparable amounts of externalizing behavior (Dishion & Andrews, 1995), referred girls are more deviant in relation to their same-age, same-sex peers than are boys (Webster-Stratton, 1996; Zoccolillo, 1993). This is because boys typically engage in more rough and tumble play, bullying, fighting, and noncompliance than girls (Achenbach, 1991a; Maccoby, 1986). Since overt antisocial behavior is more common in boys, their symptoms are more noticeable at a younger age. This could account for the reported earlier age of onset of conduct problems in boys. Since early displays of antisocial behavior are less visible in girls, lower thresholds or different diagnostic criteria may be needed to detect girls with CD at a young age (Zoccolillo, 1993). However, this could have the effect of stigmatizing girls, if low levels of aggression or nonaggressive behaviors were to result in a diagnosis of CD (Zahn-Waxler, 1993).

Girls may display different developmental pathways to delinquent behavior. One pathway describes girls who exhibit antisocial behavior during childhood, associate with deviant peers, and exhibit delinquent behavior and drug use during adolescence. A second pathway describes girls who do not show a history of antisocial behavior; rather, they have an early menarche, which indirectly heightens their delinquent behavior through increasing their involvement with deviant peers (Caspi, Lynam, Moffitt, & Silva, 1993; Moffitt, Caspi, Belsky, & Silva, 1992). Interestingly, early onset of menarche predicts increased delinquency primarily for girls who attend mixed-gender rather than all-girl schools. In mixed-gender schools, girls' exposure to boys who model antisocial behavior and place pressure on them for early sexual relations may interact with early physical maturation. Such exposure may lead to antisocial behavior in these girls, who are more likely to find rewards and opportunities for antisocial activities in the company of boys than girls (Caspi et al., 1993).

Developmental Pathways for Antisocial Behavior

Given the many different types of antisocial behaviors and children that we have described, one can't help wondering if we might be describing the same behaviors or children, but just at different points in their development or from different vantage points. For example, is covert rule breaking (such as stealing or using alcohol) in adolescents just a more advanced form of earlier childhood antisocial tendencies, a form that results from increasing maturity and opportunity? Or is adolescent covert rule breaking a new and different problem? It is now well established that *patterns* of antisocial behavior maintain a certain degree of consistency over time, even though these behaviors may look quite different at different points in development. Recent longitudinal studies have greatly advanced the understanding of antisocial patterns, by revealing both a general developmental progression for conduct problems, as well as important variations on this theme.

A General Progression for the Development of Conduct Problems. An approximate ordering of the emergence of different forms of disruptive and antisocial behavior is shown in Figure 6.5 (Loeber, 1990). The earliest signs of antisocial behavior may be a *difficult temperament* in the first few years of life. Difficult temperament may be expressed as fussiness, irritability, irregular sleeping and eating patterns, or upset and frustration in response to new and challenging events. Possible underlying neurological impairments may lead to noticeable hyperactivity as the child gains mobility, and a heightened risk for overt oppositional and aggressive behaviors during the preschool and early school years. Oppositional and aggressive behaviors are often accompanied by poor social skills and social-cognitive deficits, predisposing the child to poor peer relationships, rejection by other children, and social isolation. With school entry, impulsivity and attention problems may result in reading difficulties and academic failure. Covert conduct problems, such as truancy or substance abuse, also begin to appear during the elementary school years, and increase in early adolescence. Adolescence is characterized by a growing association with deviant peers, and by increasing rates of arrest, re-arrest, and conviction as the age of criminal responsibility is met.

In this sequence, we see considerable continuity in the child's antisocial behaviors over time, even though the form of these behaviors changes dramatically with age (Patterson, 1993). In addition, most children with conduct problems show *diversification,* by adding new forms of antisocial behavior over time rather than just replacing old ones. Does this mean that every young

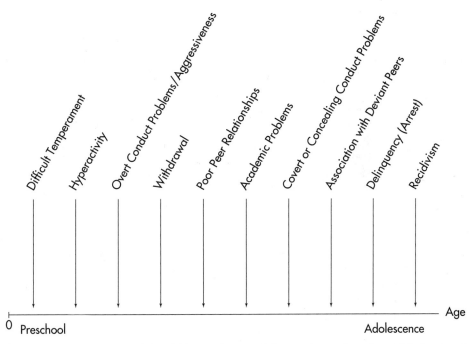

FIGURE 6.5 Approximate ordering of the different forms of disruptive and antisocial behavior from childhood through adolescence. (Loeber, 1990)

child with a difficult temperament goes on to become a delinquent adolescent? Definitely not. The sequence in Figure 6.5 represents a *maximum* progression for conduct problems that begins early in life and continues through adolescence. Although some children display this maximum progression, others will desist from their antisocial activity at a young age, and others may not display any problems until adolescence. Not all children display the full range of difficulties described in this maximum progression, which leads to the consideration of two important variations on this general progression.

Two Developmental Pathways. There are as many unique developmental pathways to antisocial behavior as there are children. However, the weight of evidence supports two common pathways: the life-course-persistent path and the adolescent-limited path (Caspi & Moffitt, 1995; Moffitt et al., 1996).

The **life-course-persistent (LCP) path,** which occurs in about 7% of children, describes those who engage in antisocial behavior at an early age and who continue to do so into adulthood. These youngsters may display "biting and hitting at age 4, shoplifting and truancy at age 10, selling drugs and stealing cars at age 16, robbery and rape at age 22, and fraud and child abuse at age 30" (Moffitt, 1993a, p. 679). Their underlying disposition remains, but the way in which it is expressed changes with new opportunities at different points in development. This path is similar, but not identical, to early-onset CD as specified in DSM-IV. In addition to early onset, the LCP path includes overlap with ADHD,

neuropsychological deficits, and family discord. For these children, antisocial behavior starts early because subtle neuropsychological deficits may interfere with their development of language, memory, and self-control, resulting in cognitive delays and a difficult temperament by age 3 or younger. These deficits heighten the child's vulnerability to antisocial elements in his or her social environment, such as abuse or poor parenting, which in turn lead to oppositional and conduct problems (Moffitt, 1993a).

Only about half of the children who display early antisocial patterns continue on the LCP path by engaging in serious delinquent activities in adolescence. They are the teens most likely to commit violent crimes and to drop out of school. LCP youth display consistency in their behavior across situations, for example, by lying at home, stealing from stores, and cheating at school. As young adults, LCP individuals have difficulties forming lasting relationships, and may display a hostile mistrust of others, aggressive dominance, impulsivity, and psychopathy. Complete spontaneous recovery is rare after adolescence, occurring in only about 6% of LCP youngsters. The LCP pattern is often perpetuated by the progressive accumulation of its own consequences. For example, poor self-control and diminished intellect may lead to irreversible decisions, such as dropping out of school or abusing drugs, behaviors that serve to limit opportunities further (Caspi & Moffitt, 1995).

The **adolescent-limited (AL) path** describes youngsters whose antisocial behavior begins around puberty and continues into adolescence, but who later desist from these behaviors in young adulthood (Farrington, 1986). About 30% of youngsters fall into the AL category (Hamalainen & Pulkkinen, 1996; Moffitt et al., 1996). This path includes most juvenile offenders whose antisocial behavior is limited primarily to the teen years. AL youths display less extreme forms of antisocial activity than those on the LCP path, are less likely to drop out of school, and have stronger family ties. Delinquent activity in the AL path is often related to temporary situational factors, especially peer influences. The behavior of AL youngsters is not consistent across situations—they may use drugs or shoplift with their friends while continuing to follow rules and do well in school.

The attractiveness of still forbidden adult privileges, such as drinking alcohol, driving a car, and having sex, may motivate some youths who otherwise have few risk signs to engage in antisocial behavior as they enter adolescence. These youngsters may observe their LCP peers obtaining desired adult privileges via illicit means and mimic their delinquent activities. Eventually, when access to adult privileges becomes available, AL youngsters cease their law-breaking, relying instead on the more adaptive and prosocial behaviors and values they learned prior to adolescence (Moffitt, Lynam, & Silva, 1994).

Marcus: Adolescent Rule Breaker

I grew up in a real poor family. My mom was on welfare all my life, we never had much. As soon as I got to the age of maybe 11 years old, I was interested in other kids who were breaking the rules. I used to see what they used to do, what they had. There was one kid who smoked PCP . . . He used to jump out of trees, and act like he was Superman and stuff. I used to look at him, and say, "That's what I want to be." . . . He was my role model. (Adapted from Goldentyer, 1994)

Marcus joined a gang when he turned 13. Two years later, after a number of arrests and four detentions in a juvenile facility, he became disillusioned with gang life and managed to turn his life around. He is now 17 and works as a youth minister for a church dedicated to helping other young people like himself (Goldentyer, 1994).

Some AL youngsters may continue to display antisocial activity well into their twenties before they eventually stop. This persistence is often the result of *snares*, which are outcomes of antisocial behavior that close the door on getting a good job, pursuing higher education, or attracting a supportive partner. Common snares include unplanned parenthood, school dropout, addiction to drugs or alcohol, disabling injuries, unemployment, erratic work history, severed family connections, imprisonment, bad reputation, and a delinquent self-image (Moffitt et al., 1994).

Determining whether adolescents are in the LCP or AL paths cannot be done on the basis of most indicators of antisocial activity, including self- and official reports of offending, peer delinquency, substance abuse, practice of unsafe sex, and dangerous driving. However, the two groups are easily distinguished when examined over a longer time frame, by taking into account differences in early temperament, violent activity in adolescence, and psychopathy (Moffitt, 1993a). Therefore, any attempt to understand conduct problems in children must consider these two and possibly other pathways rather than adopt one all-encompassing definition.

The identification of the LCP and AL pathways helps us understand why adult antisocial behavior is almost always preceded by antisocial behavior during childhood, while most antisocial adolescents do not go on to become antisocial adults (Robins, 1978). At the crossroads of early adulthood, LCP and AL adolescents go different ways. Antisocial behavior is remarkably stable for youngsters on the LCP path, who continue on the same road, but clearly unstable for those on the AL path (Dishion et al., 1995). Inconsistent findings in prior research on prevalence, causal factors, underlying mechanisms, and response to treatment in children with conduct disorders may be the result of lumping together a small group of children who display a persistent developmental pattern of antisocial behavior with a much larger group who engage in time-limited antisocial activity during adolescence.

Course and Adult Outcomes

Although there are isolated reports, such as that of a 9-month-old infant being expelled from day care for punching other children (Kazdin, 1995, p. 27), early signs of conduct problems are usually not so obvious. Infant irritability, overactivity, or fussiness often precede later conduct problems, but are not specific to them. Preschoolers with oppositional defiant disorder display stubbornness, temper tantrums, defiance of adults, irritability, arguing, blaming others, annoying others, anger, and spitefulness (Campbell, 1990). These kinds of externalizing problems are stable from 2 to 5 years, and discipline problems and poor self-regulation in early childhood are strong indicators that the oppositional child will continue to experience problems (Campbell, Pierce, March, Ewing, & Szumowski, 1994). From ages 8 to 12, behaviors such as fighting, bullying, fire setting, use of a weapon, vandalism, cruelty to animals and people, and stealing begin to emerge. From ages 12 to

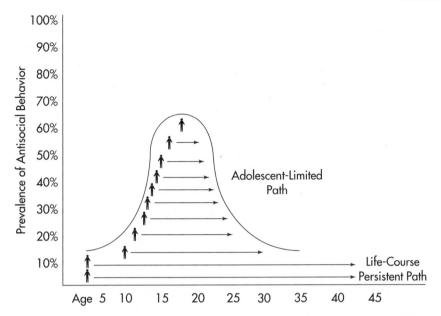

FIGURE 6.6   The changing prevalence of participation in antisocial behavior across the life span. (Moffitt, 1993a)

14, problems such as substance abuse, sexual assault, property destruction, running away from home, truancy, mugging, breaking and entering, and forced sex occur with increasing frequency. By age 18, many children with conduct disorder display behaviors that forecast an antisocial future, including substance dependence, unsafe sex, dangerous driving habits, delinquent friends, delinquent perceptions, and unemployment (Moffitt et al., 1996).

Across cultures, conduct problems are more frequent during adolescence than childhood. Delinquent behavior shows a dramatic increase in middle adolescence that peaks around the age of 17, followed by an equally dramatic decrease in late adolescence and young adulthood (Hirschi & Gottfredson, 1983). By the early twenties, the number of active offenders decreases by about half, and by age 28, almost 85% of former delinquents desist from offending (Caspi & Moffitt, 1995). This general relationship between age and crime applies to males and females, for most types of crimes, during recent historical periods, and in numerous Western nations (Caspi & Moffitt, 1995). However, this general age trend obscures the important differences between the LCP and AL paths. As shown in Figure 6.6, a small number of children show a stable pattern of antisocial conduct throughout their lives, whereas a majority do not.

Adult outcomes for children and adolescents with conduct problems depend on the type and variety of conduct problems displayed in childhood and adolescence, in combination with the number of risk and protective factors in the child, family, and community. Even when antisocial behavior decreases in adulthood, coercive interpersonal styles may sometimes persist, along with family, health, and work difficulties. Many children with conduct problems go on as adults to display criminal behavior, psychiatric problems, social maladjustment, health problems, lost productivity, and poor parenting of their own children. Adults with a history of ill temper are more likely to be downwardly socially mobile than their family of origin and to display an erratic work history. This may be due to both lower skill attainment and difficulties in getting along with co-workers and supervisors. As adults, individuals with conduct problems have higher rates of divorce and are more likely than others to select partners with similar antisocial characteristics. One follow-up study of adult women who displayed severe conduct problems in adolescence found that most continued to display conduct problems as adults. A majority had depressive and anxiety disorders, 6% had died a violent death, many had dropped out of school, one-third were pregnant before the age of 17 years, half were re-arrested, and many had suffered traumatic physical injuries (Zoccolillo & Rogers, 1991, 1992).

The unrestrained stages of growth of conduct problems over the life span are graphically depicted in "The Vile Weed," shown in Figure 6.7.

CAUSES OF CONDUCT PROBLEMS

Efforts to identify simple or single causes of conduct problems in children oversimplify the issue, since such problems are diverse and the range of potential influences many. Consider the Wideman brothers—one brother, John Edgar, is an award-winning author

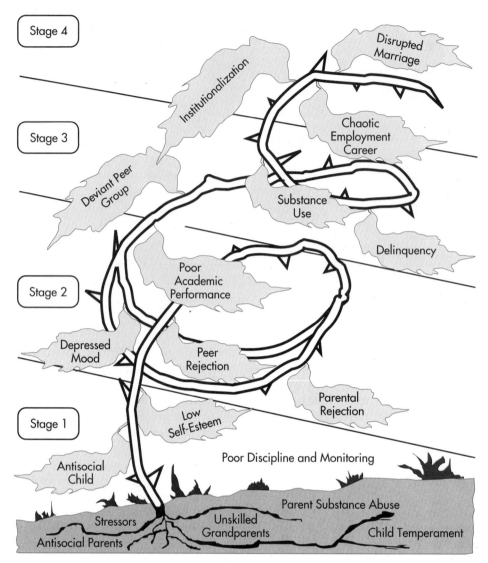

Stage 4

Stage 3

Stage 2

Stage 1

Disrupted Marriage

Chaotic Employment Career

Institutionalization

Deviant Peer Group

Substance Use

Delinquency

Poor Academic Performance

Depressed Mood

Peer Rejection

Parental Rejection

Low Self-Esteem

Antisocial Child

Poor Discipline and Monitoring

Parent Substance Abuse

Stressors

Unskilled Grandparents

Child Temperament

Antisocial Parents

FIGURE 6.7   The Vile Weed: The unrestrained growth of conduct problems over the life span. (Patterson et al., 1992)

("Brothers and Keepers"), while his brother Robbie is in prison for murder. How can we account for this difference? Similarly, how would you explain the following differences in the behavior of 6-year-old fraternal twin boys, one with conduct problems, and one without conduct problems?

Mike and Brian: Bad Twin, Good Twin

Although only 7, Mike had already run away twice and on numerous occasions had wandered from home, having been picked up by the police several times. On one occasion he made a serious attempt to set the house on fire. Mike was truant from

school and had repeatedly stolen from teachers as well as his parents. He had also stolen money from a neighbor's apartment, a hospital, and a gas station. Moreover, Mike's parents complained of his disobedience, impudence to his mother, and his temper tantrums. In general he was regarded as being extremely troublesome at school and incorrigible at home. In sharp contrast, Mike's twin brother, Brian, was described as an even-tempered, obedient, thoroughly well-behaved "model child."

The twins were the result of a welcomed pregnancy; Brian was born first and without instruments; Mike was delivered by instruments during a difficult labor. They weighed about 6 pounds each and both were bottle-fed from the time of birth. Mike was a fussy crying baby; Brian was not. They both had an uneventful health history. Mike had an IQ of 82, although the examiner commented that he would have done considerably better if his attention could have been fully held. Brian's IQ was 95. Mike was exceedingly restless, active, impulsive, and uninhibited. He frequently acted as a "show-off" with other children. He was especially proud of his grinning picture in the newspapers, which appeared once he had been found by the police. At home he was said to be extraordinarily inquisitive, "into everything." Brian was an amenable, pleasant youngster, much quieter than Mike, self-reliant, and easily amused at home. (Adapted from Healy & Bronner, 1926, pp. 95–97)

How do we account for such striking differences between children in the same family? Are they due to differences in genetic makeup, neurobiological functioning, birth complications, temperament, intellectual competence, treatment by parents, peer influences, difficulties in school, or some combination of these or other factors?

Early explanations of conduct problems in children focused mainly on aggression, invoking a primary cause, such as an aggressive drive, frustration, poor role models, reinforcement, or deficits in social cognition. However, most single-cause or "smoking gun" explanations can be challenged on one point or another. For example, not all children behave aggressively as would be predicted by aggressive-drive theory, and frustration sometimes leads to cooperation rather than aggression. In addition, single-cause theories have not been effective in predicting why the amount and type of aggressive behavior changes as a function of the child's age and situation (Patterson, 1996). Although each theory of antisocial behavior highlights a potentially important determinant, no single theory can explain all forms of antisocial behavior.

More recently, comprehensive models have emerged that incorporate the many different forms of antisocial behavior and associated characteristics of children with conduct problems. These newer theories view conduct problems as resulting from the interplay among predisposing child, family, community, and cultural characteristics, and ongoing experiences. The causal mechanisms or risk factors that underlie conduct problems are seen as multifaceted and transactional. For example, antisocial behavior may result from individual child factors, such as impulsivity, impaired avoidance conditioning, a diminished response to punishment, poor early socialization practices, family criminality, exposure to environ-

mental toxins such as lead, exposure to deviant conditions in the community, poverty, or some combination of these (Farrington, 1995; Sutker, 1994). An illustrative framework for the ecology of antisocial behavior, which includes individual and interpersonal factors, relationship processes, behavior settings, and community contexts, is shown in Figure 6.8.

The sections that follow consider several proposed causes of antisocial behavior in children. Examining causes separately, however, misrepresents the real state of affairs with regard to etiology—namely, that antisocial behavior in children is best accounted for by multiple causes, or risk and protective factors, that operate in a transactional fashion over time (Hinshaw & Anderson, 1996; Shaw & Bell, 1993).

Biological Factors

Early Temperament.   Difficult early temperament is reflected in the child's impulsivity, emotional lability, lack of persistence in problem solving, restlessness, negativity, and sensitivity to stress (Caspi, Henry, McGee, Moffitt, & Silva, 1995). Although it is difficult to distinguish between early temperament and early behavior problems, several studies support the link between a difficult early temperament and risk for the development of later conduct problems (Caspi et al., 1995). Difficult temperament at 6 months has been shown to predict externalizing problems in both boys and girls in middle childhood (Bates, Bayles, Bennett, Ridge, & Brown, 1991). Restless, impulsive, risk-taking, and emotionally labile behaviors at age 3 have been shown to differentiate adolescents with antisocial disorders from those displaying other disorders or no disorders at all (Block et al., 1988; Caspi et al., 1995; White, Moffitt, Earls, Robins, & Silva, 1990). Other studies have found that a childhood temperament involving impulsivity, risk-taking behavior, and lack of concentration is specifically associated with convictions for violent offenses in late adolescence and adulthood (Farrington, 1989; Henry, Caspi, Moffitt, & Silva, 1996).

Genetic Influences.   The pervasiveness of aggressive and antisocial behavior in humans, and the fact that such behavior runs in families within and across generations, suggests the importance of genetic influences on antisocial behavior. Although antisocial behavior is not inherited, a number of biologically based traits, such as difficult temperament or impulsivity, may underlie the heritability for this behavior by predisposing children to develop antisocial patterns of behavior.

Until recently, evidence for the genetic mediation of antisocial behavior in children has been relatively weak (Rutter, MacDonald, et al., 1990). However, newer

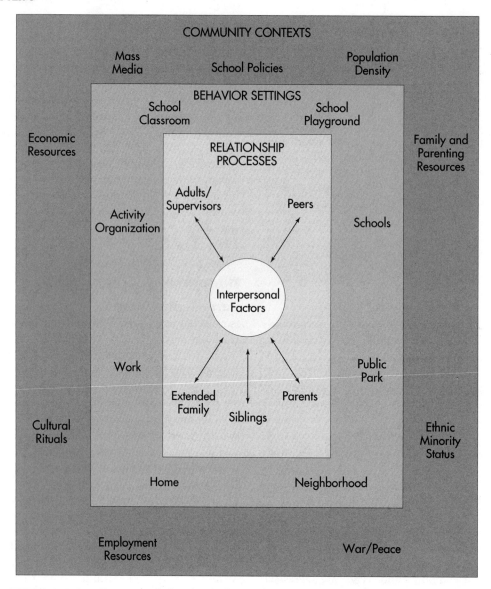

FIGURE 6.8 Framework for the ecology of antisocial behavior. (Dishion et al., 1995)

findings from adoption and twin studies provide growing support for a genetic contribution to antisocial and criminal behavior, with about half of the variance in antisocial behavior attributable to heredity (Mason & Frick, 1994). The strongest evidence for a genetic contribution to antisocial behavior has been found for adults, with evidence for genetic contributions to antisocial behavior in adolescents and children being far less consistent (Gottesman & Goldsmith, 1994; Raine, 1993). Genetic contributions to overt forms of antisocial behavior such as aggression are stronger than those for covert behaviors such as stealing or lying (Edelbrock, Rende, Plomin, & Thompson, 1995). Interestingly, children who display LCP patterns show double the genetic risk for antisocial behavior as those displaying AL patterns (Frick & Jackson, 1993). Since LCP patterns are

more likely to be detected among adult criminals than in mixed groups of delinquent or oppositional children, weak or age-inconsistent findings regarding genetic influences in children and adolescents may be partly due to an insensitivity of prior research to subtypes of behavior and subgroupings of children.

Adoption and twin studies. There are genetic contributions to differences in the trait of aggressiveness in adults (Tellegen et al., 1988), and to adult criminality (DiLalla & Gottesman, 1989). Findings from longitudinal studies of adopted-at-birth offspring of biological parents with antisocial personality disorder or substance abuse/dependency or both show that when adopted offspring are assessed as adults, their rates of conduct disorder, antisocial personality disorder, and drug abuse are more strongly related to their biological

Table 6.4 Correlation in Personality Traits for Twins Reared Apart and Together

Personality Dimension	MZ Apart	MZ Together	DZ Apart	DZ Together
Constraint	.57	.58	.04	.25
Negative emotionality	.61	.54	.29	.41
Positive emotionality	.34	.63	−.07	.18

DZ = Dizygotic
MZ = Monozygotic
Source: Tellegen et al., 1988.

than adoptive backgrounds (Cadoret, Yates, Troughton, Woodworth, & Stewart, 1995a, 1995b). Such findings support the role of genetic influences on antisocial behavior in adults.

Personality traits such as high *negative emotionality* and low *constraint* are associated with antisocial behavior in adults (Krueger et al. 1994). Individuals with high negative emotionality have a low threshold for negative emotions, such as fear, anxiety, and anger, and tend to break down under stress. Those low on constraint reject conventional social norms, seek dangerous situations, and act impulsively. As shown in Table 6.4, genetic influence is suggested by the finding that identical (monozygotic) twins reared apart and those reared together are quite similar on these personality characteristics, whereas fraternal (dizygotic) twins are not.

Average concordance rates for adolescent delinquency are approximately 85% for MZ twins and 70% for DZ twins, respectively (DiLalla & Gottesman, 1989; Raine, 1993). This similarity in concordance rates for identical and fraternal adolescent twins suggests that shared environmental influences contribute a great deal to antisocial behavior. These findings for adolescents can be contrasted with average concordance rates for adult criminality, which are sufficiently different for identical and fraternal twins to suggest a genetic component for criminality, in adulthood (Raine, 1993). However, remember that studies of adolescent delinquents group together LCP and AL youngsters, obscuring possible differences in the role of genetic factors for each group.

Twin studies of conduct problems in childhood have yielded a much less consistent pattern of genetic influence, with reported heritability estimates ranging from .24 to .94 (Plomin, Nitz, & Rowe, 1990). Thus, although genetic factors have been found to influence some child characteristics that are associated with antisocial patterns, the role of genetic influences on conduct problems during childhood awaits further study (Caspi & Moffitt, 1995).

Adoption and twin studies suggest that genetic factors contribute to antisocial behavior across the life span as do environmental factors. The studies do not, however, specify the mechanisms by which the process occurs. It is likely that genetic influences contribute to a difficult temperament, impulsivity, and neuropsychological deficits, creating an antisocial predisposition that makes the likelihood of criminal behavior higher in those who have these behavioral tendencies than in those who do not (Eme & Kavanaugh, 1995; Gottesman & Goldsmith, 1994).

Direct genetic influences. It has been proposed that antisocial individuals, particularly those with psychopathic features, are more likely to seek rewards than are other individuals, a tendency referred to as **reward dominance** (O'Brien & Frick, 1996). The reward dominance of individuals with conduct problems has been linked to a possible genetic aberration that is associated with alterations in the reward pathways of the brain. Individuals with impulsive disorders (and addictive and compulsive disorders such as alcoholism, polysubstance abuse, smoking, and obesity) are believed to suffer from what Kenneth Blum has referred to as a *reward deficiency syndrome*. These individuals may have a biochemical inability to derive reward from ordinary, everyday activities, which leads them to turn to persistent stimulus-seeking behavior to gain rewards (Blum, Cull, Braverman, & Comings, 1996). The hypothesized genetic aberration involves a variant form of the gene for the dopamine D_2 receptor, called the A_1 allele. This genetic aberration has been identified in a significant proportion of adolescents diagnosed as pathologically violent (Blum et al., 1996).

It has also been suggested that a mutation in the gene for an enzyme called monoamine oxidase A (MAOA) may underlie aggressive and sometimes violent behavior. One genetic linkage study found an X-linked transmission of impulsive violence and lower IQ in five affected males in a single Dutch family (Brunner, Nelen, Breakfield, Ropers, & Van Oost, 1993). This transmission was linked to a specific point mutation in the monoamine oxidase (MAOA) gene. With further research, this genetic finding for a rare subtype of CD in a single family may help increase the understanding of neurobiological mechanisms in a larger group of children with CD.

Neurobiological Factors. Jeffrey Gray (1982, 1987) proposed that people's behavioral patterns are related to two subsystems of the brain, a behavioral activation or reward system and a behavioral inhibition system, with each of these subsystems having distinct neuroanatomical regions and neurotransmitter pathways (McBurnett, 1992; Quay, 1993). The **behavioral inhibition system (BIS)** produces anxiety and inhibits ongoing behavior in the presence of novel events, innate fear stimuli, and signals of nonreward or punishment. The **behavioral activation system (BAS)** activates behavior in response to cues of reward or nonpunishment. The operation of the BAS is thought to be antagonistic to the operation of the BIS; thus specific behavioral patterns result from the relative balance or imbalance of these two neural systems. You might think of the BAS as similar to the gas pedal and the BIS as similar to the brakes—some individuals ride one more heavily than the other.

It has been proposed that antisocial and undersocialized patterns of behavior result from a dominant BAS relative to BIS, with the opposite pattern resulting in anxious and avoidant behavior (Quay, 1988, 1993). These patterns are determined primarily by genetic predisposition. Consistent with an overactive BAS, children with conduct problems show a heightened sensitivity to rewards (O'Brien & Frick, 1996). In addition, they show perseverative responding under conditions of no reward, and they fail to respond to aversive stimuli—patterns that are consistent with an underactive BIS. The relative balance or imbalance between the BAS and BIS systems and the proposed behavior patterns associated with each are shown in Figure 6.9.

The role of neurobiological influences on conduct problems in children, particularly aggressive behavior, is suggested by studies of neurochemistry, neuroimagery, neurodevelopmental risk factors, peripheral psychophysiology, and neuropsychology (McBurnett & Lahey, 1994; Raine, 1993). Children and adolescents diagnosed with conduct disorder who show an early onset of aggressive symptoms and undersocialized patterns of symptoms differ from normal and clinical comparison groups in two important ways (Hinshaw & Anderson, 1996):

❖ They demonstrate low psychophysiological and/or cortical arousal. For example, consistent with a pattern of underarousal, aggressive boys show lower basal levels of adrenaline in their urine than nonaggressive boys (Magnusson, 1988).

❖ They display low autonomic reactivity on a variety of measures, such as heart rate and skin conductance. For example, children with conduct disorder display lower electrodermal activity and poorer skin conductance conditioning (Pennington & Ozonoff, 1996; Raine, 1993).

Low arousal and autonomic reactivity in early-onset and LCP children with conduct problems may lead to a diminished avoidance learning to usual socialization practices, such as warnings or reprimands, and a poor response to punishment, which in turn may result in an overall pattern of undersocialized behavior, a failure to

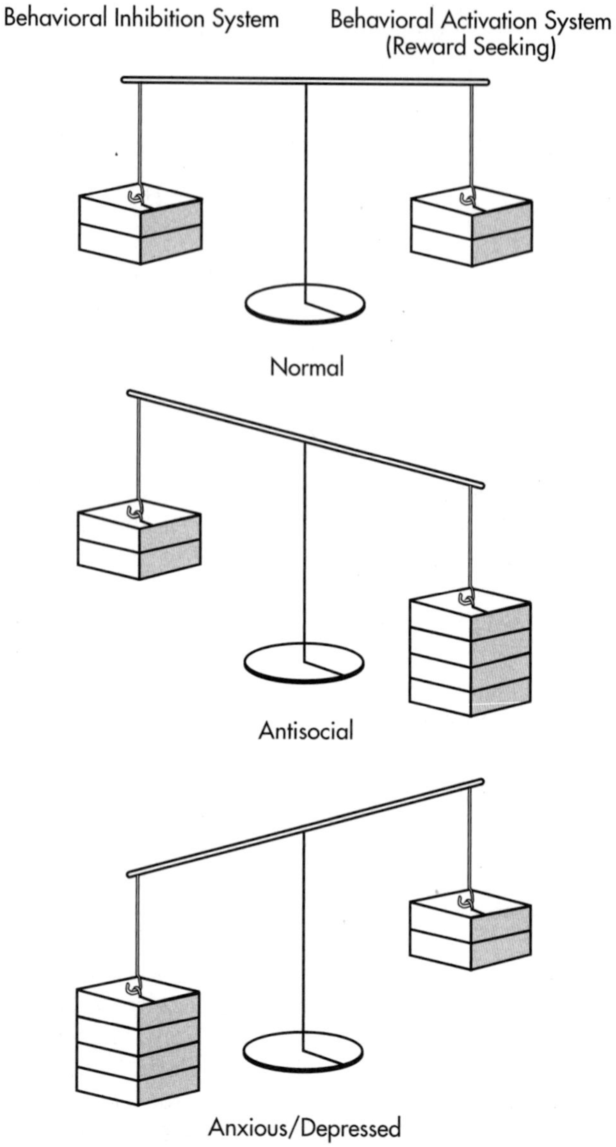

FIGURE 6.9 Three neurological profiles and their associated behavior patterns. (Dishion et al., 1995)

develop the anticipatory fear needed to avoid antisocial behavior, and a lack of conscience. Most children respond to discipline and punishment by reducing their antisocial behavior. Often, just the opposite occurs with children who have conduct problems—they may *increase* their antisocial behavior when they are punished and become even more defiant.

Other findings from studies related to the influence of neurobiological factors on conduct problems can be summarized as follows (Lahey et al., 1993; McBurnett & Lahey, 1994; Quay, 1993):

❖ There is some evidence of lower levels of serotonin and norepinephrine in antisocial adolescents, and for an association between low levels of serotonin in boys at risk for antisocial behavior and parental histories of incarceration, substance abuse, and use of harsh parenting (Pine et al., 1996). In general, however, the association between serotonergic abnormalities and antisocial behavior is stronger for adults than for children (Zubieta & Alessi, 1993).

❖ Findings for a relationship between sex-linked hormonal influences such as testosterone levels and aggression are inconsistent, with testosterone levels being more highly correlated with reactive than with unprovoked forms of aggression (McBurnett & Lahey, 1994; Olweus, 1987).

❖ There is some evidence from neuroimaging studies of frontal lobe activation differences between individuals with and without conduct problems.

❖ Children with conduct problems have somewhat higher rates of neurodevelopmental risk factors such as birth complications and closed head injuries.

❖ Childhood exposure to lead, a neurotoxin that interferes with the child's ability to inhibit impulsive behavior, is associated with higher rates of conduct problems in early adolescence (see Box 6.3).

❖ Children with conduct problems display neuropsychological deficits as suggested by lower IQ, especially verbal IQ, and deficits in verbal reasoning and executive functions (Moffitt, 1993b; Moffitt & Lynam, 1994).

Children who show late-onset and nonaggressive forms of CD show higher levels of arousal and reactivity than early-onset children with conduct disorder (McBurnett & Lahey, 1994). In addition, antisocial adolescents who desist from adult crime show better classical conditioning and enhanced processing of emotion-relevant events at age 15 compared with antisocial adolescents who go on to become criminals (Raine, Venables, & Williams, 1996). Taken together, these findings suggest that neurobiological influences such as low arousal and autonomic reactivity play a more central role for early-onset than for late-onset CD, and that an absence of these neurobiological deficits may constitute a protective factor against the development of later criminal behavior in antisocial teens.

Social-Cognitive Factors

Several theories have made the connection between children's thinking and their aggressive behavior. These include cognitive-structural approaches that emphasize immature forms of thinking, such as egocentrism and a lack of perspective taking (Selman, Beardslee, Schultz, Krupa, & Poderefsky, 1986; Selman et al., 1992); cognitive-behavioral models that emphasize **cognitive deficiencies,** such as the child's failure to use verbal

---

Box 6.3

Lead's Legacy: Childhood Exposure to Lead Is Related to Later Conduct Problems

Herbert Needleman and his colleagues have found that boys with relatively high levels of lead in their bones are more likely to be rated by their parents and teachers as aggressive and delinquent than are those with less lead in their bones. Although exposure to lead is not the cause of conduct problems, such exposure may increase the likelihood of these problems for some children by interfering with brain functions related to impulse control.

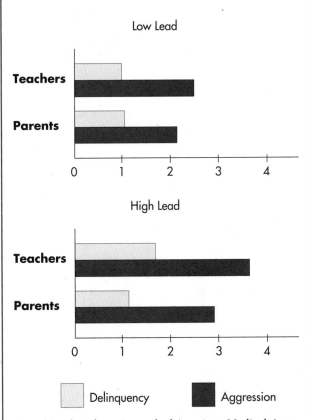

Based on data from *Journal of American Medical Association;* Herbert L. Needleman, M. D.; *New York Times.*

Children with higher levels of lead in their bones show more delinquent and aggressive behavior. Data for graph from *New York Times Service,* Thursday, February 8, 1996.

Source: Adapted from Needleman et al., 1996.

---

mediators to regulate behavior (Meichenbaum, 1977); and social information-processing approaches that focus on **cognitive distortions,** such as interpreting a neutral event such as being bumped into by another child as an act of hostility (Crick & Dodge, 1994).

Table 6.5 Steps in the Thinking and Behavior of Aggressive Children in Social Situations

Step 1: Encoding—searching for and focusing one's attention on pertinent stimuli

Socially aggressive children use fewer cues before making a decision. When defining and resolving an interpersonal situation, they seek less information about the event before acting (Slaby & Guerra, 1988).

Step 2: Interpretation—the derivation of meaning from cues that previously became the focus of one's initial attention

Socially aggressive children attribute hostile intentions to ambiguous events.

Step 3: Response Search—the generation of response alternatives

Socially aggressive children generate fewer and more aggressive responses and have less knowledge about social problem solving.

Step 4: Response Decision—the selection of a specific response

Aggressive children are more likely to choose aggressive solutions.

Step 5: Enactment—the performance of the most appropriate response

Aggressive children use poor verbal communication and strike out physically.

Source: Crick & Dodge, 1994.

Kenneth Dodge and his colleagues have presented the most elaborate social-cognitive theory to account for the behavior of socially aggressive boys (Crick & Dodge, 1994). In this theory, a series of thought processes are presumed to occur during the course of appropriate social interactions and to be absent or distorted during inappropriate social interactions. The thinking and behavior of aggressive children in social situations are characterized by deficits in one or more of the steps described in Table 6.5.

Recently, Dodge and his colleagues have reformulated their conceptual framework to include the reciprocal interactions between the child's information-processing skills and the child's social schemas, memories, social knowledge, and cultural values or rules, referred to as the child's *data base* (Crick & Dodge, 1994; Dodge & Crick, 1990). Parent-child interactions and the quality of early attachments are important contributors to the ongoing formulation of this data base. The reformulated model also gives increased recognition to the influence of peer appraisals and reactions and of emotional processes as contributors to social adjustment. The expanded model of Crick and Dodge addresses criticisms that cognitive processes alone are insufficient to explain aggression without also including the emotional and social-interaction processes that are known to mediate the relationship between cognition and aggressive behavior (Graham, Hudley, & Williams, 1992; Patterson, 1996).

Family Factors

I am convinced that increasing rates of delinquency are due to parents who are either too careless or too busy with their own pleasure to give sufficient time, companionship, and interest to their children.

J. Edgar Hoover,
The New York Times,
December 6, 1947

Many aspects of dysfunctional family settings have been implicated as causes of children's antisocial behavior. Among these are marital conflict; family isolation; violence in the home; the use of harsh, lax, erratic, or inconsistent discipline practices; a lack of parental supervision or emotional support; and excessive dominance by one family member (Frick, 1993; Hinshaw & Anderson, 1996).

Although the association between family factors and conduct problems is well documented, the nature of this association and the possible causal role of family factors in the development of antisocial behavior continues to be a matter of some debate (Deater-Deckard & Dodge, 1997). Since so many aspects of the family have been implicated, findings differ depending on which aspect is being examined and on the sample under investigation. Some investigators find consistent support for family process variables, such as negative communication patterns, as predictors of later antisocial behavior (e.g., Patterson, 1996), whereas others do not (e.g., Henry et al., 1996). Although family difficulties are related to the development of both CD and ODD, the association is stronger for CD than for ODD, and for children on the LCP versus the AL path (Lahey et al., 1992). The combination of extreme deficits in family management skills and individual child risk factors, such as a difficult temperament or neuropsychological deficits, likely accounts for the more persistent and severe forms of antisocial behavior (Caspi & Moffitt, 1995).

Family influences are related to children's antisocial behavior in complex ways, and cannot be understood independent of factors in the child and environment that mediate their effects. For example, the impact of marital hostility and conflict on children's aggressive behavior may be mediated by the parents' unavailability and negativity toward the child (Olweus, 1979), or by the way in which the child interprets conflict between parents (Grych & Fincham, 1993). A broken home is not by itself related to antisocial activity (Rutter & Giller, 1983), since the effect of divorce on CD in boys is strongly related to the co-occurring presence of antisocial personality disorder in the parents (Lahey, Hartdagen, et al., 1988). Other factors associated with divorce such as stress, depression, loss of a prosocial role model, financial hardship, and greater responsibility at home may also contribute to antisocial behavior. Similarly, early physical abuse is a strong risk factor for later aggressive behavior, with deficits in social information processing that result from abuse mediating this relationship (Dodge, 1991; Dodge, Bates, & Pettit, 1990; Dodge, Pettit, Bates, & Valente, 1995).

> *Nick's mother says. . . .*
>
> *Nick hit a neighborhood kid on the head with a two-by-four; the injured child required 16 stitches. Then he killed another kitten by jumping on it from his bunk bed. I lost control. I told him I hated him, I grabbed him by the cheek, I pinched it a little too hard. I didn't know what to do. (Colapinto, 1993, p. 150)*

Nick's aggressive and cruel behaviors lead to strong reactions in others, such as the angry and harsh response by his mother. An important concept for understanding the role of family influences on antisocial behavior is that of **bidirectional influence,** or **reciprocal influence,** in which the child's behavior is both influenced by and influences the behavior of other family members. Negative parenting practices may lead to antisocial behavior, but such practices may also be a reaction to the difficult, oppositional, and aggressive behaviors displayed by children with conduct problems (Lytton, 1990). In an interesting study of reciprocal influence, mothers of conduct disorder and comparison boys were asked to interact with their own sons, another boy with conduct disorder, and another comparison boy (Anderson, Lytton, & Romney, 1986). In support of a child-to-parent effect, all mothers were more demanding and negative when interacting with a child with conduct disorder. However, mothers of boys with conduct disorder responded most negatively to their own sons, suggesting that a history of negative interactions with their child also plays an important role. In the context of ongoing development and interaction, reciprocal influence is the most accurate way to describe the mutual interplay between family influences and antisocial behavior. We should also recognize the possibility that some aspects of the family environment could be related to childhood antisocial behavior as the result of a common genetic predisposition that leads to certain behavior patterns (Frick & Jackson, 1993).

Coercion Theory. One of the most influential developmental theories of family contributors to antisocial behavior is the **coercion theory,** presented by Gerald Patterson of the Oregon Social Learning Centre (Patterson, 1982). Patterson has provided a simple yet enormously powerful model to describe the way in which **coercive parent-child interactions** serve as a training ground for the development of antisocial behavior (Patterson et al., 1992). This process occurs through a four-step escape-conditioning sequence in which the child learns how to use increasingly intense forms of noxious behavior to escape and avoid unwanted parental demands. The coercive parent-child interaction described in Box 6.4 begins when a mother finds her son Paul, who is failing in school, watching TV rather than doing his homework. These coercive patterns of parent-child interaction are made up of well-practiced actions and reactions that usually occur with little awareness on the part of the family members involved. This process has been called a **reinforcement trap** because, over time, coercive family members find themselves trapped by the consequences of their own behavior. For example, mothers of antisocial children are 8 times *less* likely to enforce demands as mothers of nonproblem children (Patterson et al., 1992).

The relationship between the quality of parenting a child receives and conduct problems appears to be moderated by the child's level of callous-unemotional traits, such as lack of empathy, lack of guilt, and manipulativeness. Ineffective parenting has been found to be related to conduct problems *only* in children *without* significant levels of these traits. In contrast, children high on these traits have been found to display significant conduct problems regardless of the quality of parenting they experience (Wootton, Frick, Shelton, & Silverthorn, 1997). In addition, it has been noted that the relationship between parental discipline and conduct problems may be nonlinear (both too much or too little discipline can have adverse effects), and may vary across cultural groups, the broader relational context in which discipline is used, and the gender of the parent-child dyad (that is, discipline is most effective in same-gender dyads; Deater-Deckard & Dodge, 1997).

Attachment Theories. Attachment theories emphasize that the quality of the child's attachment to parents will determine his or her eventual identification with parental values, beliefs, and standards. Secure bonds with parents promote a sense of closeness, shared values, and identification with the social world. Attachment theory proposes that most children refrain from antisocial behavior because they have a stake in conformity. Children with conduct problems are believed to show little internalization of parent and

Box 6.4

Four-Step Escape-Conditioning Sequence

Step 1
Mother Scolds

Step 2
Child Argues

Step 3
Mother Talks

Step 4
Child Stops
Arguing

No
Homework

Punishment

Negative
Reinforcement

Negative
Reinforcement

Short-Term Outcome

Mother
less likely
to scold

Child
more likely
to argue
when mother
scolds

Mother
more likely
to submit

Long-Term Outcome

No Homework

Step 1: Raising her voice, Paul's mother scolds, "Why are you sitting in front of the TV when you should be doing your homework?"

Step 2: Paul snaps back, "School is boring, my teachers are stupid, and I don't have any homework to do." Paul's arguing has the immediate effect of punishing his mother for her scolding and over time, may reduce her efforts to do something about his homework and school problems.

Step 3: Paul's mother withdraws her demand for him to complete his homework, allowing herself to be satisfied that he does not have any homework to do. She lowers her voice and says, "Does Mrs. Smith still put everyone to sleep in her English class?" The mother's withdrawal of her demand for homework negatively reinforces Paul's arguing and increases the chances that the next time she makes an issue of homework, he will argue with her. Over time Paul may also turn up the volume of his negative reactions by shouting or throwing things.

Step 4: As soon as Paul's mother withdraws her demand, Paul withdraws his counterattack. He stops arguing and engages in neutral or even positive behavior, saying, "You're sure right about Mrs. Smith, Mom. It's tough to keep your eyes open in her class." Paul, by ceasing his noxious behavior, negatively reinforces his mother for giving in and increases the likelihood that she will do so again in response to his arguing and protests in the future.

Source: Patterson et al., 1992.

societal standards. Even when such children comply with parental requests, they do so because of perceived threats to their freedom or physical safety (Shaw & Bell, 1993). When these threats are not immediately present, such as when the child is unsupervised, antisocial behavior is likely to occur. Weak bonds with parents may lead the child to associate with deviant peers, which in turn may lead to patterns of delinquency and substance abuse (Elliott, Huizinga, & Ageton, 1985; Elliott et al., 1989).

Studies generally support the relationship between insecure early attachments and antisocial behavior in children (Greenberg, DeKlyen, Speltz, & Endriga, 1997). Insecure attachments are frequently reported in clinical samples of preschool boys (but not girls) with ODD (Greenberg, Speltz, DeKlyen, & Endriga, 1991; Speltz, Greenberg, & DeKlyen, 1990). Many children who are insecurely attached display symptoms similar to children with disruptive behavior disorders (Greenberg, Speltz, & DeKlyen, 1993). Insecure avoidant and disorganized/disoriented attachments have been linked to early hostile behavior problems (Lyons-Ruth, Alpern, & Repacholi, 1993), preschool oppositional defiant behavior (Erickson, Sroufe, & Egeland, 1985), and aggression in elementary school boys (Easterbrooks, Davidson, & Chazan, 1993; Renken, Egeland, Marvinney, Mangelsdorf, & Sroufe, 1989).

The relationship between avoidant attachment and antisocial behavior has been found to be stronger in high-risk samples of children than in low-risk samples (Greenberg et al., 1993), suggesting the possibility of two types of children with insecure avoidant attachments: one characterized by high cognitive competence and relatively few problem behaviors, and the other by low cognitive competence and externalizing problem behaviors (Fagot & Pears, 1996). In a hospitalized psychiatric sample, adolescents with a dismissing/avoidant attachment were more likely than other children to display a conduct or substance abuse disorder, narcissistic or antisocial personality disorder, and self-reported narcissistic, antisocial, and paranoid personality traits (Rosenstein & Horowitz, 1996). A relation between dismissing attachment and criminal behavior in young adults has also been found (Allen, Hauser, & Borman-Spurrell, 1996). Thus, insecure attachment appears to be related to antisocial behavior during childhood, adolescence, and young adulthood. It is likely that this relationship is mediated by many factors, including the child's gender and temperament, family factors, and parent management practices. For example, a child with an insecure avoidant attachment could develop either a coercive or a defensive style depending on whether the family environment is threatening or demanding.

General Family Disturbances. As we saw earlier in the cases of Steve and Greg, families of children with conduct problems may experience numerous sources of dysfunction and stress. The following description illustrates multiple sources of family disturbance, including single-mother status, maternal depression, suicide attempts, child abuse, spousal violence, family instability, and a lack of resources.

Multiple Sources of Family Disturbance

A single mother with two young boys (ages 2 and 4) sought treatment because her older son was engaging in relatively severe and uncontrollable aggressive behaviors, including hitting, kicking, and biting the younger sibling. The mother was currently diagnosed as clinically depressed and, at the time of intake, was at risk for suicide. Her boyfriend is the father of the two children. He lives nearby and demands that she come over so he can see the children. During these visits, he engages her in what she referred to as "forced sex" (i.e., rape), and he demands that the two children remain with them and watch. In principle, the mother could have refused the visits. However, the boyfriend threatened that if she did not comply, he would stop paying child support, take the children away in a custody battle, kill himself, or come over to the house and kill her and the two children. These threats of violence were to be taken seriously as the boyfriend had a prior arrest record for assault and brandished a gun. (Adapted from Kazdin, 1995, p. 17)

Family structure and transitions. Families of children with conduct problems are often characterized by an unstable family structure with frequent transitions, including changes in parents, residence changes, geographic mobility, and family disruptions (Dishion et al., 1995). These family factors are related to a generalized heightened risk for antisocial behavior, criminal conviction, academic problems, low self-esteem, depression, peer rejection, and association with deviant peers (Capaldi & Patterson, 1991; Henry et al., 1996; Kasen, Cohen, Brook, & Hartmark, 1996). Stepfamily status appears to be associated specifically with disruptive behavior disorders, whereas having a single custodial mother is associated with both disruptive behavior disorders and anxiety disorders (Kasen et al., 1996). In most cases, the impact of marital breakup on children's antisocial behavior is secondary to the family disruption and conflict that accompanies it. Moreover, in some cases, the child's antisocial behavior can increase the chances of divorce (Block, Block, & Gjerde, 1986).

Family stress. High levels of family stress are associated with negative child behavior in the home, and family stress may be both a cause and an outcome of antisocial behavior. Among family stressors, poverty and deprivation are among the strongest predictors of conduct disorder and high rates of crime (Farrington, 1989; Kolvin, Miller, Fleeting, & Kolvin, 1988; Rutter et al., 1974; Sampson & Lauritsen, 1994). Unemployment, low SES, and multiple family transitions have been found to relate specifically to early-onset conduct disorder, but not to adolescent-onset conduct disorder. But what constitutes the "active ingredient" in the link between poverty and antisocial behavior? In this regard, the family instability, family disruption, residential mobility, and disruptions in parenting practices that are associated with poverty have all been found to be important (Dodge, Petit, & Bates, 1994; Elder, Robertson, & Ardelt, 1994; Snyder, 1991). The **amplifier hypothesis** states that stress may serve to amplify the maladaptive predispositions of parents, thereby disrupting family management practices and compromising parents' ability to be supportive of their children (Elder, Caspi, & Van Nguyen, 1986; Conger, Ge, Elder, Lorenz, & Simons, 1994).

Parental criminality and psychopathology. Aggressive and antisocial tendencies run in families, within and across generations (Eron & Huesmann, 1990; Frick & Jackson, 1993). In fact, children's aggression is associated with their parents' childhood aggression at the same age (Huesmann, Eron, Lefkowitz, & Walder, 1984). Parents of antisocial children have higher rates of arrests, motor vehicle violations, license suspensions, and substance abuse (Patterson, 1996). Antisocial individuals are likely to be poor parents, especially during discipline confrontations, where they display an irritable, explosive style of interaction. Certain types of parental psychopathology, such as antisocial personality disorder, are strongly and specifically related to conduct disorder in children (Faraone, Biederman, Keenan, & Tsuang, 1991). This relationship is particularly clear for fathers (Frick et al., 1992), as is the link between paternal criminal behavior and substance abuse and child antisocial patterns (Lahey, Piacentini, et al., 1988). The strong association between paternal antisocial personality disorder and child antisocial patterns has been found to exist independent of the father's being in the home or of the degree of contact between the father and child (Tapscott, Frick, Wootton, & Kruh, 1996). For mothers, *histrionic personality* (excessive emotionality and attention seeking) and depression are related to children's

"*Like grandfather, like father, like son...*"

From Patterson et al., 1992.

antisocial behavior, although these findings are not as consistent as those for fathers. Mothers of children with conduct disorder also display other personality problems as reflected in high scores on the hypomania and psychopathic deviate scales of personality inventories (Patterson, 1996).

Antisocial family values. Antisocial family values may serve to directly encourage antisocial behavior in children. To illustrate, a mother who was referred to a clinic by her son's school because of his frequent fighting and repeated school suspensions explained why she had missed a previously scheduled first appointment several months ago:

> *Never Shoot Someone in Public*
>
> *The mother apologized for not showing up for her prior appointment, stating that she was unable to come in because she "broke a family rule." The mother reported that she and her husband, and for that matter a number of their relatives, would often shoot each other (with guns). However, they had one family rule: "You never shoot someone in public." The mother said she broke this rule; some neighbors saw her shoot her husband, and she spent 3 months in prison. Now that she is out of prison, she said, she is ready for her son to begin treatment. (Kazdin, 1995)*

Societal Factors

Causes of antisocial behavior at the level of the individual and family tell only part of the story, since the larger societal and cultural context interacts with more immediate conditions as determinants of conduct problems (Sampson, 1992). The structural characteristics of the community provide a backdrop for the emergence of antisocial behavior by giving rise to community conditions that interfere with the adoption of prevailing social norms and the development of productive social relations (Caspi & Moffitt, 1995; Sampson, Raudenbush, & Earls, 1997). Sociological studies of crime leave little doubt that poverty, immigration concentration, neighborhood crime, family disruption, and residential mobility are related to crime and delinquency in children and adolescents. However, studies have not identified the specific mechanisms by which these structural variables lead to crime and delinquency. Recent theories of social disorganization have suggested that community structures affect the child's adjustment because of their impact on family processes (Sampson, 1992; Sampson & Laub, 1994).

Adverse contextual factors such as low SES are associated with poor parenting skills, particularly coercive and inconsistent discipline and poor monitoring, which are in turn associated with the early onset of antisocial acts in childhood, early arrest, and chronic juvenile offending during adolescence (Capaldi & Patterson, 1994; Patterson, Forgatch, Yoerger, & Stoolmiller, in press; Shaw & Vondra, 1994). A vicious cycle of adaptational failure and added stress places downward pressure on both the parent and the child. The antisocial individual is more vulnerable and at greater risk of entering a class of divorced, unemployed, and disadvantaged people (Patterson, 1996). For example, social disadvantage, economic cycles, and increased motility, along with societal changes related to divorce, early sexual activity, and working-mother status may lead to an increase in never-married adolescents or mothers in divorce transition who are at greater risk for antisocial parenting practices. Also, less skilled antisocial mothers may drift into areas of large cities that isolate them from family and neighbors and lead them to function in an atmosphere of mistrust and minimal communication. When these women become pregnant again they may have reduced access to public health services. Poor diet and drugs may result in a higher incidence of low birth weight, prematurity, and birth defects in their offspring, which in turn make their infants and toddlers more difficult to raise. The combination of a difficult infant and an unskilled parent increases the likelihood of antisocial behavior and subsequent onset of arrest (Patterson, 1996). And so, around and around the generation of conduct problems go.

Neighborhood and School Influences.

Antisocial behavior in youth is disproportionately concentrated in neighborhoods characterized by a criminal subculture that supports activities such as drug dealing and prostitution, frequent transitions and mobility, and low social support from neighbors or religious groups (Caspi & Moffitt, 1995). In addition, antisocial people tend to select neighborhoods with other people like them. The **social selection hypothesis** states that people who move into different neighborhoods differ before they arrive, and those who remain differ from those who leave. Thus, consistencies at the community level lead to stability in antisocial patterns of behavior. Low SES, family disruption, ethnic/immigration concentration, and residential instability may give rise to a community organization that minimizes productive social relations and effective social norms (Caspi & Moffitt, 1995; Sampson et al., 1997).

Skogan (1990) has proposed the concept of a **neighborhood disorder**, involving graffiti, broken windows, litter-strewn lots, loitering youth, and other visible signs of social and physical decay. The effects of community structural characteristics, such as low SES, on crime and delinquency are likely mediated by neighborhood social disorganization characterized by an inability to supervise and control teenage peer groups, low amount and density of local friendship and acquaintance networks, and low local participation rates in formal and voluntary community organizations (Sampson & Groves, 1989). The ways in which community social disorganization and neighborhood characteristics are related to antisocial behavior in youth are highlighted in Figure 6.10 (Caspi & Moffitt, 1995).

In high-risk neighborhoods, enrollment in a poor school is associated with antisocial and delinquent behavior, whereas a positive school experience can be a protective factor for the development of these behaviors (Rutter, 1989). A good school environment characterized by clear requirements for homework completion, high academic expectations, clear and consistent discipline policies, and incentives for appropriate school behavior and achievement may partially compensate for poor family circumstances. Systematic interventions to promote these school characteristics have resulted in school-wide reductions in children's conduct problems (Gottfredson, Gottfredson, & Hybel, 1993).

Media Influences.

Controversy abounds concerning the impact of media violence on young people. Consider these two contrasting opinions by experts:

> I believe that this kind of vicarious adventure, escape, excitement, even blood and thunder is necessary and important to most children as outlets for their own emotions, particularly their feelings of aggression.
> —Josette Frank, Media Consultant

> Programs interestingly depicting antisocial conduct, crime, murder, influence children to antisocial attitudes and lead to aggression.
> —Judge Jacob Panken, New York City Children's Court

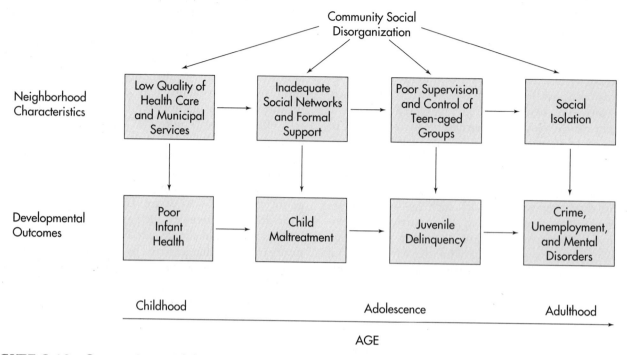

FIGURE 6.10 Community social disorganization and the development of antisocial behavior. (Caspi & Moffitt, 1995)

You may be surprised to learn that these comments by experts were made more than 50 years ago (*The New York Times*, April 14, 1946)—in reference to the influence of *radio* on children. The controversy regarding media influences on aggression in young people rages on. Some researchers claim that TV violence verges on child maltreatment and that we can reduce murders by pulling the plug (Huesmann, Eron, Berkowitz, & Chaffee, 1992); others argue that there is little evidence for a causal relation between TV violence and aggressive behavior (Freedman, 1984, 1992).

Weapons signs such as this one in the Los Angeles area are routinely posted outside schools.

By the time a child in the United States reaches sixth grade, he or she has seen 8,000 murders on TV and over 100,000 other acts of violence (Leland, 1995). The concern is that this steady diet of violence leads children to think of violence as normal, to become desensitized to the suffering of real people, or to become aroused by images they see and to mimic these violent acts. For example, one 5-year-old boy, after watching his favorite cartoon characters pull one of their famous arson stunts, set his house ablaze. His younger sister was killed in the fire. Children between the ages of 6 and 10 who are prone to aggression, especially boys, may be the most susceptible to the influence of violent messages on the media (Eron, Huesmann, Lefkowitz, & Walder, 1996).

The correlation between TV violence and aggression is indisputable—but does TV violence *cause* aggression? The answer to this question remains elusive despite decades of research and a pressing government and societal concern to act on research findings through social policies such as requiring TV manufacturers to equip new TVs with the V-chip and requiring networks to implement a TV ratings system (Zoglin, 1996). Exposure to media violence may reinforce preexisting antisocial tendencies in some children. In one series of studies spanning a decade, children with conduct problems were found to view relatively large amounts of violent material, prefer aggressive characters, and believe fictional content to be true (Gadow & Sprafkin, 1993).

Calvin and Hobbes

by Bill Watterson

Calvin and Hobbes © Watterson. Reprinted with permission of Universal Press Syndicate. All rights reserved.

However, they were not more likely to behave aggressively in social situations after viewing material with aggressive content than they were after viewing material with nonaggressive content (Gadow & Sprafkin, 1993). It is unlikely that media influences alone can account for the substantial amount of antisocial behavior in young people (Rutter & Smith, 1995). Like the other risk factors we have discussed, media influences likely interact with other individual, family, community, and cultural factors in contributing to conduct problems.

Cultural and Ethnic Factors

Cultural differences in the expression of aggressive behavior are dramatic. Across cultures, socialization of children for aggression has been found to be one of the strongest predictors of aggressive acts such as homicide and assault. As illustrated in the following examples of contrasting socialization practices, aggression may be an inadvertent consequence of a culture's emphasis on training "warriors":

The Kapauku of Western New Guinea

At about 7 years of age, a Kapauku boy begins to be under the father's control, gradually sleeping and eating only with the men and away from his mother. . . . His training [to be a brave warrior] begins when the father engages his son in mock stick fights. Gradually the fights become more serious and possibly lethal when the father and son shoot real war arrows at each other. Groups of boys play at target shooting; they also play at hitting each other over the head with sticks." (C. R. Ember & M. Ember, 1994, p. 639–640)

The Lepcha of the Indian Himalayas

The Lepcha are very clear about what they expect from their children. "Good children help out with the work, tell the truth, listen to teaching from elders, help old people, and are peaceable. Bad children quarrel with and insult people, tell lies, draw their knives in anger when reprimanded, and do not do their share of the work." (C. R. Ember & M. Ember, 1994, p. 641)

The homicide rate among the Kapauku in 1953 to 1954 was estimated at 200 per 100,000, approximately 20 times current United States murder rates. In contrast, interviews with the Lepcha people revealed that the only authenticated murder in their culture had occurred about 200 years ago (C. R. Ember & M. Ember, 1994).

Rates of antisocial behavior vary widely across cultures, and not necessarily in relation to technological gains, material wealth, or population density. For example, some Third World countries that value interdependence are characterized by high rates of prosocial behavior, and some places with high population density, such as Singapore, have very low rates of violence. The United States is by far the most violent of all industrialized nations.

Minority status is associated with antisocial behavior in the United States, with elevated rates of antisocial behavior in African-American, Hispanic-American, and Native American youth and adults (Elliott et al., 1985). Studies that have included a small number of African-American children in their samples report higher rates of externalizing problems for this group (Costello, 1989; Velez, Johnson, & Cohen, 1989). However, other studies with much larger national samples that included non-

Table 6.6 Summary of Causal Influences and Outcomes of Early-Onset Antisocial Behavior

CAUSAL INFLUENCES

Biological/Constitutional	Developmental	Family/Environmental
Male gender	Disruptions in attachment	Marital discord
Genetic risk	Early-stage social-cognitive deficits and	Discordant parent-child interactions
Neuropsychological deficits	distortions (reactive aggression type)	Child abuse
Lowered verbal IQ and verbal deficits	Later-stage social-cognitive patterns	Low SES
Lowered arousal and reactivity	(proactive aggression subtype)	Poor neighborhood
Attention deficits/hyperactivity		

OUTCOMES

Academic underachievement
Rejection by peers
Neuropsychological deficits secondary to violence/head injury
Altered psychophysiological parameters—arousal, reactivity—secondary to violent lifestyle

Source: Adapted from Hinshaw & Anderson, 1996.

Hispanic white, African-American, and Hispanic children have reported either no or very small differences in antisocial behavior related to race or ethnicity when SES, gender, age, and referral status were controlled for (Achenbach & Edelbrock, 1981; Achenbach et al., 1991; Lahey et al., 1995). So, although externalizing problems have been reported to be more frequent among minority-status children, this finding is likely related to economic hardship, limited employment opportunities, or residence in high-risk urban neighborhoods.

Summary of Causal Influences

A summary of causal influences and outcomes for conduct problems in children is presented in Table 6.6. These risk factors apply primarily to children with early-onset or LCP conduct problems. The most common risk factor associated with AL conduct problems is the association with antisocial peers.

TREATMENT

Despite considerable efforts over the past century to help children and adolescents with conduct problems, continuing high rates of antisocial behavior provide sobering testimony to an absence of clearly effective interventions (Kazdin, 1995). Many different forms of treatment will be tried throughout the life of a child with severe conduct problems. This process may begin during the preschool years or, more typically, when behavior problems at school lead to referral for treatment. Ongoing contacts with the educational system, mental health services, and the judicial system may lead to referrals for any one of a wide range of treatment options, including counseling, cognitive behavior therapy, medication, family therapy, peer interventions, school intervention, inpatient hospitalization, and out-of-home placements (Tolan & Guerra, 1994).

Unfortunately, none of these treatments has proved very effective in eliminating serious conduct problems in children and adolescents. In fact, if antisocial behavior is not changed by the time the child has completed the third grade, such behavior might best be treated as a social disability or chronic condition, much like diabetes, which cannot be cured but can be managed or contained through the provision of ongoing interventions and supports (Kazdin, 1995). This chronic treatment model of conduct disorder suggests the need for a comprehensive and ongoing intervention strategy to help youngsters and their families cope with the many social, emotional, and academic problems that are associated with this disorder throughout childhood and adolescence.

Most people understand that abuse, family dysfunction, school expulsion, association with drug-using peers, residence in a high-crime area, and minimal parental supervision contribute to serious conduct problems in youth (Henggeler, 1996). Despite this recognition, however, typical, and often court-mandated, treatments such as psychotherapy, group therapy, tutoring, punishment, or boot camps fail to meaningfully address these determinants and thus are among the least effective approaches for treating children with conduct problems (Henggeler, 1996; Henggeler, Schoenwald, & Pickrel, 1995; Lipsey, 1995). Group treatments that bring together antisocial adolescents may make the problem worse, since associating with like-minded youngsters encourages antisocial activities. Despite their lack of effectiveness in treating serious antisocial behavior, office-based individual counseling and family therapy are often provided because they are relatively inexpensive (Tate, Reppucci, & Mulvey, 1995). More restrictive approaches, such as residential treatment, psychiatric hospitalization, and incarceration, also show little effectiveness and have the additional disadvantage of being extremely expensive (Henggeler & Santos, 1997). Nevertheless, approximately 70% of mental health dollars for children and adolescents in the United States are still spent on restrictive out-of-home placements that may do more harm than good (Sondheimer, Schoenwald, & Rowland, 1994). Incarceration may not even serve a community protection function, since youth who are incarcerated and then released often commit more crimes than those kept at home and given treatment (Henggeler, 1996).

Not surprisingly, the most promising interventions are those that use a combination of treatments that are applied across individual, family, school, and community settings. In addition, treatment frequently requires that related family difficulties, such as maternal depression, marital discord, or abuse, be addressed if gains are to be made and maintained (McMahon & Wells, 1998).

The degree of success in treating antisocial behavior depends on the type and severity of the child's conduct problem and related risk and protective factors in the child, family, and community. The classic work with delinquents conducted in the 1920s by Healy and Bronner (1926) reported success rates of 72% for delinquents with no major personality problems and no gross abnormalities in their social situation; 38% for cases with deviant family and peer situations only; and *only 3%* for those cases showing extreme deviations in personality and social circumstances. These findings have been echoed in study after study over the past 70 years—children from mostly healthy middle-class families who display mild conduct problems are likely to benefit from parent, family, and school interventions, whereas those from highly dysfunctional families and poor neighborhoods who display severe and persistent problems are likely to benefit very little, if at all. Although small, short-term gains for children with *severe* conduct problems have been achieved using family and school interventions, the degree of normalization and long-term impact of these approaches have proved minimal for this group.

Since children's conduct problems often show a developmental progression, diversification, and escalation over time, treatments must be sensitive to where a child is in this trajectory, and will differ in methods and goals for preschoolers, school-age children, and adolescents. In general, the farther along the child is in the progression of antisocial behavior, the greater the need for intensive interventions and, unfortunately, the poorer the prognosis. This troubling situation of high treatment efforts and costs with less return for older children has led to a reevaluation of priorities, and a growing emphasis on the need for programs of early intervention and prevention.

Since many of the treatments used for children with conduct problems have little supportive evidence, in the sections that follow we highlight three of the approaches for which there is some empirical support: parent management training, cognitive problem-solving skills training, and multisystemic treatment. We also discuss psychopharmacological interventions and promising new preventive interventions for young children. As you will see, almost all treatment programs attempt to provide corrective interpersonal experiences with parents, siblings, and peers, a reflection of the fact that most antisocial acts, including violence, occur between the child and family members or peers.

Parent Management Training

The focus of **parent management training (PMT)**, which we described in Chapter 5, is on teaching parents to change their child's behavior in the home (Eyberg, 1988; Forehand & McMahon, 1981). The underlying assumption of PMT is that maladaptive parent-child interactions are at least partially responsible for producing and sustaining the child's antisocial behaviors, and that changing the way parents interact with their child will lead to improvements in the child's behavior (Dishion, Patterson, & Kavanagh, 1992; McMahon & Wells, 1989, 1998). Although coercive exchanges in the family are seen as the joint outcome of parent and child behavior, the easiest and most desirable point of entry in modifying these interactions is by changing parent behavior. The goal of PMT is for the parent to learn specific new skills. Although there are many variations of PMT, such as individual versus group training, training in the clinic versus in the home, or the use of live versus videotaped training materials, all parent management training approaches share several features (Kazdin, 1995). These are presented in Table 6.7.

Parent management training has a number of strengths and limitations (McMahon & Wells, 1989). On the positive side, many excellent treatment manuals and training materials have been developed that facilitate its widespread use (e.g., Forehand & McMahon, 1981). In addition, PMT has been evaluated more than any other treatment for conduct problems. These evaluations have repeatedly demonstrated the short-term effectiveness of PMT in producing changes in both parent and child behaviors, with the average child whose parents participate in PMT showing better adjustment after

Table 6.7 Common Features of Parent Management Training (PMT)

- There is minimal or no direct intervention of the therapist with the child.
- The parent learns to use specific procedures to change parent-child interactions, promote prosocial child behavior, and decrease deviant child behavior.
- Therapists use a variety of teaching methods in the home or clinic, including interactive discussion, direct instruction, modeling, behavioral contracting, behavior rehearsal, shaping, feedback, role playing, and structured homework assignments.
- Parents learn to identify, define, and observe their child's problem behaviors in new ways.
- Treatment sessions cover social learning principles, including the effective use of commands; ways of setting clear rules; use of differential attention; use of praise, tangible rewards, or tokens for desired behavior; use of mild punishment such as time-out from reinforcement or loss of privileges; negotiation; and contingency contracting.
- Sessions provide opportunities for parents to see how the new techniques are implemented, to practice using the techniques, and to review progress in the home.
- Homework assignments and other tactics are used to promote generalization of the skills learned in the treatment sessions to the home.
- Progress in treatment is carefully monitored, and ongoing modifications in treatment are made as needed.

Source: Adapted from Kazdin, 1995, pp. 83–84.

treatment than 80% of children whose parents do not participate (Serketich & Dumas, 1996). In addition to changes in the referred child, PMT has also been associated with reductions in the problem behaviors of siblings, and reduced stress and depression in the parents.

However, a number of limitations of PMT can also be identified (Kazdin, 1995, 1997; McMahon & Wells, 1998). First, although PMT produces short-term gains, its long-term effectiveness is less clear. Second, some families do not respond to treatment. PMT makes numerous demands on parents, such as mastering and implementing procedures in the home, attending meetings, and maintaining phone contacts with the therapist. For families with few resources who are under stress, these demands may be too great to continue in treatment and they simply stop coming (Armbruster & Kazdin, 1994). Third, PMT has been used mostly with parents of children younger than 12 years of age. Although PMT has had some success with adolescents, it is generally more effective with younger children (Bank, Marlowe, Reid, Patterson, & Weinrott, 1991; Dishion & Patterson, 1992). It is possible that age-related differences in outcome are due to the greater problem severities of older children prior to entering treatment (Ruma, Burke,

& Thompson, 1996). Fourth, the application of PMT is rarely straightforward. The use of coercion may not be recognized by parents who believe that difficulties occur because their child is stubborn, their marriage is bad, work is interfering with their spending time together, or school personnel are unfair. In fact, parents of children with conduct problems frequently believe they use good parenting practices but their child fails to respond. Unless such parental beliefs and concerns are addressed in treatment, it is unlikely that training procedures will be learned or implemented (Johnston, 1996; Miller & Prinz, 1990; Prinz & Miller, 1996). Finally, PMT has not been sensitive to the changing ethnic profile in the U.S. population. The embeddedness of many parenting practices (e.g., the use of punishment) in cultural beliefs and values dictates that PMT will need to be more sensitive to such issues (Deater-Deckard, Dodge, Bates, & Pettit, 1996; Forehand & Kotchick, 1996).

In response to some of the limitations of PMT, treatment efforts have increasingly focused not just on teaching parents behavior management techniques, but also on teaching general problem-solving strategies and play skills to enhance the parent-child relationship, and on parent cognitions, marital and social support, therapy style and engagement, and ethnic and cultural factors.

Cognitive Problem-Solving Skills Training

Cognitive problem-solving skills training (PSST) focuses on the cognitive deficiencies and distortions displayed by children and adolescents with conduct problems in interpersonal situations, particularly by those children who are aggressive (Dodge, 1989; Kazdin, 1996). The underlying assumption of PSST is that the child's antisocial and aggressive responses are triggered by his or her perceptions and appraisals of environmental events, and that changes in the child's faulty thinking will lead to changes in overt behavior. As illustrated in Box 6.5, children are taught to identify their thoughts, feelings, and behaviors in problem social situations, using a series of five problem-solving steps.

During the course of PSST the therapist, who plays an active role in treatment, uses instruction, practice, and feedback to help the child discover different ways of handling social situations by learning how to appraise the situation, identify self-statements and reactions, alter the types of attributions made about other children's motivations, be more sensitive to how other children feel, anticipate others' reactions, generate alternative and more appropriate solutions to interpersonal problems, and examine the effects of personal behavior on others and him- or herself. The primary elements of PSST are outlined in Table 6.8.

Box 6.5

Problem-Solving Steps and Self-Statements of Cognitive Problem-Solving Skills Training

Problem situation: Jason, one of the kids in your class, has taken your Nintendo game. You want to get it back. What do you do?

Step 1: What am I supposed to do? This step asks the child to identify and define the problem.

I want to get my Nintendo game back from Jason.

Step 2: I have to look at all my possibilities. This step asks the child to come up with alternative solutions to the problem.

I can beat him up and take it back, ask him to give it back, or tell my teacher.

Step 3: I had better concentrate and focus in. This step instructs the child to concentrate and evaluate the solutions that he or she comes up with.

If I beat him up, I would get into trouble. If I asked him, he might give it back.

Step 4: I need to make a choice. In this step, the child chooses the solution that he or she thinks is the most effective.

I'll try asking him, and if that doesn't work, I will tell my teacher.

Step 5: I did a good job or I made a mistake. In this final step, the child evaluates the solution: whether it was the best of those available, whether the problem-solving process was followed correctly, whether a mistake or less than desirable solution was selected (if so, the five-step process starts anew).

I made a good choice. I won't get into trouble. Jason and I can still be friends if he returns my Nintendo game. If not, I did my best to get it back before asking my teacher for help. I did a good job!

Source: Adapted from Kazdin, 1996, p. 383.

Table 6.8 Primary Elements of Cognitive Problem-Solving Skills Training (PSST)

❖ An emphasis on the child's thinking, although the behaviors that result from thinking are also viewed as important; children are taught a step-by-step approach to solve interpersonal difficulties.

❖ Self-statements are used to direct attention to aspects of the problem that lead to effective solutions.

❖ Treatment uses structured tasks, which include games, school activities, or stories.

❖ The child learns to apply the cognitive problem-solving skills that are learned to real-life situations.

❖ The therapist plays an active role in treatment, giving examples of the cognitive processes through verbal statements, applying the sequence of statements to problems, giving cues to prompt the use of the skills, and providing feedback and praise for the correct use of these skills.

❖ Treatment combines modeling, practice, role playing, behavioral contracts, reinforcement, and mild punishments, such as the loss of points or tokens.

❖ Treatment emphasizes the extension of problem solving to the child's everyday life through the use of homework assignments. In addition, parents are trained to help the child use the steps and to practice joint assignments with the child at home.

Source: Adapted from Kazdin, 1995.

have revealed that the alteration of cognitive processes may not necessarily lead to changes in behavior (Dodge, 1989). Finally, although consistent changes have resulted from PSST, the magnitude and clinical significance of these changes remain in question. Many children improve, but they continue to display problems far in excess of those of their nondeviant peers (Kazdin, Siegel, & Bass, 1992).

Multisystemic Treatment

Multisystemic treatment (MST) is based on a family systems approach that emphasizes the reciprocity of interpersonal relations and the view that child conduct problems typically reflect dysfunctional family relations (Henggeler & Borduin, 1990; Henggeler, Schoenwald, Borduin, Rowland, & Cunningham, 1998). MST views the child with conduct problems as functioning within interrelated social systems, such as the family, school, neighborhood, and court and juvenile services. The underlying assumption of MST is that antisocial behavior results from or can be maintained by transactions within or between any of those systems (Henggeler, 1991). Thus, treatment is carried out with all family members, school personnel, peers, juvenile justice staff, and other individuals in the child's life. MST is an

PSST has achieved some success with children and youth who are clinically referred for conduct problems, especially with older children and children with milder problems from relatively functional families (Kazdin, 1993, 1995, 1996). Research continues to support the relationship between maladaptive cognitions and aggressive behavior on which PSST is based, and PSST procedures are carefully specified in treatment manuals (Finch, Nelson, & Ott, 1993; Shure, 1992). Although the evidence in support of PSST is suggestive, it is not clear if there is a pattern of cognitive deficits that is specific to children with conduct problems, or if changes in cognitive processes are responsible for behavioral improvements. Indeed, studies of the treatment of aggression

Box 6.6

Principles of Multisystemic Intervention and Specific Treatment Strategies

Albert was referred for treatment after punching the school principal, who wanted him permanently expelled. Albert had a long history of assaulting other children, as did his siblings. His mother was also quite aggressive—she had previously assaulted the same principal. Factors that contributed to Albert's aggression included poor discipline skills on both the part of Albert's mother, who used inconsistent discipline and relied on physical punishment, and Albert's teacher, who inadvertently gave positive attention to Albert's aggression. Moreover, the situation was worsened by the considerable conflict between the mother and school personnel, Albert's relatively low intellectual abilities (IQ = 65), peer reinforcement of Albert's aggression (i.e., he was respected as the strongest and toughest boy in his grade), and the rough neighborhood where the family lived. Thus, although the presenting problem was relatively specific, numerous factors contributed to Albert's aggression.

Principle 1: The purpose of assessment is to understand the 'fit' between the identified problems and their broader context.

Albert's assault on the principal closely fit his social context. He (a) was modeling maternal and sibling aggression, (b) lived in a neighborhood that required toughness, (c) was reinforced for aggression by his peers, and (d) possessed few intellectual strengths from which to obtain status in a school. In addition, his mother and the school personnel were mishandling their efforts to discipline Albert effectively.

Principle 2: Interventions should be present-focused and action-oriented, targeting specific and well-defined problems.

All parties agreed that the primary goal of treatment was to greatly reduce Albert's interpersonal aggression. In addition, the therapist targeted several secondary goals aimed at achieving the primary goal: (a) Albert's mother needed to develop more effective and less aggressive discipline strategies; (b) Albert's brothers needed to stop reinforcing his aggressive behavior; (c) the teacher needed to learn better discipline strategies, especially the effective use of time-out; (d) the teacher's demands for academic performance needed to be consistent with Albert's ability level; (e) Albert's mother and teacher needed to develop a cooperative and supportive working relationship; and (f) Albert needed to be provided with a socially accepted mechanism for maintaining his high peer status.

Principle 3: Interventions should focus on behavioral transactions within or between multiple systems.

The primary goal and each of the secondary goals described under principles 1 and 2 met this criterion. The primary goal targeted Albert's transactions with others. Secondary goal (a) targeted the mother-child relationship; (b), sibling interactions; (c) and (d), teacher-child interactions; (e), the family-school relationship; and (f), peer relations.

Principle 4: Interventions should be developmentally appropriate and should fit the developmental needs of the youth.

Interventions focused on improving the control strategies of the adults in Albert's life. This thrust is appropriate for an 11-year-old with serious behavior problems. In addition, interventions attempted to maintain Albert's peer status by conferring high-status classroom privileges

---

intensive approach that draws on other techniques, such as PMT, PSST, and marital therapy, as well as specialized interventions, such as special education placements and referral to substance abuse treatment programs or legal services. In effect, MST attempts to address the multiple determinants of severe antisocial behavior.

Box 6.6 presents the basic principles of this approach along with examples of how they were implemented to help Albert, an 11-year-old boy with conduct problems, and his family and teacher.

Outcome studies of MST conducted with extremely antisocial, aggressive, and violent youths have reported this approach to be superior to usual services, individual counseling, and community services in reducing delinquency, decreasing aggression with peers, improving family warmth and cohesion, and reducing long-term rates of criminal behavior for periods as long as 5 years after treatment. In addition, MST has been shown to be

cost-effective, with costs estimated at one-fifth of those for more conventional interventions (Henggeler, 1992; Henggeler et al., 1998). Since studies of MST have not differentiated between adolescents who show life-course-persistent versus adolescence-limited patterns of antisocial behavior, it is difficult to know whether successful outcomes reported for this approach apply equally to both groups. It is possible that part of the success of MST may be in helping AL adolescents decrease their association with deviant peers and by doing so lowering the age at which they desist from delinquent behavior.

Medications

A variety of medications have been used to treat the aggressive symptoms of conduct problems in children and adolescents, including neuroleptics, lithium carbonate, and anticonvulsants (Gadow, 1991; Stewart, Myers,

Box 6.6
Principles of Multisystemic Intervention and Specific Treatment Strategies—cont'd

(e.g., class monitor) contingent on positive behavior, and by facilitating Albert's involvement in organized athletics, at which he excelled. Thus, interventions were sensitive to Albert's developmental needs.

Principle 5: Interventions require daily and weekly effort by family members.

Albert's mother agreed to monitor and record his noncompliance and aggression, and to implement, daily contingencies based on his performance. The teacher sent a note home each day that rated Albert's aggressive and prosocial behavior and academic efforts, and the mother implemented prearranged contingencies. Weekly, the therapist discussed the mother's changes in disciplinary practices and her son's involvement in prosocial peer activities such as sports. The therapist provided considerable support for Albert, his mother, and the teacher.

Principle 6: Intervention efficacy is evaluated continuously from multiple perspectives.

The structured and active nature of the intervention tasks enabled the ready evaluation of intervention efficacy. Moreover, the views of at least three respondents, Albert, his mother, and his teacher, were obtained on a regular basis.

Principle 7: Interventions should be designed to promote treatment generalization and long-term maintenance of therapeutic change.

All interventions were carried out by individuals in Albert's natural environment who will remain in place after the therapist leaves. Interventions were designed with the future in mind. For example, the development of the mother's disciplinary skills may have substantial long-term benefit for the sons. The development of a positive working relationship between the mother and the teacher set an example for future mother-teacher relationships. Finally, Albert's involvement in organized athletics had the potential to develop his capacity for cooperative teamwork, self-discipline, and goal attainment, as well as providing considerable peer status and self-esteem.

Principle 8: Therapeutic contacts should emphasize the positive, and interventions should use systemic strengths as levers for change.

Albert was a strong and athletic boy who, in spite of low intellectual abilities, was putting considerable effort into academics and was actually achieving above expectations. Albert's mother was an assertive and demanding woman who was not afraid to stand up for her rights. Moreover, she and her sons loved Albert very much and had only his best interests at heart. Albert's teacher was a very warm person who wanted the best for Albert. She also placed considerable demands on his academic performance, believing that he was not achieving up to his abilities. These strengths provided the levers for change.

Principle 9: Interventions should be designed to promote responsible behavior and decrease irresponsible behavior.

Overall, the therapist prompted the mother to behave as a mature and responsible parent. Her support and implementation of the treatment plan as well as her willingness to meet with the teacher were instrumental in decreasing Albert's irresponsible and immature aggressive behavior.

Source: Adapted from Henggeler, 1991.

Burket, & Lyles, 1990). **Neuroleptics,** particularly haloperidol and pimozide, are the most commonly used drugs to treat aggressive behavior. The former is more potent; the latter has less frequent side effects. However, the long-term use of neuroleptics needs to be carefully considered because they may cause side effects including cognitive deficits, movement disorders, drowsiness, weight gain, and gastrointestinal upsets. Lithium carbonate is a mood stabilizer that reduces aggressive behavior, usually taking 2 to 3 weeks to achieve effectiveness. Side effects, which are fewer than those of the neuroleptics, include weight gain, stomachache, headache, and tremors. The anticonvulsant carbamazepine helps reduce aggressive and manic behaviors while having minimal effect on cognitive functions. The most common side effect is allergic skin rash, although at higher levels there is an increased risk of seizure activity and worsening of original symptoms.

Few controlled studies have evaluated the effectiveness of medications for treating conduct problems, and findings are mixed. These medications may reduce explosive aggressive and destructive acts, but they are not likely to do much for covert symptoms such as stealing or lying (Campbell, Gonzalez, & Silva, 1992). If used to reduce aggressive behavior, medication alone is rarely sufficient and should always be used in combination with interventions that teach appropriate social behaviors and self-control.

Preventive Interventions

Until very recently, there has been an overemphasis on the treatment of older children with conduct problems and an underemphasis on early-intervention and prevention programs that can compete with the child's negative developmental history, poor environment, and deviant peer associations (Tolan, Guerra, & Kendall, 1995). The underlying assumptions of preventive interventions include the following (Webster-Stratton, 1996):

❖ Conduct problems can be treated more easily and more effectively in younger children.

❖ By counteracting risk factors and strengthening protective factors at a young age, one can limit or prevent the escalating developmental trajectory of increased aggression, peer rejection, low self-esteem, conduct disorder, and academic failure that is commonly observed in children with early-onset conduct problems.

❖ In the long run, preventive interventions will reduce the substantial costs to the educational, criminal justice, health, and mental health systems that are associated with conduct problems.

Carolyn Webster-Stratton has developed an intensive early-intervention program for parents of 4- to 8-year-old children with oppositional defiant disorder and conduct disorder (Webster-Stratton, 1994, 1995, 1996). A strength of this program is its emphasis on the use of interactive videotapes in training, an approach that permits widespread use at a relatively low cost. In addition to teaching parents child management skills, the program also addresses the associated individual, family, and school difficulties that accompany conduct problems. Parents are taught personal self-control strategies for managing anger, depression, and blame; effective communication skills; strategies for coping with conflict with spouses, employers, extended family members, employers, and children; and ways of strengthening social supports.

Approximately 65% of children whose parents are involved in these early interventions show sustained improvements in their behavior. However, high rates of relapse for some families and a lack of generalization of behavioral improvements to school and peer relationships suggest that additional interventions that treat the child directly are needed. As a result, an additional component of this program teaches developmentally appropriate problem-solving and social skills to 3- to 8-year-old children. Treatment sessions take place in small groups and focus on rules, empathy training, problem-solving training, anger control, friendship skills, communication skills, and school training (Webster-Stratton, 1996). Because of the young age of the children, practice, play, role playing, cartoons, drawing, and other exercises are used to keep children involved. Follow-up studies have found that these procedures are effective, especially when combined with the parent training intervention (Webster-Stratton, 1995).

An innovative effort designed to prevent serious chronic antisocial behavior is the FAST Track program (Conduct Problems Prevention Group, 1992). This early intervention provides an excellent example of the integration of developmental findings with clinical practice and the kind of comprehensive effort needed to treat children with serious conduct problems (Bierman, Greenberg, & Conduct Problems Prevention Group, 1996; Zigler, Taussig, & Black, 1992). FAST Track is directed at high-risk kindergarten children who are identified in terms of their disruptive behavior and poor peer relations at home and at school. The goals of FAST Track are to reduce disruptive behaviors in the home and improve the quality of the parent-child relationship; to reduce aggressive, disruptive, and off-task behaviors in school; to promote the social-cognitive skills needed for effective interpersonal problem solving and emotion regulation; to improve peer relations; to strengthen academic skills, especially reading; and to improve the quality of the relationship between family members and school personnel.

Five integrated treatment components are used to achieve these goals: parent training, home visiting/case management, social skills training, academic tutoring, and teacher-based classroom intervention. FAST Track interventions are implemented with close collaboration among parents, teachers, and project staff. The strengths of the program are that it targets the deficits and determinants that research has shown to be important in children with conduct problems and uses treatment procedures for which there is already some empirical support. The outcomes of FAST Track are just now being evaluated. Preliminary reports suggest improvements in peer relations and school performance, decreases in disruptive behavior, and enhanced parenting attitudes and values (Coie, 1997; Conduct Problems Prevention Research Group, 1997). However, these effects are modest and vary across intervention sites, informants, and the methods used to assess them. The preliminary findings are promising, but only time will tell whether this all-out intervention effort will achieve its intended long-term goal to prevent serious chronic antisocial behavior.

SUMMARY

Perspectives on Conduct Problems

1. Conduct problems are age-inappropriate actions and attitudes that violate family expectations, societal norms, and the personal or property rights of others.

2. Most commonly, conduct problems in children are defined from legal, psychological, and psychiatric perspectives.

DSM-IV Defining Features

3. Oppositional defiant disorder (ODD) is diagnosed in children who show an age-inappropriate and persistent pattern of irritable, hostile, oppositional, and defiant behavior.

4. Conduct disorder (CD) describes children who display severe aggressive and antisocial acts involving inflicting pain on others or interfering with others' rights.

5. Psychopathy refers to a pattern of deceitful, callous, manipulative, and remorseless behavior.

Associated Characteristics of Conduct Problems

6. Children with conduct problems have interpersonal difficulties with peers, although they may form friendships with other antisocial children.

7. Families of children with conduct problems show high rates of conflict among family members relative to rates in nonproblem families, poor communication patterns, low support, and disorganization.

8. Children with conduct problems engage in behaviors that place them at high risk for health-related problems such as drug overdose and sexually transmitted diseases.

9. Children with conduct problems usually have one or more other disorders, most typically attention-deficit/hyperactivity disorder, depression, and anxiety.

Prevalence, Gender, and Developmental Pathways

10. Prevalence estimates of conduct disorder range from 2% to 6% of all children. Estimated rates of oppositional defiant disorder range from 10% to 22%.

11. Rates of conduct problems are about 3 or 4 times higher for boys than for girls during childhood. This disparity decreases or disappears completely by age 15, mainly due to an increase in covert nonaggressive antisocial behaviors by girls.

12. There is a maximum progression of antisocial behavior from difficult early temperament and hyperactivity, to oppositional and aggressive behavior, to social difficulties, to school problems, to delinquent behavior in adolescence, to criminal behavior in adulthood. There are also important variations on this general progression.

13. The life-course-persistent (LCP) path describes children who display antisocial behavior at an early age and who continue to do so into adulthood. The adolescent-limited (AL) path describes youngsters whose antisocial behavior begins around puberty and continues into adolescence, and who later desist from these behaviors in young adulthood.

14. Delinquent behavior shows a dramatic increase in middle adolescence that peaks around the age of 17, followed by an equally dramatic decrease in late adolescence and young adulthood.

Causes of Conduct Problems

15. Conduct problems in children are best accounted for by multiple causes, or risk and protective factors, operating in a transactional fashion over time.

16. Adoption and twin studies suggest the importance of genetic influences on antisocial behavior in adults and adolescents, although findings for children are less clear.

17. The structural characteristics of the community provide a backdrop for the emergence of conduct problems by giving rise to community conditions that interfere with the adoption of prevailing social norms and the development of productive social relations.

Treatment

18. Despite considerable efforts to help children and adolescents with conduct problems, there is an absence of clearly effective interventions.

19. The focus of parent management training is on teaching parents to change their child's behavior in the home.

20. The underlying assumption of cognitive problem-solving skills training is that the child's antisocial responses are triggered by faulty perceptions and appraisals of interpersonal events. The focus is on changing behavior by changing the way the child thinks in social situations.

21. Multisystemic treatment is an intensive approach that is carried out with all family members, school personnel, peers, juvenile justice staff, and other individuals in the child's life.

22. Recent efforts have focused on preventing conduct problems through early intervention.

KEY TERMS

conduct problems, 185

antisocial behavior, 185

delinquent, 190

status offenses, 190

index offenses, 190

externalizing dimension, 190

undercontrolled, 190

overt–covert dimension, 190

destructive–nondestructive dimension, 190

aggression, 191

verbal aggression, 191

physical aggression, 191

instrumental aggression, 192
hostile aggression, 192
direct aggression, 192
indirect aggression, 192
reactive aggression, 192
proactive aggression, 192
bullying, 193
disruptive behavior disorders, 194
oppositional defiant disorder (ODD), 194
conduct disorder (CD), 194
antisocial personality disorder (APD), 194
psychopathy, 194
childhood-onset conduct disorder, 196
adolescent-onset conduct disorder, 196
antisocial personality disorder (APD), 197
callous-unemotional interpersonal style, 198
trait confluence, 201
life-course-persistent (LCP) path, 207

adolescent-limited (AL) path, 207
reward dominance, 213
behavioral inhibition system (BIS), 213
behavioral activation system (BAS), 214
cognitive deficiencies, 215
cognitive distortions, 215
bidirectional influence, 217
reciprocal influence, 217
coercion theory, 217
coercive parent-child interactions, 217
reinforcement trap, 217
amplifier hypothesis, 220
social selection hypothesis, 221
neighborhood disorder, 221
parent management training (PMT), 225
cognitive problem-solving skills training (PSST), 226
multisystemic treatment (MST), 227
neuroleptics, 229

Anxiety Disorders

Separation Anxiety: Nine-year-old Brad is terrified of being separated from his mother. He follows her around the house constantly, always needing to know where she is.

Generalized Anxiety: Ten-year-old Alesha "worries about everything"—What others think of her, how she is doing in school, events in the news, and family finances.

Social Anxiety: Thirteen-year-old Dante feels completely isolated at school. He doesn't interact with anyone. Dante is totally preoccupied with what others think of him.

Obsessive-Compulsive Disorder: Ten-year-old Wayman can't stop thinking about not being able to sleep. Every night before bedtime he goes through the same routine of opening and closing the closet door and making and remaking his bed.

Panic Attack: Sixteen-year-old Claudia describes her sudden attack of overwhelming anxiety. "My heart started pumping so fast I thought it would explode. I thought I was going to die."

All children experience fear, worry, anxiety, or shyness as a normal part of growing up. However, children like Brad, Alesha, Dante, Wayman, and Claudia suffer from anxiety that is excessive and debilitating. These children have **anxiety disorders,** one of the most common mental health problems in children and adolescents (Fleming, Offord, & Boyle, 1989; Kashani & Orvaschel, 1990; Lewinsohn, Hops, Roberts, Seeley, & Andrews, 1993). Despite their high frequency and associated problems, anxiety disorders in children often go unnoticed, undiagnosed, and untreated. This is partly due to the frequent occurrence of fears and anxiety in normal development, the invisible nature of many anxiety disorder symptoms (e.g., a knot in the stomach or feelings of apprehension), and the fact that anxiety is not nearly as damaging to people or property as are other childhood disorders,

for example, conduct problems (Albano, Chorpita, & Barlow, 1996).

Although the study of children's fears, in both psychology and medicine, has a long tradition, the systematic study of anxiety disorders in children is relatively recent. For many years anxiety in children was thought to be a mild and transitory disturbance. The resulting short-term distress was expected to fade over time as a result of normal life experiences. Contrary to this once popular belief, many children with anxiety disorders, and others who experience anxiety symptoms to a lesser degree, continue to display problems in adjustment well into adolescence and adulthood (Ollendick & King, 1994a). Although isolated symptoms of fear and anxiety are usually short-lived, anxiety disorders have a more chronic course. In fact, nearly half of those children with anxiety disorders have an illness duration of 8 years or more (Keller et al., 1992).

DESCRIPTION

Anxiety disorders come in many different forms. Some children, like Brad, feel anxious whenever they are separated from their mother or are away from home. Others, like Alesha, worry about almost everything and feel anxious most of the time for no apparent reason. Some children feel anxious only in certain situations, such as when they have to travel by airplane, or, like Dante, when they do something that makes them the focus of other people's attention. Other children, like Wayman, experience repeated, intrusive, and unwanted thoughts that produce anxiety, and spend hours in ritualized behavior in an effort to alleviate that anxiety. Some children, like Claudia, have unpredictable bouts of anxiety that are so sudden and intense that they become terrified and immobilized. Still others have persistent and frightening thoughts as a result of experiencing a traumatic event, such as a flood or sexual abuse.

These diverse forms of anxiety disorder share certain common features, and possess others that make them distinct. Moreover, many children with anxiety disorders suffer from more than one type, either at the same time or at different times during their development (Eisen, Kearney, & Schaefer, 1995). In view of the substantial overlap among the different anxiety disorders, we begin by discussing the general features and mechanisms of anxiety that apply across all types (Barlow, 1988). The common occurrence of fears and anxieties in childhood and adolescence requires that we also consider the role of these emotions in normal development. We then examine each anxiety disorder and discuss what makes it unique.

Although much of what is currently known about anxiety disorders in children is derived from research with adults, recent studies involving children indicate that childhood anxiety can be serious and persistent (March, 1995a; Ollendick, King, & Yule, 1994).

The Experience of Anxiety

When 7-year-old Billy saw a dog running loose in front of his house, he became "pale, sweaty, cold, and trembly." His "thoughts raced so fast that he couldn't think. He froze. His heart pounded, he felt tense, and he found it difficult to breathe."

On his first day at a new school, 12-year-old Eric experienced "intense feelings of fear and dread, uncontrollable crying, nausea, bowel disturbance, headache, and fever."

When 8-year-old Charlotte saw a spider crawl out from under her bed, she experienced "feelings of unreality, a sense that sounds were louder than usual, blurred vision, feelings that her hands were swollen and numb, palpitations, nausea, and tightness in her chest."

Why do these children have the symptoms just described and an overwhelming desire to flee the situation they are in? They are experiencing anxiety in response to events they see as potentially threatening or dangerous—a dog, a new school, a spider. Anxiety is a feeling we all recognize and can relate to. As humans we are programmed to detect and react to signs of anxiety in ourselves and in others. Although no single definition covers every aspect of anxiety, we all know what it's like to be anxious—the butterflies in the stomach before giving a speech or the tension that grips us just before a final exam; the jitters we feel before an important job interview, and the panic of waking up in the middle of the night, certain that we heard a strange noise in the basement. Masters of suspense use this to their advantage, making us jump when the villain suddenly appears.

When children become anxious, they are experiencing one of the oldest and most basic of all human emotions. As reflected in these quotes from the fourth-century, losing sleep over money or growing old with worry are hardly new concerns:

Wakefulness over wealth wastes away one's flesh, and anxiety about it removes sleep.

Jealousy and anger shorten life, and anxiety brings on old age too soon.
(Son of Sirach, Vulgate, 31:1.9; 30:24.7)

Most of us experience some anxiety every day of our lives—it is both expected and normal at certain ages and in certain situations. One-year-old infants become distressed when separated from their mothers, and almost all young children have short-lived specific fears of the dark, storms, animals, monsters, or strangers. What would you make of a 2-year-old who showed no reaction to her mother's leaving her with a complete stranger in an unfamiliar setting? Or a 5-year-old with absolutely no fear of heights? These reactions are not normal—we want and expect children to be anxious in these kinds of situations. It's fine to be "calm, cool, and collected," but a child who shows no anxiety in the face of real or potential danger may find it difficult to survive. The child's world can be a strange and menacing place—full of unknown dangers and developmental land mines, some real, others imagined. Although no one likes to feel anxious, the alternative of not feeling anxious when the situation calls for it is far worse.

Why does a feeling as disagreeable as anxiety seem to hit us whenever we do something important? Paradoxically, the answer seems to be that some anxiety is a good thing. Following the classic inverted U shaped function, anxiety in moderate doses helps us think and act more effectively. You will probably be better prepared for your next exam in this course if you're just a little bit nervous about taking it. Similarly, some anxiety may help a child prepare harder for an upcoming oral report or athletic event. Anxiety helps children plan for the future and anticipate things that could go wrong so they will be prepared to deal with problems should they arise. In this sense, anxiety is a highly adaptive emotion that readies children both physically and psychologically for coping with people, objects, or events that could be dangerous to their safety or well-being (Barlow, 1988).

Although some anxiety is good, too much is not. Excessive, uncontrollable anxiety can have unfortunate consequences. For example, children may fail a test because they can't focus on the questions, or they may spend too much time thinking about how awful it would be to fail, making it nearly impossible to think about anything else (like how to solve a math problem). Other children may have difficulty making friends because they feel so sick, nervous, or worried about how they come across in social situations that they can't think of a single thing to say. Thus, for children with anxiety disorders, this normally useful emotion can work against them.

When children continue to experience fears and anxieties beyond a certain age, feel intense anxiety in situations that pose no real threat or danger, and suffer significant distress that seriously interferes with daily activities such as going to school, making friends, or separating from parents, anxiety can be a serious problem. Children with anxiety disorders do not seem to get the idea that there is really nothing to be anxious about. Even if they know there is little to be afraid of in a feared situation, they are terrified nonetheless, and do everything they can to escape or avoid the situation. In other words, these children cannot easily abandon their self-defeating behaviors. This pattern of self-defeating behavior, known as the **neurotic paradox** (Mowrer, 1950), can become self-perpetuating—much like Sisyphus pushing the rock endlessly up the hill, only for it to roll back down on him again.

David Barlow, a world-renowned anxiety researcher, has defined _anxiety_ as a mood state characterized by strong negative affect and bodily symptoms of tension in which an individual apprehensively anticipates future danger or misfortune (Barlow, 1988). This definition captures two key components of anxiety—strong negative affect and an element of fear. First and foremost, anxiety is an immediate reaction to perceived danger or threat. Technically, this reaction is known as the **fight/flight response** because all its effects are aimed at protecting children against potential harm, either by confronting the source of danger (fight), or by removing them from the situation (flight). Back when our ancestors were living in caves and cavorting with saber-toothed tigers it was essential that humans had a rapid and automatic way of readying ourselves for immediate action when confronted with danger. Such a mechanism was necessary for our survival back then, and it still is today. If you looked up to see a grand piano about to fall in your direction and experienced no anxiety whatsoever, the clean-up crew would soon be scraping your remains off the sidewalk and depositing them on top of a large pile of evolutionary wannabees. To avoid such a fate, your fight/flight response would kick in to overdrive and you would jump out of harm's way (Barlow, 1988).

Think of a recent situation that made you anxious. Perhaps a test for which you didn't have enough time to prepare (hopefully not in this course)? An oral presentation? Asking someone out on a date? What is it about this situation that made you anxious? What physical symptoms did you notice? What were you thinking? What did you do? Describing what it's like to be anxious

Fight/flight response

is not easy because anxiety is a complex reaction with many symptoms. As shown in Table 7.1, the symptoms of anxiety are abundant. How many of these symptoms did you experience? What do these many symptoms have in common? The best way to think about the different symptoms of anxiety is to remember that all are directed at preparing a person for rapid action to protect against actual or perceived threat or harm (Barlow, 1988).

The symptoms of anxiety shown in Table 7.1 are expressed through three interrelated response systems: the **physical system**, the **cognitive system**, and the **behavioral system**. It is essential to understand how the three sets of symptoms, or response systems, of anxiety work, since one or another of them may be more evident in different children with the same anxiety disorder. Also, different response systems are especially conspicuous for certain anxiety disorders. For example, the physical symptoms of physiological hyperarousal and bodily tension, called anxious arousal, become central in panic because they are most easily mistaken for signs of a serious disease; cognitive symptoms such as excessive worry about future events, called anxious apprehension, are a central feature of generalized anxiety; and avoidance behavior is a primary feature of compulsions. Because of their importance for understanding anxiety disorders in children, let's take a closer look at how each of the response systems of anxiety works.

Physical System. When danger is perceived or anticipated, the brain sends messages to the sympathetic nervous system, the part of the nervous system that discharges energy and mobilizes the body for action (fight/flight system). The activation of this system produces

Table 7.1 The Many Symptoms of Anxiety

Physical

Increased heart rate	Dry mouth	Flushes/Chill
Fatigue	Muscle tension	Breathlessness
Increased respiration	Heart palpitation	Headache
Nausea	Blushing	Urination
Stomach upset	Vomiting	Labored breathing
Defecation	Numbness	Dizziness
Blurred vision	Sweating	

Cognitive

Thoughts of being scared	Blanking out	Thoughts of being hurt
Thoughts or images of monsters or wild animals	Forgetfulness	Thoughts of danger
Self-deprecatory or self-critical thoughts	Thoughts or images of bodily injury	Thoughts of appearing foolish
Thoughts of incompetence or inadequacy	Thoughts of imminent death	Difficulty concentrating
Thoughts racing	Thoughts of going crazy	Images of harm to loved ones
	Thoughts of contamination	

Behavioral

Avoidance	Immobility	Trembling voice
Crying	Twitching	Screaming
Nail biting	Thumb sucking	Rigid posture
Eyes shut	Avoidance of eye contact	Clenched jaw
Stuttering	Physical proximity	White knuckles
Trembling lip	Certain verbalizations	Gratuitous arm, hand, and leg movements
Swallowing	Fidgeting	

Source: Adapted from Barrios & Hartmann, 1997.

many important chemical and physical effects through-out the body (Rapee, Craske, & Barlow, 1996):

❖ **Chemical effects.** Two chemicals, adrenalin and noradrenalin, are released from the adrenal glands on the kidneys.

❖ **Cardiovascular effects.** Heart rate and the strength of the heart beat increase. This readies the body for action by speeding up blood flow and improving delivery of oxygen to the tissues.

❖ **Respiratory effects.** The speed and depth of breathing increase, which brings oxygen to the tissues and removes waste. This may lead to feelings of breathlessness, choking or smothering, or chest pains. Blood supply to the head may decrease, leading to unpleasant but harmless symptoms such as dizziness, blurred vision, confusion, and hot flushes.

❖ **Sweat gland effects.** Sweating increases, which cools the body and makes the skin slippery.

❖ **Other physical effects.** The pupils widen to let in more light, which may lead to blurred vision or spots in front of the eyes. Salivation decreases, resulting in a dry mouth. Decreased activity in the digestive system may lead to nausea and a heavy feeling in the stomach. Muscles tense up in readiness for fight or flight, leading to subjective feelings of tension, aches and pains, and trembling.

These physical symptoms—such as a racing heart, rapid breathing, sweating, or muscle tension—are familiar signs of anxiety. Overall, the fight/flight response produces general activation of the entire body metabolism. As a result, the individual often feels hot and flushed, and because this activation takes a lot of energy, afterwards he or she feels tired and drained (Rapee et al., 1996).

Cognitive System. Since the main purpose of the fight/flight system is to alert the individual to possible danger, the activation of this system produces an instant and automatic shift in attention to a search of the surroundings for potential threat. For children with anxiety disorders, focusing on everyday tasks at home or school is difficult because their attention is consumed by a constant search for threat or danger. They have trouble concentrating and are easily distracted from their daily chores, homework, or classroom assignments. Distraction is a normal part of the fight/flight response, which is designed to get us to stop attending to what we are doing so that we can scan our surroundings for possible danger. For example, how adaptive would it be for you to continue to study if you thought there was an intruder at your back door? Naturally, you're going to be distracted!

The problem for children with anxiety disorders is that even though they are on constant vigil, there is usually no obvious threat to be found. When they can't come up with a reason for their anxiety, they may turn their search inward: "If nothing is out there to make me feel anxious, then something must be wrong with me." Or they may distort the situation: "Even though I can't find it, there's still something out there to be afraid of." Or they may do both. Children with an anxiety disorder invent explanations for their anxiety: "I must be a real jerk"; "Everyone will think I'm a dummy if I say something"; "Even though I can't see them, there are germs all over the place" (Rapee et al., 1996). Activation of the cognitive system often leads to subjective feelings of apprehension, nervousness, difficulty concentrating, and panic.

Behavioral System. The fight/flight response readies the body to act at once—to attack or to flee. Not surprisingly then, the overwhelming urges that accompany this response are aggression and a desire to escape the situation. However, social constraints may prevent the individual from doing either. For example, just before writing a final exam, you may feel like attacking your professor or not showing up at all—but fortunately, for your professor and for your grade in the course, you are likely to inhibit these urges! When this happens, however, the urges may show up as foot tapping, fidgeting, or irritability (consider the number of teeth marks in pencils during a difficult final exam), or as escape or avoidance of the exam by getting a doctor's note, requesting a deferral, or even faking illness. The overall feeling is one of being trapped and needing to escape or avoid the situation—pacing, fidgeting, and avoidance are common symptoms. Unfortunately, avoidance is the very thing that keeps anxiety going. Avoiding or getting out of doing something that is anxiety-provoking usually brings instant relief. Avoidance behaviors are negatively reinforced; that is, they are strengthened when they are followed by the removal of an unpleasant event—in this case a rapid reduction in feelings of anxiety. As a result, the next time a child is confronted with an anxiety-producing situation, she or he tries to get out of it more quickly, the anxiety drops off more quickly, and the more that person learns to avoid. As children with anxiety disorders engage in more and more avoidance, carrying out normal everyday activities can become exceedingly difficult (Rapee et al., 1996).

Chantelle: Home Alone

When Chantelle realized that she was at home alone, she became terrified. Her thoughts raced so fast that it was impossible for her to think clearly. She forgot all the right things to do. Her heart pounded and she tensed up. She felt like she couldn't breathe, and she began to sob. She wanted to run but felt completely immobilized.

Being *Home Alone* (described as a family movie without the family) may have made 8-year-old Macaulay Culkin famous, but it was a terrifying experience for Chantelle. Chantelle's reactions illustrate the three response systems of anxiety and how they interact and feed off one another. At a physical level, Chantelle's heart pounded, she became tense, and she had difficulty breathing. At a cognitive level, she could not think clearly and forgot all the right things to do. At a behavioral level, she became completely immobilized.

Anxiety versus Fear and Panic

It is important to distinguish anxiety from two closely related emotions—fear and panic. **Fear** is an immediate alarm reaction to current danger or life-threatening emergencies. Although fear and anxiety have much in common, the fear reaction differs both psychologically and biologically from anxiety. Fear is a *present-oriented* emotional reaction to current danger, marked by strong escape tendencies and an all-out surge in the sympathetic nervous system. The overriding message is one of alarm: "If I don't do something right now, I might not make it at all." In contrast, anxiety is a *future-oriented* mood state accompanied by feelings of apprehension and lack of control over upcoming events that could pose a threat. Fear and anxiety both serve to warn of danger or distress. However, unlike fear, anxiety is frequently felt even when no realistic danger is present (Barlow, 1988).

Panic can be seen as a group of unexpected physical symptoms of the fight/flight response that occur in the absence of any obvious threat or danger. With panic, the individual experiences the alarm reaction of fear when there's nothing to be afraid of. In the absence of an explanation for the physical symptoms (e.g., a pounding heart), the individual may invent one: "I'm dying." In the case of panic, the physical sensations themselves can become threatening and may trigger further fear, apprehension, anxiety, and panic (Barlow, 1988).

All children experience some fear, anxiety, and worry as a normal part of growing up.

Normal Fears, Anxieties, Worries, and Rituals

Since fear and anxiety in moderate doses are adaptive emotions, it is not surprising that fear, anxiety, worry, and rituals that increase feelings of control are common during childhood and adolescence. Most fears and anxieties in children are normal and typically not associated with severe disturbance. It is only when fears and anxieties become excessive, or occur in a developmentally inappropriate context, that they are of concern.

Normal Fears. Understanding which childhood fears are abnormal requires that we know which ones are normal at certain ages. Since children and their environments constantly change, fears that are normal at one age can be debilitating a few years later. For example, a fear of strangers may serve a protective function for infants and young children, but when it persists beyond a certain age, it can seriously interfere with the development of peer relations. Determining whether or not a specific fear is normal will also depend on its effect on the child and how long it lasts. If a fear has little impact on the child's daily activities or lasts only a few weeks or a month, then it is likely a part of normal development.

Fears are quite common in children, with the number and type changing with age (Barrios & Hartmann, 1997). There is a general age-related decline in number of fears for both referred and nonreferred children. Even so, specific fears are still frequent in adolescents, with as many as 20% to 30% of parents reporting fears as a problem for their teens (Achenbach, 1991). Many teens report that their fears cause them considerable distress and significantly interfere with daily activities (Ollendick & King, 1994b). Girls tend to have more fears than boys at almost every age—they also rate themselves as more

Table 7.2 Common Fears in Infancy, Childhood, and Adolescence

Age	Objects of Fear
0–6 months	Loss of support, loud noise
7–12 months	Strangers; sudden, unexpected, and looming objects
1 year	Separation from parent, injury, toilet, strangers
2 years	Loud noises, animals, dark room, separation from parents, large objects or machines, change in personal environment
3 years	Masks, dark, animals, separation from parent
4 years	Separation from parent, animals, dark, noises
5 years	Animals, "bad" people, dark, separation from parent, bodily harm
6 years	Supernatural beings (e.g., ghosts or witches), bodily injuries, thunder and lightning, dark, sleeping or staying alone, separation from parent
7–8 years	Supernatural beings, dark, media events, staying alone, bodily injury
9–12 years	Tests and examinations in school, school performance, bodily injury, physical appearance, thunder and lightning, death
Adolescence	Personal relations, personal appearance, school, political issues, future, animals, supernatural phenomena, natural disasters, safety

Source: Adapted from Klein & Last, 1989.

fearful and report fears that are more intense and disabling than do boys (Ollendick, Yang, Dong, Xia, & Lin, 1995).

Type of fear is important when examining developmental trends. Although many fears decline with age, some, such as school-related fears, remain stable, and others, such as social fears, may increase. The most common fears of infants, children, and adolescents are shown in Table 7.2. Young children are more afraid of the dark than older children, whereas older children are more likely to be afraid of dying than younger children, who don't yet understand that death is an irreversible condition. In general, infants fear loss of support and loud noises. Fear of strangers begins at 6 months to a year and usually continues until the age of 2 or 3. Fear of separation from parents begins at about 12 months and may persist until 7 to 8 years. Common fears in preschool children include fear of the dark, small animals, imaginary creatures, large objects, changes in the environment, and sleeping alone. Older children may fear social situations, exams, events in the news such as bombings or kidnappings, injury, illness, or death. Adolescents have many social and sexual fears, most of which are usually mild and transient.

Normal Anxieties. Like fears, anxieties are very common during childhood and adolescence. About 10% to 30% of parents of nonreferred children report that their child is too nervous, fearful, or anxious (Achenbach, 1991). This number jumps to 40% to 80% of children referred for treatment. Isolated symptoms of anxiety are also commonly reported by children themselves, with about 10% to 30% of nonreferred children reporting symptoms of anxiety. The most common symptoms of anxiety in normal samples are test anxiety, an overconcern about competence, an excessive need for reassurance, anxiety about harm to a parent, and anxiety about physical complaints (Barrios & Hartmann, 1997).

Younger children generally experience more anxiety symptoms than older children, most often about separation from parents (Beidel, Silverman, & Hammond-Laurence, 1996; Bell-Dolan, Last, & Strauss, 1990). Girls display more anxiety than boys, but generally the types of symptoms experienced by boys and girls are quite similar. Although some specific anxieties, such as separation anxiety, decrease with age, nervous and anxious symptoms do not show the age-related decline observed for many specific fears. Anxious symptoms may reflect a stable trait that predisposes children to develop time-limited fears that reflect their stage of development. The disposition to be anxious may remain stable over time, even when the object of the child's fears change (Silverman & Nelles, 1989).

Normal Worries

> *"Don't worry about the future. Or worry, but know that worrying is as effective as trying to solve an algebra equation by chewing bubble gum. The real troubles in your life are apt to be things that never crossed your worried mind, the kind that blindside you at 4 P.M. on some idle Tuesday."* (Mary Schmich, Chicago Tribune, *1997*)

If worrying about the future is so unproductive, why do we all do so much of it? Part of the reason seems to be that the process of worry, which involves thinking about all possible negative outcomes, serves an extremely useful function in normal development. In moderate doses, worry can help children prepare for the future—for example, by checking their homework before they hand it in or by rehearsing for an upcoming class play. Worry is also a central feature of anxiety, and anxiety is related to both the number of children's worries and their intensity (Silverman, La Greca, & Wasserstein, 1995; Vasey, 1993). Children of all ages worry, but the form and expression of children's worries change with age. Older children report a greater variety and complexity of worries, and are better able to elaborate on the

possible outcomes of their worries than are younger children (Chorpita, Tracey, Brown, Collica, & Barlow, 1997; Vasey & Daleiden, 1994; Vasey, Crnic, & Carter, 1994).

Children with anxiety disorders do not necessarily have a greater number of worries than other children, but seem to experience worries that are more intense (Perrin & Last, 1997). Some intense worries, such as being around strangers, dying, going to school, or having bad things happening to the child or parents, occur frequently in children with anxiety disorders and rarely in other children. Other intense worries, such as personal safety, doing a good job, and being embarrassed, occur in both groups, but much more so in children with anxiety disorders. Still other intense worries, such as schoolwork, aches and pains, or performance in sports, are equally common in children with and without anxiety disorders.

Normal Rituals and Repetitive Behavior.
Understanding normal ritualistic behaviors is important to our discussion because some children with anxiety disorders engage in excessive amounts of these behaviors as a way of avoiding thoughts or situations that provoke anxiety. Ritualistic, repetitive, and compulsivelike activity is extremely common in young children. One common example is a child's bedtime ritual of saying good night to people in precisely the same way—addressing people in a certain order or giving a certain number of hugs and kisses. Ritualistic behaviors in young children include preferences for sameness in the environment (e.g., watching the same video over and over again), repetitive behavior, rigid likes and dislikes, preferences for symmetry and wholeness (e.g., carrying a toy in each hand), awareness of minute details or imperfections in toys or clothes (e.g., being bothered by a minuscule thread on a jacket sleeve), and arranging things so they are "just right" (e.g., insisting that peas be carefully put on one part of the plate and not touch any of the other food). These rituals help young children gain control and mastery over their social and physical environments and make their world a more predictable and safer place in which to live (Evans et al., 1997). Any parent who has ever violated these rituals and paid the price can appreciate how important they are to the young child.

Despite their frequent occurrence, surprisingly little is known about the onset, prevalence, or developmental course of rituals in normal young children. This situation is changing. Several common routines of young children and their average age of onset are shown in Table 7.3. The routines of young children fall into two distinct categories, repetitive behaviors and doing things "just right." Although these categories are strikingly similar to those found for older individuals with obsessive-compulsive disorder (OCD) (Carter, Pauls, & Leckman,

Table 7.3 Average Age of Onset for Several Common Childhood Routines

Routine	Average Age of Onset
Being very attached to one favorite object	14 months
Repeating certain actions over and over	18 months
Preferring to have things done in a particular order or in a certain way	21 months
Arranging objects or performing certain behaviors until they seem "just right"	23 months
Collecting or storing objects	26 months

Source: Adapted from Evans et al., 1997.

1995), it is not known whether OCD is an extreme point on a continuum of normal developmental rituals or a totally different problem (Evans et al., 1997).

The Anatomy of Anxiety: From Symptoms to Disorders

Researchers have never really agreed on how to classify children's fears and anxieties (Barrios & Hartmann, 1997). This state of affairs is reflected in the many different, and at times confusing, terms used to describe children's fears and anxieties. These terms vary with respect to two important issues. The first relates to the severity of anxiety symptoms and their impact on the child's life. For example, a specific fear is usually seen as a normal reaction. However, as a child's fear becomes more severe, irrational, or disruptive, it may be labeled a clinical fear or phobia and viewed as abnormal. Since the boundary between what constitutes a normal fear versus an abnormal clinical fear is frequently blurred, terms such as *subclinical fear* have been used to describe reactions that fall into these gray areas of severity and impairment.

A second critical issue is whether we view anxiety as a specific symptom, a group of symptoms that co-occur, or a disorder. As we have seen, the specific symptoms of fear and anxiety in children are plentiful—if we were to classify children on the basis of these isolated symptoms alone we would have an instant anxiety epidemic! However, symptoms of anxiety tend to co-occur, and a child who has some anxiety symptoms is likely to have others. Children differ in the extent to which they display one group of symptoms versus another, for example, their degree of worry versus that of physical arousal. These clusters of symptoms are referred to as *dimensions* of anxiety, which are typically identified by grouping symptoms using statistical procedures such as factor

analysis. Several consistent dimensions of anxiety emerge by means of these procedures (March, Parker, Sullivan, Stallings, & Conners, 1997). For example, one study identified five dimensions of anxiety (Birmaher et al., 1997). The five dimensions and some expressions of the symptoms associated with each are as follows:

❖ **Somatic/Panic.** People tell me I look nervous. When frightened, I feel like things aren't real. My heart beats fast. I get shaky. I get really frightened for no reason. When frightened, I feel like I'm choking. I'm afraid of having panic attacks. I feel dizzy.

❖ **General Anxiety.** I worry about others liking me. I am nervous. I am a worrier. People tell me I worry too much. I worry about the future. I worry about things in the past.

❖ **Separation Anxiety.** I get scared if I sleep away from home. I follow my parents wherever they go. I have nightmares about bad things happening to me. I'm afraid to be alone at home.

❖ **Social Phobia.** I don't like to be with people I don't know. I feel nervous with people I don't know. I find it hard to talk with people I don't know. I'm shy with people I don't know well.

❖ **School Phobia.** I get headaches when I am at school. I get stomachaches at school. I worry about going to school. I'm scared to go to school.

(Adapted from Birmaker et al., 1997)

Finally, some children display distinct and persistent patterns of anxiety, such as extreme reactions to separation, social avoidance, or generalized worries. These patterns are referred to as anxiety disorders. Often these patterns are thematic and based on the nature of the perceived threat, for example, separation from parents or social encounters. Most anxiety disorders are exaggerated, prolonged, or disabling versions of normal childhood fears and anxieties, or dimensions of anxiety, and the boundaries between the many different disorders are not always clear.

AN OVERVIEW OF DSM-IV ANXIETY DISORDERS

Anxiety disorders in DSM-IV are divided into categories that closely define the cause of the child's reaction and avoidance. These categories mirror several of the dimensions of anxiety that have emerged from the factor analytic studies. According to DSM-IV, children may be diagnosed with one or more of nine anxiety disorders (American Psychiatric Association, 1994). We will discuss each of these disorders in the sections that follow.

Box 7.1

Main Features of Nine DSM-IV Anxiety Disorders

SEPARATION ANXIETY DISORDER (SAD)

Age-inappropriate, excessive, and disabling anxiety about being apart from parents or away from home.

GENERALIZED ANXIETY DISORDER (GAD)

Chronic or exaggerated worry and tension; almost constant anticipation of disaster even though nothing seems to provoke it (apprehensive expectation). Worrying is often accompanied by physical symptoms, such as trembling, muscle tension, headache, and nausea.

SPECIFIC PHOBIA

Extreme and disabling fear of specific objects or situations that pose little or no danger. Fears may include animals, heights, or injections.

SOCIAL PHOBIA

Fear of being the focus of attention or scrutiny or of doing something that will be intensely humiliating.

OBSESSIVE-COMPULSIVE DISORDER (OCD)

Repeated, intrusive and unwanted thoughts that cause anxiety, often accompanied by ritualized behavior to relieve this anxiety.

PANIC DISORDER (PD)

Characterized by panic attacks, sudden feelings of terror that strike repeatedly and without warning. Physical symptoms include chest pain, heart palpitations, shortness of breath, dizziness, or abdominal stress. Persistent concern about having another attack and the possible implications and consequences.

PANIC DISORDER WITH AGORAPHOBIA

In the context of a panic disorder, anxiety about being in places or situations from which escape might be difficult (or embarrassing), or in which help might not be available in the event of having a panic attack or paniclike symptoms. Common situations include being outside the home or in a crowd of people.

POSTTRAUMATIC STRESS DISORDER (PTSD)

Persistent, frightening thoughts that occur after undergoing a frightening and traumatic event.

ACUTE STRESS DISORDER

Anxiety and other symptoms develop after exposure to an extreme traumatic stressor; symptoms do not persist for more than 4 weeks after the trauma.

Source: Based on DSM-IV 1994 by APA.

However, to give you the overall picture, brief descriptions of the main features of each disorder are shown in Box 7.1.

With the appearance of DSM-IV in 1994, anxiety disorders in children took on a new look. Previously, the categories of *overanxious disorder (OAD)* (roughly corresponding to generalized anxiety disorder in DSM-IV), *avoidant disorder* (roughly corresponding to social phobia in DSM-IV), and *simple phobia* (corresponding to specific phobia in DSM-IV) were among those used to diagnose children with anxiety disorders. Since a great deal of our knowledge about anxiety disorders in children is based on research with youngsters who received these earlier diagnoses, some confusion exists in attempts to compare current findings using the newer diagnoses with previous research. For the sake of consistency we use the descriptors for current DSM-IV anxiety disorders throughout this chapter. Keep in mind, however, that findings from studies conducted prior to the appearance of DSM-IV are for children diagnosed using the older categories of OAD, avoidant disorder, and simple phobia. Fortunately, research suggests that the older and newer diagnoses are virtually interchangeable (Kendall & Warman, 1996).

Now that we understand the mechanisms involved in fear and anxiety, the role of fear and anxiety in normal development, and the way in which anxiety is defined and classified, let's reacquaint ourselves with some of the children we met earlier in the chapter and meet some new children with other anxiety disorders. In the sections that follow, we describe the characteristic features of each anxiety disorder and present information about its prevalence, comorbidity, and developmental course. Following our discussion of individual disorders we examine the associated characteristics and causes of anxiety disorders, and the treatments used to help children with these problems.

SEPARATION ANXIETY DISORDER

Brad: Separation Anxiety

Nine-year-old Brad is unable to enter any situation that involves his being separated from his parents, for example, playing in the backyard, going to other children's homes, or staying at home with a baby-sitter. When pushed to be separated from his parents, Brad responds with crying or a full-blown tantrum. When Brad's mother does plan to leave the house, he states all the horrible things that might happen to her, in an endless series of what-if questions. She then becomes frustrated and angry, making Brad even more anxious. The more anxious he gets, the more he argues with his mother not to leave, and the angrier she gets. Brad has also threatened to hurt himself (e.g., jump out of the classroom window) if forced to go to school.

Brad's separation problems began about a year ago. At that time his father was having problems with alcohol and was frequently absent from the home for long periods of time. Brad's problem gradually worsened over the course of the year, resulting in a complete refusal to go to school. Help had been sought but Brad continued to deteriorate. He developed significant depressive symptoms, including a sad mood, guilt about his problems, occasional wishes to die, and frequent early morning wakening. (Adapted from Last, 1988)

Anxiety about separation from one's primary caregiver is important for the young child's survival and is normal at certain ages. From about age 7 months through the preschool years, almost all children fuss at times of separation from their parents or others with whom they are close. In fact, an absence of separation anxiety at this age may suggest an insecure attachment or other problems. Unfortunately, as happened with Brad, some children continue to display anxiety about separation long after the age when such behavior is typical or expected. When this anxiety becomes severe and begins to interfere with normal daily routines, such as going to school or participating in recreational activities, the child may have a separation anxiety disorder. The DSM-IV criteria for SAD are presented in Table 7.4.

Children with **separation anxiety disorder** (SAD) display age-inappropriate, excessive, and disabling anxiety about being apart from their parents or away from home. These fears may show up in young children as vague feelings of anxiety or as repeated nightmares about being kidnapped or killed, or about the death of a parent. Older children may have specific fantasies of

---

Table 7.4 | **Diagnostic Criteria for Separation Anxiety Disorder (SAD)**

A. Developmentally inappropriate and excessive anxiety concerning separation from home or from those to whom the individual is attached, as evidenced by three (or more) of the following:
   (1) recurrent excessive distress when separation from home or major attachment figures occurs or is anticipated
   (2) persistent and excessive worry about losing, or possible harm befalling, major attachment figures
   (3) persistent and excessive worry that an untoward event will lead to separation from a major attachment figure (e.g., getting lost or being kidnapped)
   (4) persistent reluctance or refusal to go to school or elsewhere because of fear of separation
   (5) persistently and excessively fearful or reluctant to be alone or without major attachment figures at home or without significant adults in other settings
   (6) persistent reluctance or refusal to go to sleep without being near a major attachment figure or to sleep away from home
   (7) repeated nightmares involving the theme of separation
   (8) repeated complaints of physical symptoms (such as headaches, stomachaches, nausea, or vomiting) when separation from major attachment figures occurs or is anticipated

B. The duration of the disturbance is at least 4 weeks.

C. The onset is before age 18 years.

D. The disturbance causes clinically significant distress or impairment in social, academic (occupational), or other important areas of functioning.

E. The disturbance does not occur exclusively during the course of a Pervasive Developmental Disorder, Schizophrenia, or other Psychotic Disorder and, in adolescents and adults, is not better accounted for by Panic Disorder with Agoraphobia.

Specify if:
   Early Onset: If onset occurs before age 6 years.

Source: DSM-IV Copyright © 1994 by APA.

illness, accidents, kidnapping, torture, or murder. For example, one 10-year-old girl with SAD feared that a kidnapper would sneak into her house at night, take her to the basement, and keep her tied up, with a stream of water slowly dripping down her forehead.

The anxiety associated with SAD is so intense that it interferes with normal daily living. Children with SAD may have difficulty being in a room by themselves, sleeping alone at home, running errands, going to school alone, going to camp, or staying at home with a babysitter. Young children with SAD frequently display excessive demands for parental attention, clinging to and shadowing their parents' every move, trying to climb into their parents' bed at night, or sleeping on the floor just outside their parents' bedroom door. Older children with SAD are fearful of entering new situations, want ready access to their mother when at home, and may display physical complaints, an unwillingness to go to school, and refusal to sleep away from home.

To avoid separation, children with SAD may fuss, cry, scream, have severe tantrums, or make suicidal gestures ("I'll slash my wrists") or threats ("I'm going to kill myself") if their parent leaves (although serious symptoms of suicide are rare in children with SAD). In anticipation of separation these children may also develop physical symptoms and complaints, such as panic, rapid heart beat, dizziness or fainting, headaches, stomachaches, nausea, and vomiting. Not surprisingly, parents of children with SAD, especially mothers, become highly distressed by their child's extreme reluctance or inability to be separated from them. When separation does occur, young children with SAD may show sadness, apathy, or difficulty paying attention, and may become preoccupied with morose fears that harm will befall them or their parents.

In older children, specific physical complaints or expressions of general malaise ("I don't feel so good") are common in school and frequently result in the child's being sent home. Children with SAD may become desperate when separated from parents, making up almost any excuse, no matter how elaborate and far-fetched, to avoid or escape the separation situation. The child may sneak away from school or run away from camp in an effort to return home. Over time, as we saw with Brad, children with SAD may become increasingly withdrawn, apathetic, and depressed (Albano, Miller, Zarate, Cote, & Barlow, 1996).

Prevalence and Comorbidity

SAD is the most common anxiety disorder of childhood, occurring in about 6% to 12% of all children. In addition, one-third or more of those children who are referred for anxiety problems are referred because of SAD. SAD seems to be equally common in boys and girls, although when gender differences are reported, they tend to favor girls (Albano et al., 1996; Last, Perrin, Hersen, & Kazdin, 1992).

Approximately 80% to 90% of children with SAD have another disorder. Usually, this is another anxiety disorder, the most common one being generalized anxiety disorder, which occurs in about 1 in 3 children with SAD. About one-third of children with SAD also develop a depressive disorder within several months following the onset of SAD. Children with SAD may also display specific fears of getting lost, or of the dark, insects, or ghosts even when they don't meet diagnostic criteria for a specific phobia. School reluctance or refusal is common in clinic-referred children with SAD, occurring in as many as 75% or more of older children. Children who show school refusal as a result of SAD tend to be younger, female, of lower SES, from single-parent families, and more likely to have another disorder than children who show school refusal as a result of a specific school phobia (Albano et al., 1996; Last, Francis, Hersen, Kazdin, & Strauss, 1987; Last et al., 1992).

Age of Onset, Developmental Course, and Outcome

In children referred for anxiety disorders, SAD has the earliest reported age of onset at 7 to 8 years, and the youngest age of referral at around 10 to 11 years (Keller et al., 1992; Last et al., 1992). The early age of onset for SAD is consistent with the early occurrence of separation fears in normal development. Younger children with SAD display fewer clinically significant symptoms than older children, and children display different symptoms of SAD at different ages. For example, younger children with SAD are more likely to have nightmares about separation or worries about getting lost than older children, whereas adolescents with SAD almost always show school reluctance or refusal and physical complaints on school days (Francis, Last, & Strauss, 1987).

Separation anxiety disorder generally progresses from mild to severe avoidance. This process may begin with the child making harmless requests or complaints. Complaints of restless sleep or nightmares may allow the child to sleep with his or her parents from time to time, a pattern which may rapidly escalate to the child's sleeping with one or both parents almost nightly. Similarly, getting ready for school may be accompanied by physical complaints or an occasional absence from school, followed by excuses or delays in leaving for school in the morning, which escalate into a daily ritual of severe tantrums about leaving for school and outright school refusal. Initially, mild avoidance may take the form of wanting parents to be near a phone during school hours or at other times. The child may become increasingly concerned about their mother's daily routine and whereabouts (Albano et al., 1996).

Separation anxiety disorder may have a chronic onset or may appear suddenly in a child who has shown no prior signs of a problem. Often, SAD occurs after a child has experienced a major stressor, such as a move to a new neighborhood, attendance at a new school, the death of a parent, illness of a relative, entry into elementary school, school transitions, or an extended vacation from school. For example, Brad's SAD emerged following his father's problem with alcohol and subsequent absence from the home. The symptoms of SAD may also fluctuate over the years as a function of stressors and transitions in the child's life. Why do you think there is a relationship between SAD and life transitions and stress? We'll return to this question in a later section on causes.

Children with SAD may drop out of sports activities or clubs if their parents are not present, even when they are eager to participate. Although they may lose friends as a result of their repeated refusal to participate in activities away from home, children with SAD are reasonably socially skilled, get along with others, and are not disliked by their peers. School performance in children with SAD may suffer as a result of frequent requests to leave class, preoccupation with separation, and repeated school absences. As a result, the child may require special school assignments just to keep up, and in extreme cases may have to repeat the school year or be remanded to the legal system to enforce school attendance (Albano et al., 1996).

Almost all children with SAD recover from this condition, although many go on to develop a different anxiety disorder or another kind of disorder (Last, Perrin, Hersen, & Kazdin, 1996). Although SAD is mostly a disorder for children that is eventually outgrown, you may be surprised to learn that even some college students experience this problem. Not surprisingly, those who experience SAD as young adults show more problems in their general adjustment than those who experienced SAD only as children (Ollendick, Lease, & Cooper, 1993). Although anxiety about separating from your mother has adaptive value during the preschool years, it does not during young adulthood. Asking someone you have just met to go to a rock concert with you *and* your mother could put a real crimp in your social life!

Since school reluctance and refusal are quite common in children with SAD, this seems like an opportune time to discuss these problems. However, it is critical to recognize that school reluctance and school refusal can occur for many different reasons, with anxiety about separation from parents being just one of these. While we are attending to matters related to school, we follow our discussion of school refusal with a comment on test anxiety, another school-related problem that is common in children and adolescents but does not fit easily into the DSM categories for anxiety disorders.

SCHOOL RELUCTANCE AND REFUSAL

Eric: Won't Go to School

Eric is a 12-year-old boy who was referred by a school psychologist and his parents for his intense school refusal behavior. Upon entering seventh grade and a new school building, Eric began to experience a variety of negative symptoms, such as hyperventilation, anxiety, sad mood, and somatic complaints. Although school attendance was not a problem at first, by mid-September Eric began to report severe headaches in the morning prior to school. School attendance then became intermittent. By late September, Eric's aversion toward school had worsened and he was staying at home on most days. Following several discussions between Eric and his parents he was allowed to stay home on a regular basis. (Adapted from Kearney, 1995)

Starting school is normally an exciting and enjoyable event for most children, a clear sign that they are growing up. But many children are reluctant to go to school, and for a few, school may bring so much fear and anxiety that they won't go at all. Such children can become sick with worry about going to school, "play sick," or let minor physical complaints keep them at home. **School refusal behavior** is defined as the child's refusal to attend classes or difficulty remaining in school for an entire day. It includes youngsters who resist going to school in the morning but eventually attend, those who go to school but leave at some point during the day, those who attend with great dread that leads to future pleas for nonattendance, and those who miss the whole day (Kearney, 1995).

School refusal behavior is equally common in boys and girls and occurs most often between the ages of 5 and 6 and 10 and 11 years. Excessive and unreasonable fears of school usually first occur in preschool, kindergarten, or first grade, and peak in the second grade.

However, school refusal behavior can occur at any time and can have a sudden onset at a later age, as happened with Eric. Children who refuse school may complain of a headache, upset stomach, or sore throat just before it's time to leave for school, then begin to "feel better" when permitted to stay at home, only to feel sick again the next morning. As the time for school draws near, the child may plead, cry, refuse to leave the house, and even have a full-blown panic reaction. School refusal often begins following a period at home during which the child has spent more time with a parent than usual (e.g., brief illness, holiday break, or summer vacation). At other times school refusal may follow a stressful event such as a change of schools or teachers (as happened with Eric), a move, an accident, or the death of a relative or family pet.

It is important to recognize that children refuse to attend school for a variety of reasons. Most children who refuse to go to school are of average or above average intelligence, suggesting that it is not a difficulty with academics that leads to this problem. Sometimes a fear of school may be associated with submitting for the first time to authority and rules outside the home, being compared with unfamiliar children, and experiencing the threat of failure. Some children fear school because they are afraid of being ridiculed, teased, or bullied by other children or being criticized or disciplined by their teacher. For many children a fear of going to school is really a fear about leaving their parents—separation anxiety. In other cases the child's fear may result from an excessive or irrational fear of being socially evaluated or embarrassed—having to recite in class or undress in front of unfamiliar people in a gym class. Eric was extremely anxious about meeting new people, being late for class, moving from class to class, classes involving public speaking, and gym class. He was refusing school mainly to escape situations in which he was being socially evaluated, and to a lesser extent, for the attention he received from his parents (Kearney & Silverman, 1993, 1996).

The possible long-term consequences are serious for a child with a persistent pattern of school refusal behavior who does not receive help. Academic or social problems may develop as a result of missed instruction and opportunities for peer interaction. Help for school refusal usually emphasizes an immediate return to school and other routines (Chorpita, Albano, Heimberg, & Barlow, 1996). Treatments also need to consider the specific functions being served by school refusal behaviors, for example, the avoidance of anxiety-provoking situations or gaining attention or rewards, and family dynamics such as detachment, overinvolvement, or conflict, that might be contributing to the problem (Kearney & Silverman, 1993, 1995).

TEST ANXIETY

We can all relate to test anxiety. Imagine that you are about halfway through writing an important exam and another student stands up and confidently walks to the front of the room and hands in her paper. How do you react? You might think, "She couldn't possibly write good answers to these questions so quickly," and simply continue writing your exam. If you reacted in this way, you're probably not test-anxious. Alternatively, you might think, "Oh no. She's already done and I've barely begun. I must be really stupid for taking so long. I'll never finish this test in time." You may become so rattled by this event that you feel your heart beating fast, your hands starting to sweat, and your mind going blank. You have great difficulty thinking, much less continuing to write the test. If you responded in this way, you might be test-anxious. People who are test-anxious are more likely to report this type of negative thinking, subjective distress, and physiological arousal when taking a test than are non–test-anxious individuals.

Like school refusal, test anxiety is one of the most common problems in children and adolescents (King, Ollendick, & Gullone, 1991b). Similarly, it is a problem that is poorly defined and understudied, and one that can occur for a variety of reasons. About 40% to 50% of school-age children experience test anxiety, with rates being similar for African-American and White children, and for children from different social classes. Since test anxiety usually interferes with test performance, it is not surprising that the academic achievement of children who are test-anxious is significantly lower than that of their non–test-anxious counterparts. In addition, children who are test-anxious view themselves as less cognitively and socially competent, express more negative feelings of general self-worth, and also report significantly more general worries and non–test-related fears than other children (Beidel & Turner, 1988; Turner, Beidel, Hughes, & Turner, 1993).

Test-anxious children and adolescents frequently report a fear of being negatively evaluated when taking a test (e.g., "My teacher will think I'm stupid"). For many of these children, their fear of negative evaluation is not confined to the test situation but also occurs in nonacademic settings. The high comorbidity rate of 24% between test anxiety and social phobia is consistent with the idea that many children with test anxiety suffer from a more generalized fear of being scrutinized by others. About one-quarter of children with test anxiety also have a generalized anxiety disorder, suggesting that for other children, test anxiety may be part of a widespread pattern of excessive worry. For a smaller percentage of children, test anxiety may reflect a specific phobia of test situations (4%) or an anxiety reaction to being separated from their parents (4%). Thus, many children who are test-anxious also meet DSM criteria for an anxiety disorder. However, at least 40% do not meet criteria for *any* DSM diagnosis, suggesting that test anxiety is a complex problem with a variety of expressions, severities, and causes (Beidel & Turner, 1988). A combination of approaches has been used to help children and adolescents overcome their test anxiety, including systematic desensitization, cognitive restructuring, and educational approaches such as study skills training and modeling.

GENERALIZED ANXIETY DISORDER

Alesha: Perpetual Worrywart

Alesha, a 10-year-old girl, was referred because of her excessive anxiety, worry, and somatic complaints. Her mother describes Alesha as overly concerned about everything. Alesha says she worries about most things, but especially about not being good enough for her parents, being teased by other kids, not doing well at school, making mistakes, and being in an accident in which she or her parents are injured. Alesha ruminates for days about things that have already occurred, such as what she said in class the previous day or how she did on last week's test. Once she begins to worry, she says, "I just can't stop, no matter how hard I try." Alesha reports several physical complaints, including headaches, stomachaches, and a rapid heart beat, when she is worrying or anticipating an upcoming event at home or school. Her mother also worries a lot, but not nearly as much as Alesha. Her mother reports that Alesha is extremely self-critical, and needs constant reassurance.

Some worry is a part of normal development. However, like Alesha, children with a **generalized anxiety disorder (GAD)** are incessant worrywarts—they worry about almost everything, even when there's nothing obvious to provoke the worrying. The technical term for this type of excessive anxiety and worry is **apprehensive expectation.** For children with GAD, episodes of worrying can vary from a few times a week to almost continuous rumination. Often the worrying is accompanied by feelings of being uptight and unable to relax, and by physical symptoms such as muscle tension, headache, or nausea. Other symptoms may include irritability, a lack of energy, difficulty falling asleep, and restless sleep.

Although the other anxiety disorders are also characterized by intense worry and anxiety, for those other disorders, anxiety converges on specific situations or objects, such as separation, social performance, animals or insects, or bodily sensations, and may be compounded by other symptoms, such as panic. In contrast, the anxiety experienced by children with GAD is widespread, general, and focuses on a variety of everyday life events. The DSM-IV criteria for GAD are presented in Table 7.5.

It was once thought that children who were generally anxious did not focus their anxiety on anything—a condition referred to as free-floating anxiety. However, these children do in fact focus their anxiety—but on many different things. Hence, the term *generalized anxiety* is more accurate than *free-floating anxiety*. Children with GAD are likely to pick up on every frightening event in a book, in a movie, or on TV and relate it to themselves. If they see a news report on TV about a car accident in another city, they may begin to worry about being in a car accident themselves. Children with GAD always expect the worst possible outcome and underestimate their ability to cope with situations or events that are less than ideal. They don't seem to realize that the events they worry about have an extremely low likelihood of actually happening (Silverman et al., 1995). Thus, their thinking is often permeated by what-if statements: "What if the school bus breaks down?" "What if they don't like me?" "What if I get hit by lightning?" Children with GAD do not restrict their worries just to frightening or catastrophic events; they also worry excessively about minor everyday occurrences, such as what to wear or what to watch on TV. This generalized worry about *minor* events is one of the characteristics that distinguishes children with GAD from those with other anxiety disorders.

Like Alesha, children with GAD are often very self-conscious, self-doubting, and worried about meeting others' expectations. They seek constant approval and reassurance from adults and fear people whom they perceive as unpleasant, critical, or unfair. These children tend to set extremely high standards for their own performance. When they fail to meet these standards, they become highly self-critical. Moreover, they continue to worry even when evidence is available to contradict the reason for their concern. For example, a child with GAD who has received an A grade on every previous class assignment may continue to worry about failing on the next assignment (Albano et al., 1996; Silverman & Ginsburg, 1995).

Once children with GAD begin to worry, they can't seem to stop—even when they recognize how unhappy their worry is making themselves and others. This characteristic is what makes pathological worry different from the typical worries that all children experience from time to time. A child who is worried about an important upcoming sports competition can temporarily set aside

Table 7.5	Diagnostic Criteria for Generalized Anxiety Disorder (GAD)

A. Excessive anxiety and worry (apprehensive expectation), occurring more days than not for at least 6 months, about a number of events or activities (such as work or school performance).

B. The person finds it difficult to control the worry.

C. The anxiety and worry are associated with three (or more) of the following six symptoms (with at least some symptoms present for more days than not for the past 6 months).

Note: Only one item is required in children.

(1) Restlessness or feeling keyed up or on edge
(2) Being easily fatigued
(3) Difficulty concentrating or mind going blank
(4) Irritability
(5) Muscle tension
(6) Sleep disturbance (difficulty falling or staying asleep, or restless unsatisfying sleep)

D. The focus of the anxiety and worry is not confined to features of an Axis I disorder, e.g., the anxiety or worry is not about having a panic attack (as in panic disorder), being embarrassed in public (as in social phobia), being contaminated (as in obsessive-compulsive disorder), being away from home or close relatives (as in separation anxiety disorder), gaining weight (as in anorexia nervosa), having multiple physical complaints (as in somatization disorder), or having a serious illness (as in hypochondriasis), and the anxiety and worry do not occur exclusively during posttraumatic stress disorder.

E. The anxiety, worry, or physical symptoms cause clinically significant distress or impairment in social, occupational, or other important areas of functioning.

F. The disturbance is not due to the direct physiological effects of a substance (e.g., a drug of abuse, a medication) or a general medical condition (e.g., hyperthyroidism) and does not occur exclusively during a Mood Disorder, a Psychotic disorder, or a Pervasive Developmental Disorder.

Source: DSM-IV Copyright © 1994 by APA.

this worry to concentrate on other tasks at home and school, and will stop worrying once the competition is over. However, for children with GAD their worries never seem to stop—one "crisis" is followed by another in a vicious and never-ending cycle. The uncontrollability of worry is an important clinical feature of GAD (Chorpita et al., 1997).

A diagnosis of GAD requires at least one somatic symptom. In fact, children with GAD are frequently first identified by a doctor as a result of their physical complaints. The physical symptoms that accompany GAD involve muscle tension and agitation rather than the autonomic arousal (e.g., heart rate increases, sweating) that characterizes some of the other anxiety disorders. Headaches, stomachaches, muscle tension, and trembling are among the most commonly reported symptoms (Eisen & Engler, 1995; Last, 1991).

Prevalence and Comorbidity

Along with SAD, GAD is one of the most prevalent anxiety disorders of childhood, occurring in approximately 3% to 6% of all children (Albano et al., 1996). In general, the disorder is equally common in boys and girls, and in young children and adolescents, with perhaps a slightly higher prevalence rate in older adolescent females (Strauss, Lease, Last, & Francis, 1988). Children with GAD present with a high rate of other anxiety disorders and depression. For children ages 5 to 11, comorbid separation anxiety and ADHD are most frequent, whereas major depression and specific phobias are the most common comorbidities in older children. Not only is GAD associated with major depression, it is also related to an increased risk for suicide, impaired social adjustment, and low self-esteem. GAD also appears to be more common in smaller families and in higher social classes (Keller et al., 1992; Strauss, Last, Hersen, & Kazdin, 1988).

Children with GAD represent about half of children referred for treatment for anxiety disorders. This proportion is higher than for adults, where the disorder is more common, but where fewer adults seek treatment. It is possible that children are more likely to be referred than adults because of associated impairments such as depression or suicidal ideation (Keller et al., 1992). Or, it may be that excessive worry is viewed as a normal part of being an adult, not something that requires treatment. Alternatively, adults may have more control over their lives than children—they have more options for coping with anxiety-arousing situations, in contrast with children who have to go to school "regardless" (Albano et al., 1996).

Age of Onset, Developmental Course, and Outcome

The average age of onset for GAD is about 10 to 14 years (Albano et al., 1996). Older children present with a higher total number of symptoms of generalized anxiety and report higher levels of anxiety and depression than younger children, but these symptoms may later diminish with age (Strauss, Last et al., 1988). In a community sample of adolescents with GAD, the likelihood of their having GAD at follow-up was higher if symptoms at the time of initial assessment were severe (Cohen, Cohen, & Brook, 1993). Nearly half of severe cases were rediagnosed after 2½ years, suggesting that *severe* generalized anxiety symptoms persist over time, even in children who have not been referred for treatment.

A Model for Generalized Anxiety Disorder.

David Barlow has presented an integrative conceptual model to account for the symptoms of GAD. Although the model is based on research with adults, we present it here because of its potential applicability to children and adolescents. The model begins with the finding that physiological reactivity in most individuals with anxiety disorders consists of strong sympathetic nervous system arousal—a rapid heart beat and blood flow indicate a readiness for threat or challenge. However, adults with GAD do not show this pattern to as great a degree and, in fact, appear to be *less* responsive on measures of arousal such as heart rate, blood pressure, skin conductance, and rate of breathing than are adults with other anxiety disorders. For this reason individuals with GAD have been referred to as autonomic restrictors (Borkovec & Hu, 1990). When compared with nonanxious adults, the measure that most distinguishes adults with GAD is chronic muscle tension. Adults with GAD startle easily and are highly sensitive to threat in general, especially when there is personal relevance. As a result, they notice and attend to threat much more readily than others who are not anxious, a tendency that is automatic and unconscious.

So how does this cognitive characteristic of hypersensitivity to threat relate to autonomic underresponsiveness? Although peripheral autonomic arousal is restricted in people with GAD, their worry may lead them to engage in intense cognitive processing in the frontal lobes of the brain, especially in the left hemisphere (reflected in increased brain activity in this area). It has been proposed that adults with GAD engage in hurried and intense thinking without experiencing the accompanying images associated with right hemisphere activity (Borkovec & Inz, 1990). In other words, they are so busy thinking about upcoming problems that they don't have any attentional resources to devote to producing the images of threat that are needed to elicit intense negative affect and autonomic activity. Thus, they avoid negative emotion—but in doing so fail to process the images and emotions associated with anxiety. So although they don't experience most of the unpleasantness and pain that go along with negative imagery, they never have a chance to confront their emotions and problems and find solutions. They become chronic worriers, with autonomic inflexibility and extreme muscle tension (Borkovec, 1994; Borkovec & Inz, 1990). In this model, worry may serve the same dysfunctional purpose as behavioral avoidance does for people with phobias. This theory will need to be tested further, especially with respect to its applicability for children. However, as summarized in Figure 7.1, the model integrates much of what we know about the characteristics of individuals with GAD.

SPECIFIC PHOBIA

Charlotte: Arachnophobia

For two years, 8-year-old Charlotte has complained of an intense fear of spiders. "Spiders are disgusting," she says. "I'm scared to death that one will crawl on me, especially when I'm sleeping. When I see a spider, even a little one, my heart pounds, my hands feel cold and sweaty, and I start to shake." Charlotte's mother says that her daughter goes completely pale when she sees a spider, even at a distance, and tries to avoid any situation where she thinks there might be one. Charlotte's fear is beginning to seriously interfere with her daughter's daily activities. For example, she won't play in the backyard and refuses to go on a class or family outing where she might encounter a spider. Her mother reports that now Charlotte is becoming afraid to go to sleep at night because she thinks a spider might crawl on her.

As we have seen, many children have specific fears that are mildly troubling, come and go rapidly up until about 10 years of age, and rarely require special attention. However, if the child's fear occurs at an inappropriate age, persists, is irrational or exaggerated, leads to avoid-

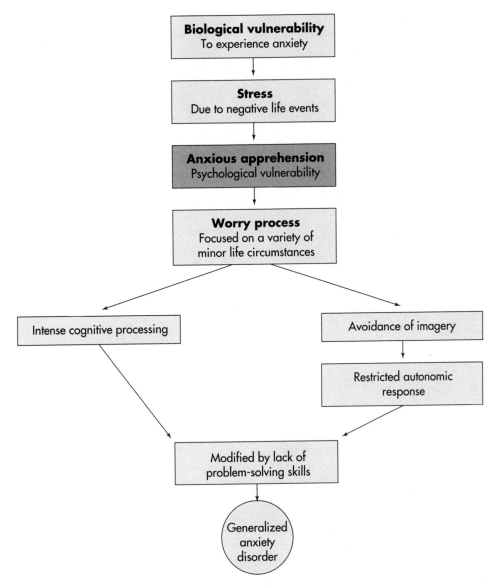

FIGURE 7.1 An integrative model of generalized anxiety disorder. (Barlow & Durand, 1995)

ance of the object or event, and causes impairment in normal routines, it is called a **phobia**. Like Charlotte, children with a **specific phobia** display a marked and persistent fear of clearly discernible, circumscribed objects or situations. Although arachnophobia may have entertained us in the Steven Spielberg produced sci-fi thriller of the same name, for Charlotte, facing or even thinking about facing spiders brings on intense anxiety. Charlotte is also disgusted by spiders, which is a common feature of girls with a spider phobia (De Jong, Andrea, & Muris, 1997).

Children with a specific phobia show an extreme and disabling fear of something that poses little or no danger or threat, and go to great lengths to avoid these objects or situations. Like Charlotte, they experience extreme fear or dread, physiological arousal to the feared stimu-

lus, and fearful anticipation and avoidance when confronted with the object of their fear. The DSM-IV criteria for specific phobia are shown in Table 7.6.

Children's beliefs regarding the danger of the feared stimulus are likely to persist despite presentation of disconfirming evidence or efforts to reason with the children. Unlike most adults with a specific phobia, children often do not recognize that their fears are extreme and unreasonable. If the object of the child's fear is rarely encountered, the phobia may not lead to serious impairment. However, if the feared object is encountered on a regular basis or if the fear seriously interferes with important life events, the child's phobia can become a serious problem (Albano et al., 1996).

Children with specific phobias often think that something dreadful will happen to them if they are

Table 7.6 | Diagnostic Criteria for Specific Phobia

A. Marked and persistent fear that is excessive or unreasonable, cued by the presence or anticipation of a specific object or situation (e.g., flying, heights, animals, receiving an injection, seeing blood).

B. Exposure to the phobic stimulus almost invariably provokes an immediate anxiety response, which may take the form of a situationally bound or situationally predisposed Panic Attack.

   Note: In children, the anxiety may be expressed by crying, tantrums, freezing, or clinging.

C. The person recognizes that the fear is excessive or unreasonable.

   Note: In children, this feature may be absent.

D. The phobic situation(s) is avoided or else is endured with intense anxiety or distress.

E. The avoidance, anxious anticipation, or distress in the feared situation(s) interferes significantly with the person's normal routine, occupational (or academic) functioning, or social activities or relationships, or there is marked distress about having the phobia.

F. In individuals under age 18 years, the duration is at least 6 months.

G. The anxiety, Panic Attacks, or phobic avoidance associated with the specific object or situation are not better accounted for by another mental disorder, such as Obsessive-Compulsive Disorder (e.g., fear of dirt in someone with an obsession about contamination), Posttraumatic Stress Disorder (e.g., avoidance of stimuli associated with a severe stressor), Separation Anxiety Disorder (e.g., avoidance of school), Social Phobia (e.g., avoidance of social situations because of fear of embarrassment), Panic Disorder with Agoraphobia, or Agoraphobia without history of Panic Disorder.

Source: DSM-IV Copyright © 1994 by APA.

exposed to the object of their fear. Their thinking usually focuses on threats to their personal safety, such as being stung by a bee, or struck by lightning. Anticipatory anxiety is also common. For example, a child who is dog phobic may think: "What if a big dog is running loose on my way to school and I get attacked and bitten in the face." Children with a specific phobia may be preoccupied with these worries to such an extent that they cause severe distress and disrupt everyday activities. These children are also constantly on the lookout for the feared stimulus and, as we saw with Charlotte, go to great lengths to avoid possible contact (Albano et al., 1996).

The kinds of phobias that can develop in children seem limitless, and include fears of telephones, water, menstruation, newspapers, mathematics, haircuts, and bowel movements, to name just a few. Although it is possible to develop a phobia of almost any object, situation, or event from A ("Apiphobia"—a fear of bees) to Z ("Zemmiphobia"—a fear of the great mole rat), certain fears are much more likely to develop in children than others, such as fear of snakes.

Eunice: What if it's in the bathroom?

Fritz: Impossible, madam. Snakes, as you know, live in mortal fear of . . . tile.

[From *What's Up, Doc?* (1972)]

One reason that this exchange may strike us as odd is that we usually think of people as being afraid of snakes, rather than what snakes are afraid of. According to evolutionary theory, human infants are biologically "prepared," or predisposed as a result of natural selection, to learn certain fears rather than others (Seligman, 1971). The majority of children's phobias have sources of natural danger during human evolution, objects such as snakes, the dark, predators, heights, blood, loud noises such as thunder, or unfamiliar places. It's not just by chance that the most common specific phobia in children is a fear of animals, particularly dogs, snakes, insects, and mice. Although evolutionary theory explains a "readiness" to acquire specific types of fears, it doesn't explain why children differ in their fearfulness or why some children develop pathological anxiety.

DSM-IV groups specific phobias into five subtypes that closely define the cause of the phobic reaction and avoidance. These subtypes and the focus of fear of each are as follows:

❖ *Animal.* Animals or insects.
❖ *Natural Environment.* Objects in the natural environment, such as heights, darkness, storms, or water.
❖ *Blood–Injection–Injury.* Seeing blood or an injury, or receiving an injection or other invasive medical procedure.

❖ *Situational.* A specific situation, such as flying in airplanes, riding in elevators, going through tunnels or over bridges, driving, or being in enclosed places.

❖ *Other.* Phobic avoidance of loud sounds or costumed characters, or of situations that may lead to choking, vomiting, or contracting an illness.

(DSM-IV Copyright © 1994 by APA)

Prevalence and Comorbidity

Between 2% and 4% of children in the general population experience clinical levels of fear that would qualify as specific phobias. However, only a very small proportion of these children are referred for treatment, suggesting that parents may not view phobias as sufficiently harmful to their children's development to seek help for the problem. Findings regarding gender differences for specific phobias in clinic-referred children are generally inconclusive, although some phobias (e.g., blood phobia) are clearly more common in girls than boys (Albano et al., 1996). The most common comorbid disorder for children with a specific phobia is another anxiety disorder. Although comorbidity is frequent for children with specific phobias, it tends to be lower than for other anxiety disorders. For example, children with a specific phobia report lower levels of fearfulness, loneliness, and depression, and are less likely to have SAD or GAD when compared with children with a social phobia (Strauss & Last, 1993).

Age of Onset, Developmental Course, and Outcome

Although we know a great deal about the age of onset and natural course of normal fears, we know far less about these factors for specific phobias. Phobias involving animals, darkness, insects, blood, and injury typically have their onset at around 7 to 9 years, which is similar to the age of onset for these kinds of fears in normal development. However, clinical phobias are much more likely to persist over time than are normal fears, even though both show a decline with age. Symptoms of anxiety remain stable for approximately 5% to 15% of children with specific phobias. However, it is not yet known why these symptoms persist for some children and disappear in others (Albano et al., 1996). Among a group of adolescents referred for treatment for anxiety disorders, those with a specific phobia were younger at the time of their referral and had an earlier onset of their phobia than those with a social phobia. Adolescents with a specific phobia were referred approximately 3 years following the onset of their phobias. Specific phobias can occur at any age but seem to peak between ages 10 to 13 years (Strauss & Last, 1993).

SOCIAL PHOBIA

Timidity. . . . a mistaken virtue, even when accompanied by substantial qualities, will always be an obstacle in the path leading to the Best. . . .
Yoritomo-Tashi, Japanese Samurai Philosopher

Your playing small does not serve the World. There is nothing enlightening about shrinking so that other people won't feel insecure around you.
Nelson Mandela, 1994, Inaugural Speech

❖ Dante, a 13-year-old, is terrified to use the phone because, he says, he doesn't know how to have a conversation and would be embarrassed by the long periods of silence.

❖ Gene, a 14-year-old, is too embarrassed to use a public rest room.

❖ Hazel, a 15-year-old, is terrified of speaking in front of her class—she's afraid of being humiliated.

In the words of Nelson Mandela, all of these children are "playing small." Although nearly half of all people admit to being shy in some situations, the children in these examples are painfully shy and anxious in social situations.

Each of these children has a **social phobia**—a marked and persistent fear of social or performance situations with adults and peers in which they are exposed to possible scrutiny and embarrassment. As a result, they go to any lengths to avoid such situations, or they may enter the situation with great effort, trying to conceal their fear with a mask of fearlessness. Long after the age when a fear of strangers is considered normal, children with social phobias continue to shrink from people they don't know. When in the presence of other children or adults, they may blush, fall silent, cling to their parents, or try to hide. The DSM-IV criteria for social phobia are shown in Table 7.7.

Previous versions of DSM used a separate category of "avoidant disorder" to describe children who displayed an excessive pattern of shrinking from contact with unfamiliar people. Since children diagnosed with avoidant disorder and those with social phobia are strikingly similar, avoidant disorder was not included as a separate category in DSM-IV (Francis, Last, & Strauss, 1992). Most likely, avoidant disorder and social phobia represent the same disorder on a developmental continuum, with a fear of unfamiliar people developing at an earlier age than a fear of scrutiny by others (Bernstein, Borchardt, & Perwien, 1996).

Have you ever been really nervous before speaking in front of a group? If so, you're not alone. One of the most common social phobias is a fear of speaking in public. Performing in public can produce extreme

Table 7.7 Diagnostic Criteria for Social Phobia

A. A marked and persistent fear of one or more social or performance situations in which the person is exposed to unfamiliar people or to possible scrutiny by others. The individual fears that he or she will act in a way (or show anxiety symptoms) that will be humiliating or embarrassing.

Note: In children, there must be evidence of the capacity for age-appropriate social relationships with familiar people and the anxiety must occur in peer settings, not just in interactions with adults.

B. Exposure to the feared social situation almost invariably provokes anxiety, which may take the form of a situationally bound or situationally predisposed Panic Attack.

Note: In children, the anxiety may be expressed by crying, tantrums, freezing, or shrinking from social situations with unfamiliar people.

C. The person recognizes that the fear is excessive or unreasonable.

Note: In children, this feature may be absent.

D. The feared social or performance situations are avoided or else are endured with intense anxiety or distress.

E. The avoidance, anxious anticipation, or distress in the feared social or performance situation(s) interferes significantly with the person's normal routine, occupational (academic) functioning, or social activities or relationships, or there is marked distress about having the phobia.

F. In individuals under age 18 years, the duration is at least 6 months.

G. The fear or avoidance is not due to the direct physiological effects of a substance (e.g., a drug of abuse, a medication) or a general medical condition and is not better accounted for by another mental disorder (e.g., Panic Disorder with or without Agoraphobia, Separation Anxiety Disorder, Body Dysmorphic Disorder, a Pervasive Developmental Disorder, or Schizoid Personality Disorder).

H. If a general medical condition or another mental disorder is present, the fear in Criterion A is unrelated to it, e.g., the fear is not of Stuttering, trembling in Parkinson's disease, or exhibiting abnormal eating behavior in Anorexia Nervosa or Bulimia Nervosa.

Source: DSM-IV Copyright © 1994 by APA.

---

anxiety—even for well-known entertainers who do it all the time! Carly Simon, Aretha Franklin, Sir Laurence Olivier, Nicholas Cage, Roseanne Barr, Naomi Judd, Sissy Spacek, Johnny Depp, Alanis Morisette, Burt Reynolds, Kim Basinger, and Barbra Streisand are among many performers who have reported suffering from severe anxiety at one time or another in their lives.

Have you ever felt uncomfortable about looking or not looking at another person? Again, you're not alone. Many people avoid eye contact. Women say they avoid eye contact because they don't want to appear unintentionally seductive, and men because they don't want to appear unintentionally confrontational. Children and adolescents with social phobias have an especially difficult time with eye contact. They may feel uncertain or anxious about where to look or how to respond when others look at them. Any look may be seen as a threatening stare. Some children and adolescents with social phobias may avoid eye contact completely because they fear that others will "see" their true feelings and reject them. Interestingly, they are usually surprised to learn that others see them as aloof and uninterested.

In addition to their extreme anxiety in social situations that make many people anxious (e.g., giving a speech), youngsters with social phobias may experience anxiety about the most mundane activities—handing out papers to the class, buttoning a coat in front of others, or ordering a Big Mac and fries at McDonalds. If they speak in public, they fear they may stumble over their words; if they ask a question they may sound stupid; if they eat in public, they may spill food; or, if they enter a room, they may trip and look awkward. Not surprisingly, these children become especially anxious in the presence of people in authority or peers with high social status (Vasey, 1995). Children with a social phobia have a discrete fear, similar to those children with a specific phobia. However, the two groups of children differ markedly in the *object* of their fears. Children with a social phobia are most likely to fear school, public speaking, blushing, crowds, or eating/drinking in front of others, whereas those with a specific phobia are most likely to fear the dark, small animals, heights, insects, or elevators.

Obviously, no one likes to be embarrassed and most of us will avoid it if we can. In fact, about one in five

THE FAR SIDE
By GARY LARSON

"Look. If you're so self-conscious about it, get yourself a gorilla mask."

people say they've tried to avoid giving a talk or eating in a restaurant due to embarrassment. However, the fear of acting in a way that may be embarrassing or humiliating is so intense and pervasive in children and adolescents with a social phobia that it severely interferes with social opportunities and other activities, often leading to loneliness and suffering. Although children with a social phobia have a desire to be liked by others, their constant worry about being scrutinized, or doing something that will make themselves look foolish, prevents them from forming the very relationships they so desire. If other people attempt to encourage or push these children into social situations they may cry, freeze, have a tantrum, or withdraw even further. In the most severe cases, children may develop a **generalized social phobia**. These children fear most social situations, are afraid to meet or talk with new people, avoid contact with anyone outside their family, and find it extremely difficult to attend school, participate in recreational activities, or socialize at all (Albano et al., 1996).

The anxiety associated with social phobia can be so severe that it produces blushing, stammering, sweating,

stomach upset, a rapid heart beat, trembling, or a full-scale panic attack. Adolescents with a social phobia frequently believe that their visible physical reactions will expose hidden feelings of inadequacy and become a further source of humiliation. This belief that others are acutely aware of their nervousness makes these children even more anxious. In a vicious cycle, children with a social phobia begin to anticipate their resulting awkwardness and poor performance, an expectation that triggers further anxiety as they approach the feared situation, which only further increases their nervousness and physical symptoms in the situation. As a result, these children come to avoid social situations and activities such as calling a classmate for missed homework, asking the teacher to explain something, answering the telephone, or dating (Albano, 1995). Extreme forms of timidity in young people have been documented for some time. Consider this adolescent boy's behavior at a social gathering that took place centuries ago in Japan, as described by the Japanese samurai/philosopher Yoritomo-Tashi:

> At these social gatherings he (the young man) became noted for his awkwardness, and his maladroitness. If offered a cup of tea he would take hold of it in such a way as to spill the contents on his clothing, and this incident would plunge him into still deeper confusion. At meals he would handle his chop-sticks so clumsily as to obtain only a few grains of rice, his bowl remaining three-quarters full a long while after every one else had emptied his. If he was obliged to salute any one, he would advance blushing, hesitating, apparently seeing nothing around him, striking against objects that came across his path, stumbling in the interstices of the matting; in fact, appearing at the very greatest disadvantage. (Yoritomo-Tashi, 1916)

Most adolescents experience heightened self-consciousness, doubts, and worries related to their appearance, social prowess, and what others may think of them. How to walk, what to say, or how to dress are ever-present in the minds of most teens, and often exploited by advertisers. Common sources of anxiety for normal adolescents include consolidation of identity, sexuality, social acceptance, and conflict around independence. Among the symptoms of anxiety most frequently reported in normal adolescents are fears of public speaking, blushing, excessive worry about past behavior, and self-consciousness (Bell-Dolan et al., 1990).

Most social phobias first occur in adolescence. Although transitory social anxiety and self-consciousness are part of normal development, adolescents with a social phobia, like the young man in our example, experience persistent anxiety. Often their anxiety is associated with an exaggerated self-focus which, in turn, heightens self-critical thinking and intensifies emotional symptoms. This downward-spiraling process can lead to severe problems in social competence and to difficulties making friends (Albano, 1995; Rubin & Stewart, 1996). Consider the painful interchange that follows, which is replete with the social anxiety and self-focused and self-critical thinking that is typical of adolescents with a social phobia. It's the first day of school. In the school yard two students, Anne and Patty, happen to be sitting near each other. They've never met before today.

> *Anne:* (To herself: I can't just sit here and look stupid, I have to say hello.) Hi, are you new here?
>
> *Patty:* (To herself: Oh no, don't talk to me. I don't know what to say.) No, I was here last year. (To herself: Sure, nobody ever notices me.)
>
> *Anne:* (To herself: Great, now I look like a jerk for not recognizing her. Now what do I do?) Oh, I guess we've never met. I'm Anne.
>
> *Patty:* (To herself: When is the bell going to ring?) I'm Patty. I've seen you before.
>
> *Anne:* Oh, weren't you in my study hall? With Mr. Holt? (To herself: I hope she doesn't remember when I got sick in there. Why did I bring up study hall!)
>
> *Patty:* (To herself: She was so popular, I can't talk to her. She thinks I'm a nerd 'cause I sat by myself all year.) Yes, I was in there. I have to go now. (To herself: I have to get out of here. I can't take this anymore.)
>
> *Anne:* (To herself: Oh boy, she thinks I'm weird, she does remember. I'm so embarrassed. I bet my face is all red.) Okay, see you. (To herself: I'm glad that's over.)
>
> (Adapted from Albano et al., 1991)

Prevalence, Comorbidity, and Course

Social phobia occurs in about 1% to 3% of children, affecting girls slightly more than boys (Vasey, 1995). Among children referred for treatment for anxiety disorders, as many as 20% have social phobia as their primary diagnosis, and it is the most common secondary diagnosis for children referred for other anxiety disorders (Albano et al., 1996). Even so, many cases of social phobia in young people are overlooked because shyness is common in our society and because these children are not likely to call attention to their problem even when they experience severe distress. About two-thirds of children and adolescents with a social phobia have another anxiety disorder, most commonly a specific phobia or panic disorder. In some cases, severe social phobia may create a vulnerability for the development of panic disorder and agoraphobia. About 20% of adolescents with a social phobia also have a major depressive disorder. Adolescents with a social phobia may also use alcohol and other drugs as a form of self-medication, a way of reducing their anxiety in social situations (Albano et al., 1996).

Social phobias generally develop after puberty, with the most common age of onset in early to mid-adolescence (Strauss & Last, 1993). The disorder is extremely rare in children under the age of 10. The prevalence of social phobia appears to increase with age, although there is little information available to describe the natural course of the disorder or its long-term outcome.

Selective Mutism

Keisha: Mum's the Word

Keisha is a 6-year-old girl in kindergarten who doesn't speak at school to teachers or peers and has not done so during her two previous years in preschool. Two years ago Keisha had difficulties being left at preschool and it took about two months before she could be left without crying. Although she doesn't talk to other children, she interacts with them and participates in school activities. Keisha speaks openly to all family members at home but does not speak to them in public if others might hear her. Keisha says that she does not know why she doesn't talk, but has told her mother that she feels scared. Her mother says Keisha is shy and is a worrier. (Adapted from Leonard & Dow, 1995)

Children with **selective mutism** fail to talk in social situations, even though they may speak loudly and frequently at home or in other settings. Although selective mutism is presently classified under "other disorders of childhood" in DSM-IV, current studies suggest that selective mutism shares much in common with anxiety disorders (Leonard & Dow, 1995). For example, a study of young children with selective mutism found that 90% of them met diagnostic criteria for a social phobia in ways other than their reluctance to speak. Parents and teachers rated these children as having high levels of social anxiety without other psychiatric symptoms

(Black & Uhde, 1995). Although studies are not conclusive, selective mutism may be a type of social phobia rather than a unique disorder.

OBSESSIVE-COMPULSIVE DISORDER

Paul: Stuck in a Doorway

At almost any hour, Paul, age 16, could be found in a doorway, slightly swaying back and forth, with his eyes fixed at the upper corner of the door frame. "What are you doing?" a ward attendant would ask. "I'm stuck," Paul whispered back, without moving. "I have to do it over again to get it right; I have to do it a certain, special way." "Have to do what?" the attendant would ask. "Get through the door right," Paul would answer. (Adapted from Rapoport, 1989)

Paul has an **obsessive-compulsive disorder** (OCD), an unusual disorder of ritual and doubt. Although OCD is a severe condition, certain elements of OCD are present in everyday life. For example, we all know people who we would describe as obsessive or compulsive. These people are overly concerned with neatness, punctuality, keeping the house spotlessly clean, or with rigidly adhering to an exact schedule. We tend to see people like this as uptight or controlling and not much fun to be around. Who wants to hang out with someone who spends most of his or her time at a party worrying about putting coasters under drinks? Similarly, many people engage in superstitious behaviors, such as carrying a lucky charm, knocking on wood, not walking under ladders, or playing a lucky number in the lottery. Although many common superstitious thoughts and habits occur from time to time for most people, these are considered obsessions or compulsions only if they cannot be controlled, if they significantly interfere with daily functioning, or if excessive effort is expended fighting them off.

Children and adolescents with OCD experience recurrent and disturbing obsessions and compulsions. **Obsessions** are persistent and intrusive thoughts, ideas, impulses, or images, described by one 7-year-old girl with OCD as "having minds." Although most children describe their obsessions as being a lot like worries, obsessions are much more than heightened worries about everyday problems such as homework or popularity with peers. They are excessive and irrational, and they focus on improbable or unrealistic events or on real-life events that are greatly exaggerated. Children

with OCD may complain about being unable to stop "hearing" recurring rhymes or songs, or about experiencing fears of having a serious disease such as cancer, or about being attacked by intruders entering their house. The most common obsessions in children and adolescents focus on germs and contamination, followed by fears of harm to self or others, concerns with symmetry, and excessive moralization or religiosity. Since these and other obsessions create considerable anxiety and distress for children with OCD, they go to great lengths to try to neutralize them with some other action, known as a compulsion (Henin & Kendall, 1997).

Compulsions are repetitive, purposeful, and intentional behaviors (e.g., handwashing) or mental acts (e.g., repeating words silently) that are performed in response to an obsession. For example, as a result of an obsession of being contaminated by germs, a child with OCD may feel compelled to clean, check for dirt, or engage in some other ritual as a way of decreasing anxiety. One 6-year-old boy for example, felt compelled to wash his homework! Multiple compulsions are the norm, with the most common ones being excessive washing and bathing (occurring in about 85% of cases), repeating, checking, touching, counting, and ordering or arranging (Swedo, Rapoport, Leonard, Lenane, & Cheslow, 1989). The process that drives OCD is similar to the children's game "Step on a crack, break your mother's back" and similar rituals and superstitions. In the case of this game, the child's troubling thought or obsession is of harming mother. The repetitive behavior or compulsion is to meticulously avoid stepping on all cracks in the sidewalk to prevent harm to mother. Paul, the young boy with OCD who got stuck in doorways, reported that "cracks in the sidewalk were also big problems." "Not the little way they are for some kids," he said, "but in a very big way" (Rapoport, 1989, p. 75). The DSM-IV criteria for OCD are shown in Table 7.8.

Many compulsive behaviors are directly related to obsessive thoughts, for example, checking to make sure that the stove is turned off in response to an obsessional thought about leaving the stove on. Sound familiar? Some checking rituals are adaptive in attending to health or safety concerns. However, these nonclinical rituals are usually brief in duration and we experience relief once we've performed them. In contrast, pathological forms of compulsions persist, are excessive, are often carried out in a rigid and stereotyped manner or sequence for which the child is unable to provide a rationale, and do not provide lasting relief.

Most children with OCD have multiple obsessions and compulsions. However, some children may experience either compulsions or obsessions only. Compulsions alone account for most of these cases, because obsessions are almost always accompanied by compulsions (Last &

Table 7.8 | Diagnostic Criteria for Obsessive-Compulsive Disorder

A. Either obsessions or compulsions:

Obsessions as defined by (1), (2), (3), and (4):

(1) recurrent and persistent thoughts, impulses, or images that are experienced, at some time during the disturbance, as intrusive and inappropriate and that cause marked anxiety or distress

(2) the thoughts, impulses, or images are not simply excessive worries about real-life problems

(3) the person attempts to ignore or suppress such thoughts, impulses, or images, or to neutralize them with some other thought or action

(4) the person recognizes that the obsessional thoughts, impulses, or images are a product of his or her own mind (not imposed from without as in thought insertion)

Compulsions as defined by (1) and (2):

(1) repetitive behaviors (e.g., hand washing, ordering, checking) or mental acts (e.g., praying, counting, repeating words silently) that the person feels driven to perform in response to an obsession, or according to rules that must be applied rigidly

(2) the behaviors or mental acts are aimed at preventing or reducing distress or preventing some dreaded event or situation; however, these behaviors or mental acts either are not connected in a realistic way with what they are designed to neutralize or prevent or are clearly excessive

B. At some point during the course of the disorder, the person has recognized that the obsessions or compulsions are excessive or unreasonable.

   Note: This does not apply to children.

C. The obsessions or compulsions cause marked distress, are time consuming (take more than 1 hour a day), or significantly interfere with the person's normal routine, occupational (or academic) functioning, or usual social activities or relationships.

D. If another Axis I disorder is present, the content of the obsessions or compulsions is not restricted to it (e.g., preoccupation with food in the presence of an Eating Disorder; hair pulling in the presence of Trichotillomania; concern with appearance in the presence of Body Dysmorphic Disorder; preoccupation with drugs in the presence of a Substance Use Disorder; preoccupation with having a serious illness in the presence of Hypochondriasis; preoccupation with sexual urges or fantasies in the presence of a Paraphilia; or guilty ruminations in the presence of a Major Depressive Disorder).

E. The disturbance is not due to the direct physiological effects of a substance (e.g., a drug of abuse, a medication) or a general medical condition.

   Specify if: **With Poor Insight:** if, for most of the time during the current episode, the person does not recognize that the obsessions and compulsions are excessive or unreasonable.

Source: DSM-IV Copyright © 1994 by APA.

Strauss, 1989b). Compulsions in the absence of anxious obsessions are most typically found in very young children or in children with comorbid tic disorders, who describe their rituals as being performed because of a vague sensation or an irresistible urge (Piacentini & Graae, 1997).

Certain compulsions are commonly associated with specific obsessions. For example, washing and cleaning rituals are likely to be associated with contamination obsessions, such as a concern or disgust with body wastes or secretions (e.g., urine, feces, saliva), a concern with dirt or germs, or an excessive concern about chemical or environmental contamination. Compulsions involving counting over and over to a certain number are frequently related to a concern about harm—that something terrible might happen (e.g., death of a parent or a fire). Obsessions with symmetry, exactness, or order are often associated with arranging and ordering compulsions, such as repeatedly packing and unpacking a suitcase or rearranging drawers (Piacentini, 1997). Why are the links between some obsessions and compulsions more likely than others? It's probably related to our evolutionary past, in the same way that we are more likely to develop phobias of animals than we are of vegetables or minerals.

How can children with OCD be so reasonable about some things yet seem so disturbed with respect to their obsessions and compulsions? Most children over age 8

Haunted by their habits: washing, checking, and symmetry.

(and virtually all adults) persist in their obsessions or compulsions even though they recognize them as being excessive and unreasonable (children ordinarily use the word *dumb* or *stupid* to describe their thoughts and rituals). However, something about OCD makes it extremely resistant to reason, even when the child recognizes the "silliness" of his or her routines. For example, one of 10-year-old Emilio's obsessive thoughts is that there is a long, flexible, pipelike structure issuing from his chest. He knows this is only a thought and that there is no pipe coming out of his chest, but he must behave as if the pipe is there and move in such a way that no one, or no object, crosses the midline in front of him (Despert, 1955).

Children with OCD often involve family members in their rituals, for example, demanding that their clothes or other belongings be washed two or three times a day, not allowing the family to eat certain foods for fear of illness or contamination, or having a parent get up at 5 A.M. to assist them in dressing rituals that may take hours to complete (Piacentini, 1997). Some children with OCD insist that certain phrases be repeated or that questions be answered in a certain way by their parents. Consider this exchange between 11-year-old Heather and her mother.

> *Heather: You said before that we were having dessert. Now you say we're having ice cream. Which one is it?*
>
> *Mother: Ice cream is dessert.*
>
> *Heather: But which one is right?*
>
> *Mother: Both*
>
> *Heather: But are we having ice cream or dessert?*
>
> *Mother: We're having ice cream.*
>
> *Heather: So why did you say we were having dessert?*

Heather became so argumentative, insistent, and persistent in getting her mother to answer her questions in just a certain way that her mother thought Heather had a severe behavior problem. However, with further assessment, it became clear that Heather's "oppositional" behavior was an expression of OCD. When interviewed about her problem, Heather said: "I can't help it. When I'm with my mother, I have to make her say things 'just right' or I feel terrible."

Compulsions are intended to neutralize or reduce anxiety and tension or to prevent some dreaded event or situation from happening. Although compulsive rituals may provide temporary relief from anxiety, because they are excessive and not clearly related to the thought or event that provoked them, in the long run these rituals fail to achieve their intended purpose of decreasing anxiety. As a result, children with OCD increasingly become trapped in a time-consuming and never-ending cycle of obsessions and compulsions. For these children, many hours each day are taken up by disabling, sometimes ridiculous, and alarming thoughts that have been likened by some to having "mental hiccups," and by repeated compulsions such as handwashing or checking to see if a door is closed. The child's preoccupation with obsessions and rituals makes it extremely difficult, if not impossible, to focus on anything else. As we saw with Paul, even a simple activity such as walking into a room may become an insurmountable problem for a child with OCD.

As a result of such excessive preoccupations, normal activities of children with OCD are reduced, and health, interpersonal and family relations, and school functioning can be severely disrupted (Carter et al., 1995). Cleaning or washing rituals may lead to health problems, such as eczema of the hands and forearms as a result of prolonged washing or use of abrasive cleaners, or to gum lesions as a result of prolonged toothbrushing. Dressing or washing rituals may result in lateness to school. Counting and checking rituals and intrusive thoughts may result in a lack of focus and concentration at school that interferes with schoolwork. Homework may become a daily struggle, with the child spending hours repeatedly checking and correcting his or her work, or erasing answers so often that there are holes in the paper and his or her fingers are raw from rubbing. Checking rituals may require the child to check and recheck every answer on a test so often that he or she is unable to finish it. Bedtime rituals may preclude inviting friends to sleep over and embarrassment related to a repeated refusal to accept similar invitations from friends. Contamination fears may interfere with school attendance or with social activities, such as going to see movies or participating in sports (Piacentini, 1997).

As children with OCD grow older, their rituals may interfere with the normal milestones of adolescence and young adulthood, such as driving a car, dating, or going away to college. Consider how 17-year-old Charlie's checking ritual interfered with his driving a car.

Charlie: A Different Kind of Check Stop

I tried driving for a few months, but whenever I hit a bump in the road, even a small stone, I had to stop to make sure I hadn't run over someone. I would check my rearview mirror and then circle around the block over and over again. When I didn't see anyone, I thought the person I hit may have been thrown off the road by the collision. So I'd back up, get out of the car, and search the ditch next to the road. But it didn't end there. I'd check the newspaper every day to make sure I hadn't killed someone and I'd worry about this for weeks—so I stopped driving.

Because of the odd and senseless nature of OCD symptoms, many children try to mask or hide their rituals, especially in social situations or at school. In less severe cases, teachers, friends, and family members may be unaware of the child's OCD for months or even years. However, as the child's rituals become more elaborate and time-consuming, they become increasingly difficult to conceal. With considerable effort, children with OCD may muster the energy to inhibit their symptoms for brief periods of time. However, these efforts to suppress commonly lead to a rebound effect, with increased symptoms once the child is in a safe place or at home with family members. As the child becomes too overwhelmed by anxiety to cope, or when specific events in the family, such as magazine articles or TV shows about OCD, bring the problem into focus, others become more and more aware of its seriousness (Piacentini, 1997).

A rare disorder of impulse control characterized by the unusual compulsion to pull one's own hair is **trichotillomania**. Victims of this disorder feel an irresistible urge to pull their hair, and experience a sense of relief after the hair has been plucked. The hair pulling may involve any part of the body where hair grows, with the most common sites being the scalp, eyebrows, and eyelashes. The child's hairpulling results in a noticeable hair loss; in some cases complete baldness may result. This disorder occurs 7 times more frequently in children than adults, and may be much more common than previously thought. Although trichotillomania is not exactly the same thing as OCD, its presentation may help us understand OCD and other disorders that involve excessive grooming behaviors (Swedo & Leonard, 1992; Swedo & Rapoport, 1991).

Prevalence and Comorbidity

The prevalence of OCD in children and adolescents is 2% to 3%, suggesting that OCD occurs about as often in young people as in adults (Piacentini & Graae, 1997). Clinic-based studies of younger children suggest that OCD is about twice as common in boys as girls. However, this gender difference has not been observed in community samples of adolescents, which may be a function of age differences, referral bias, or both (Albano et al., 1996). Comorbidity in children with OCD is common, with 60% to 80% of children having at least one other disorder and 50% or more experiencing multiple comorbid conditions. The most common comorbidities are other anxiety disorders (25% to 75%); depressive disorders, especially in older children with OCD (25% to 62%); and disruptive behavior disorders (18% to 33%) (Last & Strauss, 1989a; Piacentini & Graae, 1997). Substance use disorders, learning disorders, and eating disorders are also overrepresented in children with OCD. Finally, motor and vocal tics and Tourette's Syndrome (TS) occur in about 20% to 30% of children with OCD. Children with both OCD and tic disorders are more likely to engage in compulsions to achieve a sense of completion or perfection and are less

likely to describe their compulsions as anxiety-driven or to report compulsions related to contamination, cleaning, or checking (Piacentini & Graae, 1997).

Age of Onset, Developmental Course, and Outcome

The mean age of onset of OCD is about 9 to 12 years, with two peaks, one in early childhood and another in early adolescence (Hanna, 1995). Children with an early onset of OCD (age 6 to 10) are more likely to have a family history of OCD than those with a later onset, suggesting a greater role of genetic influences in such cases (Swedo et al., 1989). These children have prominent motor patterns, engaging in compulsions without obsessions and displaying odd compulsions, such as finger licking or walking compulsively in geometric designs. In addition, 20% or more have chronic motor tics and there is a strong familial association with Tourette's disorder.

Examining the developmental course of OCD in young children indicates that they typically have obsessions that are more vague than those of older children, and they are less likely to feel that their obsessions are abnormal. Young children with OCD often ask their parents endless questions related to their obsessions and make no effort to hide their discomfort. Most children over age 8 are aware that their obsessions are abnormal, and they commonly use the word *stupid* or *dumb* to describe them. Because of this awareness, children 8 or older are usually embarrassed and uncomfortable talking about their obsessions. They may try to hide or minimize them, or deny they have them, although their extreme avoidance suggests otherwise. Parents can find it very frustrating to know that something is wrong and try to help, only to have the child deny that there is a problem.

The symptom pattern in most children with OCD changes over time. Parents may report that their child began by checking locks and closet doors, but subsequently replaced these actions with counting or arranging rituals. OCD in children seems to follow a chronic but fluctuating course (Swedo et al., 1989). The untreated symptoms of OCD may vary over a period of years, going away, remaining the same, or worsening. Obsessions usually change over time for unknown reasons. Some obsessions seem to decrease and lose their importance while others grow. For example, it is not uncommon for a child at age 9 to be obsessed with having the doors locked, and then gradually replace this obsession at age 14 with an obsession about germs.

One-half to two-thirds of children with OCD continue to meet the criteria for the disorder 2 to 14 years

Table 7.9 Diagnostic Criteria for a Panic Attack

A discrete period of intense fear or discomfort, in which four or more of the following symptoms developed abruptly and reached a peak within 10 minutes:

(1) palpitations, pounding heart, or accelerated heart rate
(2) sweating
(3) trembling or shaking
(4) sensations of shortness of breath
(5) feeling of choking
(6) chest pain or discomfort
(7) nausea or abdominal distress
(8) feeling dizzy, unsteady, lightheaded, or faint
(9) derealization (feelings of unreality) or depersonalization (being detached from oneself)
(10) fear of losing control or going crazy
(11) fear of dying
(12) paresthesias (numbness or tightening sensations)
(13) chills or hot flashes

Note: A panic attack is not, in and of itself, a diagnosable disorder.

Source: DSM-IV Copyright © 1994 by APA.

later. Although most children, including those treated with medication, show some improvement in symptoms, fewer than 10% show complete remission. Predictors of poor outcome include a poor initial response to treatment, a lifetime history of tic disorder, and parental psychopathology at the time of referral. Thus, OCD remains a serious and chronic disorder for a significant number of children (Albano, Knox, & Barlow, 1995).

PANIC ATTACKS AND PANIC DISORDER

Panic Attacks

The word *panic* originates from the goatlike Greek god Pan, the god of nature. Pan terrified travelers in the countryside who dared to disturb his nap by surprising them with a bloodcurdling scream. So intense was this scream that it sometimes scared the intruders to death. This unexpected and devastating feeling of terror and fright came to be known as panic. Comments about panic include the following:

❖ "When my heart starts pounding, I feel like I'm going to die."
❖ "No one really knows how terrified I am when I have these attacks."
❖ "I can't help being so frightened. My dad says I should snap out of it. I wish I could."

A **panic attack** is a sudden and overwhelming period of intense fear or discomfort that is accompanied by four

or more physical and cognitive symptoms characteristic of the fight/flight response. These symptoms are listed in Table 7.9. Panic attacks seem to come without warning and with no obvious trigger. Usually, an attack is short, with symptoms reaching maximal intensity in 10 minutes or less and then diminishing slowly over the next 30 minutes or the next few hours. Panic attacks are accompanied by an overwhelming sense of imminent danger or impending doom, and by an urge to escape. Although panic attacks are brief, they can occur several times a week or month, and when they do occur, the symptoms are severe. It is important to remember that although these symptoms are uncomfortable and frightening, they are not physically harmful or dangerous.

Panic attacks are easily identified in adults, but some controversy exists over how often they occur in children and adolescents (Kearney & Allan, 1995). Although panic attacks are extremely rare in young children, they are common in adolescents (Ollendick, Mattis, & King, 1994). Why this age difference in occurrence? One idea is that young children lack the cognitive ability to make the kinds of catastrophic misinterpretations that usually accompany panic attacks (Nelles & Barlow, 1988). These misinterpretations involve the belief that bodily sensations are much more serious than they actually are—for example, that a rapid heart beat signals a heart attack, or that shakiness is a sign of losing control and going crazy. However, a study of children in the third, sixth, and ninth grades found that although third-graders' conceptions of panic attacks were less well developed than those of sixth and ninth graders, there were no differences across grade levels in children's

Panic

tendency to make catastrophic versus noncatastrophic attributions in response to somatic symptoms of panic. In fact, when presented with panic-inducing imagery, children of all ages were likely to make internal and *non*catastrophic attributions. Internal catastrophic cognitions were most likely to be made by children who attributed negative outcomes to something about themselves and who believed that anxiety causes illness, embarrassment, or additional anxiety (Mattis & Ollendick, 1997a).

If a limited cognitive capacity is not the primary reason that panic attacks are so rare in young children, what is? In a revealing study, the relationship between the occurrence of panic attacks and pubertal stage was assessed in 754 girls in the sixth and seventh grades. About 5% of the girls reported having had at least one four-symptom panic attack. None of the 94 girls who were at an early stage of puberty reported experiencing panic attacks. Rates of panic attacks increased with increasing sexual maturity, up to a rate of 8% for girls who were at the highest stage of pubertal development. Importantly, increasing rates of panic were related to pubertal development—not to increasing age (Hayward et al., 1992). The significance of pubertal development and anxiety disorders in females more generally is suggested by recent findings that sixth- to eighth-grade females who developed internalizing symptoms were on average 5 months earlier in their pubertal development than females who were asymptomatic (Hayward, Killen, Wilson, & Hammer, 1997). Given that spontaneous panic attacks are rare before puberty and are related to

pubertal stage, and that adolescence is the peak time for the onset of the disorder, the physical changes that take place around puberty seem critical to understanding panic, although the specific biological processes are not known.

Why do the physical symptoms of the fight/flight response occur, if an adolescent is not frightened in the first place? One possibility is that these symptoms can be produced by other things besides fear. A youngster may be distressed for some other reason (e.g., an accident or illness), and this stress can increase production of adrenalin and other chemicals that from time to time produce physical symptoms of the fight/flight response. Increased adrenalin may be maintained chemically in the body even after the stressor is no longer present. Another possibility is that some youngsters may breathe a little too fast (subtle hyperventilation) and this also can produce symptoms. Because the overbreathing is very slight, the child gets used to it and doesn't realize that he or she is hyperventilating. A third possibility is that some youngsters are experiencing normal bodily changes but, because they are constantly monitoring and keeping a check on their bodies (as adolescents are prone to do), they notice these sensations far more readily than they would otherwise (Barlow, 1988).

Panic Disorder

Claudia: Panic

Sixteen-year-old Claudia was watching TV after a noneventful day at school. She suddenly felt very "strange" and was overwhelmed by an intense feeling of lightheadedness and a smothering sensation, as if she couldn't get any air to breathe. Her heart started to pound rapidly, as if it would explode. The attack came on so fast and was so intense that Claudia panicked and thought that she must be having a heart attack that would kill her. She began to sweat and tremble, and she felt like the room was spinning. These feelings reached a peak within 2 minutes—but this was the seventh attack that Claudia had experienced this month. She frantically ran to her mother and pleaded to be taken to the hospital emergency room—again.

Some adolescents who experience repetitive, severe panic attacks have no other symptoms. Others, like Claudia, may begin to experience a progression of distressing symptoms and develop a **panic disorder (PD)**. Adolescents with PD display recurrent, unexpected panic attacks followed by at least 1 month of persistent concern about having another panic attack, constant worry about the ramifications or consequences of having the attacks, or a significant change in their behavior related to the attacks. Those who have suffered a number of panic attacks develop considerable secondary anxiety, and may begin to feel anxious most of the time, even when they are not having panic attacks. They worry about when or where the next attack will occur and if they will live to tell about it. This kind of worry is called **anticipatory anxiety**.

Adolescents with PD may begin to avoid situations in which they've had a panic attack in the past, similar situations or activities in which they fear an attack might occur, or situations where help may not be available. Usually, this is because the adolescent feels it would be especially dangerous or embarrassing to have a panic attack in that situation. An adolescent with PD such as Claudia might think:

"It would be bad enough to have an attack at all, but it would be really dangerous if I had one while riding my bike to school. I'd be totally preoccupied with the attack and would have an accident. I'd probably destroy my bike and wind up seriously hurting myself or someone else in the process!" Claudia's avoidance of riding a bike to school could be misinterpreted as a fear of bike riding when it really is a fear of having a panic attack while riding the bike.

If not recognized and treated, PD and its complications can seriously interfere with relationships at home and school, and with school performance. Some adolescents with PD may be reluctant to go to school or be separated from their parents. The unpredictability of panic attacks leads the adolescent to expect future panic attacks and therefore to fear any situation in which an attack may occur. In severe cases, the tendency to avoid everyday life circumstances may increase and generalize, to the point that the older adolescent with PD becomes terrified to leave the house at all, and normal activities are severely restricted.

This extensive pattern characterized by a fear of being alone in and of avoiding certain places or situations is called **agoraphobia**. In agoraphobia, the adolescent's anxiety is related to a fear of having a panic attack in situations where escape would be difficult or help unavailable if he or she were incapacitated. Some of the more common situations that are avoided are going to school, movies, restaurants, crowded shopping malls, or public assemblies; riding in elevators; and traveling in a car, bus, or airplane. If an adolescent with agoraphobia dares to venture into a feared situation, he or she does so only with great distress, or when accompanied by a family member or a friend. It is not clear why panic disorder progresses to agoraphobia in some individuals. When a first panic attack occurs in public and is accompanied by

---

Box 7.2

Did Darwin Have a Panic Disorder?

Charles Darwin (1809–1882) was an outgoing and daring traveler and outdoorsman in his college days. However, in his late twenties—just a year after returning to England after a 5-year voyage to South America and the Pacific aboard HMS *Beagle*—he started to complain of an "uncomfortable palpitation of the heart." The symptoms arose shortly after he began keeping a secret notebook that, 22 years later, would become his book-length elaboration of the theory of evolution, *On the Origin of Species*. Over the years his affliction was described as a case of bad nerves, a tropical disease, intellectual exhaustion, arsenic poisoning, suppressed gout, and a host of other complaints. However, in his journal Darwin described his malady as a "sensation of fear . . . accompanied by troubled beating of the heart, sweat, trembling of muscles."

Source: Desmond & Moore, 1991.

---

feelings of embarrassment, the risk for developing agoraphobia is heightened. In general, agoraphobia has received little systematic study in children and adolescents, since most cases develop between ages 18 and 35.

Prevalence and Comorbidity

Whereas panic attacks are common among adolescents in community samples (about 35% to 65%), PD is much less common, affecting only 0.6% to 4.7% of teens (Ollendick et al., 1994). Adolescent females are more likely to experience panic attacks than are adolescent males, and a fairly consistent association has been found between panic attacks and stressful life events (King, Ollendick, & Mattis, 1994; Last & Strauss, 1989b). About half of adolescents with PD have no other disorder, and for the remainder, an additional anxiety disorder and depression are the most common secondary diagnoses (Kearney, Albano, Eisen, Allan, & Barlow, 1997; Last & Strauss, 1989b). After months or years of unrelenting panic attacks and the restricted lifestyle that results from avoidance behavior, adolescents and young adults with PD may develop severe depression and may be at risk for suicidal behavior. Others may begin to use alcohol or drugs as a way of alleviating their anxiety.

Age of Onset, Developmental Course, and Outcome

The average age of onset for a first panic attack in adolescents with PD is around 15 to 19 years, and 95% of adolescents with the disorder are postpubertal

(Bernstein et al., 1996; Kearney & Allan, 1995). PD occurs in otherwise emotionally healthy youngsters about half the time. The most frequent prior disturbance when there is one is a depressive disorder (Last & Strauss, 1989b). Unfortunately, children and adolescents with panic disorder have the lowest rate of remission for any of the anxiety disorders (Last et al., 1996).

Although panic attacks are extremely rare in children, it has been proposed that SAD may be a possible early form of panic attacks and that SAD could develop into PD in later adolescence and adulthood (King et al., 1994; Mattis & Ollendick, 1997b). About 20% of adults with panic attacks had separation anxiety or school phobias as children. However, research does not currently support SAD as a *specific* precursor for PD, since SAD is a precursor for a number of later conditions, including other anxiety disorders and depression.

POSTTRAUMATIC STRESS DISORDER

Marcie: Trauma

While accompanying her mother to a neighbor's farm, 6-year-old Marcie was viciously attacked and mauled in the face by a large German shepherd. Marcie's 7-year-old brother Jeff and her two younger sisters, Cathy (age 4) and Susan (age 2), were present and observed the incident. The family was approached by the barking dog while walking up the driveway. Although the mother warned the children to keep away from the dog, Marcie and Jeff let the dog approach and Jeff was able to pet the dog. Upon seeing this, Marcie then bent toward the dog to pet it, and at that point the dog attacked. The mother immediately applied pressure to the bleeding wound, as the brother attempted to chase the dog away. The two youngest children clung to their mother's legs. The dog's owner (who had followed the dog down the driveway) panicked and ran to the children's home to get their father, leaving the dog unleashed and barking at the frightened family for about 20 minutes. Upon his arrival, the father took the family back to their home, cleaned Marcie's wound, and then took her for emergency medical treatment. As a result of the attack, Marcie received stitches in her face, which were applied while she was strapped down and in extreme distress.

Following the incident, all the children displayed some fear and reverted to behaviors displayed at a younger age, such as bed-wetting and finger sucking. They also displayed irritability and anger outbursts following the trauma. In addition, all the children developed varying degrees of sleep disturbances and nightmares. Moreover, Marcie developed an intense fear of medical procedures or any situation that reminded her of a medical procedure. Thus, follow-up visits to the plastic surgeon were accompanied by intense fear and panic reactions. Excessive distress was evidenced in everyday first-aid situations such as caring for a minor scratch or scrape. (Adapted from Albano et al., 1997)

Children with **posttraumatic stress disorder (PTSD)** display persistent anxiety following exposure to or witnessing of an overwhelming traumatic event that is outside the range of usual human experience. When the diagnosis of PTSD was first developed, the reference points were catastrophic events, such as war, torture, rape, and both natural disasters (e.g., earthquakes and hurricanes) and disasters of human origin (e.g., fires and automobile accidents). A distinction is made between these types of trauma and other very stressful life events such as illness or family breakup; the traumatic experiences associated with PTSD are likely to exceed and overwhelm the coping abilities of most humans. The experiences associated with PTSD involve actual or threatened death, injury, or threat to one's physical integrity. The DSM-IV diagnostic criteria for PTSD are shown in Table 7.10.

PTSD is most common among children exposed to major accidents, natural disasters, kidnapping, brutal physical assaults, or physical or sexual abuse (see Chapter 14). Symptoms of PTSD following exposure to trauma are both conspicuous and complex. Reactions to the trauma include intense fear, helplessness, and horror, which in children can be expressed as agitated behavior and disorganization. The three core features of PTSD are persistent reexperiencing of the traumatic event, avoidance of stimuli associated with the trauma and numbing of general responsiveness, and persistent symptoms of extreme arousal. Children with PTSD show many of the same symptoms that were previously identified in combat soldiers exposed to the horrors of war. They may be extremely agitated and have nightmares, fears, and panic attacks for many years following their traumatic experience. They may regress developmentally and display age-inappropriate behaviors, such as a fear of strangers. They avoid situations that could remind them of the traumatic event or they may reenact the event in play. Common symptoms include pessimism, feelings of vulnerability, sleep disturbances, school difficulties, and emotional numbness. The main features of PTSD are

Table 7.10 Diagnostic Criteria for Posttraumatic Stress Disorder

A. The person has been exposed to a traumatic event in which both of the following were present:
   (1) the person experienced, witnessed, or was confronted with an event or events that involved actual or threatened death or serious injury, or a threat to the physical integrity of self or others
   (2) the person's response involved intense fear, helplessness, or horror

   Note: In children this may be expressed instead by disorganized or agitated behavior

B. The traumatic event is persistently reexperienced in one (or more) of the following ways:
   (1) recurrent and intrusive distressing recollections of the event, including images, thoughts, or perceptions

   Note: In young children, repetitive play may occur in which themes or aspects of the trauma are expressed

   (2) recurrent distressing dreams of the event

   Note: In children, there may be frightening dreams without recognizable content.

   (3) acting or feeling as if the traumatic event were recurring (includes a sense of reliving the experience, illusions, hallucinations, and dissociative flashback episodes, including those that occur on awakening or when intoxicated)

   Note: In young children, trauma-specific reenactment may occur.

   (4) intense psychological distress at exposure to internal or external cues that symbolize or resemble an aspect of the traumatic event
   (5) physiological reactivity on exposure to internal or external cues that symbolize or resemble an aspect of the traumatic event

C. Persistent avoidance of stimuli associated with the trauma and numbing of general responsiveness (not present before the trauma), as indicated by three (or more) of the following:
   (1) efforts to avoid thoughts, feelings, or conversations associated with the trauma
   (2) efforts to avoid activities, places, or people that arouse recollections of the trauma
   (3) inability to recall an important aspect of the trauma
   (4) markedly diminished interest or participation in significant activities
   (5) feeling of detachment or estrangement from others
   (6) restricted range of affect (e.g., unable to have loving feelings)
   (7) sense of a foreshortened future (e.g., does not expect to have a career, marriage, children, or a normal life span)

D. Persistent symptoms of increased arousal (not present before the trauma), as indicated by two (or more) of the following:
   (1) difficulty falling or staying asleep
   (2) irritability or outbursts of anger
   (3) difficulty concentrating
   (4) hypervigilance
   (5) exaggerated startle response

E. Duration of the disturbance (symptoms in Criteria B, C, and D) is more than 1 month.

F. The disturbance causes clinically significant distress or impairment in social, occupational, or other important areas of functioning.

   Specify if:
      Acute: if duration of symptoms is less than 3 months
      Chronic: if duration of symptoms is 3 months or more

   Specify if:
      With Delayed Onset: if onset of symptoms is at least 6 months after the stressor

Source: DSM-IV Copyright © 1994 by APA.

exposure to trauma, intrusive recollection and reexperiencing, avoidance and numbing, hyperarousal, persistent symptoms, and distress and impairment.

Some of the key symptoms of PTSD, such as intrusive reexperiencing of the traumatic event, are expressed differently in children than in adults. For example, instead of experiencing flashbacks and waking recall of the traumatic event, young children are more likely to reexperience trauma in nightmares. Initially, the nightmares may reflect the traumatic event, but over time they may become more nonspecific. Similarly, daytime recall of the trauma may be expressed in play or through reenactment of the event or themes related to the event. Trauma reactions of preschool children may include repetitive drawing and play focused on trauma-related themes, regressive behavior, antisocial or aggressive behavior, and destructive behavior (Yule, 1994).

The occurrence of symptoms in Marcie and her siblings illustrates how PTSD may result from direct, witnessed, or verbal exposure to a traumatic event (Saigh, 1991). Marcie's case also shows that it is sometimes difficult to distinguish between a traumatic specific phobia and PTSD. Typically, the nature of the event is much more extreme in PTSD, as are the range and pattern of symptoms.

Prevalence and Comorbidity

PTSD prevalence rates are 5% to 10% for adults in the United States (Kessler, Sonnega, Bromet, Hughes, & Nelson, 1996). Although prevalence rates are not available for children, PTSD appears to be common, and there is some evidence that rates are increasing (Amaya-Jackson & March, 1995). What is known is that the prevalence of PTSD is greater in children who are exposed to life-threatening events as compared with those who are not. For example, 37% of 179 children aged 2 to 15 who were exposed to the Buffalo Creek dam collapse in 1972 showed probable PTSD symptoms 2 years after the disaster (Fletcher, 1996). PTSD in children is also strongly correlated with degree of exposure. In a study of children exposed to a schoolyard sniper attack, proximity to the attack was linearly related to the risk for developing PTSD symptoms (Pynoos et al., 1987). Traumatized children frequently exhibit symptoms of disorders other than PTSD, and children with other disorders may have PTSD as a comorbid diagnosis (Famularo, Fenton, Kinscherff, & Augustyn, 1996). The PTSD that occurs in children traumatized by fires, hurricanes, or chronic maltreatment may worsen or lead to disruptive behavior disorders (Amaya-Jackson & March, 1995).

Age of Onset, Developmental Course, and Outcome

PTSD can strike a child at any age. The course of PTSD depends on the age of the child when the trauma occurred and the nature of the trauma. Since the traumatic experience is filtered cognitively and emotionally before it can be appraised as an extreme threat, how trauma is experienced will depend on the child's developmental level. Furthermore, some children appear to have different trauma thresholds: Some seem more protected; others seem more vulnerable to developing clinical symptoms after exposure to extremely stressful situations. Despite these differences, exposure to horrific events, such as war-zone stress, torture, or rape, are experienced as traumatic by nearly all children. Among the specific traumatic events that have been associated with the onset of PTSD in children are Hurricane Hugo, the Jupiter cruise ship disaster, and the Oklahoma City bombing. Other events, such as criminal violence, serious accidents, and painful medical procedures, have also been connected with PTSD.

As many as 30% of children who experienced Hurricane Andrew reported severe levels of PTSD symptoms. In fact, many children thought they might die during the storm. Although PTSD symptoms declined over time following the hurricane, a significant number of children continued to report many symptoms at the end of the school year. About 12% of the children continued to report severe to very severe levels of PTSD symptoms nearly a year following the disaster, most commonly those related to reexperiencing the trauma. Even among the 90% of the children who were on the road to recovery, more than 75% reported at least one PTSD symptom 10 months after the hurricane (La Greca, Silverman, Vernberg, & Prinstein, 1996). Several factors appear to be important in predicting children's course of recovery from PTSD following exposure to a natural disaster: exposure to traumatic events during and after the disaster; children's prior demographic characteristics; the occurrence of major life stressors; the availability of social support; and the types of strategies used to cope with disaster-related distress (La Greca, Silverman, Vernberg, & Prinstein, 1996). These factors are highlighted in Figure 7.2.

Efforts to help children cope with their feelings and reactions following a disaster often focus on these same factors (see Box 7.3).

Longitudinal findings suggest that PTSD can become a chronic psychiatric disorder, persisting for decades and sometimes for a lifetime (Fletcher, 1996; Nader, Pynoos, Fairbanks, & Frederick, 1990; Terr, 1983). Children

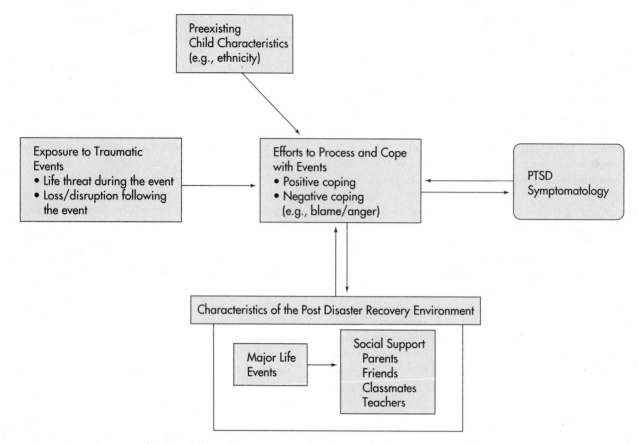

FIGURE 7.2 Predicting children's reactions to Hurricane Andrew. (Adapted from La Greca et al., 1996)

with chronic PTSD may display a developmental course marked by remissions and relapses. In a delayed variant of PTSD, individuals exposed to a traumatic event may not exhibit PTSD until months or years afterwards. A situation that resembles the original trauma in a significant way triggers the onset of PTSD. For example, dating violence at a later age may contribute to the development of PTSD in a survivor of childhood abuse.

ACUTE STRESS DISORDER

The essential feature of an **acute stress disorder** is the development of characteristic anxiety, dissociative, and other symptoms that occur within 1 month following exposure to an extreme traumatic stressor. Either while experiencing the traumatic event or after the event, the individual has at least three of the following dissociative symptoms: a subjective sense of numbing and detachment or an absence of emotional responsiveness; derealization; a reduced awareness of surroundings; depersonalization; or dissociative amnesia. Following the trauma, the event is persistently reexperienced, and the child displays marked avoidance of stimuli that arouse memo-

ries of the trauma. These disturbances last for at least 2 days, but do not persist beyond a month following the trauma (APA, 1994). The major distinction between an acute stress disorder and PTSD is that the former is short-lived, whereas the latter has long-lasting effects.

ASSOCIATED CHARACTERISTICS OF ANXIETY DISORDERS

Cognitive Disturbances

For most children, growth in cognitive maturity is associated with a reduction in fears. However, children with anxiety disorders continue to evaluate nonthreatening events as threatening, suggesting a disturbance in how these children perceive and process information.

Intelligence and Academic Achievement. Children with anxiety disorders are typically of normal intelligence, and there is little evidence for a strong relationship between anxiety and overall IQ. Although not related to general intelligence, excessive anxiety may be related to deficits in specific areas of cognitive

Box 7.3
Helping Children Following a Disaster

❖ A catastrophe such as an earthquake, hurricane, tornado, fire, or flood is frightening to children and adults alike. It is important to acknowledge the frightening parts of the disaster when talking with a child about it. Falsely minimizing the danger will not end a child's concerns.

❖ The way children see and understand their parents' response is very important. Children are aware of their parents' worries most of the time, but they are particularly sensitive during a crisis. Parents should admit their concerns to their children, and also stress their abilities to cope with the situation.

❖ A child's reaction also depends on how much destruction he or she sees during and after the disaster. If a friend or family member has been killed or seriously injured, or if the child's school or home has been severely damaged, there is a greater chance that the child will experience difficulties.

❖ A child's age affects how the child will respond to the disaster. For example, six-year-olds may show their concerns about a catastrophe by refusing to attend school, whereas adolescents may minimize their concerns but argue more with parents and show a decline in school performance.

Source: American Academy of Child and Adolescent Psychiatry, 1995. Adapted from *Facts for Families #36: Helping Children After a Disaster.*

functioning, such as memory, attention, and speech or language. High levels of anxiety can interfere with academic performance. A study of over 1000 first-grade children found that children with high anxiety were about 4 times as likely to be in the lowest 25% of their class in reading and twice as likely to be in the lowest 25% in math as those with low anxiety (Ialongo, Edelsohn, Werthamer-Larsson, Crockett, & Kellam, 1994). A follow-up study of these children found that anxiety in the first grade predicted anxiety in the fifth grade, and significantly influenced fifth-grade achievement (Ialongo, Edelsohn, Werthamer-Larsson, Crockett, & Kellam, 1995). These findings establish a connection between anxiety and academic functioning but do not identify the specific mechanisms involved. These could include anything from frequent absences to direct interference on cognitive tasks, such as writing a test or solving a math problem.

Attentional Biases.
Children with anxiety disorders selectively attend to information that may be potentially threatening, a tendency referred to as anxious vigilance or hypervigilance. High-anxious children have been found to selectively shift their attention toward threatening stimuli, in contrast to low-anxious children (especially boys), who shift their attention away from threatening stimuli. This attentional bias is not specific to the content of the threat (social versus physical), suggesting that the bias extends across a wide class of potentially threatening stimuli (Vasey, El-Hag, & Daleiden, 1996). The bias of anxious children to attend to threatening stimuli may seem inconsistent with their extreme avoidance behavior. However, although these children are quick to notice threatening stimuli, they are equally quick to avoid these stimuli once detected. In one study, the extent of looking away (gaze aversion) by children as they watched videotapes of positive, neutral, or negative (threatening) cues (face of another child looking happy, neutral, or afraid) was evaluated. Children with low perceived control, a characteristic associated with anxiety, showed greater attentional disengagement when exposed to threatening cues (Cortez & Bugental, 1994, 1995). Thus, attention allocation in anxious children seems to occur in two stages. The first involves a rapid and involuntary process that shifts the child's attention toward threatening stimuli; the second reflects a somewhat slower and more voluntary process of avoidance, in which attention is shifted away from the perceived threat once it is detected. Anxious vigilance is maintained because it permits the child to avoid potentially threatening events via early detection, with minimal anxiety and effort. Although this may benefit the child in the short term, it has the unfortunate long-term effect of maintaining and heightening anxiety by interfering with the elaborative information-processing and coping responses that are needed for the child to learn that many potentially threatening events are not so dangerous after all (Vasey et al., 1996).

Cognitive Errors and Biases.
A variety of cognitive errors and biases have been identified in children with anxiety disorders (Bell-Dolan, 1995; Bell-Dolan & Wessler, 1994). In the context of a clear general threat, both normal and anxious children use rules to confirm information about danger and play down information about safety. However, high-anxious children often do this in the face of less obvious threats, suggesting that their perceptions of threat are sufficient to activate a danger-confirming reasoning strategy. In one study, school-age children were read words that could have two meanings—one negative, the other neutral. Examples of such homophones (i.e., words that sound alike but have different meanings) are *die* and *dye*, *pain* and *pane*. Children were asked to write the word exactly as they heard it. Children with higher levels of general anxiety showed

a bias toward selecting threatening interpretations of homophones (Haldwin, Frost, French, & Richards, 1997). Anxious children are also more likely to interpret ambiguous social situations with adults and peers as threatening (Bell-Dolan, 1995; Chorpita, Albano, & Barlow, 1996). You may recall from our discussion of children with conduct problems in Chapter 6 that they too put a negative spin on ambiguous social situations. The main difference is that anxious children select avoidant solutions in response to perceived threat whereas children with conduct problems select aggressive ones.

Anxious children generally engage in more negative self-talk than do nonanxious children—for example, "If I speak, everyone will know how stupid I am" or "I won't be able to handle this." However, positive self-talk does not distinguish anxious children from controls, suggesting that anxious children have an internal dialogue that is more negative, but not necessarily less positive, than that of other children (Treadwell & Kendall, 1996).

Physical Symptoms

As we have seen, many children with anxiety disorders have somatic complaints, such as stomachaches or headaches. These complaints are more common in youngsters with PD and SAD, and less common in those with a specific phobia. Somatic complaints are also more frequent in adolescents than in younger children, and in children who display school refusal. Children with anxiety disorders also experience sleep disturbances. Some children may experience **nocturnal panic,** or an abrupt waking from sleep in a state of panic that is similar to a daytime panic attack. Nocturnal panic attacks usually occur in adolescents who suffer from PD. These attacks interfere with a return to sleep and are vividly recalled the next day (Craske & Rowe, 1997).

Can excessive worry and anxiety actually stunt a child's growth? Or are children who are short likely to experience anxiety because of the premium that our society places on height? Most likely, it's an interaction. It is possible that some individuals with a growth hormone deficiency may be at high risk for the development of anxiety disorders, particularly social phobia and panic disorder, but further research is needed to confirm this (Uhde, 1994). A recent study found that girls with anxiety disorders were about half as likely as other girls to reach an adult height of greater than 5 feet 2 inches (Pine, Cohen, & Brook, 1997). However, there was no relation between anxiety and height in boys, suggesting different biological responses to stress for the two sexes. These findings suggest that anxiety disorders in girls may be related to growth hormone abnormalities, but the mechanisms underlying this relationship are not known at this time.

Social Deficits

Since social expectancies of anxious children are distorted toward seeing threat and danger in social situations such as entering a new peer group, it's not surprising that they may anticipate difficulties in their interactions with other children (Chansky & Kendall, 1997). In fact, children with anxiety disorders report negative social expectancies, low social competence, and high social anxiety, and their parents and teachers are likely to view them as socially maladjusted (Chansky & Kendall, 1997; Strauss, Frame, & Forehand, 1987; Strauss et al., 1989). Relative to their peers, these children are more likely to see themselves as shy and socially withdrawn, and to report low self-esteem, loneliness, and difficulties in starting and maintaining friendships. Findings regarding how children with anxiety disorders are viewed by other children are mixed (Kendall, Panichelli-Mindel, Sugarman, & Callahan, 1997). It appears that childhood anxiety disorders are most likely to be associated with diminished peer popularity when these disorders coexist with depression (Strauss, Lahey et al., 1988).

Accompanying Disorders and Symptoms

We have already discussed comorbidities in relation to each anxiety disorder, and it is important to keep in mind that a child's risk for accompanying disorders will vary with the type of anxiety disorder (Kendall & Brady, 1995). The frequent association of anxiety and depression (see Chapter 8) merits further discussion.

Anxiety and Depression. The relationship between anxiety and depression in children is undeniable. But how are they related? For example, are anxiety and depression the same disorder with different clinical features, are they on a continuum of severity, or are they distinct disorders with different causes but some overlapping features?

Children with concurrent anxiety and depression are older at age of presentation, and in most cases the symptoms of anxiety precede those of depression (Brady & Kendall, 1992). However, this may depend on type of depression. For example, anxiety disorders are 6 times more likely to precede major depression than dysthymia (Curry & Murphy, 1995). Recent work suggests that anxiety and depression form a single indistinguishable dimension in younger children, but become increasingly distinct in older children and children with at least one diagnosable disorder (Gurley, Cohen, Pine, & Brook, 1996). There is an extremely high correlation between anxiety and depression in third-graders but a much smaller one in sixth-graders (Cole, Truglio, & Peeke,

1997). Depression is also more likely to be diagnosed with certain types of anxiety disorders than with others—social phobia, GAD, and SAD are more commonly associated with depression than is specific phobia. Depression is also more commonly diagnosed in children with multiple anxiety disorders and in those who show severe impairments in their everyday functioning (Bernstein, 1991).

The concept of negative affectivity is useful in understanding the nature of the link between anxiety and depression (King, Ollendick, & Gullone, 1991a; Wolfe & Finch, 1987). **Negative affectivity** refers to a persistent negative mood, as reflected in nervousness, sadness, anger, and guilt. In contrast, **positive affectivity** includes states such as joy, enthusiasm, and energy. Negative affectivity correlates with both anxiety and depression, whereas positive affectivity is negatively correlated with depression but unrelated to anxiety symptoms and diagnoses (Watson, Clark, & Carey, 1988). In general, depressed and anxious children do not differ in their degree of depressed affect (e.g., being sad and lethargic, or feeling alone and isolated), suggesting that a general underlying dimension of negative affectivity is common to both anxiety and depression. The difference between children who are anxious and those who are depressed may be the presence of greater positive affectivity in children who are anxious (Lonigan, Carey, & Finch, 1994). Studies into the negative emotional symptoms of children who are clinically anxious generally support three distinct constructs—anxiety, depression, and fear—with anxiety corresponding to negative affect, depression to low positive affect, and fear to physiological over-arousal (Chorpita, Albano, & Barlow, 1998; Joiner, Catanzaro, & Laurent, 1996).

GENDER, ETHNICITY, AND CULTURE

Recent studies of community samples have found a preponderance of anxiety disorders in girls as compared with boys during childhood and adolescence (Lewinsohn, Gotlib, Lewinsohn, Seeley, & Allen, 1998). By age 6, twice as many girls as boys have experienced an anxiety disorder, and this discrepancy persists through childhood and adolescence. In adolescents, gender differences in symptoms and diagnoses of anxiety cannot be accounted for solely by psychosocial factors (e.g., stress, self-perceived social competence, emotional reliance), suggesting a female vulnerability to anxiety related to genetic influences rather than purely environmental ones (e.g., differing social roles and experiences) (Lewinsohn et al., 1998). These findings need to be interpreted cautiously, however, since the possibility that girls are more likely than boys are to *report* anxiety cannot be ruled out as an alternative explanation. Interestingly, few differences between male and female adolescents in symptoms of anxiety are found among youngsters who have never experienced a diagnosable anxiety disorder—the gender difference occurs only when females who are vulnerable to an anxiety disorder are included in the sample (Lewinsohn et al., 1998).

Research into the relationship between ethnic and cultural factors and childhood anxiety disorders is quite limited. The underrepresentation of minorities and lower SES children for certain anxiety disorders (e.g., OCD) could reflect a bias in which minority children are less likely to be referred for treatment (Neal & Turner, 1991). Although early studies reported differences in fears in African-American versus white youngsters, more recent findings suggest that the number and nature of fears are more similar than different across groups (Ginsburg & Silverman, 1996; Treadwell, Flannery-Schroeder, & Kendall, 1994). Among children *referred* for anxiety disorders, whites are more likely to present with school refusal and higher severity ratings, while African-Americans are more likely to have a history of PTSD and a somewhat greater number of fears (Last & Perrin, 1993). Although anxiety may be similar in the two groups, patterns of referral, help-seeking behaviors, diagnoses, and treatment processes are likely to differ. For example, African-Americans may be more likely to turn to members of their informal social network, such as clergy, or to medical personnel than to mental health professionals, for help with their child's OCD symptoms and to have family members who are less likely to be drawn into the child's OCD symptoms (Hatch, Friedman, & Paradis, 1996). Although ethnicity is not related to outcomes in the treatment of anxiety disorders, it may be related to premature termination of treatment (Kendall & Flannery-Schroeder, in press).

Research comparing phobic and anxiety disorders in Hispanic and white children finds marked similarities on most measures, including age at intake, gender, primary diagnoses, proportion of school refusal, and proportion with more than one diagnosis. Hispanic children are more likely to have a primary diagnosis of SAD and are more likely to come from families with lower incomes. Hispanic parents also rate their children as more fearful than do white parents (Ginsburg & Silverman, 1996).

Studies of Native American children are virtually nonexistent. Recent prevalence estimates from a study of American Indian youth in Appalachia (mostly Cherokee) indicate rates of anxiety disorders similar to those for white youth, with the most common disorder for both groups being SAD. Rates of SAD were slightly higher for American Indian youth, especially for girls (Costello, Farmer, Angold, Burns, & Erkanli, 1997).

Although cross-cultural research into anxiety disorders in children is limited, specific fears in children have been studied and documented in virtually every culture. Cross-cultural comparisons have found that species-related developmental fears (e.g., a fear of loud noises or of separation from the primary care-giver during infancy) occur in children of all cultures at about the same age. The details may vary from culture to culture, but in general the number of fears in children tends to be highly similar across cultures as does the presence of gender differences in the pattern and content of children's fears. Nevertheless, the expression and developmental course of fear and anxiety may be affected by culture. For example, cultures that favor inhibition, compliance, and obedience serve to increase levels of fear in children (Ollendick, Yang, King, Dong, & Akande, 1996). For example, the pressures of Chinese cultural values (e.g., human malleability and self-cultivation) may cause heightened levels of general distress and increased levels of specific fears (e.g., social evaluative) (Dong, Yang, & Ollendick, 1994).

THEORIES AND CAUSES

All children experience fears and anxiety as a normal part of growing up—some to an extreme. Why do some children outgrow or cope with their fears and anxieties while others do not? Over the years numerous theories and causes have been proposed to explain the origins of fear and anxiety in children, including anxious and harsh parenting practices, conditioning, and instinct. The study of fear and anxiety in children dates back to Freud's (1909/1953) classic account of the case of Little Hans, Watson and Rayner's (1920) conditioning of a fear in Little Albert, and Bowlby's (1973) monumental works on early attachment and loss. Although each of these theories and its usefulness to understanding fear and anxiety in children has been debated since it was introduced, all have had a lasting impact on how we think about anxiety.

Early Theories

Classical psychoanalytic theory viewed anxieties and phobias as defenses against unconscious conflicts that are rooted in the child's early upbringing. Certain drives, memories, and feelings are so painful that they must be repressed and displaced onto an external object or symbolically associated with the real source of anxiety. Thus, anxiety and phobias protect the child against unconscious wishes and drives. Freud's most famous case of a phobia was little Hans, a 5-year-old boy who feared horses. According to Freud, little Hans unconsciously felt that he was in competition with his father for his mother's love and feared his father's revenge (the Oedipus complex). Hans's fear was repressed and displaced onto horses, a symbol of his castrating father. Having something specific to fear—a horse—was less stressful for Hans than suffering from anxiety without any awareness of the source.

Behavioral and learning theories emphasized that fears and anxieties were learned via classical conditioning. In the case of Little Albert (described in Chapter 1), Watson and Rayner (1920) had created what looked very much like a rat phobia, thereby claiming that fears were learned by association. Operant conditioning, another type of learning, has been used to explain why fears persist once they are established. The principle is that behavior will continue if it is reinforced or rewarded. Once something has become frightening, there is the automatic reward of instant relief whenever the child avoids the feared object or situation. Thus, through a process of negative reinforcement, avoidance of a feared stimulus becomes a learned response, which serves to maintain the child's fear even in the absence of exposure. The combination of classical and operant conditioning in the learning and maintenance of fears is called the "two-factor theory" (Mowrer, 1947).

Bowlby's theory of attachment (1973) presents a very different explanation for children's fears. According to attachment theory, fearfulness in children is biologically rooted in the emotional attachment needed for survival. Infants must be close to their care-givers if their physical and emotional needs are to be met. Attachment behaviors, such as crying, fear of strangers, and distress, represent active efforts by the infant to maintain or restore proximity to his or her care-giver. Separation gradually becomes more tolerable as the child gets older. However, children who are separated from their mothers too soon, who are treated harshly, or who fail to have their needs met in a consistent way show atypical reactions to separation and reunion, or insecure attachments. These early insecure attachments become internalized as working models of how children see the world and people in it. Children who come to view the world and people as undependable, unavailable, hostile, or threatening may develop later anxiety and avoidance behavior.

These different theories call attention to the many factors that contribute to fears and anxieties in children. No single theory is sufficient to explain the many different forms of anxiety disorder in children, the differences among children in the expression of these disorders, or the variations in outcomes over time. Current models of anxiety emphasize the importance of interacting biological and environmental influences (Albano et al., 1996; Barlow, 1988). It is also important to recognize that different causal models may be needed for different anxiety disorders. For example, the mechanisms in disorders such as panic appear to be different from those for GAD. Clearly articulated causal models for anxiety disorders in children are just beginning to emerge.

Temperament

One of the authors of this book was recently visiting with a group of preschool children from the campus day care center when he noticed a little Caucasian boy slowly sneaking up behind a little Chinese girl who was walking in front of him. The boy came to within 2 feet of the girl, his presence still undetected, stopped, and then screamed at the top of his lungs, "Boo!" Even though I saw it coming, the intensity of the boy's scream startled me a bit. However, much to my surprise, the intended victim showed hardly any reaction. Instead, this pint-sized version of Xena the Warrior Princess *paused for a moment, slowly turned, looked at the boy (who appeared dumbfounded by this unexpected display of fearlessness), and with a relaxed smile on her face, calmly said, "I'm used to that sort of thing." She then turned and continued on her way, with the little boy trailing behind like a puppy dog (I think he was in love).*

The lesson of this story is that children (and adults) differ markedly in their reactions to novel or unexpected events, perhaps because of their wiring, gender, cultural background, prior experience (in this example, perhaps with a pesky little brother?), or a combination of these and other factors. How would you react if someone snuck up behind you and yelled "BOO!!"?

A readiness to react to unfamiliar or discrepant events (like someone sneaking up behind you and yelling) is a distinguishing feature of all mammals. Orienting, attending, vigilance, wariness, and motor readiness in response to the unfamiliar are important mechanisms for survival. From an evolutionary perspective, abnormal fears and anxieties are partly rooted in variation among infants in their initial behavioral reactions to novelty. As noted by Jerome Kagan, of Harvard University:

The behavioral reactions to unfamiliar events are basic phenomena to all vertebrates. Four-month-old infants who show a low threshold to become distressed and motorically aroused to unfamiliar stimuli are more likely than others to become fearful and subdued during early childhood, whereas infants who show a high arousal threshold are more likely to become bold and sociable. (Kagan, 1997, p. 139)

This variation is a reflection of inherited differences in the neurochemistry of structures in the brain that are thought to play an important role in detecting discrepant events (Kagan, Snidman, Arcus, & Reznick, 1994). These include the excitability of the amygdala and its projections to the motor system, the cingulate and frontal cortex, the hypothalamus, and the sympathetic nervous system. As described in Box 7.4, children who have a high threshold to react to novelty with fear, such as the little girl in the story, are presumed to be at low risk for developing anxiety disorders. In contrast, those who display a low threshold to novelty, and react with fear and distress, avoidance, cessation of ongoing activity, and crying may be at risk for the development of later anxiety disorders. These children have been called high-reactive, inhibited, timid, or shy.

Is there any evidence to link early temperament with later anxiety symptoms or anxiety disorders? One study

Early differences in temperament may predispose some children to develop anxiety disorders.

Box 7.4

Born to Be Fearful? Infant Reactivity and Fearful Behavior

In a groundbreaking study, Jerome Kagan found that about 20% of 4-month-old infants became very active and distressed to presentations of brightly colored toys moved in front of their faces, recordings of voices speaking brief sentences, and cotton swabs dipped in alcohol that were applied to their noses. These infants were described as **high reactive–inhibited**. In contrast, 40% of the infants remained relaxed and did not fuss or cry in response to the same unfamiliar events. These infants were described as **low reactive–uninhibited**. The differences between these two groups were interpreted as a reflection of variation in the excitability of the amygdala and its projections to other areas of the brain.

When high and low reactive infants were observed in a variety of unfamiliar laboratory situations at 14 and 21 months, about one-third of the high reactives were highly fearful. In contrast, only 4% of the low reactive group displayed high levels of fear. When these children were 4 and 5 years old, the high reactives talked less and smiled less often in a novel laboratory situation than did the low reactives, indicating higher levels of fear.

However, only a small proportion of children maintained their extreme reactions from 4 months to 4–5 years. For example, only about 20% of the high reactives show a high level of fear at both 14 and 21 months and low comments and smiles at 4–5 years. Presumably this lack of stability was due to intervening family influences. In stark contrast, not one low reactive infant showed a consistently fearful and emotionally subdued profile and only one low reactive infant manifested a consistently uninhibited profile. Thus it was very uncommon for one temperament type to develop and maintain the core features of the other type, but quite common for each type to develop a profile characteristic of the less extreme child who is neither timid nor very bold.

High reactive-inhibited infants who become very inhibited 4-year-olds (about 20% of all high reactives) have a low threshold for developing a state of fear to unfamiliar events and people. Are these children at higher risk for developing an anxiety disorder when they become adolescents or adults? If so, which type? Interviews with 13–14 year-old adolescents suggested that social phobia was more frequent among inhibited than uninhibited adolescents, whereas specific phobias, separation anxiety, or compulsive symptoms did not distinguish the two groups.

Source: Adapted from Kagan, 1997.

---

examined the relationship between early temperament and the development of anxiety symptoms over a 12-year period in 800 children. Boys who were confident and eager to explore new situations at age 5 were the least likely to show anxiety in childhood and adolescence. In contrast, 3- to 5-year-old girls who were passive, fearful, and shy, and who avoided novel situations were the most likely to experience anxiety at a later age (Caspi, Henry, McGee, Moffitt, & Silva, 1995). Other research has found that children initially classified as behaviorally inhibited are more likely to develop multiple psychiatric disorders and to have two or more anxiety disorders (Biederman et al., 1993a, 1993b), most commonly social phobia, SAD, and agoraphobia (Rosenbaum, Biederman, Hirshfeld, Bolduc, & Chaloff, 1991a; Rosenbaum et al., 1992). It seems clear that some babies are born with a tendency to become overexcited in response to novel stimulation, that this tendency to withdraw is an enduring trait for some children, and is a possible risk factor for the development of anxiety disorders (Rubin & Stewart, 1996).

However, the road from an inhibited temperament in infancy to a later anxiety disorder is neither direct nor straightforward. Although inborn infant reactivity may contribute to later anxiety disorders, it is not an inevitable outcome. Such an outcome for an inhibited child likely depends on whether or not the child grows up in an actualizing environment (Kagan, Snidman, & Arcus, 1992). For example, at age 2 over 40% of highly reactive infants are typically behaviorally inhibited. However, Kagan's research found that *not one* of the highly reactive excitable infants whose parents imposed firm limits on his or her behavior became fearful at age 2. Thus, firm limits that teach children how to cope with stress may reduce their risk for anxiety. In contrast, it is possible that well-meaning but overprotective parents who shield their sensitive child from stressful events may inadvertently encourage a continuation of inhibited tendencies by preventing the child from confronting her or his fears and, by doing so, eliminating them. Such a tendency in the parents of inhibited children may become more common, since, compared with parents of uninhibited children and normal controls, these parents have a higher risk for multiple anxiety disorders, social phobia, continuing anxiety disorders (both a child and adult anxiety disorder in the same parent), and a history of childhood avoidant and overanxious disorders (Hirshfeld et al., 1992; Rosenbaum et al., 1991b). Thus, the child-rearing environment (and no doubt other environmental influences) plays an important role in mediating the developmental pathway from early inhibition to later anxiety disorders. Nevertheless, inhibited children may be at high risk not only because of their inborn temperament, but also because of their elevated risk of being exposed to a pattern of anxious, overprotective parenting (Turner, Beidel, & Wolff, 1996).

Genetic and Family Risk

Family and twin studies suggest a biological vulnerability for the development of anxiety disorders, suggesting that children's general tendencies to be inhibited, tense, fearful, or uptight are inherited (DiLalla, Kagan, & Reznick, 1994). However, little research exists at present to support a direct link between specific genetic markers and specific types of anxiety disorders. However, contributions from multiple genes do seem to contribute to a proneness to develop anxiety when certain psychological and social factors are also present.

Genetic Risk. Twin studies have found that the overall concordance rates for anxiety disorders are significantly higher for monozygotic (MZ) twins than for dizygotic (DZ) twins (Andrews, Stewart, Allen, & Henderson, 1990). However, MZ twin pairs do not typically have the same types of anxiety disorders. This finding is consistent with the view that what is being inherited is a disposition to become anxious, with the form that the disorder takes being a function of environmental influences. Among specific anxiety disorders in adults, a heritability estimate of about 30% has been reported for GAD (Kendler, Neale, Kessler, Heath, & Eaves, 1992a), and GAD tends to run in families (Noyes et al., 1992). Studies of OCD, also with adults, support the heritability of a dimension of neurotic anxiety, but not specifically of OCD (Rasmussen & Eisen, 1992). Similarly, the family aggregation of agoraphobia, social phobia, situational phobia, and specific phobia in adults is most consistent with the notion of a general phobia proneness (Kendler, Neale, Kessler, Heath, & Eaves, 1992b).

Variants in the serotonin transporter gene (5-HTT) have recently been implicated in anxiety-related personality traits in adults. Although they account for only a small amount of inherited variance, these variants are of interest because transporter-facilitated uptake of serotonin has been implicated in anxiety in humans and in animal models, and is the site of action of widely used antianxiety and antidepressant medications (Lesch et al., 1996).

Family Risk. Two lines of evidence suggest that anxiety disorders run in families. First, parents of children with anxiety disorders have increased rates of current and past anxiety disorders. Second, children of parents with anxiety disorders have an increased risk for these anxiety disorders. There is an increased risk of anxiety disorders in the relatives of children with anxiety disorders when compared with relatives of normal con-

trol children and with relatives of children with other psychiatric disorders (Last, Hersen, Kazdin, Finkelstein, & Strauss, 1987). For example, up to 20% of youths with OCD have parents who also have the disorder, with an additional 50% of parents displaying some OCD symptoms (Piacentini & Graae, 1997). In general, family studies of children with anxiety disorders clearly show a relationship between the disorder in the child and the presence of anxiety disorders in first-degree relatives. However, even though there is a higher prevalence of these disorders, they are not necessarily the *same* anxiety disorders. In other words, there is no one-to-one correspondence between the type of disorder displayed by the child and the one displayed by the parent. Once again, what is carried in families seems to be a general disposition for anxiety.

Children of parents with anxiety disorders are about 5 times more likely to have anxiety disorders than are children of parents without anxiety disorders (Beidel & Turner, 1997). However, the risk is not for one specific type (e.g., the one displayed by the parent). Whereas children of parents with anxiety disorders have primarily anxiety disorders (most commonly GAD), children of parents who are depressed, or who suffer from mixed anxiety and depression, have a variety of disorders. For example, children of parents with a social phobia may develop GAD (30%), social phobia (24%), SAD (20%), specific phobia (13%), or PTSD (7%) (Mancini, van Ameringen, Szatmari, Fugere, & Boyle, 1996).

Nearly 70% of children of parents with agoraphobia meet diagnostic criteria for internalizing disorders, such as anxiety and depression, and report more fear and anxiety and less control over various risks than do children of comparison parents. Mothers with agoraphobia report more separation anxiety than comparison mothers, and maternal separation anxiety is negatively correlated with children's perceived control. However, the fears of parents with agoraphobia and the fears of their children are no more closely aligned than those of nonanxious parents and their children, once again supporting the view that it is a general predisposition for anxiety that is perpetuated in families (Capps, Sigman, Sena, & Henker, 1996).

Neurobiological Factors

Anxiety is associated with specific brain circuits and neurobiological processes (Sallee & Greenawald, 1995). The part of the brain most often connected with anxiety is the limbic system, which acts as a mediator between the brain stem and the cortex. Potential danger signals are monitored and sensed by the more primitive brain stem, which then relays these potential danger signals to the higher cortical centers via the limbic system. There is a brain circuit leading from the septal and hippocampal areas in the limbic system to the frontal cortex. The septal-hippocampal system is innervated by noradrenergic circuits originating in the locus ceruleus, and by serotonergic circuits originating in the raphe nucleus, both located in the brain stem. This brain system has been referred to as the behavioral inhibition system and is believed to be overactive in children with anxiety disorders (Barlow & Durand, 1995).

The potential underlying vulnerability of children at risk for anxiety is most likely localized to the locus ceruleus/sympathetic system and the hypothalamic-pituitary-adrenal (HPA) axis. The HPA axis and the locus/ceruleus sympathetic system work together to provide homeostasis in the sympathetic nervous system. The locus ceruleus is the major nucleus for brain noradrenergic activity. Overactivation is presumed to lead to a fear response, and underactivity to inattention, impulsivity, and risk taking. Dysregulation of these systems appears to be related to anxiety states in children (Sallee & Greenawald, 1995).

The neurotransmitter system that has been implicated most often in anxiety disorders is the γ-aminobutyric acid-ergic (GABA-ergic) system. Other neurotransmitter systems, including the noradrenergic and serotonergic systems, have also been implicated, with some evidence that the serotonergic system may be strongly involved in anxiety. Recent evidence also implicates neuropeptides, which are generally viewed as anticipatory stress modulators whose abnormal regulation may play a role in anxiety disorders (Sallee & Greenawald, 1995).

Obsessive-Compulsive Disorder. The onset of OCD after such conditions as head trauma, encephalitis, and epilepsy suggests the role of neurobiological factors for this disorder. Additionally, there is an association between OCD and abnormal birth events, Tourette's syndrome, and toxic brain lesions. There is also a subgroup of children who develop OCD or tic symptoms following streptococcal infection. This reaction may be related to an autoimmune system response triggered when antibodies produced to counter the strep infection mistakenly attack healthy cells in the basal ganglia of the brain. This sets up an inflammatory response leading to OCD and tic disorder symptoms, a syndrome labeled pediatric autoimmune neuropsychiatric disorders and associated disorders, or PANDAS (Swedo et al., 1997).

Neuroimaging studies have also identified potential neuroanatomic substrates for OCD. Primary attention has been given to the orbitofrontal cortex, basal ganglia (specifically, the caudate nucleus), and related areas such as the cingulate. Positron-emission tomography (PET) studies have found increased glucose metabolism in the orbitofrontal and prefrontal cortex, right caudate nucleus, and anterior cingulate gyrus. Successful treatment of OCD using medication or behavior therapy has resulted in decreased activity in these areas of the brain. OCD may be associated with abnormalities in central nervous system (CNS) serotonergic activity or sensitivity for some children. This association is suggested by the effectiveness of medications that block serotonin reuptake in treating OCD and also by a relation between peripheral markers of serotonergic functioning and OCD severity and outcome (Piacentini & Graae, 1997).

Panic Disorder. Panic disorder is now generally recognized to be a physical problem with metabolic causes. Three distinct areas of the brain have been implicated: the brain stem (particularly the locus ceruleus), the limbic system, and the frontal cortex. One view is that panic attacks are triggered by stimulation of areas of the brain that control the release of adrenalin. Stimulation of the locus ceruleus produces many of the symptoms of panic, and certain antidepressants block panic attacks by reducing the rate of activity in the locus ceruleus. The limbic system is believed to mediate anticipatory anxiety. This area of the brain is rich in benzodiazepine receptors. Paths that link the brain stem with the limbic system can produce anticipatory anxiety following a panic attack. The limbic system is also sensitive to changes in blood flow caused by hyperventilation. Deep-breathing exercises and relaxation decrease anticipatory anxiety by quieting the limbic system and blocking a potential trigger for panic. (So, "take a deep breath" is good advice!) Agoraphobia is likely related to activity in the frontal cortex. Discharges from the brain stem may be interpreted by the frontal cortex as dangerous or life-threatening, and an association is made between the panic attack, environment, and thoughts. Descending pathways from the frontal cortex may enable catastrophic thoughts to stimulate the brain stem and cause further panic attacks (Papp & Gorman, 1995).

Family Influences

Surprisingly little is known about the relation between parenting styles or family factors and anxiety disorders. In early studies, parents of anxious children were described as overinvolved, intrusive, or limiting of their child's independence. Recent observations of interactions between 9- to 12-year-old children with anxiety disorders and their parents found that parents of children with anxiety disorders were rated as granting less autonomy to their children. The children rated their mothers and fathers as being less accepting (Siqueland, Kendall, Steinberg, 1996). Other studies have found that mothers of children previously identified as behaviorally inhibited are more likely to use criticism when interacting with their children, and that emotional overinvolvement is associated with an increased occurrence of SAD in these children (Hirshfeld, Biederman, Brody, & Faraone, 1997; Hirshfeld, Biederman, & Rosenbaum, 1997). These findings generally support the notion of excessive parental control as a parenting style associated with anxiety disorders in children, although the causal role of such a style is not yet known (Rapee, 1997).

Not only do parents of children with anxiety disorders seem to be more controlling, they also have different expectations for their children. For example, mothers of children with anxiety disorders expected their children to become more upset and had lower expectations for their children's coping when they thought their child was being asked to give a videotaped speech (Kortlander, Kendall, & Panichelli-Mindel, 1997). These findings suggest that mothers of children with anxiety disorders may hold rigid beliefs with limited explanations for why their child might cope effectively. It is likely that these maternal beliefs shape, and are shaped by, interactions with the child, during which both parent and child revise their expectations and behavior as a result of feedback from the other. This mutual shaping process is supported by studies indicating that parents of anxious children may amplify their children's avoidant problem solving by reciprocating avoidant behavior during family interactions (Barrett, Rapee, Dadds, & Ryan, 1996; Dadds, Barrett, & Rapee, 1996).

Parental anxiety disorder alone may not lead to an elevated risk of anxiety disorders in children of high or middle SES parents, but may increase risk in children of low SES parents. (Beidel & Turner, 1997). These findings are consistent with the idea that some children have a general vulnerability for developing anxiety, which may be actualized in the context of specific life circumstances—in this case, the stressful conditions that often occur in low SES families. Children with an initial disposition to develop high levels of fear may be especially vulnerable to power-assertive parenting of the type frequently used by low SES parents. These children may be particularly sensitive to punishment and when exposed to physical discipline, may become hypervigilant to hostile cues and develop a tendency to react aggressively or defensively (Colder, Lochman, & Wells, 1997).

Insecure early attachments may be a risk factor for the development of later anxiety disorders (Bernstein et al., 1996; Manassis & Bradley, 1994). Mothers with anxiety disorders have been found to have insecure attachments themselves, and 80% of their children are also insecurely attached (Manassis, Bradley, Goldberg, Hood, & Swinson, 1994). Infants who are ambivalently attached have more anxiety diagnoses in childhood and adolescence (Bernstein et al., 1996). Although a risk factor, insecure attachment may be a nonspecific one in that many infants with insecure attachments develop disorders other than anxiety (e.g., disruptive behavior disorder), and many do not develop any disorders.

Developmental Pathway

In the absence of integrative models to account for the development of anxiety disorders in children, we present the following possible pathway (shown in Figure 7.3). A child begins this developmental pathway to anxiety disorder by inheriting a disposition to be anxious or fearful. This disposition interacts with early child-rearing environments and may result in an insecure early attachment. Overcontrolling and overprotective parenting styles and rigid parenting beliefs may heighten the child's risk for the development of an anxiety disorder. Children with a disposition for anxiety and an actualizing environment may feel uncertain about themselves and their ability to deal with current or upcoming events in their lives. Danger-laden beliefs in combination with a lack of confidence in one's coping ability may increase the child's vulnerability to later stressors. In effect, the child's sense that the world is not a safe or controllable place or that he or she cannot deal with events that go wrong may create a psychological vulnerability to be anxious. When the child is faced with stress, these cognitions are likely to activate tendencies to become aroused and to avoid the situation. Once anxiety occurs, it begins to feed on itself. As anxiety leads to avoidance behaviors that provide short-term relief, the process becomes self-perpetuating. The anxiety and avoidance continue long after the stressors that may have initially provoked them are gone.

TREATMENT

Candy: Dehydrated

Eleven-year-old Candy was hospitalized for dehydration. Her voice trembled and her eyes widened with fear as she described being rushed to the emergency room in an ambulance after she had fainted. She felt embarrassed that something as simple as eating was so hard for her, but it terrified her to even think about trying. Candy detested being thin, and desperately wanted to be "just like other kids." After talking with Candy, it became apparent that she dreaded eating because she was afraid of vomiting in public. Her fear began when she couldn't eat in front of other kids in the school cafeteria, but advanced quickly to her not being able to eat at all. Candy doesn't have an eating disorder—she has a severe social phobia.

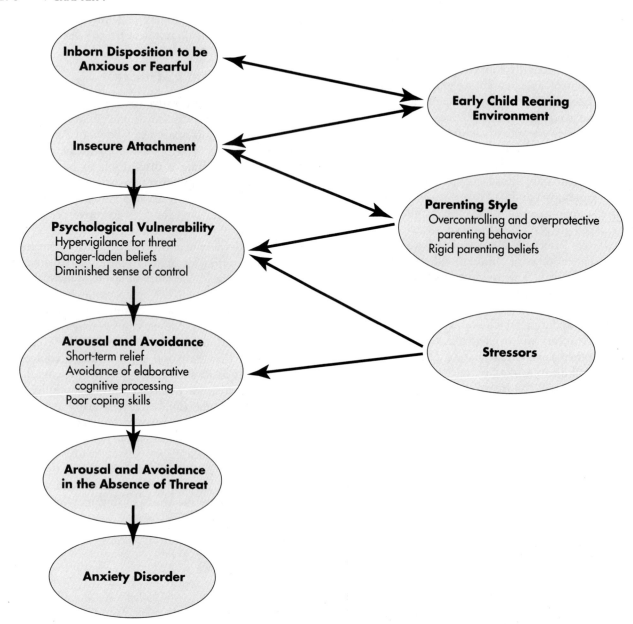

FIGURE 7.3 A possible developmental pathway for anxiety disorders.

Since most fears and anxieties of childhood are ordinary and not associated with serious disturbances, deciding when a child's anxiety is serious enough to warrant treatment is seldom easy. Although anxiety disorders are extremely disabling for the child and family, they are rarely life-threatening. If a feared object or situation is easy to avoid, children and adolescents with phobias are not likely to be brought for treatment. Because most specific childhood fears go away, few children who suffer from fears or even mild phobias get treatment. Sometimes a severe disruption to a normal routine may be needed before a parent seeks help. If a child is so afraid of spiders or dogs that she is terror-stricken when going outside, regardless of whether a spider or dog is nearby, then treatment may be needed. Treatment may also be required when families repeatedly make important decisions that interfere with family functioning in order to avoid a child's feared object or situation, such as not going camping, not traveling by airplane, or not driving on holidays. Thus, unless a child's anxiety becomes severe, as happened when Candy's social phobia led to her fear of eating, or disrupts family, school, and social functioning, anxiety may easily be overlooked and left untreated. In addition, because children with anxiety disorders can be extremely quiet, shy, compliant, eager to please, or secretive, their distress may go unnoticed.

Unlike children who provoke or offend others, children with anxiety disorders typically don't cause trouble, and as a result receive far less professional attention than children with disruptive behavior disorders. This is unfortunate, because many of these children can be helped with treatment.

In 1924, Mary Cover Jones showed that a 3-year-old boy named Peter's fears of a rabbit could be eliminated by gradually exposing Peter to the rabbit while Peter was relaxed; by having Peter watch other children play with a rabbit, and by rewarding Peter for approaching the rabbit. Many of these treatment techniques are still used today. Cognitive-behavioral treatments and, to a lesser extent, medications have enjoyed considerable success in helping children with anxiety disorders. Family-based interventions also show promise (King & Ollendick, 1997). Teaching children to use cognitive and behavioral coping skills as ways of reducing anxious avoidance also serve to increase the child's options and opportunities (Kendall, 1992). In this regard, early intervention may prevent future problems such as loss of friends, failure to reach social and academic potential, low self-esteem, and depression (Spence & Dadds, 1996).

Overview of Treatments

"Timidity will always diminish if the occasions that produce it be skillfully repeated, until they cease to cause surprize, for the timid apprehend the unexpected." (Yoritomo-Tashi, 1916)

Decades of research from almost every perspective imaginable corroborate the popular adage that the best way to defeat your fears is to face them. As noted by Yoritomo-Tashi, although the specific procedures may vary, exposing children to the situations, objects, and occasions that produce their anxiety is the main line of attack in any treatment for anxiety disorders. Reassurance, understanding what may have caused the fear, coping strategies, and mental routines can all help build confidence, but it is only by facing their fears that children become less fearful. When three-time world heavyweight boxing champion Evander Holyfield was just 17 years old, he faced his fears—and was never afraid again (see Box 7.5).

Treatments designed to help children confront their fears and anxieties are directed at modifying four primary problems (Barlow, 1988):

❖ excessive escape and avoidance behaviors
❖ emergency physiological reactions to perceived threat
❖ sense of a lack of control

Box 7.5

Evander Holyfield: The Best Way to Defeat Fear Is to Face It

Evander Holyfield, a three-time world heavyweight boxing champion, now has the reputation of having no fear of failure or injury. Was he always this way? Apparently not. In fact, Holyfield is amazed by his courage, since he used to be paralyzed by fear. From age 8, when he began boxing, until he was 17, he knew nothing but the constant anxiety of being bullied. "I was scared at everything I did, but especially boxing," he says. "I don't know how I ever got started, but I was scared. I don't know why I stayed. But I won a lot of fights, never got hurt, and as much torment as I was living in, I just assumed I would quit before I got to, say, 18. From watching the older kids box, I knew there came a time when you could get hurt, your nose would be bloody, your eye cut. I'd quit before that happened to me."

However, at 17, he suddenly found himself looking at a left hook from nowhere. Holyfield, then a slim 147 pounds of quivering nerves, was knocked unconscious, more or less, but he rose from the deck and charged his opponent. It was quite a little amateur fight.

The fight came back to him in a dream that night, after his head had cleared. He had been knocked down, yes, but he had gotten up and fought, after a fashion. Amazingly, he remembered nothing more from that experience than a numbness; it hadn't hurt at all. "I was never afraid again" he says.

Source: Adapted from *Sports Illustrated*, June 30, 1997.

❖ distorted information processing such as hypervigilance for threat and cognitive avoidance

All treatments for anxiety disorders focus on changing these central problems, but they come at them from somewhat different directions. We first present an overview of the primary treatments for anxiety disorders. Then we consider the application of these general approaches in relation to several of the specific types of anxiety disorders that we have been discussing. It is important that interventions be matched to the kinds of anxiety symptoms that each child is experiencing (Eisen & Silverman, 1993).

Primary Treatments for Children with Anxiety Disorders

Behavior Therapy. The main technique of behavior therapy for treatment of anxiety disorders is **exposure,** a procedure that bares children to what frightens them, while providing them with ways of coping with their fears other than by escape and avoidance. About 75% of children with anxiety disorders are helped by this type of treatment (Silverman & Kurtines, 1996b). Usually exposure is gradual, a procedure referred to as **graded exposure.** The child and therapist generate a list of feared situations from least to most anxiety-producing, and the child is asked to rate the amount of distress caused by each situation on a scale from 1 to 10 (called a SUDS [Subjective Units of Distress] scale or fear thermometer). The child is then exposed to each of the situations, beginning with the least distressing and moving up the hierarchy as her or his level of anxiety permits. An example of a fear hierarchy, this one for 10-year-old Wayman, who has OCD, is presented in Box 7.6.

Following is part of an exposure procedure that was used with Wayman, who included leaving his bedroom closet door open as an anxiety-provoking situation with a SUDS rating of 8. In this case, exposure was achieved by asking Wayman to imagine being in this bedtime situation. However, as we shall see, imaginal exposure is just one way of exposing the child to his or her fears.

Therapist: It is nighttime. Your parents have tucked you in and have gone to bed themselves. You reach over to shut off the light on the nightstand, and you notice that your bedroom closet door is cracked just a bit, just enough for something to crawl out and into your room. It's dark in that corner, and you think you see something. You shut off the light and lie down. You hear a strange, scratching noise coming from the closet. It sounds like something is moving. What's your SUDS rating?

Wayman: (Points to fear thermometer.) It's a seven.

Therapist: Stay with it. Tell me about what happens next.

Wayman: The closet door creaks open a bit more, and now I know that something is there. It can come get me. It's a monster.

Therapist: You begin to sweat. You want so badly to go and shut that door, but you stay in bed. You close your eyes, but the sound doesn't stop. It seems to be getting closer. You look over and see a horrible face, with red eyes staring at you. You want to scream, but you know you can't. What's your SUDS rating now?

Wayman: Eight. This is the worst part.

Therapist: Okay, good, stay with the image. Tell me what happens next.

(Adapted from Albano et al., 1995)

Another behavior therapy technique for treating children's fears and anxiety is **systematic desensitization.** This procedure consists of three steps: teaching the child to relax; constructing an anxiety hierarchy; and presenting the anxiety-provoking stimuli sequentially while the child remains relaxed. With repeated presentation, the child feels relaxed in the presence of stimuli that previously provoked his or her anxiety.

Exposure may also be carried out in prolonged and repeated doses, a procedure called **flooding.** Throughout the flooding process the child remains in the anxiety-provoking situation and provides anxiety ratings until levels of anxiety diminish. Flooding is typically used in combination with **response prevention,** which prevents the child from engaging in escape or avoidance behaviors. More than other approaches, flooding may create distress, especially during the early stages of treatment. This procedure must be used carefully, especially with younger children, who may not understand the rationale for the procedure.

In using exposure-based therapies, the feared object can be confronted in a number of different contexts, including real-life, role playing, and imaginal contexts, or by observing others come into contact with the feared object or situation (modeling). There is even evidence that exposure via virtual reality works (Rothbaum et al.,

---

Box 7.6
Sample Fear Hierarchy

Wayman: OCD

Situation	SUDS Rating
Checking class schedule	10
Leaving bedroom closet door open	8
Arranging books in bookbag	7
Arranging items in bathroom	6
Rewriting homework	5
Flipping light on and off three times	3

Source: Adapted from Piacentini, 1997.

THE FAR SIDE

By GARY LARSON

Professor Gallagher and his controversial technique of simultaneously confronting the fear of heights, snakes and the dark.

The Far Side © 1986 *Farworks, Inc.* Used by Universal Press Syndicate. All rights reserved.

1995). Although all exposure procedures are effective, real-life exposure, or **in vivo exposure**, is the *most* effective, although not always the easiest to implement. Because children actually confront their fears in real-life situations, rather than in their imagination or by watching others, in vivo exposure provides them with the most convincing evidence that they can face their fears. In effect, the child has already faced his or her fear at least once in a real-life situation with no adverse consequences, which raises confidence that he or she can do it again when the situation occurs.

Other useful behavior therapy procedures are directed at reducing the physical symptoms of anxiety. These include teaching the child muscle relaxation or special breathing exercises. One technique, for example, trains children to take slow, deep breaths to reduce anxiety. This is useful because children who are anxious often take rapid shallow breaths (hyperventilation) that can produce increased heart beat, dizziness, and other symptoms. These and other relaxation procedures are often used in conjunction with gradual exposure so that the child is better able to confront his or her fears.

Cognitive-Behavioral Therapy.

Cognitive-behavioral therapy teaches children to understand how their thinking contributes to their anxiety symptoms and how to modify their maladaptive thoughts to decrease their symptoms (Kendall & Treadwell, 1996). For example, an adolescent who becomes lightheaded during a panic attack and fears she is going to die can be helped by using the following clinical strategy: The therapist asks the child to spin in a circle until she becomes dizzy. When the child becomes alarmed and begins to think, "I'm gonna die," she learns to replace this thought with one that is more appropriate (i.e., a coping self-statement)—for example, "It's just a little dizziness—I can handle it." Giving the child an awareness of thought patterns and alternative ways of thinking is typically combined with exposure and other behavior therapy procedures, such as positive reinforcement and relaxation. Since cognitive-behavioral treatments are almost always used in conjunction with exposure based treatments, we shall discuss these further when we talk about combined interventions.

Medications.

A variety of medications have been used to treat the symptoms of anxiety in children and adolescents (Bernstein, 1994; Kutcher, Reiter, & Gardner, 1995). These medications are often used in combination with behavior therapy and cognitive-behavioral treatments. Commonly used medications for reducing anxiety symptoms include tricyclic antidepressants, benzodiazepines, and selective serotonin reuptake inhibitors (SSRIs) (Allen, Leonard, & Swedo, 1995). The demonstrated effectiveness of medications for the treatment of anxiety disorders in children is limited by the small number of controlled studies to date. However, clinical trials and studies are beginning to provide some knowledge regarding how these compounds may be used to treat anxiety in children (Kutcher et al., 1995). Findings from a recent open trial of 9- to 18-year-old youngsters with mixed anxiety disorders found that fluoxetine (Prozac) was particularly effective for the treatment of SAD and social phobia, and not very effective in treating generalized anxiety disorder (Fairbanks et al., 1997).

To date, the strongest evidence for the effectiveness of medication to treat anxiety disorders in children and adolescents is for OCD. Although the research is limited, SSRIs such as fluvoxamine and setraline have been used with some success in treating children with OCD (Piacentini & Graae, 1997). Controlled trials using SSRIs have found treatment response rates from 50% to 75%, with average symptom reductions ranging from 20% to 50%. It has been suggested that treatments that combine SSRIs with exposure plus response prevention may be most effective, since children treated with either of these alone continue to experience some OCD symptoms.

Combined approaches may also increase compliance and minimize relapse when medication is terminated (Piacentini & Graae, 1997).

Findings regarding the effectiveness of medications for treating anxiety disorders other than OCD have been inconsistent in controlled studies to date (Popper, 1993). Although clinical trials suggest the potential utility of medications in managing the symptoms of anxiety, the overall status of medications for treating specific anxiety disorders in children (other than OCD) is uncertain at this time (Kendall et al., 1997).

Family Interventions. Anxiety disorders often occur in a family context of parental anxiety and problematic family relationships, a situation that may influence the effectiveness of any of the treatment approaches. In some cases, child-focused treatment may have spillover effects into the family. For example, as children come to view themselves as more competent and less avoidant, parents' perceptions about what their child can and can't do change as well. As a result, parents may begin to respond differently to their child, and their own feelings and functioning are improved (Kendall & Flannery-Schroeder, in press). Approaches that attempt to address children's anxiety disorders in a family context may result in more dramatic and lasting effects than approaches that focus only on the child (Ginsburg, Silverman, & Kurtines, 1995; Silverman & Kurtines, 1996a). In one study it was found that nearly 70% of the children with anxiety disorders who completed individual or family treatment did not meet criteria for any anxiety disorder at post-treatment. The addition of a family component that focuses on interactions, managing emotion, communication, and problem solving significantly enhances short-term outcome and long-term maintenance (Barrett, Dadds, & Rapee, 1996). There is growing support for the utility of family-based approaches to the treatment of anxiety disorders in children (Howard & Kendall, 1996b, 1996a).

Combined Cognitive-Behavioral Treatments for Specific Disorders

Social Phobia, GAD, and SAD. The cognitive-behavioral therapy model developed by Philip Kendall and his colleagues is one of the most well-developed and carefully evaluated treatments for children and adolescents with social phobia, GAD, and SAD (Flannery-Schroeder & Kendall, 1996; Kendall & Treadwell, 1996). The approach emphasizes the role of learning processes and the influence of contingencies and models in the environment, as well as the pivotal role of information processing. Treatment is directed at decreas-

ing negative thinking, increasing active problem solving, and providing the child with a functional coping outlook. The intervention creates behavioral experiences with emotional involvement while at the same time addressing thought processes. Skills training and exposure are used to combat the problematic thinking that contributes to anxious distress and the behavioral avoidance that serves to maintain it. The training and exposure consist of a variety of techniques including modeling, role play, exposure, relaxation training, and contingent reinforcement. The therapist uses social reinforcement throughout to encourage and reward the children, and children are also taught to reward their own successful coping efforts. Through these general techniques, children learn to deal with their anxiety using the following four steps of a FEAR plan (Kendall & Treadwell, 1996):

F = Feeling frightened?
recognizing anxious feelings and somatic reactions to anxiety
E = Expecting bad things to happen?
clarifying anxious cognitions in anxiety-provoking situations (unrealistic or negative expectations)
A = Actions and attitudes that can help
developing a plan for coping (modifying anxious self-talk into coping self-talk, and identifying which coping actions might be effective)
R = Results and rewards
evaluating performance and administering self-reinforcement as appropriate

Children attend 16 to 20 sessions over a period of 8 weeks, and to enhance the skills learned in therapy, they practice using them in anxiety-producing situations at home and school. Controlled evaluations of this approach have found it to be extremely effective in the short term, with most children showing reductions in anxiety, 71% of children not having their primary diagnosis at end of treatment, and 54% not meeting criteria for any anxiety disorder at all. These gains have been maintained for periods of 1 to 3 years following treatment. Interestingly, at the time of follow-up, children's memories of the specific procedures used in the FEAR approach were correlated with successful outcomes (Kendall, 1994; Kendall & Southam-Gerow, 1996; Kendall et al., 1997).

Obsessive-Compulsive Disorder. In cognitive behavior therapy for OCD, children learn to confront their worst fears gradually while being prevented from engaging in their rituals (graded exposure plus response prevention) (Knox, Albano, & Barlow, 1991). For example, a child who is a chronic hand washer would be prevented from washing his or her hands. A hoarder would be encouraged to throw things out, starting with small amounts and working up to larger ones. A child with obsessive thoughts about violence might be asked to record the thoughts and then listen to the recordings repeatedly until they no longer make him or her anxious. The goal is to break the link between the fear and the compulsive behavior that arises from it, or between the obsessive thought and the anxiety it produces.

Initial stages of treatment focus on helping the child define obsessions and compulsions, and on developing a rank-ordered list of all the child's symptoms along with the situations in which they are most likely to occur (Piacentini & Jacobs, 1997). The child is then systematically exposed to these situations, going from least to most difficult, while being instructed *not* to engage in the compulsive behaviors. After repeated exposures, the anxiety that is associated with the situation disappears, through a process of autonomic habituation. In addition, when the feared consequences of not performing a ritual fail to occur, the child's expectations of harm disappear, which further reduces anxiety.

Treatments for OCD take from 3 to 21 months to implement, with about half the children showing a reduction in their OCD symptoms (March, 1995b). Recent approaches emphasize strategies to enhance the child's compliance with exposure tasks, including relaxation training, cognitive restructuring to increase the child's understanding of OCD, constructive self-talk, breathing techniques, positive coping strategies, therapist modeling, feedback on progress, and rewards for compliance with in-session and homework tasks (March & Mulle, 1996, 1998; Piacentini & Jacobs, 1997).

Several case reports suggest that exposure + response prevention is most effective when combined with parental involvement, and current treatments for OCD have increasingly emphasized the involvement of the family (Knox, Albano, & Barlow, 1996). Family treatment builds on the basic treatment program by actively involving family members and also by dealing with feelings that family members may be experiencing, such as helplessness in not being unable to relieve the child's pain, frustration that the child cannot "just stop," resentment that the child may be manipulating the entire family, jealousy about the amount of attention the child with OCD may be getting, and disappointment that the child is not "normal" (Piacentini, Jacobs, & Maidment, 1997).

Cognitive-Behavioral Group Treatment for Adolescent Social Phobia.

Ann Marie Albano and her colleagues have developed a group treatment program for adolescents with a social phobia (Albano & Barlow, 1996; Albano et al., 1991). Treatment is carried out in small groups of 4 to 6 teens aged 13 to 17 years and involves 16 sessions of 90 minutes duration.

The treatment includes a number of important elements. In the psychoeducational phase, children are provided with information about the nature of anxiety. A model emphasizing the cognitive, physiological, and behavioral symptoms of anxiety is presented to increase children's awareness and understanding of what provokes and maintains their anxiety. Children are taught self-monitoring to facilitate the identification of anxiety triggers and reactions. As a way to help children identify the symptoms of anxiety, they are presented with anxiety-provoking situations, such as entering a classroom late, and asked to describe their physical, cognitive, and behavioral reactions, as follows:

Therapist: What would you be feeling? (physical)

Child: Butterflies, dizziness, shortness of breath.

Therapist: What would you be thinking? (cognitive)

Child: Everyone will be looking at me. "What if the teacher yells at me? My face will be all red; they'll see it.

Therapist: What would you do? (behavioral)

Child: Skip the class. Not look up at anyone. Go to the nurse's office instead.
(Adapted from Albano et al., 1991)

In the next phase of treatment, *skill building,* teens learn *cognitive restructuring,* social skills, and problem-solving skills. With cognitive restructuring, adolescents are taught to identify cognitive distortions, or errors in thinking, that perpetuate anxiety. Systematic rational responses are developed to replace these cognitions. Modeling, role playing, and systematic exposure exercises are used.

Specific *social skills* for interpersonal interactions, maintenance of relationships, and assertiveness are identified and taught via modeling and role playing. Adolescents first identify behaviors that negatively influence social interactions, such as not smiling, turning away from the other person, making nervous gestures, not showing interest or asking questions, speaking too low or softly, criticizing others often, or ignoring others. Youngsters then practice ways of engaging in more skilled forms of social interaction (Marten, Albano, & Holt, 1991).

In the next phase of treatment, problem solving, a model for identifying problems and developing realistic goals is presented and rehearsed. In this phase, the child is taught how to cope by using a proactive approach rather than avoidance. Two therapists role-play a social anxiety producing situation, while verbalizing their automatic thoughts and rational coping responses in order to model stages of cognitive restructuring. In this role-play, one therapist verbalizes the automatic thoughts, while the second therapist acts as the "rational responder," as illustrated in the following example:

Scene: You have been called on to give a brief impromptu talk in front of your class.

T1: Oh no, I can't do this!

T2: Okay, calm down, stay cool. Don't think so negative.

T1: Everyone will be looking at me. I'll mess up.

T2: They have to do this too. We're all a little nervous.

T1: What will I say? I can't think!

T2: Okay, I can say things clearly, I know this stuff.

T1: My heart is beating so fast, I'm gonna be sick.

T2: I feel nervous, but it will pass. I'll be fine.

T1: Boy, I'm glad that's over, I'll never do this again.

T2: All right! I did it! That was okay. I made it!
(Adapted from Albano et al., 1991)

Therapists then discuss the role play with the group while drawing on the group members' experiences with similar situations.

In the *exposure* phase of treatment, children develop a fear and avoidance hierarchy of social situations, which serves as the focus of in-session exposures. Group members and therapists simulate the situations. Exposures target the behavioral avoidance and cognitive component of anxiety, showing that anxiety will dissipate via habituation. The prosocial and coping behaviors that the child learns in the group are modeled and practiced during snack-time sessions, and to enhance generalization and maintenance of treatment effects the group treatment program also includes a component for active parent participation (Marten et al., 1991).

SUMMARY

Description

1. Anxiety disorders are among the most common mental health problems in children and adolescents, but they often go unnoticed and untreated.

2. Anxiety is an adaptive emotion that prepares youngsters for coping with potentially threatening people, objects, or events. It is characterized by strong negative emotions and bodily symptoms of tension, in which a youngster apprehensively anticipates future danger or misfortune.

3. The symptoms of anxiety are expressed through three interrelated response systems: the physical system, the cognitive system, and the behavioral system.

Normal Fears, Anxieties, Worries, and Rituals

4. Fears, anxieties, worries, and rituals in children are common, change with age, and follow a predictable developmental pattern with respect to type.

The Anatomy of Anxiety: from Symptoms to Disorders

5. Specific symptoms of fear and anxiety are prevalent in children. Common groupings of symptoms, such as somatic symptoms or social fears, are referred to as dimensions of anxiety. Persistent patterns of extreme symptoms of anxiety or of generalized worries are called anxiety disorders.

An Overview of DSM-IV Anxiety Disorders

6. Anxiety disorders in DSM-IV are divided into nine categories that closely define the cause of the child's reaction and avoidance.

Separation Anxiety Disorder

7. Children with separation anxiety disorder (SAD) display age-inappropriate, excessive, and disabling anxiety about being apart from parents or away from home.

School Reluctance and Refusal

8. School refusal behavior refers to the child's refusal to attend classes or difficulty remaining in school for an entire day. It may occur for many reasons, including a fear of separation from parents or of being scrutinized by others.

Test Anxiety

9. Children who are test-anxious have a fear of being negatively evaluated when taking a test, a fear that may also occur in nonacademic settings.

Generalized Anxiety Disorder

10. Youngsters with a generalized anxiety disorder (GAD) experience chronic or exaggerated worry and tension, often accompanied by physical symptoms.

Specific Phobia

11. Children with a specific phobia exhibit an extreme and disabling fear of specific objects or situations that in reality pose little or no danger.

Social Phobia

12. Children with a social phobia have a fear of being the focus of attention or scrutiny, or of doing something that will be intensely humiliating.

Obsessive-Compulsive Disorder

13. Youngsters with obsessive-compulsive disorder (OCD) experience repeated, intrusive, and unwanted thoughts or obsessions that cause anxiety, often accompanied by ritualized behaviors or compulsions to relieve the anxiety.

Panic Attacks and Panic Disorder

14. A panic attack is a sudden and overwhelming period of intense fear or discomfort accompanied by physical and cognitive symptoms. Adolescents who experience repeated panic attacks and persistently worry about the possible implications and consequences of having another attack have a panic disorder (PD).

Posttraumatic Stress Disorder

15. Youngsters with posttraumatic stress disorder (PTSD) experience persistent, frightening thoughts that occur after undergoing a frightening and traumatic event.

Associated Characteristics of Anxiety Disorders

16. Children with anxiety disorders display deficits in specific areas of cognitive functioning, and selectively attend to information that may be potentially threatening.

17. Children with anxiety disorders report being socially withdrawn and lonely, and may be viewed as socially maladjusted by others.

18. Children with anxiety disorders frequently have other disorders, most commonly another anxiety disorder or depression.

Theories and Causes

19. Theories have viewed anxiety as a defense against unconscious conflicts, a learned response, or an adaptive mechanism needed for survival. No single theory can explain the many different forms of anxiety disorder in children.

20. Family and twin studies suggest a biological vulnerability for the development of anxiety disorders.

21. Anxiety is associated with specific brain circuits and neurobiological processes. The potential underlying vulnerability of children at risk for anxiety is most likely localized to brain circuits involving the brain stem, the limbic system, and the frontal cortex.

22. A parenting style characterized by overcontrol and rigid beliefs is the one most often associated with anxiety disorders in children.

Treatment

23. Cognitive-behavioral treatments and, to a lesser extent, medications have enjoyed considerable success in helping children with anxiety disorders. Family-based interventions also show promise.

24. Exposing youngsters to the situations, objects, and occasions that produce their anxiety is the main line of attack in treating anxiety disorders.

25. Cognitive-behavioral treatments teach children to understand how their thinking contributes to anxiety, how to change maladaptive thoughts to decrease their symptoms, and how to cope with their fears and anxieties other than by escape and avoidance.

KEY TERMS

anxiety disorder, 233

neurotic paradox, 235

anxiety, 235

fight/flight response, 235

physical system, 235

cognitive system, 235

behavioral system, 235

fear, 237

panic, 237

separation anxiety disorder (SAD), 242

school refusal behavior, 244

generalized anxiety disorder (GAD), 246

apprehensive expectation, 246

phobia, 249

specific phobia, 249

social phobia, 251

generalized social phobia, 253

selective mutism, 254

obsessive-compulsive disorder (OCD), 255

obsessions, 255

compulsions, 255

trichotillomania, 259

panic attack, 260

panic disorder (PD), 261

anticipatory anxiety, 262

agoraphobia, 262

posttraumatic stress disorder (PTSD), 263

acute stress disorder, 266

nocturnal panic, 268

negative affectivity, 269

positive affectivity, 269

high reactive-inhibited, 272

low reactive-uninhibitive, 272

exposure, 278

graded exposure, 278

systematic desensitization, 278

flooding, 278

response prevention, 278

in vivo exposure, 279

Mood Disorders

Some are unhappy through illness,
some are ill through unhappiness.
                        —Sir Walter Langdon Brown

David: Depressed

Eleven-year-old David says, "Sometimes I feel like jumping off the roof or finding some other way to hurt myself." Over the past 3 months David has become more and more withdrawn, and his feelings of sadness, worthlessness, and self-hatred scare him. David's teacher describes him as "a loner who seems very troubled and unhappy." David has always been a good student, but he is now having difficulty concentrating on schoolwork, is failing tests, and feels totally unmotivated. At home, David is having trouble sleeping, has no appetite, and frequently complains of headaches. Most days he stays in his room and does nothing. When his mother asks him to do something, David becomes extremely upset. His mother says that David is "moody and irritable most of the time."

Beth: Sad Since Childhood

"You can see it in the old family photo album when Beth was just 8 years old. That vacant stare, that sunken emptiness. She had that depressive look in her face, especially in her eyes, even then," her mother says, now almost 20 years later. "But we didn't recognize it. It was only when she was in Grade 11 and would come into our room at night crying that my husband said we had to get help for her. . . . I remember her being very withdrawn. She was very difficult to get out of bed and she refused to eat. It was extremely difficult to get her stimu-lated. She didn't want to do anything. And the summer prior to her treatment we were at the lake and Beth was crying all the time. And she was very clingy. She always had her arms around me and never wanted me to leave." (Adapted from Owen, 1993)

Mick: Sad and Manic

Sixteen-year-old Mick is moody all of the time. Sometimes he is sad, sullen, and apathetic, sometimes full of life and energy, and sometimes intensely angry. When full of energy, Mick can go with little or no sleep for days without feeling tired. His attention moves constantly from one thing to another. He talks incessantly and cannot be interrupted. These extreme changes in mood make Mick feel out of control, and sometimes he thinks about hurting himself. He is frightened by his thoughts and drinks or uses drugs when they are available to reduce the pain.

Perhaps you have known a child or adolescent who is constantly unhappy, shows little enthusiasm for anything, is moody, or, at worst, thinks that life just isn't worth living. Like David, Beth, and Mick, such a child may have a **mood disorder** (also called an affective disorder), in which a disturbance in mood is the central feature. *Mood* is generally defined as a feeling or emotion—for example, sadness, happiness, anger, elation, or crankiness. Children with mood disturbances usually suffer from extreme, persistent, or poorly regulated emotional states, such as excessive unhappiness or wide swings in mood from sadness to elation. Mood disorders come in several brands. At one end of the spectrum are children who experience a negative mood such as depression. Like David and Beth, these children suffer from prolonged bouts of sadness, referred to as dysphoria. They feel little joy in anything they do and lose interest in nearly all activities—a state known as anhedonia. In the words of one depressed teen:

> "Depression makes you lose interest in all the stuff you used to think was fun. You might quit playing guitar or drop out of yearbook, and claim that you just don't have the energy or desire to pursue extracurricular activities—or curricular activities, for that matter." (Solin, 1995, p. 156)

Many youngsters with depression express these combined feelings of sadness and loss of interest. However, you may be surprised to learn that others with depression don't report feeling sad at all. Rather, their depression is expressed through their irritable mood. "Irritability" is easy to recognize but not so easy to define. Terms used to describe children who are irritable include *cranky, grouchy, moody, short-fused,* or *easily upset.* Being around children like this is difficult because any little thing can set them off. Irritability is one of the most common symptoms of depression, occurring in about 80% of clinic-referred youngsters with depression (Goodyer & Cooper, 1993).

At the opposite end of the spectrum from depression is a smaller number of youngsters, those like Mick, who also experience episodes of mania, an abnormally elevated or expansive mood, and feelings of euphoria (an exaggerated sense of well-being). These youngsters suffer from an ongoing combination of extreme highs and extreme lows, a condition known as manic-depressive illness or bipolar disorder. Their highs may alternate with lows, or they may feel both extremes at about the same time.

Although a disturbance in emotion involving extreme lows and/or extreme highs is the hallmark of mood disorders, it is evident from the wide range of problems displayed by David, Beth, and Mick that these disorders involve much more than disturbed mood. Youngsters with mood disorders display numerous other symptoms and impairments, including cognitive disturbances, major changes in eating or sleeping patterns, poor concentration, and difficulties in daily functioning at home and school.

Although mood disorders in young people are frequent and serious problems, they often go undetected. Children with mood disorders, especially those who are depressed, may not be troublesome for their parents and teachers. Because adults may not recognize signs of mood disturbance, a child can easily fall between the cracks for a number of reasons. First, because symptoms of mood disorders may be expressed differently in children than in adults, a child with depressive or manic symptoms may be seen as quiet, irritable, or hyperactive. Second, mood disorders in children are frequently accompanied by other more visible conduct problems that make the mood disturbance more difficult to observe. Third, because mood disorders usually begin in adolescence, a turbulent time in development for most youngsters, it is difficult to know whether a teen is experiencing the normal emotional storms of this period or something more serious. Finally, many parents and teachers don't recognize mood disorders in children because they perceive these problems as adult illnesses—not something that children experience. In fact, mood disorders in children have only recently received recognition.

AN OVERVIEW OF DSM-IV MOOD DISORDERS

Mood Episodes

Four types of **mood episodes** provide the basis for diagnosing mood disorders in children and adolescents:

❖ *Major depressive episode.* A period of at least 2 weeks during which there is either a depressed mood or the loss of interest or pleasure in nearly all activities, as well as other depressive symptoms. In children, the mood may be irritable rather than sad.

❖ *Manic episode.* A distinct period of at least 1 week (or less, if hospitalization is required) in which there is an abnormally and persistently elevated, expansive, or irritable mood and other symptoms of mania.

❖ *Mixed episode.* A period of time lasting at least 1 week in which the criteria are met for both a depressive and a manic episode nearly every day. The child experiences rapidly alternating moods, from sadness to irritability to euphoria.

❖ *Hypomanic episode.* A distinct period during which there is an abnormally and persistently elevated, expansive, or irritable mood that lasts at least 4 days, accompanied by other symptoms. A hypomanic episode is not severe enough to cause marked impairment in social or occupational functioning, or to require hospitalization.

Mood Disorders

The presence or absence of one or more of the above mood episodes is used to define each of the primary mood disorders in DSM-IV (APA, 1994). Mood disorders are divided into two general categories—**depressive**

Box 8.1
Main Features of Primary Mood Disorders

DEPRESSIVE DISORDERS

Major Depressive Disorder (MDD). Characterized by one or more major depressive episodes accompanied by additional symptoms such as sleep disturbances or thoughts of suicide.

Dysthymic Disorder (DD). Characterized by at least 1 year of depressed mood (2 years in adults) for more days than not, accompanied by additional depressive symptoms that do not meet criteria for a major depressive episode.

BIPOLAR DISORDERS

Bipolar I Disorder. Characterized by one or more manic or mixed episodes, usually accompanied by major depressive episodes.

Bipolar II Disorder. Characterized by one or more major depressive episodes, accompanied by at least one hypomanic episode.

Cyclothymic Disorder. Characterized by at least 1 year (2 years in adults) of numerous periods of hypomanic symptoms that do not meet criteria for a manic episode, and numerous periods of depressive symptoms that do not meet criteria for a major depressive episode.

MOOD DISORDER DUE TO A GENERAL MEDICAL CONDITION

Characterized by a prominent and persistent disturbance in mood that is judged to be a direct physiological consequence of a general medical condition.

SUBSTANCE-INDUCED MOOD DISORDER

Characterized by a prominent and persistent disturbance in mood that is judged to be a direct physiological consequence of a drug of abuse, a medication, another somatic treatment for depression, or toxin exposure.

RELATED MOOD DISTURBANCES

Adjustment Disorder with Depressed Mood. Not a mood disorder but related. Sometimes depressive symptoms are a reaction to a stressor such as parental divorce, a move, or serious illness or accident involving the child's parent. These symptoms usually occur shortly after the stressful event, within 3 months. Although such reactions are normal, they are considered to be a disorder when they are in excess of the usually experienced reaction and when they cause significant impairment in everyday functioning. The symptoms usually remit after a period of adjustment to the new circumstances.

Bereavement. This is not a disorder but may become a focus of clinical attention in some circumstances. Bereavement following the death of a loved one is often associated with several depressive symptoms or a full depressive disorder and temporary impairment in school and social functioning. The reaction is regarded as significant if the symptoms last past a reasonable period or recur long after the loss.

Source: Based on DSM-IV 1994 by APA.

---

disorders and **bipolar disorder (BP)**. The two types of depressive disorders are **major depressive disorder (MDD)** and **dysthymic disorder (DD)**. Additionally, two other mood disorders are included in DSM-IV, when the disturbance in mood is due to either a general medical condition or to the use of a substance. Although not technically a mood disorder, adjustment disorder with depressed mood is another type of mood disturbance in which excessive depressive symptoms follow an identifiable psychosocial stressor, such as family breakup.

We discuss each of the primary mood disorders in the sections that follow. However, to give you an overall picture, the main features and a brief description of each disorder are presented in Box 8.1. The course of episodes (e.g., single episode or recurrent episodes) and the nature of the most recent episode (e.g., depressed or manic) are used to diagnose subtypes of the main mood disorders.

DEPRESSION
Description of the Disorder

"And how are you?" said Winnie-the-Pooh.
Eeyore shook his head from side to side.
"Not very how," he said. "I don't seem to have felt at all how for a long time."

A. A. Milne, Winnie-the-Pooh (1926)

Depression generally refers to a pervasive unhappy mood, the kind of gloomy feeling displayed by Eeyore, the sad and indecisive old grey donkey in *Winnie-the-Pooh*. The symptoms of depression are so universal that depression is sometimes called the "common cold of psychopathology." All of us have felt sad, blue, glum, out of sorts, or "down in the dumps" at times. (Even reading or writing about depression can be a real downer—can anyone think of a way to put a positive spin on feelings of dejection, hopelessness, worry, loneliness, or self-blame?). Sometimes our feelings of sadness are normal reactions to an unfortunate event in our lives such as the loss of a friend or a job. At other times we may feel depressed without really knowing why. These feelings soon pass, however, and we resume our normal activities. Clinical depression, in contrast, is much more than the occasional blues or mood swings that everyone gets from time to time.

Childhood is usually thought of as a happy and care-free time, a period unfettered by the worries, burdens, and responsibilities of adulthood. We tend to think of young people as having a natural tendency to be positive and upbeat, not depressed. In fact, a common reaction to hearing that a child is depressed is, "What does she have to be depressed about?" Even when children experience disappointment, disapproval, or negative events in their daily lives, as inevitably happens, their sadness, frustration, and anger are expected to be short-lived. When children become sad, irritable, or upset, parents often attribute such negative moods to temporary factors, such as a lack of sleep or not feeling well, and expect the moods to pass. So, for a long time it was thought that children didn't get depressed, and when they did, it would be short-lived. We now know differently.

Unlike most children who bounce back quickly when they are sad, children who are depressed can't seem to shake their sadness, and it begins to interfere with their daily routines, social relationships, school performance, and overall functioning. In addition to their sad mood, psychological symptoms, and impairments, depressed youngsters often experience accompanying problems, such as anxiety or conduct disorders. Thus, although clinical depression may resemble the normal emotional dips of childhood, for many youngsters, it is a pervasive, disabling, long-lasting, and life-threatening disorder.

Depression affects children and adolescents in a number of areas of functioning, including mood, behavior, changes in attitude, thinking, and physical condition (Oster & Montgomery, 1995, pp. 47–48):

❖ _Mood_. Children with depression experience feelings of sadness that are more exaggerated and more persistent than normal sad feelings. Other feelings that frequently accompany depression include irritability, guilt, shame, and oversensitivity to criticism.

❖ _Behavior_. Children with depression may display increased restlessness and agitation, reduced activity, slowed speech, and sometimes, excessive crying. These behaviors are a change from usual behavior, persist for a long time, and interfere with everyday functioning. Along with decreased activity comes a reduction in social contact. At times, youngsters who are depressed may express their sadness through aggressive or negative acts, such as verbal sarcasm, screaming, or destructive behavior. Adolescents with depression may abuse alcohol or other drugs as a way to feel better.

❖ _Changes in attitude_. Children with depression experience feelings of worthlessness and low self-esteem. They see themselves as inadequate and believe others also view them in this fashion. Worries and fears dominate their lives. Their attitudes toward school may change, and their school performance may suffer. They begin to dread the future and are convinced they are doomed to failure. "Why should I even bother?" and "What's the use in trying?" are common questions. When these thoughts and feelings intensify, the risk for suicidal behavior may increase.

❖ _Thinking_. Children with depression are preoccupied with their inner thoughts and tensions. They have a self-focus and may feel extremely self-critical and self-conscious. Thought patterns slow down, reasoning is distorted, and pessimistic views about the future are expressed. They may have difficulty concentrating, remembering, and making decisions. These children may also blame themselves for every bad outcome.

❖ _Physical changes_. Many children with depression experience disruptions in eating and sleeping. Appetite loss and early morning or frequent awakening are common, as are reports of feeling tired all the time. Comments such as, "she's always dragging" or "I feel exhausted all the time" are typical. Complaints of physical illness, such as headaches and stomachaches, nausea, aches and pains that don't go away, and loss of usual energy, also occur.

Although the primary features of mood disorders are the same in children as in adults, children may express their symptoms differently. Rather than talking directly about their feelings, children may express them through their behavior. Thus, without the more recognizable pattern of unhappiness and withdrawal that makes diagnosis relatively easy in adults, knowing when a child is depressed is not always easy. Some children with depression may look generally sad or unhappy, but do not complain of unhappiness or even seem to be aware of it. Their most noticeable symptom may be withdrawal or irritability. A child who used to play with friends may now spend most of the time alone and without interests. Activities that were once fun now bring little pleasure. The child's apathy and listlessness may appear as boredom. Depression may also be expressed in physical symptoms, as noted above.

We may think of children with depression as being tearful and quietly sobbing away alone in their rooms, but the reality is that many youngsters show their depression in other ways. As mentioned earlier, they may be irritable or cranky, and become upset by even little disappointments, such as a broken date or a lost article of clothing. Children with depression can be extremely argumentative, moody, and tearful, making it difficult for others to be around them. Some children express their disturbed mood by having temper tantrums or lashing out in anger, behaviors that may elicit anger in others, and scapegoating of the child. Acting out may be a way of avoiding the painful feelings of depression. Because the youngster may not seem sad, parents and teachers don't realize that bothersome behavior could be a sign of depression. In the words of one mother:

> "My son attempted to gain some control over his life by becoming the bad guy at school and at home.... He lashed out at everyone who came near, and we were too angry to think about the possibility that he was depressed." (Levine, 1995, pp. 42, 44)

The potpourri of negative symptoms has led some researchers to suggest, rather facetiously, that a better term for depression in young people might be "miserable mood disorder of childhood" (Reynolds & Johnston, 1994b, p. 4). The chronicity, disability, and damage associated with depression may result in lifelong struggles and even in death for some youngsters. Such a severe condition is clearly not part of normal development (Kovacs & Devlin, 1998).

Historical Background

> The hypothesis that depressive disorder exists in children awaits confirmation.... At this juncture it seems prudent to remain skeptical about the existence of adult-type major depressive disorder in children. (Quay & Werry, 1986, p. 74)

The preceding quote appeared just over 10 years ago in an authoritative textbook on childhood disorders, and attests to the fact that it was not very long ago that people doubted the very existence of depression in children. The mistaken belief that depression didn't exist in children in a form comparable to that in adults was rooted in traditional psychoanalytic theories. These theories viewed depression as resulting from hostility and anger that was turned inward, usually as a result of actual or perceived loss. However, since children lacked sufficient superego development to permit aggression to be directed against the self, it was believed that they were incapable of experiencing depression (Rochlin, 1959).

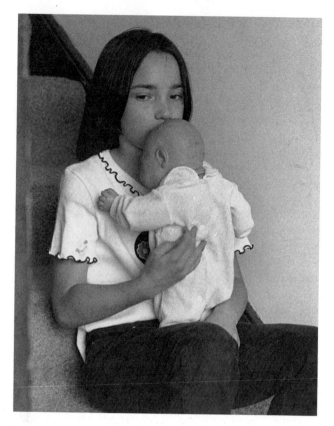

Depression in children goes well beyond normal mood swings.

Another mistaken view was that symptoms of depression were normal and passing expressions of certain stages of development or related to teenage *angst*—a belief that also has proved false. Depression in young people is a recurrent problem, just as it is for adults.

As the existence of depression in children came to be acknowledged, a popular view emerged that depression was expressed completely differently in children than in adults, often in an indirect and hidden fashion. This idea came to be known as *masked depression*. It was thought that children with depression did not display negative affect or the cognitive, psychomotor, or physical symptoms of depression. Rather, their depression was thought to be concealed by a wide array of other behaviors, referred to as *depressive equivalents*. Virtually any known clinical symptom occurring during childhood, including aggression, hyperactivity, learning problems, bed-wetting, separation anxiety, sleep problems, and running away, could be taken as a sign of an underlying but masked depression (Cytryn & McKnew, 1974). Because these concepts are too broad to be of much use, the once popular notions of masked depression have been rejected. Research has shown that depression in children isn't masked, but rather may simply be overlooked because it frequently co-occurs with other more visible disorders, such as conduct problems (Carlson &

Cantwell, 1980; Hammen & Compas, 1994). The controversy over the existence of depression in children and adolescents is now over—depression in children exists and can be diagnosed using criteria quite similar to those used for adults.

The Significance of Depression in Young People

A significant number of young people display lasting depressed mood in the face of real or perceived distress, and show other symptoms of disturbances in their thinking, physical functioning, and social behavior (Harrington, Fudge, Rutter, Pickles, & Hill, 1990). Depression in young people is also an extremely disabling disorder. For example, in one large community sample nearly 90% of 8- to 16-year-old youngsters with depressive symptoms showed a significant degree of impairment in their functioning. By contrast, although as many or more youngsters in this sample displayed symptoms of anxiety, their associated degree of impairment was substantially less than that for depressed youngsters (Simonoff et al., 1997).

Almost all children and teenagers experience some symptoms of depression, and as many as 5% of prepubertal children and 10% to 20% of adolescents experience significant depression that may not get better on its own (Reynolds & Johnston, 1994b). Suicide among teenagers, which is frequently associated with depression, has skyrocketed by 200 percent in the last decade. Even when children recover from their depression, they are likely to experience continued impairments and recurrent bouts of depression usually within a year or two (Lewinsohn, Roberts et al., 1994). The long-lasting emotional suffering of children with depression, their problems in everyday living, disruptions to their development, possible heightened sensitivity to recurring depression, and the heightened risk for substance abuse, bipolar disorder, and suicide make depression in young people a very serious concern (Reynolds & Johnston, 1994a).

The apparent rise in depression in young people (Cross-National Collaborative Group, 1992) is also a significant concern. Individuals born in the latter part of the 20th century have a greater risk for developing depression than those born earlier. Not only is depression increasing, it is also occurring at a younger age, with individuals born in the later decades of the 1900s reporting progressively younger ages of onset for their first episode of major depression than those born in earlier decades (Cross-National Collaborative Group, 1992; Kovacs & Gatsonis, 1994; Lewinsohn, Rohde, Seeley, & Fischer, 1993). The increase in prevalence and age of onset of depression appears to be primarily for mild to moderate depressions, not for the more severe melancholic types with psychomotor and physical symptoms (Birmaher et al., 1996b). Although the precise reasons for the increase in depression in young people are not known, one factor that has been implicated is rapid social change. Overcrowded cities, family breakup, increased drug use, and shifts in occupational and employment patterns may create increasing levels of stress for young people. In addition, these changes may make children more vulnerable to stress due to a loss of protective factors such as family support (Kovacs, 1997). In general, depression in young people is prevalent, disabling, increasing in frequency, occurring at an earlier age, and often underreferred and undertreated.

Depression at Different Developmental Periods

The ways in which children express and experience depression are related to their level of physical, emotional, and cognitive development. An infant may show sadness by being passive and unresponsive; a preschooler may appear withdrawn and inhibited; a school-age child may be argumentative and combative; and a teenager may express feelings of guilt and hopelessness (Herzog & Rathbun, 1982). These are not different types of depressions but likely represent different stages in the developmental course of the same process.

No one pattern fits all children within a particular age group or developmental period, and not until children get older does depression become clearly recognizable as a clinical disorder. Depression in children under the age of 7 tends to be diffuse and less easily identified than depression in older children and adolescents (Cantwell, 1990). However, it is important to be aware of depressive symptoms in young children since youngsters who develop depressive disorders in late childhood or early adolescence may experience subclinical symptoms of depression at a younger age.

We know the least about depression in infants. In the 1940s, Renee Spitz described a condition he called **anaclitic depression,** in which infants raised in a clean but emotionally cold institutional environment displayed reactions that resembled a depressive disorder, including weeping, withdrawal, apathy, weight loss, sleep disturbance, overall decline in development, and in some cases, death (Spitz & Wolf, 1946). Although Spitz attributed this depression to an absence of "mothering" and the subsequent lack of opportunity to form an attachment, other factors, such as physical illness and deprivation, may also have played a role. It also became clear that similar symptoms could occur even when infants remained in their own homes but failed to thrive because of a severely disturbed family environment in which their

Depression in institutionalized infants: a physical appearance that in an adult might be described as depression.

mother was depressed (Weissman et al., 1987), psychologically unavailable (Pianta, Egeland, & Erickson, 1989), or physically abusive (see Chapter 14). The varying symptoms occurring in infants who experience these disturbed family environments include sleep disturbances, increased clinging, crying, sadness, apprehension, decreased contact with care-givers, difficulties self-quieting, stupor, and loss of appetite.

Preschool children who are depressed may appear extremely somber and tearful. They generally lack the exuberance, bounce, and enthusiasm in their play that characterize most children of this age. These children may display excessive clinginess and whiny behavior around their mothers, as well as fears of separation or abandonment. In addition to getting upset when things don't go their way, preschool children who are depressed may also be irritable for no apparent reason. Negative and self-destructive verbalizations may occur, and physical complaints such as stomachaches are common.

In addition to the symptoms of preschoolers, children between the ages of 6 and 12 may show increasing irritability, disruptive behavior, temper tantrums, combativeness, and argumentativeness. A parent may say, "Nothing ever pleases my child—she hates herself and everything around her." School-age children may look sad, but are often unwilling to talk about their sad feelings. Other complaints may include weight loss, difficulty concentrating, headaches, and sleep disturbances. Academic difficulties, peer problems, and suicide threats may also occur. These children may complain of not having any friends or of being picked on by other children. Frequent fights with peers and inappropriate behavior in school may also occur.

In addition to the symptoms of preschoolers and school-age children, preteens may show increasing self-blame and expressions of low self-esteem, persistent sadness, and inhibition. A child may say, "I'm bad," or "I'm stupid," or "Nobody likes me." Feelings of isolation from family are also common. The preteen may experience an inability to sleep or may sleep excessively. Disturbances in eating are also common. Teenagers who are depressed often show increased irritability, loss of feelings of pleasure or interest, and worsening school performance. Angry discussions with parents regarding normal parent-teen issues, such as choice of friends or curfew, are also common. Other symptoms include a negative body image and low self-esteem and self-consciousness, excessive fatigue and energy loss, difficulty tolerating routines, physical symptoms and illness, restlessness, loneliness, self-blame and guilt, feelings of worthlessness, and suicidal thoughts and attempts.

The disturbances in mood and other behavioral symptoms that characterize youngsters with depression are summarized in Table 8.1. Since many of the symptoms and behaviors presented in this table may also occur in children who are developing normally, or in children with other disorders or conditions, the presence of dysphoric mood, loss of interest, or irritability is essential for diagnosing depression. In addition, whatever the child's age, the symptoms must reflect a change in behavior, persist over time, and cause significant impairment in functioning if they are to be used to diagnose depression.

The Anatomy of Depression: Symptom, Syndrome, and Disorder

The term *depression* has been used in different ways, sometimes referring to a specific symptom such as sadness and at other times to a clinical disorder involving a broad range of symptoms and impairments. It is important to distinguish between depression as a symptom, depression as a syndrome, and depression as a disorder (Cantwell, 1990).

As a *symptom,* depression refers to feeling sad or miserable. Depressive symptoms often occur without the existence of a serious problem and are relatively common at all ages, occurring in 15% to 40% or more of children and adolescents (Rutter, Tizard, & Whitmore, 1970). For most children, symptoms of depression are temporary, related to events in the environment, and not part of any disorder. The single symptom of "unhappy, sad, or depressed" is also one of the best discriminators of youngsters who are referred to clinics versus those who are not, suggesting that the symptom of depression occurs across a wide range of childhood problems.

As a *syndrome,* depression is more than a sad or dysphoric mood. A syndrome refers to a group of symptoms that occur together more often than by

Table 8.1 Mood Disturbances and Possible Behavioral Symptoms of Depression and Related Disorders in Children of Different Ages

Dysphoric Mood, Loss of Interest, and/or Irritability	Possible Behavioral Symptoms
0 TO 36 MONTHS	
Sad or expressionless facial appearance, gaze aversion, blank staring, bland affect, irritability	1. Somatic disorders (failure to thrive, rumination) 2. Lack of social play/responsiveness 3. Persistent irritability or lethargy 4. Separation and/or attachment problems, inability to separate, separation without reaction 5. Behavior difficulties 6. Developmental delays (especially speech and gross motor) 7. Feeding difficulties 8. Sleep difficulties
3 TO 5 YEARS	
Sad facial expression, woeful eyes, irritability, somber or labile affect	1. Somatic disorders (encopresis, enuresis, asthma, failure to thrive, stomachaches) 2. Social withdrawal 3. Excessive activity or lethargy 4. Separation problems, including school refusal 5. Aggressive behavior or passive-compliant behavior 6. Self-endangering behavior (accident-proneness, head banging) or morbid play 7. Feeding difficulties 8. Sleep difficulties
6 TO 8 YEARS	
Prolonged unhappiness, irritability, somber affect	1. Somatic complaints (vague complaints, abdominal pain) 2. Diminished socialization 3. Excessive activity or lethargy 4. Phobic behavior and/or separation problems 5. Aggressive behavior, lying, or stealing 6. Self-endangering behavior or morbid preoccupations 7. Appetite or weight changes 8. Sleep difficulties 9. School difficulties
9 TO 12 YEARS	
Sadness, apathy, helplessness, or irritability; loss of pleasure in usual activities	1. Somatic symptoms 2. Restlessness or lethargy 3. Phobic behavior and/or separation problems 4. Antisocial behavior 5. Self-endangering behavior or morbid thoughts 6. Appetite or weight changes 7. Sleep difficulties 8. Decreased ability to concentrate 9. Excessive guilt, self-deprecation 10. Low self-esteem

Source: Adapted from Herzog and Rathbun, 1982.

Continued

chance. Sadness may occur as part of a larger constellation of symptoms that includes reduced interest in activities, cognitive changes, changes in motivation, and somatic and psychomotor changes. The occurrence of depression as a syndrome is far less common than the occurrence of isolated depressive symptoms. A depressive syndrome may occur following certain kinds of life events—for example, as a normal grief reaction following the loss of a loved one. However, bereavement is regarded as a clinically significant syndrome only if the

Table 8.1 Mood Disturbances and Possible Behavioral Symptoms of Depression and Related Disorders in Children of Different Ages—cont'd

Dysphoric Mood, Loss of Interest, and/or Irritability	Possible Behavioral Symptoms
	13 TO 18 YEARS (POSTPUBERTAL)
Sadness, apathy, helplessness, or irritability; loss of pleasure in usual activities	1. Somatic symptoms (eating disturbances)
	2. Restlessness or lethargy
	3. Phobic behavior, anxiety, and/or separation problems
	4. Antisocial behavior
	5. Recurrent thoughts of death or suicide
	6. Appetite or weight changes
	7. Sleeping difficulties
	8. Decreased ability to concentrate
	9. Excessive guilt, self-deprecation
	10. Low self-esteem and self-consciousness

Source: Adapted from Herzog and Rathbun, 1982.

symptoms remain well beyond a reasonable adjustment period or begin to reoccur long after the loss has occurred. The syndrome of depression can also occur along with or secondary to other disorders, such as anxiety, conduct disorder, ADHD, and schizophrenia.

As you may recall from our discussion in Chapter 7, the symptoms of anxiety and depression show much overlap in young people (Seligman & Ollendick, 1998), and often cluster on a single dimension of negative affect. As shown in Table 8.2, empirically derived syndromes of depression often include mixed symptoms of anxiety and depression.

When viewed as a *disorder,* depression involves a depressive syndrome that has a minimum duration and is associated with significant impairments in functioning. As a disorder, depression is characterized by a common clinical picture, and may also be associated with a characteristic course, outcome, response to treatment, common etiologic factors, and associated biological, family, or environmental characteristics. Depression as a disorder is usually defined using the DSM-IV diagnostic criteria for major depressive disorder and for dysthymia.

MAJOR DEPRESSIVE DISORDER

Nine-year-old Joey: "I Feel Worthless"

Joey's mother and teacher have shared their concerns about his irritability and temper tantrums displayed both at home and at school. With little provocation, he bursts into tears and yells and throws objects. In class he seems to have difficulty concentrating and seems easily distracted. Increasingly shunned by his peers, he plays by himself at recess—and at home, spends most of his time in his room watching TV. His mother notes that he has been sleeping poorly and has gained 10 pounds over the past couple of months from constant snacking. A consultation with the school psychologist has ruled out learning disabilities or attention-deficit disorder; instead she says he is a deeply unhappy child who expresses feelings of worthlessness and hopelessness—and even a wish that he would die. These feelings began about 6 months ago, when Joey's father—divorced from his mother for several years—remarried and moved to another town and now spends far less time with Joey. (Adapted from Hammen & Rudolph, 1996)

Seventeen-year-old Alison: "I Couldn't Take It Anymore"

Alison gets high grades, is a talented musician, and is attractive. However, for the past 3 years she has been fighting to stay alive. "There are times when I was in school and I would start to cry—I had no idea why. My friends would say, 'What have you got to be depressed about, Alison? You're smart, talented, and can have any boy you want.' When my closest friend moved away 3 years ago, I was really lonely," says Alison. "I'd write notes about suicide and talk about killing myself. I couldn't eat and was tired most of the time. Even the smallest decision was overwhelming. Some days I'd never get out of bed I was so depressed—I couldn't stand school and hated everyone." Alison's feelings of hopelessness continued for days, then weeks, then months. Finally, "I couldn't take it anymore," says Alison. "I wanted to die—so I tried to kill myself."

Although Joey and Alison differ widely in age and symptoms, both display the key features of major depressive disorder (MDD)—sadness, loss of interest or pleasure in nearly all activities, irritability, plus a number of additional specific symptoms that are present for at least 2 weeks. These symptoms and the other diagnostic criteria for a major depressive episode are presented in Table 8.3.

A major depressive episode can be further specified as mild, moderate, or severe (on the basis of the severity of symptoms and the degree of functional impairment), with or without psychotic features, and with or without melancholic features.

The presence of a major depressive episode is the stepping-stone for diagnosing MDD. A diagnosis of MDD depends on the presence of a depressive episode *plus* the exclusion of other conditions, such as a psychotic disorder or the prior occurrence of a manic episode (in which case a diagnosis of bipolar disorder would be made). If there is just a single episode of major depression, then MDD, single episode is diagnosed. When there are two or more episodes of major depression, a diagnosis of MDD, recurrent is made. In the latter case, for the episodes to be considered distinct, they must be separated by at least 2 or more months in which the criteria for a major depressive episode are not met. A diagnosis of MDD also requires ruling out organic factors that may have caused or maintained depression, depression that is part of normal bereavement, the presence of delusions or hallucinations in the absence of mood symptoms, and underlying thought disorders.

The examples of Joey and Alison highlight three important points about the diagnosis of MDD in children and adolescents (Hammen & Rudolph, 1996). First, the same DSM criteria can be used to diagnose children, adolescents, and adults, and the main features of the disorder are as discernible in younger children, like Joey, as they are in older adolescents, like Alison. Second, because children's disruptive behaviors attract more attention or are more easily observed in comparison with internal, subjective suffering, depression can be easily overlooked. Third, some features of depression are likely to be more common in children and adolescents than in adults, notably, irritable mood (Hammen & Rudolph, 1996).

Table 8.2 Anxious/Depressed Syndrome in Young People

Symptoms Rated by Parents, Children, and Teachers

Complains of loneliness
Cries alot
Fears he or she might think or do something bad
Feels he or she has to be perfect
Feels or complains that no one loves him or her
Feels others are out to get him or her
Feels worthless or inferior
Nervous, high-strung, or tense
Too fearful or anxious
Feels too guilty
Self-conscious or easily embarrassed
Suspicious
Unhappy, sad, depressed
Worries

Symptoms Rated by Children

Harms self
Thinks about suicide

Symptoms Rated by Teachers

Overconforms
Hurt when criticized
Anxious to please
Afraid to make mistakes

Source: Achenbach, 1993.

Using the same diagnostic criteria for children and adults has the advantage of creating greater developmental continuity between depressive disorders in children and adults. However, as you might expect, there are some differences between children and adults with MDD in the expression of various symptoms. Depressed appearance, separation anxiety, phobias, somatic complaints, and behavioral problems occur more frequently in young people than in adults. In contrast, symptoms of anhedonia, psychomotor retardation, psychosis, suicide attempts, lethality of suicide attempts, and impairment of functioning increase with age (Carlson & Kashani, 1988; Hammen & Rudolph, 1996). For the most part, children and adults with MDD display similar symptoms and have comparable rates of comorbidity and recurrence. However, relative to adults, clinically referred youngsters with MDD are almost exclusively first-episode depressions, recover somewhat faster from their index episode of MDD, and are at greater risk for developing a bipolar disorder. Children who develop MDD suffer from their disorder for many more years than adults, making very early onset MDD a particularly serious form of affective illness (Kovacs, 1996; Mitchell, McCauley, Burke, & Moss, 1988).

| Table 8.3 | DSM-IV Diagnostic Criteria for Major Depressive Episode |

A. Five (or more) of the following symptoms have been present during the same 2-week period and represent a change from previous functioning; at least one of the symptoms is either (1) depressed mood or (2) loss of interest or pleasure.

Note: Do not include symptoms that are clearly due to a general medical condition, or mood-incongruent delusions or hallucinations.

(1) depressed mood most of the day, nearly every day, as indicated by either subjective report (e.g., feels sad or empty) or observations made by others (e.g., appears tearful).
   Note: In children and adolescents, can be irritable mood.
(2) markedly diminished interest or pleasure in all, or almost all, activities most of the day, nearly every day (as indicated by either subjective account or observation made by others).
(3) significant weight loss when not dieting or weight gain (e.g., a change of more than 5% of body weight in a month), or decrease or increase in appetite nearly every day.
   Note: In children, consider failure to make expected weight gains.
(4) insomnia or hypersomnia nearly every day.
(5) psychomotor agitation or retardation nearly every day (observable by others, not merely subjective feelings of restlessness or being slowed down).
(6) fatigue or loss of energy nearly every day.
(7) feelings of worthlessness or excessive or inappropriate guilt (which may be delusional) nearly every day (not merely self-reproach or guilt about being sick).
(8) diminished ability to think or concentrate, or indecisiveness, nearly every day (either by subjective account or as observed by others).
(9) recurrent thoughts of death (not just fear of dying), recurrent suicidal ideation without a specific plan, or a suicide attempt or a specific plan for committing suicide.

B. The symptoms do not meet criteria for a Mixed Episode.

C. The symptoms cause clinically significant distress or impairment in social, occupational, or other important areas of functioning.

D. The symptoms are not due to the direct physiological effects of a substance (e.g., a drug of abuse, a medication) or a general medical condition (e.g., hypothyroidism).

E. The symptoms are not better accounted for by Bereavement (i.e., after the loss of a loved one, the symptoms persist for longer than 2 months or are characterized by marked functional impairment, morbid preoccupation with worthlessness, suicidal ideation, psychotic symptoms, or psychomotor retardation).

Source: DSM-IV Copyright © 1994 by APA.

Differential Diagnosis

Certain symptoms of depression, such as sadness, excessive worry, sleep disturbances, somatic complaints, apathy, and social withdrawal, occur with many disorders, including other mood disorders, such as dysthymic disorder and bipolar disorder. They may also occur in the context of parental separation and other anxiety disorders, or in children who have been abused. Depressive symptoms can also occur as a side effect or direct physical consequence of various medications (e.g., anticonvulsants, steroids, narcotics/analgesics), substance abuse, or exposure to a toxin. Symptoms of depression may also be associated with a variety of physical illnesses, such as endocrine problems, infectious disease, and autoimmune disorders (Duffy, Manion, & Davidson, 1994).

Prevalence

The overall prevalence rate of MDD for children ages 4 to 18 is between 2% and 8% (Poznanski & Mokros, 1994). However, estimates vary widely with the age of the child. Depression is rare among preschool children (less than 1%) and school-age children (about 2%) (Kashani & Carlson, 1987). By adolescence, however, the prevalence of MDD increases two- or threefold, to about 2% to 8% (Birmaher et al., 1996b). Since depression is episodic (i.e., it comes and goes), prevalence estimates will vary with the length of the time period in which symptoms are assessed. For example, in 14- to 18-year-old adolescents, prevalence rates for depression are about 3% when taken at a single point in time and about 8% when taken over a 1-year period. However, the lifetime prevalence in adolescents—whether or not a youngster has *ever* been depressed—is as high as 15% to 20%. This rate is similar to that for adults and suggests that depression in adults may originate in adolescence (Harrington, Rutter, & Fombonne, 1996; Lewinsohn, Hops, Roberts, Seeley, & Andrews, 1993). The high lifetime prevalence of MDD indicates that about 1 in every 5 or 6 youngsters experiences diagnosable depression at some time during childhood or adolescence (Birmaher et al., 1996b; Lewinsohn, Clarke, Seeley, & Rohde, 1994). As high as these rates are, they may underestimate the problem. First, rates estimated via formal diagnostic criteria may be lower than self-reported rates of depression. Second, many youngsters who come close but fail to meet diagnostic criteria for MDD still show significant impairments in their social competence, cognitive attributions, coping skills, family relations, and experience of stress. These youngsters are also at greater risk for the development of future depression and other disorders, such as substance abuse, than youth without subclinical symptoms (Gotlib, Lewinsohn, & Seeley, 1995; Herman-Stahl & Petersen, 1996; Lewinsohn, Hops, et al., 1993).

The modest increase in the prevalence of depression from preschool to elementary school is likely not biologically based, but rather a reflection of the school-age child's growing self-awareness, cognitive capacity to conceptualize, verbal ability to report symptoms, and increased performance and social pressures. In contrast, the sharp increase in depression in adolescence appears to be the result of biological maturation at puberty interacting with important developmental changes that occur during this tumultuous time period. This hypothesis is supported by the postpubertal emergence of bipolar disorder, the rapid increase in suicide attempts and completions in adolescence, the relative stability in rates of depressive disorder through adolescence, and the sex differences in depression that emerge after puberty (Birmaher et al., 1996b).

Comorbidity

Raymond: Sad and Aggressive

Raymond is a 16-year-old boy who lives alone with his single mother. For the past few months he has been persistently sad and unhappy, overcome with feelings of personal worthlessness. He is socially withdrawn, spending most of his time alone at home or avoiding contact with his peers on those days when he manages to attend school. He is constantly tired but still finds it difficult to sleep, lying awake at night for hours and then struggling to drag himself from bed in the morning. Both he and his mother are concerned about his weight, which has increased substantially due to his inability to control his appetite for chips, candy, and soda. Even if he makes it to school, he finds he is unable to concentrate on his work. Raymond's listlessness and withdrawal are countered, however, by his repeated outbursts of anger and aggression. He frequently lashes out in rage at his mother, recently punching his fist through a wall and a door at home. He also has been involved in several fights with other students at school as a result of being teased by his peers. He rarely complies with rules and limits either at home or at school, leading to frequent conflicts with his mother and with school authorities. The event that precipitated Raymond's current referral was his arrest for shoplifting at a local store. (Adapted from Compas & Hammen, 1994)

Like Raymond, who has MDD and a comorbid conduct disorder, about 40% to 70% of youngsters with MDD have another disorder, with at least 20% to 30% having two or more combined diagnoses (Simonoff et al., 1997). The most frequent comorbid conditions in *clinic-referred* youngsters with MDD are anxiety disorders, particularly, generalized anxiety disorder (55%), phobias (45%), and separation anxiety disorder (9%); dysthymia (between 30% and 80%); conduct problems and ADHD (estimates vary widely—between 10% and 80%); and substance use disorder (20% to 30%) (Birmaher et al., 1996b; Simonoff et al., 1997). The pattern of comorbidity is also related to age—children and preadolescents with MDD are more likely to display comorbid separation anxiety disorder than are adolescents, whereas adolescents are more likely to display comorbid substance use disorders (Fleming & Offord, 1990). Depression and anxiety commonly co-occur, but become increasingly visible as *separate* disorders as the severity of the child's problems increases and as the child gets older (Gurley, Cohen, Pine, & Brook, 1996; Rohde, Lewinsohn, & Seeley, 1991).

Although lower than in clinic samples, rates of comorbidity in community samples of adolescents with MDD are also quite high for anxiety disorders (18%), disruptive behavior disorders (8%), and substance use disorder (14%) (Lewinsohn, Rohde, Seeley, & Hops, 1991). Further, more than 60% of adolescents with MDD have been found to have comorbid personality disorders, most commonly borderline personality disorder (characterized by instability of interpersonal relationships, self-image, affects, and marked impulsivity). However, symptoms of personality disorder are no longer present following an adolescent's depressive episode, underscoring the importance of making only interim diagnoses of personality disorder in cases of acute depression (Birmaher et al., 1996b). Unlike studies with clinic samples, findings regarding the comorbidity of depression and ADHD in community samples are mixed. One recent study of 8- to 16-year-old youth found that depression was comorbid with all other disorders *with the exception* of ADHD (Simonoff et al., 1997). This discrepancy in findings in clinic versus community samples may reflect an increased likelihood of referral in those youngsters with depression who also have ADHD.

MDD in young people is more likely to occur *after* rather than before the onset of all other psychiatric disorders except alcohol or substance abuse, whereas MDD has been found to precede the onset of substance abuse by an average of 4.5 years. In addition, conduct problems may sometimes develop as a complication of depression and continue after the depression remits. Not only is the child's comorbid diagnosis usually present before MDD, it is likely to persist even after the child is no longer depressed (Birmaher et al., 1996b).

The presence of a comorbid disorder is significant because it affects the youngster's risk for recurrent depression, possibly the duration of the depressive episode, suicide attempts or behavior, outcomes, response to treatment, and utilization of mental health services. For example, youngsters with MDD and dysthymic disorder have more severe and longer depressive episodes, a higher rate of other comorbid disorders, more suicide attempts, and worse social impairment than those with either MDD or DD alone. MDD with an accompanying anxiety disorder may increase the severity and duration of the youngster's depressive symptoms, and the risk for psychosocial problems, substance abuse, and suicide. Finally, youngsters with MDD and a comorbid disruptive behavior disorder tend to have poorer outcomes, a higher incidence of adult criminality, higher levels of family criticism, and more suicide attempts than those with MDD alone (Birmaher et al., 1996b; Harrington et al., 1990).

Age of Onset, Course, and Outcome

Most adults report having had their first depressive episode when they were between the ages of 15 to 19 years (Burke, Burke, Regier, & Rae, 1990). However, prospective studies of children and adolescents usually find earlier ages of onset (11 to 15 years), most commonly between age 14 and 15 (Lewinsohn, Hops, et al., 1993). About 7% to 14% of children experience an episode of major depression before they are 15 years old, and an early age of onset predicts a more serious illness

and a greater likelihood that depressive episodes will recur. Onset of depression during adolescence may be gradual or sudden. Either way, a youngster typically has a history of subthreshold episodes of depression (Gotlib & Hammen, 1992).

The average episode of MDD in children and adolescents lasts about 7 to 9 months. For children identified through a community sample, the first episode of major depression lasted 26 weeks on average, with a median duration of 8 weeks (Lewinsohn, Clarke, Seeley, & Rohde, 1994). This finding suggests a bimodal distribution in which a first episode is relatively brief (2 months or less) for half the children with MDD but much longer for the remainder. MDD that is severe enough to result in referral for treatment usually lasts about a year. About 90% of children recover from their episode of MDD within 1½ to 2 years following onset, but the rest may experience a prolonged episode and remain depressed (Birmaher et al., 1996b; Kovacs, Obrosky, Gatsonis, & Richards, 1997).

Although almost all youngsters eventually recover from their initial depressive episode, their disorder does not go away. Unfortunately, MDD is a recurrent condition with a cumulative chance of recurrence of about 25% by 1 year, 40% by 2 years, and 70% by 5 years. A significant proportion of youngsters develop a chronic relapsing disorder that persists into young adulthood, with recurrence rates of around 60% to 70% and an average of 5 or 6 lifetime episodes (Birmaher et al., 1996b). For youngsters hospitalized for their depression, nearly half will be rehospitalized within 2 years following remission. In addition, about 20% to 40% of adolescents with MDD develop bipolar I disorder within 5 years after the onset of their depression (known as a bipolar switch) (Kovacs, Akiskal, Gatsonis, & Parrone, 1994; McCauley et al., 1993). These youngsters are more likely to have an early onset of MDD (before the age of 10), display depression accompanied by psychomotor retardation or psychotic features, and have a family history of mood disorders (Birmaher et al., 1996b; Kovacs, 1996).

The following comments by the mother of a depressed teen paint a bleak picture of the long-term outcome for a child who suffers from MDD and, unfortunately, one that is not too far off the mark:

> "Depression in kids, when it hits them in their teens, leaves a hole in their lives. When they're young and just starting out in life, they're supposed to become independent. But that doesn't happen with depressed kids. They're out of synch and get left behind. And they never really catch up. That leaves a permanent scar." (Adapted from Owen, 1993, p. C1)

Youngsters with early-onset depression experience many more episodes of depression than individuals whose first episode occurs in adulthood, compounding the developmental disruptions and functional impairments associated with depression and creating a long-term social, emotional, and economic burden for the child and family (Kovacs, 1997). What happens to youngsters with depression as they get older? First, for most adolescents, their depressive episode is likely to continue for about 5 to 6 months (Strober, Lampert, Schmidt, & Morrell, 1993). As we have seen, rates of recovery are high, with about 75% of youngsters experiencing a significant reduction in symptoms of depression within a year and the remainder within 2 years (Goodyer, Germany, Gowrusankur, & Altham, 1991). So the good news is that rates of recovery are high for most youngsters with depression. The bad news is that rates of relapse are also very high—depression is a condition that endures over the course of development.

Why do depressive episodes keep recurring, and why does the length of time between episodes get progressively shorter? One possibility is that the first episode may sensitize the youngster to future episodes. According to this idea, the first episode of depression may be linked to a particular stressor, and is accompanied by lasting changes in biological processes and alterations in responsibility to future stressors (Post et al., 1996). In addition, the initial externally produced changes in the brain can be conditioned so that following the first depressive episode, even minor events that resemble loss or stress experiences may result in depression, a phenomenon referred to as "kindling" (Kovacs, 1997; Post, 1992).

Even after recovery from their depression, many youths continue to show subclinical symptoms of depression and experience many adjustment and health problems (Birmaher et al., 1996b; Rohde, Lewinsohn, & Seeley, 1994). This is a significant concern because functional impairment is a risk factor for the occurrence of future depressive episodes (Lewinsohn, Seeley, Hibbard, Rohde, & Sack, 1996). In addition to recurring bouts of depression, the immediate and long-term prospects for children with MDD include many other negative outcomes. For example, adolescents who are depressed have a greater-than-normal risk for delinquency, arrest and conviction, school dropout, and unemployment (Lewinsohn, Roberts, et al., 1994). A history of depression during the school years also increases the risk for later substance use disorder, suicidal behavior, poor work record, marital problems, and other relationship difficulties into adulthood (Harrington & Vostanis, 1995). Adolescents with two or more depressive episodes have poorer outcomes whereas those who experience only a single episode of depression have reasonably good psychosocial outcomes (Birmaher et al., 1996b). In summary, the overall outcome for young people with MDD is not good—these youngsters continue to be at high risk for later episodes of affective and other disorders and for impaired social and academic functioning.

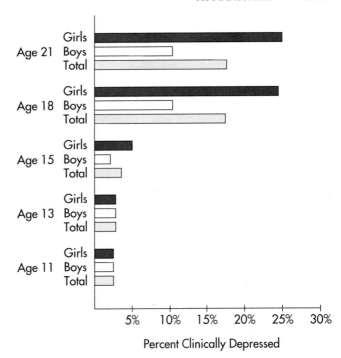

FIGURE 8.1 The overall rate of depression and the proportion of females with depression increases dramatically during adolescence. (Data from Hankin et al., 1998)

Gender and Ethnicity

In what has been called depression's double standard, women are twice as likely to suffer from depression as males, and are also more susceptible to milder mood disorders. However, this gender difference is not present among younger children. Depression in preadolescent children is equally common in boys and girls, with a prevalence of about 2.6% for boys and girls ages 6 to 11 years (Speier, Sherak, Hirsch, & Cantwell, 1995). Boys may even show a decrease in their depressive symptoms between the ages of 8 and 11 years (Angold, Erkanli, Loeber, & Costello, 1996). Gender differences in depression begin between the ages of 13 and 15, when the rate rises for girls (Nolen-Hoeksema & Girgus, 1994). As shown in Figure 8.1, findings from a recent follow-up study of a large community sample found that rates of depression as well as gender differences in rates increase dramatically between the ages of 15 and 18 (Hankin et al., 1998). The ratio of girls to boys is about 2:1 to 3:1 after puberty, a pattern that continues throughout adolescence and adulthood.

Gender differences in depressive symptoms are even more evident in children referred for treatment than in community samples (Compas et al., 1997; Hinden, Compas, Howell, & Achenbach, 1997; Lewinsohn, Hops, et al., 1993). Since rates of anxiety are higher for girls with depression than they are for boys, the higher reported incidence of depression in clinically referred girls may be related to the presence of comorbid anxiety disorders (Silverstein, Caceres, Perdue, & Cimarolli, 1995; Simonoff et al., 1997).

The increase in the prevalence of depression in adolescence and the emergence of gender differences in rates at this time has led to an interest in this developmental period and in challenges to self-worth as being particularly salient for depression (Petersen et al., 1993). Not only do cognitions about the self, others, and future become more prominent during adolescence, many biological (e.g., hormones), intrapersonal (e.g., identity concerns, autonomy), and interpersonal (e.g., intimate relationships) changes also occur at this time. Changes during adolescence may diminish self-worth, lead to dysphoric mood, and evoke self-focused attention. It is thought that females may be at even greater risk because they have more aspects of self invested in other people than do males, have a greater orientation toward cooperation and sociality, and use ruminative coping styles to deal with stress, especially stress that involves interpersonal loss and disruptions. These characteristics put girls at a disadvantage in adolescence, when they face somewhat greater biological and stressful role-related challenges than boys do (Avison & McAlpine, 1992; Hammen & Rudolph, 1996; Huston & Alvarez, 1990).

Women may also have a biological tendency for developing depression. Hormones and sleep cycles, which can alter mood, differ dramatically between men and women. A recent study of blood flow in regions of the brain during periods of sadness in men and in women found that although men and women considered themselves to be equally sad, their brain activity differed. When asked to feel sad, both sexes activated regions of the left prefrontal cortex, but women showed a much wider activation of the limbic system than did males. Significantly, the brain regions activated during transient sadness were ones that may function abnormally during clinical depression. It is hypothesized that the overactivity of the limbic system in women experiencing sadness has the effect over time of exhausting this region and

leading to the underactivity in this region of the brain during clinical depression (George, Ketter, Parekh, Herscovitch, & Post, 1996). These findings with adults suggest that gender differences in depression may be partly rooted in biological differences in the brain processes that regulate emotions.

Although the incidence of depression has been found to vary across regions worldwide (Culbertson, 1997; Leutwyler, 1997), few studies have examined ethnocultural differences in children and adolescents. A recent study compared the prevalence of major depression across nine ethnic groups in a large community sample of children in grades six to eight (Roberts, Roberts, & Chen, 1997). Of these groups, African-American and Mexican-American youths both had significantly higher rates of depression without impairment, but only Mexican-American youths were at elevated risk for depression with impairment.

In the next section we discuss dysthymic disorder, a milder but more chronic form of depression about which we know relatively little in comparison to MDD. Dysthymia and MDD are related, since many children with dysthymia eventually develop MDD.

DYSTHYMIC DISORDER

Deborah: A Childhood without Laughter

A few months ago, my mother unearthed some pictures of me as a baby, which I had never seen before. One showed me at about eight to ten months old, crawling on the grass of Golden Gate Park. I was looking directly at the camera, my tongue sticking out of the corner of my mouth, and I was laughing happily. My face was lit from within, and looked more than a little mischievous. I was absolutely transfixed by that photograph for days. I would continually take it out of my wallet and stare at it, torn between laughter and tears. For a while I couldn't figure out what it was about the picture that drew me. Finally it hit me; this was the only picture of myself as a child that I had seen which showed me laughing. All the photos I had ever seen depicted a child staring solemnly or smiling diffidently, but never laughing. I looked at the Golden Gate Park picture and wished that I had remained that happy, and that depression had not taken away my childhood. When I first was diagnosed with depression in 1990, I discussed my childhood with my doctor. Although it is hard to diagnose a child twenty years in the past, it seemed

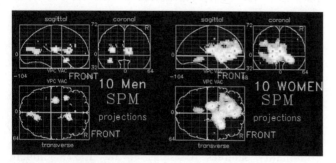

PET scans reveal that during sadness, the limbic system in women's brains (right) becomes metabolically more active than that area does in men's brains (left).

clear to both of us that I had suffered from dysthymia (mild, long-term depression) probably from the time I was a small child. (Deren, 1997)

Like Deborah, youngsters who suffer from dysthymic disorder (DD) are unhappy or irritable most of the time. Although their symptoms are chronic, they are less severe than those of children with MDD. Children with a diagnosis of DD display depressive symptoms on most days, for at least 1 year—this is in contrast to a duration of 2 weeks for a diagnosis of a major depressive episode. The DSM-IV criteria for DD are presented in Table 8.4.

Relative to children with MDD, those with dysthymia generally show lower rates of melancholic or neurovegetative symptoms (e.g., restlessness, agitation, and sleeplessness) and the virtual absence of anhedonia and social withdrawal. Impaired concentration, thoughts of dying, and somatic complaints are also less common (Kovacs et al., 1994). Relative to those with MDD, children with DD are characterized by their poor emotion regulation, including constant feelings of sadness, feelings of being unloved and forlorn, self-deprecation,

---

Table 8.4 | **DSM-IV Diagnostic Criteria for Dysthymic Disorder**

A. Depressed mood for most of the day, for more days than not, as indicated by either subjective account or by observation by others, for at least 2 years.

   Note: In children and adolescents, mood can be irritable and duration must be at least 1 year.

B. Presence, while depressed, of two (or more) of the following:
   (1) poor appetite or overeating
   (2) insomnia or hypersomnia
   (3) low energy or fatigue
   (4) low self-esteem
   (5) poor concentration or difficulty making decisions
   (6) feelings of hopelessness

C. During the 2-year period (1 year for children or adolescents) of the disturbance, the person has never been without the symptoms in Criteria A and B for more than 2 months at a time.

D. No Major Depressive Episode has been present during the first 2 years of the disturbance (1 year for children and adolescents); i.e., the disturbance is not better accounted for by chronic Major Depressive Disorder, or Major Depressive Disorder, In Partial Remission.

   Note: There may have been a previous Major Depressive Episode provided there was a full remission (no significant signs or symptoms for 2 months) before development of the Dysthymic Disorder. In addition, after the initial 2 years (1 year for children and adolescents) of Dysthymic Disorder, in which case both diagnoses may be given when the criteria are met for a Major Depressive Episode.

E. There has never been a Manic Episode, a Mixed Episode, or a Hypomanic Episode, and criteria have never been met for Cyclothymic Disorder.

F. The disturbance does not occur exclusively during the course of a chronic Psychotic Disorder, such as Schizophrenia or Delusional Disorder.

G. The symptoms are not due to the direct physiological effects of a substance (e.g., a drug of abuse, a medication) or a general medical condition (e.g., hypothyroidism).

H. The symptoms cause clinically significant distress or impairment in social, occupational, or other important areas of functioning.

Specify if:
   Early Onset: if onset is before age 21 years
   Late Onset: if onset is age 21 years or older
Specify (for most recent 2 years of Dysthymic Disorder):
   With Atypical Features

Source: DSM-IV Copyright © 1994 by APA.

low self-esteem, anxiety, irritability, anger, and temper tantrums (Renouf & Kovacs, 1995).

Although the boundaries between DD and MDD may seem blurry, they can be reliably drawn. In fact, some children have **double depression,** where a major depressive episode is superimposed on the child's previous DD so that the child presents with both disorders. Among a community sample of adolescents with a depressive disorder, 85% had a pure episode of MDD, 10% had pure dysthymia, and about 5% had both (Lewinsohn et al., 1991). Rates of double depression are much higher in clinic samples and follow two common paths. First, a child with DD may develop new symptoms that meet criteria for MDD. For example, in addition to the dysthymic symptoms, the child develops appetite and sleep problems. Second, the child's dysthymic symptoms may change in severity and/or previous subclinical symptoms may worsen so as to reach criteria for a depressive episode. For example, the child's lack of a pleasurable response to praise develops into pervasive anhedonia (Renouf & Kovacs, 1995).

The chronic nature of DD raises the issue of whether DD should be considered a chronic form of mood disorder or a general personality style? We've all known people whom we would describe as a "sad sacks"— nothing ever seems to make them happy. Is this a mood disorder or is it their personality? Recent work suggests that DD follows a chronic course that is typical of mood disorders, and there is growing evidence for its existence in young people. Thus, dysthymia in young people is related to MDD and appears to be a mood disorder rather than a personality disorder (Renouf & Kovacs, 1995).

Prevalence and Comorbidity

Rates of DD are low, with estimates ranging from 0.6% to 1.7% in children and 1.6% to 8.0% in adolescents (Birmaher et al., 1996b; Lewinsohn, Hops, et al., 1993; Polaino-Lorente & Domenech, 1993). In general, about 1% of children and adolescents have DD during any 1-year period, and about 5% of children and adolescents have an episode of dysthymia by the end of adolescence (lifetime prevalence) (Renouf & Kovacs, 1995).

DD occurs with other affective as well as nonaffective disorders. Superimposed MDD is the most prevalent comorbid diagnosis during childhood and adolescence (Renouf & Kovacs, 1995). Rates of comorbidity vary depending on whether children are identified because of depression or dysthymia and the point in the course of the disorder that children are identified. When children are identified as having MDD, about 30% have comor-

bid DD (in both clinic and nonclinic samples). When children are identified on the basis of DD, comorbid MDD occurs at a higher rate—from 40% to 60%. During the course of their DD, as many as 70% of children may have an episode of major depression (Renouf & Kovacs, 1995). About half of children with DD also have nonaffective disorders that preceded dysthymia and were present at the time of diagnosis, such as anxiety disorders (40%), conduct disorder (30%), ADHD (24%), and enuresis or encopresis (15%), with 15% of children having two or more comorbid conditions (Kovacs et al., 1994).

Age of Onset, Course, and Outcome

Compared to MDD, DD can develop at a relatively early age, most commonly around 11 to 12 years. In a clinic sample of children with DD, the *earliest* age of onset was 5 years and the mean age of onset was about 9 years (Kovacs et al., 1997). DD begins about 3 years earlier than MDD and could be a precursor to the development of MDD—dysthymia almost always precedes major depression (Lewinsohn et al., 1991; Lewinsohn, Hops, et al., 1993).

Childhood-onset DD has a prolonged duration in both clinic and community samples, with an average episode length of 2½ to 5 years. In one clinic sample, half of the children with this disorder took 4 years or longer to recover. Time to recovery was related not to whether children had received treatment, but to the presence of a comorbid externalizing disorder—DD lasts about 2½ years longer when an externalizing disorder is present than when it is not (Kovacs et al., 1997). In a community sample of children ages 14 to 18 years, the episode length was 2.5 years for those with pure dysthymia and 3.4 years for those with dysthymia and MDD (Lewinsohn et al., 1991). Its early onset and its protracted duration make DD a serious problem: Youngsters who develop DD at age 9 and recover 4 years later will have spent more than 30% of their entire lives and over half of their school-age years being depressed. Since depression is associated with many other academic, cognitive, family, and social problems, these long-lasting episodes of dysthymia can have extremely harmful effects on a young child's development (Renouf & Kovacs, 1995).

Long-term outcomes for children with DD are variable. Almost all youngsters eventually recover from their dysthymia. On the other hand, they also have an extremely high risk of developing other disorders, especially MDD, anxiety disorders (particularly separation anxiety disorder and generalized anxiety disorder), and conduct disorder. About 70% to 80% of individuals with early-onset DD will develop a first episode of major depression within 8½ years of the onset of dysthymia, with the second and third years being of particularly high risk. Youngsters with DD are also at increased risk for the subsequent development of bipolar disorder (about 20%) and substance abuse disorder (15%) (Kovacs et al., 1994). Of children hospitalized with dysthymia, 40% are rehospitalized within the first year of discharge (Asarnow et al., 1988).

Adolescents with a history of DD report receiving less social support from friends (fewer friends, lower frequency of interactions, and lower quality of relationships), a finding that is *specific* to children with dysthymia when compared with children with MDD (Klein, Lewinsohn, & Seeley, 1997). Children who have recovered from their DD have not been found to differ from comparison groups on any measure of family relationships, school functioning, or cognitive variables (e.g., pessimism and attributional style) that are characteristic of depressive episodes (Klein et al., 1997). Following recovery, the only area that continues to be affected is psychosocial functioning. However, it is not known if deficits in psychosocial functioning precede or follow DD. Psychosocial dysfunction may be a predisposing factor for the development of DD, or a lasting scar of the illness.

In summary, our knowledge of DD in young people is limited. We know far less about this disorder than we do about MDD. However, what we do know seems to be consistent across studies (Renouf & Kovacs, 1995, p. 22):

❖ DD is characterized by psychological, rather than the neurovegetative symptoms (e.g., restlessness, agitation, and sleeplessness) that often accompany MDD.
❖ DD has an earlier age of onset than MDD.
❖ DD has a prolonged duration.
❖ DD has a high frequency of comorbidity both during a dysthymic episode and subsequently.
❖ DD has a chronic course marked by repeated episodes of affective illness.
❖ DD is associated with elevated levels of depressive symptoms and significant difficulties in psychosocial functioning, even after recovery (Klein, et al., 1997).

Since early-onset DD is almost always followed by a depressive episode, and sometimes by a bipolar disorder, the early identification of DD may assist in the identification of youngsters at risk for later affective disorders and may have important implications for prevention. Now that we have a basic understanding of MDD and DD, we next consider the associated characteristics and possible causes for these disorders.

ASSOCIATED CHARACTERISTICS OF DEPRESSIVE DISORDERS

In addition to their mood disturbances and other symptoms, youngsters with depression experience numerous cognitive and psychosocial difficulties. Among these are deficits in intellectual performance and academic achievement, and disturbances in self-perceptions, self-esteem, social problem solving, actual social behavior, coping skills, and life stressors (Kovacs & Goldston, 1991). Since depression often occurs with other disorders, it's hard to know if these associated deficits are specific to depression or related to the presence of psychopathology in general (Lewinsohn, Gotlib, & Seeley, 1997). For example, many of the cognitive errors and distortions associated with depression in young people are also associated with anxiety and other disorders, suggesting that negative thinking may not be *specific* to depression (Garber, Weiss, & Shanley, 1993). In addition, we don't know whether cognitive and psychosocial deficits are an outcome or a cause of depression. In one study, depression at the beginning of the school year did not predict changes in either academic or social competence over time in sixth-graders. However, children's level of social competence at the start of the school year predicted depression at the end of the school year, suggesting that social dysfunction may be a vulnerability factor for later depression in youngsters of this age (Cole, Martin, Powers, & Truglio, 1996).

Intellectual and Academic Functioning

Certain depressive symptoms—difficulty concentrating, loss of interest, and psychomotor slowing—are particularly likely to have a harmful effect on a youngster's intellectual functioning and academic achievement. Depressed youngsters may experience problems with attention that can interfere with learning new or complex academic assignments, and their reduced motivation and energy make it nearly impossible for them to take on demanding tasks. Psychomotor retardation can slow the rate at which a child acquires and consolidates information for long-term memory, and may lead to poor test performance. This may result in academic failure, which may in turn undermine self-esteem and lead to further negative learning experiences (Kovacs & Goldston, 1991).

Intellectual Functioning. The overall intellectual potential of depressed youngsters is comparable to those who are not depressed, with no apparent cognitive deficits prior to the onset of their depression. It is not clear how the onset of depression affects intellectual functioning over time. In general, the relation between children's severity of depression and overall intelligence is weak, suggesting that the effects of depression on cognitive functions may be selective, and associated with impairments on nonverbal intellectual performance tasks that require attention, coordination, and psychomotor speed, but not necessarily on those that require verbal skills or verbal intellectual performance. However, depressed youngsters show mild declines in verbal intellectual performance over time, which may reflect a disruption in their learning of academic skills (Kovacs & Goldston, 1991).

Academic Functioning. Depression can directly interfere with academic achievement and school performance. Compared with nondepressed youngsters, those with MDD perform more poorly in school, display a greater variety of academic difficulties, score lower on standardized achievement tests, are rated by their teachers as doing less well academically, and have lower levels of grade attainment (Cole, 1990; Cole et al., 1996; Nolen-Hoeksema, Girgus, & Seligman, 1986). Poor concentration and thinking ability, psychomotor retardation or agitation, fatigue, insomnia, and somatic complaints may lead to grade repetition, being late for or skipping school, failure to complete homework, and dissatisfaction with or refusal of school (Kearney, 1993; Lewinsohn, Roberts, et al., 1994). Jennifer, a 15-year-old girl with MDD, and her mother had this to say about school:

> "School is a big waste of time," says Jennifer. "I don't want to be there. I don't have the energy or motivation for school. I just say I'm sick so I can stay at home in bed and sleep all day." Jennifer's mother says, "We used to fight about school so much that eventually I'd let her stay home—just to avoid having another fight."

Youngsters with a longer history of depression receive poorer grades over time, and the greater proportion of time that the child has major depression during the school year, the lower the child's grade point average (Kovacs & Goldston, 1991). However, it is unclear whether MDD has an enduring effect on school performance. Some studies report that school difficulties of depressed children go away following their recovery from depression, while others report that academic problems continue even after recovery (Kovacs & Goldston, 1991; Puig-Antich et al., 1985b). In general, the association between depression and school difficulties is not as strong as the one between depression and social dysfunction (Lewinsohn et al., 1997).

Cognitive Disturbances

> "Good morning, Pooh Bear," said Eeyore gloomily. "If it is a good morning," he said. "Which I doubt."
> —A. A. Milne, Winnie-the-Pooh (1926)

Fifteen-year-old Ellie: Feels Worthless

". . . like everything's worthless, like it's just not worth it to even be. . . .It's—it seems like it's a silly thing to even go through life and exist. And from one day to the next you're always wondering if you're going to make it to the next day if it's—if you can stand it, if it's worth trying to get to tomorrow. . . . It's just—just, I feel like—I feel mostly like I'm worthless, like there's something wrong with me. It's really not a pleasant feeling to know that you're a total failure, a complete nothing, and I get the feeling that I never do nothing right or worthwhile or anything." (Adapted from McKnew et al., 1983)

Like Ellie, many youngsters with depression experience deficits and distortions in their thinking (Kaslow, Brown, & Mee, 1994). Some cognitive disturbances, such as Ellie's painful feelings of worthlessness, are part of the diagnosis of depression. Other cognitions, such as negative beliefs (e.g., "I never do nothing right") and attributions of failure ("I'm a total failure"), are not part of the diagnosis but typically accompany the disorder. Self-critical automatic negative thoughts, such as "I'm no good," "I'm so disappointed with myself," "I'm a real loser," "I'm ugly," "I'm stupid," "I can't do it," or "I'm gonna fail," are common (Garber et al., 1993; Kazdin, 1990; Stark, Humphrey, Laurent, Livingston, & Christopher, 1993). Unfortunately, these thoughts can't simply be swept aside by suggesting to a depressed youngster that she or he "look at the bright side," or "not take things so seriously," or "try to be more positive."

During their depressed states, youngsters with depression frequently make inaccurate interpretations of their experiences and are consistently negative and self-critical (Fichman, Koestner, & Zuroff, 1996). They are more likely to attend to and focus narrowly on negative events for longer periods of time, referred to as a **depressive ruminative style** (Nolen-Hoeksema, Girgus, & Seligman, 1992). They misread situations, feeling slighted by otherwise harmless remarks, and may feel defeated, deprived, or rejected. They are easily frustrated—small setbacks are seen as major catastrophes. Depressed youngsters often devalue their own performance by not acknowledging their accomplishments and dismissing praise when it is given. They view themselves as ineffective in most areas of their lives and make self-directed disparaging comments when faced with further failure or rejection (e.g., "It must be my fault"). Negative and faulty conclusions are generalized across situations, so the depressed youngster sees no hope of gaining any pleasure or satisfaction. These negative thoughts and feelings often lead to further frustration, maintain depressive symptoms, and undermine the youngster's confidence and initiative.

It is also not unusual for youngsters with depression to feel that no one can help them out of their suffering. They become isolated and feel detached, even when they are with family or friends. Their lives are dominated by an ever-present gloomy and pessimistic outlook, feelings of hopelessness, and self-blame. Thus, youngsters with depression experience a vicious downward cycle in which self-defeating negative thoughts become pervasive and severely impair performance at school and home. As performance deteriorates, they perceive more failure and receive further negative feedback. These outcomes maintain their isolation and feelings of being unable to change, which in turn lead to a further loss of motivation and greater social withdrawal.

Youngsters with depression have a *pessimistic* outlook, seeing themselves as unable to cope with even minor setbacks and as no longer having any attainable goals. The smallest demand may feel overwhelming and make even the most minor obstacle seem insurmountable. They are also completely convinced that there will be no end to their troubles, feeling helpless to alter the downward cycle in which they find themselves. Youngsters with such a pessimistic cognitive style are at greater risk for the development of depressive symptoms, especially in response to stressful life events (Nolen-Hoeksema, Girgus, & Seligman, 1992; Robinson, Garber, & Hilsman, 1995). Their pessimistic outlook may continue even after remission of depressive symptoms, thus placing them at risk for future depressive episodes (Gotlib, Lewinsohn, Seeley, Rohde, & Redner, 1993). Moreover, about 65% report hopelessness, or negative expectations about the future, as a symptom (Mitchell et al., 1988). Hopelessness has been found to be related to suicide ideation and attempts, and to diminished self-esteem (Kazdin, French, Unis, Esveldt-Dawson, & Sherick, 1983; Marciano & Kazdin, 1994).

"It's snowing still," said Eeyore gloomily.
"So it is."
"And freezing."
"Is it?"
"Yes," said Eeyore. "However," he said, brightening up a little, "we haven't had an earthquake lately."
—A. A. Milne, *The House at Pooh Corner* (1928)

Depressed youngsters display distortions in how they process information and also a depressive attributional style (Joiner & Wagner, 1995). For example, they may overgeneralize from a single experience (e.g., "I didn't get a date for the party, so no one will *ever* want to go out with me") or catastrophize (e.g., "My friend didn't call, so my whole life is falling apart"). When negative things happen, they believe they are to blame (Gladstone & Kaslow, 1995). We will talk more about distortions in information processing and negative attributional styles in a later section on cognitive theories of depression.

Self-Esteem and Self-Perceived Personal Competence

Eeyore, the old grey Donkey, stood by the side of the stream and looked at himself in the water.
"Pathetic," he said. "That's what it is. Pathetic."
—A. A. Milne, *Winnie-the-Pooh* (1926)

Farah: Never Quite Good Enough

Fifteen-year-old Farah's mother says that Farah is a "model daughter" who is near the top of her class at school, active in school activities, and extremely popular. Her mother is concerned about "how hard Farah is on herself, thinking that she has to be perfect." If Farah doesn't get the highest grade on a test, she won't allow herself to see her friends for a week, and spends most of the time in her room studying. Farah acknowledges that she sets very high standards for herself and if she fails to meet these standards becomes extremely self-critical and self-punitive. She has even slapped herself in the face after what she saw as academic "failure" (getting an A– rather than an A). Farah's accomplishments bring her little satisfaction, and any perceived failure leads to immediate self-condemnation. Farah's overall self-worth is low and her sense of self, which is based on competency in academic achievement, is highly vulnerable.

Peanuts Reprinted by permission of United Feature Syndicate.

Low self-esteem or self-perceived personal competence is a crucial element of depression. As many as 95% of youngsters with depression experience low self-esteem (Mitchell et al., 1988), and a significant relation exists between low self-esteem and both depressed affect and other depressive symptoms, such as low energy level (Renouf & Harter, 1990). Not only is low self-esteem nearly universal among depressed youngsters, it is the symptom that is most *specifically* related to depression in adolescents (Lewinsohn et al., 1997). Instability in self-esteem may also be a vulnerability factor for depression. The self-esteem of youngsters who are depressed is highly reactive to daily life events, and such daily reactivity in self-esteem appears to be related to depression following exposure to major life stresses (Roberts & Gotlib, 1997). Thus, both low self-esteem and unstable self-esteem seem to play important roles in depression.

Differences among youngsters in self-esteem are related to two principal factors: their experience of support from others and their sense of self-competence in areas that are important to them. Young people differ in whether they base their self-esteem on support from others, a sense of self-competence, or various combinations. For some youngsters, like Farah, self-esteem is rooted mainly in academic competence. For others, it may be based on physical appearance, behavioral conduct, support from parents, or support from peers. Various sources of support and their combinations result in numerous possible pathways to self-esteem. Thus, low or unstable self-esteem can come about in many different ways—which raises the question of whether certain types of low or unstable self-esteem are more likely to result in depression than others. For example, if physical appearance and approval from peers are especially important as sources of self-esteem, as they are for most adolescents, perceived incompetence in these areas may heighten the risk for depression in this age group. Problems in self-esteem in adolescent girls are often related to distress over a negative body image, which may partly explain

the higher risk for depression in this group (Allgood-Merten, Lewinsohn, & Hops, 1990; Petersen, Sarigiani, & Kennedy, 1991).

Despite its significance for depression, self-esteem has proved to be an elusive concept (Shirk & Harter, 1996). Current views are moving away from a unitary model of self-esteem and recognizing that self-esteem or self-perceived personal competence encompasses multiple domains. One developmental model of self-esteem and depression hypothesizes that children seek and receive feedback from others about their competence or incompetence in various domains of functioning—academics, social relations, behavior, sports, conduct, physical appearance. Self-perceptions are constructed from this feedback, and the outcome may be a complex and positive self-view leading to optimism, energy, and enthusiasm, or a simplistic and negative self-view leading to pessimism, a sense of helplessness, and possibly, depression (Jordan & Cole, 1996; Seroczynski, Cole, & Maxwell, 1997). Positive or negative self-esteem in different domains may have cumulative, competitive, or compensatory effects. For example, positive self-esteem in one area may compensate for negative in another, or negative self-esteem in one area may reverse competency in another (Seroczynski et al., 1997). Youngsters who have self-views that are negative and narrowly focused, such as Farah's overinvestment in academic achievement, may show greater instability in their self-esteem because they lack alternative compensatory areas of functioning (e.g., athletics, social relationships). This may make them vulnerable to developing depression when faced with stress in their primary domain of functioning (Jordan & Cole, 1996).

Interpersonal Difficulties

Social Withdrawal and Peer Difficulties.
Youngsters who are depressed experience a broad range of social difficulties. They may have few close relationships, feel lonely and isolated, feel that others do not like

them (which, unfortunately, often becomes a reality), and have few friends to play with or talk to at school. Feelings of loneliness and isolation and poor peer relations are reflected in social rejection and lower popularity (Kaslow et al., 1994). One study found that nearly 25% of youngsters referred for depression reported poor friendships at the time of referral, and none of these recovered at follow-up (Goodyer, Herbert, Tamplin, Secher, & Pearson, 1997).

The loss of interest and social withdrawal of youngsters with depression can seriously limit normal interactions with other children. They often spend significant amounts of time alone, show little interest in seeing friends, and engage in few activities. Social withdrawal occurs in about 75% to 95% of depressed youngsters and, other than dysphoric mood, is the symptom that most distinguishes depressed from nondepressed children with a diagnosable disorder (Goodyer & Cooper, 1993; Kovacs, 1987; Mitchell et al., 1988). The social withdrawal of depressed youngsters may reflect their inability to maintain social interactions, possibly related to negative, irritable, and aggressive behavior toward others; deficiencies in social functioning, such as initiating conversations or making friends; and socially unskilled interpersonal behavior (Altmann & Gotlib, 1988).

Although misery may love company, company does not seem to like being with people who are miserable. In fact, many of the social problems of depressed youngsters may relate to the impact of their depressed behavior on others. For example, when observing a film of a depressed child and a nondepressed child of similar age, young schoolchildren rate the child with depression more negatively and less likable or attractive (Peterson, Mullins, & Ridley-Johnson, 1985). Thus, even when children with depression make social overtures, their irritability and nonverbal expressions of depression, such as avoidance of eye contact, may be viewed by others as negative, leading to a decrease in social initiations by others, and to further social isolation. This combination of social withdrawal and a low rate of social initiation which results in negative reactions from others, can seriously interfere with depressed children's social development. As a result, they may fail to experience the social exchanges that lead to healthy social skills and the effective management of social relationships and situations (Kovacs & Goldston, 1991; Kovacs, 1997).

Youngsters with depression often display interpersonal dependency, a lack of social competence and confidence, and inappropriate assertiveness (e.g., fewer socially assertive and more hostile solutions to social problems). They lack social skills, feel uncomfortable during social exchanges, and are especially sensitive to perceived interpersonal slights. Their lack of social competency may lead to a lack of rewards for social behavior, which in turn results in a sad mood and self-blame. There is also a relationship between depression and the use of less effective styles of coping in social situations. For example, relative to nondepressed youngsters, those who are depressed show less active problem solving or problem-focused coping, and use more passive avoidant, ruminative, or emotion-focused coping (Hammen & Rudolph, 1996). Some depressed teens may make poor problem-solving choices, such as getting drunk, as a solution to dealing with a break-up with a boy- or girlfriend. In the words of 17-year-old Page:

> I was so unhappy that I didn't care about myself—even about being safe. I was out drinking a lot, doing a lot of pot. Sometimes I would just black out and not know what was happening. One night I think a bunch of guys had sex with me when I passed out, I don't know. I never remembered anything, it was all hearsay the next day. I made some really bad boyfriend choices. I would date guys who reinforced my view of myself as ugly, stupid, and uncool. I dropped my preppy boyfriend and started dating a 20-year-old guy who was living in his own apartment and playing in a band. He had tattoos on his arms and stomach and was a Hare Krishna. I would date guys just so I could get a ride, even though I didn't like them. I would pick boyfriends who were depressed or ones that my parents really didn't like." (Solin, 1995)

Interestingly, the basic social-cognitive understanding needed for appropriate social relations appears to be relatively intact in youngsters with depression. They are generally as capable as their nondepressed counterparts of providing cognitive solutions to interpersonal problems and show a normal progression on Piagetian tasks of social cognition. However, in sharp contrast to their social understanding, as evident in Page's case, are their social-interpersonal behaviors. In social situations youngsters with depression are less socially adept; are preferred less often as play- or workmates; have poor peer relations, including less contact and fewer best friends; and are rejected, more isolated, less liked, and less assertive than nondepressed youngsters. Importantly, some of these social impairments appear to persist even after recovery from depression (Kovacs & Goldston, 1991).

Family Relationships. In both clinic and community samples, children and adolescents with depression experience poor relations with their parents and siblings (Chiariello & Orvaschel, 1995). They feel more socially isolated from their families and prefer to be alone rather than with their families (Larson, Raffaelli, Richards, Hamm, & Jewell, 1990). In family situations, the child's social isolation may not be a skills deficit but rather a reflection of the child's desire to avoid conflict. Many of these family relationship difficulties have been found to persist, even when children are no longer depressed (Giaconia et al., 1994).

Young children are realistically dependent on their parents until middle or late adolescence. Thus, although the child with depression may not appear dependent, this pattern may emerge later on when issues of autonomy and emancipation come to the fore (Poznanski, 1979). The inappropriate behavior of children with depression may also disrupt normal attachment processes between parent and child. Children with depression may be quite negative toward their parents when interacting, and their parents in turn may respond in a negative, dismissing, or harsh manner (Coyne, Downey, & Boergers, 1992). Parents of children with depression may be similar to parents of nondepressed children in reacting positively to their children's positive behavior; however, they exhibit more negative and neutral behaviors as well (Messer & Gross, 1995). When repeated over time, these interactions may adversely affect the relationship between parent and child in a way that interferes with later development. Children with depression who are irritable, unresponsive, and unaffectionate provide little positive reinforcement for their parents and frustrate their parent's desire for satisfaction in the parenting role (Kovacs, 1997).

THEORIES AND CAUSES OF DEPRESSION

Since depressive disorders come in different forms and show differences in symptoms and severities within the same disorder, it is likely that many processes operate and interact in leading to depression. Asking what *the* cause of depression is, is similar to asking what *the* cause of fever is, or what *the* cause of car accidents is. The road to depression is paved with interactions among vulnerability, risk, and protective factors. Several of the more significant influences are family factors, a lack of rewarding experiences, negative thinking, poor self-regulatory skills, deficits in interpersonal skills, genetic factors, neurobiological deficits, and stressful life events, such as illness, divorce, or maltreatment (Birmaher et al., 1996b). Depression is likely a final common pathway for interacting influences that predispose a child to develop the disorder (Cicchetti & Toth, 1998; Hammen & Rudolph, 1996).

Theories of Depression

Many theories have been proposed to explain the onset and course of depression. Until recently, most were developed to explain depression in adults, then directly applied to children with minimal regard for developmental differences.

Psychodynamic Theory. Early psychodynamic theories viewed depression as the conversion of aggressive instinct into depressive affect. Depression, according to these theories, results from the loss of a love object that is loved ambivalently. Such loss can be actual, in the case of the death of a parent, or symbolic, as a result of emotional deprivation, rejection, or inadequate parenting. The individual's subsequent rage toward the love object is then turned against the self. Since children and adolescents were believed to have inadequate superego development, the hostility and rage directed against internalized love objects that have disappointed or abandoned them do not yet produce guilt and depression, so children and adolescents do not become depressed (Bemporad, 1994; Poznanski, 1979). The fact that depression occurs in many youngsters who do not experience loss or rejection, and doesn't occur in many children who do, casts doubt on the psychodynamic model. Furthermore, contrary to psychodynamic notions, many children do experience clinical depression.

Attachment Theory. Attachment theory focuses on parental separation and disruption of an attachment bond as predisposing factors for depression. John Bowlby hypothesized that a child confronted with unresponsive and emotionally unavailable care-giving experiences goes through a typical sequence (Bowlby, 1961, p. 485):

❖ *Protest.* The child actively tries to recover his or her mother. "At first, with tears and anger he demands his mother back and seems hopeful he will succeed in getting her."

❖ *Despair.* The child feels preoccupied with and remains vigilant for the mother's return, but hope fades. "Later he becomes quieter, but to the discerning eye it is clear that as much as ever he remains preoccupied with his absent mother and still yearns for her return; but his hopes have faded. . . ."

❖ *Detachment.* Emotional disinterest develops as a defense against painful feelings. "Often these two phases [protest and despair] alternate: hope turns to despair and despair to renewed hope. Eventually, however, a greater change occurs. He seems to forget his mother so that when she comes for him he remains curiously uninterested in her and may seem even not to recognize her."

A parent's consistent failure to meet the child's needs is associated with the development of an insecure attachment, a view of self as unworthy and unloved, and a view of others as threatening or undependable—these in turn may place the child at risk for the development of later depression (Cicchetti, Ganiban, & Barnett, 1991). Furthermore, attachments serve to regulate biological and behavioral systems that are related to emotional experience—for example, when a secure attachment relationship can be used to reduce distress. Insecure attachments may lead to difficulties in regulating emotional experience, which may become a risk factor for later depression. Children with insecure attachments who show poor patterns of social relatedness are more likely to display symptoms of depression (e.g., Toth & Cicchetti, 1996).

Behavioral Theories. Behavioral views emphasize the importance of learning, environmental consequences, and skills and deficits in the onset and maintenance of depression. Depression is related to *a lack of response-contingent positive reinforcement* that may occur for several reasons (Lewinsohn, 1974). First, the youngster may be unable to experience available reinforcement, often due to interfering anxiety. Second, changes in the environment—for example, the loss of a significant person in the child's life—may result in a lack of availability of rewards. Third, a youngster may lack the skills needed to have rewarding and satisfying social relationships. Children may also receive sympathy for their sadness, which produces desired attention and concern. However, this sympathy is usually short-lived because even people who care about the youngster begin to avoid him or her, leading to a reduction in attention that may then lead to withdrawal, functional impairment, and heightened feelings of depression. Few studies have tested specific behavioral hypotheses with children, and this model seems incomplete in the light of what is known about other factors that may lead to a vulnerability to depression. Nevertheless, the behavioral model highlights the importance of learning processes in the emergence, expression, and outcome of depression in young people.

Cognitive Theories

Twelve-year-old Lorna: Dear Diary

January 7: Hi Di. How are you? I'm awful. Why do things have to go wrong all the time. I can't stand it. My friend Lisa's back from her trip. I wish I could go on a trip—but I'll never get to go anywhere. I'm so depressed. I just feel like life's not worth living.

Until recently, cognitive models of depression in children were derived almost exclusively from theories based on cognitive processes in depressed adults (Hammen, 1992). Cognitive theories focus on the relation between negative thinking and mood. The underlying assumption is that how young people view themselves and their world will influence their mood and behavior. Distortions in thinking, such as Lorna's extreme statement that she will "never get to go anywhere," are related to depressed mood. A variety of negative cognitions, attributions, misperceptions, and deficiencies in cognitive problem-solving skills have been related to depression in young people (Kaslow et al., 1994). Although there are several different versions, all cognitive theories of depression emphasize the negative perceptual and attributional styles and beliefs associated with depressive symptoms—referred to as **depressogenic cognitions.**

Learned helplessness. The original model of **learned helplessness** proposed that exposure to uncontrollable aversive events resulted in a sense that one could not control important outcomes in one's life—a state of helplessness (Seligman, 1975). This model has since been revised to say that depression-prone individuals tend to make **internal, stable, and global attributions** for the causes of negative events. In other words, when something *bad* happens, depressed individuals think they are responsible (internal attribution), the reason they are to blame won't change over time (stable attribution), and the reason that something bad happened applies to most things they do and in most situations (global attribution) (Abramson, Seligman, & Teasdale, 1978).

Individuals who are depression-prone also attribute positive events to something outside themselves (external), that is not likely to happen again (unstable), and is seen as unique to this event (specific). A negative attributional style results in the individual's taking personal blame for negative events in his or her life and leads to helplessness and avoidance of these events in the future. Helplessness may in turn lead to hopelessness about the future, which promotes further depression (Abramson, Metalsky, & Alloy, 1989).

Beck's cognitive model. The cognitive model of Aaron Beck (1967) proposes that depressed individuals make negative interpretations about life events because they use biased and negative beliefs as interpretive filters for understanding these events. Depressed individuals show cognitive problems in three areas. First, they display *information-processing biases,* or errors in their thinking in specific situations, called negative automatic thoughts. They selectively attend to negative information, assume blame for negative events, maximize and exaggerate negative events, and minimize positive events. They also assign negative labels to events and then react

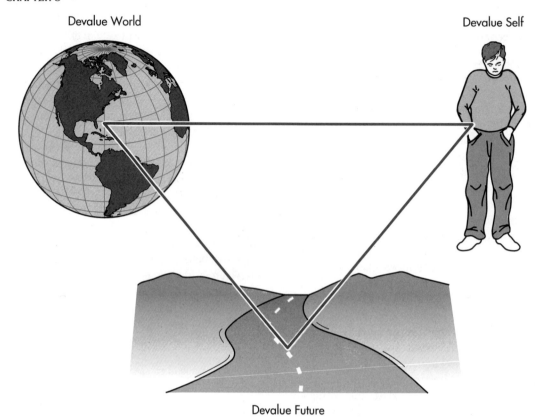

Devalue World

Devalue Self

Devalue Future

FIGURE 8.2 The negative cognitive triad: Depression is related to a devaluation of self, the world, and the future. (D. Murdoch, 1997)

emotionally to the label rather than the event. For example:

❖ *Event:* Child didn't receive an invitation to Henry's party.
❖ *Label:* "I didn't receive an invitation because Henry doesn't like me. Nobody likes me."
❖ *Emotional reaction:* Unhappiness and depression.

Second, depression is believed to be associated with a negative outlook in three areas, referred to as the negative **cognitive triad** (D. Murdoch, personal communication, November 11, 1997) (see Figure 8.2). Youngsters with depression see themselves as worthless or inadequate, the world as mean or unfair, and the future as hopeless. For example:

❖ Negative views about oneself (e.g., "I'm no good," "I'm boring")
❖ Negative views about the world (e.g., "They're no good," "It's too hard")
❖ Negative views about the future (e.g., "It's always going to be this bad," "I'll never graduate")

These negative perceptions serve to maintain feelings of helplessness and to undermine the youngster's mood and energy level, and are related to the child's severity of depression (Stark, Schmidt, & Joiner, 1996).

Third, depressed youngsters have **negative cognitive schemata,** which are stable structures in memory that guide information processing, including self-critical beliefs and attitudes. These cognitive schemata are rigid and resistant to change even in the face of contradictory evidence, and may heighten the youngster's sensitivity to depression, especially when activated by stress.

Comment on cognitive theories. Applying cognitive theories to depression in young people raises questions about the cognitive capacities of children at various stages of development, and the development and stability of cognitive structures that may be involved in depressive thinking. A well-developed sense of self and a time perspective for the future would be needed in order to experience depression. However, in children, the cognitive processes that may ultimately serve to predispose or protect them from depression are still developing. In fact, many of the cognitive errors and distortions discussed so far, such as illogical thinking or faulty attributions, are normal ways of thinking in young children!

These cognitive errors and distortions need to be considered in relation to the child's developing sense of personal competence, not as factors that predispose the child to depression (Seroczynski et al., 1997). For example, during the transition from preoperational to concrete operational thinking in middle childhood, children begin to develop the capacity to reflect on their own thinking (metacognition). Before this age, children can make social comparisons, but not as a basis for making self-evaluations. With the emergence of concrete operational thinking, however, children begin to compare themselves to others in a self-evaluative way. Also around this time depression begins to be characterized by low self-esteem as well as mood disturbance (Rehm & Carter, 1990). A vulnerability for depressogenic thought processes may begin during middle childhood in the context of emerging views of personal competence, and once developed, may remain relatively stable throughout adolescence (Garber et al., 1993).

Although higher rates of depressogenic cognitions are found in youngsters with depression, there are still many unanswered questions regarding the relation between cognition and depression (Kaslow et al., 1994). Is attributional style associated with depression in the presence, but not in the absence, of negative life events (Joiner & Wagner, 1995)? Are low self-concept, decreased self-worth, cognitive biases, and negative attributional styles unique to depression, or are they an indication of psychopathology in general? Are depressed youngsters' cognitions different from those of youngsters with other disorders? For example, anxiety may relate to low self-competence (e.g., "I'm not good at doing anything"), and depression to low self-worth (e.g., "I'm worthless"). Do negative cognitions represent distortions in thinking or accurate appraisals by a child who is experiencing actual impairments in functioning? We also need more information about how negative cognitions develop. Are they the result of parental rejection and the use of negative forms of parental control, such as scorn and withdrawal of affection? Is there a relation between maternal cognitions and child cognitions, as suggested by findings that mothers' cognitive triads are related to their children's cognitive triads (Stark, Schmidt, & Joiner, 1996)? How does a cognitive vulnerability for depression interact with stress to result in depression (Hammen & Rudolph, 1996)? Longitudinal studies are needed to answer these and other questions.

Self-Control Theory. Self-control theories view individuals with depression as having difficulty organizing their behavior in relation to long-term goals. They display deficits in self-monitoring, self-evaluation, and self-reinforcement. As a result they selectively attend to negative versus positive events and to immediate rather than delayed consequences of behavior, set excessively high standards and expectations for performance, make negative causal attributions, administer insufficient self-rewards to motivate effective behavior, and use excessive self-punishment, which serves to further decrease effective behavior. Evidence suggests that children with depression display some of these deficits, although research findings are limited (Rehm & Sharp, 1996).

Interpersonal Theories. Interpersonal models view disruptions in interpersonal relationships, especially within the family, as the basis for the onset and maintenance of depression (Bemporad, 1994; Coyne, 1976; Gotlib & Hammen, 1992). The depressed individual engages in behaviors that are aversive to others, leading family members to become more annoyed and frustrated. As the depressed person becomes more aware of how others are reacting, he or she feels even more needy, and unthinkingly increases the annoying behaviors. Interpersonal models also assume that child depression serves some function in the family—for example, to decrease marital conflict.

Biological/Neurobiological Theories.
Biological models of depression in young people have focused on the role of genetic vulnerabilities and neurobiological processes and correlates, including neuroanatomical, neuropsychological, neurochemical, and neuroendocrine factors, as well as sleep architecture. Abnormalities in each of these areas have been identified, although findings for depressed children and adolescents are far less clear and less consistent than they are for adults (Emslie, Weinberg, Kennard, & Kowatch, 1994). We discuss possible biologic factors in the next section on causes.

Socioenvironmental Theories. Socioenvironmental models focus on the relationship between stressful life events and depression. Research with children and adolescents has pointed to the significant role of such events in the onset of depressive episodes (Compas, Grant, & Ey, 1994). A number of models regarding this relation have been proposed. Stress reaction models link depression directly with the occurrence of stressful life events, such as the loss of a parent. In **diathesis-stress models of depression** the impact of stress is moderated by individual risk factors such as genetic risk, and the occurrence of depression depends on the interaction between the youngster's personal vulnerability and life stress. The match between the vulnerability and nature of the stressor may determine whether or not depression will occur. For example, for a child with low self-worth in the area of academic competence, failure in school may be particularly likely to lead to depression. Mediational models propose that negative environmental events are internalized as negative cognitions, which then predispose the child to develop depression. Stress generation models propose that depression results in impaired

Table 8.5 Overview of Theories of Depression

Psychodynamic	Introjection of the lost object; anger turned inward; excessive severity of the superego; loss of self-esteem
Attachment	Insecure early attachments; distorted internal working models of self and others
Behavioral	Loss of reinforcement or quality of reinforcement; deficits in skills needed to obtain reinforcement
Cognitive	Depressive schemata; distorted or maladaptive cognitive structures, processes, and products; negative view of self, world, and future; poor problem-solving ability
Self-Control	Problems in organizing behavior toward long-term goals; deficits in self-monitoring, self-evaluation, and self-reinforcement
Interpersonal	Impaired interpersonal functioning related to grief over loss; role dispute and conflict, role transition, interpersonal deficit, single parenting; social withdrawal; interaction between mood and interpersonal events
Neurobiological	Neurochemical and receptor abnormalities; neurophysiological abnormalities; neuroendocrine abnormalities
Socioenvironmental	Stressful life circumstances and daily hassles as vulnerability factors; social support, coping, and appraisal as protective factors

Source: Adapted from Dozois, 1997.

functioning that contributes to the occurrence of stressful circumstances that in turn lead to depressive reactions. A number of environmental influences and stressors that may be important to the onset of depression have been identified, including social disadvantage, unemployment, remarriage, single-parent status, large family, and poor social support (Hammen & Rudolph, 1996).

An overview of the primary theories of depression is presented in Table 8.5.

Causes of Depression

Genetic and Family Risk. Genetic influences account for about half of the variance in the transmission of mood disorders in adults. Environmental factors are also important, especially nonshared experiences such as differences in the way parents treat each of their children (Kendler, 1995; Plomin, 1994). For example, a chaotic family environment is associated with an increased risk for depression in the offspring of parents who have MDD (Warner, Mufson, & Weissman, 1995). Children of parents with affective disorder have 2 to 3 times the risk of having depression compared with children of parents having no psychiatric disorders (Beardslee, Keller, Lavori, Staley, & Sacks, 1993). Children with a parent who suffered from depression as a child are 14 times more likely than controls to become depressed themselves before they reach the age of 13 (Weissman, Warner, Wickramaratne, & Prusoff, 1988).

The earlier the onset of depressive illness, the greater the risk in first-degree relatives (Harrington et al., 1996). For example, rates of depressive disorder in the first-degree relatives of youngsters with depression range from about 45% in relatives of children with depression

to 25% in relatives of adolescents with depression. The lifetime prevalence of depressive disorder in mothers of children with depression ranges from 56% to 73%. In general, the increased risk of depression in the families of youngsters with depression has been greatest when comparisons are with children who have no disorder. However, the aggregation of depression in families of children with depression is also higher than in families of children with other psychiatric disorders (Kovacs, 1997).

Although depression in young people appears to be a family disorder, the mechanisms and modes of transmission and the nature of the vulnerability are not known at present (Kovacs, 1997). It is unclear whether the transmission in families is genetic, psychosocial, or both. Depression could be transmitted either directly or indirectly through psychosocial processes. For example, youngsters may learn depressive symptoms through modeling or differential reinforcement, through interactions with a depressed mother that lead to depression, or by living in a world of social isolation created by a depressed parent that limits access to resources outside the family. The link between parent and child depression may also be related to common influences, such as stress, marital discord, or family adversity (Fergusson, Horwood, & Lynskey, 1995). In general, family and twin studies suggest that what may be inherited is a vulnerability to depression and anxiety, and that certain environmental stressors may be required for these disorders to be expressed (Kendler, 1995). Some evidence suggests that the family loading may be for anxiety disorder, and that anxiety disorder may be a risk factor for later depression. For example, the family resemblance of siblings or offspring of parents with depression is substantially higher for anxiety disorders than for depression (Weissman, Warner, Wickramaratne, Moreau, & Olfson, 1997).

Neurobiological Influences. Some of the new work emerging from the labs of those who study neurobiological processes of depression is too recent to provide a basis for firm conclusions, but it seems to be saying that youngsters with depression may have heightened reactions to stress that increase their vulnerability to depression. In one scenario neurobiological influences on depression may be direct. Alternatively, psychological experiences may produce biochemical and neurological changes that form and perpetuate a lasting basis for depressive disorder (Cytryn & McKnew, 1996; Post et al., 1996). Regardless of their origin, neurobiological factors play a critical role in depression. The frontal lobe of the brain plays a primary role in regulating mood and affect (Stuss, Gow, & Hetherington, 1992). Infants of mothers with depression show less frontal lobe electrical activity and higher levels of salivary cortisol (the stress hormone) than infants of mothers without depression (Dawson, Frey, Panagiotides, Osterling, & Hessl, 1997). Other studies have found that infants who display greater right than left frontal lobe activity experience more distress upon separation from their mothers (Davidson & Fox, 1989; Dawson, 1994). Emotions related to social engagement and exploration may trigger left frontal lobe activity, whereas feelings associated with social withdrawal, flight, and negative affect may strengthen right frontal activity (Field, Fox, Pickens, & Nawrocki, 1995). This pattern of right frontal activation may be a biological marker for infant vulnerability toward an anxious or fearful disposition that predicts later difficulties in mood and behavior.

These findings concerning brain organization and activity in the infants of mothers with depression suggest the possibility of ontogenetic sculpting (Kolb, 1989), in which interactions between mothers and their infants change brain physiology by selectively strengthening and weakening certain neural networks related to emotion regulation. As a result of this process, some children may develop a dissociation between their physiological and behavioral reactions. Although they are inwardly distressed, they appear passive and unresponsive. It's as if these children have no sense of how they are feeling, or no way to access or express their feelings. Although research strongly indicates the importance of early mother-infant interactions in the development of neurobiological systems, more information is needed about critical periods for neural development and their relation to the development of emotion regulation (Kazdin & Marciano, 1998).

Studies of neurobiological correlates of depression have focused on the hypothalamic-pituitary-adrenal axis (HPA), sleep architecture, growth hormones, and serotonergic function (Emslie et al., 1994; Hammen & Rudolph, 1996). There has been much interest in the relation between functioning of the brain HPA axis—the brain-endocrine system that regulates reactions to stressful events—and depression. Studies of HPA regulation and depression take two approaches. The first assesses baseline plasma cortisol secretion, for example, over a period of 24 hours. Studies using this approach generally fail to find differences between youngsters with and without depression in baseline levels of cortisol (Emslie et al., 1994). The second approach assesses youngsters' responses to challenges such as the dexamethasone suppression test (DST). Dexamethasone is a substance (glucocorticoid) that suppresses cortisol secretion in normal individuals. However, when given to adults with depression, much less suppression occurs, or if it does occur, it doesn't last very long. About half of adult patients with depression show reduced suppression (Carroll et al., 1980). Presumably, individuals with depression are already secreting so much cortisol that it overrides any suppressive effects of the dexamethasone. Findings for the DST in children and adolescents are generally inconclusive relative to those for adults (Birmaher et al., 1996b), possibly because of differences between children and adults in dexamethasone metabolism. In general, findings related to HPA functions are far less consistent for children than they are for adults (Hammen & Rudolph, 1996).

A variety of sleep abnormalities have been found in depressed adults, including delayed sleep onset and decreased sleep efficiency (see Chapter 12). Although youngsters with depression frequently complain of sleep disturbances, EEG studies have not found consistent sleep abnormalities similar to those for adults. However, few studies have been conducted with children (Birmaher et al., 1996b; Emslie et al., 1994; Williamson, Dahl, Birmaher, Goetz, & Ryan, 1995). Children with depression have been found to undersecrete growth hormone (GH) following various drug challenges (e.g., growth hormone-releasing hormone) (Ryan et al., 1994). The persistence of lowered GH responses following recovery from MDD suggests that this reaction may be a trait marker for MDD. Findings related to nocturnal GH secretion without drug challenge are inconsistent, although recent findings suggest that stressful life events may be related to increased nocturnal GH secretion in adolescents with depression (Birmaher et al., 1996b). Serotonin, acetylcholine, and dopamine levels in adults with depression have been studied at length because these neurotransmitters control how people feel and play a major role in the regulation of several areas of functioning related to depression. Research with adults suggests that dysregulation of central serotonergic function may be a risk factor for depression. However, findings with children are less consistent (Birmaher et al., 1996b). In general, studies of the neurobiological correlates of depression in children and adolescents suggest that youngsters with depression have an increased sensitivity to stress rather than a chronic dysregulation. Repeated neuroendocrine activation related to stress may increase youngsters' susceptibility to depressive disorders, and chronic depressive symptomatology may lead to further extreme biological activation and to psychosocial stress (Birmaher et al., 1996b).

Family Influences

"I was always able to explain away my daughter's symptoms," says the mother of a 12-year-old. "When she was 10 and fought with me about everything, I just wrote it off as preadolescent hissy fits. When she dropped out of gymnastics—which had been her raison d'etre—and started losing weight, I told myself she was just searching for a new identity. But when her best friend came to me and told me that my daughter was talking about suicide, I was forced to face the truth. I keep blaming myself. What did I do to cause this depression? What could I have done to prevent it?" (Levine, 1995, p. 44)

Several parent and family characteristics have been associated with depression in children and adolescents (Hammen, 1991). One way of examining these characteristics considers the family environment of children with depression; the second considers the family environment of parents who are depressed.

Families of children with depression. The families of youngsters with depression display more negative and punitive behavior toward the depressed child (compared with other children in the family); less warmth; more anger, conflict, and control; less support; poorer communication; overinvolvement; and more criticism (Asarnow, Tompson, Hamilton, Goldstein, & Guthrie, 1994; Chiariello & Orvaschel, 1995; Kaslow et al., 1994; Lewinsohn, Roberts, et al., 1994). These families often experience high levels of adversity and stress, disorganization, marital discord, and a lack of social support (Messer & Gross, 1995; Slavin & Rainer, 1990). Youngsters with depression describe their families as less cohesive and more disengaged. These children display emotional separateness and a lack of closeness to their families as compared with children without depression (Kashani, Allan, Dahlmeier, Rezvani, & Reid, 1995).

Research points strongly to the link between childhood depression and family dysfunction. One longitudinal study found that less supportive and more conflictual family environments were associated with more depressive symptoms in adolescents both concurrently and prospectively over a 1-year period. In contrast, adolescent depressive symptoms did not predict a worsening of family relationships over the same time period. Thus, quality of the family environment may be related to the development of depressive symptoms (Sheeber, Hops, Alpert, Davis, & Andrews, 1997). However, a number of issues regarding the nature of this relationship exist. First, family difficulties of the type described above are related to various child and adolescent disorders and may not be specific to depression (Downey & Coyne, 1990; Goodyer et al., 1997). Second, it is difficult to know the extent to which family problems are related to the presence of a comorbid condition, and many studies have failed to take comorbidity into account. Finally, most studies are correlational, making it impossible to determine the direction of influence. Certainly, an adverse family environment can lead to depression, but as we have seen, depression may also evoke negative and critical reactions from family members and produce distress in parents and others (Bell-Dolan, Reaven, & Peterson, 1993). It may be that family conflict represents a coping strategy (albeit an ineffective one) for attempting to control the disruptive behaviors of a depressed youngster (Asarnow et al., 1994). Children in dysfunctional families may also learn to give up when faced with stress and may not develop adaptive ways to regulate negative emotions (Garber & Hilsman, 1992). It is also possible that some other factor, such as genetic risk, may account for both depression and family disturbances. Some support exists for all these mechanisms of family influence in child depression.

Children of parents with depression. Children of parents with depression are at a higher risk for MDD and other impairments (Weissman et al., 1987; Weissman et al., 1997). Overall, these children are 3 times more likely to have lifetime episodes of MDD than are children of nondepressed parents, with a lifetime risk for MDD of between 15% and 45% (Hammen, Burge, Burney, & Adrian, 1990). These children also have an earlier age of onset for their depression (by about 3 years) and are more likely to show a prepubertal onset than children of nondepressed parents (Weissman et al., 1997). An early onset and recurrence of depression in the parent are associated with the highest risk for the child. Risk for depression is also higher for the child when *both* parents have a mood disorder. Not only are the children of parents with depression at risk for developing depression, but they are also at elevated risk for developing other forms of psychopathology, including anxiety disorders, disruptive behavior disorders, and related disturbances (Stoleru, Nottelmann, & Ronsaville, 1997).

The study of parent-child interaction patterns among mothers with depression and their children has suggested precursors of depression and the possible processes leading to depression (Hammen, 1991). When interacting with their children, mothers with depression tend to be less responsive, affectionate, and contingent, as well as more irritable, hostile, and critical than mothers who are not depressed. They also display less energy in stimulating play, less consistency in following through with discipline, less involvement, poor communication, lack of affection, and more criticism and resentment of their children than well mothers (Kovacs, 1997). As illustrated in the following example, interactions between mothers with depression and their children are frequently characterized by dysphoria, withdrawal, negative verbal and nonverbal behavior, and a lack of physical affection and emotional expressiveness:

Mrs. D.

Mrs. D., the mother of 5-year-old Maria, is depressed and has been helpless and needy for most of Maria's life. She moves ever so slowly to prepare breakfast for Maria and herself. Wringing her hands, she pays little attention to events around her. Maria has been tugging at her mother for some time, apparently wanting food. Mrs. D. mumbles something, sobs continuously, and wipes tears from her cheek as she moves between the cupboard and kitchen table. Maria persists in trying to gain her mother's attention, and finally Mrs. D. hugs her and strokes her hair. At first Maria pulls back; then she snuggles against her mother's legs. Finally Maria's mother fills a bowl with cereal, and she and Maria sit down to eat in total silence, during which Mrs. D. looks sadly at her daughter. Deep bouts of depression periodically incapacitate Mrs. D., and any problem that Maria has sends her to bed. Mostly, Maria is left on her own to handle problems. (Adapted from Radke-Yarrow & Zahn-Waxler, 1990)

Depression clearly interferes with the ability of the parent to meet the needs of the child. Mothers who suffer from depression, like Mrs. D., create a child-rearing environment teeming with negative mood, irritability, helplessness, and unpredictable displays of affection—an extremely inconsistent emotional environment. There is also a greater likelihood of marital conflict and family discord and high levels of stress in the home when a parent is depressed (Beardslee & Wheelock, 1994; Kaslow et al., 1994). Children of mothers with depression attempt to cope with the unpredictability of their environment in different ways, often maladaptive, showing reactions ranging from aggressive and hurtful behavior, to withdrawal, to school refusal, to failure to thrive, to depression (Philips, 1979).

Children of mothers with depression must take care of themselves and must learn how to handle their own

problems. It is not surprising that infants and toddlers of mothers who are depressed show emotional delays, separation difficulties, and insecure attachments. Children of mothers with depression tend to be self-critical and have difficulties regulating their own emotions. As a result, these children are ill equipped to cope effectively with stressful events, which may subsequently place them at risk for depressive disorder and other impairments (Radke-Yarrow & Zahn-Waxler, 1990).

Long-term follow-up studies of children of parents with depression confirm the risks associated with growing up in a family with a depressed parent. Over a 10-year period children of depressed parents had increased rates of MDD (3 times the risk), particularly before puberty, and phobias (3 times the risk), panic disorder, alcohol dependence (at a fivefold risk), and a greater degree of social impairment (Weissman et al., 1997). Relative to controls, offspring of depressed parents received more outpatient treatment over 10 years and had poorer overall functioning in work, family, and marital relationships. The findings from this study are sobering in documenting serious long-term negative outcomes and impairments in the offspring of depressed parents.

Stressful Life Events

Thirteen-year-old Carline

I don't feel depressed all the time. It comes and goes. Usually it takes something to set it off. It could be something big, like when we moved, but anything, no matter how small, can really get to me, and then I start feeling bad and can't do anything. So today things are OK and I don't feel so bad. But tomorrow, or the next day, something might happen, no matter how minor, and I just might not want to get out of bed, or do anything.

Depression is often associated with negative life events, such as a move to a new neighborhood, a change of schools, the death of a loved one, a serious accident or family illness, an extreme lack of family resources, a violent family environment, or parental conflict or divorce (Goodyer et al., 1997; Kovacs, 1997). These events may occur alone or in combination with other risk factors, such as a lack of social support or inadequate parental care. At times, minor stressful events, or **daily hassles,** such as a poor grade on a test, an argument with a parent, criticism from a teacher, a fight with a boyfriend, or a broken date, may also result in depression. Relative to nondepressed youngsters, those who become depressed experience significantly more severe *and* nonsevere stressful events in the year preceding their depression—

especially in areas related to romantic relationships, education, relations with friends or parents, work, and health (Birmaher et al., 1996b).

Depressive triggers often involve actual or perceived personal losses, such as the death of a loved one, abandonment, disappointment, rejection, or a threat to one's self-esteem. Sadness and depression following loss are common. In children ages 5 to 12 who had recently suffered the most horrible loss, the loss of a parent, all experienced sadness and grief, and about 40% developed major depression (Weller, Weller, Fristad, & Bowes, 1991). Yet depressive disorder is not an inevitable outcome or even the most common reaction—more than 60% of children who experience the loss of a parent do not develop major depression. Thus, objective loss is neither necessary nor sufficient to cause a depressive disorder.

Exposure to suicide is a grim stressful event that is associated with a threefold increase in MDD in friends, siblings, and mothers of victims. In a group of adolescents who had lost a friend or peer through suicide, 30% developed a depressive disorder within 6 months following the loss (Brent et al., 1992). The risk of developing depression following loss through suicide is related to the closeness of the youngster to the victim and the intensity of exposure. Other factors, such as a history of interpersonal losses, additional stressors, a history of psychiatric illness in the family, and prior psychopathology of the child, including depression, increase the youngsters' risk for depression following loss through suicide (Birmaher et al., 1996b). Although loss and other negative life events can trigger depression, these events are nonspecific risk factors for many different disorders. For example, not only do adolescents who experience the suicidal death of a sibling or peer have a heightened risk for MDD, they also are at increased risk for developing anxiety disorder and post-traumatic stress disorder within 6 to 12 months following the suicidal death (Pfeffer et al., 1997). Thus, bereavement related to suicide may result in a wide range of symptoms and impairments, including, but not restricted to, depression.

In general, the relation between stressful life events and depression in young people is significant, but modest. Stressful major life events tend to be nonspecific factors that are related to a variety of problems besides depression. It is also possible that elevated levels of stressful life events among adolescents with depression are related to the co-occurrence of other disorders, such as conduct disorder. In fact, one study found that adolescents with depression only (and no other disorder) did not differ from controls in the number of negative life events they reported experiencing (Lewinsohn et al., 1997). It would appear that triggering negative life events interact with individual vulnerabilities to result in depression in some youngsters, and some stressful events

that do not end in depression may still become risk factors for the later development of other disorders (Kovacs, 1997). Understanding the processes by which negative life events may lead to depression for some children is an important next step in research (Ge, Conger, Lorenz, & Simons, 1994).

Cognitive Factors. We have seen that depression is related to a negative cognitive style that includes low self-esteem, cognitive distortions, negative attributions, hopelessness, excessive self-criticism, and a perceived lack of control over negative life events. However, it is not clear if a negative cognitive style is specific to depression, or if it is a stable trait or a temporary characteristic that is associated with the depressive episode. The specific processes by which youngsters come to develop negative styles of thinking are not yet known. However, some factors that may be important include modeling by significant others, perfectionistic standards, excessive criticism, rejection, and exposure to uncontrollable stressful life events (Hammen & Rudolph, 1996). The fact that a negative cognitive style seems to emerge in adolescence suggests that it may result from repeated subclinical or clinical episodes of depression (Turner & Cole, 1994). After children recover from depression, they may continue to have low self-esteem, which in turn places them at risk for a future episode of depression. The cognitive-diathesis model proposes that youngsters who experience stressful events, such as a poor report card or peer rejection, and who have negative styles of interpreting and coping with stress may be at high risk for developing a depressive disorder (Garber, 1992; Garber & Hilsman, 1992; Hilsman & Garber, 1995).

Emotion Regulation. Interest is growing in the role of emotion regulation and dysregulation in understanding affective disorders in young people. **Emotion regulation** refers to the processes by which emotional arousal is redirected, controlled, or modified to facilitate adaptive functioning (Cicchetti et al., 1991), and to the balance maintained among positive, negative, and neutral mood states (Kopp, 1992). Youngsters demonstrate wide differences in regulating their emotions and managing their negative mood states. For example, if a favorite playmate cannot be found, one child may cry and cannot be comforted, another may cry for a short time and then find someone else to play with, and another child may look to an adult for comfort. Children's strategies for self-regulation play a crucial role in overcoming, maintaining, or preventing negative emotional states (Garber, Braafladt, & Zeman, 1991). Young children who experience prolonged periods of emotional distress and sadness may have problems in regulating negative emotional

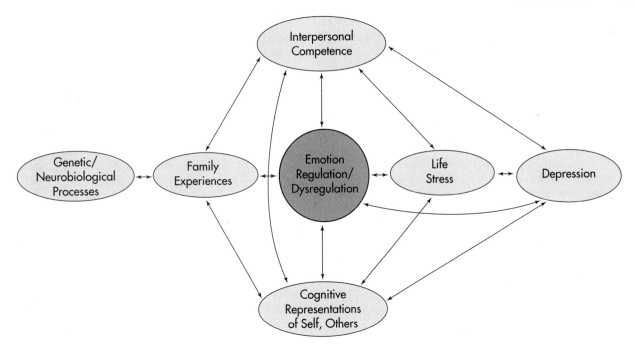

FIGURE 8.3 A developmental framework for depression in young people.

states and may be prone to the development of depression (Kovacs, 1997).

A variety of skills are needed to manage one's own emotions, including recognizing that changes have occurred in affect that require regulation, accurately interpreting the conditions that led to one's mood change, setting goals for what is needed to change one's affect, and generating, evaluating, and implementing effective coping responses (Kazdin & Marciano, 1998). Youngsters with depression may show deficits in one or more of these regulatory skills and, as a result, have difficulty overcoming their negative moods. They may use avoidance or negative behavior to regulate their distress rather than more problem-focused and adaptive coping strategies. Their use of ineffective emotion regulation strategies may in turn contribute to social isolation and distress (Garber et al., 1991). Children with depression are often negative and hostile during social interactions and display more anger and sadness than children who are aggressive (Kovacs, 1997). They report more daily feelings of unhappiness and irritability, and more emotional variability than nondepressed youngsters (Larson et al., 1990). Since emotion regulation encompasses neurobiological regulatory processes, acquired behavioral and cognitive strategies, and external resources for coping (Thompson, 1994), depression may result from difficulties in any one or more of these areas.

Summary of Causes. As we have seen, depression may be due to numerous factors affecting the child's early development and sense of self. The potentially large number of risk factors for depression and their interaction over time require an integrative framework to account for not only the development of depression in young people, but also its nonoccurrence in the presence of risk. Recently, developmental models of depression have taken a multidimensional, interactive perspective (Cicchetti & Toth, 1998; Hammen & Rudolph, 1996). A possible developmental framework for depression in young people is presented in Figure 8.3. This framework highlights the interplay among genetic, neurobiological, family, cognitive, emotional, interpersonal, and environmental factors over time.

Within this framework, genetic risk influences neurobiological processes and is reflected in such child characteristics as arousability and temperament. Early temperament or personality may be displayed as a general oversensitivity to negative stimuli, referred to as neuroticism, high negative emotionality, or negative affectivity (Clark, Watson, & Mineka, 1994). These early dispositions both direct and are shaped and organized by experiences within the family, and continue to exert influence throughout development. Core beliefs about the self and others and expectations about future interpersonal interactions develop as a result of interactions within the family. Insensitive and rejecting parenting leads to a view of self as incompetent, other people as threatening or unresponsive, and relationships as negative and unpredictable. Negative family experiences may also provide an inconsistent emotional and social environment, which makes it difficult for the child to effectively regulate her or his emotions and interpersonal behavior. These cognitive, emotional, and interpersonal problems may lead directly to depression. Or they may result in negative social behaviors and emotional cues that elicit conflict, rejection by others, and social isolation, resulting in depression. In other instances, negative cognitive representations, poor social relationships, and emotion dysregulation may create a vulnerability that makes children more prone to develop depression when they encounter negative life events. In any of these scenarios the child's depression may then interfere with future development by disrupting social relationships, damaging existing competencies, producing further emotion dysregulation, creating additional stress, and confirming the child's already negative views of self, the world, and the future (Hammen & Rudolph, 1996).

BIPOLAR DISORDER

"In a sense, depression is a view of the world through a dark glass, and mania is that seen through a kaleidoscope—often brilliant but fractured. (Jamison, 1997, p. 48)

Ben: Highs and Lows

Fourteen-year-old Ben was living in a residential treatment center. He had a history of moodiness, hyped-up activity, sleeplessness, and a sexual preoccupation with girls in his class—he had even approached his teacher with offers of sexual intimacy. Ben showed the racing thoughts and the fast or "pressured" speech characteristic of mania and had wide mood swings. At the high extreme Ben rarely slept, yelled, sang, and disturbed everyone—charging about the residence day and night with a seemingly endless supply of energy. He felt "absolutely terrific" at these times and thought he could fly. The low extreme found Ben curled up in a ball beneath a stack of blankets, a withdrawn and hopeless young man who expressed feelings of worthlessness and thoughts of suicide.

Although bipolar disorder (BP) is generally thought of as an adult illness, it is considered here because of its emergence during adolescence. If you've seen the movie *Shine*, chances are you have a clear image of Australian piano prodigy David Helfgott racing through the Rachmaninoff Third Piano Concerto ("Rach 3") as if there were no tomorrow. Until recently, BP in young people received very little attention (Carlson, 1994). This lack of attention is partly related to the difficulties in identifying BP in young people, including its low base rate of

occurrence, variability of clinical presentation within and across episodes, overlap in symptoms with more common childhood disorders such as ADHD, and the developmental constraints placed on symptom expression at different ages (Bowring & Kovacs, 1992). Although extremely rare in young children, BP increases significantly after puberty. It is at once remarkable and almost inconceivable how a young person with this disorder, like Ben, can be so manic, elated, and wild at one moment, so depressed and immobile the next, and at other times seem so normal (Geller & Luby, 1997). Ben displays the essential features of BP—a striking period of abnormally and persistently elevated, expansive, or irritable mood, alternating with or accompanied by one or more major depressive episodes. The mood states associated with BP are elation and euphoria. However, these feelings can quickly change to anger and hostility if the youngster is impeded in his or her behavior. Since many youngsters with BP have simultaneous feelings of depression and dysphoria, they are easily reduced to tears.

Youngsters with BP show severe and cyclical mood changes and outbursts. Mania typically occurs in episodes, with an onset and offset. Thus, in its fully developed state it is clearly different from a youngster's usual condition (Carlson, 1995). During a manic episode, youngsters with BP might display intense symptoms such as irritability and rage. Or they may show silly, giddy, overexcited, overtalkative behavior coupled with expansive, grandiose beliefs (e.g., a teen who feels he or she has a special connection to God). It is normal for children to pretend to have special powers or abilities, but a youngster with BP, during a manic episode, will actually believe that he is Hercules, or Jackie Chan, or the President, and that he is all-powerful. He might believe he can walk on water, fly, control traffic, or jump off buildings without hurting himself—and kill himself in the process. Grandiosity is extremely rare in young children with BP, but begins to appear around the age of 9 or 10 years (Carlson, 1994).

Restlessness, agitation, and sleeplessness are also typical of youngsters with BP. Sexual disinhibition (like Ben's propositioning his teacher) in which the youngster becomes uncharacteristically preoccupied with sexual themes, sexually touching others, or "talking dirty" may also occur. Youngsters with BP may experience unrealistic elevations in self-esteem and vast surges of energy; they may have the ability to go with little or no sleep for days without feeling tired. They may be able to concentrate for hours on an activity that interests them, such as drawing, playing a musical instrument, or becoming engrossed in a mentally demanding fantasy game. At the same time, they may be highly distractible, constantly jumping from one thing to another (Geller & Luby, 1997).

Table 8.6   DSM-IV Criteria for Manic, Mixed, and Hypomanic Episodes

DSM-IV Criteria for a Manic Episode

A **manic episode** is the hallmark characteristic of bipolar disorder and is defined as follows:

A. A distinct period of abnormally and persistently elevated, expansive, and/or irritable mood, lasting at least 1 week (or any duration if hospitalization is necessary).

B. During the period of mood disturbance, three (or more) of the following symptoms have persisted (four if the mood is only irritable) and have been present to a significant degree:
   (1) inflated self-esteem or grandiosity
   (2) decreased need for sleep (e.g., feels rested after only 3 hours of sleep)
   (3) more talkative than usual or pressure to keep talking
   (4) flight of ideas or subjective experience that thoughts are racing
   (5) distractibility (i.e., attention too easily drawn to unimportant or irrelevant external stimuli)
   (6) increase in goal-directed activity (either socially, at work or school, or sexually) or psychomotor agitation
   (7) excessive involvement in pleasurable activities that have a high potential for painful consequences (e.g., engaging in unrestrained buying sprees, sexual indiscretions, or foolish business investments)

C. The symptoms do not meet criterion for a Mixed Episode.

D. The mood disturbance is sufficiently severe to cause marked impairment in occupational functioning or in usual social activities or relationships with others, or to necessitate hospitalization to prevent harm to self or others, or there are psychotic features.

E. The symptoms are not due to the direct physiological effects of a substance (e.g., a drug of abuse, a medication, or other treatment) or a general medical condition (e.g., hypothyroidism).

Note: Manic-like episodes that are clearly caused by somatic antidepressant treatment (e.g., medication, electroconvulsive therapy, light therapy) should not count toward a diagnosis of Bipolar I Disorder.

DSM-IV Criteria for a Mixed Episode

A mixed episode is diagnosed when criteria are met for both a manic episode and a major depressive episode over at least a 1-week period. The requirement for significant impairment and the exclusion or organic causes are the same as for a manic episode.

DSM-IV Criteria for a Hypomanic Episode

A hypomanic episode has similar features to a manic episode but differs in the severity, duration, and degree of impairment criteria. The symptoms must be present for at least 4 days and must produce an unequivocal change in functioning that is uncharacteristic of the person when not symptomatic. However, by definition, there is no marked deterioration in functioning, need for hospitalization, or psychotic symptoms; otherwise a diagnosis of manic episode applies. The requirement for exclusion of organic causes are the same as for manic episode.

Source: Adapted from DSM-IV 1994 by permission of APA.

The elated mood of manic youngsters may (erroneously) give them the appearance of being happy and cheerful people. Like Ben, they may say, "I feel absolutely terrific." It is difficult to recognize that a laughing, happy youngster also has a history of misery and distress. For this reason evaluating a youngster's current mood in relation to his or her developmental history is essential, particularly when there is an inconsistency between the child's elated mood and his or her history of trouble in school, family conflict and adversities, or problems with the law (Geller & Luby, 1997).

The diagnosis of BP in young people is made using the same DSM-IV criteria used for adults. Current research suggests that BP with an onset prior to age 18 is essentially the same disorder as in adults, although possible differences in long-term outcomes and associated characteristics are not known. There are several subtypes of BP, based on whether the youngster displays a manic, mixed, or hypomanic episode. The DSM-IV criteria for each of these episodes are presented in Table 8.6, and the criteria for the different types of BP are presented in Table 8.7. A diagnosis of BP requires evidence for a manic or mixed episode in the case of **bipolar I disorder,** a hypomanic episode in the case of **bipolar II disorder,** or subthreshold manic symptoms in the case of **cyclothymic disorder.**

Characteristic stages of mania have been described in older persons. Initially, the individual may display euphoria, increased psychomotor activity, and mood lability. A second stage is characterized by irritability,

Table 8.7   Subtypes of Bipolar Disorder

❖ **Bipolar I Disorder**

To have a bipolar I disorder, the individual has a clinical course characterized by one or more manic or mixed episodes, and one or more major depressive episodes.

❖ **Bipolar II Disorder**

Individuals with bipolar II disorder have a clinical course of one or more major depressive episodes accompanied by at least one hypomanic episode. The presence of a manic or mixed episode precludes the diagnosis of a bipolar II disorder.

❖ **Cyclothymic Disorder**

For children and adolescents, cyclothymia is diagnosed when there have been periods of 1 year or more (2 years in adults) where there are numerous hypomanic and depressive symptoms that do not meet full criteria for either a manic espoused, mixed episode, or major depressive disorder. The symptoms must be present for most of the defined 1-year period, with no more than 2 consecutive symptom-free months, and must cause significant distress or impairment in functioning.

Exclusionary criteria. None of the above disorders is diagnosed if the symptoms are better accounted for, or are superimposed on, schizoaffective disorder, schizophrenia, schizophreniform disorder, delusional disorder, or a psychotic disorder not otherwise specified.

Specification of course. The diagnosis of both bipolar I and bipolar II require specification of whether there is a seasonal pattern or rapid cycling. With a seasonal pattern major depressive episodes occur consistently at a particular time of year (see section on seasonal affective disorder). Rapid cycling is diagnosed when there have been at least four episodes of a mood disturbance (major depression, mania, mixed, or hypomania) over a 1-year period.

Source: Based on DSM-IV 1994 by APA.

racing thoughts, dysphoria, and disorganization. Finally, cognitive status deteriorates, with significant confusion and elaborate psychotic symptoms. Significant depressive symptoms may precede, co-occur, and/or follow mania within the same episode. In BP, depressive episodes are usually characterized by psychomotor retardation, suicide attempts, and psychotic symptoms (Goodwin & Jamison, 1990). However, in contrast to adults, youngsters with mania often present with atypical symptoms (Bowring & Kovacs, 1992). Changes in mood, psychomotor agitation, and mental excitation are often volatile and erratic rather than persistent. Irritability, belligerence, and mixed manic-depressive features are more common than euphoria. In addition, developmental limitations and the social environment place constraints on children's reckless behaviors, which are characterized by school failure, fighting, dangerous play, and inappropriate sexual activity. Thus, the classic manic symptoms of grandiosity, psychomotor agitation, and reckless behavior must be differentiated from those of other more common childhood disorders such as ADHD, and from normal childhood behaviors such as bragging, imaginary play, overactivity, and youthful blunders (American Academy of Child and Adolescent Psychiatry [AACAP], 1997).

How are some of the more notable symptoms of mania expressed in youngsters with BP? When in a manic state, youngsters show great conviction about the correctness or importance of their ideas. Adolescents may show grand delusions, illogical and strong beliefs that lead to action. Such grandiosity may lead to poor judgment and impulsive behavior (Jamison, 1997). One common expression of grandiosity in youngsters with BP is to badger their teachers about how to teach the class. This badgering may become so intense that teachers contact the child's parents, pleading with them to ask their child to cease. Youngsters with BP may even fail subjects on purpose, acting on their illogical belief that children can choose what to pass or fail, because they believe they are being taught wrongly. Another common symptom of grandiosity is stealing expensive items and being totally unresponsive to efforts by police or parents to explain that their actions are wrong and illegal. Although these youngsters know that stealing is illegal for others, they believe they are above the law. A common grandiose delusion in adolescents with BP is based on the illogical belief that they will achieve great fame, for example, as a surgeon, even though they are failing every one of their classes at school. If asked how this might be, the adolescent might say, "I just know that I will." Similarly, a youngster with BP who is short, clumsy, and lacking any athletic ability may practice basketball with great fervor, and strongly believes that he will be recruited for a basketball scholarship at North Carolina and become the next Michael Jordan (Carlson, 1994; Geller & Luby, 1997).

In contrast to youngsters with depression, who can't fall asleep and may lie in bed fretting and brooding for hours, those with mania show high levels of activity at bedtime, spend very little time in bed, and require very little sleep. For example, a child with mania might spend several hours at bedtime rearranging clothes in a dresser or closet, or an adolescent may wait until his or her parents are asleep and then sneak out of the house to party.

For children with mania, words, thoughts, and actions are in fast motion. Increased verbal production, with puns, word plays, and incessant speech, are common. At all ages, children with mania show pressured speech—they talk too much and too fast, change topics too quickly, and cannot be interrupted. Children with mania also have racing thoughts that they may describe in very concrete terms, for example, by saying they can't do their schoolwork because their thoughts keep interrupting. In the words of one teen, "I wish I had a switch on my forehead so I could turn off my racing thoughts" (Geller & Luby, 1997). Like adults with BP, youngsters with the disorder also show a flight of ideas, illogically jumping from one idea to another. For example, in reply to the question, "Do you live in Los Angeles?" the child may reply, "Some people like to swim in the ocean. Do you have a dog?" For manic children of all ages, even slight changes in their surroundings can lead to significant distractibility. Heightened psychomotor agitation and goal-directed actions resemble normal activities carried out in excess with a seemingly endless supply of energy. In a brief period of time a manic youngster might draw several pictures, read a book, work on the computer, prepare a snack, make multiple phone calls, write a letter, and vacuum the house.

Accepting dares is common for youngsters with BP. In older adolescents this may appear as reckless driving that results in multiple tickets for speeding or driving under the influence. In preadolescents it may be expressed as grandiose delusions of being able to jump out the window because they believe they can fly, or pushing the envelope on usual childhood climbing on things, based on the strong belief that they are above the possibility of danger (Geller & Luby, 1997). In extreme cases, the youngster may experience violent agitation with delusional thinking as well as visual and auditory hallucinations.

The following statement captures the wide array of moods, symptoms, and feelings experienced by youngsters who suffer from BP:

> The constant transitions in and out of constricted and then expansive thoughts, subdued and then violent responses, grim and then ebullient moods, withdrawn and then outgoing stances, cold and then fiery states—and the rapidity and fluidity of moves through such contrasting experiences—can be painful and confusing. (Jamison, 1997, p. 48)

Prevalence

BP is far less common than MDD in young people, with lifetime prevalence estimates of 0.4% to 1.2% (Lewinsohn, Klein, & Seeley, 1995). Since manic symptoms in young people often do not last long enough to meet the 1-week duration requirement of DSM-IV for a manic episode, the most common diagnoses are the milder bipolar II disorder and cyclothymic disorder, rather than bipolar I disorder (Lewinsohn et al., 1995). Children are also likely to present with rapid cycling episodes, with about 80% of children showing this course (Geller et al., 1995). Despite anecdotal accounts of the onset of mania in children as young as 5 or 6 years, the incidence of BP prior to puberty is extremely rare, but increases during adolescence (Lewinsohn et al., 1995). In fact, the prevalence of BP during adolescence is at least as high as it is for adults and, like depression, may be on the rise (Geller & Luby, 1997). The graph in Figure 8.4 compares two groups of relatives of bipolar patients—one group born prior to 1940, the other born later. At each age, the

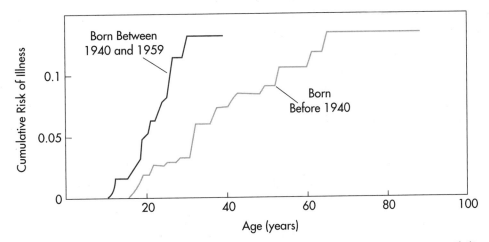

FIGURE 8.4 Bipolar disorder: incidence and age of onset in individuals with a genetic susceptibility. (*Scientific American*, September 1992, p. 131)

later-born individuals are at far higher risk of developing BP or a related psychosis. These findings suggest that some as yet unknown environmental factor is increasing the incidence and age of onset of bipolar illness or related psychosis in individuals with a genetic susceptibility.

Comorbidity and Differential Diagnosis

Some youngsters with BP have normal histories prior to the onset of their illness. However, preexisting behavior problems, such as ADHD and disruptive behavior disorders, are present in a significant number of cases. Premorbid anxiety and emotional problems are also common, as is prior experience of a major depressive episode (Akiskal, 1995). The most common forms of comorbidity are ADHD, disruptive behavior disorders, anxiety disorders, and substance abuse.

Youngsters with BP frequently display symptoms of ADHD, such as poor judgment, distractibility, inattention, irritability, hyperactivity, argumentativeness, anger, poor impulse control, demandingness, and the tendency to jump from one topic or activity to another. For children first seen because of symptoms of BP, about 90% of prepubertal children and 30% of adolescents also have ADHD. However, the reverse is not true—children with ADHD do not show increased rates of BP. For some children, hyperactivity may represent an early age-related manifestation of prepubertal-onset BP, which is consistent with the finding of a higher prevalence of ADHD in prepubertal-onset BP versus adolescent-onset BP. However, for other children with BP, ADHD and BP may be comorbid conditions (Geller & Luby, 1997). Youngsters with ADHD don't typically show the goal-directed behaviors of children with BP, nor do their symptoms have the episodic nature that is characteristic of BP. Children with ADHD also do not display psychotic symptoms, excitability, rapid mood swings, and inappropriate affect.

Oppositional and conduct disorders occur in about 20% of children and adolescents with BP. Symptoms of grandiosity and poor judgment in BP may be confused with symptoms of conduct disorder. For example, one 11-year-old boy with BP, who believed he would be a famous rock star, stole several hundred dollars worth of CDs and was totally unaffected when questioned by the police. Conduct disorder overlaps with BP on symptoms such as running away, driving under the influence, substance abuse, sexual promiscuity, and stealing. Features that may distinguish BP from conduct disorder include antisocial behavior with elevated or irritable mood and lack of peer group involvement. Like youngsters with MDD, those with BP also have multiple comorbid anxiety disorders which occur in about 33%

of prepubertal children and 12% of adolescents (Geller & Luby, 1997).

The symptoms of BP during childhood and adolescence may also be confused with schizophrenia, sexual abuse, and substance use disorders. Symptoms common to schizophrenia and BP may include grandiose and paranoid delusions and hallucinations. During adolescence, youngsters with BP show growing perceptual distortion, and at the peak of their illness, mania can appear very psychotic and disorganized. Thus, there can be serious confusion in distinguishing these two disorders at the extreme end of the manic spectrum in young people. In fact, youngsters with BP may have more psychotic symptoms than adults with BP; 72% of youngsters with mania (onset prior to age 20) were originally judged to be schizophrenic, versus just 24% of individuals with onset after age 30. In general, a family history of mania is more likely for adolescents with BP than for those with schizophrenia (Carlson, 1994).

Since the manic hypersexuality displayed by youngsters with BP may be expressed in frequent masturbation or sexual preoccupations, a history of sexual abuse also needs to be considered as a possible factor before making a diagnosis of BP. Symptoms of mania may also occur in adolescents with substance use disorders. For example, marijuana use may lead to laughing fits and giddiness characteristic of elation; amphetamine highs followed by withdrawal crashes may resemble very rapid cycling; and hallucinogenics may mimic the perceptual distortions of children with BP (Carlson, 1994).

Age of Onset, Course, and Outcome

About 20% of all patients with BP have their first episode during adolescence, with a peak age of onset between 15 and 19 years of age (AACAP, 1997). Onset prior to age 10 occurs in only 0.3% to 0.5% of patients with BP. Individuals with a prepubertal onset of BP have family members with early onset and a high rate of positive family history. Various phases and patterns are associated with BP. Individuals may first present with either depressive or manic episodes. Most of those with an onset of BP during childhood and adolescence report that their first mood episode was major depression. This is consistent with the reported high rates of switching from depression to mania in both children and adolescents (Geller & Luby, 1997). In children with MDD who go on to develop either mania or hypomania, 80% are 12 years or younger at the time of onset of their depression (Geller, Fox, & Clark, 1994). The risk factors for eventual mania include a major depressive episode characterized by rapid onset, psychomotor retardation, and psychotic features; a family history of affective disorders, especially BP; and a history of mania or hypomania following treatment with antidepressants (AACAP, 1997). When a young person presents with a first episode of obvious mania, it's very likely that further manic episodes will follow. Although the time to recurrence may be difficult to predict, a course of BP is likely. Bipolar episodes are generally shorter than major depressive episodes, lasting between 4 and 6 months if left untreated. About 75% of adolescents will have recovered within 6 months (Carlson, 1994).

There are two patterns of BP in young people. Youngsters with onset before puberty or in early adolescence present with a continuous, mixed manic, rapid cycling of multiple brief episodes. They show an initial episode of MDD, rapid cycling of mixed episodes, a pattern of chronic and continuous cycling, and poor interepisode functioning. This pattern is reported by many parents. These youngsters may be laughing and cheerfully playing a computer game when, without apparent provocation, they suddenly become miserable and actively suicidal, and talk about slashing their wrists. BP that has an onset before puberty appears to be a chronic, rapid cycling, mixed manic state that may co-occur with ADHD and conduct disorders or have features of these other disorders as initial signs. In the second pattern onset is in later adolescence. These youngsters show an initial episode of mania, with discrete episodes that have sudden onsets and offsets, the duration of episodes is for weeks, and the youngster shows improved functioning between episodes (Geller & Luby, 1997).

Adolescents with mania often have complex presentations that include psychotic symptoms, such as mood-incongruent hallucinations, paranoia, and thought disorder; unstable moods, with mixed manic and depressive features; and severe deterioration in behavior. These diverse forms of presentation may result in an underdiagnosis of BP in teens (often with a misdiagnosis of schizophrenia). Because of the difficulty in recognizing symptoms of BP in young people, it is not unusual for the symptoms to be noticed long before a youngster is treated or hospitalized. A look back at the histories of adults with bipolar symptoms often shows that mood swings began around puberty; however, there is frequently a 5- to 10-year lag between the onset of symptoms and display of the disorder serious enough to be recognized and require treatment (Carlson, 1994).

An early onset and course of BP in adolescents is chronic and resistant to treatment, with a poor long-term prognosis similar to that in adults (AACAP, 1997). In a 5-year prospective follow-up study of 54 adolescents with BP, two patients never achieved complete remission (Strober et al., 1995). Of the remaining patients, 44% had a relapsing course (either MDD or mania), and 21% had two or more further episodes. Recovery from the index episode was about twice as long for patients with depression than for either mania or mixed episodes (Strober et al., 1995). Compared with adults, adolescents with BP may have a more prolonged early course and poorer response to treatment. Many adolescents with BP present with mixed features, psychotic symptoms, comorbid behavior, and substance abuse problems, all of which predict poorer response to lithium therapy. However, long-term prognosis appears to be similar to that for adults, with about half of patients showing significant functional impairment relative to premorbid functioning. The long-term impact of BP on development is likely to be great, but has not received systematic study to date (AACAP, 1997; Geller & Luby, 1997).

Gender and Ethnicity

In sharp contrast to depression, BP affects males and females equally. However, in studies of youngsters with early-onset BP, boys seem to be affected more often than girls, especially when the age of onset is before 13 years. Rates of BP have not been found to differ by ethnicity or culture, but few studies have investigated this issue in children and adolescents (AACAP, 1997).

Associated Characteristics of Bipolar Disorder

Ninety percent of youth with BP have normal intellectual functioning. Nevertheless, BP, including rapid cycling, can occur in youngsters with moderate to severe MR, autism, and Down syndrome. Although depressed mood is fundamental to BP, youngsters with this disorder may not describe or even view themselves as depressed. They may feel awful but view their incomprehensible mood as something that no one has ever experienced. This total state of apathy and numbing of all feelings may be mistaken for flat affect and sometimes confused with schizophrenia. Although a loss of interest in usually pleasurable activities is not always present with BP, its occurrence is nevertheless more common than in MDD (Carlson, 1994). Other symptoms associated with depression in BP include slowed thinking and vegetative symptoms. Slowed thinking interferes with the youngster's concentration, and he or she may appear to be in a foggy or dazed state. In adolescents, this symptom may result in dramatic drops in school grades in previously good students, and in skipping classes because the schoolwork is so overwhelmingly difficult to concentrate on and to complete. Slowed physical behavior may result in hypersomnia (including napping); slowed, monotonous speech; lack of spontaneous speech; and long latencies to respond (Carlson, 1994). Risk of suicide is higher among adolescents with BP compared with adolescents with other diagnoses (Brent et al., 1993). In one sample, 20% of patients with BP made at least one serious suicide attempt. Males and those in the depressed phase of their illness are at highest risk for suicide (Strober et al., 1995).

Causes of Bipolar Disorder

Gabrielle: A Family Disorder

"Gabrielle's father had been an alcoholic and a manic depressive," says her mother, probably since he was an adolescent. He died of dehydration that occurred during a manic episode. His illness had been a mystery to us. Growing up, Gabrielle knew her father was ill, and when she was older, she began to worry about what his sickness might mean for her. I worried too," says Gabrielle's mother. "By the time Gabrielle was in her early twenties, something was clearly wrong. At first, I noticed only that she had become less reliable—forgetting things, arriving late, occasionally missing appointments with me. Frequently, she complained of fatigue, a cold, flu, or a stomachache. Increasingly, her responses were brief, perfunctory. Though we didn't know it then, Gabrielle was experiencing a huge mood shift that was taking months to complete itself. Gabrielle had MDD, without the manic swings of the bipolar disorder her father had suffered from." (Adapted from Dowling, 1992)

Very few studies have examined the causes of BP in children and adolescents. Findings from familial and gene studies with adults indicate that BP is the result of a genetic vulnerability in combination with environmental factors, such as life stress or disturbances in the family. Although BP can affect anyone, it has definitely been shown to be a familial disorder. If one or both parents have BP, the chances are much greater that their children will also develop BP or, like Gabrielle, some other mood disorder. Besides mood disorder, children at risk for BP by virtue of having parents with the disorder also display a wide range of psychopathology, particularly conduct problems and ADHD. Relatives of youngsters with BP also have a higher incidence of BP. Family incidence is highest in cases of early-onset BP, with lifetime prevalence rates of about 15% in first-degree relatives (AACAP, 1997). This rate is 15 times greater than the prevalence of the disorder in the general population. Increasing evidence suggests that BP stems from multiple genes. There is likely a complex mode of inheritance rather than a single dominant gene. Individuals with a genetic predisposition do not necessarily develop BP, since environmental factors play an important role in determining how genes are expressed (Geller & Luby, 1997).

SUICIDE AND DEPRESSION

Oh, that this too too solid flesh would melt,
Thaw, and resolve itself into a dew!
Or that the Everlasting has not fix'd
His canon 'gainst self-slaughter! Oh, God! God!
How weary, stale, flat, and unprofitable
Seem to me all the uses of this world!

—Shakespeare, Hamlet

The following poem was written by 17-year-old Cheryl, 3 days prior to her suicide attempt:

A Plea

My world is a lonely world
A world devoid of love, laughter, and life
A world full of despair and darkness . . .
A world in need of a knife

My life is a lonely life
No more friends or happiness do I have
The only thing left in my life
is cold, dark loneliness and sadness

No need for worry
No need for despair
Don't worry for her life
For Cheryl is already dead inside
The job has been done by her knife

(Adapted from Berman & Jobes, 1991)

Carla: "It Became Too Much"

Carla, age 12, was admitted to the intensive care unit unconscious and unstable after ingesting eight of her mother's 50-mg Elavil tablets, an unknown quantity of antidepressants, and approximately 20 tablets of Tylenol 3. This suicide attempt, her first, came after arguing with her father over chores and restrictions imposed because her grades were so bad. Carla said she went to the medicine cabinet and ingested everything she could find because "it became too much" and she "did not want to live." For the previous month, she had displayed a noticeable change of mood, behaving with more instability and depression, feeling worthless and

Table 8.8   Child Suicide Potential Scale

Nonsuicidal	No evidence of self-destructive thoughts and actions
Suicidal ideation	Thoughts or verbalization of causing injury or death to oneself (e.g., "I don't want to live")
Suicidal threat	Verbalization of impending suicidal action and/or precursor action that if fully carried out would lead to harm (e.g., "I'm going to get a gun and shoot myself")
Mild attempt	Actual self-destructive action that realistically would not have endangered life and did not necessitate intensive care (e.g., superficial slashing of wrists)
Serious attempt	Actual destructive action that realistically could have led to the child's death and may have necessitated intensive care (e.g., ingestion of potentially fatal dose of drugs)

Source: Pfeffer, 1986.

hopeless. In this period she had lost her appetite and had dropped two dress sizes. She increasingly had isolated herself, staying alone in her room. Her school performance, for which her father had restricted her, had declined from B's the previous term to D's. Both her mother and maternal grandmother had histories of affective disorder. (Adapted from Berman & Jobes, 1991)

The preceding examples illustrate the profound feelings of pain, hopelessness, helplessness, and despair that often lead a youngster with depression to attempt suicide. Many of the signs of suicidal thoughts and feelings are similar to those of depression, including loss of interest in pleasurable activities, changes in eating and sleeping patterns, social withdrawal, drug and alcohol use, antisocial behavior, sudden personality change, difficulty concentrating, decline in schoolwork, and physical complaints (Reynolds & Mazza, 1994). In addition, a youngster who is contemplating suicide may say things like "What's the use," "I'll never see you again," "I won't be a problem for you much longer," or "Nothing matters." Such a youngster may also abruptly become cheerful after a bout of depression, and begin to put her affairs in order by giving away favorite things, cleaning her room, or throwing away important possessions. Although suicide is extremely rare in young children, some signs may include morbid play themes, dangerous and reckless behavior (e.g., running into traffic), and breaking, discarding, or losing preferred toys (Pfeffer, 1986).

Suicide in older children and adolescents has occurred for centuries (Murphy, 1986), but the idea that young people actually kill themselves has only recently gained acceptance. An estimated 2000 teens commit suicide each year in the United States, making it the third leading cause of death in young people after accidents and homicide. Suicidal behavior can be defined as any self-destructive act that has the intent to seriously dam-

age oneself or cause death (Pfeffer, 1985). As shown in Table 8.8, suicidal ideation and actions can be rated on a scale that ranges from no evidence for either ideation or actions at the low end, to serious attempts at the high end.

Jenna: "I Wish I Could Sleep Forever . . . "

"I wish I could sleep forever, nothing matters anymore, they'll be sorry when I'm gone, I want to die, I'm afraid I'll drive the car off the road, there has to be a better place in the world, my father is dead. I must be with him, take all my clothes I won't need them anymore, the seasons come and go and so do I, I took some pills, Yes I cut my wrists. My mother will feel bad now. The angels were calling me to be in heaven, just let me die." (Hagerty, 1984)

Like Jenna, about 60% to 70% of depressed youth report suicidal ideation (Mitchell et al., 1988). One depressed young girl's suicidal ideation is illustrated in the drawings from her journal, shown in Figure 8.5. It is important to recognize that ideation and attempts are not interchangeable as indices of suicidality. Between 16% and 30% of clinically referred youths who think about killing themselves actually attempt it (Kovacs, Goldston, & Gatsonis, 1993). The most common methods used by children who *complete* suicide are firearms (about 60%), hanging (about 25%), and poisoning (about 10%), with methods varying somewhat with age (Kachur, Potter, James, & Powell, 1995). Overdose and wrist-cutting are the most common means for those adolescents who *attempt* suicide.

Suicide and suicide attempts almost never occur in children who are free of any mental disorder. In fact, more than 90% of adolescents who commit suicide have a psychological disorder. However, because a youngster is suffering from a psychological disorder or from

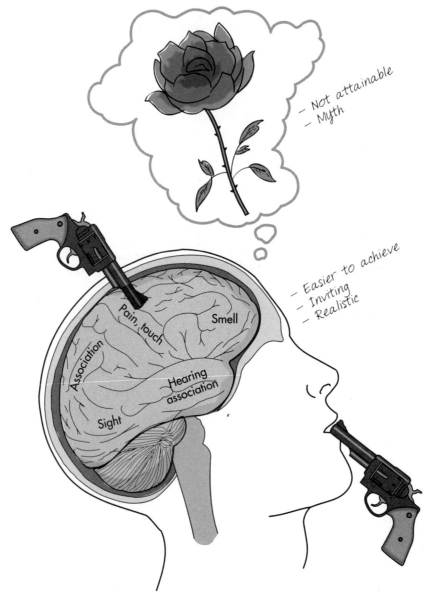

Not attainable
- Myth

- Easier to achieve
- Inviting
- Realistic

How do I go about obtaining a gun?

FIGURE 8.5 Suicidal ideation: How do I go about obtaining a gun? (Berman & Jobes, 1991)

clinical depression doesn't mean that she is about to kill herself—not all adolescents who are depressed are suicidal, and not all children who attempt suicide are depressed (Feldman & Wilson, 1997). Nevertheless, the link between mood disorders and suicide is undeniable, strong, and sobering. In one study of adults who had been depressed as children, nearly 5% had committed suicide by early adulthood, compared with none in the control groups (Wolk & Weissman, 1996). Between 25% and 34% of children and adolescents who are clinically depressed attempt suicide (Ryan et al., 1987). Young people with MDD and DD have similar high rates of suicidal behavior, rates that are higher than for adults.

Interestingly, adjustment disorder with depressed mood is associated with rates of suicide ideation and attempts that are intermediate to the rates for affective disorders and nondepressive disorders, suggesting that even a few depressive symptoms may increase a youngster's risk for suicidal behavior. Among inpatient samples, children who attempt suicide tend to be more depressed and hopeless and may be more aggressive than their nonsuicidal counterparts. Sadly, about half of all youngsters who attempt suicide eventually make further attempts (Kovacs et al., 1993).

Although suicidal ideation (e.g., thinking about killing oneself) is common across many different types of

Box 8.2

Depressive Disorder Is Associated with Suicide Thoughts and Suicide Attempts
Teri: What's the Use ?

Teri, age 15, had been depressed since her father died when she was 11. According to her mother, over the past 14 months her behavior had gone from "moody" to sullen. She had disobeyed restrictions imposed as punishments, and had run away from home on several occasions. She labeled herself as "stupid," spoke and wrote often of death and suicide (see accompanying figure), and on three occasions had cut her wrists, albeit only superficially. Her school performance had declined and she spoke now of hating school. Her peer associations were almost exclusively with other alienated teens, described by her as "punks and other anarchists."

What's the use?

I look erott around here and all
I see,
Is a school and a world
that could do without me.
I've gotten here but only by
fate.
My death, I'm sure, will not come
late.
I try each day to see the use
of being here.
There is none.
I try to find a meaning,
But the wars have been fought,
my battle is yet to come.
When I close my eyes the pain
goes.
When I open them again the
pain. snows.
I try to not cry aloud,
Wouldn't matter anyway I'm lost
in this crowd.
You can pretend I don't live,
But I'll keep living 'till my
life gives.

Teri's note.

Source: Berman & Jobes, 1991.

Kurt Cobain in concert.

disorders with depressive features, including MDD, DD, or adjustment disorder with depressed mood (Shaffer et al., 1996). The suicide attempts of youngsters with MDD or DD almost never occur during times when they are symptom-free—more than 90% have depressive features at the time of their suicidal episode. About one-third of youngsters with MDD and/or DD are at risk for a first suicide attempt by 17 years of age (Kovacs et al., 1993). Depression in young people is also a significant contributor to suicides that result in death, with about 60% to 80% of all adolescents who commit suicide having a history of depressive disorder or BP. For example, Kurt Cobain, the leader of the rock group Nirvana, was suffering from bouts of depression compounded by substance abuse when he killed himself on April 5, 1994. The odds of having major depression are 27 *times higher* among youngsters who kill themselves than among controls (Brent et al., 1993; Shaffer et al., 1996).

Prevalence and Comorbidity

Mirroring the increase in MDD, rates of suicide in adolescents have quadrupled since 1950 from 2.5 to 11.2 per 100,000. This represents 12% of the total number of deaths in this age group (Lewinsohn, Rohde, & Seeley, 1993). Similarly, suicide attempts by adolescents have also increased and have been found to have 1-year and lifetime prevalence rates of 2% to 6% and 3% to 7%, respectively (Centers for Disease Control, 1994). The prevalence of suicide in young people may be underestimated because many suicides can and do pass for accidents. In addition, because of social stigma associated with suicide, many families try to cover it up.

In addition to mood disorders, suicide also occurs with conduct disorders and substance use disorders. Comorbidity of these disorders further increases the risk of suicide attempts (Kovacs et al., 1993). Anxiety is not associated with suicide when these other comorbid

disorders (see Box 8.2), actual suicide attempts seem to be specific to depression. For example, in one 7- to 9-year follow-up of children with psychiatric disorders, 84% of all suicide attempts were found to occur for

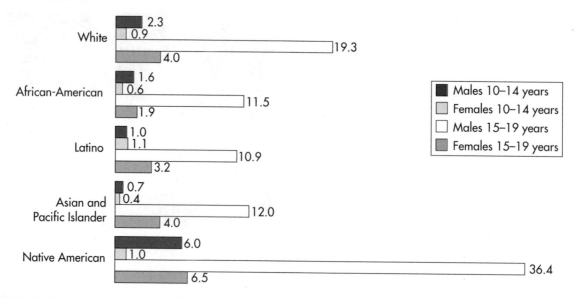

FIGURE 8.6 Estimated rate of suicide per 100,000 children and adolescents ages 10 to 14 and 15 to 19 years in five ethnic groups. (Adapted from Kachur et al., 1995)

conditions are taken into account (Beautrais, Joyce, & Mulder, 1996).

Age of Onset, Developmental Course, and Outcome

Suicidal attempt and completion are rare before puberty, but increase markedly in adolescence (Hawton, 1986). For youngsters who are depressed, ages 13 and 14 are peak periods for a first suicide attempt, usually by drug ingestion. In adolescents with depression, rates of suicidal ideation have been found to remain stable over time, but suicide attempts double during the teen years, reaching 24% by the average age of 17 years. However, rates of suicide attempts in teens with depression show an abrupt decline after age 17 to 18. It is possible that as young people mature, they are better able to tolerate their negative mood states and acquire more resources for coping, thus making it less likely that they will attempt suicide during periods of sadness (Kovacs et al., 1993).

Gender and Ethnicity

In general, young females show more suicidal ideation and attempt suicide about 9 times more often than young males, with drug overdose and wrist-cutting being the most common means. Since girls typically don't use guns (although this may be changing), they are usually less successful in completing suicide than boys (about 1% for female versus 1% to 9% for male adolescent attemptors) (Kovacs et al., 1993; Shaffer, Garland, Gould, Fisher, & Trautman, 1988). The male-to-female ratio of attempts

increases with age from ages 15 to 19 years. Interestingly, interpersonal loss has been found to increase the risk of suicide in boys but not in girls (Gould, Fisher, Parides, Flory, & Shaffer, 1996). As reflected in the following comments by a 19-year-old gay male, rates of suicide are particularly high in gay and lesbian teenagers:

> *"We grow up hating ourselves like society teaches us to. If someone had been 'out' about their sexuality. If the teachers hadn't been afraid to stop the 'fag' and 'dyke' jokes. If my human sexuality class had even mentioned homosexuality. If the school counselors would have been open to a discussion of gay and lesbian issues. If any of those possibilities had existed, perhaps I would not have grown up hating what I was. And, just perhaps, I wouldn't have attempted suicide." (Sattler, 1998, p. 447)*

Rates of suicidal ideation, suicide plans, and suicide attempts vary across different ethnic groups of adolescents in the United States. After adjusting for the effects of age, gender, and SES in a comparison of Anglo, Mexican, Pakistani, and Vietnamese American adolescents, only Pakistani and mixed-ancestry youths had an elevated risk for suicidal ideation (Roberts, Chen, & Roberts, 1997). As shown in Figure 8.6, rates of adolescent suicide also vary across ethnic groups, being generally higher in Native American youth and lower in African-American youth (Centers for Disease Control and Prevention, 1996). However, suicide rates for African-American adolescent boys may be increasing (Shaffer, Gould, & Hicks, 1994). One study found that disciplinary crises and failing a grade increased the likelihood of suicide for Caucasian and African-American but not Hispanic youths, suggesting that some factors contributing to suicide may vary by ethnic background (Gould et al., 1996). Nevertheless, mood disorder is a common antecedent for suicide across ethnic groups and cultures (Cheng, 1995).

Risk Factors

The increase in suicide rates in children and adolescents has been attributed to reduced family influence, economic stress, peer pressure, alcohol and substance use and abuse, sexual pressures, fear of AIDS, media, and gang influences (DeSpelder & Strickland, 1992). Suicidal behavior in young people has many causes, and completed suicides are often the endpoint in a negative life path of unhappiness, misery, hopelessness, low self-esteem, family discord, mental disturbance, and substance abuse (Asarnow & Carlson, 1988). A family history of mood disorders and suicidal behavior, sociodemographic disadvantage, exposure to family violence, substance abuse, impulsivity, school problems, and the availability of guns or other methods have all been associated with increased suicide risk (Beautrais et al., 1996; Berman & Jobes, 1991; Gould et al., 1996; King, 1997).

A family history of suicidal behavior suggests the possibility of genetic factors. One study found that rates of suicidal behavior were about 4 to 5 times higher in first-degree relatives of 58 adolescent suicide victims, even after adjusting for differences in familial rates of psychiatric disorders (Brent, Bridge, Johnson, & Connolly, 1996). Adoption and twin studies have also found a concordance between biological relatives for suicide. For example, of 150 sets of twins in which at least one twin committed suicide, all 10 pairs in which both committed suicide were identical twins—half of these were concordant for the same psychiatric illness, usually a mood disorder (Brent et al., 1996).

The overall picture to emerge of serious suicide attemptors is that of a group of young people who have many disadvantages. Their childhood and teen years are characterized by poor parental care and unhappy family circumstances. As a group, they lack formal educational qualifications and are poorer, more residentially mobile, and more likely to have depressive disorder, to be abusing alcohol or drugs, and to exhibit antisocial behaviors. Life-threatening suicide attempts among young people represent the endpoint of a troubled life course marked by childhood adversity, limited life opportunities as a young person, and significant psychiatric disorder. It is likely that completed suicide is the end of a lifelong path of difficulties and dysfunction (Beautrais et al., 1996).

TREATMENT OF MOOD DISORDERS
Treatment of Depression

Leeta: Feeling Better

Thirteen-year-old Leeta sat slumped in her chair. Disheveled and distracted, she answered questions in a vague and unfocused manner. This was her second extended psychiatric hospitalization for depression, suicidal thoughts, and destructive gestures. She was first admitted to the hospital after she slit her wrists with a knife; this time she had become despondent, irritable, and out of control at home. The night before our interview, she had slammed her hand against the wall in an outburst of anger and frustration stating "I can't stand it anymore!" As in most periods of depression, Leeta's thoughts and reasoning were distorted. She expressed a pervasive sense of hopelessness and was certain that she would remain in hospitals for the rest of her life. Fortunately, this was not the case. She became involved in cognitive-behavior therapy that focused on accurate reasoning, a more positive self-image, and ways to lessen family turmoil, and was also treated with antidepressant medication. One year later, Leeta entered our office for a follow-up interview with energy and excitement. "I never thought that I would feel like hanging out with friends and taking dance lessons. I started tap dancing three months ago, and I love it! It's not that I don't get sad once in a while, but it doesn't take over my whole life." (Adapted from Oster & Montgomery, 1995)

Unfortunately, young people with depression often don't receive help for their distress. In one community sample only 20% to 30% of 14- to 18-year-old children who were diagnosed with MDD and/or DD had received treatment (Lewinsohn et al., 1991). In a study of adolescents who killed themselves, the majority of whom had an affective disorder, only 7% had been in treatment prior to their suicide (Brent et al., 1988). An onset of MDD before the age of 15 places youngsters at great risk for experiencing multiple episodes of major depression throughout their lives. Therefore it is critical that treatment begins as soon as possible—very early and aggressive intervention is warranted in order to prevent a lengthy depressive episode, minimize associated impairments in functioning, and reduce the risk of suicide.

Overview of Treatments

The high comorbidity of MDD with other disorders, the recurrent nature of the problem, and the many associated deficits that often persist following a depressive episode require that a combination of treatments be used, with a major emphasis on maintaining treatment effects and preventing relapse (Birmaher, Ryan, Williamson, Brent, & Kaufman, 1996a; Kazdin & Marciano, 1998; Stark et al., 1996). Cognitive-behavioral therapy (CBT) has shown the most short- and long-term success, with about 70% of youngsters with MDD responding to treatment. CBT is also more effective than either family therapy or nondirective supportive therapy in treating the symptoms of depression in adolescents with MDD (Brent et al., 1997). In addition, when used as a maintenance therapy following the remission of depression, CBT has also been found to reduce the likelihood of a relapse of depression (Kroll, Harrington, Jayson, Fraser, & Gowers, 1996).

Although antidepressant medications have had some reported success in clinical trials, controlled studies have generally not found these medications to be nearly as effective for children as they are for adults. Treatments that emphasize interpersonal relationships, the remediation of social and academic dysfunctions, and family intervention may be useful. Involvement of parents in treatment may serve to strengthen positive parenting behavior, increase treatment involvement, and establish more positive parent-child relationships. In addition, a parent may need separate treatment if he or she is suffering from a depressive or other mood disorder (Birmaher et al., 1996a; Kovacs, 1997).

A very small number of adolescents who suffer from *extremely severe depression* that has not responded to other treatments may receive electroconvulsive therapy (ECT). ECT is a highly controversial treatment with a history of unfortunate abuse. Although its use has changed considerably today, it is still seldom used with young people. There is a general lack of systematic evidence regarding ECT use with adolescents, but available findings suggest effectiveness (about 60% improvement) and side effects (minor and transient) similar to those found in adults (Rey & Walter, 1997; Walter & Rey, 1997). An overview of the main approaches to treatment for youngsters with depression is presented in Table 8.9.

Table 8.9   An Overview of Treatment Approaches for Youngsters with Depression

Behavior Therapy	The main goal is to increase behaviors that elicit positive reinforcement and reduce punishment from the environment. Behavior therapy may involve teaching social and other coping skills and using anxiety management training and relaxation training.
Cognitive Therapy	The primary goal is to help the youngster with depression become more aware of pessimistic and negative thoughts, depressogenic beliefs and biases, casual attributions of self-blame for failure, and a lack of self-acknowledgment for success. Once these depressogenic thought patterns are recognized, the child is taught to change from a negative, pessimistic view to a more positive, optimistic one.
Self-Control Therapy	The main goal is to teach youngsters with depression to organize their behavior in relation to long-term goals. Self-control therapy emphasizes self-monitoring of thoughts and moods, long-term rather than short-term goals, more adaptive attributional styles, more realistic standards for self-evaluation, and increased self-reinforcement and decreased self-punishment.
Cognitive Behavior Therapy (CBT)	The most common form of psychosocial intervention, CBT combines elements of behavioral, cognitive, and self-control therapies in an integrated approach. Attribution retraining may also be used to challenge the youngster's pessimistic beliefs (Jaycox, Reivish, Gillham, & Seligman, 1994).
Interpersonal Therapy	Family interactions that maintain depression are explored. Family sessions are supplemented with individual sessions in which youngsters with depression are encouraged to understand their own negative cognitive style and the effects of their depression on others, and to increase pleasant activities with family members and peers.
Supportive Therapy	Provides therapeutic support to create a safe and supportive environment that allows depressed youngsters to feel connected to and supported by others. Attempts to increase adolescents' self-esteem and to decrease depressive symptoms (Fine, Forth, Gilbert, & Haley, 1991).
Medications	Treats mood disturbances and other symptoms of depression using antidepressants (e.g., imipramine, amitryptyline, desipramine), monoamine oxidase inhibitors (MAOIs), and the newer selective serotonin reuptake inhibitors (SSRIs) such as fluoxetine and sertraline.

Psychosocial Interventions

Most psychosocial treatments for depression in young people have used an integrated cognitive-behavioral approach derived from two traditions—cognitive therapy and behavior therapy. These two approaches were originally developed for depressed adults, but have since been adapted and applied with children and adolescents.

Cognitive therapy maintains that persons with depression hold beliefs and use information-processing styles that lead to and maintain negatively biased views of self, the world, and the future (Beck, Rush, Shaw, & Emery, 1979). Youngsters with depression learn to identify, challenge, and modify dysfunctional cognitive processes, such as misattributions, negative self-monitoring, short-term focus, excessively high performance standards, and a failure to self-reinforce. They are taught to identify and eliminate negative thoughts, such as "It's my fault," or "What's the point?" or "I can't do that," and to replace them with positive thoughts, such as "She really likes me," or "That's really neat," or "I'm an interesting person." For example, a child who has been rejected by a friend might be encouraged to think, "She was in a bad mood" rather than "She hates me." The youngster may be presented with specific situations and examples of irrational negative thinking, and taught to substitute alternative logical explanations that are more positive. For example:

> *Situation:* Two girls, Diana and Colleen, both ask friends to get together with them after school. Both girls' friends say they can't because they have too much homework to do.
>
> *Irrational thinking:* Diana feels rejected and thinks, "Because my friend won't get together with me, she doesn't like me, and she'll never want to do anything with me again."
>
> *Rational thinking:* In contrast, Colleen thinks, "Well, my friend is busy today, but we can get together some other time. She's still my best friend."

Behavior therapy maintains that depression results from and is sustained by a lack of reinforcement due to a restricted range of potential reinforcers, few available reinforcers, or inadequate skills for obtaining rewards (Lewinsohn, 1974). The focus is on increasing pleasurable activities and events, and providing the youngster with the skills needed to obtain more reinforcement. Interventions such as social skills training teach children assertiveness, communication, ways of accepting and giving feedback, social problem solving, and conflict resolution skills in order to increase the frequency of positive social interactions (e.g., Fine et al., 1991). In practice, cognitive and behavioral strategies are integrated into a unified treatment approach in which more adaptive cognitions are hypothesized to lead to more adaptive behavior and vice versa. Examples of these integrated treatment approaches follow.

Interventions for School-Age Children

Primary and Secondary Control Enhancement Training. John Weisz and his colleagues at UCLA have developed an eight-session treatment program for elementary school children with mild to moderate depressive symptoms. The Primary and Secondary Control Enhancement Training (PASCET) program has two main components:

- *Primary enhancement.* Enhancing reward or reducing punishment by changing the objective conditions to fit one's wishes (e.g., activity selection and goal attainment)
- *Secondary control.* Enhancing reward or reducing punishment by changing oneself to buffer the impact of objective conditions (e.g., altering depressogenic thinking, or learning to relax), thereby influencing the subjective impact of these conditions.

The focus of this program is to help the child change conditions that are changeable and to change the subjective impact of those that are not (Weisz, Thurber, Sweeney, Proffitt, & LeGagnoux, 1997).

Taking Action. Kevin Stark, Philip Kendall, and their colleagues have developed a comprehensive cognitive-behavioral intervention for children with depression and their families (Stark & Kendall, 1996). The Taking Action program uses a holistic approach that involves both the child and family. The ACTION acronym is used to nourish the idea that youngsters can have an impact on their moods and is presented to them as follows (Stark & Kendall, 1996, p. 14):

A = Always find something to do to feel better.
C = Catch the positive.
T = Think about it as a problem to be solved.
I = Inspect the situation.
O = Open yourself to the positive.
N = Never get stuck in the negative muck.

Multiple treatment procedures are used to reduce the child's mood disturbances, behavioral deficits, and cognitive symptoms. For example, the child's dysphoria, anger, anhedonia, and excessive anxiety are treated by educating the child about the relation between mood, thinking, and behavior; the use of anger-management procedures; scheduling pleasant activities; and relaxation training. Social skills training is used to remediate

FIGURE 8.7 Exercise teaching effective coping responses. (Adapted from Stark et al., 1996)

interpersonal deficits. Maladaptive schemata, distortions in information processing, negative automatic thoughts, and negative and self-critical thinking are addressed through the use of cognitive-restructuring procedures and training in effective problem solving, adaptive attributions, and self-control procedures, including self-monitoring, self-evaluation, and self-reward. These interventions are carried out in both individual and group formats and make use of a workbook that includes a variety of exercises. An exercise similar to those used in the Taking Action program, and designed to teach children effective coping responses to counter their negative thinking, is presented in Figure 8.7.

Interventions with family members are used to support work with the depressed child, to facilitate the child's use of effective coping strategies outside the treatment setting, and to change events and circumstances that may be contributing to and maintaining the child's problems. Since critical feedback and punitive parent-child interactions may result in negative cognitive schemata that lead to negative information processing, the modification of maladaptive patterns within the family is an integral feature of the Taking Action program. Several methods are used to change parental and family cognitions and behavior, including teaching parents more positive behavior management techniques, the use of noncoercive discipline, ways to manage anger, more effective communication strategies, ways to change dysfunctional cognitions, and ways to increase pleasant activities. Interventions with the entire family teach negotiation and conflict resolution skills, recreational planning, effective problem solving, and family communication (Stark, Swearer, Kurowski, Sommer, & Bowen, 1996). The Taking Action program is a promising intervention built on a sound theoretical and research base, but requires further evaluation as a comprehensive treatment package for depression. However, many of the individual components of this program have already been found to have some success in treating children with depression.

Interventions for Adolescents

Adolescent Coping with Depression Course.
Among the most well-established and comprehensive CBT programs for the treatment of depression in adolescents is the Adolescent Coping with Depression Course (CWD-A) (Clarke, Lewinsohn, & Hops, 1990). CWD-A is a nonstigmatizing psychoeducational approach that emphasizes skills training to promote adolescents' control over their moods and enhancement of their ability to cope with problematic situations. Treatment is provided in 16 two-hour sessions over an 8-week period for groups of up to ten adolescents. Adolescents use a workbook that includes brief readings, short quizzes, structured learning tasks, and forms for homework assignments for each session. In addition to the core treatment sessions with adolescents that involve group activities and role playing, complementary therapy with the youngsters' parents is carried out to accelerate and support the learning of new skills, and to assist in the application of the skills learned in the group to everyday life situations. Periodic "booster sessions" are provided to maintain the skills taught during treatment (Lewinsohn, Clarke, & Rohde, 1994; Lewinsohn, Clarke, Rohde, Hops, & Seeley, 1996).

During the initial session adolescents learn that depression can result from many causes:

- ❖ Experiencing stressful situations that are difficult to resolve
- ❖ Losing contact with someone close
- ❖ Thinking many negative thoughts
- ❖ Having no one to confide in
- ❖ Not having friends
- ❖ Being around other depressed people
- ❖ Inherited tendencies
- ❖ Changes in brain chemistry

After they are given a rationale for treatment, relaxation training is administered in order to quickly provide a successful experience and to supply immediate relief. Next, teens learn self-change skills, such as self-monitoring of mood and behavior, as well as ways of establishing realistic goals. In addition, pleasurable activities and opportunities for reinforcement based on behavior are increased. Later sessions are more cognitively oriented and attempt to increase positive thinking by identifying, challenging, and changing negative cognitions. Social skills training is integrated throughout the program, and specific sessions are designed to teach the adolescents conversational skills, ways to plan social activities, and ways to make friends. They are also instructed in general communication, which includes conflict-resolution and negotiation skills. Final sessions emphasize integrating the skills learned and making plans for the future (Lewinsohn, Clarke, et al., 1996).

Interpersonal Therapy. Interpersonal Psychotherapy for Adolescents (IPT-A) is a brief treatment that attempts to decrease depressive symptoms by helping adolescents understand current problems within the context of ongoing interpersonal relationships. The model assumes that an improvement in family interactional processes will lead to a corresponding improvement in an adolescent's affective, behavioral, cognitive, and interpersonal functioning (Kaslow & Racusin, 1988; Racusin & Kaslow, 1991). Treatment strategies include self-monitoring of mood, exploratory questioning, problem clarification, identification of the link between affect and events in the environment, and communication skills. During therapy, real-life situations are role-played and the therapist gives feedback regarding the adolescent's interpersonal style. Some promising results have been reported for IPT-A in uncontrolled studies, but controlled investigations are needed (Moreau, Mufson, Weissman, & Klerman, 1991; Mufson, Moreau, Weissman, & Klerman, 1993; Mufson et al., 1994; Mufson, Moreau, & Weissman, 1996).

Summary of Psychosocial Interventions.
Psychosocial interventions have produced significant reductions in depressive symptoms in youth from middle childhood through adolescence when compared with controls receiving no treatment and those on a wait list (Kaslow & Thompson, 1998). CBT has been found to have both short-term and long-term effects as compared with no treatment (Reinecke, Ryan, & DuBois, 1998). However, differences in the efficacy of active treatments such as CBT and relaxation training have not always been found, and when they are found, they often disappear by follow-up (e.g., Wood, Harrington, & Moore, 1996). This could be due to the short-term nature and low intensity of the treatments that have been used and the likely presence of comorbid conditions. In addition, few treatments have been sensitive to developmental factors that are known to be related to depression and that vary with age, such as cognitive processes and relations with other children (Kazdin & Marciano, 1998).

Several factors have been found to predict outcomes for youngsters with depression who receive psychosocial interventions. A greater severity of depression, comorbid anxiety disorder, lack of support, parental psychopathology, family conflict, exposure to stressful life events, and low socioeconomic status predict poorer response to treatment and poorer outcomes (Kazdin & Marciano, 1998). Better outcomes have been reported for males, younger cases, youngsters with lower initial levels of depression and anxiety, and youngsters who display more rational thinking and engage in more pleasant activities prior to treatment (Jayson, Wood, Kroll, Fraser, & Harrington, 1998; Lewinsohn, Clarke, et al., 1996). Since comorbid anxiety disorders predict poorer outcomes, precede depression, and persist after recovery from a major depressive episode, it is essential to treat anxiety as well as depression.

Medications

"I kept hearing about Prozac in the news," says one father, "and when we finally brought my 9-year-old to a psychiatrist, I thought he could just give her this pill and change our lives. After a year, I can say that things are a bit better. But it took lots of trials with lots of different pills." (Levine, 1995, p. 45)

Many of the medications used with adults have been applied with children and adolescents with depression, particularly the tricyclics imipramine and amitryptyline (Kutcher, 1997). Although the risk appears to be remote, the sudden deaths of several children under the age of 14 treated with desipramine have appropriately raised concerns about its safety with children (Biederman, Thisted, Greenhill, & Ryan, 1995). The causes are seemingly related to cardiac side effects, especially during periods of exertion that may occur during normal athletic activities at school (Tingelstad, 1991). For some youngsters, antidepressant medications can shorten a depressive episode and by doing so return them to the important developmental tasks of childhood and adolescence (Ambrosini, Bianchi, Rabinovich, & Elia, 1993). However, although antidepressants have been shown to be very effective with adults, controlled studies with children have been far less conclusive. In fact, antidepressants consistently fail to demonstrate *any* advantage over placebo in treating depression in young people. Most studies find about a 50% response rate for both tricyclics and placebo (Ambrosini et al., 1993; Dujovne, Barnard, & Rapoff, 1995; Harrington, 1993; Johnston & Fruehling, 1994; J. Sommers-Flanagan & R. Sommers-Flanagan, 1996). Despite the limited evidence and problems, it may be premature to conclude that antidepressants do not work

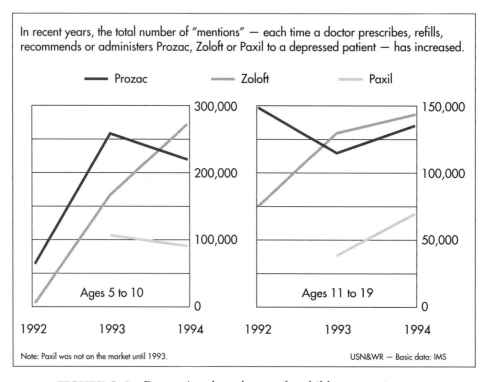

FIGURE 8.8 Depression drug therapy for children. (Brophy, 1995)

with children and adolescents. The few studies that have been conducted were limited to small numbers of patients with mild to moderate depression, and used short-term administration of medications or insufficient doses (Birmaher et al., 1996a; Kovacs, 1997).

Newer SSRI drugs, such as fluoxetine (Prozac), sertraline (Zoloft), and paroxetine HCL (Paxil), are being used to treat depression in children with increasing (and perhaps alarming) frequency despite a lack of scientific evidence that they are safe and effective for children. Prozac now comes in peppermint flavor, and nearly three-quarters of a million prescriptions for SSRIs for children ages 6 to 18 were written in 1996—an increase of 80% in just 2 years (*APA Monitor*, December, 1997). As shown in Figure 8.8, the number of times that Prozac was prescribed, refilled, recommended, or administered by physicians for children ages 5 to 10 quadrupled from 1992 to 1994.

Some have claimed that SSRI drugs are the first line of treatment for depression owing to fewer side effects, equal effectiveness, and greater convenience of use than antidepressants. *Clinical trials* report a 70% to 90% response to fluoxetine for treatment of depression in adolescents with MDD (Birmaher et al., 1996a). However, as with antidepressants, findings from controlled studies have reported no differences. One exception is a recent double-blind study of nearly 100 youngsters with MDD aged 7 to 17 years, which found significant improvement in patients taking fluoxetine (56%) over those taking placebo (33%) (Emslie et al., 1997). Despite the statistically significant response rate, many youngsters had only partial improvement, suggesting that variation in drug dose or length of treatment as well as combined interventions may be needed (Birmaher et al., 1996a). Furthermore, this drug appears to be effective for about only half of the youngsters treated.

Prevention

In view of the recurring nature of depression, efforts during childhood and adolescence to prevent the onset of depression may reduce a lifelong risk. Studies of adolescents with depressive symptoms have found that group CBT with relaxation and group problem-solving therapy may prevent the recurrence of depression for up to 2 years following treatment (Lewinsohn, Clarke, Hops, & Andrews, 1990; Lewinsohn, Clarke, & Rohde, 1994). Similar studies of grade school and high school students with *subclinical* symptoms of depression have also found that CBT is effective in reducing depressive symptoms and lowering risk for developing depression up to 2 years after treatment (Clarke, Hawkins, Murphy, & Sheeber,

off the mark   by Mark Parisi

THAT'S THE WAY, UH, HUH UH, HUH... I LIKE IT! UH, HUH UH, HUH...

EEYORE WHEN *HE* REMEMBERS HIS PROZAC

www.offthemark.com

ATLANTIC FEATURE © 1996 MARK PARISI

©Mark Parisi/Atlantic Feature Syndicate. Reprinted by permission.

1993; Clarke et al., 1995; Jaycox et al., 1994). Finally, interventions aimed at families with parents with an affective illness have reported increased family communication, better adaptation, and greater understanding of the parent's illness by their children following intervention (Beardslee, 1997; Beardslee, Wright, Salt, & Drezner, 1997). A high priority needs to be given to the development and continued refinement of prevention efforts for young people who are at risk for depressive disorders.

Treatment of Bipolar Disorder

The treatment of BP in children and adolescents is an understudied area. BP generally requires a multimodal treatment plan with education of the patient and the family about the illness, medications such as lithium, and psychotherapeutic interventions to address the youngster's symptoms and related psychosocial impairments. The general goals of treatment are to decrease BP symptoms and to prevent relapse while also reducing long-term illness and enhancing the youngster's normal health and development (AACAP, 1997). Clinical trials of medication have had some success. Medications are typically used to address manic or mixed symptoms and depressive symptoms or to prevent relapse. Nevertheless, at this time, controlled studies of medication treatment for children and adolescents with BP are limited. Currently recommended treatments are based on findings with adults, and, as with tricyclic antidepressants, such an extrapolation may not be warranted (Carlson, 1994; Geller & Luby, 1997). There is currently little information concerning recommended treatments in the psychosocial realm.

In general, lithium is the first agent of choice in the treatment of BP, although other medications have been used, including SSRIs, anticonvulsant mood stabilizers (e.g., sodium valproate), benzodiazepines (especially for agitated manic states), and neuroleptics. Lithium is a common salt that is widely present in the natural environment, for example, in drinking water, usually in amounts too small to have any effects. The side effects of therapeutic doses of lithium, however, can be serious, and may include toxicity (poisoning), renal and thyroid problems, and substantial weight gain. However, lithium can be given to young people with the same safety precautions and similar careful monitoring used for adults. A review of anecdotal reports of lithium treatment of BP in young people suggests a range of responses similar to that found for adults, although overall response rates are lower (Carlson, 1994). A recent report found lithium to be significantly more effective than placebo for adolescents with BP who were also substance-dependent (Geller, 1997). In one study, more than 90% of adolescents who discontinued medication relapsed, in contrast to just 37% of those who were compliant with medication (Carlson, 1994). These findings suggest that long-term maintenance use of lithium may be warranted. Because of its potentially serious side effects, lithium is not a drug that can be given to children in chaotic families or those who are unable to keep multiple appointments for monitoring of lithium levels and of renal and thyroid functioning. Since cycling and abrupt onset of depression and suicidality can occur, medications that are safer than lithium if taken in overdose may need to be considered. Adolescents with BP and premorbid behavior or personality disorders generally show much poorer responses to lithium than those without these other problems (Carlson, 1994; Geller & Luby, 1997).

Medications may decrease symptoms of BP but do not help with the associated functional impairments, which include preexisting or comorbid substance abuse disorders, learning problems, and family- and peer-related issues. Once the affective episode has been stabilized with medications, the disruptions that emerge as a result of the disorder need to be addressed. Psycho-social interventions focus on providing information to the child and family about the disorder, symptoms and course, possible impact on family functioning, and heritability. Nonadherence to medication has been shown to be a major contributor to relapse in adults (Carlson, 1994; Geller & Luby, 1997); thus, the family also needs to be educated about the negative effects of nonadherence to medications and to recognize emerging symptoms of relapse, such as sleep deprivation or substance abuse. Psychosocial interventions may help promote medication compliance and avoid relapse. Unfortunately, there is little research on psychosocial interventions for children with BP and no psychotherapy that is specific to the treatment of mania.

SUMMARY

An Overview of DSM-IV Mood Disorders

1. Mood disorders are divided into two categories—depressive disorders and bipolar disorder (BP)—on the basis of the presence or absence of one or more different types of mood episodes.

Depression

2. Depression in children and adolescents involves numerous and persistent symptoms, including impairments in mood, behavior, attitudes, thinking, and physical functioning.

3. For a long time it was mistakenly believed that depression didn't exist in children in a form comparable to that in adults. It is now known that depression in young people is prevalent, disabling, increasing in frequency, and often underreferred and undertreated.

4. The way in which children express and experience depression changes with development. It is important to distinguish between depression as a symptom, syndrome, and disorder.

Major Depressive Disorder

5. The key features of major depressive disorder (MDD) are sadness, loss of interest or pleasure in nearly all activities, irritability, plus a number of additional specific symptoms that are present for a duration of at least 2 weeks.

6. The overall prevalence rate of MDD for children ages 4 to 18 is between 2% and 8%, with rates being low during childhood but increasing dramatically in adolescence. Depression in preadolescent children is equally common in boys and girls, but the ratio of girls to boys is about 2:1 to 3:1 after puberty.

7. The most frequent accompanying disorders in youngsters with MDD are anxiety disorder, dysthymia, conduct problems and ADHD, and substance use disorder.

8. Almost all youngsters recover from their initial depressive episode, but about 70% have another episode within 5 years and many develop bipolar disorder.

Dysthymic Disorder

9. Children with dysthymic disorder (DD) display depressive symptoms on most days for at least 1 year. About 5% of children and adolescents have an episode of dysthymia by the end of adolescence.

10. The most common accompanying disorders with DD are superimposed MDD, anxiety disorders, conduct disorder, and ADHD.

11. The most common age of onset for DD is between 11 and 12 years, with an average episode length of between 2 and 5 years. Almost all youngsters eventually recover from their dysthymia, but many will develop MDD.

12. Children who recover from their DD don't differ from other children on any measures except psychosocial functioning.

Associated Characteristics of Depressive Disorders

13. Youngsters with depression experience numerous cognitive and psychosocial difficulties, including deficits in intellectual and academic performance, and disturbances in self-perceptions, self-esteem, social problem solving, actual social behavior, coping skills, and life stressors.

Theories and Causes of Depression

14. Many theories of depression have been proposed, including psychodynamic, attachment, behavioral, cognitive, self-control, interpersonal, neurobiological, and socioenvironmental.

15. Depression is likely a final common pathway for interacting influences that predispose a child to develop the disorder. These influences include genetic risk, neurobiological factors, family conditions, stressful life events, cognitive factors, and deficits in emotion regulation.

Bipolar Disorder

16. Youngsters with BP show periods of abnormally and persistently elevated, expansive, and/or irritable mood and may display symptoms such as an inflated self-esteem, decreased need for sleep, pressured speech, flight of ideas, distractibility, and reckless behavior.

17. BP is far less common than MDD in young people, with prevalence estimates of 1% or lower. It has a peak age of onset in late adolescence and affects males and females about equally. The most common accompanying disorders are ADHD, conduct disorders, anxiety disorders, and substance abuse.

Causes of Bipolar Disorder

18. Very few studies have examined the causes of BP in children and adolescents. Family and gene studies with adults indicate that BP is the result of a genetic vulnerability in combination with environmental factors, such as life stress or disturbances in the family.

Suicide and Depression

19. Suicidal behavior is any self-destructive act that has the intent to seriously damage oneself or cause death. Suicidal attempt and completion are rare before puberty, but increase markedly in adolescence. Suicide represents about 12% of the total number of deaths in this age group.

20. More than 90% of adolescents who commit suicide have a psychological disorder. A strong link exists between mood disorders and suicide—about one-third of youngsters who are clinically depressed attempt suicide.

21. Suicidal ideation and attempts are 9 times more common in girls than boys, but boys complete suicide more often than girls.

22. A family history of mood disorders and suicidal behavior, sociodemographic disadvantage, exposure to family violence, substance abuse, impulsivity, school problems, and the availability of guns have all been associated with increased risk for suicide in young people.

Treatment of Mood Disorders

23. Cognitive-behavioral therapy has had the most success in treating depression in young people. A high priority also needs to be given to programs aimed at preventing depression in young people.

24. BP in young people requires a multimodal treatment plan with education of the patient and the family about the illness, medication, and psychotherapeutic interventions to address the youngster's symptoms and related psychosocial impairments.

KEY TERMS

mood disorder, 284
dysphoria, 285
anhedonia, 285
mania, 285

euphoria, 285
mood episodes, 285
depressive disorders, 285
bipolar disorder (BP), 286
major depressive disorder (MDD), 286
dysthymic disorder (DD), 286
anaclitic depression, 289
double depression, 300
depressive ruminative style, 302
depressogenic cognitions, 302

learned helplessness, 307
internal, stable, and global attributions, 307
cognitive triad, 308
negative cognitive schemata, 308
diathesis-stress models of depression, 309
daily hassles, 313
emotion regulation, 314
bipolar I disorder, 317
bipolar II disorder, 317
cyclothymic disorder, 317

Mental Retardation

> *What is retardation? It's hard to say. I guess it's having problems thinking. Some people think that you can tell if a person is retarded by looking at them. If you think that way you don't give people the benefit of the doubt. You judge a person by how they look or how they talk or what the tests show, but you can never really tell what is inside the person.*
>
> *—Ed, 27 years old, who was labeled mentally retarded by his family, teachers, and others and placed in a state institution at age 15. (Bogdan & Taylor, 1982)*

> The scientific history of idiocy has yet to be produced; its data are scarce, and the study has not many charms.
> —P. M. Duncan & W. Millard, 1866

So lamented the authors of one of the first professional books on the topic of mental retardation, or "idiocy," as it was called almost one and a half centuries ago. The term *idiot* is based on the Greek word for "a private person" (Kanner, 1964). Until the mid-19th century, children and adults who today would be diagnosed as having mental retardation were often lumped together with those suffering from mental disorders (the "insane") or medical conditions (those with severe hypothyroidism, or "cretins"). They were typically ignored or feared, even by the medical profession, because their differences in appearance and ability were so poorly understood. Such misunderstandings resulted in the segregation of children as well as adults, who were subjected to treatment that today would be considered inhumane.

Although age-old fears, resentment, and scorn continue to overshadow many important discoveries about subnormal intelligence, the field of mental retardation has experienced monumental gains over the past century, in terms of both determining causes and providing services. Advances in understanding the development of children with mental retardation, along with research in genetics, psychopathology, and other areas, have changed the face of this field dramatically. An appreciation of the rapid improvements in knowledge and treatment of mental retardation, as well as an understanding of the prejudice and ignorance that had to be overcome, can be gained by looking at how the disorder has been interpreted over the years.

PERSPECTIVES ON INTELLIGENCE AND MENTAL RETARDATION

Early references to persons with intellectual impairments have been traced to the Romans, who sometimes kept "fools" for the amusement of the household and its guests (Kanner, 1964). Kept by the wealthy, these individuals were generally treated well. Throughout recorded history, however, the vast majority of persons with intellectual and other disabilities received scorn, not assistance, from fellow townspeople. Martin Luther, the German theologian who initiated the Protestant Reformation in 1517, explained how the odd appearance and behavior of a child (one with mental retardation, unknown at the time) was attributed to possession by the devil:

> He was twelve years old, had the use of his eyes and all his senses, so that one might think that he was a normal child. But he did nothing but gorge himself as much as four peasants or threshers. He ate, defecated, and drooled and, if anyone tackled him, he screamed. If things didn't go well, he wept. . . . For it is in the Devil's power that he corrupts people who have reason and souls when he possesses them. The Devil sits in such changelings where their soul should have been! (cited in Kanner, 1964)

The prevailing misunderstanding and mistreatment of those with mental retardation began to change toward the end of the 18th century, fueled by the discovery of feral or "wild" children such as Victor, the "wild boy of Aveyron" (discussed in Chapter 1), and by the expansion of humanitarian efforts to assist other oppressed or neglected groups, such as slaves, prisoners, the mentally ill, and those with physical disabilities. A few professionals and laypersons offered private dwellings to care for the crippled and the feebleminded. By the mid-19th century, the concept had spread from France and Switzerland to much of Europe and North America. Also during the mid-19th century, Dr. Samuel G. Howe, after convincing his contemporaries that training and educating the feebleminded was a public responsibility, opened the first humanitarian institution in North America for persons with mental retardation—The Massachusetts School for Idiotic and Feeble-Minded Youth.

By the late 19th century, treatment of persons with intellectual disabilities and special educational needs had become the responsibility of state-run schools and institutions. However, initial optimism for curing mental retardation was fading. As admissions multiplied, it became clear that many individuals had no prospect of returning to their families or communities. Within a span of approximately two decades, institutional inmates were seen as lifelong residents, and an emphasis on teaching basic occupational skills (to be used in service to the institution, in many cases) replaced basic academic education and training in self-support (Kuhlmann, 1940).

Parents of children with mental retardation can be credited with advancing a perspective and response completely different from that of the prevailing public and professional opinions. By the 1940s, parents began to meet in groups and create local diagnostic and guidance centers to increase the availability of humane care. These groups organized in 1950 to become the National Association for Retarded Children, which quickly established a scientific board made up of representatives from every specialty that could possibly assist in the study, prevention, and care of persons with mental retardation (Kanner, 1964). These efforts gained momentum when President John F. Kennedy, who had a sister with mental retardation, formed the President's Panel on Mental Retardation in 1962 and called for a national program to combat mental retardation, especially in such areas as maternal and child health.

By the mid-1960s, the deplorable conditions in institutions for persons with mental retardation were exposed by both a young New York reporter named Geraldo Rivera and U.S. Senator Robert Kennedy. The ensuing controversy inspired Professor Burton Blatt to ask his friend, freelance photographer Fred Kaplan, to accompany him on a tour of the back wards of similar institutions. With a hidden camera strapped to Kaplan's waist, they were able to take pictures of what they

---

Box 9.1
The Infamous Kallikaks

Psychologist Henry Goddard, who began one of the largest training schools for the mentally retarded in the early 20th century, was also a proponent of the popular degeneracy theory and eugenics movement. In his book *The Kallikak Family: A Study in the Heredity of Feeble-Mindedness* (1912), Goddard traced two lines of descendants from a Revolutionary War soldier, Martin Kallikak. Kallikak (a name invented by Goddard from a combination of two Greek words: *kalos*, meaning "attractive, pleasing," and *kakos*, meaning "bad, evil") fathered a child by a feebleminded barmaid during the war, which began the first line, and then fathered other children by a "respectable girl" he married after the war. Goddard reported that many descendants of the first union were feebleminded, delinquent, poor, and alcoholic, whereas those of the second were of good reputation. He claimed this outcome was evidence for the inheritance of intelligence, although he overlooked the two families' obvious environmental differences (Achenbach, 1982). A closer look at the disclaimer (from the preface to the book) is telling: "It is true that we have made rather dogmatic statements and have drawn conclusions that do not seem scientifically warranted by the data."

---

observed. Their photographs brought the plight of many residents in such institutions to the attention of the public. Administrators attributed the use of solitary confinement and restraints to staff shortages: "What can one do with those patients who do not conform? We must lock them up, or restrain them, or sedate them, or put fear into them." (Blatt & Kaplan, 1966). With these exposés, public awareness of and outrage at the treatment of persons with mental retardation reached an all-time high.

The Eugenics Scare

Degenerationism, or **evolutionary degeneracy theory**, a pervasive 19th-century phenomenon, confused symptoms with causes in explaining medical and social problems (Bowler, 1989). Accordingly, the intellectual and social problems of persons with mental retardation were attributed to regression to an earlier period in the development of humankind. In fact, mental deficiency experts in the 19th century believed they had found the "missing link" between humans and lower species (Gelb, 1995). J. Langdon H. Down, best known for the clinical description of the genetic syndrome that bears his name, interpreted the "strange anomalies" among his medical sample of persons with mental retardation as an evolutionary throwback to the Mongol race (Down, 1866). Down believed that parents in one racial group might give birth to a child with mental retardation who was a "retrogression" to another group. Grounded in speculation and misinformed conclusions, evolutionary degeneracy theory and its notion of moral defect (see Box 9.1) received growing support as an explanation for insanity, mental deficiency, and social deviance by the late 19th century.

By 1910, the eugenics movement was gaining momentum. **Eugenics** was first defined by Sir Francis Galton (Charles Darwin's cousin) in 1883 as "the science which deals with all influences that improve the inborn qualities of a race" (cited in Kanner, 1964, p. 128). Public and professional emphasis shifted away from the needs of persons with mental retardation toward a consideration of the needs of society; society was to be protected from the presumable harm done by the presence in the community of persons with mental problems. Leo Kanner, a pioneer in the study of autism and mental retardation, aptly describes the prevailing sentiment:

> A feeling that society was in serious danger created an atmosphere of growing alarm. The mental defectives were viewed as a menace to civilization, incorrigible at home, burdens to the school, sexually promiscuous, breeders of feebleminded offspring, victims and spreaders of poverty, degeneracy, crime, and disease. (Kanner, 1964)

Consequently, persons with mental retardation were often blamed for the social ills of the time, which is a powerful example of how labeling a problem can quickly become an explanation for it (see Box 9.2). The appearance, ability, and behavior of persons with mental retardation were considered evidence of their lack of moral fiber, a belief that led to the use of the diagnostic term *moral imbecile*, or *moron*, to describe and explain their differences. This concept became a straightforward explanation for acts of deviance, and justified wide-ranging attempts to identify and control such individuals. Morons, considered the least intellectually impaired (roughly comparable to mild mental retardation today) were seen as a threat to society because, unlike the insane, they could easily pass for normal (Gelb, 1995). The intellectually impaired and other "undesirables" were once again seen as a public menace, to be feared and ostracized.

With little scientific evidence to challenge degeneracy theory, early developmental psychologists proposed that children pass through an "ancestral stage" between the ages of 8 and 12, years in which moral reasoning emerges. As G. Stanley Hall, a prominent psychologist who was instrumental in the development of educational psychology, described it, children of this age were "mature savages" who required strong social forces to ensure

---

Box 9.2

Early 20th Century Perspectives on Mental Retardation— a Newspaper Account

WEAK-MINDED FILL RANKS OF CRIMINALS
DR. HENRY STODDARD SAYS SOCIAL PROBLEMS CAN BE SOLVED BY SEGREGATING THEM
WOULD NOT LET THEM MARRY
THIS POLICY WOULD IN TIME LARGELY REDUCE CRIMES, DISEASE, AND DRUNKENNESS, HE BELIEVES

From the army of 300,000 feeble-minded persons in the United States come the recruits that swell the ranks of the drunkards, criminals, paupers, and other social outcasts. Twenty-five per cent of the girls and boys in our reformatories are lacking in mental fibre and are unable to discern the difference between right and wrong or are too weak in character to do right whenever there is any inducement to do wrong. Sixty-five per cent of the children have a mother or a father, or both, who are feeble-minded. This country has so far taken no steps to segregate these irresponsible persons, so the number of them is constantly increasing.

These facts, and many more equally startling, are set forth in an article written for The Survey by Dr. Henry H. Stoddard, director of the department of research of the training school at Vineland, N. J. . . .

"Three hundred thousand persons in the United States are feeble-minded. Five hundred thousand have not sufficient intelligence to manage their affairs with ordinary prudence, are unable to compete with their fellows on equal terms, and thereby to earn livelihoods. This army furnishes the ranks of the criminals, paupers, drunkards, the ne'er-do-wells, and others who are social misfits. Their incapacity would be a priori cause of believing that they eventually will become public charges in one form or another, and investigation, in fact, proves that the groups of criminals, paupers, etc., actually do contain large percentages of people mentally irresponsible."

Source: The New York Times, March 10, 1912.

---

that they advanced beyond this stage and became fit for civilized life (Gelb, 1995). Persons with different abilities or less social status—especially members of minority groups, women, children, and the physically and mentally challenged—were considered less capable of judgment or reasoning, which of course provided further justification for restricting their rights and opportunities for advancement. In fact, under English common law, mental incompetents, as well as all individuals under the age of 18 years and married women were considered incompetent for purposes of entering into a legal contract.

Defining and Measuring Children's Intelligence and Adaptive Behavior

Competing with the eugenics movement and degeneracy theory were simultaneous efforts to develop scientific criteria for evaluating intellectual abilities more objectively, and to devise ways to meet the academic needs of children more compassionately. Around the turn of the century, the pioneering work of two French educators, Alfred Binet and Theophile Simon, led to some of the first major advancements in the field of children's intellectual functioning. Binet and Simon were asked to develop a way to identify schoolchildren who might need special help. They approached this monumental task by developing the first measures of judgment and reasoning, which they believed were basic processes of higher thought. To reduce the effect of previous education and knowledge, they developed test items that did not require academic skills such as reading and writing; rather, these early test questions asked children to manipulate unfamiliar objects, such as blocks or figures, and to solve puzzles and match familiar parts of objects. In 1916, psychologist Lewis Terman of Stanford University revised the Binet-Simon scale and developed norms for Americans from age 3 to adulthood. The Stanford-Binet scale, revised and renormed about every 25 years since, remains one of the most widely used intelligence tests.

The Binet-Simon scale had a profound, worldwide impact on children's education and the emerging definitions of intelligence and mental retardation. An upswing in professional and public attention to the needs of individuals with mental retardation reemerged, as greater optimism was expressed for helping those with varying degrees of mental retardation. The availability of a formal testing procedure led Henry Goddard to propose a new classification system for mental retardation based on the Binet-Simon concept of **mental age (MA)**, which is a measure of a child's mental attainment in terms of the number of years it takes an average child to reach the same level. Those with MAs below 2 years were designated "idiots"; from 3 to 7 years, "imbeciles"; and from 7 to 10 years, "morons." Widely adopted, this terminology remained in use for many years (Achenbach, 1982).

From these beginnings in intellectual testing, **general intellectual functioning** is now defined by an intelligence quotient (IQ or equivalent) based on assessment with one or more of the standardized, individually administered intelligence tests, such as the Wechsler Intelligence Scales for Children-III (WISC-III), the Stanford-Binet-IV, and the Kauffman Assessment Battery for Children. These tests assess different verbal and visual-spatial skills in the child, such as knowledge of the world, similarities and differences, and mathematical concepts, which together are presumed to constitute the general construct

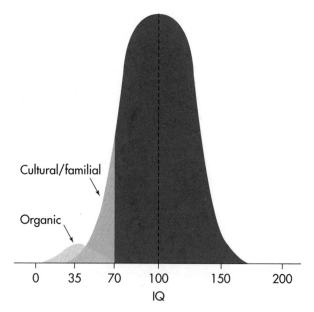

FIGURE 9.1 The approximate distribution of Stanford-Binet IQs. In practice, more children get low IQs than is predicted by this distribution. The excess of very low IQs has important implications for the "two-group" explanations of MR—cultural-familial and organic—discussed later. (Adapted from Ziegler & Hodapp, 1986)

known as intelligence. By convention, intelligence test scores are converted to a scale in which the mean is 100 and the standard deviation is 15. Originally, intelligence quotient (IQ) was formed by dividing the obtained mental age score by chronological age and multiplying by 100 (for example, a 48-month-old child with an assessed mental age of 36 months would obtain an IQ of 75 (36/48 × 100). However, this procedure has been replaced by the *deviation IQ*, which uses standardized tables that cross-reference a person's age and test score to a particular IQ score (Neisser et al., 1996). Because intelligence is defined along a normal distribution (see Figure 9.1), approximately 95% of the population has scores within 2 standard deviations of the mean (that is, between 70 and 130). Subaverage intellectual functioning is defined, accordingly, as an IQ of about 70 or below (approximately 2 standard deviations below the mean).

Defining mental retardation includes not only measuring intelligence but also evaluating the skills involved in **adaptive functioning**. In general terms, adaptive functioning refers to how effectively individuals cope with ordinary life demands and how capable they are of living independently and abiding by community standards (Hodapp & Dykens, 1996). Two of the many tests available to assess adaptive abilities in children are the Vineland scales and the Adaptive Behavior scales, which address about ten content areas of adaptive abilities.

Table 9.1 Content Areas within Adaptive Behavior Assessment

Content Area	Examples
Basic developmental skills	Sensory development, motor development
Survival numerics	Basic mathematics, time management
Survival reading	Basic academics, functional reading
Communication	Expressive language, receptive language, writing and spelling skills
Knowledge of self	Self-awareness, self-concept
Emotional and personal adjustment	Coping, entering a new school or job, interpersonal conflict
Social and interpersonal skills	Basic interaction skills, group participation, play activities and skills
	Social amenities, sexual behavior, responsibility
Self-help skills	Dressing, eating, toileting, personal hygiene and grooming
Consumer skills	Money handling, banking, budgeting, purchasing
Domestic skills	Kitchen skills, household cleaning, household management, maintenance and repair, laundering and clothing care
Health care	Treatment for various health problems, preventive health measures, use of medications, corrective devices
Knowledge of community	Independent travel skills, community expectations, awareness and use of community resources, telephone use

Source: Halpern et al., 1982.

Table 9.1 gives examples of content areas that are evaluated.

Factor analytic studies show that the structure of adaptive behavior among samples of persons with and without mental retardation is best represented by one large dimension (McGrew & Bruininks, 1989). Several secondary dimensions have been identified as subsets of primary adaptive behavior, such as social responsibility, academic and physical development, and community and vocational functioning. As shown throughout this chapter, the factors associated with low IQ may differ from those associated with adaptive functioning. That is, some children and adolescents may learn to adapt quite well to their environment despite their lowered intelli-gence as measured by the IQ test, and would therefore not be considered mentally retarded.

The Controversial IQ

> There is nothing in the intellect that
> was not first in the senses.
> —Aristotle

If intelligence is relatively stable over time, it would be tempting to conclude that it is largely innate and immu-table. On the other hand, if intellectual and cognitive development are significantly shaped by environment, perhaps cognitive growth can be stimulated at an early age and the level of mental retardation decreased.

Because intelligence is measured in relation to age-mates, IQ is generally stable from childhood through adult development. One exception to this general rule is when IQ is measured in early infancy, because consider-able fluctuation can still occur. For typically developing children, IQ measured prior to the first birthday has virtually no correlation with the IQ score achieved at age 12 (Vernon, 1979). But by the time children are 4 years old, the correlation with IQ 12 years later is high (r = .77) (Neisser et al., 1996).

The picture is dramatically different, however, for in-fants and children with developmental delays or mental retardation. At the lower IQ levels (say, below 50), even the youngest infants show IQ stability over time, with correlations between infant and childhood test scores ranging from .50 to .97 (Sattler, 1988). Researchers have discovered a similar pattern of IQ stability among chil-dren with mild to moderate intellectual delays as well, with very high IQ correlations (.70 to .90) between ages 3 and 8 (Bernheimer & Keough, 1988). Among persons with mental retardation, such stability usually continues into adulthood (Ross, Begab, & Dondis, 1985).

Even though the IQ of cognitively delayed infants and young children is unlikely to change, proper envi-ronmental circumstances help children reach their fullest potential. Since the early 1960s, researchers in child development and retardation have been investigating ways to provide early stimulation programs that help children with developmental delays and environmental disadvantages build on their existing strengths. Although intelligence is genetically influenced to a significant degree, mental ability is always modified by experience. Moreover, contrary to many people's expectations, stud-ies of both normal and mentally retarded populations indicate that genetic influences on intelligence and prob-lem solving tend to increase with age, both during childhood and in adult life, probably as a result of the stabilization of brain development (Simonoff, Bolton, & Rutter, 1996). The best window of opportunity for

Table 9.2   Intelligence Testing: Pro and Con

Pro	Con
1. The IQ has a larger collection of correlates predictive of success in a wide variety of human endeavors than does any other variable.	1. Intelligence tests limit our understanding of intelligence and sample only a limited number of conditions under which intelligent behavior is revealed.
2. Intelligence testing is the primary leveler preventing the classes from hardening into castes.	2. IQs are used to sort children into stereotyped categories, thereby limiting their freedom to choose fields of study.
3. Intelligence testing has revealed unsuspected talents in many individuals and has improved educational opportunity.	3. Knowledge of their IQs may inhibit children's level of aspiration and affect their self-concept.
4. Intelligence tests provide standardized ways of comparing a child's performance with that of other children observed in the same situations represented by test items.	4. Intelligence tests fail to measure the process underlying the child's responses and are limited in the extent to which they reveal the underlying cognitive processes needed for successful test performance.
5. IQs may be regarded as a measure of the child's ability to compete in our society in ways that have economic and social consequences.	5. IQs are misused as measures of innate capacity.
6. Intelligence tests provide a profile of strengths and weaknesses.	6. The single IQ does not do justice to the multi-dimensional nature of intelligence.
7. IQs are excellent predictors of scholastic achievement.	7. IQs are limited in predicting occupational success.
8. IQs measure the effects of changes associated with special programs, treatment, and training.	8. IQs are limited in predicting nontest or nonacademic intellectual activity; the standard question format cannot capture the complexity and immediacy of real-life situations.
9. Intelligence tests assess individual differences and provide useful reflections of cultural and biological differences among individuals.	9. Intelligence tests are culturally biased against ethnic minorities.
10. Intelligence tests are valuable tools in working with handicapped children.	10. Nonconventional, original, or novel responses are penalized on intelligence tests.

Source: Sattler, 1988.

influencing intellectual ability, therefore, is from infancy through early childhood (Ramey & Ramey, 1992). Between early childhood and adolescence, the IQ is generally stable, with the correlation between childhood and adult IQ reaching its maximum (of about .80) by the early high school years (McCall, 1977).

The importance of genetic makeup notwithstanding, IQ can and does change for some individuals by 10 to 20 points between childhood and adolescence (Simonoff et al., 1996). Differences in outcome vary widely in relation to opportunities to learn and develop. Children who live in healthy environments, where care-givers provide appropriate levels of stimulation and help them manage ambient levels of stress, are most likely to reach their full potential. Moreover, tests sample only a limited spectrum of intellectual ability and are incapable of accounting for each individual's unique learning history (see pros and cons of intelligence testing in Table 9.2).

Are We Getting Smarter?   Scores have risen
sharply since the beginning of IQ testing: 27 points in Great Britain since 1942 and 24 points in the United States since 1918, with similar gains reported throughout Western Europe, Canada, Japan, Israel, urban Brazil, China, Australia, and New Zealand. When James Flynn brought this phenomenon to the attention of scientists in 1987, it became known as the "Flynn effect." The gain has averaged about 3 IQ points per decade, adding up to more than a full standard deviation since the 1940s. This increase in IQ scores implies that the above-average schoolchild today—with an IQ, say, of 116—is as bright as the near-geniuses (IQ greater than 130) of yesteryear. If IQ is a measure of innate intelligence, either a large percentage of today's children are gifted or, as Flynn himself puts it, "almost half of white Americans during World War I had IQs so low [below 76] that they lacked the intellectual capacity to understand the basic rules of baseball" (cited in Begley, 1996; p. 70).

In attempting to explain the Flynn effect, scientists have considered rising standards of living, better schooling, better nutrition, medical advances, more stimulating environments, even the influence of computer games and complex toys. IQ tests themselves have once again come under scrutiny, as have children's exposure to problems similar to those on the tests—such as the mazes and puzzles appearing on cereal boxes and fast-food bags. Yet the consistent IQ gains are too large to seem the result simply of increased familiarity with testing methods.

Although the exact cause of the effect remains unknown, experts on children's intelligence suspect the gains are reflecting a very meaningful aspect of intellectual growth and development. A relatively child-focused parenting style has emerged during recent decades, and one result may be that children have greater facility with language and stronger overall cognitive capacity. Moreover, unprecedented cultural differences exist between successive generations, as daily life and occupational experiences are far more complex today than in the early years of the 20th century. Because children are very adaptive, changes in everyday life may have produced corresponding changes in cognitive abilities (Neisser et al., 1996).

Are IQ Tests Biased or Unfair? Concern has been expressed from many quarters over the relatively low mean of the distribution of intelligence test scores of African Americans. Although studies using different tests and samples yield a range of results, the mean of African Americans is typically about 1 standard deviation (about 15 IQ points) below that of whites (Neisser et al., 1996). In a controversial article entitled "How Much Can We Boost IQ and Scholastic Achievement?" Arthur Jensen (1969) argued that the heritability of IQ was high among both white and black populations (in the neighborhood of 80%), and therefore the mean IQ difference between them was probably primarily genetically determined. This conclusion led to critical analysis of the environmental enrichment programs that were just beginning to gain foothold in various communities. Many academics viewed Jensen's findings and conclusions (which, in retrospect, were premature and based on incomplete studies) as poor science at best and racism at worst. The recent book *The Bell Curve* (Herrnstein & Murray, 1994) keeps this controversial discussion alive in academic as well as public arenas.

In spite of the continuing controversy, economic and social inequality—not test bias or racial differences (Neisser et al., 1996)—is the simplest explanation for existing group differences in test performance between Blacks and Whites in North America. Any person, regardless of race or intelligence level, can benefit from appropriate environmental interventions (Rutter, 1991), which do have meaningful effects on IQ. However, a much higher proportion of African Americans and other ethnic minorities are poor, and poverty is linked to poor nutrition, inadequate prenatal care, fewer intellectual resources, and similar realities that can have negative effects on children's developing intelligence (Neisser et al., 1996).

Nevertheless, the differential in IQ scores appears to be diminishing. Since 1980, the mean score of African Americans has consistently been over 90, and the differential has been in single digits. Some of the gains can be attributed to the many programs implemented during the past two decades that were geared to the education of minority children (Neisser et al., 1996).

FEATURES OF MENTAL RETARDATION

Mental retardation encompasses perhaps the widest variation in cognitive and behavioral abilities of any childhood disorder. Some children function quite well in school and the community, whereas others, those with significant physical and cognitive impairments, require daily supervision and assistance. The situations of Matthew, age 6, and Vanessa, age 8, illustrate some of the unique challenges children with mental retardation face every day.

Matthew: Gaining at His Own Pace

Matthew was almost 6 years old when he was referred for a psychological assessment. His brief school record described him as "developmentally delayed," and the school was concerned that his speech and social skills were very limited. He also had temper tantrums at home, and his new first-grade teacher had expressed concerns about his aggressive behavior with children in his class.

I first met with Matt in his home. "Show me some of your favorite toys or games," I suggested, unsure of how comfortable he was with a stranger at his home. He was a thin boy, with curly hair and a cautious, reserved expression. He looked me over for what must have been several minutes while I spoke with his mother and father. Although he said "OK," I wasn't sure he meant it—he stayed put and seemed uninterested in my request. Matt had turned 6 a few months ago, but I noticed that his clothes, games, and vocabulary were closer to those of my 3-year-old daughter. "I don't want to talk about school stuff!" he exclaimed, quite loudly, when I asked about his favorite subjects. "I only like recess and lunchtime—the stuff they won't let you do till the bell rings!" There was a certain degree of truth, and humor, to his statement, although I don't think he intended it as such. . . .

Matt became a bit more interested when I brought out some testing materials. He completed with ease a puzzle designed for toddlers, and was able to make the sounds of animals in the puzzle. But his emotional expression remained subdued, with little spontaneous laughter or joy. He seemed watchful and cautious. "Tell me about this story," I said to Matt, holding up a card showing some animals arguing over a ball. "What do you think is going on in this picture, and what are the characters, like the elephant and the zebra, thinking and feeling?" Matt started right in: "He's mad 'cuz the zebra grabbed the ball and ran away with it into the woods. That's all I see." My attempts to elicit more detail were met with only an inquisitive look.

After a few minutes of this, we took a break and brought out his toys. "Do you like Star Wars?" he asked. We found some common ground among the ewoks and the battlestars, and under these "ideal" conditions, Matt's communication became more at ease and spontaneous. He expressed a wide range of emotion throughout the interview, and settled in to his own comfortable level of relating. Gradually, his language production increased as we continued with the more relaxed play sessions.

In private, Matt's mother told me about his behavior problems around other children, such as hitting, biting, throwing objects, and demanding attention. I saw a brief episode of it myself, when his 3-year-old sister came into the room: "Get out! This man is here to play with me!" Overall, Matt behaved much like a younger child, for example, by shouting or pushing when he couldn't get his way immediately. When we met for the second time, in my office, Matt's WISC-III full-scale IQ was assessed at 64, and his adaptive abilities score was 68, based on mother's report on the Adaptive Behavior Scales. Despite his mild mental retardation, however, Matt has been gaining over the past year in school, and he is showing a healthy gain in his developmental milestones as well.

Vanessa: Gaining at Home

Vanessa is an 8-year-old girl with moderate mental retardation (IQ = 52) and limited communication skills. She was diagnosed prior to her fourth birthday, after medical and psychological examinations were undertaken to determine why she was not making many speech sounds or learning basic self-help skills. Vanessa's mother told us about how her daughter's special needs were poorly met while she was a resident in a special school for the mentally retarded, and how this led to their deci-

sion to raise Vanessa at home with the help of their community:

"When our family moved here in 1990, we were told that we would receive $55 per month to care for her at home, or she could live at the Children's Training Center. Vanessa had been diagnosed with moderate mental retardation prior to her fourth birthday, and we knew that we could not care for her daily needs at home with the limited assistance being offered. So we made the difficult decision to place her at the training center. But, even though Vanessa came home every weekend, we felt there was something missing from her life; something beyond staff care and attention was needed to foster her growth.

"About 2 years later, things changed dramatically. Vanessa was injured by another resident, and we decided that she should return home once and for all. We made every effort to find services she needed for her training and education in our own community. She now attends an integrated classroom at the same school as her older brother, and her teachers have noticed strong gains in her behavior and language. She participates in recreational programs, and has become an accomplished swimmer and basketball player."

Matthew was diagnosed as having *mild mental retardation*. Although delayed in his speech and language development, he was developing effective verbal skills and was capable of attending a regular classroom. Establishing friendships with children at school was sometimes problematic, because he was often slow at understanding the rules of games and was teased by some because of his slowness. Vanessa was diagnosed as having *moderate mental retardation*. She could feed and dress herself with minimum assistance, and she communicated in short sentences, although her speech was not always discernible to people outside her family. Vanessa required more daily assistance to complete her routines, but she too was able to attend a local school during part of the day. As these cases show, the special needs of both children were sometimes overshadowed by economic and educational limitations, which required creativity and coordinated assistance on the part of parents, teachers, and other professionals.

Clinical Description

When the psychiatrist interviewed me he had my records in front of him—so he already knew I was mentally retarded. It's the same with everyone. If you are considered mentally retarded there is no way you can win. There is no way they give you a favorable report.

—*Ed, describing part of his intake interview at the state institution. (Bogdan & Taylor, 1982)*

Children with mental retardation show a considerable range of abilities and interpersonal qualities. With proper assistance, children with mild intellectual impairments, like Matthew, can carry out their daily routine much like other children. They can attend a regular classroom, adjust to the demands of physical and intellectual challenges, and develop meaningful and lasting relationships with peers and adults. Many show normal physical development and can learn to ride a bike. Others, like Vanessa, who have more severe impairments, will require greater daily supervision and care throughout their childhood and sometimes into early adulthood, at which time they may have developed the necessary skills to live more independently.

Both Matthew and Vanessa, however, experience limitations that cut across most areas of daily living. Their most obvious difficulties have been learning to communicate well, due to their limited speech and language skills. Although Matthew eventually learned effective verbal communication, Vanessa had to rely for several years on sign language and nonverbal expressions or gestures to express her needs. Both children had problems developing friendships with other children because of their limited ability to comprehend what other children were expressing, especially during games and social activities that require stamina and formal rules.

Because mental retardation affects many different cognitive abilities, such as language and problem solving, most children have difficulty with some aspect of learning. The degree of difficulty depends on the extent of cognitive impairment, which is the primary reason current definitions of mental retardation emphasize this aspect. Table 9.3 lists the DSM-IV diagnostic criteria for mental retardation.

The DSM-IV criteria for mental retardation consist of three core features that are thought to best describe this disorder in both children and adults. First, such individuals must have "significantly subaverage intellectual functioning," determined on the basis of formal intelligence testing or clinical judgment (in the case of an infant or an untestable subject). An individual must have an IQ score of approximately 70 or below to meet this first criterion, which falls 2 standard deviations below the average IQ score of 100 and thereby includes roughly 2% to 3% of the population. The American Association on Mental Retardation (AAMR), in contrast, chose to define "significantly subaverage" as being equivalent to an IQ score of approximately 70 to 75 or below, rather than 70 or below. This relatively small (5 IQ points) upward adjustment in the score that determines mental retardation essentially changes the IQ criteria from below 70 to below 75, an issue that has created considerable controversy. As noted by Macmillan, Gresham, and Siperstein (1993), "*Twice as many people are eligible* [for a diagnosis of mental retardation] when the cutoff is IQ 75 and below as when it is IQ 70 and below" (p. 327, italics in original). Thus, if this criterion was widely adopted, the number of children and adults

---

Table 9.3 DSM-IV Diagnostic Criteria for Mental Retardation

A. Significantly subaverage intellectual functioning: an IQ of approximately 70 or below on an individually administered IQ test (for infants, a clinical judgment of significantly subaverage intellectual functioning).

B. Concurrent deficits or impairments in present adaptive functioning (i.e., the person's effectiveness in meeting the standards expected for his or her age by his or her cultural group) in at least two of the following areas: communication, self-care, home living, social/interpersonal skills, use of community resources, self-direction, functional academic skills, work, leisure, health, and safety.

C. The onset is before age 18 years.

Code based on degree of severity reflecting level of intellectual impairment:

Mild Mental Retardation:	IQ level 50–55 to approximately 70
Moderate Mental Retardation:	IQ level 35–40 to 50–55
Severe Mental Retardation:	IQ level 20–25 to 35–40
Profound Mental Retardation:	IQ level below 20 or 25

Mental Retardation, Severity Unspecified: When there is strong presumption of mental retardation but the person's intelligence is untestable by standard tests.

Source: DSM-IV, Copyright © 1994 by APA.

eligible for special services would drastically increase and the number of minority children identified as mentally retarded could expand disproportionately (Jacobsen & Mulick, 1992).

The second criterion for diagnosing mental retardation, adopted in both the DSM-IV and the AAMR definitions, requires "concurrent deficits or impairments in adaptive functioning," which refers to the ability to perform daily activities. In effect, an IQ score of 70 or below is not sufficient to receive a diagnosis of mental retardation; one must also show significant limitations in at least two areas of adaptive behavior: communication, self-care, home living, social/interpersonal skills, use of community resources, self-direction, functional academic skills, work, leisure, health, and safety. This aspect of the definition is important because it specifically excludes persons who may function well in their own surroundings, yet for various reasons may not perform well on standard IQ tests.

Controversy surrounds this part of the definition as well, largely because some areas of adaptive behavior are seldom tested and may even be unnecessary, especially among children, such as leisure, health and safety, use of community resources, and self-direction. Most clinicians cannot test all areas of children's adaptive functioning, simply because measures are not available to cover them all adequately (Hodapp & Dykens, 1996). Moreover, whether a child or adolescent exhibits these various adaptive skills is related not only to ability but also to experience and opportunity (Evans, 1991). Using public transportation, walking to a neighborhood store, and even making simple purchases can all be affected by the individual's place of residence (urban versus rural, for example), concerns about neighborhood safety, and so forth. Clinicians and educators must make educated guesses regarding a person's potential for performing a certain task, in the event the person has not had any experience with a particular skill on the test. Such estimates clearly reduce the reliability of the test and, in turn, the degree of faith one can place on the diagnosis of mental retardation for that particular individual.

The final criterion for mental retardation stipulates that the above two characteristics—below-average intellectual and adaptive abilities—must be evident prior to age 18. The purpose of establishing this upper limit for the age of onset is twofold. First, it acknowledges that mental retardation is a developmental disorder that is evident during childhood and adolescence. Problems in learning and comprehension are most likely to occur during this time of rapid brain development. Second, this age criterion rules out persons who may show mental deficiencies caused by adult-onset degenerative diseases, such as Alzheimer's disease, or by head trauma.

The definition of mental retardation continues to be somewhat inaccurate and arbitrary, largely because it is based on a statistical concept—a cutoff IQ score—rather than on the nature or qualities of the person who supposedly has mental retardation (Barlow & Durand, 1995). Cutoff scores, however, whether for IQ, high blood pressure, or high cholesterol, are valid constructs because they help identify a need for early intervention. A diagnosis of mental retardation is less likely to be imprecise and arbitrary among those with more severe cognitive impairments; however, since the majority of persons diagnosed with mental retardation fall into the mild range, the ramifications of identifying someone as mentally retarded bear significance. As Ed described so well, a careful balance must be struck between identifying the special needs of persons with intellectual disabilities, and labeling them as mentally retarded on the basis of somewhat arbitrary criteria.

Additionally, the definition and identification of mental retardation depend to some degree on our social institutions. Entry into the school system becomes a major point at which children's abilities are compared and deficiencies are most likely to be detected. If a child is placed in a poorly matched learning environment, his or her developmental progress can be disrupted. Following the school years, persons with mild mental retardation often blend back into the larger population, and their "diagnosis" no longer has as much meaning to either their education or training (Hodapp & Dykens, 1996).

Levels of Functioning

Children with mental retardation vary widely in their degree of disability. Some show cognitive impairments, such as limited vocalizations or poor self-regulation, from early infancy, whereas others may go relatively unnoticed through the elementary school years. Because of the wide variation in cognitive functioning and impairment, classification systems for mental retardation have always attempted to delineate various degrees of intellectual impairment in some manner. The DSM-IV has continued the tradition by designating retardation as **mild, moderate, severe,** or **profound**; these designations are based primarily on IQ scores. The AAMR, in contrast, has restructured its description of different degrees of mental retardation, choosing to base its categories on the level of support or assistance the person needs, rather than on IQ.

Degrees of Impairment (DSM-IV). Those with **mild mental retardation** (IQ level of 50–55 to approximately 70) constitute the largest number of persons with mental retardation, estimated to be as many as 85% of persons with the disorder (APA, 1994). Children with mild mental retardation often show small delays in development during the preschool years, but typically are not identified until academic or behavior problems emerge in the early·elementary years. This category also has an overrepresentation of minority group members.

As a group, children with mild mental retardation typically develop social and communication skills during the preschool years (ages 0–5 years), perhaps with modest delays in expressive language. They usually have minimal or no sensorimotor impairment, and engage with peers readily. Like Matthew, however, some may find school and peer relationships to be challenging. By their late teens, these children can acquire academic skills up to approximately the sixth-grade level. During their adult years, they usually achieve social and vocational skills adequate for minimum self-support, but may need supervision, guidance, and assistance, especially when under unusual social or economic stress. With appropriate supports, individuals with mild mental retardation can usually live successfully in the community, either independently or in supervised settings.

Persons with **moderate mental retardation** (IQ level of 35–40 to 50–55) constitute about 10% of those with mental retardation. Individuals at this level of impairment are more intellectually and adaptively impaired than those with mild mental retardation, and are usually identified during the preschool years as a result of delays in reaching early developmental milestones. By the time they enter school, they may communicate through a combination of single words and gestures, and show self-care and motor skills similar to those of an average 2- to 3-year-old. Many persons with Down syndrome and fragile-X syndrome function at the moderate level of retardation. Some of these individuals may require only a few supportive services to get along on a daily basis, but others may continue to require some help throughout life.

Like Vanessa, most individuals with this level of mental retardation acquire limited communication skills during their early years, and by age 12 may be using practical communication skills. They benefit from vocational training and, with moderate supervision, can attend to their personal care. They can also benefit from training in social and occupational skills but are unlikely to progress beyond the second-grade level in academic subjects. Adolescents with moderate mental retardation often have difficulties in recognizing social conventions, such as appropriate dress or humor, which interferes with peer relationships. By adulthood, the majority of persons with moderate mental retardation adapt well to living in the community and are able to perform un-

skilled or semiskilled work under supervision in sheltered workshops (specialized manufacturing facilities that train and supervise persons with mental retardation) or in the general workforce.

Those with **severe mental retardation** (IQ level of 20–25 to 35–40) constitute approximately 3% to 4% of persons with mental retardation. Most of these individuals suffer one or more organic causes of retardation, and are identified during infancy (i.e., birth to age 2) because of substantial delays in development and visible physical features or anomalies. Milestones such as standing, walking, and toilet training may be markedly delayed, and basic self-care skills are usually acquired by about age 9 (Editorial Board, 1996). In addition to intellectual impairment, they may have problems with physical mobility or other health-related problems, such as respiratory, heart, or physical complications.

Most persons functioning at this severe level of mental retardation require some special assistance throughout their lives. During the early childhood years they acquire little or no communicative speech; by age 12 they may use some two- to three-word phrases. Between 13 and 15 years of age their academic and adaptive abilities are similar to those of an average 4- to 6-year-old. They profit to a limited extent from instruction in preacademic subjects, such as familiarity with the alphabet and simple counting, and can master skills such as learning sight reading of some "survival" words, such as *hot, danger,* and *stop.* In their adult years, they may be able to perform simple tasks in closely supervised settings. Most adapt well to life in the community, in group homes or with their families, unless they have an associated disability that requires specialized nursing or other care.

Persons with **profound mental retardation** (IQ level below 20 or 25) constitute approximately 1% to 2% of those with mental retardation. Such individuals are typically identified as infants because of marked delays in development and biological anomalies such as asymmetrical facial features (Editorial Board, 1996). During early childhood they show considerable impairments in sensorimotor functioning; by the age of 4 years, for example, their responsiveness is similar to that of a typical 1-year-old. They are able to learn only the rudiments of communication skills, and intensive training is required to teach them basic eating, grooming, toileting, and dressing behaviors.

Persons with profound mental retardation require lifelong care and assistance. Almost all these individuals show organic causes for their retardation, and many have severe co-occurring medical conditions, such as congenital heart defect or epilepsy, that sometimes lead to death during childhood or early adulthood. Most of

Table 9.4 American Association on Mental Retardation: Definition of Needed Supports

Intermittent

Support on an as-needed basis; episodic in nature, with the person not always needing the support(s) required during life-span transitions (e.g., job loss or an acute medical crisis). Intermittent support may be high or low intensity when provided.

Limited

Support characterized by consistency over time; time-limited but not intermittent. This level may require fewer staff members and less cost than more intense levels of support (e.g., time-limited employment training or support during the school-to-adult transition period).

Extensive

Support characterized by regular involvement (e.g., daily) in at least some environments (such as work or home) and not time-limited (e.g., long-term support and long-term home living support).

Pervasive

Support characterized by constancy and high intensity; provided across environments; potentially life-sustaining in nature. Pervasive support typically involves more staff members and intrusiveness than does extensive or time-limited support.

Source: Luckasson et al., 1992.

these individuals live in supervised group homes or small, specialized facilities. Optimal development may occur in a highly structured environment with constant aid and supervision and an individualized relationship with a care-giver. Motor development as well as self-care and communication skills may improve if appropriate training is provided. For example, over half of persons with profound mental retardation can perform simple tasks, such as washing their hands and changing their clothes, provided they have close supervision.

Level of Needed Supports (AAMR). The AAMR, rather than using the traditional IQ-based levels of impairment, categorizes persons with mental retardation according to their need for supportive services: **intermittent, limited, extensive,** and **pervasive** (Luckasson et al., 1992). Table 9.4 defines these AAMR categories. Although similarities do exist between these levels of support and the DSM-IV levels of impairment, the major difference concerns the AAMR emphasis on the *interaction* between the person and the environment in determining his or her level of functioning. Defined in this manner, mental retardation is determined not so much by the ability of the person alone (as in the DSM-IV definition), but by the level of supports the

person needs to function adaptively in the community (Hodapp & Dykens, 1996).

The AAMR approach underscores the areas of assistance the child needs, which can be translated into specific training goals. Instead of a diagnosis of moderate mental retardation, Vanessa might receive the following AAMR diagnosis: "Vanessa is a child with mental retardation who needs limited supports in home living, academic skills, and development of self-help skills." Matthew's diagnosis might state: "Matt is a child with mental retardation who requires support on an as-needed basis, especially during stressful or demanding times—for example, during the transition to school, when making new friends, and when faced with new academic challenges." Despite its attractiveness in terms of emphasizing needed assistance rather than disability, the recently developed AAMR system has yet to be evaluated over time to determine its practical value.

Educational System of Classification. Because the terms still appear, it is worthwhile to mention an additional classification method that has been long used in the educational system to identify the level of services needed for students with mental retardation. Three categories have been defined: *educable mental retardation* (based on an IQ ranging from 50 to approximately 70–75), *trainable mental retardation* (IQ of 30 to 50), and *severe mental retardation* (IQ below 30) (Cipani, 1991). These categories were used under the assumption that students diagnosed with educable mental retardation—which corresponds to mild mental retardation—could be taught basic academic skills such as reading, writing, and math, but perhaps at an individually paced rate. Students diagnosed with trainable mental retardation (similar to moderate mental retardation) were viewed as not being able to master academic skills, but being able to learn basic vocational and self-help skills for independent living. Finally, those diagnosed with severe mental retardation were seen as being unlikely to benefit from either academic or vocational instruction, and would by necessity require more custodial care. Current trends have moved away from this educational system of classification, largely because of concerns that it inadvertently provided teachers with a negative expectation of their students, and set limits as to the types of training or education a student might receive.

Both the educational and the DSM-IV categories have been criticized as being potentially stigmatizing and limiting because of their emphasis on degree of impairment. This criticism provided the major impetus for the AAMR focus on levels of needed support and assistance (Luckasson et al., 1992). This approach no doubt will

Table 9.5 Observed Prevalence and Causes of Mental Retardation

	Mild Mental Handicap	Moderate to Profound Mental Handicap
Prevalence per hundred*	0.70	0.32
Reported range	0.37–0.92	0.31–0.39
Genetic (%)	14	45
Environmental (%)	10	19
Idiopathic (%)	76	36

*These figures do not add up to the expected prevalence of ≈2%, because prevalence of mild mental retardation is not fully reported in all studies.
Source: Raynham et al., 1996.

face similar challenges in surmounting the unfortunate pressures of stigmatization.

PREVALENCE

Based on available evidence and estimates, the total number of children and adults with mental retardation most likely falls between 1% and 3% of the entire population (Hodapp & Dykens, 1996). Recall that the number of persons diagnosed with mental retardation depends on the point at which the line is drawn for cutoff scores for IQ and adaptive behavior. Even with a stable IQ criterion of 70 and below, however, the number of persons with mental retardation is open to debate, because each person applies his or her own cognitive abilities in unique ways that may be more or less adaptive in her or his own environment.

Table 9.5 presents recent prevalence rates for different subtypes of mental retardation. These rates are based on selected, as opposed to fully representative, samples, so they reflect the more conservative prevalence estimate of 1% to 2% of the general population. Notice that the range in estimates is broader for mild mental retardation (.37% to .92%) than for more severe forms of mental retardation (.31% to .39%). The range for more severe forms is narrower because intellectual functioning at these levels is influenced less by *cultural and familial* factors and more by *organic* factors (Raynham, Gibbons, Flint, & Higgs, 1996). (This distinction between **organic** and **cultural-familial** mental retardation, known as the two-group approach, is discussed in detail later in the chapter.) Also apparent in the table is the vast difference between those with moderate to profound and those with mild mental retardation in terms of known and unknown causes. Unknown causes are most likely **idiopathic**—that is, unique to a particular individual's development.

Slightly more males than females are currently considered to fall within the range of mental retardation (APA, 1994; Murphy, Yeargin-Allsopp, Decoufle, & Drews, 1995). Similar to racial differences in diagnosis of mental retardation, however, this gender difference may be an artifact of identification and referral patterns. Boys are referred more often than girls for psychometric testing (usually in relation to behavioral disturbances) and are somewhat more likely than girls to fail on adaptive functioning tests (Richardson, Katz, & Koller, 1986). Moreover, investigators who administer IQ tests to *nonreferred* samples have found no differences between boys and girls in the rates of mild mental retardation (Reschly & Jipson, 1976; Richardson et al., 1986). If a true male excess of mental retardation does exist, researchers suspect this may be due to the occurrence of X-linked genetic disorders, such as fragile-X syndrome (discussed below), which affect males more prominently than females (Anderson, 1994).

It is a well-established finding that mental retardation is more prevalent among children of lower socioeconomic status (SES) and those from minority groups. This link is found primarily among children in the mild mental retardation range; children with more severe levels are identified almost equally in different racial and economic groups. Whether or not signs of organic etiology are present, diagnoses of mild mental retardation increase sharply from near zero among children from higher SES to about 2.5% in the lowest SES category (Birch, Richardson, Baird, Horobin, & Illsley, 1970). These figures indicate that SES factors play a suspected role both in the cause of mental retardation and in the identification and labeling of persons with mental retardation.

The overrepresentation of minority and low SES children in the group with mild mental retardation is a complicated and unresolved issue (Artiles & Trent, 1994). In many studies, average IQ levels for the African-American population are lower than those found in the White population. As a result, more African-American children are found among the mild mental retardation samples (Macmillan et al., 1993). What specific environmental circumstances might create such an imbalance in IQ findings between Black and White children? To answer this question, Brooks-Gunn, Klebanov, and Duncan (1996) tested the theory that such differences can be explained on the basis of social and economic disadvantage. They accounted for initial Black versus White child IQ differences of over 17 points by the independent effects of economic deprivation, home environment, and maternal characteristics. Their findings are graphed in Figure 9.2.

Brooks-Gunn et al. (1996) showed that initial IQ differences were 17.8 points between a sample of 483

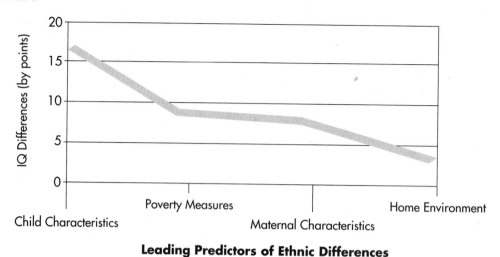

Leading Predictors of Ethnic Differences

FIGURE 9.2 Accounting for IQ differences between White and Black children. (Data from Brooks-Gunn et al., 1996)

black and white children at 5 years of age, controlling for gender, birth weight, and length of neonatal stay. However, these differences were almost completely eliminated by adjusting for differences in poverty (a reduction of 52%, from 17.8 to 8.5 IQ points) and home environment (a further reduction of 28%, resulting in a nonsignificant difference of 3.4 IQ points). Notably, differences in maternal education, age, and verbal ability did not add significantly to the explanation of ethnic differences once the effects of poverty were taken into account.

DEVELOPMENTAL COURSE AND ADULT OUTCOMES

To appreciate the manner in and extent to which children with mental retardation achieve various developmental milestones, consider for a moment how typically developing children express themselves. An infant exploring his or her world relies on primitive sensorimotor functions—such as touching, tasting, and manipulating objects—to learn about the environment. At this stage of development everything is new, and the brain is establishing literally millions of new connections each day. Then, between 18 and 24 months, the toddler begins to acquire language and to draw on memories of past experience to aid in understanding the present. Among intellectually normal children, this is the stage in which the child's environmental conditions and opportunities are known to play a crucial role in fostering enthusiasm for learning and in establishing the roots of intellectual sophistication. Although the majority of children with mental retardation progress through each developmental milestone in roughly the same manner as their nonretarded counterparts, important differences in their developmental accomplishments are evident.

Dan, a 15-year-old with Down syndrome, describes how his early development was similar to, but much slower than, that of his younger brother.

Dan: With His Brother's Help

When I was almost 3 and my sister was 5½, we had a baby brother. I helped feed him and take care of him until he was almost 3. I was 5 by then, and could do most of the things he could do, but about that time he caught up to me. I could still do some things he couldn't, but not many. He could do some things I had trouble with. We became good friends. Every time he learned a new skill, I would either learn it with him, or he would teach me later. I was really little for my age, so we were pretty close in size. We shared a bunk bed, toys, and clothes. We learned to do a lot of things together. When he learned to ride a bike, and I wasn't ready to learn yet, mom and dad got me a Powerwheel motorized bike so I could ride, too. When he learned to read, he taught me how, too. When he played baseball and football, he took me with him.

In those days, I still went to school in another district, so most of my friends were his friends. Now that we go to the same school it is sometimes hard for him to remember that I have my own friends, too. I have to tell him I am the big brother. He sometimes gets teased at school because he is my brother, but he is learning to explain instead of fight. Mostly, the kids are all nice to us.

Dan, with moderate mental retardation, is describing how his younger brother Brian, with normal intelligence, caught up with him by the time Brian was 2, and progressed through developmental milestones at a faster pace. Does Dan's development follow the same organized sequence as his brother's? Will his development show specific deficits in certain intellectual abilities, or will he eventually catch up? This case illustrates the **developmental-versus-difference controversy** (Weiss, Weisz, & Bromfield, 1986), an issue that has intrigued those in the field of child development and mental retardation for some time. Simply stated, the issue is this: Do all children—regardless of intellectual impairments—progress through the same developmental milestones in a similar sequence, but at different rates? Or does the development of children with mental retardation proceed in a different, less sequential and less organized, fashion?

The developmental position (which applies primarily to individuals not suffering from organic impairment) argues that *all* children, with or without mental retardation, pass through Piagetian stages of cognitive development in an identical (invariant) order; they differ only in their rate and upper limit of development (Hodapp & Zigler, 1995). This perspective consists of two related hypotheses regarding underlying cognitive development. The **similar sequence hypothesis** posits that children with or without mental retardation pass through cognitive developmental stages in the same order. In addition, the **similar structure hypothesis** suggests that children with mental retardation will demonstrate the same behaviors and underlying processes as will typically developing children who are at the same level of cognitive functioning (such as Dan and his younger brother were at ages 5 and 2, respectively). That is, if children with mental retardation are matched to nonretarded children by their mental age, then the children with mental retardation will show equivalent performance on cognitive tasks, such as problem solving, spelling, and moral reasoning. The developmental position rejects the notion of a specific deficit or difference among children with mental retardation, and instead places importance on how such children traverse the stages more slowly and attain a lower developmental ceiling than typically developing children (Hodapp & Zigler, 1995; Zigler & Hodapp, 1986).

In contrast, the difference viewpoint argues that cognitive development of children with mental retardation differs from that of children without mental retardation in more ways than merely differences in developmental rate and upper limit. According to this position, even when his mental age is matched to his younger brother's, Dan will show qualitatively different reasoning and problem-solving strategies, and he may never be able to accomplish some tasks beyond a certain level.

Although this issue has not been entirely resolved, ample evidence supports the developmental hypotheses for children with *familial*, as opposed to *organic*, types of retardation (these two major types of mental retardation are discussed in the section on causes). Specifically, children with familial mental retardation by and large follow developmental stages in an invariant order, the same as nonretarded children (Hodapp & Zigler, 1995; Weiss et al., 1986). The exceptions are some children with co-occurring severe organic impairments, such as EEG abnormalities, and autistic children (Hodapp & Zigler, 1995). The similar structure hypothesis has also been supported for children with familial mental retardation, with some exceptions. Children with familial MR show slight deficits in memory and information processing when compared with MA-matched, nonretarded children (Weiss et al., 1986), but the deficits may be due to their difficulty staying motivated to perform repetitive, boring tasks (Weisz, 1990).

The picture for children with organically based mental retardation is more straightforward: They often have one or more specific deficit areas that cause them to perform worse than MA-matched, nonretarded children. Thus, Dan will most likely pass through the same developmental sequences as his younger brother, but at a slower pace. He is likely to show some differences in his performance in certain areas of development, however, such as his expressive language.

Motivation

Many children who fall within the mild range of mental retardation are bright enough to learn and attend regular schools and classrooms, yet they are more susceptible to a sense of helplessness and frustration, which places additional burdens on their social and cognitive development. As a consequence, they begin to expect failure, even for tasks they can master; in the absence of proper instruction, their motivation to tackle new demands decreases (Hodapp & Zigler, 1995). Ed, describing his memory of comments made by his teacher in elementary school, expresses this phenomenon well:

> Her negative picture of me stood out like a sore thumb. That's the problem with people like me—the schools and teachers find out we have problems, they notice them, and then we are abandoned. That one teacher was very annoyed that I was in her class. She had to put up with me. (Bogdan & Taylor, 1982)

Consequently, compared with typically developing children of their same mental age, children with mental retardation expect little success, set low goals for themselves, and settle for minimal success when they could do better (MacMillan & Keough, 1971). This learned helplessness may be unwittingly condoned by adults. When

"Acknowledge our children's differences but respect their uniqueness."—parent of a child with Down syndrome.

told a child is "retarded," for example, adults are less likely to urge the child to persist following failure than they would for a normal child of the same level of cognitive development (Weisz, 1982). This process accounts for some of the increasing performance deficits found among children with mental retardation as they grow older, especially with tasks that involve verbal processing skills (Weiss et al., 1986), such as reading, writing, and problem solving.

Much of the knowledge about other issues involved in developmental course and adult outcomes for children with mental retardation is derived from studies of children with Down syndrome. These children, along with their parents, have frequently participated in studies comparing their development with that of their nonretarded peers.

Changes in Developmental Progress

Mental retardation is not necessarily a lifelong disorder. Although it is a relatively stable condition from childhood into adulthood, any given individual can have considerable change in IQ—either up or down—in relation to level of impairment and type of retardation. Children who have mild mental retardation, such as Matthew, may, with appropriate training and opportunities, develop good adaptive skills in other domains and may no longer have the level of impairment required for a diagnosis of mental retardation (APA, 1994).

The major cause of a child's mental retardation certainly affects the degree to which his or her IQ and adaptive abilities may change. Children with Down syndrome, who are *not* representative of the course of mental retardation in general, may plateau during the middle childhood years, and then decrease in IQ over

time. For example, from 1 to 6 years of age, children with Down syndrome often show significant age-related gains in adaptive functioning; but as they grow older, their pace of development levels off or even declines. Similarly, as they grow older, a deceleration is often seen in their rate of social development (Brown, Greer, Aylward, & Hunt, 1990). This observation has been termed the **slowing and stability hypothesis** (Gibson, 1966; Hodapp & Dykens, 1996), and affirms that children with Down syndrome may alternate between periods of gain and functioning and periods of little or no advance. Although these children continue to develop in intelligence, they do so at slower and slower rates throughout the childhood years (remember that the IQ score is based on age-related norms). In fragile-X syndrome, boys show steady or near steady IQs until approximately 10 to 15 years of age, at which point their development slows considerably (Dykens et al., 1989). These age-related slowdowns in IQ suggest some link to pubertal development.

Related Developmental Disabilities

Many children with mental retardation, especially those with moderate to profound retardation, suffer other physical and developmental disabilities, which can affect their health and development in pervasive ways. Epilepsy is commonly associated with mild as well as more severe forms of mental retardation (Health and Welfare Canada, 1988). Speech and language problems, behavioral disturbances, and sensory impairments (hearing and vision) are also commonplace among this population, and are related to the degree of intellectual impairment. Figure 9.3 shows how often some of the more common developmental disabilities are noted among children with mild and severe mental retardation, based on a large sample of schoolchildren in Atlanta (Murphy et al., 1995). Overall, 12% of the children with mild mental retardation and 45% of those with severe mental retardation had at least one other disability, such as a sensory impairment, cerebral palsy, or epilepsy.

Despite such major co-occurring physical and intellectual disabilities, children and adults with mental retardation, including those with Down syndrome and other chromosomal disorders, now have greater life expectancy than ever before. For example, the life expectancy in 1929 for a person with Down syndrome was only 9 years, but by 1980 it had increased to over 55 years for men and 52 years for women because of improved services and early detection (Cooper & Collacott, 1995). In addition, Baird and Sadovnick (1987) found that 70% of individuals with Down syndrome will survive beyond 30 years of age, largely as a result of better medical treatments for respiratory infections and

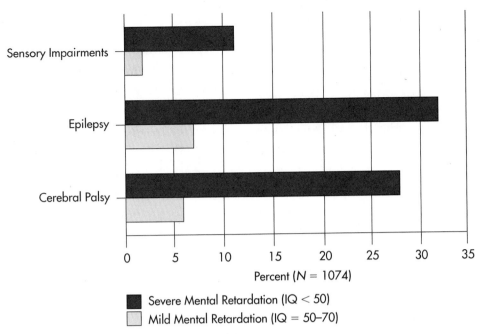

FIGURE 9.3   Developmental disabilities among children with mental retardation. (Data from Murphy et al., 1995)

congenital heart disorders that have plagued adults with Down syndrome. However, most individuals with Down syndrome who live beyond the age of 40 also demonstrate Alzheimer's disease–like cognitive decline due to gene damage on chromosome 21 (Lendon, Ashall, & Goate, 1997).

Language and Social Behavior

Language development and social functioning among children and adolescents with Down syndrome have been the focus of considerable research (Cicchetti, Toth, & Bush, 1988; Dykens, Hodapp, & Evans, 1994), revealing that development follows a largely predictable and organized course. Cognitive development, play, language, self-knowledge, and knowledge of others are interrelated in organized and meaningful ways, suggesting that symbolic abilities in children with Down syndrome are largely intact (Cicchetti et al., 1988). Such symbolic abilities are at the foundation of speech and language which, in turn, influence the rate and extent of cognitive development.

Important differences in language development exist between children with Down syndrome and their typically developing age-mates. Perhaps the most striking difference is the considerable delay in children with Down syndrome in expressive language development, which is necessary to establish independent living skills. Expressive language is often much weaker than receptive language, especially as children with Down syndrome attain communication abilities beyond the 24-month level.

In addition to the development of symbolic and language skills, a major milestone of infancy and early childhood development concerns the ability to form a secure attachment relationship with one's primary care-givers. A healthy attachment relationship is a valuable precursor to cognitive, emotional, and behavioral competence throughout toddlerhood and well into childhood (Erickson, Sroufe & Egeland, 1985; Sroufe, 1989). Fortunately, many, if not the majority of, children with Down syndrome form secure attachment relationships with their care-givers by 12 to 24 months of developmental age (Cicchetti et al., 1988).

Attachment is a process seemingly designed by nature to ensure proximity, contact, and interactions that form the foundation of the adult-child relationship. However, because many children with Down syndrome exhibit less emotional expression than other children, this natural process is sometimes subverted. Vaughn, Contreras, and Seifer (1994) discovered that over 40% of their sample of children with Down syndrome were classified as insecure, primarily because many were unclassifiable according to the traditional "strange situation" for assessing attachment quality (Ainsworth, Blehar, & Waters, 1978). Children with Down syndrome were not picked up and held by either the mother or the stranger in the strange situation to the extent seen for nondelayed children. Even when these children made approaches with appropriate signals for contact, mothers and strangers rarely completed the contact, presumably because the children did not show distress signals, such as crying, reaching, or holding on, that typically tell the parent "I want to be picked up!" This finding has important implications for parents of young children with Down syndrome: Even though they may show few signals of distress or desire for contact, these infants and toddlers need to be held and nurtured just as any others.

Following the attachment period the next important developmental milestones have to do with the emergence of a sense of self, which establishes the early foundations of personality. Like other children, toddlers with Down syndrome begin to delight at recognizing themselves in mirrors and photos, although this milestone is often delayed. The experience of self-recognition in most infants is immediately met with smiles and laughter, a finding that is repeated among toddlers with Down syndrome as well (Mans, Cicchetti, & Sroufe, 1978). Such positive affect accompanying their visual self-recognition suggests that these children feel good about themselves (Cicchetti et al., 1988). However, as toddlers and preschoolers, children with Down syndrome show delayed and aberrant functioning in their *internal state* language, the language that reflects the emergent sense of self and others (through the use of words such as "mad" and "happy"). Because internal state language is critical to the regulation of social interaction and provides a foundation for early self–other understanding, these children may be at increased risk for subsequent problems in the development of the self-system (Beeghly & Cicchetti, 1997).

Children with mental retardation, especially those with moderate to mild impairments, learn symbolic play, such as games, puppets, and sports, in much the same manner as other children. Nevertheless, they often fail to gain the acceptance of their peers in regular education settings, often because of deficits in social skills and social-cognitive ability (Cullinan, Sabornie, & Crossland, 1992; Taylor, Asher & Williams, 1987). Siperstein and Leffert (1997) compared the social behavior and social-cognitive skills of 20 socially accepted (mean IQ = 66.5) and 20 socially rejected (mean IQ = 68.0) 12-year-old students with mental retardation attending regular classrooms. As expected, those who were accepted by their peers were more outgoing and skilled at engaging others in activities.

As a result of delayed social development, some children with mental retardation are slower in learning to interpret social cues and to respond appropriately to their peers. However, they are not more likely to resort to aggression (see Box 9.3). Their situation can be compared with the relationship between siblings. The younger child may want to play with his older brother and his friends, yet he may not be able to understand or may not be skilled at the games the older ones are playing, resulting in their avoiding or teasing him.

Box 9.3
Peers and Problems

It's a part of growing up—learning how to face common challenges to personal integrity and choices without resorting to aggression in one form or another. Because children with mental retardation often attend the same schools as other children, educators have been particularly interested in how they handle everyday conflicts with peers, especially if teased or provoked. This issue was studied among school-age children with mild mental retardation by posing hypothetical conflict situations with peers (Leffert & Siperstein, 1996). The children were asked how they would respond to social conflict situations presented on videotape, involving peer group entry and peer provocation. Children with mental retardation were consistently accurate in interpreting hostile intentions, such as when the peer snatched a pencil away. However, they had difficulty interpreting benign intentions, such as the peer saying, "Oops, I didn't see you there!" Similar to children without mental retardation, the more aggressive children with mental retardation frequently misinterpreted benign intention cues and generated aggressive strategies, whereas those who were described as being more socially sensitive or isolated often generated preferred solutions that involved avoidance or an appeal to someone for help.

It is noteworthy that children with mental retardation were most likely to generate nonaggressive strategies even when faced with a situation involving provocation from a peer. They perceived such provocation with a high degree of accuracy, yet they were still 3 times as likely to generate nonaggressive as aggressive strategies. The study indicated that only aggressive children—regardless of mental retardation—consistently misinterpreted peer cues. The low frequency of aggressive strategies generated by children with mental retardation is congruent with other observational studies, which find that these children are no more aggressive than other children (Kaufman, Agard, & Semmel, 1985; Roberts, Pratt, & Leach, 1991).

Such concerns about the social development of children with mental retardation are increasing because of the movement toward inclusion of children with different levels of ability in regular classrooms and schools, rather than in institutions or specialized facilities. Because typically developing children seem to prefer playing with other typically developing children, children with mental retardation still end up being socially isolated from other children their age (Guralnick, Connor, Hammond, Gottman, & Kinnish, 1995). Their mere physical presence in the class does not seem to enhance the social competence of children with mental retardation (Leffert & Siperstein, 1996). Consequently, the social outcomes of placing students with mental retardation in regular education classrooms have been disappointing.

Emotional and Behavioral Problems

Pattie: Disturbed or Disturbing?

Pattie was labeled mentally retarded and lived in over 20 homes and institutions before being committed to a state school at age 10. At the age of 20, she discussed some of her experiences and feelings:

"I guess I was very disturbed. I call it disturbed, but it was when I was very upset. A lot of people at (the institution) . . . told me I was disturbed—that I was disturbed and that I was retarded—so I figure that all through my life I was disturbed. Looking at the things I done, I must have been disturbed. . . . Upset and disturbed are the same in my mind. Crazy to me is something else. It is somebody that is really gone. I mean really out. Just deliberately kill somebody just to do it. That is what I call crazy. I guess what I was was emotionally disturbed—yeah. Emotionally disturbed is a time when too many things are bothering me. They just build up till I get too nervous or upset. My mind just goes through all these changes and different things. So many things inside that were bothering me." (Bogdan & Taylor, 1982)

Pattie's description of her feelings while living in different institutions illuminates how "disturbing" her behavior could be. But are her feelings a function of her environment and personal limitations? Many children and adolescents with mental retardation have to face a number of obstacles related to their intellectual, physical, and social impairments, and often they have little control over their own lives. So it is not surprising that an estimated 10% to 40% of children with mental retardation display significant emotional or behavioral problems (Nezu, Nezu, & Gill-Weiss, 1992; Rojahn & Tassé, 1996). These estimates amount to a rate of emotional and behavioral disturbances 4 to 6 times greater than in the general population (McLean, 1993).

However, these problems do not necessarily constitute psychiatric disorders. When specific psychiatric diagnoses are given to children with mental retardation, they most frequently involve impulse control disorders (such as conduct disorder or self-injurious behavior), anxiety disorders, and mood disorders (King, DeAntonio, McCracken, Forness, & Ackerland, 1994; Volkmar,

Burack, & Cohen, 1990). Although these problems are sometimes severe and often require intervention, they are considered part of the spectrum of problems coexisting with mental retardation, rather than indicators of other psychiatric illness (Hodapp & Dykens, 1996). Therefore, adjustments are usually needed in how DSM-IV diagnostic criteria for other mental disorders are applied. The frequency at which certain problems, such as temper tantrums, hyperactivity, and mood disorders, are seen among these children requires consideration of what is normal or typical for other children with similar levels of retardation. For example, recall that the diagnosis of ADHD requires "behavioral disturbance that is excessive for an individual's mental age." Among individuals with profound mental retardation, attention span, distractibility, and on-task behavior vary considerably. An individual with profound mental retardation must be compared with other children with profound mental retardation for the purpose of diagnosing any other psychiatric disturbance.

Note that mental retardation is an Axis II disorder. Remember that the purpose of separating disorders by axes is to distinguish the ones that are more chronic and less amenable to treatment (Axis II) from those that are linked to environmental circumstances and have a greater potential for improvement (Axis I). The axes are intended as well to remind clinicians to consider whether such chronic disorders are present and may be affecting the presentation of some other problem. Children as well as adults can be diagnosed on both Axis I and Axis II.

Estimates of coexisting emotional and behavioral disorders among children with mental retardation often rely on the observations of care-givers, rather than on psychiatric diagnoses. Thus, the estimates of emotional and behavioral disturbances reflect what parents and teachers see on a day-to-day basis when caring for children with mental retardation. In the early 1970s a major study was conducted on the Isle of Wight off the coast of England (Rutter, Tizard, Yule, Graham, & Whitmore, 1976) to gain some understanding of the extent of psychiatric disorders among children and adults with and without mental retardation. Ratings by parents and teachers each revealed that about one-third of the children with mild mental retardation and one-half of the children with more severe forms of mental retardation showed major signs of emotional disturbance, suggesting that such problems are common. In contrast, a lower prevalence rate, 10%, is found when estimates are determined specifically from psychiatric disorders based on reports from mental health agencies (Jacobson, 1982).

Children and adults with mental retardation may show additional symptoms that can be particularly troublesome. Pica (discussed in Chapter 13), which can result in the ingestion of caustic and dangerous substances, is seen in its more serious forms among children and adults with mental retardation. **Self-injurious behavior (SIB)** is a serious and sometimes life-threatening disorder that affects about 10% of persons with severe and profound mental retardation (Matson & Frame, 1986). Some of the common forms of SIB include head banging, eye gouging, severe scratching, rumination, some types of pica, and inserting objects under the skin. The long-term prognoses for pica and SIBs are not favorable. An 18-year study indicates that emotional withdrawal, stereotypies (e.g., head banging, hand or body movements), and avoidance of eye contact were still evident 18 years later among persons with severe mental retardation (Reid & Ballanger, 1995).

ADHD-related symptoms are commonly reported by teachers and parents of children with mental retardation, requiring adjustments in instruction and child management strategies (Epstein, Cullinan, & Gadow, 1986). As is the case with nonretarded children with ADHD, when a teacher is present to prompt appropriate behavior and participate in the activity, children with mental retardation with and without ADHD generally remain on task. However, differences between those with and without ADHD emerge during independent tasks, when they are instructed to work on their own without teacher assistance (Handen, McAuliffe, Janosky, Feldman, & Breaux, 1994). When children with mental retardation and ADHD are placed on stimulant medication, they are able to remain on task for longer periods, although their work accuracy is not significantly affected (Handen et al., 1992).

Children and youth with mental retardation are also capable of self-harm and suicidal behavior, especially when mood or thought disorders are present. Although suicidal attempts or threats are relatively rare among persons with mental retardation in general, such behaviors as cutting oneself, running into vehicles, and jumping from heights are seen in about half of the referrals of children and youth with mental retardation to psychiatric facilities (Walters, Barrett, Knapp & Borden, 1995). Sadly, physical and sexual abuse, parental psychiatric disturbance, and familial loss are often noted in the backgrounds of these children, at rates similar to those of their nonretarded counterparts. Additionally, these high rates of suicidal behavior among psychiatrically disturbed children and youth with mental retardation may be connected to their limited ability to communicate effectively about their distress and thereby receive proper attention (Walters et al., 1995).

So we see that children with mental retardation may show emotional and behavioral problems that require special recognition and learning strategies. By and large

such problems do not constitute major psychiatric disorders, but rather, reflect the greater challenges these children may have in learning to express their needs and adapt to their surroundings. A 7-year-old girl with mild mental retardation, for instance, may be at a developmental level comparable to a typically developing 4-year-old. In the classroom, therefore, she may have difficulty sitting in her seat and remaining on task. She may not always control her emotions or her behavior as well as other 7-year-olds in the class, leading to occasional outbursts of laughter or anger. It is important to keep these problems within a developmental perspective. We would not expect a 4-year-old to behave as well in the classroom as an older child, and expectations and teaching methods have to be adjusted accordingly. As expressed so well by Ed and Pattie, labeling a child with a diagnostic term implying pathology or inability is often ill-conceived and counterproductive. Such terms must be used sparingly—only in those instances, such as suicidal risk, where special attention is warranted.

CAUSES

It is astounding to consider that there are now over 1000 different known organic causes of mental retardation (Moser, 1992), a *fivefold* increase since 1983. Yet, despite this rapid growth in the number of known causes, scientists cannot account for mental retardation in the majority of cases, especially the milder forms. As noted in Table 9.5, a genetic or environmental cause is known in almost two-thirds of individuals with moderate to profound mental retardation, whereas only about a quarter of those causes are known for mild mental retardation. Some of the causes happen prenatally, as is the case with all the genetic disorders and accidents in utero. Other types of mental retardation are caused by perinatal insults, such as prematurity or anoxia at birth. Still other types occur as a result of meningitis, head trauma, and other postnatal factors.

To make sense of these different causes, researchers have proposed a two-group approach to mental retardation. The definitions, characteristics, and causes of mental retardation as viewed from the two-group approach are summed up in Table 9.6. The organic group (sometimes referred to as pathological) has a clear organic cause and is usually associated with severe and profound mental retardation, whereas the *cultural-familial* group has no clear organic cause and is usually associated with mild mental retardation (Zigler, 1967; Zigler & Hodapp, 1986).

Considerable knowledge exists about organic mental retardation because of the strong biological factors involved. In stark contrast, the cultural-familial group

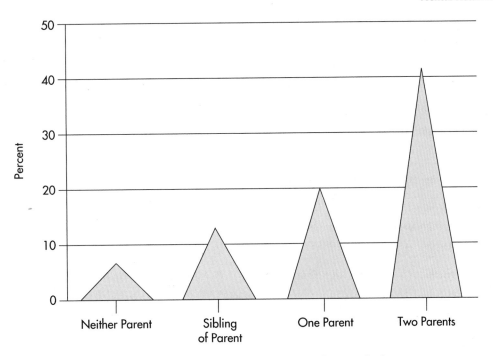

Family Members with Mental Retardation

FIGURE 9.4   Chance of mental retardation occurring in the same family. (Data from Reed & Reed, 1965)

remains somewhat of a mystery, even though it comprises one-half to two-thirds of all persons with mental retardation (Hodapp & Dykens, 1996). Environmental and situational factors, such as poverty, inadequate child care, and parental psychopathology, which affect the psychological (as opposed to biological) development of the child, are prime suspects, yet more specific cause-and-effect relationships have not been determined. Certainly, genetic factors still play some role in cultural-familial forms of mental retardation, as suggested by the family histories of children with mental retardation, shown in Figure 9.4. The chance of mental retardation increases geometrically if both parents have normal IQ but one has a sibling with mental retardation (13%), if one parent has mental retardation (20%), and if both parents have mental retardation (42%). Accordingly, both genetic and environmental factors are implicated in milder forms of mental retardation, but in a manner as

Table 9.6   The Two-Group Approach to Mental Retardation

	Organic	Cultural-Familial
Definition	Individual shows a clear organic cause of mental retardation.	Individual shows no obvious cause of retardation.
		Sometimes other family member has mental retardation.
Characteristics	More prevalent in moderate, severe, and profound mental retardation.	More prevalent in mild mental retardation.
	Equal or near-equal rates across all ethnic and SES levels.	Higher rates within minority groups and low SES groups.
	More often associated with other physical disabilities.	Few associated physical and medical disabilities.
Causes[1]	Prenatal (genetic disorders, accidents in utero).	Polygenic (i.e., parents of low IQ).
	Perinatal (prematurity, anoxia).	Environmentally deprived.
	Postnatal (head trauma, meningitis).	Undetected organic conditions.

[1]Causes are suspected for cultural-familial mental retardation.
Source: Hodapp & Dykens, 1996.

yet to be determined (Burack, 1990; Zigler & Hodapp, 1986).

The two-group distinction also contends that mild mental retardation should be conceptualized along a continuum that varies from lesser to greater degrees of intellectual ability, similar to a bell curve. The more severe forms of mental retardation, in contrast, are considered categorical—present or absent—due to unusual events that have powerful influences on development. Refer to Figure 9.1, which shows that an unexpected excess of very low-range IQ scores opposes the assumption of a normal distribution. These scores are believed to be accounted for by the organic group.

The relative importance of the environment also stands out in this distinction. The socioeconomic background of the organic group is about the same as the general population, which fits with the notion that severe forms of mental retardation can affect anyone, regardless of SES. The familial group, on the other hand, is overrepresented by those of lower SES and social disadvantage, and is significantly related to a family history of mental retardation. This fits with the assertion that an impoverished social environment can influence intellectual growth and ability in subtle, yet crucial, ways.

For the most part the two-group approach has been supported empirically, with some adjustments (Moser, Raimey, & Leonard, 1990; Simonoff et al., 1996). The previous assumption that mild mental retardation is not due to organic causes had to be tempered by findings that epilepsy, cerebral palsy, and other organic disorders are found among persons with mild mental retardation (Hagberg, Hagberg, Lewerth, & Lindberg, 1981; McClaren & Bryson, 1987; Rao, 1990; Sabaratnam, Laver, Butler, & Pembrey, 1994). Additionally, organic pathology cannot be determined in about 10% or so of persons with severe mental retardation (Hodapp & Dykens, 1996). Even after factoring in the overlap between the two groups, however, this approach to the etiology of mental retardation has stood the test of time.

Heritability and the Role of the Environment

The study of human intelligence has received the lion's share of attention in terms of the underlying processes involved in genetic makeup and the environmental factors that influence genetic expression. Still, the long-standing debate concerning the relative contributions of genes and environment is far from being fully resolved (McGue, 1997). This debate is clearly not an either/or position—gene action requires at least a biochemical environment, and often an ecological one. Conceivably, genetic influences on development are potentially modifiable by environmental input, though the practicality of

The Buckets reprinted by permission of United Feature Syndicate, Inc.

such modifications is another matter. Similarly, environmental influences on development involve the genes or structures to which the genes have contributed (Neisser et al., 1996). Simply stated, children do not inherit an IQ—they inherit a collection of genes referred to as a **genotype** for intelligence. The expression of the genotype in the environment—the gene-environment interaction—is referred to as the **phenotype**. The **heritability** of a trait describes the proportion of the variation of a trait that is attributable to genetic influences in that population (Sattler, 1988). The degree of heritability of any given trait, therefore, can range from none at all (0%) to 100% genetically determined.

So can we estimate the heritability of intelligence as defined by IQ and, by implication, the heritability of mental retardation? This intriguing question can now be answered with some degree of confidence, but little fanfare. The overwhelming evidence points to a heritability of intelligence of roughly 50%; that is, both genetic and nongenetic factors play a powerful role in the makeup and expression of intelligence (McGue, Bouchard, Iacono, & Lykken, 1993; Plomin & Neiderhiser, 1991).

There are so many specific genetic causes of mental retardation that some skepticism about the importance of environmental effects still remains. The difficulty of identifying, pinpointing, and measuring specific, nongenetic variables certainly adds to this dilemma (Plomin, 1995; Rowe, 1994). Considerable evidence has demonstrated, however, that major environmental variations do affect cognitive performance in children from disadvantaged backgrounds (Rutter, 1991). For example, children who are born to socially disadvantaged parents and then adopted into more privileged homes have significantly higher IQ scores than their siblings reared by their disadvantaged, biological parents (Capron & Duyme, 1989; Schiff & Lewontin, 1986). Even the *prenatal* environment may influence IQ to a greater extent than previously appreciated. On the basis of a meta-analysis of studies of twins and nontwin siblings, Devlin, Daniels, and Rodin (1997) found that the shared prenatal environment (that is, all children shared the same mother) accounted for 20% of IQ similarity in twins, but only 5% among nontwin siblings. Such findings imply that prenatal influences, such as nutrition, hormone levels, and toxic substances, may be misconstrued as genetic when in fact they are environmental (McGue, 1997). The practical benefits of this research are important to consider: If early environmental (prenatal) influences have a significant impact on intellectual functioning, expansion of fledgling public health initiatives aimed at improving maternal nutrition and reducing prenatal exposure to toxins may not only improve maternal prenatal care but have the unexpected benefit of improving children's intellectual and cognitive functioning as well.

Genetic and Constitutional Factors

Despite the rapid expansion of knowledge regarding genetic mechanisms underlying conditions associated with mental retardation, the actual biological mechanisms that cause impaired intellect are poorly understood (Simonoff et al., 1996). Identification of abnormal genes, or genes involving an increased risk for particular disorders, is invaluable for genetic screening and counseling, but such identification does not specify a more effective treatment mode for mental retardation.

Because there are so many conditions causing mental retardation, the focus here will be on several different disorders or classes of disorder. These include Down syndrome; fragile-X syndrome; Prader-Willi and Angelman syndromes; and single-gene conditions, such as PKU. Each of these disorders illustrates different aspects of genetic mechanisms. The various ways in which genes may interact with environmental influences are also highlighted.

Chromosome Abnormalities.

Chromosome abnormalities are the single most common cause of severe mental retardation. **Down syndrome**, or trisomy 21, is the most common disorder resulting from such abnormalities. Abnormalities can also occur in the number of sex chromosomes, resulting in mental retardation syndromes such as Klinefelter's (XXY, a disorder in which males have an extra X chromosome) and Turner's (XO, a disorder in which women are missing a second X chromosome). These latter disorders are somewhat common—about 1 in 400 live births—but they are generally less devastating in their effects on intellectual functioning than irregular formation of autosomes (Simonoff et al., 1996).

Down syndrome occurs at a rate of about 1.5 per 1000 births (deGrouchy & Turleau, 1990). The syndrome produces several distinguishing physical features, including a small skull; a large tongue protruding from a small mouth; almond-shaped eyes with sloping eyebrows; a flat nasal bridge; a short, crooked fifth finger; and broad, square hands with a simian (monkeylike) crease across the palm. These physical features are sometimes inconspicuous, and children with Down syndrome can be quite attractive.

In most Down syndrome cases, the extra chromosome results from the failure of the 21st pair of the mother's chromosomes to separate during meiosis, an abnormality termed **nondisjunction**. When the mother's two chromosomes join with the single 21st chromosome from the father, the result is three number 21 chromosomes instead of the normal two. Because nondisjunction is strongly related to maternal age, the incidence of Down syndrome increases from less than 1 per 1000 live births for mothers less than 33 years old to 38 per 1000 when the mother is 45 years of age or older (Trimble & Baird, 1978) (see Figure 9.5). Although nondisjunction of maternal chromosomes accounts for the vast majority of Down syndrome cases, scientists are investigating the possibility that environmental toxins from the father's workplace can affect sperm development and in rare cases lead to Down syndrome (Olshan, Baird, & Teschke, 1989).

Although the chromosomal basis of Down syndrome is well understood, the cause of mental retardation is not known. One view is that the chromosome imbalance may create "critical regions" of genetic material which, when unbalanced, give rise to particular phenotypic characteristics (Epstein, 1990). Another theory is that trisomy 21 causes developmental instability, and as a result, the formation of important neural tissue is abnormal (Blum-Hoffman, Rehder, & Langenbeck, 1987). Once the genes responsible for the various abnormalities and trisomy 21 are identified and their mode of action is specified, this puzzle will be solved (Simonoff et al., 1996).

The anomaly found in **fragile-X syndrome** is the most common cause of *inherited* mental retardation (Down syndrome is more frequent but is rarely inherited). This disorder affects about 1 in 1500 to 2000 males and 1 in 2000 to 2500 females (Kahkonen et al., 1987). Physical features are more subtle than in Down syndrome, and may include a large forehead, a prominent jaw, and low, protuberant ears. Mental retardation is generally in the mild to moderate range, although some children are profoundly handicapped and others have normal intelligence (Simonoff et al., 1996).

Although the gene for fragile-X syndrome, known as the FMR-1 gene, is located on the X chromosome, this syndrome does not follow a traditional X-linked inheritance pattern. About one-third to one-half of the females who carry and transmit the disorder are themselves affected with a variant of the syndrome and show a slight degree of cognitive or emotional impairment. Further, about 20% of males with the FMR-1 gene transmit the disorder but are themselves unaffected (Anderson, 1994). The behavioral characteristics of fragile-X

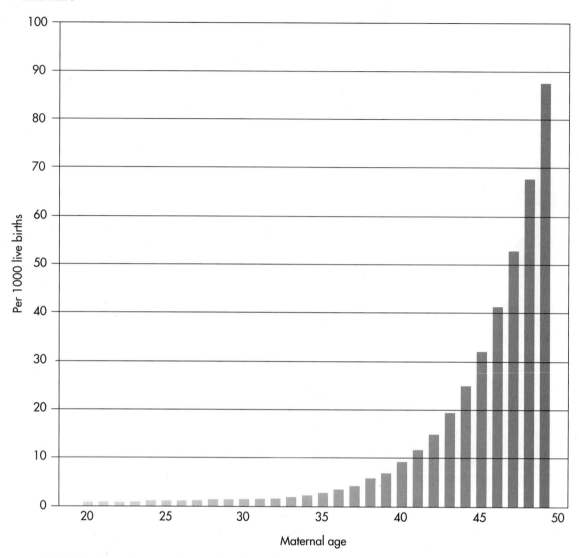

FIGURE 9.5 Rates of Down syndrome births by maternal age. (Data from Hook, 1982)

syndrome are often subtle, but distinctive. The majority of affected males have unusual social and communication patterns marked by shyness and poor eye contact. A minority show extreme social anxiety, and less than 5% meet criteria for autism (Flint & Yule, 1994).

Prader-Willi syndrome is a complex genetic disorder that includes short stature, mental retardation or learning disabilities, incomplete sexual development, low muscle tone, and an involuntary urge to eat constantly. The syndrome is rare, estimated to affect only about 5 to 10 per 100,000 births (Butler, 1990). Children with Prader-Willi syndrome may make extreme attempts to obtain food, because the area of their struggle with controlling food intake is the fact that they need fewer calories than normal to maintain an appropriate weight, which leads to obesity. **Angelman syndrome** is associated

with mental retardation (usually moderate to severe), but with rather different features. Behavior is characterized by ataxia (awkward gait), jerky movements, hand flapping, seizures, and the absence of speech. Distinctive facial features include a large jaw and an open-mouthed expression.

Both Prader-Willi and Angelman syndromes are associated with an abnormality of chromosome 15, but they are not considered inherited conditions. Rather, they are believed to be spontaneous genetic birth defects that occur at or near the time of conception. For reasons that are still not well understood, genes in the affected region on the mother's chromosome 15 are not expressed (functional). This lack of a gene or genes that are very close to each other appears to be the cause of the related syndromes. The origin—whether maternal or

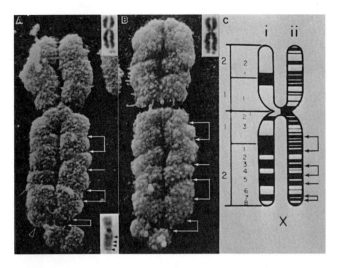

Micrograph showing the "pinched chromosome" found in fragile-X syndrome.

paternal—of the genetic material that is *absent* is the likely cause of the marked phenotypic differences.

Much is being discovered about the genetic influences on intelligence and adaptive abilities. Because these influences are by no means uniform or exact, a challenge remains in accounting for the mechanisms causing these effects on intelligence and the variations in phenotypic expression. Even with Down syndrome, for example, the range in IQ extends into mild mental retardation, and some individuals have an IQ within the normal range. Molecular genetic and biological techniques are beginning to make it possible to understand why such variation occurs, although knowledge to date is extremely limited (Simonoff et al., 1996).

Single-Gene Conditions.

Other syndromes affecting intelligence and cognitive functioning can result from genetically based metabolic defects, known as **inborn errors of metabolism**. Such defects cause excesses or shortages of certain chemicals that are necessary during particular stages of development. Inborn errors of metabolism account for some 3% to 7% of cases of severe mental retardation (Moser et al., 1990). One of the best understood examples of such a single-gene condition is **phenylketonuria (PKU)**, a rare disorder occurring in approximately 1 in 10,000 individuals (DiLella & Woo, 1987). Unlike chromosomal abnormalities (the cause of Down syndrome), the cause of PKU is a recessive gene transmitted by typical Mendelian mechanisms. Children receive the gene from both parents—neither of whom need have PKU—which results in a lack of liver enzymes necessary for converting the amino acid phenylalanine into another essential amino acid, tyrosine. Tyrosine is normally converted into other chemicals needed for physical development. Because the individual is unable to metabolize phenylalanine, which is found in many foods, it accumulates in the body and is converted to phenylpyruvic acid, another abnormal metabolite. This metabolite, in turn, causes brain damage, mental retardation, musty body odor, hyperactivity, seizures, and dry, bleached skin and hair.

PKU is a good example of a genetic disorder that can be treated successfully by environmental changes. All infants are now screened at birth for the presence of the defect, and immediately placed on a restricted diet if necessary. However, now that affected individuals have received early treatment, young women have begun to reproduce, resulting in high rates of birth defects and subsequent mental retardation in offspring. Severe dietary restriction, begun prior to conception, is currently the best precaution for these problems (Simonoff et al., 1996).

Neurobiological Influences

Fetal and infant development also can be affected by adverse biological conditions such as malnutrition, exposure to toxic substances, and various prenatal and perinatal stressors. These conditions directly or indirectly cause lowered intelligence and mental retardation in some, but by no means all, circumstances, often depending on the degree of insult to the fetus and the time of fetal development (the first trimester being the period of greatest susceptibility). Pregnancy and delivery are times of greatest susceptibility to trauma, infections, or other complications, and such problems account for about 10% of mental retardation overall (APA, 1994). Other general medical conditions acquired in infancy or childhood, such as infections, traumas, and accidental poisonings, account for another 5% or so of suspected or known causes of mental retardation (APA, 1994).

One of the most widely recognized causes of preventable mental retardation is prenatal exposure to alcohol, especially if the mother drinks heavily during pregnancy. Extensive exposure can cause **fetal alcohol syndrome (FAS)**, denoted by mental retardation as well as a range of physical symptoms, but even small amounts of prenatal alcohol may have negative effects on intelligence even though the full syndrome does not appear. The relationship between alcohol exposure and IQ is convincing. Mothers who consume more than 1.5 ounces of alcohol daily during pregnancy were found to have children who scored some 5 IQ points below controls by age 4 (Streissguth et al., 1991). Prenatal exposure to aspirin and antibiotics had similar negative effects in this study.

Although somewhat rare, fetal alcohol syndrome is considered a leading *known* cause of mental retardation because of its clear link to intellectual impairment. Its incidence is estimated at about .7 per 1000 live births in the United States (Centers for Disease Control, 1995), with much higher incidence rates among African Americans and, particularly, among Native Americans, where fetal alcohol syndrome occurs almost 4 times as often as in the general U.S. population (2.7 per 1000 live births). Fetal alcohol syndrome is characterized by central nervous system (CNS) dysfunction, cranial feature defects, and growth retardation below the 10th percentile. The mechanism causing such abnormalities is not clear but is believed to involve the *teratogenic* (referring to damage to fetal development) effects of alcohol on the development of the central nervous system as well as related damage stemming from metabolic and nutritional problems associated with alcoholism (Steinhausen, Willms, & Spohr, 1994). In addition to intellectual deficits, children with fetal alcohol syndrome often have long-term difficulties that resemble ADHD, including attention deficits, poor impulse control, and serious behavior problems. On average, their IQ is in the mild range of mental retardation (Streissguth et al., 1991).

Several other teratogens besides alcohol are known to increase the risk of mental retardation because of their effect on CNS development. Viral infections such as rubella (German measles), contracted by the mother during the first 3 months of pregnancy, can cause severe defects in the fetus. However, immunization has virtually eliminated this cause of retardation in most developed countries. Syphilis, scarlet fever, tuberculosis of the nervous system, degenerative diseases of the nerves, and sometimes measles and mumps can also lead to mental retardation. Retardation can also be caused by X rays and certain drugs taken by the mother during pregnancy, by mechanical pressure on the child's head during birth, by anoxia owing to delays in breathing at birth, by poison such as lead and carbon monoxide, and by tumors and cysts in the head (Hodapp & Dykens, 1996). In essence, any biochemical or infectious substance that cannot be destroyed or regulated by the mother's immune system or regulatory system can pose a risk to fetal development and, in turn, intellectual ability.

Social and Psychological Dimensions

The final group of factors causing mental retardation, or occurring in association with it, is perhaps the least understood and most diverse. Broadly defined, these factors cover a wide range of environmental influences, such as deprived physical and emotional care and stimulation of the infant, as well as other mental disorders that are often accompanied by mental retardation, such as autistic disorder. Together these events account for about 15% to 20% of mental retardation (APA, 1994). Although quite broad in scope, these influences are largely

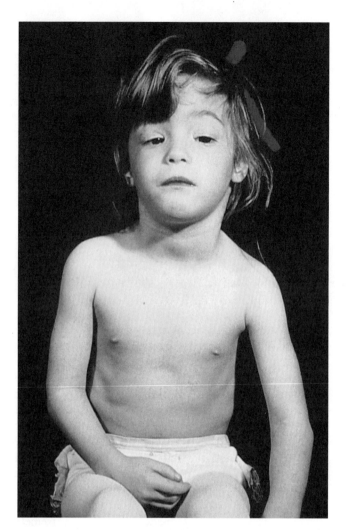

Characteristics of children with fetal alcohol syndrome include skin folds at the corner of the eye, low nasal bridge, short nose, groove between nose and upper lip, small head circumference, small eye opening, small midface, and thin upper lip.

indirect and unproven because they are often embedded in different layers and degrees of individual and family circumstances. Here we focus on the role of the caregivers and the family in supporting the development of a child with mental retardation, as well as the stress and challenges that may interfere with such a role. Parental deviance, such as abuse or neglect, and how it can affect intellectual and behavioral development are dealt with in greater detail in Chapter 14.

Parents provide their children not only with their genes, but also with a child-rearing environment and atmosphere that serve to direct and shape the child's psychological development right from the beginning. Consider the comments by the father of a young child with Down syndrome, who had to learn how to ask for proper assistance and to connect with other families of Down syndrome children:

> *I will never forget when the nurse told us how much these children can achieve. Her advice to contact a local association for children with Down syndrome was an important beginning. Other parents at the association helped me understand that Down syndrome was a chromosomal aberration and not a disease, and [gave advice on] how to look for help. My son was hardly a month old when he began physiotherapy to help him learn and interact with others. Jake is three years old now and he is full of life. He walks, repeats several words, and understands directions. (Adapted from Martin, 1995)*

How do families who have a child with mental retardation contribute to the child's healthy development or, alternatively, to his or her decline? The field of mental retardation in recent years has shown a major change in how this question is being addressed. Rather than focusing only on the family's negative influence, researchers are interested in learning more about the successful ways some families cope with the additional stress and demands of raising a child with mental retardation. As is the case when dealing with other stressors, individual members and the family unit itself can be affected both negatively as well as positively, such as when the couple is brought closer together by caring for a difficult child.

One way parents adapt successfully to a child with special needs is to use social supports and community resources, although individual preferences regarding type of support may vary—supports that help mothers may not help fathers. Mothers seem to prefer more emotional support, information about the child's condition, and help in child care (Bailey, Blasco, & Simeonsson, 1992), whereas fathers request ways to find assistance in the financial cost of raising the child with mental retardation (Price-Bonham & Addison, 1978). Mothers are often concerned about how raising a child with mental retardation may affect their personal relationships with their husbands and about the restrictions the child's care may place on their role in the family, whereas fathers worry about not feeling close to the child or being reinforced by the child (Krauss, 1993). Thus, mothers and fathers differ in how they understand and relate to the child with mental retardation, which aspects of raising the child they see as stressful, and which factors best alleviate stress.

An understanding of the social and independent functioning of young people with Down syndrome has helped us understand what factors affect their adjustment to community living. Not surprisingly, early cognitive development is a strong predictor of developmental progress and self-sufficiency among such children, as shown in areas such as language (Sloper & Turner, 1996). However, family factors are also important, particularly mothers' strategies for coping with their children's problems and the families' level of social support.

PREVENTION, EDUCATION, AND TREATMENT

We plead for those who cannot plead for themselves.
—Motto of Highgate, the first public institution for persons with mental retardation, established in London, England, October 1847

As we turn our discussion toward treatment methods for children with mental retardation, consider for a moment how you would apply your knowledge of psychological and educational treatments to best assist a child like Vanessa or Matthew. Would you start with Matthew's behavior problems and try to get them under control first, and then teach him other skills? Would Vanessa likely benefit from individualized treatment, emphasizing gradual speech training and self-help skills?

As is the case with several other disorders we have discussed, such as autism, ADHD, and some types of conduct disorders, the primary presenting problems—in this case, intellectual retardation and limited adaptive abilities—are chronic conditions that pose limitations across many important areas of development. Consequently, programs often have to be designed to fit the educational and developmental level of each individual child even more so than, say, treatment programs for children with behavior or anxiety problems. It is useful to begin this task with an overview of major environmental and individual characteristics that either increase the risk of adjustment problems or serve to protect the child from such problems. Figure 9.6 shows these major factors.

As you can see, the child's overall adjustment is a function of parental participation, family resources, and social supports (on the environmental side) combined with his or her level of intellectual functioning, basic temperament, and other specific deficits (on the individual side). Treatment can be designed to build on the child's existing resources and strengths in an effort to bolster particular skill areas or learning abilities. In other words, attention does not have to be focused primarily on what the child *lacks,* but more so on how best to match teaching and therapeutic methods to the child's own levels and abilities to accomplish realistic, practical

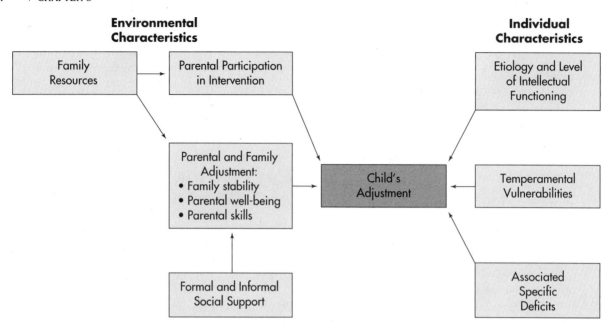

Environmental Characteristics

Individual Characteristics

FIGURE 9.6 Risk and protective factors affecting the psychological adjustment of intellectually disabled children. (Based on Lacharité et al., 1995)

goals. Thus, treatment and education for children with mental retardation involves a multicomponent, integrated strategy that considers children's needs within the context of their individual development, their family or institutional setting, and their community.

Mental retardation can be prevented or reduced in severity in some instances if proper precautions are taken. Therefore, we begin this section by discussing current health care practices involving parental education and prenatal screening. These procedures, implemented in many communities, are designed to inform parents of proper prenatal care and risks, and to detect abnormal fetal development. We then turn to psychosocial treatments for children with mental retardation and their families, which have become a common part of many treatment and education plans. In short, treatment focuses on teaching the necessary skills and abilities to the child, such as language, personal care and hygiene, and social skills, as well as teaching skills and providing supports to parents and other care-givers.

Psychopharmacological interventions with children and adults with mental retardation are presently very limited. The effective use of medications with this population has been hindered somewhat by both professional and public perceptions that psychotropic drugs are used to *control* behavior, a view based historically on unfortunate, inappropriate use and on the drugs' major side effects (Lewis, Aman, Gadow, Schroeder, & Thompson,

1996). Although many newer classes of compounds, which reduce unpleasant side effects, have become available over the past decade, these compounds have not been systematically studied with people with mental retardation. Nevertheless, drug treatment is beneficial in some cases. As with other childhood disorders, drug treatment can be targeted at desirable changes in specific behaviors or dimensions, such as compulsions, aggression, or self-injury, rather than at treating the underlying disorder itself (Lewis et al., 1996). Children with ADHD and mental retardation often benefit from either fluoxetine (Prozac) or methylphenidate (Ritalin), although the former drug has to be monitored carefully because of the possibility of such side effects as drowsiness, dizziness, and anorexia (Aman, Kern, Osborne, & Tumuluru, 1997).

Prenatal Education and Screening

One of the best opportunities to promote healthy child outcomes is during prenatal development (Devlin et al., 1997). Although not all forms of mental retardation can be prevented prenatally, many debilitating forms of retardation, such as those related to fetal alcohol syndrome, lead poisoning or rubella, can be easily prevented if proper precautions are taken. A much larger number of children are affected by prenatal education and health care if one includes not only the prevention of specific risks, but also the promotion of proper child care, especially during the child's first two years (Olds, Henderson, & Kitzman, 1994).

Not too long ago, a pregnant woman would have seen her doctor for several visits prior to childbirth, and may have gained additional knowledge through reading and from family members. The focus was largely on the medical needs of the pregnancy, with little opportunity to consider what it means to raise a child and to prepare for the added stress and complexity that child care involves. Fortunately, almost all communities today have prenatal programs for parents, and fathers have taken on a much larger role as well. These programs, often run by public health nurses, community colleges, churches, and other community organizations, have filled much of the gap in services between basic medical care and basic child care that parents need prior to the birth of a baby. Parents are provided with information about the different periods of fetal development, and cautioned about the use of alcohol, tobacco, nonprescribed drugs, and caffeine during pregnancy. The stresses of childbirth and postnatal adjustment are described, with opportunities for parents to consider the additional supports they may need and the changes they may need to make to ensure the child's health and safety. Many programs also include discussion of children with special needs, so that parents are not left feeling confused and alone.

A recent development in the delivery of these important prenatal services is the increasing multicultural focus, which sensitively and appropriately considers the cultural background of recipients (Coates & Vietze, 1996). We now recognize that a family is at least bicultural and perhaps multicultural, and that family members make choices on the basis of cultural influences. To be of most help, prenatal and postnatal services must be *culturally diverse* and *culturally sensitive*. Meeting this goal involves working with informal support and helping networks, such as churches, community and spiritual leaders, and community organizations, in ways that extend self-determination (Issacs & Benjamin, 1991). More and more, prenatal programs are breaking away from a set curriculum and being modified to establish a better fit with each cultural group or community, for example, by providing information on ways to access health care and family services with limited transportation, limited income, and so forth. In this manner, issues germane to infant care and family social support are of much greater relevance to recipients.

Prenatal screening constitutes a particular form of genetic screening that is used to determine whether a fetus has some genetic abnormality, such as Down syndrome, that would lead to a seriously handicapping condition. Ultrasound scanning can detect many conditions associated with physical defects, and both amniocentesis (ordinarily performed at 16 to 18 weeks) and chorionic villus sampling (ordinarily performed at 9 to 12 weeks) allow prenatal diagnosis of chromosomal abnormalities and genetic diseases identifiable at the DNA level (Cooley & Graham, 1991). The next decade will probably see substantial advances in **genetic screening** (Simonoff et al., 1996), which will allow for much greater precision in genetic counseling. Ethical and practical guidelines must first be developed, however, because there is a fundamental difference between using genetic information to prevent an illness or disease and altering genetic material to promote desired (or get rid of undesired) personal characteristics (Sutton, 1995).

Psychosocial Treatments

The first psychosocial treatment we consider involves intensive, broad-ranging early-intervention services for families with young children, designed to reduce risk factors and promote healthy child development. Although expensive to deliver, these services are proving to be of considerable benefit to children and families over the long term, and accomplish a great deal more than a reduction in intellectual deficits alone. We then take a close look at the existing educational and therapeutic methods that have successfully benefited children with various levels of mental retardation. The application of behavioral, cognitive-behavioral, and family-oriented interventions is discussed, with an emphasis on the task of integrating known treatments that best match the different needs of these children.

As a prelude to the discussion of psychosocial treatments, we acknowledge the importance of community-based activities that offer persons with disabilities a choice of ways to develop their interpersonal and practical skills and self-confidence. For example, a study involving over 100 athletes who participated in the 1993 Special Olympics World Games in Austria found that athletes scored higher on measures of social competence and had more positive self-perceptions than a matched, nonathlete comparison group (Dykens & Cohen, 1996).

Early Intervention. For over 25 years, one of the most promising methods for enhancing the intellectual and social skills of young children with developmental disabilities, including those with mental retardation, learning disabilities, and lack of environmental stimulation, has been the involvement of care-givers and other adults in intensive, child-focused activities from an early point in time. Many of these children would be described

Social and sports events are an important way of fostering independence, social competence, and self-esteem in persons with mental retardation.

as disadvantaged or high-risk, synonymous terms referring to family circumstances (such as low income, insufficient health care, poor housing), child characteristics (such as low IQ, poor adaptive abilities, physical or health disabilities), or a combination of both (C. T. Ramey, Mulvihill, & Ramey, 1996). Early educational intervention consists of systematic efforts to provide high-risk children with supplemental educational experiences before they enter school, and frequently includes other family and child services.

One of the more successful examples of an early educational intervention is the Carolina Abecedarian project (Campbell & Ramey, 1995). The intervention is offered to children of poor families, who are provided with enriched environments from early infancy through preschool years. Results show that by age 2, test scores of children in the enrichment-group are already higher than those of controls, and they remain some 5 points higher at age 15, 10 years after the end of the program. At age 15, members of the treated group are less likely to score in the mentally retarded or low-normal range of intellectual functioning. The enrichment group also outperformed the controls in academic achievement through 10 years in school for both reading and mathematics, and there were fewer instances of grade retention or special education classes.

Based on these and related findings, the optimal timing for intervention appears to be during the preschool years (C. T. Ramey et al., 1996). Early education programs such as the Abecedarian project are highly relevant to the issue of environmental effects in mental retardation, because they involve children from socially disadvantaged backgrounds, who have a much higher risk of retardation. Although the programs clearly are effective, lasting benefits depend on the stability and continuation of environmental changes that foster healthy child development.

C. T. Ramey and S. L. Ramey (1992) offer a set of practical recommendations for enhancing children's lives through early intervention:

1. *Encouragement of exploration.* Children are encouraged by adults to explore and gather information about their environments.
2. *Mentoring in basic skills.* A trusted, familiar adult teaches children basic cognitive skills such as labeling, sorting, sequencing, and comparing.
3. *Celebration of developmental advances.* Family and others who know the child celebrate and reinforce each of the child's accomplishments.
4. *Guided rehearsal and extension of new skills.* Responsible others assist the child in rehearsing and extending newly acquired skills.
5. *Protection from harmful displays of disapproval, teasing, or punishment.* Constructive criticism and negative consequences for unacceptable behaviors are used.
6. *A rich and responsive language environment.* Adults provide a predictable and understandable environment for communication. Spoken and written language is used to convey information, provide social awards, and encourage the learning of new material and skills.

Dan's mother added some additional ideas, based on her own experiences:

> Be creative. He learns by repetition, so the more closely you follow the "house" system and coordinate all the topics of all the classes, the easier he and the other students can learn. He can learn spelling words of items he touches in science lab. He can learn history related to his library book of the week. Combine the lesson plans to touch all phases of the subject.

Behavioral Treatments. As noted earlier, for many years the mode for dealing with problems faced by persons with mental retardation was to isolate them from society through institutionalization or separate schools, a practice that curtailed their ability to interact with typically developing peers. Behavioral interventions first emerged in the context of these restricted settings, and were initially seen primarily as a means to control or redirect negative behaviors, such as aggression or self-injurious behavior. Through the efforts of concerned behavior therapists, important principles were established concerning the implementation of behavioral methods with children and other persons who are unable to provide fully informed consent. The Association for Behavior Analysis (ABA) Task Force stipulated that each individual has the right to the least restrictive effective treatment, as well as a right to treatment that results in safe and meaningful behavior change (Van Houten et al., 1988). These efforts, coupled with continued input from parents and educators, led to a greater emphasis on positive methods for teaching basic academic and social skills in both academic and community settings to help children and adolescents with mental retardation adapt in the most normal fashion.

Vanessa's treatment plan typifies how several important behavioral methods are successfully applied. Language training is often considered a fundamental starting point for teaching more advanced skills to children with mental retardation, and behavioral methods are well suited for this purpose (Matson & Coe, 1991). The plan developed for Vanessa offers a useful example of how these methods are applied (based on Morris, 1978).

Vanessa participated in one-to-one therapy sessions, in which she was reinforced (by edibles and praise) for emitting sounds that imitated the therapist's sounds. The speech therapist used a **shaping** procedure, which began by forming a list of responses (such as "ge," "ga," "oh") that were more and more similar to the target response (in this case, the word "go"). After she mastered the first sound, she was reinforced only for attempts at the next sound on the list, and so on until the desired sound or word was gradually shaped. Then, to encourage her speech sounds and simple words to become functional speech and language, the therapist taught her to imitate the names of pictures shown to her. If she said the name of the picture—such as "dog"—within a few seconds, she received social rewards and, if necessary, tangible rewards such as candy. As she became more adept at naming the pictures, the therapist began to use some of the trained words in response to questions he would pose, such as "What is this?" Gradually, Vanessa's mother and father were brought into the sessions with the therapist, to begin asking her similar questions and promoting her use of functional speech. As her speech grew, new words and short sentences were introduced—ones that would be of most use to Vanessa on a daily basis at home and at the cafeteria, and when asking to use the bathroom.

Vanessa's behavior during mealtimes also presented considerable problems for her parents. She had difficulty getting food onto her utensil, so her parents were taught to use simple methods of **modeling** and **graduated guidance** to assist. After demonstrating for her how to hold a spoon, they would show her how to pick up her food and bring it to her mouth. They carefully demonstrated the steps involved, from dipping the spoon to placing it in the mouth, each time praising her for her attempts. As required, they would guide her hand to show her how each step was done. Unfortunately, without much warning, Vanessa would sometimes throw or spit her food, so her parents were also taught how to respond to such outbursts. Their first attempt to stop this problem was to remove her food for half a minute or so. If this tactic did not settle the behavior, or if she became more aggressive, they used time-out from reinforcement. They provided a short reprimand ("Don't throw food!") and told her why she was in time-out. Without ceremony, they turned her chair into the corner for about a minute. At the first sign of settling her behavior, they turned Vanessa around to face them and returned to a positive, guided method of helping her to learn to feed herself.

In addition to training in basic skills to promote language and readiness to learn, many older children and adolescents with mental retardation benefit from specific **social skills training** to promote their integration into regular classrooms and other activities. As mentioned previously, individuals with mental retardation have various degrees of difficulty in communication, self-control, anger management, correct recognition and labeling of affect in others, social problem solving, and a host of other interpersonal limitations (Matson & Hammer, 1996). Tailored to each student's individual needs, social skills training has succeeded in improving such important interpersonal skills as smiling, sharing, asking for help, attending, taking turns, following directions, and solving problems (McEvoy, Shores, Wehlby, Johnson, & Fox, 1990), largely through the use of positive reinforcement strategies that teach and reward such actions. Nondisabled peers can also be taught ways to increase opportunities for social interaction of children with mental retardation, a method known as *social network intervention*. This method is successful in increasing the quantity and quality of interactions between children with disabilities and their nondisabled peers, and promoting the development of friendships (Haring & Breen, 1992).

Cognitive-Behavioral Therapy

The greatest discovery of my generation is that human beings can alter their lives by altering their attitudes of mind.
—William James

The same theories that led to the development of cognitive therapy techniques for children with other types of learning and behavior problems generally apply to children with mental retardation as well. These methods are most effective for children with some receptive and expressive language skills, such as Vanessa acquired after careful and prolonged training through the use of visual and physical prompts. Once children are able to follow adult verbal directives and to describe their own actions verbally, they are in a position to benefit from verbal **self-regulation training** programs (Whitman, Scherzinger, & Sommer, 1991). Self-instructional training is most beneficial for children who have developed some language proficiency but who still have difficulty understanding and following directions. Such training teaches children to use verbal cues to process information, which are initially taught by the therapist or teacher, to keep themselves on task ("I'm not gonna look. I'm gonna keep working.") and to remind themselves of how to approach a new task ("What do I have to do here?" First, I have to . . . ").

Education of children with mental retardation has been plagued by the fact that, although specific cognitive skills can be taught, children often lack the higher-order (metacognitive) capabilities to apply these skills in new situations. Children with mental retardation use fewer, simpler, and more passive cognitive strategies in memory and learning task situations than do nonretarded children (Butterfield & Ferretti, 1987); therefore instructional methods developed to assist the average or above-average learner are often ineffective. Coupled with this concern is the continued reliance on verbal instruction to teach behavioral and cognitive skills to normal and exceptional children. Because of language problems, verbal instructional techniques sometimes need to be replaced by methods that capitalize on a particular child's strongest learning channels. Such methods often rely less on verbal, symbolic representation and more on perceptual, visually oriented techniques such as modeling and picture cuing.

Metacognitive training is a good example of how more specific learning techniques can be used to improve memory and learning (Campione, 1987). This training method, also known as *executive functioning* training, has expanded the value of specific self-management skills by coordinating such skills across learning situations. For example, in addition to being taught various basic math skills, students learn to identify the type of math problem with which they are confronted, and then to choose the appropriate strategy for solving the problem. The goal of such training is, first of all, to teach the child to be *strategical*—to use cognitive strategies—and then to be *metastrategical*—to make discriminations regarding how to apply different strategies in different situations (Whitman et al., 1991).

Cognitive-behavioral intervention strategies have also been applied to another major problem faced by many children with mild mental retardation: peer acceptance and social competence. The increase in inclusion and mainstreaming programs in most communities has led to the need to assist these children in negotiating effective interactions with their typically developing peers. In the main, typically developing children appear to be unaffected by the presence of children with disabilities; they continue to associate primarily with each other and to ignore the less-skilled child (Buysse & Bailey, 1993). Researchers are finding that mainstream settings are more supportive of the peer interactions of children with developmental delays than are specialized settings, especially for younger children (Guralnick et al., 1995). For some children, additional training procedures that directly address the social cognitive processes of encoding, interpreting cues, generating strategies, and evaluating consequences in typical peer situations appear to be beneficial (Vaughnn & Bos, 1991). Teaching the child to encode properly ("What happened?"); to interpret social cues appropriately ("Is the child [on the tape or in the story] being mean or not being mean?"); to generate different strategies for the problem ("What would you do if this happened to you?"); and to evaluate the consequences of his or her choices seem to be reasonable and effective methods for assisting children with mild mental retardation who also show social adjustment problems (Rosenthal-Malek & Yoshida, 1994).

Family-Oriented Strategies. The presence in the family of a child with mental retardation is a challenge, but not an insurmountable problem. Families are central to the development of any child, but for families of a child with mental retardation, child care involves an expanded commitment of time, energy, and skills (Baker, 1996). The needs of the child often dictate that the family participate in various community services and educational systems with which they may be quite unfamiliar. In the end, the majority of parents of children with mental retardation come to see their child as a positive contributor to their family and quality of life (Behr & Murphy, 1993), although the family experiences a higher-than-average level of stress and parental depressive symptoms (Singer & Irvin, 1990). This view of the child as a positive contributor is reassuring, given the finding that individual services provided for the child are usually more effective when family members are active participants (Floyd, Singer, Powers, & Costigan, 1996).

What exactly do the parents of a child with mental retardation need in order to be most effective? Family members need support and guidance, access to necessary services and respite care (opportunities for a short care-giving break, such as a weekend), and the availability of goal-oriented counseling to deal with the practical difficulties that they may encounter: demanding care-giving tasks, sleep disruption, marital discord, and restricted leisure and social opportunities (Floyd et al., 1996). Short-term, problem-focused behavior therapy for the parents is one of the most successful approaches for helping parents deal with the practical difficulties. Each family's treatment goals are developed individually; then parents are provided with solutions that are matched to their needs. For example, parents may be taught assertiveness skills or behavior management techniques (see below). In some instances, the solutions involve obtaining new resources from teachers or day care staff, or from informal sources such as neighbors and extended family.

Parent training has been widely used to assist parents of children with mental retardation. As opposed to the focus of many other applications of parent training, the primary focus on behavior change when the child has mental retardation is skill acquisition rather than behavior problem reduction (Baker, 1996). The parents' roles as primary teachers often continue well past the normal childhood years, so parent training often entails a developmentally relevant focus to prepare the family to tackle each new challenge. One illustrative program is the Portage Project, which has now been implemented in several countries (Shearer & Loftin, 1984). Children with mental retardation are taught at home by their parents, from infancy through age 6 or so. A therapist visits the family each week in the home to observe, give feedback, evaluate progress, and model ways to teach new behaviors. The program is set up in a series of sequenced behaviors in the five skill areas of cognition, language, self-help, motor skills, and socialization. Because each of these skills is broken down into very small and discrete steps, the program is relatively easy to learn and implement, and both the parents and the child increase their competence.

There are commonly three critical, but not exclusive, periods in the family life cycle in which parent training and family counseling are most beneficial. The first of these periods is during the child's infancy and toddlerhood, when parents are coming to terms with the child's disability and may need assistance in learning ways to provide adequate stimulation of early language formation and similar developmental skills. A second critical time is during the preschool and school years, when parents often want to know more about the best way to teach their child basic academic and social skills. Intensive programs, which demand a considerable amount of the parents' time, are usually best suited during the preschool years when the family is most focused on child developmental issues (Cunningham, Bremner, & Secord-Gilbert, 1993). Finally, parental concerns reemerge during their child's emergence into young adulthood. At this age, their child is no longer eligible for funded schooling, and new issues of housing, employment, relationships, and financial planning associated with independent living become concerns. To date, most services for families of an older child with mental retardation have not been as well established as those for the younger child. This remains an important area for future development (Baker, 1996).

Some children and adolescents with mental retardation benefit from an out-of-home placement, known as **residential care**, which carries with it unique responsibilities of family members as well. Residential care services are seldom a full replacement for the love and attention of the family, yet they may be necessary and beneficial under some circumstances, such as aggressive behavior of the child or the need for specialized language or social skills training that cannot be provided adequately in the home or regular school setting. Residential care may range from part-time care, whereby the child returns home each evening or weekend, to full-time care, where home visits are less frequent. Some residential programs may serve only a few children at a time, much like a group home; others may be large, multidisciplinary tertiary care facilities serving persons of all ages with various disabilities. Regardless of the structure of the residential program, research has determined that family involvement plays a critical role in children's adaptation to and benefit from such settings. Facilities that offer ways to promote family involvement, such as weekend visits and participation in classroom activities, strengthen the important attachment between children with mental retardation and their families (Baker & Blacher, 1993).

Whether the child or adolescent with mental retardation lives at home or in a community residential setting, he or she is likely to attend a regular school, at least for a part of each day. The inclusion movement calls for integration of individuals with disabilities in regular classroom settings, regardless of the severity of the disability. This movement has raised anew the issue of how the person with disabilities is perceived and treated by nonretarded professionals and peers. Mental health professionals seeking to maximize the chances of social acceptance of such individuals must contend with the myriad issues that emerge in integrated settings (Podell, Kastner, & Kastner, 1996). Unfortunately, individuals with mental retardation continue to suffer high levels of rejection by the community (Sandler & Robertson, 1981), due mostly to ignorance and preconceived bias. Adults and children with mental retardation are still sometimes perceived to be socially incompetent and behaviorally disordered (Antonak, Fiedler, & Mulaick,

1989). As they have for the past 100 years and beyond, biases and misinformation held by the public remain one of the important challenges to the field.

SUMMARY

Perspectives on Intelligence and Mental Retardation

1. The early history of mental retardation was plagued by ignorance and blame. By the mid-20th century, however, progress toward understanding mental retardation moved more rapidly, as parents, researchers, politicians, and the general public sought better answers regarding its causes and ways to assist both children and adults with mental retardation.

2. Mental retardation refers to limitations in intelligence and adaptive behavior. However, many persons with this disorder are capable of learning and of living fulfilling lives.

3. Despite its drawbacks, the IQ has become a principle standard for diagnosing mental retardation, in combination with other skills and abilities of the child.

Features of Mental Retardation

4. The DSM-IV criteria for mental retardation consist of subaverage intellectual functioning (defined as an IQ of 70 or below), deficits or impairments in adaptive functioning, and onset before age 18.

5. Mental retardation is described in reference to levels of functioning. The DSM-IV defines these levels as mild, moderate, severe, or profound. A recent, alternative approach, set forth by the American Association on Mental Retardation (AAMR) is based on needed levels of support or assistance, rather than on IQ. The AAMR levels are intermittent, limited, extensive, and pervasive.

Prevalence

6. Mental retardation occurs in an estimated 1% to 3% of the population, more often among males than females, and more often among children from lower socioeconomic and minority groups. Economic disadvantage and discrimination practices often account for the latter findings.

Developmental Course and Adult Outcomes

7. Children with mental retardation follow developmental stages in the same order as typically developing children. However, their goals and motivation are reduced over time, because of feelings of frustration, which often lead to expectations of failure.

8. Adaptive skills and level of impairment may improve over time, especially for children with mild mental retardation, if appropriate training and opportunities are provided.

9. Related developmental disabilities are common, such as epilepsy, speech and language problems, sensory impairments, and behavioral disturbances. Emotional and behavioral problems are considered part of the spectrum of problems coexisting with mental retardation, rather than indicators of mental disorder.

Causes

10. The two-group approach emphasizes the important etiological differences between organic and cultural-familial causes of mental retardation.

11. Causes of organic forms include genetic and constitutional factors, such as chromosome abnormalities, single gene conditions, and neurobiological influences.

12. Suspected causes of cultural-familial forms include economic deprivation and genetic inheritance of intelligence.

13. Social and psychological causes of mental retardation include diverse environmental influences, focusing particularly on the quality of physical and emotional care and stimulation of the infant and small child.

Prevention, Education, and Treatment

14. Intervention efforts are most successful when offered at the earliest point in time, include behaviorally based training and educational components, are matched to the child's individual needs and abilities, and are integrated with the school and community.

KEY TERMS

evolutionary degeneracy theory, 338
eugenics, 338
mental age (MA), 340
general intellectual functioning, 340
adaptive functioning, 340
degrees of impairment: mild, moderate, severe, profound, 346–347
level of needed supports: intermittent, limited, extensive, pervasive, 348
organic mental retardation, 349
cultural-familial mental retardation, 349
idiopathic, 349
organic mental retardation, 349
cultural-familial mental retardation, 349

developmental versus difference controversy, 351
similar sequence hypothesis, 351
similar structure hypothesis, 351
slowing and stability hypothesis, 352
self-injurious behavior (SIB), 356
genotype, 358
phenotype, 358
heritability, 358
Down syndrome, 359
nondisjunction, 359
fragile-X syndrome, 359
Prader-Willi syndrome, 360

Angelman syndrome, 360
inborn errors of metabolism, 361
phenylketonuria (PKU), 361
fetal alcohol syndrome (FAS), 361
genetic screening, 365
shaping, 367
modeling, 367
graduated guidance, 367
social skills training, 367
self-regulation training, 368
metacognitive training, 368
residential care, 369

Autism and Childhood-Onset Schizophrenia

Autistic disorder, or autism, is one of several **pervasive developmental disorders (PDDs)**. These disorders are characterized by severe and widespread impairments in social interaction and communication skills, and stereotyped patterns of behaviors, interests, and activities. We devote most of this chapter to autism because it is the most common and most studied PDD. Other PDDs have recently received increased attention, and we consider each of these in the section on differential diagnosis. For most of this century, autism and schizophrenia in childhood were lumped together as a single condition; it is now clear, however, that they are separate disorders. Since the two disorders share a common past and show some overlapping symptoms, we also devote part of this chapter to childhood-onset schizophrenia.

AUTISM

> *It wasn't just that she didn't understand language. She didn't seem to be aware of her surroundings. She wasn't figuring out how her world worked, learning about keys that fit into doors, lamps that turned off because you pressed a switch, milk that lived in the refrigerator. . . . If she was focusing on anything, it was on minute particles of dust or hair that she now picked up from the rug, to study with intense concentration. Worse she didn't seem to be picking up anyone's feelings. (Maurice, 1993a, pp. 32–33)*

This mother's compelling description of her 2-year-old daughter offers a first glimpse into the mystery of **autism**, perhaps the most captivating and telling of all childhood disorders. Autism is a severe disorder characterized by abnormalities in social functioning, language, and communication, and by unusual interests and behaviors.

The disorder affects every aspect of the child's interaction with his or her world, involves many parts of the brain, and undermines the very traits that make us human—our social responsiveness, ability to communicate, and feelings for other people. Imagine yourself the parent of an infant or toddler who won't cuddle, look into your eyes, or respond to your affection or touching. Unlike other children, your child doesn't form a loving relationship with you as you interact with him. In fact, he seems incapable of forming a normal relationship or communicating with anyone. As he grows older, he rarely speaks. When he does speak, he talks in unusual ways, for example, by parroting what you say to him or blurting out seemingly meaningless phrases, such as "dinosaurs don't cry." Your child doesn't use facial expressions or gestures to communicate his needs or to tell you how he feels—no smiles, no nods, no head shakes, no holding up toys for you to look at. Nor does he seem to understand the smiling faces that you and others make as you try to engage him socially. Your child shows little interest in sharing pride or pleasure with you or anyone else. Over the first few years of life he becomes more and more isolated, caught up in his own little world of obsessive rituals and interests, which when interrupted, cause him to become extremely upset. Something is seriously wrong.

Historical Background of Autism

The term *autism* was first used by the Swiss psychiatrist Eugen Bleuler in 1911 to describe individuals with schizophrenia who lost contact with reality (Bleuler, 1911/1950). **Schizophrenia** is a devastating disorder involving characteristic disturbances in thinking (**delusions**), perception (**hallucinations**), speech, emotions, and behavior. In the early 1940s two psychiatrists, Leo

Kanner (1943) and Hans Asperger (1944/1991), independently described children who displayed social impairments, abnormal language, and restricted and repetitive interests. These children were thought to experience a loss of contact with reality without having schizophrenia. In his initial report, Kanner described 11 children who, in the first few years of life, withdrew into a shell, disregarded people for objects, avoided eye contact, lacked social awareness, had limited or no language, and displayed stereotyped motor activities including an obsessive insistence on the **preservation of sameness**. The children were described by their parents as "like in a shell," "a lone wolf," "happiest when left alone," "acting as if people weren't there," and "perfectly oblivious to everything around him" (Kanner, 1943, p. 242).

Kanner (1943, 1944) called this disorder **early infantile autism** (*autism* literally means "within oneself"). He viewed the core feature of autism as the children's "inability to relate themselves in the ordinary way to people and situations from the beginning of life" (1943, p. 242). There is, said Kanner, "an *extreme autistic aloneness* that, whenever possible, disregards, ignores, shuts out anything that comes to the child from outside" (p. 242). The early onset of this disorder led Kanner to conclude that autism resulted from an inborn inability to form loving relationships with other people.

Kanner described the parents of the children he observed as highly intelligent and obsessive people who were cold, mechanical, and detached in their relationships—the so-called refrigerator parents. Thus, although he clearly saw autism as an inborn deficit, he also planted the seeds for the **psychogenic theory** that "the precipitating factor in infantile autism is the parent's wish that his child should not exist" (Bettelheim, 1967, p. 125). This early view that autism was the result of a child's defensive withdrawal from an intellectual, cold-hearted, and hostile parent has found no support. Children with autism have not withdrawn from reality because of a mental disorder—rather, they have failed to enter reality because of widespread and serious disturbances in their development (Rutter, 1991). Or, as Clara Clark, the mother of a child with autism, put it, "You can't say autistic children are withdrawn, because they were never there" (Adler, 1994, p. 248). Since Kanner's original report more than a half century ago, autism has increasingly come to be recognized as a biologically based lifelong developmental disability that is present in the first few years of life (Rimland, 1964).

Description

Autism walks with Jay like a shadow, growing and diminishing. Intangible but persistent, it retreats only in the dark as he sleeps. (Swackhamer, 1993, p. 312)

The three main behavioral features of autism are social abnormalities, abnormalities in language and communication, and restricted patterns of behaviors and interests. The following description by the mother of Jay, a high-functioning 8-year-old boy with autism, illustrates many typical features of this disorder:

Jay: Not Normal

My 8-year-old son, Jay, is autistic. Autism is blatantly wrong. It is maladaptive. I know it; Jay knows it. He wants out. "Are you normal yet?" he says, as his hands flap in wing beats below his chin. He toe-steps in place. "'Am I,'" I correct. "Am I normal yet?" His high-pitched voice is raspy. Blue eyes probe me with intensity. "Not when you scream, kick, and bite people," I say. "You want to be normal!" he screeches. Flopping to the floor, he flails his legs in the air. "Normal, normal. This program has also been made possible with financial support of viewers like you. This program has also been made possible by . . . Stop! No more." I hold my ears and rock slightly, modeling his technique.

When he awakens, Jay charges out of bed to the stereo where he slips on headphones and listens intently to *Phantom of the Opera*. If the selection on the CD player is anything other than *Phantom*, he shrieks while kicking tables, flipping chairs, and striking out at anyone within reach. Then abruptly he begins to weep, a timeless wailing, unchildlike in its profound grief. Later he adds and subtracts numbers in his workbooks or obsessively lists the previous day's events. With his uneven motor control, he inscribes letters and numbers hieroglyphic-like on endless pages. Throughout the day he searches for apostrophes. He locates them on signs, cereal boxes, books. "Is that an apostrophe?" His body trembles; his eyes wet with joy. But his real friends are the newscasters. He tracks their appearance and mourns their absence. For special occasions his conversations with them include Spanish. "Jane Pauley will be sitting in for Tom Brokaw tomorrow. Tom, are you sick? See you Lunes. See you mañana, Jane Pauley." His vision of order is sacred. I never dare trespass on it. (Adapted from Swackhamer, 1993)

Like Jay, most children with autism behave in bizarre, unusual, and frequently puzzling ways. They may squeal with excitement at the sight or sound of a wheel spinning on a toy car, yet ignore or have a full-blown tantrum over someone's attempts to turn playing with this car into a two-way social activity. Children with autism may sometimes look through you as if you are a pane of glass, but at other times stare directly into your face or tug on your arm to lead you to something they want. When you speak to a child with autism, she may act as if she is deaf, but then quickly turn in the direction of the faint sound of crinkling of a candy wrapper in another room.

Many children with autism display extreme fear or avoidance of noisy or moving objects, such as running water, swings, elevators, battery-operated toys, or even the wind. One child was so afraid of a vacuum cleaner that he would not go anywhere near the closet where it was kept. When it was used, he ran to the garage and covered his ears with his hands. Yet this child was oblivious to the sounds of traffic roaring by him on a dangerous freeway. Although children with autism fear many things, they are also attracted to and preoccupied with other objects and activities—for example, a rotating fan, a flickering light, or in Jay's case, TV newscasters. These children often develop unusual attachments or reactions to odd objects, such as a rubber band, a piece of sandpaper or string, or, like Jay, apostrophes.

Children with autism may scream, kick, and lash out at others if a chair is moved from its usual location in their room, if a stuffed giraffe isn't lined up just so between a doll and a teddy bear on their bed when they get home, or, like Jay, if something other than a favorite musical selection is on the CD player. They may spend hour after hour playing in a corner of their room, engaged in stereotyped or repetitive motor activities, such as rocking, lining up objects, tearing paper into confetti, or repeatedly flapping their hands and fingers as they flip through pages of a magazine without ever looking at the pictures. Rather than seeing the big picture, children with autism are much more likely to fixate on a minuscule object or event in their world, such as a tiny spot on their shirt. Whereas most of us see the hugeness of trees in the forest, a child with autism is more likely to fixate on a pine needle.

Higher-functioning adults with autism have provided us with fascinating glimpses into what it might be like growing up with autism. Here is one reconstruction by Jerry, a 31-year-old man with autism and normal intelligence:

Jerry: Fear and Order

According to Jerry, his childhood experience could be summarized as consisting of two predominant experiential states: confusion and terror. The recurrent theme that ran through all of Jerry's recollec-

tions was that of living in a frightening world presenting painful stimuli that could not be mastered. Noises were unbearably loud, smells overpowering. Nothing seemed constant; everything was unpredictable and strange. Animate beings were a particular problem. Dogs were remembered as eerie and terrifying. As a child, he believed they were somehow humanoid (since they moved out of their own volition, etc.), yet they were not really human, a puzzle that mystified him. They were especially unpredictable; they could move quickly without provocation. To this day, Jerry is phobic of dogs.

He was also frightened of other children, fearing that they might hurt him in some way. He could never predict or understand their behavior. Elementary school was remembered as a horrifying experience. The classroom was total confusion and he always felt he would "go to pieces."

There were also enjoyable experiences. He liked going to grocery stores with his mother so he could look at the labels of canned goods as well as the prices of objects. He also remembered liking to spin objects but could not describe the pleasure this activity gave him. His life seemed to have markedly changed when he discovered multiplication tables at around age 8. He denied that arithmetic helped give his world a sense of order; he said he simply liked working with numbers. Similarly, he could give no reason for his need for sameness or rituals beyond stating that was how things should be. It is significant that he did not mention any relationship to family members when reconstructing his childhood; they seemed of little importance. (Bemporad, 1979)

DSM-IV: Defining Features of Autism

The DSM-IV criteria for **autistic disorder** are presented in Table 10.1. In addition to the core symptoms of the disorder, the child must also evidence delays or abnormal functioning in either social interaction, language as used in social communication, or symbolic or imaginative play with onset *prior to age 3 years*.

Autism Across the Spectrum

When we hear the term *autism* many of us think of Raymond, the young man with an encyclopedic memory and amazing math skills portrayed by Dustin Hoffman in his Academy Award–winning performance in the

Table 10.1	**DSM-IV Diagnostic Criteria for Autistic Disorder**

A. A total of six (or more) items from (1), (2), and (3), with at least two from (1), and one each from (2) and (3).

   (1) qualitative impairment in social interaction, as manifested by at least two of the following:

      (a) marked impairment in the use of multiple nonverbal behaviors such as eye-to-eye gaze, facial expression, body postures, and gestures to regulate social interaction

      (b) failure to develop peer relationships appropriate to developmental level

      (c) a lack of spontaneous seeking to share enjoyment, interests, or achievements with other people (e.g., by a lack of showing, bringing, or pointing out objects of interest)

      (d) lack of social or emotional reciprocity

   (2) qualitative impairments in communication as manifested by at least one of the following:

      (a) delay in, or total lack of, the development of spoken language (not accompanied by an attempt to compensate through alternative modes of communication such as gesture or mime)

      (b) in individuals with adequate speech, marked impairment in the ability to initiate or sustain a conversation with others

      (c) stereotyped and repetitive use of language or idiosyncratic language

      (d) lack of varied, spontaneous make-believe play or social imitative play appropriate to developmental level

   (3) restricted repetitive and stereotyped patterns of behavior, interests, and activities, as manifested by at least one of the following:

      (a) encompassing preoccupation with one or more stereotyped and restricted patterns of interest that is abnormal either in intensity or focus

      (b) apparently inflexible adherence to specific, nonfunctional routines or rituals

      (c) stereotyped and repetitive motor mannerisms (e.g., hand or finger flapping or twisting, or complex whole-body movements)

      (d) persistent preoccupation with parts or objects

B. Delays or abnormal functioning in at least one of the following areas, with onset prior to age 3 years: (1) social interaction, (2) language as used in social communication, or (3) symbolic or imaginative play.

C. The disturbance is not better accounted for by Rett's Disorder or Childhood Disintegrative Disorder

Source: DSM-IV Copyright © 1994 by APA.

movie *Rain Man.* Although a few individuals with autism may possess special talents like Raymond's, most do not. Autism is a **spectrum disorder,** which means that its symptoms and characteristics are expressed in many different combinations and in any degree of severity. At one end of the spectrum we may find a mute child, crouched in a corner of his room, spinning a paper clip over and over again for hours; at the other, a university researcher who has also held corporate jobs—so long as they didn't require interacting with customers.

Not only do children with autism vary widely in their cognitive, language, and social abilities, they also display many features not specific to autism, most commonly, mental retardation and epilepsy. Thus, two children with a diagnosis of autism can be vastly different from one another. To illustrate this point, let's contrast two children, Lucy and John. Both are diagnosed with autism:

Dustin Hoffman with Tom Cruise in *Rain Man:* Although some individuals with autism display the special talents that are portrayed in the movies, most do not.

Lucy: Autism with Mental Retardation

Lucy's parents watched her development right from the start, because there had been so many difficulties during pregnancy and delivery. On the ultrasound scan, they were so excited to see their baby moving about that it was a hard blow to hear she was "small for dates." Labor began three weeks early, and lasted 23 hours, so that forceps were needed to assist the delivery. Lucy had to have oxygen to revive her, she spent four days in the special-care unit, and received ultraviolet-light treatment for jaundice. Understandably, Lucy's parents felt she was "delicate" from the start.

Indeed, it seemed in comparison to her older brother that everything in Lucy's development was troubling. Feeding Lucy was one of the problems. She was always too distressed to feed or she fed so ravenously and quickly that minutes later she vomited. Lucy's mother doesn't remember a single "easy" feed. Nights were no better, as Lucy took hours to settle, and always woke early. The feeding and sleeping difficulties continued for years.

By Lucy's first birthday she had only just started to sit up, and was still not crawling. Everyone else's baby seemed to be at the stage of pulling themselves up on the furniture, and some had even taken their first steps. Their family physician said that she was indeed delayed in her development. At 14 months Lucy began to crawl (6 months is typical), and at 19 months she pulled herself up on the furniture (most children do this around 12 months); she made little progress in other areas.

At two years Lucy still did not use any words, and was unresponsive to her parents' attempts to engage her in simple games like peek-a-boo. A pediatrician thought the delay in her development might be due to the difficulties with her delivery and suggested that Lucy be checked every 12 months.

At 30 months Lucy started to walk (most children walk by 14 months). However, her main sounds were a strange clicking noise made with the back of her tongue, and a variety of screams. Lucy still seemed oblivious to people around her (including her parents) unless they had something she wanted. For example, she loved to play with a particular blue and red rattle. If anyone picked this up, Lucy leapt on them; stared directly into their eyes with her face very close; and then grabbed the rattle and ran off to a corner. There she would shake it or spin it round and round. Once she had the rattle she did not look at anyone, and if someone tried to take it from her she screamed and banged her head on the floor. Understandably, this devastated her parents. To prevent the head-banging, they tried to see that other people never touched the rattle. Gradually, they began to feel that their lives were totally controlled by Lucy.

Lucy took great interest in odors, sniffing food, toys, clothes, and (to her parents' embarrassment) people. She even tried to smell strangers in the street. She also liked to feel things—she insisted on carrying a small piece of sandpaper in her pocket. She often tried to stroke stockings on women's legs, even of complete strangers. If they tried to stop her, she had a tantrum.

When Lucy was four, the pediatrician suspected Lucy suffered from autism, and suggested the family attend a child psychiatric clinic for a detailed assessment. The diagnosis was confirmed, and her parents were told that Lucy was generally delayed in her development. They were heartbroken, but they felt that finally Lucy would get the help she desperately needed. (Adapted from Baron-Cohen & Bolton, 1993)

John: Autism with Average Intelligence

John, an only child, was born after a normal pregnancy and delivery. As an infant, he was easy to feed and slept well. He seemed happy and content to lie in his crib for hours. He sat unsupported at six months (which is within the normal range), and soon after, he crawled. His parents saw John as independent and willful. However, his grandmother thought John showed an undue preference for his own company, as if he lacked interest in people.

John walked on his first birthday (in sharp contrast to Lucy, who did not walk until she was 30 months old); yet during his second year he did not progress as well as expected. Although he made sounds, he did not use words. Indeed, his ability to communicate was so limited that even when he was three years old his mother still found herself trying to guess what he wanted (as if he were a much younger child). Often she tried giving him a drink or some food in the hope that she had guessed his needs correctly. Occasionally he would grab hold of her wrist and drag her over to the sink, yet he never said anything like "drink," or pointed to the tap.

At this time his parents also became concerned about John's extreme independence. Even when he fell down and hurt himself, John would not come to his parents for help. He never became upset when his mother had to go out and leave him with a neighbor or relative. In fact, he seemed to be more interested in his toy bricks than people. He spent hours lining them up in exactly the same way and in precisely the same sequence of colors.

At times, his parents wondered if John were deaf, particularly as he often showed no response when they called his name. However, at other times he would turn his head at the slightest sound of a plane going over the house. After his third birthday his parents became increasingly concerned, despite reassurances from their doctor. John used no words to express himself, and showed no interest in playing with other children. He did not wave bye-bye or show any real joy when they tried to play peek-a-boo. John always wriggled away from his mother's cuddles, and only seemed to like rough-and-tumble play with his father. His mother worried that she had done something wrong, and felt depressed, rejected, and guilty.

[When John was three and a half years old], the family doctor referred [him] to a child psychiatrist who told [his parents] that John had autism, but added that John's abilities in spatial tasks (such as jigsaw puzzles) suggested normal intellectual abilities in these areas. Although still too early to tell how John would progress, the psychiatrist said there were some indications he would do better than most children with autism. John was sent to a special play group, and received speech therapy. A psychologist visited the family at home and helped the parents plan ways of encouraging the development of communication, and reducing the frequency of his temper tantrums.

At age four, John suddenly began to speak in complete sentences. His parents were greatly relieved, and for a time actually believed he had finally "grown out" of the problem. However, his speech was quite unusual. For example, he often repeated back word for word whatever his parents had said. So, if they asked him "Do you want a drink?" he would say "you want a drink" in reply. At other times, John made rather surprising remarks. For instance, he would say "You really tickle me" in a tone of voice exactly similar to that of a family friend who had first used the expression some days before. However, his use of this phrase, and most of his speech, was usually inappropriate to the setting, and lacked any clear meaning. (Adapted from Baron-Cohen & Bolton, 1993)

Lucy and John are similar in that they both display the core features of autism. They both failed to develop normal two-way social relationships and communication in the first few years of life, and both display unusual and repetitive interests and preoccupations. When Lucy was young, she was described by her parents as "living in a glass bubble." Such extreme social unresponsiveness is typical of many children with autism. John, on the other hand, is more socially outgoing and talkative when he approaches others. Whenever he meets new people, he inevitably asks the same precise questions in exactly the same way, "Why do people wear wristwatches?" or "How did you get to work today?" Although John approaches others, his efforts at social contact are repetitive and unnatural. John's abnormalities in communication are less obvious than his social deficits, and consist of speaking in a one-sided and stereotyped way. In contrast, Lucy is seriously lacking in her ability to communicate and is silent most of the time (Baron-Cohen & Bolton, 1993).

In addition to their abnormalities in social and language development, John and Lucy both display ritualistic behavior. Lucy checks the location of little pieces of thread that she has tied on all the chairs in her house, and John insists on taking exactly the same route to school each day. John and Lucy also have repetitive interests: John likes nothing better than counting lampposts, while Lucy, if allowed to do so, watches the same video over and over again. Both children can spend hours absorbed in nothing but these narrow interests. Such obsessions may lead to other problems. For example, John or Lucy may scream intensely if even a minor change occurs in one of their daily routines (Baron-Cohen & Bolton, 1993).

Despite the similarities shown by John and Lucy, their stories also show how children with autism can be quite different from one another. Three critical factors contribute to these differences. First, children with autism may possess any level of intellectual ability, from profound retardation to above-average intelligence. John is of average intelligence, whereas Lucy has severe mental retardation. Because of her mental handicap, Lucy was slow to develop in all areas. As a result of Lucy's limited overall level of functioning, she shows a much narrower range of interests and activities than John. Second, children with autism vary in the severity of their language problems. John has quite a bit of speech, whereas Lucy is mute. Children with autism can fall anywhere between these two extremes. Third, the behavior of children with autism changes with age. Some children make little progress, while others develop speech or become more outgoing. When significant gains are made, they are usually made by children, like John, who are not mentally retarded and who acquire speech at a young age.

CORE CHARACTERISTICS

Considerable debate still exists about the core features of autism, despite more than 50 years of research by professionals from many disciplines. Because autism is a rare disorder and can affect children in vastly different ways, it is a difficult problem to study. Findings from studies of small samples of children who differ widely in their levels of language and intellect are hard to interpret. Contributing to the difficulty is the interrelatedness during the first few years of life of the child's social, language, cognitive, and emotional development; a disturbance in one area is likely to affect all other areas as well. For example, a problem in social development may lead to an impairment in language, or vice versa. Rather than one primary deficit, autism more likely consists of several deficits that affect the child's socioemotional, language, and cognitive development. As we discuss each of the core characteristics of autism, we need to keep in mind that these abilities are interconnected—they do not develop in isolation (Klinger & Dawson, 1996).

Social Impairments

Children with autism experience profound difficulties in relating to other people. From a young age, they show deficits in many of the skills that are crucial for early social development—imitating others, orienting to social stimuli, sharing a focus of attention with others, understanding other people's emotions, and engaging in make-believe play. As they grow older, children with autism initiate few social behaviors and seem unresponsive to other people's feelings. Social expressiveness and sensitivity to others' social cues are limited, and little sharing of experiences or emotions with other people takes place. Children with autism generally have great difficulty integrating social, communicative, and emotional behavior, as would be required when greeting a familiar person who enters the room. Their lack of understanding of people as social agents may lead to their treating people as objects or to actions directed at the body parts of people, as when the child attacks a restraining hand rather than the person (Carr & Kemp, 1989; Phillips, Gomez, Baron-Cohen, Laa, & Riviere, 1995).

Children with autism display impairments in all aspects of **joint social attention,** which is the ability to coordinate one's focus of attention on another person and an object of mutual interest. Joint social attention, which normally develops by 12 to 15 months of age, involves getting on the same wavelength with another person by directing that person's attention to objects or people by pointing, showing, and looking, and by communicating shared interest. Although children with autism may bring an object to a person, or point to an object when they want someone to do something with that object or to get it for them, they show little desire to share interest and attention with another person for the sheer pleasure of doing so.

Children with autism process social information in unusual ways. At a young age, they may have greater difficulty than other children with imitation of body actions versus toy actions (Smith & Bryson, 1994; Stone, Ousley, & Littleford, 1997), or in orienting to social versus nonsocial stimuli (Dawson, 1996). In processing information about the human face, they may focus on parts of the face, such as the mouth or nose, rather than its overall shape (Boucher & Lewis, 1992). They may not show the typical preference of most children for speech over nonspeech sounds (Klin, 1991).

Although it was once thought that children with autism failed to form a social bond with their parents or that they could not tell the difference between their parents and other adults, research has proved this wrong. Most children with autism *do* respond differently to their care-givers than to unfamiliar adults, directing more social behavior and seeking to be closer to them than to strangers after a brief separation (Sigman & Mundy, 1989). In addition, the proportion of children with autism who display a secure attachment to their mother (40% to 50%) is slightly lower than but comparable to that of normal controls (65%), once the children's disoriented and disorganized repetitive motor behaviors are taken into account in making the attachment rating (Capps, Sigman, & Mundy, 1994). Children with a secure attachment show a preference for their mother over a stranger, use their mother as a secure base for exploration, and are comforted by their mother when distressed. Thus, children with autism do not suffer from a global deficit in their ability to form an attachment. Rather, the deficit seems to be in their ability to understand and respond to social information (Rogers, Ozonoff, & Maslin-Cole, 1993). As shown in Box 10.1, a child with autism will likely notice when his or her mother leaves the room and will look for her, both signs of attachment. However, unlike a normal child, a child with autism may have little understanding of the event or how to respond in order to change the situation, making it seem as if the child has no attachment.

In addition to their social difficulties, children with autism also show problems in processing emotional information contained in body language, gestures, facial expressions, or the voice. Preschool-age children with autism do not look for or attend to the emotional or

Box 10.1

Children in a Social Situation

This young boy with autism notices that his mother has left the room. He wanders around the room looking for her, but there's essentially no change in his expression. He doesn't seem to know what to do to change the event.

A child of his age without autism is likely to react like this:

This child's facial expression goes in ten seconds from "Oh no, they're not really leaving me" to "You gotta be kidding" to "Oh my god, they're gone." He's crying, but as soon as his parents come back in, he's comforted and he's fine.

Source: Behavior Disorders of Childhood, produced by Alvin H. Perlmutter, Inc.

attentional cues provided by other people—for example, whether the other person is happy, sad, interested, or annoyed. In contrast to control children of the same mental age, children with autism may sort pictures of people according to the type of hat these people are wearing rather than their emotional expressions (Weeks & Hobson, 1987).

It has been suggested that the primary psychological deficit in autism is an early failure to directly perceive bodily expressions, including emotions (Hobson, 1993). However, deficits in emotional understanding have not always been found, especially when children with autism are compared with control children of equivalent verbal, rather than nonverbal, ability. Nevertheless, children with autism do experience great difficulty understanding emotional information. In addition, their own bodily expressions of emotion are very different from those of normal children, often characterized by limited spontaneous use of expressive gestures, and bizarre, rigid, or mechanical facial expressions. Thus, children with autism both process and express emotional information in unusual ways. It is not yet known if they also *experience* emotions differently than do other children (Attwood, Frith, & Hermelin, 1988; Loveland et al., 1994; Macdonald et al., 1989).

As children with autism become older, they continue to have difficulty reading the social cues, emotions, and subjective experiences of other people. As seen in John's case, these qualitative impairments in social interaction and social understanding are present even in children with autism who have average or above-average intelligence.

Communication Impairments

For two years the mother of a young man with autism would correct her son by saying, "Don't do that. It doesn't look normal." The son would stop the inappropriate behavior. Then she would add, "You want to look normal, don't you?" The son would say, "Yes." Then one day it occurred to the mother to ask her son, "Do you know what normal means?" "Yes," he said, and the mother was impressed. She pushed for his definition. He said, "It's the second button from the left on the washing machine." (Donnellan, 1988)

Children with autism display serious abnormalities in communication and language that appear early in life and persist over time. Since the main motivation to communicate comes from a desire to share intentions, thoughts, and feelings with other people, it is not surprising that the impairments in social interaction and social understanding of children with autism also have a profound negative impact on the development of communication skills (Tager-Flusberg, 1996).

Before children learn to talk, they have at their disposal a rich array of facial expressions, vocalizations, and gestures to communicate their needs, interests, and feelings to others. One of the first signs of language impairment in children with autism is their *inconsistency* in using these early preverbal communications. For example, a child with autism may point to a stuffed animal she wants that is out of reach. By doing this, she is demonstrating the ability to use **protoimperative gestures**—gestures or vocalizations that are used to express needs. However, this child will fail to use **protodeclarative gestures**—gestures or vocalizations that direct the visual attention of other people to objects of shared interest. The primary purpose of protodeclarative gestures is to engage other people in interaction; for example, a toddler excitedly points to a dog to direct her mother's attention to this fascinating little creature that she sees. The use of protodeclarative gestures requires shared social attention and an implicit understanding of what other people are thinking, abilities that are lacking in children with autism. Other declarative gestures are also missing in children with autism—for example, the **showing gesture**, which normal young children use to show someone else something of interest, like a newly discovered object (or a handful of shaving cream; see Box 10.2).

Box 10.2
Early Communication

When a dab of shaving cream is put in the hand of this child with autism, he pays attention to the shaving cream, and that's all he pays attention to. He is oblivious to the fact that his father is a foot away and his mother is close by. He shows no signs of wanting to share his experience with others.

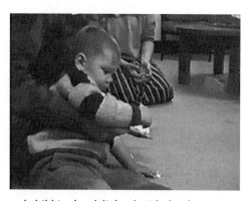 

This normal child is also delighted with the shaving cream, and immediately incorporates everybody into his experience by showing his mother what he has in his hand. He has something to communicate and wants to let everyone in on it. He gets to be the star of the show, which is his major function at this age.

Source: *Behavior Disorders of Childhood*, produced by Alvin H. Perlmutter, Inc.

As many as half of children with autism do not develop any useful language. This includes some children who begin to speak and then regress in their speech development, usually between 12 and 30 months of age. Children with autism with no speech or with limited speech do not use gestures to communicate. Instead, they rely on primitive forms of communication, such as pulling their mother's hand in a desired direction or bringing her an orange to be peeled or a box to be opened. Children with autism may use **instrumental gestures** to get someone else to do something for them immediately. However, they fail to use **expressive gestures** to convey feelings (Frith, 1989). These two types of gestures are illustrated in Figure 10.1.

In some cases, it is possible that the limited use of speech is related to impairments in the child's ability to execute the motor movements necessary for speech, in addition to his or her social and cognitive deficits. Motor speech impairments are suggested by the fact that some nonspeaking children with autism learn to communicate using nonspeech systems, such as sign language, picture symbols, or writing. In addition, some nonspeaking children with autism display symptoms suggesting oral motor deficits, such as limited independent movement of the tongue, lips, or jaw; a history of feeding problems; and in some cases, low facial tone or drooling. Other nonspeaking children with autism display significant limitations in speech intelligibility that are consistent with a difficulty in executing oral/verbal movements, including limited use of consonants, difficulty sequencing sounds in multisyllabic productions, reduced length of utterance, or a relative lack of intelligibility in spontaneous versus stereotyped speech (Prizant, 1996).

Children with autism who develop language usually do so before the age of 5 years. Although almost all children with autism show delays in their language development, it is their use of *qualitatively deviant* forms of communication that is most striking. Most noticeable is their lack of social chatter—their failure to use language for interpersonal communication. Parents and teachers of children with autism describe their communications as nonsensical, silly, incoherent, and irrelevant, having little meaningful connection with the situation in which they occur. Such meaningless communication is illustrated in the following interview with Jerry, a 5½-year-old boy with autism who has a great deal of expressive language (Bemporad, 1979, pp. 183–184):

Interviewer: Would you draw a man or a woman?

Jerry: A man was business to a lady.

Interviewer: What does that mean?

Jerry: No, a man is present to a lady, yes, yes, yes. A radio. Lady gives the pedal. Great big handkerchief

Instrumental Gestures

Expressive Gestures

FIGURE 10.1 Instrumental and expressive gestures. Children with autism may use gestures to get others to do things for them, but not to convey feelings. (Based on Frith, 1989)

and napkin, all tucked in. So see, there it is. We'll paint the picture and put it in a frame.

Although difficult to confirm, at least some of the seemingly irrelevant speech of children with autism may

FIGURE 10.2 Children with autism have difficulty with the pragmatic use of language. (Based on Frith, 1989)

take on meaning when traced to earlier sources. Such meaning may be rooted in concrete, specific, and personal experiences rather than in accepted or acceptable substitutions of meaning. For example, one child's nonsensical use of the phrase "Peter eater" was traced to his association of the nursery rhyme "Peter, Peter, pumpkin eater" with his mother's dropping a saucepan when he was 2 years old, resulting in his saying "Peter eater" in response to anything in his environment that resembled a saucepan (Kanner, 1946).

In addition to their use of idiosyncratic, unusual, and seemingly irrelevant verbalizations, other common qualitative language impairments in children with autism include pronoun reversals and echolalia. **Pronoun reversals** occur when the child repeats personal pronouns exactly as heard, without changing them to suit the situation. For example, a child named Tim when asked, "What's your name?" answered, "Your name is Tim," rather than "My name is Tim." **Echolalia,** which can be either immediate or delayed, refers to the child's parrot-like repetition of words or word combinations that she or he has heard. A child who is asked the question "Do you want a cookie?" responds by repeating "Do you want a cookie?" Although echolalia was once thought to be pathological, it may actually be a critical first step in language acquisition for many children with autism. Echolalia and other unconventional verbal behavior, such as **perseverative speech** (going on and on about the same topic) and incessant questioning, may serve a variety of communicative and developmental functions

for children with autism, and reflect the child's desire to communicate, although in a very primitive way (Prizant, 1996; Prizant & Wetherby, 1989).

The primary difficulty of children with autism who develop language is not so much with the computational (sounds, words, and grammar) or semantic (meaning) use of language. Rather, these children display profound impairments in **pragmatics,** or the appropriate use of language in social and communicative contexts. An example of pragmatics, or in this case the lack of it, is shown in Figure 10.2. The point of the question "Can you get the phone?" is a request that an action be taken, not a request for information about one's ability to pick up a receiver. To understand this, a child needs to know more than what words mean—he or she must "read" the context in which words are used. Lacking in pragmatic competence, children with autism have difficulty understanding nonliteral statements or adjusting their language to fit the situation (Dawson, 1996; Tager-Flusberg, 1993).

Children with autism rarely use language to share information with others or to ask for new information. This failure to use language to exchange information reflects a lack of recognition that each individual possesses unique information and ideas, and that language is a critical tool for understanding what others are thinking. Because children with autism restrict their use of language to expressing their needs or obtaining things they want, their conversational abilities are limited. They show little progress in initiating, expanding, or elaborating on a topic, even when they develop good vocabulary and grammar skills. It has been suggested that the common element underlying all the communication deficits in autism is a general failure to understand that language can be used to inform and influence other people (Tager-Flusberg, 1996).

Children with autism often fail to establish joint attention to sounds with the person they are speaking to, and as a result may speak too loudly or too softly, with very little intonational inflection. Normal children vary their tone of voice to make their speech more interesting and audible to the listener, and to communicate social and emotional information. However, children with autism fail to do this, perhaps because they lack a concept of the other person as an interested listener.

Children with autism also use language in a literal fashion. Often the meaning of a word becomes inflexible and cannot be used apart from its original acquired meaning. For example, a child with autism who learns to use the word *yes* when put on his father's shoulders, may take the word *yes* to mean *only* the desire to be put on his father's shoulders. The child does not detach the meaning of the word *yes* from the specific context and has difficulty using it as a general affirmation. Or, the word *normal* may be used only in reference to a button on the washing machine!

This tendency to associate word meanings with highly specific situations is captured in the following recollection of her childhood experiences by Donna Williams (1992), an adult with autism:

> The significance of what other people said to me, when it sank in as more than just words, was always taken to apply only to that particular moment or situation. Thus, when I once received a serious lecture about writing graffiti on Parliament House during a class trip, I agreed that I'd never do this again and then, ten minutes later, was caught outside writing different graffiti on the school wall. To me, I was not ignoring what I had been told, nor was I trying to be funny; I had not done *exactly* the same thing as I had done before. My behavior puzzled others, but theirs puzzled me too. It was not so much that I had no regard for their rules as that I couldn't keep up with the many rules for each specific situation. (p. 69)

Even high-functioning children with autism who have mastered word order and have large vocabularies continue to display impairments in the pragmatic functions of language. In addition, they continue to show both verbal and nonverbal deficits that reflect a basic failure to recognize the thoughts, feelings, and intentions of other people. At a nonverbal level, their monotone voice and lack of gestures suggest difficulty in communicating emotions. At a verbal level, they display problems with narrative discourse, including impoverished stories and difficulty using nonliteral language or providing sufficient information to others. As they get older, children with autism make little use of language for social convention—for example, to greet others or to be polite.

Repetitive Behaviors and Interests

Jerry, a high-functioning 15-year-old boy with autism, wrote the following poem (Bemporad, 1979, p. 188):

> I prayed to the Lord
> That he show me a path
> I waited for his word
> He guided me to the subject of math
>
> The people envy me now
> As the Lord guided me thru his thunderous world
> I like numbers, decimal points and fractions
> Many equations, I learn to create
> With multiplications, additions and subtractions
> I see mathematics will be my fate

Children with autism often display narrow patterns of interests such as Jerry's fascination with arithmetic, repetitive behaviors such as lining up objects, or stereotyped body movements such as rocking. They seem driven to engage in and maintain these behaviors. Some may perform stereotyped movements, such as rocking or flapping their hands and arms, with such intensity that they begin to perspire; others may react explosively to even a minor change in their routine. Stereotyped and repetitive behaviors often occur at times when children with autism are not explicitly directed to engage in some other activity, suggesting a possible deficit in their ability to generate alternative actions. Other stereotyped behaviors occur in novel, unpredictable, or demanding situations, and may serve to provide the child with a sense of control over the environment and a way of coping with changes that are not understood. Consistent with this idea is the finding that children with autism are much more responsive in social situations that are highly predictable (Klinger & Dawson, 1995).

Self-stimulatory behaviors are repetitive body movements or movements of objects—for example, hand flapping or pencil spinning. Although self-stimulatory behaviors occur in children with other forms of developmental disability, they are especially common and persistent in children with autism. A particular behavior, such as moving the fingers in front of the eyes, may persist from childhood through adulthood. In the accompanying photos of Pamela, taken 20 years apart, her self-stimulatory behavior looks amazingly similar.

As the examples that follow illustrate, self-stimulation may involve one or more of the senses, and the same stereotyped behavior, such as spinning a spoon on a table, may involve more than one sense—seeing

Pamela engaging in self-stimulation as a child and as an adult. (*Behavior Treatment of Autistic Children,* produced by E. L. Anderson)

the movement of the spoon and hearing the sound that it makes.

Common Forms of Self-Stimulation in Children with Autism

Visual: Repetitive blinking, staring at lights, hand flapping, moving fingers in front of eyes

Auditory: Snapping fingers, making vocal sounds, tapping ears, spinning an object on a table

Tactile: Scratching, rubbing the skin with the hands or with an object

Vestibular: Rocking front to back, rocking side to side

Taste: Placing body parts or objects in the mouth, licking objects

Smell: Smelling objects, sniffing people

The reasons that children with autism engage in self-stimulatory behaviors are not known, although several theories have been advanced. One theory is that these children crave stimulation, and self-stimulation serves to excite their nervous system. Another is that the environment may be too stimulating for them, and they engage in repetitive self-stimulation as a way of blocking out and controlling unwanted stimulation. In the case of an individual child, either may be possible.

ASSOCIATED CHARACTERISTICS OF AUTISM

Intellectual Deficits and Strengths

Like Lucy and John, children with autism vary widely in intelligence—from profound mental retardation to superior ability. Although children with superior abilities are often the ones that capture media attention, in reality,

about 80% of children with autism also have mental retardation, with approximately 60% having IQs less than 50, and 20% having IQs between 50 and 70. About 20% of children with autism have average intelligence or above, with IQs higher than 70. As illustrated in Table 10.2, the social impairments associated with autism are most common in children with the lowest level of intellectual functioning.

Unlike children with mental retardation without autism, who show a general delay across all areas of intellectual functioning, the performance of children with autism on IQ tests tends to be strikingly uneven across different subtests. Although the pattern of unevenness is not the same for all such children, one of the more common ones is a relatively low score on the verbal Comprehension subtest (e.g., What's the thing to do if you hurt yourself?) and a relatively high score on the nonverbal Digit Span (short-term memory for strings of numbers) and Block Design (arranging blocks to form a specific pattern) subtests of the Wechsler Intelligence Scales (Happe, 1994b). Low verbal IQ in particular seems to be strongly associated with the severity of symptoms of autism, whereas nonverbal IQ does not

Table 10.2	**The Close Link Between Autism and Mental Retardation**
IQ Range	Proportion of Children Who Display Social Impairments Typical of Autism
0–19	86 percent of 44 children
20–49	42 percent of 96 children
50–69	2 percent of 700 children
70+	0.013 percent of 34,100 children

Source: Data from Lorna Wing, Medical Research Council, London.

show this relationship to the same degree (Bolton et al., 1994). Low intellectual ability in children with autism is generally associated with poorer long-term outcomes, and only those children with average intelligence or above are likely to achieve independent living status as adults. IQ scores of children with autism are typically stable over time and are good predictors of their level of educational attainment. However, as we will discuss, recent reports of intensive early intervention suggest that intelligence in children with autism may be more malleable than once thought.

Despite their many intellectual deficits, a small but significant number of children with autism develop **splinter skills,** or **islets of ability,** of the kind displayed by Raymond in the movie *Rain Main.* Their special talents may be in spelling, reading, arithmetic, music, or drawing. As many as 25% of children with autism with an IQ greater than 35 display a special cognitive skill that is above average for the general population, and well above their own general level of intellect (Goode, Rutter, & Howlin, 1994). Although splinter skills do not occur in all children with autism, and are not exclusive to autism, they are especially common in children with autism (Frith, 1989).

In addition, about 5% of children with autism develop an isolated and often remarkable talent that is *far* in excess of that found even in normal children of the same age. These children, referred to as **autistic savants,** display supernormal abilities in such areas as calculation, memory, jigsaw puzzles, music, or drawing. One boy with autism had an IQ of 60 but could recite the daily lottery numbers for the past 5 years. Another learned to play the piano by reproducing any tune he heard on the radio, from Brahms to Bacharach. Psychologists who studied him figure he had more than 2000 tunes in his head (Gzowski, 1993, p. 91). The incredible memory skills of Trevor Tao, an autistic savant with abilities in music and chess, are captured in the following description by his music teacher:

Trevor: Autistic Savant

I stumbled across Trevor's phenomenal chess memory during a music lesson when he was 9 years old. I asked for the whereabouts of his theory book and Trevor jerked his thumb over his shoulder to the bookshelf behind. I noticed a dozen or so books on advanced chess mastery, and Trevor casually remarked, "I know all those books backwards." I opened a book at random, cited the game number and its master players, and Trevor reeled off every move of both players on a page of complicated play. Even though practice naturally played a considerable part in that memory feat, it was still a token of unique memory power. I noticed at one of the family mealtimes that Trevor's mother put a chess book in front of him as a kind of pacifier. (Adapted from Hendrickson, 1996)

Nadia, a girl with autism, was obsessed with horses; she drew hundreds of pictures of them with incredible vividness and accuracy when she was only 3 to 6 years old. Two of Nadia's drawings are reproduced in Figure 10.3. After seeing a picture of a horse in a story, Nadia could generate endless images of what this horse would look like in any posture. Interestingly, as Nadia began to speak, around the age of 11, she produced fewer and fewer drawings (Baron-Cohen & Bolton, 1993).

The development of the fascinating skill of an autistic savant is related to the presence of unusual preoccupations and repetitive behavior, and the degree of the skill is related to the child's IQ. It is not clear whether such skills of children with autism reflect intact abilities or are signs of a cognitive deficit. One idea is that autistic savants have a tendency to segment information into parts rather than looking at the whole, which leads to exceptional performance in certain domains (Pring, Hermelin, & Heavey, 1995). Another is that children with autism think in images rather than abstract ideas, which allows them to remember material in a camera or recorderlike fashion (Hurlbert, Happe, & Frith, 1994). Unfortunately, despite the fascination and appeal of the skills of autistic savants or the more common splinter skills, in most cases neither are used constructively by children with autism to enhance their everyday living.

Sensory and Perceptual Impairments

Many sights, sounds, smells, or textures that don't bother most children can be confusing or even painful to children with autism. A child with autism may perceive and react to a specific person's voice as a loud shriek, to a gentle stroke on the arm as a sharp pain, or to a ringing telephone as the sound of a power drill next to the ear. Such sensory abnormalities and deficits, which are common in children with autism, include oversensitivities or undersensitivities to certain stimuli, overselective and impaired shifting of attention to sensory input, and impairments in mixing across sensory modalities—for example, simultaneously seeing the movement and hearing the sound of a person's clapping.

Early theories of autism examined such related sensory-perceptual deficits as sensory dominance and stimulus overselectivity. **Sensory dominance** is the tendency to focus on certain types of sensory input over others—for example, a preference for sights over sounds.

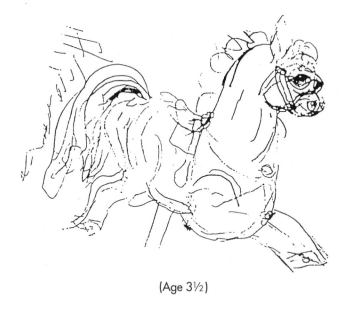

(Age 3½)

(Age 5)

FIGURE 10.3 Drawings of horses by Nadia at age 3½ and at age 5. (Selfe, 1977)

Stimulus overselectivity is the tendency to focus on one feature of an object or event in the environment while ignoring other equally important features. For example, in learning to respond to a request from her mother, such as "Come here," a child with autism might selectively attend to either her mother's lip movements or the sound of her mother's voice. If the child focuses only on lip movements and not voice, she may not come when her mother's head is turned away, because lip movements are not visible. Alternatively, if the child focuses on just her mother's voice and not lip movements, she may not respond if noise in the room muffles the sound of her mother's voice, even when her mother is looking directly at her, saying "Come here," and motioning for her to come. Children with autism may display stimulus overselectivity because they have difficulty shifting their attention from one stimulus to another. Stimulus overselectivity, common among children with autism, is also displayed by children with mental retardation who do not have autism.

A selective focus on one narrow part of the environment while ignoring other important features gives children with autism the appearance of having tunnel vision or tunnel hearing and makes it very difficult for them to learn about their world. For example, in learning the difference between a red car and a blue truck, a child with autism may selectively focus on the color difference and totally ignore shape, size, and other attributes of the objects. Learning about the concept of vehicles will be very difficult if based on color alone. Attending to multiple stimuli is critical to such cognitive processes as forming associations among many different elements of a complex environment, developing general concepts, and making inferences about new situations based on past experiences. Children with autism have difficulties in all these areas (Klinger & Dawson, 1995).

Cognitive Deficits

In addition to their IQ deficits and sensory-perceptual impairments, children with autism display many other cognitive limitations. Two types of dysfunctions that have been proposed to underlie autism are specific cognitive impairments in processing social and emotional information and more general cognitive impairments in information processing, planning, and attention.

Specific Deficits. The social and communication deficits of children with autism have generated much interest in how children with autism process social, emotional, and personal information, such as emotional expressions, facial cues, and internal mental states. The odd social behavior of children with autism suggests a significant impairment in their social sensitivities (Sigman, 1995). It is not that social interaction is totally absent or impaired in these children, but rather that they have great difficulty in situations that require social understanding.

At around 12 months of age, most normal infants can tell when they and another person are attending to the same thing. They begin to recognize that people's actions are driven by desires and directed at goals. In the second year of life, this ability contributes to the emergence of pretend, or "as if," play. Children with autism, however, don't understand pretense, nor do they engage in pretend play. For example, a normal child may give a doll a drink of water from an empty cup while making the appropriate slurping sounds, whereas a child with autism may simply spin the cup repetitively (Frith, 1993). It is this absence of shared attention and lack of pretend play that often create nagging doubts in parents about their ability to engage their child.

The absence of spontaneous pretend play in young children with autism led to the hypothesis that these children would also display impairments in their understanding of mental states—other people's and their own—that cannot be seen directly, such as beliefs and desires. This is referred to as the **theory of mind (ToM)** hypothesis of autism, which has received a great deal of research attention over the past decade (Baron-Cohen, 1989). By the age of 4, most children can figure out what others might know, think, and believe, something that even older individuals with autism have great difficulty doing (Baron-Cohen, 1995). Although children with autism can think about physical events and characteristics that they can see, they have great difficulty forming higher-order representations about invisible mental states (Dawson, 1996).

The ToM hypothesis of autism begins with the premise that the ability to read the intentions, beliefs, feelings, and desires of others from their external behavior has adaptive significance in an evolutionary sense. ToM proposes that all humans are, by nature, mind readers. We spend our waking lives reading subtle cues that enable us to fill in the blanks about other people's beliefs and intentions. We do this automatically and with little conscious effort.

Suppose, for example, that a student walked into one of your classes about 10 minutes after it began, looked around the room, and then left. How would you explain the student's behavior? As a mind reader, you may have thought: "Maybe she was *trying* to find a book she lost, and she *thought* she left it in this classroom," or "Maybe she *wanted* to find a friend who was taking this class, but *realized* that her friend was not in class that day." No doubt you can come up with lots of explanations for this student's behavior, and most of them will

be based on her mental states (the words in italics). You may not be 100% certain of the reason, but chances are you can easily generate many possibilities. The development of such an awareness of others' mental states and one's own is referred to as **mentalization** or theory of mind (Baron-Cohen, 1995; Morton & Frith, 1995). It has been proposed that the primary problem of individuals with autism stems from a deficit in their ToM mechanism. In other words, children with autism suffer, to varying degrees, from "mindblindness"; that is, "they fail to develop the capacity to mindread in the normal way" (Baron-Cohen, 1995, p. 5).

For a person who lacks a ToM, even a simple behavior sequence, such as someone's walking into a classroom, looking around, and then walking out, can be a real puzzle. Now imagine the following more typical and more complex social situation:

> *A child is sprawled out on the floor of the living room staring into space while his mother watches TV and his father reads the newspaper. Without saying a word, his mother motions to his father with her hand. The father then looks at his son, looks at his watch, and then looks at the mother and nods, and she nods back. Next, the father puts down his newspaper and moves toward his son as the mother gets up from her chair and moves toward the TV.*

How would you make sense out of this situation? Chances are that any explanations you come up with will be full of mental-state concepts and terms to describe the thoughts and intentions of the people in this situation—the mother *thought* her child was getting tired and it was time to go to bed, or the father *realized* it was getting late, or the parents *decided* it was time to go somewhere. Now, imagine that the child in the situation has autism and an impaired ToM. How would he make sense of this situation without using mental-state concepts or terms? Why did his mother motion to his father? Why were his mother and father nodding at one another? What did their smiles mean? Why did they get up at the same time? Not being able to mind-read, this child would find it extremely difficult or even impossible to make sense of his parents' behavior. Interestingly, when asked what brains do, most 5-year-olds say that brains are for thinking, dreaming, keeping secrets, and so on. But when children with autism are asked this question, they may say that the brain is what makes people move—expressing nothing about mental activity (Baron-Cohen, 1995). Thus, almost any social situation, even the simplest one, can be mysterious, confusing, or frightening for a child with ToM deficits.

Trying to imagine what the world would be like for someone who cannot mentalize may be an impossible task for those who do. Here is one attempt to imagine what sitting around the dinner table might look like through the eyes of a child who is mind-blind:

> *At the top of my field of vision is a blurry edge of a nose, in front are waving hands. . . . Around me, bags of skin are draped over chairs and stuffed into pieces of cloth; they shift and protrude in unusual ways. . . . Two dark spots near the top of them swivel restlessly back and forth. A hole beneath the spots fills with food and from it comes a stream of noises. The noisy skin-bags suddenly move toward me, and their noises grow louder. I don't know why they are moving toward me, I can't explain it, nor can I guess what they will do next. (Adapted from Gopnik, 1993; cited in Baron-Cohen, 1995, pp. 4–5)*

A child with ToM deficits may be able to learn, remember, and know things about the social world but would have little understanding of their meaning.

The original test used to determine children's ability to detect mental states of others was called the Sally-Anne Test. A similar test is described in Box 10.3. This test, which is extremely simple, illustrates what it means to have an everyday ToM.

Although most children with autism fail tests of understanding false beliefs, the findings are not clear-cut. A small but significant number of children with autism (estimates range widely, from 15% to 60%) demonstrate some knowledge of ToM—they pass the Sally-Anne Test or tests like it (Happe, 1995a). In contrast to the children with autism who do not pass false-belief tests, those children who do pass display insightful and interactive behavior and have better verbal and communication abilities (Frith & Happe, 1994). They also display far more verbal knowledge (they have a higher verbal mental age) than other children of the same chronological age, suggesting that they may work out ToM tasks in a conscious and logical way (Happe, 1995a, 1995b). Children who succeed at ToM tasks, including children with autism, usually understand metaphors, irony, and a range of speaker emotions, such as the intention to lie or tell a joke. However, youngsters with autism who understand false belief give laborious explanations for their insights, suggesting the use of conscious and deliberate strategies to discern mental states. In contrast, understanding a false belief may be so natural, automatic, and unconscious for most children that they may have difficulty explaining how they come up with their answer (Happe, 1995a). Even youngsters with autism who pass ToM tests tend to show impairments on complex tests that use more real-life situations (Happe, 1994a).

Box 10.3

The Sally-Anne Test: What It Means to Have a Theory of Mind

Two dolls, Sally and Anne, are used as props. Sally has a basket; Anne, a box. Sally puts a marble in her basket and covers it, then leaves the room. Anne takes the marble from the basket and hides it in her own box. Next, Sally comes back from her walk and wants to play with her marble. The critical question is: where will Sally look for her marble?

Most normal kids of about 4 years can answer this question reliably: Sally will look for her marble in her basket where she put it. Even children with mental retardation realize that Sally will think that the marble is where she had left it. They also indicate that Sally did not know what Anne did because she was out of the room when Anne moved the marble.

This understanding demonstrates that young children have attributed a mental state to another person. They grasp that someone can have a false belief about a situation. The **false belief** [boldface added] is a mental state, not a physical state, and can very helpfully explain and predict behavior, for instance, that Sally will look for her marble in her basket. Understanding false belief naturally implies an understanding of true belief, of knowledge and ignorance, and of intentions and feelings. This is a theory of mind.

Most children with autism, even of a mental age far in excess of 4 years, find the simple Sally-Anne test a great puzzle and tend to get it wrong. They say that Sally will look for the marble in Anne's box (where it really is)—even though they remember correctly that Sally had put the marble into her basket and was not present when Anne transferred it to her box. Despite remembering the simple sequence of events, they cannot make sense of them by inferring that Sally has a false belief—so they do not take into account at all what Sally thinks; they miss the important change (her previously correct belief is now wrong). Thus they cannot predict Sally's behavior. Their lack of understanding of false belief reflects a lack of understanding of other mental states. Hence the claim that individuals with autism do not have a theory of mind.

Source: Adapted from Frith, 1996.

Interesting preliminary findings from neuroimaging studies suggest that the brain regions that are activated when normal individuals are engaged in tasks requiring them to make attributions about other people's mental states differ from the regions activated for tasks that do not require such attributions (Fletcher et al., 1995). In view of the difficulties displayed by children with autism, these findings may have implications for understanding the neural basis of autism, which we will return to in a later section. Although specific socioemotional cognitive deficits such as ToM are very common in children with autism, the fact that they do not occur in all children with autism suggests that other mechanisms besides ToM may be needed to explain the cognitive deficits in autism.

General Deficits. It has recently been suggested that children with autism display a general deficit in higher-order planning and regulatory behaviors. These processes, called executive functions, are believed to be mediated by the frontal regions of the brain (see Chapter 5). Executive functions permit us to maintain an effective problem-solving framework by inhibiting inappropriate behaviors, engaging in thoughtful actions, sustaining task performance, self-monitoring, using feedback, and flexibly shifting attention from one task to another. In support of a general deficit in executive functioning, children and adults with autism have difficulties planning and organizing; changing to a new cognitive set; disengaging from salient stimuli; processing information in novel, unpredictable environments; and generalizing previously learned information to new situations (Bryson, Landry, & Wainwright, 1997; Klinger & Dawson, 1995; Ozonoff, 1994; Ozonoff, Pennington, & Rogers, 1991).

Another general cognitive deficit hypothesized to underlie autism is a weak drive for **central coherence** (Frith, 1993), which refers to the strong tendency of humans to interpret stimuli in a relatively global way that takes the broader context into account. By doing this, we can extract meaning from diverse and complex sets of information and remember the main points rather than the precise details. It has been proposed that individuals with autism have a weak tendency for central coherence and tend to process information in bits and pieces rather than looking at the big picture (Frith & Happe, 1994). Understanding other peoples' words, gestures, or feelings can be extremely difficult for someone lacking in central coherence, as reflected in this statement by Donna Williams, an adult with autism who has written extensively about what it is like to have this disorder:

> It is hard to care or be interested in what a person feels when you perceive a body and then a hand and an eye and a nose and other bits all moving but not perceived in any connected way, with no perception of the context. (Memeth, 1994, p. 49)

Social communication may also be very limited in individuals who lack central coherence, because each statement is treated as a separate unit, without any overall effort for continuity or coherence. In language tasks, most individuals read words both individually and

in context (e.g. *lead*, related to guiding, versus *lead*, the metal). Weak central coherence would predict the relative independence of words from context. This prediction is supported by telltale errors made by individuals with autism in their pronunciation of certain words—for example, saying "lead," as in the metal, when context demands "lead" as in guiding somebody (Frith, 1993).

Consistent with a general deficit in central coherence, individuals with autism perform surprisingly well on tasks in which a focus on parts of a stimulus rather than the overall pattern or design serves to facilitate performance. Examples of two such tasks, the Block Design subtest of the WISC and the Embedded Figures Test (Jolliffe & Baron-Cohen, 1997) are shown in Figure 10.4. The relative advantage of individuals with autism on these tasks may be due to their spontaneous mental segmentation of the designs into unconnected and meaningless units, which just happens to facilitate the reproduction of the overall design with the given blocks, or the identification of the figure that is embedded in the whole pattern.

Key Questions about Cognitive Deficits. *Are these deficits specific to autism?* Of the cognitive deficits that we have described, ToM seems to be the one most specific to children with autism compared with those with mental retardation or specific language deficits. However, ToM has not been studied extensively in children with other conditions, such as ADHD and conduct disorder, and, as we know, these children also have difficulties in accurately interpreting other people's intentions. Deficits in processing socioemotional information appear to be less specific to autism than ToM deficits, occurring in a number of other conditions, including schizophrenia and mental retardation. There is even less specificity for deficient executive functioning, which occurs in many other clinical groups of children, including those with ADHD, conduct disorder, and treated phenylketonuria (see Chapter 9). However, because *executive functioning* is a general term that encompasses many different processes, further work is needed to determine if the kinds of deficits in executive functioning for children with autism differ from those in children with other problems.

Are the cognitive deficits we have described found in all individuals with autism? As we have noted, some individuals with autism pass ToM tests. However, it is not yet clear whether normal-IQ individuals with autism have actually developed a ToM. The fact that many of these individuals still display severe social impairments in everyday life suggests that they have not developed a ToM, but rather, may have learned to use an alternative strategy to solve ToM tasks.

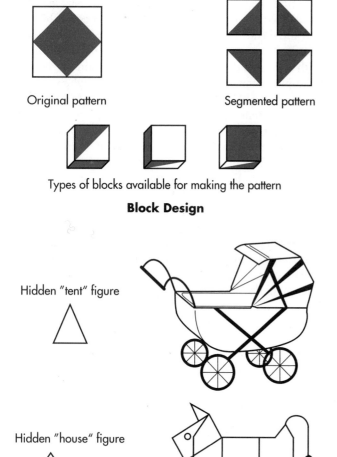

Block Design

Embedded Figures

FIGURE 10.4 Block Design subtest and Embedded Figures Test: Children with autism perform relatively well on tasks that require attention to details of a figure rather than to the overall pattern or design. (Witkin et al., 1971)

How are the various cognitive deficits associated with autism related? It is possible that deficits in executive function are primary and lead to ToM problems, or vice versa. Perhaps broad cognitive deficits in executive function and specific ones related to social and emotional information processing exist independently, with each having a unique neurobiological substrate. Or executive functions and ToM are related and interdependent, with a similar underlying neurobiological substrate. The fact that ToM and executive functions are seriously deficient in autism, improve little with development, never reach normal levels, and appear to hit a developmental ceiling

in adolescence suggests that they are related rather than independent types of deficits in cognitive functioning (Ozonoff & McEvoy, 1994). It has also been proposed that ToM problems and weak central coherence may exist independently in autism, with the deficits in autism involving impairments in two different cognitive systems—a specific system dedicated to processing mental states and a more general system that determines the individual's overall style of processing information (Bailey, Phillips, & Rutter, 1996; Frith & Happe, 1994a).

Following the initial enthusiasm for a single cognitive deficit, such as ToM, to explain the core features of autism, research efforts have widened considerably. Currently, it seems unlikely that a single cognitive abnormality can explain all the deficits present in children with autism. The presence of multiple cognitive deficits, some specific and some general, may help us explain why autism exists in so many different forms and levels of severity.

Physical Characteristics

About 20% to 30% of individuals with autism also develop epilepsy. In contrast to individuals with mental retardation, in whom epilepsy is often present at a younger age, individuals with autism show a distinctive and relatively high onset of epilepsy in late adolescence or early adulthood. Epilepsy in youngsters with autism that begins in the preschool years is most likely to be associated with profound mental retardation. However, apart from this latter association, the risk of epilepsy in children with autism is not strongly associated with IQ. For example, the risk of epilepsy is 18% among individuals with autism and a nonverbal IQ greater than 70, compared with 16% in the 50 to 69 IQ range, and 20% in the 35 to 49 IQ range (Bailey et al., 1996).

Children with autism are usually described as having a normal or attractive physical appearance. Clearly, these children do not display the visible physical deviations that often accompany severe mental retardation that is unassociated with autism. Children with autism may have more subtle but distinctive minor physical anomalies, such as facial asymmetries. Minor anomalies suggest the influence of genetic or other prenatal factors in autism. However, although children with autism have an elevated risk for these minor anomalies, they also occur in children with other developmental disorders (Bryson, 1996).

In his original description, Kanner (1943) noted that 5 of the 11 children he observed had relatively large heads. This observation is consistent with more recent reports that about 25% of individuals with autism have a larger-than-normal head circumference that places them in the upper 3% of the general population. This characteristic distinguishes children with autism from those with mental retardation or language disorders (Woodhouse et al., 1996). It is not yet known if the group of children with autism who have a larger-than-normal head circumference are different from other children with autism, although findings to date suggest that they are not (Bailey et al., 1996).

Characteristics of Family Members

Kanner first observed that the parents of all 11 children he studied were highly intelligent individuals, with all but three of the families represented in *Who's Who in America* or in *American Men of Science*. It was later determined, however, that the families who were referred to Kanner's clinic were a select and unrepresentative sample. The once popular view that autism is more prevalent in highly educated or upper social class families has not generally been supported, particularly when contemporary criteria are used to make the diagnosis (Wing, 1980).

Similar Deficits in Relatives.

Nonautistic identical twins, siblings, and parents of individuals with autism, particularly male relatives, display higher-than-normal rates of social, language, and cognitive deficits. These deficits are similar in quality to those found in autism but less severe, and suggest a general family risk for autisticlike features (e.g., aloofness, lack of tact, obsessiveness) that is likely genetically mediated (see the later section on genetic contributions) (Piven et al., 1994). Language deficits in family members are mostly pragmatic in nature and involve mixes of overcommunicativeness and undercommunicativeness, excessive caution, and inhibition. Language-related cognitive deficits such as poor verbal comprehension have also been reported in family members, but mental retardation or general cognitive impairments have not been found to occur at an elevated rate. Taken together, these findings suggest that the risk for autism in other family members and the expression of autism in general are likely to extend well beyond a formal diagnosis of autism. The so-called lesser variant of expression of autism in family members differs from autism in that it is typically diagnosed by its lack of association with atypical language such as echolalia or reversal of pronouns, its less-stereotyped repetitive behavior, its association with subtle social deficits, and especially by its lack of association with mental retardation and epilepsy (Bailey et al., 1996).

Affective Disorder in Relatives.
Several studies have reported an increased risk for affective disorder in family members of children with autism, with major affective disorder being 3 times more common in the first-degree relatives of children with autism than in first-degree relatives of control children. Social phobia is also more common in family members in cases where autism is not accompanied by mental retardation. It seems plausible that the increased risk of depressive disorders is related to the stress that goes along with raising a child with autism. However, an increased risk of depressive disorder has been found to occur not only in first-degree relatives, but also in second-degree relatives who would not have had as much exposure to the child with autism. The increased risk also applies to affective disorders in family members that have an onset *prior* to the birth of the child with autism. Thus, although further research is needed to clarify the mechanisms underlying the association between autism and affective disorder in the family, it is possible that this link reflects a common genetic predisposition (Bailey et al., 1996).

Stress in the Home.
Life for the parents of a child with autism can be a daily grind, a totally draining, sleepless, relentless effort to prevent their child from harming herself, guess their child's needs, and search for ways of preventing their child from withdrawing from them forever. The exhausting demands of raising a child with autism are captured in the following description:

Emilie: Hard on the Family

Four-year-old Emilie can spend the whole day flipping the pages of a catalogue, never looking at the pictures, just staring into space. Or she'll twirl her skipping rope in the air, over and over again, her crystal blue eyes wandering, never noticing the bins of brightly colored blocks and puzzles and little plastic animals her mother has collected for her. She is driven to climb—onto the stove, the fridge, the highest dresser. Twice she has brought the television set down on top of herself. All the doors in the house have hooks on them. If she's not strapped into the stroller, she'll dart out into traffic—if the front door is left open, she'll bolt out. Emilie is a whirlwind in need of constant attention. She gets up in the middle of the night several times a week, wide awake, humming loudly, tossing toys, laughing and tugging on her sleeping brother in the upper bunk. (Adapted from Semenak, 1996)

Parents of children with autism may also experience social ostracism from friends who find it difficult to be around such demanding children, or from strangers who may be unaware of the context for the child's disruptive behavior or the parent's efforts to control these behaviors.

> *In the midst of these tantrums that come 5, 10, 20 times a day, strangers stare at her and shake their heads. "What a spoiled brat," they mutter so she can hear. (Adapted from Semenak, 1996)*

Subtypes

Lorna Wing has presented an interesting way of grouping children with autism based on behavioral domains that include the child's social interaction, cognitive functioning, communication skills, and other behaviors (Wing & Gould, 1979). As described below, three subtypes of children with autism have been identified—aloof, passive, and active-but-odd—with the amount and quality of social interaction being the primary distinguishing feature.

> *Aloof.* Child rarely displays spontaneous social approach to others (except to satisfy wants or needs) and tends to reject unsolicited social and physical contact.
> *Passive.* Child displays a lack of spontaneous social approach, but typically engages another person when approached, provided the other person structures the interaction.
> *Active-but-odd.* Child shows a willingness to approach others but does so in a peculiar, naive, or one-sided manner.

There is some support for the distinctness of these three subgroups, with the aloof children showing a greater severity of autism and lower IQ scores, and the active-but-odd group being generally less severely impaired and of higher intellectual and language functioning than the other two groups (Castelloe & Dawson, 1993). In addition, preliminary findings suggest that patterns of brain activity may differ for the passive and active-but-odd subtypes (Dawson, Klinger, Panagiotides, Lewy, & Castelloe, 1995).

Accompanying Disorders and Symptoms

The disorders that most often accompany autism are mental retardation and epilepsy. Additional behavioral and psychiatric symptoms in children with autism may include hyperactivity, obsessive rituals, stereotyped mannerisms, anxieties, fears, and compulsive behavior. Some children with autism also engage in extreme and sometimes potentially life-threatening **self-injurious behavior** (SIB)—that is, any self-inflicted behavior that can cause tissue damage to the child's own body. The most com-

mon forms of SIB are head banging, hand or arm biting, and excessive scratching and rubbing. Self-inflicted punching, pinching, or face slapping may lead to swelling and bruises. SIBs such as head banging, if not prevented, can be so severe as to produce bleeding or even brain injury. SIB may occur for a variety of reasons—as a form of self-stimulation, a way to gain attention, or a way to eliminate unwanted demands and other aversive stimuli. SIB may also be related to the presence of a subclinical seizure or middle ear infection (Carr, 1977). Like self-stimulatory behavior, SIB is not specific to autism—it also occurs in children with other severe developmental disabilities (see Chapter 9).

Differential Diagnosis and Other Pervasive Developmental Disorders

In a number of developmental and mental disorders other than autism, children display language, cognitive, social, or behavioral characteristics similar to those of autism. At the low end of intelligence, the social deficits of children with autism may be difficult to distinguish from those of children with severe or profound mental retardation without autism. However, even children with profound mental retardation show simple social behaviors, such as smiling, eye contact, and social approach, that are appropriate to their mental age. Children with mental retardation do not display the specific deficits in joint attention, motor imitation, or theory of mind abilities that are observed in children with autism (Charman et al., 1997). Children with autism as well as those with mental retardation display simple stereotyped motor behaviors, including self-stimulation and SIBs. These behaviors appear to be more a function of the child's mental age than of diagnosis.

Distinguishing between autism and developmental language disorders (see Chapter 11) can sometimes be difficult, especially in young children. Both groups show similar delays in babbling, language acquisition, length of utterance, and grammatical complexity. However, children with autism use more deviant forms of language, such as echolalia, pronoun reversal, stereotyped utterances, and literalness; display less spontaneous social conversation; and show greater impairment in nonverbal communication, including gestures and pretend play (Cantwell, Baker, Rutter, & Mawhood, 1989). In contrast, children with developmental language problems may show more difficulties in articulation (Bishop, 1992).

It sometimes can be difficult to distinguish children with autism from those with other pervasive developmental disorders. When a diagnosis of autism is being considered, four other PDDs may need to be taken into account: **Asperger's disorder (AD)**, **Rett's disorder**, childhood disintegrative disorder, and pervasive developmental disorder not otherwise specified (PDD-NOS). Although all PDDs have some clinical features in common, their possible neurobiological relatedness to each other is not yet known. In general, the other PDDs have received much less study than autism.

Asperger's Disorder.

This disorder was originally described in 1944 by Hans Asperger, who labeled it "autistic psychopathy." Asperger described several cases whose clinical features resembled Kanner's description of autism, but differed in that speech was less commonly delayed, motor deficits were more common, and the age of onset appeared to be somewhat later. Asperger reported unusual circumscribed interests (e.g., memorizing bus schedules) in these children and in other family members, particularly their fathers.

AD is a severe developmental disorder characterized by major difficulties in social interaction and unusual patterns of interest and behavior in children with relatively intact cognitive and communication skills (Volkmar et al., 1996). Children with AD display the same kinds of social impairments and restricted, stereotyped interests as children with autism but not their general delays in language, cognitive development, development of age-appropriate self-help skills, adaptive behavior (other than social interaction), or curiosity about the environment. Although not required for a diagnosis of AD, delayed motor milestones and motor clumsiness are commonly reported in children with AD (Wing, 1981). In contrast to young children with autism, whose motor development is often a relative strength, children with AD may experience delays in such motor abilities as catching or throwing a ball or riding a bike.

In many ways AD and autism are very similar; there is ongoing debate about whether or not AD is a variant of autism or simply describes higher-functioning individuals with autism (Schopler, Mesibov, & Kunce, 1998). To some extent the resolution of this debate will depend on how the AD diagnosis is used, since no "official" definition for AD existed until it was recently introduced in DSM-IV (Volkmar & Klin, 1998). One recent report found few clinical differences between individuals with AD and those with autism. Individuals with autism showed greater language delay, but as many as 43% of those with AD also had a delayed onset of language. The main differences between AD and autism appear to be higher verbal mental age, less language delay, and greater interest in social contact in children with AD (Eisenmajer et al., 1996).

Generally, individuals with AD tend to be egocentric, socially inept, and preoccupied with highly abstract, circumscribed interests that make them appear eccentric. Other common clinical features of AD include clumsy and ill-coordinated movements; odd posture; a lack of empathy; naive, inappropriate, one-sided social interaction; little ability to form friendships; social isolation; pedantic and flat speech; poor nonverbal communication; and preoccupation with topics such as the weather, facts about TV stations, or maps, which are learned in rote fashion and reflect poor understanding. The speech of individuals with AD is noticeably odd, and they may ramble on about topics that have little interest to anyone but themselves. Older children and adults with AD display marked difficulties with nonliteral language, conversational skills, and other pragmatic abilities even when other aspects of language are intact (Volkmar et al., 1996). Some evidence suggests that individuals with AD, like those with autism, describe their inner experiences in terms of visual images or photographs rather than in terms of feelings (Hurlbert, Happe, & Frith, 1994).

Our knowledge of AD is still very limited (Lincoln et al., 1998). Although boys are more likely to be affected than girls, information about the ratio of boys to girls is lacking. We also know little about possible genetic links that increase the likelihood of finding similar conditions in other family members. The higher intellectual functioning in children with AD suggests a better long-term outcome than is typically seen in autism.

Rett's Disorder.

Rett's disorder was discovered just over 25 years ago by Andreas Rett in his clinic in Vienna, Austria, when he observed two girls in his waiting room making identical stereotyped hand-washing movements. After examining these children, he noted a remarkably similar pattern of early development and symptoms. Girls with Rett's disorder have a normal head circumference at birth. However, following a period of apparently normal prenatal and early development for the first 6 to 12 months of life, they begin to display a specific pattern of deficits that include the following characteristics:

❖ deceleration of head growth between ages 5 months and 48 months
❖ loss of previously acquired purposeful hand skills between ages 5 months and 30 months with the subsequent development of stereotyped hand movements (e.g., hand-wringing or hand washing)
❖ loss of social engagement early in the course (although often social interaction develops later)
❖ appearance of poorly coordinated gait or trunk movements
❖ severely impaired expressive and receptive language development with severe psychomotor retardation (DSM-IV copyright © 1994 by APA)

Rett's disorder is a severe neurological developmental disorder whose cause is presently unknown. Only female cases have been reported to date, although some variants of the disorder have recently been described in males (Christen & Hanefeld, 1995). Girls with Rett's disorder have brains that are 12% to 34% smaller than other children's (Armstrong, 1992; Bauman, Kemper, & Arin, 1995). They experience a variety of serious problems, including severe or profound mental retardation, epileptic seizures, motor handicaps, and difficulties with communication (Hagberg, 1995). **Apraxia,** the inability to execute desired movements, is common in girls with Rett's—25% may never walk, and about half of those who do walk will lose the ability. Rett's disorder is rarer than autism and occurs at a rate of about 1 in 10,000 females. The symptoms of Rett's disorder are similar to autism, but the prognosis is poorer. In addition, in autism the symptoms may or may not have occurred following a period of early normal development. Girls with Rett's are severely impaired and are likely to need assistance with all activities of daily living, including feeding, dressing, and toileting.

Childhood Disintegrative Disorder.

Childhood disintegrative disorder, formerly called Heller's disease (Heller, 1954), describes children who evidence a significant loss of previously acquired skills prior to the age of 10. Following a period of apparently normal development in verbal and nonverbal communication, social relationships, play, and adaptive behavior for the first 2 years of life, children with childhood disintegrative disorder show losses in at least two of the following areas: expressive or receptive language, social skills or adaptive behavior, bowel or bladder control, play, or motor skills. In addition, abnormalities in two of the following three areas of functioning are also present:

❖ qualitative impairment in social interaction (e.g., impairment in nonverbal behaviors, failure to develop peer relationships, lack of social or emotional reciprocity)
❖ qualitative impairments in communication (e.g., delay or lack of spoken language, inability to initiate or sustain a conversation, stereotyped and repetitive use of language, lack of varied make-believe play)
❖ restricted, repetitive, and stereotyped patterns of behavior, interests, and activities, including motor stereotypes and mannerisms
(DSM-IV copyright © 1994 by APA)

In order for this diagnosis to be made, the disturbances cannot be better accounted for by another specific PDD or by schizophrenia. The characteristics of children with this disorder are quite similar to those for children with autism with the exception of the period of normal development in the first 2 years of life. For this reason, clinicians sometimes refer to childhood disintegrative disorder as regressive autism.

Pervasive Developmental Disorder Not Otherwise Specified.

A final category of pervasive developmental disorder, PDD-NOS, describes children who display the social, communication, and behavioral impairments associated with PDD, but do not meet criteria for PDD, schizophrenia, or other disorders. PDD-NOS might better be called atypical autism, since the category is often used for children who fail to meet criteria for autistic disorder because of their late age of onset, atypical symptoms, subthreshold symptoms, or a combination of these symptoms.

PREVALENCE AND COURSE
Prevalence

Autism is a rare disorder, affecting approximately 4 to 5 children per 10,000. However, recent reports suggest that autism may be more prevalent than previously thought, with some estimates running as high as 15 to 20 children per 10,000 (Wing, 1993). These higher estimates are likely related to changes in the criteria that have been used to diagnose autism and to a greater recognition of milder forms of autism that occur in higher-functioning individuals (Bryson, 1996). Changing diagnostic criteria and the lack of a clear consensus on how autism should be defined make it difficult to compare prevalence rates across studies. Autism is found in all social classes and has been identified in every country in which it has been sought.

Autism is 3 to 4 times more common in boys than in girls. This ratio has remained fairly constant, even with increasing prevalence estimates. The greater number of boys is most apparent in the group of children with autism and IQs in the normal range, and least apparent among children with autism and profound mental retardation, where the numbers of boys and girls are similar. Thus, although girls are less often affected by autism than boys, when they are affected, they tend to be more severely cognitively impaired.

Age of Onset

Anne-Marie: First Birthday

"She's so serious!" said her father Marc, with a puzzled laugh. We were celebrating Anne-Marie's first birthday and had just paraded in, bearing the cake with much fanfare. Daniel, her big brother, almost two and a half years old, and greatly excited, joined us in singing. Anne-Marie, in her high-chair, gazed solemnly at the cake, her baby body still, her mouth unsmiling. . . . I couldn't help once again making a silent comparison to her brother, who at his first birthday party had squealed with delight. . . . Who knows, really, what the first sign was, at what point Anne-Marie began to slip away from us? Was it around that first celebration, or after or before? (Maurice, 1993b)

The age at which the symptoms of autism first appear is uncertain. Most parents of children with autism become seriously concerned in the months preceding their child's second birthday. At this time, their child's lack of progress in social relations, language, and imaginative play stands in sharp contrast to rapid developments in these areas by children close in age. Although the deficits of autism become increasingly noticeable around age 2 years, elements are probably present at a much earlier age, as reflected in Anne-Marie's solemn reaction to her first birthday party. In fact, about half of parents of children with autism report suspecting that something was wrong before their child's first birthday.

When parents of older children with autism are asked to recall early child behaviors, such as anticipating being picked up, using eye-to-eye gaze as a social signal, reaching for a familiar person, exhibiting joint attention, or imitating other people's actions such as hand clapping or waving bye-bye, abnormalities in these behaviors by 12 months of age seem evident, although often not reported at the time they occurred. In a revealing study, Julie Osterling and Geraldine Dawson (1994) coded home videotapes of the first birthday of children who were later diagnosed with autism and of normal controls. Global judgments made by a pediatrician and observer ratings of specific child behaviors, such as pointing, showing, failing to orient to a spoken name, and especially, looking at the face of another person, accurately predicted which children had autism and which did not.

Baron-Cohen, Allen, and Gillberg (1992) developed and administered a checklist designed to screen for autism, the **Checklist for Autism in Toddlers (CHAT)**, to parents of forty-one 18-month-old toddlers with an older brother or sister with autism, and to fifty age-matched controls. Four children, all younger siblings of those with autism, were later diagnosed with autism when they were 30 months of age. These four children were the only ones in the entire sample to have failed on *two or more* of five key behaviors when they were 18 months old. The five key behaviors and questions from the CHAT that were used to assess each of them were the following (Baron-Cohen et al., 1992):

❖ *Pretend play:* Does your child ever pretend, for example, to make a cup of tea using a toy cup and teapot, or pretend other things?

❖ *Joint attention:* Does your child ever bring objects over to you (parent) to show you something?
❖ *Protodeclarative pointing:* Does your child ever use his or her index finger to point, to indicate interest in something?
❖ *Social interest:* Does your child take an interest in other children?
❖ *Social play:* Does your child enjoy playing peek-a-boo/hide-and-seek?

Further study of a large random population sample of 16,000 children found that the consistent failure of the three key items of pretend play, protodeclarative pointing, and gaze monitoring from the CHAT at 18 months of age carried an 83.3% risk of receiving a diagnosis of autism (Baron-Cohen et al., 1996). The CHAT has promise as an instrument for identifying children with autism at a young enough age so that early intervention can begin. At present, the period from 12 to 18 months seems to be the earliest point in development that autism can be reliably detected (Johnson, Siddons, Frith, & Morton, 1992). However, with increasing research into key early social indicators, it is possible that autism can be detected much earlier than it is at present.

Course and Outcome

The symptom profiles in children with autism change over time. Most children with autism show a gradual improvement of their symptoms with age, even though they continue to experience many problems. What happens to children with autism when they become adolescents or adults? This question is very difficult to answer because existing outcome studies span different time periods with respect to treatment, diagnosis, and educational opportunity; use different predictors and measures of outcome; vary widely in details regarding diagnosis and treatment; and rarely extend beyond adolescence. During adolescence, some symptoms, such as hyperactivity, self-injury, and compulsivity, may worsen in about 35% of individuals with autism. In later adolescence and adulthood, abnormalities such as stereotyped motor movements, unexpressiveness, anxiety, and socially inappropriate behaviors are common, even in high-functioning individuals with autism. For higher-functioning individuals, feelings of loneliness, social ineptness, and work difficulties are common, and adaptive behavior remains at or below mental age. Complex obsessive-compulsive rituals may develop, and speech may resemble that of individuals with schizophrenia, including idiosyncratic and concrete usages, perseverative speech, monotonous tone, repeated questions, and self-talk (Newsom, 1998).

In summarizing later outcomes for the children he studied, Kanner (1973) reported that only 11 out of 96 children were "sufficiently integrated into the texture of society to be employable, to move among people without obvious behavior problems, and be acceptable to those around them at home, at work, and in other modes of interaction" (p. 190). All 11 of these children had speech by age 5 and remained at home. However, these factors were also true of many of his children who did not fare as well. Kanner (1973) also noted that the children who did well seemed to become aware of their peculiarities during adolescence and began to make a conscious effort to do something about them.

In other early studies describing outcomes for children with autism who received limited help, only 1% to 2% of them became normal in the sense of being indistinguishable from others. About 10% had good outcomes, meaning that they achieved near-normal functioning in their social behavior and language, progressed in school or work, but continued to display oddities of speech or personality. Another 20% had fair outcomes, making social and educational gains despite significant handicaps in areas such as speech. The overwhelming majority, 70%, showed poor outcomes with limited progress and continuing handicaps that did not permit them to lead an independent existence (Lotter, 1978).

Notably, the two strongest predictors of adult outcomes in children with autism are IQ and language development. Children with autism who have an IQ below 50 are likely to show the poorest levels of later social adjustment, while those with higher IQs show better long-term adjustment. Children who display language by age 5 are also more likely to show better long-term outcomes. For most individuals, especially those with severe or profound mental retardation, autism is a chronic and lifelong condition. Perhaps the most reliable statement that can be made about outcomes is that without intensive early intervention, most children with autism show some degree of gradual improvement in their symptoms with age, but will continue to display cognitive, language, and social impairments that make them different from others throughout their lives (Piven, Harper, Palmer, & Arndt, 1996).

CAUSES OF AUTISM

No single abnormality is likely to explain all the impairments associated with autism. The existence of multiple causes is a more realistic alternative to account for the many different forms of autism, ranging from mild to severe. Although the causes of autism are still not known, our understanding of possible mechanisms has increased dramatically over the past decade. These advances are evident when we consider that only 10 years ago, autism was thought to be due to a single brain abnormality, and not that long ago, autism was being attributed to cold and unloving parents.

It is now generally accepted that autism is a biologically based neurodevelopmental disorder. As we have noted, many children with autism who show no clinically detectable neurological abnormalities develop epilepsy as they grow older, a finding that suggests some form of brain dysfunction (Rutter, 1970). Understanding the biologic bases of autism requires that we look at early development, genetic influences, and neuropsychological and neurobiological findings.

Problems During Pregnancy and Birth

Children with autism experience more health problems during pregnancy, at birth, or immediately following birth than normal children. Risk factors such as the mother's age, prematurity, bleeding in pregnancy, toxemia (blood poisoning), viral infection or exposure, and a lack of vigor after birth have been identified in about 25% of children with autism. However, there is little evidence that these problems occur consistently across all children with autism, that they predict different outcomes, or that they are specific to autism. We know that many of these early health problems occur in children with other disorders, such as reading disorder or developmental language problems (see Chapter 11). Few differences in pre-, peri-, and neonatal factors are apparent between individuals with autism and their unaffected siblings. Pregnancy and birth complications are not the primary cause of autism, but they do suggest that fetal or neonatal development has been compromised in some general way (Bryson, Smith, & Eastwood, 1988; Nelson, 1991; Piven et al., 1993).

Genetic Contributions

Evidence from specific gene disorders, chromosomal conditions, and family and twin studies strongly indicates that autism is a genetic condition, although the specific genetic regions that contribute directly to the disorder have yet to be identified.

Specific Disorders. About 10% of children with autism have an identifiable medical condition, with even higher rates for those with autism and profound mental retardation (Rutter, Bailey, Bolton, & Le Couteur, 1994). The discovery of the fragile-X anomaly and its identification in a substantial minority of individuals with autism led to increased attention to fragile-X and other chromosomal defects that might be related to autism. Recall from Chapter 9 that fragile-X gets its name from the appearance of a fragile site on the long arm of the X chromosome. This syndrome occurs at a rate similar to that of autism and is associated with mental retardation ranging from mild to severe. Early reports suggested that as many as 15% of all cases of autism had fragile-X, but technological advances and better research now put the true rate at 2% to 3% or lower (Lincoln, Courchesne, Mascarello, Yeung-Courchesne, & Schreibman, 1996). In addition, although individuals with fragile-X may display the typical core features of autism, more often their cognitive and social deficits are uncharacteristic of autism. Any association that exists between autism and fragile-X may be secondary to the presence of mental retardation, since most individuals with autism and fragile-X have mental retardation. Thus, the relationship between fragile-X and autism appears to be a weak one that does not point to genetic mechanisms specific to autism (Bailey et al., 1996).

Clinical reports suggested that some cases of autism were associated with single-gene disorders such as **tuberous sclerosis,** a condition that occurs in about 1 in 7000 individuals. Gene sites for this disorder have been identified on chromosomes 9 and 16. About 75% of cases of tuberous sclerosis are derived from new mutations, with no family history of the disorder. The manifestations of this disorder can vary widely from mild to severe, and may include abnormalities such as skin lesions, neural deficits, seizures, and learning disabilities. Approximately 25% of children with tuberous sclerosis have autism and a further 19% show autistic-like characteristics. It has also been estimated that about 3% to 9% of individuals with autism have tuberous sclerosis, making its association with autism higher than that of any other genetically based medical condition. The main association between autism and tuberous sclerosis seems to be for individuals with mental retardation and epilepsy. Autism is much less common when these conditions are not present. These findings suggest that the risk for autism may be due to a brain disorder that accompanies tuberous sclerosis rather than to an association between autism and the specific gene sites known to be linked to this condition (Bailey et al., 1996).

It is likely that individuals with autism have an elevated risk of about 5% for other chromosomal anomalies (Gillberg & Coleman, 1992). Unfortunately, the chromosomal anomalies associated with autism do not indicate the gene sites underlying the disorder, because autism has been associated with anomalies involving almost all chromosomes (Hotopf & Bolton, 1995).

Family Risk. For the 90% of cases of autism not associated with a known medical condition, family and twin studies provide strong evidence for genetic influences (Le Couteur et al., 1996). Family studies indicate that up to 3% to 7% of siblings and extended family members of individuals with autism have the disorder and that many others display autisticlike features and social deficits. Although these numbers may seem small, they indicate a likelihood that autism will occur twice in the same family that is 50 to 100 times greater than would be expected by chance alone (Bolton et al., 1994). Twin studies have reported concordance rates for autism in monozygotic (MZ) twins ranging from approximately 40% to 90%, in contrast to near zero rates for same-sex dizygotic (DZ) twins (Bailey et al., 1996).

Possible nongenetic explanations for the high concordance rates of autism in MZ twins have included shared environmental events, such as birth complications, infectious diseases (e.g., rubella) during pregnancy, and environmental pathogens during pregnancy. However, these explanations have received minimal support, and at best may account for autism in rare cases. As noted, psychosocial environmental risk factors, such as parental neglect, rejection, or indifference, have received no support, and numerous studies have failed to find any association between child-rearing conditions or stress experiences and autism. Some children raised in grossly deprived conditions, such as those that existed in orphanages in Romania prior to 1990, have been found to display autisticlike behaviors. However, many of these behaviors were found to decrease with age, and most children with autism do not experience this kind of severe physical and psychological deprivation. In general, psychological and family stressors and adversities have not been found to play a significant role in the etiology of autism and cannot account for the high concordance rates in identical twins. Genetic factors are likely to account for the great majority of cases (Bailey et al., 1996).

Conclusions and Speculations. Based on our knowledge of medical genetics and other disorders, it seems likely that several genetic factors are associated with autism. The findings that autism may be associated with fragile-X and tuberous sclerosis provide some support for the idea that different genetic abnormalities may result in the same clinical picture. Is there evidence of genetic variability in cases of autism that are not associated with a known medical condition? In this regard, even though concordance rates of autism for MZ twins are very high, considerable variation exists between MZ twin pairs in their autistic symptoms and IQ scores, with reported IQ differences of up to 50 points (Le Couteur et al., 1996). In fact, there is almost as much variability within MZ twin pairs as between MZ twin pairs. The variable expression of symptoms and IQ in MZ twin pairs provides little information about possible indicators of genetic variability. Thus, although genetic heterogeneity underlying autism seems likely, there is presently no way to determine this from the clinical expression of the disorder.

Given the evidence that autism is a genetically based disorder, what is the mode of genetic transmission? Although we don't know for sure, current findings

Table 10.3 Neuropsychological Findings in Autism

Domain	Impaired Function	Spared Function
Intelligence	Verbal, abstract, sequential processing	Visuospatial organization
Attention	Orienting	Sustained attention
	Shifting/disengaging	
	Selective attention	
Memory	Mild long-term memory, especially for complex	Paired associate learning
Higher-functioning children	information	Auditory rote memory
	Strategies for encoding complex information	Cued recall
	Sequential, abstract information	
Memory	Short- and long-term memory	Discrimination learning
Lower-functioning children	Declarative memory	Operant learning
Language	Pragmatics	Phonology
Higher-functioning children	Intonation, stress, rhythm	Syntax
	Comprehension of complex verbal information	
Language	Severe expressive and receptive language (e.g., mutism)	
Lower-functioning children		
Executive functions	Working memory	
	Inhibition	
	Planning/organization	
	Flexibility/set shifting	

Source: Adapted from Klinger & Dawson, 1996.

suggest that multiple interacting genes are a far more likely cause than is a single gene. The evidence for multiple interacting genes comes from several sources. First, consistent with this model are marked reductions in concordance rates from MZ twins to DZ twins or siblings, with further reductions in both autism and autisticlike symptoms from first- to second-degree relatives. Second, estimates point to a three-gene model as the most likely, although the range could be anywhere from two to ten genes. Finally, the likelihood of other family members' having autism increases with the severity of the disorder. The increased prevalence of mental retardation and specific cognitive deficits in the siblings of children with autism also suggests that what is inherited is a polygenic disorder that increases the child's risk for a variety of cognitive impairments including autism (Bailey et al., 1996).

Neuropsychological Findings

Given the many cognitive, language, and socioemotional deficits in children with autism, an equally wide array of deficits in performance on tests of neuropsychological functioning would be expected. As summarized in Table 10.3, neuropsychological impairments in autism occur in many domains, including intelligence, attention, memory, language, and executive functions. The widespread nature of these deficits suggests the involvement of multiple regions of the brain at both the cortical and subcortical levels (Happe & Frith, 1996). The fact that

there are both affected and unaffected areas of functioning within each domain, with the possible exception of executive functions, suggests that within each affected area some brain functions remain intact (Dawson, 1996).

Neuropsychological findings suggest that frontal lobe impairments are common in most individuals with autism, with greater variability in areas of the brain associated with language and memory, which may explain why language problems may range from no language to mild pragmatic difficulties. Within the same domain of functioning, large differences exist in the types of neuropsychological deficits found across children with autism, often as a function of the severity of the child's disorder. For example, lower-functioning children with autism may show impairments in basic memory functions, such as visual recognition memory, which are mediated by the brain's medial temporal lobe, including the hippocampus and amygdala (Barth, Fein, & Waterhouse, 1995). In contrast, higher-functioning children may have more subtle deficits in working memory or in encoding complex verbal material, suggesting the involvement of higher cortical functions (Dawson, 1996).

Neurobiological Factors

Although no known biological marker for autism has been determined, impressive advances have been made in documenting the biological basis of the disorder (Bauman & Kemper, 1994b; Gillberg & Coleman, 1992). Several brain abnormalities have been identified that are generally consistent with an early disturbance in neural development that occurs prior to 30 weeks before birth. Unfortunately, many findings regarding brain abnormalities in autism have varied across studies, a point that needs to be kept in mind in the discussion that follows (Filipek, 1996).

Brain Abnormalities.   Brain imaging studies and postmortem investigations have looked for structural abnormalities in brain development or consistently localized brain lesions associated with the symptoms of autism (Kemper & Bauman, 1993; Minshew & Dombrowski, 1994). These studies have most consistently identified structural abnormalities in the cerebellum and the medial temporal lobe and related limbic system structures (Courchesne, Chisum, & Townsend, 1994; Courchesne et al., 1994). The cerebellum, a relatively large part of the brain located near the brain stem, is most frequently associated with motor movement. However, growing evidence suggests that the cerebellum is also partially involved in nonmotor functions such as language, learning, emotion, thought, and attention (Courchesne, Townsend, & Chase, 1995). Specific areas of the cerebellum have been found to be significantly smaller than normal in a majority of individuals with autism, a condition known as *cerebellar hypoplasia* (Courchesne et al., 1995). It has been proposed that cerebellar abnormalities may underlie the problem that children with autism have in rapidly shifting their attention from one stimulus to another. Although the cerebellar findings and hypotheses are suggestive, they have not been replicated across all studies (Piven et al., 1992). In addition, the presence of cerebellar hypoplasia in some individuals without autism raises questions regarding the specificity of these findings for autism (Bailey et al., 1996).

A second localized brain abnormality is in the medial temporal lobe and related limbic system structures. These areas of the brain are closely connected to one another via neural circuits and are associated with functions known to be disturbed in children with autism—for example, emotion regulation, learning, and memory. The amygdala seems to play an especially important role in the recognition of the emotional significance of stimuli, in the formation of associations for understanding the relation between social behavior and rewards, in the perception of body movements and eye gaze direction, in orienting toward social stimuli, and, with the hippocampus, in long-term memory. Damage to these brain areas in animals may lead to behaviors similar to those observed in autism, such as social withdrawal, compulsive behaviors, failure to learn about dangerous situations, difficulty retrieving information from memory, and difficulty adjusting to novel events or

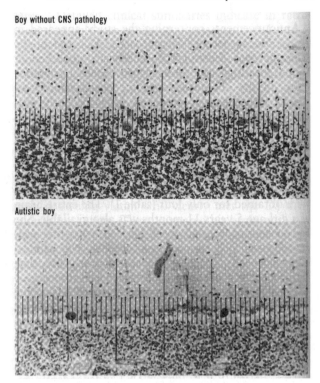

FIGURE 10.5   Studies point to a greatly reduced density of Purkinje cells in the cerebellums of individuals with autism. (Ritvo et al., 1986)

situations. However, we must be extremely cautious in generalizing from these findings directly to autism.

Postmortem studies for a rare disorder such as autism are difficult to conduct, and autopsy findings are few. The focus of these studies has been primarily on microscopic abnormalities in the cerebellum and the medial temporal lobe and related structures. As shown in Figure 10.5, greatly reduced Purkinje cell density has been reported in the cerebellum of individuals with autism. Purkinje cells are rich in the neurotransmitter serotonin and may modulate output from the cerebellum to other brain regions, thus playing a role in selective attention (Courchesne et al., 1995). Abnormally small and densely packed neurons have been reported in the medial temporal structures (Bauman & Kemper, 1994a). However, as with the neuroimaging data, findings concerning these regions have been variable from study to study (Bailey et al., 1996).

Recent findings suggest increased head circumference, higher-than-expected brain weight (megalencephaly) of 100 to 200 grams, and increased brain volume in individuals with autism (Bailey et al., 1993), particularly in males (Piven et al., 1996). These findings for children with autism are in contrast to the lower-than-expected brain weight found in nonautistic individuals with mental retardation and older individuals with

Child with autism

Comparison children

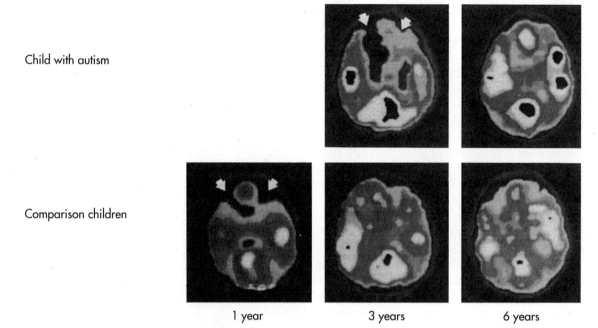

1 year   3 years   6 years

FIGURE 10.6 Regional blood flow images illustrate the transient frontal hypoperfusion (reduced cerebral blood flow) observed in children with autism. *Top row:* A child with autism at 3 and 6 years of age. SPECT examination at 3 years showed a clear bilateral frontal hypoperfusion (white arrows), while the exam at 6 years revealed normal frontal perfusion. *Bottom row:* Three normal comparison children. SPECT images show frontal hypoperfusion at 1 year (white arrows) but normal perfusion by age 3. These differences suggest a possible delay in frontal brain maturation in children with autism, a finding that is consistent with findings related to deficits in executive functions. (Zilbovicius et al., 1995)

autism (Bauman, 1996; Cole, Neal, Fraser, & Cowie, 1994). Findings related to increased brain weight and volume suggest that the overgrowth and pruning (thinning out or reduction) of neurons that are integral features of normal brain development may be disrupted in children with autism, with more neuron growth, less neuron death, or more nonneuronal brain tissue all being possibilities (Minshew, 1996).

Far less is known about the brain abnormalities underlying Asperger's and Rett's disorders than autism. Preliminary findings for Asperger's suggest that brain abnormalities are similar to those for autism in being primarily in the cerebellar circuits and limbic system, but that the extent of abnormality is more limited (Bauman, 1996). This selective involvement may underlie the prominent social and pragmatic language difficulties of individuals with Asperger's, despite their strong cognitive skills. Individuals with Rett's disorder have smaller brains than other children, with reduced size and increased density of neuronal cells found extensively throughout the forebrain (Armstrong, 1992; Bauman et al., 1995). Decreased length and complexity of dendritic branching have been found in all areas of the cortex, suggesting deficiencies in dendritic and synaptic development (Armstrong, 1992). As in autism, there is also a reduced number of Purkinje cells in the cerebellum. The brain abnormalities in Rett's disorder appear to be diffuse, suggesting a reduction in brain maturation prior to birth (Bauman, 1996).

Neurophysiological and Neurochemical Findings. Elevated rates of epilepsy and the occurrence of EEG abnormalities in about half of individuals with autism provide strong general evidence of abnormal brain functioning. Neuroimaging studies of brain metabolism in individuals with autism using PET and single photon emission computed tomography (SPECT) suggest decreased blood flow in the temporal and frontal lobes. Other studies have found a decrease in the functional connections between cortical and subcortical regions and a delay in the maturation of the frontal cortex, as indicated by reduced cerebral blood flow in the frontal brain regions of preschool-age children with autism (see Figure 10.6). These findings suggest a possible delay in the maturation of the frontal lobes that is consistent with clinical findings related to deficits in executive functions in autism (Zilbovicius et al., 1995). Perhaps the most consistent findings from studies of brain function are of extremely variable metabolic rates in the context of a normal global brain metabolism (Bailey et al., 1996).

Numerous hypotheses concerning neurotransmitter abnormalities in autism have been advanced (Cook, 1990; Narayan, Srinath, Anderson, & Meundi, 1993). No consistent abnormalities in the dopaminergic, noradrenergic, and neuropeptide systems have been identified, and there is little support for the hypothesis that elevated brain opioids inhibit the development of social attachments in children with autism (Gillberg, 1995). The most consistent finding of a neurotransmitter abnormality is that about one-third of individuals with autism show elevated levels of whole blood serotonin that place them in the upper 5% of the general population (Cook, 1990; Cook & Leventhal, 1996). Findings of elevated serotonin levels in the relatives of individuals with autism suggest that this abnormality may be more than a general indicator of abnormal brain development, although its significance is yet unclear. The role of serotonergic system abnormalities in autism is also suggested by recent genetic findings of linkage between autistic disorder and the serotonin transporter gene (hydroxytryptamine transporter, or HTT) (Cook et al., 1997).

In general, neurobiological findings support the presence of a pervasive abnormality in brain development in autism, with more localized lesions, such as cerebellar and medial temporal abnormalities, being one consequence of the more general impairment in development. Abnormal brain function in individuals with autism does not appear to be a highly localized phenomenon.

Autism as a Disorder of Brain Development

Collectively, the findings presented above suggest that autism is a developmental disorder at the neural systems level of brain organization that produces generalized impairments in complex information-processing abilities subserved by these systems. Several events in neuronal brain organization have been implicated, including dendritic and axonal development, the establishment of synaptic contacts, and programmed cell death and selective elimination of neuronal processes (Minshew, 1996). Given the many difficulties that children with autism have with processing social information, it has been suggested that autism may involve dysfunction of a brain system that is specialized for social cognition. Parts of the medial temporal lobe (amygdala, hippocampus, and entorhinal cortex) and orbital frontal lobe have been suggested as such a system. With regard to the hypothesized neural substrates for the early symptoms of autism, the amygdala in particular seems to be connected with early deficits in orienting to social stimuli, motor imitation, joint attention, and empathy (Dawson, 1996). Findings implicating frontal lobe deficits, as well as those related to medial temporal lobe dysfunction, suggest that autism involves both a general cognitive dysfunction caused by problems in distributed neural systems and specific social dysfunctions. These social dysfunctions are related to abnormalities in a brain system subserving social and emotional behaviors, which have evolved specifically in humans to deal with social interactions (Baron-Cohen, 1995; Voeller, 1996).

In summary, any explanatory model of autism will ultimately need to integrate behavioral, cognitive, and biological findings. With respect to behavior, diagnosis is becoming less controversial, although recent findings on subtypes of autism have sparked new interest. Cognitive impairments in ToM, weak central coherence, and executive functions have all been implicated, although the relation and degree of overlap among these impairments are not known. There is strong support for genetic contributions, although the precise mechanism is not known. Recent advances in gene mapping and brain imaging should help to enhance our understanding of the biological mechanisms in autism and their interaction with the child's cognitive, emotional, and behavioral functioning (Happe & Frith, 1996).

TREATMENT

I have not counted the trials of medication, the diets, the neurosurgery, the behavioral programs. If they total five hundred, there are five hundred fewer to try. . . . I'm a believer. . . . I believe my son can get well. (Swackhamer, 1993, p. 312)

Autistic people suffer from a biological defect. Although they cannot be cured, much can be done to improve their lives. (Frith, 1997, p. 92)

These two sentiments, the first by the mother of a child with autism, the second by an autism expert, underscore the promise, pain, and uncertainty that surround efforts to help children with autism and their families. Although behavioral, educational, and medical treatments may improve learning and behavior, and may even permit a small number of children to achieve near-normal functioning, there is no known cure for autism. Most treatments are directed at maximizing the child's potential and helping the child and family cope more effectively with the disorder. Many forms of treatment have been tried. Some treatments, such as medication, dietary modifications, and sensory integration, have not lived up to their claims, and others, such as facilitated communication, have not stood the test of close scientific scrutiny (Jacobson, Mulick, & Schwartz, 1995; Spitz, 1996). The recent emergence of promising programs of early intervention, community-based educational programs, supported employment opportunities, and varied community living options are all reasons for optimism about improving the outcomes for children with autism. However, these newer approaches are not yet widely available, so many children with autism continue to be placed in less than optimal treatment or educational environments that have little chance of making much of a difference in their lives (Dawson & Osterling, 1997; Newsom, 1998).

Different Children, Different Treatments

Given the large variability in severity of symptoms, in language impairments, and in intellectual functioning found in children with autism, it should not be surprising that variations in these factors relate to expected gains in

---

Box 10.4

Pamela and Ricky: Living with a Lifelong Disorder

In 1964, psychologist Ivar Lovaas started a long-term research and treatment program at UCLA. Pamela and Ricky were among the first children with autism to receive intensive behavioral interventions.

At ages seven and eight, Pam and Ricky had made significant improvements, but still had language and social skill deficits. Unfortunately, after 14 months, they had to be discharged to a State Hospital, so that the treatments could be offered to other children. The staff at the State Hospital did not have the resources to follow through with the behavioral treatment. Sadly, both Pam and Ricky lost most of their gains. In recent years, however, the State Hospital has developed behavioral treatment programs, and Pam and Ricky have both benefited.

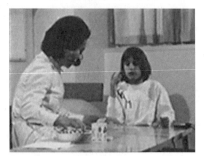

Pamela at age seven.

Pamela at age twenty-seven.

Pam has remained in the State Hospital. She is able to carry out some basic household tasks, though she has lost much of her appropriate speech.

Ricky lives in a small teaching home in the community. He has lost most of his language skills and spontaneity.

Ricky at age eight.

Ricky at age twenty-eight.

Unlike Pamela, Ricky has developed some recreational skills, such as rug hooking. With assistance, he participates in the community.

Source: Behavior Treatment of Autism, produced by E. L. Anderson.

treatment. The stories of Pamela and Ricky illustrate this point (see Box 10.4). Both received intensive treatment when they were 7 to 8 years old. As a child, Ricky had higher intellectual ability and more language than Pamela, and his adult outcome and living arrangements are consistent with his higher overall level of functioning. Pamela, in contrast, had lower intellectual ability and less language as a child than Ricky, and as an adult requires a more closely supervised living arrangement. These two cases illustrate how treatment strategies, goals, and expectations vary considerably for different children with autism.

Treatment for Low-Functioning Children.

Children with autism and profound or severe mental retardation will likely require supervised living and work arrangements throughout their lives. The prognosis is especially poor for low-functioning children who do not develop speech by age 5 years, display profound social impairments, show clear signs of neurological problems, have confirmed chromosomal abnormalities, or have significant delays in their motor development. Treatment strategies for lower-functioning children generally emphasize the elimination of harmful behavior and efforts to teach the child self-help skills, compliance with simple requests and rules, basic social and emotional behaviors, communication of needs, and appropriate play. As these children get older, an increasing emphasis is placed on teaching domestic and work-related skills to prepare them for supervised living or work settings. Work with the parents of low-functioning children must walk a fine line between avoiding expectations for dramatic improvement and not creating excessive pessimism. The emphasis is on rewarding progress, no matter how gradual, and on enjoyment of the child for his or her uniqueness (Newsom, 1998).

Treatment for High-Functioning Children.

The long-term outlook for children with autism who function within the moderately retarded to normal range of intelligence seems to depend on when treatment begins and how intensive it is. High-functioning children who receive concentrated doses of early intervention are the ones most likely to achieve normal or near-normal outcomes. In general, the treatment strategy for these children consists of an all-out effort. Time is assumed to be of the essence so as to maximize any advantage related to the plasticity of neural and behavioral processes in early development (Newsom, 1998). In addition to the goals for low-functioning children, goals for high-functioning children include teaching language fluency, age-appropriate social interactions with normal peers, and the behaviors and skills that are expected in typical preschool and elementary school classrooms.

The mother of Emilie, a 4-year-old girl with autism, spends hours each day on the floor in face-to-face communication with her daughter.

Extensive parental involvement and support, including the use of in-home therapy aides, are common. Children who are most likely to reach near-normal functioning as a result of intensive early intervention usually show rapid learning during the first few months of treatment. For high-functioning older children who have not received early intervention, goals include successful functioning in their special education classrooms and elaboration of their language, social, community, and work skills. In general, outcomes for high-functioning children can be extremely variable depending on the child, family, quality of early treatment and education, and later opportunities (Newsom, 1998).

Overview of Treatments

Autism has touched the lives of many individuals, including such well-known people as actor Sylvester Stallone, football quarterback Dan Marino, and musicians Wynton and Bradford Marsalis, who have all described their experiences with a family member with autism. The demands, frustrations, hopes, and aspirations of a family trying to do the best possible for their child with autism are captured in the experiences of the mother of 4-year-old Emilie:

Emilie: A Full-Time Job

. . . [W]hen Emilie was 2½ she was diagnosed with autism, Emilie's mother recalled, her eyes brimming with tears. "We've been relying on ourselves ever since." Treatment center staff are trying to teach Emilie but progress has been slow. Emilie's mother says if she could afford it she would hire a speech therapist or specialized trained educators to work with Emilie all day long.

Emilie's mother and her husband have read about children with autism who become accomplished scientists and musicians. Two months ago they hired a specialist who came to the house to teach them a new one-on-one approach for getting through to Emilie with a reward system. Pictures of food are taped to hallway walls. On the fridge is a cut-out of a glass of milk. Emilie is learning to express her needs after four years of shrieking and kicking for what she wanted. When she points to what she wants, she gets a reward—a potato chip, half a cookie, or an extra 10 minutes twirling her beloved skipping rope. Every afternoon mother and daughter spend two hours on the floor, face to face, their legs interlocked. "Listen to maman, Emilie. Look at me. Look at me. Say 'yes'. Say 'yes'. Do you like chips, Emilie? You can have one if you just say the word, 'yes'."

Emilie's mother coaxes patiently, firmly, holding out a bowl of chips. But Emilie runs to the radiator and climbs it, teetering there. When her mother pulls her down she shrieks and kicks, then throws herself to the floor crying. In a minute the episode is over, the lessons begin again and this time Emilie is ready to fit the puzzle pieces into their box. She completes her task and holds out her hand for a chip. "Bravo, sweetheart. You did it. I knew you could," her mother beams. "There are lots of things Emilie can do." Emilie's mother has used the reward system to build Emilie's vocabulary to 22 words. When she wants to, Emilie can say toast, milk, maman, papa, cake, baby, poopoo, peepee. And that, to her parents, has been a monumental breakthrough.

". . . [W]e have to motivate her," says her mother, whose only respite is an evening out once or twice a month with her husband. "If we let her be, she'd just climb or hide under the cover all day long. That's my nightmare, that she'll end up in a psychiatric hospital, withdrawn from the world. I can see that we are slowly beginning to get through to her," Emilie's mother says with a deep sigh. "She didn't pay any attention to us at all before. She never showed any affection or made eye contact. But now she looks at me and says maman. Sometimes she hugs me. It doesn't happen every day. But it grabs my heart when it does." (Adapted from Semenak, 1996)

Numerous treatments have been used to help children like Emilie and their families. The most effective ones involve highly structured skills-oriented treatments that are tailored to the individual child and that provide the family with education and supportive counseling. These treatments, elements of which are highlighted in the overview that follows, lead to significant gains in the child's social adjustment, language, and preacademic and academic achievement, and produce other positive outcomes for both the child and family.

Overview of Treatments for Children with Autism
❖ *Initial Stages of Treatment*
  Building rapport with the child
  Teaching learning readiness skills
  Reducing or eliminating disruptive behavior
❖ *Teaching Appropriate Social Behavior*
  Teaching imitation and observational learning
  Expressing affection
  Social play and social skills groups
  Peer-mediated interventions
    Peer-initiated procedures
    Child-initiated procedures
    Sibling-mediated procedures
❖ *Teaching Appropriate Communication Skills*
  Operant speech training
    Verbal imitation
    Receptive labeling
    Expressive labeling
    Incidental teaching
  Sign language training
❖ *Family Intervention*
  Behavioral parent training
  Parent counseling
    Emotional difficulties
    Interpersonal difficulties
❖ *Early Intervention*
  Preschool programs
  Home-based programs
❖ *Educational Interventions*
❖ *Psychopharmacological/Somatic Interventions*
  (Data from Newsom, 1998)

Treatment programs for children with autism usually include general strategies for engaging children in treatment; specific techniques to decrease or eliminate self-injurious behavior, self-stimulation, and other disruptive behaviors that interfere with learning; teaching of appropriate social behavior and communication skills; interventions that enable parents to participate fully in their child's treatment and to cope with the substantial demands associated with raising a child with a severe developmental disorder; and comprehensive programs of early intervention (Newsom, 1998; Schreibman & Koegel, 1996). In addition, educational regimens are commonly included in programs for children with autism, and for some children, medications may be of benefit in improving interfering behavioral symptoms (McDougle et al., 1997). Examples of some of the more commonly used treatments for children with autism are highlighted in the sections that follow.

Treatment programs generally target the specific social, communication, cognitive, and behavioral deficits of children with autism that we have been discussing throughout this chapter. Because children with autism have great difficulty making changes and generalizing previously acquired skills to new environments, these areas must be directly addressed in treatment. It is also critical that any treatment approach be tailored to meet the needs of the individual child and family, thus making it possible for each child to meet his or her full potential.

Initial Stages. Early stages of treatment focus on building rapport and teaching the child learning-readiness skills. A variety of procedures have been used to help the child with autism feel comfortable being physically close to the therapist and to identify possible rewards that can help strengthen the child's social behavior, affection, and play. Imitating the child's use of toys may increase eye contact, touching, and vocalizations directed toward the therapist, and prompting the child to engage in play with a preferred toy may decrease social avoidance. These and similar procedures are used throughout treatment.

Children with autism must learn to sit in a chair, come when called, and attend to their teacher if they are to progress in treatment. These **readiness skills** are taught in small steps. For example, the sequence of steps presented below may be used to teach a child to look directly at an adult. This sequence describes procedures commonly used throughout treatment, such as prompts, rewards, and generalization training. Some procedures involve a step-by-step approach to presenting a stimulus and requiring a specific response, called **discrete trial training.** Other procedures attempt to strengthen behavior by capitalizing on naturally occurring opportunities, referred to as **incidental training.** Successful interventions usually use a combination of these approaches.

Sequence of Steps Used in Teaching a Child with Autism to Look at Other People

1. The teacher provides a brief instruction, such as "Look at me."
2. The teacher may prompt the response to increase the chances that it will occur, for example, by holding a treat in the line of gaze between the child and the teacher.
3. Prompts are eliminated as soon as the child begins to respond on his or her own.

4. When the child responds correctly, he or she is rewarded; alternatively, if the child responds incorrectly, he or she is ignored, reprimanded, or corrected.
5. This process is repeated, often hundreds of times, until the child looks at the teacher consistently.
6. The child is then taught to generalize this behavior to persons other than the teacher and to other settings in the child's environment.
7. The use of the behavior to access naturally occurring rewards is increased—for example, by requiring the child to look directly at the parent when turning on the TV or going out to play.
8. The behavior may be used to facilitate the acquisition of other more complex forms of learning—for example, looking at the teacher's hands during signed communication or at objects or pictures when learning to identify and discriminate between them.

Reducing or eliminating disruptive behavior. Young children with autism display many disruptive and interfering behaviors, such as tantrums, yelling, screaming, or throwing or destroying objects, as well as self-stimulation, aggression, and self-injury. Such behaviors are common reactions to demands that are made of the child early in treatment and must be eliminated if the child is to learn more adaptive forms of social interaction and communication. A variety of procedures have been used effectively to eliminate disruptive behavior in children with autism, including rewarding competing behaviors, ignoring, and administering mild forms of punishment. An innovative approach that was used to eliminate disruptive behavior in Nile, a 3-year-old boy with autism, is described below:

Nile: Learning to Communicate Nondisruptively

At the time of referral Nile was a 3-year-old boy with autism and developmental delay who didn't speak. When family members tried to interact with him, he lashed out at them by biting, pinching, or scratching; engaged in self-injurious behaviors such as biting his arm, slapping his face, or banging his head; and had severe tantrums in which he screamed or broke toys.

We began our assessment by observing Nile's behavior under different conditions, for example, when he was given more or less attention or asked to work on tasks that were more or less demanding or more or less preferred. Although Nile displayed some inappropriate behavior in all conditions, his behaviors were most severe when he was required to perform demanding tasks. Our observations were consistent with those of Nile's parents, and suggested that his disruptive behaviors were being maintained because they worked to eliminate unwanted demands.

To explore this, we assessed Nile during alternate conditions in which no demands were placed on him during side-by-side play with his mom or in which he was required to play in a certain way, but was permitted to briefly escape this task if he displayed inappropriate behaviors such as screaming or throwing toys. Nile's inappropriate behaviors increased when they led to the removal of the unwanted demands. However, once these demands were removed he immediately stopped his inappropriate behavior. This assessment supported our hypothesis that Nile's disruptive actions were maintained because they worked to get rid of unwanted requests and demands.

We then began functional communication training to teach Nile to ask for breaks from demanding tasks by signing "done," a much more appropriate way of communicating when he had enough than by having a full-blown tantrum. This training consisted of three parts. First, breaks were provided from demanding tasks when Nile signed the word "done." Second, Nile was required to continue the activity when he engaged in inappropriate behavior. Third, positive parent attention was paired with access to reinforcement. During treatment, Nile was prompted first by his mother, then by his brother and father, to complete part of a play activity. As soon as he complied with the first step of this activity, Nile was prompted to sign "done," the task was removed, and he was permitted to take a break. On his breaks, Nile's parents followed him and played with him but did not attempt to direct him to other activities. Our hope was that, over time, social interactions with his family would become rewarding to him. Following his break, Nile was required to finish another step of the task and to sign "done." If he displayed inappropriate behavior at any time, he was not allowed to take a break, but rather was required to continue with the task.

We progressively increased the time he remained on task before asking for a break. After about 3 months, Nile began to sign "done" on his own and even began to say "done." Within 6 months, there was a dramatic reduction in his disruptive behavior, and equally important, he started to play with his mother, father, and brother and to say other words. (Adapted from Wacker et al., 1996)

Teaching Appropriate Social Behavior.

Teaching children with autism to increase the amount and appropriateness of their social behavior receives a high priority in treatment. A variety of methods have been used to increase the salience of social cues by associating the therapist, teacher, and parents with actions, activities, and events that the child finds pleasant or useful. For example, children may be taught to imitate simple movements of objects, such as banging a spoon or stacking blocks, then to imitate the body movements of other people, such as raising their hand or opening their mouth, and then to play "follow the leader" in the context of social play with peers. Children are also taught ways to express affection through smiling, hugging, tickling, patting, or kissing—behaviors that enable them to return the affection they receive from others. Direct efforts to teach children with autism appropriate displays of verbal and facial affect may also be used (Gena, Krantz, McClannahan, & Poulson, 1996).

Further efforts to enhance social interaction have included teaching the child with autism social toy play, social pretend play, and such specific social skills as initiating and maintaining interactions, giving and receiving compliments, taking turns and sharing, helping others and asking for help, and including others in activities. One study by Ozonoff and Miller (1995) attempted to increase social skills in adolescents with autism and normal intelligence by focusing on training an understanding of states of knowledge, beliefs, deception, and intention in the context of perspective-taking and false-belief tasks like those used to test for theory of mind. Efforts were made to generalize these concepts from the group setting in which they were taught to more natural settings, such as games, parties, and field trips. Although the children who received treatment showed considerable improvement on ToM tests relative to children who had not received treatment, there were no changes in their social behavior. It remains to be seen whether direct efforts to remediate ToM deficits will increase the child's social skills in everyday life.

One of the most common strategies for teaching appropriate social behavior to children with autism involves teaching normal or mildly handicapped peers to interact with them. Peers are taught to initiate age-appropriate social behaviors, such as initiating toy play, establishing mutual attention, commenting about ongoing activities, or acknowledging or rewarding their partner's responses. Teachers may signal and reward the peers' social initiations with the child with autism. Other strategies have used prompts and rewards for teaching the child with autism to initiate interactions with others, and in some cases to involve siblings of children with autism as peer trainers.

These strategies have shown some success in increasing the social relatedness of children with autism (Strain,

Kohler, & Goldstein, 1996). However, efforts are needed to integrate these efforts to enhance social behavior with those directed at the child's affect and communication skills, since these areas are highly interrelated. Moreover, effective social interaction requires that the child learn to use social behaviors spontaneously, selectively, and flexibly in relation to the changing demands of specific social situations.

Teaching Appropriate Communication Skills.

Several strategies have been used to help children with autism use language more appropriately. **Operant speech training** is a step-by-step approach that successively increases the child's vocalizations, teaches the child to imitate sounds and words, teaches the meanings of words, and teaches the child to use language expressively to label objects, make verbal requests, and express desires. The emphasis is on teaching the child to use language more spontaneously and more functionally in everyday life situations to influence others and to communicate better. The early stages of operant speech training focus on teaching the child new forms of language whereas the later stages emphasize new functions of language as a way to communicate (Newsom, 1998). Engaging the child with autism as an active communication partner is essential. This can be achieved by teaching spontaneous communication strategies, self-initiated communication skills to replace disruptive behaviors, self-management skills to enhance the use of learned behaviors, and strategies to improve intelligibility of communication (L. K. Koegel & R. L. Koegel, 1996).

Another approach to teaching language to children with autism is **sign language training**. Many of the specific steps in teaching sign language are similar to those for operant speech training: first teaching the child signs, then teaching the meaning of signs, and finally,

A child receiving speech therapy.

teaching the functional use of signs in everyday situations. Many children with autism find it easier to learn through nonverbal training methods. However, since verbal communication is the norm, speech training is recommended first for most children who are beginning language training. If the child does not progress using verbal communication methods alone, then simultaneous communication training (verbal plus signing) can be implemented. Mute children who are poor verbal imitators are initially more likely to learn language via simultaneous communication training or sign-only training than with verbal training. Simultaneous communication training may facilitate the emergence of verbal language in a small proportion of children, usually in those children with good verbal imitation skills.

Early Intervention.

As standardized methods to recognize autism at a very young age are developed, possibilities for early intervention increase dramatically. The promise of early intervention derives from the plasticity of neural systems early in development and the yet-to-be-tested hypothesis that providing very young children with autism with intensive and highly structured experiences may alter their developing brains in ways that permit outcomes that would not otherwise be possible. The average age of children with autism entering early-intervention programs has been 3½ to 4 years or younger. Children in these programs have an average IQ in the mid 50s, although many are not testable at the time of intake. Early intervention provides direct one-to-one work with the child for 15 to 40 hours per week, and active involvement of the family in the child's treatment. Programs are carried out at home and in the preschool, and efforts are made to include the child in interactions with normal peers, especially later in treatment. Early-intervention programs target many of the specific deficits that we have described for children with autism and uses procedures similar to those that were developed with older children. The core elements of these programs are described below (Dawson & Osterling, 1997).

Curriculum content that emphasizes basic skills. The curriculum emphasizes core skills such as paying attention to people and complying with requests, imitating others, attending to elements of the environment (especially to people) that are essential for learning, and complying with requests from others. Also emphasized are verbal and motor imitation, language, functional and symbolic play with toys, and social interactions with others.

Supportive teaching environment. Core skills are first established in a highly structured and focused one-on-one learning environment designed to maximize attention and reduce distractions.

Teaching generalization. Gradual and systematic fading of the high-support environment is implemented to facilitate the spontaneous occurrence of core skills and their generalization to more natural, complex environments.

Predictability and routine.

The child is assisted with the inevitable changes in routine and activities that occur during a typical day by using visual and verbal cues and photographs, signaling the child well in advance of changes, walking the child through transitions, providing a transitional object, or carrying out a familiar ritual during the transition.

Functional approach to problem behaviors.

The likelihood that problem behaviors will occur is minimized by enhancing the child's interest and engagement in preferred activities and providing a high level of structure. Any problem behavior that occurs is dealt with by analyzing the functions that the behavior serves (e.g., requesting help, getting rid of unwanted demands), changing the environment to support appropriate behavior, and teaching the child more appropriate ways of coping with the situation.

Transition from the preschool classroom.

A great deal of time and attention is devoted to helping children make a successful transition from preschool to kindergarten or first grade by teaching them survival skills that will enable them to function as independently as possible in the classroom. These survival skills include complying with adult requests, taking turns, listening to directions from afar or near, sitting quietly during activities, volunteering, raising the hand to gain attention, waiting and walking in line, using toilets in classroom versus in the hallway, picking up toys and materials after use, and communicating basic needs. Post-preschool placements are sought that provide the best match for the child with respect to class size, structure, and teaching style. Then the skills needed to maximize the child's success in this placement are identified and systematically taught—for example saying the new teacher's name.

Family involvement.

Parent involvement is viewed as a critical component in treatment, although the nature and extent varies with the needs of individual families. To varying degrees, parents are trained in the treatment methods, contribute to their development, and are included in the educational process at home, at school, or both. Programs are sensitive to the stresses encountered by families who have a child with autism and provide parent groups and other types of support.

Intensive intervention.

Programs average nearly 30 hours per week of school-based intervention, substantially more hours than are typically provided by most public school systems for preschoolers with disabilities. In addition, since all programs involve parent training, the number of hours of treatment that children receive is substantially higher than that of other pre-schools, and programs include many hours of treatment in the home.

Other elements.

Programs may include other treatments—for example, speech therapy or sign language, occupational therapy, specific social skills training, peer-mediated training, and the development of independent initiative and choice-making skills.

A comprehensive review of data for about 150 children completing early-intervention programs found that a substantial number of them were able to function in regular educational placements, although the type of setting and amount of support services needed varied considerably. In addition, most children showed developmental gains, as reflected in improvements in their IQ scores, scores on developmental tests, and classroom observations (Dawson & Osterling, 1997).

Several anecdotal accounts and research reports claim that some children with autism can achieve normal functioning if given intensive intervention before the age of 3 years (Maurice, 1993b; McEachin, Smith, & Lovaas, 1993). The UCLA Young Autism Project, begun about 25 years ago under the direction of Ivar Lovaas, has received considerable attention. This program includes the core elements of early intervention, is the most detailed and labor-intensive of the early interventions, begins the earliest, and is the only program whose outcomes have been evaluated against a control group of similar-age children receiving less intensive intervention (McEachin et al., 1993; Smith & Lovaas, 1998).

The program consists of a step-by-step approach based on principles of applied behavioral analysis, including the use of shaping by successive approximation and of rewards and punishment. Parents are taught to be the primary therapists for their children, with direction and help from graduate and undergraduate students who work with them in the home. The average age of children entering the program is 32 months. During the initial phases, children receive 40 hours a week of intensive one-to-one discrete trial training. Parents are trained in the use of treatment procedures so that intervention can take place during most of the child's waking hours. In the first year of the program, the emphasis is on reducing self-stimulatory behavior and aggressive behaviors while at the same time building competing behaviors, such as compliance, imitation, and appropriate toy play. The second year emphasizes expressive and abstract language and interactive play with other children. Children are also taught how to function in a preschool group and are enrolled in regular education preschool, if possible. The third year of the program emphasizes the appropriate expression of emotions, preacademic tasks, assertiveness, and observational learning. Throughout the program, self-stimulatory and aggressive behaviors are dealt

Table 10.4a The UCLA Young Autism Project: Classroom Placements at Age 7

	Experimental Group	Control Group 1	Control Group 2
Regular classroom	9	0	1
Special education classroom for children with language delays	8	8	10
Special education classroom for children with autism/mental retardation	2	11	10

Source: Data from Newsom, 1998.

Table 10.4b The UCLA Young Autism Project: Mean IQ Changes

	Mean IQ at Age 3	Mean IQ at Age 7	Mean IQ at Age 13
The nine children with the best outcomes of those in the experimental group	70	107	112
Entire experimental group, including the nine children with the best outcomes	53	83	86
Control group 1	46	52	56
Control group 2	59	58	

Source: Data from Newsom, 1998. Children in control group 2 were not assessed at 13 years.

with by ignoring, placing the child in time-out, rewarding competing behaviors, and as a last resort, using mild punishment such as a loud "no."

In a landmark research investigation, children with autism were assigned to one of three groups. Although this assignment was not carried out randomly, the groups were found to be comparable with respect to age, language, intellectual functioning, and other measures prior to intervention. The experimental group of 19 children received 40 hours a week of intensive intervention. Control Group 1 consisted of 19 children who attended special education classes and received 10 hours a week of one-to-one instruction. Control Group 2 consisted of 21 children from a larger study who also attended special education classes but received no one-to-one instruction. The first outcome data were obtained when the children were 7 years old. Findings are presented in Tables 10.4a and 10.4b.

Remarkably, 47% of the children in the experimental group were found to be educationally and intellectually normal. They had successfully completed a regular first-grade class without support, had been recommended for promotion by their teachers to a regular second-grade class, and had scored at or above average on standardized IQ tests. The average IQ scores of these children increased by 37 points from 70 to 107; overall, the experimental group children showed an increase in mean IQ from 53 to 83. Children in the two control conditions did not fare nearly as well, with only 1 of 40 children being placed in a regular first-grade class; overall, these children showed only minimal increases in IQ scores. The experimental group children were assessed again when their average age was 13 years, with similar results. The 9 children who were placed in regular classrooms were virtually indistinguishable from same-age normal peers.

All children with autism benefit from early intervention, but it remains unclear how much the rate of progress depends on the child's IQ and language ability, and what the long-term outcomes will be (Rogers, 1998; Smith, Eikeseth, Klevstrand, & Lovaas, 1997). The question of whether young children with autism can achieve full recovery following early intensive intervention continues to be hotly debated (Gresham & MacMillan, 1997a, 1997b; Smith & Lovaas, 1997), and further controlled research is needed before this issue can be resolved. The range of outcomes for three children who were treated in the UCLA Young Autism Project is described in Box 10.5.

Training and Counseling Family Members.
The uncertainties surrounding the causes, diagnosis, and treatment of autism have led many parents to become self-taught experts on their child's disorder. Given the wide range of services that are typically needed to meet the needs of children with autism, parents must be more than just parents. As one mother of a child with autism put it, "parents have to be spokespersons, lobbyists, coordinators, counselors, realists, and dreamers, and very often . . . they have to be downright obnoxious" (Randall, 1993, p. 10). Since parents are the ones who spend the most time with their children, their knowledge and insights into their child's behavior contribute directly to the formulation of treatment plans and to the maintenance and generalization of skills learned in treatment. Active parental involvement in treatment may also serve to increase parents' feelings of connectedness with their child and their sense of competence as parents, to reduce stress, and to facilitate their own feelings of well-being (Dawson & Osterling, 1997).

Parent training gives parents of children with autism the specific skills needed to reduce their child's disruptive

Box 10.5

Chris, Val, and Neils: The UCLA Young Autism Project

CHRIS: AUTISM WITH MODERATE MENTAL RETARDATION

PRETREATMENT

Chris stopped talking at 18 months. At pretreatment he would not respond to his name. He had no toy play, no peer play, spun tops and knobs and sifted sand. He had frequent temper tantrums. If angry, Chris would bite his mother or brother.

CURRENT FUNCTIONING

During a ten-year period, Chris received over 15,000 hours of one-to-one instruction. However, Chris's IQ remained unchanged. But his adaptive and self-help skills improved, so that now he is actively involved in family life.

LANGUAGE SKILLS

Mother: *Language skills are very difficult for Chris, so we pair up the signed word and the spoken word. Over the last ten years Chris has learned about 200 words. We chose these words because we felt they were important for him to use in his everyday living.*

FUTURE PLANS

Mother: *We've been working very hard over the last ten years, some of which has been a struggle. We hope that by the age of 20 Chris will be employed as a bus boy or a chef's helper, or perhaps a gardening job. He could live in our home, or he could live in a community group home; it's still open.*

VAL: AUTISM WITH MILD MENTAL RETARDATION

PRETREATMENT

Val was echolalic, was very aggressive, had no toy play or peer play, and rejected affection. He excessively flapped his hands while gazing at them, smelled objects, and paced in patterns across the floor.

CURRENT FUNCTIONING

After treatment, Val's IQ rose 23 points, from 34 to 57, and he improved sufficiently to be placed in classes with language or mildly delayed children.
Mother: *His language is pretty good now but I know that he needs to improve more. . . . Because when he talks. . . he has a hard time to get the words together.*

LANGUAGE SKILLS

Val converses with his therapist.
V: *What did you do—the weekend?*
T: *I went to Disneyland.*
V: *And what did you ride?*
T: *What did I ride? Let's see. I went on Pirates of the Caribbean, and the Matterhorn.*
V: *I didn't ride on Matterhorn.*
T: *You didn't? Why?*
V: *Cause I'm scared.*

FUTURE PLANS

Mother: *I don't know about school, if he'll be able to finish school, but I have the feeling he'll probably be able to work. For the kind of work my husband does, he doesn't need to know a lot of things. The only thing he needs to know how to do—math, is he has to know how to charge. But you know, to set up tile, I think, it's not too hard. And I think he'll be able to do that.*

NEILS: AUTISM WITHOUT MENTAL RETARDATION

PRETREATMENT

Neils had no toy play or peer play, acted as if blind and deaf, and rejected adult attention. He stared at rotating fans, paced, spun himself, and lined objects. His mother was particularly concerned that he did not speak or interact with any other children.
Mother: *He was nonverbal, or didn't talk. He just sort of lived in his own little world. He'd sit out in the sand box and sift sand.*

CURRENT FUNCTIONING

Following intensive treatment, Neils' IQ rose from the retarded to the superior range.
Mother: *He is going to gifted and talented classes here in school and they consider him gifted in the areas of mathematics and science. Neils is one of these three boys. Nine years after treatment at age 14 he is indistinguishable from other boys his age.*

LANGUAGE SKILLS

Neils' language skills appear to be normal:
Interviewer: *Are there any things that bother you, that you worry about?*
Neils: *I guess, uh, not making very good grades and not being able to get into a place I want to go after I graduate from high school. . . . I think I'm a more outgoing person, because of the therapy. And if I didn't have the therapy I'd be clammed up, hiding in a corner all my life.*

FUTURE PLANS

Neils: *When I graduate from high school the reason I want to go to the air force academy is my dad served in the air force for over 20 years, and I think I have a pretty good chance of getting in.*

Source: Behavior Treatment of Autistic Children, produced by E. L. Anderson.

behavior and to increase adaptive behavior, communication, and social responsiveness. Parent training may include lectures, readings, demonstrations of treatment techniques, practice with feedback, tests of mastery, home visits, telephone consultations, and follow-up contacts directed at maintaining progress in treatment. Parents often participate in face-to-face group discussions with other parents of children with autism that focus on solving practical problems at home and school, and on sharing information about professionals, resources, and services, such as respite care or short-term residential treatment. Research has found that parents' mastery of specific skills, such as "shaping" behavior, and the number of hours parents spend working with their child are predictive of the child's progress in specific areas, such as language, and the maintenance of this progress over time (Newsom, 1998). Although parents continue to use reinforcement and behavior management procedures informally, most eventually stop using structured teaching sessions in the home because of employment, illness, other demands on their time, and the needs of other family members. Although parent training clearly results in progress, it is not yet clear whether such efforts appreciably alter long-term outcomes for the child with regard to residential placement or employment prospects (Howlin & Rutter, 1987).

In addition to specific skill training, work with families of children with autism typically provides support and guidance for the practical, emotional, and interpersonal problems associated with raising a severely handicapped child. Such problems represent a potential source of stress for parents, which can be reduced through the availability of social support and counseling. Practical concerns may include lack of community resources, difficulty locating appropriate educational and health services, the burden of extra medical expenses and costs of summer programs, and difficulty finding time away from the daily demands of caring for a severely disturbed child. At an emotional level, most parents of children with autism experience guilt, depression, anger, and feelings of helplessness at one time or another. These may be normal reactions to difficult circumstances that can be attenuated with counseling, or in some cases, they may be severe enough to require more intensive therapy. Interpersonal family problems related to raising a child with autism may include marital difficulties and strain, and the normal siblings' feelings of resentment or embarrassment about their sibling with autism, restricted opportunities for participating in activities, perceived burden in caring for or interacting with their sibling, and reduced parental attention. Friends, grandparents, coworkers, or even strangers may sometimes provide criticism or unsolicited advice. Counseling and support groups may help parents cope with these kinds of interpersonal problems. Many parents also find support outside the family on the Internet, where they can participate in on-line discussion groups, and find sources of information and mailing lists, allowing them to share ideas and resources and providing mutual emotional support.

A critical factor in helping families adapt to the demands associated with raising a child with autism is avoiding an exclusively negative focus. Emphasizing small gains, endowing the child's disorder with a higher significance through faith or a focus on improvement, developing a close supportive relationship with one's spouse, focusing on relationships in the family, and developing interests and activities not directly related to their child are all methods that parents perceive as important in helping them maintain a more positive focus in coping with their child with autism (Bristol, 1984).

CHILDHOOD-ONSET SCHIZOPHRENIA

> I have a special power in my nose and I can control what's on TV and what people say or do. (Nichols, 1995, p. 73)

This statement by a young girl with schizophrenia highlights the seriousness of this disorder. The term *childhood schizophrenia* has previously been applied to a highly diverse mix of children with little in common other than their experience of a profound and chronic disturbance in early childhood (Rutter, 1972). The label was often applied to children who displayed borderline or no psychotic symptoms and who by today's standards would likely be diagnosed with autism, PDD, or some other disorder. Unlike children with autism, those with schizophrenia typically have a later age of onset of their problem, show less intellectual impairment, display less severe social and language deficits, develop hallucinations and delusions as they get older, and experience periods of remission and relapse. Earlier approaches to diagnosis attempted to construct a category for childhood schizophrenia that was distinct from schizophrenia in adults. However, it has now been shown that the criteria used to diagnose schizophrenia in adults can be used reliably to diagnose schizophrenia in children (Werry, 1992). Thus, rather than being a distinct form of schizophrenia, early-onset or **childhood-onset schizophrenia (COS)** appears to be a more severe form of adult-onset schizophrenia.

Schizophrenia in children and adults is one of several **psychotic disorders** characterized by severe symptoms, such as bizarre delusions, hallucinations, disturbances in thinking, grossly disorganized or catatonic (motor dysfunctions ranging from wild agitation to immobility) behavior, extremely inappropriate or flat affect, and significant deterioration or impairment in functioning. In the initial stages of the disorder the afflicted individual may have difficulty concentrating, sleeping, or doing schoolwork, and may start to avoid friends. As the illness progresses, the individual may begin to speak incoherently and see or hear things that no one else does. Periods of improvement may be followed by terrifying relapses characterized by disordered thinking, in which the individual leaps illogically from one idea to another. The individual may experience hallucinations, paranoia, and delusions. In their psychotic phases individuals with schizophrenia may be convinced that they have godlike powers or that people are spying on them. When in the grips of a psychosis, the individual may behave unpredictably and may become violent and suicidal.

Several of the clinical features of COS are illustrated in the case of Mary, a girl who first began to display symptoms of the disorder when she was about 10 years old:

Mary: Depressed, Disorderly, Doomed

Mary had always been a very shy child. At times, she would become mute, had severe difficulties making friends, was frequently oppositional, and occasionally wet the bed. By the time she reached roughly 10 years of age, Mary showed academic difficulties in addition to continuing social isolation. She became depressed, felt that the devil was trying to make her do bad things, believed that her teacher was trying to hurt her, and became preoccupied with germs. Her behavior became increasingly disorganized; she talked of killing herself, appeared disheveled, and ran in front of a moving car in an apparent suicide attempt.

This episode precipitated an inpatient psychiatric evaluation where Mary continued to show bizarre behavior. She lapsed into periods of intense anxiety and had one episode of uncontrolled screaming. At times she would stare blankly into space and was frequently mute. Although Mary's functioning improved during hospitalization and she returned to her family, throughout her childhood and adolescence she was tormented by fears, hallucinations, the belief that others were out to get her, and occasional bouts of depression often accompanied by suicide attempts. She continued to be socially isolated and withdrawn, and to perform poorly at school. At age 17, after several brief inpatient hospitalizations, Mary was admitted to a state hospital where she remained until the age of

19. During this period her affect was increasingly flat, and her psychotic symptoms persisted. One week after discharge from the hospital, Mary went into her room, locked the door, and overdosed on her medications. She was found dead the next morning. (J. R. Asarnow & R. F. Asarnow, 1996)

Mary's tragic story illustrates several key features of COS. First, although most cases have their onsets in late adolescence or early adulthood, schizophrenia does occur in childhood. Second, COS has an insidious rather than an acute onset in childhood, with the child displaying a wide range of impairments that precede his or her psychotic symptoms. Third, when the disorder is present in childhood, the child's symptoms are likely to persist into adolescence and adulthood. Fourth, when the disorder occurs in childhood, it has a profound negative impact on the child's developing social and academic competence. And finally, Mary's futile struggle with schizophrenia underscores the tremendous pain and personal suffering experienced by children and adolescents with this illness (J. R. Asarnow & R. F. Asarnow, 1996).

DSM-IV: Defining Features of Schizophrenia

DSM-IV criteria for schizophrenia include the following (DSM-IV Copyright © 1994 by APA):

A. *Characteristic symptoms:* At least two or more of the following symptoms are present for a significant portion of time during a 1-month period.

   (1) delusions
   (2) hallucinations
   (3) disorganized speech (e.g., frequent derailment or incoherence)
   (4) grossly disorganized or catatonic behavior
   (5) negative symptoms, i.e., affective flattening, alogia, or avolition

   If delusions are bizarre or if hallucinations consist of a running commentary about the person or two or more conversing voices, then just one of these symptoms is required to make the diagnosis.

B. *Social/occupational dysfunction:* Since the onset of the disturbance there is a significant decrement in one or more areas of functioning or a failure to achieve expected level of interpersonal, academic, or occupational achievement.

C. *Duration:* Continuous signs of disturbance must persist for at least 6 months.

In addition, the disorder cannot be attributable to mood disorder or schizoaffective disorder and is not due to substance use or a general medical condition. If there is a history of autistic disorder or another PDD, the additional diagnosis of schizophrenia is made only if prominent delusions or hallucinations are also present for at least a month.

The use of the same diagnostic criteria for children and adults facilitates comparisons between cases of early- and later-onset schizophrenia and the identification of continuities in the disorder over the course of development. However, schizophrenia may be expressed differently at different ages. For example, hallucinations, delusions, and formal thought disturbances are extremely rare and difficult to diagnose before the age of 7; when they do occur, they may be less complex and reflect childhood themes (Caplan, 1994). A failure to adjust diagnostic criteria for developmental changes may overlook children who show early signs of schizophrenia but may not develop the full-blown adult type until a later age. Other developmental considerations may also come into play in making a diagnosis. For example, it is sometimes difficult to distinguish between pathological symptoms such as delusions and the rich, imaginative fantasies that are typical of many young children. One difference between children and adults with schizophrenia is that young children may not experience their psychotic symptoms as distressing or disorganizing. Thus, when psychotic symptoms appear early in development, children may have difficulty distinguishing them from normal experience (Russell, 1994).

Psychotic Symptoms

The most common presenting symptom for children with schizophrenia is auditory hallucinations, which have been found to occur in approximately 80% of documented cases with an onset prior to age 11. About 40% to 60% of children with schizophrenia also experience visual hallucinations, delusions, and thought disorder (Caplan, 1994; Russell, Bott, & Samons, 1989). Examples of psychotic symptoms reported by children with schizophrenia are presented in Box 10.6.

Related Symptoms and Comorbidities

Children with schizophrenia often display other symptoms and disorders, such as depression, ADHD, oppositional and conduct problems, and suicidal tendencies. About 68% meet criteria for another diagnosis, most commonly conduct/oppositional disorder (31%) or depression (37%) (Russell, Bott, & Sammons, 1989). Given links that have historically been made between autism and schizophrenia, it is of interest that children

with schizophrenia do not show an elevated risk of autism or PDD. The rate of schizophrenia in children with autism is approximately 0.6%, which is comparable to the rate of schizophrenia in the general population. Thus, autism and COS are distinguishable syndromes.

For a majority of children with COS, the onset of their disorder is gradual rather than acute, with nearly 90% exhibiting a clear history of behavioral and psychiatric disturbance before the onset of psychosis (Russell, 1994). For example, Mary was oppositional and had difficulty making friends well before she began to display psychotic symptoms. Given this kind of developmental history, it is difficult to determine whether the related symptoms of COS are precursors of schizophrenia, early manifestations of the disorder, or co-occurring conditions (J. R. Asarnow & R. F. Asarnow, 1996).

PREVALENCE

Schizophrenia is extremely rare in children under 12 years of age, increases in frequency in adolescence, and has a modal age of onset between 20 and 25 years. Prevalence estimates of schizophrenia in childhood have ranged from .14 to 1.0 child in 10,000 (Burd & Kerbeshian, 1987; Remschmidt, Schulz, Martin, Warnke, & Trott, 1994). Although preliminary, these estimates suggest that schizophrenia occurs 100 times more frequently in adults than in children. COS has an earlier age of onset in boys, and is about twice as common in boys as in girls, although the gender difference disappears in adolescence (Frazier et al., 1997; Remschmidt et al., 1994). The reasons for the excess of males with COS are not known; a greater general biological vulnerability of males for neurological disorders and different etiological processes have both been suggested as possibilities. For adults, rates of schizophrenia are higher in lower socioeconomic groups. However, there is little information regarding the relationship between social class and schizophrenia in childhood. In a related vein, the incidence rates and pattern of symptoms in adults with schizophrenia are quite similar across cultures and countries, but again, little information regarding cross-cultural patterns is available for children (J. Asarnow & R. Asarnow, 1994).

CAUSES

Current views regarding the causes of schizophrenia are based on a **vulnerability-stress model** that emphasizes the interplay among vulnerability, stress, and protective factors. Vulnerability factors are predisposing conditions, such as genetic risk, central nervous system impair-

Box 10.6

Psychotic Symptoms in Children with Schizophrenia

HALLUCINATIONS

Auditory: Unrelated to affective state. A 7-year-old boy stated, "Everything is talking, the walls, the furniture, I just know they're talking."

Auditory: Command. An 8-year-old boy stated, "I once heard a noise coming from the south and the east; one told me to jump off the roof and one told me to smash my mom."

Auditory: Conversing. An 8-year-old boy stated, "I can hear the devil talk—God interrupts him and the devil says 'shut up God.' God and the devil are always fighting."

Auditory: Religious. An 11-year-old boy heard God's voice saying, "Sorry D., but I can't help you now, I am helping someone else." He also reported hearing Jesus and the devil.

Auditory: Persecutory. A 9-year-old boy reported voices calling him bad names, and threatening that if he doesn't do what he is told something bad will happen to him.

Auditory: Commenting. An 8-year-old girl reported an angel saying things like, "You didn't cry today" and "You've been a very nice girl today."

Visual. A 12-year-old boy saw a ghost (man) with red, burned, scarred, and cut face on multiple occasions and in different locations. He had been seeing this since age 5.

Tactile. An 8-year-old boy felt the devil touching him and moving his body "so he can make me come and live with him."

Somatic. An 8-year-old girl reported feeling an angel, babies and devil inside her arm, and that she could feel them fighting.

DELUSIONS

Bizarre. A 9-year-old boy was convinced he was a dog (his parents were German Shepherds) and was growing fur, and on one occasion, refused to leave a veterinarian's office unless he received a shot.

Persecutory. A girl believed that the "evil one" was trying to poison her orange juice.

Somatic. An 11-year-old boy described "waste" produced when the good and bad voices fought with each other; the "waste" came out of his feet when he swam in chlorinated pools.

Reference. An 8-year-old girl believed that people outside of her house were staring and pointing at her trying to send her a message to come outside. She also believed that people on the TV were talking to her because they used the word "you."

Grandiose. An 11-year-old boy had the firm belief that he was "different" and able to kill people. He felt that when "God zooms through me [him]" he became very strong and developed big muscles.

THOUGHT DISORDER

"I used to have a Mexican dream. I was watching TV in the family room. I disappeared outside of this world and then I was in a closet. Sounds like a vacuum dream. It's a Mexican dream. When I was close to that dream earth, I was turning upside down. I don't like to turn upside down. Sometimes I have Mexican dreams and vacuum dreams. It's real hard to scream in dreams."

Source: Adapted from Russell, 1994.

---

ment, inadequate learning opportunities, or deviant patterns of family interaction. Stressors are events that heighten the likelihood of a schizophrenic episode and may include major life-change events such as the death of a parent, or chronic stressors such as ongoing child abuse. Protective factors are conditions that reduce the risk of a schizophrenic episode in individuals who are at risk and may include intelligence, social competence, or supportive family relationships.

A vulnerability-stress model recognizes the complex and diverse pathways that may lead to schizophrenia. For example, a child who has a genetic risk for schizophrenia may experience central nervous system impairments that lead to deficits in attention and information processing. Such deficits in a child of low intelligence who is exposed to a deviant family environment may increase the risk of a schizophrenic episode, whereas the same impairments in a child of high intelligence with a

supportive family environment may not. Thus, the onset of schizophrenia will depend on the interactions among enduring psychobiological vulnerabilities, environmental and biological stressors, and the protective effects of child and family competencies and resources for coping. Although there is a genetic predisposition for schizophrenia, schizophrenic episodes are likely to occur only in vulnerable individuals who are exposed to certain levels and types of stressors, and who possess few resources for coping (J. R. Asarnow & R. F. Asarnow, 1996).

Biological Factors

Preliminary evidence suggests a strong genetic loading for schizophrenia in childhood. The rate of schizophrenia among relatives of youngsters with COS is about twice that for family members of adults with schizophrenia. One early twin study found concordance rates of

88% and 23%, respectively, for identical versus fraternal twins with schizophrenia with an onset prior to 15 years of age (Kallman & Roth, 1956). Although better-controlled research is needed, these findings suggest that preadolescent schizophrenia may represent a more severe form of adult schizophrenia with virtually complete penetrance (Rosenthal, 1970). Although a variety of genetic anomalies have been reported for schizophrenic adults (De Lisi & Lovett, 1991), similar data are not yet available for children, although there has been one reported case of a translocation involving chromosomes 1 and 7 (Gordon, Krasnewich, White, Lenane, & Rapoport, 1994).

The presence of central nervous system dysfunction among individuals with schizophrenia and the dramatic improvements associated with medication suggest that schizophrenia is a disorder of the brain. However, no unitary brain lesion has been identified in all cases, and the lesions that have been found in some cases are not specific to schizophrenia. Weinberger (1987) has presented a neurodevelopmental model of schizophrenia in which a fixed brain lesion involving the limbic system and prefrontal cortex is believed to be present early in life. This lesion does not lead to active psychotic symptoms until a certain level of normal maturation of the dopaminergic neural mechanisms involved in the activation of the prefrontal cortex has taken place. A breakdown in these mechanisms increases susceptibility to stress in individuals with schizophrenia. The hypothesis that dopaminergic dysfunction is involved in schizophrenia is supported by findings that drugs, such as the phenothiazines, that block dopaminergic transmission reduce psychotic symptoms in adults, whereas those that produce an excessive release of dopamine, such as amphetamine or L-dopa, are associated with a heightening of psychotic symptoms. A model of early-occurring neural pathology in schizophrenia is consistent with findings that children with this disorder display developmental impairments well before the onset of their psychotic symptoms—for example, in their expressive language and in gross and fine motor skills. Early difficulties in social behavior are also common, characterized by a lack of social responsiveness during infancy, and extreme moodiness, inappropriate clinging, and unexplained rage reactions during early childhood (J. R. Asarnow & R. F. Asarnow, 1996).

Few autopsy, brain imaging, or neurochemical studies of children with schizophrenia have been conducted. However, consistent with findings for adults, the limited evidence that is available suggests the presence of diverse anatomical and neurological anomalies. For example, an autopsy study of a man who died at age 22 and had his first onset of schizophrenia when he was about 10 years old found abnormalities in several brain regions, including the brain stem, thalamus, and frontal cortex (Casanova, Carosella, & Kleinman, 1990). MRI and PET scan findings suggest increased size of the left ventricular horn and abnormalities in glucose metabolism (Gordon, Frazier, et al., 1994; Hendren, Hodde-Vargas, Vargas, Orrison, & Dell, 1991). Recent MRI studies have reported smaller total cerebral volume and a strong relationship between smaller cerebral volume and negative symptoms in children with schizophrenia (Alaghband-Rad, Hamburger, Giedd, Frazier, & Rapoport, 1997; Frazier et al., 1996). Such findings are highly suggestive of disrupted early brain development in children with schizophrenia.

Neuropsychological and other test findings have found that children with schizophrenia show many of the same deficits in attention and information processing found in adults with schizophrenia. The performance of children with schizophrenia on information-processing tasks is disrupted by increasing the amount of information to be processed. Moreover, recordings of brain activity during task performance suggest limitations in resources available for cognitive processing, findings which are consistent with those for adults with schizophrenia (Strandburg, Marsh, Brown, Asarnow, & Guthrie, 1994). Neuropsychological findings for children with schizophrenia may be summarized as follows (R. F. Asarnow et al., 1994):

❖ impaired performance when required to attend to, remember, and respond to sequences of verbal and nonverbal stimuli that make excessive demands on processing capacity
❖ impairments on tests of visual perception, but only when memory demands are added to the task, such as holding a sample stimulus in short-term memory before responding
❖ impairments in visual-motor coordination and fine motor speed
❖ impairments in executive functions

These findings suggest a deficit in central nervous system structures involved in recruiting and allocating resources for processing information.

Environmental Factors

COS is a familial disorder, but the less than 100% concordance rates for identical twins suggest that nongenetic influences contribute to the likelihood that a child will develop schizophrenia. The elevated risk of psychiatric illness in parents of children with schizophrenia will likely have a negative effect on parental role functioning. Higher rates of prenatal and perinatal complications have been found among adults with schizophrenia and in high-risk children of schizophrenic parents who developed schizophrenia (Cannon, Barr, & Mednick, 1991; McNeil, 1988). The possible causal influence of such early environmental stressors in some cases of schizophrenia is also suggested by reports of elevated rates of adult schizophrenia among those exposed to viral infection during the second trimester of pregnancy (Mednick, Machon, Huttunen, & Bonett, 1988).

The influence of psychosocial stress in the etiology of schizophrenia is most apparent in studies of high-risk samples in which the onset of schizophrenia is associated with significant psychosocial stress on the family. However, because of its rarity, very few cases of COS have been identified in high-risk samples. There was one report of two high-risk children who developed schizophrenia at age 10. Although no conclusions can be drawn from such a small sample, it is of interest that these were the only children in the sample who had been physically abused, both were raised by schizophrenic mothers, and both showed transient lags and disorganization in their gross motor and/or visual motor development occurring with delays in physical growth (Fish, 1987). A study of the home environments of siblings and fraternal twins of children with schizophrenia found that disturbed child-rearing environments were more likely to be associated with schizophrenia-spectrum outcomes (Kallman & Roth, 1956); 82% of the homes of twins and siblings diagnosed as schizoid or schizophrenic included a disturbed or inadequate parent, economic distress, or a broken home, in contrast to 65% of the homes of twins and siblings with healthy outcomes. The generally high level of difficulties in these families may reflect the fact that all included at least one child with schizophrenia.

A series of interesting studies have been conducted describing the family environments of children with schizophrenia and those with **schizotypal personality disorder (SPD)** (J. R. Asarnow, Tompson, & Goldstein, 1994). Individuals with SPD show social and interpersonal deficits marked by acute discomfort with close relationships and by cognitive and perceptual distortions and eccentricities. Although the diagnosis of SPD is controversial in childhood, schizotypal symptoms such as social isolation and thought disturbance may be precursors of schizophrenia (J. R. Asarnow, 1988). For example, raters can distinguish between children who later developed schizophrenia as adults and their healthy siblings by observing home movies that were made before the age of 8 years (Walker & Lewine, 1990).

Parents of children with schizophrenia or SPD score higher than parents of children who are depressed on **communication deviance**, a measure of interpersonal signs of attentional and thought disturbance. Children from families with high communication deviance showed the most severe impairment and the poorest attentional functioning. These findings suggest that communication deviance may be associated with a severe form of schizophrenia or that family interaction may worsen the severity of dysfunction (J. R. Asarnow, Goldstein, & Ben-Meir, 1988). Parents of children with schizophrenia are also more likely to use harsh criticism of their children relative to parents of depressed children or normal controls.

In general, family findings highlight the stress, distress, and personal tragedy that is often experienced by families of children with schizophrenia (J. R. Asarnow & R. F. Asarnow, 1996). In the words of June Beeby, the mother of 17-year-old Matthew, who was diagnosed with schizophrenia and believed that God wanted his mother and his sister to die: "It's quite horrendous. First of all, you've got somebody that you love, a child that you've raised. And then suddenly, the child becomes a crazy person" (Nichols, 1995, p. 70). On a dark and cold winter day, June Beeby arrived home to find her son dead in a pool of blood. "He had taken two ordinary dinner knives . . . and plunged them into his eyes until they pierced his brain" (p. 70). In a diary entry that he had made 2 years before he took his life, Matthew had described an encounter with God: "He used his power and he controlled my brain for nine months. . . . God wanted me to feel that I would die, in order for individuals to live forever in heaven" (p. 74).

TREATMENT

> As a parent you feel you have a tremendous responsibility to keep a son or daughter safe. . . . But when your child is schizophrenic you can't do that, because the person doesn't want help. (Nichols, 1995, p. 73)

Schizophrenia is a chronic disorder with a bleak long-term outcome for most sufferers. However, the outcome for most afflicted individuals is vastly improved over what it once was, with antipsychotic drugs making the difference. Although we know far less about the use of these drugs with children than with adults, pharmacological treatments, particularly **neuroleptics,** are widely used to treat children with schizophrenia. Neuroleptics are dopamine agonists that increase neurotransmitter activity and diminish delusions, hallucinations, and aggressive behavior in psychotic individuals. However, they sometimes have serious side effects. Preliminary reports indicate that alternative medications such as haloperidol and clozapine (a weak dopamine antagonist) may be effective in treating psychotic symptoms in previously untreatable children and adolescents, with fewer serious side effects. Further research that compares the relative efficacy of alternative medications, various side effects, and possible complications is needed (J. R. Asarnow &

R. F. Asarnow, 1996). Although medications may help control psychotic symptoms in children with schizophrenia, the need for psychosocial treatments, such as social skills training, family intervention, and special school placement, is also widely recognized in clinical practice. Many advances have occurred in the psychosocial treatment of adults with schizophrenia; however, few controlled studies have been conducted with children.

SUMMARY

Autism

1. Autistic disorder (autism) is one of the pervasive developmental disorders (PDDs). PDDs are characterized by severe and widespread impairments in social interaction and communication skills, and stereotyped patterns of behaviors, interests, and activities.
2. Autism and schizophrenia in childhood were previously lumped together as a single condition; now, however, it is recognized they are separate disorders.
3. Autism has increasingly come to be recognized as a biologically based lifelong developmental disability that is present in the first few years of life.

Core Characteristics

4. Children with autism experience profound difficulties in relating to other people, including deficits in orienting to social stimuli, imitating others, sharing a focus of attention with others, and noticing and understanding other people's feelings.
5. Children with autism display serious abnormalities in communication and language, including deficits in the use of preverbal vocalizations and gestures, language oddities such as pronoun reversal and echolalia, and difficulties with the appropriate use of language in social contexts.
6. Children with autism display stereotyped and repetitive patterns of behaviors, interests, and activities that include obsessive routines and rituals, abnormal preoccupations, insistence on sameness, or stereotyped body movements.
7. About 80% of children with autism also have mental retardation; approximately 60% have IQs less than 50, and 20% have IQs between 50 and 70. About 20% of children with autism have average intelligence or above, with IQs higher than 70.
8. Sensory-perceptual abnormalities and deficits are common in children with autism and include oversensitivities or undersensitivities to certain stimuli, overselective and impaired shifting of attention to sensory input, and impairments in mixing across sensory modalities.
9. Children with autism display a deficit in theory of mind (ToM)—the ability to understand other people's and one's own mental states, including beliefs, intentions, feelings, and desires.
10. Children with autism display a general deficit in higher-order planning and regulatory behaviors (e.g., executive functions).

Family Characteristics

11. Nonautistic relatives of individuals with autism display higher-than-normal rates of social, language, and cognitive deficits that are similar in quality to those found in autism, but are less severe and are not associated with intellectual deficits or epilepsy. The risk for affective disorder in family members of children with autism is about 3 times greater than for family members of normal children.

Prevalence

12. Autism is a rare disorder that affects approximately 4 to 5 children per 10,000, and is 3 to 4 times more common in boys than girls. Autism is found across all social classes and has been identified in every country in which it has been sought.
13. Autism is most often identified around age 2 years or older, although elements are probably present at a much earlier age. Most children with autism show gradual improvement of their symptoms with age, although they continue to display social impairments that make them different from others throughout their lives.
14. The two strongest predictors of adult outcomes in children with autism are IQ and language development.

Causes

15. It is now generally accepted that autism is a biologically based neurodevelopmental disorder that may result from multiple causes.
16. Autism is a genetic condition, although the specific genetic sites have yet to be identified.
17. Neuropsychological impairments occur in many areas of functioning, including intelligence, attention, memory, language, and executive functions.
18. Structural abnormalities in the cerebellum and the medial temporal lobe and related limbic system structures have been found.

Treatment

19. Most treatments are directed at maximizing the child's potential and helping the child and family cope more effectively with the disorder.

20. The most effective treatments for children with autism use highly structured skills-oriented strategies that are tailored to the individual child, and that provide education and supportive counseling for the family.

Childhood-Onset Schizophrenia

21. Unlike children with autism, those with schizophrenia have a later age of onset, show less intellectual impairment, display less severe social and language deficits, develop hallucinations and delusions as they get older, and experience periods of remission and relapse.

22. Childhood-onset schizophrenia is a more severe form of adult-onset schizophrenia, rather than a different disorder.

23. Schizophrenia in children is a psychotic disorder characterized by severe symptoms, such as bizarre delusions, hallucinations, disturbances in thinking, grossly disorganized behavior, extremely inappropriate or flat affect, and significant deterioration or impairment in functioning.

24. Schizophrenia is extremely rare in children under 12 years of age, occurring much less often than in adolescents and adults.

25. Current views regarding the causes of schizophrenia are based on a vulnerability-stress model that emphasizes the interplay among vulnerability, stress, and protective factors.

26. Neuroleptics are commonly used to treat children with schizophrenia but often have serious side effects. Although medications may help control psychotic symptoms in children with schizophrenia, psychosocial treatments, such as social skills training, family intervention, and special school placement, are also needed.

KEY TERMS

pervasive developmental disorders (PDDs), 372
autism, 372
schizophrenia, 372
delusions, 372
hallucinations, 372

preservation of sameness, 373
early infantile autism, 373
psychogenic theory, 373
autistic disorder, 374
spectrum disorder, 375
joint social attention, 378
protoimperative gestures, 380
protodeclarative gestures, 380
showing gestures, 380
instrumental gestures, 381
expressive gestures, 381
pronoun reversal, 382
echolalia, 382
perseverative speech, 382
pragmatics, 382
self-stimulatory behaviors, 383
splinter skills, 385
islets of ability, 385
autistic savants, 385
sensory dominance, 385
stimulus overselectivity, 386
theory of mind (ToM), 387
mentalization, 387
false belief, 388
central coherence, 389
self-injurious behavior (SIB), 392
Asperger's disorder (AD), 392
Rett's disorder, 392
childhood disintegrative disorder, 392
pervasive developmental disorder not otherwise specified (PDD-NOS), 393
apraxia, 394
Checklist for Autism in Toddlers (CHAT), 395
tuberous sclerosis, 397
readiness skills, 405
discrete trial training, 405
incidental training, 405
operant speech training, 407
sign language training, 407
childhood-onset schizophrenia (COS), 411
psychotic disorders, 411
vulnerability-stress model, 413
schizotypal personality disorder (SPD), 416
communication deviance, 416
neuroleptics, 416

Communication and Learning Disorders

Picture yourself having important needs and ideas you want to express but not being able to get them across. Sights and sounds may surround you, but you cannot focus your attention enough to make sense of them. When you are shown how to read or add numbers, you find the letters and numbers look too much alike. Although different from person to person, these difficulties make up the common daily experiences of many children, adolescents, and adults with communication and learning disorders. Everyday tasks, like reading homework assignments, can become confusing and frustrating, leading sometimes to a cycle of academic failure and lowered self-esteem.

Children and adults with communication or learning disorders can learn, and they are as intelligent as others. The disorders usually affect only certain limited areas of learning; rarely are they severe enough to impair a person's pursuit of a normal life, but they can make life very stressful. Consider the experiences of James and Francine:

James: Fear and Frustration

James, age 9, was a growing concern for his teacher: "James is obviously a very bright boy, and he wants to do well, I can tell. I've noticed that he likes art, and is always wanting to draw. But he gets really upset when I ask him to do some work in class. He looks like he dreads going to school. And he complains that some words he tries to read don't make sense to him. I'm worried that his increasing frustration is going to cause other problems in school or with friends. Sometimes he gets mad at something and he has trouble calming down. If he is trying to create something that doesn't turn out the way he envisioned it, he explodes, slams his fist on something, or hits his head against the wall."

What James's mother was hearing from his teacher was all too familiar. All summer he had been anxious about starting school, and he would fuss about being in day camp or at soccer practice. She knew that her son would get involved in something only if he could do it his own way. Her mind wandered briefly to when he was a toddler and would sometimes get so anxious and worried about something that he had trouble sleeping or felt sick. She shared with his teacher her frustration at trying to find out what the problem was: "Getting him to read at home is like pulling teeth, and he will not read at all on his own because he knows he can't read many of the words."

Francine: Alone and Withdrawn

Francine, age 7, was entering a new school, for the second time in 2 years. Her first school proved to be too challenging for her, and the other kids teased her because she "doesn't know what 2 plus 2 is." She is content to play for hours by herself and is not interested in the things that other kids her age are doing. "Most of the time," her mother explained, "Francine seems humorless and in a bit of a fog." Although school performance was a major concern, her mother was also quite worried about Francine's lack of friends and the way other children treated her.

Her mother and father were proud sharing their daughter's early childhood history and developmental milestones with me during our first interview. "Francine walked before she was a year old, and was a very talkative baby and toddler, who picked up new words quite quickly. She was a healthy and normal baby—we can't figure out why she seems so uninterested in school and other kids." They went on to explain: "When she entered preschool and kindergarten, she seemed uninterested in making friends. The other kids basically ignored her, even though she didn't do anything to bother them. My husband and I didn't think much of it at first. In fact, we bragged about how our daughter took an early interest in reading and would spend a lot of her time alone with a book or magazine, even when she was 4 or 5, although she didn't usually understand what she read. But we grew more concerned around age 5 because she paid little attention to popular movies, toys, and things other kids her age played with. When she was a preschooler, we also noticed that she had trouble with numbers and understanding concepts like 'more,' 'less,' or 'bigger.' She knows what these words mean now, but she is still confused when we ask her to count something. Yesterday I gave her her allowance and just for the heck of it, I used pennies, nickels, and dimes to see if she could add them up. No matter how hard we tried, she became confused switching from one coin to the other, and she thought she had a bigger allowance if I stacked the pennies up! And if you ask her to arrange something, like setting the table for dinner, you never know what you'll end up with!"

James and Francine have different learning problems. James's difficulties are with language and reading. His ability to appreciate the different sounds (phonemes) of language is underdeveloped, which is the primary reason for his poorly developed word recognition and poor written spelling ability. Francine's problems, in contrast, are mostly in the *nonverbal* learning areas, such as math. She can read quite well, although she has difficulty understanding some of the more subtle aspects of what she has read. She also confuses terms and instructions that describe spatial or numerical relationships, like setting the table in a certain order or understanding number conservation.

The field of learning and communication disorders, broadly referred to as learning disabilities, has changed dramatically over the past decade. For many years the poorly understood and diverse learning problems reported by persons with difficulties reading or comprehending speech were often attributed to poor motivation on the part of the child or poor instruction on the part of the teacher. Fortunately, recent breakthroughs in neuroimaging techniques have led to increased recognition of the existence of differences in the neurological makeup and development of children and adults who present with problems in language and related cognitive tasks, such as reading. With recent advances in detection and intervention aimed at early language development, children with signs of communication problems are being detected at an early age and provided with alternative teaching methods that build on their developmental strengths.

This chapter emphasizes the relationship between language development and the subsequent appearance of a learning problem once the child attends school. Therefore, communication disorders, which are diagnosed primarily in early childhood, and learning disorders, which are identified most often during early school years, are considered from the standpoint of their interconnected features and underlying causes. This connection is supported by the finding that 85% of children with language impairments at age 4 had a form of learning disability at age 8, even though their language abilities improved as they got older (Tallal, Townsend, Curtiss, & Wulfeck, 1991). The chapter puts these problems in a developmental context; learning disabilities are described and the historical background is presented, followed by an overview of normal development of language and communication, and concluding with a discussion of the clinical features, causes, and treatment of communication and learning disorders.

DESCRIPTION

Learning disability is a general term that refers to learning problems that occur in the absence of other obvious conditions, such as mental retardation or brain damage. The term has been replaced in the DSM-IV by the more specific reference to learning or communication disorders, but its common usage warrants some clarification of how the concept of learning disabilities emerged and how learning disabilities are defined today.

A learning disability affects the manner in which individuals with normal or above-average intelligence take in, retain, or express information. Incoming or outgoing information can become scrambled as it passes between the senses and the brain. Unlike most physical disabilities, a learning disability is a hidden handicap, which often goes undetected in young children (National Institute of Mental Health [NIMH], 1996). Thus children and adults with learning disabilities often have to deal not only with their limitations in reading, writing,

Slowly but surely, most children learn the letters of the alphabet and how to use them to write words. For children with certain learning disabilities, however, the shapes and sounds of different letters continue to be confusing.

or math, but also with the frustration of having to convince others that their invisible disabilities are as legitimate a concern as visible disabilities.

Learning difficulties often show up in schoolwork and can impede learning to read or write or to do math, but they also can affect many other parts of a person's life, including work, daily routines, family life, and friendships. For some, problems in learning are relatively specific and affect a narrow range of ability, whereas others may be challenged almost daily across many different tasks and social situations. Each type of learning disability, whether it is related to reading, writing, math, or language, is characterized by its own distinct definitional and diagnostic issues.

Although precise definitions and full understanding still have a way to go, knowledge of communication and learning disorders is growing by leaps and bounds as a result of increased scientific interest and support for these diverse problems. We now recognize that learning disabilities, though challenging, do not have to be a handicap—many well-known persons with known or suspected learning disabilities used their talents in ways that were exceptional (Orton Dyslexia Society, 1996):

Thomas Edison, inventor
Albert Einstein, physicist
Winston Churchill, British Prime Minister
Woodrow Wilson, U.S. President
George Bush, U.S. President
Tom Cruise, actor

Children with learning disabilities constitute about one-half of all children receiving special education services in the United States today. Prior to 1968, however,

these problems went largely unrecognized as a federally designated handicapping condition (U.S. Department of Education, 1989). Although relatively common, learning disabilities are one of the least understood and most debated groups of problems affecting children.

The field still struggles to decide on an adequate definition of learning disabilities because of their many forms and overlapping symptoms. As a preview to the remainder of the chapter, take a minute to study the following list of major terms. Note especially how the terms and categories related to communication and learning disorders overlap or are connected, as well as how they differ.

Learning disabilities: A general, nondiagnostic term that refers to significant problems in mastering one or more of the following skills: listening, speaking, reading, writing, reasoning, mathematics. Learning disabilities do not include learning problems that are due primarily to visual, hearing, or motor handicaps; to mental retardation; to emotional disturbance; or to environmental disadvantage. Emotional and social disturbances and other adaptive deficiencies may occur along with learning problems, but they do not by themselves constitute a learning disability (adapted from the National Joint Committee on Learning Disabilities, 1988).

Chapter 9 describes intelligence as involving basic underlying cognitive abilities that affect problem solving, verbal skills, and mental reasoning. A discussion of communication and learning disorders needs to go beyond the traditional ways of thinking about intelligence. To a degree, we all have areas of learning and performance that are stronger than others (we enjoy writing and reading, but don't ask us to program your VCR). Similarly, we know that children with these disorders, although they have normal intelligence, show a pattern of relative strengths and weaknesses that can make some learning tasks, such as reading, much more difficult than others. This pattern is noteworthy mostly because it is so extreme and unexpected for a child who otherwise shows normal cognitive and physical development. Recall how Francine had developed normally throughout her early childhood and was able to read quite well; nevertheless, she struggled with numerical and informal mathematical concepts.

The concept of *multiple intelligence* recognizes the diverse forms of intelligence, also referred to as skills or competencies, and suggests that each

Box 11.1
Aspects of Multiple Intelligence

❖ *Linguistic intelligence:* A sensitivity to the meaning, function, and grammatical rules of words, as in writing an essay.

❖ *Musical intelligence:* A sensitivity and creativity in hearing and manipulating tones, rhythms, musical patterns, pitch, and timbre, as in composing a symphony.

❖ *Logical/mathematic intelligence:* The ability to solve problems and see abstract relationships, as in calculus or engineering.

❖ *Spatial intelligence:* A sensitivity to the perception, manipulation, and creation of different forms and contexts, as in painting.

❖ *Bodily/kinesthetic intelligence:* The ability to use the body and the relevant part of the brain to coordinate movements in special and highly coordinated ways, as in dance and athletics.

❖ *Intrapersonal intelligence:* The ability to recognize, define, and pursue inner feelings and thoughts, as in poetry and self-knowledge.

❖ *Interpersonal intelligence:* The ability to sense the moods, feelings, and actions of other people, as in teaching, parenting, and politics.

Source: Based on Gardner, 1993.

type of intelligence is just as important as the others, but for different reasons (see Box 11.1). Broadening the concept of intelligence to include more than logical, mathematical, or language abilities does not make any child smarter than before, but it does help focus attention on individual strengths and uniqueness. Teachers are finding new ways to apply this knowledge in their approach to learning by using the child's strengths to build up the areas of relative weakness.

Communication disorders: A diagnostic term that refers to difficulty producing speech sounds (phonological disorder) or with speech fluency (stuttering); using spoken language to communicate (expressive language disorder); or understanding what other people say (mixed expressive-receptive language disorder). These disorders are developmentally connected to the later onset of learning disorders.

Learning disorders: A diagnostic term that refers to specific problems in reading (disorder of reading, also referred to as **dyslexia**), math (disorder of mathematics), or writing ability (disorder of written expression), as determined by achievement test results that are substantially below what

would be expected for the child's age, schooling, and intellectual ability.

For all intents and purposes, the terms *learning disorders* and *learning disabilities* are often used interchangeably.

Simply stated, the main characteristic shared by all children with learning disabilities is that they do not perform up to their expected level in school. Otherwise, the presentation of symptoms varies tremendously (Taylor, 1988). Despite controversy over definition and scope, the concept of learning disability has brought needed attention to a sizeable number of children and adults who are unable to acquire academic-related skills at a normal rate.

HISTORICAL BACKGROUND

The field of learning disabilities emerged from a need to understand learning and performance problems of children and adults who displayed *specific* deficits in using spoken or written language while maintaining the integrity of their general intellectual functioning. This unexpected pattern of strengths and specific weaknesses in learning was first noted and studied by physicians in the late 19th century who were treating patients with medical injuries (Hammill, 1993). Franz Joseph Gall, a pioneer of language disorders, was struck by what he observed among some of his brain-injured patients: They had lost the capacity to express their feelings and ideas clearly through speech, yet they did not seem to suffer any intellectual impairments. One of his patients could not speak at all, even though he had no problem writing his thoughts on paper. Because he knew that this patient had normal speech before the head injury, Gall reasoned that the problem must have resulted from brain damage that had disrupted the neurological processes related to speech. For the first time, scientists were beginning to pinpoint areas in the brain that control the ability to express and receive language processes.

These early observations, based on known (organic) medical injuries, raised the possibility that persons with learning disabilities may differ from those with mental retardation in terms of *relative strengths and deficits;* that is, such individuals had normal intellectual processes in most areas, but were relatively weaker in others, such as reading or math. This basic premise, now referred to as an **unexpected discrepancy** between measured ability and actual performance, remains at the foundation of today's definition of learning disorders. However, debate now focuses on whether such a discrepancy is *necessary* for distinguishing children with learning disabilities from those without.

The relationship between mental retardation, organic brain damage, and learning problems continued to fascinate scientists, who had a firmer understanding of brain-behavior relationships by the 1940s. But the question still remained as to why some children who did not fit the definition of mental retardation based on IQ nonetheless had significant problems in learning. Could mental retardation be restricted to certain intellectual abilities but not others? Were academic problems the same as those assessed by measures of general intelligence? Straus and Werner (1943) shed light on this issue by pointing out how children learn in their own individual ways, challenging the concept that learning is a relatively uniform, predictable process among nonretarded children. Three important concepts emerged from their work, which continue to influence the field to this day (Lyon, 1996):

1. Children approach learning in different ways, so each child's individual learning style and uniqueness should be recognized and used to full advantage.
2. Educational methods should be tailored to an individual child's pattern of strengths and weaknesses; one method should not be imposed on everyone.
3. Children with learning problems might be helped by teaching methods that strengthen existing abilities rather than emphasize weak areas.

By the early 1960s the modern learning disabilities movement was beginning to take shape. Parents and educators were dissatisfied with the notion that some children with clearly observable learning problems could not receive a suitable diagnosis or treatment (until this time a child often had to be diagnosed with mental retardation to receive special education services). A category was needed to describe those children whose learning problems could not be explained on the basis of mental retardation, lack of learning opportunities, psychopathology, or sensory deficits (Lyon, 1996). Thus, the emerging concept of learning disabilities made intuitive sense to many who were familiar with the varied needs of children, and was welcomed as states and provinces began to support special education programs and services. The domination of physicians and psychologists in the field simultaneously gave way to greater input from educators, parents, and clinicians in meeting the special educational needs of those youngsters. Teacher training programs expanded to develop new ways to teach youngsters who did not respond to typical classroom methods. Professionals trained in speech and language pathology became an important part of school-based services because of the growing awareness of the link between language disorders and problems in reading and writing.

With the wider availability of school programs, the focus of the learning disabilities movement shifted from the clinic to the classroom. Parents and educators assumed a major role in programming and placement, encouraged by the fact that the term *learning disabled* did not stigmatize children, but rather brought them needed services (Hammill, 1993). Receiving a diagnosis of learning disabled did not imply low intelligence, behavioral problems, or sensory handicaps. To the contrary, children with learning disabilities had difficulties in learning *despite* having average to above-average intelligence and intact hearing, vision, and emotional status. The fact that these children had normal intelligence gave parents and teachers hope that difficulties in reading, writing, and math could be overcome if only the right set of instructional conditions and settings could be identified (Lyon, 1996).

So, with the collaborative leadership of parents, educators, and other specially trained professionals, the field of learning disabilities emerged from its beginnings in the 1960s to become a major aspect of educational services today.

LANGUAGE DEVELOPMENT AND DISORDERS

From the start, infants selectively attend to parental speech sounds and soon learn to communicate with basic gestures and sounds of their own. Usually, by their first birthday they can recognize several words and are using a few words of their own to express their needs and emotions. Over the next 2 years their language development proceeds at a geometric pace, and their ability to formulate complex ideas and express new concepts is a constant source of amazement and amusement for parents. Parents and care-givers play an important role in encouraging such speech development, by providing clear examples of speech and enjoying their child's expressions.

In the world of a newborn, sounds are the building blocks of language. Sounds in the English language consist of **phonemes**, such as sharp *ba's* and *da's* and drawn-out *ee's*, *ll's*, and *ss's*. When children hear a phoneme over and over, receptors in the ear stimulate the formation of dedicated connections to the brain's auditory cortex. A perceptual map is formed in the brain; the map represents the similarity between sounds and helps the infant learn to discriminate different phonemes. These maps are formed quickly; 6-month-old infants in English-speaking homes already have auditory maps different from those of infants in Swedish-speaking homes, as measured by neuron activity in response to different sounds (Kuhl, 1995). By the first birthday, the

From an early age, children love to express themselves.

maps are completed, and infants have lost the ability to discriminate sounds that are not important in their own language.

This rapid development of a perceptual map explains why learning a second language after, rather than with, the first is so difficult—brain connections are already wired for English, and the remaining neurons are less able to form basic new connections for, say, Swedish. Once the basic circuitry is established, infants are able to turn sounds into words, and the more words they hear, the faster they learn language. The sound of words serves to strengthen and expand neural connections that can then process more words. Similar cortical maps are formed for other highly refined skills, such as music. Children who take up a musical instrument at a younger age may strengthen the neural circuits underlying not only music, but spatial reasoning and mathematics as well (Hancock, 1996).

Phonological Awareness

Not all children progress normally through the milestones of language development. Some are quite delayed, continuing to use gestures or sounds rather than speech to communicate their needs. Others progress normally in some areas of speech and language, such as following spoken directions and attending to commands, but have trouble finding the words to express themselves clearly. Although the development of language is one of the best predictors of school performance and overall intelligence (Sattler, 1988), delays or differences in development by no means are a definitive sign of intellectual retardation or cognitive disorder. Rather, such deviations from normal may be just that—deviations—and may be accompanied by superior abilities in other areas of cognitive functioning. Albert Einstein, considered an intellectual genius, began speaking late and infrequently, causing his parents to worry that he was "subnormal." According to

family members, when his father asked his son's headmaster what profession his son should adopt, the answer was simply, "It doesn't matter, he'll never make a success of anything" (Clark, 1971, p. 10).

Since language development is an indicator of general mental development (Sattler, 1988), children who fail to develop language or who show severe delay in acquiring language are considered at risk of having a language-based learning disability. Albert Einstein notwithstanding, early language problems are considered highly predictive of subsequent communication and learning disorders (Benasich, Curtiss, & Tallal, 1993).

Phonology refers to the ability to learn and store important sounds in the language (called phonemes) as well as the rules for combining the sounds into meaningful units such as words. Deficits in phonology have been identified as a major factor explaining why most children and adults with communication and learning disorders have problems in language-based activities such as learning to read and spell (Catts, 1986; Frost, 1998).

A young child has the difficult task of recognizing that speech is segmented into phonemes (the English language contains 44 phonemes, such as *ba, ga, at,* and *tr*). What makes this task very difficult for many children is the fact that speech does not consist of separate phonemes produced one after another. Instead, the sounds are **co-articulated** (overlapped with one another) to permit rapid communication of speech, rather than sound-by-sound pronunciation (Blachman, 1991; Liberman & Shankweiler, 1991).

About 80% of children can segment words and syllables into their proper phonemes by the time they are 7 years old (Blachman, 1991; Lyon, 1996). Unfortunately, the remainder continue to have difficulty understanding the alphabetic principle underlying the ability to segment words and syllables into phonemes. It is these children who have the greatest difficulties learning to read (B. Shaywitz & S. Shaywitz, 1994).

School entry generally marks the time at which earlier language problems surface as learning problems, as children begin to connect spoken and written language. Those who do not easily learn to read and write often have difficulty learning the alphabetic system—the relationship of sounds to letters. Nor can they manipulate sounds within syllables in words. This lack of **phonological awareness** is a precursor to reading problems (Frost, 1998). Primary-grade teachers detect such phonological awareness as they ask children to rhyme words and manipulate sounds. For example, the teacher can say "hat" and ask the child to say the word without the *h* sound, or say "trip" and have the child say the word without the *p*. To assess the child's ability to blend sounds, teachers can say, for example, the three sounds *t, i,* and *n* and see if the child can pull the sounds together to say "tin."

In addition to serving as a prerequisite for basic reading skills, phonological awareness and processing also appear highly related to expressive language development. Readers with core deficits in phonological processing problems have difficulty segmenting phonemes, retrieving the names of common objects and letters, storing phonological codes in short-term memory, categorizing phonemes, and producing some speech sounds. For the most part, reading and comprehension depend upon the rapid and automatic ability to decode single words. Children who are slow and inaccurate at decoding have the most difficulties in reading comprehension (Lyon, 1996).

COMMUNICATION DISORDERS

Children with communication disorders, formerly known as developmental speech and language disorders, have difficulty producing speech sounds, using spoken language to communicate, or understanding what other people say. In DSM-IV, communication disorders include the diagnostic subcategories of expressive language disorder, phonological disorder, mixed receptive-expressive disorder, and stuttering. These subcategories differ mostly in terms of the exact nature of the communication impairment. Recall that phonological problems appear developmentally prior to problems in language expression or reception. Because of these strong connections, the following discussion focuses on expressive language disorder in an effort to highlight problems of expression that emerge in early childhood and that represent the common, fundamental features of communication disorders. Stuttering has a more unique clinical feature and developmental course, so it is discussed separately.

Consider Jackie's communication problems at age 3½ years:

Jackie: Screaming, Not Talking

Jackie's mother expressed her reasons for asking for help with no hesitation: "My 3½-year-old daughter is a going concern. Since she was a baby, she has been plagued by ear infections and sleep problems. Some nights she screams for hours on end, usually because of the ear infections. She has violent temper outbursts and refuses to do simple things that I ask her to do, like get dressed or put on her coat." The child, waiting in the playroom, could be heard screaming over her mother's voice. Jackie was asking my assistant for something, but she could not make out what Jackie was saying. It was pretty obvious how frustrated both the child

and her mother must feel on occasion. Her mother went on to explain how she and Jackie's father had divorced when Jackie was less than 2 years old, and following weekend exchanges it sometimes took a few days for Jackie's routine to return to some degree of normalcy.

I opened the letter she had brought from Jackie's preschool teacher, someone who I knew had a great deal of experience with children of this age. "Jackie is a bright and energetic child," the letter began, "but she is having a great deal of difficulty expressing herself with words. When she gets frustrated, she starts to give up or becomes angry—she won't eat her meals or she fights with staff at nap time, even if she is hungry or tired. If a new teacher at day care is introduced, it takes Jackie a long time to get used to the new person. Jackie seems to understand what she is being asked, but can't find the words to express herself, which understandably leads to an emotional reaction on her part."

Jackie's language problems met criteria for an **expressive language disorder.** Her understanding of speech was normal, but she had significant deficits in expression, which caused her to express her frustration in loud and inappropriate ways at times.

Children's language development follows specific steps, but individual differences in ability and acquisition are the norm rather than the exception. These normal variations can make it difficult to predict whether a given child's early communication problems will pose major problems in learning later on. When their child is young, parents may learn to "read" the child's unique pattern of communication and a potential problem can go unnoticed. A common example is the child who points to different objects and makes grunting or squealing noises that the parent quickly recognizes as "more milk" or "fewer peas." Prior to age 3 or so, many children are inclined to communicate in this way unless parents actively encourage the use of words and discourage inappropriate nonverbal communications. Nevertheless, despite plenty of verbal examples and proper language stimulation, some children fail to develop in some areas of speech and language, leading to later problems in academic skills. This developmental connection makes the study of communication disorders highly pertinent to the understanding and treatment of subsequent learning problems.

Like those with other forms of learning disability, by definition, children with communication disorders have normal intelligence, normal sensory processes, and nonexceptional home environments. Moreover, as discussed in Chapters 9 and 10, children with pervasive develop-

| Table 11.1 | DSM-IV Diagnostic Criteria for Expressive Language Disorder |

A. The scores obtained from standardized individually administered measures of expressive language development are substantially below those obtained from standardized measures of both nonverbal intellectual capacity and receptive language development. The disturbance may be manifest clinically by symptoms that include having a markedly limited vocabulary, making errors in tense, or having difficulty recalling words or producing sentences with developmentally appropriate length or complexity.

B. The difficulties with expressive language interfere with academic or occupational achievement or with social communication.

C. Criteria are not met for Mixed Receptive-Expressive Language Disorder or a Pervasive Developmental Disorder.

D. If Mental Retardation, a speech-motor or sensory deficit, or environmental deprivation is present, the language difficulties are in excess of those usually associated with these problems.

Source: DSM-IV Copyright © 1994 by APA.

mental disorders such as mental retardation or autism often have major communication problems. Such differential diagnosis would not require the additional diagnosis of a communication disorder, however.

Expressive Language Disorder

Some children with communication disorders have problems using words to express their thoughts, desires, and feelings. They understand what is being said to them, but show significant impairments in how they respond verbally. Children with an expressive language disorder, like Jackie, are not mentally retarded, nor do they suffer from one of the pervasive developmental disorders that affect speech and language. One of the defining characteristics of expressive language disorder, in fact, is the discrepancy between what children understand (receptive language) and what they are able to say (expressive language), as shown in the diagnostic criteria in Table 11.1. For example, when asked by her parents to go upstairs, find her socks, and put them on, Jackie was quite capable of understanding and complying with these directions. When asked by her mother to describe what she has just done, however, she might respond simply, "find socks." The linguistic abilities of children with expressive language disorders vary significantly, depending on the severity of the disorder and the age of the child. Most often these children begin speaking late and progress slowly in their speech development. Their speech is also limited in vocabulary and marked by short sentences and simple grammatical structure, as in Jackie's response. To fit the diagnostic criteria, these problems have to be of such severity that they interfere with academic, or in the case of small children, preacademic, achievement or the ability to communicate in everyday social situations.

Two other types of communication disorders that are closely related to expressive language disorder de-

serve clarification. If the above problems in expressive language are coupled with difficulty *understanding* some aspects of speech, a **mixed receptive-expressive language disorder** may be present. Although their hearing is normal, children with this disorder cannot make sense of certain sounds, words, or sentences they hear. They may have difficulty understanding particular types of words or statements, such as complex if-then sentences. In more severe cases the child's ability to understand basic vocabulary or simple sentences may be impaired, and deficits in auditory processing may be present, such as discrimination of sounds and symbols, storage, recall, and sequencing (APA, 1994). Understandably, these problems make the child seem inattentive or noncompliant, and the disorder can be easily misdiagnosed.

Imagine how it would feel to be in Greece with an English-speaking host and her Greek husband. Unless your host is present, the simplest of acts—like engaging in friendly conversation (in Greek)—can be frustrating and uncomfortable. Even if both you and the husband can understand a few words that the other is saying, you probably cannot respond appropriately. If you have ever faced such a communication barrier, you probably have a greater appreciation of the frustration and discomfort that often accompany an expressive language disorder.

When the developmental language problem is one of articulation or sound production, rather than word expression, a diagnosis of **phonological disorder** may be more appropriate. Children with this disorder may have trouble controlling their rate of speech, or they may lag behind playmates in learning to make certain speech sounds (problems in articulation). The most frequently misarticulated sounds are the ones acquired later in the developmental sequence, such as *l, r, s, z, th,* and *ch* (APA, 1994). Depending on the severity of the disorder, the speech quality of these children may be unusual or even unintelligible. For example, at age 6 James still said "wabbit" instead of "rabbit" and "we-wind" for "rewind." Preschoolers, of course, often mispronounce words or confuse the sounds that they hear, which is a normal part of learning to speak. When these problems persist beyond the normal developmental range previously discussed, or if they begin to interfere with academic and social activities, they deserve separate attention.

Prevalence and Developmental Course.

Children commonly show problems in speech articulation and expression as they attempt to tackle new sounds and express concepts in their own ways. Even though prevalence estimates take into account normal variation in language development and are based on those individuals who meet the specific diagnostic criteria, the degree of severity can vary considerably. For example, in early childhood, milder forms of phonological disorder are relatively common, affecting close to 10% of preschoolers. However, many of these children outgrow their earlier difficulties, so by the time they reach first or second grade (ages 6 to 7 years) only 2% to 3% would meet the criteria for phonological disorder. Similarly, expressive language disorder (affecting 2% to 3%) and mixed expressive-receptive disorder (affecting less than 3%) are both relatively common among younger school-age children (APA, 1994).

Fortunately, by mid- to late adolescence, most children with a developmental type of communication disorder have acquired normal language (APA, 1994). About one-half fully outgrow their problems, whereas the other half may show considerable improvement but still have some degree of impairment until late adolescence. In contrast to the *developmental type,* the course and prognosis for children with an *acquired type* of communication disorder (caused by some event unrelated to development, such as brain lesions, head trauma, or stroke) depend highly on the severity and location of the brain injury, the age at the time of the event, and the extent of the language development at that time (APA, 1994).

Even though language problems usually disappear or diminish with time, children with communication disorders often have higher than normal rates of negative behaviors from an early age (Caulfield & Fischel, 1989). Associated behavior problems, such as hyperactivity, can add to their existing communication problems, further altering the course of development in terms of how they relate to peers or keep up with educational demands. As educators became more aware of the importance of providing children with special needs with the opportunity to interact with typically developing children, school systems have begun to **mainstream** children with different developmental and educational needs into regular,

---

Box 11.2

Which Peer Setting—Specialized or Mainstreamed?

Educators and researchers are interested in understanding the capabilities of children with expressive language disorder and similar communication disorders when these children are playing with their peers. Do they progress more rapidly when placed with other children with similar problems, or do they benefit from opportunities to interact with normally developing peers? Guralnick, Connor, Hammond, Gottman, and Kinnish (1996) addressed this question by observing the peer interactions of these two groups of children across different settings. They found many similarities between the two groups, including sustained interactive play, successful peer group entry, conflict resolution, and responsiveness to the social bids of peers, among other things. Important differences emerged between these two groups as well. Regardless of setting, children with communication disorders engaged in fewer instances of active conversation, had a lower rate of positive social behaviors, and were less successful in gaining an appropriate response to their social bids.

As expected, normally developing children were more successful at engaging their peers in play than were children with communication disorders, regardless of the peer group setting. However, children with communication disorders were relatively more successful when interacting with the normally developing peer group than with other children with communication disorders. This finding provides support for the inclusion of children with special needs in settings with normally developing peers, so long as the special needs of these children are addressed.

---

rather than segregated, classrooms. This approach is based on the premise that children with special needs will benefit from associating with normally developing peers and be spared the effects of labeling and special placements (see Box 11.2). The effects of peer interactions on social competence remind us of the powerful environmental factors that influence the course of development of exceptional children.

The actual prevalence of communication disorders is similar for boys and girls (S. Shaywitz, B. Shaywitz, Felton, & Escobar, 1990). However, because of the presence of more behavior problems, boys are referred and diagnosed with communication disorders (and learning disorders) more often than girls (Wood & Felton, 1994)—an example of how some children, especially aggressive and noncompliant boys, are referred for help more often because they behave in ways that arouse anger and frustration. Girls, too, can have communica-

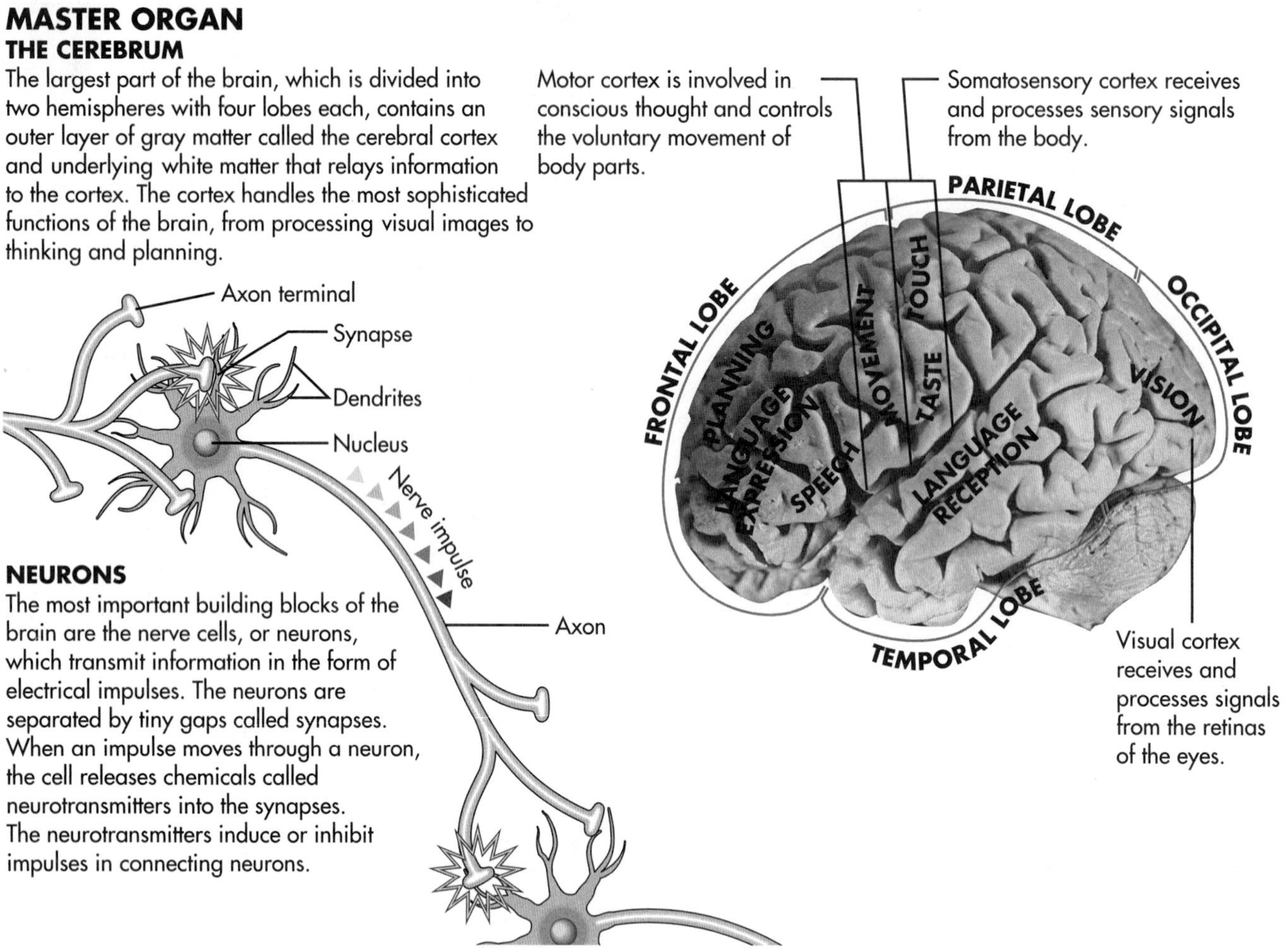

MASTER ORGAN
THE CEREBRUM

The largest part of the brain, which is divided into two hemispheres with four lobes each, contains an outer layer of gray matter called the cerebral cortex and underlying white matter that relays information to the cortex. The cortex handles the most sophisticated functions of the brain, from processing visual images to thinking and planning.

Motor cortex is involved in conscious thought and controls the voluntary movement of body parts.

Somatosensory cortex receives and processes sensory signals from the body.

PARIETAL LOBE

FRONTAL LOBE

OCCIPITAL LOBE

PLANNING

LANGUAGE EXPRESSION

SPEECH

MOVEMENT

TOUCH

TASTE

LANGUAGE RECEPTION

VISION

TEMPORAL LOBE

Visual cortex receives and processes signals from the retinas of the eyes.

Axon terminal

Synapse

Dendrites

Nucleus

Nerve impulse

Axon

NEURONS

The most important building blocks of the brain are the nerve cells, or neurons, which transmit information in the form of electrical impulses. The neurons are separated by tiny gaps called synapses. When an impulse moves through a neuron, the cell releases chemicals called neurotransmitters into the synapses. The neurotransmitters induce or inhibit impulses in connecting neurons.

FIGURE 11.1   Areas of the brain involved in language functions. (*Time,* July 5, 1995, p. 36.)

tion disorders that merit attention, regardless of the presence or absence of other presenting problems.

Causes and Treatment. Language functions, along with many related brain functions, develop rapidly in children. The language functions are housed primarily in the left temporal lobe of the brain (see Figure 11.1). A circular feedback loop helps strengthen the developmental process of language reception and expression. The better children are at comprehension of spoken language (language reception), the better they will become at expressing themselves well. Feedback from their own vocalizations, in turn, helps shape their subsequent expression. Lack of comprehension and feedback reduces verbal output, thus interfering with the development of articulation skills (Spreen, Risser, & Edgell, 1995).

How much does the home environment contribute to communication disorders? Could some parents fail to provide adequate or proper language examples to stimu-

late their children's language? Because of the important role parents play in stimulating language development, psychologists have studied this issue carefully. We noticed when we first visited the home of Jackie that her stepfather was a very quiet man who often communicated using nonverbal means—a gesture, a frown, a short phrase. Her mother used very simple speech when talking to Jackie, but at the same time, we noticed how her speech was quite different when talking with Jackie's 6-year-old sister. These observations match those of Whitehurst and his colleagues (1988), who compared verbal interactions of families with and without a child with an expressive language disorder. They found that parents changed the way they spoke to their children, depending on their children's abilities. When their child spoke in simple, two- or three-word sentences, the parents adjusted their speech accordingly. Thus, except in extreme cases of child neglect or deprivation, it is unlikely that communication disorders are caused by parents' speech patterns. Parental speech and language stimulation may affect the pace and range of language development, but not the specific impairments that characterize these disorders (Tallal et al., 1996).

Many recent discoveries of the causes of language-based disorders, including different forms of communication and learning disorders, are the result of advances in assessing brain functioning in children and adults. Anatomical studies and neuroimaging studies show that deficits in phonology, particularly those in phonological awareness and segmentation, are related to problems in brain functioning within the posterior left hemisphere, particularly in the region of the perisylvian fissure (Lyon, in press). Regional cerebral blood flow studies indicate that poor performance on tasks demanding phonological awareness is associated with less activation than normal in the left temporal region (Wood, Felton, Flowers, & Naylor, 1991). Thus, phonological problems may stem from neurological deficits or deviations in posterior left-hemisphere systems that control the ability to process these sounds.

One specific biological cause of expressive language impairment for a subset of children with expressive language disorder may be recurrent otitis media, or middle ear infections, in the first year of life, because of the hearing loss that accompanies frequent or long bouts of otitis media. This link is supported by evidence that 2- to 3-year-olds with expressive language disorder who show the best improvement in language are more likely to have had longer episodes of otitis media as toddlers (12 to 18 months of age) (Lonigan & Fischel, 1992). Thus, otitis media during a critical period for the development of expressive language may cause early language problems that improve relatively quickly, whereas in the absence of such a history, the causes are likely to be more central and long lasting (Lonigan & Fischel, 1992). Children with chronic otitis media still face some delays in their social development, however, as they attempt to catch up to their peers in learning appropriate forms of verbal communication (Vernon-Feagans, Manlove, & Volling, 1996).

Language processes appear to be heritable to a significant degree (Miller & Tallal, 1995), although the specific genetic underpinnings are difficult to pinpoint. Clinical studies of children with specific language disorders and their families find that 70% of these children show a positive family history of some type of learning disability (Tallal, Ross, & Curtiss, 1989a; 1989b). Twin studies also suggest a genetic connection, illustrated by the finding that 3- to 5-year-old monozygotic twin pairs misproduce the same sounds on an articulation test significantly more often than dizygotic twin pairs or unrelated children (Locke & Mather, 1989). Based on convergent findings from family and twin studies, the transmission rate of communication disorders appears to follow an *autosomal dominant* mode of transmission, meaning that about half the offspring from an affected parent will be affected (Tallal et al., 1991). Coupled with the previously noted finding that males and females are equally likely to have such problems, the likelihood of a sex-linked mode of genetic transmission can largely be ruled out (Miller & Tallal, 1995).

Scientists are even zeroing in on the specific deficits in brain functioning that may be heritable and lead to communication disorders. Studies comparing language-impaired children with or without an affected parent suggest that a profile of *temporal processing deficits* occurs significantly more often in children with a positive family history for a language-based learning disability (Merzenich et al., 1996; Tallal et al., 1991). That is, affected children have more difficulty deciphering certain speech sounds, which is due to subtle but important differences in the way neurons fire in response to different sounds. Temporal processing deficits, which likely have a familial or genetic basis, result in language patterns that reflect problems in deciphering different speech sounds and patterns (Miller & Tallal, 1995).

Although biological findings point to abnormal brain *functioning,* how such abnormality originates is still unclear. The best guess is that communication disorders result from an interaction of genetic influences, slowness or abnormalities of brain maturation, and possibly, minor brain lesions that escape clinical detection (Bishop, 1987). Fortunately for us left-handed persons, "abnormal hand preference" and brain lateralization do not relate to language or learning disabilities, despite many attempts to find such a connection!

The treatment of children with expressive language disorder and similar communication disorders must be balanced with the knowledge that many of these problems are self-correcting by the age of 6 and may not require intervention. Fortunately, ongoing brain development, exposure to examples of normal speech, and ample opportunities to use language in describing feelings and needs serve to overcome these initial problems for many children. Even so, parents may seek help and advice to understand their child's speech delays and to ensure that they are doing everything possible to stimulate their child's language development. For this reason, short-term psychological treatment often consists of a home-based parent training package that teaches parents different ways to improve the child's expressive speech (Whitehurst, Fischel, Arnold, & Lonigan, 1992). Such an approach was taken in assisting Jackie and her parents. We designed ways that her parents and day care teachers could build on her existing strengths. Her day care teacher had an excellent idea: Use Jackie's interest in drawing to increase her interest and enthusiasm for speaking, because Jackie loved to draw and to talk about her artwork. When I visited her class, she ran up to show me her drawing, exclaiming, "I draw picture of mom, dad, kitty, and lake." We agreed that her behavior problems could be managed by simple forms of ignoring and distracting and the occasional use of time-out. Jackie became attached to computer graphics and images, and soon was able to identify letters and small words and to move shapes around the screen. All the while, her expressive language improved and by age 5, she could pronounce all the letters of the alphabet and was eager to start kindergarten.

Stuttering

It is quite normal for children to go through a period of nonfluency, or difficult-to-understand speech, as part of their development. Young children are still learning to speak, and it takes practice and patience to develop the coordination to make the tongue, lips, and brain work in unison to produce unfamiliar or difficult combinations of sounds. For most children, this period of speech development passes without notice, and to most parents it is a period of wonder and amusement as their children wrestle with new words. Some children, however, progress slowly through this stage, repeating (wa-wa-wa) or prolonging (n-ah-ah-ah-o) sounds to the point where they struggle to continue or they develop ways to avoid or compensate for certain sounds or words. Consider 4½-year-old Sayad:

Sayad: Family Legacy

Sayad's parents had received a lot of informal advice from friends and relatives about their son's speech problems, but most of the advice was worrisome. "He'll struggle with this for most of his life," his grandmother had warned. "If something isn't done right away, he'll become a stutterer, and be so self-conscious that he won't be able to keep up in school or with his friends." Sayad first started repeating and prolonging some of his words when he was about 2½, but by now his problem had grown more noticeable. As he spoke, he pursed his lips, closed his eyes, and shortened his breathing, seeming to tense up his face. Yet his interactions with me were friendly and at ease. "M-m-m-m-y words get stuck in m-m-m-m-y m-m-mouth," he explained, "and I-I-I-I talk t-t-t-too fast. Wh-wh-wh-why can't I talk right?" I discovered soon

thereafter why his grandmother was so concerned: The child's great-grandfather and great-uncle both stuttered, and her son (Sayad's father) had been a stutterer until he was a teenager.

Sayad's mother had been trying to ignore the problem and not draw attention to it, but she was growing more aware of Sayad's peers' teasing and imitating him. She explained why she came for an assessment: "We were on the way to the store when Sayad kept saying 'where' over and over. After I stopped the car and unfastened his seatbelt, he finished his question—'is daddy?' After that, I gave up on my 'leave it alone' notion and began trying ways to slow Sayad down a bit."

Prevalence and Developmental Course.
Sayad's speech problems fit the criteria for **stuttering**. He had repeated and prolonged pronunciations of certain syllables, and this interfered with his communication. Stuttering has a gradual onset between the ages of 2 and 7 years, with age 5 being the peak age, and affects males about 3 times more often than females (APA, 1994). The DSM-IV criteria for stuttering are shown in Table 11.2. Few children (less than 1% of the child population; APA, 1994) receive this diagnosis, however, because stuttering tends to be something from which most children recover. This developmental course is important for treatment considerations, because almost 80% of children who stutter before age 5 will no longer stutter once they have been in school a year or so (Yairi & Ambrose, 1992).

Causes and Treatment.   Many myths and falsehoods surround this communication disorder. The widely held view that stuttering is caused by an unresolved emotional problem or by anxiety, for example, has been put to rest as a result of a lack of supportive evidence (Barlow & Durand, 1995). Because this speech problem runs in families, researchers have focused on family characteristics as the major causes of stuttering. But it is not likely that such behavior is acquired primarily as a function of the child's linguistic environment. Sayad's grandmother and mother would be relieved to know that the communicative behavior of mothers does not significantly contribute to the development of stuttering (Kloth & Janssen, 1995).

Genetic factors play a strong role in the etiology of stuttering. According to one major study, heritability accounts for over two-thirds (71%) of the variance in the causes of stuttering, with the remaining third or so (29%) being the result of the environment (Andrews, Morris-Yates, Howie, & Martin, 1991). Genetic factors

Table 11.2	DSM-IV Diagnostic Criteria for Stuttering

A. Disturbance in the normal fluency and time patterning of speech (inappropriate for the individual's age), characterized by frequent occurrences of one or more of the following:
   (1) sound and syllable repetitions
   (2) sound prolongations
   (3) interjections
   (4) broken words (e.g., pauses within a word)
   (5) audible or silent blocking (filled or unfilled pauses in speech)
   (6) circumlocutions (word substitutions to avoid problematic words)
   (7) words produced with an excess of physical tension
   (8) monosyllable whole-word repetitions (e.g., "I-I-I-I see him")

B. The disturbance in fluency interferes with academic or occupational achievement or with social communication.

C. If a speech-motor or sensory deficit is present, the speech difficulties are in excess of those usually associated with these problems.

Source: DSM-IV Copyright © 1994 by APA.

most likely influence speech in terms of the location of the most prominent speech centers in the brain. For instance, findings from imaging scans of the brains of adult stutterers reveal that they use the "wrong side" of their brains to speak—stutterers were found to be using much more of the right hemisphere during speech (DeNil, 1997). While both sides of the brain are involved in the speech process, the left side normally plays a more significant role. Moreover, when they were talking or reading, people who stutter were on the lookout for difficult words that might trigger stuttering (DeNil, 1997). This biological source for stuttering explains many of its clinical features, including why the speech of stutterers may lose its spontaneity, and why stutterers report that when they need to communicate, stuttering makes them anxious, rather than the other way around, because of anticipated difficulty in expressing their thoughts (Miller & Watson, 1992).

Since most children outgrow stuttering, one of the most frustrating problems for parents and therapists is determining whether therapy is intervention or interference. Therapy is usually recommended if sound and syllable repetitions begin to happen more often, if the parent or child is concerned or anxious about the speech problem, or if the child shows signs of facial or vocal tension, as we saw in Sayad's case. A common psychological treatment for children who stutter is to counsel parents on how to speak to their children more slowly, use shorter and less complex sentences, and basically remove the pressure the child may feel about speaking (Blood, 1988). In cases where this simple approach is not effective or the problem is interfering with academic and peer activities, a behavioral treatment method called the

regulated breathing method may be useful. The child is instructed to stop speaking when a stuttering episode occurs and to take a deep breath, inhaling and exhaling, before proceeding (Gagnon & Ladouceur, 1992).

LEARNING DISORDERS

> People do not understand what it costs in time and suffering to learn how to read. I have been working at it for eighty years, and I still can't say that I've succeeded.
> —Goethe (1749–1832)

Whether we are studying Roman history or calculus, applying ourselves to the task of learning new information and concepts requires exertion and concentration. Similar to physical activities, some learning activities are more difficult than others, especially for younger children who have not as yet developed a foundation of good study habits and successful learning experiences. Parents and teachers may begin to notice that a child is struggling unusually hard with a particular activity, such as reading, and wonder why. At this point the problem may be formally assessed by an individual administration of an IQ test and various achievement tests that assess abilities in specific academic areas. When achievement on one of these standardized tests in reading, math, or writing ability is substantially below what would be expected for the child's age, schooling, and intellectual ability, he or she may be diagnosed with a **learning disorder**. In practice, *substantially below* means a discrepancy of more than 2 standard deviations between the

IQ findings and the actual achievement test findings. In other words, children with a learning disorder are bright enough to learn the subject material, but they are not showing evidence of being able to do so.

Let's return to James, the 9-year-old boy with reading problems:

James: Strong Points Shine

The look on the 9-year-old's face said it all—he did not want to be here. "I'm tired of talking to people" was his terse greeting. I wondered for a moment whether he would talk to me at all, but as soon as he saw my computer, he brightened a bit. Determined to allow time for him to feel more comfortable, I invited James to play a quick game or two. His skill at the action games told me a lot about his basic energy and problem-solving ability—he was a whiz at figuring out the rules of each game and getting a high score. We spoke casually during the computer game warm-up, but it was clear to me that he preferred to concentrate on the game.

A half hour passed, with little more than a few sentences exchanged between us. A quick trip to the snack bar gave us the common ground we needed to open up and talk a bit. "Why does my teacher want me to come here?" he reasonably asked. As he listened and replied to my explanation, his language problems stood out. His sentences were short and simple, and were often spoken at a rapid rate. Here is an example:

"James, tell me something about your favorite story or a recent movie you've seen."
"I like the movie. Lots of dogs."
"What movie is that, James?"
"Dog movie."

During testing, James often tried to start before I had even finished telling him what I wanted him to do. He was eager to do what I asked, but he stopped abruptly as soon as he ran into frustration or failure. James could focus on only one sound at a time, so if he missed early cues or initial instructions, he would become disoriented, frustrated, and uncooperative. James wanted to do well, but I could see he was struggling with many of the sounds and words as I spoke. He completed the WISC-III in less than an hour, seeming to hurry almost as if to escape from his own mistakes. His measured general intelligence was within the normal range, but his performance abilities (performance IQ = 109) were much stronger than his verbal abilities (verbal IQ = 78). It was obvious as well that the test was likely an underestimation of his true ability, a result of his eagerness to finish and his difficulty with understanding some of the instructions.

To my surprise, James was willing and ready to continue on to the next test after only a short computer game break. He explained why this was so: "I put things together, like puzzles. I make cars and planes at my house." As long as I gave him some small breaks on the computer, he seemed to be willing to tackle the material on the tests. Some of his spelling errors stood out immediately, such as *skr* for *square*, and *srke* for *circle*. When asked to write the sentence *he shouted a warning*, he wrote *he shtd a woin*. He read *see the black dog* as "see the black pond," and *she wants a ride to the store* as "she was rid of the store." He seemed to use a "best guess" strategy in tackling reading, based on the sounds that he knew: When asked to write the word *bigger*, he wrote just *her*. But I noticed that James's enthusiasm picked up a bit as he began telling stories from pictures he was shown, and he marveled at his own ability to rotate shapes on the computer in order to complete a picture. He left my office more animated and talkative than when he arrived, which indicated to me how nice it must have felt for him to experience success.

Compare James's reading problems with those of Tim, a 7-year-old boy who is having a great deal of trouble with math and drawing:

Tim: Warming with Interest

When I first saw Tim at age 7, he seemed aloof and disinterested. His eyes stayed focused on the floor, and his body remained expressionless, as if to say, "Leave me alone, and let me outta here." As I searched for something to say, I asked Tim to tell me a little about his family: "Do you have any brothers or sisters? Does your family like to do anything special together?" His tired response, "I have two brothers, my father works all day, mom plays piano. We want a boat," sent me a clear message as to his mood and interest in this activity. My usual ploy of turning on the computer games fell flat—"I hate computers" was Tim's preemptive response. I wondered, "Is he depressed, angry, hurt, frustrated? Just what is going on here?" Having looked at his school record, I knew he was struggling, especially in math and physical sciences, but his speech and affect expressed more than academic problems alone. His school records flashed the news that Tim had a learning disorder, as evidenced by his WISC-III performance score, which fell in the borderline- to low-average range (79), and his verbal score, which fell in the average range (108). The test administrator had politely described Tim's test-taking approach as "reluctant." Notes by teachers indicated that he commonly had problems on tasks involving drawing, particularly if they involved memory, and his math skills and social skills were far below those of others in his class.

I pulled out my *Where's Waldo?* book and we began looking at it together. In addition to being fun, looking for Waldo and his friends (small figures buried amidst millions of figures and colors) required Tim to be quick at identifying the hidden figures. At first he balked, but I noticed that he improved if he used his own verbally mediated strategy to solve the problem. Tim talked to himself as he thought aloud: "Look around the edges first, then start to look closer and closer to the middle of the page. Look for Waldo's red and white shirt—look closely at each section!" The more interested he was, the more he would talk. Once he warmed up, his smile appeared, along with his admission that "this sure beats math lesson."

Tim has problems in areas of spatial orientation and mathematical reasoning, and further achievement testing confirmed that his problems fit the diagnostic criteria for a learning disorder in mathematics. But his academic problems were surrounded and almost masked by his frustration and low self-esteem. Such emotional problems are commonly seen among children who are bright enough to recognize that their performance is below that of others, but who experience mostly failure and little success in the classroom.

James's pattern of strengths and weaknesses shows that although he has problems recognizing and articulating unfamiliar words while he reads, he has other strengths that can be drawn upon to compensate for this disability. He has a strong talent for figuring out how things work and drawing ideas on paper. Tim has several strengths, too, especially in the area of linguistic skills such as word recognition, sentence structure, and reading. In contrast to James's problems, Tim's problems are primarily in the visual-spatial-organizational spheres, which show up as difficulties with tactile (touch) perception, psychomotor activity (such as throwing and catching), and nonverbal problem solving (such as figuring out math problems and assembling things). Both children's limitations can affect every aspect of their educational goals as well as their interpersonal abilities, and will require comprehensive and ongoing treatment plans.

To get a better feel for the nature of learning disorders, picture yourself asking for directions at a gas station in an unfamiliar town. The attendant says: "Go out the driveway and turn right. Go till you reach the second light, turn left, and look for the sign to Amityville. It's about 3 miles down the road. You'll pass a cemetery and a red schoolhouse, and go under a railroad trestle before you get to Highway 18. When you see the sign, turn right." We all have some difficulty processing such information and recalling it accurately; we drive away, repeating to ourselves, "Stop light, go left, cemetery, highway, turn at schoolhouse?" Our driving companions, who heard the same instructions, may recall a different route. This situation demonstrates that even simple things, like verbal instructions, can be easily jumbled. Children or adults with learning disorders experience similar confusion in everyday situations, such as processing new information or understanding what they are reading. Such learning problems can be difficult to recognize because for most of us, the material in question is straightforward and simple. The child may be blamed for not listening, not paying attention, or for being "slow," which further disguises the true nature of the learning problems.

Clinical Description

This section describes learning disorders in reading, mathematics, and written expression. The diagnostic criteria for these disorders are listed in Table 11.3. These disabilities are characterized by performance that is below that expected for someone the same age. The performance problems must significantly interfere with academic achievement or daily living; some children and adults have found their own ways to compensate for their learning problems and therefore do not in fact have a disability, despite test findings of poor achievement. Finally, the disability cannot be related to a sensory problem such as hearing or sight, unless it goes well beyond what such children typically experience.

Because many aspects of speaking, listening, reading, writing, and arithmetic overlap and build on the same functions of the brain, it is not surprising that children and adults can have more than one form of learning disorder. Recall that the ability to understand language (phonological awareness) facilitates the ability to speak and, later on, to read and write. A single gap in the

For children with learning disorders, following simple instructions can be confusing and frustrating.

Reading Disorder. Children are naturally attracted to reading, and its importance in our society is unparalleled by any other academic accomplishment. Children are surrounded by written signs and messages, and by about age 5 or so, most want to know what these signs mean. (Capitalizing on this natural curiosity, advertisers have become expert in pairing recognizable symbols with the names of their product or establishment so that children can "read" more quickly.) By the first grade, this natural interest and developmental readiness are channeled by the school into a formal attempt to learn how to read. For many children this process is difficult and tedious; for a sizeable minority, however, learning to read can be frustrating, confusing, and upsetting. The role of parents in this process is critical, for children need to have positive feedback and feel satisfied with their performance, regardless of their speed and accuracy.

When you consider what is involved in learning the basics of reading, such as associating shapes of letters (graphemes) with sounds (phonemes), it is not surprising that some children have difficulty and can quickly fall behind in many subject areas. To gain an understanding of what is involved in the process, read the following sentence: "I believe that abnormal child psychology is one of the most fascinating and valuable courses I have taken." As you read the sentence, did you notice that you had to simultaneously

❖ focus attention on the printed marks and control your eye movements across the page?
❖ recognize the sounds associated with letters?
❖ understand words and grammar?
❖ build ideas and images?
❖ compare new ideas with what you already know?
❖ store ideas in memory?

Most of us have forgotten all the effort that goes into reading, especially in the beginning. Not surprisingly,

brain's functioning can disrupt many types of cognitive activity. These disruptions, in turn, can interfere with the child's development of important fundamental skills and compound the learning difficulties over a short time period. Moreover, as we saw with both James and Tim, numerous secondary problems can emerge, such as temper outbursts and withdrawal from social situations, as a result of frustration and lack of success.

Problems in the development of *motor skills* in young children (described in DSM-IV as developmental coordination disorder) are sometimes associated with communication and learning disorders as well (Spreen et al., 1995). These delays or deficits—which include marked delays in achieving motor milestones such as sitting, crawling, and walking; clumsiness; poor performance in sports; and poor handwriting—can affect the child's learning ability and rate of progress. Most affected children outgrow these coordination problems by late adolescence.

Table 11.3 | **DSM-IV Diagnostic Criteria for Learning Disorders: Reading Disorder, Mathematics Disorder, and Disorder of Written Expression***

A. Reading achievement/mathematical ability/writing skill, as measured by individually administered standardized tests, is substantially below that expected given the person's chronological age, measured intelligence, and age-appropriate education.

B. The disturbance in criterion A significantly interferes with academic achievement or activities of daily living that require reading skills/mathematical ability/composition of written texts.

C. If a sensory deficit is present, the reading/mathematical/writing difficulties are in excess of those usually associated with it.

*Because the basic criteria are identical, the three separate learning disorders are combined here, with the exception of the specific ability that is affected.
Source: Adapted from DSM-IV 1994 by APA.

children's initial attempts to read are laboriously slow and monotonous as they wrestle with the sounds and complexities of the combined letters. Such mental processing requires a complex and intact network of nerve cells that connect the brain's centers of vision, language, and memory (NIMH, 1996). A small problem in any one of those areas can lead to reading difficulties. The most common underlying feature associated with reading disorder, however, is an inability to distinguish or to separate the sounds in spoken words. This deficit is critical because the phonological skills are fundamental to learning to read.

Reading disorders have been studied more than any other type of learning disability. The DSM-IV definition and criteria for reading disorder specify that the condition is marked by subaverage reading ability in the presence of average to above-average intelligence. The diagnosis also adheres to the other two major criteria cited in Table 11.3. Basically, the core diagnostic issue is the degree to which an individual's reading accuracy, reading speed, or reading comprehension differs from what is expected with regard to chronological age or measured intelligence (Lyon, 1996).

Many of the clinical signs of reading disorders are first evident only to a trained eye. Some of the methods developed by teachers and school psychologists in this regard are illustrative of the way children with reading disorders function in the classroom. They often have trouble learning basic sight words, especially those that are phonetically irregular and must be memorized, such as *the, who, what, where, was, laugh, said,* and so forth. Such children show particular error patterns that point to their idiosyncratic approach to reading and spelling; that is, they have developed their own unique and peculiar reading patterns, which signal the need for additional teaching methods. Typical errors include *reversals (b/d; p/q), transpositions* (sequential errors such as *was/saw, scared/sacred*), *inversions (m/w; u/n),* and *omissions* (reading "place" for *"palace"* or "section" for *selection*). To assess a child's need for additional practice in certain areas, teachers may log the types of errors the child makes as he reads out loud. In addition to decoding of words, reading comprehension is assessed by having the student retell a story she has read or suggest the next episode. Whereas average readers rely heavily on auditory and visual modalities for gathering new information, children with a reading disorder may prefer a different mode, such as touch or manipulation, to assist them in learning. These different patterns of strengths and weaknesses, if adequately assessed, can then be used to the child's advantage in planning additional teaching methods, such as computer-based learning (Henry, 1996).

The core deficits underlying reading disorders relate primarily to difficulties in **decoding**—breaking down a word into parts rapidly enough to read the whole word—coupled with problems reading single, small words (Olson, Foresberg, Wise, & Rack, 1994; Stanovitch, 1994). When a child lacks the ability—usually acquired in infancy and early childhood—to detect the phonological structure of language and to recognize simpler words automatically, reading development is very likely to be impaired (Adams, 1990; Blachman, 1991; Perfetti, 1985; Shankweiler & Liberman, 1989). The slow and labored decoding and recognition of single words require substantial effort and detract from the child's ability to retain the core meaning of a sentence, much less that of a paragraph or a passage. The child with a reading disorder lacks the critical language skills that are necessary for basic reading, reading comprehension, spelling, and written expression.

Mathematics Disorder.   In their preschool years, children are not as naturally drawn to mathematical concepts as they are to reading. This changes rapidly as they discover that they need to count and add to know how much money it takes to buy something or how many days remain until summer vacation. As in reading, the need to know propels children to learn new and difficult concepts, and little by little their new skills help them understand their world better.

For some children, like Tim and Francine, this curiosity about numbers is compromised by their inability to grasp the abstract concepts inherent in many forms of numerical and cognitive problem solving. Francine's problems with numbers and basic math concepts began to show up well before she attended school, which is typically the case. As she began to encounter math concepts in grade two that required some abstract reasoning, she fell further and further behind.

Any or all of the skills involved in arithmetic—recognizing numbers and symbols, memorizing facts such as the multiplication table, aligning numbers, and understanding abstract concepts such as place value and fractions—may be difficult for children with a **mathematics disorder** (NIMH, 1996). The DSM-IV criteria for mathematics disorder, like the criteria for learning disorders in oral language, reading, and written expression, are based on assumptions of normal or above-average intelligence (as assessed by IQ), normal sensory function, adequate educational opportunity, and absence of developmental disorders and emotional disturbance. Children and adults with this disorder not only have problems in math, but also may experience problems in the comprehension of abstract concepts or in visual-spatial ability. Historically, these characteristics were

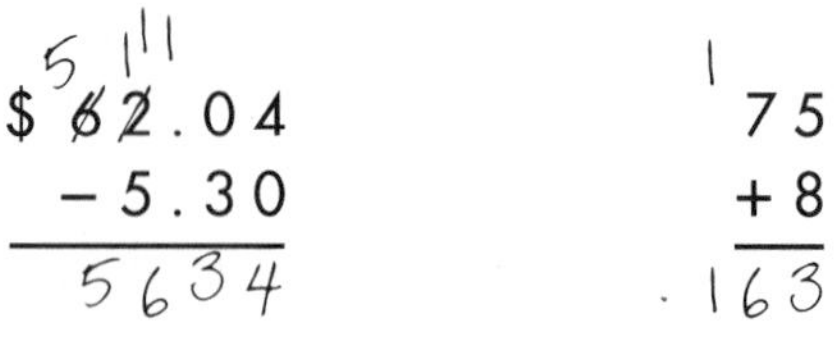

$$\begin{array}{r}^{5}\cancel{6}\overset{1\ \ 1}{2}.04\\-5.30\\\hline 5634\end{array}\qquad\begin{array}{r}^{1}75\\+8\\\hline .163\end{array}$$

FIGURE 11.2 Errors in math computation for a 10-year-old girl with a mathematics disorder. (Taylor, 1988)

termed *developmental dyscalculia,* meaning the failure to develop arithmetic competence, a term that is seldom used today. Examples of calculation errors typical of children with a mathematics disorder are shown in Figure 11.2. The example in this case points out that the errors suggest spatial difficulties and directional confusion.

Children with mathematics disorders typically have core deficits in arithmetic calculation and/or mathematics reasoning abilities. These problems may be expressed as difficulties in naming mathematical amounts or numbers; an inability to enumerate, compare, and manipulate objects; problems reading and writing mathematical symbols; understanding mathematical concepts and performing calculations mentally; and performing computational operations (Lyon, 1996; Taylor, 1988). These deficits are connected to neuropsychological development and functioning, implying that the mental processes underlying mathematical reasoning and calculation are underdeveloped or impaired. Children with low arithmetic performance relative to reading and spelling performance often have high scores on auditory verbal measures and low scores on visual-perceptual and visual-spatial measures (this was the case with Tim). From a neuropsychological perspective, this unexpected discrepancy supports the long-held belief that mathematics disorders are associated with deficiencies in visual-perceptual and visual-spatial domains (Rourke, 1985).

Writing Disorder

Carlos: Slowly Taking Shape

Carlos, age 7, was about to finish grade two when his teacher and parents met to discuss his difficulties in handwriting. The year had gone generally well, but his parents were bracing for bad news. Smiling and pulling out some workbooks, Carlos's teacher lined up examples of how he had gradually become able to shape and print some letters over the course of the year. But what his parents saw was self-explanatory: His shapes were very poor and looked more like those of his 3½-year-old sister. Sensing both parents' apprehension, his teacher clarified: "Carlos is having a few problems in his fine motor coordination, in activities such as artwork, putting puzzles together, and similar tasks. He goes too fast when trying to do these tasks, and he forgets to be careful or to follow the pattern. He makes a half-hearted attempt on his writing assignments and then starts talking to his classmates. I'd like him to be seen by a psychologist for testing, and hopefully next fall his new teacher can strengthen his writing and fine motor skills with some additional exercises."

When Carlos attended the initial interview, he took an immediate interest in our computer games, exclaiming how easy it was to use the mouse to draw figures. When asked to switch to using a pencil and paper, however, Carlos balked. We asked him to copy by hand some of the figures he had been drawing on the computer, after first printing them for him on paper. In doing so, he switched his preferred hand in the middle of the task. He also showed several letter reversals (b/d; p/q), and would push down very hard on the pencil in an attempt to trace or draw the figures. Throughout these tasks he talked freely and asked a lot of questions, making us wonder at times who was assessing whom.

Carlos showed evidence on neuropsychological testing of finger agnosia (he could not tell which finger I touched when his hand was behind his back), especially with his left hand. He also had considerable difficulty copying a triangle, a circle, and a square based on examples shown to him (see Figure 11.3). On the WISC-III he obtained a performance score in the low-average range (91), and a verbal IQ score in the high-average range (117). On performance subtests he had particular problems with block design and puzzles, such as object assembly. He had more difficulty with verbal IQ subtests involving concentration and attention, such as math and digit-span tasks. Throughout the testing we found Carlos to be impulsive and sometimes quite defiant: If he didn't want to do something, he simply would not do it. These observations were consistent with his parents' frustration at his immature behavior and defiance at home.

Carlos has a learning disorder related to written expression. He has strong language and reasoning abilities, as well as reasonable problem-solving skills for his age. Yet he is considerably weaker in his visual-motor

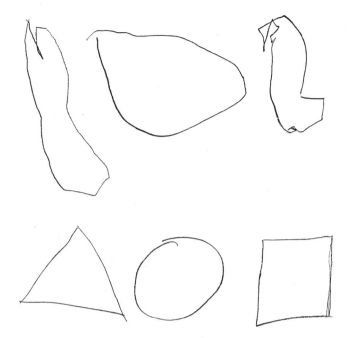

FIGURE 11.3 *Top:* Drawings produced by Carlos when asked to copy a triangle, a circle, and a square; *Bottom:* Examples of a triangle, circle and square from a normally developing 7-year-old boy.

abilities, as shown by his writing, figure copying, and ability to rotate figures. Like reading and math, writing involves several brain areas that must be in good working order, with interconnections underlying the functions that produce vocabulary, grammar, hand movement, and memory.

Children with **writing disorders** not only have problems with writing and drawing, but often experience other fine visual-motor problems with tasks that require eye/hand coordination, despite their normal gross motor development. Carlos could draw and type well on the computer, yet his ability to produce written output and to manipulate objects was significantly impaired. Teachers most often notice that, compared with children with normal writing skills, children with a writing disorder produce shorter and less interesting essays, produce poorly organized text, and are less likely to review spelling, punctuation, grammar, or the body of their text to increase clarity (Hooper et al., 1994). In addition, problems in written expression signal the possibility of other learning disorders because the same metacognitive processes are involved: planning, self-monitoring, self-evaluation, and self-modification (Wong, 1992).

Knowledge about writing disorders lags behind that of the other learning disorders. Children with this disability have problems with at least one component of writing (Hooper et al., 1994); most, if not all, however, show a combination of core deficits related to written

output, including grammatical or punctuation errors, poor paragraph organization, multiple spelling errors, and very poor handwriting (APA, 1994). Spelling errors or poor handwriting, in the absence of any significant interference in daily activities or academic pursuits, does not qualify a child for this diagnosis. As expected, writing disorders are commonly found in combination with learning disorders in reading or mathematics, because of underlying core deficits in language and neuro-psychological development.

Prevalence and Developmental Course

Estimates of the prevalence of learning disorders range from 2% to 10% of the entire population, depending on how the problems are specifically defined and measured (APA, 1994). This range fits with the finding that about 5% of students in public schools in the United States are identified with learning disorders (Lyon, 1996). Most prevalence estimates are based on reading disorders, because they are by far the most common and overlap considerably with math and writing disorders. These estimates are probably very conservative, however, because they are based only on identified cases.

Reading difficulties may be part of a continuum of reading abilities rather than a discrete, all-or-none phenomenon, which would mean that children with reading disorders are essentially those who fall at the lower end of the continuum (B. Shaywitz, Escobar, S. Shaywitz, Fletcher, & Makuch, 1992). This is a useful and important consideration, because, clearly, there are strong readers and weak readers, and no definitive cutoff point easily distinguishes the two (Lyon, 1996). Moreover, if prevalence estimates are based on a continuum of reading problems rather than a diagnostic category, reading disabilities are estimated to affect at least 10 million U.S. children, or about 1 in 5 (S. Shaywitz et al., 1992).

Estimates of the prevalence of disorders related to mathematics and written expression are even more approximate, due to a lack of epidemiologic studies. Again we find highly discrepant prevalence estimates. Estimates from clinical studies put the prevalence of mathematics disorder at about one-fifth of all children with learning disorders, which translates to about 1% of school-age children who receive this diagnosis (APA, 1994). If prevalence is estimated on the basis of test scores, however, about 6% of school-age children would be included (Lyon, 1996). Like reading disorder, mathematics disorder usually becomes apparent during second or third grade, once formal mathematics instruction begins. Therefore, prevalence estimates based solely on diagnoses may be unduly conservative.

Finally, disorder of written expression is considered to be rare *when not associated with other learning disorders* (APA, 1994); however, given the high rate of developmental language disorders in the general population (8% to 15%) and the significantly high rate of disorders in reading skills noted above, written language disorders probably affect at least 10% of the school-age population (Lyon, 1996). Because of their high comorbidity, disorders in math and written expression may best be construed as related features of a generalized problem in learning, rather than selective impairments (Lyon, 1996).

Cultural, Class, and Gender Variations.

Social and cultural factors have less of an influence on the prevalence of learning disorders than they have on other types of cognitive and behavioral problems of children. In fact, the diagnostic criteria for learning disorders state that they cannot be attributed to social and cultural factors. Nevertheless, some cultural and racial issues may be an important part of how children with learning disorders are identified and treated.

Language development is highly influenced by its context (Bates, 1993), so it is necessary to consider how cultural and ethnic differences in the home may influence a particular child's language development. Wood et al. (1991) did an interesting study to illustrate the point that deficits in phonological awareness occur more frequently among populations that use nonstandard English. They followed a random sample of 485 Caucasian (55%) and African-American (45%) children from first grade through third grade, and found that although African-American youngsters read at the same grade level as Caucasian children at the beginning of the first grade, they show marked declines in reading by the third grade and severe declines by the fifth grade.

Why this difference in reading ability becomes evident for some children and not others over these critical 2 years of schooling leads to a consideration of the important interaction between children's needs and environmental opportunities. As emphasized throughout this text, many childhood disorders reflect an *interaction* between the child's inherent abilities and resources and the opportunities that exist in the child's local environment. In the case of learning to read, some teaching approaches that do not explicitly emphasize specific sound-symbol relationships may interact poorly with the nature of African-American children's dialect (Wood et al., 1991). Greater attention to such differences can lead to better learning opportunities.

Whereas attention to cultural and ethnic issues pertaining to learning disorders is very recent, gender differences have a long and contentious history. Males are more often diagnosed with learning disorders than are females, accounting for 60% to 80% of children with such diagnoses (APA, 1994). As is the case with commu-

nication disorders, reasons for referral can distort the fact that boys and girls actually have very similar rates of reading problems. Schools are a prime source of referral for children suspected of having learning disorders, so it comes as no surprise that schools identify about 4 times as many boys as girls as having learning disorders in reading, largely because boys are more likely to also show behavior problems. When male-female ratios are derived from epidemiological estimates rather than referrals, boys and girls are represented equally among children with learning disorders in reading, *so long as attention-related disorders are taken into account* (De-Fries, Olson, Pennington, & Smith, 1991; Moats & Lyon, 1993; S. Shaywitz et al., 1990). Boys are often identified sooner than girls as well, because teachers are trained to identify students with learning difficulties on the basis of visible behavior problems (Henry, 1996). Girls who are having learning problems are often quiet, rather than loud and attention-seeking, and thereby may be overlooked unless educators and parents are well informed.

Development.

The course of development for children and adolescents with learning disorders is much better understood than it was a decade ago, because of the increase in well-designed studies and more careful diagnostic criteria. Some of the misconceptions, including placing the blame on the child, that characterized earlier work have given way to better recognition of underlying patterns and coexisting symptoms. Although learning disorders are considered lifelong, recent studies have also shown that adult outcomes are more positive and adaptive than previously believed.

Children with learning disorders often absorb what others thoughtlessly say about them. Hearing themselves described as "slow," "different," or "behind," they may perceive themselves in terms of their disabilities rather than their strengths. Most often they do not know how or why they are different, but they do know how it feels to be unable to keep up with others in their classroom. These daily experiences may cause some children with learning disorders to act out in various ways, either withdrawing from others or becoming angry and noncompliant. Like James, they may stop trying to learn and keep up. Or, like Francine, they may become isolated and limit their participation in activities that their peers enjoy.

What can be expected of Francine, James, Tim, and Carlos over the course of their school years, and are such expectations subject to fluctuation? Realistic expectations assist in proper planning and goal setting, and are the cornerstone of strategies to assist children through enhanced educational and family assistance. Learning disorders are not a transient, easily outgrown childhood disorder, but there is reason for optimism based on recent developments in detection, etiology, and intervention. First and foremost, developmental expectations and educational planning must be ongoing, in recognition of the chronicity of learning problems (Francis et al., 1994): About three-fourths of children who are diagnosed with reading disorder in the third grade still have major reading problems in high school (Fletcher, Francis, Rourke, S. Shaywitz, & B. Shaywitz, 1993; Francis et al., 1994; S. Shaywitz et al., 1992; S. Shaywitz, Fletcher, & B. Shaywitz, 1994).

In view of the ongoing nature of learning problems, researchers, parents, and educators alike are asking: Are these continuing problems a direct and unchangeable result of the disability, or are they the result of a failure to identify the learning problem in time to affect its course? The need to show a discrepancy between IQ and performance is considered one of the forces slowing down early identification of children, because this assessment often is not done until the child has attempted and failed at reading, usually by the third grade. By that time, the child's achievement may have suffered enough to demonstrate the required discrepancy, but the child has failed for 2 to 3 years in reading progress and may have developed other problems as a result of such failure (Lyon, 1996). Furthermore, the discrepancy requirement for the diagnosis of learning disorder may not be necessary or meaningful, given that researchers are finding very few differences between discrepant and nondiscrepant readers across a wide range of factors, such as information processing, genetic variables, neurophysiological response, and so forth (Fletcher et al., 1994; Stanovich & Siegel, 1994).

Some researchers speculate that the diagnosis of learning disorders will soon be made in relation to associated language-based and neuropsychological features rather than the historical notion of a discrepancy between potential and performance (Kraus et al., 1996). Until practical alternatives are found, however, it is likely that the discrepancy criteria will continue to be used in eligibility decisions. Nevertheless, the limitations of this approach should be kept in mind when it is necessary to meet local regulations for determining a child's eligibility for special services.

The following sections examine the particular psychological and social problems of children and adolescents with learning disorders and the possible outcomes for these children when they reach adulthood. Both children and adolescents are more likely to express problems related to depression, lower self-worth and perceived competence, and externalizing behaviors than are their peers (Boetsch, Green, & Pennington, 1996). The range and type of problems are generally similar for both younger and older age groups. Accordingly, issues pertaining to both younger and older children and adolescents with learning disorders are considered jointly unless particular developmental differences warrant attention. Many of these issues are common to all types of learning disorders unless otherwise noted.

Psychological and social adjustment.

Children with learning disorders are more likely to show increased anxiety, withdrawal, depression, and low self-esteem when compared with their nonhandicapped peers, although accurate percentages for these various problems are unavailable (Bruck, 1986; Lyon, 1996). Teachers often note these children's attention-seeking and acting-out behaviors, as well as their low self-confidence and frustration over their scholastic abilities (Spreen et al., 1995). Conflict with parents and teachers over homework, grades, and attendance is common. Not surprisingly, the school dropout rate for adolescents with learning disorders is nearly 40%, or approximately 1½ times the average (APA, 1994).

The connection between learning disorders and behavioral/emotional disorders has generated considerable interest, but only cautious conclusions. Common sense suggests that children with learning disorders are faced with considerable challenges that are likely to take a toll on self-esteem and, in time, their social relationships. Indeed, students with reading disorders feel less supported by their parents, teachers, and peers than do normal readers, and are more likely to express poor academic or scholastic self-concepts (Boetsch et al., 1996). Children's self-concepts in areas such as sports and appearance, however, are usually less affected (Renick & Harter, 1989; Chapman, 1988).

Parents and teachers describe children with learning disorders from an early age as being more difficult to manage than typically developing children. Although overall reports of behavior problems increase considerably for *all* children between early and middle childhood (Achenbach, Howell, Quay, & Conners, 1991), reported rates of behavior problems for children with learning disorders are about 3 times higher than the norm by 8 years of age (Benasich et al., 1993) (see Figure 11.4). Most of these problems are not specific to learning disorders, but cover a broad range of problems that overlap 10% to 25% with features of conduct disorder, oppositional defiant disorder, attention-deficit/ hyperactivity disorder, and major depressive disorder across all ages (APA, 1994). These co-occurring problems are often interpreted as individual reactions and coping styles in response to failure, frustration, and in some instances, punishment and negative attention. In terms of development, however, it is hard to say which comes first: Behavior problems may precede learning problems, follow them, or occur at the same time (Spreen et al., 1995). One explanation for the higher rate of behavior problems

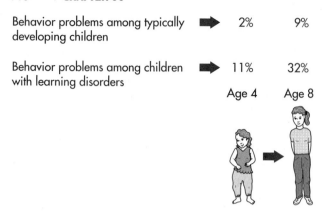

Behavior problems among typically developing children ➡ 2% 9%

Behavior problems among children with learning disorders ➡ 11% 32%

Age 4 Age 8

FIGURE 11.4 Percent of clinically significant behavior problems among children with and without learning disorders, at 4 years and 8 years of age. (Data from Benasich et al., 1993)

in children with learning disorders as they enter school is their slower overall intellectual development (Beitchman, Hook, Rochon, & Paterson, 1989; Tallal et al., 1989a, 1991). Slower cognitive development creates additional pressure relating to their academic and social progress, thereby causing frustration and lack of motivation across different learning situations.

As a group, children with learning disorders are more socially isolated and less popular among peers than are other children, and they make more negative impressions on others (Kavale & Forness, 1996; Taylor, 1988). Their difficulties developing friendships are related to deficits in social skills and social perceptiveness. Like Francine, who was described by her mother as "humorless and in a bit of a fog" and mostly ignored by other children her age, most children with learning disorders have difficulty grasping the nuances of social interaction and may not know how to greet others, make friends, or join in playground games. Subtle cues of social interaction, such as taking turns and waiting in line, may be missed or ignored by children with learning disorders (Ozols & Rourke, 1985). They may not always interpret correctly or respond appropriately to the frequent nonverbal—but very expressive—communication of other children, such as rolling the eyes to show dislike or disinterest. When children with learning disorders misunderstand the situation and act inappropriately, other children turn away.

Social skills deficits seem to be an integral part of learning disorders. According to a meta-analysis of over 150 studies (Kavale & Forness, 1996), about three of every four students with learning disorders have significant social skills deficits. These students, as well as their teachers, describe their social skills deficits largely in terms of poor school performance, a defining feature of this disorder. In addition, peers and teachers describe

children with learning disorders as being less accepted and more rejected by classmates. Thus, although behavior and social skills problems are by no means characteristic of all children with learning disorders, they are common enough to warrant careful attention, because they likely contribute to the academic challenges already faced by these children.

Having a child with a learning disorder can also be an emotional burden for family members. Parents may experience a range of emotions, including denial, guilt, blame, frustration, anger, and despair. Brothers and sisters often feel annoyed or embarrassed by or jealous of the attention their sibling receives. Because attention-seeking and acting-out problems are usually highly salient, a child's underlying distress and emotional needs may easily be overlooked; in fact, parents are often more aware of their children's acting-out problems than of their underlying feelings of sadness and self-doubt (Boetsch et al., 1996).

Adult outcomes. Unfortunately, the social and emotional difficulties connected to communication and learning disorders may continue to pose a challenge into adulthood, largely because of inadequate recognition and services (Lyon, 1996). Adults with learning disorders may avoid pleasure reading and may find ways to cover up their problems, such as watching television news rather than reading newspapers. On the other hand, many adults with reading disorders excel in nonacademic subjects, such as art, music, dance, or athletics. Still others may become outstanding architects and engineers, or they may have extraordinary interpersonal skills (NIMH, 1996), like the examples shown at the chapter's beginning. Each child and adolescent has many other strengths that can be developed to compensate for known deficits. Knowledge of strengths can also lead to ways of teaching that build on existing abilities and individual needs. Thus, despite having been at risk for academic failure and psychosocial problems, many adults with learning disorders lead successful and productive lives (Werner, 1993).

Perhaps the change in environmental pressures and expectations, along with the opportunities that open up once compulsory education has ended, can account for the ability of individuals with learning disorders to become productive and valued members of society. Once they are no longer restricted by the demands of school, adults presumably are freer to pick a niche that does not emphasize their academic problems, but instead capitalizes on their strengths. This explains why men with reading disorders do not differ from their peers with regard to feelings of global self-worth; symptoms of depression; feelings of competency and satisfaction with jobs, marriages, and other relationships; or frequency of antisocial behavior (Boetsch et al., 1996). However, men still perceive lower levels of social support from parents and relatives—the only people still in their lives who knew of their problems as children—an indication of the indelible impressions left by early experiences of failure and criticism.

One adult who developed his own way of compensating for learning problems describes it in his own words:

> I faked my way through school because I was very bright. I resent most that no one picked up my weaknesses. Essentially I judge myself on my failures. . . . [I] have always had low self-esteem. . . . A blow to my self-esteem when I was in school was that I could not write a poem or a story. . . . I could not write with a pen or pencil. The computer has changed my life. I do everything on my computer. It acts as my memory. I use it to structure my life and for all of my writing since my handwriting and written expression has always been so poor. (Polloway et al., 1992. p. 521)

Whereas the long-term outlook for men with learning disorders is generally positive, the troublesome question of sexism arises when considering how adult women with learning disorders fare over time. As a group, women with learning disorders have more adjustment problems than men as they leave the school environment and face the demands of adult life. Problems and breakdowns in relationships are common, which are seen as indicators of continued vulnerability for these women (Bruck, 1985). These problems could very well result from the relative lack of opportunity these women have to achieve in areas that capitalize on strengths. Reading problems result in poor qualifications at completion of school; such qualifications, in turn, lead to relatively undemanding and less rewarding early employment options. In addition, women who lack competitive job skills and strong career options due to school failure tend to get involved at an earlier age in intimate relationships, and these relationships are generally unsupportive (Maughan & Hagell, 1996). Young men, in contrast, have more wide-ranging options once they leave school, which facilitates more positive social functioning in adulthood. So, *if* they are able to select their own environments in adulthood (and women have more obstacles in this regard than do men), both men and women with learning disorders can build on their existing strengths, skills, and talents (Maughan & Hagell, 1996).

It is safe to say that even though learning disorders do not disappear, given proper educational experiences, people have a remarkable ability to learn throughout the life span (see Box 11.3). Adults with reading disorders can still learn to read, though it becomes more difficult because of a slowdown in brain development after puberty. Current gains in knowledge of the causes and

---

Box 11.3
Factors That Increase Resiliency and Adaptation

Several personal characteristics and circumstances aid those with learning disorders in their successful adaptation from childhood, through adolescence, to young adulthood. As part of a longitudinal study of all children born in 1955 on the island of Kauai, Hawaii, E. E. Werner followed 22 children with learning disabilities and 22 matched controls throughout their childhood, adolescence, and adulthood. She found, first of all, that most children with learning disabilities made a successful adaptation to adult life. In addition, those who showed the greatest resiliency and adaptation over time were described as having (1) a basic temperament that elicited positive responses from others; (2) a well-developed sense of efficacy, planning ahead, and self-esteem that guided their lives; (3) competent care-givers and supportive adults in their lives; and (4) opportunities for a second chance if they made mistakes or got into trouble with the law. Although some of the characteristics are present from birth (e.g., temperament), many of the other protective factors can be increased through the efforts of family members, schools, and communities.

Source: Based on Werner, 1993.

---

early signs of learning disorders are likely to have a positive impact on early recognition and proper instruction. Ways to detect potential learning problems based on nonintrusive electrophysiological measurements of brain reactivity, for example, may permit the diagnosis of learning disorder to be based on underlying deficits in phonological processing rather than on performance alone (Kraus et al., 1996). Thus, early identification and intervention may hold the key to preventing the long-term consequences of these disorders.

Causes

Some children have considerable problems learning to read and write, many of which are correctable. Having limited exposure to reading materials in the home, for example, will slow a child's interest in and acquisition of basic reading skills, as will poor teaching methods and distracting classrooms. For the 5% to 10% of children with learning disorders, however, learning problems seem to be caused by difficult-to-detect neurological problems that run in families (Frith & Frith, 1996). What may be inherited are deficits in how certain areas of the brain work, which, singly or in combination, result in poor discrimination of sounds or symbols and limited ability to process such information accurately and rapidly.

Most types of learning disorders do not stem from problems in a single, specific area of the brain, but from difficulties in bringing together information from various brain regions into "convergence zones," where the information is integrated and understood (Damasio, Gabowski, Tranel, Hichwa, & Damasio, 1996). Minute disturbances are suspected to exist in brain structures and functions that underlie phonological processing abilities, the most significant deficits related to communication and learning disorders. In addition, underlying abnormalities in cognitive processing may be present, such as deficits in visual perception, linguistic processes, attention, memory, or some combination of factors. Such abnormalities precede or cause learning disorders. Emerging evidence points to the conclusion that, in many cases, these subtle disturbances begin very early in development, perhaps prenatally (Miller & Tallal, 1995).

Genetic and Constitutional Factors.

Studies tracing relatives of adults with reading problems confirm that such difficulties run in families. Children who lack some of the skills needed for reading, such as hearing the separate sounds of words, are likely to have a parent with a related problem. Around the turn of the 20th century this problem was studied largely by physicians, who considered reading disorders to be an inherited condition called *congenital word blindness* (Morgan, 1896). Today, estimates based on behavioral genetic studies indicate that heritability accounts for 60% of the variance in reading disorders (DeFries et al., 1991), although the exact mode of transmission remains undetermined (Pennington et al., 1991; Spreen et al., 1995).

Most of the attention paid to heritability of learning disorders is aimed at genetic transmission of critical brain processes underlying phonetic processing, either through polygenetic or single-gene processes (Pennington et al., 1991). Because a parent's learning disorder may take a slightly different form in the child—the father may have a writing disorder and his child an expressive language disorder—it seems unlikely that specific types of learning disorders are inherited *directly* as an autosomal dominant form of transmission (Plomin, 1989; Pennington et al., 1991). More likely, what is inherited is a subtle brain dysfunction that in turn can lead to a learning disorder. For example, an area has been identified on chromosome 6 that predisposes children to reading disorder (Cardon et al., 1994). Such a genetic mode of transmission provides a plausible explanation for the high rate of 35% to 45% among family members for learning disorders in reading, which are considerably higher than the estimated base rate of 5% to 10% in the population (Pennington et al., 1991).

Behavioral genetic studies, where behavioral outcomes can be studied in relation to known or suspected genetic influences, indicate that deficits in phonological processing abilities are strongly influenced by hereditary factors. Siblings of children with severe phonological disorders, for example, have problems related to phonological abilities such as rhyming and segmentation, which suggests that they have inherited a similar underlying deficit (Lewis, 1990). As expected, given the critical role of phonology in learning to read, those family members who had linguistic phonological deficits also had higher rates of reading disorders.

Neurobiological Factors.

The understanding of learning disorders, particularly reading and language-based problems, took an important new direction in the mid-1980s following the discovery that the brains of persons with these problems were characterized by cellular abnormalities in the left hemisphere that involved important language centers (Galaburda, Sherman, Aboitiz, & Geschwind, 1985). The fact that these cellular abnormalities could occur only during the fifth to seventh month of fetal development strengthened the view that learning disorders evolved from subtle brain deficits present from birth (Lyon, 1996). These initial autopsy findings have now been confirmed by sophisticated brain imaging technology that makes it possible to observe the brain directly at work and to detect subtle malfunctions that could never be seen before. The suspected deficits, which likely are genetically based, involve specific discrimination tasks, such as detecting visual and auditory stimuli, as well as more pervasive visual-organizational deficits associated with reasoning and mathematical ability (Hynd & Semrud-Clikeman, 1989). One of the most likely locations of these deficits is a brain structure called the *planum temporale,* a language-related area found in both sides of the brain. In a normal brain, the left side of the planum temporale is usually larger than the right side; however, in the brain of an individual with a reading disorder, both sides are the same size (Hynd, Marshall, & Gonzalez, 1991). As discussed below, these discoveries are leading to promising new teaching methods that help children with learning disorders learn alternative methods for discriminating sounds.

Language-based learning disorders.

We have stressed that most children with reading and writing disorders have difficulty distinguishing phonemes that occur rapidly in speech. But why is this so? Consider what is involved as the brain goes about processing speech (see Figure 11.5). The sound must be processed by different brain areas as it is carried by nerve impulses from the ear to the thalamus to the nerve cells

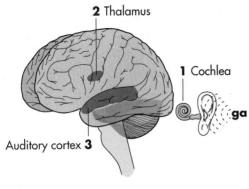

Making sense of spoken words

1. A sound, like the phonic syllable *ga*, hits the ear and is sent as nerve impulses to the brain.

2. In the brain, the thalamus processes incoming signals and sends them to the auditory cortex.

3. The nerve cells within the auditory cortex match incoming signals with patterns the cortex has previously stored.

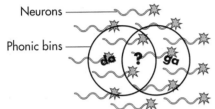

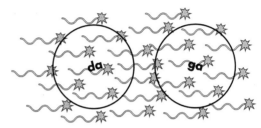

Why do language-impaired children confuse sounds?

By repeated exposure to spoken language, the neurons in the brain form patterns, or phonic bins, associated with particular sounds. When children have difficulty distinguishing between rapid acoustic cues, like the consonants in *ga* and *da*, those bins may overlap. Some scientists believe this overlap may be the key to language-based learning disabilities.

Can you retrain the brain?

Researchers at Rutgers and the University of California at San Francisco found that when children are taught to distinguish sounds that have been slowed down and exaggerated, their brains form new phonic bins. The scientists hypothesize that these new bins may be larger and no longer overlap. Eventually, the children learn to distinguish *ga* and *da* in ordinary speech.

FIGURE 11.5 How the brain processes speech. (*Time*, January, 29, 1996)

---

within the auditory cortex. As a nerve impulse arrives, it is matched by nerve cells in the auditory cortex to existing patterns, or phonic bins, that have been previously formed and stored.

To better understand the processing of speech, compare it to listening to music. When you first hear a new song, do you recognize aspects that resemble other recordings by that group or recordings by another group? Can you distinguish one group's music from that of other groups? As we listen to music, we tend to cluster sounds into various categories, acquiring our taste for music as we store more and more collections and melodies into memory. Each time we hear new music, it is matched to what we already know and appreciate. Young people are particularly adept at assimilating new sounds, thereby broadening their tastes for various types of music. In contrast, those who have already formed specific musical tastes tend to stick to what they know, rejecting sounds that are unpleasant or unrecognizable. This "gap" in music appreciation is analogous to the gap

researchers describe in the phonic abilities of children with learning disorders—these children do not possess certain auditory sites that would allow certain sounds to be recognized, so their appreciation of certain words is compromised.

Each neuron in the brain has immense specificity when it comes to processing language, and fascinating patterns of neuronal firings can be seen by probing the brain with electrodes. Some neurons fire when you silently name an object but not when you read the object's name, and vice versa. In bilingual persons certain neurons are activated when the individuals speak one language but not when they speak the other (Ojemann, 1991). The discovery of such neuronal specificity serving language functions explains why someone can have an expressive language problem despite full comprehension; neurons that are active when a person hears a word are not active when that person expresses it.

Two major strands of evidence converge with regard to the specific neurobiological deficits underlying learning disorders in phonological processing and, subsequently, reading. As a result, the long-held assumption that language functions are located primarily in two separate areas of the brain—one for speech production (Broca's area) and the other for speech comprehension (Wernicke's area)—is no longer valid. The first of these strands, previously mentioned in relation to communication disorders, is the well-established finding that children with reading disorders have subtle problems with language—specifically, phonological processing—even before learning to read. The streams of sounds (phonemes) that compose spoken language are not fully processed by these children. (These deficits often show up in word-repetition tasks.) Children who have problems splitting the sounds of words into their component phonemes are at a major disadvantage when it comes time to learn to read.

The picture thus far provides a valid explanation at the cognitive level, but does not explain where these problems originate. Very recently, a second strand of evidence has emerged that pinpoints the underlying physiological problem. The brain is organized in such a way that different functions are located in specific areas. This organization is referred to as *functional segregation* (Frith & Frith, 1996). The visual system provides a good illustration of functional segregation. Different aspects of what you see, such as form, color, and motion, are routed to different regions of the visual cortex. When something moves in your visual field, the region that responds to visual motion—labeled "V5"—is activated. Eden et al. (1996) discovered that adults with reading disorders show no activation in this V5 area when asked to view randomly moving dots.

Together, these two major findings implicate specific biological underpinnings of reading disorders: (1) the language problems of persons with a reading disorder are specifically associated with the understanding of phonology; and (2) behavioral and physiological abnormalities are found in the processing of visual information. It is not surprising, therefore, that phonological and visual processing problems often coexist among those with reading disorders (Eden et al., 1996).

What does visual discrimination have to do with auditory processing of sounds? Possibly the connection is mostly coincidental and not causally related; the lack of activity in the V5 area could simply be a marker of a genetic deviation that shows up in a number of different ways. A more intriguing, but still speculative, possibility is that the V5 defect in perception of visual motion is a marker of a more general deficit in *timing*, which affects many different brain functions (Frith & Frith, 1996). Consider that in order to detect differences between consonant sounds—such as *b* or *t*—we must be able to distinguish between very rapid changes in sound fre-

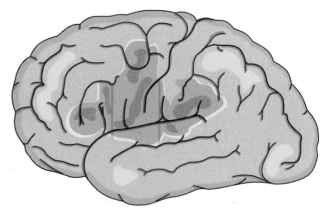

Normal (control) brain

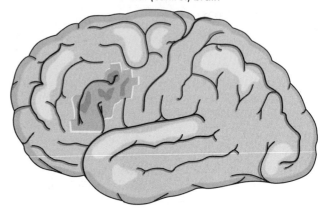

Dyslexic brain

FIGURE 11.6 Left-hemisphere brain activity of controls and dyslexics during a simple rhyming activity. (C. Frith & U. Frith, 1996)

quency. A subtle neurological deficit in sensitivity could lead to a problem in such distinction, which would then show up clinically as problems in reading and phonological processing. Figure 11.6 depicts left-hemisphere brain activity in controls and in dyslexics during a simple rhyming task. The task involved the visual presentation of two letters at a time; subjects had to indicate whether the letters rhymed (B and T) or did not rhyme (B and K). For example, for the letters B and T, subjects needed to evoke the names or the letters internally (*bee* and *tee*) and to separate out the beginning phonemes (*b* and *t*) from the rhyming part *(ee)*. When controls performed the task, three areas of the brain were activated—Broca's area, Wernicke's area, and the insula, a part of the cortex that lies between various language areas. In dyslexics, in contrast, only one area—Broca's area—was activated. Presumably, in more challenging language tasks this reduced amount of activation would impair performance. As noted earlier, Eden et al. (1996) now demonstrate that dyslexics also show reduced brain activation when carrying out nonlanguage tests: The visual area V5 is not activated when moving dots are observed. Also important is the fact that the V5 area of the brain becomes fully myelinated before birth, which argues for the viewpoint that its connections are already matured at birth (Frith & Frith, 1996).

Auditory processes show similar evidence for physiologically based problems in timing. Because vowel sounds resonate for about 100 milliseconds, they are easier to distinguish than fast consonants, such as *k*, that fly by at speeds of 40 milliseconds or so. Although children with language impairments have difficulty with fast consonants, they are better at identifying them when the sounds are slowed to half their normal speed (Tallal et al., 1996). Again, these problems are often present at birth; 6-month-old babies who have problems detecting changes in the sequence of tones when the tones are spaced closely together do poorly at distinguishing between speech sounds (Benasich et al., 1993). As mentioned earlier, the ability to make fine acoustic distinctions is a critical factor in language development.

One final point: These problems in auditory and visual discrimination occur at the level of the nervous system, not at the level of consciousness or awareness. Therefore, children with learning disorders often have no conscious perception of certain sounds, shapes, and movements because their brains do not process them at a subcortical level and make them available to higher centralized brain functions. Thus certain visual and auditory stimuli that would normally be heard or seen by others escape detection in those with learning disorders. To demonstrate the neurophysiology that precedes conscious detection of sounds, Kraus et al. (1996) first controlled for children's attention by diverting them with a movie, and then introduced auditory signals and measured electrophysiologic responses to small acoustic changes. They found that children with learning disorders, relative to controls, showed no discrimination of rapid speech changes, such as *ba* versus *wa*, indicating that some discrimination deficits originate in the auditory pathway before conscious perception.

Nonverbal learning disability.

Studies of the causes of learning disorders mostly involve children with reading disorders, but the findings overlap to those with disorders in written expression and mathematics as well. Many—but not all—disabled writers show deficits in reading (Lyon, 1996), and some mathematical concepts require reading and writing as well as mathematics skills. In contrast to these language-based disorders, however, are various **nonverbal learning disabilities** (Casey, Rourke, & Pickard, 1991; Rourke, 1987, 1988, 1993), a nondiagnostic term describing deficits related to right-hemisphere brain functioning. These deficits involve social skills, spatial orientation, problem solving, and the recognition of nonverbal cues such as body language. Recall that Francine's pattern of central processing

abilities and deficits was marked by well-developed word recognition and spelling, but significantly worse mechanical arithmetic skills. Mathematics disorder, and perhaps that of written expression as well, are known to be associated with brain deficits that differ from those described for language-based learning disorders. These deficits are largely found in areas not related to verbal ability, which has led to use of the term *nonverbal learning disorders*.

In addition to math deficiencies, nonverbal learning disorders are characterized by several neuropsychological patterns (Lyon, 1996):

❖ *Bilateral tactile deficits*—that is, problems with touch sensation that occur more on one side of the body than the other. In the case of nonverbal learning disorders, they are found more on the left side of the body. Carlos, for example, had finger agnosia (an inability to detect which finger was being touched) on his left hand.

❖ *Bilateral psychomotor coordination deficiencies*, again more often showing up as coordination problems on the left side.

❖ *Deficiencies in visual-spatial-organizational abilities*, often shown as problems orienting and assembling objects correctly (recall Carlos's problems earlier in the chapter), misalignment of numbers in columns, and similar difficulties with math-related functions.

❖ *Deficits in nonverbal problem solving, judgment, and reasoning.* Children with nonverbal learning disorders often attempt to resolve math problems that are clearly beyond their ability, resulting in unreasonable solutions.

❖ *Relative strengths in verbal abilities and reading.*

❖ *Difficulties adapting to novel and complex situations,* which may be related to the visual-spatial deficits.

❖ *More social problems than occur with other types of learning disorders,* as shown by problems in social perception (understanding subtle body language and facetious behavior) and social interaction with peers.

❖ *A tendency to communicate in a rote and repetitive manner.*

The search for suspected causes for this nonverbal pattern of learning disabilities—characteristic of children who perform considerably worse at math than reading—focuses on neurological diseases of childhood and developmental disabilities impairing brain functioning. Fetal alcohol syndrome, insulin-dependent diabetes, autism, irradiation (for treatment of various forms of cancer), and several other fetal and early childhood diseases and trauma have been linked to nonverbal learning disorders (Rourke & Del Dotto, 1994). The common element among these various diseases and traumas—the final common pathway leading to the nonverbal learning disorder syndrome—is their impairment of development and functioning of white matter of the brain. (Rourke, 1987, 1989).

Social and Psychological Factors.

James, Francine, and Carlos each had problems at school in addition to academic difficulties. James became easily frustrated, which led to attention seeking and classroom disturbances. Carlos, too, was impulsive and inattentive and engaged in diversion tactics to avoid schoolwork. Francine, on the other hand, avoided other children (and vice versa) because she lacked the skills needed to interact. Parents and teachers of children with learning disorders commonly report such problems, and understandably, experience their own frustration and impatience at times. Could the behavior problems have caused the learning disorders, or did the learning disorders cause the behavior problems? Could both problems—learning and behavior—be related to some third factor, such as intellectual deficits or environmental influences, that causes them both (Barkley, 1990; Shelton & Barkley, 1994)?

As noted previously in the definition of learning disorders, emotional disturbances and other signs of poor adaptive ability may arise in conjunction with academic problems because the underlying causes may be the same. The best example of this overlap is ADHD. Like James, Francine, Carlos, and Tim, some children with learning disorders behave in a manner that resembles features of ADHD, including inattention, restlessness, and hyperactivity (Boetsch et al., 1996; Hinshaw, 1992; Pennington, Groisser, & Welsh, 1993). Let's first put the issue in perspective. The actual overlap between learning disorders and either ADHD or conduct disorder is less than 20% (Hinshaw, 1992), which is far lower than previously thought. This degree of overlap, while significant, suggests that although behavioral and learning problems have certain common aspects, *they are still distinct and separate disorders* (Lyon, 1996). Reading disorder is commonly associated with deficits in phonological awareness, whereas ADHD has more variable effects on cognitive functioning, especially in areas of rote verbal learning and memory. ADHD, moreover, is relatively unrelated to phonological awareness tasks (Wood et al., 1991).

A developmental perspective helps explain possible ways that learning disorders may be connected to behavioral and attentional problems, and highlights the progressive, interactive nature of this connection. Figure 11.7 considers three possibilities, or developmental pathways, for explaining this connection (Rutter & Yule, 1970). The developmental periods noted across the top of the figure correspond roughly to the emergence of the learning and behavior problems described below.

As depicted in part A of Figure 11.7, the first possibility is that early developmental deficits lead to behavior problems such as inattentiveness, noncompliance, disruptiveness, and so forth, which in turn lead to learning disorders because they disrupt the learning process. Some evidence indicates that when behavior problems appear during the preschool years and continue into school entry, they are a significant risk factor in the development of reading disorder, particularly for boys: About one-quarter of children who have behavior problems at school entry, especially attentional and hyperactivity problems, show reading disorders 2 years later (Alexander, Entwisle, & Dauber, 1993; Smart, Sanson, & Prior, 1996). According to this pathway, therefore, early onset of behavior problems—such as those commonly associated with ADHD—may interfere with preschoolers' ability to grasp prelearning skills, such as attending, listening, and concentrating.

Part B of Figure 11.7 depicts the second possibility: Problems in early language development and the presence of communication and learning disorders cause the child to act out, be disruptive, or experience symptoms of anxiety and depression in relation to frustration and failure. Recall that prenatal problems, organic damage and genetic/constitutional factors can lead directly to learning and communication disorders in early childhood, such as phonological processing and speech and language problems. According to this pathway, these early learning problems increase the likelihood of hyperactivity and inattention problems in childhood and adolescence, which may be further accompanied by lower perceived competence in scholastic ability and lower self-concept (Casey, Levy, Brown, & Brooks-Gunn, 1992; Renick & Harter, 1989). Not surprisingly, inattention and hyperactivity are the most consistent correlates of underachievement among kindergarten and grade-school children (Hinshaw, 1992), which is reflected in both of the above explanations.

The third, and most likely, possibility for explaining the connection between learning and behavior problems is shown in part C of Figure 11.7: Learning disorders and behavior problems, although distinct disorders, interact in some manner, thereby increasing the potency of either or both problems over time (Hinshaw, 1992). It is difficult to determine if one causes the other, but if both are present, they are likely to intensify problems in both learning and behavior. These early, co-occurring problems in learning and behavior set the stage for further problems in childhood and adolescence (Boetsch et al., 1996). Underachievement in school and learning disorders in reading, in particular, become part of the picture. Again, if behavior problems coexist, they are likely to interact with these school problems in such a manner that failure and frustration continue to grow. By adolescence the picture changes further. Earlier problems in

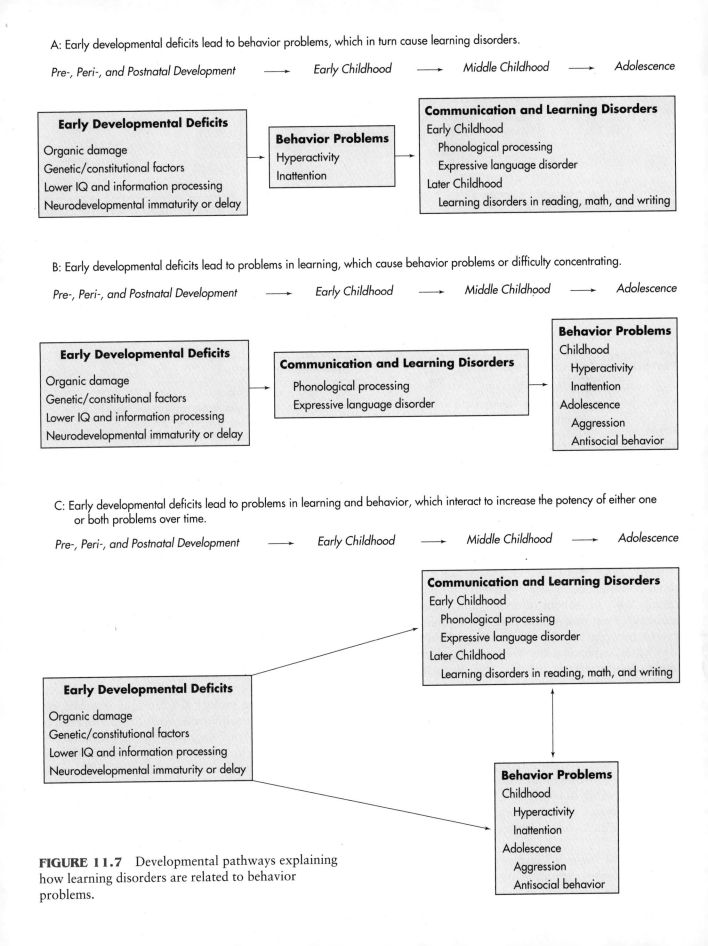

A: Early developmental deficits lead to behavior problems, which in turn cause learning disorders.

Pre-, Peri-, and Postnatal Development ⟶ *Early Childhood* ⟶ *Middle Childhood* ⟶ *Adolescence*

Early Developmental Deficits

Organic damage
Genetic/constitutional factors
Lower IQ and information processing
Neurodevelopmental immaturity or delay

Behavior Problems

Hyperactivity
Inattention

Communication and Learning Disorders

Early Childhood
    Phonological processing
    Expressive language disorder
Later Childhood
    Learning disorders in reading, math, and writing

B: Early developmental deficits lead to problems in learning, which cause behavior problems or difficulty concentrating.

Pre-, Peri-, and Postnatal Development ⟶ *Early Childhood* ⟶ *Middle Childhood* ⟶ *Adolescence*

Early Developmental Deficits

Organic damage
Genetic/constitutional factors
Lower IQ and information processing
Neurodevelopmental immaturity or delay

Communication and Learning Disorders

    Phonological processing
    Expressive language disorder

Behavior Problems

Childhood
    Hyperactivity
    Inattention
Adolescence
    Aggression
    Antisocial behavior

C: Early developmental deficits lead to problems in learning and behavior, which interact to increase the potency of either one or both problems over time.

Pre-, Peri-, and Postnatal Development ⟶ *Early Childhood* ⟶ *Middle Childhood* ⟶ *Adolescence*

Communication and Learning Disorders

Early Childhood
    Phonological processing
    Expressive language disorder
Later Childhood
    Learning disorders in reading, math, and writing

Early Developmental Deficits

Organic damage
Genetic/constitutional factors
Lower IQ and information processing
Neurodevelopmental immaturity or delay

Behavior Problems

Childhood
    Hyperactivity
    Inattention
Adolescence
    Aggression
    Antisocial behavior

FIGURE 11.7 Developmental pathways explaining how learning disorders are related to behavior problems.

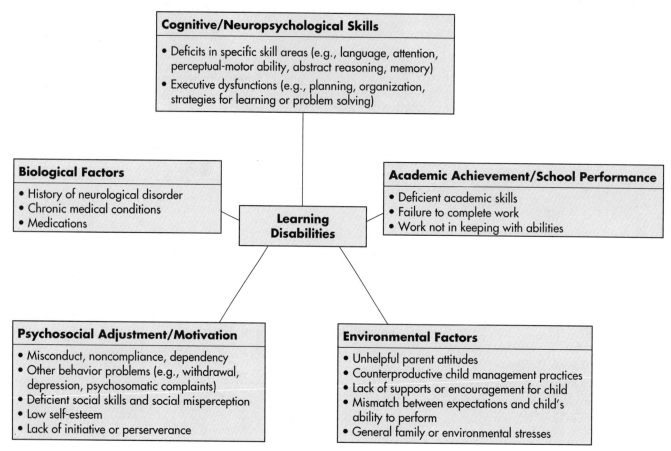

FIGURE 11.8 A behavioral systems model of major areas influencing the development and expression of learning disorders. (Taylor, 1989)

learning and achievement are strongly associated with delinquent behavior, even more so than with low verbal IQ (Brier, 1989; Hinshaw, 1992). Such behavior drives school performance further downward, resulting in increased risk of school dropout and limited self-sufficiency. Even though this pathway accounts for the overlap between learning and behavioral disorders in many cases, explaining the overlap is not a matter of simply choosing one of the three different pathways—pathways may differ for different children.

In short, academic underachievement, including learning disorders, in early and middle childhood overlaps with behavior problems such as hyperactivity and inattention. By adolescence, underachievement and learning disorders overlap with aggressive and antisocial acts. However, we cannot say with certainty whether one precedes the other in some causal manner. In all likelihood they interact with one another to increase the level of adjustment and academic difficulties a particular child will show.

In view of the many factors that contribute to the development and expression of learning disorders, a comprehensive model can provide a helpful integration and summation. Figure 11.8 shows the interacting influ-

ences of biological, cognitive, academic, environmental, and psychosocial factors touched on throughout the discussion of the developmental course and causes of learning disorders (Taylor, 1989).

TREATMENT AND PREVENTION

Although learning disorders have strong biological underpinnings, intervention methods for problems in learning rely primarily on educational and psychosocial methods rather than on biological treatments. Psychosocial treatments for James, Francine, Carlos, and Tim must be comprehensive and ongoing, with each new task broken down into manageable steps involving examples, practice, and ample feedback. In conjunction with proper teaching strategies, these children and their families may benefit from counseling aimed at helping the children develop greater self-control and a more positive attitude toward their own abilities. Support groups for parents can also fill an important gap between the school and the home by being a source of information, practical suggestions, and mutual understanding.

Breakthroughs in brain research may soon lead to new medical interventions and drugs, but at present no biological treatments exist for the speech, language, and academic disabilities shown by these children. Biological treatments for children with communication and learning disorders are typically limited to situations where significant problems coexist in concentration and attention. In these instances, some children respond favorably to stimulant medications. As discussed in Chapter 5, stimulant medications temporarily improve children's attention, concentration, and ability to control their impulsivity. Typically, the child takes the medication so that the drug is active during peak school hours, such as when reading and math are taught (NIMH, 1996).

Consider the coordinated planning and effort that went into the treatment programs for Francine:

Francine: Slowly but Surely

To approach the difficulties that Francine was having with math and, especially, with peer relationships, we considered several factors. First, we decided that teaching methods should be primarily verbal, with an understanding that she will have more difficulty in subjects such as math and science. Her teachers were in favor of allowing Francine to use a calculator and a computer to assist her in learning new concepts. An emphasis on physical education was also planned, to help her with her visual motor coordination. Her math teacher agreed that using graph paper might help her visualize numerical relationships, which led to noticeable improvements in her schoolwork.

Francine's problems in making friends was a major concern to everyone, and we believed that this problem was directly linked to her learning disability. A cognitive-behavioral intervention plan was developed in conjunction with her school-based educational plans. Because of Francine's strong verbal skills, we decided to use a self-guidance program involving problem solving for social situations. We taught her some problem-solving skills using role playing, and encouraged her mother to invite one child at a time over for her to play with so that she could "practice" her skills. Francine had drifted into being a loner and seemed disinterested in looking after herself, so we also discussed ways of developing better self-care at home by giving her an allowance for completing household chores. We spent considerable time explaining to her parents the nature of these problems, and this guidance led to relief and understanding of her learning strengths and weaknesses. We saw the family once again 1 year later; although some of her problems still existed, her social abilities had improved. She still had difficulties in developing friendships and tended to prefer being alone, but the problem had clearly lessened from the year before.

Francine was able to get help because the problem was detected; recall, however, that by the time she was referred, she had already begun to fail at formal schooling. The first step in solving any problem is realizing that a problem exists. The nature of learning disorders makes this step a difficult one for many children and parents. Even though many of the signs of language-based learning disorders are present from early childhood, sophisticated means of assessing such problems are not presently available until children are old enough to be formally tested.

Regrettably, this often means that they have already begun schooling, and persistent difficulties in reading, writing, or arithmetic are obvious to the classroom teacher. Some problems are not so obvious, however. Children who are quiet and polite often go unnoticed, and those with above-average intelligence may maintain passing grades despite their specific disability. Children with hyperactivity, on the other hand, are more often identified quickly as a result of their impulsive behavior and heightened activity level.

These issues of identification are quite important, because a relatively brief window of opportunity may exist for the most successful treatment of learning disorders. If the problem is detected in early childhood, say, by kindergarten age, language-based deficits can often be remediated successfully. If the problem is not detected until age 8 or so, response to treatment is much worse (Fletcher & Foorman, 1994). This is why prevention of reading difficulties has become a hot topic: Training children in phonological awareness activities at an early age may prevent subsequent reading problems among those at risk (Blachman, Ball, Black, & Tangel, 1994; Foorman, Francis, Beeler, Winikates, & Fletcher, 1997). These activities consist of games in the areas of listening, rhyming, identifying sentences and words, and analyzing syllables and phonemes. For example, the child might analyze *sand* as *s-and* and then synthesize it into *sand,* or colored blocks might be used to break the word into separate phonetic sounds *(s-a-n-d)* (Lyon & Cutting, 1998).

Before turning to specific remediational methods for assisting school-age children with communication and learning disorders, we take a brief look at how knowledge of these disorders has played leapfrog with the philosophy and practice of classroom instruction over the last decade. Recent discoveries, such as those in neurosciences noted above, challenged some of the prevailing educational practices, and even today considerable disagreement remains as to the "best" way to assist children with learning disorders.

The Regular Education Initiative

Inclusion of children with special educational needs into the regular classroom has become the norm throughout North America in recent years. The groundwork for this *inclusion movement* began in the 1950s and was based on studies showing that segregated special classes for students with disabilities were ineffective and possibly harmful (Baldwin, 1958). A new educational philosophy gained momentum, based on the belief that children with special needs should be placed in the least restrictive environment possible and provided with a full range of "pull-out" services (Reynolds, 1962). Resource rooms and specially trained teachers replaced the special classes that had been in vogue, a change that had the further advantage of removing the need to label and categorize children. The Education for All Handicapped Children Act of 1975 in the United States (Public Law 94-142) and the Education Act of 1982 in Canada (Bill 82) mandated that children with special needs be afforded access to all educational services, regardless of their handicaps.

By the late 1980s, this inclusion movement expanded to become the **regular education initiative (REI)**, whereby students with disabilities are placed in general classrooms with general and special education teachers sharing responsibility for student instruction. Most prominently, the programs—rather than the children—are labeled (Hammill, 1993). In principle, the REI is attractive and promising, because it allows children with special needs to receive services without being diagnosed or labeled mentally retarded, learning disabled, and so forth. However, implementation and teacher training, as well as the question of whether the REI meets the special needs of students, continue to be unresolved and hotly debated topics (Kauffman, 1989; Wang, Walberg, & Reynolds, 1992).

Instructional Methods

Although controversy remains over the practical aspects of including all children in regular classrooms, educators generally agree over the best instructional methods. Most educators today favor **direct instruction** for children with learning disorders. This straightforward approach to teaching is based on the premise that to improve a skill, the instructional activities have to approximate those of the skill being taught (Hammill, 1993). But what is the best way to go about this? Would you begin by directly teaching specific phonetic subskills and proceed to words and sentences, or vice versa (Lyon & Cutting, 1998)? Do children with learning disorders need to break down each word into each sound before they can adequately grasp the meaning of the word and put it in context?

On the one hand, say advocates of a **code-emphasis approach,** specific instruction in word structure is necessary because of the child's phonological deficits (Mather, 1992). Reading needs to be decontextualized, goes the argument, because if children with a reading disorder have too much trouble with basic word recognition, their cognitive abilities are too overtaxed to permit comprehension as well (Stanovich, 1994). This approach is similar to having to look up every other word in the dictionary as you read this text. Do you think you would gain enough understanding to pass the next test? On the other hand, say advocates of **whole language methods,** instruction in basic phonics is too far removed from what reading is all about. Teaching practices that fragment language into small parts are seen as counterproductive (Goodman, 1986). You may not grasp every detail, but by reading whole words and sentences, you gain a greater appreciation of the overall content and meaning.

Code emphasis is based on the notion that the ability to decode and recognize words accurately and rapidly is essential to reading comprehension (Hallahan, Kauffman, & Lloyd, 1996). Intervention methods derived from this view involve cognitive, behavioral, and task-analytic approaches that focus in detail on helping the child understand the main sound-symbol relationships and the application of phonic skills to reading. A whole-language advocate, in contrast, places emphasis on the teaching of wholes: whole person, whole words, whole idea, and so on. Rather than teaching isolated words or sounds, whole-language methods get the student involved in the entire text; this approach is based on the premise that children—even those with learning disorders—will learn the language rules essential for reading (King & Goodman, 1990). Instruction is planned in consideration of a particular child's needs and abilities, such as the child's motivation, particular strengths and weaknesses, and the setting. The student is immersed in reading activities, and only meaningful units—words or sentences—are taught (Hammill, 1993).

By and large, research findings favor the code-emphasis model as the more viable strategy for teaching basic reading (Foorman, 1995; Lyon & Cutting, 1998). Whole-language approaches are effective at improving children's *attitudes* toward reading, but reading *achievement* is less affected unless specific phonics training is included (Stahl, McKenna, & Pagnucco, 1994). In everyday use, both approaches are often blended to keep the task rewarding and successful for the child (Hammill, 1993).

We now turn to some practical examples of how the tasks of reading, writing, and math can be taught by applying well-established principles of learning. Behavioral and cognitive-behavioral strategies have been highly beneficial in remediating the problems of children with communication and learning disorders (Lyon & Cutting, 1998). In addition, new methods based on the use of technology offer some children additional ways to acquire basic and advanced academic skills.

Behavioral Strategies.

Many problems that children with communication and learning disorders have stem from the fact that the material is simply presented too fast for them (Rourke & Del Dotto, 1994). Thus, a strategy that provides children with a set of verbal rules that can be written out and re-applied may be more beneficial than a strategy that relies on memory or on grasping the concept all at once. Tried-and-true behavioral principles of learning are well suited to this task of teaching in a systematic, step-by-step fashion. Not only academic concepts can be mastered in this way; as we saw with Francine, some of the associated problems with peers can be addressed in like fashion. A simple, gradual approach is more beneficial than one that tries to solve the problem all at once. Children also need help learning how to generalize new information to different situations. An individualized, skills-based approach does not have to be boring or routine; in fact, speech and language therapists are skilled at providing a stimulating but structured environment for hearing and practicing language patterns. During an engaging activity with a younger child, the therapist may talk about toys, then encourage the child to use the same sounds or words. The child may watch the therapist make the sound, feel the vibration in the therapist's throat, then practice making the sounds before a mirror.

Behavioral methods are often used in conjunction with a complete program of direct instruction, which typically proceeds in a cumulative, highly structured manner (Rosenshine & Stevens, 1986) (see Box 11.4). Notice how this method places a strong emphasis on the behavior of the teacher in terms of explicit correction, reinforcement, and practice opportunities. Because of this emphasis, it is sometimes referred to as "faultless instruction": Each concept should be so clearly presented that only one interpretation can be made (Englemann & Carnine, 1982). Each lesson is structured according to field-tested scripts. Teachers work with a small group of students at a time, and shoot questions at them at a rate as high as 10 to 12 per minute. Box 11.5 offers a cogent example.

This highly structured, repetitive method for assisting students with learning disorders is clearly effective (Gersten, White, Falco, & Carnine, 1982). Students who

> ### Box 11.4
> ## Steps in Direct Instruction Using Behavioral Methods
>
> 1. Review child's existing abilities.
> 2. Develop a short statement of goals at the beginning of each lesson.
> 3. Present new concepts and material in small steps, each followed by student practice.
> 4. Provide clear and detailed instructions and explanations.
> 5. Provide considerable practice for all students.
> 6. Check student understanding of concepts continually, in response to teacher questions.
> 7. Provide explicit guidance for each student during initial practice.
> 8. Provide systematic feedback and corrections.
> 9. Provide explicit instruction and practice for exercises completed by students at their desks.
>
> *Source:* Lyons & Cutting, 1998.

receive behaviorally based direct instruction typically outperform those who receive standard classroom instruction by almost 1 standard deviation on various learning measures (White, 1988).

Cognitive-Behavioral Interventions.

Cognitive-behavioral interventions are also highly suited for children with learning disorders. Like behavioral methods, these procedures actively involve students in learning, particularly in monitoring their own thought processes. Considerable emphasis is placed on self-control, by using such strategies as self-monitoring, self-assessment, self-recording, self-management of reinforcement, and so on (Lloyd, Hallahan, Kauffman, & Keller, 1991). Essentially, children are taught to ask themselves several questions as they progress, to make them more aware of the material (Wong, Harris, & Graham, 1991). Try it yourself: "Why am I reading this? What's the main idea the authors are trying to get across? Where would I find the answer to this question? How does this follow from what I learned a minute ago?"

Carlos's treatment program shows how some of these procedures were applied to his particular writing problems:

Carlos's PLANS

In grade three, Carlos's treatment plan was to integrate a cognitive-behavioral approach into regular teaching methods. Rather than using one-

Box 11.5

Sample Teaching Script from a Direct Instruction Program: Thinking Operations

EXERCISE 1: ANALOGIES
TASK A

The first thinking operation today is analogies.

1. We're going to make up an analogy that tells how animals move. What is the analogy going to tell? Signal: *How animals move*. Repeat until firm.

2. The animals we're going to use in the analogy are a hawk and a whale. Which animals? Signal. *A hawk and a whale*.

3. Name the first animal. Signal. *A hawk*. Yes, a hawk. How does that animal move? Signal. *It flies*. Yes, it flies.

4. So, here's the first part of the analogy: A hawk is to flying. What's the first part of the analogy? Signal. *A hawk is to flying*. Yes, a hawk is to flying. Repeat until firm.

5. The first part of the analogy told how the animal moves. So, the *next* part of the analogy must tell how another animal moves.

6. You told how a hawk moves. Now you're going to tell about a whale. What animal? Signal. *A whale*. How does that animal move? Signal. *It swims*. Yes, it swims.

7. So, here's the second part of the analogy: A whale is to swimming. What's the second part of the analogy? Signal. *A whale is to swimming*. Yes, a whale is to swimming.

8. Repeat steps 2 to 7 until firm.

9. Now we're going to say the whole analogy. First, we're going to tell how a *hawk* moves and then we're going to tell how a *whale* moves. Say the analogy with me. Signal. Respond with the students. A hawk is to flying as a whale is to swimming. Repeat until the students are responding with you.

10. All by yourselves. Say that analogy. Signal. *A hawk is to flying as a whale is to swimming*. Repeat until firm.

11. That analogy tells *how those animals move*. What does that analogy tell? Signal. *How those animals move*.

12. Repeat steps 10 and 11 until firm.
    Individual test: Call on individual students to do step 10 or 11.

Source: Engelmann et al., 1978.

ways of using computers and tape recorders to help him learn the materials. He seemed to like these methods, and they helped him bypass some of his disability. We discussed practice strategies for visual motor integration, such as drawing and tracing, and gradually added more complexity to the task. Because cursive writing is often easier for children than printing, we suggested to his teacher that he bypass learning to print and work more on cursive writing. This approach was suggested because a continuous pattern of output is easier for Carlos to plan and produce than is a discrete form of output, such as printing.

To assist Carlos in writing a paper for school, we adopted a basic planning strategy from Graham, MacArthur, Schwatz, and Voth (1992), which helped him structure the writing tasks into related subproblems: The acronym *PLANS* helps him to remember to

> **P**ick goals (related to length, structure, and purpose of the paper)
> **L**ist ways to meet goals
> **A**nd
> **M**ake Notes
> **S**equence notes

This mnemonic was used in a three-step writing strategy to assist Carlos to (1) do PLANS, (2) write and say more, and (3) evaluate if he is successful in achieving his goals.

Computer-Assisted Learning. For some children with language-based communication and learning disorders, computer games may be their ticket to a brighter future (Reinking & Bridwell-Bowles, 1991). One problem in reading instruction is maintaining a balance between the basic but dull word decoding and the complex but engaging text comprehension (Perfetti, 1985). Not all the issues have been resolved, but computer-assisted methods for spelling, reading, and math provide more academic engagement and achievement than traditional pencil-and-paper methods (MacArthur, Haynes, Malouf, & Harris, 1990).

Computers have been used as simple instructional tools to deliver questions and answers for some time. Following the recent discoveries of phonological awareness and timing problems in the brain, researchers are now testing whether computers can *remedy* some of the basic auditory problems. Some children with communication and learning disorders are unable to process information that flashes by too quickly, such as the

to-one instruction, we discussed with his teacher ways of blending some behavioral methods into the classroom. For example, his strengths are in the areas of speaking and thinking, so we discussed

New research raises cautious hope that computer games and exercises can help children with learning disabilities develop key mental skills.

Box 11.6

Critical Elements for a Successful Beginning Reading Program

1. *Provide direct instruction in language analysis.* Identify at-risk children early in their school careers—preferably in kindergarten—and teach phonological awareness skills directly.

2. *Provide direct teaching of the alphabetic code.* Code instruction should be structured and systematic, in a sequence that goes from simple to more complex. Teach the regularities of the English language before introducing the irregularities. Nothing should be left to guesswork—be as explicit as possible. If a child is overly reliant on letter-by-letter decoding, teach him or her to process larger and larger chunks of words.

3. *Teach reading and spelling in coordination.* Children should learn to spell correctly the words they are reading.

4. *Provide intensive reading instruction.* Children may need 3 or more years of direct instruction in basic reading skills to ensure competency. As they progress, they should practice more and more reading that is contextualized. Reading materials should have controlled vocabularies that contain mostly words the children can decode. As children develop a core sight vocabulary, introduce only those irregular words that can be read with high accuracy. Guessing is counterproductive.

5. *Teach for automaticity.* Once basic decoding is mastered, children must be exposed to words often enough that the words become automatically accessible. This usually requires a great deal of practice, which should be as pleasant and rewarding as possible.

Source: Felton, 1993.

---

consonant sounds *ba* and *da*. This deficit interferes with vital speech processes. In a test to determine whether computers could help these children by delivering the sounds more slowly, 5- to 10-year-olds played simple computer games in which they won points for distinguishing various sounds (Tallal et al., 1996). Computers stretched consonant sounds to half normal speed. As the children improved, the games got harder, with sounds becoming shorter in duration and spaced closer together. The results were striking: Children who were 1 to 3 years behind in language ability improved by a full 2 years after only 4 weeks. These gains remained 6 weeks later. The training did not simply supply the children with tricks for performing exercises, but actually improved their language understanding. Whether this approach will hold up under further scientific scrutiny remains to be seen.

In sum, treatment methods for communication and learning disorders are varied and beneficial. For many of these children who for so long received very little attention or help, choices are beginning to be available. Box 11.6 reviews some of the basic elements for a successful reading program, elements that apply to other disabilities as well. For children with reading disorders to learn how to read, they must receive a balanced intervention program composed of direct and explicit instruction in phonemic awareness, a systematic way to generalize this learning to the learning of sound-symbol relationships (phonics), and many opportunities to practice these coding skills within the context of reading meaningful, interesting, and controlled texts. The sooner in schooling this intervention occurs, the better (Lyon & Cutting, 1998).

SUMMARY

The Concept of Learning Disabilities

1. *Learning disabilities* is a general term that encompasses communication and learning problems that occur in the absence of other obvious conditions, such as mental retardation or brain damage.

2. Children and adults with learning disabilities show *specific* deficits in using spoken or written language, often referred to as relative strengths and weaknesses.

Language Development and Disorders

3. Language development, which is based on innate ability and environmental opportunities to learn, store, and express important sounds in the language, proceeds very rapidly in infancy.

4. Deficits in phonology have been identified as a major cause underlying both communication and learning disorders.

Communication Disorders

5. Speech and language problems emerging in early childhood include difficulty producing speech sounds, speech fluency, using spoken language to communicate, or understanding what other people say.

6. Even though most children with communication disorders acquire normal language by mid- to late adolescence, communication disorders are developmentally connected to the later onset of learning disorders.

7. Expressive language disorder is a type of communication disorder defined as a discrepancy between receptive language and expressive language.

8. Stuttering, or speech dysfluency, occurs mostly in younger children, peaking around age 5. Recovery usually occurs once the child enters school.

9. Causes of communication disorders include genetic influences and slowness or abnormalities of brain maturation. Ear infections from an early age may play a causal role in some cases.

10. Treatment of children with communication disorders is often unnecessary, since many of these problems are self-correcting soon after school entry.

Learning Disorders

11. These disorders consist of specific problems in reading, mathematics, or writing ability, of which reading disorders are by far the most common. Mathematics and writing disorders overlap considerably with reading disorders.

12. Although learning disorders overlap with behavioral disorders, they are distinct problems. Opportunities to develop and use particular strengths lead to more successful adult outcomes.

13. Learning disorders in reading may be caused by phonological problems arising from behavioral and physiological abnormalities in the processing of visual information in the brain. These deficits are believed to be largely inherited.

Treatment and Prevention

14. Treatments for children with communication and learning disorders involve educational strategies that capitalize on existing strengths, such as behavioral strategies involving direct instruction. Cognitive-behavioral techniques and computer-assisted instruction are also used successfully.

KEY TERMS

learning disability, 420
dyslexia, 422
unexpected discrepancy, 422
phonemes, 423
co-articulated, 424
phonological awareness, 424
expressive language disorder, 425
mixed receptive-expressive language disorder, 426
phonological disorder, 426
mainstream education, 427
stuttering, 430
learning disorder, 431
reading disorders, 435
decoding, 435
mathematics disorder, 435
writing disorder, 437
nonverbal learning disabilities, 445
regular education initiative (REI), 450
direct instruction, 450
code-emphasis approach, 450
whole-language methods, 450

Health-Related Disorders

We are not ourselves
When nature, being oppress'd, commands the mind
To suffer with the body.

—Shakespeare, King Lear

Jeremiah: Breath Is Life

Jeremiah Jager, four, loves blue. He drinks blue soda pop, picks the blue marshmallows out of his Magic Stars cereal and grabs the blue crayon. But when he got croupy and turned his favorite color this past winter—lips, cheeks, nose—his mother panicked. It was Jeremiah's eighth visit to the ER. And the scariest. "When he turned blue, I said 'I want some answers,'" says Cathy, who figured that, like relatives on both sides of his family, Jeremiah was developing asthma. She called the 800 number for Lung Line at the National Jewish Medical and Research Center in Denver. "This is going to cost twice as much as our car," says Cathy. "But why give birth to them if you're not going to do all you can for them?" Within a week, the Jagers left Alliance, Nebraska, for the long drive to Denver. They had to find out what was wrong with their child. (Dowling & Hollister, 1997)

Anita: Too Worried to Sleep

Anita, age 12, had considerable difficulty falling asleep. Each night it would take her an hour or two to fall asleep, which made it very difficult for her to get up for school at 6:00 the next morning. Her typical nighttime routine was to watch television downstairs until 9:00 P.M. and then get ready for bed. Once in bed, she read for a while before turning out the lights. She explains:

> I start to get sleepy when I'm reading, but as soon as I turn off the lights I'm wide awake. I can't stop from thinking about things, especially stuff that bothers me at school, like homework and making friends. My dad told me I would get sick because I don't sleep enough, and now I'm afraid I'll catch "mono" like a friend of mine has at school. No matter what I do, I can't seem to just fall asleep like I used to. (Adapted from Bootzin & Chambers, 1990)

What do Jeremiah and Anita have in common? On a regular basis, these children face situations that affect their health and well-being; as a result, they and their family members are continually distressed and worried. Jeremiah's parents want answers for his breathing problems, which seem to occur without warning. Because doctors are unable to explain his episodes, Jeremiah's parents secretly wonder sometimes if his breathing problems may be due to psychological causes. Similarly, Anita's sleep problems are intermingled with worries, brought on by her father's comments about her failing to get enough sleep. What role, if any, do psychological factors play in Jeremiah's and Anita's development and adaptation to their health-related problems?

Children, parents, and other family members are all deeply affected by children's health-related problems, which is why they have considerable psychological importance. Problems discussed in this chapter are not typically viewed as mental health disorders, but rather as health-related problems and medical stressors. Some

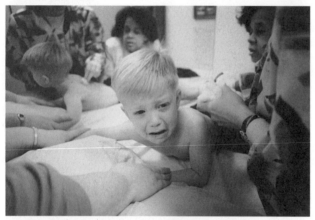

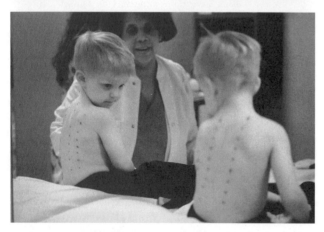

Jeremiah and Fire Bear (top) wait for a test. The boy's back is dotted with solutions of common allergens to see if he gets raised bumps, but he does not.

stressors are mild, like Anita's problems falling asleep and sleeping through the night, but others, like Jeremiah's asthma, can be life-threatening and highly disruptive, and involve complicated and intrusive medical interventions.

Pediatric health-related disorders cover a broad yet distinct area of specialization, ranging from relatively minor concerns like **enuresis** (bed-wetting) and **encopre-** sis (soiling), to **chronic illnesses** like cancer and diabetes (Olson, Mullins, Gillman, & Chaney, 1994). Health-related disorders are often viewed differently from child psychopathology in general because children's adjustment problems are more directly connected to the impact of the physical illness. Moreover, the field of pediatric health-related problems stresses the interaction between physical and mental health, since the various disorders and developmental problems all share medical, psychological, and psychosocial components (Harbeck-Weber & Peterson, 1996). The involvement of psychologists and other mental health professionals in children's health-related problems has led to many highly successful ways to assist children and family members in coping with and adapting to their circumstances.

HISTORICAL DEVELOPMENTS

Although psychological approaches to aiding children with health-related problems have gained considerable momentum over the past two decades, a long history preceded these developments. Ever since Greek philosophers first suggested that pain and disease were caused by an imbalance in the body's basic elements of fire, air, water, and earth, various cultures have been fascinated and perplexed by the interrelationship between the mind and the body. These early ideas took a giant step backward during the medieval period, however, when mental and physical illnesses were often seen as demonic possession, requiring a quick and gruesome dispatch of the afflicted person.

Scientific interest in the relationship between emotional and physical well-being remained largely dormant until the late 19th century, when Charcot and Freud brought forth their theories on the nature of hysteria and conversion disorders. Psychodynamic theory and the emerging discoveries of modern medicine often clashed during the early years of the 20th century, however, as debates emerged over the relative importance of the mind-body dichotomy (L. J. Siegel, Smith, & Wood, 1991). Partially as a result of these developments, an early distinction emerged between disorders caused by physical factors and those caused by emotional or psychological factors (Harbeck-Weber & Peterson, 1996). Disorders stemming from psychological and social factors affecting physical disorders were referred to as *psychosomatic* and, later on, *psychophysiological* disorders, which meant that psychological factors were affecting somatic (physical) function. These terms are no longer used, however, because they wrongly implied that a person's physical symptoms were caused solely by mental problems, especially if no medical evidence could be found.

Until 50 years ago or so, attention was rightfully placed on the acute, infectious diseases, such as smallpox, tuberculosis, diphtheria, and typhus, which claimed the lives of one in four children before their ninth birthday (Pollock, 1987). This statistic—simple, unemotional, impartial—belies the emotional toll this high infant and child mortality rate must have had on our ancestors. In fact, some historians argue that prior to the mid-19th century, children's highly unpredictable lifespans contributed to a diminished emotional investment in children among parents and society at large (Garrison & McQuiston, 1989). It is difficult to conceive of such circumstances today in Western society, even though high child mortality rates still exist in other countries around the world.

The problems addressed in this chapter—sleep disorders, elimination disorders, and chronic illness—are good examples of how poorly understood physical symptoms can sometimes be misattributed primarily to psychological causes. Moreover, these diverse realities of childhood underscore how reliance on fashionable cures and untested folk wisdom, as opposed to scientific findings, can be viewed by subsequent generations as unwise and sometimes traumatic.

Consider children's sleep and elimination problems. For centuries, these relatively common afflictions were unfairly attributed to children's inherent stubbornness and laziness. Similar to the responses elicited by mental retardation, societal attitudes varied from severe to lenient. By the turn of the 20th century, professional and public opinion held that enuresis, like childhood masturbation, was a potential sign of emotional and behavioral disturbance and characterological weakness. Early psychodynamic theory, gaining in popularity, proposed that toileting difficulties reflected unconscious conflicts that, if unresolved, could turn into troublesome personality styles. Sources of the underlying conflict were numerous: lack of parental love, the guilt value of feces, separation anxiety, fear of loss of feces, pregnancy wishes, aggression against a hostile world, response to family problems, and traumatic separation from mother between the oral and anal stages of psychosexual development (Fielding & Doleys, 1988).

By the 1920s the *Infant Care Bulletin*, the official publication of the U.S. Children's Bureau, reflected the harsh stance of society toward children's developmental problems. It advised parents to force their children to have bowel movements on a strict, regular schedule, and to complete toilet training by 8 months of age at the latest! If the baby did not go along with this plan, elimination was induced by inserting a stick of soap into the rectum (Achenbach, 1982). Fortunately, by the 1940s this advice mellowed toward more natural, developmentally sensitive approaches that allowed children's matu-

rity to dictate when parents could shift from diapers to toileting, anywhere between 12 and 30 months of age. Some of you may also be aware of how toilet training issues once again emerged during the rebellious 1960s, when pediatrician Benjamin Spock was blamed for many social problems in North America because his advice on toileting and early childhood discipline from the 1940s on was considered too lenient. Spock had made it clear, though, that "the child supplies the power but the parents have to do the steering" (1955).

How children adapt to the many situational, developmental, and chronic stressors affecting their health and well-being is a primary interest of pediatric health psychology. We begin by discussing sleep disorders, pausing to consider how important sleep is to our psychological and physical development and regulation from birth. From there we discuss elimination disorders and chronic illness in children and adolescents, areas in which monumental gains have been made in recent years in helping children overcome or adapt to these challenges. How health-related problems interact with children's and adolescents' psychological well-being, and how they and their families adapt in response, are central themes throughout this chapter.

SLEEP DISORDERS

It must be difficult for a student to understand sleep problems in children, since you have lectures, textbooks, and many other sleeping aids to rely on! Nonetheless, we all have problems sleeping at one time or another. Most often the problem is not serious and does not interfere with the next day's activities, but sometimes sleep problems can have a major effect on our physical and psychological health and well-being. As any parent, sibling, or roommate can attest, these problems can have a major impact on them as well. In fact, problems related to sleep, such as resistance at bedtime, difficulty settling at bedtime, night waking, difficulty waking up, and fatigue, are among the most common complaints or concerns expressed by parents of young children (Blader, Koplewicz, Abikoff, & Foley, 1997).

Arguably, sleep is the *primary* activity of the brain during the early years of development. Consider this: By 2 years of age the average child has spent almost 10,000 hours (nearly 14 months) asleep, and approximately 7500 hours (about 10 months) in waking activities (Anders, Sadeh, & Appareddy, 1995). In those 2 years, the brain has reached 90% of adult size, and the child has attained remarkable complexity in areas such as cognitive skills, language, concept of self, socioemotional development, and physical skills (Dahl, 1996; Cicchetti & Beeghly, 1990). Yet, during most of the time these maturational advances were occurring, the child was asleep.

Gradually, by age 5 or so, a more even balance emerges between sleep and wakefulness. Still, by the time they begin school, children have spent more time asleep than in social interactions, exploration of the environment, eating, or any other single waking activity. Why has evolution favored sleep over these other important activities? Wouldn't it be to our advantage to have more waking time to learn language, acquire knowledge, and develop similar adaptive skills? Apparently, sleep serves a fundamental role in brain development and regulation (Dahl, 1996). This role explains why sleep disturbances can affect overall physical and mental health and well-being, and why sleep disorders are important to abnormal child psychology.

Perhaps you have noticed how sleep problems co-occur with many different disorders, especially ADHD, depression, and anxiety, a connection that raises an important consideration: Do sleep problems *cause* or *result from* other disorders? The answer to this question requires an understanding of how sleep problems interact with a person's psychological well-being. Because our own experience has been that sleep problems commonly arise from particular stressors, like an upcoming exam or a relationship problem, we tend to think that sleep difficulties are secondary symptoms of a more primary problem. However, the relationship between sleep problems and psychological adjustment is not unidirectional. Sleep problems may themselves cause emotional and behavioral problems among children and adolescents, and they also can be caused directly by a psychological disorder. In some circumstances, sleep problems might result from some underlying factor that is common to both sleep problems and other disorders. Remember in the chapter on anxiety how problems in the brain's arousal and regulatory systems can cause increased anxiety? Such problems can affect sleep patterns as well. Simply stated, sleep disorders can cause other psychological problems or can result from other disorders or conditions. Sleep disorders have considerable importance to abnormal child psychology because they mimic or worsen many of the symptoms of major disorders (Dahl, Pelham, & Weirson, 1991).

The link between sleep and emotions is familiar to us all. Lack of sleep is associated with irritability, impulsivity, and difficulty focusing attention. In fact, parents often attribute almost any malady to their child's being overtired, and naturally assume that emotional distress underlies most transient sleep disturbances in their child or adolescent. The early stages of an intense romantic relationship or the anticipation of an exciting event, for example, can disrupt sleep. In addition, such problems as separation anxiety and fear of "monsters" can cause nighttime awakenings, nightmares, or fear of going to bed (not to mention what effect they have on the *child . . .*). By and large these transient sleep problems are normal, and are usually alleviated by reducing stress, ensuring safety, and providing reassurance, support, firm and consistent limits, and positive reinforcement for improvement as children "outgrow" or master their fears (Ferber, 1985).

In brief, emotional disturbance can cause temporary disruptions in sleep and can produce changes in sleep regulation, and disrupted or insufficient sleep can disrupt regulation of emotional and attentional processes. This reciprocal relationship between sleep disturbances and emotional distress explains why sleep problems are common symptoms associated with many of the other disorders covered in this text. Until recently, however, sleep disorders in children were seldom studied, and techniques of assessment and treatment were borrowed from efforts with adults. Fortunately, behavioral interventions are now available that help parents deal more readily with the particular sleep problems experienced by children of all ages.

Normal Stages of Sleep

Like adults', children's levels of activity and attention go through regular cycles during the day. Sometimes children are active and alert; at other times, disengaged and inattentive. During sleep this cyclical pattern of brain activity—referred to as *sleep architecture*—continues, fluctuating between **rapid eye movement (REM) sleep** and **nonrapid eye movement (NREM) sleep**. REM sleep is when brain activity is highest, and is accompanied by autonomic arousal, loss of muscle tone, and rapid eye movements. Most dreaming occurs during this period of brain activity, which is why REM sleep is often thought of as dream sleep. During REM sleep, things seem real and the mind responds to images with emotional and physiological reactions as if they indeed were happening, yet the body lies still and uninvolved while this incredible production is going on. In contrast, during NREM sleep the brain is relatively quiet, slow, and synchronized. Pulse and respiration are slow and regular, and muscle tone is maintained (Bootzin & Chambers, 1990).

NREM sleep is subdivided into four stages, on the basis of brain wave patterns measured with an electroencephalogram (EEG). These stages correspond roughly to how deep sleep is. For children over a year old, a normal night's sleep begins with NREM stage 1. Sleep gradually deepens through stage 2 until, by stages 3 and 4 (also called delta or slow-wave sleep), the child does not respond to external stimuli and is difficult to awaken. If awakened from slow-wave sleep, the child is likely to be groggy and disoriented, and not be dreaming. Children have extremely long periods of deep slow-wave sleep. Delta sleep levels peak between 3 and 6 years of age

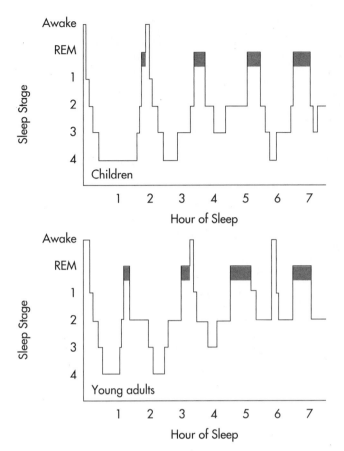

FIGURE 12.1 Sleep cycles: a representative night for a child and a young adult. (Adapted from A. Kales & J. Kales, 1974)

(usually at the point when children give up daytime naps), and subsequently decrease across school age and adolescence, and throughout adulthood (Dahl, 1996).

Figure 12.1 depicts typical sleep cycles for a child and a young adult, showing how they go through NREM and REM stages of sleep several times throughout the night (Carskadon, 1990). Children begin by entering the four stages of NREM sleep, which takes an hour or so in young adults, but considerably less time in infants and children (Hauri, 1982). During the first 1 to 3 hours, infants and children spend the longest time in deep, slow-wave sleep. The length of this deep delta sleep increases in proportion to how long the child has been awake, and becomes even deeper if he or she needs to recover from sleep loss or chronic sleep disturbances. It is during this deep, slow-wave stage of sleep that confused partial arousals, such as sleepwalking and sleep terrors, usually emerge.

Following the progressive stages of NREM sleep, children and adults move into REM sleep. If you watch a child (or a cat, for that matter) sleeping, eventually her eyelids will twitch as her eyes rapidly move about. This time when the brain is active but the body is not is in

contrast to that of NREM sleep, when the brain is relatively inactive but the body is not. REM sleep is believed to provide a restorative function for the brain, allowing new information to be sorted and stored into memory (Smith & Lapp, 1991). If a person is deprived of REM sleep, the brain will try to compensate by entering this sleep stage more frequently and more quickly over the next few nights. Because the majority of REM sleep occurs in the second half of the night, REM-related disorders, like nightmares, occur more often in the early morning hours.

Maturational Changes. Our sleep patterns and needs change dramatically during the first few years of life, then gradually settle into a stable pattern by adulthood. Newborns sleep about 16 to 17 hours each day, and 1-year-olds sleep about 13 hours a day, including daytime naps that range from 1 to over 2 hours (Anders & Eiben, 1997). These maturational changes partially explain why infants and children have sleep problems different from those of older children, adolescents, and adults. Infants and toddlers have more night-waking problems; pre-schoolers, more falling-asleep problems; and younger school-age children, more going-to-bed problems (Anders, Halpern, & Hua, 1992); sleep problems among adolescents and adults typically involve difficulty going to or staying asleep (insomnia).

Maturational changes also influence sleep architecture and how long a person remains in each stage of sleep, especially during adolescence. Following puberty the amount of REM sleep decreases slightly and delta sleep (stages 3 and 4) declines significantly (Dahl, 1996). At the same time, teens are often sleepier during the day, even if they continue getting as much sleep as they did before puberty (Carskadon et al., 1980). Paradoxically, adolescents have an increased physiological need for sleep, but many get significantly *less* sleep than they used to. This results in many teens' being chronically sleep-deprived and having daytime symptoms of inadequate sleep: fatigue, irritability, emotional lability, difficulty concentrating, and falling asleep in class (Carskadon et al., 1989). The bottom line? Let sleeping teens lie—they need to catch up on their sleep!

Situational and Cultural Influences

[Being a] conscientious parent . . . is a responsibility which most of us, including me, avoid most of the time because it's too hard.

—John Lennon

By the time their infant or toddler is tired, parents are usually exhausted too, which can lead to irregular or unintentional bedtime routines. Additionally, infants who begin their night's sleep outside their cribs more often wake up and demand a repetition of their routine

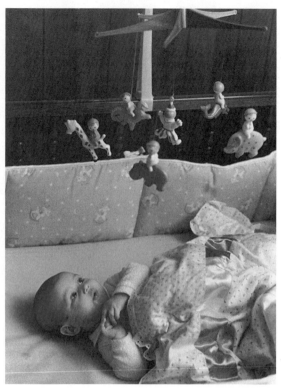

Different cultures have different views about the way children should sleep at night, including whether they sleep in their parents' room (left) or alone in their cribs.

in the middle of the night, whereas those who fall asleep in their own cribs from the beginning are more likely to return to sleep on their own during the night (Anders et al., 1992). Parents are faced with the daunting task of establishing and maintaining a regular bedtime routine, despite pressures of busy schedules, child illness, or shared custody. Yet, successful maintenance of such a routine is a strong protective factor against sleep-related problems that can persist for years.

Cultural influences and family expectations also play a significant role in children's developing sleep patterns. Compare Western and North American expectations that infants sleep in their own bed, preferably in a separate room, with those of some Eastern and South American cultures that expect young children to spend their first few years sharing mothers' room and bed. You may be surprised to learn that families in these cultures report fewer bedtime problems and closer bonds with their children (Morelli, Rogoff, Oppenheim, & Goldsmith, 1992). These cultural patterns, whether they involve young children's sleeping with parents or not, have one aspect in common: the importance of maternal sensitivity and response to infant and toddler cues and signals of distress (Benoit, Zeanah, Boucher, & Minde, 1992). Young children establish their own self-regulatory patterns, including eating, elimination, and sleep, with the help of parental sensitivity and attentiveness (Lyon-

Ruth, 1996). Remember, nighttime can be a scary time for small children.

Sleep's Regulatory Function. We tend to think that sleep is a time when not much is happening— the "lights are on but nobody's home." This lack of activity and nearly complete loss of awareness during sleep gives us the impression that sleep regulation has little to do with psychological processes such as attention, arousal, emotions, and behavior. So why does the brain—particularly, the developing brain—require long periods of relative inactivity?

Opposing the popular image of sleep as simply rest is the growing awareness that sleep, arousal, affect, and attention are all closely intertwined in a dynamic regulatory system (Dahl, 1996). If the central nervous system (CNS) regulatory system has to increase arousal in response to possible danger, the system has to recover soon thereafter and restore the balance between sleep and arousal. It is fascinating how the system changes with development: During infancy the balance is skewed in favor of more sleep, because safety and other needs are largely looked after by caretakers. As children mature, they start looking after their own needs, becoming more alert and attentive to danger. Gradually, the cycle between sleep and arousal becomes skewed more in favor of arousal, which by then is adaptive and necessary, and the dynamic patterns of sleep help restore a balance once again.

Most students suffer sleep loss or disruption as a result of all-night study sessions or late night partying, so you are probably familiar with sleep's important role in regulating states of emotional arousal and restoration (Horne, 1993). The giddiness, silliness, and impulsive behaviors children and adults show if sleep-deprived signify that prefrontal cortex functions are impaired. As noted in earlier chapters, the prefrontal cortex is an important *executive control* center in the brain—it's in charge of processing emotional signals and making critical decisions as to how to respond—so its impairment results in signs of decreased concentration and diminished ability to inhibit, or control, basic drives, impulses, and emotions (if Freud's concept of the *ego* has a location, this is probably it). The prefrontal cortex is uniquely situated in the brain to allow it to integrate thoughts (higher cortical functions) with emotions (more basic CNS functions). If a person is sleep-deprived or otherwise impaired, the first functions to be affected are the more complex, demanding tasks, which require integrating cognitive, emotional, and social input rapidly and accurately (Dahl, 1996). Ask any parent or teacher and they can tell you: Children with disrupted or inadequate sleep show less executive control the next day; they are more cranky, impulsive, distractible, and emotionally labile, meaning they switch abruptly from, say, laughing to crying. These symptoms are easily confused with those of ADHD, although sleep problems usually self-correct within a day or two (Dahl et al., 1991).

The physiology of sleep also has a fascinating connection to developmental problems occurring during childhood, and further underscores the crucial role of sleep in restoring balance. Specific stages of sleep are believed to produce an active *uncoupling,* or disconnection, of neurobehavioral systems (Dahl, 1996). In effect, separate aspects of the central nervous system take a break from their constant duty. Think about how your nervous system constantly has to maintain an active, close connection all the time you are awake, which is achieved through electrical signals. As we noted in our discussion of learning disabilities, these signals require that we maintain precise timing and frequency (Singer, 1993). Sleep researcher R. E. Dahl (1996) describes the uncoupling process by comparing sleep's role to that of tuning instruments in a large orchestra: Tuning cannot be accomplished while the instrument is continuously playing, or "coupling," with the other instruments in the orchestra. Likewise, retuning or recalibration of the components of the CNS may require temporary uncoupling, or disconnection from other systems. Further, such uncoupling may be particularly critical for children.

As they mature, regions of the brain rapidly differentiate and establish specific functions and patterns of interconnection within the CNS (Levitt, 1995), which requires considerable recalibration or retuning. In Dahl's music analogy, a new instrument must be retuned more often than one that has been broken in.

We now look at how the two major types of sleep disorders—dyssomnias and parasomnias—originate from these key sleep processes.

Features of Sleep Disorders

Primary sleep disorders are presumed to be a result of abnormalities in the body's ability to regulate sleep-wake mechanisms and the timing of sleep, as opposed to sleep problems related to a medical disorder, a mental disorder, or the use of medications. The DSM-IV divides primary sleep disorders into two major categories: dyssomnias and parasomnias (APA, 1994). **Dyssomnias** are disorders of initiating or maintaining sleep, characterized by difficulty getting enough sleep, not sleeping when you want to, not feeling refreshed from sleeping, and so forth. The American Sleep Disorders Association (ASDA, 1990) further distinguishes between *extrinsic dyssomnias,* in which sleep problems are produced and maintained by extrinsic factors, such as noise or staying up late, and *intrinsic dyssomnias,* in which sleep problems originate from causes within the body, such as pain or illness.

Parasomnias, in contrast, are sleep disorders in which behavioral or physiological events intrude upon ongoing sleep. Whereas dyssomnias involve *disruptions* in the sleep process, parasomnias involve physiological or cognitive *arousal* at inappropriate times during the sleep-wake cycle, which can result in sleepwalking or in nightmares that jolt someone from sleep. Persons suffering from parasomnia sleep disorders often complain of unusual behaviors during sleep, rather than sleepiness or insomnia.

DSM-IV criteria for sleep disorders typically are not met in full by younger children because of the transitory nature of their sleep problems (Anders & Eiben, 1997). Refer to Tables 12.1 and 12.2, in lieu of the specific DSM-IV criteria for children, to aid in understanding the major features of and the differences between the various sleep disorders. Also, please note two considerations concerning diagnostic criteria: In addition to the symptoms pertaining to each sleep disorder, as listed in Tables 12.1 and 12.2, DSM-IV diagnostic criteria for all sleep-related disorders emphasize (1) the presence of clinically significant distress or impairment in social, occupational, or other important areas of functioning; and (2) the requirement that the sleep disturbance cannot be better accounted for by another mental disorder, the direct

The Buckets reprinted by permission of United Feature Syndicate, Inc.

physiological effects of a substance, or a general medical condition (other than a breathing-related disorder) (APA, 1994). These considerations apply to all the disorders discussed in this chapter.

Dyssomnias. Dyssomnias, many of which are quite common during certain times of development, are disturbances in the amount, timing, or quality of sleep. Anita, for example, suffered from a common form of childhood insomnia in which she had difficulty getting to sleep. Fortunately, many of these sleep problems resolve themselves as the child matures, especially if parents are given basic information and guidance, such as refraining from yelling at the child to go to sleep and adhering to a bedtime routine (Blader et al., 1997).

Table 12.1 notes that the dyssomnias include **protodyssomnia** (also known as primary insomnia in adults), **hypersomnia** (excessive sleepiness), **narcolepsy** (sleep attacks), **breathing-related sleep disorders,** and **circadian rhythm disorders** (disruption in the sleep-wake cycle). For the most part, dyssomnias are common childhood afflictions. A major exception is narcolepsy, which is rare and affects mostly adolescents and adults. Breathing-related sleep disorders are somewhat less common than other dyssomnias and can affect children of various ages as a result of allergies, asthma, or swollen tonsils and adenoids that interfere with breathing during sleep. Although relatively common, dyssomnias can sometimes have a significant impact on children's behavior and emotional state, much like they do for adults.

Protodyssomnia and Hypersomnia. These two sleep problems entail difficulties getting to sleep and sleeping too much. Because sleep patterns among younger children normally vary with development, the term *protodyssomnia* (*proto* means "resemblance or similarity") is often preferred over primary insomnia by sleep researchers (Anders & Eiben, 1997). This term recognizes that children's problems of falling and staying asleep are common and mostly transitory, and should be

distinguished from primary insomnia, a significant DSM-IV sleep disorder that affects mostly adults. Infants and toddlers tend to have problems getting to and staying asleep (protodyssomnia), whereas preschoolers are more likely to have occasional problems staying awake (hypersomnia). Usually, these problems resolve themselves on their own, but intervention can be helpful for some families in which situational stress or unfamiliarity with developmental norms plays a role.

The primary features of hypersomnia in children are excessive daytime sleepiness and extended periods of nighttime sleep. These problems become quite noticeable if they continue once the child begins school. Children may fight to stay awake, and in fact they may have short periods of sleep known as **microsleep.** These unintentional sleep episodes usually occur in situations of low stimulation and low activity, like sitting in a classroom or watching TV (sound familiar?). During microsleep, a person's eyes usually remain open but take on a glassy, "unseeing" look, a look that is quite familiar to teachers, professors, and dull comedians. The child may be able to answer a simple question ("Did you do your math homework, Freddy?") with a short reply ("yes"), but more elaborate answers are likely to be incoherent and inappropriate ("homework saw last night did math on TV"). Needless to say, the amount of new information children are able to obtain is about nil. Moreover, some children with excessive daytime sleepiness related to hypersomnia may be misdiagnosed with mild mental retardation because of their diminished learning ability and performance (Bootzin & Chambers, 1990).

Both of these common sleep disturbances affect boys and girls, as well as those from different social class backgrounds, about equally (Anders & Eiben, 1997). Protodyssomnia is often caused by events that would normally disrupt or reduce sleep, such as ear infections, colds, and teething, so parents usually recognize why their child is sleepy or fussy. Likewise, hypersomnia in children can usually be traced to disrupted sleep sched-

Table 12.1　Dyssomnias

Sleep Disorder	Description	Prevalence and Age	Treatment
Protodyssomnia	Difficulty initiating or maintaining sleep, or sleep that is not restorative; in infants, repetitive night waking and inability to fall asleep.	25% to 50% of 1- to 3-year-olds.	Behavioral treatment, family guidance.
Hypersomnia	Complaint of excessive sleepiness that is displayed as either prolonged sleep episodes or daytime sleep episodes.	Common among young children.	Behavioral treatment, family guidance.
Narcolepsy	Irresistable attacks of refreshing sleep occurring daily, accompanied by brief episodes of loss of muscle tone (cataplexy).	0.04% to 0.07% of children and adolescents.	Structure, support, psychostimulants, antidepressants.
Breathing-related sleep disorder	Sleep disruption leading to excessive sleepiness or insomnia that is caused by sleep-related breathing difficulties.	1% to 2% of children; preschool, elementary ages.	Removal of tonsils and adenoids.
Circadian rhythm sleep disorder	Persistent or recurrent sleep disruption leading to excessive sleepiness or insomnia due to a mismatch between the sleep-wake schedule required by a person's environment and his or her internal sleep cycle (circadian rhythm); late sleep onset (after midnight), difficulty awakening in morning, sleeping in on weekends, resistance to change.	Unknown; possibly 7% of adolescents.	Behavioral treatment, chronotherapy.

ules or inadequate sleep opportunities, whereas in adults this problem may have biological and genetic roots (Barlow & Durand, 1995). Despite their common occurrence, the general course of early childhood protodyssomnia and hypersomnia has not been well documented by longitudinal studies. Infants and toddlers with significant sleep problems are more likely to have sleep difficulties as they reach the preschool and school-age years (Zuckerman, Stevenson, & Bailey, 1987), but whether or not children with these early forms of sleep disorder are more likely to develop dyssomnias later on in life is unknown (Anders & Eiben, 1997).

Narcolepsy.　Narcolepsy is a dyssomnia in which *sleep attacks,* consisting of bouts of REM sleep, intrude upon wakefulness for 10 to 20 minutes, sometimes close to an hour if uninterrupted. Instead of progressing through the four NREM stages before reaching REM sleep, people with narcolepsy periodically progress right to the dream sleep stage, almost directly from a state of being awake (remember how we described REM sleep as a stage when the brain was active but the body isn't?). The person begins dreaming, and some will actually go about their activities—driving, talking, attending class—in a state of partial awareness. The individual feels refreshed after each episode, but sleepiness returns 2 to 3 hours later. Full-blown narcoleptic symptoms are rarely seen before age 10 (Dahl, Holttum, & Trubnick, 1994). The following synopsis of an actual case is an interesting exception:

Mario: Troubled by Sleep Attacks

Mario, a 7½-year-old boy, was referred to the sleep disorders center by his mother, who complained of his excessive daytime sleepiness and a tendency to fall asleep in almost any situation, despite 10 hours of nocturnal sleep and two daily naps of 1 to 1½ hours each. It was also reported that during episodes of laughter or excitement, Mario would experience sudden weakness, occasionally falling down, although never losing consciousness. Mario also claimed to see faces of people in his bedroom at night, and during these hallucinations he found himself unable to move.

Mario's past medical history was unremarkable, with the exception of chicken pox and a tonsillectomy, both at about age 6. Family medical history was equally free of major medical disorders. His mother, however, stated that she frequently fell asleep with inactivity and spoke of "losing her balance" with laughter. Following an assessment of his day and nighttime sleep patterns, narcolepsy was diagnosed and medications prescribed. Within a week, Mario's cataplexy (muscle weakness) had disappeared, and he was more alert, and he found it easier to stay awake in school. After several months, his mother attempted to discontinue his medication, but medication was resumed because the symptoms returned. (Adapted from Wittig et al., 1983)

Mario shows several major symptoms of narcolepsy. First, he had recurring, irresistible attacks of sleep that seemed to refresh him briefly. Second, Mario experienced **cataplexy,** or sudden weakness due to loss of muscle tone, whereby he sometimes fell but never lost consciousness. Muscle weakness can be subtle, such as a sagging jaw or drooping eyelids, or more dramatic, like Mario's fall. It is usually triggered by some strong emotion, such as anger or laughter. Third, Mario claimed to see faces of people in his bedroom at night and found himself unable to move. These symptoms are indicative of intrusions of REM sleep during his transition from sleep to wakefulness. Most children complain of such symptoms from time to time, but if they are recurrent, they may be indicative of two features associated with the REM intrusions of narcolepsy: **sleep paralysis** and **hypnagogic hallucinations.** Sleep paralysis, occurring at the beginning or end of sleep episodes, entails a brief period of time in which the child can't move or speak. You can imagine how frightening this would seem, especially to a child or adolescent. Equally unnerving are hypnagogic hallucinations—intense, dreamlike images said to be unbelievably realistic because they incorporate elements of the person's environment into the dream, somewhat like virtual reality. Sometimes children like Mario not only see a face, but also believe that the "dream person" is moving and speaking from a picture on the wall or is pulling at their pajamas. Could such phenomena account for the realistic and frightening stories of persons who claim to have been kidnapped by aliens (Spanos, Cross, Dickson, & DuBreuil, 1993)?

Narcolepsy is rare among children and adolescents, affecting only 4 to 7 out of 10,000. It usually first appears during the late teens and early twenties (Anders & Eiben, 1997). However, it may be underdiagnosed among children and younger adolescents, especially offspring of narcoleptic parents (Carskadon, 1990). The disorder tends to be chronic and lifelong in adults,

although some of the associated neurological symptoms may diminish over time (Anders & Eiben, 1997).

You can see how easy it would be to confuse Mario's symptoms of narcolepsy with those of a mental disorder. Hypnagogic hallucinations, especially in a young or frightened child, can mimic psychotic symptoms, and cataplexy can be mistaken for a somatoform disorder— that is, a disorder that resembles or suggests a medical condition but has no organic basis (Dahl et al., 1994). For this reason, narcolepsy was previously assumed to be caused by biological events similar to those that cause major mental illness, such as a neurotransmitter imbalance. However, narcolepsy appears to be an inherited, neurological disorder that affects the person's ability to go in and out of REM sleep (Dahl et al., 1994). Skeletal muscles are inhibited during normal REM sleep, which is a good thing because otherwise we might injure ourselves or our bed partner during over-excited dreams. Cataplexy and sleep paralysis, however, are *inappropriate* activation of muscle paralysis while the person is awake (J. M. Siegel et al., 1991). Likewise, hypnagogic hallucinations are very similar to normal REM dream imagery; the difference is that persons with narcolepsy experience these symptoms before they are fully asleep. Narcolepsy, simply put, is a disturbance of REM sleep physiology; REM sleep, rather than being limited to specific times of the night, intrudes on the person at the wrong time and the wrong place (Dahl et al., 1994).

Breathing-Related Sleep Disorder.

Some children suffer sleep loss or disruption simply because their breathing is impaired. We have all experienced occasional disrupted and fragmented sleep as a result of a bad cold; breathing is blocked and we are aroused over and over again to restore adequate breathing. Some children and adults, however, because of physical abnormalities, regularly suffer such sleep disturbances. If breathing stops altogether, for periods lasting 10 seconds up to 2 minutes, the person is said to have **obstructive sleep apnea syndrome (OSAS),** the most common form of breathing-related sleep disorder in children (Hansen & Vandenberg, 1997). OSAS is caused by collapse of the airway and obstruction of air flow, and is thought to affect 1% to 2% of both children and adults (ASDA, 1990). Men are afflicted with this disorder much more often than women, but such gender differences are not found among prepubertal children (APA, 1994).

OSAS is characterized by loud snores or gasps for air, alternating with episodes of silence that usually last 20 to 30 seconds. Children may also become agitated and restless, wet the bed, or assume unusual sleep postures, such as sleeping on their hands and knees, to aid their breathing (APA, 1994). The diagnosis is usually aided by placing an audiotape recorder next to the

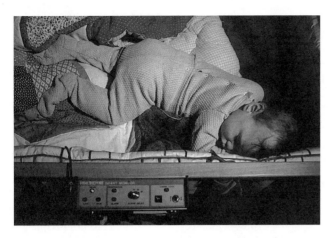

Sudden infant death syndrome (SIDS) is a mysterious disorder that strikes only infants and toddlers, mostly during sleep. Children are considered to be at risk of SIDS if a sibling died of the disorder or they have breathing difficulties at night. Sensors may be used to alert parents immediately if a child stops breathing.

sleeping child to detect these abnormal breathing patterns. In toddlers and young children, OSAS is most often caused by enlarged tonsils and adenoids, which can be removed to restore normal breathing patterns.

As a result of disturbed sleep, children with OSAS—and their parents and teachers—often complain of daytime tiredness and inattention, restless and sometimes hyperactive behavior, and impairments in learning and cognitive functions. For these reasons, the diverse symptoms related to pediatric OSAS can easily be confused with those of other childhood disorders, such as oppositional disorder, learning disorders, and, in particular, ADHD, although studies have not addressed these co-morbidities (Hansen & Vandenberg, 1997). Furthermore, some toddlers may experience growth retardation resembling failure to thrive; their fragmented sleep is possibly related to insufficient growth hormone secretion (Anders & Eiben, 1997).

Circadian Rhythm Sleep Disorder.

This sleep problem, believed to be common but transitory among adolescents, involves an inability to fall asleep at the customary bedtime and an inability to rise at a reasonable hour. As you'd expect, parents start to get upset by the late bedtimes, the morning struggles, the daytime sleepiness, and the frequent napping. Teens say they can't get to sleep for 1 to 1½ hours after going to bed even if they have stayed up until after midnight. Once asleep, they stay asleep—well past an appropriate morning hour.

Circadian rhythm sleep disorder is essentially a mismatch between the internal sleep cycle (circadian rhythm) and external opportunities or demands. Circa-

dian rhythms—the daily patterns governing the regularity and intensity of drowsiness and wakefulness—indicate when a person needs to sleep, but they may be disrupted by restricted opportunities for sleep. If untampered, these rhythms are maintained internally by a biological "clock" located in the hypothalamus, which is adjusted daily by the light of morning and the decreasing light of nightfall. But, like other bodily functions, these rhythms can become irregular if we force ourselves to ignore or alter them. Disruptions of circadian rhythms are part of the daily life of some adolescents, university and college students, globe-trotters, shift workers, and parents of newborns, which can lead to a chronic problem for some.

Interference with circadian rhythms is nothing to yawn about, however. Prolonged periods of sleep deprivation or persistent irregularities in sleep hygiene can get out of control and turn into a circadian rhythm sleep disorder that lasts from months to years. Staying up later and later can become habit-forming. Adolescents often attempt to make up the sleep debt on the weekend, which, as noted earlier, is all right in moderation; however, this pattern can upset the biological clock if continued in excess beyond short periods and within narrow limits. Once the circadian clock is damaged or abused, the delayed sleep phase syndrome can persist even when normal amounts of sleep are restored and the sleep debt is no longer significant (Anders & Eiben, 1997).

Parasomnias. Imagine that you are just falling to sleep after an evening of celebrating New Year's Eve with friends when suddenly you are awakened by a terrifying scream from Jenny, your 3-year-old daughter. You run in to see what's the matter, and she flails her arms at you, yelling "Get away, get away!" Getting out of bed, she looks at you but somehow doesn't seem to know who you are. Sensing her fear, you try to pick her up to comfort her and she strikes you in the face, scratches you, and in an angry, belligerent tone of voice tells you, "Put me down!" She seems terrified, but everything you try to do just makes matters worse. By the next morning Jenny disavows any memory of her stark fear during the night. (This example was an actual experience for one of the authors.) As a young preschooler, Jenny experienced several episodes of troublesome sleep arousal, or parasomnia, which she soon outgrew.

The parasomnias are somewhat common afflictions of early to mid-childhood and, we might add, a bit easier to understand because of their more familiar terms and our own experiences. They include **nightmares** (repeated awakenings, with frightening dreams that you usually remember), **sleep terrors** (abrupt awakening, accompa-

Table 12.2   Parasomnias

Sleep Disorder	Description	Prevalence and Age	Treatment
	REM PARASOMNIA		
Nightmare disorder	Repeated awakenings with detailed recall of extended and extremely frightening dreams, usually involving threats to survival, security, or self-esteem; generally occurs during the second half of the sleep period.	Common between ages 3 and 8.	Provide comfort, reduce stress.
	AROUSAL PARASOMNIAS		
Sleep terror disorder	Recurrent episodes of abrupt awakening from sleep, usually occurring during the first third of the major sleep episode and beginning with a panicky scream; Autonomic discharge, racing heart, sweating, vocalized distress, glassy-eyed staring, difficult to arouse, inconsolable, disoriented; no memory of episodes in morning.	3% of children; ages 18 months to 6 years.	Reduce stress and fatigue; add late afternoon nap.
Sleepwalking disorder	Repeated episodes of arising from bed during sleep and walking for periods of 5 seconds to 30 minutes, usually during the first third of the major sleep episode; poorly coordinated, difficult to arouse, disoriented; no memory in morning.	15% of children have one attack; 1% to 6% have one to four attacks per week; age 4 to 12 years, rare in adolescence.	Take safety precautions, reduce stress and fatigue, add late afternoon nap.

nied by autonomic arousal but no recall), and **sleepwalking** (getting out of bed and walking around, but with no recall the next day). Nightmares are referred to as *REM parasomnias* because they occur during REM (dream) sleep, usually during the second half of the sleep period. Sleep terrors and sleepwalking, in contrast, are referred to as *arousal parasomnias* because they occur during deep sleep in the first third of the sleep cycle, when the person is so soundly asleep that he or she is difficult to arouse and has no recall of the episode the next morning (ASDA, 1990). Fortunately, as with the dyssomnias, children typically grow out of parasomnias or recover from sleep disruption or loss without developing a chronic condition that interferes with daily activities. Characteristics of parasomnia sleep disorders are shown in Table 12.2.

Nightmares (REM Parasomnias).
Nightmares are sudden arousals from REM sleep, associated with frightening or disturbing dreams. As you might suspect, the intensity and frequency of nightmares are often affected by stress, especially traumatic or emotionally arousing experiences. Nightmares usually start between the ages of 3 and 6 years, and affect 10% to 50% of children in that age group severely enough to disturb themselves or others.

Nightmares of preschool children often relate to a fear of being punished or devoured (J. D. Kales, Soldatos, & A. Kales, 1980). Ever wonder, then, why so many nursery rhymes and children's stories focus on these fears? Child psychologist Bruno Bettelheim (1976) explains how such stories may help children express and cope with their fears and fantasies:

> Fairy tales are loved by the child not because the imagery he finds in them conforms to what goes on within him, but because—despite all the angry, anxious thoughts in his mind to which the fairy tale gives body and specific content—these stories always result in a happy outcome, which the child cannot imagine on his own (p. 123)

Sleep Terrors and Sleepwalking (Arousal Parasomnias).
Sleep terrors (like Jenny's) and sleepwalking are clustered as *arousal disorders* by the ASDA (1990) because they share many common features: automated behavior, relative nonreactivity to external stimuli, difficulty in being aroused, fragmentary or absent dream recall, mental confusion or disorientation when awakened, and retrograde amnesia (no memory for the event) the next morning. Arousal disorders occur at a particular point in the sleep cycle, usually in the first 1 to 3 hours after sleep onset. This is the time when a

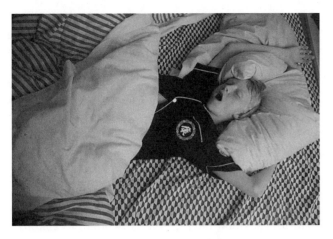

Children and teens can usually recover from sleep deprivation or loss if given the opportunity to add more rest.

person's sleep undergoes a transition from NREM stage-4 sleep to REM sleep. Instead of making the usual smooth transition to REM sleep, the child suddenly becomes agitated and frightened, and like Jenny, may sit up in bed screaming and staring with glassy, unseeing eyes and rapid breathing.

During a sleep terror episode, children are inconsolable and difficult to awaken; if they are awakened, they may be quite disoriented and confused. Typically, after a few minutes they calm down and continue to sleep, and remember nothing about the episode the next day. About 3% of children experience sleep terrors, although the prevalence is probably higher as a result of underreporting (Anders & Eiben, 1997). Sleepwalking, which typically occurs at an older age than sleep terrors, between the ages of 4 and 12 years, is very similar in presentation to sleep terrors and occurs at the same transition in the sleep cycle. When walking occurs, body movements are poorly coordinated and the sleepwalker's direction is purposeless (it's a myth, or at least very rare, for someone to unintentionally raid the fridge at night). Because these arousal disorders occur during NREM sleep, the person is not dreaming and usually has no recall. About 15% of children have one sleepwalking attack sometime during childhood, whereas 1% to 6% have several attacks each week (Anders & Eiben, 1997).

Sleepwalking and night terrors are due to CNS arousal—specifically, motor and autonomic nervous system activation. Children probably inherit this tendency, since a family history for sleep terrors or sleepwalking is reported in up to 80% of individuals presenting with such problems (APA, 1994). Sleep terror disorder is more common among boys than girls, but the gender ratio evens out by adulthood. Fortunately, arousal disorders are seldom associated with psychopathology in children or adolescents, and they usually disappear on their own as the child matures, especially when aided by appropri-

ate reassurance and understanding by parents. If these sleep disorders first appear in adulthood, however, the person may be suffering from another stress-related disorder, such as PTSD or generalized anxiety disorder, or a personality disorder, such as dependent, schizoid, or borderline personality disorder (APA, 1994).

Nightmares are easily differentiated from sleep terrors (see Table 12.3). Sleep terrors occur early on in sleep and are not accompanied by mental imagery—the child in the midst of a sleep terror attack is soundly asleep and does not remember anything in the morning. Nightmares, on the other hand, occur later in the night, usually in the last third of the sleep period, when REM sleep predominates.

Treatment

Protodyssomnias in infants and toddlers often subside on their own, but any parent who has been awakened night after night by a screaming child can attest that "waiting for them to grow out of it" seems like forever. If going to sleep or staying asleep becomes a problem, the goal of behavioral interventions is to teach parents to attend to the child's need for comfort and reassurance, but to gradually withdraw more quickly from the child's room after saying goodnight (this is an example of extinction, since parental attention is being removed). Parents can also be taught how to establish good sleep hygiene appropriate to their child's developmental stage and the family's cultural values. Once established, positive reinforcement methods, such as praise or star charts, can be used to reward the child for efforts to follow the bedtime routine (Bootzin & Chambers, 1990).

Sleep hygiene may involve identifying suspected causes of disrupted sleep and involving other family members in maintaining a chosen routine. For example,

Table 12.3 Comparison of Sleep Terrors and Nightmares

	Sleep Terrors	Nightmares
Time of night	Early, usually within 4 hours of bedtime	Late
State on waking	Disoriented, confused	Upset, scared
Response to parents	Unaware of presence, not consolable	Comforted
Memory of events	None, unless fully awakened	Vivid recall of dream
Return to sleep	Usually rapid, unless fully awakened	Often delayed by fear
Sleep stage	Partial arousal from deep NREM sleep	REM sleep

Source: Blum & Carey, 1996.

individualized bedtime rituals, such as reading, singing, or playing a quiet game, establish a positive transition to bedtime, and regular bedtimes and waking times establish a consistent routine (Blum & Carey, 1996). Children should be put to bed while they are still awake whenever possible, with parents remaining close by until children fall asleep. Although many parents find bedtime a struggle, if the separation problem at naptime and bedtime can be resolved, middle-of-the-night wakenings usually disappear (Anders & Eiben, 1997). Anita's treatment plan, for example, was implemented using a behavioral intervention (stimulus control and relaxation) that established a bedtime routine geared to reducing thoughts and activities, like worrying, that would interfere with sleep onset:

Anita's Bedtime Routine

Anita's treatment began by reassuring her that she would not catch a serious illness just from lack of sleep. She was provided with a plan to manage her bedtime routine (stimulus-control instructions), and told to keep a daily sleep diary to track her progress. As it turns out, her father had been pressuring her every night about her sleep, which of course was having the opposite effect he intended: she worried more about getting in trouble if she didn't fall asleep.

Stimulus-control instructions were tailored to Anita's proper bedtime routine. First, she was told not to read, do her homework, or worry in bed: her bed was only for sleeping. She went to bed each night at 9:00, and if she couldn't fall asleep within a half hour, or if she woke up for 15 to 30 minutes in the middle of the night, she was to get out of bed and go into the living room until she felt sleepy or until 30 minutes had passed. Then she was to return to bed and practice relaxation exercises. If she still couldn't fall asleep, she was to repeat getting out of bed as often as necessary. She was also told to get up at about the same time every day. After 3 weeks of this program Anita began to fall asleep usually in less than 20 minutes, and she no longer worried about getting sick or in trouble with her father. (Adapted from Bootzin & Chambers, 1990)

Narcolepsy is the only dyssomnia that often requires drug therapy in addition to behavioral intervention, as noted in Mario's case. Tricyclic antidepressants may be used to control the REM-related symptoms of cataplexy, hypnagogic hallucinations, and sleep paralysis, because these medications tend to suppress REM sleep (Bootzin & Chambers, 1990). Psychostimulant medications such as Ritalin may also be used to control excessive daytime sleepiness and sleep attacks (Anders & Eiben, 1997). In addition, setting consistent bedtimes and rise times, as well as regularly scheduled naps (20 to 30 minutes, 2 to 3 times a day) is important. Finally, psychosocial support and counseling, especially self-help groups, help patients and family members understand and cope effectively with the symptoms of narcolepsy.

Treatment of circadian rhythm sleep disorders requires a highly motivated adolescent and a supportive family, because there are no shortcuts or medications that can easily restore an abused sleep-wake cycle. The goal of behavioral intervention is twofold: to eliminate the sleep debt and to restore a more normal sleep and wake routine. After gaining the cooperation of all family members, the adolescent is asked to keep a sleep-wake and daily activity log. Regular bedtimes and rise times are agreed upon, and the teen is assisted in managing stress or other demands that infringe on this new routine. If begun early in the disorder, such supportive behavioral methods are often effective. However, in more severe cases, **chronotherapy**—resetting the biological clock—is indicated (Bootzin & Chambers, 1990). *Phase delay treatment* is one method of chronotherapy, in which both sleep and rise times are delayed by 1 to 2 hours each day. Over several weeks this delay shifts the sleep-onset time around the clock to a more appropriate time. Treatment is stopped when bedtime and sleep-onset time approach 10:00 to 11:00 P.M. However, you can see the obvious drawback to phase delay treatment while an adolescent is in school, so treatment usually has to be done during a lengthy vacation period (a further drawback). *Phase advance treatment,* or advancing the biological clock, can also restore the circadian rhythm by very gradually shifting to an earlier bedtime by 15 minutes a day, every few days. Although this approach is less grueling than phase delay treatment, improvement in sleep onset by advancing bedtime is very gradual, perhaps 15 to 30 minutes per week (Anders & Eiben, 1997).

In contrast to treatment for some of the dyssomnias, prolonged treatment of child and adolescent parasomnias is usually not necessary, particularly if the episodes of sleep intrusion occur infrequently. Treatment of nightmares consists of providing comfort at the time of occurrence and making every attempt to reduce daytime stressors. If nightmares or sleep terrors are intense and persistent, daytime stresses at school, family conflicts, or emotional disturbance may be implicated (Bootzin & Chambers, 1990). If sleepwalking is suspected, parents are usually first asked to record episodes at home using a camcorder. If sleepwalking is confirmed, parents have to take precautions in order to reduce the chance of a child's being injured by falling or by bumping into objects. Because of the possibility of fire or other emergencies, children should *never* be locked in their rooms. Because excessive fatigue or unusual stresses during the daytime often precipitate sleepwalking, brief afternoon naps can also benefit some children.

ELIMINATION DISORDERS

"Step 1: Before you begin, remove all stubbornness from the child." These instructions were provided by a popular toilet training manual years ago, apparently without a hint of irony. For generations, parents have half-jokingly referred to the bathroom, and toilet training in particular, as the "combat zone," where parental right meets child's might (Levine, 1982). Teaching toddlers how to use the toilet is one of the more significant challenges of parenting, but whether it truly deserves the disproportionate amount of attention it received in the early psychopathology literature is unlikely.

Although challenging, toileting and bed-wetting problems are not considered the source of psychopathology that they once were. Nor do they result in lengthy battles for most children and their parents—the child gradually makes the transition from having no control of elimination functions to recognizing and responding to cues. Thanks to a better understanding of the biological and psychological underpinnings of elimination disorders, attention has been directed away from the child's personality or emotional trauma. However, for a significant minority the problems associated with toileting continue well past the age when most children have achieved freedom and independence. Elimination problems can turn into distressing and chronic difficulties, and can affect children's participation in educational and social activities, camps, sleepovers, and so forth. In extreme cases, toileting accidents can precipitate physical child abuse (R. C. Herrenkohl, E. C. Herrenkohl, & Egolf, 1983).

The two types of elimination problems of childhood and adolescence are enuresis, the involuntary discharge of urine during the day or night, and encopresis, the passage of feces into inappropriate places, such as clothing or the floor. Child psychologists have studied and treated these elimination problems among children because they can have strong implications for young children's developing senses of self-competence and self-esteem. Even though most children eventually outgrow problems of enuresis or encopresis by age 10 or so, they may have suffered years of embarrassment and peer rejection that remain troublesome. Fortunately, in most instances the problems can be alleviated through education and retraining efforts involving both parents and children, making these disorders one of the few areas of abnormal child psychology where early referral and treatment can virtually eliminate long-term consequences.

Enuresis

As many as 7 million children in the United States and Canada go through the same routine each night—turn off the lights, go to sleep, wet the bed. These children suffer from enuresis, the involuntary discharge of urine during the day or night. Most of the time the child cannot control the discharge, but on occasion it may be intentional. Although the problem is relatively common, it is stressful for parents and children. Understandably, enuresis can become a major embarrassment to children and adolescents. Parents, moreover, cannot disguise their mixed feelings of concern and growing irritation, as they wonder if their children are somehow doing this on purpose or out of laziness, or if they themselves are somehow to blame.

Concerns about correcting children's bed-wetting have perplexed professionals and parents for generations. Here is how Thomas Phaer, "the father of English pediatrics," explained the early cure to physicians in his *Boke of Children* (1544):

> Of Pyssying in the Bedde
> Many times for debility of vertus retentive of the reines or blader, as wel olde men as children are oftentimes annoyed, whan their urine issueth out either in theyre slepe or waking against theyr wylles, having no power to reteine it whan it cometh, therfore yf they will be holpen, fyrst they must avoid al fat meates, til ye vertue be restored againe, and to use this pouder in their meates and drynkes. (cited in Glicklich, 1951, p. 862)

The "pouder" was derived from the trachea of a cock or the "stones of a hedge-hogge" (the authors do not suggest you try this remedy at home). This remedy seems tame in view of more "enlightened" mechanical and surgical approaches to enuresis that emerged by the 18th century: yokes made of iron (mercifully covered with velvet) that prevented urination, steel spikes placed on the child's back to prevent lying on the back, which was believed to stimulate bladder function during sleep. If you didn't want your child to be outfitted for one of these devices, other forms of treatment were available: Medicinals like strychnine, belladonna, sacral plasters, and chloral hydrate were used presumably to stimulate the bladder (regardless of poisonous side effects), or the orifice of the urethra could be cauterized (partially closed) with silver nitrate to make it more tender and responsive to passage of urine (Glicklich, 1951). In many respects, the treatment of childhood bed-wetting throughout history reflects society's generally poor

Table 12.4 DSM-IV Diagnostic Criteria for Enuresis

A. Repeated voiding of urine into bed or clothes (whether involuntary or intentional).

B. The behavior is clinically significant as manifested by either a frequency of twice a week for at least 3 consecutive months or the presence of clinically significant distress or impairment in social, academic (occupational), or other important areas of functioning.

C. Chronological age is at least 5 years (or equivalent developmental level).

D. The behavior is not due exclusively to the direct physiological effects of a substance (e.g., a diuretic) or a general medical condition (e.g., diabetes, spina bifida, a seizure disorder).

Specify type:
Nocturnal Only
Diurnal Only
Nocturnal and Diurnal

Source: DSM-IV Copyright © 1994 by APA.

understanding and sensitivity to children's needs and problems at the time.

Because almost all children have bed-wetting accidents until age 5 or so, DSM-IV has narrowed the criteria to reflect the developmental nature of this disorder. The criteria stipulate that the problem be frequent (at least twice a week for 3 consecutive months), or accompanied by significant distress or impairment in social, academic, or other important areas of functioning. A chronological age of 5 years or equivalent developmental level was arbitrarily chosen as a developmental benchmark for the point at which most children have achieved urinary continence. Finally, the voiding of urine into bed or clothes must not be due exclusively to a general medical condition or the result of a diuretic (drug that reduces water retention). DSM-IV criteria for enuresis are described in Table 12.4.

DSM-IV distinguishes between three subtypes of enuresis (APA, 1994). *Nocturnal only* is the most common, in which wetting occurs only during sleep at night, typically during the first third of the night. Sometimes the child is dreaming of urinating, which indicates that the voiding took place during REM sleep. *Diurnal only* is defined as the passage of urine during waking hours, most often during the early afternoon on school days (APA, 1994). Diurnal enuresis is more common in females than males, and is uncommon after age 9. Because of these features, suspected causes of diurnal enuresis often point to a reluctance to use the toilet because of social anxiety or a preoccupation with a school event. Finally, nocturnal and diurnal can exist in combination.

Prevalence and Course. About 7% of all 8-year-old children wet their beds (Fergusson, Horwood, & Shannon, 1986), boys more often than girls, which makes enuresis a relatively common problem among younger school-age children. But the prevalence of enuresis declines rapidly with maturity: By age 10, only 3% of males and 2% of females are affected, and this evens out to 1% of males and less than 1% of females by late adolescence (Houts, Berman, & Abramson, 1994). Diurnal enuresis is much less common: About 3% of 6-year-olds are estimated to suffer from diurnal enuresis (Harbeck-Weber & Peterson, 1996). However, prevalence of both forms of enuresis is higher among less educated, lower socioeconomic groups as well as institutionalized children, perhaps due to less daily structure of their routines and added environmental stressors (APA, 1994).

Approximately 80% of children with enuresis disorder have *primary enuresis,* because they have never attained at least 6 months of continuous nighttime continence. By definition, primary enuresis starts at age 5. *Secondary enuresis,* in contrast, refers to children who have previously established urinary continence but then relapse, usually between the ages of 5 and 6 years (APA, 1994). Secondary enuresis is less common than primary. Children with secondary enuresis often took a longer time establishing initial nighttime continence, or face a higher dose of stressful life events (Houts et al., 1994). Most children do eventually stop bed-wetting, but for those who do not remit on their own, treatment is particularly beneficial in preventing a lengthy and disruptive problem.

You can imagine how younger children are treated when peers discover that they have wet themselves in class or while sleeping over. Teasing, name calling, and social stigmatization are common peer reactions to this unfortunate problem. Thus, even though enuresis is a physical condition, it is often accompanied by some

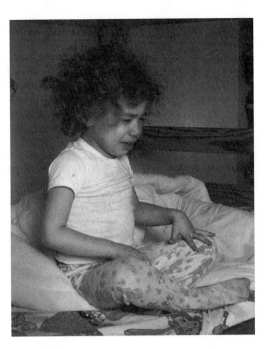

Waking up to a wet bed is upsetting, and can affect a young child's self-confidence if poorly managed.

degree of psychological distress. The impact of this distress often depends on three features related to the nature of the enuresis: (1) limitations imposed on social activities, such as sleeping away from home, (2) effects on self-esteem, including the degree of social ostracism imposed by peers, and (3) parental reactions, such as anger, punishment, and rejection (Houts et al., 1994). Parents are often poorly informed of the nature of enuresis and may respond with punishment or humiliation. Fortunately, these consequences are not inevitable or long-lasting. Many children with enuresis are able to establish their self-esteem and peer relationships despite the occasional embarrassment or anxiety about their problem. For others, treatment for bed-wetting usually has a positive impact on their self-concept and peer relations (Moffatt, Kato, & Pless, 1987).

Causes and Treatment. Children with nocturnal enuresis need to urinate at night, but they don't wake up when they need to urinate. By age 5 or so, most children have made the transition from urinating around the clock, as they did in infancy, to urinating only during waking hours. Children who continue to need to urinate at night may have a deficiency during sleep of an important hormone known as **antidiuretic hormone (ADH)**. ADH helps concentrate urine during sleep hours, meaning that the urine contains less water and is therefore of decreased volume. For normal children, this decreased volume usually means that their bladders do not overfill while they are asleep, unless they drank excessive fluids

before bed. But some children with enuresis do not show the usual increase in ADH during sleep (Norgaard, Pederson, & Djurhuus, 1985). They continue to produce more urine during the hours of sleep than their bladders can hold, and if they fail to wake up, bed-wetting results. Why children with enuresis fail to wake up when they need to urinate can also be explained by developmental and biological factors. Older children and adolescents have the ability to sense a full bladder at night, which activates a nerve impulse from the bladder to the brain. This signal may initiate dreams about water or going to the toilet, which usually alerts the reticular activating system to wake them up. This signaling mechanism matures during early childhood, so infants understandably have very little ability to detect the need to urinate.

Primary enuresis, the most common type, is decidedly not due to stress or child obstinence. To the contrary, this trait appears to be inherited. If both parents were enuretic, 77% of their children are too; if only one parent was enuretic, 44% of their offspring are. If neither parent had this problem, only about 15% of their children develop enuresis. Concordance rates of enuresis for monozygotic (68%) and dyzygotic (36%) twins also verify this connection (Bakwin, 1973). An autosomal dominant inheritance pattern was recently identified by a specific gene (on the 13th chromosome), which is present in those members of families who wet the bed and not present in those who don't (Eiberg, Berendt, & Mohr, 1995). Presumably, this gene affects whether children will need to urinate at night or how easily they can wake up when their bladders are full.

Treatments for children with nocturnal enuresis have perhaps the most comprehensive evaluation track record of any psychological intervention for childhood problems (Houts et al., 1994). Dozens of promising behavioral methods have been investigated by literally hundreds of studies over several decades; they are joined by many other studies of pharmacological agents. Fortunately, these efforts have led to some rather strong conclusions as to what works best (which, as an aside, provides a good lesson in how long it often takes to verify successful treatment methods for psychological disorders). We consider the two most successful forms of intervention, which are often combined in clinical practice: behavioral training methods using either an alarm (classical conditioning) or reinforcement contingencies (operant conditioning) to teach bladder control, and pharmacological treatment involving a nasal spray that increases the availability of ADH at night.

The standard behavioral intervention, based on classical conditioning principles, is the use of an alarm that sounds at the first detection of urine. Bed-wetting alarms have been around since O. H. Mowrer and W. M. Mowrer (1938) first invented the "bell and pad" (a battery-operated device that produced a loud sound as soon as a drop of urine closed the electrical circuit), and they are among the safest and most effective treatments. The alarms have a simple moisture sensor that snaps into a child's pajamas, with a small speaker attached to the shoulder to awaken the child. A single drop of urine completes the electronic circuit, setting off a piercing alarm that causes the child to tense and reflexively stop urinating. The one drawback to this method is the alarm's unpopularity with other household members. Some children actually sleep through the alarm, but as long as someone helps them in the beginning, these deep sleepers often benefit the most from this procedure. For the alarm to be effective, an adult must wake the child up, which usually isn't easy, walk him to the bathroom, get him to finish urinating in the toilet, and then reset the alarm. If this ritual is carefully followed, the alarm will begin to wake the child directly within 4 to 6 weeks, and by 12 weeks he will likely master nighttime bladder control and no longer need the alarm.

Another behavioral method, based on operant conditioning principles, involves variations of *dry-bed training*. Children, like adults, wake up more easily when the day holds promise and excitement, and reward systems, such as star charts or other tokens, capitalize on this anticipation. Dry-bed training was originally developed as a brief but intensive intervention in response to parents' frustration over the more intrusive and drawn-out urine alarm (Azrin & Foxx, 1974). Parents were instructed, during a single office visit, in bladder retention control training by having their child drink more and more fluids during the day and then delay urination for longer periods (in an effort to strengthen bladder control), hourly wakings for trips to the toilet, a cleanup routine for accidents (overcorrection, or having the child clean more than just the sheets), and positive reinforcement contingent on dry nights. This routine was practiced nightly for 1 or 2 weeks. An early study of this method reported very low dropout and relapse rates (Azrin, Thienes-Hontos, & Besalel-Azrin, 1979), but subsequent investigations found that the urine alarm is often a necessary adjunct to establish initial continence rapidly (Bollard & Nettelbeck, 1981).

The flurry of studies on dry-bed training and its variations in the early 1980s resulted in the conclusion that the effectiveness of the urine alarm conditioning procedure was increased by the addition of close professional supervision provided by dry-bed training (Graziano & Mooney, 1984). Thus, dry-bed training methods combined with an alarm (referred to today as *full-spectrum home training*) are still in common use, resulting in a success rate of about 3 in 4 children, and a relapse rate of 21% after 1 year (Whelan & Houts, 1990). In less severe or prolonged cases of primary enuresis, a simple incentive such as earning "stars" or similar tokens for dry nights is often enough to make children responsive to nighttime bladder fullness; others, however, may require the alarm to get the message firmly implanted, coupled with close professional monitoring to help parents adhere to the training methods.

Psychopharmacological interventions for bed-wetting have also been around for some time. The use of tricyclic antidepressants, such as imipramine, to treat enuresis grew in popularity following the serendipitous finding that an incontinent adult being treated for depression became continent as a side effect of the medication (MacLean, 1960). The mechanism by which this medication works remains unknown, and children often relapse soon after it is withdrawn. An additional issue is the questionable practice of keeping children on antidepressant medication simply for bed-wetting. In the mid-1980s, desmopressin, a synthetic ADH, became available as a treatment for enuresis. Desmopressin is a simple nasal spray administered before bedtime. Within a few days, about 70% of children using desmopressin can avoid bed-wetting, with another 10% or so showing significant improvement in the number of dry nights (Rappaport, 1993). Although desmopressin works very well while children are on the medicine, the difficulty comes in keeping them dry when they stop. Unlike alarm systems, which have most children cured of bed-wetting within 12 weeks, treatment with medication often requires some additional behavioral treatment before children are able to go completely off the medicine (Thompson & Rey, 1994).

Psychological and psychopharmacological treatments for enuresis have been widely used, but how effective are they? On the basis of a review of 78 published studies involving active treatments, such as psychological and pharmacological approaches, and no-treatment control groups, psychological treatments were determined to be generally more effective than pharmacological treatments (Houts et al., 1994). In particular, urine-alarm treatment was found to be superior to any other type of intervention. At the end of treatment, which generally lasts 12 weeks, children treated with a urine alarm or with desmopressin were equally likely to have ceased bed-wetting; however, at 3-month follow-up, children treated with a urine alarm were almost twice as likely to have ceased bed-wetting than were children who received other treatments, including desmopressin. The longer children were treated with a urine alarm, the higher the rates were for cessation of bed-wetting. At follow-up, on average, almost half of children treated with alarms remained dry, compared with about one-third treated with other behavior therapies and one-quarter treated with tricyclic medications (Houts et al., 1994). Notably, some children who received tricyclic

Table 12.5 DSM-IV Diagnostic Criteria for Encopresis

A. Repeated passage of feces into inappropriate places (e.g., clothing or floor)

B. At least one such event a month for at least 3 months.

C. Chronological age is at least 4 years (or equivalent developmental level).

D. The behavior is not due exclusively to the direct physiological effects of a substance (e.g., laxatives) or a general medical condition except through a mechanism involving constipation.

Source: DSM-IV Copyright © 1994 by APA.

medications actually became *worse* the longer they took these medications. Age, gender, or type of enuresis (primary versus secondary) had little influence on the outcome, although children who wet less frequently before treatment and children who wet only at night tended to have greater success. Treatment of enuresis is one of the few treatments in which psychological interventions are clearly superior to drug therapies, and should be used instead of waiting for the child to grow out of the problem because of the distress it causes the child and family (Harbeck-Weber & Peterson, 1996).

Encopresis

Encopresis refers to the passage of feces into inappropriate places, such as clothing or the floor. Like enuresis, this act is usually involuntary, but may occasionally be done on purpose. The diagnostic criteria stipulate that this event must occur at least once per month for at least 3 months, and that the child be 4 years old or older (if the child is developmentally delayed, a mental age of at least 4 years is used). Fecal incontinence must not be due to an organic or general medical condition. DSM-IV criteria for encopresis are described in Table 12.5.

Two subtypes of encopresis are described in DSM-IV: with or without constipation and overflow incontinence. Essentially, encopresis results from constipation that produces fecal impaction. Liquid stool above the impaction gradually develops sufficient pressure to leak around the impaction, thereby producing overflow incontinence in the majority of cases (Cox, Sutphen, Ling, Quillian, & Borowitz, 1996). Children with encopresis without constipation and overflow incontinence are more likely to deposit feces in a prominent location, a behavior that is usually associated with oppositional defiant disorder or conduct disorder (APA, 1994).

Prevalence and Course. Similarities exist between enuresis and encopresis in their clinical features, prevalence, and course. On the basis of parental reports and clinic referrals, an estimated 1.5% to 3% of children

have encopresis (Sprague-McRae, Lamb, & Homer, 1993). Again, this disorder is more common—5 to 6 times—in boys than in girls (Schroeder & Gordon, 1991). The frequency of encopresis decreases with age, and shows a spontaneous remission rate of about 28% per year (Schaefer, 1979). Like enuresis, encopresis can be categorized as primary or secondary. Children with primary encopresis have reached age 4 without having established fecal continence, whereas children with secondary encopresis have had an established period of continence before the current episode of encopresis began.

As many as one in five children with encopresis show significant psychological problems, but these problems are more likely to result from, rather than initially cause, the encopresis (Abrahamian & Lloyd-Still, 1984; Harbeck-Weber & Peterson, 1996). Understandably, they may feel ashamed and try to avoid situations, like camp or school, that might lead to embarrassment. As with enuresis, the degree of children's impairment and associated psychological distress is partially a function of social ostracism by peers, as well as anger, punishment, and rejection on the part of care-givers.

Causes and Treatment. Overly aggressive or early toilet training, family disturbance and stress, and child psychopathology have all been thought to cause encopresis at one time or another (Harbeck-Weber & Peterson, 1996). However, like enuresis, encopresis is a physical disorder that can lead to, but seldom results from, psychological factors alone. The sooner it is diagnosed and treated, the less likely that the child will suffer any lasting emotional scars or disruptions in social relationships. Exceptions, of course, are those children with oppositional defiant and conduct disorders (discussed in Chapter 6), in which encopresis and enuresis may occur as secondary symptoms of broader behavior patterns.

Understanding the etiology of encopresis leads to a discussion of toilet training, where children first learn how to control bowel movements. Children have to learn how to recognize signals from the muscles and nerves that tell them when it is time for a bowel movement. Sometimes they try to avoid or suppress these signals, especially if something more enjoyable is going on. Naturally, accidents happen, which the child and others find unpleasant. Some children attempt to suppress their feces to avoid such accidents, which allows feces to build up in the colon over a period of time, causing *megacolon*. If uncleared, the feces that stay in the bowel become large, hard, and dry, which causes further bowel movements to be painful. Over time, the stretched muscles and nerves give fewer and fewer signals to the child about the need to have a bowel movement. This decrease in signals results in stool accidents, and the colon and rectum often do not empty as they should.

About half of children who develop this pattern of avoidance also have abnormal *defecation dynamics*, that is, they contract rather than relax the external sphincter when they attempt to defecate (Harbeck-Weber & Peterson, 1996). Combined with avoidance tactics, an increased risk of chronic constipation and encopresis develops. In case you're wondering how such dynamics develop, consider how some children (and adults) avoid using a bathroom if they are in a strange place, or if they have been told that public toilets are to be avoided because they are germ-infested. Anxiety about defecating in a particular place, or because their toileting experiences were stressful and harsh, can cause chronic constipation. Unless this pattern of retention is reversed, the child becomes less able to perform the many skills required for successful toileting, including recognizing body cues, undressing, going into the bathroom, sitting on the toilet chair, and relaxing the appropriate muscles (Harbeck-Weber & Peterson, 1996).

Optimal treatment of encopresis involves both medical and behavioral interventions to help the child learn to empty the colon so that it can return to normal size and function (Sprague-McRae et al., 1993). To get the process moving, fiber, enemas, laxatives, or lubricants may be given to disimpact the rectum. Then, to establish a better routine and healthy pattern of elimination, behavioral methods are used in combination with laxatives or similar agents. Laxatives alone do not address the underlying behavioral mechanisms. Children who have large and impacted stools will find defecation frightening and painful, which encourages them further to ignore early rectal distention cues (the urge to defecate) and avoid going to the toilet. Some children can create quite a mess for their parents when they smear feces in an attempt to clean or hide the accident. This is when parents' patience may break down, leading them to become more forceful and coercive which, once again, teaches the child to associate toileting with fear and avoidance.

Behavioral methods involve teaching a toilet-training procedure that encourages detection of and response to rectal distention cues, parental efforts to praise the child's clean pants and toilet use, and regularly scheduled toilet times after meals. During these times, children practice tensing and relaxing their external anal sphincter for several minutes; the practice time is often followed by "fun time" of reading or playing games to desensitize children to sitting on the toilet. They are then taught to strain and attempt to have a bowel movement. For children who have paradoxically learned to contract their external anal sphincter to avoid pain or embarrassment, biofeedback procedures may also be used to train them how to relax the sphincter during attempted defecation (Cox et al., 1996). With biofeedback, children can watch on a video display how their efforts to tighten and relax their anal sphincter muscle control a moving "basket" that catches a "falling egg" (psychologists are a clever bunch, especially when they team up with designers of video games). Once they master this connection, the video display changes to a circle that constricts when the sphincter is tightened and opens when the muscle is relaxed. This teaches them to recognize when to strain while keeping their anal canal open. With a combination of laxatives and behavioral treatment, most children improve significantly within the first 2 weeks of treatment, and over 75% maintain these improvements (Cox et al., 1996; McClung et al., 1993; Nolan, Debelle, Oberklaid, & Coffey, 1991).

CHRONIC CHILDHOOD ILLNESS

A Mother's Reflection

When does the pain go away? I don't think ever. It is a lifetime mourning for what could have been. It has nothing to do with lack of acceptance or understanding and everything to do with things we hold close in our hearts; the celebrations never realized. Sharing in the joy of watching others trying out for sports, having a first date, graduate, get accepted at university, or watch a beloved daughter walk down the aisle to be married, will never be experienced. Different experiences are ours. Instead of reflecting on what could have been, look for what's right with your child, not what's wrong. Be proud of all accomplishments. Different joys are ours. Celebrate each achievement, each milestone. They are great motivators for yourself, your child, and others. (Greey, 1995, p. 97)

Who has not feared that the very worst could somehow single out a family member? Who does not worry as a toddler wanders toward the curb, a preschooler climbs a playground ladder, or a teenager suddenly begins having severe headaches and dizziness? Chronic illnesses and medical conditions affect over 11 million children and adolescents in North America, so it is likely that we will hear about these sad events quite often. A chronic illness is one that persists longer than 3 months in a given year, or requires a period of continuous hospitalization of more than 1 month (Pless & Pinkerton, 1975). Chronic medical conditions—the wide range of complications relating to physical growth, function, and development, such as a visual or hearing impairment—are part of this picture as well. About one-fifth of children with chronic illness or medical conditions are severely limited in their daily activities and face numerous obstacles to forming friendships, attending school, and simply pursuing a normal quality of life (Thompson & Gustafson, 1996).

Children and adolescents whose health and functional ability is compromised by a chronic medical condition face numerous challenges to their development and adjustment. Each day, children with insulin-dependent diabetes must monitor their blood glucose level and diet, and administer insulin through injections; children with asthma cautiously navigate new situations, on the alert for an attack that can literally leave them breathless; and children with cancer must cope with the stares or comments from peers, who have little understanding or compassion for why another child looks different or seems frail. Like other developmental disorders, these conditions have an impact not only on the child but on peers and family members as well. This impact, in turn, affects the child's ability to adapt to the condition.

The DSM-IV addresses the mental health issues pertaining to health-related disorders in children and adults indiscriminantly, relying mainly on two quite distinct categories: somatoform disorders and psychological factors affecting physical condition. These DSM-IV categories are briefly discussed to provide an understanding of their meaning and limited applicability to pediatric populations.

Somatoform disorders are a group of related problems involving physical symptoms that resemble or suggest a medical condition, but lack organic or physiological evidence (APA, 1994). Somatization, hypochondriasis, and pain disorders are examples of somatoform disorders. The diagnostic criteria involve a clustering of complaints with pain, gastrointestinal, sexual, and pseudoneurological symptoms existing at any time during the course of the disturbance. These symptoms are not intentionally produced or feigned, and they are real enough to cause significant distress or impairment to the individual. For some somatoform disorders, especially

conversion disorder, a strong presumption of a psychological component to the symptom is required for the diagnosis.

Somatoform disorders have been defined and studied largely with adult populations, especially because they imply a chronic, established pattern that is often not detected until young adulthood (Harbeck-Weber & Peterson, 1996). Thus, their diagnostic applicability in reference to children and adolescents is questionable and seldom used (Fritz, Fritsch, & Hagino, 1997). Nonetheless, we raise this topic primarily because children's multiple somatic complaints, especially recurrent abdominal pain, may be developmental precursors to adult somatoform disorders (Ernst, Routh, & Harper, 1984; Fritz et al., 1997; Walker, Garber, Van Slyke, & Greene, 1995).

The second category, **psychological factors affecting physical condition,** refers to disorders in which psychological factors are presumed to cause or exacerbate a physical condition (Harbeck-Weber & Peterson, 1996). The DSM-IV criteria for this disorder are shown in Table 12.6. Notice that these criteria primarily address situations in which a person's medical condition is adversely affected by psychological factors, such as a person with diabetes who is depressed and refuses to monitor and regulate her glucose level. However, this diagnostic category does not apply to most children with chronic health conditions, because it is the *medical condition* and its limitations that affect their psychological adjustment, not the other way around. That is, psychological symptoms develop in response to the stress of having or being diagnosed with a general medical condition. Rather than depression affecting the course of diabetes, as in the example above, it is more likely the case that diabetes causes adjustment difficulties, which sometimes (but by no means always) include clinical disorders, such as depression. Thus, some children and adolescents with chronic illness accompanied by significant adjustment or behavioral problems may receive a diagnosis of Adjustment Disorder, which better accounts for the nature of the stressor (APA, 1994).

Progress in the development of effective medical treatments and cures for children with chronic illness has been spectacular over the past three decades, greatly prolonging the lives of many who previously would have died in infancy or childhood. Remarkably, the cure rate for certain types of cancer, such as acute lymphoblastic leukemia, has increased from about one in five children in the 1950s to four in five children today (Cecalupo, 1994). At the same time, however, these advances and improved survival rates have led to greater child and adult **morbidity.** Morbidity refers to the various forms of physical and functional consequences and limitations resulting from an illness. Increased morbidity implies

Table 12.6 DSM-IV Psychological Factor* Affecting Medical Condition

A. A general medical condition (coded on Axis III) is present.

B. Psychological factors adversely affect the general medical condition in one of the following ways:
  (1) the factors have influenced the course of the general medical condition as shown by a close temporal association between the psychological factors and the development or exacerbation of, or delayed recovery from, the general medical condition
  (2) the factors interfere with the treatment of the general medical condition
  (3) the factors constitute additional health risks for the individual
  (4) stress-related physiological responses precipitate or exacerbate symptoms of the general medical condition

*Note: *Choose* name based on the nature of the psychological factors:

mental disorder affecting . . . (e.g., an Axis I disorder, such as major depressive disorder delaying recovery from an illness)
psychological symptoms affecting . . . (e.g., anxiety exacerbating asthma)
personality traits or coping style affecting . . . (e.g., pathological denial of the need for surgery in a patient with cancer)
maladaptive health behaviors affecting . . . (e.g., overeating, lack of exercise, unsafe sex)
stress-related physiological response affecting . . . (e.g., stress-related exacerbations of ulcer, hypertension, tension headache)
other or unspecified psychological factors affecting . . . (e.g., interpersonal, cultural, or religious factors)

Source: DSM-IV Copyright © 1994 by APA.

---

that more children and adolescents are adapting to the challenges of a chronic illness. For these children, illness has become a chronic life situation and stressor. As children's survival has improved and life-threatening illnesses are better controlled, attention has moved away from the acute, infectious diseases to a broader emphasis on promoting children's health and development, and assisting in the care of those with chronic illness or handicapping conditions (Garrison & McQuiston, 1989). Pediatric health psychologists are particularly active in helping children with chronic health disorders successfully adapt and attain an optimal quality of life.

To increase our awareness of the ways children with chronic disease learn to cope and adapt to physical and social challenges, we take a look at how children normally think of and express health concerns. This awareness provides a developmentally sensitive context for distinguishing between adaptive and maladaptive coping reactions among children with chronic illness. We then discuss the nature and course of childhood diabetes and cancer, to illustrate the nature of the challenges faced by children with different chronic health disorders.

Normal Variations in Children's Expression of Health Concerns

Picture this common scene: Since age 6, Jackie has informed her parents from time to time that she was "too sick" to go to school. She would then carefully provide them with a list of her symptoms: "My tummy hurts, I feel hot, my throat hurts, I can't feel my toes." Careful questioning would usually result in a further list of symptoms—in fact, most of the ones suggested by one of her parents "Does your leg hurt too?" [yes]; "How does your head feel?" [achey]; "What does your skin feel like?" [stingy]). The astute reader might note that these symptoms emerged at about the time Jackie was entering the first grade. Would you consider this situation to be typical of how children learn about physical symptoms and their connection to life's responsibilities?

We now recognize that children are able to communicate about their pain and discomfort about as well as adults can, but this was not always so. It was thought that infants did not experience pain at all, and that children were far less sensitive to pain than adults. Because children seemed less able to communicate about their pain, it was wrongly concluded that they had higher pain thresholds than adults. However, children do have a good concept of what pain is, and how to express it (McGrath & McAlpine, 1993). Their concepts of pain and its causes, their descriptions of pain, and their specific pain experiences seem remarkably well formed by an early age, both for boys and girls (D. M. Ross & S. A. Ross, 1984).

Consider these comments:

It [stomachache] was like bees in your stomach—stinging your stomach, yellow jackets going ping, pong, bop inside—like something just chopped down your stomach.

[6-year-old boy]. It [earache] felt like something is inside your ear like a sticker from a rose bush poking deep inside your ear, like way harder than just pricking. [9-year-old boy] (D. M. Ross & S. A. Ross, 1984, p. 184)

Further, it is unlikely that children simply pick up pain descriptions from their parents or others. Consider the childlike imagery used by a 7-year-old boy in describing a headache:

Like there's this big monster in there, see, and he's growing like crazy and there's no room and he's pulling the two sides of my head apart he's getting so big. (D. M. Ross & S. A. Ross, 1984, p. 189)

Are somatic complaints in children (such as those expressed by Jackie) normal and commonplace? As we noted in Chapter 7, children and adolescents often express their fears, worries, and anxiety by somatic complaints. About a third of typical 5- to 12-year-olds report using pain for secondary gains, such as increased parental and peer attention and avoidance of school and athletic activities. One 8-year-old girl says it straight: "Whenever I don't want to go to swimming practice I grab my stomach and make a face like eating a lemon and I say, 'Gee, mom, I *hope* I don't have to miss *swimming.*'" (D. M. Ross & S. A. Ross, 1984, p. 188). Undeniably, one of the most common ways children express their fears, dislikes, and avoidance is to complain of aches and pains, often of uncertain or dubious origin. And girls and boys show interesting differences in this respect. Girls report more symptoms of pain and anxiety than do boys, when asked. Under stressful circumstances, girls are more likely to cry, cling, and seek emotional support, and boys are more likely to be uncooperative, avoidant, and stoic. Does this imply that girls are somehow more sensitive to pain or less able to manage their fear and anxiety than boys? (OK, a loaded question). Not likely. These gender differences probably stem from socialization expectations, not physiological differences. We are all familiar with the ways boys are encouraged to adopt stoic attitudes about pain, whereas girls are reinforced for passive, affective expression (McGrath, 1993). Both boys and girls are reactive to distress, but they express it in accordance with how they have been taught and what they wish to receive. Therefore, such complaints are developmentally within the normal range and do not merit a psychiatric label.

Some children may be more likely than others to experience recurrent pain and physical symptoms because of family influences, including not only genetic predispositions but also social learning processes based on the family's emphasis on health and illness (Peterson, Harbeck, Farmer, & Zink, 1991). Remember how children mimic behaviors that they have observed? Social learning theory contends that whether or not children imitate behaviors they observe depends in part on the consequences experienced by the model. Children will repeat the behaviors they imitate if the consequences for them are rewarding, which can involve positive reinforcement, such as attention, or negative reinforcement, such as staying home from school. This explanation has been empirically supported: Children with functional abdominal pain and similar forms of recurrent unexplained pain are more likely to identify someone in their family who often expresses pain than are children whose pain is due to known organic causes (Osborne, Hatcher, & Richtsmeier, 1989; Routh & Ernst, 1984). These unexplained, recurrent pain symptoms among children, therefore, seem to originate primarily from family *pain models* (Harbeck-Weber & Peterson, 1996). But children also learn healthy adaptational patterns at home and elsewhere: Children with well-developed social and academic competence, for instance, are less likely to respond to negative life events, like divorce or hospitalizations, with amplified stress and pain reactions (Walker, Garber, & Greene, 1994).

Representative Chronic Childhood Illnesses

Let's turn our attention now to those children who have chronic health problems or conditions. Each chronic illness has unique challenges. Children with diabetes face daily medical routines, but they have a relatively predictable prognosis; children with cancer experience unpleasant side effects of treatment, and must also cope with the uncertain prognosis of their illness. The one important thing that all chronic illnesses and medical conditions have in common is that they constitute a major stressor that challenges and absorbs both the child's and the family's available coping resources. Viewing chronic illness in this way—as a form of major stress requiring adaptation—has allowed researchers to identify factors that promote successful adaptation to chronic illness. This view has also advanced new ways to assist children in coping with these challenges, as we will see.

The number of children with *any* chronic health-related disorder or condition is quite high, varying from 10% to 20% of the child population (Gortmaker & Sappenfield, 1984). Of these children, about two-thirds have mild conditions; the remainder have conditions that result in moderate to severe activity restrictions and bothersome treatment regimens (Harbeck-Weber & Peterson, 1996). Asthma is the most common chronic illness in childhood, followed by neurological and developmental disabilities and behavioral disorders. Fortunately, severe forms of chronic illnesses—those which pose major physical and intellectual limitations that interfere with children's daily lives—are relatively rare.

Table 12.7 Estimated Population Prevalence of Selected Chronic Diseases and Conditions in Children, aged 0 to 20, in the United States

	Prevalence Estimates per 1000	Percent Surviving to Age 20
Moderate to severe asthma	10.0	98
Congenital heart disease	7.0	65
Cystic fibrosis	.20	60
Diabetes mellitus	1.8	95
Hemophilia	.15	90
Leukemia	.11	40
Muscular dystrophy	.06	25
Sickle-cell anemia	.28	90

Source: Adapted from Gortmaker & Sappenfield, 1984; Gortmaker, 1985.

Their combined rates are sizeable, however: About 2 out of every 100 children in the general population are significantly affected by a chronic illness or medical condition (Thompson & Gustafson, 1996).

Table 12.7 shows the prevalence of selected chronic childhood diseases and medical conditions. As mentioned briefly, survival rates for many of these illnesses have risen rapidly since the 1950s, so prevalence rates now reflect a large proportion of children who have survived these childhood illnesses until age 20 or longer. Many of these illnesses are approaching their maximum (100%) survival rates (Gortmaker, 1985). The impact of new diseases, such as AIDS, will likely be a major health issue in the years to come.

Chronic childhood illnesses do not discriminate in terms of social class and ethnicity—they affect all children equally. The only exceptions are those specific conditions that are genetically determined by racial or ethnic descent. For example, cystic fibrosis affects primarily Caucasians, and sickle-cell disease affects primarily persons of African descent (Thompson & Gustafson, 1996). However, a troubling connection exists between socioeconomic status (SES) and *survival* rates, among children and adults with cancer, in particular (Mackillop, Zhang-Salomons, Groome, Paszat, & Holowaty, 1997). Despite attempts to achieve more equitable health care delivery, residents of poorer communities still may receive inferior quality of care, even in publicly funded, single-tier health care systems like that in Canada. In addition, the poor may have other ailments that make cancer survival more difficult, or parents may be less inclined to seek medical attention because of other major life stressors or their lack of awareness of critical symptoms (Mackillop et al., 1997). People with adequate means generally enjoy a greater degree of empowerment—self-guidance and choices—over their lives, which translates into greater opportunity for proper medical care for their children. Later in this chapter we consider some ways to empower families and achieve a greater balance in their roles and resources.

We now take a closer look at two specific illnesses, diabetes mellitus and childhood cancer, that are representative of the course and patterns of adaptation that children with chronic illness face. These representative illnesses convey the adaptive illness-related tasks that confront children and their families, and how these tasks interact with normal development.

Diabetes Mellitus

Amanda: Daily Struggle with Diabetes

Amanda, age 14, was diagnosed with insulin-dependent diabetes mellitus about a year ago. Like most teenagers, she leads an active life, and eating the proper foods is difficult enough even without the added burden of daily glucose monitoring and insulin injections. She shared with us some of the ways this disease has affected her life, and how she copes with its demands and limitations:

Becoming diabetic has completely changed my life. My best friend is the insulin I take and the machine. I use the machine to test my blood sugar four times a day by poking my finger and putting blood on a test strip. From the reading I am able to adjust my insulin and what I must eat. I am forced to eat a healthy balanced meal regularly about six times every day. I try not to have a negative attitude because I now realize just how lucky I am. I do not know what I would do if I did not have my machine or all of the sugar-free foods that are now available.

Not only did diabetes change my physical life, but it altered my mental life as well. It helped me look at my life and realize what was important to me. My close friend, Germaine, helped me get through the first year at school, when some of the other kids wondered why I had to use needles and couldn't eat the same things that they do. My parents have been great, and even my younger brother lays off me when he knows I'm having a particularly bad day. In a way, I'm more aware of how important health is to us than most kids at school, and I don't take things for granted the same way I used to.

Amanda suffers from **insulin-dependent diabetes mellitus (IDDM)**, a lifelong metabolic disorder in which the body is unable to metabolize carbohydrates as a result of inadequate pancreatic release of insulin. This lack of insulin has a domino effect on the body's ability to regulate appetite, metabolize carbohydrates into necessary energy, and maintain a balance of blood chemistry. First, the lack of insulin prohibits glucose from entering the cells, forcing glucose to accumulate in the bloodstream and cause *hyperglycemia*. Glucose also tells the regulatory cells of the hypothalamus when a person is hungry or full, so without such information, the person tends to eat constantly but does not gain weight (Thompson & Gustafson, 1996). A treatment regimen consisting of insulin injections, diet, and exercise is necessary to approximate a normal metabolic state. Although current treatment regimens have greatly improved the health status of people with IDDM, the condition is still associated with significant morbidity and mortality.

IDDM affects boys and girls equally (Johnson, 1988). Initial symptoms often include fatigue, thirst, hunger, frequent urination, and weight loss despite excessive eating. IDDM is a progressive disease, with the more chronic complications occurring in young adulthood or beyond, including circulatory problems that can lead to blindness, kidney failure, and accelerated cardiovascular disease (Arslanian, Becker, & Drash, 1995). Life expectancy is one-third less than that of the general population (Silverstein, 1994). Given the seriousness of the illness and the long-standing, intrusive treatment requirements, it is understandable that children with diabetes and their families have an increased risk for conflict and adjustment problems (Northam, Anderson, Adler, Werther, & Warne, 1996).

Children with IDDM face daily treatment tasks to maintain their **metabolic control,** such as blood glucose monitoring, dietary restraints, insulin injections, and learning how to balance energy demands and insulin needs (Thompson & Gustafson, 1996). Metabolic control is the degree to which the patient's glucose levels are maintained within the normal range. Children and adolescents must monitor their insulin levels carefully because too little insulin can result in a diabetic coma; too much insulin can result in an insulin reaction called *hypoglycemia*. Hypoglycemic episodes are extremely unpleasant and can include irritability, headaches, and shakiness. Adding to the complexity is the fact that illness and stress can upset the relationship between glucose and required insulin levels (Arslanian et al., 1995; Hanson, Henggeler, & Burghen, 1987).

Children and teens must carefully follow the instructions given to them by their physician; that is, they must practice careful *regimen adherence*. Good regimen adherence and metabolic control are linked to individuals' correct knowledge about their disease and its treatment, their belief that adherence is important, and adequate problem-solving skills (Harbeck-Weber & Peterson, 1996). As we saw with Amanda, adolescence is a particularly difficult period because of the impact that the illness can have on self-esteem and social and educational experiences—adolescence is difficult enough without the added burden of these daily treatment tasks. For these reasons, psychologists have become active in developing ways to promote regimen adherence and metabolic control by helping family members adapt favorably to the demands of the condition (Hanson, Henggeler, Harris, Burghen, & Moore, 1989). Behavioral strategies have been quite successful in this regard—increasing compliance by as much as 85% (Haynes, 1976)—especially methods that reinforce symptom reduction or medication use, and self-control methods that teach patients to regulate dosage and monitor their symptoms, blood glucose, and medications (Delamater, 1988; Epstein & Cluss, 1982; Meichenbaum & Turk, 1987).

Childhood Cancer

> How I hate this world. I would like to tear
> it apart with my own two hands if I could. I
> would like to dismantle the universe star
> by star, like a treeful of rotten fruit.
> —Peter De Vries, *after his daughter died of leukemia*

Chen: A Determined Boy Fighting Leukemia

Chen, age 9, explains his feelings about childhood leukemia and its impact on his family and peer relations:

I've had cancer now for three years. They're still trying to fight it with the right medicine but nothing has worked yet. My friends come visit me—they're pretty OK with everything. But sometimes if you try and tell other kids about it they don't understand because they don't have it. To them we're normal. They don't have any kind of problems that hold them back from doing things. They don't have to worry about being in the hospital, checkups and things, to see how you're doing. You can tell your friends why you have to stop and rest awhile, but they don't really understand—they don't really want to—they want to keep on going.

I've got lots of family who care about me and I worry for them. I guess I'm used to all the doctors and medicines I take. Not that I like them but I know it's the only thing that might help. But I liked having the ability to do anything with my friends (or even my parents). I want to be able to get up and go. I'd tell someone else going through this to stay strong and keep the faith. And speak up when you need something!

Chen's mother explains the ordeal he and his family have undergone since his diagnosis:

Chen received a bone marrow transplant from his brother over a year ago and, thankfully, his leukemia went into remission. But when we went back one year later for a checkup we were told Chen had suffered a relapse—the cancer had overtaken the bone marrow, and his prognosis is poor. Now our family focuses on enjoying our time together and doing things with Chen. We are fortunate—my employer has gone out of their way to help me stay at home with Chen. Their support over the past year has been incredible. In fact, our whole community has shown tremendous support to our family. But his turn for the worst has made it difficult for us to do the things we have done over the past few weeks. We are angry, hopeful, depressed, joyous, saddened all the time. It is the worse roller coaster that we have ever ridden. Yet, Chen's medical condition has made us more determined to do more than we had ever hoped for, and the kindness shown toward our family has been overwhelming.

It is difficult for most of us to imagine what Chen and his family have experienced. Their words acknowledge the importance of human kindness when faced with a serious childhood illness, which in this case was terminal, and their strength and determination. Cancer can strike children very suddenly, more so than with adults. Children are also often at a more advanced stage of cancer when they are first diagnosed: Whereas only 20% of adults with cancer show evidence that the disease has spread at the time of diagnosis, this figure is fourfold in children (National Childhood Cancer Foundation, 1997).

The most common form of childhood cancer is **acute lymphoblastic leukemia (ALL)**, which accounts for close to half of all forms of childhood cancer (Thompson & Gustafson, 1996). ALL is actually a group of heterogeneous diseases in which there is a malignancy of the bone marrow that produces blood cells. The bone marrow produces malignant cells called *lymphoblasts* that progressively replace normal bone marrow with fewer red blood cells and more white blood cells, causing anemia, infection, and easy bruising or excessive bleeding (Friedman & Mulhern, 1992). Childhood cancer used to be fatal, but advances in medical treatment have resulted in dramatic improvements in survival rates. Still, long-term

complications such as recurrent malignancy, growth retardation, neuropsychological deficits, cataracts, and infertility, pose a risk.

Like those with diabetes, children with cancer undergo complicated medical treatment regimens, especially during the first 2 to 3 years. In addition, they face school absences, significant treatment side effects, and an uncertain prognosis. Chemotherapy and radiation therapy can cause hair loss and weight changes, as well as nausea, vomiting, increased fatigue, endocrine and growth retardation, and a depressed immune system (Friedman & Mulhern, 1992). Children with cancer must also cope with painful medical procedures, such as venipuncture, bone marrow aspirations, and lumbar punctures. Treatment also requires children to be away from friends and some family members, which hinders their psychosocial development. For these reasons, the psychosocial aspects of pediatric cancer have focused on management of distress related to the multiple diagnostic and treatment procedures these children face. We consider these issues in the section on enhancing adaptation.

Development and Course

Are children with chronic illnesses more likely to suffer emotional and behavioral adjustment problems stemming from the burden of their disease and its treatment? Findings of large-scale epidemiological studies and controlled clinical studies have shed considerable light on this issue.

The Ontario Child Health Study (Cadman, Boyle, Szatmari, & Offord, 1987) was a major undertaking designed, in part, to determine the connection between medical conditions and psychological adaptation among a representative sample of 4- to 16-year-olds. Parents and teachers completed a mental health survey containing information on children's illnesses and psychological adjustment. Children were then classified into one of three levels of physical health: chronic illness with physical disability ($n = 110$), chronic illness without disability ($n = 418$), and physically healthy ($n = 2360$). Psychiatric disorders, if any, were also determined from parent and teacher data.

Figure 12.2 shows the percentages of children with at least one psychiatric disorder across these three groups. Overall, children with chronic illness, regardless of degree of disability, had a risk for psychiatric disorder that was 2.4 times that of healthy children. However, notice from the figure that children with chronic illness *accompanied by disability* were at greatest risk for other disorders. These disorders appeared primarily in the form of internalizing problems, such as anxiety and depression, but externalizing problems, such as ADHD, were evident as well. Understandably, children whose

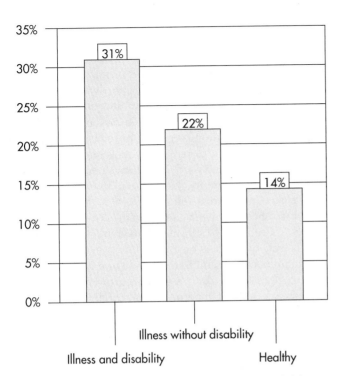

FIGURE 12.2 Psychiatric disorders among children with chronic illness with or without disability, and healthy children. (Data from Cadman et al., 1987)

normal functional abilities are limited face the greatest challenges in everyday activities, which in turn increases behavioral, social, and school adjustment difficulties. These findings were mirrored by the U.S. National Health Survey, where chronic physical conditions posed a significant risk factor for behavior problems, above and beyond socioeconomic status effects (Gortmaker, Walker, Weitzman, & Sobol, 1990).

Therefore, the answer to the earlier question is yes; children with chronic physical illnesses, especially those with physical disabilities, have an *increased risk* of secondary psychological adjustment difficulties (Goldberg, Gotowiec, & Simmons, 1995; Lavigne & Faier-Routman, 1992). Secondary psychological adjustment difficulties refer to problems that are suspected to be due to the primary medical condition, rather than the reverse. These problems are most often expressed as internalizing symptoms, such as anxiety and depression, or a combination of both internalizing and externalizing problems (Lavigne & Faier-Routman, 1992; Thompson & Gustafson, 1996).

To keep these symptoms in perspective, though, one must recognize that adjustment of children with chronic illness is typically better than that of other children referred to mental health clinics for non-health-related problems (Wallander, Varni, Babani, Banis, & Wilcox, 1988). For the most part, these children are exhibiting

stress-related symptoms; the incidence of DSM-IV–type disorders among children with chronic illness is actually low. For example, the prevalence of depression among children with various chronic health conditions averages only 9% across studies, an encouraging indication of successful adaptation among the vast majority of these children (Bennett, 1994). Moreover, when followed several years later, children with diabetes (Kovacs et al., 1990) as well as those with cancer (Greenberg, Kazak, & Meadows, 1989) on average report symptoms of anxiety, depression, and low self-esteem that are within the normal range for their age and gender.

Although chronically ill populations of children have increased risk of initial adjustment difficulties, it is difficult to say what causes particular symptoms, or why some children adapt more successfully than others. When one considers how these children must cope with unpredictable events and challenges almost every day, it is understandable that they would show an increase in stress-related symptoms. It is especially encouraging to know that most are able to adapt successfully to the course and consequences of their illness. Much like the adjustment problems faced by children with mental retardation and those who have been abused or neglected, symptoms of anxiety, depression, and anger can be thought of as normal responses to stressful experiences associated with the long-term illness and treatment regimens, rather than psychiatric disorders (L. J. Siegel et al., 1991). Most children with chronic illness show considerable resilience in the face of stressful experiences associated with their condition, and we should exercise caution in applying psychiatric labels or descriptors that fail to capture the context and nature of their circumstances.

Effect on Family Members

> The more I read and the more I talked to other parents of children with disabilities and normal children, the more I found that feelings and emotions about children are very much the same in all families. The accident of illness or disability serves only to intensify feelings and emotions, not to change them. (Weatherly, 1984).

The field of pediatric health psychology has clearly adopted a focus on the important role of family functioning in the adjustment of children with chronic illness. The child's circumstances may result in family cohesion and support, as we saw in Amanda's and Chen's families, or family disruption and crisis. As parents try to understand and cope with the news of their child's diagnosis, they must at the same time start to accept that their child might always be different from other children. How they react and accept these realities determines, to a large extent, how their child and other siblings will react and adapt. Parents who fail to resolve this crisis are more likely to have problems with attachment and child-rearing (Goldberg et al., 1995; Sheeran, Marvin, & Pianta, 1997), which further complicates the stressful nature of the child's illness.

Learning that a child has a life-threatening disease causes trauma and stress to all family members and, in fact, qualifies as a traumatic event that can precipitate PTSD (APA, 1994). A mother of an infant born with a chronic disability describes her initial reaction:

> I felt like I was bouncing around on a raft in the middle of a terrible storm. I didn't know where I was, where I was going, or what wave was going to break over my head next. Most of the time, I just hung on. Hanging on, I discovered, is the key to survival. (Medvescek, 1997, p. 67)

Many parents of children with chronic illness report that their fears resurface and memories return whenever their child has even a common illness like a cold or flu. About 10% of mothers and fathers suffer severe symptoms of PTSD, a rate that is comparable to other types of traumatic stress exposure (Kazak et al., 1997). Fortunately, the children themselves do not typically suffer PTSD-related symptoms connected to learning of their disorder, probably because they were very young at the time of diagnosis. However, some survivors of childhood cancer recall disturbing memories of the medical procedures as much as 12 years later (Stuber, Christakis, Houskamp, & Kasak, 1996).

Families exert a significant impact on the behavior of children with chronic health problems, just as they do with healthy children. No one type of chronic illness poses a significantly greater risk of adjustment than any other. This implies that factors associated with children's situations—like family stress and resources—may be more critical to their adaptation than the challenges posed by their particular illness alone (Lavigne & Faier-Routman, 1992). In general, stress factors parents face are quite similar across all types of pediatric chronic illness: financial and physical burdens, changes in parenting roles, sibling resentment, child adjustment problems, social isolation, frequent hospitalizations, and grief (Pless & Perrin, 1985). It comes as no surprise, therefore, that couples with chronically ill children report more marital distress, such as conflict, poor communication, role incongruity, and a lack of intimacy and positive affect (Gordon-Walker, Johnson, Manion, & Cloutier, 1996).

The point is worth repeating: Despite these psychological and tangible repercussions, many children with chronic illness adapt favorably to these challenges, as do their families. Perceived social support and parental adaptation are key components aiding such adaptation (Kazak et al., 1997), since primary care-givers play an important role in their children's stress and coping abilities. Specifically, mothers who perceive lower levels of illness-related stress, who use more adaptive and active ways to cope with stress and problems, and who perceive their families as more supportive rather than conflictual are more likely to show normal adjustment levels themselves (Thompson & Gustafson, 1996). We often see this connection regardless of the circumstances: When maternal abilities remain intact, child and family functioning is less impaired. This illustrates the reciprocal relationship between children's adjustment and parental stress and distress—healthy *parental* adjustment is related to healthy *child* adjustment, and vice versa (Banez & Compas, 1990) (most research has considered only the role of mothers on child adjustment, but fathers' specific influence on children's coping and adaptation to chronic illness may also be prominent). Thus, parental adjustment is one of the important correlates of adjustment of children with chronic illness.

Social Adjustment and School Performance. Children's adjustment to chronic illness is reflected not only in terms of psychological distress, but also through developmental accomplishments, such as social adjustment, peer relationships, and school performance. Because chronic illness results in lifestyle interruptions that interfere with opportunities for social interaction (La Greca, 1990), children with more severe, disruptive illnesses tend to suffer most in terms of social adjustment (Graetz & Schute, 1995).

Consider child cancer patients' peer relationships. Chen explained how the other children basically did not understand why he could not join in or behave the same as they did—to them he looked normal, so he must be okay. Negative or ill-informed reactions from peers and others are, unfortunately, a fact of life for some children with chronic illness. In a longitudinal study of children with cancer, adolescents were perceived by their teachers as being less sociable, less prone toward leadership, and more socially isolated and withdrawn than their peers (Noll, Bukowski, Rogosch, LeRoy, & Kulkarni, 1990; Noll, LeRoy, Bukowski, Rogosch, & Kulkarni, 1991). Similar problems in social adjustment are evident among those children who have illnesses that affect primarily the CNS, such as cerebral palsy, spina bifida, and brain tumors, because of the impact of these disorders on cognitive abilities such as social judgment (Breslau, 1985; Mulhern, Carpentieri, Schema, Stone, & Fairclough, 1993).

School adjustment and performance is yet another domain in which children and adolescents with chronic illness are at increased risk for adjustment difficulties. Such risk may stem from two sources: primary effects of the illness or its treatment, and secondary consequences

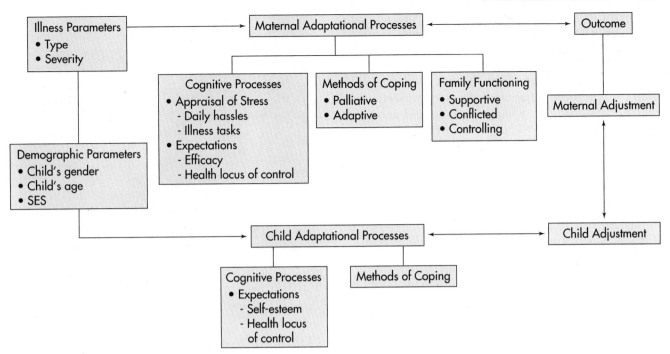

FIGURE 12.3 The transactional stress and coping model for chronic childhood illness. (Adapted from Thompson et al., 1994)

of the illness, such as fatigue, absenteeism, or psychological stress (Thompson & Gustafson, 1996). Primary effects of the illness on school performance are especially evident among children with brain-related illnesses, who must undergo aggressive treatment regimens that put a heavy toll on the CNS, especially for younger children (Friedman & Mulhern, 1992). The most common neurocognitive effects appear in nonverbal abilities and attention or concentration functions (Fletcher & Copeland, 1988). Short-term memory, speed of processing, visuomotor coordination, and sequencing ability are also frequently affected (Cousens, Ungerer, Crawford, & Stevens, 1991). For these reasons, about half of the children with brain-related illnesses are placed in special education settings or do not attend school (Rutter, Tizard, & Whitmore, 1970). In contrast, children with physical, non-brain-related illnesses tend to have normal educational placements; however, they still have problems in reading, which may be one of the indirect effects of chronic illness and school absence (Cadman et al., 1987; Gortmaker et al., 1990).

A Biopsychosocial Model of Children's Adaptation to Chronic Illness

We described the adjustment difficulties of children with chronic illness in general terms, but we know that each child's illness and family situation is different. Some children, like Amanda and Chen, have a supportive family, but others may not. Countless events can influence children's adaptation to chronic illness; no single factor explains why some children adjust more readily than others. So how do we make sense of the numerous factors influencing children's adjustment? When a single-factor theory is not sufficient to explain something, researchers often develop multifactorial theories that link the most important variables in conceptual and meaningful ways. Figure 12.3 depicts the *transactional stress and coping model* developed by Thompson and colleagues (Thompson, Gil, Burbach, Keith, & Kinney, 1993; Thompson, Gustafson, George, & Spock, 1994), which shows how children's adaptation to chronic illness is influenced not only by the nature of the illness itself, but also by personal and family resources. This model helps make sense of the complicated processes that shape children's outcomes.

The transactional stress and coping model emphasizes the stressful nature of chronic illness, which compels the child and family members to adapt. How they accomplish such adaptation is a key factor in children's outcomes. *Illness parameters* encompass the type of illness and its severity, including visible disfigurement and functional impairment (MacLean et al., 1992; Mulhern et al., 1993). *Demographic parameters* include gender, age, and SES, which also can affect the impact of the illness. The model then proposes that important child and family processes *mediate* the illness-outcome relationship, beyond illness and demographic factors.

Important psychological mediators involve parental adjustment, child adjustment, and their interrelationship, as described below.

Illness Parameters.

One would expect that children's psychosocial adjustment varies as a function of their medical condition. Some illnesses have an uncertain course and others have dire effects on everyday activities, adding stress along the way. Different chronic illnesses have many features in common, though, so it often makes sense to study children's adjustment in relation to illness-related dimensions, or parameters, rather than specific illnesses. This is known as a *noncategorical* approach. The common dimensions that vary among different illnesses include such things as the extent to which the illness (Thompson & Gustafson, 1996):

❖ is visible to others, or involves physical deformity
❖ is severe and life-threatening
❖ has a worsening or fatal prognosis versus a stable or improving prognosis
❖ requires intrusive or painful procedures
❖ affects the child's functional status, such as physical or cognitive impairments that affect performance of everyday tasks

Children with chronic illness face different challenges along each of these dimensions, so naturally their adjustment may be affected accordingly. Across all medical conditions, the illness parameters that play the most significant role in children's adjustment are *severity, prognosis,* and *functional status* (Lavigne & Faier-Routman, 1993). Functional status seems to be especially important in terms of cognitive impairments. As noted, children with conditions that involve the brain and CNS are most likely to show behavior problems and poor social functioning. Psychological adjustment has a logical connection to the nature and extent of stressful circumstances children face, reinforcing the notion that efforts to assist in coping with these stressful circumstances may enhance quality of life and overall adaptation.

Child Characteristics.

Chronic medical conditions require children and family members to accept and cope with considerable stress and uncertainty. What child characteristics and resources might favor successful adaptation? Gender is one consideration: Boys with chronic illness show more adjustment problems overall than girls. But this gender difference depends on the dimension of adjustment and who is doing the reporting. Boys are described by parents and teachers as having more behavior problems than girls (Gortmaker et al., 1990; Perrin, Ayoub, & Willett, 1993; Wallander et al., 1988). However, girls are more likely than boys to

Jeremiah's arms are in temporary restraints so he can't remove the tube through his nose measuring stomach acid reflux.

self-report symptoms of distress, such as anxiety, depression, and negative perceptions of physical appearance (La Greca, Swales, Klemp, Madigan, & Skyler, 1995; Ryan & Morrow, 1986), and to describe themselves as less socially competent (Holden, Chmielewski, Nelson, & Kager, 1997). This gender difference likely is a reflection of two common findings: Girls are more willing to acknowledge and report symptoms than are boys (Achenbach, McConaughy, & Howell, 1987), and girls react to stress with internalizing symptoms, whereas boys react with more externalizing symptoms (Compas, 1987). Other than gender, however, children's overall adjustment seldom differs as a function of current age or age at the onset of the illness (Thompson & Gustafson, 1996).

Not surprisingly, children with greater intellectual ability and acquired strengths in terms of self-concept and coping also show more positive psychological adjustment, regardless of medical condition (Lavigne & Faier-Routman, 1993). Specifically, children's accurate appraisal of perceived stress—how they interpret and react to daily events and hassles associated with illness management—leads to a better sense of well-being and fewer symptoms of distress and maladjustment (Thompson & Gustafson, 1996). Chen states this well:

> I now realize that life is full of a series of tests. You never know what is around the corner, but you have to take it as it comes. A positive attitude, and remembering that I have friends and family for support, helps me get through some of the rough days.

His acquired wisdom attests to the important role of cognitive processes in children's adjustment (an issue addressed in a later section).

Parental Adaptation and Family Functioning.

If chronic illness is considered a stressor affecting all family members to a greater or lesser extent, then child adjustment depends in part on the degree of stress and symptoms experienced by other family members, especially the primary care-giver. Undeniably, the family environment assumes greater importance in the lives of children with a chronic illness, in part because a closer parent-child interaction often is necessary to manage the disease. Notice how the transactional model considers parental adaptation to be a key mediator of the relationship between child illness and both child and parent adjustment. But how does a parent "adapt" in a way that favors healthy outcomes? According to the model, parental adaptation is a function of three major processes: (1) their cognitive appraisal of stress, that is, how they manage daily stress and view their self-efficacy, as seen with Chen's mother (Gil, Williams, Thompson, & Kinney, 1991); (2) their ways of coping—that is, whether they use active, solution-focused coping or passive, palliative coping methods; and (3) family functioning and perceived support. Successful parental adaptation, in turn, leads to better parental adjustment (Barakat & Linney, 1992) and healthier family communication and conflict resolution skills (Wysocki, 1993). Ultimately, of course, parents' positive adjustment greatly increases the likelihood of more positive child outcomes.

Chen's mother relied on her family's support network to carry her through some of the difficult times. Family process is a critical part of children's adaptation to chronic illness, because the family provides the context for problem solving, support, and belongingness. Fortunately, most families of chronically ill children maintain a normal level of family functioning, although their support networks tend to be smaller and more dense as a result of their efforts to seek out other parents who are undergoing similar forms of stress (Kazak, Christakis, Alderfer, & Coiro, 1994). Supportive, cohesive family relationships contribute both to parental adaptation and, indirectly, to less behavioral symptoms and more competent psychological functioning among children with chronic illness. In contrast, problematic family qualities, like conflict, generally are associated with children's diminished social competence and increased adjustment problems (Drotar, 1997).

Family functioning is often defined in terms of the availability of two types of primary family resources—*utilitarian* and *psychological*. Utilitarian family resources relate to the practical demands of caring for a child with a disability, such as financial resources (an obvious pressure) and parental education, which influences their ability to understand the illness and seek proper assistance for their child. Psychological resources, on the

Jeremiah struggles (top, middle) as EKG electrodes are placed on his chest to monitor his heart rate. "It's tough," says his mother. "You try to hide the tears and cry later."

other hand, are less tangible but often considered far more important: how family members support one another, relate to each other and to persons outside the family, and resolve conflicts. Together these two types of family resources account for considerable variance in behavioral and social adjustment of chronically ill children (Wallander, Varni, Babani, Banis, & Wilcox, 1989).

Intervention

The psychological impact of chronic illness occurs through the disruption of normal processes of child development and family functioning. Fortunately, this impact can be lessened and adaptation strengthened by psychosocial interventions that reduce stress, enhance social problem-solving skills, and promote effective child-rearing methods. These various methods often entail stress management and skill-building components to assist children and family members in their continuous process of adaptation.

The basic goal of intervention is to enhance the quality of life for children with chronic illness and their families. Ways to achieve this goal have taken a dramatic shift over the past two decades, given the strong interest of pediatric and health psychologists. Prior to the mid-1970s intervention efforts were based primarily on a child-centered, medically based model. The health professional was the expert, the child was the patient, and parents were passive observers. However, the passage of the Education for All Handicapped Children Act in 1975 (described in Chapter 11) created new expectations for parents to be part of the decision-making process and their child's educational planning. This started a philosophical shift from child-centered to family-centered intervention, which was furthered by the 1986 Handicapped Infant and Toddler Program (Bazyk, 1989). For the first time this century, families were properly recognized as the constant in children's lives, and their role as consumers of services and decision makers was deemed worthy of support and assistance.

Empowering Families. These and other developments eventually led to the current trend toward health promotion and **empowerment** for families and children, which refer to ways of encouraging changes, opportunities, and competence to achieve one's health potential (Millstein, Petersen, & Nightingale, 1993). This perspective recognizes the importance of attaining a balance between the abilities of the individual or family and the challenges and risks of the environment. The role of health care provider thus began to shift from being the expert to being more of a consultant—someone who seeks to establish a collaborative relationship that supports parents in meeting their goals (Bazyk, 1989). In effect, families are now recognized as important resources and are seen as part of the solution; they are kept in the forefront of children's intervention needs, not the background.

This underlying philosophy of family empowerment reduces dependency and enables families to obtain information to help them make informed decisions and take competent actions (Dunst, Trivett, Davis, & Cornwell,

1988). Chen's family members, for example, took an active role in enhancing his quality of life and were not frightened away or kept uninformed of his needs and their opportunities. His mother explains:

> Physiotherapy has helped Chen be less dependent on mom and dad. The goal is for him to think ahead and be prepared to do things on his own. An example is at bedtime getting his clothes out and onto the bed for the following morning. Then in the morning he can get himself dressed and transferred into his chair by himself.

As part of the trend toward empowering families, support groups and educational programs of various types have been of considerable benefit to both the children and other family members. Helping families connect with one another and share their common experiences and concerns generates both personal power and important resources for change (Wallerstein, 1992). Participation is the active agent in empowerment, and a cooperative health professional–family model encourages individuals to support one another while providing a venue for modeling positive attitudes and values. A support group serves as a forum for problem identification and solution, information sharing, and discussions related to medical treatment (L. J. Siegel et al., 1991). Similarly, educational programs that provide information and skills training to family members are often beneficial, especially those that promote knowledge and self-management of the illness, reintegration of children into the school setting, and support and coordination of care among parents of children with chronic illness (Bauman, Drotar, Leventhal, Perrin, & Pless, 1997). Gaining more knowledge about their child's disease promotes greater parental understanding of the child and the overall effect of the disease on the family.

In short, treatment-related activities for children with chronic illness are often based on the needs of the entire family. However, these efforts must fit the degree to which parents want to be, and realistically can be, involved in their child's overall care. Examples of intervention methods that favor these adaptive processes include adherence to medical regimens and psychologically based approaches to helping children cope with the pain associated with invasive medical procedures and illness, as described below.

Enhancing Children's Coping with Hospitalization and Medical Procedures.

Throughout our discussion of children with chronic illness we have seen how they have to cope with numerous stressful circumstances, ranging from painful medical procedures to peer rejection and functional limitations. For this reason, considerable effort has been placed on ways to enhance their successful coping (see

Box 12.1
Virtual Support Groups

In her private room at New York City's Mount Sinai Medical Center, 12-year-old Lauren peers intently into the colorful screen of a computer monitor, using a mouse to navigate the on-screen avatar representing her through a virtual space called the Build Your Own zone. Early in 1995 Lauren was diagnosed with a malignant tumor in her right wrist; nine months of chemotherapy followed, and the radius bone in her right forearm was replaced with a metal rod. But today her mischievous brown eyes and smile light up the room as she plays. Finally tiring of the game, she clicks her way out and uses the computer to place a video call to one of her friends—another seriously ill child at Lucille Salter Packard Children's Hospital at California's Stanford University. "I've had bothersome moments," Lauren says after completing the call. "Like when I was in intensive care, and I wasn't allowed to do anything or see anyone. But this system lets me talk to kids from other hospitals who have the same thing as I do. I realized I'm not alone, and that made me feel better."

The system that cheers Lauren and children like her is an interactive network called Starbright World, after its namesake, the not-for-profit Starbright Foundation. For some of the children, Starbright World helps speed their recovery; for those less fortunate, it helps provide a measure of pleasure, comfort, diversion, and solace in their last months and weeks. "We've made tremendous technological advances in diagnosis and treatment," says Dr. John Rowe, MD, president and CEO of Mount Sinai Medical Center. "But we haven't used new technology to advance the nonmedical aspects of our patients' lives in the hospital—until now. Through our creative partners and their genius, children can escape from the trap that's caused by their illness or treatment."

Source: Tannert, 1996.

Box 12.1). Much of this work has focused on painful medical procedures; however, these methods are also applicable to other settings and circumstances, like school or home routines. Parent involvement and maternal adaptation are, once again, key components in children's coping; to assist their child, parents need to maximize their sense of control over the outcome and progress of their child's health (Baine, Rosenbaum, & King, 1995).

> As soon as I get in the chair I pretend he's the enemy and I'm a secret agent and he's torturing me to get secrets and if I make one sound I'm telling him secret information and I never do. I'm going to be a secret agent when I grow up so this is good practice. (D. M. Ross & S. A. Ross, 1984, p. 186)

This 10-year-old boy visiting the dentist is describing how he copes with one of life's unpleasant necessities—dental work. As any dentist can attest, one of the first challenges faced in children's dental care is simply getting the child to comply with instructions in the chair and adhere to a cavity-fighting routine at home. Enhancing adaptation and quality of life of children with chronic illness similarly requires that they comply as much as possible with medical regimens, both in- and outside the doctor's office. Since children often don't comply with even simpler things, like following directions, eating what they should, or getting ready for school, how can we expect them to comply with the unpleasant demands of medical procedures? Because of the significance of these procedures, the emphasis in pediatric health psychology has shifted to helping children and their parents cope with necessary protocols, rather than developing ways to make them comply.

Imagine that you have to undergo an unfamiliar medical procedure. Would you prefer to be told all about it first, to be shown exactly what is going to be done? Or would you prefer to be told and shown nothing, so you can get it over with? Which of the different ways of coping described in Box 12.2 would you most likely engage in? Evidence suggests that most children and adults do best if the procedure is explained first and they are given an opportunity to see what is going to happen. Accordingly, interventions for reducing stress and managing pain during pediatric procedures have applied behavioral and cognitive approaches that emphasize **coping and stress management.** Children who actively seek information about impending painful events show improved adjustment and less distress (Rudolph, Dennig, & Weisz, 1995). In addition, maternal and family functioning, effective child-rearing strategies to reinforce desired behaviors, and a positive doctor-patient relationship all contribute to children's improved adherence to the requirements of monitoring and treating their illness (Meichenbaum & Turk, 1987; Thompson & Gustafson, 1996).

In general, there are two main psychological approaches to helping children cope with stressful medical procedures and chronic and recurrent pain: providing information and training in coping skills (Thompson & Gustafson, 1996). *Information strategies* offer verbal explanations and demonstrations as well as modeling the procedure, which reduce distress because the procedure is more predictable (Dahlquist, 1992). Inexperienced patients often prefer modeling and receiving information about the unfamiliar medical procedure to alleviate their anxiety, whereas experienced children prefer specific training in ways to cope with bothersome procedures (Dahlquist, 1989). *Coping strategies* involve the teaching of various coping skills, such as deep breathing, attention

Box 12.2
Pediatric Coping Strategies Scale

Pretend that you are going to the doctor's office, and you know that they have to do something to you that will hurt (like giving you a shot). I am going to tell you some things that some children either do or say to themselves to make themselves feel better. I want you to tell me which of these things you think you might say or do to make yourself feel better. There are no right or wrong answers. Would you:

❖ tell yourself it's not that bad?
❖ tell yourself you'll feel better when it's over?
❖ try to understand why the nurse has to do it?
❖ make a fist or tense some other part of your body?
❖ want your parents there to make you feel better?
❖ do some things so you don't think about it (like counting things or talking to someone else) while it's happening?
❖ think about other things to take your mind off the hurt (like good times you've had)?
❖ tell yourself that it won't hurt at all?
❖ pretend you are somewhere else?
❖ tell yourself that it could be worse?
❖ try to be calm?
❖ get angry and fight the nurse to keep her from doing it?
❖ look away?
❖ laugh about it?
❖ cry?

Source: Adapted from Routh & Sanfilippo, 1991.

Box 12.3
Reducing the Stress of Medical Procedures

I wish they'd stop poking me so much and crammin' breathing instruments in my face. Someone's always coming in and out of my room. If I'm supposed to rest then I'm not gettin' much of it.

This quote from a 12-year-old boy who was suffering from severe asthma aptly expresses what it's like to be hospitalized for medical assessment and treatment. Many children have to undergo repeated invasive procedures, such as lumbar punctures or the insertion of respiratory tubes, as part of their medical regimen. These procedures are painful and frightening for children and parents alike, which has prompted psychologists to develop stress-reduction methods for this purpose.

Kazak et al. evaluated both child and maternal distress during an invasive procedure involving children with leukemia. They first trained parents to assume a primary role in teaching their child how to cope, which was individually tailored based on the child's age and ability to concentrate on concrete versus abstract concepts. Play activities were usually used with younger children under 6, such as bubbles, video games, and musical books; older children received more abstract methods, such as guided imagery, counting, and breathing. Guided imagery is a way of helping children imagine they are going to a special place or doing something special, such as visiting an enchanted forest, feeling the warm sun relaxing their muscles, or planning how to prepare a terrific meal. The psychological coping intervention, combined with pharmacologic pain relievers, was equal or superior to pain relievers alone across different measures of child and parent distress. More and more, medical facilities are seeing the value of active parental involvement in teaching children ways to cope with their illness.

Source: Based on Kazak et al., 1996.

distraction, muscle relaxation, relaxing imagery, emotive imagery, and behavioral rehearsal. For example, children may be asked to imagine themselves as superheroes undergoing a test of their powers, similar to the strategy used by the boy in the dentist chair (Dahlquist, 1992). Children are encouraged to identify specific stressors associated with their illness—like giving themselves an injection—and to learn ways to handle those stressors and prevent distress or failure. Amanda, for instance, coped with her injections by thinking of positive things in her life. Parents can serve as coaches during the stress and coping procedures and help their children rehearse coping skills both at home and in the clinic (Powers, Blount, Bachanas, Cotter, & Swan, 1993). Box 12.3 describes such a procedure.

Does it always help to have parents present during painful medical procedures, or do some parents make matters worse? Just as you might imagine, their presence helps in reducing child distress—so long as they reinforce the child's coping behaviors rather than stress behaviors, and control their own emotions (Blount, Davis, Powers, & Roberts, 1991). To help their child cope with invasive medical procedures, parents should be encouraged to use distraction, contingent praise, and active directives to cope ("take a deep breath now"), but they should avoid explanations, reassurance, or criticism (Blount et al., 1989; Gonzalez, Routh, & Armstrong, 1993). Because of its demonstrated benefit, cognitive-behavioral therapy for children with chronic medical conditions that require painful medical procedures has become routine. However, parents still experience these procedures as highly traumatic; they too may benefit from similar methods to reduce stress and increase successful coping strategies (Jay & Elliott, 1990).

SUMMARY

1. Health-related disorders differ from other types of child psychopathology because children's adjustment problems are more directly connected to the impact of the physical illness or problem.
2. The field of children's health-related problems stresses the interaction between physical and mental health, because children's psychological disorders and developmental problems all share medical, psychological, and psychosocial components.

Historical Developments

3. For centuries, poorly understood physical symptoms have been misattributed to psychological causes. Today, pediatric health psychologists study how children's health-related problems interact with their psychological well-being, and how they and their families adapt in response.

Sleep Disorders

4. Sleep disorders can cause psychological problems or result from other disorders. They are important to abnormal child psychology because they mimic or worsen many of the symptoms of major disorders.
5. The normal stages of sleep involve a cyclical pattern of brain activity that fluctuates between rapid eye movement (REM) sleep and nonrapid eye movement (NREM) sleep. Brain activity is highest during REM sleep, and relatively quiet, slow, and synchronized during NREM sleep.
6. Dyssomnias are disorders of initiating or maintaining sleep, and include protodyssomnia, hypersomnia, narcolepsy, breathing-related sleep disorders, and circadian rhythm disorder. Narcolepsy has a genetic component, and breathing-related sleep disorders are connected to breathing obstructions. Other dyssomnias emerge in the course of child and adolescent development.
7. Parasomnias are sleep disorders in which behavioral or physiological events intrude upon ongoing sleep, arousing the sleeper. They include nightmares, sleep terrors, and sleepwalking. A genetic predisposition is often found for these disorders of arousal and REM sleep.
8. Although most dyssomnias and parasomnias of childhood are common and often disappear with maturity, it is important to determine if they are having an impact on the child's daily activity and adjustment. Effective psychological treatments for most childhood sleep disorders involve the establishment and regulation of bedtime routines.

Elimination Disorders

9. Enuresis is the involuntary discharge of urine during the day or night, and encopresis is the passage of feces into inappropriate places, such as clothing or the floor.
10. Primary enuresis has a strong genetic component, whereas encopresis results from children's efforts to avoid defecation, resulting in chronic constipation. Combined pharmacological and psychological treatments of elimination problems are often very successful.

Chronic Childhood Illness

11. Children with chronic illness are at increased risk for psychosocial problems, which generally reflect their attempts to cope with stress.
12. Children respond to the stress of chronic conditions very differently, and adjustment problems are more likely among those who have increased disability. Adjustment problems may appear in the form of behavioral and emotional distress symptoms, such as low self-esteem, lack of social competence, poor school performance, and sometimes, psychiatric disorders.
13. Many children and their families adapt favorably to the challenges associated with chronic illness. Perceived social support and maternal adaptation are key components aiding such adaptation.
14. Recent shifts to greater family empowerment and parental involvement have resulted in innovative ways to help children cope with the challenges of chronic illness. Psychosocial interventions assist children's adaptation to chronic illness by enhancing social problem-solving skills and coping skills, and reinforcing effective child-rearing methods.

KEY TERMS

enuresis, 456
encopresis, 456
chronic illness, 456
rapid eye movement (REM) sleep, 458
nonrapid eye movement (NREM) sleep, 458
dyssomnias, 461
parasomnias, 461
protodyssomnia, 462
hypersomnia, 462
narcolepsy, 462
breathing-related sleep disorders, 462
circadian rhythm disorders, 462
microsleep, 462

cataplexy, 464

sleep paralysis, 464

hypnagogic hallucinations, 464

obstructive sleep apnea syndrome (OSAS), 464

nightmares, 465

sleep terrors, 465

sleepwalking, 466

chronotherapy, 468

antidiuretic hormone (ADH), 471

somatoform disorders, 475

psychological factors affecting physical condition, 475

morbidity, 475

insulin-dependent diabetes mellitus (IDDM), 478

metabolic control, 479

acute lymphoblastic leukemia (ALL), 480

empowerment, 486

coping and stress management, 487

Eating Disorders and Related Conditions

Can we ever have too much of a good thing?
—Miguel de Cervantes

Although eating disorders have only recently been viewed as symptomatic of a mental disorder, bizarre and unusual eating habits have been documented for many centuries. The ancient Egyptians believed that illness could be avoided through monthly purges. The ancient Romans built the aptly described "vomitorium," where men purged their stomachs after overindulging in a heavy banquet—before returning to eat more. For centuries, voluntary as well as forced starvation has had both saintly and evil guises, whether in the form of religious fasting or as a way to put an end to individuals who seemed possessed and bewitched. Today, as always, eating and starvation are connected to mental health problems and unusual cultural practices (Vandereycken & Van Deth, 1996).

This chapter is divided into two sections that address different types of eating disorders and related conditions. The first section includes disorders that occur during infancy or childhood: pica, rumination disorder, and feeding disorder of infancy or early childhood. We also look at two associated growth disorders, failure to thrive and psychosocial dwarfism, which are related to feeding problems and have psychological importance. Eating disorders occurring prior to age 2 are typically referred to as *feeding disorders,* to emphasize the social context of an infant's or a toddler's eating disturbance. Important in their own right, early feeding disorders have little or no known connection to adolescent and adult eating disorders discussed in the second section. Lastly, the developmental significance of childhood obesity is considered. We emphasize from the outset that obesity is not a psychiatric disorder nor is it associated with greater psychopathology (Brownell & Wadden, 1992). How-

ever, children with obesity are at risk of establishing unhealthy dieting patterns, due largely to social discrimination, that sometimes lead to chronic health problems and eating disorders.

The second section addresses the major eating disorders of adolescence and young adulthood: anorexia nervosa and bulimia nervosa. A person with **anorexia nervosa** refuses to maintain even a minimally normal body weight. The disorder, which emerges primarily among adolescent girls and may continue into young adulthood, is often marked by such an obsession with food and a drive for thinness that the person loses sight of what is healthy. It is not unusual for adolescents suffering from anorexia to lose weight drastically by reducing their food intake, counting calories, exercising excessively, using laxatives, and/or inducing vomiting. **Bulimia nervosa** is characterized by binge eating, followed by an effort to compensate, usually through self-induced vomiting, but sometimes by misusing laxatives, diuretics, or other medications; by fasting; or by exercising excessively. Individuals with bulimia are also obsessed with food and with losing weight, but they do not have the excessive weight loss associated with anorexia. Most persons with bulimia are within 10% of their normal weight, whereas individuals with anorexia refuse to maintain even a minimally normal weight.

Eating disorders, along with disorders of growth, have traditionally been a medical concern. Studies of their etiology and treatment have focused on physiological mechanisms and the serious biological consequences associated with these disorders. As mental health professionals began to study psychosocial factors over the last quarter century, however, they discovered that many of the same factors underlying other major childhood disorders play a major role in early feeding and eating disorders, such as genetic makeup, cognitive and social development, and everyday experiences between infant and care-givers. We now recognize that eating disorders emerge in relation to an individual's biological makeup, ongoing experiences, and current opportunities and social patterns (Attie & Brooks-Gunn, 1995).

How anorexia and bulimia relate to abnormal development can be considered in many ways, from disturbances in early parent-child relations to problems in the formation of self-identity. Overlapping cultural, familial, and biological influences affect eating patterns; however, societal norms linking beauty, success, and happiness to a thin body shape have had an unprecedented effect on the behavior and health of many young women in recent years (Killen et al., 1996). The desire to appear thin may be responsible for the near-epidemic rates of referral of young people with eating disorders, especially bulimia, since the mid-1970s throughout the Western world (Garner & Fairburn, 1988; Hay & Hall, 1991; J. H. Lacey, 1992). What makes these disorders of adolescence and early adulthood particularly unusual is that they are so closely linked to Western culture, where food is plentiful and physical appearance, especially among young women, is so highly valued. Unlike most of the other disorders of childhood and adolescence described in this text, the causes of major eating disorders are disproportionately related to sociocultural, rather than psychological and biological, influences.

Until quite recently, society had not been kind to people with eating disorders. At the turn of the 20th century, individuals who could eat unusual substances or amounts of food, or perform other feats involving ingestion and regurgitation, could earn a living as exhibitionists in fairs, circuses, and sideshows (Vandereycken & Van Deth, 1996). Children who suffered from growth failure or obesity were considered undesirable or mentally defective, which justified their being displayed in sideshows as well. Fortunately, considerable light has been cast on these problems in recent years, leading to better identification, treatment, and prevention.

We begin by reviewing how most infants and young children develop normal eating habits and by describing the biological mechanisms that regulate appetite and energy expenditure, and their developmental and psychological implications.

DEVELOPMENT OF EATING PATTERNS

Anyone who has ever watched a 2-year-old eat spaghetti knows that learning to feed oneself is not a simple process. In fact, feeding and eating problems are a

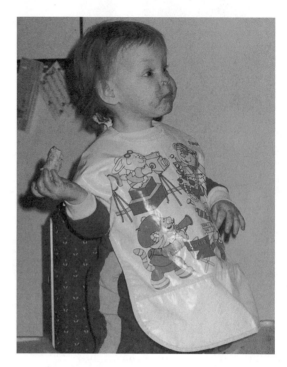

Eating disorders should not be confused with disorderly eating, a normal part of early development.

normal part of development for most children as they learn through gradual approximations.

Normal Development

Troublesome eating habits and limited food preferences are among the most distinguishing characteristics of early childhood. Almost a third of young children (under age 10) are described as picky eaters by their mothers. Picky eating is more common among girls than boys (Rydell, Dahl, & Sundelin, 1995; Marchi & Cohen, 1990), and is connected to the later emergence of eating disorders. By late childhood and early adolescence, girls are much more anxious about losing weight than are boys (Marchi & Cohen, 1990).

These normal developmental patterns are in part, especially for girls, a function of societal norms and expectations, as portrayed through images of thinness and attractiveness in books, magazines, television, and movies. In addition, normal concerns about weight and appearance can be either reduced or increased by the comments of parents, friends, and romantic partners. The effects of the early parent-child relationship on such fundamental biological processes as eating and growth patterns is of paramount importance. Entering school is the next significant landmark because of increasing social pressure to conform to narrow perceptions of

Developmental Periods

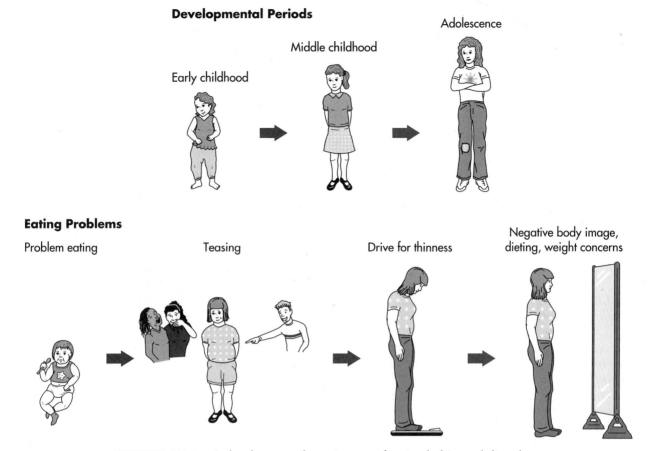

FIGURE 13.1 A developmental continuum of eating habits and disorders.

desirable body type. The desire to achieve an ideal image can turn into an obsession during adolescence.

Developmental Risk Factors

A developmental perspective of eating problems and eating disorders raises the intriguing possibility of a continuum of "eating pathology," from dieting to clinical syndromes, across developmental periods (Attie & Brooks-Gunn, 1995) (see Figure 13.1). Several connections are emerging in support of such a continuum. For example, even though most normal dieters do not go on to develop eating disorders, they share many of the characteristics of eating-disordered individuals, such as weight preoccupation, concern with appearance, and restrained eating (Garner, Olstead, Polivy, & Garfinkel, 1984; Polivy & Herman, 1987). The increasing challenges faced by children and adolescents, coupled with immense social pressure and expectations, provide important clues for understanding the nature of this continuum, and how some individuals manage to avoid the most dire consequences.

Early Eating Habits, Attitudes, and Behaviors. Eating habits in young children are at one end of the hypothetical continuum of eating pathology. A 10-year comprehensive study of risk factors related to the later onset of an eating disorder traced the eating habits of 659 children (Marchi & Cohen, 1990). The findings, shown in Figure 13.2, indicate that many problem eating behaviors showed significant stability over the 10-year period, including pickiness, bingeing, and problems at mealtime, which should not surprise those of you with children or younger siblings. Weight-reduction efforts, understandably, changed dramatically throughout the course of adolescence. An important finding of this study was that early childhood pica and problems at mealtime were both connected to the onset of bulimia in adolescence. Although speculative, this connection suggests an underlying relation of bulimia to self-control and family struggles. Children who were picky eaters or had digestive problems were at greater risk for developing anorexia, suggesting a biological substrate that predisposes certain children to refrain from eating.

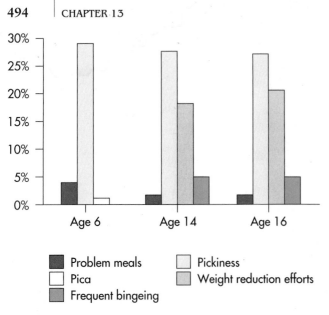

FIGURE 13.2 Troublesome eating behaviors. (Data from Marchi & Cohen, 1990)

Researchers following samples of children and adolescents over several years have documented the continuity between eating problems in childhood and the subsequent onset of a disorder. Graber, Brooks-Gunn, Paikoff, and Warren (1994) examined patterns of eating problems over 8 years among 116 normal adolescent girls and discovered that about one-quarter of the sample showed signs of a serious eating problem at each of the three times of assessment. These teens were distinguishable by their earlier pubertal maturation, higher percentages of body fat, concurrent psychological problems (especially depression), and poorer body image. A study of 877 high school–aged girls similarly found that weight concerns, indicated by such factors as fear of weight gain, worry over weight and body shape, diet history, and perceived fatness, were significantly related to the onset of partial-syndrome eating disorders 4 years later (Killen et al., 1996).

Apparently, disturbed eating patterns and attitudes start at a young age. Even among third-graders (8- to 10-year-olds), concerns about weight, dieting, and physique are not uncommon, suggesting that Western sociocultural values and preoccupation with body weight and dieting—factors that lead to eating disorders among vulnerable adolescents—may be internalized and expressed at a very early age (S. Shapiro, Newcomb, & Loeb, 1997). Girls, in particular, seem unduly afraid of becoming fat, are unhappy because of their weight, and wish they were thinner.

This constellation of physical and psychological factors, linked to early eating problems and distorted beliefs, signifies a considerable risk pattern for the development of persistent and possibly severe eating problems (Attic & Brooks-Gunn, 1995). We now consider how these risk factors are connected to adolescent development and the emergence of unhealthy dieting patterns.

Transition into Adolescence. Passage from childhood to early adolescence is full of unexpected challenges, not the least of which is undergoing significant changes in body shape that require major adjustments in self-image. Younger adolescents also have to move gradually away from parental expectations and develop autonomy, including learning how to confide in others and how to express their emerging sexuality (Crockett & Peterson, 1993). Older adolescents are faced with the challenges of establishing intimacy, pursuing their educational and occupational goals, and establishing their identity apart from their family (Attie, Brooks-Gunn, & Petersen, 1990). Their ability to organize new experiences, especially during these critical transitions, predicts how well they will adapt to current and future challenges.

In conjunction with changes related to pubertal development, dieting and weight concerns intensify during early adolescence and may set the stage for more serious problems later on (see Box 13.1). Adolescent girls experience a "fat spurt" associated with puberty, adding an average of 11 kilograms of body fat (Brooks-Gunn & Warren, 1985). The timing of maturation also affects dieting behavior, because girls who mature early are likely to be heavier than their late-maturing peers (Brooks-Gunn, 1988).

Important gender differences are evident during these adolescent transitions. As we saw with younger children, girls report feeling worse about themselves than do boys, most likely because girls place greater emphasis on their self-image, including their body image. Although they readily acknowledge their interpersonal and social abilities, over 40% of girls say they frequently feel ugly and unattractive (Offer & Ostrov, 1981). In contrast, boys see themselves in a more positive light with respect to achievement, academic aspirations, self-assertion, and body image (Bakken & Romig, 1992). Contradictory societal messages implying that women must be successful in traditionally feminine *and* traditionally masculine roles place added pressure on young women to aspire to some elusive "superwoman" caricature (Levine & Smolak, 1992). Female adolescents who describe themselves in superwoman terms are more likely to associate thinness with autonomy, success, and recognition for their independent achievements; however, they are also significantly more at risk for eating disorders (Steiner-Adair, 1990).

Box 13.1

Female Adolescent Development: Changes and Challenges

Although no single explanation exists for the onset of eating disorders, many developmental changes and social pressures may explain the increased risk for young women during adolescence:

1. *Physical maturation.* Physical maturation for boys involves the development of muscle and lean tissue, whereas girls experience weight gain in the form of increased fat tissue. Early menarche is a specific risk factor for bulimia (Fairburn, 1994). Young adolescent girls who gain weight sooner than their peers may go on diets; they may also suffer from adjustment problems because of their parents' reactions to their early sexual maturation (Hsu, 1990).

2. *Development of sense of self.* Identity formation is a fundamental issue of early adolescence. Young girls whose identities are insecure and dependent on the views of others are more likely to rely on physical appearance as a concrete way of constructing their identity (Striegel-Moore, 1993).

3. *Dieting.* Dieting has been criticized not only in relation to eating disorders (Pyle et al., 1990) but also because of its ineffectiveness for maintaining proper weight for any substantial length of time. When faced with opportunities to binge, the chronic dieter is simply less likely to maintain restraint, a phenomenon known as the counter-regulation effect (Polivy & Herman, 1993). Such a reaction may be triggered by the sight of food and may also occur when the person is feeling depressed or guilty because of overeating.

Source: Based on Wilson et al., 1996.

The all-too-familiar interaction of pubertal weight gain, emergence of social dating, and threats to achievement status promote body dissatisfaction, distress, and perceived loss of control in young adolescents, especially because they occur cumulatively over a relatively short period of time (Levine & Smolak, 1992). (The importance of body image reemerges later on in our discussion of anorexia and bulimia.)

Dieting. Restrictive dieting has become a North American pastime, especially among youth, who are choosing to diet at very young ages. A large-scale survey of public school students in grades 5 through 8 found that almost one-third had dieted and 45% wanted to lose weight (Childress, Brewerton, Hedges, & Jarrell, 1993), which is consistent with the notion that such concerns often begin as early as elementary school and increase steadily throughout adolescence (Moreno & Thelen,

1995). A significant number of these students report feeling depressed after overeating and choose strict dieting as a form of weight control.

Chronic dieting seems strongly related to both gender and developmental factors. By mid-adolescence, the number of girls reporting being on a diet during the previous year climbs to twice what it was in grades 5 through 8, to about two-thirds of girls sampled. Story et al. (1991) found that among those who diet, about 1 girl in 9 (12%) was a chronic dieter—that is, someone who remains on a diet all the time or diets off and on more than 10 times during the year. In contrast, only 2% of boys were chronic dieters. Chronic dieters were not distinguished on the basis of where they lived (urban, suburban, or rural) or by their socioeconomic status. However, African-American girls were less likely to diet than Caucasian girls. Excessive dieting was strongly related to bulimic symptoms among these youth: Chronic dieters were 7 to 13 times more likely to use purging techniques than were nonchronic dieters (Story et al., 1991).

Why does dieting sometimes lead to overeating? Decreasing caloric intake reduces metabolic rate, so weight loss is in fact impeded. This failure to lose weight sets the stage for a vicious cycle of increased dieting and vulnerability to binge eating. Psychological consequences also contribute to this cycle by creating a sense of deprivation, further increasing the tendency to lose control. Once binge eating begins, purging may be seen as a way of counteracting the perceived effects of binge eating on weight gain. But purging is invariably followed by disgust and self-recrimination, prompting renewed vows of abstinence and setting the stage for the whole cycle of dieting, overeating, dietary failure, and affective distress to begin again (Heatherton & Polivy, 1992).

Although dieting is clearly a risk factor in relation to early-adolescent maturity, it should be viewed in perspective: Many young persons diet in order to influence body weight and shape, yet only a small minority develop eating disorders (Garner, 1993a). Dieting can be harmful or beneficial, depending on the individual and the conditions. For some individuals, especially those with obesity, proper diet and exercise is a potential solution to a serious medical problem; for others, chronic, severe dieting can lead to eating disorders (Wilson, 1993). Thus, it is important to distinguish between dieting in individuals (especially children) who are not overweight from dieting in those whose excess weight increases medical or psychological risk (Brownell & Rodin, 1994). There is a critical difference between watching your weight as part of a health-conscious lifestyle, and chronic, unrealistic dieting that upsets your body's natural rhythm and balance.

Biological Regulators

How do you know when to eat and how much to eat? For most of us, eating, like sleeping, is a natural process, controlled by biorythms that have adapted successfully over time to the stress and strain of our individual lives. However, normal patterns of eating and growth, as well as the disorders based on disturbances in these patterns, are influenced by both physical and psychological processes that interact constantly. In essence, your particular growth and weight pattern is based on the relation between your genes and your constitution, which governs your ability from early infancy to self-regulate your sleep and elimination patterns, appetite, and past and current nutritional patterns.

Metabolic rate, or balance of energy expenditure, is established on the basis of individual genetic and physiological makeup as well as eating and exercise habits. Individual metabolism, in turn, serves to self-monitor and self-regulate behavior, which is why we may have trouble maintaining changes in weight or exercise. If you burn more energy than you take in, a state of chronic negative energy balance, or hypocaloric malnutrition, can occur. Malnutrition, even for brief periods of time, is followed by physical attempts to adapt, which can produce significant biological, behavioral, and psychological effects, including loss of circadian rhythm, increase in the release of growth hormones, various anemias, dermatological changes (such as loss of fatty tissue or hair pigmentation), and emotional and behavioral changes, such as lethargy, depression, and apathy (Woolston, 1991). Feeding and eating disorders thus merit careful study, for they can be overlooked when they are accompanied by more pronounced emotional and behavioral problems.

Body Weight. Anyone who has tried dieting knows just how hard it is to lose weight and keep it off. Weight loss is rapid for the first few weeks, but most of the lost weight returns with time. In fact, 90% to 95% of those who lose weight regain it within several years (Garner & Wooley, 1991). Why is body weight so resistant to change? For years the blame was placed largely on the dieter's weak resolve or lack of willpower, but today researchers place more credence in the view that each person is biologically and genetically programmed to weigh within a certain, natural weight range. A person's natural weight is regulated around his or her own *set point,* a comfortable range of body weight that the body tries to "defend" and maintain (Garner, 1997).

In effect, people who gain or lose weight experience metabolic changes that strive to bring the body back to its natural weight. If fat levels decrease below our body's normal range, the brain (specifically, the hypothalamus) compensates by slowing metabolism. We begin to feel lethargic and increase our sleep, and our body temperature decreases slightly to preserve energy (which is why many persons with anorexia complain of being cold). In this state of relative deprivation, uncontrollable urges to binge are common because our bodies are telling us that they need more food than they are getting in order to function properly. Similarly, the body fights back against weight gain by increasing metabolism and raising body temperature in an effort to burn off extra calories (admittedly, this valiant effort is seldom enough to conquer the force of holidays and other feasts). Because of its responsivity to change, researchers often compare the body's set point to the setting on a thermostat that regulates room temperature. When room temperature falls below a certain range, the thermostat automatically goes to work to increase the heat level until it again reaches the established temperature setting. Human bodies respond similarly to deviations in body weight by turning the metabolic "furnace" up or down (Garner, 1997).

Growth. Growth normally occurs in a predictable but shifting pattern from infancy through adolescence. Growth in height and weight (*cumulative*) and pace of growth (*velocity*) wax and wane through the periods of development. Through the first trimester of prenatal development, for example, growth occurs at the highest velocity in the course of human development. The peak velocity occurs at the beginning of the second trimester of pregnancy, when it approaches the postnatal equivalent of 144 centimeters (about 4½ feet) per year (Woolston, 1991). Not only does growth occur rapidly during the first year of life, but the pattern of growth changes in important ways. Adipose (fatty) tissue increases considerably during the first year, when infants typically triple their birth weight and grow an additional 25 centimeters (10 inches). By 2 years of age, the growth pattern typically stabilizes; growth will continue at that rate throughout childhood (MacGillivray, 1987). Adolescence is the last period of major growth, and it is during that time that the most pronounced and chronic forms of eating disorders emerge, perhaps because rapid physical growth coincides with increased social pressures.

Under normal conditions, the biological mechanisms of growth are like the well-orchestrated ecosystem of a forest or a lake: a system of feedback loops, messenger signals, and major organs that work together to maintain a healthy balance. For humans, the biology of growth fundamentally involves the manner in which circulating hormones interact with available nutritional resources to produce changes throughout the skeletal system. Major hormonal determinants of growth rate during childhood are the *growth hormone* (GH) and *thyroid hormone*

(T4), with additional gonadal steroids kicking in during adolescence to produce a further growth spurt and skeletal maturation. From 50% to 75% of growth hormone production occurs after the onset of deep sleep in children and young adults (Woolston, 1991), which may explain why eating and sleep disorders coexist in some younger children (Lyons-Ruth, Zeanah, & Benoit, 1996).

Thus, individual growth depends on GH circulating throughout the body. The release of GH from the pituitary gland is determined by the hypothalamus and the higher brain structures that affect it (the limbic cortex and amygdala). These higher brain structures are involved in emotional sensation and response, which may account for the connection between eating and emotional disorders (discussed below). Just as a thermostat determines the need to increase or decrease temperature, the hypothalamus senses the need to release more or less GH throughout the body. To accomplish this task, the hypothalamus releases two controlling hormones that exert opposite effects. The *growth hormone inhibiting factor* (also known as somatostatin) essentially inhibits the GH response to internal signals of hunger, so we stop eating. In contrast, the *growth hormone releasing factor* has the specific function of telling our body when, how, and where to grow by releasing growth hormone from the pituitary.

Familiarity with these biological processes makes it easier to understand how the biological substrates of growth and metabolism can be thrown off balance by numerous factors, causing behavioral and physiological changes in children or young adults. However, the question has not been suitably resolved whether the majority of eating disorders are caused by biological abnormalities, or whether the disorder itself creates a biological disruption.

The Biochemistry of Eating. Will dieting and weight-loss programs someday be a thing of the past? Recent discoveries have led to greater understanding of some of the brain chemicals that inhibit and stimulate eating. In addition to the short-acting neurotransmitters, researchers have discovered long-acting proteins known as neuropeptides in regions of the brain that affect mood and appetite, as well as in the digestive tract (Erickson, 1991). Neuropeptide Y begins stimulating the appetite for carbohydrates within minutes after appearing in the brain in the early morning and continues up to 24 hours. Scientists believe this molecule gets carbohydrates into body systems to provide quick energy during the early waking hours. Our taste for fat increases gradually throughout the day, as galanin, another neuropeptide, increases and stimulates fat intake. Pharmaceutical companies are hungry to be the first to market an artificial drug that will regulate these proteins and hormones (Erickson, 1991).

FEEDING AND EATING DISORDERS OF INFANCY AND EARLY CHILDHOOD

Feeding and eating disorders of infancy or early childhood constitute a general category that includes several different developmental and behavioral problems associated with eating and growth that are evident from a very young age. Pica, in which the infant or toddler persists in eating inedible substances, such as hair, insects, or chips of paint, is one of the more common and usually less serious eating disorders found among very young children. However, pica is sometimes seen in older children and adolescents as well, especially among persons with mental retardation. Rumination disorder, characterized by regurgitating and reswallowing food with obvious enjoyment, is much rarer and potentially more serious than pica. Feeding disorder of infancy or early childhood is marked by a sudden or rapid deceleration of weight gain and a disruption in major developmental milestones, which can lead to physical and mental retardation and even death.

Pica

Infants and toddlers typically put things into their mouths, because throughout much of the first year of life, taste and smell are their preferred ways of exploring the physical world. However, an infant or young child who actually eats inedible, nonnutritive substances for a period of 1 month or more may be showing a form of eating disorder known as **pica**. Infants may eat such things as paint, dirt, fabric, or hair; older children may eat animal droppings, sand, insects, leaves, or similar objects. Although children with pica are interested in eating and like food, they persist in consuming nonedible items as well. In most reported cases, the disorder begins in infancy and lasts for several months, at which time it remits on its own or in conjunction with added infant stimulation and improved environmental conditions. For individuals with mental retardation, however, pica may continue into adolescence before it begins to diminish gradually. The DSM-IV diagnostic criteria for pica are described in Table 13.1.

Prevalence and Development. Because pica is an uncommon diagnosis among noninstitutionalized children and adults, prevalence and epidemiological estimates in the general population have been curtailed. However, among institutionalized persons with mental

Table 13.1 | **DSM-IV Diagnostic Criteria for Pica**

A. Persistent eating of non-nutritive substances for a period of at least 1 month.

B. The eating of non-nutritive substances is inappropriate to the developmental level.

C. The eating behavior is not part of a culturally sanctioned practice.

D. If the eating behavior occurs exclusively during the course of another mental disorder (e.g., Mental Retardation, Pervasive Developmental Disorder, Schizophrenia), it is sufficiently severe to warrant independent clinical attention.

Source: DSM-IV Copyright © 1994 by APA.

retardation, prevalence estimates range from 9.2% (McAlpine & Singh, 1986) to 16.7% (Danford & Huber, 1982). Subclinical forms of pica (symptoms that do not quite fit the criteria) may be common among certain populations, including pregnant women and normally developing preschoolers. The degree of severity is often related to the degree of environmental deprivation and mental retardation in individuals suffering from the more extreme forms.

Causes. Historically, pica was sometimes encouraged by fashions and social pressures of the day, similar to those affecting body image and appearance today. During the 18th and 19th centuries, for example, young girls sometimes ate lime, coal, vinegar, and chalk, because these substances were believed to produce a fashionably pale complexion (W. L. Parry-Jones & B. Parry-Jones, 1994).

Although specific causes of pica have not been isolated, researchers have identified three distinct subpopulations based on available clinical studies (Woolston, 1991):

1. Pica may appear in the first and second years of life even among otherwise normally developing infants and toddlers. The only distinguishing characteristic of these children is that they typically have poor stimulation in their home environment and may be poorly supervised. Because of the risk of lead poisoning or of obstruction in their intestine, pica can become a very serious and substantial problem for this group of infants or toddlers.

2. A small subset of adolescent and young adult pregnant women have been known to eat a variety of substances voluntarily, including clay and starch. Although voluntary, such behavior may be governed by certain superstitious beliefs, such as preventing a curse on the fetus, reducing the side effects of pregnancy, or eliminating the possibility of syphilis (Halmi, 1985). Again, such eating practices may result in serious consequences to the mother or fetus,

including metal poisoning, nutrient deficiency, or intestinal obstruction.

3. Individuals with more severe degrees of mental retardation are more likely to show signs of pica. Among persons with mental retardation, moreover, the risk of eating poisonous substances also poses a considerable danger to health, and requires institutionalized supervision in most instances.

Researchers have also suspected and in some cases discovered vitamin or mineral deficiencies among persons with pica, although no specific biological abnormalities have shown a causal link to the disorder (Vyas & Chandra, 1984). One prominent theory proposes that cultural and family factors influence young pregnant women to eat specific substances, especially clay and starch (E. P. Lacey, 1990). Similarly, poor supervision and understimulation of infants or children are often associated with pica. There is no evidence, except in cases of mental retardation, that genetic factors play a role in the etiology of the disorder. As mentioned earlier, however, pica in childhood constitutes a risk factor for the development of bulimia in adolescence (Marchi & Cohen, 1990).

Treatment. Because of the limited number of treatment studies, no conclusions can be drawn about the relative success of any treatment for pica (K. E. Bell & Stein, 1992). Most clinical interventions for children with pica emphasize operant conditioning procedures in which care-givers are shown how to reinforce the child for desirable behaviors, such as exploring the room or playing with objects. Positive forms of attention, including smiling, laughing, and tickling, provide additional stimulation and are especially beneficial, because the disorder is often related to inadequate interaction with care-givers. Care-givers may be taught how to keep the child's environment tidy and to remove or safely store dangerous substances. However, reinforcement procedures sometimes take too long for such a high-risk behavior, and therefore differential reinforcement of

Infants and toddlers with pica may develop the disorder as a result of poor stimulation and supervision. They are at considerable risk of lead poisoning or intestinal obstruction.

voluntary regurgitation, rechewing, and reswallowing of food. What is particularly striking is that the infant appears to enjoy the act of regurgitation, and engages in deliberate activities, such as putting fingers down the throat, to bring up the food. Rather than showing signs of distress, the infant often shows signs of pleasure and contentment. However, the infant loses considerable amounts of food in the process and may become seriously malnourished; the mortality rate attributed to chronic rumination ranges from 12% to 20% of identified cases (Rast, Johnston, Drum, & Conrin, 1981). Diagnostic criteria are presented in the Table 13.2.

Prevalence and Development. This disorder is so rare that what we know about it has been derived primarily from single case reports and a small number of case studies. For an otherwise normally developing infant, the onset of rumination usually occurs in the first year of life; in persons with mental retardation, the age of onset can extend well into adulthood (Mayes et al., 1988). In infants, the disorder usually remits on its own.

Causes. There is considerable uncertainty as to how this pattern of disturbed eating originates and is maintained. The three current explanations reflect both medical and psychological viewpoints, and emphasize the importance of the interaction between biology and learned behavior: (1) Medical practitioners emphasize the relationship between rumination and anatomical abnormalities. Seeking attention or other forms of reinforcement (Woolston, 1989), some children may gain partial voluntary control of the gastroesophageal reflex (GER), which normally causes vomiting and an unpleasant sensation. Such control eventually can lead to an abnormal GER. (2) Others point to the social learning process. Parents may unwittingly respond to their infant's regurgitation in a manner that provides positive or negative reinforcement. Holding and soothing the baby if she or he regurgitates can be a form of positive attention or stimulation that increases such behavior.

other behaviors may be combined with an aversive technique, under supervised conditions. For example, when a child engages in pica, a therapist may give a loud verbal reprimand ("No!") and hold an aromatic ammonia capsule under the child's nose to suppress the behavior. When the behavior is inactive, there are more opportunities for reinforcement of appropriate behavior (Fultz & Rojahn, 1988).

Rumination Disorder

Rumination disorder is a relatively rare eating disorder that generally affects young infants and persons with mental retardation. Rumination is characterized by the

Table 13.2	DSM-IV Diagnostic Criteria for Rumination Disorder

A. Repeated regurgitation and rechewing of food for a period of at least 1 month following a period of normal functioning.

B. The behavior is not due to an associated gastrointestinal or other general medical condition (e.g., esophageal reflux).

C. The behavior does not occur exclusively during the course of Anorexia Nervosa or Bulimia Nervosa. If the symptoms occur exclusively during the course of Mental Retardation or a Pervasive Developmental Disorder, they are sufficiently severe to warrant independent clinical attention.

Source: DSM-IV Copyright © 1994 by APA.

Table 13.3	DSM-IV Diagnostic Criteria for Feeding Disorder of Infancy or Early Childhood

A. Feeding disturbance as manifested by persistent failure to eat adequately with significant failure to gain weight or significant loss of weight over at least 1 month.

B. The behavior is not due to an associated gastrointestinal or other general medical condition (e.g., esophageal reflux).

C. The disturbance is not better accounted for by another mental disorder (e.g., Rumination Disorder) or by lack of available food.

D. The onset is before age 6 years.

Source: DSM-IV Copyright © 1994 by APA.

Similarly, parents unknowingly may negatively reinforce regurgitation by removing something the infant finds unpleasant or aversive, such as a particular food. (3) From a developmental perspective, rumination, like other eating disorders, reflects an unsatisfactory parent-infant relationship marked by lack of stimulation or even by child neglect. Such a relationship may be a function of the infant's temperament, the parent's disposition, or, in all likelihood, a mismatch between the two. For example, ruminating infants are described as being irritable and hungry between episodes of regurgitation. A caregiver may not sufficiently nurture a fussy infant, so the child may seek some other source of gratification or stimulation. Lack of attention may itself make an infant demanding and irritable. This view does not fully explain why an infant chooses this particular form of expression, so the social learning paradigm must also be considered.

In sum, evidence points to three factors in the development of rumination disorder: (1) an inability of the infant or person with mental retardation to regulate his or her internal state of satisfaction; (2) a propensity to regurgitate food, which may be related to the GER; and (3) a paradigm in which the infant learns that regurgitation helps relieve the internal state of dissatisfaction and may bring additional pleasures to bear (Woolston, 1991).

Treatment. Learning-based explanations have inspired successful behavioral treatments for chronic or serious rumination disorder. The least restrictive interventions typically involve changing the antecedents to the behavior, such as altering food texture and quality (Rast et al., 1981), or using differential reinforcement of other behavior and ignoring ruminative responding (Mulick, Schroeder, & Rojahn, 1980). When these methods are ineffective, they may be combined with an aversive procedure, such as squirting lemon juice into the mouth, to prevent the ruminative behavior (Sajwaj, Libet, & Agras, 1974).

Feeding Disorder of Infancy or Early Childhood

Feeding disorder of infancy or early childhood is characterized by a sudden or marked deceleration of weight gain in an infant or a young child and a slowing or disruption of emotional and social development. Onset must occur prior to age 6. Diagnostic criteria for feeding disorder are shown in Table 13.3.

Confusion and controversy have existed throughout the near century-long period that this eating disorder has been studied. The number of labels that have been used interchangeably for feeding disorder is daunting: hospitalism, anaclitic depression, institutionalism, environmental retardation, maternal deprivation syndrome, psychosocial deprivation dwarfism, deprivational dwarfism, deprivation syndrome, environmental failure to thrive, and nonorganic failure to thrive syndrome. These labels reflect the changing perspectives and uncertainty about the unique patterns and causes of feeding disorder (Woolston, 1991).

Prevalence and Development. Feeding disorders and failure to gain weight are relatively common, affecting up to 35% of young children (Lyons-Ruth et al., 1996) and accounting for approximately 1% to 5% of all pediatric hospital admissions (Hannaway, 1978). However, failure to gain weight is disproportionately more common among children from disadvantaged environments: Nearly 10% of low-income children are below the 5th percentile for their weight or length (Trowbridge, 1984). Feeding disorder is particularly troublesome because if it is not identified early, it can have lasting effects on growth and development. Feeding disorders are equally common among males and females.

There is no typical developmental outcome among children with feeding disorders, probably because many of the factors that led to the problem in the first place also affect the course of the illness over time. However, onset of feeding disorder during the first 2 years of life, which is the common pattern, can lead to malnutrition and thus have serious developmental consequences. If there is no medical reason for the failure to gain weight, such early onset is often associated with poor care-giving, including abuse and neglect (APA, 1994). For this reason, feeding disorder can lead to, or be the result of, failure to thrive. As expected, the factors that lead to more serious problems over time include the degree and chronicity of malnutrition, the degree and chronicity of developmental delay, the severity and duration of the problems in the infant–care-giver relationship, and such other problems as physical abuse, neglect, or social isolation of the family (Drotar, 1991).

Causes and Treatment.

The etiology of feeding disorder has been studied from both biological and psychosocial perspectives, and the best conclusion at present is that many interacting risk factors influence how a child adapts to a certain level of caloric intake and shows normal or abnormal behavioral development. Because feeding disorder has long been associated with family disadvantage, poverty, unemployment, social isolation, and parental mental illness, considerable attention has been focused on those concerns.

Maternal eating disorders have been identified as a specific risk factor for an infant's eating or feeding disorder. Brinch et al. (1988) studied a group of women with a history of anorexia nervosa and found that 17% of their children had a diagnosis of failure to thrive by their first birthday. In a well-controlled study involving 32 children with feeding disorders, Stein et al. (1995) found a direct association between such problems and disturbed eating habits and attitudes among mothers. Because of the critical nature of the mother-child relationship during the early stages of attachment, eating disorders shown by infants and young children may be symptomatic of a fundamental problem in this relationship (Lyons-Ruth et al., 1996). For these reasons, treatment regimens involve a detailed assessment of feeding behavior and other forms of parent-child interaction, such as smiles, talking, and soothing, while allowing the parents to play a role in the infant's recovery (Wolfe & St. Pierre, 1989).

Associated Disorders

Two growth disorders associated with early feeding disturbances—failure to thrive and psychosocial dwarfism—can have severe consequences for a child's physical and psychological development. Like feeding disorder, these associated disorders are embedded in social and economic disadvantage, and are often connected to inadequate or abusive care-giving originating in early infancy. Failure to thrive is considered the final common pathway for multiple biological, psychological, and social factors that influence growth and viability of the infant or toddler (Attie & Brooks-Gunn, 1995). Psychosocial dwarfism applies to severe growth disturbances that have their onset during the preschool or school-age years.

Failure to Thrive.

The eating and feeding disorders of early childhood described above can lead to, coexist with, or be the result of failure to thrive. **Failure to thrive** is characterized by weight below the 5th percentile for age, and/or deceleration in the rate of weight gain from birth to the present of at least 2 standard deviations, using standard growth charts for comparison (Budd et al., 1992; Lyons-Ruth et al., 1996).

A prominent controversy has to do with the significance of emotional deprivation (love) and malnutrition (food). Investigators have argued that the infant with failure to thrive has been deprived of maternal stimulation and love, which results in emotional misery, developmental delays, and eventually, physiological changes. In one study, mothers of infants who were diagnosed with failure to thrive were found to be more insecure with respect to attachment than their matched counterparts, who were mothers of normal infants. Mothers of failure-to-thrive infants were also more passive and confused, and either became intensely angry when discussing past and current attachment relationships or dismissed such attachments as unimportant and noninfluential (Benoit, Zeanah, & Barton, 1989). These findings support the notion that eating and growth disorders during early infancy are highly related to the poor quality of the mother-child attachment, which is likely to reflect the mother's own childhood treatment by insensitive care-givers. Poverty, family disorganization, and limited social support contribute to the likelihood of malnutrition and growth failure as do infants who are difficult to feed and nurture (because of such factors as temperament and acute physical illnesses) (Budd et al., 1992; Drotar, 1991).

Evidence of failure to thrive is considered a strong indicator of major problems in the formation of the early parent-child relationship, resulting in a failure to meet the child's dependency needs. Follow-up studies of children diagnosed with failure to thrive have shown that child welfare intervention may be necessary later on as a result of early maltreatment (Haynes, Cutler, Gray, & Kempe, 1984). Furthermore, hospitalization to achieve weight gain, without consideration of the parent-child relationship, is often insufficient to protect the child from further harm.

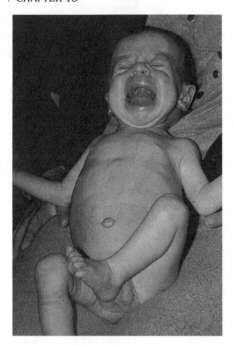

This four-month-old infant stopped gaining weight and developed failure to thrive.

Psychosocial Dwarfism. Psychosocial dwarfism is a rare disorder. No figures are available regarding incidence, prevalence, gender ratio, or sociodemographic features. Although it is easily confused with failure to thrive and related eating disorders, there are important differences. The stunting associated with failure to thrive is secondary to malnutrition; with **psychosocial dwarfism,** it is the primary syndrome. Deceleration of linear growth is combined with other behavior disturbances. Children with psychosocial dwarfism may form bizarre eating habits, drinking stagnant water or drinking out of toilet bowls, gorging, vomiting, stealing and hoarding food, and eating garbage and animal food (Woolston, 1991). Sleep disturbances have also been reported, including difficulty falling asleep, insomnia, and night wandering (Green et al., 1984). These sleep disturbances are probably related to growth delay because growth hormones are released during sleep.

What is particularly striking about both psychosocial dwarfism and failure to thrive is that developmental outcome is highly related to the child's home environment. A child who is removed from a disturbed home experiences reversals in many neuroendocrine, growth, and behavioral problems (Hopwood & Becker, 1979). Normalization takes from several weeks to 2 years, depending on the degree of endocrine disturbance (Green et al., 1984; Silver & Finkelstein, 1967). However, if the child is returned to the problematic environment, the gains are often arrested or reversed. For these reasons,

much of the etiology has focused on parental psychopathology that results in maltreatment of the child. In short, these associated feeding disorders may be a biological outcome of child abuse and neglect.

Obesity

Ellen, an 18-year-old who first became aware of her obesity when she was 9, describes her thoughts and feelings with respect to her weight. This entry was taken verbatim from the journal she kept as part of her individual therapy, with only the names changed:

Ellen: Changes in Self-Image

It does matter to me what people say and think about my size. I guess the whole self-esteem thing began when I was little and other kids made fun of me for being fat—which basically I feel has continued until about a year ago. OK, fine, that is other people's rudeness and lack of sensitivity about someone's problem. Because of these a--holes I have always had to try harder at everything to prove I wasn't just a fat blob—there was a person living, breathing, caring inside that has to be dealt with. . . .

. . . I fell into the trap from about age 5–? of letting others' images of a fat me be my own self-image. I have now let myself get to the point of only accepting others' concept of my new getting-thin person and don't allow myself to think thin. There are times when I get what I need—either trying a smaller-sized outfit, having a total stranger compliment me or a friend tell me I'm looking nice that day—I get high on those compliments and I can be fueled on them for a day or so and then I'm back to square one—who is this person in the picture?

I am scared. All my life I have wanted to be thin. . . . I know the day I weigh 170 there won't be fireworks and a prince on a white horse. It will be a personal landmark celebrated by close friends who can pat me on the back and say good job—you finally did it. . . . I guess the closer I get and the more confused/emotional I get about the whole thing and realize the number isn't going to make my mind snap into line and make me happy with my accomplishment.

The whole self-esteem thing seems as difficult if not more so than the actual weight loss. To lose weight you eat the right foods and exercise—the weight falls off—but to change how you feel about yourself is a whole different ball of wax. How do you change approximately 18 years of thinking about yourself one way when you are really no longer that person? In computer terms—I have changed the hardware and the software is no longer compatible. I don't know where to begin to write my new software program. And there I go again—it's not where do I go—it's what do I tell myself. How do I convince myself—do I write 500 times a day I am thin, worthwhile, nice, organized, good worker, pleasant personality, pretty, smart, logical mind, good advice giver? I know all these things about myself, but they are shadows of the tower of this whole f-ing weight thing. I need a bulldozer to knock over that tower. Where does the bulldozer come from—from inside? But where is it buried, where are the good feelings, the easiness with myself, the self-confidence that I do look nice and desirable? (Foreyt & Cousins, 1987)

Ellen's self-disclosure captures the social and emotional conundrum that overweight children and adolescents so often face, which she characterizes as "the self-esteem thing." Many obese children and adults suffer the consequences of Western cultural attitudes that equate attractiveness and competence with thinness. As early as first grade, children are less likely to befriend overweight peers (Goldfield & Chrisler, 1995), and such attitudes intensify during adolescence (Foreyt & Cousins, 1989). Although her weight losses were slow, with the help of group and individual therapy, Ellen defeated the critical messages that had plagued her since childhood, allowing her to maintain her realistic goal of 170 pounds.

Contrary to popular belief, obesity is not a disorder of weight regulation. Furthermore, obesity does not reflect a failure of will or behavior nor is it a mental disorder, although it can affect a child's psychological development in diverse ways. It is a chronic medical condition, similar to hypertension or diabetes (Weigle, 1990). Persons with obesity regulate their weight appropriately, but their set point is elevated. As we have seen, more and more children and adolescents are caught up in a dieting cycle. The reasons for wanting to lose weight are compelling: Obesity is severely stigmatized in North American society and carries many social and health hazards.

Prevalence and Development. Obesity in childhood and adolescence is often defined as a body mass index of 30 or more [derived from the formula: weight (in kilograms)/height (in meters)^2]. Based on this index, obesity seems to be increasing: 11% of today's children between 6 and 17 years of age are obese compared with 5% only two decades ago (Gortmaker, Dietz, Sobol, & Wehler, 1987; Troiano, Kuczmarski, Johnson, Flegal, & Campbell, 1995). And the percentages don't improve with age: Approximately one-third of North American adults are obese (Troiano et al., 1995).

Obesity is linked to the socioeconomic situation of one's parents (Goldblatt, Moore, & Stunkard, 1965) and to lower income and educational achievement, especially for women (Stunkard, D'Aquill, Fox, & Fillion, 1972). Over an 8-year period spanning late adolescence and early adulthood, women who were obese finished fewer years of school, were less likely to be married, and had lower household incomes and higher rates of household poverty than those who were not obese. Men who were obese were less likely to be married (Gortmaker, Perrin, Sobol, & Dietz, 1993). To a large extent, eating habits and dietary choices are determined by educational level and cultural background. However, obesity is also a stigma that results in discrimination and, consequently, fewer socioeconomic opportunities (Gortmaker et al., 1993). Thus, the relationship between obesity and SES works both ways: Obesity can be caused by SES factors, but it can also result in lower levels of income and education as a result of discrimination.

There has been considerable disagreement during the past two decades about the developmental course of children with obesity. Until recently, scientists believed that infant or early **childhood obesity** was a chronic and steadily progressive disorder that was unlikely to change in young adulthood. Researchers speculated that fat-cell production in early childhood, due to both biological and environmental factors, had a deleterious impact on appetite and weight gain later in life (Nisbett, 1972). However, subsequent studies revealed a low correlation between obesity in infancy and obesity in later childhood. L. R. Shapiro, Crawford, and Clark (1984) followed 450 infants (from age 6 months) for 8 years, 26 of whom were considered obese. Fewer and fewer of those infants who had been obese remained so at subsequent measurements. By the age of 9, only 1 of the original 26 obese children was still considered obese. It is now believed that existing fat cells increase in size rather than in number, and that very little multiplication of fat cells takes place in infancy (Poskitt, 1980).

Although obesity in infancy and obesity in later childhood are not strongly related, *childhood-onset* obesity is more likely to persist into adolescence and adulthood (Troiano et al., 1995; Woolston, 1991). If obesity continues throughout adolescence, the odds against a child's achieving normal weight as an adult are approximately 28 to 1 (Stunkard & Burt, 1967). Even in their youth, individuals with obesity risk a number of health concerns, such as cardiovascular problems and elevated cholesterol and triglycerides (Hayman, Meininger, Coates, & Gallagher, 1995).

One troubling finding is that preadolescent obesity is a risk factor in the later emergence of eating disorders, especially for females, largely because of the manner in which peers ignore or tease children who are obese. Thompson, Coovert, Richards, Johnson, and Cattarin (1995) examined the causal sequences leading to eating disturbances by following 87 girls (10 to 15 years old) for 3 years. Obesity was strongly correlated with teasing by age-mates at an early age; teasing, in turn, predicted overall dissatisfaction with appearance and body image, and set in motion a chain of restrictive and high-risk eating practices (Cattarin & Thompson, 1994). Overweight children and adolescents may require assistance at an early age in developing a healthy, acceptable body image so that they are able to resist the harmful and cruel pressures of early adolescence.

Causes. Body weight, like height and hair color, is to a large extent a function of pedigree. By age 17, a child of two obese parents has 3 times the chance of being obese as a child of lean parents; moreover, if one sibling is obese, there is a 40% chance that a second sibling will be obese as well (Garn & Clark, 1976). Yet, even though heritability may account for a substantial proportion of the variance in obesity, other individual and family-related factors, such as dietary and lifestyle preferences, play a role.

Very recently researchers discovered one of the principle genetic underpinnings of severe obesity, which has triggered a burst of research into obesity's biochemical underpinnings. Laboratory investigators identified an obesity gene among mice that carries instructions to make a protein called *leptin* (Friedman & Burley, 1995). Soon thereafter, leptin deficiencies were found among children with severe obesity (Montague et al., 1997). Scientists believe that when the obesity gene is defective, leptin is not synthesized in the fat cells or no leptin receptors are present in the hypothalamus. In either case, leptin does not communicate properly to the brain to signal an end to eating. Persons with obesity actually have higher levels of leptin than normal-weight persons, yet they are somehow resistant to leptin's effect (this situation is similar to that of adult diabetes, in which a person usually produces insulin but it fails to work properly, causing sugar levels to go out of control). The brain signals the body to make more leptin, but it does not reduce eating as it should (Friedman & Maffei, 1995). Paradoxically, leptin levels decrease with dieting (so it is even less likely to provide feedback to the hypothalamus), which may explain why dieting can increase hunger and slow metabolism, resulting in gaining back the weight that was lost (Lowe, 1993).

Despite strong biological forces, proper diet and exercise still play a critical role in determining a child's level of obesity. Not only do we inherit our biochemical makeup from our parents, we also look to our parents as routine instructors and models as we develop attitudes toward food and eating. Parents determine what food is available, and they model an approach to exercise and diet. Parents of obese children sometimes have greater difficulty setting limits, which has obvious implications for the child's tendency to overeat. Any decrease in physical activity relative to food intake, such as eating while viewing television, results in increased prevalence rates of obesity (Dietz, 1987).

As with the feeding disorders mentioned earlier, family disorganization and parental inadequacy are also related to poor eating habits and weight gain among children (Sherman et al., 1995). For inexperienced or highly pressured parents, any sign of distress in the infant or toddler may be responded to by attempts to feed, by neglect, or by both reactions. Such responses are likely to occur in the context of parental conflict or separation, alcohol or drug abuse, or failure to maintain a stable and constant living environment. Childhood obesity, therefore, may be associated with poor medical care, failure to follow through with recommended health care plans, and similar issues indicative of poor setting of limits and reduced parental competence (Favaro & Santonastaso, 1995; Woolston & Foreyt, 1989).

Treatment. Several important directions for the assessment of childhood obesity and for intervention have been developed during the past decade. Obesity associated with an acute onset in the first 12 months of life has an excellent prognosis because, in most cases, simply reducing the infant's caloric intake to the recommended level for height and age will return weight to a normal level and rate (Woolston, 1991). This simple solution, however, can be complicated by other risk factors, such as severe family dysfunction, a strong family history of obesity, or a medical syndrome.

Because of the combination of health and social consequences, prevention or intervention efforts that take into account not only the individual's health but also the family's resources are often desirable. In many cases, except when there are serious medical complications, pediatricians recommend proper nutrition to arrest weight gain until the child's height and weight are proportional. This approach does not involve putting the child on a diet by restricting calories to below the recommended amount for height, age, and sex. Severely energy-restricted or unbalanced diets can lead to deficiency syndromes, chronic fatigue, impaired concentration, mood changes, and similar side effects that could place a child in jeopardy of medical or learning problems. Calorie restriction can also restrict the growth of lean muscle mass, which could contribute to obesity later on (Weigle, 1990).

Family functioning not only influences level of obesity, but also can be instrumental in its prevention and treatment. Families that are disorganized or inattentive to children's needs often promote a sense of poor self-esteem, which can lead to unlimited use of food (Sherman et al., 1995). When children's eating is an attempt to fulfill emotional needs, a pattern may form of enormous caloric intake and rapid onset of severe obesity, usually between ages 3 and 5 (Woolston, 1991).

On the other hand, children whose family history of overweight is their primary risk factor respond favorably to brief, behaviorally based interventions. L. H. Epstein, Valoski, Wing, and McCurley (1990) demonstrated at the end of a 10-year follow-up that an 8-week behavioral intervention program involving parents as well as children had significantly reduced the children's obesity. By and large, obese and overweight children need parental encouragement to avoid too much inactivity, so teaching parents and children ways to be more active and less sedentary is effective. In a study in which obese children 8 to 12 years old were randomly assigned to one of three conditions (increased exercise, decreased sedentary behaviors, or a combination of both), L. H. Epstein et al. (1995) found that children who were taught to be active and reinforced for being less sedentary (such as playing outdoors and watching less television) increased their liking for high-intensity activity. Importantly, 1 year after treatment, children who received both forms of intervention had a greater decrease in percentage overweight and body fat than children who received either method alone. Treatment methods, therefore, do not have to involve demanding exercise or diet regimens, but rather should instill active, less sedentary routines.

Other behavioral interventions focus on the goal of making the child's eating behaviors and physical activity patterns more adaptive and self-managed. Self-control procedures encourage children to set their own goals for diet, weight, and exercise, and teach them the necessary skills to achieve these goals with minimal outside directives from parents or therapists. For example, children may be taught to monitor the quantity and nature of their food, when they eat it, and who shared the meal; similar self-monitoring is encouraged for exercise goals (Foreyt & Cousins, 1989). Even if some children are unable to reach or maintain their intended goal of weight loss, self-control training still encourages a greater sense of perceived control among children with obesity (Israel, Guilem Baker, & Silverman, 1994).

A related behavioral intervention involves stimulus control, in which an attempt is made to modify the factors that may trigger inappropriate eating. The all-too-familiar pitfalls of weight-control plans have to be anticipated and removed so that the child's environment and daily routines can be altered. For example, parents may be advised not to bring high-calorie snack foods into the house and to monitor what they eat in front of their children. Since parents must help the child maintain changes in weight once a treatment program has ended, including them in the child's weight-loss program is encouraged. Stable changes in weight may depend on family factors that either support or sabotage children's efforts to improve their eating and exercise patterns.

Some researchers (and drug companies) predict that molecular biology will ultimately provide the cure for obesity. In the meantime, however, proper food choices and regular, light aerobic exercise (especially walking) are preferable to calorie restriction. Even if pharmaceutical interventions become more safe and acceptable than they are today, overweight children will still likely require additional behavior modification techniques to strengthen their commitment to activity and weight management.

EATING DISORDERS OF ADOLESCENCE

Eating disorders, as well as such eating-related problems as dieting and bingeing, are most likely to appear during two important periods of adolescent development: the early passage into adolescence and the movement from later adolescence to young adulthood (Attie & Brooks-Gunn, 1995). Early- and middle-childhood risk factors, such as eating problems, dieting patterns, and negative body image, clash with the ongoing challenges confronting adolescents. Unfortunately, this clash leads some teens, particularly girls, to exert excessive control over their eating in a misguided effort to manage stress and physical changes. In some instances this controlled pattern of eating, coupled with other ill-conceived efforts to overcompensate for eating and weight changes (such as excessive exercise) leads to major eating disorders, such as anorexia nervosa and bulimia nervosa.

Anorexia nervosa gained medical attention in 1873, when two doctors first described the disorder. Sir William Gull, an English physician, named the malady and described it for the first time as a specific disease; about the same time, in Paris, psychiatrist Charles Laségue described anorexia from a social and psychological standpoint. Both investigators observed that the disease was most prevalent in the wealthiest social classes, which prompted Laségue to propose a connection between a lack of parental affection (believed to be relatively common among wealthy families) and a preoccupation with food. Conflict between parents and children could drive some teenage girls to refuse food as a way of expressing their feelings of rejection. Accordingly, by the turn of the century, the prescribed treatment for anorexia was a "parentectomy," the removal of the child from the family home, which was combined with forcefeeding by whatever means necessary (R. Epstein, 1990).

References to what we now refer to as bulimia date back to sixth-century descriptions of more than 40 individuals who displayed symptoms described as "insatiable voracity, morbid or canine appetite, with or without vomiting" (W. L. Parry-Jones & B. Parry-Jones, 1994, p. 288). Interestingly, these historical cases almost all described males, perhaps because overeating was socially accepted as a sign of wealth or success, a reversal of the pattern today.

Ideal body sizes change with the times and with cultural preferences. Rubenesque figures were considered highly attractive and desirable until the late 19th century, when body image preferences were usurped by major cultural changes. During the Victorian period refusing food was in keeping with prevailing social pressures. A hearty appetite was seen as a wanton expression of sexuality and lack of self-restraint; women were expected to be passively uninterested in both sex and food. Thus, it became morally, spiritually, and socially desirable for women to refuse food, largely on the basis of spiritual, rather than physical, beauty (Brumberg, 1988). Anorexia nervosa, according to physicians around the turn of the 20th century, was a symptom of inappropriate romantic choices, blocked educational or social opportunities, and conflicts with parents. Slimness symbolized asexuality and gentility, which implied a respectable amount of social distance from the working classes (Attie & Brooks-Gunn, 1995). Originating in the 1930s, today's attitudes and beliefs about women's ideal body size and appearance have been shaped by advertisers, film stars, clothing designers, and similar forces, resulting in a prevailing cultural preference for slimness.

The meaning of food and eating for female identity, the role of family and social class in determining body image and food choices, and the use of weight regulation as a substitute for self-regulation and control in adolescence remain salient causes of eating disorders to this day (Brumberg & Streigel-Moore, 1993). Within the last quarter century, additional aspects of eating disorders, such as the chronic refusal of food, emphasis on overactivity, and bulimic symptoms of bingeing and purging, have gained recognition as significant and potentially dangerous complications (Attie & Brooks-Gunn, 1995).

Anorexia Nervosa

Martha: Obsessed with Food and Weight

At 14, Martha was five-foot-two and 69 pounds. And she thought that was normal. "I feel like I don't need to gain weight, like I'm at a reasonable weight now," reads her journal entry. Martha was in the hospital's Eating Disorders Program because her dieting, which had begun six months earlier as a health kick, had evolved into anorexia: an obsession with food and weight that was consuming her life and threatening to kill her.

"It started when I was 13," Martha explains. "Before I left for camp I had a physical, and the doctor said I should start eating more because I hadn't started menstruating. She said 'Eat more dairy products because we want to get your body going.'" At camp, Martha started eating "kind of the way a dieter would. In the morning I would eat a bowl of peaches. And at first I'd eat the hot entrées, but then I started just having salads. My friends would say, 'Gosh, you're a healthy eater.' I lost three pounds that summer. Nothing serious."

But it was the start of something serious. Martha staved off her period, but she embarked on a food fixation that would stay with her for years. Along with the new eating regimen came a strict exercise program. "It was gradual, but I really got into it: get home, no snack, do homework. In the afternoon, jump rope for ten minutes. Eat dinner. Every night I would do situps, leg lifts and jumping jacks. Fifty of each—no more, no less."

Her mother tried everything to get her daughter to eat. "We tried saying 'You *have* to eat this,' but she would just burst into tears and leave the room." The dinner table became a nightly battleground as everyone focused on Martha's stubborn refusal to eat. "I wanted to eat, to be like other people, but I couldn't," she explains. "I thought a lot about the things that I wasn't going to allow myself to eat each day. I felt like eating was something I had total control of, and I didn't want to let go of that control."

No one was able to convince Martha that she was in danger. Finally, her doctor insisted that she be hospitalized and carefully monitored for treatment of her illness. It took a lengthy hospitalization and a good deal of individual and family outpatient therapy for Martha to face and solve her problems.

Today, at age 16, she weighs 100 pounds and [is] gaining. Martha is able to focus on some long-term goals—she plans to attend medical school and go into pediatrics—undaunted by the fact that she'll be in school for many, many years to come. "I'm not afraid to work really hard," she says. "I'm good at that." (Solin, 1995)

Martha at age 16, on the road to a full recovery from anorexia nervosa.

Martha is suffering from the restricting type of anorexia nervosa. As her story shows, this is a severe eating disorder, with serious health and mental health consequences if left untreated. It is characterized by the refusal to maintain a minimally normal body weight, an intense fear of gaining weight, and a significant disturbance in the individual's perception and experiences of his or her own size. One of the most notable features of the psychopathology of the disease is that persons with anorexia deny that they are too thin or that they have a weight problem. As a result, friends or family members often must insist on taking them to see a physician. Diagnostic criteria for anorexia nervosa are shown in Table 13.4.

Although the word *anorexia* literally means "loss of appetite," that definition is misleading because the person with this disorder rarely suffers appetite loss. Weight loss is accomplished deliberately through a very restricted diet, purging, or exercise. Although many persons occasionally use these methods to lose weight, the individual with anorexia is intensely afraid of obesity and pursues thinness relentlessly.

Young persons who suffer from anorexia show a major distortion in how they experience their weight and shape. Some individuals feel overweight all over, whereas others realize they are thin but believe that certain body

---

Table 13.4 | **DSM-IV Diagnostic Criteria for Anorexia Nervosa**

A. Refusal to maintain body weight at or above a minimally normal weight for age and height (e.g., weight loss leading to maintenance of body weight less than 85% of that expected; or failure to make expected weight gain during period of growth, leading to body weight less than 85% of that expected).

B. Intense fear of gaining weight or becoming fat, even though underweight.

C. Disturbance in the way in which one's body weight or shape is experienced, undue influence of body weight or shape on self-evaluation, or denial of the seriousness of the current low body weight.

D. In postmenarcheal females, amenorrhea, i.e., the absence of at least three consecutive menstrual cycles. (A woman is considered to have amenorrhea if her periods occur only following hormone, e.g., estrogen, administration.)

Specify type:

Restricting Type: during the current episode of Anorexia Nervosa, the person has not regularly engaged in binge-eating or purging behavior (i.e., self-induced vomiting or the misuse of laxatives, diuretics, or enemas)
Binge-Eating/Purging Type: during the current episode of Anorexia Nervosa, the person has regularly engaged in binge-eating or purging behavior (i.e., self-induced vomiting or the misuse of laxatives, diuretics, or enemas)

Source: DSM-IV Copyright © 1994 by APA.

parts are too fat. They may become obsessed with measuring themselves to see if the "fat" has been eliminated. Thus, how they see themselves and how they relate to others is often a function of their perceived shape and weight. To such an individual, weight loss is a triumph of self-discipline. Martha expressed this perfectly: "When I lose weight, I look better and I feel better." But with anorexia there is never enough weight loss: The person always wants to lose more weight to be on the safe side, and if not enough weight is lost one day, the person may panic and work extra hard to lose weight the next day.

The DSM-IV specifies two subtypes of anorexia based on the methods used to limit caloric intake. This distinction has to do with possible differences in etiology and treatment avenues. In the **restricting** type, individuals seek to lose weight primarily through diet, fasting, or excessive exercise; in the binge-eating/purging type, the individual regularly engages in episodes of binge eating or purging, or both. In comparison to persons with bulimia, those with the binge-eating/purging type of anorexia eat relatively small amounts of food and commonly purge more consistently and thoroughly. Approximately half of the individuals meeting criteria for anorexia engage in binge eating and purging behavior (APA, 1994). The significantly different characteristics exhibited by the two subtypes have clinical implications. Individuals who regularly binge and purge tend to have stronger personal and family histories of obesity and higher rates of so-called impulsive disorders, including stealing, drug misuse, self-harm, and mood problems. In contrast, the restricting subtypes are highly controlled, rigid, and often obsessive individuals (Garner, 1993a).

Finally, the initial clinical presentation of persons with anorexia is usually quite distinctive, as serious medical complications due to malnutrition are imminent. By the time most individuals are brought to a professional, their average weight is 25% to 30% below normal for their age and height (Hsu, 1990). Accordingly, many physical symptoms of starvation are usually evident. Cessation of menstrual cycle (amenorrhea) is invariably present in postmenarcheal young women, as are dry and sometimes yellowish skin; fine downy hair (lanugo) on the trunk, face, and extremities; a sensitivity to cold; and cardiovascular and gastrointestinal problems. The American Anorexia/Bulimia Association (1996) provides the following list of anorexia danger signals:

❖ losing a great deal of weight in a relatively short period
❖ continuing to diet, although bone-thin
❖ reaching a diet goal and then immediately setting another for further weight loss
❖ being dissatisfied with appearance, even after reaching a weight-loss goal

❖ preferring to diet in isolation rather than with a group
❖ experiencing the loss of monthly menstrual periods
❖ engaging in strange eating rituals and/or eating extremely small amounts of food
❖ becoming a secret eater
❖ being obsessive about exercising
❖ experiencing long-lasting depressions
❖ engaging in bingeing and purging

Bulimia Nervosa

Phillipa: A Well-Kept Secret

Phillipa developed bulimia nervosa at 18. Like Martha, her strange eating behavior began when she started to diet. But Phillipa began gaining weight because she was eating a lot at night. With the extra weight came self-loathing. "I felt like my body was in the way of me being successful at school, and getting dates. I looked in the mirror several times a day, thinking 'I don't even want to be in this body.' There wasn't a minute in my life that I didn't think about some aspect of how I looked."

Although Phillipa dieted and exercised to lose weight, unlike Martha she regularly ate huge amounts of food and maintained her normal weight by forcing herself to vomit. Phillipa often felt like an emotional powder keg—angry, frightened, and depressed. Unable to understand her own behavior, Phillipa thought no one else would either. She felt isolated and lonely. Typically, when things were not going well, she would be overcome with an uncontrollable desire for sweets. She would eat pounds of candy and cake at a time, and often not stop until she was exhausted or in severe pain. Then, overwhelmed with guilt and disgust, she would make herself vomit.

Her eating habits so embarrassed her that she kept them secret until, depressed by her mounting problems, she attempted suicide. Fortunately, she didn't succeed. While recuperating in the hospital, Phillipa was referred to an eating disorders clinic where she became involved in group therapy. There she received medications to treat the illness and the understanding and help she so desperately needed from others who had the same problem. With a smile, Phillipa explains: "It taught me that my self-worth is not absolutely correlated with my appearance or what others may think of me." (National Institute of Mental Health [NIMH], 1994)

Table 13.5	DSM-IV Diagnostic Criteria for Bulimia Nervosa

A. Recurrent episodes of binge eating. An episode of binge eating is characterized by both of the following:
   (1) eating, in a discrete period of time (e.g., within any 2-hour period), an amount of food that is definitely larger than most people would eat during a similar period of time and under similar circumstances
   (2) a sense of lack of control over eating during the episode (e.g., a feeling that one cannot stop eating or control what or how much one is eating)

B. Recurrent inappropriate compensatory behavior in order to prevent weight gain, such as self-induced vomiting; the misuse of laxatives, diuretics, or enemas, or other medications; fasting; or excessive exercise.

C. The binge eating and inappropriate compensatory behaviors both occur, on average, at least twice a week for 3 months.

D. Self-evaluation is unduly influenced by body shape and weight.

E. The disturbance does not occur exclusively during episodes of Anorexia Nervosa.

Specify type:

Purging Type: during the current episode of Bulimia Nervosa, the person has regularly engaged in self-induced vomiting or the misuse of laxatives, diuretics, or enemas

Nonpurging Type: during the current episode of Bulimia Nervosa, the person has used other inappropriate compensatory behaviors, such as fasting or excessive exercise, but has not regularly engaged in self-induced vomiting or the misuse of laxatives, diuretics, or enemas.

Source: DSM-IV Copyright © 1994 by APA.

Of the two major forms of eating disorders afflicting adolescents and young adults, bulimia is far more common than anorexia. The DSM-IV diagnostic criteria listed in Table 13.5 note that the primary hallmark of the disorder is binge eating. Because most of us overeat certain foods at certain times, you may ask "What exactly is a *binge?*" As noted in the criteria, a **binge** is an episode of overeating that must involve both an objectively large amount of food (more than most people would eat under the circumstances), and lack of control. Thus, no particular quantitative amount of food constitutes a binge. The context of the behavior must also be considered: Overeating at celebrations or holiday feasts, for example, is excluded. Although most binge eaters report overeating junk food rather than fresh fruits and vegetables, the amounts of food they consider a binge vary widely. On average, eaters consumed roughly 1500 calories during a binge, about 5 times more than they normally ate at one time (Rosen, Leitenberg, Fisher, & Khazam, 1986).

Persons with bulimia attempt to conceal binge eating out of shame. Thus, although binges are not planned, a ritual may form wherein the person, sensing no one around, makes a split-second decision (on the way home from a late-night party, for example) to stop, purchase, and consume massive quantities of food. Typically, binge eating follows changes in mood or interpersonal stress, but it may also be related to intense hunger due to dieting, or to feelings about personal appearance or body shape. Although these feelings may dissipate for a period of time, the depressed mood and self-criticism usually return.

The second important part of the diagnostic criteria involves the individual's attempts to compensate somehow for a binge. The criteria subdivides bulimia into **purging** type, in which there is regular self-induced vomiting or regular misuse of laxatives or diuretics (that is, overuse of these drugs to reduce fluids and solids), and nonpurging type, in which the individual uses other forms of compensation, such as fasting or excessive exercise. Approximately two-thirds of persons with bulimia engage in purging. By far the most common compensatory technique after an episode of binge eating is induced vomiting—stimulating the gag reflex with the fingers or some instrument—a method reported by 80% to 90% of individuals with bulimia who seek treatment. Vomiting produces immediate relief from physical discomfort and reduces fear of gaining weight.

A different pattern of **compensatory behavior** is reported among community samples of individuals who fit criteria for bulimia. These are individuals who have not sought help but are identified through random phone or in-person interviews. Figure 13.3 shows the various compensatory behaviors of males and females who met all criteria for bulimia nervosa, on the basis of their responses to part of the Ontario Health Survey, in which over 8000 individuals were interviewed in person about their health habits. Among these nonreferred subjects,

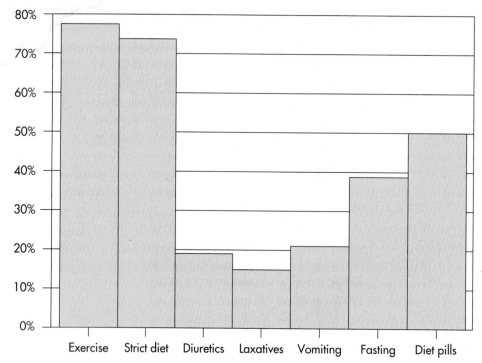

FIGURE 13.3 Compensatory behaviors of full-syndrome bulimia nervosa among community samples. (Data from Garfinkel et al., 1995)

vigorous exercise and strict diet are the preferred means of compensating for bingeing. In contrast to clinical samples, only 21% reported vomiting as a compensatory behavior (Garfinkel et al., 1995).

Research with community (nonclinical) samples has not identified any significant differences between persons with bulimia who purge and those who do not. A study by Walters et al. (1993) is particularly intriguing because it involved 54 persons who purged and 69 who did not; the study was based on interviews with over 1000 pairs of identical twins to permit greater control over the underlying biological component. Although both groups of persons with bulimia showed significant signs of major depression, alcoholism, and anorexia, there were no differences between the two groups on any variables related to personality or weight. Studies have not yet followed individuals who purge or do not purge long enough to determine the long-range consequences, but it is clear that bulimia involves a core disorder whether or not purging is present (Woolston, 1991).

Like those with anorexia, adolescents and adults with bulimia are often described as rigid and absolutistic (displaying an all-or-nothing attitude) in their thinking (Butow, Beumont, & Touyz, 1993). They see themselves as either completely in control or completely out of control, and view everyday events in extremes of either black or white. Martha revealed such thinking by her

comment, "I felt like eating was something I had total control of, and I didn't want to let go of that control." Phillipa also expressed absolutistic thinking, attributing her woes to one thing and one thing only: "I felt like my body was in the way of me being successful at school, and getting dates." Such beliefs relate to the DSM-IV criteria, which stress the importance of body shape and weight to self-evaluation. Women with bulimia, as well as those with anorexia, have greater dissatisfaction with their body proportions and distort their true body size, compared with women without these disorders. A meta-analysis of 66 studies of this issue revealed that body dissatisfaction and distortion are more strongly connected to cognitive factors, such as biases in attention, memory, and selective interpretation or judgment, rather than any actual problem with perceptual ability (Cash & Deagle, 1997).

The medical consequences of chronic bulimia can be significant, although they are not as severe as those that result from anorexia. Common physical complaints include fatigue, headaches, puffy cheeks (due to enlarged salivary glands), and permanent or significant loss of dental enamel, especially from the inside surface of the front teeth (due to the contact of the acidic stomach contents with the teeth). Among females, menstrual irregularity or amenorrhea sometimes occurs, although it is not clear whether these disturbances are related to weight fluctuations, to other nutritional deficiencies, or to stress. Electrolyte imbalances due to purging behavior are sometimes severe enough to cause significant medical problems.

The American Anorexia/Bulimia Association (1996) provides the following list of bulimia danger signals:

❖ regular bingeing (eating large amounts of food over a short period of time)
❖ regular purging (by vomiting, using diuretics or laxatives, strict dieting, or excessive exercising)
❖ retaining or regaining weight despite frequent exercise and dieting
❖ not gaining weight but eating enormous amounts of food at one sitting
❖ disappearing into the bathroom for long periods of time to induce vomiting
❖ abusing drugs or alcohol or stealing regularly
❖ experiencing long periods of depression
❖ having irregular menstrual periods
❖ exhibiting dental problems, swollen cheek glands, bloating, or scars on the backs of the hands from forced vomiting

PREVALENCE AND DEVELOPMENT OF ANOREXIA AND BULIMIA

Distinguishing between the two major eating disorders of adolescents and young adults can be difficult, because anorexia and bulimia share many features. Members of both groups have distorted body image and feel nervous after eating. Whereas persons with anorexia are 15% or more below normal weight, persons with bulimia are within 10% of normal. Also, persons with anorexia engage in binge eating only occasionally and typically avoid forbidden food, whereas those with bulimia binge frequently on forbidden food and purge to control their weight. Moreover, eating disorders overlap so much with other mental disorders, including depression and schizophrenia, that some features can be obscured and the disorder misdiagnosed (Foreyt & Mikhail, 1997). However, in terms of cognitive beliefs and self-image, only patients with anorexia show an intense **drive for thinness** and a disturbance in their perception of body image.

Among female adolescents and young adults, studies have estimated the prevalence of anorexia nervosa at 0.5% to 1.0% (Hoek, 1993; Hsu, 1990), and bulimia nervosa at 1% to 3% (APA, 1994; Garfinkel et al., 1995). Clinicians and researchers have drawn public and scientific attention to evidence that major eating disorders have increased during the past two or three decades (Fairburn, Hay, & Welch, 1993). The number of children under age 14 presenting for treatment of an eating disorder appears to be increasing as well (Lask & Bryant-Waugh, 1992).

Curiously, eating disorders are among the few mental health problems in children and youth that affect females far more than males. There are too few cases of males with anorexia to determine a reliable prevalence rate, but the rate of occurrence of bulimia among males is about one-tenth that of females (Lucas, Beard, O'Fallon, & Kurland, 1991). Young men with eating disorders show the same clinical features as young women; however, men show less of a preoccupation with food or a drive for thinness, and place more emphasis on athletic appearance or attractiveness as the rationale for their disturbed eating behavior (Carlat & Camargo, 1991). Because eating disorders are considered a problem affecting primarily women, researchers believe they are underdiagnosed among young men (Lask & Bryant-Waugh, 1992).

Cross-Cultural Considerations

Eating disorders are highly culturally specific. In North America, for example, the incidence of anorexia is considerably lower among immigrant and minority populations than in the majority population (Dolan, 1991). These cross-cultural differences are particularly noticeable when youths from other cultures are exposed to Western ideals of weight and appearance: In short order, the rates of eating disorders and disturbances increase significantly (Fairburn & Beglin, 1990; Pate, Pumariega, Hester, & Garner, 1992). Minority adolescents from upper-middle-class families are particularly at risk, because of their motivation to be accepted into the dominant White culture, or as a result of their being caught between two different sets of cultural values (Yates, 1989). As already discussed, eating patterns, including disorders, are closely connected to child-rearing patterns and cultural values, and an emphasis on thinness and restraint pervades North American culture.

Why the incidence of bulimia (but not anorexia) is more than 5 times higher in large cities than in rural areas (Hoek et al., 1995) cannot be readily explained; perhaps urbanization increases pressure on young women to be thin. The stress associated with city living may also play a causal role, as might the fact that more stimuli are available to provoke binge eating, such as billboards and fast-food restaurants (Hoek et al., 1995). Certain subgroups of adolescents are more likely to develop the disorders, including young women of higher socioeconomic status (Jones, Fox, Babigian, & Hutton, 1990) or those who are seeking specific career paths, such as dance or modeling.

Paula Abdul has raised awareness of bulimia, based on her own struggle.

Development and Course

Anorexia nervosa usually strikes during adolescence, between the ages of 14 and 18, although it does occasionally affect older women, men, and prepubertal children. The disorder is usually related to a stressful life event, such as parental divorce or changes in family or school. Although the symptoms of anorexia are quite specific and well defined, its developmental course and outcome are highly variable. The relapse and chronic course of anorexia are evident in the findings averaged across 31 studies of persons with anorexia, shown in Figure 13.4: Just over half show full recovery, less than one-third show fair improvement, and one-fifth continue

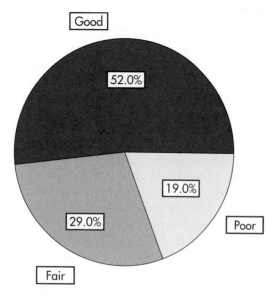

FIGURE 13.4 Outcome of anorexia. (Data from Steinhausen, 1997)

on a chronic course (Steinhausen, 1997). Most common is a fluctuating pattern involving a restoration of normal weight followed by relapse (Eckert, Halmi, Marchi, Grove, & Crosby, 1995). As the individual loses weight and becomes dangerously malnourished, she is hospitalized and begins to show signs of improvement. Sadly, a significant number of patients—between 6% (Sullivan, 1995) and 10% (APA, 1994)—die from medical complications or suicide. Although the disorder itself is rare, those individuals who are afflicted have a mortality rate that is more than *12 times higher* than the annual death rate from all other causes for females 15 to 24 years old in the general population (Sullivan, 1995).

Bulimia nervosa also mostly affects adolescents and young adults, but its onset is typically in late adolescence. A noteworthy aspect of this disorder is that binge eating often develops during or after a period of restrictive dieting (Hsu, 1990). Because of the guilt and discomfort caused by binge eating, purging follows as compensation (Wilson et al., 1996).

Bulimia can either follow a chronic course or occur intermittently, with periods of remission alternating with binge eating and purging. However, it is not easy to reverse the developmental course. Because the habits and cultural influences that led to the disorder in the first place are so powerful, a chronic pattern of disturbed eating may be established, such as secretive bingeing at social gatherings, which in turn leads to further problems. A 10-year follow-up of 50 patients with bulimia revealed that over half (52%) had recovered fully and fewer than 10% continued to suffer the full syndrome (Collings & King, 1994). The best predictors of a more favorable outcome were younger age at onset, higher social class, and a family history of alcohol abuse (the latter suggesting that once the teen left the negative family circumstances, improvement was made). Importantly, bulimia responds favorably to treatment that disrupts its cyclical course.

Similar to the above study of long-term outcomes of persons with bulimia, studies of eating behaviors and attitudes among college student populations suggest that maturing into adulthood and getting away from powerful social pressures that emphasize thinness help many women escape from chronic dieting and abnormal eating. A 10-year follow-up of body weight, dieting, and symptoms of eating disorders among male and female college students found both encouraging and discouraging results (Heatherton, Mahamedi, Striepe, Field, & Keel, 1997). On a positive note, women reduced their eating disorder behaviors and increased their body satisfaction ratings; however, body dissatisfaction and desires to lose weight still remained relatively high, and one-fifth of the women who met clinical criteria for an eating

cathy®

disorder in college also met criteria 10 years later. Men, on the other hand, were prone to weight gain after college, and many reported increased dieting or disordered eating in the 10 years following college. Thus, although disordered eating tends to decline during the transition to early adulthood, body dissatisfaction remains an issue for many young adults (Heatherton et al., 1997).

CAUSES OF ANOREXIA AND BULIMIA

Why would people starve themselves to near emaciation or eat to the point of illness? The dramatic effects on physical and psychological well-being that can result from eating disorders have inspired many theories. No single factor has been isolated as the major cause of any type of eating disorder, and searching for causes is complicated by the "chicken and egg" problem of causation: Do neurobiological processes disrupt eating patterns, or do eating problems lead to changes in neurobiology?

Explaining the gradual degenerative process of forming an eating disorder requires acknowledging the contribution of all three major etiological domains—biological, sociocultural (including family and peers), and psychological—which can operate singly or in combination to disturb self-regulation in any given individual. We are all familiar with the cultural emphasis on thinness, self-control, and exercise, which creates idealized images that define attractiveness (for women especially, but for men as well). We'll see that these sociocultural aspects play a very powerful role in initiating disturbed eating patterns.

Biological Dimension

There is reasonably good agreement that neurobiological factors play only a minor role in *precipitating* anorexia and bulimia. However, such factors may contribute to the *maintenance* of the disorder, because of their effects on appetite, mood, perception, and energy regulation (Kaplan & Woodside, 1987; Wilson et al., 1996).

It makes sense to suspect that biological mechanisms (a gene? a neurochemical process?), acting together or alone, are responsible for corrupting normal regulatory functions. A slight twist places the problem on the individual who disrupts his or her normal regulatory processes in an ill-conceived attempt to achieve weight or diet goals. This disruption may cause biological changes throughout the central nervous and neuroendocrine systems that, in turn, create more disruption. Thus, it also makes sense that success at controlling such important bodily functions as hunger or appetite may lead to unnatural eating habits that result in an abusive eating pattern.

Genetic and Constitutional Factors. Eating disorders tend to run in families. Research conducted over the past decade has found that relatives of patients with anorexia or bulimia, especially female relatives, are 4 to 5 times more likely than those in the general population to develop an eating disorder themselves (Hudson, Poke, Jonas, & Yurgelun-Todd, 1983; Strober & Humphrey, 1987; Strober, Lampert, Morrell, Burroughs, & Jacobs, 1990). Twin studies, in which genetic factors are better controlled, indicate that the concordance rate for a major eating disorder among monozygotic twins runs between 30% and 50%, whereas the rates for dizygotic twins are typically 10% or less (Hsu,

Chesler, & Santhouse, 1990). In a major study, 2163 female twins were interviewed to determine the prevalence of bulimia (Kendler et al., 1991): 23% of individual monozygotic twins both had the disorder, compared with 9% of dizygotic twins.

If bulimia and anorexia are connected to genetic factors, what exactly is being inherited? Hsu (1990) suggests that some people have a biological vulnerability that interacts with social and psychological factors to increase the chances of their developing an eating disorder. For example, inherited personality traits, such as emotional instability and poor self-control, would predispose an individual to be emotionally reactive to stress, which, in turn, could lead to impulsive eating in an attempt to relieve the feelings associated with stress.

Neurobiological Factors. Norepinephrine decreases eating at some sites of the hypothalamus but increases eating at other sites (Schlundt & Johnson, 1990), and is abnormal—either too low or too high— among patients with anorexia nervosa (Fava, Copeland, Schwaiger, & Herzog, 1989). Lower levels of norepinephrine have also been found among patients with bulimia, although it is not clear whether these changes cause bulimia or result from it (Kaye & Weltzin, 1991). Norepinephrine levels usually return to normal once the patient begins to gain weight. Researchers believe, therefore, that low norepinephrine concentrations are due to low body weight, and that high norepinephrine concentrations may result from excessive exercise or dieting (Lesem et al., 1989).

Among patients with bulimia, a disregulation in either one or both neuroendocrine systems may cause the bingeing behavior that precedes purging (Kaye & Weltzin, 1992). Because **serotonin** regulates hunger and appetite, this neurotransmitter has been focused on as a possible cause of both anorexia and bulimia. Essentially, the presence of serotonin leads to a feeling of fullness and a desire to decrease food intake, so a decrease in serotonin leads to continuing hunger and greater consumption of food at one time: the perfect condition for bingeing.

One of the strongest findings in support of the serotonin explanation for bulimia comes from studies investigating the relationship of diet to the availability in the brain of the serotonin precursor tryptophan. Meals that are rich in protein or low in carbohydrates decrease tryptophan; carbohydrate-rich meals increase it. Put another way, bingeing on sweet and starchy foods creates conditions in the brain that produce more serotonin, which, eventually, leads to a sense of fullness.

To illustrate this process, Cowen, Anderson, and Fairburn (1992) compared the dietary habits of healthy subjects and of patients with bulimia and found that the patients with bulimia had unusually large drops in plasma levels of tryptophan after eating protein-rich meals. Moreover, women in the study were more sensitive to the tryptophan-depleting effects of low-carbohydrate diets than were men. Thus, binge eating (which usually involves high-carbohydrate food), especially for women, increases the availability of tryptophan, thereby temporarily increasing brain serotonin and forestalling the compensatory response (Jimmerson et al., 1992). It is still not known, however, whether problems related to the availability of serotonin in the brain are due to dieting or are a premorbid characteristic. Wilson et al. (1996) go further in stating that dieting may be a major factor in *altering* brain serotonin levels, and that once the resulting changes in eating patterns occur, a self-maintaining cycle may begin.

An interesting but as yet unproven theory explains the alternation of starvation and bingeing as a function of the release of endogenous opioid peptides (EOPs). To understand the role of EOPs, think back to the last time you skipped a meal and continued to study energetically or to work at some other intense activity. For some of us, the strongest feelings of hunger subside 1 or 2 hours after we would normally have eaten, and at least for a while, we continue to feel energized. EOPs, which reside naturally in the body and are released in response to the need for food, are part of the opiate system, and their release helps decrease pain and increase the pleasure of eating in general. (Their evolutionary purpose may have been to provide the energy necessary to hunt for food.) Could a person with an eating disorder become addicted to the release of EOPs? Skipping meals (a form of starvation) forces the body to release these opiates, the increased pleasure of eating resulting from their release leads to bingeing, and the cycle of starvation and bingeing continues. Although intriguing, this addiction model of eating disorders remains unconfirmed (Wilson, 1991).

In addition to connections between depression and eating disorders, scientists have found biochemical similarities between people with eating disorders and those with obsessive-compulsive disorder (OCD). Just as serotonin levels are known to be abnormal in people with depression and people with eating disorders, they are also abnormal in patients with OCD. Moreover, many persons with bulimia show obsessive-compulsive behavior as severe as that shown among patients diagnosed with OCD, and patients with OCD often have abnormal eating behaviors. One clue to this connection may be the hormone **vasopressin**, another brain chemical that is abnormal in people with eating disorders and in those with OCD. Levels of vasopressin are elevated in patients with anorexia, bulimia, and OCD. Normally released in response to physical (and possibly emotional) stress, vasopressin may contribute to the obsessive behavior seen in some patients with eating disorders.

In summary, these prominent biological theories indicate that some neurobiological and endocrinological abnormalities are found among persons with eating disorders, although these problems are probably the result, rather than the primary cause, of semistarvation or the binge/purge cycle. Understanding how normal eating patterns may initially become disturbed requires a close look at the cultural and psychological components of eating disorders.

Social Dimension

Features of contemporary Western culture are almost prerequisites for eating disorders. Personal freedom, an emphasis on instant gratification, the availability of food any time of night or day, lack of supervision, and the cultural ideal of diet and exercise for weight loss add up to powerful influences (Attie & Brooks-Gunn, 1995). These factors contribute to what some call a drive for thinness, a key motivational variable underlying dieting and body image, among young females in particular (Polivy & Herman, 1993).

Sociocultural Factors. Adolescents' concerns about undereating and overeating are legendary (Mueller et al., 1995), which causes us to question: What aspects of Western culture drive someone, most likely a young woman, to overcome the body's natural rhythm and force it into a punishing and dangerous routine of semistarvation or frequent purging? It is well known that for most young White females in middle- and upper-class society, self-worth, happiness, and success are determined to a large extent by physical appearance, and most eating disorders represent an attempt to feel good with respect to personal appearance and self-control. In reality, body size itself has little or no long-term correlation with personal happiness and success; one's self-concept and self-efficacy are more important. However, as Brownell (1991) explains, a collision may be occurring between our culture and our physiological boundaries, because the average North American woman between 17 and 24 years old is heavier by 5 to 6 pounds than 20 years ago, and she is not satisfied with her body image.

Dieting and "fast and easy" weight-loss programs are further cultural phenomena, so it is not surprising that as many as 80% of adolescent girls diet to control weight (Wilson et al., 1996). Concerns about physical attractiveness have also been discovered in children as young as 7 or 8 years old (Hsu, 1990). In addition, more females in higher SES groups than in lower SES groups want to be thin. Boarding schools and colleges, where social contagion increases the vulnerability of adoles-

The look that launched a thousand diets.

cents, are settings that illustrate the relationship between SES and eating disorders (Steiner-Adair, 1990).

Few would argue that eating disorders are more common in women because of sex-role identification. Late 20th-century images of women and assumptions about what it is to be feminine are based largely on the idea that girls must be pretty (i.e., not fat) to draw attention and praise from others, while boys are admired for their accomplishments. Body build and self-esteem are correlated for girls, but not for boys, by the time they reach the fourth grade (Striegel-Moore, Silberstein, & Rodin, 1986). This finding endorses the view that the relationships on which young women's identity and self-worth depend are overly influenced by physical attractiveness and body image (Miller, 1976). Even lesbians, who generally reject sociocultural expectations of women, do not differ significantly from heterosexual women in their attitudes about weight and in the prevalence of bulimia (Heffernan, 1996), which again points to societal pressures as powerful contributors to eating disorders.

Sex-role identification is closely tied to cultural norms and expectations, so it is not surprising that women in different cultures do not share the same perception of ideal body weight. Cogan, Bhalla, Sefa-Dedeh, and Rothblum (1996) looked at cross-cultural trends in attitudes toward obesity and thinness and how they affect dieting patterns in young women from the United States and from Ghana. Ghanaian women, compared with American women, rated larger body sizes as

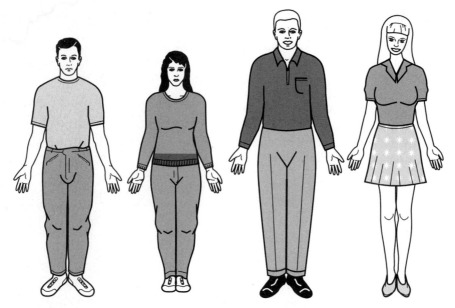

FIGURE 13.5 Comparison of life-size Barbie and Ken to their normally proportioned human counterparts. (Based on Brownell & Napolitano, 1995)

ideal for both sexes. American women scored higher on measures of eating restraint and eating-disordered behavior, and perceived the experience of being overweight as interfering with social acceptance. A disturbing trend indicates that a greater drive for thinness is emerging among young African-American girls in the United States in relation to increased peer criticism about weight and appearance (Striegel-Moore, Schreiber, Pike, Wilfley, & Rodin, 1995). The forces of culture, combined with gender-based expectations, are powerful determinants of one's perception of ideal body size and associated eating and dieting patterns.

The finding that the weight of Miss America contestants since the 1950s has been falling below healthy norms for adult females (Garfinkel & Garner, 1982; Wiseman, Gray, Mosimann, & Ahrens, 1992) illustrates the pressures of social conformity. To prove that children are exposed to distorted images that affect their self-appraisals, Brownell and Napolitano (1995) calculated the changes necessary for a young, healthy adult woman and man to attain the same body proportions as Barbie and Ken dolls (see Figure 13.5). On average, the female would have to grow 2 feet taller, add 5 inches to her chest, and lose 6 inches from her waist; the male would have to grow 20 inches taller and add 10 inches to his waist and 11 inches to his chest. As the researchers aptly surmise, if children and younger adolescents use such models as standards, discontent and despair are likely outcomes.

Fortunately, these sociocultural patterns may be gradually shifting toward more healthy norms of eating behaviors and lifestyle choices. Eating disorder symp-

toms, dieting, and body dissatisfaction declined significantly on college campuses between 1982 and 1992 (Heatherton, Nichols, Mahamedi, & Keel, 1995). The increase in public health advertisements, talk shows and television shows devoted to discussions of eating disorders and to healthy lifestyles, and noted celebrity sufferers (Princess Diana) and celebrity deaths (Karen Carpenter) may be responsible for raising awareness and prevention of these various disorders and dieting patterns (Heatherton et al., 1995). Perhaps as a further result of these awareness efforts, sociocultural messages about the importance of proper nutrition and body satisfaction are changing as well.

Family Influences. Researchers and clinicians have placed considerable importance on the role of the family, and parental psychopathology in particular, in considering causes of eating disorders. They have argued convincingly that alliances, conflicts, or interactional patterns within a family may play a causal role in the development of eating disorders among some individuals (Minuchin, Rosman, & Baker, 1978; Selvini Palazzoli, 1974). Accordingly, a teen's eating disorder may be functional in that it directs attention away from basic conflicts in the family, such as marital discord, to the teen's more obvious (symptomatic) problem.

Because of the importance of the family in shaping a young adolescent's values, it is understandable that family processes may contribute to an overemphasis on weight and dietary control. For example, a mother who is critical of her daughter's weight or who diets frequently herself and encourages her daughter to diet may

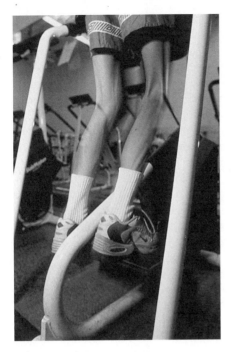

Excessive exercise can become a compulsion for persons suffering from anorexia nervosa.

unintentionally become a coconspirator in the development of an eating disorder (Attie & Brooks-Gunn, 1989; Fairburn, 1994; Pike & Rodin, 1991). Similarly, parents who drink heavily or abuse drugs (Garfinkel et al., 1995) or who are often absent, uninterested, demanding, or critical (Fairburn, 1994) may lay the groundwork for the later emergence of bulimia and other disorders in their children. Parents who deny the significance of severe marital distress by pretending their relationships are positive and healthy also may deny the effect this has on their children, especially if avoidance diverts attention from their troubled marriages (Humphrey, 1988).

In addition to general family dynamics, childhood obesity, problems in parent-child relations, and child sexual abuse have gained attention as possible contributors to eating disorders in adolescence. In a 10-year follow-up of children ages 6 to 12 who had received prior treatment for obesity, L. H. Epstein, Klein, and Wisniewski (in press) found the occurrence of bulimia to be 6% among the girls, a two- to sixfold increase over the rate in the general population. Thus, a childhood pattern of being overweight may make it more difficult during adolescence and adulthood to achieve or maintain the culturally valued degree of thinness, and the individual may engage in the more extreme weight-control measures that may lead to an eating disorder. Similarly, families of adolescents with eating disorders show higher incidents of negative, contradictory communication and less trust and helping behavior. For example, inappropriate parental pressure was significantly

greater for girls with eating disorders even when compared with girls with psychiatric disorders (as well as healthy controls) (Horesh, Apter, & Ishal, 1996). The specific role of such patterns in the etiology or course of this disorder remains unclear, however (Wonderlich, 1992).

Early clinical suspicions that child sexual abuse could be an underlying cause of bulimia among some individuals led to several recent investigations of the issue, but the connection remains uncertain. Epidemiological studies of a general population sample revealed that women with bulimia were about 3 times more likely to have been sexually abused as children than were women without the disorder (35% and 12.5%, respectively) (Garfinkel et al., 1995). Other studies, however, have not found a higher prevalence of childhood sexual abuse specific to eating disorders (Pope, Mangweth, Negrao, Hudson, & Cordas, 1994; Rorty, Yager, & Rossotto, 1994). An explanation for these inconsistent findings is suggested by a study of a community sample of young women with bulimia who had not been referred for treatment, and who were compared with matched normal controls and psychiatric controls. Childhood sexual abuse was shown to be a *general* risk factor for psychopathology but not a *specific* risk factor for bulimia, because it was a common feature in the background of individuals with bulimia as well as those with other psychiatric disorders (Fairburn, 1994). Presumably, childhood sexual abuse is associated with many undesirable adolescent and adult outcomes, of which eating disorders are prominent. (These issues are discussed further in Chapter 14.)

The importance of family factors has led to valuable treatment approaches, as we will see later on. Nonetheless, family factors must be considered in conjunction with individual and sociocultural factors to explain why the particular features of eating disorders emerge in some families with such dynamics but not others.

Psychological Dimension

Understanding the role of psychological processes in the expression of eating disorders requires keeping in mind the powerful social and cultural forces noted above. External pressures to look thin and be in control of one's weight and appearance interact with certain psychological characteristics to increase the risk of an eating disorder, especially during important developmental transitions. This is a complex, interactive process embedded in multiple layers of biological, familial, personality, and environmental factors. Understandably, this complexity makes causal connections difficult to pinpoint.

Consideration of the psychological dimensions related to eating disorders grew out of the pioneering efforts of Hilda Bruch (1962, 1973), who was the first to propose that self-starvation among persons with anorexia was related to their struggle for autonomy, competence, control, and self-respect. She linked this struggle most closely to parental failure to recognize and confirm their child's emerging independent needs, which sets in motion further confusion that can lead to the principal symptoms of anorexia: disturbance in body image; inability to recognize and respond to internal sensations such as hunger and satiety, and to emotions; and all-pervasive feelings of ineffectiveness and loss of self-control. Her early work set the stage for the cognitive-behavioral interventions used today. She proposed gradual but deliberate relabeling of misconceptions and errors in thinking resulting from faulty developmental experiences, and encouraged patients to learn healthy ways of expressing their thoughts and feelings in a genuine and more direct fashion (Silverman, 1997).

Arthur Crisp, another pioneer in the understanding and treatment of eating disorders, considers anorexia to be a type of phobic avoidance disorder in which the phobic objects are normal adult body weight and shape. He describes this fear metaphorically as a flight from growth (Crisp, 1997). As a result of family and cultural influences, a young female may begin to perceive herself as being fat as she reaches puberty and starts to change into a more adult size and weight. In response, she tries to pursue and maintain her prepubertal weight as a way of avoiding the unwelcome aspects of her own growth. This pursuit becomes a vicious cycle, of course, because trying to maintain one's prepubertal body weight meets powerful biological resistance, so she continues her pursuit of weight loss as "insurance" against these unrelenting forces of nature. In effect, a person with anorexia fears loss of control over her attempts to avoid growth, which often translates into a fear of weight gain above 95 to 100 pounds. Like Hilda Bruch's insights, this explanation has led to important treatment efforts.

Young persons with anorexia are clinically described as being obsessive and rigid, showing emotional restraint, preferring the familiar, having a high need for approval, and showing poor adaptability to change (Casper, Hedeker, & McClough, 1992). The psychological dimensions underlying such clinical features can be collapsed into a triad of personality features: avoidance of harm, low novelty seeking, and reward dependence (Strober, 1991). Such features render persons vulnerable to developmental events, like puberty, that disrupt their carefully maintained sense of self. These dimensions help explain the finding that about one-third of persons with anorexia seeking treatment receive a comorbid diagnosis involving one or more Axis II personality disorders, the most common being compulsive and avoidant personality (Herzog, Keller, Sacks, Yeh, & Lavori, 1992).

Depression and anxiety are cofeatures of eating disorders, usually emerging close to the development of the disorder (Herzog et al., 1992). A study of all known Swedish 16-year-olds with anorexia revealed that only 6% (compared with 75% of matched age-mates) had *not* been depressed at some time before or after the onset of anorexia. Depression, however, was more likely to occur *following* the onset of the eating disorder (Rastam, 1992), suggesting that it may be a consequence of the failed attempts to manage stress and developmental changes. A personality characteristic known as *perfectionism* may be a common link between depression and eating disorders. Persons who are high on the need for perfectionism and who also experience high levels of daily stress are more likely to exhibit symptoms of depression (Hewitt & Flett, 1993). Similarly, individuals who score high on perfectionism and also perceive themselves as being overweight have a greater risk of bulimic symptoms (Joiner, Heatherton, Rudd, & Schmidt, 1997). Simply stated, a discrepancy between one's actual self (in this case, perceived weight) and ideal self (a strive toward perfectionism) increases the likelihood of bulimic symptoms, especially among women (Joiner et al., 1997).

The adolescent with bulimia is likely to exhibit a pattern of personality characteristics involving mood swings or fluctuations and poor impulse control (C. Johnson & Connors, 1987). In the study by Garfinkel et al. (1995) noted previously, persons with bulimia had a threefold increase in the lifetime occurrence of major depression, and at least a doubling of the rate for anxiety disorders. Specific phobias, agoraphobia, panic disorder, generalized anxiety disorder, and alcohol dependence were all more elevated among bulimic individuals than among nonbulimic community members. Moreover, abuse of alcohol or stimulants to control appetite is also present in about one-third of the clinical samples of adolescents with bulimia (APA, 1994) and about 10% of community samples of high school students who meet criteria for bulimia (Timmerman, Wells, & Chen, 1990). In addition to major depression, some patients with bulimia (less than 10%) fit criteria for Axis II personality disorders, such as borderline, histrionic, or avoidant personality (Herzog et al., 1992).

Recently, a seasonal pattern of affect disturbance has been identified among some individuals with bulimia. In reports from 60 outpatients, Lam, Goldner, and Grewal (1996) found two seasonal peaks in which binge-purge symptoms worsen: a large peak of about one-third of patients who binge and purge the most in winter, and a smaller peak of about one-fifth who suffer more in the summer months. These studies and others like it raise the possibility of a common diathesis (a similar genetic predisposition) of bulimia and major affective disorders, which expresses itself according to environmental circumstances, such as seasonal changes in light and degree of psychosocial stress.

Let's look at a practical example of how the preceding information can be put into dynamic perspective. The adolescent with bulimia or anorexia feels her efforts to restrict her diet and lose weight are ways of gaining control over her life and of becoming a better person, beliefs that were formed in childhood and become operational when she faces the challenges of early adolescence. What develops into the rigidity of anorexia or the battle for control of bulimia may start out as a moderate diet. A teenager may unwittingly begin a dangerous eating pattern because of dissatisfaction with body weight and shape, and her efforts initially are rewarded by weight loss and a sense of greater control and self-worth, such as former gymnast Erica Stokes describes in Box 13.2. The transition from dieting to an eating disorder may be prompted by the extra attention from peers for what appears to be dramatic willpower and weight loss. Powerful psychological needs may therefore be at the root of many eating disorders, because the disorder itself is a way of dealing with powerful feelings that the person otherwise does not know how to express or resolve, especially in relation to the turmoil of adolescence (Maloney & Kranz, 1991). This dynamic process accounting for the many determinants of eating disorders is depicted visually in Figure 13.6.

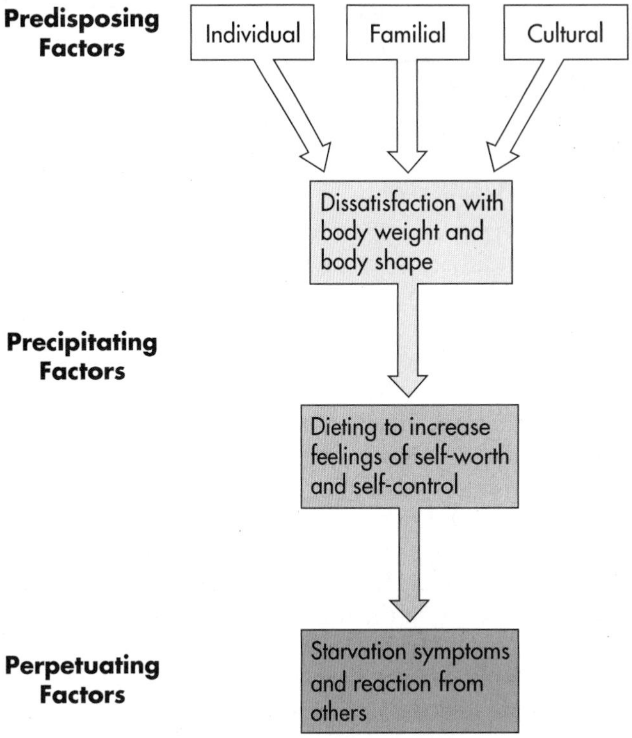

FIGURE 13.6 A dynamic perspective on the determinants of eating disorders. (Adapted from Garner, 1993b)

Because of recent high-profile cases of gymnasts and other performers with eating disorders, a common misunderstanding is that competitive sports and performing arts are to blame for such problems. Both types of activities emphasize appearance, so involvement in them has been often cited as a risk factor for developing an eating disorder because of the pressure to be thin (Owens & Slade, 1987). Recent findings cast some doubt on the strength of this relationship, however. The most parsimonious explanation accounting for the noted association may be the previously mentioned psychological and social factors. French, Ferry, Leon, and Fulkerson (1994) found among their sample of 1494 adolescents that sports participation was a weak predictor of symptoms of eating disorders. The psychological, social, and environmental variables we have reviewed, such as self-esteem and the pressure to dress and behave in a certain manner, explain a larger proportion of the variance for being at risk than do dietary and physical activity variables. Taub and Blinde (1994) likewise found no difference between female athletes and nonathletes among their sample of 650 high school females (of whom two-thirds were engaged in athletic activities); yet they did find that the responses *of one in every five* students in their total sample reflected disturbed eating patterns, regardless of athletic involvement. Once again, these findings confirm the influence of social pressures on

Box 13.2
Success—At What Price?

Former gymnast Erica Stokes clearly remembers the first time she threw up. The 14-year-old Olympic hopeful and National Team member had just eaten lunch and was feeling, as usual, fat. Living and training year-round at an elite gymnast camp in Houston, she was under constant pressure to maintain her tiny 4-foot 10-inch, 90-pound frame. Food was the enemy. And today, she decided on a solution to beat the foe. She marched into the bathroom and threw up. She didn't use her fingers—just her will and her strong stomach muscles to force out the food.

"My whole insides burned, it was the worst feeling," she remembers. "But afterwards, there was a sense of relief. I felt my stomach go down a little bit."

This started for Erica what was to be a vicious 2-year cycle of eating—sometimes bingeing—then vomiting. "It was my way of maintaining the weight," she reflected. It was also her way of succeeding—and surviving—in an obsessively weight-conscious sport where only the very few, and the very thin, have a shot at becoming a star.

Source: A. Bell, 1996.

eating behavior and appearance, especially during early- to mid-adolescence.

TREATMENTS FOR ANOREXIA AND BULIMIA

The difficulty lies not in the new ideas but in escaping the old.

—John Maynard Keynes

Treatment methods for major eating disorders have improved a great deal since attempts in the 1930s to treat anorexia through Freudian psychoanalysis. It was then believed that persons with anorexia refused to eat because of fixated unconscious conflicts regarding oral-sadistic fears, oral impregnation, and primitive fantasies (Foreyt & McGavin, 1989), with obesity being viewed as a sort of pregnancy. Effective treatment of the disorder required uncovering the fears through insight into emotional traumas. It is now recognized that treatment usually involves considerably more than insight and should begin as soon as possible.

Today's treatment options, especially psychological interventions, are leading to more and more successful outcomes for adolescents and adults with eating disorders. For anorexia, psychologically based therapies often include other family members, and draw from advances in cognitive-behavioral therapy (CBT) as well as more traditional person- and family-centered psychotherapy (Garner & Needleman, 1997). For bulimia, cognitive-behavioral approaches have shown considerable benefit (Compas, Haaga, Keefe, Leitenberg, & Williams, 1998; Dare & Eisler, 1997). In many cases these psychological interventions are delivered in conjunction with hospitalization or medical supervision. Pharmacological treatments are also gaining recognition, especially if combined with cognitive-behavioral treatments aimed specifically at the attitudes, beliefs, and behaviors supporting dieting, binge eating, or purging.

The first major treatment consideration is whether or not a person with an eating disorder is in sufficient medical danger to require hospitalization. Conditions warranting hospitalization include excessive and rapid weight loss, serious metabolic disturbances, clinical depression or risk of suicide, severe binge eating and purging, and psychosis (NIMH, 1994). In the majority of cases, inpatient treatment can be brief, as long as psychological counseling and outpatient psychotherapy are made available. In more severe cases, a patient must remain in the hospital for weeks or months to reach at least 90% of her expected weight (Garner & Needleman, 1997).

Pharmacological

Because of the strong association between anorexia and bulimia and the affective disorders, several psychotropic drugs have been used for treatment purposes, including neuroleptics, tricyclic antidepressants, monamine oxidase inhibitors, and serotonin-reuptake inhibitors. The serotonin-reuptake inhibitor *fluoxetine* (Prozac) has become a common drug for treating these eating disorders, and for some forms of obesity. The weight-loss benefits of this drug were discovered serendipitously during clinical trials of its ability to regulate mood. It was believed that people with obesity load up on carbohydrates to elevate mood and that a sense of well-being could be achieved artificially by regulating serotonin levels.

To date, however, no drug has proved useful or effective for treating symptoms of anorexia; none has consistently improved long-term weight maintenance, changed a distorted self-image, or prevented relapse (Craighead & Agras, 1991; Garner & Needleman, 1997; Hoffman & Halmi, 1993; W. G. Johnson, Tsoh, & Vanrado, 1996). In contrast, there is a consensus that antidepressants have a useful role in the treatment of bulimia, but probably not as the initial treatment of choice (Compas et al., 1998; W. G. Johnson et al., 1996). Persons with bulimia may respond favorably to antidepressants and serotonin-reuptake inhibitors, so long as they are continued for 6 months or so and are accompanied by psychosocial treatments with proven effectiveness, as described below (Agras et al., 1994; Leitenberg et al., 1994; Wood, 1993). Although drug therapy has its use, especially in cases that are not responding to psychological therapy, CBT remains a more effective choice than medication alone (Goldstein et al., 1995; W. G. Johnson et al., 1996).

Psychosocial

The presence of both emotional and physiological problems in eating disorders requires a comprehensive treatment plan. Ideally, a treatment team consisting of an internist, a nutritionist, a psychotherapist, and a psychopharmacologist will work together in all the aspects of the disorder that can threaten recovery or cure. Once an eating disorder has been diagnosed and any other illness has been medically ruled out, the clinician determines whether the individual can be treated as an outpatient. Family engagement then may become important, both to assist family members in managing their fears and worries as well as to enlist their cooperation. For younger patients, family involvement is often necessary and practical, since parents are responsible for their child's well-being and can offer important directives and guidance that increase successful treatment (Dare & Eisler, 1997). In some cases, resolution of family problems like those we mentioned earlier, such as parental psychopathology, family isolation, and a poor parent-child relationship, are crucial to the recovery from an eating disorder. Convincingly, recovered patients consider the resolution of family and interpersonal problems as pivotal to their recovery (Hsu, Crisp, & Challender, 1992).

Anorexia. The etiology and course of anorexia result in a disorder that is less responsive to treatment than bulimia; nevertheless, inroads are certainly being made. The initial phase of treatment must involve the restoration of weight, which may require inpatient hospitalization as a precaution against medical complications that might arise (Baran, Weltzin, & Kaye, 1995). But restoring weight may be the easier part of the process. Many patients regain weight while in the hospital, but the pattern of weight loss and distorted beliefs continues once they are released from the hospital, unless careful attention is paid to family and individual factors that led to the overemphasis on control of eating in the first place.

Given its critical importance, what should psychosocial therapy involve for those with anorexia? Whereas bulimia has undergone many clinical treatment trials that have resulted in a clear understanding of what methods work best, fewer studies have been conducted with anorexic patients. This is likely due to the much lower prevalence of the disorder, as well as the difficulty of randomly assigning patients with life-threatening disorders to control group conditions. An alternative to a treatment–control group comparison is to assign patients to two different treatment conditions and compare their relative effectiveness. Robin, Siegel, and Moye (1995) offer an excellent example of such a strategy. Behavioral family systems therapy (BFST) was compared with ego-oriented individual therapy (EOIT) over a 16-month treatment regimen with 22 adolescents with anorexia. BFST emphasized parental control over eating, cognitive restructuring, and problem-solving communication training, whereas EOIT emphasized building ego strength, adolescent autonomy, and insight. Both treatments led to improvements in body mass and restoration of menstruation, and produced significant reductions in negative communication and parent-adolescent conflict. Importantly, these changes were maintained 1 year later, a critical period for recovery.

As mentioned, family therapy is the initial treatment of choice for persons with anorexia who are younger and living at home. The facade of togetherness expressed by family members of girls with anorexia is often seen by clinicians as an attempt to disguise covert or overt aggression and avoid conflict. Family-based interventions, therefore, are often required to restore healthy communication patterns (Shugar & Krueger, 1995). By involving the whole family, therapists can attend to the family's attitudes toward body shape and body image that, to an adolescent, can be perceived as subtle but critical judgments. Once weight is restored to within acceptable levels and family support becomes more available, cognitive-behavioral methods similar to those described previously can focus more specifically on the patient's rigid beliefs, self-esteem, and self-control processes.

Family therapy does not necessarily mean that all family members are seen at the same time (conjoint family therapy); sometimes seeing family members separately is the best approach. For instance, instead of challenging family members' negative interaction patterns, such as conflict avoidance and alliances (similar to the early work of Minuchin et al., 1978), the therapist can encourage parents to take control of their adolescent's eating patterns in an effort to prevent hospital admission, can raise the parents' morale, and can engage parents in further therapy. Focusing on the nature of the illness and its treatment avoids further criticizing the child and placing blame on family members as well (Dare & Eisler, 1997). Working with parents separately from their teenaged daughters (which of course makes it impossible to challenge interaction patterns and alliances) has been shown to be as effective as conjoint methods, and even more beneficial for families who had high levels of critisism and hostility (Le Grange, Eisler, Dare, & Russell, 1992; Eisler et al., 1998).

Similar findings have been shown in studies that combine individual outpatient psychotherapy with family therapy. Three months of outpatient individual and family psychotherapy sessions were as effective as intensive inpatient treatment at one-year follow-up on measures of weight gain, return of menses, and key psychological variables (Crisp et at., 1991). Two years later, the individually treated outpatient population was still doing especially well (Gowers, Norton, Halek, & Crisp, 1994).

Bulimia. The most effective current therapies for bulimia involve CBT delivered individually or involving the family unit (Fairburn, Jones, Peveler, Hope, & O'Connor, 1993; Schlundt & Johnson, 1990). Cognitive-behavioral therapists change eating behaviors by rewarding or modeling appropriate behaviors, and help patients change distorted or rigid thinking patterns that may contribute to their obsession. CBT has become the standard treatment for bulimia nervosa, and forms the theoretical base for much of the treatment for anorexia as well (Garner & Needleman, 1997). This method is the treatment of choice for patients whose age does not mandate family therapy, and whose symptoms are moderate to severe.

The clinical application of CBT has been expanded to address specific cues that trigger the urge to binge or to vomit, as well as to address the underlying interpersonal issues that bother some patients. The goals of CBT are to modify abnormal cognitions regarding the importance of body shape and weight, and replace efforts at dietary restraint and purging with more normal eating and activity patterns (W. G. Johnson et al., 1996). CBT for treatment of bulimia includes several components (Fairburn, Marcus, & Wilson, 1993). First, patients are taught to self-monitor their food intake and bingeing and purging episodes, as well as any thoughts and feelings that trigger these episodes. This is combined with regular weighing; specific recommendations on how to achieve desired goals, such as the introduction of avoided foods and meal planning, designed to normalize eating behavior and curb restrictive dieting; cognitive restructuring aimed at habitual reasoning errors and underlying assumptions that are relevant to the development and maintenance of the eating disorder; and regular review and revision of these procedures to prevent relapse.

Some evidence indicates that the effectiveness of standard CBT can be improved by adding components. One approach is to offer interpersonal therapy that addresses situational and personal issues contributing to the development and maintenance of the disorder. In a treatment study in which patients were randomly assigned to receive behavior therapy, CBT, or interpersonal therapy, those who received either CBT or interpersonal therapy showed similar improvements over the course of the 1- and 6-year follow-ups (Fairburn et al., 1993, 1995). Another modification of CBT is a method known as **exposure plus response prevention (ERP)**, which is sometimes used to prevent self-induced vomiting (Rosen & Leitenberg, 1985). This is a therapist-assisted, in-session exposure treatment used in cases where patients cannot comply with instructions to eat forbidden foods or when even small meals lead to purging. Patients are instructed to eat their typical binge foods to the point at which they would ordinarily induce vomiting. The therapist then guides the patient in ways to resist vomiting and to cope with the anxiety they experience. Although the addition of ERP to CBT has received some support (Leitenberg, Rosen, Gross, Nudelman, & Vara, 1988), other studies have not found an added benefit of ERP (Wilson, Eldredge, Smith, & Niles, 1991). Thus, the value of ERP in the treatment of bulimia is currently unknown. A related exposure method is to focus on the cues that trigger binge eating rather than vomiting. The

patient eats a small amount of forbidden food, which would typically lead to uncontrolled overeating; she is then guided by the therapist in preventing a subsequent binge (Jansen, Broekmate, & Heymans, 1992).

Treatment of bulimia has progressed rapidly over the course of two decades, and CBT has emerged as a strong treatment of choice for this disorder (Compas et al., 1998). Nevertheless, on average, just over half (55%) of persons with bulimia who are treated with CBT remain in complete remission at follow-up (Agras, 1991). Even though the success of psychological interventions for bulimia and related forms of eating disorders is exemplary, considerable room for improvement still exists.

SUMMARY

Development of Eating Patterns

1. Troublesome eating habits are common among children. Normal concerns about weight and appearance can become unduly influenced by parents and peers, sometimes resulting in eating disturbances.

2. Several physical and psychological factors, linked to early eating problems, constitute a risk pattern for the development of eating disorders. These risk factors are connected to adolescent development and the emergence of unhealthy dieting patterns.

3. Normal patterns of eating and growth, as well as eating disorders, are influenced by the interaction of both biological and psychological processes.

Childhood Disorders

4. Pica refers to eating inedible substances. It affects mostly infants, toddlers, and some children with mental retardation.

5. Rumination disorder involves regurgitating and reswallowing food. It is relatively rare and affects mostly younger children.

6. Feeding disorder of infancy or early childhood is denoted by a sudden or rapid deceleration of weight gain and a disruption in major developmental milestones. The disorder can have serious consequences.

7. Feeding disorder of early childhood can lead to or result from failure to thrive, characterized by weight below the 5th percentile for age. Psychosocial dwarfism applies to severe growth disturbances that occur in children of preschool age or older.

8. Obesity, body weight greater than 20% above normal for height and age, poses a risk for unhealthy dieting patterns, chronic health problems, and later-onset eating disorders.

9. The causes for eating disorders and related conditions during childhood include genetic predisposition (especially for obesity), as well as inadequate parental care and nurturance.

Adolescent Disorders

10. Anorexia nervosa is characterized by a refusal to maintain body weight, an intense fear of gaining weight or becoming fat, a distorted body image, and amenorrhea.

11. Bulimia nervosa involves recurrent episodes of binge eating, followed by an effort to compensate by self-induced vomiting or other means. Individuals with bulimia are also unduly influenced by body shape and weight, and are obsessed with food.

Prevalence and Development of Anorexia and Bulimia

12. Anorexia affects 0.5% to 1.0% of the population and usually strikes during adolescence (ages 14 to 18). Bulimia affects 1% to 3% of mostly older adolescents. If untreated, both disorders can become chronic and pose serious threats to health.

Causes of Anorexia and Bulimia

13. Biological factors do not precipitate eating disorders, but their effects on appetite, mood, perception, and energy regulation contribute to the maintenance of the disorder.

14. Features of Western culture and family life play a significant causal role in eating disorders. Emphasis on dieting and physical appearance can lead to a drive for thinness.

15. The psychological dimensions associated with anorexia can be described in terms of a triad of personality features: avoidance of harm, low novelty seeking, and reward dependence. Bulimia is associated with mood swings and poor impulse control.

Treatments for Anorexia and Bulimia

16. Psychosocial treatments for anorexia emphasize the importance of changes in family communication patterns. Recovery can occur, but ongoing treatment is essential.

17. Psychosocial and pharmacological treatments for bulimia are successful for the majority. Most beneficial are cognitive-behavioral treatments that focus on the attitudes, beliefs, and behaviors supporting dieting, binge eating, or purging.

KEY TERMS

anorexia nervosa, 491
bulimia nervosa, 491
metabolic rate, 496
pica, 497
rumination disorder, 499
feeding disorder of infancy or early childhood, 500
failure to thrive, 501
psychosocial dwarfism, 502
childhood obesity, 503
restricting, 508
binge, 509
purging, 509
compensatory behavior, 509
drive for thinness, 511
norepinephrine, 514
serotonin, 514
vasopressin, 514
exposure plus response prevention (ERP), 522

Child Abuse and Neglect

Peace in society depends upon peace in the family.
—Augustine

Mary Ellen's Legacy

She is a bright little girl, with features indicating unusual mental capacity, but with a care-worn, stunted, and prematurely old look. Her apparent condition of health, as well as her scanty wardrobe, indicated that no change of custody or condition could be much for the worse.

. . . On her examination [in court] the child made a statement as follows: ". . . I don't know how old I am. . . . I have never had but one pair of shoes, but I cannot recollect when that was. I have had no shoes or stockings on this winter. . . . I am never allowed to play with any children, or to have any company whatever. Mamma has been in the habit of whipping and beating me almost every day. She used to whip me with a twisted whip—a raw hide. The whip always left a black and blue mark on my body. I have now the black and blue marks on my head which were made by mamma, and also a cut on the left side of my forehead which was made by a pair of scissors. She struck me with the scissors and cut me; I have no recollection of ever having been kissed by any one. . . . I have never been taken on my mamma's lap and caressed or petted. . . . I do not know for what I was whipped—momma never said anything to me when she whipped me." (*New York Times*, April 10, 1874)

The heart-breaking and tragic story of Mary Ellen led to the formation of the New York Society for the Preven-

tion of Cruelty to Children in the winter of 1874, when citizens discovered that animals were protected from mistreatment, but children were not. Sadly, it took another 100 years before legislation was passed that clearly defined and mandated the reporting of child abuse and neglect, launching new efforts to identify and assist abused and neglected children in North America. Despite these efforts, child abuse and neglect remain one of the most common causes of nonaccidental child deaths, as Nadine's sorrowful story reveals:

Nadine: What Went Wrong?

Prison was only the last stop on Carla Lockwood's miserable family journey, one that over the years brought the troubled mother and her children into contact with far more institutions than just the city's child welfare agency. Before her daughter, Nadine, 4, was found starved to death last week, there were public schools, hospitals and welfare offices, among other social-service agencies, that touched the family. . . . In the end, the mix of bad fortune and good intentions, blessings, mistakes and a mother's apparent act of malice, did not prevent Nadine from dying. (Sexton, *The New York Times*, Sept. 5, 1996)

Reports of abuse and neglect have doubled in the United States in less than a decade—from 1.4 million children in 1986 to 2.8 million in 1993—and the lives of some children, like Nadine, end tragically and without purpose. Unfortunately, Nadine is not alone in her tragic end—in fact, about 1600 children in the United States die each year at the hands of their parents (Sedlak & Broadhurst, 1996).

Words hit as hard as a fist.

"You're pathetic. You can't do anything right!"

"You disgust me! Just shut up!"

"Hey stupid! Don't you know how to listen."

"Get outta here! I'm sick of looking at your face."

"You're more trouble than you're worth."

"Why don't you go find some other place to live!"

"I wish you were never born."

Children believe what their parents tell them. Next time, stop and listen to what you're saying. You might not believe your ears.

Take time out. Don't take it out on your kid.

 Write: National Committee for Prevention of Child Abuse, Box 2866E, Chicago, Illinois 60690

This dramatic rise in the incidence of child abuse and neglect over the past decade has reached such startling proportions that the U.S. Advisory Board on Child Abuse and Neglect (1990) labeled it a national epidemic. In North America, before they grow up, about one in every five girls and one in nine boys will experience some form of sexual abuse (Finkelhor, 1994; Finkelhor, Hotaling, Lewis, & Smith, 1990), and each year about one of every ten children are the victims of severe physical violence by a parent or other care-giver (Straus & Gelles, 1986). Countless other children suffer the effects of emotional abuse and neglect, which, like physical and sexual abuse, can cause known harm to their psychological development.

Violence against children and other family members has been viewed as a private matter for generations, and its significance continues to be poorly acknowledged. Until very recently, violence against members of one's own family was considered in the eyes of the law to be less consequential, less damaging, and less worthy of society's serious attention than was violence between strangers. Today we know better: Family violence occurs in numerous forms, from mild acts such as frightening or yelling at children, to severe acts like assaulting with fists and weapons. Violence and abuse, moreover, wax and wane in a cyclical manner that creates tension and fear in children, forcing them to cope with harsh realities and fearful demands (Jaffe, Lemon, Sandler, & D. A. Wolfe, 1996).

We devote an entire chapter to maltreatment because severe disturbances in the parent-child relationship or the family are common causes of abnormal child development (Garmezy, 1983). This chapter departs from the traditional taxonomic approach to abnormal child psychology, and considers how disturbed child-rearing environments or unsafe communities play an important role in abnormal development during childhood and adolescence.

Child maltreatment is a generic term referring to four primary acts: physical abuse, neglect, sexual abuse, and emotional abuse. Maltreatment can take many forms, including acts experienced by the majority of children, such as corporal punishment, sibling violence, and peer assault, as well as acts experienced by a significant minority, such as physical abuse (Finkelhor & Dziuba-Leatherman, 1994). It cuts across all lines of gender, national origin, language, religion, age, ethnicity, disability, and sexual orientation.

Child abuse and neglect have considerable psychological importance, because they occur within ongoing relationships that are expected to be protective, supportive, and nurturing. Children from abusive and neglectful families grow up in environments that fail to provide consistent and appropriate opportunities that guide development; instead, these children are placed in jeopardy of physical and emotional harm (D. A. Wolfe & Jaffe, 1991). Yet, their ties to their families—even to the abuser—are very important, so child victims may feel torn between a sense of loyalty and a sense of fear and apprehension. A child victim of sexual abuse expressed it this way: "I was afraid. When it happened, [my father] behaved as if it never happened—he made me doubt myself. I was afraid that I would embarrass my father [the abuser] and be a shame to his family" (Sas et al., 1993, p. 68). Because children are dependent on the people who harm or neglect them, they face other paradoxical dilemmas as well (Report of the American Psychological Association, 1996):

❖ *The victim wants to stop the violence but also longs to belong to a family.* Loyalty and strong emotional

ties to the abuser are powerful opponents to the victim's desire to be safe and protected.

❖ *Affection and attention may coexist with violence and abuse.* A recurring cycle may begin, whereby mounting tension characterized by fear and anticipation ultimately gives way to more abusive behavior. This may be followed by a period of reconciliation, with increased affection and attention. Children are always hopeful that the abuse will not recur.

❖ *The intensity of the violence tends to increase over time, although in some cases physical violence may decrease or even stop altogether.* Abusive behavior may vary throughout the relationship, taking verbal, sexual, emotional, or physical forms, but the adult's abuse of power and control remains the central issue.

As a result of increased recognition of these psychological effects, a significant shift is under way in how child maltreatment is defined and in how its effects are studied. In the past, abuse was defined primarily by visible physical injuries. However, today we recognize that physical injuries are only one of many consequences. Maltreatment can also damage individuals' developing relations with others and their fundamental sense of safety and self-esteem.

We begin our discussion of child abuse and neglect by considering the role of the family in children's healthy socialization, and how boundaries between appropriate and inappropriate actions toward children need to be more clear and well-established.

PERSPECTIVES ON CHILD-REARING AND MALTREATMENT

Society's view of child-rearing and intolerance of abuse and neglect has evolved over a very short period of time. Child abuse has always existed, and most likely was even more commonplace in previous generations than it is today (Radbill, 1974), but it was seldom identified as a problem or concern. For generations, children were viewed as the exclusive property and responsibility of their parents. This right was unchallenged by any countermovement to seek more humane treatment for children up until the time of Mary Ellen, just over 100 years ago.

Values and laws governing the treatment and care of children have always been up to the discretion of adults, and harsh forms of discipline have for some time been considered part of parental rights and responsibilities.

Children in Tudor England were expected to recite a penitential verse at the end of each day:

> *If I lie, backbite, or steal*
> *If I curse, scorne, mock, or swear,*
> *If I chide, fight, strive, or threat*
> *Then I am worthy to be beat.*
> *Good mother or mistress of mine*
> *If any of these nine*
> *I trespass to your knowledge*
> *With a new rod and a fine*
> *Early naked before I dine*
> *Amend me with a scourging.*
> (Powell, 1917, pp. 109–110)

Massachusetts' Stubborn Child Act of 1654 gave the strong patriarchal view of children as possessions an absurd status: Parents (fathers, actually) could petition a magistrate to put their child to death if he or she was deemed stubborn or rebellious (Radbill, 1974). Although no sentences were carried out, the implications of such a prerogative no doubt shaped parents' attitudes and behavior toward their children. Sadly, this view of children as personal property to be managed however the parent wishes is still echoed by parents who proclaim, "They're my kids, and I'll treat them any way I see fit!"

Children, because of their social and psychological immaturity, are highly dependent on adults, which creates a vulnerability for **victimization** (Finkelhor & Dziuba-Leatherman, 1994). Thus, we have to balance parental rights and the rights of children. As parents ourselves, we recognize that children require considerable direction and control, and sometimes behave in ways that challenge our decisions and interfere with our plans. If you've not experienced this yourself, ask a parent you know if you can take their young child grocery shopping! Adults who are ill-prepared for the vital and challenging role of being parents may rely heavily on child-rearing methods from their own childhood, without question or modification. Although this approach to parenting is natural and often appropriate, it can also perpetuate undesirable child-rearing methods, such as physical coercion, verbal threats, and neglect of the child's needs (D. A. Wolfe, 1999).

Family Context

It is difficult to talk about child abuse and neglect without talking about the importance of families. Family relations are the earliest and most enduring social relationships, and they significantly affect a child's competence, resilience, and sense of well-being. For most of us, family influences are positive and beneficial, offering a primary source of support and nurturance that sets the stage for lifetime patterns of relationships and well-being. But for others, family events and experiences are profoundly negative and harmful, providing the context for some of the most severe violence in society (Gelles & Straus, 1988). Understanding the dire effects of abuse and neglect on the mental health of children and adults must begin with a discussion of what children should expect from a healthy family environment.

Healthy Families. For healthy development, children need a care-giving environment that balances their need for control and direction, or "demandingness," with their need for stimulation and sensitivity, or "responsiveness" (Maccoby & Martin, 1983). Determinants of healthy parent-child relationships and family roles derived from these two primary developmental needs include:

❖ adequate knowledge of child development and expectations, including knowledge of children's normal sexual development and experimentation
❖ adequate skill in coping with stress related to caring for small children, and ways to enhance child development through proper stimulation and attention
❖ opportunities to develop normal parent-child attachment and early patterns of communication
❖ adequate parental knowledge of home management, including basic financial planning, proper shelter, and meal planning
❖ opportunities and willingness to share the duties of child care between both parents, when applicable
❖ provision of necessary social and health services

These healthy patterns depend, to a large extent, not only on parental competence and developmental sensitivity, but also on family circumstances and community resources. The family situation itself, including the parents' marital relationship and the child's characteristics, such as temperament, health, and developmental limitations, provides the basic context for child-rearing. Also playing an important role are the availability of such community resources as education and child-rearing information, as well as social networks and supports.

Although we would expect a considerable range in ability and resources among North American families, certain features of a child's environment should be fundamental and expectable (Scarr, 1992). Infants require protective and nurturant adults, as well as opportunities for socialization within a culture. For older children, an **expectable environment** includes a supportive family, contact with peers, and ample opportunities to explore and master the environment (Cicchetti & Lynch, 1995). Responsible parenting, moreover, involves a gradual shifting of control from the parent to the child and the community. Seldom is this process a smooth one, but healthy families learn to move gradually from nearly complete parental control, through shared control, to the child's growing self-control and eventual independence as an adult.

Family Stress and Disharmony

You know the only people who are always sure about the proper way to raise children? Those who've never had any.
—Bill Cosby

Children are amazingly adaptable to changing demands, an ability that is essential for healthy development. Nevertheless, they need a basic expectable environment to adapt successfully; otherwise their development may be compromised. All children must cope with various degrees of stress, and such experiences can be strengthening if they do not exceed the child's coping ability (Garmezy, 1983). Most children can tolerate single chronic stressors or risk factors, such as poor housing, parental separation, or school disruption, with little or no apparent harm. As additional stressors accumulate, however, children become less able to resist the harmful effects, a situation that can lead to **adaptational failure** (Rutter, 1979; Sroufe, 1989). In other words, a child's method of adapting to current environmental demands (such as avoiding an abusive care-giver) may later compromise the child's ability to form relationships with others or to be flexible in his or her style of adaptation.

Children who face numerous episodes of unresolved anger and aggression between family members on a regular basis show signs of adaptational failure in their abilities to cope with parental anger and tension. They remain uncertain as to the outcome of the conflict and sensitive to new outbreaks. Signs of stress appear, such as increased illness, symptoms of fear and anxiety, and problems with peers or school. Even infants as young as 3 months have been found to react with changes in their heart rate to adults' arguing (Cummings, 1997). Children are more capable of coping with family conflict and stress, however, if parents communicate to them about how they resolved the conflict (Hennessy, Rabideau, Cicchetti, & Cummings, 1994), by saying, for instance: "We apologize for upsetting you, and we want to let you know that we solved the problem. Dad is going to help out at mealtimes more often, and I'm going to cut back my hours at work so I can get home earlier." Unfortunately, children from violent and disturbed families rarely have such opportunities to learn about appropriate conflict resolution.

Stressful events in the family affect each child in different and unique ways. However, certain situations trigger more intense stress reactions and consequences than others (consider, for example, the difference between the stress of moving to a new school and that of being bullied by an older child). Child maltreatment is among the worst and most intrusive forms of stress. It impinges directly on the child's daily life, may be ongoing and unpredictable, and is often the result of actions or inactions of persons the child trusts and depends on. Keep in mind, however, that even traumatic events like abuse, neglect, emotional deprivation, and related forms of maltreatment do not affect children in a predictable, characteristic fashion. Rather, their impact depends on many factors, especially the child's makeup and available supports (Zahn-Waxler, Cole, Welsh, & Fox, 1995).

A prime factor in how children respond to various forms of stress is the degree of support and assistance they receive from their parents to help them cope and adapt. Parents provide a model for the child that teaches them how to exert some control even in the midst of confusion and upheaval (Garmezy, 1983). Understandably, a warm relationship with an adult who provides a predictable routine and consistent, moderate discipline, and who buffers the child from unnecessary sources of stress, is a valuable asset. Maltreated children may have the hardest time adapting appropriately to any form of stress to the extent that they are deprived of positive adult relationships, effective models of problem solving, and a sense of personal control or predictability.

Categories of Care

Most of us agree that children who lack the basic necessities of life—food, affection, medical care, education, and intellectual and social stimulation—are placed in jeopardy, but different cultural values, community standards, and personal experiences make one person's abuse another person's discipline or education (Korbin, 1994). The child care continuum below, which depicts a hypothetical range of child care from healthy to abusive and neglectful, provides some guidelines and boundaries for acceptable behavior between parents and children (Wolfe, 1991):

Continuum of Parental Emotional Sensitivity and Expression

Child-Centered

❖ provides a variety of sensory stimulation and positive emotional expressions

❖ engages in highly competent, child-centered interactions

❖ communicates to child about normal sexuality and healthy relationships

❖ makes rules for safety and health

- ❖ occasionally scolds, criticizes, interrupts child activity
- ❖ uses emotional delivery and tone that are sometimes harsh

Borderline
- ❖ shows rigid emotional expression and inflexibility in responding to child
- ❖ uses verbal and nonverbal pressure to achieve unrealistic expectations
- ❖ frequently uses verbal and nonverbal coercive methods and minimizes child's competence
- ❖ is insensitive to child's needs
- ❖ makes unfair comparisons
- ❖ takes advantage of or ignores child's dependency status
- ❖ impinges on the child's personal need for privacy

Inappropriate/Abusive/Neglectful
- ❖ denigrates, insults child
- ❖ expresses conditional love and ambivalent feelings towards child
- ❖ emotionally or physically rejects child's attention
- ❖ uses cruel and harsh control methods
- ❖ shows no sensitivity to child's needs
- ❖ intentionally seeks out ways to frighten, threaten, or provoke child
- ❖ responds unpredictably with emotional discharge
- ❖ takes advantage of child's dependency status through coercion, threats, or bribes
- ❖ is sexually or physically coercive and intrusive

At the child-centered end of this continuum we see appropriate and healthy forms of child-rearing actions that promote child development. Competent parents encourage their child's development in a variety of ways, and match their demands and expectations to the child's needs and abilities. Of course, parents are human, and many on occasion scold, criticize, or even show insensitivity to the child's state of need; in fact, discipline often requires such firm control, with accompanying verbal statements and affect. The borderline actions represented along this continuum, however, represent greater and greater degrees of irresponsible and harmful child care. Parents who show any measurable degree of these actions toward their child often need instruction and assistance in effective child care methods. Finally, those who violate their child's basic needs and dependency status in a physical, sexual, or emotional manner are engaging in inappropriate and abusive behavior. Similarly, failure to respond to a child's needs is the cornerstone of neglect.

In sum, child maltreatment represents one of the greatest failures of the child's expectable environment. Maltreating families fail to provide many of the expected emotional and physical necessities, and offer few supports and opportunities for children to explore and master their environment. The boundaries between appropriate and inappropriate behavior toward children are not always clear or well established, but an awareness of what is right and what is wrong can go a long way in preventing maltreatment.

DESCRIPTION

Have you ever baby-sat a younger child or been in charge of a group of children at a camp or school? Imagine that you saw bruises on a child—what would you do? You should be aware that all states and provinces in North America have civil laws, or statutes, which obligate persons who come in contact with children as part of their job or volunteer work (bus drivers, day care workers, teachers, baby-sitters, and so forth) to report known or suspected cases of abuse to the police or child welfare authorities. These statutes also provide criteria for removing children who are suspected of being maltreated from their homes. Criminal statutes further specify the forms of maltreatment that are criminally punishable.

Such situations that affect children's health and well-being involve abuse and neglect by adults, not abnormal child behavior or psychological disorders. Thus, specific definitions of types of child maltreatment do not appear in DSM-IV. Instead, DSM-IV considers severe maltreatment (of an adult or a child) under the Axis I category "Other conditions that may be a focus of clinical attention." If a child who was abused was also suffering from a clinical disorder, such as depression (Axis I), the maltreatment would be noted on Axis IV (psychosocial and environmental problems), because it may affect the diagnosis, treatment, and prognosis of the child's depression.

Maltreatment situations are classified into four major types—physical abuse, child neglect, sexual abuse, and emotional abuse. The definition of each type has been established by three National Incidence Studies (NIS) conducted by the U.S. Department of Health and Human Services in 1980, 1986, and 1993. NIS estimates are derived from official reports of abuse and neglect as well as a nationally representative sample of professionals who come in contact with maltreated children in a variety of settings. To account for the fact that maltreatment affects children regardless of actual physical injuries, the NIS definitions of maltreatment allow for two different sets of definitional standards: the harm standard, whereby the child has suffered demonstrable harm as a result of maltreatment, such as a broken bone; and the endangerment standard, which includes all children covered by the harm standard, but adds in those whose maltreatment experiences put them in *danger* of being harmed, such as witnessing parental violence. Approximately 3 times as many children are endangered as harmed each year (Sedlak & Broadhurst, 1996).

Physical Abuse

Milton: Abused and Abusive

Four-year-old Milton's rambunctious nature and his mother's hair-trigger temper were an explosive mix. He was constantly in trouble at home and was often spanked, yelled at, and locked in his room. One evening his baby-sitter took him to the emergency department because she thought he had a bad cold. During examination the doctor discovered that Milton had a fracture to his left forearm that was a couple of weeks old or so. There was a goose egg on Milton's forehead and multiple bruises on his face that were at various stages of healing, as well as bruises on his back.

Several people had noticed Milton's aggressive behavior—pushing other children or hitting them with something at preschool—but no one had realized that he was being abused. His preschool teacher told investigators, "I'm never sure from one minute to the next how Milton will react to the other children. He could be playing and suddenly become angry at something and start to destroy things or hit someone. I've also seen him become frightened—at what I don't know—and withdraw into a corner. I've tried several times to discuss these things with his mother, but she says he's just trying to get his way all the time."

Milton has been physically abused. His behavior is indicative of growing up in an environment where punitive disciplinary methods are the norm, to the detriment of child-centered stimulation and appropriate limit setting. **Physical abuse** includes acts such as punching, beating, kicking, biting, burning, shaking, or otherwise harming a child. In most cases the injuries are not intentional, but they occur as a result of overdiscipline or physical punishment. The severity and nature of injuries resulting from physical abuse vary considerably, as shown by these sobering examples of physical abuse from the NIS (Sedlak et al., 1996):

❖ a 1-year-old child who died of a cerebral hemorrhage after being shaken by her father
❖ a teen whose mother punched her and pulled out her hair

❖ a child who sustained second- and third-degree "stocking" burns to the feet after being held in hot water
❖ a preteen whose grandfather gave her a black eye
❖ a teen who sustained bruises after being beaten with an extension cord
❖ a 3-year-old who had welts and bruises from being beaten with a belt by his father

As a result of their harsh and insensitive treatment, physically abused children like Milton are often described as more disruptive and aggressive than their age-mates, with disturbances reaching across a broad spectrum of emotional and cognitive functioning (Aber & Cicchetti, 1984). Physical injuries may range from minor (bruises, lacerations), to moderate (scars, abrasions), to severe (burns, sprains, or broken bones). Sadly, these physical signs represent only the visible injuries; we will see later on that the psychological development of physically abused children is often impaired in less visible, but very serious, ways as well. We ask you to keep Milton's case in mind, since we refer to him several times throughout the chapter.

Neglect

Jane and Matt: Used to Neglect

Although Janet had worked for child protective services for over 10 years, she still cringed when she described the conditions of the home from which she had just removed two young siblings. "Neighbors and relatives have complained about the parents' never being around much, and how they often hear children crying," Janet explained during our interview. "I've been to the home before, and usually it stays clean for a few days after my visit. But this time the children were left with a teenaged baby-sitter, who went off to play in an arcade. They walked out of the home, and had to be returned by the police. What I saw this time was worse than before. Little Matt, who's almost 3 years old, was running around in soiled diapers, crawling across broken dishes and spilled food, putting things in his mouth. His sister Jane, who turns 6 next month, was dressed in dirty clothes and looked like she hadn't eaten in a week. The odor from the house forced me to step outside for air. The children seemed used to it—they just moved things out of their way and didn't seem to care."

I met with both children once they were settled into a foster home, and offered ways for the foster parents to manage Jane's strong-willed behavior and Matt's delay in speech and toileting. The foster mother noted how both children seemed to need "constant attention and control," and how neither one had knowledge of typical routines like sitting down together for dinner, cleaning up, bed times, basic hygiene, and the need to wear clean clothing.

These two children suffered the effects of physical and emotional neglect, characterized by a failure to provide for their basic physical, educational, or emotional needs. **Physical neglect** includes refusal of or delay in seeking health care, abandonment, expulsion from the home or refusal to allow a runaway to return home, and inadequate supervision. **Educational neglect** involves actions such as allowing chronic truancy, failing to enroll a child of mandatory school age in school, and failing to attend to a special educational need. **Emotional neglect,** one of the most difficult categories to define, includes such actions as marked inattention to the child's needs for affection, refusal of or failure to provide needed psychological care, spousal abuse in the child's presence, and permission of drug or alcohol use by the child.

The determination of child neglect requires consideration of cultural values and standards of care, as well as recognition that the failure to provide the necessities of life may be related to poverty. Below are actual cases of these forms of neglect (Sedlak et al., 1996):

Physical Neglect
❖ a teen whose mother refused to provide needed medication for his seizures
❖ a preteen whose mother threw him out of their home and told him not to return
❖ a 2-year-old who was found wandering in the street late at night, naked and alone
❖ an infant who had to be hospitalized for near-drowning after being left alone in a bath
❖ children living in a home contaminated with animal feces and rotting food

Educational Neglect
❖ an 11-year-old and a 13-year-old who were chronically truant
❖ a young teen, previously adjudicated as truant, whose parents did not send him to school
❖ a 12-year-old whose parents permitted him to decide whether to go to school, how long to stay there, and in which activities to participate
❖ a young teen whose mother did not enroll him in school after he was returned from foster care to her custody

Child neglect, the most common form of maltreatment, is tied to poverty, substance abuse, and parental indifference.

❖ a special education student whose mother refused to believe he needed help in school

Emotional Neglect
❖ siblings who were subjected to repeated incidents of family violence between their mother and father
❖ a 12-year-old whose parents permitted him to drink and use drugs
❖ an 8-year-old whose parents permitted him to smoke
❖ a child whose mother helped him shoot out the windows of a neighbor's house
❖ a 4-year-old whose caretakers refused to permit evaluation and treatment of his severe behavior problems

Neglected children may suffer physical health problems, limited growth, and increased complications arising from other health conditions, such as diabetes and allergies. They may also show patterns of behavior that vacillate between undisciplined activity and extreme passivity (Crittenden & Ainsworth, 1989), due to their ways of adapting to an unresponsive care-giver. As toddlers, they show little persistence and enthusiasm; as preschoolers, neglected children show poor impulse control and are highly dependent on teachers for support and nurturance (Erickson, Egeland, & Pianta, 1989).

Note that emotional neglect also includes children who witness parental violence. Passive recipients of violence and abuse are affected in much the same way as other victims of maltreatment. Younger ones are fearful, and often show regressive and somatic signs of distress, such as sleep problems, bed-wetting, headaches, stomachaches, diarrhea, ulcers, and enuresis. Older boys tend to be more aggressive with peers and dating partners;

girls tend to be more passive, withdrawn, and low in self-esteem (McCloskey, Figueredo, & Koss, 1995; D. A. Wolfe, Jaffe, Wilson, & Zak, 1985).

Sexual Abuse

Rosita: No Haven at Home

Rosita was not quite 4 years old when her family doctor suspected that something was going on that troubled her. His concerns were expressed to child welfare, and Rosita reenacted several sexual acts for them, using dolls depicting her father and herself. "Daddy said I can play a game, and it's OK 'cause grownups do it," she hesitantly explained. Rosita made the dolls kiss, then the male doll rubbed the female doll's vagina. "But he hurt me, and it made me scared. I didn't want to get in trouble." To make matters worse, her mother became furious with Rosita and the agency when she heard the accusations, and was unwilling to ensure her protection and safety at home. "Rosita just wants a lot of attention—she's said this stuff before and I don't believe her one minute," was her mother's only comment.

Rosita was sexually abused by her father and disbelieved by her mother; as a result, she faces many ongoing psychological complications. Because Rosita was seen several times throughout the course of her childhood and adolescent development, her case is discussed further in a later section on the course of development of children and adolescents who have been sexually abused.

Sexual abuse includes fondling a child's genitals, intercourse, incest, rape, sodomy, exhibitionism, and commercial exploitation through prostitution or the production of pornographic materials. Sexual abuse may be underreported because of the secrecy or "conspiracy of silence" that so often characterizes these cases. The following are cases of sexual abuse reported in the NIS (Sedlak et al., 1996):

❖ a 10-year-old girl who was raped by her father
❖ two sisters and a brother who were sexually molested by their mother's live-in boyfriend
❖ a teen whose mother prostituted her
❖ a preteen who had to lie next to her father with his body pressed against her after he watched a pornographic movie, and who was afraid to sleep in her room as a result

❖ a 17-year-old who had emotional problems and ran away as a result of being fondled by her stepfather
❖ a 4-year-old who was fondled by his father during weekend visitations

The behavior and development of sexually abused children may be affected significantly, especially in relation to the longer duration or greater frequency of abuse, the use of force, penetration, and a closer relationship to the perpetrator (Finkelhor & Browne, 1988; Kendall-Tackett, Williams, & Finkelhor, 1993). The physical health of these children may be compromised by urinary tract problems, gynecological problems, sexually transmitted diseases (including AIDS), and pregnancy (National Research Council, 1993). About one-third of sexually abused children report or exhibit no visible symptoms, and about two-thirds of those who do show symptoms recover significantly during the first 12 to 18 months following the abuse (Kendall-Tackett et al., 1993). Nonetheless, the possibility of delayed emergence of symptoms is becoming more widely recognized (Williams, 1994).

Children's reactions to and recovery from sexual abuse vary, depending on the nature of the sexual assault and the response of their important others, especially the mother. Many of the acute symptoms of sexual abuse resemble children's common reactions to stress, such as fears, increased anger, anxiety, fatigue, depression, passivity, difficulties focusing and sustaining attention, and withdrawal from usual activities. It is common for younger children to regress temporarily in reaction to an abusive incident, such as becoming enuretic or easily upset, or to have problems sleeping. In later childhood and early adolescence, these signs of distress may take the form of acting-out behaviors, such as delinquency, drug use, promiscuity, or self-destructive behavior (Wekerle & D. A. Wolfe, 1996). Some sexually abused children behave in a "sexualized" manner with other children and/or with toys. Such behavior may include excessive masturbation, age-inappropriate knowledge of sexual activity, and/or pronounced seductive or promiscuous behavior. Any of these symptoms of distress may be associated with a decline or sudden change in school performance, behavior, and peer relations.

Unlike physical abuse and neglect, sexual abuse has no connection to child-rearing, discipline, or inattention to developmental needs. Rather, it constitutes a breach of trust, deception, intrusion, and exploitation of a child's innocence and status. Whereas all types of maltreatment share a common ground in relation to the abuse of power by an adult over a child, sexual abuse stands out from physical abuse and neglect in terms of these specific dynamics.

Emotional Abuse

Evan: If This Is Love . . .

Evan described himself as "an eleven-year-old boy who can be good when he tries really hard, but most of the time he makes bad choices." One of these bad choices was to put paint in the teacher's coffee cup, leading to his suspension from school. Evan also started stealing and drinking beer. The school says he was threatening other kids, wanting their money. To document their plight, his parents volunteered to have a television documentary made about their "trouble with Evan," using motion-sensitive cameras in two rooms in their home. What emerged from the tapes, however, were repeated episodes of emotional abuse toward Evan by his stepfather and mother. Below are some illustrative conversations:

Evan's stepfather: "I would like to lock you up in a cage and let everybody look at you like you are an animal. I am fed up with this sh——. I can't put up with it no more and neither can your mother. And if you think I am talking to the wall, I am talking to you, beef head. If you'd of been me, you'd of been dead because my father would have killed you. Your insubordination is going to get you a hook on the side of your f——ing head. If you don't like it the door is right there."

Evan's parents were convinced that he was stealing money from them, and his mother's confrontation follows: "We already know that you are lying so you f——ing tell me the truth NOW! Everything. Go take a look in the mirror. Go take a look in the mirror and then come back here. You look guilty as sin. [Turns to husband] I am going to hit him. Now that is not how you normally look, is it? That is not a normal look for a child, is it? You have got great big letters written all over your face that spell guilty." Evan's mother then discovered she had miscounted the money. (*Trouble with Evan*, 1994)

Evan experienced very harsh, emotionally abusive threats and put-downs from his parents, which can do as much harm to his development as physical abuse or neglect. **Emotional abuse** includes acts or omissions by the parents or care-givers that have caused, or could cause, serious behavioral, cognitive, emotional, or mental disorders. For example, the parents or caregivers may use extreme or bizarre forms of punishment, such as confinement of a child in a dark closet. Emotional abuse also includes verbal threats and put-downs like those Evan experienced, as well as habitual scapegoating, belittling, and name-calling. Emotional abuse exists, to some degree, in all forms of maltreatment, so the specific psychological consequences of this form of maltreatment are poorly understood (Garbarino, Guttman, & Seeley, 1986). The following actual cases reported in the NIS tend to be more severe forms of emotional abuse because of the definitional requirement that the acts have caused, or could cause, serious harm (Sedlak et al., 1996):

❖ a young child strapped in a high chair all day while her parents went to work

❖ a child forced by her parents to live in a basement, to use the floor as a toilet, and then to clean it up, and who suffered emotional problems, including acting-out, that required counseling as a result

❖ a 4-year-old who was locked in a closet as a means of discipline

❖ children traumatized when their father took them to a store to buy a gun with which he threatened to kill them and their mother

❖ a child who ran away because his mother punished him by refusing to feed him, by feeding him spoiled food, and by putting him out of the house without a coat or shoes

❖ siblings whose emotional problems were a result of their mother's constant verbal abuse

PREVALENCE AND CONTEXT

When the *battered child syndrome* (the early term for physical abuse) was first described in the early 1960s by Kempe, Silverman, Steele, Droegemueller, and Silver (1962), they estimated that this phenomenon applied to fewer than 300 children in the United States. Today, state child protective services agencies investigate over 3 million suspected cases of child abuse and neglect *each year.*

Childhood isn't a peaceful time for many. Because of their age and dependency status, many children and adolescents face events that, when considered together, add up to considerable risk and victimization. Finkelhor and colleagues (1994) listed these events in rough order of magnitude, based on various U.S. statistics on crimes against children:

1. *Pandemic victimizations,* everyday events experienced by a majority of children in the course of growing up, include assaults by siblings, physical punishment by parents, and theft, as well as peer assault, vandalism, and, to a lesser extent, robbery.

Deborah Eappen holds a photo of her 8-month-old son, Matthew, during the trial of the boy's nanny, Louise Woodward. The nanny was found guilty of manslaughter stemming from shaken baby syndrome.

2. *Acute victimizations,* which occur less often but are generally of greater severity, include physical abuse, neglect, and family abduction.

3. *Extraordinary victimizations,* which occur to a very small number of children but attract a great deal of attention, include homicide, child abuse homicide, and nonfamily abduction.
(Based on Finkelhor et al., 1994)

Certain common victimization experiences, especially assaults by siblings and physical punishment by parents, are typically treated as relatively inconsequential, even though from the child's point of view they may not be. Perhaps you'll recognize that considerably more public and professional attention is paid to the extraordinary and acute forms of victimization than to the pandemic ones. Yet most people have vivid memories of their victimization experiences, no matter how seemingly trivial. This confirms the importance of these various forms of victimization in creating a spectrum of childhood victimization, of which abuse and neglect are a major part.

Incidence of Abuse and Neglect

There are two ways of considering how common child abuse and neglect are. The first is based on *incidence* rates, which tell how many new cases are reported to officials each year; the second is based on *prevalence* estimates, which indicate the number of people who are maltreated prior to 18 years of age. (Both estimates are divided by the total population from which the cases are identified, such as the number of children or adults in

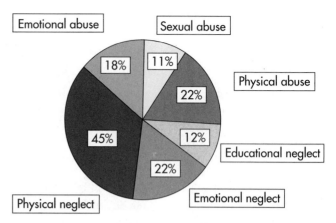

FIGURE 14.1 Incidence of maltreatment. (Data from Sedlack & Broadhurst, 1996)

the population.) Current incidence figures indicate that almost 3 million children are harmed or endangered by abuse or neglect each year in the United States, amounting to a total yearly incidence rate of 42 out of every 1000 children (Sedlak & Broadhurst, 1996). Figure 14.1 shows the proportion of each subtype of abuse and neglect, a pattern that has remained fairly constant over the past decade. Child neglect continues to be a worrisome problem, affecting almost 30 children out of every 1000 in the United States and accounting for 70% of all incidents. Physical, sexual, and emotional abuse affect another 18 children per 1000, or 43% of the total. (The percentages exceed 100% because of overlap.) Moreover, a study of children exposed to domestic violence in five major U.S. cities found that the youngest age group (0 to 5 years old) was disproportionately exposed to multiple incidents of interparental violence, and in nearly one of every five households, the child (as a result of his or her illness, need for lunch money, and so forth) was considered to be a factor in the eruption of the dispute (Fantuzzo, Boruch, Beriama, Atkins, & Marcus, 1997).

Although official incidence rates provide a useful year-to-year comparison of *reported rates* of child maltreatment, they have been criticized as being a significant underestimate of the actual prevalence of severe abuse by parents throughout the country (Straus, 1994). Incidence of maltreatment can also be estimated from large-scale community or nationwide surveys that are representative of society at large, and which avoid some of the factors that may inhibit children or adults from reporting maltreatment to officials. Consequently, asking representative samples of parents about their various child-rearing methods anonymously results in much higher estimates of the number of children at risk of maltreatment each year than those provided by official reports. Based on telephone interviews with over 3500 families in the United States, 10.7% of parents (which translates to 107 per 1000 children) admitted having used some method in the past year to control their child that amounted to a severe violent act, such as hitting with an object, pushing, or scalding their child (Straus & Gelles, 1986).

Lifetime prevalence estimates of maltreatment are derived by asking adults if they ever experienced particular forms of maltreatment as children. Oddly, such studies have been conducted almost exclusively on sexual abuse, perhaps because discrete sexual acts are more readily defined than are other forms of abuse and neglect. A notable exception is the recent Ontario Health Supplement, a general population survey of nearly 10,000 residents of Ontario, Canada, in which persons 15 years and older were asked about physical and sexual abuse in childhood (MacMillan et al., 1997). A history of child physical abuse was reported more often by males (31.2%) than females (21.1%), while sexual abuse during childhood was more commonly reported by females (12.8%) than males (4.3%). Keep in mind that these figures are estimates only. Retrospective reports of childhood experiences are inexact, and it is rarely possible to corroborate episodes of maltreatment to get precise accounts. Nevertheless, on the whole, these incidence and prevalence data indicate a substantial problem that, until quite recently, was disregarded.

The Increasing Rate of Child Maltreatment

It's difficult to ignore the finding that the total number of abused and neglected children reported to authorities has nearly doubled since 1986. Physical abuse nearly doubled; sexual abuse more than doubled; and emotional abuse, physical neglect, and emotional neglect are all more than 2½ times greater. A disturbing trend indicates that the total number of children *seriously injured* and the total of those endangered by maltreatment has quadrupled since 1986.

Are these dramatic increases in estimated numbers of maltreated children real, or are they due to greater awareness and reporting than in previous generations? The answer is, both. The increased number of abused and neglected children is most likely real, attested to by the fact that there were four times as many *seriously injured* children in 1993 than in 1986. Serious injuries would not have escaped notice, even prior to improved laws and professional training (Sedlak & Broadhurst, 1996). However, the capability of community professionals to recognize abuse and neglect has also improved since 1986, so more of the subtle cues indicative of abuse and neglect may now be receiving attention and increasing the number of reported cases.

We now consider how characteristics of the child and family may influence the likelihood of maltreatment.

Characteristics of Victimized Children

Are some children more likely to be abused or neglected than others because of their age, race, or gender? The NIS studies have consistently found that children's sex and age are related to risk of maltreatment, but racial background is not (Sedlak & Broadhurst, 1996).

Child maltreatment occurs at all ages, but there is correspondence between certain types of maltreatment and children's age. Younger children, who have the greatest need for care and supervision, are the most common victims of physical neglect. Along with young adolescents, toddlers and preschoolers are the most common victims of physical and emotional abuse, which corresponds to the emergence of greater independence and parental conflict at these developmental periods. Sexual abuse incidence, in contrast, is relatively constant from age 3 on, which attests to children's vulnerability from early preschool years throughout childhood (Sedlak & Broadhurst, 1996).

Gender differences in maltreatment rates are generally few, with the important exception of specific types of abuse. Although girls are 25% more likely to be victims of any form of abuse than boys, this essentially reflects the fact that they account for about 80% of the victims of sexual abuse (Finkelhor, 1993). Moreover, the dynamics of sexual abuse differ considerably for boys and girls. Although boys as well as girls are more likely to be abused by someone they know and trust, boys are more likely to be abused by male nonfamily members—camp staff, teachers, scout leaders—whereas girls are more likely to be sexually abused by male family members (Finkelhor, 1995). This finding suggests different patterns of vulnerability for boys and girls, and has implications for safety and prevention.

Characteristics of Family and Perpetrator

Family characteristics remind us of the cultural and social forces that shape child-rearing methods. Most significant is the well-established finding that maltreatment is more common among the poor and disadvantaged (Gelles, 1983). Consider that the incidence rate for overall maltreatment rises from 42 in 1000 to 99 in 1000 children among those from the poorest families (earning less than $15,000 per year). This rate is 3 times greater than that of children from moderate-income families ($15,000 to under $30,000 per year), and 25 times higher compared with children in families in the highest income bracket (over $30,000 per year). This finding is not likely due to a reporting bias, since it has not changed for the past 20 years despite increased awareness and reporting (Pelton, 1994). What it does imply, however, is that the economically based context of maltreatment—restricted child care opportunities, crowded and unsafe housing, lack of health care, to name a few conditions—is a powerful backdrop to the high incidence rates.

Family structure is also connected to the probability of child maltreatment. Children living with a single parent are at significantly greater risk of both physical abuse and neglect. Those living in father-only homes are almost twice as likely to be physically abused than those living with mothers alone (Sedlak & Broadhurst, 1996). Maltreatment—especially physical and educational neglect—is more common in larger families, where additional children in the household mean additional tasks, responsibilities, and demands.

Who commits these acts? It shouldn't surprise you that the child's birth parent is the perpetrator about 80% of the time, across all forms of maltreatment. However, there are important exceptions, as well as key gender differences in the nature of abuse or neglect. Nearly one-half of sexually abused children are abused by persons other than parents or parent figures, compared with only a fraction in other categories. Child neglect is committed predominantly—about 90% of the time—by mothers, which fits with the fact that mothers and mother substitutes tend to be primary caretakers. In contrast, sexual abuse is committed more often—about 90% of the time—by males, about half of whom are the child's father or father figure. Males are also the offender in the majority of emotional (63%) and physical abuse (58%) incidents as well (Sedlak & Broadhurst, 1996).

Cross-Cultural Comparisons

How do children fare in other Western countries and in other countries around the world? Although it is difficult to draw comparisons between countries because of differences in defining and reporting child maltreatment, what little is known about the prevalence of maltreatment in other countries suggests, unfortunately, that physical and sexual abuse are at epidemic proportions in many societies worldwide.

According to the World Health Organization (1997), child abuse is found in all societies and is almost always a highly guarded secret wherever it occurs. Studies in which children or young adults were interviewed about their childhood experiences further confirm that rates of child sexual abuse in other Western societies around the world are comparable to North American rates, clustering around 20% for females and between 3% and 11% for males (Finkelhor, 1994) (estimates of child sexual abuse for African, Middle Eastern, or Far Eastern countries are not available, however). The United Nations Children's Fund estimates that nearly 2 million children worldwide are being sexually abused, including many who are forced into prostitution and pornography.

A comparison of incidence rates of abuse and neglect in two North American societies suggests how such rates are influenced by their broader social context. Canadian estimates, extrapolated from the Province of Ontario (Trocmé, McPhee, Tam, & Hay, 1994), suggest that the United States has about double Canada's overall rate of maltreatment (42 in 1,000 versus 21 in 1000). Similar findings are reported for Australia (16 in 1000; Broadbent & Bentley, 1997). Higher U.S. rates of child neglect are primarily responsible for differences between otherwise similar countries, which in turn may reflect the higher poverty rate in the United States and the more limited access to social, medical, and educational services for many U.S. families (Trocmé et al., 1994).

DEVELOPMENTAL COURSE AND PSYCHOPATHOLOGY

> The child trapped in an abusive environment is faced with formidable tasks of adaptation. She must find a way to preserve a sense of trust in people who are untrustworthy, safety in a situation that is unsafe, control in a situation that is terrifyingly unpredictable, power in a situation of helplessness. (Herman, 1992, p. 98)

This statement by prominent clinician and researcher Judith Herman captures the essence of the world of maltreated children and youth. Abuse and neglect are much more than physical pain and transitory fear; to a child or adolescent, such events often represent threats to their emerging sense of self, their world, and their feelings of safety and well-being. We return to Rosita's case to illustrate this dramatic impact:

Rosita: Feeling Trapped

At age 6, Rosita was brought to the hospital following two suicidal/self-harm gestures. While camping, she wrapped a rope that hung from a tree around her neck and her foster mother grabbed it and untangled it. She did not appear to be hurt, but she sat and cried for a long time while her foster mother cuddled her. The next morning she played with a stick in the campfire and deliberately tried to burn her leg. When stopped and asked why, she replied, "I wanted to hurt myself." She occasionally has severe nightmares involving monsters and threats of harm.

"Rosita is preoccupied with themes of death and self-harm, in her drawings, stories at school, and even with her classmates," her teacher explained. "She has problems making friends, because she acts silly when she tries to join their games. More than once she's asked other children to touch her vagina, and she has tried to put her finger in one girl's vagina. Needless to say, this has alarmed other parents and teachers. But she's such a needy child—she'll go from a temper tantrum to becoming clingy in a matter of seconds."

Rosita's life became more settled, and by age 9 her school performance had improved noticeably. However, at age 15 her psychological condition rapidly grew worse. She made suicide attempts and began cutting her arm with glass and other sharp objects. When I saw her following her release from the hospital she was very distraught, and felt unloved and abandoned. Her feelings of depression and anxiety were evident: "I'll jump or get really scared, for no reason. I just want to go somewhere and hide, and get away from people," she explained. "I can't trust anybody except for my friend Mary—but even she thinks I'm weird when I get like this. It's like I'm trapped or caught, and can't get away." My interview went on to reveal Rosita's sleeping problems and her constant crying and sadness.

Rosita had never forgotten the abuse she experienced as a child, and sometimes had intrusive reminders of what happened. "I feel tied in a knot, and I feel like I'm going crazy or something. That's when I might start cutting on my arm or something, just to feel like I'm not dreaming, that I'm real." Sometimes she even blamed herself for losing her family years ago, explaining that "no matter how bad it was I wish no one had ever found out, because it wasn't worth all the pain I'm going through."

Rosita lacks a sense of self-esteem and a sense of the future. She is very vulnerable to recurring victimization, as a result of her lack of self-awareness and her limited self-protection skills. She feels a terrible loss and ambivalence over her family, sometimes blaming herself for the abuse or wishing it had never been discovered. Although she is a verbal and insightful young woman, she is often overcome with worries, anxiety, fear, and emotional distress related to her current circumstances.

What happens to the development of children who were abused or neglected during important formative years? Recall how normal development follows a predictable, organized course, beginning with the mastery of physiological regulation (eating, sleeping), and continu-

ing throughout the development of higher skills, such as problem solving and peer relationships. But under abnormal and unusual circumstances, especially abuse and neglect, predictability and organization are disrupted and thrown off course, resulting in developmental failure and limited adaptation. Because this issue has important implications for understanding the effects of maltreatment, we examine important factors that serve to protect some children from serious harmful effects. Then we discuss some of the known risk factors that pose serious challenges to development.

Resilience and Adaptation

Maltreated children experience ongoing, uncontrollable events that challenge their successful development and adaptation in a pervasive manner and pose a threat to their core psychological well-being (Cicchetti & Lynch, 1995). They not only have to face acute and unpredictable parental outbursts or betrayal, but also have to adapt to environmental circumstances that pose developmental challenges. These influences include the more dramatic events, such as marital violence and separation of family members, as well as the mundane but important everyday activities that may be disturbing or upsetting, such as unfriendly interactions, few learning opportunities, and chaotic lifestyle. Children who are sexually abused undergo pronounced interruptions in their developing view of themselves and the world, resulting in significant emotional and behavioral changes indicative of their attempts to cope with such events. Because the source of stress and fear is centralized in their family, children who are maltreated are challenged on a regular basis to find ways to adapt that pose the least risk and offer maximum protection and opportunity for growth.

Until recently, the impact of abuse on the child's development was assumed to be invariably negative and disruptive, but the issue is not that straightforward. On the basis of numerous indicators of academic and social adjustment collected over 3 years, about 12% of a large sample (N = 133) of maltreated school-aged children showed significant resilience despite adversity (Cicchetti & Rogosch, 1997). Even though this percentage was about half that of nonmaltreated children from similar low-income disadvantaged backgrounds, it certainly attests to the fact that some maltreated children (about one in eight) accomplish important developmental milestones regardless of their plight. Personality characteristics such as positive self-esteem and sense of self were the best predictors of resilience among maltreated children, whereas relationship factors such as emotional availability of the mother were key factors among nonmaltreated disadvantaged children (Cicchetti & Rogosch, 1997). This latter finding makes sense if one considers the disturbed parent-child relationships that maltreated children have known. Nevertheless, we still have a poor understanding as to how some maltreated children manage to adapt successfully. Are resilient children born with these positive personality traits, such as an optimistic outlook? Do these traits develop from some other experience, such as positive relations with other caregivers or family members? The answers to these important questions simply are not known. Thus, instead of revealing maltreatment as a uniform stressor, these data demonstrate how the effects of maltreatment on development are dynamic and unpredictable. Whether or not a particular child shows demonstrable harm, however, does not detract from the fact that child maltreatment is harmful and poses significant risk to each child's development.

This leads to an important principle: Child maltreatment, like other forms of adversity and trauma during childhood, does not affect each child in a predictable or consistent fashion. To the contrary, the impact of maltreatment depends not only on the severity and chronicity of the events themselves, but also on how such events interact with the child's individual and family characteristics. In effect, the impact of any stressor, including all types of maltreatment, depends to a large extent upon the characteristics of the individual who must cope with the stressor (Kagan, 1983). Children may face various sorts of stress and risk in their lives, some chronic and pervasive, yet they learn to negotiate these situations in many different ways and with many different outcomes (Radke-Yarrow & Brown, 1993). Young children who may have initially achieved normal developmental milestones can show a dramatic downturn in their developmental progress as a result of chronic or acute maltreatment and similar types of stress (Farber & Egeland, 1987). Consequently, core developmental processes are impaired, resulting in emotional and behavioral problems ranging from speech and language delays to criminal behavior.

As we mentioned earlier, children in general have a remarkable ability to adapt to their circumstances—good or bad—and many can often resist or recover from the negative effects of maltreatment once they are given proper opportunities and protection. So, even though maltreated children are at an increased risk for many adjustment and criminal problems, these problems are not inevitable (Widom, 1989a).

What factors may protect children from serious psychological harm? Children may be protected in part from the effects of maltreatment by a positive relationship with at least one important and consistent person in their lives who provides support and protection (Kendall-Tackett et al., 1993; National Research Council, 1993). This person is typically the mother in cases of

Young Jason never goes unarmed. Grabbing his plastic gun and rubber knife, he tells his mother, "If daddy comes, I'll be able to stop him." (From *Living with the Enemy*, photo © Donna Ferrato)

child sexual abuse (Alessandri & Lewis, 1996), but he or she could also be the identified maltreating parent, a notion that at first may be hard to comprehend. However, children do not think of their parents as "abusive"—they just adapt to their own experiences as best as possible. Loyalty to one's parents is a powerful emotional tie, so from the child's point of view, a parent who at times yells, hits, and castigates may at other times be a source of connection, knowledge, or love (Wekerle & D. A. Wolfe, 1996). As noted earlier, this is one of the paradoxical dilemmas faced by maltreated children.

Simply stated, if children are raised in environments where love and positive attention are expressed rarely or inconsistently, they have no other standard of comparison. Their natural inclination is to distort their view of their parents as being more like others'—positive, well-meaning, and all-important. It may be more adaptive for children to focus on what their parents provide, rather than on what they don't, because this permits them to see themselves as normal and accepted. This view has important implications for intervention efforts, because some interventions, such as removing children from their families, can become another source of stress and disruption that has undesired side effects (Melton, 1990).

Developmental Consequences

Although children's development follows a course, based on centuries of genetic and species-specific processes, that is normally quite organized and adaptive, certain environmental events can interfere with this established pattern, causing an individual to proceed along an unusual and less predictable course. Child maltreatment is one such event. The diverse actions or inactions that are described collectively as maltreatment usually occur in such a pervasive manner that children's development is thrown off its normal course (Cicchetti & Lynch, 1995).

Understanding the major consequences of maltreatment of children requires consideration of the basic developmental processes that are impaired or delayed among this population. We begin this discussion by focusing on early attachment and affect regulation—the building blocks of the development of important self-regulatory and interpersonal competencies.

Early Attachment and Affect Regulation.

Child maltreatment is known to disrupt the important process of attachment (Cicchetti, Toth, & Bush, 1988). Recall that attachment is a critical, ongoing process—typically beginning between 6 and 12 months of age—that provides infants with a secure, consistent base from which to explore and learn about their worlds. We referred earlier to these important opportunities as part of children's expectable environment that provides them with human contact and assists in the regulation of physical and emotional processes. Episodes of child abuse and neglect, whether chronic or sporadic, can disrupt this natural process and interfere with children's ability to seek comfort and to regulate their own physiological and emotional processes. As a result, maltreated children are more likely than other children to show an absence of an organized attachment strategy (Cicchetti et al., 1988; Main & Solomon, 1990).

Without consistent stimulation, comfort, and routine to aid in the formation of secure attachment, maltreated infants and toddlers have considerable difficulty establishing a reciprocal, consistent pattern of interaction with their care-givers. Instead, they show a pattern described as insecure-disorganized attachment, characterized by a mixture of approach and avoidance, helplessness, apprehension, and a general disorientation (Carlson, Cicchetti, Barnett, & Braunwald, 1989; Schneider-Rosen, Braunwald, Carlson, & Cicchetti, 1985). This insecure-disorganized pattern occurs much more often among maltreated than non-maltreated infants and their mothers—as many as four out of five (Carlson et al., 1989), which is especially striking given that this pattern is very uncommon among non-maltreated, middle-class samples (Main & Solomon, 1990).

Because children's beliefs about themselves and others follow from their initial attachment experiences, an insecure-disorganized pattern can have significant repercussions on later stages of development (Aber, Allen, Carlson, & Cicchetti, 1989). Children's early relationships provide a basis for the formation of their interpersonal style, so it makes sense that infants who adapt to hostile or unavailable care-givers by withdrawing or

being constantly on alert will use similar methods with peers and other adults. Failure in early attachment results in a model of relationships that will further impair future relationships (Sroufe & Fleeson, 1986). The lack of a secure, consistent basis for relationships places maltreated children at greater risk of falling behind in their cognitive and social development, and can result in their having problems regulating their emotions and behavior with others.

Because of their unpredictable and at times fearful circumstances, some maltreated infants and toddlers become hypervigilant—looking for any cue related to a possible verbal or physical outburst (Crittenden & DiLalla, 1988). Hypervigilance includes not only constantly scanning the environment, but also developing the ability to detect subtle variations in adult behavior, such as facial, intonational, and body language changes, that alert them to possible danger (Herman, 1992). Sometimes they learn to placate angry parents to avoid becoming the target (Hennessy et al., 1994). But as disorganized toddlers become preschoolers, hypervigilance and similar ways of adapting to their environment give way to various forms of controlling behavior toward the parents. Controlling behavior may take the form of pseudomaturity, such as looking after the parent and the household, or emotional immaturity, such as excessive tantrum-throwing and noncompliance. This developmental transition from hypervigilance to controlling behavior among maltreated children—which differs significantly from the developmental patterns of nonmaltreated children—is believed to compensate for the absence of an expectable environment by controlling and organizing the parent (Main & Hesse, 1989).

Parent-child attachment and the home climate play a critical role in emotion regulation, another early developmental milestone. Emotion regulation refers to the ability to modulate or control the intensity and expression of feelings and impulses, especially intense ones, in an adaptive manner (Cicchetti, Ganiban, & Barnett, 1990). Emotions serve as important internal monitoring and guidance systems that are designed to appraise events as being beneficial or dangerous, and provide motivation for action. Emotions serve interpersonal regulatory functions as well. Most of us can interpret someone else's emotional state by reading facial, gestural, postural, and vocal cues, a process known as *social referencing*. Social referencing serves an important survival and learning function for infants and young children, because they rely on an adult's affective interpretation of an event (Bretherton, Fritz, Zahn-Waxler, & Ridgeway, 1986). In effect, emotional reactions and perceptions help young children understand their world.

Because emotions provide important signals about our internal and external worlds, children must learn how to interpret and respond to them appropriately. Most children learn this naturally through the emotional expressions and explanations given by their care-givers. Maltreated children, on the other hand, live in a world of emotional turmoil and extremes, making it very difficult for them to understand, label, and regulate their internal states. Expressions of affect, such as crying or signals of distress, may trigger disapproval, avoidance, or abuse, so maltreated youngsters have a greater tendency to inhibit their emotional expression and regulation (Cicchetti & Beeghly, 1987). When a new situation involving a stranger or peer triggers emotional reactions, they do not have the benefit of a caring smile or words from a familiar adult to assure them that things are okay.

Let's consider how this process works by using a laboratory analog. A recent study illustrates how cognitive processing of emotional information among maltreated children differs from that of nonmaltreated children, even at the level of brain activity associated with attention. Three pictures—of happy, neutral, and angry adult faces—were presented at the same time, and children were randomly told to attend to each one to measure how they process affective versus neutral information. Compared with nonmaltreated controls, school-aged children with maltreatment histories showed more reactivity when asked to attend to the angry faces (Pollak, Cicchetti, Klorman, & Brumaghim, 1997). A unique aspect of this study is that reactivity was measured by event-related potentials in the brain, an index of CNS functioning thought to reflect the underlying neurological processing of discrete stimuli. It was found that the situational context—being asked specifically to look at the angry face—is an important aspect of how such children attend to affective stimuli. This tendency to react more strongly to provocative stimuli may be adaptive for maltreated children in the short run, but at the same time it may create costly and maladaptive solutions that contribute to their social-cognitive problems and adjustment difficulties over time (Pollak et al., 1997).

Understandably, therefore, one of the most far-reaching effects of maltreatment is the loss or disruption of children's ability to regulate the intensity of their emotional feelings and impulses (Van der Kolk & Fisler, 1994). As they grow older and are faced with new situations involving peers and other adults, poor emotional regulation becomes more and more problematic, and may result in unusual and self-harmful behaviors, such as Rosita's attempts to cut herself. Over time, this inability to regulate emotions is associated with both internalizing disorders such as depression and fearfulness, as well as externalizing disorders such as hostility, aggression, and various forms of acting-out.

In sum, early child maltreatment has a profound effect on normal development, setting the child on a different course that further impairs normal adaptation. Failure to develop an adaptive attachment strategy sets off a chain reaction that goes in unpredictable directions. The absence of an organized attachment strategy makes the young child's behavior more difficult to manage, which in turn causes the care-giver to react with even more withdrawal or abuse. A damaging, interactive pattern may develop, which over time places the child's development in further jeopardy. Keep in mind, though, that this process is neither inevitable nor irreversible. Although exact numbers are unknown, many children who experience such events in infancy and early childhood manage to adapt successfully over the long run (Malinosky-Rummell & Hansen, 1993), which emphasizes that development is sensitive to positive as well as negative influences.

Emerging View of Self and Others. As normal development proceeds, regulation of affect and behavior becomes less dependent on the care-giver and more and more autonomous (parents often prefer the vernacular expression, "terrible twos"). Toddlers' developing self-regulation is now applied to new situations, which further strengthens their emerging view of themselves and others. Development of language and symbolic play allow them to represent their growing awareness of self and others (Cicchetti, 1990), influenced by both maturational and environmental factors. Importantly, children form complex mental representations of people, relationships, and the world during this period. Their emerging view of themselves and their surroundings is fostered by healthy parental guidance and control that invoke concern for the welfare of others. Sadly, because such opportunities are seldom available to maltreated children, emotional and behavioral problems are more likely to appear as a result of their maladaptive view of themselves and others.

Representational models of oneself and others are significant because they contain experience, knowledge, and expectations that are carried forward to new situations (Cicchetti & Lynch, 1995). For example, consider how a child's internalized belief that "my mother is usually there for me when I need her" or that "I am loved and worthy of love" shapes his basic beliefs about himself and others, and how these ideas reflect a sense of well-being and connection (Bretherton, 1990). Maltreated children, in contrast, often lack such core positive beliefs about themselves and their world (Hartman & Burgess, 1989). Instead, they may develop negative representational models of themselves and others based on a sense of inner "badness," self-blame, shame, or rage, which further impair their ability to regulate their affective responses. One male survivor of child sexual abuse explains this feeling of inferiority: "I could not see anybody loving me. I could not see anybody liking me or wanting to be with me, I could not see myself as significant to the point where I would actually be in a relationship with someone else" (Lisak, 1994, p. 542).

Feelings of powerlessness and betrayal are often described by children and adults who have experienced maltreatment—feelings which become salient components of their self-identity (Finkelhor & Browne, 1988). Powerlessness refers to the situation whereby the child's will, desire, and sense of self-efficacy are thwarted and rebuked, and it is often linked to fears, worries, and depression. In the words of a survivor, "It's as if the world was evil, it's coming to get you, and you could do almost nothing to defend from it" (Lisak, 1994, p. 533). One's sense of personal power or self-efficacy can be undermined by physical and verbal abuse as well as by physical and emotional neglect; such maltreatment devalues the child as a person. Feelings of betrayal can also challenge an individual's sense of self, because a person on whom the individual was dependent violated that trust and confidence. Such feelings may not be identified until years later, once the individual reaches an age whereby he or she can recognize this betrayal dynamic as the source of feelings of self-blame, guilt, and powerlessness (Williams, 1994). The following are typical of children's and adolescents' descriptions of having their sense of safety and self-esteem undermined by the sexual abuser (Sas et al., 1993, p. 68):

> "I was scared that if someone else found out, that my father would believe that we had told and that he would kill our mother."
> "I was embarrassed, worried, especially as I was a boy, I was being molested by a man. I thought people might think I was gay or my parents might not believe me."

Emotional reactions elicited by harsh punishment or sexual exploitation require the child to search for an answer to a fundamental question concerning responsibility and blame: "Why did this happen to me?" The quotes above illustrate how some sexually abused children feel responsible for failing to recognize the abuse, participating in the abuse, causing their families' reactions to disclosure, failing to avoid or control the abuse, and failing to protect themselves. Rather than acknowledge or believe that one's own parents or a trusted adult could be at fault, some maltreated children may ascribe nonmalevolent intentions to the offender, which can then be used to explain and justify family problems and disruption to others. Shifting the blame to themselves or to situational

factors that are less important than one's own parents serves to provide a more acceptable explanation (D. A. Wolfe, 1999). One male survivor describes this attribution of blame: "I had to make sense out of what was going on. And the sense I made out of this was that I'm not really a good person. There's something different about me and something wrong" (Lisak, 1994, p. 541).

Blaming oneself or someone else for negative events is usually accompanied by unpleasant emotional reactions, such as sadness or anger (Fincham, Bradbury, & Grych, 1990). So child victims are faced with the ongoing challenge of seeking to explain their maltreatment, while at the same time avoiding the emotional turmoil that accompanies attributions of self-blame. As a result of this predicament, emotional and behavioral signs of stress and conflict are commonplace. Girls and boys tend to differ in the ways they process and express such turmoil: Maltreated girls tend to show more internalizing signs of distress, such as shame (Alessandri & Lewis, 1996) and self-blame (Hazzard, Celano, Gould, Lawry, & Webb, 1995; D. A. Wolfe, Sas, & Wekerle, 1994); boys, on the other hand, tend to show heightened levels of physical and verbal aggression (Scerbo & Kolko, 1995). Over time, misattributions of self-blame for sexual or physical abuse are likely to result in emotional, relational, and sexual problems (Hazzard, 1993; Herzberger, Potts, & Dillon, 1981; Wyatt & Newcomb, 1990). We now take a look at how some of these beliefs and behaviors emerge in the context of adjustment to situations involving peers and school.

Peer Problems and School Adjustment. It comes as no surprise that maltreated children's relationships with their peers and teachers typically mirror the models of relationships they know best (Cicchetti & Lynch, 1995). Instead of a healthy sense of autonomy and self-respect, their models of relationships have elements of being both a victim and a victimizer—those who rule and those who submit—and during interactions with peers, maltreated children may alternate between being the aggressor and being the victim (Dodge, Pettit, & Bates, 1994). Their adaptational strategies, such as hypervigilance and fear, have evolved to become highly responsive to threatening or dangerous situations. But these strategies conflict with the new challenges of school and peer groups. As a result some maltreated children, especially those with histories of physical abuse and neglect, may be more distracted by aggressive stimuli and misread the intentions of their peers and teachers as being more hostile than they actually are (Dodge et al., 1994).

The development of empathy and social sensitivity toward others during the preschool years are prerequisites for the development of positive, reciprocal peer relationships. Physically abused and neglected children, however, show little skill at recognizing distress in others, since this has not been their experience. This is how one 2-year-old boy who had been physically abused by his parents responded to a crying child:

> He then turned away from her to look at the ground and while looking at the ground began vocalizing "Cut it out! Cut it out! with increasing agitation, each time speaking more loudly and more quickly. He patted the child on the back, but when this disturbed her he retreated from her, hissing and baring his teeth. He again began patting her on the back, but this time his patting turned into beating. He continued beating the little girl despite her screams. (Main & Goldwyn, 1984, p. 207)

Thomas, an abused 1-year-old, exhibits disturbing signs of fearful distress when he hears a child crying in the distance:

> Suddenly, Thomas becomes a statue. His smile fades and his face takes on a look of distress also. He sits very still, his hand frozen in the air. His back is straight, and he becomes more and more tense as the crying continues. . . . The (distant) crying diminishes. Suddenly Thomas is back to normal, calm, mumbling, and playing in the sand. (Main & George, 1985, p. 410)

These quotes from a study of ten physically abused and ten nonabused toddlers illustrate a lack of social sensitivity as well as a disorganized, victim-victimizer reaction to peer distress. In this study, nonabused children typically showed concern or attempted to provide comfort to the distressed child, but as shown in Figure 14.2, not one maltreated child exhibited a concerned response at witnessing the distress of another toddler. Maltreated children not only failed to show concern, but also actively responded to distress in others with fear, physical attack, or anger. Can you see the continuity between their own experiences and their behavior with peers?

The general nature of maltreated children's peer relationships can be organized into two prominent themes (Cicchetti & Lynch, 1995). First, maltreated children, particularly *physically abused* children, are more physically and verbally aggressive toward their peers (Prino and Peyrot, 1994; Feldman et al., 1995). They are more likely to respond with anger and aggression both to friendly overtures from peers and to signs of distress in other children. Understandably, they are less popular and have atypical social networks marked by

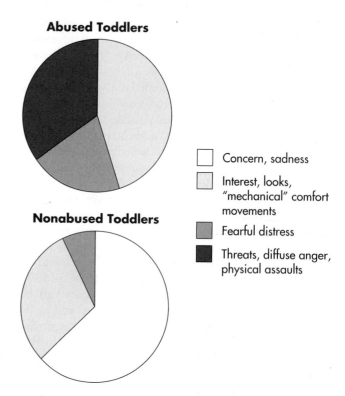

FIGURE 14.2 Responses to the distress of peers observed in abused versus nonabused toddlers in the daycare setting. (Main & George, 1985)

aggression and negative attention-seeking, which appear to grow worse over time (Haskett & Kistner, 1991; Feldman et al., 1995). Given their propensity to attribute hostile intent in others and their lack of empathy and social skill, it is not surprising that abused and neglected children are rejected by their peers.

The second theme is that maltreated children, especially *neglected children,* withdraw from and avoid peer interactions (Dodge et al., 1994; Hoffman-Plotkin & Twentyman, 1984). Neglected preschool and school-age children tend to remain isolated and passive during opportunities for free play with other children (Crittenden, 1992), and seldom display overtures of affection or initiate play with their mothers or peers (Bousha & Twentyman, 1984; Haskett & Kistner, 1991).

School entrance demands that children learn to integrate into their peer group, perform in the classroom, and develop their motivation to achieve. Physically abused and neglected children once again face considerable challenges. Low educational aspirations, lack of language stimulation, little encouragement to learn, and lack of recognition of strengths and achievements serve to undermine academic success. Moreover, maltreating families move twice as often as nonmaltreating families from similar SES backgrounds, which wreaks further havoc on academic stability and performance

(Eckenrode, Rowe, Laird, & Brathwaite, 1995). As a result of these negative experiences and of environmental deprivation, physically abused and neglected children perform at 2 years below grade level in verbal and math abilities (Salzinger, Kaplan, Pelcovitz, Samit, & Kreiger, 1984), obtain lower grades, and receive more discipline referrals and suspensions (Eckenrode, Laird, & Doris, 1993). Unfortunately, they continue to show significant differences in IQ and reading abilities into adulthood (Perez & Widom, 1994).

Children with histories of neglect stand out as having the most severe and wide-ranging problems in school. They perform worse than other maltreated children on standardized tests of reading, language, and math (Eckenrode et al., 1993; Kurtz, Gaudin, Wodarski, & Howing, 1993). They are described by teachers, who are unaware of their backgrounds, as lacking maturity and academic readiness; descriptions indicate problems completing schoolwork, lack of initiative, overreliance on teachers for help, and behavior that is both aggressive toward and withdrawn from their peers (Erickson et al., 1989). By the end of their first year of school, 65% of neglected children in a large prospective study were either referred for services or retained in first grade (Erickson et al., 1989).

Sexually abused children also have problems with peers and school adjustment, although this varies considerably. Unaware of their maltreatment status, teachers describe them as more anxious, inattentive, and unpopular, and having less autonomy and self-guidance in completing schoolwork (Erickson et al., 1989). Children with histories of sexual abuse are more likely than nonabused children to suffer in their academic performance and their ability to focus on tasks, to have histories of frequent school absenteeism, and to receive teacher ratings of shyness-anxiousness (Trickett, McBride-Chang, & Putnam, 1994).

Before discussing the clinical outcomes of abuse and neglect, let's review and summarize these major developmental implications. Child maltreatment has a demonstrable effect on children's peer- and school-related problems. Adjusting to school requires a *secure readiness to learn,* a dynamic balance between establishing secure relationships with adults and feeling free to explore their environment in ways that promote cognitive competence (Cicchetti & Lynch, 1995). Because they have little faith in their ability to succeed and are less independent in approaching novel situations (Aber et al., 1989), maltreated children try to adapt to their first major out-of-home environment (i.e., school) in the best way they know how. Thus, children with histories of neglect struggle considerably with academic tasks, because they usually have had poor academic and social preparation. Similarly, children with physical and sexual abuse histories have difficulty relating to peers and teachers, because they learned to be cautious and self-protective, and to use physical aggression or avoidance indiscriminantly. Such backgrounds not only expose children to violent or avoidant problem-solving strategies, but also deprive them of positive alternatives to interpersonal conflict and failure. Finally, keep in mind that children who are maltreated usually experience more than one form of maltreatment and family stress (D. A. Wolfe & McGee, 1994), so in practice an individual child's adjustment might vary considerably from these general conclusions.

Psychopathology and Adult Outcomes

The body mends soon enough. The broken spirit, however, takes the longest to heal.

—*Adult survivor of sexual abuse*

The developmental disruptions and impairments that accompany child abuse and neglect set in motion a series of events that increase the likelihood of failure and future maladaptation. As stated earlier, not all maltreated children who face these developmental challenges will develop psychopathology—let alone the same form of psychopathology—but they are at a much greater risk for significant emotional and adjustment problems (Cicchetti, 1990). Adolescents and adults with histories of physical abuse are at increased risk to develop interpersonal problems accompanied by aggression and violence (Malinosky-Rummell & Hansen, 1993). This relationship between being abused as a child and becoming abusive toward others as an adult supports the **cycle-of-violence hypothesis,** which infers that victims of violence become perpetrators of violence (Widom, 1989b). Those with histories of sexual abuse, in contrast, are more likely to develop chronic impairments in self-esteem, self-concept, and emotional and behavioral self-regulation (Putnam & Trickett, 1993), including severe outcomes such as PTSD, depression, and dissociative states. As adulthood approaches, these developmental impairments stemming from child maltreatment can lead to more pervasive and chronic psychiatric disorders, including anxiety and panic disorders, depression, eating disorders, sexual problems, and personality disturbances (Browne & Finkelhor, 1986; D. A. Wolfe & Jaffe, 1991).

Although little is known about emotional and behavioral problems among children with histories of neglect or emotional abuse, recent epidemiological studies of children with histories of sexual or physical abuse provide excellent detail on the extent of mental disorders and clinical symptoms among children and adolescents. In a study notable for its large and representative sample, Dutch researchers Garnefski and Diekstra (1997)

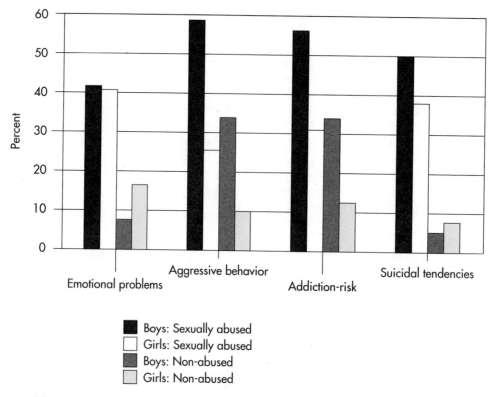

FIGURE 14.3 Problems among sexually abused and non-sexually abused boys and girls. (Data from Garnefski & Diekstra, 1997)

compared self-reported mental health problems of adolescents with sexual abuse histories (N = 745, ages 12 to 19 years; 80% female) with problems in a matched group without such histories. Their findings, shown in Figure 14.3, provide a useful overview of the mental health problems discussed in the following subsections. As expected, boys as well as girls with sexual abuse histories reported significantly more adjustment problems than their nonabused counterparts across all four areas of adjustment. However, an important new finding to emerge from this study was that boys with histories of sexual abuse reported considerably more emotional and behavioral problems, including suicidality, than their female counterparts, which could not be attributed to concurrent physical abuse these boys had experienced. These differences in how boys and girls react to and cope with the aftermath of childhood sexual abuse are just beginning to receive attention; such efforts will likely improve the ability to diagnose and treat these problems.

A similar epidemiological study of the aftermath of child physical abuse sheds light on the specific mental disorders and associated psychosocial problems experienced by these children (Flisher et al., 1997). Caretakers and children from a community-based probability sample of 9- through 17-year-olds (N = 665) in New York State and Puerto Rico were interviewed to assess a

broad range of adjustment and mental health indicators, as well as physical abuse. This study reinforces the responsibility researchers face in studying abuse: If abuse is reported by a child or parent, the interviewer is obligated to report it to authorities. Such requirements are explained to participants prior to the study, and in this particular study, researchers made arrangements to refer families to a mental health clinician. Over 25% (N = 172) of the sample had experienced some form of physical abuse (this percentage was reduced to 16.8% when persons were excluded whose only physical abuse was having been hit very hard on fewer than five occasions). A history of physical abuse was associated with significant functional impairments, such as poor social competence, as well as psychiatric problems. For example, 24% of children and adolescents with histories of physical abuse met criteria for a mood disorder, including major depression and dysthymia; 31% met criteria for one of the disruptive disorders, including ADHD, conduct disorder, and oppositional defiant disorder; and over 55% met criteria for an anxiety disorder, such as agoraphobia, overanxious disorder, and generalized anxiety disorder (Flisher et al., 1997). The odds ratios—the likelihood of having one of these disorders if physical abuse was present versus absent—are telling: Those with histories of physical abuse were about 3 times more likely to suffer a mood disorder, 4 times more likely to show a disruptive disorder, and 2 to 4 times more likely to have an anxiety disorder than their nonabused counterparts.

We now examine four prominent developmental outcomes of maltreatment—mood and affect disturbances, post-traumatic stress–related problems, sexual adjustment, and criminal and antisocial behavior—and note similarities and differences in these outcomes according to particular forms of abuse whenever appropriate.

Mood and Affect Disturbances. The following comment is from an adult survivor of sexual abuse:

> I trusted him so I think that it was confusing that he was doing this to me. I think that when I got older I was afraid more often than I was confused. I was really afraid. I really didn't want him to come near me. I'd try to avoid the situation and try to pretend that I was asleep so that he wouldn't come in to the room or anything like that, but it never worked. I felt helpless, which gradually turned into hopelessness and despair. (Suzuki, 1994)

Some say that child maltreatment affects children to their very soul, since it disrupts and impairs so many significant childhood memories and experiences. Perhaps this is why symptoms of depression, emotional distress, and suicidal ideation are common features of children with histories of physical, emotional, and sexual abuse (Kaufman, 1991; Koverola, Pound, Heger, & Lytle, 1993; Toth, Manly, & Cicchetti, 1992). Emotional trauma resulting from chronic rejection, loss of affection, betrayal, and feelings of helplessness that may accompany chronic maltreatment by one's own family members may be responsible for the emotional and behavioral disturbances shown among children, adolescents, and adults. On a more positive note, these outcomes can sometimes be avoided if children are provided with available support from nonoffending family members and opportunities to develop healthy coping strategies and social supports (Spaccarelli & Fuchs, 1997).

If symptoms of depression and mood disturbance go unrecognized, however, they are likely to increase during late adolescence and adulthood, especially among those who were sexually or physically abused since childhood (Browne & Finkelhor, 1986; Kolko, 1992). These symptoms, moreover, can lead to life-threatening suicide attempts and self-mutilating behavior (Hartman & Burgess, 1989; Kaplan, Pelcovitz, Salzinger, Mandel, & Weiner, 1997), especially among those who were sexually abused from early childhood (Van der Kolk, Perry, & Herman, 1991). In addition, PTSD-related symptoms

may co-occur with depression over time (Brand, King, Olson, Ghaziuddin, & Naylor, 1996; McLeer, Callaghan, Henry, & Wallen, 1994) (see following section). Perhaps as a result of chronic emotional pain, some teens and adults attempt to cope with unpleasant memories and current stressors by abusing alcohol and drugs, in a futile effort to temporarily reduce or avoid their distress (Herman, 1992). Substance abuse may also bolster self-esteem and reduce feelings of isolation (National Research Council, 1993).

Post-Traumatic Stress–Related Problems

Celia: Walled Away

"What I would end up doing was separating from the physical feeling and couldn't comprehend the physical pain and emotional sensation. The only word I can use now—I didn't have the word when I was five—the word I use now is rape, and the only way I could deal with that was I would separate into the wallpaper and the wallpaper was all different ballerinas and different poses and what I could see from them was that they didn't move. They were always smiling or they always had this look on their face and they couldn't be touched. They just stood still. So I would become this ballerina and I couldn't be touched and whatever he did to me I couldn't feel it because I was in the wall." (Suzuki, 1994)

A significant number of men and women who have been subjected to severe physical or sexual abuse during childhood suffer long-term stress-related disorders of the type described in Chapter 7. Like Rosita, they may be haunted by intrusive thoughts or feelings of being trapped or, like Celia, they may dissociate or become emotionally numb, as they had done originally to escape from the pain and fear. As noted in Chapter 13, child sexual abuse can also lead to eating disorders, such as anorexia and bulimia nervosa.

Almost half of children and adolescents with histories of maltreatment involving sexual abuse or combined sexual and physical abuse, meet criteria for PTSD (D. A. Wolfe et al., 1994). The prevalence may be even higher among adults: 87% of a sample of 45 women with sexual abuse histories met criteria for current PTSD, and almost all (98%) met criteria at some point in their life since the abuse (Rodriguez, Ryan, Kemp, & Foy, 1997); these results are similar to previous findings (Rowan, Foy, Rodriguez, & Ryan, 1994). The course of this disorder may begin in childhood with abuse-specific fears, such as fear of being alone and fear of men, as well as idiosyncratic fears related to specific abuse events, such as fear of sleeping (Terr, 1991; V. V. Wolfe, Gentile, & D. A. Wolfe, 1989). PTSD-related symptoms are also more likely if the abuse was chronic and the perpetrator relied on some method of coercion or trickery to force compliance (Rowan et al., 1994; D. A. Wolfe et al., 1994). The nature of sexual abuse trauma, coupled with the child's developmental stage, may lead to the development of PTSD-related symptoms among sexually abused girls, in particular. Physically abused adolescents, in contrast, are more likely to have behavioral and social difficulties rather than PTSD (Pelcovitz et al., 1994).

Because of the emotional and physical pain of abusive experiences, children may voluntarily or involuntarily induce an altered state of consciousness known as **dissociation,** which can be adaptive when neither resistance nor escape are possible (Herman, 1992). The process allows the victim to feel detached from the body or self, as if what is happening is not happening to him or her. Almost all people dissociate in minor ways, such as daydreaming, but abuse victims may have to rely on this form of psychological escape to the extent that profound disruptions to self and memory can occur. Over time, this fragmentation of experience and affect can progress into borderline or multiple personality disorders (Briere & Runtz, 1991; Weaver & Clum, 1993).

The extreme stress associated with child sexual abuse may actually cause changes in brain development and structure, which may explain some of the symptoms of psychological trauma. Changes in the hippocampus—the part of the brain that deals with short-term memory and, possibly, the coding and retrieval of long-term memory—could occur as a result of hormones flooding the brain before and after a stressful episode. The hippocampus is particularly sensitive to high levels of cortisols, which circulate for hours or days after stress. Low cortisol is linked with emotional numbing, and spasms of high cortisol coincide with disturbing memories (Wang et al., 1995). After prolonged stress, cortisol levels become depleted, and the feedback systems that control hormone levels in the brain may become dysfunctional. Stress floods the brain with cortisol; the brain, in turn, resets the threshold at which cortisol is produced, so that ultimately it circulates at a dramatically low level. The neuroendocrine system becomes highly sensitive to stress, much like it does in individuals who suffer from PTSD (De Bellis, Burke, Trickett, & Putnam, 1996). Pharmacological and psychological treatment methods show promise in reversing this process.

Sexual Adjustment. Sexual abuse can also lead to **traumatic sexualization,** in which children's sexual knowledge and behavior are shaped in developmentally inappropriate ways. About 35% of preschoolers who have been sexually abused show age-inappropriate sexual behavior, such as French-kissing, open masturbation, and genital exposure (Cosentino, Meyer-Bahlburg, Alpert, Weinberg, & Gaines, 1995; Friedrich, Jaworski, Huxsahl, & Bengston, 1997). These signs of traumatic sexualization are more likely to occur following situations in which a sexual response was evoked from the child, or he or she was enticed or forced to participate (Finkelhor & Browne, 1988). For some children, the offenders' means of enticement—gifts, privileges, affection, and special attention—teaches them that their sexual behavior is a means to an end. Thus they may attempt to sexualize interpersonal relationships by indiscriminantly hugging and kissing strange adults and children, something that is relatively uncommon among non-sexually abused children (Cosentino et al., 1995). For others, however, sexual behavior is associated with strong emotions, such as fear, disgust, shame, and confusion. These feelings may translate into distorted views about the body and sexuality, in some cases leading to weight problems, eating disorders, poor physical health care, and physically self-destructive behaviors (Springs & Friedrich, 1992).

Although sexualized behaviors are more common among younger abused children, they sometimes re-emerge during adolescence in the guise of promiscuity, prostitution, sexual aggression, and victimization of others (Beitchman et al., 1992; Kendall-Tackett et al., 1993). In fact, an early history of sexual abuse among males is a significant risk factor for inappropriate sexual behaviors, alienation, and social incompetence in adolescence (Haviland, Sonne, & Woods, 1995). Among a sample of youths being treated for psychiatric disorders (80% of whom were male), those who were sexually abused before 7 years of age engaged in sexually inappropriate behaviors, such as hypersexuality (flirtatious behaviors or touching others' private parts), exposure (public masturbation or self-exposure), or victimization of others (repeated or forcible touching against another's will, incest, or rape), about twice as often as in patients whose sexual abuse began after age 7 (McClellan et al., 1996). In contrast to these outcomes among abused males, women with childhood histories of sexual abuse are more likely to report difficulties in adulthood related to sexual adjustment, ranging from low sexual arousal to intrusive flashbacks, disturbing sensations, and feelings of guilt, anxiety, and low self-esteem concerning their sexuality (Finkelhor & Browne, 1988). Because their normal development of self-awareness and self-protection was compromised, adult survivors of child sexual abuse may become less capable of identifying risk situations or persons, or knowing how to respond to unwanted sexual or physical attention. Consequently, they are more likely to fall victim to further violence in adulthood, such as rape or domestic violence (Kendall-Tackett et al., 1993; Russell, 1986).

Criminal and Antisocial Behavior.

Does violence beget violence, as predicted by the cycle-of-violence hypothesis mentioned earlier? Although many persons convicted of heinous crimes and child abuse report significant histories of child abuse and neglect, most abused children do not go on to commit crimes. How do we reconcile this obvious, but complicated, connection between victim and victimizer roles?

Consider the developmental importance of adolescence. This stage may represent a critical transition between being a victim of child maltreatment and the future likelihood of becoming abusive or being abused as an adult (D. A. Wolfe, Wekerle, & Scott, 1997). Social dating, a favorite—and significant—adolescent pastime, can be a testing ground whereby one's knowledge and expectations about relationships are played out. Youth who have learned to adapt to violence and intimidation as a way of life, and who lack suitable alternative role models or experiences, are more likely to enter the social dating arena with inappropriate expectations about relationships. Indeed, youth (girls as well as boys) who grew up in violent homes report more violence—especially verbal abuse and threats—toward their dating partners as well as toward themselves (D. A. Wolfe, Wekerle, Reitzel-Jaffe, & Lefebvre, 1998). Dating violence during adolescence, combined with a past history of violence in their own family, are strong prerelationship predictors of intimate violence in early adulthood and marriage (O'Leary, Malone, & Tyree, 1994). Thus, adolescence may be the middle stage, or initiation period, in the formation of a violent dynamic in intimate partnerships.

As we said, many children with maltreatment histories do not become violent offenders. Yet there is a significant connection between such events and subsequent arrest as a juvenile or an adult (Widom, 1989a), or engaging in sexual and physical violence as a young adult, especially for males (Malamuth, Sockloskie, Koss, & Tanaka, 1991; Feldman, 1997). A history of maltreatment is associated with an earlier mean age at first offense and a higher frequency of offenses, as well as a higher proportion of chronic offenders (Widom, 1989b). Retrospective studies of delinquent populations find that the amount of violence in the adolescent's past is the most striking factor distinguishing violent from nonviolent delinquents (Lewis, Pincus, & Glaser, 1979; Tarter, Hegedus, Winsten, & Alterman, 1984). Keep in mind, however, that such studies have methodological shortcomings, such as relying on subjects' own recall of events from the past once they have committed offenses (Mash

& D. A. Wolfe, 1991). Box 14.1 describes a study which, while avoiding some of the major methodological limitations, links childhood violence and adult violence.

Although most child victims of maltreatment do not grow up to be perpetrators of violence, a disturbingly high number—approximately 30%—carry the pattern into adolescence and adulthood (Kaufman & Zigler, 1989). Growing up with power-based, authoritarian methods—even if they don't result in physical injuries or identified maltreatment—can be toxic to relationship and social patterns. Remarkably, the amount of routine violence—frequently being hit with objects or physically punished—one experiences as a child is significantly associated with violent delinquent behavior later on (Straus & Donnelly, 1994). This connection is especially noteworthy, given the previous description of how routine violence toward children is commonplace throughout North America.

Final Considerations.

The connection between early child maltreatment and subsequent violent or abusive acts has important implications. Early maltreatment poses major challenges to the child's cognitive, emotional, and behavioral coping strategies, yet many children and adolescents remain capable of accomplishing major developmental milestones and become well-functioning adults. The pathway from child maltreatment to violent behavior—while very significant—is by no means direct, inevitable, or irreversible. Many circumstantial events, such as the availability of a caring adult, as well as individual factors, such as strong ego control, an easygoing temperament, and social competence, may play a role in mitigating against such outcomes (Cicchetti & Lynch, 1995). Child sexual abuse often follows a developmental trajectory different from that of other forms of maltreatment, which is not surprising given the nature and dynamics of such offenses. Child sexual abuse may lead to serious psychological problems, but the vast majority of these child victims do not commit crimes.

Nevertheless, community as well as clinical studies attest to the reality that any form of child maltreatment can result in significant negative repercussions that persist into adulthood, including affect disturbances, PTSD, difficulties in sexual adjustment, and criminal and antisocial behavior (Briere, 1997; Mullen, Martin, Anderson, Romans, & Herbison, 1996). While many—perhaps most—adults with histories of maltreatment lead productive and satisfying lives, others lead lives fraught with serious psychological distress and disturbance (Jumper, 1995). Some of the elements shared by almost all maltreated children—disrupted and disturbed family background, commonly marked by alcohol abuse and high levels of violence against family members—may

Box 14.1

What Are the Long-Term Criminal Consequences of Child Maltreatment?

This important question has been plaguing the field and the general public, from therapists and educators to policy makers and criminal justice officials. Cathy Widom (1989a, 1989b; 1996) addressed this question by examining the criminal records of over 900 individuals who had been subjected as children to physical or sexual abuse or neglect prior to age 12, along with a matched cohort of nonmaltreated children. Both groups were followed into adolescence and early adulthood to determine if they engaged in criminal or delinquent behavior as adolescents or adults. The results are telling: Of the people who experienced any type of child maltreatment (physical abuse, sexual abuse, or neglect), 27% were arrested as juveniles, compared with 17% of their nonabused counterparts. The same pattern continued into adulthood: 42% of the abused/neglected group, compared with 33% of the controls, had arrest records as adults. Consistent with the cycle-of-violence hypothesis, those with histories of physical abuse (21%), neglect (20%), or both (16%) were particularly more likely to be arrested for a violent crime (Maxfield & Widom, 1996) (although not as visible, child neglect is linked to the cycle of violence because of the parent's disregard of basic child care and the violation of a child's dependency status, which may involve a parent's vehement refusal to provide for the child as well as a passive withholding of love and affection; Wekerle & D. A. Wolfe, 1996). A disturbing result is that women with histories of physical abuse and neglect were significantly more likely than nonmaltreated women to be arrested for a violent act (7% versus 4%, respectively), whereas this relationship was barely significant for men (26% versus 22%, respectively). Notably, those with histories of sexual abuse were no different from the other maltreated children in their rates of criminal offenses.

But what about sex crimes? Are persons who were sexually abused in childhood more likely to commit sexual offenses, as suggested by the backgrounds of known sexual offenders? If all types of abuse and neglect

are combined, the odds of being arrested for a sex crime were 2 times greater than for nonvictims. However, if maltreatment backgrounds were broken down by type, only those with physical abuse and neglect backgrounds were associated with increased arrests for sex crimes; those with sexual abuse backgrounds were not (this finding remained even when only male subjects were compared). Children who were sexually abused were about as likely as the controls to be arrested later for any sex crime, and less likely than victims of physical abuse and neglect (see accompanying figure). Thus, although any type of maltreatment puts victims at higher risk for criminal behavior, persons who were sexually abused in childhood are less likely than victims of physical abuse or neglect to commit a sex crime, and no more likely than demographically similar individuals.

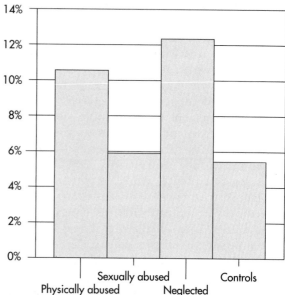

Sex crimes and maltreatment backgrounds. (Data from Wisom, 1996)

---

be operative in defining these developmental trajectories (D. A. Wolfe, 1999). We explore the interplay between these shared elements of adult, child, and family influences in the following discussion of causes.

CAUSES

My father was frightened of his mother. I was frightened of my father and I am damn well going to see to it that my children are frightened of me.
—George V (1865–1936)

Why do some family relationships give rise to pain and conflict instead of support and harmony? Because there is no simple answer to this question, we have to rely on a combination of theory, clinical observations, and empirical findings. For physical abuse and neglect, an important fact is that they are **relational disorders** (Cicchetti et al., 1988). These forms of maltreatment occur most often during periods of stressful role transitions for parents, such as the postnatal attachment period, the early childhood and early adolescence "oppositional" periods of testing limits, and times of family instability and disruption (Milner & Dopke, 1997). Care-givers' failure to provide nurturant, sensitive, available, and supportive care-giving, especially during critical periods, is a fundamental feature of maltreatment.

Notwithstanding the critical role of the adult offender, abuse and neglect are rarely caused by a single risk factor. In addition, even though risk signs and indicators are present, it is still very difficult to predict who may become abusive and who will not. Remember that child maltreatment is an event, not a uniform disorder; therefore it is necessary to consider multiple causes that interact unpredictably. Like a tornado that arises from just the right conditions of heavy wind, atmospheric pressure, and open terrain, child maltreatment may emerge in any given family if the "right" conditions exist. These causal conditions stem largely from the interaction of individual, familial, and cultural influences, but it is not possible to predict with precision where and when they will detonate (Belsky, 1984; Spaccarelli, 1995).

Stress is one of those forces of nature and humankind that can convert static conditions into dynamic, chaotic patterns. For example, physical abuse and neglect occur most often in the context of social and economic family deprivation, which can transform predisposed, high-risk parents into abusive or neglectful ones. The greater degree of stress in the social environment of the abusive parent increases the probability that violence will surface as an attempt to gain control or cope with irritating, stressful events. In the case of neglect, stress may be so great that parents withdraw from their child care responsibilities.

Sexual abuse is also influenced by cultural and familial practices as well as the dynamic forces of stress. However, unlike physical abuse and neglect, sexual abuse is primarily a premeditated act, in which the adult offender plays a purposeful and intentional role. The abuser plans ways to circumvent the child's natural resistance and self-protection, and controls the situation to avoid detection. In the following sections we address these important causal issues in relation to psychological, social, and cultural dimensions.

Social scientists have learned an enormous amount in recent years about the characteristics of abusive and neglectful parents. Still, they cannot fully explain why, under similar circumstances, some adults become abusive and others do not. In general, maltreatment is seldom caused by adult psychopathology (D. A. Wolfe, 1985) or known biological influences alone (National Research Council, 1993), although these factors can play an important role in some cases. Early explanations for child abuse and neglect were straightforward, yet narrow: Child abuse was a deviant act; therefore, the perpetrators of such acts were probably criminally inclined or psychiatrically disturbed (Spinetta & Rigler, 1972). But studies of the psychological characteristics of abusive and neglectful parents have suggested other possibilities. Fewer than 10% of maltreating parents have a primary psychiatric illness, such as paranoid schizophrenia or Munchausen by Proxy (see Box 14.2), that might cause them to harm a child (D. A. Wolfe, 1985). However, they are quite likely to have a history of learning and intellectual deficits and personality disorders that impede their day-to-day abilities to cope successfully with child-related and other stressors. Similarly, intrafamilial sexual abusers do not show evidence of psychopathology; rather, sexual abuse perpetrators are heterogeneous and impossible to classify on the basis of one or even several personality traits (Williams & Finkelhor, 1990). It's a complicated story that we begin to unravel by looking at the important psychological dimensions that contribute to these adult behaviors toward children.

Physical Abuse and Neglect

Brenda: Unhappy Childhood, Unhappy Motherhood

Milton's mother, Brenda, described her childhood as one of harsh discipline and physical abuse. "My father was an alcoholic, and when he was drunk he'd start picking on one of us—me, my older brother, or my mom," Brenda explained. "After being pushed around and beaten for so long, I took off and left home as soon as I was able to, when I was 15. I lived with friends until I was old enough to get welfare; then I hooked up with Milton's father. He was good to me at first, but it wasn't long until he started hitting me, just like my dad had done." In recounting her background, Brenda would sometimes grow quiet and sad, but this soon was overpowered by her efforts to force herself back to her complaints about her son. Her affect changed rapidly to one of hostility and annoyance, which spilled over into her actions with Milton.

To many parents like Brenda, child-rearing is a difficult and aversive event that can escalate unpredictably into a sudden abusive incident, or more gradually turn into avoidance and neglect. Lacking experience and guidance in child-rearing, and faced with overwhelming stress, these parents cannot think of ways to handle the situation. Instead, they succumb to the irritation of the moment—the child—and respond emotionally, without thinking.

Box 14.2

Munchausen by Proxy—The Deadly Game

After 22 months of unsuccessful diagnostic procedures in a hospital setting in England to determine the cause of a baby's breathing problem, staff concealed a video camera in the baby's hospital room, and a policewoman and a nurse jointly monitored the scene. The following events occurred:

Sixteen hours after the onset of video monitoring, the child was asleep in his cubicle with only his mother in attendance. She moved the chair away from the cot and lowered the cot sides. She then placed a soft garment (a T-shirt) on the bedding close to the child's face. Five minutes later she placed the garment over his nose and mouth and forced his head onto the mattress. He awoke immediately and struggled violently. After ten seconds the officer alerted the nurses who went into the cubicle. . . . In this first episode the police officer had intervened prematurely [by legal standards] because of her own distress at what she had seen. She decided to continue surveillance. Twenty minutes later, when the child was asleep on his side and the mother was again alone in the cubicle, she placed him in a supine position with his face upright and tucked his arms under the bedding. Ten minutes later she again applied the garment to his nose and mouth and forced his head onto the mat-

tress. The child struggled violently. Forty-two seconds later the nursing staff were alerted by the police and went into the cubicle. . . . The mother claimed that he had woken screaming and that she was comforting him. (Schreier & Libow, 1996, p. 40)

Munchausen is the name of an 18th-century military mercenary who became famous for his wartime tales, suspected to be fabrications. As an adult disorder, Munchausen syndrome refers to an intentional fabrication of illness. As a form of child abuse, it refers to physical and psychological harm either through direct attack by the parent (which can be life-threatening) or as a function of being subjected to painful and numerous medical assessment procedures. Although the disorder is more likely to involve the mother, the father may be a passive colluder and an uninvolved or absent parent. Little is known of this form of abuse, however, and prevalence rates have not been determined. In a 1991 U.S. survey of 316 pediatric neurologists and gastroenterologists, 273 confirmed cases and 192 suspected cases were reported.

Source: Schreier & Libow, 1996.

Brenda's history and situation is very typical: How would she know how to raise her child, given her own childhood experiences? Many abusive and neglectful parents have had little exposure to positive parental models and supports, either in their past or at present. Their own childhoods were often full of difficult, sometimes very traumatic, episodes of family violence, alcoholism, and harsh family circumstances related to frequent moves, unemployment, and poverty (D. A. Wolfe, 1985). As adults, they find daily living stressful and irritating, and they prefer to avoid potential sources of support because it takes additional energy to maintain social relationships. Chronic physical ailments and a pervasive mood of discontentment are common complaints, which are understandable in light of their circumstances and limited coping resources. What are the major adult characteristics and the child and family influences that can turn everyday problems into high-risk circumstances?

Adult Characteristics. Maltreatment doesn't happen accidentally, but it's not usually a planned or intentional act either. One parent described it this way: *"I felt I was spinning out of control. Everywhere I went, things just built up and tension mounted. When I tried to quiet my kids down, I would start shouting. When I tried*

to run away, everything followed me like a trail of debris. I just wanted the craziness to stop."

Like a chain reaction, a tragic combination of events can cause some predisposed individuals to maltreat a child in their care. Most of these events have one factor in common: They pose added stress to an individual who has already reached his or her limit.

Because abuse and neglect usually occur in relation to child-rearing demands, it is not surprising that both neglectful as well as abusive parents interact less often with their children than other parents do during everyday activities involving their children. In general, neglectful parents actively avoid interacting with their children, even when the child appropriately seeks attention, most likely because social interaction is unfamiliar and even unpleasant. Physically abusive parents, in contrast, tend to deliver a lot of threats or angry commands to their children that exceed the demands of the situation, rather than positive forms of guidance and praise.

Let's return to Brenda's situation and consider how her learning history, combined with situational events, became a recipe for disaster. When her son misbehaved, she responded with a harsh combination of emotional and physical threats, the methods most familiar to her. At first, physical punishment would stop Milton's misbehavior, but over time it led to a standoff, forcing her to increase the severity of her punishment and the child to escalate his aversiveness (Patterson & Cobb, 1973). Her cognitive perceptions and distortion of events also played a significant role in this coercive process. Because of **information-processing disturbances,** maltreating parents may misperceive or mislabel typical child behavior in ways that lead to inappropriate responses and increased aggression (Azar, 1997; Crittenden, 1993; Larrance & Twentyman, 1983; Milner, 1993). They are unfamiliar with their role as parents and what is developmentally appropriate behavior for a child at a given age. Brenda believed that her son was able to understand—at age 4—what she was thinking and feeling, and to put her needs ahead of his own.

Over time Brenda thought Milton was misbehaving intentionally, presumably because, in her mind, he should have known better ("I can never get him to listen—he's a troublemaker, and he knows how to push my buttons"). Some parents apply the same faulty reasoning to themselves as well, which results in lowered self-efficacy ("I'm not a good mother; other mothers can get their children to do these things"). Sadly, these unrealistic expectations and negative intent attributions can lead to greater punishment for child misbehavior and less reliance on explanation and positive teaching methods (Azar, 1991; Larrance & Twentyman, 1983). Children are seen as deserving of harsh punishment, and its use is rationalized as a way to maintain control. By now you can see where this process might end up.

Neglectful parents have received far less research attention than physically abusive ones, perhaps because *omissions* of proper caretaking behaviors are more difficult to describe and detect than *commissions*. Although personality characteristics and lifestyle choices of abusive and neglectful parents overlap considerably, as a group, neglectful parents have more striking personality disorders and inadequate knowledge of children's needs, and they suffer more chronic patterns of social isolation than both abusive and nonmaltreating parents (Gaines, Sandgrund, Green, & Power, 1978; D. A. Wolfe, 1985). Furthermore, neglectful care-givers typically disengage when under stress, whereas abusive parents become emotionally and behaviorally reactive (Hillson & Kuiper, 1994). Neglectful parents try to cope with the stress of child-rearing and related family matters through escape and avoidance, which can lead not only to severe consequences for the child but also to higher risk for these parents of substance abuse and similar coping failures (Harrington, Dubowitz, Black, & Binder, 1995).

Like a tropical storm with an unpredictable course, a conflict between the parent and child can suddenly increase in intensity and turn into a damaging hurricane, or it can simply blow over. Negative arousal and emotions are highly "conditionable," meaning that they are easily paired with salient events that can later trigger the same feelings. Such conditioning may occur gradually and build into uncontrollable outbursts, or occur suddenly during highly stressful, provocative episodes of conflict.

To illustrate, picture yourself trying to get your child ready for school each day, and going through the same frustrating chain of events: you're late for work and under pressure to get to a meeting when your preschooler starts to fuss about wearing his boots or combing her hair. For all but a hearty few, this combination of stress and all-too-familiar child demands spells anger and frustration. While most of us manage to control our emotions so as to deal with the situation in the best possible way, parents who have deficits in child-rearing and information-processing skills may see the child as intentionally causing them to be late. Anger and arousal are powerful emotions, so rational problem solving can quickly give way to emotional and reflexive reactions.

Anger and rage are highly dependent on situational cues, which usually stem from prior emotionally arousing events. In Brenda's case, certain "looks" that her son gave led her to believe that he wasn't going to comply. We discovered this by videotaping the two of them playing together and then having Brenda ask Milton to straighten up the room. We played the tape back and asked Brenda to tell us whenever she felt that Milton was doing something that bothered her. She stopped the tape at several different points, telling us that "he's giving me that look," or "I know what he's thinking—why should I have to do what she says?" This is when Brenda's tone of voice would become more tense and frustrated, and her instructions to Milton more forceful and abrupt. Although she could acknowledge that she was getting very angry, she was not able at first to interrupt this process and calm herself down. This demonstrates how parental arousal can be triggered by events, including past memories and current emotional tension, that may be highly specific to a particular parent-child relationship. This may lead, of course, to an overgeneralized—more angry, more aggressive—parental response, because the parent is responding to cues that have been previously associated with frustration and anger.

Child and Family Influences. Do certain child characteristics or behaviors increase the likelihood of abusive or neglectful care? Children have an uncanny ability to figure out what their parents are going to do before they actually do it, and they become amazingly accomplished at weighing the odds for desired outcomes. But even though children might do things that are annoying, adults are fully responsible for abuse and neglect. No child—no matter how difficult to manage or how challenging to teach—ever deserves to be mistreated. Children's behavior or developmental limitations may increase the potential for abuse, but only if accompanied by the other critical factors noted previously. With the important exception of the relation between gender and sexual abuse, no child characteristic—age, gender, temperament, low birth weight, hyperactivity, conduct problems, or handicapping conditions—has been associated with the risk of maltreatment, once environmental and adult factors are controlled (National Research Council, 1993; Whitmore, Kramer, & Knutson, 1993). Unintentionally, however, the child may still play a role in the continuation or escalation of an abusive or neglectful relationship.

The kind of coercive family interactions that we discussed in Chapter 6 with regard to aggressive children frequently occur in abusive families (Reid, Taplin, & Lorber, 1981; D. A. Wolfe, 1985). Physically abused or neglected children, for example, may learn from an early age that misbehaving often elicits a predictable parent reaction—even though it's negative—which gives the child some sense of control. If crying and clinging are the only ways to get a parent's attention, these behaviors may escalate in intensity over time, especially if the parent fails to provide appropriate child stimulation and control. This type of interaction explains why abusive incidents occur most often during difficult, but not uncommon, episodes of child behavior, such as disobedience, fighting and arguing, accidents, and dangerous behavior, that may produce anger and tension in some adults. Circumstances surrounding incidents of neglect, in contrast, relate more to chronic adult inadequacy, which spills over into daily family functioning (B. C. Herrenkohl, E. C. Herrenkohl, & Egolf, 1983). Neglected children's early feeding problems or irritability may place an increased strain on the parents' limited child care abilities, again setting in motion an escalation in the child's dependency needs and demandingness, accompanied by further parental withdrawal (Drotar, 1992).

Family circumstances, most notably conflict and marital violence, also have a causal connection to child maltreatment. In about 40% of the families in which adult partners are violent toward one another, one or both parents have also been violent toward a child at some point during the previous year (Straus, Gelles, & Steinmetz, 1980). Domestic conflicts and violence against women most often arise during disagreements over child-rearing, discipline, and each partner's responsibilities in child care (Edleson, Eisikovits, Guttmann, & Sela-Amit, 1991). Children may be caught in the cross fire between angry adults, or in some cases, they might instigate a marital conflict by misbehaving or demanding attention (Jaffe, D. A. Wolfe, & Wilson, 1990). In either case, an escalating cycle of family turmoil and violence

"I hate you! Never come back to my house," screamed an eight-year-old at his father as police arrested the man for attacking his wife. (From *Living with the Enemy*, photo © Donna Ferrato)

begins, whereby children's behavioral and emotional reactions to the violence create additional stress on the marital relationship, further aggravating an already volatile situation. Because of the physical and psychological consequences of violence, moreover, abused women are less capable of responding to their children's needs, which again increases pressure on the family system. Tragically, not only do marital violence and family turmoil frighten and disturb children in a direct manner, but the resulting fallout from such events—ranging from changes in financial status and living quarters to loss of family unity and safety—prolongs the stress and thus the harmful impact on children's development (D. A. Wolfe et al., 1985).

An Integrated Model. In a dynamic process, parental and situational factors interact over time to either increase or decrease the risk of physical abuse or neglect. Figure 14.4 depicts this dynamic process in relation to three hypothetical transitional stages which suggest that maladaptive interaction patterns, like adaptive ones, develop not simply because of the predilections of the parent or child. To the contrary, such behaviors are the result of complex interactions between child characteristics, parental personality and style, the history of the parent-child relationship, and the supportive or nonsupportive nature of the broader social context within which the family is embedded (D. A. Wolfe, 1999). This process, moreover, includes both destabilizing and compensatory factors that can influence the likelihood of abuse or neglect in a negative or positive fashion, respectively.

Stage 1: The integrated model first acknowledges the degree of parental preparation for their important role: How well do they cope with the demands and frustrations of child-rearing? If parents lack the ability or

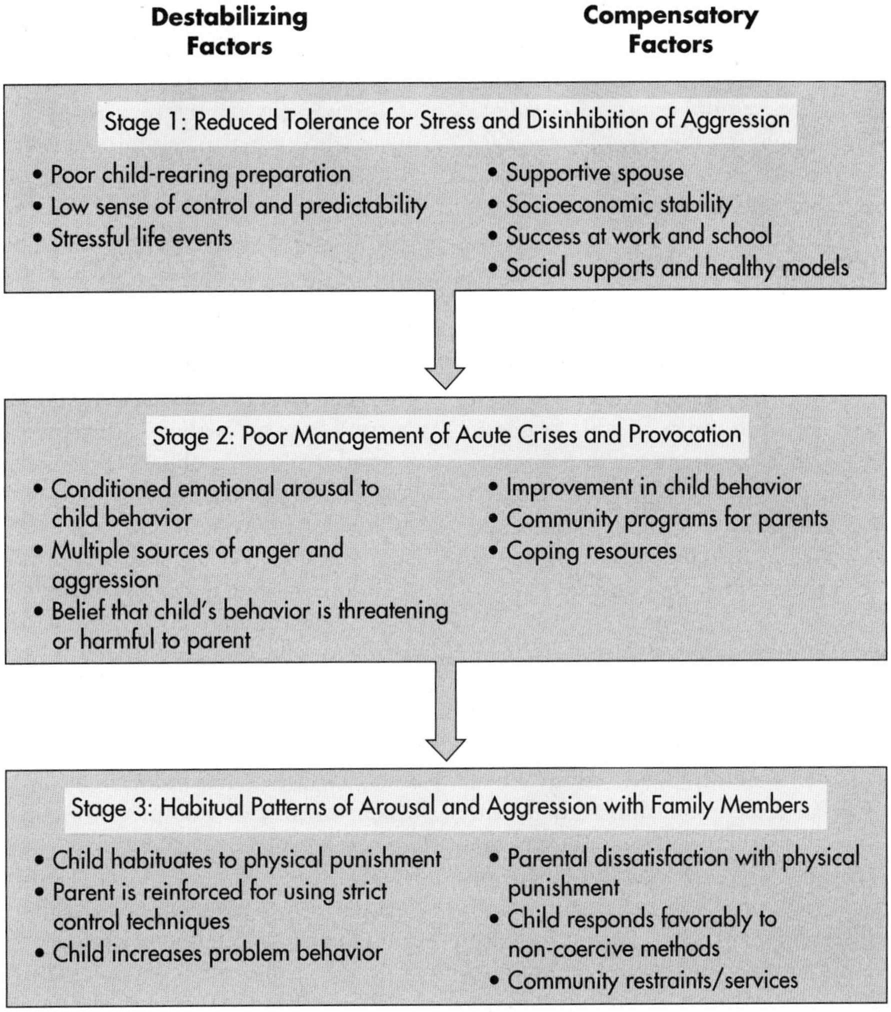

**Destabilizing
Factors**

**Compensatory
Factors**

Stage 1: Reduced Tolerance for Stress and Disinhibition of Aggression

- Poor child-rearing preparation
- Low sense of control and predictability
- Stressful life events

- Supportive spouse
- Socioeconomic stability
- Success at work and school
- Social supports and healthy models

Stage 2: Poor Management of Acute Crises and Provocation

- Conditioned emotional arousal to child behavior
- Multiple sources of anger and aggression
- Belief that child's behavior is threatening or harmful to parent

- Improvement in child behavior
- Community programs for parents
- Coping resources

Stage 3: Habitual Patterns of Arousal and Aggression with Family Members

- Child habituates to physical punishment
- Parent is reinforced for using strict control techniques
- Child increases problem behavior

- Parental dissatisfaction with physical punishment
- Child responds favorably to non-coercive methods
- Community restraints/services

FIGURE 14.4   An integrated model of physical child abuse. (Wolfe, 1999)

adequate resources to cope effectively at this initial stage (and many do, at first), the risk of poorly managing daily events and annoyances increases. Many first-time parents admit to the sometimes overwhelming and unexpected demands of parenthood, but the vast majority do not become abusive or neglectful because they have compensatory factors available, such as those mentioned in the figure. However, failure to deal effectively with the demands of their role early on, both within and outside the family context, can readily lead to increased pressure on the parent-child relationship and a concomitant increase in the probability of child maltreatment.

Stage 2:   The patterns begun in Stage 1 may progress to Stage 2, whereby the parents' inability to cope effectively with child-rearing demands further heightens their emotional arousal and strengthens their belief that their child is causing them undue stress. Because they are unfamiliar with more positive methods, and because coercive methods seem to work in the short

run (that is, the child stops misbehaving, or the parents relieve their tension or anger), parents learn to rely on coercion, threats, or avoidance as means of responding to child-related stressors. Their children, too, may learn to be more demanding, even coercive, when interacting with their parents, because this is what they have learned to do from an early age. At this point the amount and intensity of uncontrollable events can seem overwhelming to the parent, which can open the floodgates, releasing anger, frustration, or resignation that is most often directed at a child or spouse.

Stage 3:   Over weeks or years, parents may become convinced that excessive punishment and force, or avoidance and escape, are absolutely necessary to control their child's behavior. They adhere to the belief that if they let up, their child will somehow destroy much of what they have remaining and, in effect, take control of the household (D. A. Wolfe, 1999). Similarly, in cases of neglect, parents may actively avoid coming in contact with the child, as a way to escape from further stress and aggravation. Under such circumstances child behavior problems often worsen, accompanied by an increase in parental frustration and harsher attempts to control the child. Parents become caught in this vicious cycle of using coercive or avoidant methods in response to tension and irritation, which works at first but gradually becomes more and more ineffective.

Unfortunately, the dangerous consequences and serious side effects of this process can continue to go unnoticed or unresolved, leading to a habitual pattern of irritability, arousal, and/or avoidance of responsibility that perpetuates the use of power-assertive or avoidant child-rearing methods. At each stage of this process, compensatory factors, such as a supportive spouse, financial stability, and intervention services, can alter the transition from stressful to abusive and neglectful child care in a positive way. We discuss compensatory factors in greater detail later in the chapter.

Sexual Abuse

Those seeking explanations for child sexual abuse have looked for evidence of deviant sexual histories of the adult offender, as well as environmental and cultural risk factors that play a role in the exploitation of children. Yet, similar to child physical abusers, sexual abusers are a very mixed group who defy personality labels or psychiatric descriptors. Some are described as timid and unassertive, while others show a pattern of poor impulse control and domineering interpersonal style. A common ground is their preference for sexual exploitation of children and adolescents who, because of their age and innocence, cannot consent to such activities nor easily disclose the abuse to someone. We now explore these adult characteristics, along with family and situational factors.

Adult Characteristics. Child sexual abusers come from many walks of life, and they are seldom discernable on the basis of personality traits, occupation, or age (Williams & Finkelhor, 1990). About the only firm conclusion is that the vast majority of offenders are male.

Child sexual offenders usually meet DSM-IV criteria for **pedophilia,** defined as sexual activity or sexually arousing fantasies involving a prepubescent child (generally age 13 years or younger), by someone who is at least 16 years old and at least 5 years older than the child. Some persons with pedophilia are sexually attracted only to children (exclusive type), whereas others are sometimes attracted also to adults (nonexclusive type). Persons with pedophilia may limit their activities to **incest,** involving their own children, stepchildren, or other

relatives, or they may victimize children outside their families (APA, 1994). Significantly, over half of individuals with pedophilia report an awareness of their pedophilic interests before they turn 17 years old (63% of those who target male children and 50% of those who target female children), which they begin to act out on average by their late teens or early twenties (Abel, Osborn, & Twigg, 1993).

Those who frequently victimize children develop complicated techniques for gaining access to and compliance from the child (APA, 1994), which emphasizes the *sexually opportunistic* and *predatory* nature of this behavior. They may win the trust of the child's mother or marry a woman with an attractive child. They may use methods to lower a child's resistance, such as initiating a friendship, playing games or giving presents, having hobbies or interests that appeal to the child, and using peer pressure (Wekerle & D. A. Wolfe, 1996). Sexual offenders seldom resort to violence or force to gain the child's compliance; rather, they are attentive to the child's needs in order to gain the child's affection, interest, and loyalty, and to reduce the chances that the child will report the sexual activity. Typically, sexual behavior takes place only after a period of "grooming," involving a gradual indoctrination into sexual activity, which underscores how sex offenders against children are "sophisticated, calculating, and patient" (Singer, Hussey, & Strom, 1992, p. 884). As one offender asserted, "You can spot the child who is unsure of himself and target him with compliments and positive attention" (Elliott, Browne, & Kilcoyne, 1995, p. 584).

As indicated in the quote from Graham James (a former hockey coach who is now serving a prison sentence for sexually abusing a player—see the photo on page 555), a perpetrator's efforts at establishing a relationship with the child or youth, such as spending time alone, singling the child out as favored or special, may also reduce the child's internal inhibition by distorting their roles and blurring interpersonal boundaries. Graham James' public statement typifies how an offender may develop a sense of entitlement and privilege with a child and may distort his role into one of being a central part of the child's life.

Like those of physical abusers, the backgrounds of child sexual abusers reveal a link between being abused in childhood and perpetrating against others, although this link is by no means well understood or inevitable. One possibility is that negative childhood experiences—sexual abuse, as well as other forms of maltreatment—set in motion a cautious, distrustful approach to intimate relationships (Marshall, 1993). An adolescent male with a history of unhealthy or exploitative relationships, for example, may justify using coercive and abusive actions toward others who are smaller or weaker, because his

Graham James says his repeated sexual assaults on Sheldon Kennedy (on right in the photo above), a professional hockey player, were acts of friendship that he never meant to push too far. As an adult involved with a 15-year-old boy, didn't James have some idea that he was doing something wrong? "Look, I'm not here trying to justify it . . . I guess I wished it were acceptable. Maybe I thought I was living in ancient Greece or something like that." James credits himself for helping Kennedy through his admitted alcoholism. "I became the key person in his life to help with his own problem [alcoholism]." James never made the connection, however, that his predatory relationship with Kennedy caused the alcoholism, as Kennedy has stated. (Spector, 1997)

other attempts have failed (Hudson & Ward, 1997). Sexual interests and arousal become fused with his need for emotional closeness, which can lead to sexual preoccupation, promiscuity, and the possibility of increasing sexual deviancy as he escalates his attempts to gain intimacy through sexual contact (Marshall, 1993). This explains why sexual offenders, as a group, are more likely to have significant social and relationship deficits, including social isolation and difficulty forming emotionally close, trusting relationships (Smith & Saunders, 1995). Remember, however, that the majority of abused children do not become abusive adults—positive factors, such as supportive friends and family, as well as individual strengths, such as intelligence and empathy, can provide important counterbalances (Lisak, Hopper, & Song, 1996).

Family and Situational Influences.
Like offenders, incestuous families do not fit a uniform profile. The most common elements of incestuous families are those that tend to protect the "family secret" and to maintain control and domination by the abuser, such as greater social isolation, restricted personal autonomy,

and deference to strict morality and religiosity. Not surprisingly, marital couples report significant levels of relationship distress and dissatisfaction, including sexual discontentment (Faust, Runyon, & Kenny, 1995). As in other maltreating families, these characteristics reflect a climate of domination and abuse of power in which children are powerless at controlling unpleasant events. However, because these studies are almost always based on families *following* the discovery of incest, there is no way of knowing which came first—the abuse or the poor family functioning.

Certain situational factors increase children's vulnerability to being sexually abused, a fact that offenders exploit to their advantage. Offenders see children as being more vulnerable if they have family problems, spend a lot of time alone, and seem unsure of themselves; they also admit to preferring victims who are attractive, trusting, and young (Elliott et al., 1995). To gain access to the child, they look for circumstances that create lax supervision or opportunities for them to become involved, such as parental unavailability, illness, stress, spousal abuse, or lack of emotional closeness to the child. Low income and social isolation also increase a child's risk of sexual abuse, because parents may lack resources or opportunities for suitable child care and safety precautions (Finkelhor, 1984).

How children disclose sexual abuse is also a critical factor in its initiation and continuation. Children are often hesitant to disclose incidents of sexual abuse because of their close and special relationship to the abuser (Sas et al., 1993), which offenders attempt to control and manipulate to prevent discovery. As one offender explained, "Secrecy and blame were my best weapons. Most kids worry that they are to blame for the abuse and that they should keep it a secret" (Elliott et al., 1995, p. 590). Delayed disclosure—not telling anyone for a long time—is quite common, especially if the perpetrator is a family member. Consider the powerful factors that oppose disclosure (Sas et al., 1993):

* the power imbalance between children and adults
* children's belief that they should do what adults tell them to do
* the existence of a relationship involving trust and/or dependency
* exhortations to keep the secret
* implied or imagined negative consequences of telling
* feelings of guilt, self-blame, stigmatization, and isolation

These are difficult obstacles for anyone, much less a child, to overcome, which is why disclosure of abuse is often delayed or abandoned. Children's own accounts of how they disclosed sexual abuse indicate that disclosure involves a gradual decision-making process made up of four stages: recognizing the behavior as wrong, overcoming inhibitions to tell and suppressing fear, deciding when to tell, and deciding whom to tell. As one child explained, "I wanted to get it off my chest. It was eating me inside" (Sas et al., 1993, p. 69).

Social and Cultural Dimensions

What role does our culture play in the abuse and neglect of children? Intuitively, a primary focus on individual factors as causes of child abuse and neglect is very limiting, since we live in a society that not only condones violence but also glorifies it directly and indirectly (Jaffe et al., 1996). Consider how the entertainment industry, including many aspects of the media and professional sports, earns billions of dollars in profits from exploiting our interest in violence in all its forms. Equally disturbing is the portrayal of sex roles by society's envoys in the media and entertainment industry: Females are stereotypically presented as relatively powerless and passive, and men as vested with power; women are encouraged to defer to the benevolence of powerful men, and men are encouraged to challenge the autonomy of powerful and assertive women (Hedley, 1994). These cultural phenomena are ingrained through years of repeated imagery, and are presumed to be at the base of some men's motivation to maintain control and power in a relationship (R. E. Dobash & R. P. Dobash, 1992). Although a distance remains, the entertainment industry is responding to these criticisms and concerns, and in recent years has made efforts to present a more balanced picture of gender roles and expectations in films and television.

At the family level, we have noted that child maltreatment usually occurs in the context of multiproblem homes and neighborhoods, where poverty and family dysfunction have a major influence on child development. The most prominent social and cultural dimensions contributing to maltreatment stem from poverty, social isolation, and wide acceptance of corporal punishment. These factors stem from *inequality,* which is arguably the major sociocultural factor contributing to abuse and neglect not only of children, but of many adults and members of minority groups as well. The extent to which a society deems any particular group as being less worthy of recognition and economic or political support represents the extent to which that group is vulnerable to violence and a host of other indignities (Miedzian, 1995).

Poverty and Social Isolation. Although child maltreatment is certainly not limited by the boundaries of socioeconomic status, the problem must be considered in the context of poverty and environmental stress. Poverty is associated with severe restrictions in the child's expectable environment, such as lack of adequate day care, safety, and housing, which often impair or impede the development of healthy parent-child relationships. In addition, adults below poverty level suffer more individual and family problems, such as substance abuse and emotional disorders. This is sadly reflected by the fact that, on average, 40% of substantiated child maltreatment cases involve substance abuse (Lung & Daro, 1996).

Although the relationship between poverty and child maltreatment is a fact, it is not a sufficient explanation. To explain this connection requires consideration of the psychological dimensions noted above. Social and cultural disadvantage amounts to an extra burden of stress and confusion, and a limited number of alternatives. The coping abilities of family members are impaired by their circumstances and further constrained by their resources. One caution is in order, however: Despite these powerful socioeconomic forces, maltreatment appears to have a significant impact on child development above and beyond the influence of stressful socioeconomic circumstances alone (Kurtz et al., 1993; Trickett, Aber, Carlson, & Cicchetti, 1991).

Perhaps as a result of cultural and social factors, maltreating families often lack significant social connections to others in their extended families, neighborhoods, and communities, as well as to social assistance agencies (Korbin, 1994; Thompson, 1994). Unfortunately, maintaining family privacy and isolation may come at the cost of restricted access to healthier child-rearing models and social supports. Neglectful families are especially prone to such isolation and insularity, which may be tied to the parents' significant interpersonal problems (Polansky, Gaudin, & Kilpatrick, 1992). Again, rather than being a direct causal factor in the etiology of child maltreatment, social isolation may be another indicator of the degree of an individual's or family's social competence in interpersonal and child-rearing situations (Burgess & Youngblade, 1988).

Child-Rearing Practices and Family Privacy.

Child-rearing practices have been changing dramatically over the past 50 years or so. Today's parents are expected to appreciate their child's developmental strengths and limitations, and to move away from total reliance on disciplinary control methods toward ones that encourage the child's emerging independence and self-control. But hypocrisy emerges when attempting to differentiate child abuse from child discipline, because cultural norms in many countries have long accepted corporal punishment as a primary, even necessary, component of discipline. As a result, four out of five 3-year-old children in the United States are physically punished by their parents in any given year, and about one in ten receive such severe discipline that they are at considerable risk of harm (Straus & Gelles, 1990).

Many parents spank their children, even though they question its effectiveness (Gallup Organization, 1995). Does acceptance of corporal punishment, however, influence the likelihood of child abuse? The tentative answer is yes, but only indirectly. Most parents who use physical discipline are not abusing their children in either the physical or psychological sense. But a change in circumstances—increased stress, more difficult child behavior—can up the ante quite suddenly. Furthermore, acceptance of corporal punishment leaves it up to local standards and parental judgment to define what is "reasonable" punishment, because no universal standard exists. Cultural values, historical precedent, and community standards, therefore, may set the stage for one person's abuse being another person's discipline. Discipline also involves considerably more effort and planning than does punishment alone, and unfortunately, too many parents are not familiar with less coercive methods of punishment. Thus, child maltreatment occurs to a certain extent because of limited cultural opportunities to learn about appropriate child-rearing and to receive necessary education and supports, as well as long-held social customs that endorse the use of physical force to resolve child conflicts.

Cultural norms and practices influence the prevalence of sexual abuse as well. The erotic portrayal of children not only in pornography but also in mainstream advertising raises concerns about boundaries and appropriate messages. Moreover, existing criminal sanctions are inadequate at deterring offenders, and rely heavily on child victims' testimony. Paradoxically, however, laws of evidence are premised on the belief that children are inherently unreliable as witnesses, so they often face many obstacles that make the court experience very unpleasant. As one child explained, "[the defense lawyer] grilled me, twisted everything I said, made me feel like a criminal and as if [my stepfather] was the victim." (Sas et al., 1993, p. 113).

PREVENTION AND TREATMENT

Consider these obstacles to intervention and prevention services for maltreating families: (1) those most in need are least likely to seek help on their own; (2) they come to the attention of professionals as a result of someone else's concern, usually *after* they have violated expected norms or laws; and (3) parents do not want to admit to problems because of their fear of losing their children or being charged with a crime (fears that are, of course, realistic). As a result, many children and adults seeking treatment related to child abuse and neglect are under some form of legal constraint. Similar to other psychological interventions, child abuse treatments are based on the principle of beneficial assistance—but who wants assistance for something they won't admit to having? As a result, treatments for child abuse and neglect have languished because of this basic dilemma: Access to treatment and prevention depends on admitting to or recognizing one's own culpability (Azar & D. A. Wolfe, 1998).

Despite these obstacles, children and youth who have grown up with violence can make major shifts in how they relate to others, especially if treatment is begun early. As we noted in Chapter 11 with regard to children with learning disorders, those who progress from maladaptive to cooperative behavior often have been exposed to other positive individuals, such as teachers, foster parents, grandparents, and others, who promote their strengths and offer alternative experiences involving positive models and adequate resources (Cicchetti & Rogosch, 1997). Also, because the need for support, instruction, and resource linkage among new parents is universal, a window of opportunity exists to provide outreach services during pregnancy and early infancy, which sets the stage for healthy parent-child relations.

Seeing persons' strengths and abilities, rather than their deficits, is a plausible approach to preventing physical abuse, neglect, and related social problems. Fifteen years after receiving pre- and postnatal home-visitation services to establish resource linkages and learn about their child's developmental needs, first-time parents—who were initially at risk of maltreatment on the basis of either low socioeconomic status, young age (under 19 years), or unmarried status—gained over controls on important dimensions: better family planning concerning number and spacing of children, less need for welfare (on average, 60 versus 90 months of receiving government assistance), less child maltreatment (an average of .29 versus .54 verified reports), and fewer arrests of their children during adolescence (.16 versus .90) (Olds et al., 1997).

Clearly, efforts to enhance positive experiences at an early stage in the development of the parent-child relationship hold considerable promise for the prevention of child maltreatment and the reduction of its consequences. Similarly, programs that instruct children and their parents on how to avoid and report sexual abuse improve children's response to victimization, although relying on child-focused prevention alone is not sufficient (Finkelhor, Asdigian, & Dzuiba-Leatherman, 1995). Formal treatment efforts also increase the chances of overcoming the harmful effects of abuse and neglect. We discuss such treatments for physical abuse and neglect in the same section because of their close connection to child-rearing disturbances. Treatment of child sexual abuse is presented separately because of its unique nature and course.

Physical Abuse and Neglect

Treatment of child abuse and neglect can be delivered in a number of ways—to individual parents, to children, to parents and children together, or to the entire family. No matter how it is delivered, treatment of physical abuse usually attempts to change how parents teach, discipline, and attend to their children, most often by training parents in basic child-rearing skills accompanied by cognitive-behavioral methods to target specific anger patterns or distorted beliefs. Similarly, treatment for child neglect focuses on parenting skills and expectations, coupled with training in social competence, which may include home safety, family hygiene, finances, medical needs, drug and alcohol counseling, marital counseling, and similar efforts to manage family resources and attend to children's needs (Azar & D. A. Wolfe, 1998). Although most interventions emphasize the *parents'* needs, desired changes in parenting can have a pronounced effect on their children's development as well (D. A. Wolfe & Wekerle, 1993).

Because maltreating parents place too much emphasis on control and discipline or ways to avoid contact and responsibilities, they seldom know how to enjoy their child's company. Treatment, therefore, often begins with efforts designed to increase positive parent-child interactions and pleasant experiences. Parents are shown, through modeling, role playing, and feedback, how to engage in daily activities with their child that serve to strengthen the child's areas of deficiency and to promote adaptive functioning. The activities are behaviorally and developmentally specific, such as stimulating appropriate language and social interaction (D. A. Wolfe, 1991). Activities are selected to maximize the child's attention and provide ample opportunity for pleasant interchanges. Milton's treatment plan illustrates this important initial step:

Milton's Treatment—Session 1

It didn't take long to see what Brenda faced at home. Partway through our first session, Milton (age 4) wanted his mother's attention and became quite angry when she was asked to leave the room for a few minutes. During this outburst he pushed an easy chair over and tried to hit Brenda with a rolled-up poster. She happily left for the observation room, leaving him and me together for the first time. I found a game and some puppets that he liked and began the process of establishing a relationship. As soon as Milton started to lose interest, I switched to a new activity. I modeled for Brenda some ways to simply observe Milton's behavior and express my interest:

"Milton likes to explore everything! Look! I have a talking doll! Can you make him say something? Excellent—he spoke to you!" (Milton starts to go for the toy chest). "Look, Milton! I have a puppet. Would you like to hold him? Good, you're coming back to play with me. After we play with the puppet, mommy will come in and play too! When we're all done, we'll go get a drink. Can you stack these blocks? Oops, you knocked them down; that looked like fun. Let's try again; only this time, you put one on here for me." I closely guided Milton to new activities to reduce his distractibility, all the time talking aloud so that his mother could hear in the adjoining room from which she was observing the interaction.

Once parents have learned a more flexible, adaptive teaching style that suits their child's development, efforts are begun to strengthen the child's compliance and self-control. Parents observe while the therapist models positive ways to encourage the child's attention and appropriate behavior, followed by practice and feedback. Therapists model for the parent how to express positive affect—with smiles, hugs, physical affection, praise—and also how to show dismay or concern when necessary—with appropriate facial expression, firmer voice tone, and similar cues that express disapproval.

But parent training seldom goes smoothly, especially with multiproblem families. What do you do when a child just "acts himself" and doesn't follow your directions—while his parent watches? These situations are often valuable for helping a parent apply the new skills under naturalistic, this-is-what-it's-really-like, conditions. Serendipitously, the value of modeling how to handle such a challenge was discovered a few sessions later:

Milton's Treatment—Session 4

Milton was tired of following my directions. Unaware that his mother was watching, he seized the opportunity to have some fun. He picked up toys and tossed them, and turned the light switch off and on. I thought I could simply get Milton to settle by taking him down from his chair (which he was using to reach the light switch) and bringing him back to the couch. I was wrong. He started throwing a tantrum and screaming violently. With no other choice (child psychologists know when they're licked), I decided to talk above the noise so that his mother could hear how I was feeling and what I thought I might do: "I'm not sure just what to do yet. Milton seems to be uninterested in listening at the moment. Rather than getting angry, I think I'll wait a minute or two and try again. I've seen my 3-year-old do this, and I know you can't always expect kids to listen."

Brenda, familiar with such behavior at home, thought the situation was priceless—"Now you know what I have to deal with!" In lighthearted defense, I explained how there may not be an easy solution for such situations, which is why it is so important to maintain your composure and not expect or demand cooperation from Milton immediately. Tongue-in-check I reminded her of Murphy's law of child behavior—"Anything that can go wrong, will"—and its collorary, "Just because it worked last time doesn't mean it will work every time!"

From this and similar misadventures we discovered how familiar problems that emerge during treatment delivery add authenticity for parents (and conveniently happen whether or not we plan them!). These situations, as well as less stressful ones, are also used to teach parents how to manage themselves calmly, yet firmly. Therapists model how to express frustration and annoyance without becoming abusive and harsh, and parents are then encouraged to discuss and rehearse how they can handle the situation. Gradually, parents learn to replace physical punishment or apathy with more positive approaches. This process takes time, and parental frustration and impatience are to be anticipated.

Psychological characteristics of abusive and neglectful care-givers are a good fit with behavioral methods that emphasize child-rearing and self-control skills. Behavioral strategies, which are concrete and problem-focused, are often preferred over insight therapies among less motivated or educated clients (Azar & D. A. Wolfe, 1998). Interventions based on social learning theory are high in face validity and permit parents to work on the problems that are of most urgency and importance to them. Moreover, because behavioral treatments are often perceived as more "educational" and problem-focused, they are less threatening to families and make cooperation a bit easier to achieve (Azar & D. A. Wolfe, 1998).

A recent study illustrates some of the outcomes achieved from interventions focusing on skills and rela-

tionships. Kolko (1996) randomly assigned 55 physically abusive families to either individual child and parent cognitive-behavioral therapy (CBT) or family therapy (FT). A control group received routine community services. In the CBT condition, children were provided with their own therapist, who taught them ways to recognize and respond to stressful events, such as using coping and self-control skills to establish safety, supports, and methods of relaxation. Parents received a separate therapist, who taught them alternatives to physical punishment using contingency management (attention, reinforcement, time-out), challenged their tendency to blame the child for not living up to their expectations, and taught them self-control skills for controlling anger and coping with stress. The FT condition also had a social learning theory base, but was designed to enhance family functioning and relationships, to increase cooperation and motivation of all family members by promoting an understanding of coercive behavior, and to teach positive communication skills and problem-solving strategies. CBT and FT were both associated with improvements in parent-reported child behavior problems, parental distress, and family conflict and cohesion, relative to controls. Only one family in both CBT and FT showed another incident of maltreatment over a 1-year period, whereas in the control group there were three such cases.

On the whole, evaluations of interventions for physical abuse and neglect indicate that cognitive-behavioral approaches are the most widely supported methods for assisting maltreating parents, for several valid reasons (Hansen, Warner-Rogers, & Hecht, 1998). Most significantly, these methods are effective (relative to standard protective-service interventions involving brief counseling and monitoring) in modifying parental behaviors that are most relevant to child maltreatment, such as appropriate child-rearing and self-control skills (Crimmins, Bradlyn, St. Lawrence, & Kelly, 1984; Wolfe & Sandler, 1981; D. A. Wolfe, Sandler, & Kaufman, 1981; D. A. Wolfe et al., 1982). Techniques such as relaxation and self-management skills training, cognitive restructuring (viewing child behavior more appropriately), problem-solving training, and stress and anger management training are often combined with structured training in basic child-rearing skills. These methods, either singly or combined, have been successful at teaching coping and problem-solving skills to abusive (Denicola & Sandler, 1980; D. A. Wolfe et al., 1981), as well as neglectful parents (Fantuzzo, Wray, Hall, Goins, & Azar, 1986).

In addition to learning new ways to stimulate child development and structure child activities, neglectful parents often require very basic education and assistance in managing everyday demands, such as financial planning and home cleanliness. Programs such as Project 12-Ways (Lutzker, Bigelow, Doctor, Gershater, &

Greene, 1998) provide multicomponent interventions that address the various needs of neglectful and multiproblem families, such as marital counseling, financial planning, lessons on cleanliness, and similar concerns (Campbell, O'Brien, Bickett, & Lutzker, 1983; Wesch & Lutzker, 1991). Project 12-Ways stands out from other programmatic intervention research in its efforts to document recidivism among participants. Based on Illinois official records, about 1 in 5 of the 710 participating families was subsequently reported for maltreatment, compared with over 1 in 4 control families (Lutzker & Rice, 1987). Despite these relatively positive results, the sobering fact remains that families with histories of maltreatment pose significant challenges to psychological and social interventions.

Treatment services for abused or neglected children are less common than parent-oriented interventions, largely because parental behavior is often the primary concern. We have seen, however, that maltreated children often lag behind in important developmental competencies, which is a strong rationale for focusing additional attention on these areas. The programmatic efforts of John Fantuzzo and his colleagues provide an excellent example of a developmentally focused intervention for maltreated children. Day care activities are coupled with resilient peer treatment (RPT), a peer-mediated classroom intervention that involves pairing withdrawn children (some of whom have maltreatment histories) with resilient peers who are exceptionally strong at positive play activities (Davis & Fantuzzo, 1989; Fantuzzo, Stovall, Schachtel, Goins, & Hall, 1987; Fantuzzo et al., 1988; 1996). Play activities are specifically targeted in this program, because play is a primary means for younger children to develop peer relationship skills. Competent "players" are encouraged to interact with less competent children in special play areas where adults have only a minimal role. As a result, withdrawn children have the uncommon experience of being the center of another child's attention and experiencing a resilient child's repertoire of tactics for creating play and getting along with others (Fantuzzo et al., 1996). The results of this series of studies have been impressive: Relative to controls, withdrawn children with histories of abuse or neglect show improvement in social behavior, cognitive development, and self-concept, and reduction in aggressive and coercive behaviors. A further strength of this intervention is that it can be conducted in community settings, such as Head Start classrooms, that offer comprehensive services for disadvantaged children and their families (Fantuzzo, Weiss, & Coolahan, 1998).

In sum, notwithstanding diverse challenges, successful interventions for child abuse and neglect often include parent- or family-focused training components for improving child-rearing competence and stress management (Becker et al., 1995; Brunk, Henggeler, & Whelan, 1987; D. A. Wolfe & Wekerle, 1993). These parent-focused efforts also help child victims regain important developmental milestones and social competencies, especially when children also receive specific, developmentally significant guidance and training in coping and self-control skills (Kolko, 1996) or relationship skills (Fantuzzo et al., 1998).

Sexual Abuse

> What allowed this to happen was that so many people were silent about it.
> —Adult sexually abused as a child

Sexually abused children, especially incest victims, have experienced a world of secrecy, silence, and isolation. Once they have broken that silence by disclosing the abuse, or it was discovered by accident, the path toward healing can be difficult. They must access not only unpleasant memories, but also buried feelings, such as guilt, confusion, fear, and low self-worth.

Despite advances in understanding the prevalence and impact of child sexual abuse, children's treatment programs are few. Like physical abuse and neglect, sexual abuse carries a special treatment challenge: Sexually abusive experiences affect each child unpredictably, which leads to diverse short- and long-rage outcomes. As a result, treatments have to match the needs of a wide age range of children who may show all kinds of symptoms or even no symptoms at all (Finkelhor & Berliner, 1995). Moreover, sexual abuse, like many other problems of childhood, occurs in the context of other individual, family, and community problems that affect its impact and treatment. Elements of family functioning, especially maternal support and help-seeking in response to the crisis, are known to affect children's level of distress and aid in their recovery, so treatment often has to address these situational issues as well.

Treatment programs for children who have been sexually abused usually provide several crucial elements to restore the child's sense of trust, safety, and guiltlessness (Finkelhor & Berliner, 1995). One major element involves education and support to help these children understand why this happened to them, and how they can learn to feel safe once again. Information and education about the nature of sexual abuse helps clarify false beliefs that might lead to self-blame, and children's feelings of stigma and isolation are often addressed through reassurance or group therapy involving other child victims. Animated films and videos offer ways for child victims to acknowledge and validate their feelings, and help them talk about their feelings, allowing them to move toward the future with a sense of hope and empowerment. Children are also taught ways to prevent sexual abuse and restore their sense of personal power and safety, again through the use of animated films and behavioral rehearsal to learn how to distinguish appropriate from inappropriate touches (Wurtele, 1990).

Cognitive-behavioral methods are particularly valuable in achieving these goals (Cohen & Mannarino, 1996). Preferably, education and support are provided not only to the child victim, but to (nonoffending) parents as well. The secretive betrayal that underlies the nature of sexual abuse causes some parents to feel ambivalent about whether to believe their child or how they feel about the alleged perpetrator, whom they often trusted. Parents may need advice on ways to understand and manage their child's behavior, which may include regressive or sexual behaviors due to the abuse. Understandably, parents often experience their own fears and worries as a result of the disclosure, and discussion with other parents and therapists can provide valuable support.

In conjunction with education and support, sexually abused children need to express their feelings about the abuse and its aftermath—anger, ambivalence, fear—within a safe and supportive context. Younger children, for example, often cannot report their psychological reactions to the trauma unless they are asked *specifically* about aspects of the trauma (D. A. Wolfe et al., 1994). Sexual abuse elicits attempts by children to cope with powerful and confusing feelings, and it is understandable that some will use every method possible to avoid such feelings. However, attempts to escape or avoid internal states of fear and anxiety can paradoxically make them worse. For these reasons, controlled-exposure techniques, similar to those discussed in Chapter 7, have been adapted for child sexual abuse victims. The child is asked to gradually recall her memories of events, often to the point of feeling distressed, so that the powerful emotions are extinguished with repeated exposure. In addition, she learns to cope with negative thoughts and feelings about the abuse by using positive statements and imagery. Preliminary findings support the contention that gradual exposure, modeling, education, coping, and prevention skills training with the child may be important in the treatment of PTSD-related symptoms (Deblinger, McLeer, & Henry, 1990).

Unfortunately, evaluating the effectiveness of interventions for sexually abused children is challenged by methodological problems, especially the inability to assign children to a no-treatment control condition, so evidence is presently limited. However, there is strong agreement that successful interventions for sexually abused children should result in several important outcomes (Berliner, 1997). Treatment services should help children understand that what happened to them was abuse, that it was wrong, and that it may have caused them some temporary problems. Emotional and behavioral problems that may have arisen from the abuse should have subsided, and children should have the personal resources to handle future problems. Importantly, they should have supportive relationships in place, especially with parents and other care-givers who have received adequate knowledge and assistance to understand the possible impact the abuse may have on their children's behavior and adjustment. Finally, successful treatment outcome would result in children's regaining their normal rate of development.

Twenty years ago, psychology textbooks never discussed these issues, we had little knowledge of the devastating developmental, mental health, and societal consequences of abuse and neglect, and very few treatments were available. Since that time considerable progress has been made in understanding and helping children who have been abused and neglected and their families. Most importantly, broader efforts at prevention and family support may help reduce or eliminate the likelihood of such unnecessary and harmful mistreatment of children and youth.

SUMMARY

Perspectives on Child-Rearing and Maltreatment
1. Abuse and neglect represent major failures of the child's expectable environment.
2. Child care can be described along a hypothetical continuum ranging from healthy to abusive and neglectful.

Description
3. Physical abuse includes acts such as punching, beating, kicking, biting, burning, shaking, or otherwise harming a child.
4. Child neglect is a failure to provide for a child's basic physical, educational, or emotional needs.
5. Sexual abuse ranges from sexual touching to exhibitionism, sexual intercourse, and commercial exploitation (pornography, prostitution).
6. Emotional abuse includes acts or omissions that could cause serious behavioral, cognitive, emotional, or mental disorders.

Prevalence and Context
7. Child abuse and neglect are at epidemic proportions in the United States, Canada, and many other societies worldwide.
8. Physical neglect is most common among younger children. Physical and emotional abuse are most common among toddlers, preschoolers, and young

adolescents. Sexual abuse, in contrast, affects children from age 3 on.

9. Poverty and single parenthood are the most prominent demographic features of abuse and neglect.

Developmental Course and Psychopathology

10. All forms of child maltreatment have profound effects on development, setting an unpredictable course that challenges normal adaptation.

11. By early childhood, maltreated children show deficits in sensitivity to others, including problems with empathy, interpersonal trust, and affect expression.

12. Impairments in cognitive and moral development often lead to problems in social judgment, communication, and school performance, as well as problems in self-control and aggression with peers.

13. Some child victims develop a DSM-related disorder, such as PTSD, depression, or antisocial behavior. The direct causal influence of maltreatment is not firmly established.

Causes

14. Parental lack of knowledge of child-rearing and ways of coping with anger and arousal play prominent roles in physical abuse and neglect.

15. A sexual offender's preference for sexual exploitation of children and adolescents is a primary cause of sexual abuse.

16. Maltreatment also stems from poverty, social isolation, and unhealthy cultural norms concerning child-rearing practices and family privacy.

Prevention and Treatment

17. Interventions for physical abuse and neglect emphasize parent- and family-focused training in child-rearing and stress management, which also benefits the child, as a result of improved parental care.

18. Interventions for children who have been sexually abused emphasize the children's needs for safety, understanding, and expression of emotional consequences.

KEY TERMS

child maltreatment, 526
victimization, 527
expectable environment, 527
adaptational failure, 528
physical abuse, 530
physical neglect, 531
educational neglect, 531
emotional neglect, 531
sexual abuse, 532
emotional abuse, 533
attachment, 539
insecure-disorganized attachment, 539
hypervigilant, 539
emotion regulation, 539
representational models, 540
cycle-of-violence hypothesis, 543
dissociation, 546
traumatic sexualization, 546
relational disorders, 548
information-processing disturbances, 551
pedophilia, 554
incest, 554

Epilogue

The child with his sweet pranks, the fool of his senses, commanded by every sight and sound, without any power to compare and rank his sensations, abandoned to a whistle or a painted chip, to a lead dragoon, or a gingerbread dog, individualizing everything, generalizing nothing, delighted with every new thing, lies down at night overpowered by the fatigue, which this day of continual pretty madness has incurred. But Nature has answered her purpose with the curly, dimpled lunatic. She has tasked every faculty, and has secured the symmetrical growth of the bodily frame, by all these attitudes and exertions—an end of the first importance, which could not be trusted to any care less perfect than her own.

—Ralph Waldo Emerson (1803–82)

Glossary

A-B-A-B design (reversal design) A single-case experimental design in which an initial baseline phase (A) is followed by an intervention phase (B), a reversal/return-to-baseline phase (A), and finally a re-intervention phase (B). If the treatment was responsible for observed changes during the intervention phase, the behavior should revert to its baseline level during the reversal phase, and should again change when the treatment is re-introduced.

abnormal child psychology A field of psychology concerned with describing and studying disorders of childhood and adolescence in a manner that recognizes the importance of developmental processes and tasks (also see *child psychopathology*).

accelerated longitudinal design A combination of cross-sectional and longitudinal research designs in which multiple groups are followed, each at different but overlapping ages or stages of development.

acute lymphoblastic leukemia (ALL) The most common form of childhood cancer, in which the bone marrow produces malignant cells, called lymphoblasts, that progressively replace normal bone marrow with fewer red blood cells and more white blood cells, thereby causing anemia, infection, and easy bruising or excessive bleeding.

acute stress disorder A form of anxiety disorder characterized by the development of anxiety, dissociation, and other symptoms within 1 month following exposure to an extremely traumatic stressor.

adaptational failure Failure to master or progress in accomplishing developmental milestones.

adaptive functioning The ability to cope effectively with ordinary life demands, to live independently, and to abide by community standards. Adaptive functioning is a necessary component for defining levels of mental retardation.

ADHD See *attention-deficit/hyperactivity disorder.*

ADHD: combined type (ADHD-C) A subtype of attention-deficit/hyperactivity disorder characterized by a combination of inattentive symptoms and hyperactive-impulsive symptoms.

ADHD: predominantly hyperactive-impulsive type (ADHD-HI) A subtype of attention-deficit/hyperactivity disorder characterized by predominantly hyperactive-impulsive symptoms.

ADHD: predominantly inattentive type (ADHD-PI) A subtype of attention-deficit/hyperactivity disorder characterized by predominantly inattentive symptoms.

adolescent-limited path (AL) A developmental pathway to antisocial behavior whereby the child's antisocial behavior begins around puberty, continues into adolescence, and later desists in young adulthood.

adolescent-onset conduct disorder A specific type of conduct disorder, the characteristics of which are not exhibited prior to 10 years of age.

aggression Behavior that threatens, attempts, or inflicts intentional physical or psychological harm.

agoraphobia A form of anxiety characterized by a fear of being alone in, and avoiding, certain places or situations from which escape may be difficult or embarrassing, or in which help may be unavailable in the event of a panic attack.

amplifier hypothesis The premise that stress may serve to amplify the maladaptive predispositions of parents, thereby disrupting family management practices and compromising the parents' ability to be supportive of their children.

anaclitic depression A condition described by Renee Spitz in the 1940s in which infants raised in a clean but emotionally cold institutional environment displayed reactions that resembled a depressive disorder, including weeping, withdrawal, apathy, weight loss, sleep disturbance, an overall decline in development, and in some cases even death.

analogue research Research that evaluates a specific variable of interest under conditions that only resemble or approximate the situation to which one wishes to generalize.

Angelman syndrome A genetic disorder associated with an abnormality of chromosome 15. Children with Angelman syndrome typically suffer from moderate to severe mental retardation, ataxia (awkward gait), jerky movements, hand flapping, seizures, the absence of speech, and distinctive facial features such as a large jaw and open-mouthed expression.

anhedonia A negative mood state characterized by a lack of enjoyment in anything one does and a loss of interest in nearly all activities.

anorexia nervosa A severe eating disorder characterized by the refusal to maintain a minimally normal body weight, an intense fear of gaining weight, and a significant disturbance in the individual's perception and experiences of his or her own size.

anticipatory anxiety An individual's worry about when or where a subsequent panic attack will occur and if he or she will live to tell about it.

antidiuretic hormone A hormone that helps to concentrate urine during sleeping hours so that there is less volume, and thus one's bladder will not overfill. Some children who suffer from enuresis do not show the usual increase in the antidiuretic hormone during sleep.

antisocial behavior See *conduct problems*.

antisocial personality disorder (APD) An adult disorder characterized by a pervasive pattern of disregard for, and violation of, the rights of others, as well as engagement in multiple illegal behaviors.

anxiety A mood state characterized by strong negative affect, bodily symptoms of tension, and apprehensive anticipation of future danger or misfortune.

anxiety disorder A disorder in which the child experiences excessive and debilitating anxiety.

apprehensive expectation Excessive and exaggerated worry and tension in the absence of conditions that would normally provoke such a reaction.

apraxia The inability to execute desired physical movements.

Asperger's disorder (AD) A pervasive developmental disorder characterized by major difficulties in social interaction and unusual patterns of interest and behavior in children with relatively intact cognitive and communication skills.

assent Evidence of some form of agreement on the part of a child to participate in a research study without the child's having the full understanding of the research that would be needed to give informed consent.

assessment A process that helps to focus attention on behaviors, patterns of behavior, and contextual factors that relate to known psychological disorders and developmental conditions. An assessment helps to determine a diagnosis and treatment plan.

attachment The process of establishing and maintaining an emotional bond with parents or other significant care givers. This process is ongoing, typically beginning between 6 and 12 months of age, and provides infants with a secure, consistent base from which to explore and learn about their worlds.

attentional capacity The amount of information in short-term memory to which one can attend.

attention-deficit/hyperactivity disorder (ADHD) A disorder in which the subject consistently and repeatedly shows age-inappropriate behaviors in the two general categories of inattention and hyperactivity-impulsivity.

attrition Sample dropout.

autism A pervasive developmental disorder characterized by abnormalities in social functioning, language and communication, and unusual interests and behaviors. More specifically, autism affects every aspect of the child's interaction with his or her world, involves many parts of the brain, and undermines the very traits that make us human— our social responsiveness, ability to communicate, and feelings for other people.

autistic disorder DSM-IV diagnostic category used to describe children with autism.

autistic savants Children with autism who develop an isolated and often remarkable talent that is far in excess of that found in normal children of the same age.

behavior analysis (functional analysis of behavior) An effort to identify as many factors as possible that could be contributing to a child's problem behavior, thoughts, and feelings, and to develop hypotheses about which ones are the most important and/or most easily changed.

behavioral activation system (BAS) A subsystem of the brain that activates behavior in response to cues of reward or nonpunishment.

behavioral assessment The evaluation of the child's thoughts, feelings, and behaviors in specific settings, based on which hypotheses are formulated about the nature of the problem and what can be done about it.

behavioral genetics A branch of genetics that investigates possible connections between a genetic predisposition and observed behavior.

behavioral inhibition The ability to delay one's initial reactions to events or to stop behavior once it has begun.

behavioral inhibition system (BIS) A subsystem of the brain that produces anxiety and inhibits ongoing behavior in the presence of novel events, innate fear stimuli, and signals of nonreward or punishment.

behavioral system The response system of anxiety that expresses symptoms in the form of behaviors such

as avoidance, fidgeting, or a worried look.

bidirectional influence (reciprocal influence) The theory that the child's behavior is both influenced by and itself influences the behavior of other family members.

bingeing Overeating that involves both excessive amounts of food and a lack of control.

bipolar disorders (BP) One of the two general categories of mood disorders, consisting of bipolar I disorder, bipolar II disorder, and cyclothymic disorder. Bipolar disorders are characterized by striking periods of abnormally and persistently elevated, expansive, or irritable mood, alternating with or accompanied by one or more major depressive episodes.

bipolar I disorder A form of bipolar disorder characterized by one or more manic or mixed episodes, usually accompanied by major depressive episodes.

bipolar II disorder A form of bipolar disorder characterized by one or more major depressive episodes, accompanied by at least one hypomanic episode.

brain circuits Paths made up of clustering neurons that connect one part of the brain to another.

breathing-related sleep disorders Sleep disorders characterized by sleep disruption caused by sleep-related breathing difficulties, thereby leading to excessive sleepiness or insomnia. Also see *obstructive sleep apnea syndrome*.

bulimia nervosa An eating disorder characterized by binge eating coupled with inappropriate compensatory behavior in order to prevent weight gain, such as self-induced vomiting; the misuse of laxatives, diuretics, or enemas, or other medications; fasting; or excessive exercise.

callous-unemotional interpersonal style (CU) A mode of social interaction that is characterized by such traits as the absence of feelings of guilt, not showing empathy, and not showing emotions.

case study An intensive and usually anecdotal observation and analysis of an individual subject.

cataplexy Transient muscle weakness, which can be triggered by strong emotions such as intense anger or laughter.

categorical classification An approach to the diagnosis and classification of child psychopathology in which distinct categories of disorders that have little or nothing in common with one another are formulated.

central coherence The strong tendency of humans to interpret stimuli in a relatively global way that takes the broader context into account.

Checklist for Autism in Toddlers (CHAT) A measure designed to screen for autism. The CHAT assesses the following five key behaviors: pretend play, joint attention, protodeclarative pointing, social interest, and social play.

child maltreatment The abuse and neglect of children by parents or by others responsible for their welfare. Child maltreatment is a generic term used to refer to the four primary acts of physical abuse, neglect, sexual abuse, and emotional abuse of persons less than 18 years of age.

child psychopathology A branch of abnormal psychology concerned with the scientific study of children's psychological and behavioral disorders (also see *abnormal child psychology*).

childhood disintegrative disorder A pervasive developmental disorder characterized by a significant loss of previously acquired skills, as well as the presence of abnormalities in two of the following three areas of functioning: social interaction, communication, and patterns of behavior and interests and activities.

childhood obesity A chronic medical condition characterized by an excessive accumulation of body fat relative to gender- and age-based norms.

childhood-onset conduct disorder A specific type of conduct disorder whereby the child displays at least one characteristic of the disorder prior to 10 years of age.

childhood-onset schizophrenia (COS) Schizophrenia that emerges in childhood. The criteria for childhood-onset schizophrenia and adult schizophrenia are the same (except for age of onset), and as such, rather than being a distinct form of schizophrenia, childhood-onset schizophrenia appears to be a more severe form of adult-onset schizophrenia.

chronic illness An illness that is long-lasting and often irreversible.

chronotherapy A form of treatment for circadian rhythm sleep disorders that involves resetting the biological clock in order to restore the circadian rhythm.

circadian rhythm disorders Dyssomnia sleep disorders characterized by an inability to fall asleep at the customary bedtime and an inability to rise at a reasonable hour due to a mis-match between one's internal sleep cycle (circadian rhythm) and external opportunities or demands.

clinical assessment A process of differentiating, defining, and measuring the behaviors, cognitions and emotions that are of concern, as well as the environmental circumstances that may be contributing to these problems.

clinical description A summary of unique behaviors, thoughts, and feelings that together make up the features of a given psychological disorder.

co-articulated The term used to describe phonemes that overlap one another, or are combined to produce meaning. The co-articulation of sounds permits rapid communication of speech, rather than sound-by-sound pronunciation.

code-emphasis methods Approaches to reading instruction that emphasize the specific learning of word structure and the decontextualization of reading until the skill is learned. Code-emphasis methods are based on the premise that the ability to decode and recognize words accurately and rapidly must be acquired before reading comprehension can occur.

coercion theory A developmental theory proposing that coercive parent-child interactions serve as the training ground for the development of antisocial behavior. Specifically, it is proposed that through a four-step escape-conditioning sequence the child learns how to use increasingly intense forms of noxious behavior to escape and avoid unwanted parental demands.

coercive parent-child interactions Negative interchanges between a child and his or her parent(s) which may serve as a training ground for the development of antisocial behavior.

cognitive deficiencies Deficits in cognitive ability; for example, a child's failure to use verbal mediators to regulate behavior.

cognitive distortions Inaccurate thought processes. For example, interpreting an accidental event, such as being bumped into by another child, as an act of hostility.

cognitive problem-solving skills training (PSST) Instruction aimed at targeting the cognitive deficiencies and distortions displayed by children and adolescents who experience conduct problems in interpersonal situations, particularly those children who are aggressive.

cognitive system The response system of anxiety that expresses symptoms in the form of thoughts, such as "there's something wrong with me," and also subjective feelings of nervousness, anxiety, and panic.

cognitive triad The combination of three areas of evaluation: (1) views about oneself, (2) views about the world, and (3) views about the future. People suffering from depression have a negative cognitive triad, seeing themselves as worthless or inadequate, the world as mean or unfair, and the future as hopeless.

cognitive-behavioral self-control training Instruction aimed at teaching techniques for monitoring and regulating one's attention and behavior. Specifically, children are taught to keep track of their own behavior; to assess what is required of them in specific situations; to examine their thoughts and feelings in these situations; to identify their usual reactions; to generate more effective alternative responses; to manage when things do not go as planned; and to reward themselves for a job well done.

cohort A group of individuals who are followed over time and who experience the same cultural or historical events during the same time period.

communication deviance A measure of interpersonal attentional and thought disturbance observed in families of children with schizophrenia or schizotypal personality disorder. Children from families with high communication deviance show the most severe impairment and the poorest attentional functioning.

comorbidity The overlapping of two or more disorders at a rate that is greater than would be expected by chance alone.

compensatory behavior Behavior shown by persons suffering from bulimia nervosa to prevent weight gain following a binge episode. Compensatory behaviors include self-induced vomiting, fasting, exercising, and the misuse of diuretics, laxatives, enemas, or diet pills. Also see *purging*.

competence The ability to adapt to one's environment. Children's competence involves their performance relative to their same-age peers as well as to their individual course of development.

compulsions Repetitive, purposeful, and intentional behaviors or mental acts that are performed in response to an obsession.

conduct disorder (CD) A form of disruptive behavior disorder in which the child exhibits an early, persistent, and extreme pattern of aggressive and antisocial acts that involve the infliction of pain on others or interference with others' rights through physical and verbal aggression, stealing, vandalism, truancy, or running away.

conduct problems (antisocial behavior) Age-inappropriate actions and attitudes that violate family expectations, societal norms, and the personal or property rights of others.

continuity of development A theoretical position for explaining development that proposes that normal and abnormal developmental changes are gradual and quantitative. Continuity theorists argue that development is an additive process that is ongoing rather than occurring in distinct stages.

continuous performance test (CPT) A method of assessing sustained attention and impulsivity. In a CPT, the subject is presented with a series of stimuli, such as letters, that appear one at a time on a computer screen. The subject is instructed to press a button only when a certain letter follows another.

coping and stress management Programs aimed at helping children deal with stress. The child is provided with information regarding the stressor (for example, an upcoming medical procedure) that makes it more predictable, and is taught skills for coping with stress that may arise. Examples of coping skills include deep breathing, attention distraction, muscle relaxation, relaxing imagery, emotive imagery, and behavioral rehearsal.

corpus callosum The area of the brain that assists with the transfer of information between hemispheres.

correlation coefficient A number that describes the degree of association between two variables of interest.

cortisol A stress hormone produced by the adrenal glands.

cross-sectional research A method of research whereby different individuals at different ages/stages of development are studied at the same point in time.

cultural-familial mental retardation Mental retardation in which there is no evidence of organic brain damage.

cycle of violence The repetition of patterns of violent behavior across generations. For example, persons who are abused as children are more likely to be abusive towards others as adults.

cyclothymic disorder A form of bipolar disorder characterized by at least

1 year (2 years in adults) of numerous periods of hypomanic symptoms that do not meet criteria for a manic episode, and numerous periods of depressive symptoms that do not meet criteria for a major depressive episode.

daily hassles Minor stressful events encountered in the course of day-to-day life, such as receiving a poor grade on a test, having an argument with a parent, or receiving criticism from a teacher.

decoding A skill necessary for reading. It involves breaking words down into parts.

degrees of intellectual impairment (mild, moderate, severe, and profound) A method of classifying individuals with mental retardation based on the degree of impairment, as indicated by IQ scores. Mild mental retardation is characterized by an IQ level of 50–55 to approximately 70; moderate mental retardation by an IQ level of 35–40 to 50–55; severe mental retardation by an IQ level of 20–25 to 35–40; and profound mental retardation by an IQ level below 20 or 25. Also see *levels of needed support.*

delinquent The legal term used to describe antisocial behavior.

delusions Disturbances in thinking involving disordered thought content and strong beliefs that are misrepresentations of reality.

depressive disorders One of the two general categories of mood disorders, consisting of major depressive disorder (MDD) and dysthymic disorder (DD). Depressive disorders are characterized by pervasive unhappy moods that begin to interfere with the subject's daily routines, social relationships, work or school performance, and overall functioning.

depressive ruminative style A cognitive tendency of individuals suffering from depression to attend to and focus narrowly on negative events for longer periods of time than they would positive events.

depressogenic cognitions The negative perceptual and attributional styles and beliefs associated with depressive symptoms.

destructive-nondestructive dimension An independent dimension of antisocial behavior consisting of a continuum ranging from acts such as cruelty to animals or destruction of property at one end, to nondestructive behaviors such as arguing or irritability at the other.

developmental course The developmental pattern of a given disorder over time.

developmental history (family history) Information obtained from the parents about potentially significant historical milestones and events that might have a bearing on the child's current difficulties.

developmental pathways A concept to describe the sequence and timing of particular behaviors, and to highlight the known and suspected relationships of behaviors over time.

developmental psychopathology An approach to describing and studying disorders of childhood and adolescence in a manner that emphasizes the importance of developmental processes and tasks. This approach uses abnormal development to inform normal development and vice versa.

developmental tasks Psychosocial tasks of childhood that reflect broad domains of competence and tell us how children typically progress within each of these domains as they grow.

developmental versus difference controversy A debate regarding the developmental progression of children with mental impairments. The developmental position argues that all children, regardless of intellectual impairments, progress through the same developmental stages in the same sequence, but at different rates. The difference position argues that the development of children with mental impairments proceeds in a different, less sequential, and less organized fashion than that of children without impairments.

dextroamphetamine One of the more effective stimulant medications used to treat children with attention-deficit/hyperactivity disorder. Two commercial names for this medication are *Dexedrine* and *Dextrostat.*

diagnosis The identification of a disorder from an examination of the symptoms.

diathesis-stress model of depression A theory of depression proposing that the impact of stress is moderated by individual risk factors and that the occurrence of depression depends on the interaction between the subject's personal vulnerability and life stress.

differential diagnosis A process of making a diagnosis whereby the clinician rules out certain other possible disorders.

difficult temperament The term used to describe the disposition of a child who is extremely active, unpredictable, and irritable; is over- or undersensitive to stimulation; has erratic sleep patterns or feeding difficulties;

and becomes upset and frustrated in response to new and challenging events.

dimensional classification An empirically based approach to the diagnosis and classification of child psychopathology that assumes that there are a number of independent dimensions or traits of behavior and that all children possess these to varying degrees.

direct aggression Aggressive behavior that involves verbal and physical displays towards others.

direct instruction An approach to teaching children with learning disorders that is based on the premise that to improve a skill the instructional activities have to approximate those of the skill being taught.

discontinuity of development A theoretical position for explaining development proposing that normal and abnormal developmental changes are abrupt and qualitative. Discontinuity theorists, such as Piaget and Erickson, argue that children pass through developmental stages that are qualitatively different from each other.

discrete trial training A method of teaching readiness skills or other desired behaviors that involves a step-by-step approach to presenting a stimulus and requiring a specific response.

disruptive behavior disorders A DSM-IV category for persistent patterns of antisocial behavior that includes oppositional defiant disorder, conduct disorder, and the predominantly hyperactive-impulsive and combined types of ADHD.

dissociation An altered state of consciousness in which the individual feels detached from the body or self. This process may be voluntary or involuntary, and can be adaptive when resistance or escape from a life-threatening situation is not possible.

distractibility A term used to describe deficits in selective attention.

double depression An instance in which a major depressive episode is superimposed on the subject's previous dysthymic disorder.

Down syndrome A chromosomal abnormality in which there are three 21st chromosomes rather than the normal two. Children with Down syndrome typically function at the moderate level of mental retardation, have an increased likelihood of medical problems, and have unusual physical features. This syndrome is also called trisomy 21.

drive for thinness A characteristic cognitive feature of anorexia nervosa, whereby the individual refuses to maintain a minimally normal body weight and has an intense fear of gaining weight.

dyslexia Disorder of reading not due to low intelligence (also see *reading disorder*).

dysphoria A negative mood state characterized by prolonged bouts of sadness.

dyssomnias A category of sleep disorders involving difficulties initiating or maintaining sleep. Such disorders are often characterized by problems getting enough sleep, not sleeping when one wants to, and not feeling refreshed after sleeping.

dysthymic disorder (DD) A form of depressive disorder characterized by at least 1 year (2 years in adults) of depressed mood for more days than not, accompanied by additional depressive symptoms that do not meet criteria for a major depressive episode. In comparison to major depressive disorder, dythymia is milder, but more long-term.

early infantile autism Autism that presents itself in the first few years of life.

echolalia A child's immediate or delayed parrot-like repetition of words or word combinations.

eclectic approach An approach to treatment in which the clinician uses different approaches for children with different problems and circumstances.

ecological model A theoretical approach to understanding the child's social and environmental context that portrays it as a series of nested and interconnected structures. The child is seen as being central to the model and as being surrounded by various levels of influence: the microsystem, the mesosystem, the exosystem, and the macrosystem.

educational neglect Failure to provide for a child's basic educational needs, including allowing chronic truancy, failing to enroll a child of mandatory school age in school, and failing to attend to a special educational need.

electroencephalogram (EEG) An electrophysiological measure of brain functioning whereby electrodes are taped to the surface of the subject's scalp in order to record the electrical activity of the brain. EEG recordings are sensitive to changes in state and emotionality, thereby making them particularly useful for studying social and emotional processes.

emotion reactivity A dimension of emotional processes that is associated with individual differences in the threshold and intensity of emotional experience.

emotion regulation The processes by which emotional arousal is redirected, controlled, or modified to facilitate adaptive functioning.

emotional abuse Abusive behavior that involves acts or omissions by parents or care-givers that cause, or could cause, serious behavioral, cognitive, emotional, or mental disorders.

emotional neglect Failure to provide for a child's basic emotional needs, including marked inattention to the child's needs for affection, refusal of or failure to provide needed psychological care, spousal abuse in the child's presence, and permission of drug or alcohol use by the child.

empowerment An individual's general ability to achieve his or her full potential in areas such as health or behavior. Empowerment reduces dependency and enables the individual (or family) to obtain information and make informed decisions and competent actions.

encopresis The passage of feces into inappropriate places, such as clothing, whether involuntary or intentional.

endocrine system A regulatory and communication system of the body. The endocrine glands (the adrenal glands, the thyroid gland, and the pituitary gland) each produce a particular hormone that is released into the bloodstream and has specific effects on other body organs.

enuresis Involuntary discharge of urine occuring in persons over five years of age or developmental equivalent.

epidemiological research The study of the incidence, prevalence, and co-occurrence of childhood disorders and competencies in clinic-referred and community samples.

epinephrine A hormone produced by the adrenal glands that is released into the bloodstream in response to stress in order to energize and prepare the body for a possible threat. This hormone is also known as adrenaline.

equifinality The concept that similar outcomes may stem from different early experiences.

etiology The study of the causes of disorders. With respect to childhood disorders, etiology considers how biological, psychological, and environmental processes interact.

eugenics The controversial pursuit of

methods (such as sterilization or mate selection) to improve the quality of human genetic stock.

euphoria An exaggerated sense of well-being.

event-related potentials (ERPs) Electroencephalogram (EEG) waves that are time-locked to discretely presented events in the environment, such as a brief visual stimuli. Because ERPs can be time-locked to specific events, they are particularly well suited for studying cognitive processes.

evolutionary degeneracy theory A pervasive 19th century explanation for medical and social problems in which such problems were attributed to a regression toward an earlier period in the development of humankind. This theory is also referred to as degenerationism.

executive functions Higher-order mental processes that enable a child to maintain a problem-solving set in order to attain a future goal. Examples of executive functions include working memory, mental computation, flexibility of thinking, internalization of speech, response inhibition, motor coordination, self-regulation of arousal level, and mature moral reasoning, among others.

expectable environment External conditions or surroundings that are considered to be fundamental and necessary for healthy development. The expectable environment for infants includes protective and nurturant adults and opportunities for socialization; for older children it includes a supportive family, contact with peers, and ample opportunities to explore and master the environment.

exposure A behavior therapy technique for treating anxiety disorders that exposes the subject to the source of his or her fear while providing appropriate and effective ways of coping with the fear (other than through escape and avoidance).

exposure plus response prevention A therapist-assisted, in-session exposure treatment. The patient is exposed to an event or stimulus that usually leads to a problematic behavior, while the therapist provides guidance in ways to resist the problematic behavior and to cope with anxiety the patient may experience. This method is sometimes used to treat the self-induced vomiting associated with eating disorders.

expressive gestures Gestures or vocalizations used to convey feelings.

expressive language disorder A form of communication disorder characterized by deficits in expression despite normal comprehension of speech.

external validity The degree to which findings can be generalized or extended to people, settings, times, measures, and characteristics other than the ones in the original study.

externalizing dimension (undercontrolled) A statistically derived factor that is made up of a mix of impulsive, overactive, aggressive, and delinquent actions, and consists of two independent but related subdimensions commonly labeled "delinquent" and "aggressive."

failure to thrive A growth disorder associated with early feeding disturbances in which, as a result of poor nutritive intake, the child's weight is below the 5th percentile for his or her age group, and the child's rate of weight gain has decelerated from the time of birth by at least two standard deviations according to standard growth charts.

false belief An incorrect assumption about a situation. Once a child recognizes that another person may have a false belief, he or she is better able to explain and predict the other's behavior. Understanding false beliefs is central to the development of theory of mind.

familial aggregation study An approach to behavioral genetic investigation that looks for nonrandom clustering of disorders or characteristics within a given family and compares these to the random distribution of these disorders or characteristics in the general population.

family history See *developmental history*.

family systems theory Theory that the behavior of an individual can be most accurately understood in the context of the dynamics of his or her family.

fear An alarm reaction to current danger or life-threatening emergencies marked by strong escape-oriented tendencies and a surge in the sympathetic nervous system.

feeding disorder of infancy or early childhood A disorder occurring in infancy or childhood characterized by a persistent failure to eat adequately, a sudden or marked deceleration of weight gain, and a slowing or disruption of emotional and social development.

fetal alcohol syndrome A disorder stemming from extensive prenatal exposure to alcohol. Children with this disorder typically suffer from problems in intellectual functioning, central nervous system dysfunction, cranial feature defects, behavior problems, growth retardation, and physical abnormalities of the face.

fight/flight response The immediate reaction to perceived danger or threat whereby efforts are directed toward protecting against potential harm, either by confronting the source of danger (fight), or by escaping from the situation (flight).

flooding A procedure for treating anxiety that involves prolonged and repeated exposure to the anxiety-provoking situation until the subject's level of anxiety has diminished.

fragile-X syndrome A chromosomal abnormality in which one area on the X chromosome is pinched. Children with fragile-X syndrome typically suffer from moderate mental retardation.

frontal lobe One of the four areas of each cerebral hemisphere; responsible for the functions underlying much of our thinking and reasoning abilities, including memory.

frontostriatal circuitry A structure of the brain consisting of the pre-frontal cortex and the basal ganglia; it is associated with attention, executive functions, delayed response, and response organization. Abnormalities with this structure have been linked to ADHD.

functional analysis of behavior See *behavior analysis*.

general intellectual functioning One's general level of intellectual ability, defined by an intelligence quotient (IQ or equivalent) derived from an assessment with one or more of the standardized, individually-administered intelligence tests.

generalized anxiety disorder (GAD) A form of anxiety disorder in which the subject experiences chronic or exaggerated worry and tension, almost always anticipating disaster, even in the absence of an obvious reason to do so. The worrying is often accompanied by physical symptoms such as trembling, muscle tension, headache, and nausea.

generalized social phobia A severe form of social phobia in which the subject fears most social situations, is afraid to meet or talk with new people, avoids contact with anyone outside his or her family, and finds it extremely difficult to attend school, participate in recreational activities, or socialize at all.

genetic screening Tests done either prior to conception or during prenatal development to determine the likelihood or presence of a genetic abnormality.

genotype An individual's specific genetic makeup.

goodness of fit The extent to which two things are suited. For instance, with respect to child psychopathology, one might use the term to refer to the extent to which the child's early temperament and the parent's style of interaction are suited to each other.

graded exposure Gradual exposure of a subject to a feared situation.

graduated guidance A technique for teaching a desired behavior that involves carefully demonstrating each step involved in executing the behavior, providing guidance when the subject attempts the steps, and praising the subject for his or her attempts. As the behavior becomes more familiar, less guidance is required.

hallucinations Disturbances in perception in which things are seen, heard, or otherwise sensed even though they are not real or present.

health promotion An approach to the prevention of disease that involves education, public policy, and similar actions to promote health.

heritability The proportion of the variance of a trait that is attributable to genetic influences.

high reactive-inhibited Term used to describe infants/children who become very active and distressed in unfamiliar situations.

hormones Proteins that carry messages between cells throughout the body (e.g., testosterone, estrogen).

hostile aggression Aggressive behavior directed toward inflicting pain on others.

hyperactive Displaying an unusually high level of energy and an inability to remain still or quiet.

hypersomnia A type of sleep disorder characterized by excessive daytime sleepiness and extended periods of nighttime sleep.

hypervigilant Overly alert to or responsive to trouble or danger. For example, maltreated children may become hypervigilant, looking for any cue related to a possible verbal or physical outburst from their parent or caregiver.

hypnagogic hallucinations Intense, dreamlike imagery that is extremely realistic because the subject incorporates elements of his or her actual environment into the dream. Hypnagogic hallucinations are indicative of intrusions of REM sleep during the transition from sleep to wakefulness.

hypothalamic-pituitary-adrenal (HPA) axis A regulatory system of the brain made up of the hypothalamus control center and the pituitary and adrenal glands; it influences a person's response to stress and his or her ability to regulate emotions.

idiographic case formulation An approach to case formulation or assessment that emphasizes the detailed representation of the individual child or family as a unique entity. This approach contrasts the nomothetic approach, which instead emphasizes the general laws that apply to all individuals.

idiopathic The term used to describe unknown causes of a problem based on the assumption that the causes may be unique to an individual's development.

impulsive Prone to acting with little or no consideration of possible consequences. This term is frequently used to describe children who suffer from attention-deficit/hyperactivity disorder.

interdisciplinary perspective An approach to study that takes into account the contributions and interests of researchers in several separate fields.

in vivo exposure Real-life exposure to anxiety-provoking stimuli, as opposed to exposure in one's imagination, in a controlled environment, through role-play, or by watching others. In vivo exposure is considered by many to be the most effective exposure procedure.

inattentive Lacking the ability to focus one's attention.

inborn errors of metabolism Genetic metabolic defects. Such defects may cause excesses or shortages of chemicals necessary during specific stages of development, thereby affecting intelligence and cognitive functioning.

incest Sexual abuse by a relative of the victim.

incidence rates The rate at which new cases of a disorder appear over a specified period of time.

incidental training A method of teaching readiness skills or other desired behaviors that works to strengthen the behavior by capitalizing on naturally occurring opportunities.

index offense An act that is considered criminal regardless of whether the perpetrator is a child or an adult.

indirect aggression Aggressive behavior that involves getting even by third party retaliation, or by spreading rumors.

information processing disturbances Cognitive misperceptions and distortions in the way events are perceived and interpreted.

informed consent An individual's expressed willingness to participate in a research study, based on an understanding of the nature of the research, the potential risks and benefits involved, the expected outcomes, and possible alternatives.

insecure-disorganized attachment The lack of an organized pattern of early childhood attachment, characterized by a mixture of approach and avoidance, helplessness, apprehension, and general disorientation.

instrumental aggression Aggressive behavior that is directed toward achieving a specific goal other than inflicting pain.

instrumental gestures Gestures or vocalizations used to prompt action on the part of the person to whom the gestures are directed.

insulin-dependent diabetes mellitus (IDDM) A lifelong metabolic disorder in which the body is unable to metabolize carbohydrates due to inadequate pancreatic release of insulin.

interdependent Applies to the assumption that abnormal child behavior is determined by both the child and his or her environment, and that these two factors are interconnected. (also see *transaction*).

internal validity The extent to which an intended manipulation of a variable, rather than extraneous influences, accounts for observed results, changes, or group differences.

internal, stable, and global attributions Assignment of responsibility for an event whereby the child believes that he or she is responsible (internal attribution), that the event is likely to occur again, that when it does he or she will again be responsible (stable attribution), and that the reason he or she is responsible applies to most other situations (global attribution). Depending on the nature of the event in question, internal, stable, and global attributions can be either good or bad. Internal, stable, and global attributions regarding negative events are characteristic of depressed individuals.

intervention Problem-solving strategies directed at helping the child and family to adapt more effectively to their current and future circumstances.

islets of ability See *splinter-skills.*

joint social attention The ability to coordinate one's focus of attention on another person and an object of mutual interest.

learned helplessness The phenomenon whereby exposure to uncontrollable adverse events results in a sense that one cannot control important outcomes in one's life.

learning disability A learning problem that cannot be attributed to an obvious condition (such as mental retardation or brain damage) and that affects the manner in which information is taken in, retained, or expressed.

learning disorder A diagnosis applied when reading, math, or writing ability is found to be substantially below normal expectations for a person of the subject's age.

levels of needed supports (intermittent, limited, extensive, pervasive) An alternative classification of the severity of mental retardation that categorizes people according to their need for supportive services. Also see *degrees of intellectual impairment.*

life-course-persistent path (LCP) A developmental pathway to antisocial behavior in which the child engages in antisocial behavior at an early age and continues to do so into adulthood.

longitudinal research A method of research whereby the same individuals are studied at different ages/stages of development.

low reactive-uninhibited Term used to describe infants and children who remain relaxed and calm in unfamiliar situations.

macroparadigm A broad philosophical framework that combines several approaches to the study of a phenomenon.

mainstream education A strategy implemented by school systems in an attempt to give children with special needs the opportunity to interact with normally developing children. Children with different developmental and educational needs are placed into the same classrooms rather than being segregated. Also see *regular education initiative.*

maintenance Efforts to increase adherence to treatment over time in order to prevent a relapse or recurrence of a problem.

major depressive disorder (MDD) A form of depressive disorder characterized by one or more major depressive episodes that last for at least two weeks, and are accompanied by additional symptoms such as sleep disturbances or thoughts of suicide.

mania An abnormally elevated or expansive mood.

mathematics disorder A form of learning disability characterized by sub-average ability in the areas of mathematics, abstract reasoning, or visual-spatial ability, despite normal intelligence.

mediator variable The process, mechanism, or means through which a variable produces a specific outcome.

mental age (MA) An index of a child's intellectual ability in relation to other children of the same chronological age. MA is no longer used on I.Q. tests.

mental status exam An assessment of a subject's general mental functioning, typically carried out during an interview in which questions are asked and systematic observations of the subject are made in the areas of appearance and behavior, thought processes, mood and affect, intellectual functioning, and sensorium.

mentalization Awareness of other people's and one's own mental states. Also referred to as theory of mind.

metabolic control The degree to which an individual's glucose level is maintained within the normal range (in reference to diabetes mellitus).

metabolic rate The body's balance of energy expenditure. Metabolic rate is determined by genetic and physiological makeup, along with eating and exercise habits.

metacognition Awareness of one's own thought processes. Metacognition is considered a higher order mental process.

metacognitive training Instruction in techniques that help to improve memory and learning, including how to coordinate learned skills across learning situations.

methylphenidate The stimulant medication most commonly used in treating children with attention-deficit/hyperactivity disorder. It is sold under the name *Ritalin.*

microsleep A short, unintentional sleep episode that usually occurs in situations of low stimulation and low activity.

minor physical anomalies Minor physical irregularities that develop prenatally, such as a head circumference out of the normal range or eyes spaced farther apart than usual.

mixed receptive-expressive language disorder A form of communication disorder characterized by deficits in expressive language coupled with a difficulty in understanding some aspects of speech (i.e., deficits in receptive language).

modeling A technique for teaching a desired behavior in which one displays the target behavior in the presence of the subject.

moderator variable A factor that influences the direction or strength of a relationship between variables.

monosomy A genetic abnormality involving the loss of an entire chromosome or chromosomal band.

mood disorder A disorder in which the subject suffers from extreme, persistent, or poorly regulated emotional states.

mood episodes Incidents characterized by disturbances in emotion. The DSM-IV recognizes four types of mood episodes: major depressive, manic, mixed, and hypomanic.

morbidity The various forms of physical and functional consequences and limitations that result from an illness.

multiaxial system A classification system consisting of several different domains (axes) of information about the subject that may assist a clinician in planning the treatment of a disorder. The DSM-IV is an example of a multiaxial classification system.

multifinality The concept that various outcomes may stem from similar beginnings.

multiple-baseline design A single-case experimental design in which the effect of a treatment is shown by demonstrating that behaviors in more than one baseline change as a result of the institution of a treatment.

multisystemic treatment (MST) An approach to treatment that attempts to address the multiple determinants of problematic behavior by involving family members, school personnel, peers, juvenile justice staff, and others in the child's life, and by drawing on multiple techniques such as parent-management training, cognitive problem-solving skills training, and marital therapy, as well as specialized interventions such as special education placements, referral to substance abuse treatment programs, or referral to legal services.

narcolepsy A sleep disorder in which bouts of REM sleep lasting anywhere from 10 minutes to 1 hour intrude upon wakefulness.

natural experiment An experiment in

which comparisons are made between preexisting conditions or treatments (i.e., random assignment is not used).

naturalistic observation The unstructured observation of a child in his or her natural environment.

negative affectivity A persistent negative mood evidenced by nervousness, sadness, anger, and guilt.

negative cognitive schemata Stable structures in memory that guide information processing, including self-critical beliefs and attitudes, in a way that is consistent with the negative self-image of the subject. These cognitive schemata are rigid and resistant to change even in the face of contradictory evidence.

neighborhood disorder The social and physical decay of a neighborhood as evidenced by visible signs such as graffiti, broken windows, litter-strewn lots, and loitering youth.

neural plasticity The malleable nature of the brain, evidenced throughout the course of development. Although infants are born with basic brain processes, experience leads to anatomical differentiation. That is, certain synapses of the brain are strengthened and stabilized, while others regress and disappear.

neurobiological perspective An approach to the study of psychological disorders that views brain and nervous system functions as underlying causes. The role of environmental influences is also recognized.

neuroimaging A method of examining the structure and/or function of the brain. Neuroimaging procedures include magnetic resonance imaging (MRI), coaxial tomographic scan (CT), positron emission tomography (PET), and functional magnetic resonance imaging (fMRI).

neuroleptics A type of pharmacological treatment for certain disorders. Neuroleptics are dopamine antagonists that increase neurotransmitter activity, and are the most commonly used drugs to treat aggressive behavior and schizophrenia.

neuropsychological assessment A form of assessment that attempts to link brain functioning with objective measures of behavior that are known to depend on an intact central nervous system.

neurotic paradox The pattern of self-perpetuating behavior in which children who are overly anxious in various situations, even while being aware that the anxiety may be unnecessary or excessive, find themselves unable to abandon their self-defeating behaviors.

neurotransmitters Specific hormones that carry messages between nerve cells (e.g., serotonin, dopamine).

nightmares A form of parasomnia that occurs during REM sleep and is characterized by repeated awakenings with detailed recall of extended and extremely frightening dreams, usually involving threats to survival, security, or self-esteem.

nocturnal panic An abrupt waking from sleep in a state of panic.

nomothetic case formulation An approach to case formulation or assessment that emphasizes general principles that apply to all people. This approach contrasts with the idiographic approach, which instead emphasizes a detailed representation of the individual or family as a unique entity.

nondisjunction Failure of a pair of chromosomes to separate during meiosis.

non–rapid eye movement (NREM) sleep A stage of sleep during which the brain is relatively quiet, slow, and synchronized, accompanied by slow and regular pulse and respiration, and maintained muscle tone.

nonverbal learning disabilities Learning disabilities characterized by deficits relating to right hemisphere brain functioning, such as problems in social skills, spatial orientation, problem solving, and the recognition of nonverbal cues such as body language.

norepinephrine A body chemical that is both a hormone and neurotransmitter. Norepinephrine can be either excitatory or inhibitory in nature, and is found in the circuits that control arousal, wakefulness, learning, memory, and eating.

nosologies Efforts to classify psychiatric disorders into descriptive categories.

observer bias The possibility that research observers who are aware of the purpose of a study may see and record what is expected rather than what actually occurs.

obsessions Persistent, intrusive, and irrational thoughts, ideas, impulses, or images, that focus on improbable or unrealistic events or real-life events that are greatly exaggerated.

obsessive-compulsive disorder (OCD) A form of anxiety disorder in which the subject experiences repeated, intrusive and unwanted thoughts that cause anxiety, and often engages in ritualized behavior to relieve this anxiety.

obstructive sleep apnea syndrome (OSAS) The most common form of breathing-related sleep disorder in children, in which a stop in breathing lasting from 10 seconds to 2 minutes occurs due to collapse of the airway and obstruction of air flow. Also see *breathing-related sleep disorders*.

operant speech training A strategy used to help children use language more appropriately; it involves a step-by-step approach that successively increases the child's vocalizations, teaches the child to imitate sounds and words, teaches the meanings of words, and teaches the child to use language expressively to label objects, make verbal requests, and express desires. This training is often employed with children with autism.

oppositional defiant disorder (ODD) The least severe form of disruptive behavior disorder, in which children show an age-inappropriate and persistent pattern of irritable, hostile, oppositional, and defiant behavior.

optimal stimulation theory A theory of attention-deficit/hyperactivity disorder that contends that hyperactivity arises from a low level of arousal and is simply an under-aroused child's effort to maintain an optimal level of arousal through self-stimulation.

organic mental retardation Mental retardation stemming from physical causes such as brain damage or improper CNS development.

organization of development The assumption that early patterns of adaptation evolve over time and transform into higher-order functions in a structured manner. For instance, infant eye contact and speech sounds evolve and transform into speech and language.

overt-covert dimension An independent dimension consisting of a continuum of antisocial behavior ranging from overt forms such as physical aggression at one end, to covert forms (i.e., hidden or sneaky acts) at the other. The overt forms of antisocial behavior correspond roughly to those on the aggressive subdimension of the externalizing dimension, whereas the covert behaviors correspond roughly to those on the delinquent subdimension of the externalizing dimension.

panic A group of unexpected physical symptoms of the fight/flight response that occur in the absence of any obvious threat or danger.

panic attack A sudden and overwhelming period of intense fear or discomfort accompanied by four or more physical and cognitive symptoms characteristic of the fight/flight response.

panic disorder (PD) A form of anxiety disorder characterized by panic attacks and sudden feelings of terror that strike repeatedly and without warning. Physical symptoms include chest pain, heart palpitations, shortness of breath, dizziness, and abdominal stress. There is also persistent concern about having another attack and the possible implications and consequences it would bring.

parasomnias A category of sleep disorders in which behavioral or physiological events intrude upon ongoing sleep. Persons suffering from parasomnias often complain of unusual behaviors during sleep such as sleepwalking and nightmares.

parent management training (PMT) A program aimed at teaching parents to cope effectively with their children's difficult behavior and their own reactions to it.

pedophilia Sexual activity or sexually arousing fantasies involving a prepubescent child, by someone who is at least 16 years old and at least five years older than the child.

perseverative speech Talking incessantly about the same topic.

personality disorder An enduring pattern of inner experience and behavior that deviates markedly from cultural expectations and is inflexible and pervasive.

pervasive developmental disorder not otherwise specified (PDD-NOS) A disorder in which the child displays social, communication, and behavioral impairments associated with PDD, but does not meet the criteria for PDD, schizophrenia, or other disorders.

pervasive developmental disorders (PDD) A category of disorders characterized by severe and extensive impairments in social interaction and communication skills, along with stereotyped patterns of behaviors, interests, and activities.

phenotype An individual's observable characteristics or behavior.

phenylketonuria (PKU) A single-gene, recessive condition in which children lack the ability to break down the amino acid phenylalanine. Unless treated successfully early in life, children with PKU may suffer from brain damage, mental retardation, musky body odor, hyperactivity, seizures, and dry bleached skin and hair.

phobia Fear that occurs at an inappropriate age, persists, is irrational or exaggerated, leads to avoidance of the object or event, and causes impairment in normal routines.

phonemes The basic sounds that make up language.

phonological awareness A broad construct that includes recognition of the relationship that exists between sounds and letters, detection of rhyme and alliteration, and awareness that sounds can be manipulated within syllables in words.

phonological disorder A form of communication disorder characterized by difficulties in articulation or sound production, but not necessarily in word expression.

physical abuse The infliction or endangerment of physical injury as a result of punching, beating, kicking, biting, burning, shaking, or otherwise intentionally harming a child.

physical aggression A form of aggressive behavior that includes hitting, bullying, assaulting, and fighting.

physical neglect Failure to provide for a child's basic physical needs, including refusal of or delay in seeking health care, inadequate provision of food, abandonment, expulsion from the home or refusal to allow a runaway to return home, inadequate supervision, and inadequate provision of clean clothes.

physical system The response system of anxiety that expresses physical symptoms such as a racing heart, sweating, dizziness, muscle tension, chest pain, and breathlessness.

pica A form of eating disorder in which the infant or toddler persists in eating inedible, nonnutritive substances. This disorder is one of the more common and usually less serious eating disorders found among very young children.

positive affectivity A persistent positive mood as reflected in states such as joy, enthusiasm, and energy.

posttraumatic stress disorder (PTSD) A form of anxiety disorder whereby the child displays persistent anxiety following exposure to or witnessing of an overwhelming traumatic event that is outside the range of usual human experience.

Prader-Willi syndrome A complex genetic disorder associated with an abnormality of chromosome 15. Children with Prader-Willi syndrome typically suffer from short stature, mental retardation or learning disabilities, incomplete sexual development, certain behavior problems, low muscle tone, and an involuntary urge to eat constantly.

pragmatics The aspect of language that focuses on its appropriate use in social and communicative contexts.

preservation of sameness A characteristic of children with autistic disorder who show an anxious and obsessive insistence on the maintenance of sameness that no one but the child may disrupt. Changes in daily routine, arrangement of objects, or the wording of requests, or the sight of anything broken or incomplete, will produce tantrums or despair.

prevalence rates The number of cases of a disorder, whether new or previously existing, that are observed during a specified period of time.

prevention Activities directed at decreasing the chances that undesired future outcomes will occur.

proactive aggression Aggressive behavior that occurs without provocation, through domination, bullying, or threats.

proband The member of a family whose trait has been singled out for study in a behavioral genetic investigation.

prognosis The prediction of the course or outcome of a disorder.

projective tests Tests used by psychoanalytically oriented clinicians in which the subject is presented with ambiguous stimuli and is asked to describe what she or he sees, with the expectation that the subject will project his or her own personality on the ambiguous stimuli.

pronoun reversal The repetition of personal pronouns exactly as heard, without changing them according to the person being referred to. For example, if asked "Are you hungry?", one might reply "You are hungry," rather than "I am hungry."

protective factor A variable that precedes a negative outcome of interest and decreases the chances that the outcome will occur.

protodeclarative gestures Gestures or vocalizations that direct the visual attention of other people to objects of shared interest, such as pointing to a dog; done with the prime purpose of engaging another person in interaction.

protodyssomnia A sleep disorder characterized by problems falling and staying asleep. While in adults this disorder is referred to as primary insomnia, the term *protodyssomnia* is used to refer to cases involving children because, unlike those of adults, children's problems of falling and staying asleep are common and mostly transitory.

protoimperative gestures   Gestures or vocalizations used to express needs, such as pointing to an object that one desires but cannot reach.

pruning   A process occurring in early childhood in which the number of brain synapses becomes selectively reduced so as to gradually shape and differentiate important brain functions.

psychogenic theory   The theory that a given problem or disorder is of mental, as opposed to organic, origin.

psychological disorder   A pattern of behavioral, cognitive, or physical symptoms that includes one or more of the following prominent features: (a) some degree of distress in the subject; (b) behavior indicating some degree of disability; and (c) an increased risk of suffering, death, pain, disability, or an important loss of freedom.

psychological factors affecting physical condition   psychological disorders or conditions that are presumed to cause or exacerbate a physical condition.

psychopathy   A pattern of deceitful, callous, manipulative, and remorseless behavior.

psychosocial dwarfism   A rare growth disorder associated with early feeding disturbances in which stunted growth is the primary syndrome. Psychosocial dwarfism is also characterized by bizarre eating behaviors such as drinking stagnant water, gorging, vomiting, stealing and hoarding food, and eating garbage and animal food.

psychotic disorders   A category of disorders characterized by severe symptoms such as bizarre delusions, hallucinations, disturbances in thinking, grossly disorganized or catatonic behavior, extremely inappropriate or flat affect, and significant deterioration or impairment in functioning.

purging   Behavior aimed at ridding the body of consumed food, including self-induced vomiting and the misuse of laxatives, diuretics, or enemas. Also see *compensatory behaviors*.

qualitative research methods   Research for which the purpose is to describe, interpret, and understand the phenomenon of interest in the context in which it is experienced.

random assignment   The assignment of research participants to treatment conditions whereby each participant has an equal chance of being assigned to each condition. Random assignment increases the likelihood that characteristics other than the independent variable will be equally distributed across treatment groups.

rapid eye movement (REM) sleep   A stage of sleep during which brain activity is high, accompanied by autonomic arousal, loss of muscle tone, and rapid eye movement. Dreaming often occurs during this stage.

reactive aggression   Aggressive behavior that occurs in response to actions by others.

reactivity   The extent to which a research subject's performance is altered because of his or her awareness of being observed, of the measurement procedures, or of participation in the study.

readiness skills   Skills that are necessary before a child will be ready to begin treatment. Such skills may include the ability to sit, the ability to speak, or the ability to attend to a teacher or therapist.

reading disorder   A type of learning disability characterized by sub-average reading ability in the presence of normal intelligence. Also see *dyslexia*.

real-time prospective design   A research design in which the research sample is identified and then followed longitudinally over time, with data collected at specified time intervals.

reciprocal influence   See *bidirectional influence*.

regular education initiative (REI)   A program implemented by some school systems that involves the placement of children with disabilities in the same classrooms as normal students, with general and special education teachers sharing responsibility for student instruction. Also see *mainstream education*.

reinforcement trap   The process by which parents who are involved in coercive interactions with their child find themselves trapped by the consequences of their own behavior.

relational disorders   Disorders that occur in the context of relationships, such as child abuse and neglect. Relational disorders signify the connection between children's behavior patterns and the availability of a suitable child-rearing environment.

reliability   The extent to which the result of an experiment is consistent or repeatable.

representational models   Cognitive schemas of self, others, and events, that incorporate experience, knowledge, and expectations, and are applied to new situations.

research design   A strategy used to test a hypothesis.

residential care   A living arrangement in which a child whose family or school cannot adequately provide for him or her is cared for in a specialized out-of-the home setting.

resilience   The ability to avoid negative outcomes despite being at risk for psychopathology.

response prevention   A procedure used in the treatment of anxiety that prevents the child from engaging in escape or avoidance behaviors. This procedure is usually used in conjunction with *flooding*.

response-cost procedure   A technique for managing a subject's behavior that involves the loss of reinforcers such as privileges, activities, points, or tokens in response to inappropriate behavior.

restricting   Behavior exhibited by people suffering from anorexia whereby dieting, fasting, or excessive exercise is used to lose or avoid gaining weight.

retrospective design   A research design in which the research sample is asked to provide information relating to an earlier time period.

Rett's disorder   A pervasive developmental disorder characterized by a deceleration of head growth in the early years, a loss of previously acquired purposeful hand skills with subsequent development of stereotyped hand movements, a loss of social engagement, poorly coordinated gait or trunk movements, severe impairments in expressive and receptive language development, and severe psychomotor retardation.

reversal design   See *A-B-A-B design*.

reward dominance   A tendency to seek rewards that is so strong that it leads to conduct problems.

risk factor   A variable that precedes a negative outcome of interest and increases the chances that the outcome will occur.

rumination disorder   A form of eating disorder characterized by the voluntary regurgitation, re-chewing, and re-swallowing of food.

schema   A hypothetical cognitive structure that stems from a child's processing of life experiences. A schema acts as a guideline or core philosophy, influencing one's expectations and filtering information in a fashion that is consistent with the individual's philosophy.

schizophrenia   A form of psychotic disorder that involves characteristic disturbances in thinking (delusions), perception (hallucinations), speech, emotions, and behavior.

schizotypal personality disorder (SPD)   A disorder characterized by social and interpersonal deficits, acute discomfort with close relationships, and cognitive and perceptual distortions and eccentricities.

school refusal behavior   A form of anxious behavior in which the child refuses to attend classes or has difficulty remaining in school for an entire day.

screening   Identification of subjects at risk for a specific negative outcome.

selective attention   The ability to concentrate exclusively on relevant stimuli and to avoid distraction by irrelevant stimuli in the environment.

selective mutism   The inability or refusal to talk in social situations, despite the fact that the subject may talk at home or in other settings.

self-injurious behavior (SIB)   Severe and sometimes life-threatening acts that cause damage to the subject's own body, such as head banging, eye gouging, severe scratching, rumination, some types of pica, and inserting objects under the skin.

self-regulation training   Instruction aimed at teaching skills necessary to control one's own behavior.

self-stimulatory behaviors   Repetitive body movements or movements of objects, such as hand flapping or spinning a pencil.

sensitive periods   Windows of time during which environmental influences on development are heightened, thus providing enhanced opportunities to learn.

sensitivity of classification   The percentage chance that a study testing for (for example) a disorder will correctly classify a subject who has the disorder.

sensory dominance   The tendency to focus on certain types of sensory input versus others; for example, a preference for sights over sounds.

separation anxiety disorder (SAD)   A form of anxiety disorder in which the subject displays age-inappropriate, excessive, and disabling anxiety about being apart from his or her parents or away from home.

serotonin   A neurotransmitter produced in the central nervous system that can be either excitatory or inhibitory in nature, and that is found in the circuits involved in sleep and emotional arousal.

sexual abuse   Abusive acts that are sexual in nature, including fondling a child's genitals, intercourse, incest, rape, sodomy, exhibitionism, and commercial exploitation through prostitution or the production of pornographic materials.

shaping   A procedure for teaching a desired behavior whereby behaviors that are more and more similar to the target behavior are taught and reinforced in succession, until the desired behavior is achieved.

showing gesture   A gesture used to bring something of interest, such as a newly-discovered object, to the attention of someone else.

sign language training   An approach to teaching language to children that involves teaching the child nonverbal signs and their functional use in everyday situations. This training is sometimes used with children with autism who are unable to communicate verbally.

similar sequence hypothesis   The assumption that children with or without mental retardation pass through cognitive developmental stages in the same order.

similar structure hypothesis   The assumption that children with mental retardation will demonstrate the same behaviors and underlying processes as will typically developing children at the same level of cognitive functioning.

single-case experimental design   A type of research design most frequently used to evaluate the impact of a clinical treatment on a subject's problem. Single-case experimental designs involve repeated assessment of behavior over time, the replication of treatment effects upon the same subject over time, and the subject serving as his or her own control by experiencing all treatment conditions.

sleep paralysis   A brief period of time at the beginning or end of a sleep episode in which the subject cannot move or speak. Sleep paralysis is indicative of intrusions of REM sleep during the transition from sleep to wakefulness.

sleep terrors   A form of parasomnia that occurs during deep sleep and is characterized by abrupt awakening, accompanied by autonomic arousal but no recall.

sleepwalking   A form of parasomnia occurring during deep sleep in which the individual gets out of bed and walks around, but has no recall the next day.

slowing and stability hypothesis   The observation that children with Down syndrome show significant age-related gains in social and intellectual development and adaptive functioning in the early years, but as they grow older their pace of development decelerates and levels off, sometimes even declining.

social cognition   A construct to describe how people think about themselves in relation to others, and how they interpret ambiguous events and solve problems.

social learning theory   A theoretical approach to the study of behavior that is interested in both overt behaviors and the role of possible cognitive mediators that may influence such behaviors directly or indirectly.

social phobia   A marked and persistent fear of social or performance situations in which the subject is exposed to possible scrutiny and embarrassment.

social selection hypothesis   The premise that people tend to select environments in which there are other people similar to themselves.

social skills training   Instruction aimed at teaching appropriate and effective social behaviors.

somatoform disorders   Health-related disorders characterized by physical symptoms that resemble or suggest a medical condition, but lack organic or physiological evidence.

specific phobia   A marked and persistent fear of clearly discernible, circumscribed objects or situations.

specificity of classification   The percentage chance that a study testing for (for example) a specific disorder will correctly classify a subject who does *not* have the disorder.

spectrum disorders   Disorders in which the symptoms and characteristics are expressed in many different combinations and in any degree of severity.

splinter skills (islets of ability)   Specialized talents that are above average for the general population, and well above the general level of intellect of the individual who exhibits the talent. A small but significant number of children with autism develop splinter skills.

standardization   The process by which a set of standards or norms is specified for a measurement procedure so that it can be used consistently across different assessments.

status offense A delinquent act committed by a youth that would not be considered an offense if committed by an adult.

stimulant medications Drugs that alter the activity in the frontostriatal region of the brain by impacting three or more neurotransmitters important to the functioning of this region—dopamine, norepinephrine, and epinephrine, and possibly serotonin.

stimulus overselectivity The tendency to focus on one feature of an object or event in the environment while ignoring other equally important features.

structured observation Observation of a subject, usually occurring in a clinic or laboratory, in which the subject is given specific tasks or instructions to carry out, and researchers look for specific information.

stuttering Repeated and prolonged pronunciations of certain syllables that interferes with communication.

subtype A group of people with a specific disorder who have something in common, such as symptoms, etiology, problem severity, or likely outcome, that makes them distinct from people with other subtypes of the same disorder.

sustained attention (vigilance) The ability to maintain a persistent focus of attention over time or when fatigued.

synapses Axonal connections in the brain that enable electrical signals from one part of the brain to be carried to other parts of the brain.

systematic desensitization A three-step behavior therapy technique for treating anxiety whereby (1) the child is taught to relax, (2) an anxiety hierarchy is constructed, and (3) the anxiety-provoking stimuli are presented sequentially while the child remains relaxed.

target behaviors Behaviors that are the primary problems of concern.

taxonomy The grouping of psychological disorders according to their distinguishing features.

temperament The child's innately based reactivity and self-regulation with respect to the domains of emotions, activity level, and attention.

test A task or set of tasks given under standard conditions with the purpose of assessing some aspect of the subject's knowledge, skill, personality, or condition.

theory of mind (ToM) The cognition and understanding of mental states that cannot be observed directly, such as beliefs and desires, both in one's self and in others.

Tourette's disorder A rare disorder in which the subject exhibits uncontrollable movements such as tics, eye blinks, and facial twitches. Children with Tourette's may also blurt or bark out words uncontrollably.

trait confluence The phenomenon whereby through differential reinforcement, members of a group become increasingly similar in their attitudes and behavior over time.

transaction The process by which the subject and environment interact in a dynamic fashion to contribute to the expression of a disorder (also see *interdependent*).

translocation A genetic disruption involving the transfer of a piece of one chromosome onto another chromosome.

traumatic sexualization One possible outcome of child sexual abuse, whereby the child's sexual knowledge and behavior are shaped in developmentally inappropriate ways.

treatment Corrective actions that will permit successful adaptation by eliminating or reducing the impact of an undesired outcome that has already occurred.

treatment effectiveness The degree to which a treatment can be shown to work in actual clinical practice, as opposed to controlled laboratory conditions.

treatment efficacy The degree to which a treatment can produce changes under well-controlled conditions that depart from those typically used in clinical practice.

treatment planning and evaluation The process of using assessment information to generate a treatment plan and to gauge its effectiveness.

trichotillomania A rare disorder of impulse control that is characterized by the compulsion to pull out one's own hair.

trisomy A genetic abnormality involving the duplication of an entire chromosome or chromosomal band.

true experiment An experiment in which the researcher has maximum control over the independent variable or conditions of interest, and in which the researcher can use random assignment of subjects to groups, can include needed control conditions, and can control possible sources of bias.

tuberous sclerosis A single-gene disorder associated with abnormalities including skin lesions, neural deficits, seizures, and learning disabilities. Gene sites for this disorder have been identified on chromosomes 9 and 16.

undercontrolled See *externalizing dimension*.

unexpected discrepancy A basic premise of current definitions of learning disorders that denotes a disparity or discrepancy between an individual's measured ability and actual performance.

validity The extent to which a measure actually assesses the dimension or construct that the researcher sets out to measure.

vasopressin A hormone released into the brain in response to physical (and possibly emotional) stress. Elevated levels of vasopressin have been found in patients with anorexia, bulimia, and obsessive-compulsive disorder.

verbal aggression A form of aggressive behavior that includes threats, name-calling, taunts, and swearing.

victimization Abuse or mistreatment of someone whose ability to protect himself or herself is limited (e.g., the mistreatment of a child by his or her parents).

vigilance See *sustained attention*.

vulnerability-stress model An approach to understanding the development of a disorder that emphasizes the interplay among vulnerability factors (e.g., genetic risk, deviant family interactions), stressors (e.g., ongoing child abuse, death of a parent), and protective factors (e.g., intelligence, supportive family relationships). The advantage of this model is that it recognizes the many diverse and complex pathways that may lead to a disorder.

whole-language methods Approaches to reading instruction that emphasize the learning of entire words and ideas rather than isolated sounds.

writing disorders Learning disabilities characterized by problems with writing, drawing, and (often) other fine visual-motor behaviors requiring eye-hand coordination, despite normal gross motor development.

References

Abel, C. G., Osborn, C. A., & Twigg, D. A. (1993). Sexual assault through the life span: Adult offenders with juvenile histories. In H. E. Barbaree, W. L. Marshall, & S. M. Husdon (Eds.), *The juvenile sex offender* (pp. 104–117). New York: Guilford Press.

Aber, J. L., Allen, J., Carlson, V., & Cicchetti, D. (1989). The effects of maltreatment on development during early childhood: Recent studies and their theoretical, clinical, and policy implications. In D. Cicchetti & V. Carlson (Eds.), *Child maltreatment: Theory and research on the causes and consequences of child abuse and neglect* (pp. 579–619). New York: Cambridge University Press.

Aber, J. L., & Cicchetti, D. (1984). The socio-emotional development of maltreated children: An empirical and theoretical analysis. In H. Fitzgerald, B. Lester, & M. Yogman (Eds.), *Theory and research in behavioral pediatrics* (Vol. 2, pp. 147–205). New York: Plenum.

Abikoff, H., Courtney, M., Pelham, W., & Koplewicz, H. (1993). Teachers' ratings of disruptive behaviors: The influence of halo effects. *Journal of Abnormal Child Psychology, 21,* 519–533.

Abrahamian, R. P., & Lloyd-Still, J. D. (1984). Chronic constipation in childhood: A longitudinal study of 186 patients. *Journal of Pediatric Gastroenterology and Nutrition, 3,* 460–467.

Abrams, E. Z., & Goodman, J. F. (1998). Diagnosing developmental problems in children: Parents and professionals negotiate bad news. *Journal of Pediatric Psychology, 23,* 87–98.

Abramson, L. Y., Metalsky, G. I., & Alloy, L. B. (1989). Hopelessness depression: A theory-based subtype of depression. *Psychological Review, 96,* 358–372.

Abramson, L. Y., Seligman, M. E., & Teasdale, J. D. (1978). Learned helplessness in humans: Critique and reformulation. *Journal of Abnormal Psychology, 37,* 49–74.

Achenbach, T. M. (1978). *Research in developmental psychology: Concepts, strategies, methods.* New York: Free Press.

Achenbach, T. M. (1982). *Developmental psychopathology* (2nd ed.). New York: Wiley.

Achenbach, T. M. (1985). *Assessment and taxonomy of child and adolescent psychopathology.* Beverly Hills, CA: Sage.

Achenbach, T. M. (1990). Conceptualization of developmental psychopathology. In M. Lewis & S. M. Miller (Eds.), *Handbook of developmental psychopathology* (pp. 3–14). New York: Plenum.

Achenbach, T. M. (1991a). *Manual for the Child Behavior Checklist/4-18 and 1991 profile.* Burlington: University of Vermont, Department of Psychiatry.

Achenbach, T. M. (1991b). *Manual for the Youth Self-Report and 1991 profile.* Burlington: University of Vermont, Department of Psychiatry.

Achenbach, T. M. (1993a). *Empirically based taxonomy: How to use syndromes and profile types derived from the CBCL/4-18, TRF, and YSR.* Burlington: University of Vermont, Department of Psychiatry.

Achenbach, T. M. (1993b). Taxonomy and comorbidity of conduct problems: Evidence from empirically based approaches. *Development and Psychopathology, 5,* 51–64.

Achenbach, T. M. (1995). Developmental issues in assessment, taxonomy, and diagnosis of child and adolescent psychopathology. In D. Cicchetti & D. J. Cohen (Eds.), *Developmental psychopathology: Vol. 1. Theory and methods* (pp. 57–80). New York: Wiley.

Achenbach, T. M. (1997). What is normal? What is abnormal? Developmental perspectives on behavioral and emotional problems. In S. S. Luthar, J. A. Burack, D. Cicchetti, & J. R. Weisz (Eds.), *Developmental psychopathology: Perspectives on adjustment, risk, and disorder* (pp. 93–114). New York: Cambridge University Press.

Achenbach, T. M., & Edelbrock, C. (1981). Behavioral problems and competencies reported by parents of normal and disturbed children aged four through sixteen. *Monographs of the Society for Research in Child Development, 46*(Serial No. 188, Whole No. 1).

Achenbach, T. M., & Howell, C. T. (1993). Are American children's problems getting worse? A 13-year comparison. *Journal of the American Academy of Child and Adolescent Psychiatry, 32,* 1145–1154.

Achenbach, T. M., Howell, C. T., Quay, H. C., & Conners, C. K. (1991). National survey of problems and competencies among four- to sixteen-year-olds: Parents' reports for normative and clinical samples. *Monographs of the Society for Research in Child Development, 56*(Serial No. 225, Whole No. 3).

Achenbach, T. M., McConaughy, S. H., & Howell, C. T. (1987). Child/adolescent behavioral and emotional problems: Implications of cross-informant correlations for situational specificity. *Psychological Bulletin, 101,* 213–232.

Adams, M. J. (1990). *Beginning to read: Thinking and learning about print.* Cambridge, MA: MIT Press.

Adelman, H. S. (1995). Clinical psychology: Beyond psychopathology and clinical interventions. *Clinical Psychology: Science and Practice, 2,* 28–44.

Adler, T. (1994). Comprehending those who can't relate. *Science News, 145,* 248–249.

Agras, W. S. (1991). Nonpharmacologic treatments of bulimia nervosa. *Journal of Clinical Psychiatry, 52,* 29–33.

Agras, W. S., Rossiter, E. M., Arnow, B., Telch, C. F., Raeburn, S. D., Bruce, B., Koran, L. M. (1994). One-year follow-up of psychosocial and pharmacologic treatments for bulimia nervosa. *Journal of Clinical Psychiatry, 55*(5), 179–183.

Ainsworth, M. D. S., Blehar, M. C., Waters, E., & Wall, S. (1978). *Patterns of attachment: A psychological study of the strange situation.* Hillsdale, NJ: Erlbaum.

Akiskal, H. S. (1995). Developmental pathways to bipolarity: Dysthymic, cyclothymic and bipolar II disorders in the "borderline realm." *Psychiatric Clinics of North America, 4,* 25–46.

Alaghband-Rad, J., Hamburger, S. D., Giedd, J. N., Frazier, J., & Rapoport, J. L. (1997). Childhood-onset schizophrenia: Biological markers in relation to clinical characteristics. *American Journal of Psychiatry, 154,* 64–68.

Albano, A. M. (1995). Treatment of social anxiety in adolescents. *Cognitive and Behavioral Practice, 2,* 271–298.

Albano, A. M., & Barlow, D. H. (1996). Breaking the vicious cycle: Cognitive-behavioral group treatment for socially anxious youth. In E. D. Hibbs & P. S. Jensen (Eds.), *Psychosocial treatments for child and adolescent disorders: Empirically based strategies for clinical practice* (pp. 43–62). Washington, DC: American Psychological Association.

Albano, A. M., Chorpita, B. F., & Barlow, D. H. (1996). Childhood anxiety disorders. In E. J. Mash & R. A. Barkley (Eds.), *Child psychopathology* (pp. 196–241). New York: Guilford Press.

Albano, A. M., Knox, L. S., & Barlow, D. H. (1995). Obsessive-compulsive disorder. In A. R. Eisen, C. A. Kearney, & C. A. Schaefer (Eds.), *Clinical handbook of anxiety disorders in children and adolescents* (pp. 282–316). Northvale, NJ: Jason Aronson.

Albano, A. M., Marten, P. A., & Holt, C. S. (1991, January). *Therapist's Manual: Cognitive-behavioral group treatment of adolescent social phobia.* Unpublished manual, University of Louisville, Department of Psychology.

Albano, A. M., Miller, P. P., Zarate, R., Cote, G., & Barlow, D. H. (1996). *Behavioral assessment and treatment of PTSD in prepubertal children: Attention to developmental factors and innovative strategies in the case study of a family.* Paper submitted for publication.

Alessandri, S., & Lewis, M. (1996). Differences in pride and shame in maltreated and nonmaltreated preschoolers. *Child Development, 67,* 1857–1869.

Alexander, K. L., Entwistle, D. R., & Dauber, S. L. (1993). First-grade classroom behavior: Its short- and long-term consequences for school performance. *Child Development, 64,* 801–814.

Alexander, L. & James, H. T. (1987). *The Nation's report card.* Cambridge, MA: National Academy of Education.

Allen, A. J., Leonard, H. L., & Swedo, S. E. (1995). Current knowledge of medications for the treatment of childhood anxiety disorders. *Journal of the American Academy of Child and Adolescent Psychiatry, 34,* 976–986.

Allen, J. P., Hauser, S. T., & Borman-Spurrell, E. (1996). Attachment theory as a framework for understanding sequelae of severe adolescent psychopathology: An 11-year

follow-up study. *Journal of Consulting and Clinical Psychology, 64,* 254–263.

Allgood-Merten, B., Lewinsohn, P., & Hops, H. (1990). Sex differences and adolescent depression. *Journal of Abnormal Psychology, 99,* 55–63.

Altmann, E. O., & Gotlib, I. H. (1988). The social behavior of depressed children: An observational study. *Journal of Abnormal Child Psychology, 16,* 29–44.

Aman, M., Kern, R. A., Osborne, P., & Tumuluru, R. (1997). Fenfluramine and methylphenidate in children with mental retardation and borderline IQ: Clinical effects. *American Journal on Mental Retardation, 101*(5), 521–534.

Amaya-Jackson, L., & March, J. S. (1995). Posttraumatic stress disorder. In J. S. March (Ed.), *Anxiety disorders in children and adolescents* (pp. 276–300). New York: Guilford Press.

Ambrosini, P. J., Bianchi, M. D., Rabinovich, H., & Elia, J. (1993). Antidepressant treatments in children and adolescents: I. Affective disorders. *Journal of the American Academy of Child and Adolescent Psychiatry, 32,* 1–6.

American Academy of Child and Adolescent Psychiatry (1995, November). *Facts for families #36: Helping children after a disaster.* Washington, DC: Author.

American Academy of Child and Adolescent Psychiatry. (1997). AACAP official action: Practice parameters for the assessment and treatment of children and adolescents with bipolar disorder. *Journal of the American Academy of Child and Adolescent Psychiatry, 36,* 138–157.

American Anorexia/Bulimia Association. (1996, January). The fear of fatness—is it worth dying for? [On-line]. Available: http://members.aol.com/amanbu/geninfo.html.

American Psychiatric Association. (1952). *Diagnostic and statistical manual of mental disorders.* Washington, DC: Author.

American Psychiatric Association. (1968). *Diagnostic and statistical manual of mental disorders* (2nd ed.). Washington, DC: Author.

American Psychiatric Association. (1980). *Diagnostic and statistical manual of mental disorders* (3rd ed.). Washington, DC: Author.

American Psychiatric Association. (1994). *Diagnostic and statistical manual of mental disorders* (4th ed.). Washington, DC: Author.

American Psychological Association. (1992). *Ethical principles of psychologists and code of conduct.* Washington, DC: Author.

American Psychological Association. (1993). *Summary report of the American Psychological Association Commission on Violence and Youth, Vol. 1.* Washington, DC: Author.

American Psychological Association. (1996). *Violence and the family.* (Report of the American Psychological Association Presidential Task Force on Violence and the Family). Washington, DC: Author.

American Psychological Association Task Force on Psychological Intervention Guidelines. (1995). *Template for developing guidelines: Interventions for mental disorders and psychological aspects of physical disorders.* Washington, DC: American Psychological Association.

American Sleep Disorders Association. (1990). *The international classification of sleep disorders: Diagnostic and coding manual* (2nd ed.). Lawrence, KS: Allen Press.

Anastasi, A., & Urbina, S. (1997). *Psychological testing* (7th ed.). Upper Saddle River, NJ: Prentice Hall.

Anastopoulos, A. D., Guevremont, D. C., Shelton, T. L., &

DuPaul, G. J. (1992). Parenting stress among families of children with attention deficit hyperactivity disorder. *Journal of Abnormal Child Psychology, 20,* 503–520.

Anastopoulos, A. D., Spisto, M. A., & Maher, M. C. (1994). The WISC-III Freedom from Distractibility factor: Its utility in identifying children with attention deficit hyperactivity disorder. *Psychological Assessment, 6,* 368–371.

Anders, T. F., & Eiben, L. A. (1997). Pediatric sleep disorders: A review of the past 10 years. *Journal of the American Academy of Child and Adolescent Psychiatry, 36,* 9–20.

Anders, T. F., Halpern, L., & Hua, J. (1992). Sleeping through the night: A developmental perspective. *Pediatrics, 90,* 554–560.

Anders, T. F., Sadeh, A., & Appareddy, V. (1995). Normal sleep in neonates and children. In R. Ferber & M. Kryger (Eds.), *Principles and practice of sleep medicine in the child* (pp. 7–18). Philadelphia: Saunders.

Anderson, C. A., Hinshaw, S. P., & Simmel, C. (1994). Mother-child interactions in ADHD and comparison boys: Relationships with overt and covert externalizing behavior. *Journal of Abnormal Child Psychology, 22,* 247–265.

Anderson, E. (1994, May). The code of the streets. *Atlantic Monthly, 273*(5), 81–94.

Anderson, J. C., Williams, S., McGee, R., & Silva, P. A. (1987). DSM-III disorders in preadolescent children: Prevalence in a large sample from the general population. *Archives of General Psychiatry, 44,* 69–76.

Anderson, K. E., Lytton, H., & Romney, D. M. (1986). Mothers' interactions with normal and conduct-disordered boys: Who affects whom? *Developmental Psychology, 22,* 604–609.

Anderson, W. F. (1994). Gene therapy for genetic disorder. *Human Gene Therapy, 5,* 281–282.

Andrews, G., Morris-Yates, A., Howie, P., & Martin, N. G. (1991). Genetic factors in stuttering confirmed. *Archives of General Psychiatry, 48,* 1034–1035.

Andrews, G., Stewart, G., Allen, B., & Henderson, A. S. (1990). The genetics of six neurotic disorders: A twin study. *Journal of Affective Disorders, 19,* 23–29.

Angold, A., & Costello, E. J. (1996). Toward establishing an empirical basis for the diagnosis of oppositional defiant disorder. *Journal of the American Academy of Child and Adolescent Psychiatry, 35,* 1205–1212.

Angold, A., Erkanli, A., Loeber, R., Costello, E. J. (1996). Disappearing depression in a population sample of boys. *Journal of Emotional and Behavioral Disorders, 4,* 95–104.

Annin, P. (1996, January 22). Superpredators arrive. *Newsweek, 127,* p. 57.

Antonak, R. F., Fiedler, C., & Mulick, J. A. (1989). Misconceptions relating to mental retardation. *Mental Retardation, 27,* 91–97.

Applegate, B., Lahey, B. B., Hart, E. L., Biederman, J., Hynd, G. W., Barkley, R. A., Ollendick, T., Frick, P. J., Greenhill, L., McBurnett, K., Newcorn, J. H., Kerdyk, L., Garfinkel, B., Waldman, I., Shaffer, D. (1997). Validity of the age-of-onset criterion for ADHD: A report from the DSM-IV field trials. *Journal of the American Academy of Child and Adolescent Psychiatry, 36,* 1211–1221.

Aries, P. (1962). *Centuries of childhood.* New York: Vintage Books.

Armbruster, P., & Kazdin, A. E. (1994). Attrition in child psychotherapy. *Advances in Clinical Child Psychology, 16,* 81–108.

Armstrong, D. D. (1992). The neuropathology of Rett Syndrome. *Brain and Development, 14*(Suppl.), 89–98.

Armstrong, T. (1995). *The myth of the A.D.D. child: 50 ways to improve your child's behavior and attention span without drugs, labels or coercion.* New York: Dutton.

Arnold, L. E. (1996). Sex differences in ADHD: Conference summary. *Journal of Abnormal Child Psychology, 24,* 555–569.

Arnold, L. E., Abikoff, H. B., Cantwell, D. P., Conners, C. K., Elliott, G., Greenhill, L. L., Hechtman, L., Hinshaw., S. P., Hoza, B., Jensen, P. S., Kraemer, H. C., March, J. S., Newcorn, J. H., Pelham, W. E., Richters, J. E., Schiller, E., Severe, J. B., Swanson, J. M., Vereen, D., & Wells, K. C. (1997). National Institute of Mental Health Collaborative Multimodal Treatment Study of Children with ADHD (the MTA): Design challenges and choices. *Archives of General Psychiatry, 54,* 865–870.

Arnold, L. E., Abikoff, H. B., & Wells, K. C. (1997). National Institute of Mental Health Collaborative Multimodal Treatment Study of Children with ADHD (the MTA): Design challenges and choices. *Archives of General Psychiatry, 54,* 865–870.

Arslanian, S., Becker, D., & Drash, A. (1995). Diabetes mellitus in the child and adolescent. In M. S. Kappy, R. M. Blizzard, & C. J. Migeon (Eds.), *The diagnosis and treatment of endocrine disorders in childhood and adolescence* (4th ed., pp. 961–1026). Springfield, IL: Charles C Thomas.

Artiles, A. J., & Trent, S. C. (1994). Overrepresentation of minority students in special education: A continuing debate. *Journal of Special Education, 27,* 410–437.

Asarnow, J. R. (1988). Children at risk for schizophrenia. *Schizophrenia Bulletin, 14,* 613–631.

Asarnow, J. R., & Asarnow, R. F. (1996). Childhood-onset schizophrenia. In E. J. Mash & R. A. Barkley (Eds.), *Child psychopathology* (pp. 340–361). New York: Guilford Press.

Asarnow, J. R., & Carlson, G. (1988). Suicide attempts in pre-adolescent child psychiatry inpatients. *Suicide and Life-Threatening Behaviors, 18*(2), 129–136.

Asarnow, J. R., Goldstein, M. J., & Ben-Meir, S. (1988). Parental communication deviance in childhood-onset schizophrenia spectrum and depressive disorders. *Journal of Child Psychology and Psychiatry, 29,* 825–838.

Asarnow, J. R., Goldstein, M. J., Carlson, G., Perdue, S., Bates, S., & Keller, J. (1988). Childhood-onset depressive disorders: A follow-up study of rates of rehospitalization and out-of-home placement among child psychiatric inpatients. *Journal of Affective Disorders, 15,* 245–253.

Asarnow, J. R., Tompson, M., & Goldstein, M. J. (1994). Childhood-onset schizophrenia: A follow-up study. *Schizophrenia Bulletin, 20,* 599–618.

Asarnow, J. R., Tompson, M., Hamilton, E. B., Goldstein, M. J., & Guthrie, D. (1994). Family-expressed emotion, childhood-onset depression, and childhood-onset schizophrenia spectrum disorders: Is expressed emotion a nonspecific correlate of child psychopathology or a specific risk factor for depression? *Journal of Abnormal Child Psychology, 22,* 129–146.

Asarnow, R. F., Asamen, J., Granholm, E., Sherman, T., Watkins, J. M., & Williams, M. E. (1994). Cognitive/neuropsychological studies of children with a schizophrenic disorder. *Schizophrenia Bulletin, 20,* 647–670.

Asarnow, R. F., & Asarnow, J. R. (1994). Childhood-onset schizophrenia. *Schizophrenia Bulletin, 20,* 591–598.

Asperger, H. (1991). "Autistic psychopathy" in childhood. In U. Frith (Ed. and Trans.), *Autism and Asperger syndrome* (pp. 37–92). Cambridge, England: Cambridge University Press. (Original work published 1944)

Attie, I., & Brooks-Gunn, J. (1989). Development of eating problems in adolescent girls: A longitudinal study. *Developmental Psychology, 25,* 70–79.

Attie, I., & Brooks-Gunn, J. (1995). The development of eating regulation across the life span. In D. Cicchetti & D. J. Cohen (Eds.), *Developmental psychopathology: Vol. 2. Risk, disorder, and adaptation* (pp. 332–368). New York: Wiley.

Attie, I., Brooks-Gunn, J., & Petersen, A. C. (1990). The emergence of eating problems: A developmental perspective. In M. Lewis & S. Miller (Eds.), *Handbook of developmental psychopathology* (pp. 409–420). New York: Plenum.

Attwood, A., Frith, U., & Hermelin, B. (1988). The understanding and use of interpersonal gestures by autistic and Down's syndrome children. *Journal of Autism and Developmental Disorders, 18,* 241–257.

Aultman, M. (1980). Group involvement in delinquent acts: A study of offense type and male-female participation. *Criminal Justice and Behavior, 7,* 185–192.

Avison, W. R., & McAlpine, D. D. (1992). Gender differences in symptoms of depression among adolescents. *Journal of Health and Social Behavior, 33,* 77–96.

Axline, V. M. (1947). *Play therapy: The inner dynamics of childhood.* Boston: Houghton Mifflin.

Azar, S. T. (1991). Models of physical child abuse: A metatheoretical analysis. *Criminal Justice and Behavior, 18,* 30–46.

Azar, S. T. (1997). A cognitive behavioral approach to understanding and treating parents who physically abuse their children. In D. A. Wolfe, R. J. McMahon, & R. Dev Peters (Eds.), *Child abuse: New directions in prevention and treatment across the lifespan* (pp. 78–100). Newbury Park, CA: Sage.

Azar, S., & Wolfe, D. (1998). Treatment of child abuse and neglect. In E. J. Mash & R. A. Barkley (Eds.), *Treatment of childhood disorders* (2nd ed., pp. 501–544). New York: Guilford Press.

Azrin, N. H., & Foxx, R. M. (1974). *Toilet training in less than a day.* New York: Simon & Schuster.

Azrin, N. H., Thienes-Hontos, P., & Besalel-Azrin, V. (1979). Elimination of enuresis without a conditioning apparatus: An extension of office instruction of the child and parents. *Behavior Therapy, 10,* 14–19.

Baer, R. A., & Nietzel, M. T. (1991). Cognitive and behavioral treatment of impulsivity in children: A meta-analytic review of the outcome literature. *Journal of Clinical Child Psychology, 20,* 400–412.

Bailey, A., Luthert, P., Bolton, P., Le Couteur, A., Rutter, M., & Harding, B. (1993). Autism is associated with megalencephaly [letter]. *Lancet, 341,* 1225–1226.

Bailey, A., Phillips, W., & Rutter, M. (1996). Autism: Towards an integration of clinical, genetic, neuropsychological, and neurobiological perspectives. *Journal of Child Psychology and Psychiatry, 37,* 89–126.

Bailey, D., Blasco, P., & Simeonsson, R. (1992). Needs expressed by mothers and fathers of young children with disabilities. *American Journal of Mental Retardation, 97,* 1–10.

Baine, S., Rosenbaum, P., & King, S. (1995). Chronic childhood illnesses: What aspects of caregiving do parents value? *Child: Care, Health and Development, 21,* 291–304.

Baird, P. A., & Sadovnick, A. D. (1987). Life expectancy in Down's Syndrome. *Journal of Pediatrics, 110,* 849–854.

Baker, B. L. (1996). Parent training. In J. W. Jacobson & J. A. Mulick (Eds.), *Manual of diagnosis and professional practice in mental retardation* (pp. 289–299). Washington, DC: American Psychological Association.

Baker, B. L., & Blacher, J. B. (1993). Out-of-home placement for children with mental retardation. *American Journal on Mental Retardation, 98,* 368–377.

Baker, L., & Cantwell, D. P. (1992). Attention deficit disorder and speech/language disorders. *Comprehensive Mental Health Care, 2,* 3–16.

Bakken, L., & Romig, C. (1992). Interpersonal needs in middle adolescents: Companionship, leadership and intimacy. *Journal of Adolescence, 15,* 301–316.

Bakwin, H. (1973). The genetics of enuresis. In I. Kolvin, R. C. MacKeith, & R. Meadow (Eds.), *Bladder control and enuresis* (pp. 73–77). Philadelphia: Lippincott.

Baldwin, W. K. (1958). The social position of mentally handicapped children in the regular class in the public schools. *Exceptional Children, 25,* 106–108.

Bandura, A. (1977). *Social learning theory.* Englewood Cliffs, NJ: Prentice Hall.

Bandura, A. (1986). *Social foundations of thought and action: A social cognitive theory.* Englewood Cliffs, NJ: Prentice Hall.

Banez, G. A., & Compas, B. E. (1990). Children's and parents' daily stressful events and psychological symptoms. *Journal of Abnormal Child Psychology, 18,* 591–605.

Bank, L., Marlowe, J. H., Reid, J. B., Patterson, G. R., & Weinrott, M. R. (1991). A comparative evaluation of parent training interventions for families of chronic delinquents. *Journal of Abnormal Child Psychology, 19,* 15–33.

Barakat, L. P., & Linney, J. A. (1992). Children with physical handicaps and their mothers: The interrelation of social support, maternal adjustment, and child adjustment. *Journal of Pediatric Psychology, 17,* 725–740.

Baran, S. A., Weltzin, T. E., & Kaye, W. H. (1995). Low discharge weight and outcome in anorexia nervosa. *American Journal of Psychiatry, 152,* 1070–1072.

Barber, M. A., Milich, R., & Welsh, R. (1996). Effects of reinforcement schedule and task difficulty on the performance of attention deficit hyperactivity disordered and control boys. *Journal of Clinical Child Psychology, 25,* 66–76.

Barkley, R. A. (1988). The effects of methylphenidate on the interactions of preschool ADHD children with their mothers. *Journal of the American Academy of Child and Adolescent Psychiatry, 26,* 336–341.

Barkley, R. A. (1989). The problem of stimulus control and rule-governed behavior in children with Attention Deficit Disorder with Hyperactivity. In J. L. Swanson & L. Bloomingdale (Eds.), *Attention deficit disorders* (pp. 203–234). New York: Pergamon Press.

Barkley, R. A. (1990). *Attention-deficit/hyperactivity disorder: A handbook for diagnosis and treatment.* New York: Guilford Press.

Barkley, R. A. (1995). *Taking charge of ADHD: The complete, authoritative guide for parents.* New York: Guilford Press.

Barkley, R. A. (1996). Attention-deficit/hyperactivity disorder. In E. J. Mash & R. A. Barkley (Eds.), *Child psychopathology* (pp. 63–112). New York: Guilford Press.

Barkley, R. A. (1997a). *ADHD and the nature of self-control.* New York: Guilford Press.

Barkley, R. A. (1997b). Attention-deficit/hyperactivity disorder.

In E. J. Mash & L. G. Terdal (Eds.), *Behavioral assessment of childhood disorders* (3rd ed., pp. 71–129). New York: Guilford Press.

Barkley, R. A. (1997c). Attention-deficit/hyperactivity disorder, self-regulation, and time: Toward a more comprehensive theory. *Journal of Developmental and Behavioral Pediatrics, 18,* 271–279.

Barkley, R. A. (1997d). Behavioral inhibition, sustained attention, and executive functions: Constructing a unifying theory of ADHD. *Psychological Bulletin, 121,* 65–94.

Barkley, R. A. (1998). Attention-deficit/hyperactivity disorder. In E. J. Mash & R. A. Barkley (Eds.), *Treatment of childhood disorders* (2nd ed., pp. 55–110). New York: Guilford Press.

Barkley, R. A., Anastopoulos, A. D., Guevremont, D. G., & Fletcher, K. E. (1992). Adolescents with attention deficit hyperactivity disorder: Mother-adolescent interactions, family beliefs and conflicts, and maternal psychopathology. *Journal of Abnormal Child Psychology, 20,* 752–761.

Barkley, R. A., & Biederman, J. (1997). Toward a broader definition of the age-of-onset criterion for attention-deficit-hyperactivity disorder. *Journal of the American Academy of Child and Adolescent Psychiatry, 36,* 1204–1210.

Barkley, R. A., DuPaul, G. J., & McMurray, M. B. (1990). A comprehensive evaluation of attention deficit disorder with and without hyperactivity. *Journal of Consulting and Clinical Psychology, 58,* 775–789.

Barkley, R. A., Fischer, M., Edelbrock, C. S., & Smallish, L. (1990). The adolescent outcome of hyperactive children diagnosed by research criteria, I: An 8-year prospective follow-up study. *Journal of the American Academy of Child and Adolescent Psychiatry, 29,* 546–557.

Barkley, R. A., Fischer, M., Edelbrock, C. S., & Smallish, L. (1991). The adolescent outcome of hyperactive children diagnosed by research criteria, III: Mother-child interactions, family conflicts, and maternal psychopathology. *Journal of Child Psychology and Psychiatry, 32,* 233–256.

Barkley, R. A., Fischer, M., & Fletcher, K. (1997). *Young adult outcome of hyperactive children diagnosed by research criteria.* NIMH Grant, University of Massachusetts Medical Center.

Barkley, R. A., Grodzinsky, G., & DuPaul, G. J. (1992). Frontal lobe functions in attention deficit disorder with and without hyperactivity: A review and research report. *Journal of Abnormal Child Psychology, 20,* 163–188.

Barkley, R. A., Guevremont, D. G., Anastopoulos, A. D., DuPaul, G. J., & Shelton, T. L. (1993). Driving-related risks and outcomes of attention deficit hyperactivity disorder in adolescents and young adults: A 3–5 year follow-up survey. *Pediatrics, 92,* 212–218.

Barkley, R. A., Murphy, K. R., & Kwasnik, D. (1996). Motor vehicle driving competencies and risks in teens and young adults with attention deficit hyperactivity disorder. *Pediatrics, 98,* 1089–1095.

Barlow, D. H. (1988). *Anxiety and its disorders: The nature and treatment of anxiety and panic.* New York: Guilford Press.

Barlow, D. H., & Durand, V. M. (1995). *Abnormal psychology: An integrative approach.* Pacific Grove, CA: Brooks/Cole.

Barlow, D. H., & Hersen, M. (1984). *Single case experimental designs: Strategies for studying behavior change* (2nd ed.). Elmsford, NY: Pergamon Press.

Baron-Cohen, S. (1989). The autistic child's theory of mind: A case of specific developmental delay. *Journal of Child Psychology and Psychiatry, 30,* 285–297.

Baron-Cohen, S. (1995). *Mindblindness: An essay on autism and theory of mind.* Cambridge, MA: MIT Press.

Baron-Cohen, S., Allen, J., & Gillberg, C. (1992). Can autism be detected at 18 months? The needle, the haystack, and the CHAT. *British Journal of Psychiatry, 161,* 839–843.

Baron-Cohen, S., & Bolton, P. (1993). *Autism: The facts.* Oxford, England: Oxford University Press.

Baron-Cohen, S., Cox, A., Baird, G., Swettenham, J., Nightingale, N., Morgan, K., Drew, A., & Charman T. (1996). Psychological markers in the detection of autism in infancy in a large population. *British Journal of Psychiatry, 168,* 158–163.

Barrett, P. M., Dadds, M. R., & Rapee, R. M. (1996). Family treatment of childhood anxiety: A controlled trial. *Journal of Consulting and Clinical Psychology, 64,* 333–342.

Barrett, P. M., Rapee, R. M., Dadds, M. M., Ryan, S. M. (1996). Family enhancement of cognitive style in anxious and aggressive children. *Journal of Abnormal Child Psychology, 24,* 187–203.

Barrios, B. A., & Hartmann, D. P. (1997). Fears and anxieties. In E. J. Mash & L. G. Terdal (Eds.), *Assessment of childhood disorders* (3rd ed., pp. 230–327). New York: Guilford Press.

Barth, C., Fein, D., & Waterhouse, L. (1995). Delayed match-to-sample performance in autistic children. *Developmental Neuropsychology, 11,* 53–69.

Bassuk, E. L., Browne, A., & Buckner, J. C. (1996). Single mothers and welfare. *Scientific American, 275*(4), 60–67.

Bates, E. (1993, April). *Nature, nurture, and language.* Invited address presented at the biennial meeting of the Society for Research in Child Development, New Orleans, LA.

Bates, J. E., Bayles, K., Bennett, D. S., Ridge, B., & Brown, N. M. (1991). Origins of externalizing behavior problems at eight years of age. In D. J. Pepler & K. H. Rubin (Eds.), *The development and treatment of childhood aggression* (pp. 93–120). Hillsdale, NJ: Erlbaum.

Bauermeister, J. J., Alegria, M., Bird, H., Rubio-Stipec, M., & Canino, G. (1992). Are attentional-hyperactivity deficits unidimensional or multidimensional syndromes? Empirical findings from a community survey. *Journal of the American Academy of Child and Adolescent Psychiatry, 31,* 423–431.

Baum, A., Grunberg, N. E., & Singer, J. E. (1992). Biochemical measurements in the study of emotion. *Psychological Science, 3,* 56–59.

Bauman, L. J., Drotar, D., Leventhal, J. M., Perrin, E. C., & Pless, I. B. (1997). A review of psychosocial interventions for children with chronic health conditions. *Pediatrics, 100,* 244–251.

Bauman, M. L. (1996). Neuroanatomic observations of the brain in pervasive developmental disorders. *Journal of Autism and Developmental Disorders, 26,* 199–203.

Bauman, M. L., & Kemper, T. L. (1994a). Neuroanatomic observations of the brain in autism. In M. L. Bauman & T. L. Kemper (Eds.), *The neurobiology of autism* (pp. 119–145). Baltimore: Johns Hopkins University Press.

Bauman, M. L., & Kemper, T. L. (Eds.). (1994b). *The neurobiology of autism.* Baltimore: Johns Hopkins University Press.

Bauman, M. L., Kemper, T. L., & Arin, D. M. (1995). Pervasive neuroanatomic abnormalities of the brain in three cases of Rett's syndrome. *Neurology, 45,* 1581–1586.

Baumeister, A. A., & Woodley-Zanthos, P. (1996). Prevention: Biological factors. In J. W. Jacobson & J. A. Mulick (Eds.),

Manual of diagnosis and professional practice in mental retardation (pp. 229–242). Washington, DC: American Psychological Association.

Baumeister, R. F., Smart, L., & Boden, J. M. (1996). Relation of threatened egotism to violence and aggression: The dark side of high self-esteem. *Psychological Review, 103,* 5–33.

Baumgardner, T. L., Singer, H. S., Denckla, M. B., Rubin, M. A., Abrams, M. T., Colli, M. J., & Reiss, A. L. (1996). Corpus callosum morphology in children with Tourette syndrome and attention deficit hyperactivity disorder. *Neurology, 4,* 477–482.

Bayley, N. (1993). *Bayley Scales of Infant Development: Birth to two years.* San Antonio, TX: Psychological Corporation.

Bazyk, S. (1989). Changes in attitudes and beliefs regarding parent participation in home programs: An update. *American Journal of Occupational Therapy, 43,* 723–728.

Beardslee, W. R., Keller, M. B., Lavori, P. W., Staley, J., & Sacks, N. (1993). The impact of parental affective disorder on depression in offspring: A longitudinal follow-up in a nonreferred sample. *Journal of the American Academy of Child and Adolescent Psychiatry, 32,* 723–730.

Beardslee, W. R., Versage, E. M., Wright, E. J., Salt, P., Rothberg P. C., Drezner, K., & Gladstone, T. R. (1997). Examination of preventive interventions for families with depression: Evidence of change. *Development and Psychopathology, 9,* 109–130.

Beardslee, W. R., & Wheelock, I. (1994). Children of parents with affective disorders: Empirical findings and clinical implications. In W. M. Reynolds & H. F. Johnston (Eds.), *Handbook of depression in children and adolescents* (pp. 463–479). New York: Plenum.

Beardslee, W. R., Wright, E. J., Salt, P., & Drezner, K. (1997). Examination of children's responses to two preventive intervention strategies over time. *Journal of the American Academy of Child and Adolescent Psychiatry, 36,* 196–204.

Beautrais, A. L., Joyce, P. R., & Mulder, R. T. (1996). Risk factors for serious suicide attempts among youths aged 13 through 24 years. *Journal of the American Academy of Child and Adolescent Psychiatry, 35,* 1174–1182.

Beck, A. T. (1967). *Depression: Clinical, experimental, and theoretical aspects.* Philadelphia: University of Pennsylvania Press.

Beck, A. T., Rush, A. J., Shaw, B. F., & Emery, G. (1979). *Cognitive therapy of depression.* New York: Guilford Press.

Becker, J. V., Alpert, J. L., BigFoot, D. S., Bonner, B. L., Geddie, L. F., Henggeler, S. W., Kaufman, K. L., & Walker, C. E. (1995). Empirical research on child abuse treatment: Report by the Child Abuse and Neglect Treatment Working Group, American Psychological Association. *Journal of Clinical Child Psychology, 24,* 23–46.

Beeghly, M., & Cicchetti, D. (1997). Talking about self and other: Emergence of an internal state lexicon in young children with Down syndrome. *Development and Psychopathology, 9,* 729–748.

Befera, M., & Barkley, R. A. (1984). Hyperactive and normal girls and boys: Mother-child interactions, parent psychiatric status, and child psychopathology. *Journal of Child Psychology and Psychiatry, 26,* 439–452.

Begley, S. (1996, May 6). The IQ puzzle. *Newsweek,* pp. 70–72.

Begley, S., & Springen, K. (1996, May 13). Life in a parallel world. *Newsweek,* p. 70.

Behr, S. K., & Murphy, D. (1993). Research progress and promise: The role of perceptions in cognitive adaptation to disability. In A. P. Turnbull, J. M. Patterson, S. K. Behr, D. L. Murphy, J. G. Marquis, & M. J. Blue-Banning (Eds.), *Cognitive coping, families, and disability* (pp. 151–164). Baltimore: Paul H. Brookes.

Beidel, D. C., Silverman, W. K., & Hammond-Laurence, K. (1996). Overanxious disorder: Subsyndromal state or specific disorder? A comparison of clinic and community samples. *Journal of Clinical Child Psychology, 25,* 25–32.

Beidel, D. C., & Turner, S. M. (1988). Comorbidity of test anxiety and other anxiety disorders in children. *Journal of Abnormal Child Psychology, 16,* 275–287.

Beidel, D. C., & Turner, S. M. (1997). At risk for anxiety: I. Psychopathology in the offspring of anxious parents. *Journal of the American Academy of Child and Adolescent Psychiatry, 36,* 918–924.

Beitchman, J. H., Hood, J., & Inglis, A. (1990). Psychiatric risk in children with speech and language disorders. *Journal of Abnormal Child Psychology, 18,* 283–296.

Beitchman, J. H., Hood, J., Rochon, J., & Paterson, M. (1989). Empirical classification of speech/language impairment in children: II. Behavioral characteristics. *Journal of the American Academy of Child and Adolescent Psychiatry, 28,* 118–123.

Beitchman, J. H., Zucker, K. J., Hood, J. E., DaCosta, G. A., Akman, D., & Cassavia, E. (1992). A review of the longterm effects of child sexual abuse. *Child Abuse and Neglect, 16,* 101–118.

Bell, A. (1996, March). Dying to win: The shocking stories of eating disorders and female athletes. *Teen,* pp. 34–41.

Bell, K. E., & Stein, D. M. (1992). Behavioral treatment for pica: A review of empirical studies. *International Journal of Eating Disorders, 11,* 377–389.

Bellack, A. S., & Hersen, M. (Eds.). (1998). *Behavioral assessment: A practical handbook* (4th ed.). Needham Heights, MA: Allyn & Bacon.

Bell-Dolan, D. J. (1995). Social cue interpretation of anxious children. *Journal of Clinical Child Psychology, 24,* 1–10.

Bell-Dolan, D. J., Last, C. G., & Strauss, C. C. (1990). Symptoms of anxiety disorders in normal children. *Journal of the American Academy of Child and Adolescent Psychiatry, 29,* 759–765.

Bell-Dolan, D. J., Reaven, N. M., & Peterson, I. (1993). Depression and social functioning: A multidimensional study of the linkages. *Journal of Clinical Child Psychology, 22,* 306–315.

Bell-Dolan, D. J., & Wessler, A. E. (1994). Attributional style of anxious children: Extensions from cognitive theory and research on adult anxiety. *Journal of Anxiety Disorders, 8,* 79–96.

Belsky, J. (1984). The determinants of parenting: a process model. *Child Development, 55,* 83–96.

Bemporad, J. R. (1979). Adult recollections of a formerly autistic child. *Journal of Autism and Developmental Disorders, 9,* 179–197.

Bemporad, J. R. (1994). Dynamic and interpersonal theories of depression. In W. M. Reynolds & H. F. Johnston (Eds.), *Handbook of depression in children and adolescents* (pp. 81–95). New York: Plenum.

Benasich, A. A., Curtiss, S., & Tallal, P. (1993). Language, learning, and behavioral disturbances in childhood: A longitudinal perspective. *Journal of the American Academy of Child and Adolescent Psychiatry, 32,* 585–594.

Benjamin, J., Li, L., Patterson, C., Greenberg, B. D., Murphy, D. L., & Hamer, D. H. (1996). Population and familial association between the D4 dopamine receptor gene and measures of Novelty Seeking. *Nature Genetics, 12,* 81–84.

Bennett, D. S. (1994). Depression among children with chronic medical problems: A meta-analysis. *Journal of Pediatric Psychology, 19,* 149–170.

Benoit, D., Zeanah, C. H., & Barton, L. M. (1989). Maternal attachment disturbances in failure to thrive. *Infant Mental Health Journal, 10,* 185–202.

Benoit, D., Zeanah, C. H., Boucher, C., & Minde, K. K. (1992). Sleep disorders in early childhood: Association with insecure maternal attachment. *Journal of the American Academy of Child and Adolescent Psychiatry, 31,* 86–93.

Berg, B. L. (1998). *Qualitative research methods for the social sciences* (3rd ed.). Needham Heights, MA: Allyn & Bacon.

Berk, L. E. (1994). Why children talk to themselves. *Scientific American,* November, 78–83.

Berk, L. E., & Potts, M. K. (1991). Development and functional significance of private speech among attention-deficit hyperactivity disorder and normal boys. *Journal of Abnormal Child Psychology, 19,* 357–377.

Berliner, L. (1997). Trauma-specific therapy for sexually abused children. In D. A. Wolfe, R. J. McMahon, & R. Dev Peters (Eds.), *Child abuse: New directions in prevention and treatment across the lifespan* (pp. 157–176). Newbury Park, CA: Sage.

Berman, A. L., & Jobes, D. A. (1991). *Adolescent suicide: Assessment and intervention.* Washington, DC: American Psychological Association.

Bernheimer, C., & Keough, B. (1988). Stability of cognitive performance of children with developmental delays. *American Journal on Mental Deficiency, 92,* 539–542.

Bernstein, G. A. (1991). Comorbidity and severity of anxiety and depressive disorders in a clinic sample. *Journal of the American Academy of Child and Adolescent Psychiatry, 30,* 43–50.

Bernstein, G. A. (1994). Psychopharmacological interventions. In T. H. Ollendick, N. J. King, & W. Yule (Eds.), *International handbook of phobic and anxiety disorders in children and adolescents* (pp. 439–451). New York: Plenum.

Bernstein, G. A., Borchardt, C. M., & Perwien, A. R. (1996). Anxiety disorders in children and adolescents: A review of the past 10 years. *Journal of the American Academy of Child and Adolescent Psychiatry, 35,* 1110–1119.

Bettelheim, B. (1967). *The empty fortress: Infantile autism and the birth of the self.* New York: Free Press.

Bettelheim, B. (1976). *The meaning and importance of fairy tales.* New York: Random House.

Bhatia, M. S., Nigam, V. R., Bohra, N., & Malik, S. C. (1991). Attention deficit disorder with hyperactivity among paediatric outpatients. *Journal of Child Psychology and Psychiatry, 32,* 297–306.

Bickett, L., & Milich, R. (1990). First impressions formed of boys with attention deficit disorder. *Journal of Learning Disabilities, 23,* 253–259.

Bickett, L. R., Milich, R., & Brown, R. T. (1996). Attributional styles of aggressive boys and their mothers. *Journal of Abnormal Child Psychology, 24,* 457–472.

Bickman, L. (1996). A continuum of care: More is not always better. *American Psychologist, 51,* 689–701.

Bickman, L. (1997). Resolving issues raised by the Fort Bragg evaluation: New directions for mental health services research. *American Psychologist, 52,* 562–565.

Biederman, J., Faraone, S. V., Keenan, K., & Tsuang, M. T. (1991). Evidence of a family association between attention-deficit hyperactivity disorder and major affective disorders. *Archives of General Psychiatry, 48,* 633–642.

Biederman, J., Faraone, S. V., & Lapey, K. (1992). Comorbidity of diagnosis in attention-deficit hyperactivity disorders. In G. Weiss (Ed.), *Child and adolescent psychiatric clinics of North America: Attention-deficit hyperactivity disorder* (pp. 335–360). Philadelphia: Saunders.

Biederman, J., Faraone, S. V., Milberger, S., Jetton, J. G., Chen, L., Mick, E., Greene, R. W., & Russell, R. L. (1996). Is childhood oppositional defiant disorder a precursor to adolescent conduct disorder? Findings from a four-year follow-up study of children with ADHD. *Journal of the American Academy of Child and Adolescent Psychiatry, 35,* 1193–1204.

Biederman, J., Newcorn, J., & Sprich, S. (1991). Comorbidity of attention deficit hyperactivity disorder with conduct, depressive, anxiety, and other disorders. *American Journal of Psychiatry, 144,* 330–333.

Biederman, J., Rosenbaum, J. F., Bolduc-Murphy, E. A., Faraone, S. V., Chaloff, J., Hirshfeld, D. R., & Kagan, J. (1993a). A three-year follow-up of children with and without behavioral inhibition. *Journal of the American Academy of Child and Adolescent Psychiatry, 32,* 814–821.

Biederman, J., Rosenbaum, J. F., Bolduc-Murphy, E. A., Faraone, S. V., Chaloff, J., Hirshfeld, D. R., & Kagan, J. (1993b). Behavioral inhibition as a temperamental risk factor for anxiety disorders. *Child and Adolescent Psychiatric Clinics of North America, 2,* 667–684.

Biederman, J., Thisted, R. A., Greenhill, L. L., & Ryan, N. D. (1995). Estimation of the association between desipramine and the risk for sudden death in 5- to 14-year-old children. *Journal of Clinical Psychiatry, 56,* 87–93.

Biederman, J., Wilens, T., Mick, E., Faraone, S. V., Weber, W., Curtis, S., Thornell, A., Pfister, K., Jetton, J. G., & Soriano, J. (1997). Is ADHD a risk factor for psychoactive substance use disorders? Findings from a four-year prospective follow-up study. *Journal of the American Academy of Child and Adolescent Psychiatry, 36,* 21–29.

Biederman, J., Wozniak, J., Kiely, K., Ablon, S., Faraone, S., Mick, E., Mundy, E., & Kraus, I. (1995). CBCL clinical scales discriminate prepubertal children with structured-interview-derived diagnosis of mania from those with ADHD. *Journal of the American Academy of Child and Adolescent Psychiatry, 34,* 464–471.

Bierman, K. L., Greenberg, M. T., & Conduct Problems Prevention Group (1996). Social skills training in the Fast Track program. In R. Dev Peters & R. J. McMahon (Eds.), *Preventing childhood disorders, substance abuse, and delinquency* (pp. 65–89). Newbury Park, CA: Sage.

Biglan, A., Metzler, C. W., Wirt, R., Ary, D., Noel, J., Ochs, L., French, C., & Hood, D. (1990). Social and behavioral factors associated with high-risk sexual behavior among adolescents. *Journal of Behavioral Medicine, 15,* 245–261.

Bijur, P. E., Haslum, M., & Golding, J. (1990). Cognitive and behavioral sequelae of mild head injury in children. *Pediatrics, 86,* 337–344.

Biklen, D. (1990). Communication unbound: Autism and praxis. *Harvard Educational Review, 60,* 291–314.

Biklen, D., & Cardinal, D. N. (Eds.). (1997). *Contested words, contested science: Unraveling the facilitated communication controversy.* New York: Teacher's College Press.

Birch, H. G., Richardson, S. A., Baird, D., Horobin, G., & Illsley, R. (1970). *Mental subnormality in the community: A clinical and epidemiological study.* Baltimore: Williams &

Wilkins.

Bird, H. R., Canino, G., Rubio-Stipec, M., Gould, M. S., Ribera, J., Sesman, M., Woodbury, M., Huertas-Goldman, S., Pagan, A., Sanchez-Lacay, A., & Moscoso, M. (1988). Estimates of the prevalence of childhood maladjustment in a community survey of Puerto Rico: The use of combined measures. *Archives of General Psychiatry, 45,* 1120–1126.

Birmaher, B., Ryan, N. D., Dahl, R., Rabinovich, H., Ambrosini, P., Williamson, D. E., Novacenko, H., Nelson, B., Lo, E. E. S., & PuigAntich, J. (1992). Dexamethasone suppression test in children with major depressive disorder. *Journal of the American Academy of Child and Adolescent Psychiatry, 31,* 291–297.

Birmaher, B., Ryan, N. D., Williamson, D. E., Brent, D. A., & Kaufman, J. (1996a). Childhood and adolescent depression: A review of the past 10 years: Part II. *Journal of the American Academy of Child and Adolescent Psychiatry, 35,* 1575–1583.

Birmaher, B., Ryan, N. D., Williamson, D. E., Brent, D. A., Kaufman, J., Dahl, R. E., Perel, J., & Nelson, B. (1996b). Childhood and adolescent depression: A review of the past 10 years: Part I. *Journal of the American Academy of Child and Adolescent Psychiatry, 35,* 1427–1439.

Birmaher, B., Suneeta, K., Brent, D., Cully, M., Balach, L., Kaufman, J., & Neer, S. M. (1997). The Screen for Child Anxiety and Related Emotional Disorders (SCARED): Scale construction and psychometric characteristics. *Journal of the American Academy of Child and Adolescent Psychiatry, 36,* 545–553.

Bishop, D. V. M. (1987). The causes of specific developmental language disorder ("Developmental aphasia"). *Journal of Child Psychology and Psychiatry, 28,* 1.

Bishop, D. V. M. (1992). The underlying nature of specific language impairment. *Journal of Child Psychology and Psychiatry, 33,* 3–66.

Bjorklund, D. F. (1995). *Children's thinking: Developmental function and individual differences* (2nd ed.). Pacific Grove, CA: Brooks/Cole.

Bjorkqvist, K., & Niemela, P. (Eds.). (1992). *Of mice and women: Aspects of female aggression.* San Diego, CA: Academic Press.

Blachman, B. A. (1991). Getting ready to read. In J. F. Kavanagh (Ed.), *The language continuum: From infancy to literacy* (pp. 41–62). Parkton, MD: York Press.

Blachman, B. A., Ball, E. W., Black, R. S., & Tangel, D. M. (1994). Kindergarten teachers develop phoneme awareness in low-income, inner-city classrooms: Does it make a difference? *Reading and Writing: An Interdisciplinary Journal, 6,* 1–18.

Black, B., & Uhde, T. W. (1995). Psychiatric characteristics of children with selective mutism: A pilot study. *Journal of the American Academy of Child and Adolescent Psychiatry, 29,* 36–44.

Blader, J. C., Koplewicz, H. S., Abikoff, H., & Foley, C. (1997). Sleep problems of elementary school children. *Archives of Pediatric Adolescent Medicine, 151,* 473–480.

Blanck, P. D., Bellack, A. S., Rosnow, R. L., Rotheram-Borus, M. J., & Schooler, N. R. (1992). Scientific rewards and conflicts of ethical choices in human subjects research. *American Psychologist, 47,* 959–965.

Blatt, B., & Kaplan, F. (1966). *Christmas in purgatory: A photographic essay on mental retardation.* Boston, MA: Allyn & Bacon.

Bleuler, E. (1950). *Dementia praecox or a group within the schizophrenias* (J. Zinkin, Trans.). New York: International Universities Press. (Original work published 1911)

Block, J., Block, J. H., & Gjerde, P. F. (1986). The personality of children prior to divorce: A prospective study. *Child Development, 57,* 827–840.

Block, J., Block, J. H., & Keyes, S. (1988). Longitudinally foretelling drug usage in adolescence: Early childhood personality and environmental precursors. *Child Development, 59,* 336–355.

Blood, G. W. (1988). Stuttering. In M. Hersen & C. G. Last (Eds.), *Child behavior therapy casebook* (pp. 165–177). New York: Plenum.

Bloomquist, M. L., August, G. J., & Ostrander, R. (1991). Effects of a school-based cognitive-behavioral intervention for ADHD. *Journal of Abnormal Child Psychology, 19,* 591–605.

Blount, R. L., Corbin, S. M., Sturges, J. W., Wolfe, V. V., Prater, J. M., & James, L. D. (1989). The relationship between adults' behavior and child coping and distress during BMA/LP procedures: A sequential analysis. *Behavior Therapy, 20,* 585–601.

Blount, R. L., Davis, N., Powers, S. W., & Roberts, M. C. (1991). The influence of environmental factors and coping style on children's coping and distress. *Clinical Psychology Review, 11,* 93–116.

Blum, K., Cull, J. G., Braverman, E. R., & Comings, D. E. (1996). Reward deficiency syndrome. *American Scientist, 84,* 132–145.

Blum, N. J., & Carey, W. B. (1996). Sleep problems among infants and young children. *Pediatrics in Review, 17,* 87–93.

Blum-Hoffman, E., Rehder, H., & Langenbeck, U. (1987). Skeletal abnormalities in trisomy 21 as an example of amplified developmental instability in chromosomal disorders: A histological study of 21 mid-trimester fetuses with trisomy 21. *American Journal of Medical Genetics, 29,* 155–160.

Boetsch, E. A., Green, P. A., & Pennington, B. F. (1996). Psychosocial correlates of dyslexia across the life span. *Development and Psychopathology, 8,* 539–562.

Bogdan, R., & Taylor, S. J. (1982). *Inside out: The social meaning of mental retardation.* Toronto: University of Toronto Press.

Boll, T. J., & LaMarche, J. A. (1992). Neuropsychological assessment of the child: Myths, current status, and future prospects. In C. E. Walker & M. C. Roberts (Eds.), *Handbook of clinical child psychology* (pp. 133–148). New York: Wiley.

Bollard, J., & Nettelbeck, T. (1981). Comparison of dry-bed training and standard urine-alarm conditioning treatment of childhood bedwetting. *Behaviour Research and Therapy, 19*(3), 215–226.

Bolton, P., MacDonald, H., Pickles, A., Rios, P., Goode, S., Crowson, M., Bailey, A., & Rutter, M. (1994). A case-control family history study of autism. *Journal of Child Psychology and Psychiatry, 35,* 877–900.

Bond, A., & Lader, M. L. (1979). Benzodiazapines and aggression. In M. Sandler (Ed.), *Psychopharmacology of aggression.* New York: Raven.

Bootzin, R. R., & Chambers, M. J. (1990). Childhood sleep disorders. In A. M. Gross & R. S. Drabman (Eds.), *Handbook of clinical behavioral pediatrics* (pp. 205–227). New York: Plenum.

Borkovec, T. M. (1994). The nature, functions, and origins of worry. In G. C. L. Davey & F. Tallis (Eds.), *Worrying:*

Perspectives on theory, assessment and treatment (pp. 5–33). Chichester, England: Wiley.

Borkovec, T. M., & Hu, S. (1990). The effect of worry on cardiovascular response to phobic imagery. *Behavior Research and Therapy, 28,* 69–73.

Borkovec, T. M., & Inz, J. (1990). The nature of worry in generalized anxiety disorder: A predominance of thought activity. *Behaviour Research and Therapy, 28,* 153–158.

Bornstein, M. H. (1989). Sensitive periods in development: Structural characteristics and causal interpretations. *Psychological Bulletin, 105,* 179–197.

Borstelmann, L. J. (1983). Children before psychology: Ideas about children from antiquity to the late 1800s. In W. Kessen (Vol. Ed.), *Handbook of child psychology* (4th ed.): *Vol. I. History, theory, and methods* (pp. 1–40). New York: Wiley.

Boucher, J., & Lewis, V. (1992). Unfamiliar face recognition in relatively able autistic children. *Journal of Child Psychology and Psychiatry, 33,* 843–859.

Bousha, D. M., & Twentyman, C. T. (1984). Mother-child interactional style in abuse, neglect, and control groups: Naturalistic observations in the home. *Journal of Abnormal Psychology, 93,* 106–114.

Boverman, H., & French, A. P. (1979). Therapy vignettes. In A. French & I. Berlin (Eds.), *Depression in children and adolescents* (pp. 210–217). New York: Human Sciences Press.

Bowlby, J. (1961). Childhood mourning and its implications for psychiatry. *American Journal of Psychiatry, 118,* 481–498.

Bowlby, J. (1973). *Attachment and loss: Vol. 2. Separation: Anxiety and anger.* New York: Basic Books.

Bowlby, J. A. (1988). *A secure base: Parent-child attachment and healthy human development.* New York: Basic Books.

Bowler, P. J. (1989). Holding your head up high: Degeneration and orthogenesis in theories of human evolution. In J. R. Moore (Ed.), *History, humanity, and evolution: Essays for John C. Greene* (pp. 329–353). Cambridge, England: Cambridge University Press.

Bowring, M. A., & Kovacs, M. (1992). Difficulties in diagnosing manic disorders among children and adolescents. *Journal of the American Academy of Child and Adolescent Psychiatry, 31,* 611–614.

Boyle, M. H., Offord, D. R., Hoffman, H. G., Catlin, G. P., Byles, J. A., Cadman, D. T., Crawford, J. W., Links, P. S., Rae-Grant, N. I., & Szatmari, P. (1987). Ontario Child Health Study: I. Methodology. *Archives of General Psychiatry, 44,* 826–831.

Brady, E., & Kendall, P. C. (1992). Comorbidity of anxiety and depression in children and adolescents. *Psychological Bulletin, 3,* 244–255.

Brand, E., King, C., Olson, E., Ghaziuddin, N., Naylor, M. (1996). Depressed adolescents with a history of sexual abuse: Diagnostic comorbidity and suicidality. *Journal of the American Academy of Child and Adolescent Psychiatry, 35*(1), 34–41.

Brandenburg, N. A., Friedman, R. M., & Silver, S. E. (1990). The epidemiology of childhood psychiatric disorders: Prevalence findings from recent studies. *Journal of the American Academy of Child and Adolescent Psychiatry, 29,* 76–83.

Brazelton, T. B., & Cramer, B. G. (Eds.). (1990). *The earliest relationship.* Reading, MA: Addison-Wesley.

Breger, L. (1974). *From instinct to identity: The development of personality.* Englewood Cliffs, NJ: Prentice Hall.

Brent, D. A., Bridge, J., Johnston, B. A., & Connolly, J. (1996). Suicidal behavior runs in family: A controlled study of adolescent suicide victims. *Archives of General Psychiatry, 53,* 1145–1152.

Brent, D. A., Holder, D., Kolko, D., Birmaher, B., Baugher, M., Roth, C., Iyengar, S., & Johnson, B. A. (1997). A clinical psychotherapy trial for adolescent depression comparing cognitive, family, and supportive therapy. *Archives of General Psychiatry, 54,* 877–885.

Brent, D. A., Perper, J. A., Goldstein, C. E., Kolko, D. J., Allan, M. J., Allman, C. J., & Zelenak, J. P. (1988). Risk factors for adolescent suicide: A comparison of adolescent suicide victims with suicidal inpatients. *Archives of General Psychiatry, 45,* 581–588.

Brent, D. A., Perper, J. A., Moritz, G., Allman, C., Friend, A., Roth, C., Schweers, J., Balach, L., & Baugher, M. (1993). Psychiatric risk factors for adolescent suicide: A case control study. *Journal of the American Academy of Child and Adolescent Psychiatry, 32,* 521–529.

Brent, D. A., Perper, J. A., Moritz, G., Allman, C., Friend, A., Schweers, J., Roth, C., Balach, L., & Harrington, K. (1992). Psychiatric effects of exposure to suicide among the friends and acquaintances of adolescent suicide victims. *Journal of the American Academy of Child and Adolescent Psychiatry, 31,* 629–640.

Breslau, N. (1985). Psychiatric disorder in children with physical disabilities. *Journal of the American Academy of Child Psychiatry, 24,* 87–94.

Bretherton, I. (1990). Pouring new wine into old bottles: The social self as internal working model. In M. Gunnar & L. A. Sroufe (Eds.), *The Minnesota Symposia on Child Development* (pp. 1–41). Hillsdale, NJ: Erlbaum.

Bretherton, I. (1995). Attachment theory and developmental psychopathology. In D. Cicchetti & S. Toth (Eds.), *Emotion and representation in developmental psychopathology* (Rochester Symposium on Developmental Psychopathology). Rochester, NY: University of Rochester Press.

Bretherton, I., Fritz, J., Zahn-Waxler, C., & Ridgeway, D. (1986). Learning to talk about emotions: A functionalist perspective. *Child Development, 57,* 529–548.

Brier, N. (1989). The relationship between learning disability and delinquency: A review and reappraisal. *Journal of Learning Disabilities, 22,* 546–553.

Briere, J. (1997). Treating adults severely abused as children: The self-trauma model. In D. A. Wolfe, R. J. McMahon, & R. Dev Peters (Eds.), *Child abuse: New directions in prevention and treatment across the lifespan* (pp. 178–205). Newbury Park, CA: Sage.

Briere, J., & Runtz, M. (1991). The long-term effects of sexual abuse: A review and synthesis. *New Directions on Mental Health Services, 51,* 3–13.

Bristol, M. M. (1984). Family resources and successful adaptation to autistic children. In E. Schopler & G. B. Mesibov (Eds.), *Autism in adolescents and adults* (pp. 251–278). New York: Plenum.

Broadbent, A., & Bentley, R. (1997). *Child abuse and neglect Australia 1995–96.* (Child Welfare Series No. 17, AIHW Cat. No. CWS 1). Canberra: Australian Institute of Health and Welfare.

Bromfield, R., Weisz, J. R., & Messer, I. (1986). Children's judgments and attributions in response to the mental retarded label. *Journal of Abnormal Psychology, 95,* 81–87.

Bronfenbrenner, U. (1977). Toward an experimental ecology of human development. *American Psychologist, 52,* 513–531.

Brook, J. S., Whiteman, M., Finch, S. J., & Cohen, P. (1996). Young adult drug use and delinquency: Childhood antecedents and adolescent mediators. *Journal of the American Academy of Child and Adolescent Psychiatry, 35,* 1584–1592.

Brooks-Gunn, J. (1988). Antecedents and consequences of variations in girls' maturational timing. *Journal of Adolescent Health Care, 9,* 365–373.

Brooks-Gunn, J., & Duncan, G. J. (1997). The effects of poverty on children. *The Future of Children, 7*(2), 55–71.

Brooks-Gunn, J., Klebanov, P. K., & Duncan, G. J. (1996). Ethnic differences in children's intelligence test scores: Role of economic deprivation, home environment, and maternal characteristics. *Child Development, 67,* 396–408.

Brooks-Gunn, J., & Warren, M. P. (1985). Effects of delayed menarche in different contexts: Dance and nondance students. *Journal of Youth and Adolescence, 14,* 285–300.

Brown, F. R., Greer, M., Aylward, E., & Hunt, H. (1990). Intellectual and adaptive functioning in individuals with Down Syndrome in relation to age and environmental placement. *Pediatrics, 85,* 450–452.

Brown, R. T., Coles, C., Platzman, K., & Hill, L. (1993, February). *Parental alcohol exposure and its relationship to externalizing disorders: A longitudinal investigation.* Paper presented at the annual meeting of the Society for Research in Child and Adolescent Psychopathology, Santa Fe, NM.

Brown, S., & van Praag, H. M. (Eds.). (1991). *The role of serotonin in psychiatric disorders.* New York: Brunner/Mazel.

Brown, T. A., Barlow, D. H., & Liebowitz, M. R. (1994). The empirical basis of generalized anxiety disorder. *American Journal of Psychiatry, 15,* 1272–1280.

Browne, A., & Finkelhor, D. (1986). Impact of child sexual abuse: A review of the literature. *Psychological Bulletin, 99,* 66–77.

Brownell, K. D. (1991). Dieting and the search for the perfect body: Where physiology and culture collide. *Behavior Therapy, 22,* 1–12.

Brownell, K. D., & Napolitano, M. A. (1995). Distorting reality for children: Body size proportions of Barbie and Ken dolls. *International Journal of Eating Disorders, 18,* 295–298.

Brownell, K. D., & Rodin, J. (1994). The dieting maelstrom: Is it possible and advisable to lose weight? *American Psychologist, 49,* 781–791.

Brownell, K. D., & Wadden, T. A. (1992). Etiology and treatment of obesity: Understanding a serious, prevalent, and refractory disorder. *Journal of Consulting and Clinical Psychology, 60,* 505–517.

Bruch, H. (1962). Perceptual and conceptual disturbances in anorexia nervosa. *Psychosomatic Medicine, 24,* 187–194.

Bruch, H. (1973). *Eating disorders: Obesity, anorexia nervosa and the person within.* New York: Basic Books.

Bruck, M. (1985). The adult functioning of children with specific learning disabilities. In I. Sigel (Ed.), *Handbook of cognitive, social and neuropsychological aspects of learning disabilities* (pp. 361–380). Hillsdale, NJ: Erlbaum.

Bruck, M. (1986). Social and emotional adjustments of learning disabled children: A review of the issues. In S. J. Ceci (Ed.), *Handbook of cognitive, social, and neuropsychological aspects of learning disabilities* (pp. 361–380). Hillsdale, NJ: Erlbaum.

Brumberg, J. J. (1988). *Fasting girls: The emergence of anorexia nervosa as a modern disease.* Cambridge, MA: Harvard University Press.

Brumberg, J. J., & Striegel-Moore, R. (1993). Continuity and change in the symptom choice: Anorexia nervosa in historical and psychological perspective. In. G. H. Elder, J. F. Modell, & R. Parke (Eds.), *Children in time and place* (pp. 131–146). Cambridge, England: University of Cambridge Press.

Brunk, M., Henggeler, S. W., & Whelan, J. P. (1987). Comparison of multisystemic therapy and parent training in the brief treatment of child abuse and neglect. *Journal of Consulting and Clinical Psychology, 55,* 171–178.

Brunner, H. G., Nelen, M., Breakfield, X. O., Ropers, H. H., & Van Oost, B. A. (1993). Abnormal behavior associated with a point mutation in the structural gene for monoamine oxidase A. *Science, 262,* 578–580.

Bryson, S. E. (1996). Epidemiology of autism. *Journal of Autism and Developmental Disorders, 26,* 165–167.

Bryson, S. E., Landry, R., & Wainwright, J. (1997). A componential view of executive dysfunction in autism: Review of recent evidence. In J. A. Burack & J. T. Enns (Eds.), *Attention, development, and psychopathology* (pp. 232–259). New York: Guilford Press.

Bryson, S. E., Smith, I. M., & Eastwood, D. (1988). Obstetrical suboptimality in autistic children. *Journal of the American Academy of Child and Adolescent Psychiatry, 27,* 418–422.

Budd, K. S., McGraw, T. E., Farbisz, R., Murphy, T. M., Hawkins, D., Heilman, N., Werle, M., & Hochstadt, N. J. (1992). Psychosocial concomitants of children's feeding disorders. *Journal of Pediatric Psychology, 17,* 81–94.

Burack, J. A. (1990). Differentiating mental retardation: The two group approach and beyond. In R. M. Hodapp & J. A. Burack (Eds.), *Issues in the developmental approach to mental retardation* (pp. 27–48). Cambridge, England: Cambridge University Press.

Burd, L., & Kerbeshian, J. (1987). A North Dakota prevalence study of schizophrenia presenting in childhood. *Journal of the American Academy of Child and Adolescent Psychiatry, 26,* 347–350.

Burgess, R. L., & Youngblade, L. M. (1988). Social incompetence and the intergenerational transmission of abusive parental practices. In G. T. Hotaling, D. Finkelhor, J. T. Kirkpatrick, & M. A. Straus (Eds.), *Family abuse and its consequences: New directions in research* (pp. 38–60). Thousand Oaks, CA: Sage.

Burke, K. C., Burke, J. D., Regier, D. A., & Rae, D. S. (1990). Age at onset of selected mental disorders in five community populations. *Archives of General Psychiatry, 47,* 511–518.

Butcher, J. N., Williams, C. L., Graham, J. R., Archer, R. P., Tellegen, A., Ben-Porath, Y. S., & Kaemmer, B. (1992). *MMPI-A, Minnesota Multiphasic Personality Inventory— Adolescent: Manual for administration, scoring, and interpretation.* Minneapolis: University of Minnesota Press.

Butler, M. G. (1990). Prader-Willi Syndrome: Current understanding of cause and diagnosis. *American Journal of Medical Genetics, 35,* 319–332.

Butow, P., Beumont, P., & Touyz, S. (1993). Cognitive processes in dieting disorders. *International Journal of Eating Disorders, 14,* 319–330.

Butterfield, E. C., & Ferretti, R. P. (1987). Hypotheses about intellectual differences among children. In J. G. Borkowski & J. D. Day (Eds.), *Cognition in special children: Comparative approaches to retardation, learning disabilities, and giftedness* (pp. 195–233). Norwood, NJ: Ablex.

Buysse, V., & Bailey, D. B., Jr. (1993). Behavioral and developmental outcomes in young children with disabilities in integrated and segregated settings: A review of comparative studies. *The Journal of Special Education, 26,* 434–461.

Cadman, D., Boyle, M., Szatmari, P., & Offord, D. R. (1987). Chronic illness, disability, and mental and social well-being: Findings of the Ontario Child Health Study. *Pediatrics, 79,* 805–813.

Cadoret, R. J., Yates, W. R., Troughton, E., Woodworth, G., & Stewart, M. A. (1995a). Adoption study demonstrating two genetic pathways to drug abuse. *Archives of General Psychiatry, 52,* 42–52.

Cadoret, R. J., Yates, W. R., Troughton, E., Woodworth, G., & Stewart, M. A. (1995b). Gene environment interaction in genesis of aggressivity and conduct disorders. *Archives of General Psychiatry, 52,* 916–924.

Cairns, R. B., & Cairns, B. D. (1991). Social cognition and social networks: A developmental perspective. In D. J. Pepler & K. H. Rubin (Eds.), *The development and treatment of childhood aggression* (pp. 249–278). Hillsdale, NJ: Erlbaum.

Calder, J. (1980). *RLS: A life study.* London: Hamish Hilton.

Calhoun, J. A. (1992). Youth as resources: A new paradigm in social policy for youth. In G. W. Albee, L. A. Bond, T. V. C. Monsey, (Eds.), *Improving children's lives: Global perspectives on prevention* (pp. 334–341). Newbury Park, CA: Sage.

Campbell, F. A., & Ramey, C. T. (1995). Effects of early intervention on intellectual and academic achievement: A follow-up study of children from low-income families. *Child Development, 65,* 684–698.

Campbell, M., Gonzalez, N. M., & Silva, R. R. (1992). The pharmacologic treatment of conduct disorders and rage outbursts. *Psychiatric Clinics of North America, 15,* 69–85.

Campbell, R. V., O'Brien, S., Bickett, A. D., & Lutzker, J. R. (1983). In-home parent training, treatment of migraine headaches, and marital counseling as an ecobehavioral approach to prevent child abuse. *Journal of Behavior Therapy and Experimental Psychiatry, 14,* 147–154.

Campbell, S. B. (1990). *Behavior problems in preschool children: Clinical and developmental issues.* New York: Guilford Press.

Campbell, S. B., March, C. L., Pierce, E. W., Ewing, L. J., & Szumowski, E. K. (1991). Hard-to-manage preschool boys: Family context and the stability of externalizing behavior. *Journal of Abnormal Child Psychology, 19,* 301–318.

Campbell, S. B., Pierce, E. W., March, C. L., Ewing, L. J., & Szumowski, E. K. (1994). Hard-to-manage preschool boys: Symptomatic behavior across contexts and time. *Child Development, 65,* 836–851.

Campione, J. C. (1987). Metacognitive components of instructional research with problem learners. In F. E. Weinert & R. H. Klewe (Eds.), *Metacognition, motivation, and understanding* (pp. 117–140). Hillsdale, NJ: Earlbaum.

Canadian Institute of Advanced Research. (1991). *The determination of health.* (Publication No. 5.). Toronto: Author.

Cannon, T. D., Barr, C. E., & Mednick, S. A. (1991). Genetic and perinatal factors in the etiology of schizophrenia. In E. F. Walker (Ed.), *Schizophrenia: A life course developmental perspective* (pp. 9–31). New York: Academic Press.

Cantwell, D. P. (1990). Depression across the early life span. In M. Lewis & S. M. Miller (Eds.), *Handbook of developmental psychopathology* (pp. 293–309). New York: Plenum.

Cantwell, D. P., & Baker, L. (1992). Association between attention deficit-hyperactivity disorder and learning disorders. In S. E. Shaywitz & B. A. Shaywitz (Eds.), *Attention deficit disorder comes of age: Toward the twenty-first century* (pp. 145–164). Austin, TX: Pro-ed.

Cantwell, D. P., Baker, L., Rutter, M., & Mawhood, L. (1989). Infantile autism and developmental receptive dysphasia: A comparative follow-up into middle childhood. *Journal of Autism and Developmental Disorders, 19,* 19–31.

Cantwell, D. P., & Hanna, G. L. (1989). Attention-deficit hyperactivity disorder. In A. Tasman, R. E. Hales, & A. J. Frances (Eds.), *Review of psychiatry* (pp. 134–161). Washington, DC: American Psychiatric Press.

Capaldi, D. M., Crosby, L., & Stoolmiller, M. (1996). Predicting the timing of first sexual intercourse for at-risk adolescent males. *Child Development, 67,* 344–359.

Capaldi, D. M., & Patterson, G. R. (1991). Relations of parental transitions to boys' adjustment problems: I. A linear hypothesis. II. Mothers at risk for transitions and unskilled parenting. *Developmental Psychology, 27,* 489–504.

Capaldi, D. M., & Patterson, G. R. (1994). Interrelated influences of contextual factors on antisocial behavior in childhood and adolescence. In D. Fowles, P. Sutker, & S. Goodman (Eds.), *Psychopathy and antisocial personality: A developmental perspective* (pp. 165–198). New York: Springer.

Caplan, R. (1994). Communication deficits in childhood schizophrenia spectrum disorders. *Schizophrenia Bulletin, 20,* 671–684.

Capps, L., Sigman, M., & Mundy, P. (1994). Attachment security in children with autism. *Development and Psychopathology, 6,* 249–261.

Capps, L., Sigman, M., Sena, R., & Henker, B. (1996). Fear, anxiety and perceived control in children of agoraphobic parents. *Journal of Child Psychology and Psychiatry, 37,* 445–452.

Capron, C., & Duyme, M. (1989). Assessment of the effects of socioeconomic status on IQ in a full cross-fostering study. *Nature, 340,* 552–554.

Cardon, L. R., Smith, S. D., Fulker, D. W., Kimberling, W. J., Pennington, B. F., & DeFries, J. C. (1994, October 14). Quantitative trait locus for reading disability on chromosome 6. *Science, 266,* 276–279.

Carey, G. (1992). Twin imitation for antisocial behavior: Implications for genetic and family environment research. *Journal of Abnormal Psychology, 101,* 18–25.

Carlat, D. J., & Camargo, C. A. (1991). Review of bulimia nervosa in males. *American Journal of Psychiatry, 148,* 831–843.

Carlson, E. A., & Sroufe, L. A. (1995). Contribution of attachment theory to developmental psychopathology. In D. Cicchetti & D. J. Cohen (Eds.), *Developmental psychopathology: Vol. 1. Theory and methods* (pp. 581–617). New York: Wiley.

Carlson, G. A. (1990). Child adolescent mania—diagnostic considerations. *Journal of Child Psychology and Psychiatry, 31,* 331–342.

Carlson, G. A. (1994). Adolescent bipolar disorder: Phenomenology and treatment implications. In W. M. Reynolds & H. F. Johnston (Eds.), *Handbook of depression in children and adolescents* (pp. 41–60). New York: Plenum.

Carlson, G. A. (1995). Identifying prepubertal mania. *Journal of the American Academy of Child and Adolescent Psychiatry, 34,* 750–753.

Carlson, G. A., & Cantwell, D. P. (1980). Unmasking masked

depression in children and adolescents. *American Journal of Psychiatry, 137,* 445–449.

Carlson, G. A., & Kashani, J. (1988). Phenomenology of major depression from childhood through adulthood: Analysis of three studies. *American Journal of Psychiatry, 145,* 1222–1225.

Carlson, V., Cicchetti, D., Barnett, D., & Braunwald, K. (1989). Finding order in disorganization: Lesson from research on maltreated infants' attachments to their caregivers. In D. Cicchetti & V. Carlson (Eds.), *Child maltreatment: Theory and research on the causes and consequences of child abuse and neglect* (pp. 494–528). New York: Cambridge University Press.

Carr, E. G. (1977). The motivation of self-injurious behavior: A review of some hypotheses. *Psychological Bulletin, 84,* 800–811.

Carr, E. G., & Kemp, D. C. (1989). Functional equivalence of autistic leading and communicative pointing: Analysis and treatment. *Journal of Autism and Developmental Disorders, 19,* 561–578.

Carroll, B. J., Feinberg, M., Greden, J. F., Haskett, R. F., James, N. M., Steiner, M., & Tarika, J. (1980). Diagnosis of endogenous depression: Comparison of clinical, research, and neuroendocrine criteria. *Journal of Affective Disorders, 2,* 177–194.

Carskadon, M. A. (1990). Patterns of sleep and sleepiness in adolescents. *Pediatrician, 17,* 5–12.

Carskadon, M. A., Harvey, K., Duke, P., Andres, T. F., Litt, I. F., & Dement, W. C. (1980). Pubertal changes in daytime sleepiness. *Sleep, 2,* 453–460.

Carskadon, M. A., Rosekind, M. R., Galli, J., Sohn, J., Herman, K. B., & Davis, S. S. (1989). Adolescent sleepiness during sleep restriction in the natural environment. *Sleep Research, 18,* 115.

Carter, A. S., Pauls, D. L., & Leckman, J. F. (1995). The development of obsessionality: Continuities and discontinuities. In D. Cicchetti & D. Cohen (Eds.), *Handbook of developmental psychopathology* (Vol. 2, pp. 609–632). New York: Wiley.

Casanova, M. F., Carosella, N., & Kleinman, J. E. (1990). Neuropathological findings in a suspected case of childhood schizophrenia. *Journal of Neuropsychiatry and Clinical Neurosciences, 2,* 313–319.

Casey, B. J., Castellanos, F. X., Giedd, J. N., Marsh, W. L., Hamburger, S. D., Schubert, A. B., Vauss, Y. C., Vaituzis, A. C., Dickstein, D. P., Sarfetti, S. E., & Rapoport, J. L. (1997). Implication of right frontostriatal circuitry in response inhibition and attention-deficit/hyperactivity disorder. *Journal of the American Academy of Child and Adolescent Psychiatry, 36,* 374–383.

Casey, J. E., Rourke, B. P., & Pickard, E. M. (1991). Syndrome of nonverbal learning disabilities: Age differences in neuropsychological, academic, and socioemotional function. *Development and Psychopathology, 3,* 331–347.

Casey, R., Levy, S. E., Brown, K., & Brooks-Gunn, J. (1992). Impaired emotional health in children with mild reading disability. *Developmental and Behavioral Pediatrics, 13,* 256–260.

Casey, R. J., & Berman, J. S. (1985). The outcome of psychotherapy with children. *Psychological Bulletin, 98,* 388–400.

Casper, R., Hedeker, D., & McClough, J. F. (1992). Personality dimensions in eating disorders and their relevance for subtyping. *Journal of the American Academy of Child and Adolescent Psychiatry, 31,* 830–840.

Caspi, A., Elder, G. H., Jr., & Bem, D. J. (1987). Moving against the world: Life-course patterns of explosive children. *Developmental Psychology, 23,* 308–313.

Caspi, A., Henry, B., McGee, R. O., Moffitt, T., & Silva, P. A. (1995). Temperamental origins of child and adolescent behavior problems: From age three to age fifteen. *Child Development, 66,* 55–68.

Caspi, A., Lynam, D., Moffitt, T. E., & Silva, P. A. (1993). Unraveling girls' delinquency: Biological, dispositional, and contextual contributions to adolescent misbehavior. *Developmental Psychology, 29,* 19–30.

Caspi, A., & Moffitt, T. E. (1995). The continuity of maladaptive behavior: From description to understanding in the study of antisocial behavior. In D. Cicchetti & D. J. Cohen (Eds.), *Developmental psychopathology: Vol. 2. Risk, disorder, and adaptation* (pp. 472–511). New York: Wiley.

Cass, L. K., & Thomas, C. B. (1979). *Child psychopathology and later adjustment.* New York: Wiley.

Cassidy, J. (1994). Emotion regulation: Influences of attachment relationships. In N. A. Fox (Ed.), *Monographs of the Society for Research in Child Development, 59*(2–3, Serial No. 240), 228–283.

Castellanos, F. X., Giedd, J. N., Eckburg, P., Marsh, W. L., Vaituzia, A. C., Kaysen, D., Hamburger, S. D., & Rapoport, J. L. (1994). Quantitative morphology of the caudate nucleus in attention deficit hyperactivity disorder. *American Journal of Psychiatry, 151,* 1791–1796.

Castellanos, F. X., Giedd, J. N., Hamburger, S. D., Marsh, W. L., Rapoport, J. L. (1996). Brain morphometry in Tourette's syndrome: The influence of comorbid attention-deficit/hyperactivity disorder. *Neurology, 47,* 1581–1583.

Castellanos, F. X., Giedd, J. N., Marsh, W. L., Hamburger, S. D., Vaituzis, A. C., Dickstein, D. P., Sarfatti, S. E., Vauss, Y. C., Snell, J. W., Lange, N., Kaysen, D., Krain, A. L., Ritchie, G. F., Rajapakse, J. C., & Rapoport, J. L. (1996). Quantitative brain magnetic resonance imaging in attention-deficit hyperactivity disorder. *Archives of General Psychiatry, 53,* 607–616.

Castelloe, P., & Dawson, G. (1993). Subclassification of children with autism and pervasive developmental disorder: A questionnaire based on Wing's subgrouping scheme. *Journal of Autism and Developmental Disorders, 23,* 229–241.

Cattarin, J. A., & Thompson, J. K. (1994). A three-year longitudinal study of body image, eating disturbance, and general psychological functioning in adolescent females. *Eating Disorders: The Journal of Treatment and Prevention, 2,* 114–125.

Cattell, R. B. (1938). *Crooked personalities in childhood and after.* New York: Appleton-Century.

Catts, W. (1986). Speech production and phonological deficits in reading-disorder children. *Journal of Learning Disabilities, 19,* 504–505.

Caulfield, M. B., & Fischel, J. E. (1989). Behavioral correlates of developmental expressive language disorder. *Journal of Abnormal Child Psychology, 17,* 187–201.

Cecalupo, A. (1994). Childhood cancers: Medical issues. In R. A. Olson, L. L. Mullins, J. B. Gillman, & J. M. Chaney (Eds.), *The sourcebook of pediatric psychology* (pp. 90–97). Boston: Allyn & Bacon.

Centers for Disease Control. (1994). Deaths resulting from firearm- and motor-vehicle-related injuries—United States, 1968–1991. *Journal of the American Medical Association,*

271, 495–496.

Centers for Disease Control. (1995). Sociodemographic and behavioral characteristics associated with alcohol consumption during pregnancy—United States. *Morbidity and Mortality Weekly Report, 44*, 261–264.

Centers for Disease Control and Prevention. (1996). *Suicide deaths and rates per 100,000—United States, 1988–1994* (E950-E959). Atlanta: Author.

Chandler, L. A. (1990). The projective hypothesis and the development of projective techniques for children. In C. R. Reynolds & R. W. Kamphaus (Eds.), *Handbook of psychological and educational assessment of children: Personality, behavior, and context* (pp. 55–69). New York: Guilford Press.

Chandola, C. A., Robling, M. R., Peters, T. J., Melville-Thomas, G., & McGuffin, P. (1992). Pre- and perinatal factors and the risk of subsequent referral for hyperactivity. *Journal of Child Psychology and Psychiatry, 33*, 1077–1090.

Chansky, T. E., & Kendall, P. C. (1997). Social expectancies and self-perceptions in anxiety-disordered children. *Journal of Anxiety Disorders, 11*, 347–363.

Chapman, J. W. (1988). Cognitive-motivational characteristics and academic achievement of learning disabled children: A longitudinal study. *Journal of Educational Psychology, 80*, 357–365.

Charman, T., Swettenham, J., Baron-Cohen, S., Cox, A., Baird, G., & Drew, A. (1997). Infants with autism: An investigation of empathy, pretend play, joint attention, and imitation. *Developmental Psychology, 33*, 781–789.

Chen, X., Rubin, K. H., & Li, Z. Y. (1995). Social functioning and adjustment in Chinese children: A longitudinal study. *Developmental Psychology, 31*, 531–539.

Cheng, A. T. A. (1995). Mental illness and suicide: A case-control study in East Taiwan. *Archives of General Psychiatry, 52*, 594–603.

Chesney-Lind, M., & Shelden, R. G. (Eds.). (1992). *Girls: Delinquency and juvenile justice*. Pacific Grove, CA: Brooks/Cole.

Chess, S. (1960). Diagnosis and treatment of the hyperactive child. *New York State Journal of Medicine, 60*, 2379–2385.

Chess, S., & Thomas, A. (1984). *Origins and evolution of behavior disorders*. New York: Brunner/Mazel.

Chethik, M. (1989). *Techniques of child therapy: Psychodynamic strategies*. New York: Guilford Press.

Chiariello, M. A., & Orvaschel, H. (1995). Patterns of parent-child communication: Relationship to depression. *Clinical Psychology Review, 15*, 395–407.

Chilcoat, H. D., & Breslau, N. (1997). Does psychiatric history bias mothers' reports? An application of a new analytic approach. *Journal of the American Academy of Child and Adolescent Psychiatry, 36*, 971–979.

Childress, A. C., Brewerton, T. D., Hodges, E. L., & Jarrell, M. P. (1993). The kids' eating disorders survey (KEDS): A study of middle school students. *Journal of the American Academy of Child and Adolescent Psychiatry, 32*, 843–850.

Chorpita, B. F., Albano, A. M., & Barlow, D. H. (1996). Cognitive processing in children: Relation to anxiety and family in influences. *Journal of Clinical Child Psychology, 25*, 170–176.

Chorpita, B. F., Albano, A. M., & Barlow, D. H. (1998). The structure of negative emotions in a clinical sample of children and adolescents. *Journal of Abnormal Psychology, 107*, 74–85.

Chorpita, B. F., Albano, A. M., Heimberg, R. G., & Barlow, D. H. (1996). A systematic replication of the prescriptive treatment of school refusal behavior in a single subject. *Journal of Behavior Therapy and Experimental Psychiatry, 27*, 281–290.

Chorpita, B. F., Tracey, S. A., Brown, T. A., Collica, T. J., & Barlow, D. H. (1997). Assessment of worry in children and adolescents: An adaptation of the Penn State Worry Questionnaire, *Behaviour Research and Therapy, 35*, 569–581.

Christen, H. J., & Hanefeld, F. (1995). Male Rett variant. *Neuropediatrics, 26*, 81–82.

Christian, R. E., Frick, P. J., Hill, N. L., Tyler, L., & Frazer, D. R. (1997). Psychopathy and conduct problems in children: II. Implications for subtyping children with conduct problems. *Journal of the American Academy of Child and Adolescent Psychiatry, 36*, 233–241.

Cicchetti, D. (1990). The organization and coherence of socioemotional, cognitive, and representational development: Illustrations through a developmental psychopathology perspective on Down syndrome and child maltreatment. In R. Thompson (Ed.), *Nebraska symposium on motivation: Vol. 36. Socioemotional development* (pp. 259–366). Lincoln: University of Nebraska Press.

Cicchetti, D. (1993). Developmental psychopathology: Reactions, reflections, projections. *Developmental Review, 13*, 471–502.

Cicchetti, D., Ackerman, B. P., & Izard, C. E. (1995). Emotions and emotion regulation in developmental psychopathology. *Development and Psychopathology, 7*, 1–10.

Cicchetti, D., & Beeghly, M. (1987). Symbolic development in maltreated youngsters: An organizational perspective. *New Directions for Child Development, 36*, 5–29.

Cicchetti, D., & Beeghly, M. (1990). *The self in transition: Infancy and childhood*. Chicago: University of Chicago Press.

Cicchetti, D., & Cohen, D. J. (Eds.). (1995a). *Developmental psychopathology: Vol. 1. Theory and methods*. New York: Wiley.

Cicchetti, D., & Cohen, D. J. (1995b). Perspectives on developmental psychopathology. In D. Cicchetti & D. J. Cohen (Eds.), *Developmental psychopathology: Vol. 1. Theory and methods* (pp. 3–20). New York: Wiley.

Cicchetti, D., Ganiban, J., & Barnett, D. (1990). Contributions from the study of high-risk populations to understanding the development of emotion regulation. In K. Dodge & J. Garber (Eds.), *The development of emotion regulation* (pp. 1–54). New York: Cambridge University Press.

Cicchetti, D., Ganiban, J., & Barnett, D. (1991). Contributions from the study of high-risk populations to understanding the development of emotion regulation. In J. Garber & K. A. Dodge (Eds.), *The development of emotion regulation and dysregulation* (pp. 15–48). Cambridge, England: Cambridge University Press.

Cicchetti, D., & Garmezy, N. (1993). Prospects and promises in the study of resilience. *Development and Psychopathology, 4*, 497–502.

Cicchetti, D., & Lynch, M. (1995). Failures in the expectable environment and their impact on individual development: The case of child maltreatment. In D. Cicchetti & D. J. Cohen (Eds.), *Developmental psychopathology: Vol. 2. Risk, disorder, and adaptation* (pp. 32–71). New York: Wiley.

Cicchetti, D., & Richters, J. E. (1993). Developmental considerations in the investigation of conduct disorder. *Development and Psychopathology, 5*, 331–344.

Cicchetti, D., & Rogosch, F. A. (1997). The role of self-organization in the promotion of resilience in maltreated children. *Development and Psychopathology, 9,* 797–815.

Cicchetti, D., & Serafica, F. C. (1981). Interplay among behavioral systems: Illustrations from the study of attachment, affiliation, and wariness in young children with Down syndrome. *Developmental Psychology, 17,* 36–49.

Cicchetti, D., Toth, S., & Bush, M. (1988). Developmental psychopathology and incompetence in childhood: Suggestions for intervention. In B. B. Lahey & A. E. Kazdin (Eds.), *Advances in clinical child psychology* (Vol. 11, pp. 1–77). New York: Plenum.

Cicchetti, D., & Toth, S. L. (1998). The development of depression in children and adolescents. *American Psychologist, 53,* 221–241.

Cicchetti, D., & Tucker, D. (1994). Development and self-regulatory structures of the mind. *Development and Psychopathology, 6,* 533–549.

Cipani, E. (1991). Educational classification and placement. In J. L. Matson & J. L. Mulick (Eds.), *Handbook of mental retardation* (2nd ed., pp. 181–191). Elmsford, NY: Pergamon Press.

Clark, L. A., Watson, D., & Mineka, S. (1994). Temperament, personality, and the mood and anxiety disorders. *Journal of Abnormal Psychology, 103,* 103–116.

Clark, R. W. (1971). *Einstein: The life and times.* New York: World Publishing.

Clarke, G. N., Hawkins, W., Murphy, M., & Sheeber, L. (1993). School-based primary prevention of depressive symptomatology in adolescents: Findings from two studies. *Journal of Adolescent Research, 8,* 183–204.

Clarke, G. N., Hawkins, W., Murphy, M., Sheeber, L. B., Lewinsohn, P. M., & Seeley, J. R. (1995). Targeted prevention of unipolar depressive disorder in an at-risk sample of high-school adolescents: A randomized trial of a group cognitive intervention. *Journal of the American Academy of Child and Adolescent Psychiatry, 34,* 312–321.

Clarke, G. N., Lewinsohn, P. M., & Hops, H. (1990). *Adolescent Coping with Depression Course: Leader's manual for adolescent groups.* Eugene, OR: Castalia.

Clementz, B. A., & Iacono, W. G. (1993). Nosology and diagnosis. In A. S. Bellack & M. Hersen (Eds.), *Psychopathology in adulthood* (pp. 3–20). Needham Heights, MA: Allyn & Bacon.

Coates, D. L., & Vietze, P. M. (1996). Cultural considerations in assessment, diagnosis, and intervention. In J. W. Jacobson & J. A. Mulick (Eds.), *Manual of diagnosis and professional practice in mental retardation* (pp. 243–263). Washington, DC: American Psychological Association.

Cohen, J. (1988). *Statistical power analysis for the behavioral sciences* (2nd ed.). Hillsdale, NJ: Erlbaum.

Cohen, J. A., & Mannarino, A. P. (1996). A treatment outcome study for sexually abused preschool children: Initial findings. *Journal of the American Academy of Child and Adolescent Psychiatry, 35,* 42–50.

Cohen, M. A., Miller, T. R., & Rossman, S. B. (1994). The costs and consequences of violent behavior in the United States. In A. J. Reiss, Jr., & J. A. Roth (Eds.), *Understanding and preventing violence, Vol. 4: Consequences and control* (pp. 67–166). Washington, DC: National Academy Press.

Cohen, P., Cohen, J., & Brook, J. S. (1993). An epidemiological study of disorders in late childhood and adolescence: II. Persistence of disorders. *Journal of Child Psychology and Psychiatry, 34,* 869–877.

Coie, J. D. (1997, August). *Testing developmental theory of antisocial behavior with outcomes from the Fast Track prevention project.* Paper presented at the annual meeting of the American Psychological Association, Chicago.

Colapinto, J. (1993, November). The trouble with Nick. *Redbook,* pp. 121–123, 145, 151–153.

Colder, C. R., Lochman, J. E., & Wells, K. C. (1997). The moderating effects of children's fear and activity level on relations between parenting practices and childhood symptomatology. *Journal of Abnormal Child Psychology, 25,* 251–263.

Cole, D. A. (1990). The relation of social and academic competence to depressive symptoms in childhood. *Journal of Abnormal Psychology, 99,* 422–429.

Cole, D. A., Martin, J. M., Powers, B., & Truglio, R. (1996). Modeling causal relations between academic and social competence and depression: A multitrait-multimethod longitudinal study of children. *Journal of Abnormal Psychology, 105,* 258–270.

Cole, D. A., Truglio, R., & Peeke, L. (1997). Relation between symptoms of anxiety and depression in children: A multitrait-multimethod-multigroup assessment. *Journal of Consulting and Clinical Psychology, 65,* 110–119.

Cole, G., Neal, J. W., Fraser, W. I., & Cowie, V. A. (1994). Autopsy findings in patients with mental handicap. *Journal of Intellectual Disability Research, 38,* 9–26.

Cole, P. M., Michel, M. K., & Teti, L. O. (1994). The development of emotion regulation and dysregulation: A clinical perspective. *Monographs of the Society for Research in Child Development, 59*(2–3), 73–100.

Collings, S., & King, M. (1994). Ten-year follow-up of 50 patients with bulimia nervosa. *British Journal of Psychiatry, 164,* 80–87.

Comings, D. E., & Comings, B. G. (1988). Tourette's syndrome and attention deficit disorder. In D. J. Cohen, R. D. Bruun, & J. F. Leckman (Eds.), *Tourette's syndrome and tic disorders: Clinical understanding and treatment* (pp. 119–136). New York: Wiley.

Comings, D. E., Comings, B. G., Muhleman, D., Dietz, G., Shahbahrami, B., Tast, D., Knell, E., Kocsis, P., Baumgarten, R., Kovacs, B. W., Levy, D. L., Smith, M., Borison, R. L., Evans, D. D., Klein, D. N., MacMurray, J., Tosk, J. M., Sverd, J., Gysin, R., & Flanagan, S. D. (1991). The dopamine D_2 receptor locus as a modifying gene in neuropsychiatric disorders. *Journal of the American Medical Association, 266,* 1793–1800.

Compas, B. E. (1987). Coping with stress during childhood and adolescence. *Psychological Bulletin, 101,* 393–403.

Compas, B. E., Grant, K. E., & Ey, S. (1994). Psychosocial stress and child and adolescent depression: Can we be more specific? In W. M. Reynolds & H. F. Johnston (Eds.), *Handbook of depression in children and adolescents* (pp. 509–523). New York: Plenum.

Compas, B. E., Haaga, D. A. F., Keefe, F. J., Leitenberg, H., & Williams, D. A. (1998). Sampling of empirically supported psychological treatments from health psychology: Smoking, chronic pain, cancer, and bulimia nervosa. *Journal of Consulting and Clinical Psychology, 66,* 89–112.

Compas, B. E., & Hammen, C. L. (1994). Child and adolescent depression: Covariation and comorbidity in development. In R. J. Haggerty, L. R. Sherrod, N. Garmezy, & M. Rutter (Eds.), *Stress, risk, and resilience in children and adolescents: Processes, mechanisms, and interventions* (pp. 225–267). New York: Cambridge University Press.

Compas, B. E., Oppedisano, G., Hammen, C., Connor, J. K., Gerhardt, C. A., Hinden, B. R., & Achenbach, T. M. (1997). Gender differences in depressive symptoms in adolescence: Comparison of national samples of clinically referred and nonreferred youths. *Journal of Consulting and Clinical Psychology, 65,* 617–626.

Conduct Problems Prevention Research Group. (1992). A developmental and clinical model for the prevention of conduct disorder: The FAST Track program. *Development and Psychopathology, 4,* 509–527.

Conduct Problems Prevention Research Group. (1997, April). *Prevention of antisocial behavior: Initial findings from the FAST Track project.* Symposium (R. J. McMahon, Chair) presented at the biennial meeting of the Society for Research in Child Development, Washington, DC.

Conger, R. D., Ge, X., Elder, G. H., Lorenz, F. O., & Simons, R. L. (1994). Economic stress, coercive family process, and developmental problems of adolescents. *Child Development, 65,* 541–561.

Conners, C. K. (1980). *Food additives and hyperactive children.* New York: Plenum.

Consumer Reports (1997, February). *When kids can't concentrate: Attention deficit disorder,* pp. 56–57.

Cook, E. H. (1990). Autism: Review of neurochemical investigation. *Synapse, 6,* 292–308.

Cook, E. H., Courchesne, R., Lord, C., Cox, N. J., Yan, S., Lincoln, A., Haas, R., Courchesne, E., & Leventhal, B. L. (1997). Evidence of linkage between the serotonin transporter and autistic disorder. *Molecular Psychiatry, 2,* 247–250.

Cook, E. H., & Leventhal, B. L. (1996). The serotonin system in autism. *Current Opinion in Pediatrics, 8,* 348–354.

Cook, E. H., Stein, M. A., Krasowski, M. D., Cox, N. J., Olkon, D. M., Kieffer, J. E., & Leventhal, B. L. (1995). Association of attention-deficit disorder and the dopamine transporter gene. *American Journal of Human Genetics, 56,* 993–998.

Cooley, W. C., & Graham, J. M., Jr. (1991). Common syndromes and management issues for primary care physicians: Down syndrome—An update and review for the primary pediatrician. *Clinical Pediatrics, 30,* 233–253.

Cooper, S. A., & Collacott, R. A. (1995). The effect of age on language in people with Down's Syndrome. *Journal of Intellectual Disability Research, 39,* 197–200.

Corcoran, M. E., & Chaudry, A. (1997). The dynamics of childhood poverty. *The Future of Children, 7*(2), 40–54.

Corkum, P., Tannock, R., & Moldofsky, H. (1988). Sleep disturbances in children with attention-deficit/hyperactivity disorder. *Journal of the American Academy of Child and Adolescent Psychiatry, 37,* 637–646.

Cortez, V. L., & Bugental, D. (1994). Children's visual avoidance of threat: A strategy associated with low social control. *Merrill-Palmer Quarterly, 40,* 82–97.

Cortez, V. L., & Bugental, D. B. (1995). Priming of perceived control in young children as a buffer against fear-inducing events. *Child Development, 66,* 687–696.

Cosentino, C. E., Meyer-Bahlburg, H. F., Alpert, J., Weinberg, S. L., & Gaines, R. (1995). Sexual behavior problems and psychopathology symptoms in sexually abused girls. *Journal of the American Academy of Child and Adolescent Psychiatry, 34,* 1033–1042.

Costello, E. J. (1989). Developments in child psychiatric epidemiology. *Journal of the American Academy of Child and Adolescent Psychiatry, 28,* 836–841.

Costello, E. J. (1990). Child psychiatric epidemiology: Implications for clinical research and practice. In B. B. Lahey & A. E. Kazdin (Eds.), *Advances in clinical child psychology* (Vol. 13, pp. 53–90). New York: Plenum.

Costello, E. J., & Angold, A. (1995). Developmental epidemiology. In D. Cicchetti & D. J. Cohen (Eds.), *Developmental psychopathology: Vol. 1. Theory and methods* (pp. 23–56). New York: Wiley.

Costello, E. J., Farmer, E. M. Z., Angold, A., Burns, B. J., & Erkanli, A. (1997). Psychiatric disorders among American Indian and white youth in Appalachia: The Great Smoky Mountains Study. *American Journal of Public Health, 87,* 827–832.

Courchesne, E., Chisum, H., & Townsend, J. (1994). Neural activity-dependent brain changes in development: Implications for psychopathology. *Development and Psychopathology, 6,* 697–722.

Courchesne, E., Townsend, J. P., Akshoomoff, N. A., Yeung-Courchesne, R., Press, G. A., Murakami, J. W., Lincoln, A. J., James, H. E., Saitoh, O., Egaas, B., Hass, R. H., & Schreibman, L. (1994). A new finding: Impairment in shifting attention in autistic and cerebellar patients. In H. Broman & J. Grafman (Eds.), *Atypical cognitive deficits in developmental disorders: Implications for brain function* (pp. 101–137). Hillsdale, NJ: Erlbaum.

Courchesne, E., Townsend, J. P., & Chase, C. (1995). Neurodevelopmental principles guide research on developmental psychopathologies. In D. Cicchetti & D. Cohen (Eds.), *Developmental psychopathology: Vol. 1. Theories and methods* (pp. 195–226). New York: Wiley.

Cousens, P., Ungerer, J. A., Crawford, J. A., & Stevens, M. (1991). Cognitive effects of childhood leukemia therapy: A case for four specific deficits. *Journal of Pediatric Psychology, 16,* 475–488.

Cowan, C. P., Cowan, P. A., Heming, G., & Miller, N. B. (1991). Becoming a family: Marriage, parenting, and child development. In P. A. Cowan & M. Hetherington (Eds.), *Family transitions* (pp. 79–109). Hillsdale, NJ: Erlbaum.

Cowen, P. J., Anderson, I. M., & Fairburn, C. G. (1992). Neurochemical effects of dieting: Relevance to eating and affective disorders. In G. H. Anderson & S. H. Kennedy (Eds.), *The biology of feast and famine: Relevance to eating disorders* (pp. 269–284). New York: Academic Press.

Cox, D. J., Sutphen, J., Ling, W., Quillian, W., & Borowitz, S. (1996). Additive benefits of laxative, toilet training, and biofeedback therapies in the treatment of pediatric encopresis. *Journal of Pediatric Psychology, 21,* 659–670.

Coyne, J. C. (1976). Depression and the response of others. *Journal of Abnormal Psychology, 85,* 186–193.

Coyne, J. C., Downey, G., & Boergers, J. (1992). Depression in families: A systems perspective. In D. Cicchetti & S. L. Toth (Eds.), *Rochester symposium on developmental psychopathology: Vol. 4. Developmental perspectives on depression* (pp. 211–249). New York: University of Rochester Press.

Craighead, L. W., & Agras, W. S. (1991). Mechanisms of action in cognitive-behavioral and pharmacological interventions for obesity and anorexia nervosa. *Journal of Consulting and Clinical Psychology, 59,* 115–125.

Craske, M. G., & Rowe, M. K. (1997). Nocturnal panic. *Clinical Psychology: Science and Practice, 4,* 153–174.

Crick, N. R. (1995). Relational aggression: The role of intent attributions, feelings of distress, and provocation type. *Development and Psychopathology, 7,* 313–322.

Crick, N. R. (1997). Engagement in gender normative versus

nonnormative forms of aggression: Links to social-psychological adjustment. *Developmental Psychology, 33,* 610–617.

Crick, N. R., Bigbee, M. A., & Howes, C. (1996). Gender differences in children's normative beliefs about aggression: How do I hurt thee? Let me count the ways. *Child Development, 67,* 1003–1014.

Crick, N. R., & Dodge, K. A. (1994). A review and reformulation of social information-processing mechanisms in children's social adjustment. *Psychological Bulletin, 115,* 73–101.

Crick, N. R., & Dodge, K. A. (1996). Social information-processing mechanisms in reactive and proactive aggression. *Child Development, 67,* 993–1002.

Crijnen, A. A. M., Achenbach, T. M., & Verhulst, F. C. (1997). Comparisons of problems reported by parents of children in 12 cultures: Total problems, externalizing, and internalizing. *Journal of the American Academy of Child and Adolescent Psychiatry, 36,* 1269–1277.

Crimmins, D. B., Bradlyn, A. S., St. Lawrence, J. S., & Kelly, J. A. (1984). In-clinic training to improve the parent-child interaction skills of a neglectful mother. *Child Abuse and Neglect, 8,* 533–539.

Crisp, A. H. (1997). Anorexia nervosa as flight from growth: Assessment and treatment based on the model. In D. M. Garner and P. E. Garfinkel (Eds.), *Handbook of treatment for eating disorders* (2nd ed., pp. 248–277). New York: Guilford Press.

Crisp, A. H., Norton, K., Gowers, S., Halek, C., Bowyer, C., Yeldham, D., Levell, G., & Bhat, A. (1991). A controlled study of the effect of therapies aimed at adolescent and family psychopathology in anorexia nervosa. *British Journal of Psychiatry, 159,* 325–333.

Crittenden, P., & DiLalla, D. L. (1988). Compulsive compliance: The development of an inhibitory coping strategy in infancy. *Journal of Abnormal Child Psychology, 16,* 585–599.

Crittenden, P. M. (1992). Quality of attachment in the preschool years. *Development and Psychopathology, 4,* 209–241.

Crittenden, P. M. (1993). An information-processing perspective on the behavior of neglectful parents. *Criminal Justice and Behavior, 20,* 27–48.

Crittenden, P. M., & Ainsworth, M. (1989). Attachment and child abuse. In D. Cicchetti & V. Carlson (Eds.), *Child maltreatment: Theory and research on the causes and consequences of child abuse and neglect* (pp. 432–463). New York: Cambridge University Press.

Crockett, L. J., & Petersen, A. C. (1993). Adolescent development: Health risks and opportunities for health promotion. In S. G. Millstein, A. C. Petersen, & E. O. Nightingale (Eds.), *Promoting the health of adolescents: New directions for the twenty-first century* (pp. 13–37). New York: Oxford University Press.

Cross-National Collaborative Group. (1992). The changing rate of major depression: Cross-national comparisons. *Journal of American Medical Association, 265,* 3098–3105.

Cuffe, S. P., McCullough, E. L., & Pumariega, A. J. (1994). Comorbidity of attention deficit hyperactivity disorder and post-traumatic stress disorder. *Journal of Child and Family Studies, 3,* 327–336.

Culbertson, F. M. (1997). Depression and gender: An international review. *American Psychologist, 52,* 25–31.

Cullinan, D., Sabornie, E. J., & Crossland, C. L. (1992). Social mainstreaming of mildly handicapped students. *Elementary School Journal, 92,* 339–351.

Cummings, E. M. (1997). Marital conflict, abuse, and adversity in the family and child adjustment: A developmental psychopathology perspective. In D. A. Wolfe, R. J. McMahon, & R. Dev Peters (Eds.), *Child abuse: New directions in prevention and treatment across the lifespan* (pp. 1–24). Thousand Oaks, CA: Sage.

Cunningham, C. E., Bremner, R., & Secord-Gilbert, M. (1993). Increasing the availability, accessibility, and cost efficacy of services for families of ADHD children: A school-based, systems-oriented parenting course. *Canadian Journal of School Psychology, 9,* 1–15.

Cunningham, C. E., & Siegel, L. S. (1987). Peer interactions of normal and attention-deficit disordered boys during free-play, cooperative task, and simulated classroom situations. *Journal of Abnormal Child Psychology, 15,* 247–268.

Curry, J. F., & Murphy, L. B. (1995). Comorbidity of anxiety disorders. In J. S. March (Ed.), *Anxiety disorders in children and adolescents* (pp. 301–317). New York: Guilford Press.

Cytryn, L., & McKnew, D. H. (1974). Factors influencing the changing clinical expression of the depressive process in children. *American Journal of Psychiatry, 131,* 879–881.

Cytryn, L., & McKnew, D. H. (1996). *Growing up sad: Childhood depression and its treatment.* New York: Norton.

Dadds, M. R., Barrett, P. M., Rapee, R. M. (1996). Family process and child anxiety and aggression: An observational analysis. *Journal of Abnormal Child Psychology, 24,* 715–734.

Dadds, M. R., & Sanders, M. R. (1992). Family interaction and child psychopathology: A comparison of two observation strategies. *Journal of Child and Family Studies, 1,* 371–391.

Dadds, M. R., Sanders, M. R., Morrison, M., Rebgetz, M. (1992). Childhood depression and conduct disorder: II. An analysis of family interaction patterns in the home. *Journal of Abnormal Psychology, 101,* 505–513.

Dahl, R. E. (1996). The regulation of sleep and arousal: Development and psychopathology. *Development and Psychopathology, 8,* 3–27.

Dahl, R. E., Holttum, J., & Trubnick, L. (1994). A clinical picture of child and adolescent narcolepsy. *Journal of the American Academy of Child and Adolescent Psychiatry, 33,* 834–841.

Dahl, R. E., Pelham, W. E., & Wierson, M. (1991). The role of sleep disturbances in attention deficit disorder symptoms: A case study. *Journal of Pediatric Psychology, 16,* 229–239.

Dalquist, L. M. (1989). Cognitive-behavioral treatment of pediatric cancer patients' distress during painful and invasive medical procedures. In M. C. Roberts & C. E. Walker (Eds.), *Casebook of child and pediatric psychology* (pp. 360–379). New York: Guilford Press.

Dalquist, L. M. (1992). Coping with aversive medical treatments. In A. M. La Grega, L. J. Siegel, J. L. Wallander, & C. E. Walker (Eds.), *Stress and coping in child health* (pp. 345–376). New York: Guilford Press.

Damasio, H., Gabowski, T. J., Tranel, D., Hichwa, R. D., & Damasio, A. R. (1996). A neural basis for lexical retrieval. *Nature, 380,* 499–505.

Danford, D. E., & Hubert, A. M. (1982). Pica among mentally retarded adults. *American Journal of Mental Deficiency, 87,* 141–146.

Danforth, J. S., Barkley, R. A., & Stokes, T. F. (1991). Observations of parent-child interactions with hyperactive children: Research and clinical implications. *Clinical Psychology Review, 11,* 703–727.

Dare, C., & Eisler, I. (1997). Family therapy for anorexia nervosa. In D. M. Garner and P. E. Garfinkel (Eds.), *Handbook of treatment for eating disorders* (2nd ed., pp. 307–324). New York: Guilford Press.

Darwin, C. (1965). *The expression of the emotions in man and animals.* London: Murray; Chicago: University of Chicago Press. (Original work published 1872)

Davey Smith, G., Bartley, M., & Blane, D. (1990). The Black Report on socioeconomic inequalities on health ten years on. *British Medical Journal, 301,* 373–377.

Davidson, R. J. (1994). Asymmetric brain function, affective style, and psychopathology: The role of early experience and plasticity. *Development and Psychopathology, 6,* 741–758.

Davidson, R. J., & Fox, N. A. (1989). Frontal brain asymmetry predicts infants' response to maternal separation. *Journal of Abnormal Psychology, 98,* 127–131.

Davis, S., & Fantuzzo, J. W. (1989). The effects of adult and peer social initiations on social behavior of withdrawn and aggressive maltreated preschool children. *Journal of Family Violence, 4,* 227–248.

Dawson, G. (1994). Frontal electroencephalographic correlates of individual differences in emotion expression in infants: A brain systems perspective on emotions. *Monographs of the Society for Research in Child Development, 59,* 135–151.

Dawson, G. (1996). Neuropsychology of autism: A report on the state-of-the science. *Journal of Autism and Developmental Disorders, 2,* 179–181.

Dawson, G., Frey, K., Panagiotides, H., Osterling, J., & Hessl, D. (1997). Infants of depressed mothers exhibit atypical frontal brain activity: A replication and extension of previous findings. *Journal of Child Psychology and Psychiatry, 38,* 179–186.

Dawson, G., Hessl, D., & Frey, K. (1994). Social influences on early developing biological and behavioral systems related to risk for affective disorder. *Development and Psychopathology, 6,* 759–779.

Dawson, G., Klinger, L. G., Panagiotides, H., Lewy, A., & Castelloe, P. (1995). Subgroups of autistic children based on social behavior display distinct patterns of brain activity. *Journal of Abnormal Child Psychology, 23,* 569–583.

Dawson, G., & Osterling, J. (1997). Early intervention in autism: Effectiveness and common elements of current approaches. In M. J. Guralnick (Ed.), *The effectiveness of early intervention: Second generation research.* Baltimore: Paul H. Brookes.

Dean, R. R., Kelsey, J. E., Heller, M. R., & Ciaranello, R. D. (1993). Structural foundations of illness and treatment: Receptors. In D. L. Dunner (Ed.), *Current psychiatric therapy.* Philadelphia: Saunders.

Dean, R. S., & Gray, J. W. (1990). Traditional approaches to neuropsychological assessment. In C. R. Reynolds & R. W. Kamphaus (Eds.), *Handbook of psychological and educational assessment of children: Intelligence and achievement* (pp. 371–388). New York: Guilford Press.

Deater-Deckard, K., & Dodge, K. A. (1997). Externalizing behavior problems and discipline revisited: Nonlinear effects and variation by culture, context, and gender. *Psychological Inquiry, 8,* 161–175.

Deater-Deckard, K., Dodge, K. A., Bates, J. E., & Pettit, G. S. (1996). Physical discipline among African American and European American mothers: Links to children's externalizing behaviors. *Developmental Psychology, 32,* 1065–1072.

DeBellis, M., Burke, L., Trickett, P., & Putnam, F. (1996). Antinuclear antibodies and thyroid function in sexually abused girls. *Journal of Traumatic Stress, 9,* 369–378.

Deblinger, E., McLeer, S. V., & Henry, D. (1990). Cognitive behavioral treatment for sexually abused children suffering post-traumatic stress: Preliminary findings. *Journal of the American Academy of Child Psychiatry, 29,* 747–752.

De Fries, J. C., Olson, R. D., Pennington, B. F., & Smith, S. D. (1991). Colorado Reading Project: An update. In D. Duane & D. Gray (Eds.), *The reading brain: The biological basis of dyslexia* (pp. 53–87). Parkton, MD: York Press.

de Grouchy, J., & Turleau, C. (1990). Autosomal disorders. In A. E. H. Emery & D. L. Rimoin (Eds.), *Principles and practice of medical genetics* (pp. 247–272). Edinburgh, Scotland: Churchill-Livingstone.

De Jong, P. J., Andrea, H., & Muris, P. (1997). Spider phobia in children: Disgust and fear before and after treatment. *Behaviour Research and Therapy, 35,* 559–562.

DeKraai, M. B., & Sales, B. D. (1991). Liability in child therapy and research. *Journal of Consulting and Clinical Psychology, 59,* 853–860.

Delamater, A. (1986). Psychological aspects of diabetes mellitus in children. In B. B. Lahey and A. E. Kazdin (Eds.), *Advances in clinical child psychology* (Vol. 9, pp. 333–375). New York: Plenum.

De Lisi, L. E., & Lovett, M. (1991). The reverse genetic approach to the etiology of schizophrenia. In H. Hafnger & W. F. Gattaz (Eds.), *Search for the causes of schizophrenia* (Vol. 2, pp. 144–170). Heidelberg, Germany: Springer-Verlag.

Denicola, J., & Sandler, J. (1980). Training abusive parents in child management and self-control skills. *Behavior Therapy, 11,* 263–270.

Denzin, N. K., & Lincoln, Y. S. (Eds.). (1994). *Handbook of qualitative research.* Thousand Oaks, CA: Sage.

Depue, R. A., Luciana, M., Arbisi, P., Collins, P., & Leon, A. (1994). Dopamine and the structure of personality: Relation of agonist-induced dopamine activity to positive emotionality. *Journal of Personality and Social Psychology, 67,* 485–498.

Deren, D. M. (1997, June). *A childhood without laughter.* (From http://members.aol.com/depress/children.htm# Introduction). Copyright © 1996, 1997 Deborah M. Deren. Revised June 8, 1997. Retrieved October 22, 1997.

Derryberry, D., & Reed, M. A. (1994). Temperament and the self-organization of personality. *Development and Psychopathology, 6,* 653–676.

Desmond, A., & Moore, J. (1991). *Darwin.* New York: Viking Penguin.

DeSpelder, L. A., & Strickland, A. L. (1992). *The last dance: Encountering death and dying* (3rd ed.). Mountain View, CA: Mayfield.

Despert, J. L. (1955). Differential diagnosis between obsessive-compulsive neurosis and schizophrenia in children. In P. Hoch & J. Zubins (Eds.), *Psychopathology of childhood* (pp. 241–253). New York: Grune & Stratton.

Deutsch, C. K., & Kinsbourne, M. (1990). Genetics and biochemistry in attention deficit disorder. In M. Lewis & S. M. Miller (Eds.), *Handbook of developmental psychopathology* (pp. 93–107). New York: Plenum.

Devlin, B., Daniels, M., & Rodin, K. (1997). The heritability of IQ. *Nature, 388,* 468–471.

Dietz, W. H. (1987). Childhood obesity. *Annals of the New York Academy of Sciences, 499,* 47–54.

DiLalla, L. F., & Gottesman, I. J. (1989). Heterogeneity of causes for delinquency and criminality: Life span perspectives. *Development and Psychopathology, 1,* 339–349.

DiLalla, L. F., Kagan, J., & Reznick, J. S. (1994). Genetic etiology of behavioral inhibition among 2-year-old children. *Infant Behavior and Development, 17,* 405–412.

DiLella, A., & Woo, S. L. C. (1987). Molecular basis of phenylketonuria and its clinical applications. *Biology and Medicine, 4,* 183–192.

Dillon, K. M. (1993). Facilitated communication, autism, and Ouija. *Skeptical Inquirer, 17,* 281–287.

Dishion, T. J., & Andrews, D. W. (1995). Preventing escalation in problem behaviors with high-risk young adolescents: Immediate and 1-year outcomes. *Journal of Consulting and Clinical Psychology, 63,* 538–548.

Dishion, T. J., Andrews, D. W., & Crosby, L. (1995). Antisocial boys and their friends in early adolescence: Relationship characteristics, quality, and interactional process. *Child Development, 66,* 139–151.

Dishion, T. J., French, D. C., & Patterson, G. R. (1995). The development and ecology of antisocial behavior. In D. Cicchetti & D. J. Cohen (Eds.), *Developmental psychopathology: Vol. 2. Risk, disorder, and adaptation* (pp. 421–471). New York: Wiley.

Dishion, T. J., Haas, E., & Poulin, F. (1997, April). *Premature adolescent autonomy: Peer deviancy as a mediational mechanism.* Paper presented at the biennial meeting of the Society for Research in Child Development, Washington, DC.

Dishion, T. J., & Patterson, G. R. (1992). Age effects in parent training outcome. *Behavior Therapy, 23,* 719–729.

Dishion, T. J., Patterson, G. R., & Griesler, P. C. (1994). Peer adaptation in the development of antisocial behavior: A confluence model. In L. R. Huesmann (Ed.), *Aggressive behavior: Current perspectives* (pp. 61–95). New York: Plenum.

Dishion, T. J., Patterson, G. R., & Kavanagh, K. A. (1992). An experimental test of the coercion model: Linking theory, measurement, and intervention. In J. McCord & R. E. Tremblay (Eds.), *Preventing antisocial behavior: Interventions from birth through adolescence* (pp. 253–282). New York: Guilford Press.

Dishion, T. J., Spracklen, K. M., Andrews, D. W., & Patterson, G. R. (1996). Deviancy training in male adolescent friendships. *Behavior Therapy, 27,* 373–390.

Dobash, R. E., & Dobash, R. P. (1992). *Women, violence, and social change.* New York: Routledge.

Dobson, K. S., & Kendall, P. C. (1993). Future trends for research and theory in cognition and psychopathology. In K. S. Dobson & P. C. Kendall (Eds.), *Psychopathology and cognition* (pp. 475–486). San Diego: Academic Press.

Dodge, K. A. (1980). Social cognition and children's aggressive behavior. *Child Development, 51,* 162–170.

Dodge, K. A. (1986). A social information precessing model of social competence in children. In M. Perlmutter (Ed.), *Minnesota symposium on child psychology* (Vol. 18, pp. 77–125). Hillsdale, NJ: Erlbaum.

Dodge, K. A. (1989). Problems in social relationships. In E. J. Mash & R. A. Barkley (Eds.), *Treatment of childhood disorders* (pp. 222–244). New York: Guilford Press.

Dodge, K. A. (1991). The structure and function of reactive and proactive aggression. In D. J. Pepler & K. H. Rubin (Eds.), *The development and treatment of childhood aggression* (pp. 201–218). Hillsdale, NJ: Erlbaum.

Dodge, K. A., Bates, J., & Pettit, G. S. (1990). Mechanisms in the cycle of violence. *Science, 250,* 1678–1683.

Dodge, K. A., & Crick, N. R. (1990). Social information-processing bases of aggressive behavior in children. *Personality and Social Psychology Bulletin, 16,* 8–22.

Dodge, K. A., Lochman, J. E., Harnish, J. D., Bates, J. E., & Pettit, G. S. (1997). Reactive and proactive aggression in school children and psychiatrically impaired chronically assaultive youth. *Journal of Abnormal Psychology, 106,* 37–51.

Dodge, K. A., Pettit, G. S., & Bates, J. E. (1994a). Effects of physical maltreatment on the development of peer relations. *Development and Psychopathology, 6,* 43–55.

Dodge, K. A., Pettit, G. S., & Bates, J. E. (1994b). Socialization mediators of the relation between socioeconomic status and child conduct problems. *Child Development, 65,* 649–665.

Dodge, K. A., Pettit, G. S., Bates, J. E., & Valente, E. (1995). Social information-processing patterns partially mediate the effect of early physical abuse on later conduct problems. *Journal of Abnormal Psychology, 104,* 632–643.

Dolan, B. (1991). Cross-cultural aspects of anorexia nervosa and bulimia: A review. *International Journal of Eating Disorders, 1,* 67–68.

Dong, Q., Yang, B., & Ollendick, T. H. (1994). Fears in Chinese children and adolescents and their relations to anxiety and depression. *Journal of Child Psychology and Psychiatry, 35,* 351–363.

Donnellan, A. M. (1988, February). Our old ways just aren't working. *Dialect.* [Newsletter of the Saskatchewan Association for the Mentally Retarded]. Available from Saskatchewan Association for Community Living, 3031 Louise Street, Saskatoon, SK S7J 3L1.

Donohue, B., Hersen, M., & Ammerman, R. T. (1995). Historical overview. In M. Hersen & R. T. Ammerman (Eds.), *Advanced abnormal child psychology* (pp. 3–19). Hillsdale, NJ: Erlbaum.

Douglas, V. I. (1972). Stop, look, and listen: The problem of sustained attention and impulse control in hyperactive and normal children. *Canadian Journal of Behavioural Science, 4,* 259–282.

Douglas, V. I. (1988). Cognitive deficits in children with attention deficit disorder with hyperactivity. In L. M. Bloomingdale & J. A. Sergeant (Eds.), *Attention deficit disorder: Criteria, cognition, intervention* (pp. 65–82). London: Pergamon Press.

Douglas, V. I. (in press). Cognitive control processes in attention deficit hyperactivity disorder. In H. C. Quay & A. E. Hogan (Eds.), *Handbook of disruptive behavior disorders.* New York: Plenum.

Douglas, V. I., & Parry, P. A. (1983). Effects of reward on delayed reaction time task performance of hyperactive children. *Journal of Abnormal Child Psychology, 11,* 313–326.

Douglas, V. I., & Parry, P. A. (1994). Effects of reward and nonreward on frustration and attention in attention deficit disorder. *Journal of Abnormal Child Psychology, 22,* 281–302.

Douglas, V. I., & Peters, K. G. (1978). Toward a clearer definition of the attentional deficit of hyperactive children. In G. A. Hale & M. Lewis (Eds.), *Attention and the development of cognitive skills* (pp. 173–248). New York: Plenum.

Dowling, C. (1992, January 20). Rescuing your child from depression. *New York*, pp. 45–51.

Dowling, C. G., & Hollister, A. (1997, May). An epidemic of sneezing and wheezing. *Life*, pp. 76–92.

Down, J. L. H. (1866). Observations on an ethnic classification of idiots. *Clinical Lectures and Reports (London Hospital), 3*, 259–262.

Downey, G., & Coyne, J. C. (1990). Children of depressed parents: An integrative review. *Psychological Bulletin, 108*, 50–76.

Dozois, D. J. A. (1997). *A developmental cognitive model of unipolar major depression.* Unpublished manuscript, University of Calgary, Calgary, Alberta.

Drotar, D. (1991). The family context of nonorganic failure to thrive. *American Journal of Orthopsychiatry, 61*, 23–34.

Drotar, D. (1992). Prevention of neglect and nonorganic failure to thrive. In D. J. Willis, E. W. Holden, & M. Rosenberg (Eds.), *Prevention of Child Maltreatment: Developmental and Ecological Perspectives* (pp. 115–149). New York: Wiley.

Drotar, D. (1997). Relating parent and family functioning to the psychological adjustment of children with chronic health conditions: What have we learned? What do we need to know? *Journal of Pediatric Psychology, 22*, 149–165.

Duffy, A., Manion, I. G., & Davidson, S. (1994). Adolescent depression: A review. *The Canadian Journal of Pediatrics, 1*, 174–179.

Dujovne, V. F., Barnard, M. U., & Rapoff, M. A. (1995). Pharmacological and cognitive-behavioral approaches in the treatment of childhood depression. *Clinical Psychology Review, 15*, 589–611.

Dulcan, M. K. (1989). Attention deficit disorders. In C. G. Last & M. Hersen (Eds.), *Handbook of child psychiatric diagnosis* (pp. 95–128). New York: Wiley-Interscience.

Duncan, G. J., Brooks-Gunn, J., & Klebanov, P. K. (1994). Economic deprivation and early-childhood development. *Child Development, 65*, 296–318.

Duncan, P. M., & Millard, W. (1866). *A manual for the classification, training, and education of the feeble-minded, imbecile, and idiot.* London: Longmans, Green, & Co.

Dunlap, K. (1932). *Habits: Their making and unmaking.* New York: Liveright.

Dunst, C. J., Trivette, C. M., Davis, M., & Cornwell, J. (1988). Enabling and empowering families of children with health impairments. *Children's Health Care, 17*, 71–81.

DuPaul, G. J., Anastopoulos, A. D., Kwasnik, D., Barkley, R. A., & McMurray, M. B. (1996). Methylphenidate effects on children with attention deficit hyperactivity disorder: Self-report of symptoms, side-effects, and self-esteem. *Journal of Attention Disorders, 1*, 3–15.

DuPaul, G. J., & Eckert, T. L. (1997). The effects of school-based interventions for attention deficit hyperactivity disorder: A meta-analysis. *School Psychology Digest, 26*, 5–27.

DuPaul, G. J., & Ervin, R. A. (1996). Functional assessment of behaviors related to attention-deficit/hyperactivity disorder: Linking assessment to intervention design. *Behavior Therapy, 27*, 601–622.

DuPaul, G. J., Guevremont, D. C., & Barkley, R. A. (1992). Behavioral treatment of attention-deficit hyperactivity disorder in the classroom: The use of the attention training system. *Behavior Modification, 16*, 204–225.

DuPaul, G. J., & Kyle, K. E. (1995). Pediatric pharmacology and psychopharmacology. In M. C. Roberts (Ed.), *Handbook of pediatric psychology* (2nd ed., pp. 741–758). New York: Guilford Press.

DuPaul, G. J., & Stoner, G. (1994). *ADHD in the schools: Assessment and intervention strategies.* New York: Guilford Press.

Durlak, J. A., Fuhrman, T., & Lampman, C. (1991). Effectiveness of cognitive-behavior therapy for maladapting children: A meta-analysis. *Psychological Bulletin, 110*, 204–214.

Dykens, E. M. (1995). Measuring behavioral phenotypes: Provocations from the "new genetics." *American Journal of Mental Retardation, 99*, 522–532.

Dykens, E. M., & Cohen, D. J. (1996). Effects of Special Olympics International on social competence in persons with mental retardation. *Journal of the American Academy of Child and Adolescent Psychiatry, 35*, 223–229.

Dykens, E. M., Hodapp, R. M., & Evans, D. W. (1994). Profiles and development of adaptive behavior in children with Down Syndrome. *American Journal on Mental Retardation, 98*, 580–587.

Dykens, E. M., Hodapp, R. M., Ort, S. I., Finucane, B., Shapiro, L., & Leckman, J. F. (1989). The trajectory of cognitive development in males with fragile X syndrome. *Journal of the American Academy of Child and Adolescent Psychiatry, 28*, 422–426.

Early Diagnosis, Division of Child Psychiatry, Columbia University, 722 West 168th Street, New York, NY 10032.

Easterbrooks, M. A., Davidson, C. E., & Chazan, R. (1993). Psychosocial risk, attachment, and behavior problems among school-aged children. *Development and Psychopathology, 5*, 389–402.

Ebstein, R. P., Novick, O., Umansky, R., Priel, B., Osher, Y., Blaine, D., Bennett, E. R., Nemanov, L., Katz, M., & Belmaker, R. H. (1996). Dopamine D4 receptor (D4DR) exon III polymorphism associated with the human personality trait of Novelty Seeking. *Nature Genetics, 12*, 78–80.

Eckenrode, J., Laird, M., & Doris, J. (1993). School performance and disciplinary problems among abused and neglected children. *Developmental Psychology, 29*, 53–62.

Eckenrode, J., Rowe, E., Laird, M., & Brathwaite, J. (1995). Mobility as a mediator of the effects of child maltreatment on academic performance. *Child Development, 66*, 1130–1142.

Eckert, E. D., Halmi, K. A., Marchi, P., Grove, W., & Crosby, R. (1995). Ten-year follow-up of anorexia nervosa: Clinical course and outcome. *Psychological Medicine, 25*, 143–156.

Edelbrock, C. (1984). Developmental considerations. In T. H. Ollendick & M. Hersen (Eds.), *Child behavioral assessment: Principles and procedures* (pp. 20–37). New York: Pergamon Press.

Edelbrock, C., Costello, A. J., Dulcan, M. J., Kalas, R., & Conover, N. C. (1985). Age differences in the reliability of the psychiatric interview of the child. *Child Development, 56*, 265–275.

Edelbrock, C. S., Rende, R., Plomin, R., & Thompson, L. A. (1995). A twin study of competence and problem behavior in childhood and early adolescence. *Journal of Child Psychology and Psychiatry, 36*, 775–786.

Eden, G. F., VanMeter, J. W., Rumsey, J. M., Maisog, J. M., Woods, R. P., & Zeffiro, T. A. (1996, July 4). Abnormal processing of visual motion in dyslexia revealed by functional brain imaging. *Nature, 382*, 66–69.

Editorial Board. (1996). Definition of mental retardation. In J. W. Jacobson & J. A. Mulick (Eds.), *Manual of diagnosis and professional practice in mental retardation* (pp. 13–53). Washington, DC: American Psychological Association.

Edleson J. L., Eisikovits, Z. C., Guttmann, E., & Sela-Amit, M. (1991). Cognitive and interpersonal factors in woman abuse. *Journal of Family Violence, 6,* 167–182.

Egeland, B. (1991). A longitudinal study of high-risk families: Issues and findings. In R. H. Starr, Jr., & D. A. Wolfe (Eds.), *The effects of child abuse and neglect: Issues and research* (pp. 33–56). New York: Guilford Press.

Eiberg, H., Berendt, I., & Mohr, J. (1995). Assignment of dominant inherited nocturnal enuresis (ENUR1) to chromosome 13q. *Nature Genetics, 10,* 354–356.

Eiraldi, R. B., Power, T. J., Nezu, C. M. (1997). Patterns of comorbidity associated with subtypes of attention-deficit/hyperactivity disorder among 6- to 12-year-old children. *Journal of the American Academy of Child and Adolescent Psychiatry, 36,* 503–514.

Eisen, A. R., & Engler, L. B. (1995). Chronic anxiety. In A. R. Eisen, C. A. Kearney, & C. A. Schaefer (Eds.), *Clinical handbook of anxiety disorders in children and adolescents* (pp. 223–250). Northvale, NJ: Jason Aronson.

Eisen, A. R., Kearney, C. A., & Schaefer, C. E. (1995). *Clinical handbook of anxiety disorders in children and adolescents.* Northvale, NJ: Jason Aronson.

Eisen, A. R., & Silverman, W. K. (1993). Should I relax or change my thoughts? A preliminary examination of cognitive therapy, relaxation training, and their combination with overanxious children. *Journal of Cognitive Psychotherapy: An International Quarterly, 7,* 256–279.

Eisenmajer, R., Prior, M., Leekam, S., Wing, L., Gould, J., Welham, M., & Ong, B. (1996). Comparison of clinical symptoms in autism and Asperger's disorder. *Journal of the American Academy of Child and Adolescent Psychiatry, 35,* 1523–1531.

Eisler, I., Dare, C., Russell, G. F. M., Szmukler, G. I., Le Grange, D., & Dodge, E. (1998). *A controlled trial of two forms of family intervention in adolescent eating disorder.* Manuscript submitted for publication.

Elder, G. H., Jr., Caspi, A., & Van Nguyen, T. (1986). Resourceful and vulnerable children: Family influence in hard times. In R. K. Silbereisen, K. Eyferth, & G. Rudinger (Eds.), *Development as action in context: Problem behavior and normal youth development* (pp. 167–186). New York: Springer-Verlag.

Elder, G. H., Jr., Robertson, E. B., & Ardelt, M. (1994). Families under economic pressure. In R. D. Conger, G. H. Elder, Jr., F. O. Lorenz, R. L., Simons, & L. B. Whitbeck (Eds.), *Families in troubled times: Adapting to change in rural America* (pp. 79–103). New York: Aldine de Gruyter.

Ellinwood, C. G., & Raskin, N. J. (1993). Client-centered/humanistic psychotherapy. In T. R. Kratochwill & R. J. Morris (Eds.), *Handbook of psychotherapy with children and adolescents.* Needham Heights, MA: Allyn & Bacon.

Elliott, D. S., Huizinga, D., & Ageton, S. S. (1985). *Explaining delinquency and drug use.* Beverly Hills, CA: Sage.

Elliott, D. S., Huizinga, D., & Menard, S. (1989). *Multiple problem youth: Delinquency, substance use, and mental health problems.* New York: Springer-Verlag.

Elliott, M., Browne, K., & Kilcoyne, J. (1995). Child sexual abuse prevention: What offenders tell us. *Child Abuse and Neglect, 19,* 579–594.

Ember, C. R., & Ember, M. (1994). War, socialization, and interpersonal violence: A cross-cultural study. *Journal of Conflict Resolution, 38,* 620–646.

Emde, R. (1989). The infant's relationship experience: Developmental and affective aspects. In A. Sameroff & R. Emde (Eds.), *Relationship disturbances in early childhood* (pp. 33–51). New York: Basic Books.

Eme, R. F., & Kavanaugh, L. (1995). Sex differences in conduct disorder. *Journal of Clinical Child Psychology, 24,* 406–426.

Emery, R. E., & Laumann-Billings, L. (1998). An overview of the nature, causes, and consequences of abusive family relationships: Toward differentiating maltreatment and violence. *American Psychologist, 53,* 121–135.

Emslie, G. J., Rush, A. J., Weinberg, A. W., Kowatch, R. A., Hughes, C. W., Carmody, T., & Rintelmann, J. (1997). A double-blind, randomized, placebo-controlled trial of fluoxetine in children and adolescents with depression. *Archives of General Psychiatry, 54,* 1031–1037.

Emslie, G. J., Weinberg, W. A., Kennard, B. D., & Kowatch, R. A. (1994). Neurobiological aspects of depression in children and adolescents. In W. M. Reynolds & H. F. Johnston (Eds.), *Handbook of depression in children and adolescents* (pp. 143–165). New York: Plenum.

Engelmann, S., & Carnine, D. (1982). *Theory of instruction.* New York: Irvington.

Englemann, S., Haddox, P., Hanner, S., & Osborn, J. (1978). *Thinking basics: Corrective reading comprehension.* Chicago: Science Research Associates.

Epstein, C. J. (1990). The consequences of chromosomal imbalance. *American Journal of Medical Genetics, 7* (Suppl.), 31–37.

Epstein, L. H., & Cluss, P. A. (1982). A behavioral medicine perspective on adherence to long-term medical regimens. *Journal of Consulting and Clinical Psychology, 50,* 950–971.

Epstein, L. H., Klein, K. R., & Wisniewski, L. (in press). Child and parent factors that influence psychological problems in obese children. *International Journal of Eating Disorders.*

Epstein, L. H., Valoski, A. M., Vara, L. S., McCurley, J., Wisniewski, L., Kalarchian, M. A., Klein, K. R., & Shrager, L. R. (1995). Effects of decreasing sedentary behavior and increasing activity on weight change in obese children. *Health Psychology, 14,* 109–115.

Epstein, L. H., Valoski, A. M., Wing, R. R., & McCarley, S. (1990). Ten-year follow-up of behavioral, family-based treatment for obese children. *Journal of the American Medical Association, 264,* 2519–2523.

Epstein, M. H., Cullinan, D., & Gadow, K. (1986). Teacher ratings of hyperactivity in learning-disabled, emotionally disturbed, and mentally retarded children. *Journal of Special Education, 22,* 219–229.

Epstein, R. (1990). *Eating habits and disorders.* New York: Chelsea House.

Erhardt, D., & Hinshaw, S. P. (1994). Initial sociometric impressions of attention-deficit hyperactivity disorder and comparison boys: Predictions from social behaviors and from nonbehavioral variables. *Journal of Consulting and Clinical Psychology, 62,* 833–842.

Erickson, D. (1991, November). Brain food: Drugs to treat eating disorders. *Scientific American,* pp. 124–125.

Erickson, M. F., Egeland, B., & Pianta, R. (1989). The effects of maltreatment on the development of young children. In D. Cicchetti & V. Carlson (Eds.), *Child maltreatment:*

Theory and research on the causes and consequences of child abuse and neglect (pp. 647–684). New York: Cambridge University Press.

Erickson, M. F., Sroufe, L. A., & Egeland, B. (1985). The relationship between quality of attachment and relationship problems in preschool in a high-risk sample. *Monographs of the Society for Research in Child Development, 50*(Serial No. 209).

Ernst, A. R., Routh, D. K., & Harper, D. C. (1984). Abdominal pain in children and symptoms of somatization disorder. *Journal of Pediatric Psychology, 9,* 77–86.

Ernst, M., Liebenauer, M. A., King, C., Fitzgerald, G. A., Cohen, R. M., & Zametkin, A. J. (1994). Reduced brain metabolism in hyperactive girls. *Journal of the Academy of Child and Adolescent Psychiatry, 33,* 858–868.

Eron, L. D., & Huesmann, L. R. (1990). The stability of aggressive behavior—even unto the third generation. In M. Lewis & S. M. Miller (Eds.), *Handbook of developmental psychopathology* (pp. 147–156). New York: Plenum.

Eron, L. D., Huesmann, L. R., Lefkowitz, M. M., & Walder, L. O. (1996). Does television violence cause aggression? In D. F. Greenberg (Ed.), *Criminal careers, Vol. 2* (pp. 311–321). Aldershot, England: Dartmouth Publishing.

Eslinger, P. J. (1996). Conceptualizing, describing, and measuring components of executive function: A summary. In G. R. Lyon & N. A. Krasnegor (Eds.), *Attention, memory, and executive function* (pp. 367–395). Baltimore, MD: Paul H. Brookes.

Evans, D. W., Leckman, J. F., Carter, A., Reznick, J. S., Henshaw, D., King, R. A., & Pauls, D. (1997). Ritual, habit, and perfectionism: The prevalence and development of compulsive-like behavior in normal young children. *Child Development, 68,* 58–68.

Evans, I. M. (1991). Testing and diagnosis: A review and evaluation. In L. H. Meyer, C. H. Peck, & L. Brown (Eds.), *Critical issues in the lives of people with disabilities* (pp. 25–44). Baltimore: Paul H. Brookes.

Evans, I. M., & Meyer, L. H. (1985). *An educative approach to behavior problems: A practical decision model for interventions with severely handicapped learners.* Baltimore: Paul H. Brookes.

Exner, J. E. (1993). *The Rorschach: A comprehensive system* (3rd ed.). New York: Wiley.

Eyberg, S. M. (1988). Parent-child interaction therapy: Integration of traditional and behavioral concerns. *Child and Family Behavior Therapy, 10,* 33–46.

Fagot, B. I., & Pears, K. C. (1996). Changes in attachment during the third year: Consequences and predictions. *Development and Psychopathology, 8,* 325–344.

Fairbanks, J. M., Pine, D. S., Tancer, N. K., Dummit, E. S., III, Kentgen, L. M., Martin, J., Asche, B. K., & Klein, R. G. (1997). Open fluoxetine treatment of mixed anxiety disorders in children and adolescents. *Journal of Child and Adolescent Psychopharmacology, 7,* 17–29.

Fairburn, C. G. (1994, May). *The aetiology of bulimia nervosa.* Paper presented at the Sixth International Conference on Eating Disorders, New York.

Fairburn, C. G., & Beglin, S. J. (1990). Studies of the epidemiology of bulimia nervosa. *American Journal of Psychiatry, 147,* 401–408.

Fairburn, C. G., Hay, P. J., & Welch, S. L. (1993). Binge eating and bulimia nervosa: Distribution and determinants. In C. G. Fairburn & G. T. Wilson (Eds.), *Binge eating: Nature,*

assessment and treatment (pp. 123–143). New York: Guilford Press.

Fairburn, C. G., Jones, R., Peveler, R. C., Hope, R. A., & O'Connor, M. (1993). Psychotherapy and bulimia nervosa: The longer-term effects of interpersonal psychotherapy, behaviour therapy and cognitive behaviour therapy. *Archives of General Psychiatry, 50,* 419–428.

Fairburn, C. G., Marcus, M. D., & Wilson, G. T. (1993). Cognitive-behavioral therapy for binge eating and bulimia nervosa: A comprehensive treatment manual. In C. G. Fairburn & G. T. Wilson (Eds.), *Binge eating: Nature, assessment, and treatment* (pp. 361–404). New York: Guilford Press.

Fairburn, C. G., Norman, P. A., Welch, S. L., O'Connor, M. E., Doll, H. A., & Peveler, R. C. (1995). A prospective study of outcome in bulimia nervosa and the long-term effects of three psychological treatments. *Archives of General Psychiatry, 52*(4), 304–312.

Famularo, R., Fenton, T., Kinscherff, R., & Augustyn, M. (1996). Psychiatric comorbidity in childhood posttraumatic stress disorder. *Child Abuse and Neglect, 20,* 953–961.

Fantuzzo, J. W., Boruch, R., Beriama, A., Atkins, M., & Marcus, S. (1997). Domestic violence and children: Prevalence and risk in five major U.S. cities. *Journal of the American Academy of Child Psychiatry, 36,* 1408–1423.

Fantuzzo, J. W., Jurecic, L., Stovall, A., Hightower, A. D., Goins, C., & Schachtel, D. (1988). Effects of adult and peer social initiations on the social behavior of withdrawn, maltreated preschool children. *Journal of Consulting and Clinical Psychology, 56,* 34–39.

Fantuzzo, J. W., Stovall, A., Schachtel, D., Goins, C., & Hall, R. (1987). The effects of peer social initiations on the social behavior of withdrawn maltreated preschool children. *Journal of Behavior Therapy and Experimental Psychiatry, 4,* 357–363.

Fantuzzo, J. W., Sutton-Smith, B., Atkins, M., Meyers, R., Stevenson, H., Coolahan, K., Weiss, A., & Manz, P. (1996). Community-based resilient peer treatment of withdrawn maltreated preschool children. *Journal of Consulting and Clinical Psychology, 64,* 1377–1386.

Fantuzzo, J. W., Weiss, A. D., & Coolahan, K. C. (1998). Community-based partnership-directed research: Actualizing community strengths to treat child victims of physical abuse and neglect. In J. R. Lutzker (Ed.), *Handbook of child abuse research and treatment* (pp. 213–237). New York: Plenum.

Fantuzzo, J. W., Wray, L., Hall, R., Goins, C., & Azar, S. T. (1986). Parent and social skills training for mentally retarded parents identified as child maltreaters. *American Journal of Mental Deficiency, 91,* 135–140.

Faraone, S. V., & Biederman J. (1994). Genetics of attention-deficit hyperactivity disorder. *Child and Adolescent Psychiatric Clinics of North America, 3,* 285–301.

Faraone, S. V., & Biederman, J. (1997). Do attention deficit hyperactivity disorder and major depression share familial risk factors? *Journal of Nervous and Mental Disease, 185,* 533–541.

Faraone, S. V., Biederman, J., Chen, W. J., Krifcher, B., Keenan, K., Moore, C., Sprich, S., & Tsuang, M. T. (1992). Segregation analysis of attention deficit hyperactivity disorder. *Psychiatric Genetics, 2,* 257–275.

Faraone, S. V., Biederman, J., Keenan, K., & Tsuang, M. T. (1991a). A family-genetic study of girls with DSM-III attention deficit disorder. *American Journal of Psychiatry,*

148, 112–117.

Faraone, S. V., Biederman, J., Keenan, K., & Tsuang, M. T. (1991b). Separation of DSM-III attention deficit disorder and conduct disorder: Evidence from a family genetic study of American child psychiatry patients. *Psychological Medicine, 21*, 109–121.

Faraone, S. V., Biederman, J., & Milberger, S. (1996). An exploratory study of ADHD among second degree relatives of ADHD children. *Society of Biological Psychiatry, 35*, 398–402.

Farber, E., & Egeland, B. (1987). Abused children: Can they be invulnerable? In E. J. Anthony & B. Cohler (Eds.), *The invulnerable child* (pp. 253–288). New York: Guilford Press.

Farrell, A. D., & White, K. S. (1998). Peer influences and drug use among urban adolescents: Family structure and parent-adolescent relationship as protective factors. *Journal of Consulting and Clinical Psychology, 66*, 248–258.

Farrington, D. F. (1991). Longitudinal research strategies: Advantages, problems, and prospects. *Journal of the American Academy of Child and Adolescent Psychiatry, 30*, 369–374.

Farrington, D. P. (1986). Age and crime. In M. Tonry & N. Morris (Eds.), *Crime and justice: An annual review of research* (Vol. 7, pp. 189–250). Chicago: University of Chicago Press.

Farrington, D. P. (1989). Early predictors of adolescent aggression and adult violence. *Violence and Victims, 4*, 79–100.

Farrington, D. P. (1991). Childhood aggression and adult violence: Early precursors and later life outcomes. In D. J. Pepler & K. H. Rubin (Eds.), *The development and treatment of childhood aggression* (pp. 5–29). Hillsdale, NJ: Erlbaum.

Farrington, D. P. (1992). Explaining the beginning, progress, and ending of antisocial behavior from birth to adulthood. In J. McCord (Ed.), *Advances in criminological theory* (pp. 253–286). New Brunswick, NJ: Transaction Publishers.

Farrington, D. P. (1995). The development of offending and antisocial behaviour from childhood: Key findings from the Cambridge Study in Delinquent Development. *Journal of Child Psychology and Psychiatry, 36*, 929–964.

Fauber, R. L., & Kendall, P. C. (1992). Children and families: Integrating the focus of interventions. *Journal of Psychotherapy Integration, 2*, 107–123.

Fauber, R. L., & Long, N. (1991). Children in context: The role of the family in child psychotherapy. *Journal of Consulting and Clinical Psychology, 59*, 813–820.

Faust, J., Runyon, M. K., & Kenny, M. C. (1995). Family variables associated with the onset and impact of intrafamilial childhood sexual abuse. *Clinical Psychology Review, 15*, 443–456.

Fava, M., Copeland, P. M., Schweiger, U., & Herzog, D. B. (1989). Neurochemical abnormalities of anorexia nervosa and bulimia nervosa. *American Journal of Psychiatry, 146*, 963–971.

Favaro, A., & Santonastaso, P. (1995). Effects of parents' psychological characteristics and eating behaviour on childhood obesity and dietary compliance. *Journal of Psychosomatic Research, 39*, 145–151.

Federal Bureau of Investigation. (1994). *Crime in the United States: Uniform Crime Reports, 1994*. Washington, DC: U.S. Government Printing Office.

Feldman, C. M. (1997). Childhood precursors of adult interpersonal violence. *Clinical Psychology: Science and Practice, 4*, 307–334.

Feldman, M., & Wilson, A. (1997). Adolescent suicidality in urban minorities and its relationship to conduct disorders, depression, and separation anxiety. *Journal of the American Academy of Child and Adolescent Psychiatry, 36*, 75–84.

Feldman, R. S., Salzinger, S., Rosario, M., Alvarado, L., Caraballo, L., & Hammer, M. (1995). Parent, teacher, and peer ratings of physically abused and nonmaltreated children's behavior. *Journal of Abnormal Child Psychology, 23*, 317–334.

Felton, R. H. (1993). Effects of instruction on the decoding skills of children with phonological-processing problems. *Journal of Learning Disabilities, 26*, 583–589.

Ferber, T. (1985). *Solve your child's sleep problem*. New York: Simon & Schuster.

Fergusson, D. M., & Horwood, L. J. (1996). The role of adolescent peer affiliations in the continuity between childhood behavioral adjustment and juvenile offending. *Journal of Abnormal Child Psychology, 24*, 205–221.

Fergusson, D. M., Horwood, L. J., & Lloyd, M. (1991). Confirmatory factor analysis of attention deficit and conduct disorder. *Journal of Child Psychology and Psychiatry, 32*, 257–274.

Fergusson, D. M., Horwood, L. J., & Lynskey, M. T. (1993). Early dentine lead levels and subsequent cognitive and behavioural development. *Journal of Child Psychology and Psychiatry, 34*, 215–227.

Fergusson, D. M., Horwood, L. J., & Lynskey, M. T. (1995). Maternal depressive symptoms and depressive symptoms in adolescents. *Journal of Child Psychology and Psychiatry, 36*, 1161–1178.

Fergusson, D. M., Horwood, L. J., & Shannon, F. T. (1986). Factors related to the age of attainment of bladder control: An 8-year longitudinal study. *Pediatrics, 78*, 884–890.

Fernald, C. D., & Gettys, L. (1978, August). *Effects of diagnostic labels or perceptions of children's behavior disorders*. Paper presented at the annual meeting of the American Psychological Association, Toronto.

Ferrato, D. (1991). *Living with the enemy*. New York: Aperture Foundation.

Fichman, L., Koestner, R., & Zuroff, D. C. (1996). Dependency, self-criticism, and perceptions of inferiority at summer camp: I'm even worse than you think. *Journal of Youth and Adolescence, 25*, 113–126.

Field, T., Fox, N. A., Pickens, J., & Nawrocki, T. (1995). Relative right frontal EEG activation in 3- to 6-month-old infants of "depressed" mothers. *Developmental Psychology, 31*, 358–363.

Field, T. M., Morrow, C. J., Healy, B. T., Foster, T., Adelstein, D., & Goldstein, S. (1991). Mothers with zero Beck depression scores act more "depressed" with their infants. *Development and Psychopathology, 3*, 253–262.

Fielding, D. M., & Doleys, D. M. (1988). Elimination problems: Enuresis and encopresis. In E. J. Mash & L. G. Terdal (Eds.), *Behavioral assessment of childhood disorders* (2nd ed., pp. 586–623). New York: Guilford Press.

Fiese, B. H., & Bickham, N. L. (1998). Qualitative inquiry: An overview for pediatric psychology. *Journal of Pediatric Psychology, 23*, 79–86.

Filipek, P. A. (1996). Neuroimaging in autism: The state of the science 1995. *Journal of Autism and Developmental Disorders, 26*, 211–215.

Filipek, P. A., Semrud-Clikeman, M., Steingard, R. J., Renshaw, P. F., Kennedy, D. N., & Beiderman, J. (1997). Volumetric MRI analysis comparing subjects having attention-deficit hyperactivity disorder with controls. *Neurology, 48,* 589–601.

Finch, A. J., Jr., Nelson, W. M., III., & Ott, E. S. (1993). *Cognitive-behavioral procedures with children and adolescents: A practical guide.* Needham Heights, MA: Allyn & Bacon.

Fincham, F. D., Bradbury, T. N., & Grych, J. H. (1990). Conflict in close relationships: The role of intrapersonal phenomena. In S. Graham & V. S. Folkes (Eds.), *Attribution theory: Applications to achievement, mental health, and interpersonal conflict* (pp. 161–184). Hillsdale, NJ: Erlbaum.

Fine, S., Forth, A., Gilbert, M., & Haley, G. (1991). Group therapy for adolescent depressive disorder: A comparison of social skills training and therapeutic support. *Journal of the American Academy of Child and Adolescent Psychiatry, 30,* 79–85.

Fingerhut, L. A., & Kleinman, J. C. (1990). International and interstate comparisons of homicide among young males. *Journal of the American Medical Association, 263,* 3292–3295.

Finkelhor, D. (1984). *Child sexual abuse: New theories and research.* New York: Free Press.

Finkelhor, D. (1993). Epidemiological factors in the clinical identification of child sexual abuse. *Child Abuse and Neglect, 17,* 67–70.

Finkelhor, D. (1994). The international epidemiology of child sexual abuse. *Child Abuse and Neglect, 18,* 409–417.

Finkelhor, D. (1995). The victimization of children: A developmental perspective. *American Journal of Orthopsychiatry, 65,* 177–193.

Finkelhor, D., Asdigian, N., & Dzuiba-Leatherman, J. (1995). The effectiveness of victimization prevention instruction: An evaluation of children's responses to actual threats and assaults. *Child Abuse and Neglect, 19,* 141–153.

Finkelhor, D., & Berliner, L. (1995). Research on the treatment of sexually abused children: A review and recommendations. *Journal of the American Academy of Child Psychiatry, 34,* 1408–1423.

Finkelhor, D., & Browne, A. (1988). Assesesing the long-term impact of child sexual abuse: A review and conceptualization. In L. Walker (Eds)., *Handbook on sexual abuse of children* (pp. 55–71). New York: Springer.

Finkelhor, D., & Dziuba-Leatherman, J. (1994). Victimization of children. *American Psychologist, 49,* 173–183.

Finkelhor, D., Hotaling, G., Lewis, I. A., & Smith, C. (1990). Sexual abuse in a national survey of adult men and women: Prevalence, characteristics, and risk factors. *Child Abuse and Neglect, 14,* 19–28.

Fischer, M., Barkley, R. A., Edelbrock, C. S., & Smallish, L. (1990). The adolescent outcome of hyperactive children diagnosed by research criteria, II: Academic, attentional, and neuropsychological status. *Journal of Consulting and Clinical Psychology, 58,* 580–588.

Fish, B. (1987). Infant predictors of the longitudinal course of schizophrenic development. *Schizophrenia Bulletin, 13,* 395–410.

Fisher, C. B. (1991). Ethical considerations for research on psychosocial intervention for high-risk infants and children. *Register Reporter, 17*(2), 9–12.

Flannery-Schroeder, E., & Kendall, P. C. (1996). *Cognitive-behavioral therapy for anxious children: Therapist manual for group treatment.* Ardmore, PA: Workbook Publishing.

Fleming, J. E., & Offord, D. R. (1990). Epidemiology of childhood depressive disorders: A critical review. *Journal of the American Academy of Child and Adolescent Psychiatry, 29,* 571–580.

Fleming, J. E., Offord, D. R., & Boyle, M. H. (1989). Prevalence of childhood and adolescent depression in the community: Ontario child health study. *British Journal of Psychiatry, 155,* 647–654.

Fletcher, J. M., & Copeland, D. R. (1988). Neurobehavioral effects of central nervous system prophylactic treatment of cancer in children. *Journal of Clinical and Experimental Neuropsychology, 10,* 495–538.

Fletcher, J. M., & Foorman, B. R. (1994). Issues in definition and measurement of learning disabilities: The need for early intervention. In G. R. Reid (Ed.), *Frames of reference for the assessment of learning disabilities: New views on measurement issues* (pp. 185–200). Baltimore: Paul H. Brookes.

Fletcher, J. M., Francis, P. J., Rourke, B. P., Shaywitz, S. E., & Shaywitz, B. A. (1993). Classification of learning disabilities: Relationships with other childhood disorders. In G. R. Lyon, D. B. Gray, J. F. Kavanagh, & N. A. Krasnegor (Eds.), *Better understanding learning disabilities: New views from research and their implications for education and public policies* (pp. 27–56). Baltimore: Paul H. Brookes.

Fletcher, J. M., Shaywitz, S. E., Shankweiler, D., Katz, L., Liberman, I. Y., Steubing, K. K., Francis, D. J., Fowler, A. F., & Shaywitz, B. A. (1994). Cognitive profiles of reading disability: Comparisons of discrepancy and low achievement definitions. *Journal of Educational Psychology, 86,* 6–23.

Fletcher, J. M., & Taylor, H. G. (1997). Children with brain injury. In E. J. Mash & L. G. Terdal (Eds.), *Assessment of childhood disorders* (3rd ed., pp. 453–480). New York: Guilford Press.

Fletcher, K. E. (1996). Childhood posttraumatic stress disorder. In E. J. Mash & R. A. Barkley (Eds.), *Child psychopathology* (pp. 242–276). New York: Guilford Press.

Fletcher, P. C., Happe, F., Frith, U., Baker, S. C., Dolan, R. J., Frackowiak, R. S., & Frith, C. D. (1995). Other minds in the brain: A functional imaging study of "theory of mind" in story comprehension. *Cognition, 57,* 109–128.

Flicek, M., & Landau, S. (1985). Social status problems of learning disabled and hyperactive/learning disabled boys. *Journal of Clinical Child Psychology, 14,* 340–344.

Flint, J., & Yule, W. (1994). Behavioural phenotypes. In M. Rutter, E. Taylor, & L. Hersov (Eds.), *Child and adolescent psychiatry: Modern approaches* (3rd ed., pp. 666–687). Oxford, England: Blackwell.

Flisher, A. J., Kramer, R. A., Hoven, C. W., Greenwald, S., Alegria, M., Bird, H. R., Canino, G., Connell, R., & Moore, R. E. (1997). Psychosocial characteristics of physically abused chidren and adolescents. *Journal of the American Academy of Child and Adolescent Psychiatry, 36,* 123–131.

Floyd, F. J., Singer, G. H. S., Powers, L. E., & Costigan, C. L. (1996). Families coping with mental retardation: Assessment and therapy. In J. W. Jacobson & J. A. Mulick (Eds.), *Manual of diagnosis and professional practice in mental retardation* (pp. 277–288). Washington, DC: American Psychological Association.

Fonagy, P., Target, M., Steele, M., & Gerber, A. (1995). Psychoanalytic perspectives on developmental psychopathology. In D. Cicchetti & D. J. Cohen (Eds.), *Developmental psychopathology: Vol. 1. Theory and methods* (pp. 504–554). New York: Wiley.

Foorman, B. R. (1995). Research on the "Great Debate":

Code-oriented versus whole language approaches to reading instruction. *School Psychology Review, 24,* 376–392.

Foorman, B. R., Francis, D. J., Beeler, T., Winikates, D., & Fletcher, J. M. (1997). Early interventions for children with reading problems: Study designs and preliminary findings. *Learning Disabilities: A Multidisciplinary Journal, 8,* 63–72.

Forehand, R. L., & Kotchick, B. A. (1996). Cultural diversity: A wake-up call for parent training. *Behavior Therapy, 27,* 171–186.

Forehand, R. L., & McMahon, R. J. (1981). *Helping the noncompliant child: A clinician's guide to parent training.* New York: Guilford Press.

Foreyt, J. P., & Cousins, J. H. (1987). Obesity. In M. Hersen & V. B. Van Hasselt (Eds.), *Behavior therapy with children and adolescents: A clinical approach* (pp. 485–511). New York: Wiley.

Foreyt, J. P., & Cousins, J. H. (1989). Obesity. In E. J. Mash & R. A. Barkley (Eds.), *Treatment of childhood disorders* (pp. 405–422). New York: Guilford Press.

Foreyt, J. P., & McGavin, J. K. (1989). Anorexia nervosa and bulimia nervosa. In E. J. Mash & R. A. Barkley (Eds.), *Treatment of childhood disorders* (pp. 529–558). New York: Guilford Press.

Foreyt, J. P., & Mikhail, C. (1997). Anorexia nervosa and bulimia nervosa. In E. J. Mash & L. G. Terdal (Eds.), *Assessment of childhood disorders* (3rd ed., pp. 683–716). New York: Guilford Press.

Foster, S. L., & Cone, J. D. (1986). Design and use of direct observation procedures. In A. R. Ciminero, K. S. Calhoun, & H. E. Adams (Eds.), *Handbook of behavioral assessment* (2nd ed., pp. 253–324). New York: Wiley.

Foster, S. L., & Robin, A. L. (1988). Family conflict and communication in adolescence. In E. J. Mash & L. G. Terdal (Eds.), *Behavioral assessment of childhood disorders* (2nd ed., pp. 717–775). New York: Guilford Press.

Foster, S. L., & Robin, A. L. (1998). Parent-adolescent conflict and relationship discord. In E. J. Mash & R. A. Barkley (Eds.), *Treatment of childhood disorders* (2nd ed., pp. 601–646). New York: Guilford Press.

Fox, N. (1991). It's not left, it's right: Electroencephalographic asymmetry and the development of emotion. *American Psychologist, 46,* 863–872.

Fox, N. A. (Ed.). (1994). The development of emotion regulation: Biological and behavioral considerations. *Monographs of the Society for Research in Child Development, 59*(2–3, Serial No. 240).

Fox, N. A., Calkins, S. D., & Bell, M. A. (1994). Neural plasticity and development in the first two years of life: Evidence from cognitive and socioemotional domains of research. *Development and Psychopathology, 6,* 677–696.

Francis, D. H., Shaywitz, S. E., Steubing, K. K., Francis, D. J., Fowler, A. F., & Shaywitz, D. A. (1994). Measurement of change: Assessing behavior over time and within a developmental context. In G. R. Lyon (Ed.), *Frames of reference for the assessment of learning disabilities: New views on measurement issues* (pp. 29–58). Baltimore: Paul H. Brookes.

Francis, G., Last, C. G., & Strauss, C. C. (1987). Expression of separation anxiety disorder: The roles of age and gender. *Child Psychiatry and Human Development, 18,* 82–89.

Francis, G., Last, C. G., & Strauss, C. C. (1992). Avoidant disorder and social phobia in children and adolescents. *Journal of the American Academy of Child and Adolescent Psychiatry, 31,* 1086–1089.

Frank, Y., Lazar, J. W., & Seiden, J. A. (1992). Cognitive event-related potentials in learning-disabled children with or without attention-deficit hyperactivity disorder. *Annals of Neurology, 32,* 478 (abstract).

Frazier, J. A., Alaghband-Rad, J., Jacobsen, L., Lenane, M. C., Hamburger, S., Albus, K., Smith, A., McKenna, K., & Rapoport, J. L. (1997). Pubertal development and onset of psychosis in childhood onset schizophrenia. *Psychiatry Research, 70,* 1–7.

Frazier, J. A., Giedd, J. N., Kaysen, D., Albus, K., Hamburger, S., Alaghband-Rad, J., Lenane, M. C., McKenna, K., Breier, A., & Rapoport, J. L. (1996). Childhood-onset schizophrenia: Brain MRI rescan after 2 years of clozapine maintenance treatment. *American Journal of Psychiatry, 153,* 564–566.

Freedman, J. L. (1984). Effect of television violence on aggressiveness. *Psychological Bulletin, 96,* 227–246.

Freedman, J. L. (1992). Television violence and aggression: What psychologists should tell the public. In P. Suedfeld & P. E. Tetlock (Eds.), *Psychology and social policy* (pp. 179–189). New York: Hemisphere Publishing.

French, J. L., & Hale, R. L. (1990). A history of the development of psychological and educational testing. In C. R. Reynolds & R. W. Kamphaus (Eds.), *Handbook of psychological and educational assessment of children: Intelligence and achievement* (pp. 3–28). New York: Guilford Press.

French, S. A., Perry, C. L., Leon, G. R., & Fulkerson, J. A. (1994). Food preferences, eating patterns, and physical activity among adolescents: Correlates of eating disorders. *Journal of Adolescent Health, 15,* 286–294.

French, V. (1977). History of the child's influence: Ancient Mediterranean civilizations. In R. Q. Bell & L. V. Harper (Eds.), *Child effects on adults* (pp. 3–29). Hillsdale, NJ: Erlbaum.

Freud, S. (1909/1953). Analysis of a phobia in a five-year-old boy. In J. Strachey (Ed.), *The standard edition of the complete psychological works of Sigmund Freud* (Vol. 10, pp. 3–149). London: Hogarth Press.

Freud, S. (1955). *Analysis of a phobia in a five-year-old boy.* London: Hogarth Press. (Original work published 1909)

Freud, S. (1991). Civilization and its discontents. In J. Strachey (Ed. and Trans.), *The standard edition of the complete psychological works of Sigmund Freud* (Vol. 21, pp. 57–146). London: Hogarth Press. (Original work published 1930)

Frick, P. J. (1993). Childhood conduct problems in a family context. *School Psychology Review, 22,* 376–385.

Frick, P. J. (in press). Callous-unemotional traits and conduct problems: Applying the two-factor model of psychopathy to children. In D. J. Cooke, A. Forth, & R. D. Hare (Eds.), *Psychopathy: Theory, research, and implications for society.* Dordresch, Netherlands: Kluwer Press.

Frick, P. J., & Hare, R. (1997). *The psychopathy screening device.* Toronto: Multi-Health Systems.

Frick, P. J., & Jackson, Y. K. (1993). Family functioning and childhood antisocial behavior: Yet another reinterpretation. *Journal of Clinical Child Psychology, 22,* 410–419.

Frick, P. J., Kamphaus, R. W., Lahey, B. B., Christ, M. A. G., Hart, E. L., & Tannenbaum, T. E. (1991). Academic underachievement and the disruptive behavior disorders. *Journal of Consulting and Clinical Psychology, 59,* 289–294.

Frick, P. J., Lahey, B. B., Loeber, R., Stouthamer-Loeber, M., Christ, M. A. G., & Hanson, K. (1992). Familial risk factors to oppositional defiant disorder and conduct disorder:

Parental psychopathology and maternal parenting. *Journal of Consulting and Clinical Psychology, 60,* 49–55.

Frick, P. J., Lahey, B. B., Loeber, R., Tannenbaum, L, Van Horn, Y, Christ, M. A. G., Hart, E. L., & Hanson, K. (1993). Oppositional defiant disorder and conduct disorder: A meta-analytic review of factor analyses and cross-validation in a clinic sample. *Clinical Psychology Review, 13,* 319–340.

Frick, P. J., O'Brien, B. S., Wootton, J. M., & McBurnett, K. (1994). Psychopathy and conduct problems in children. *Journal of Abnormal Psychology, 103,* 700–707.

Friedman, A. G., & Mulhern, R. K. (1992). Psychological aspects of childhood cancer. In B. B. Lahey & A. E. Kazdin (Eds.), *Advances in Clinical Child Psychology* (Vol. 14, pp. 165–189). New York: Plenum.

Friedman, H. S., Tucker, J. S., Schwartz, J. E., Tomlinson-Keasey, C., Martin, L. R., Wingard, D. L., & Criqui, M. H. (1995). Psychosocial and behavioral predictors of longevity: The aging and death of the "termites." *American Psychologist, 50,* 69–78.

Friedman, J., & Burley, S. K. (1995). *Leptin helps body regulate fat, links to diet* [On-line]. Available: http://www.rockefeller.edu/pubinfo/leptinlevel.nr.html. Rockefeller University and Howard Hughes Medical Institute Press Release.

Friedman, J., & Maffei, M. (1995). *Fat, body weight regulated by newly discovered hormone* [On-line]. Available: http://www.rockefeller.edu/pubinfo/ob.rel.nr.html. Rockefeller University andHoward Hughes Medical Institute Press Release.

Friedrich, W., Jaworski, T., Huxsahl, J., & Bengston, B. (1997). Dissociative and sexual behaviors in children and adolescents with sexual abuse and psychiatric histories. *Journal of Interpersonal Violence, 12,* 155–171.

Friman, P. C., Larzelere, R., & Finney, J. W. (1994). Exploring the relationship between thumbsucking and psychopathology. *Journal of Pediatric Psychology, 19,* 431–441.

Frith, C., & Frith, U. (1996). A biological marker for dyslexia. *Nature, 382,* 19–20.

Frith, U. (1989). *Autism: Explaining the enigma.* Oxford, England: Basil Blackwell.

Frith, U. (1993, June). Autism. *Scientific American,* pp. 108–114.

Frith, U. (1997). Autism. *Scientific American* [Special Issue], pp. 92–98.

Frith, U., & Happe, F. (1994). Autism: Beyond "theory of mind." *Cognition, 50,* 115–132.

Fritz, G. K., Fritsch, S., & Hagino, O. (1997). Somatoform disorders in children and adolescents: A review of the past 10 years. *Journal of the American Academy of Child and Adolescent Psychiatry, 36,* 1329–1338.

Frost, R. (1998). Toward a strong phonological theory of visual word recognition: True issues and false trails. *Psychological Bulletin, 123,* 71–99.

Fultz, S. A., & Rojahn, J. (1988). Pica. In M. Hersen & C. Last (Eds.), *Child behavior therapy casebook* (pp. 303–316). New York: Plenum.

Fuster, J. M. (1989). *The prefrontal cortex.* New York: Raven.

Gabel, S., & Shindledecker, R. (1993). Characteristics of children whose parents have been incarcerated. *Hospital and Community Psychiatry, 44,* 656–660.

Gadow, K. D. (1991). Clinical issues in child and adolescent psychopharmacology. *Journal of Consulting and Clinical Psychology, 59,* 842–852.

Gadow, K. D., & Pomeroy, J. C. (1993). Pediatric psychopharmacotherapy: A clinical perspective. In T. R. Kratochwill & R. J. Morris (Eds.), *Handbook of psychotherapy with children and adolescents* (pp. 356–401). Needham Heights, MA: Allyn & Bacon.

Gadow, K. D., & Sprafkin, J. (1993). Television "violence" and children with emotional and behavioral disorders. *Journal of Emotional and Behavioral Disorders, 1,* 54–63.

Gagnon, M., & Ladouceur, R. (1992). Behavioral treatment of child stutterers. Replication and extension. *Behavior Therapy, 23,* 113–129.

Gaines, R., Sandgrund, A., Green, A. H., & Power, E. (1978). Etiological factors in child maltreatment: A multivariate study of abusing, neglecting, and normal mothers. *Journal of Abnormal Psychology, 87,* 531–540.

Galaburda, A. M., Sherman, G. F., Rosen, G. D., & Geschwind, A. F. (1985). Developmental dyslexia: Four consecutive patients with cortical anomalies. *Annals of Neurology, 18,* 222–223.

Gallup Organization. (1995). *Disciplining children in America: A Gallup poll report.* Princeton, NJ: Author.

Garbarino, J., Guttman, E., & Seeley, J. (1986). *The psychologically battered child.* San Francisco: Jossey-Bass.

Garber, J. (1984). Classification of childhood psychopathology: A developmental perspective. *Child Development, 55,* 30–48.

Garber, J. (1992). Cognitive models of depression: A developmental perspective. *Psychological Inquiry, 3,* 235–240.

Garber, J., Braafladt, N., & Zeman, J. (1991). The regulation of sad affect: An information-processing perspective. In J. Garber & K. Dodge (Eds.), *The development of emotion regulation and dysregulation* (pp. 208–240). New York: Cambridge University Press.

Garber, J., & Hilsman, R. (1992). Cognition, stress, and depression in children and adolescents. *Child and Adolescent Psychiatric Clinics of North America, 1,* 129–167.

Garber, J., Weiss, B., & Shanley, N. (1993). Cognitions, depressive symptoms, and development in adolescents. *Journal of Abnormal Psychology, 102,* 47–57.

Gard, M. C. E., & Freeman, C. P. (1996). The dismantling of a myth: A review of eating disorders and socioeconomic status. *International Journal of Eating Disorders, 20,* 1–12.

Gardner, H. (1993). *Multiple intelligences: The theory in practice.* New York: Basic Books.

Garfinkel, P. E., & Garner, D. M. (1982). *Anorexia nervosa: A multidimensional perspective.* New York: Brunner/Mazel.

Garfinkel, P. E., Lin, E., Goergin, P., Spegg, C., Goldbloom, D. S., Kennedy, S., Kaplan, A. S., & Woodside, D. B. (1995). Bulimia nervosa in a Canadian community sample: Prevalence and comparison of subgroups. *American Journal of Psychiatry, 152,* 1052–1058.

Garmezy, N. (1983). Stressors of childhood. In N. Garmezy & M. Rutter (Eds.), *Stress, coping, and development in children* (pp. 43–84). New York: McGraw-Hill.

Garmezy, N. (1991). Resiliency and vulnerability to adverse developmental outcomes associated with poverty. *American Behavioral Scientist, 34,* 416–430.

Garn, S. M., & Clark, D. C. (1976). Trends in fatness and the origins of obesity: Ad hoc committee to review the ten-state nutrition survey. *Pediatrics, 57,* 443–456.

Garnefski, N., & Diekstra, R. F. W. (1997). Child sexual abuse and emotional and behavioral problems in adolescence: Gender differences. *Journal of the American Academy of Child and Adolescent Psychiatry, 36,* 323–329.

Garner, D. M. (1993a). Binge eating in anorexia nervosa. In C. G. Fairburn & G. T. Wilson (Eds.), *Binge eating: Nature, assessment and treatment* (pp. 50–76). New York: Guilford Press.

Garner, D. M. (1993b). Pathogenesis of anorexia nervosa. *Lancet, 341,* 1631–1635.

Garner, D. M. (1997). Psychoeducational principles in treatment. In D. M. Garner and P. E. Garfinkel (Eds.), *Handbook of treatment for eating disorders* (2nd ed., pp. 145–177). New York: Guilford Press.

Garner, D. M., & Fairburn, C. G. (1988). Relationship between anorexia nervosa and bulimia nervosa: Diagnostic implications. In D. M. Garner & P. E. Garfinkel (Eds.), *Diagnostic issues in anorexia nervosa and bulimia nervosa.* New York: Brunner/Mazel.

Garner, D. M., & Needleman, L. D. (1997). Sequencing and integration of treatments. In D. M. Garner and P. E. Garfinkel (Eds.), *Handbook of treatment for eating disorders* (2nd ed., pp. 50–63). New York: Guilford Press.

Garner, D. M., & Wooley, S. C. (1991). Confronting the failure of behavioral and dietary treatments for obesity. *Clinical Psychology Review, 11,* 729–780.

Garrison, W. T., & McQuiston, S. (1989). *Chronic illness during childhood and adolescence: Psychological aspects.* Newbury Park, CA: Sage.

Gaub, M., & Carlson, C. L. (1997a). Behavioral characteristics of DSM-IV subtypes in a school-based population. *Journal of Abnormal Child Psychology, 25,* 103–111.

Gaub, M., & Carlson, C. L. (1997b). Gender differences in ADHD: A meta-analysis and critical review. *Journal of the American Academy of Child and Adolescent Psychiatry, 36,* 1036–1045.

Ge, X., Conger, R. D., Lorenz, F. O., Shanahan, M., & Elder, G. H., Jr. (1995). Mutual influences in parent and adolescent distress. *Developmental Psychology, 31,* 406–419.

Ge, X., Conger, R. D., Lorenz, F. O., & Simons, R. L. (1994). Parents' stressful life events and adolescent depressed mood. *Journal of Health and Social Behavior, 35,* 28–44.

Gelb, S. A. (1995, February). The beast in man: Degenerationism and mental retardation, 1900–1920. *Mental Retardation, 33,* 1–9.

Gelfand, D. M., & Hartmann, D. P. (1984). *Child behavior analysis and therapy* (2nd ed.). New York: Pergamon Press.

Geller, B. (1997, March). *Double-blind placebo-controlled study of lithium for adolescents with comorbid bipolar and substance dependency disorders.* Paper presented at the mid-year meeting of the American Academy of Child and Adolescent Psychiatry, Hamilton, Bermuda.

Geller, B., & Luby, J. (1997). Child and adolescent bipolar disorder: A review of the past 10 years. *Journal of the American Academy of Child and Adolescent Psychiatry, 36,* 1168–1176.

Geller, B., Sun, K., Zimerman, B., Luby, J., Frazier, J., & Williams, M. (1995). Complex and rapid cycling in bipolar children and adolescents. *Journal of Affective Disorders, 34,* 259–268.

Geller, V., Fox, L. W., & Clark, K. A. (1994). Rate and predictors of prepubertal bipolarity during follow-up of 6- to 12-year-old children. *Journal of American Academy of Child and Adolescent Psychiatry, 33,* 461–468.

Gelles, R. J. (1983). An exchange/social control theory. In D. Finkelhor, R. J. Gelles, G. T. Hotaling, & M. A. Straus (Eds.), *The dark side of families* (pp. 151–165). Beverly Hills, CA: Sage.

Gelles, R. J., & Straus, M. A. (1988). *Intimate Violence.* New York: Simon & Schuster.

Gelman, D. (1989, March 27). Haunted by their habits. *Newsweek,* pp. 71–72, 75.

Gena, A., Krantz, P. J., McClannahan, L. E., & Poulson, C. L. (1996). Training and generalization of affective behavior displayed by youth with autism. *Journal of Applied Behavior Analysis, 29,* 291–304.

George, M. S., Ketter, T. A., Parekh, P. I., Herscovitch, P., & Post, R. M. (1996). Gender differences in regional cerebral blood flow during transient self-induced sadness or happiness. *Biological Psychiatry, 40,* 859–871.

Gersten, R. M., White, W. A. T., Falco, R., & Carnine, D. (1982). Teaching basic discriminations to handicapped and non-handicapped individuals through a dynamic presentation of instructional stimuli. *Analysis and Intervention in Developmental Disabilities, 2,* 305–317.

Giaconia, R. M., Reinherz, H. Z., Silverman, A. B., Pakiz, B., Frost, A. K., & Cohen, E. (1994). Ages of onset of psychiatric disorders in a community population of older adolescents. *Journal of the American Academy of Child and Adolescent Psychiatry, 33,* 706–717.

Gibson, D. (1966). Early developmental staging as a prophesy index in Down's syndrome. *American Journal of Mental Deficiency, 70,* 825–828.

Giedd, J. N., Castellanos, F. X., Casey, B. J., Kozuch, P., King, A. C., Hamburger, S. D., & Rapoport, J. L. (1994). Quantitative morphology of the corpus callosum in attention deficit hyperactivity disorder. *American Journal of Psychiatry, 151,* 665–669.

Gil, K. M., Williams, D. A., Thompson, R. J., Jr., & Kinney, T. R. (1991). Sickle cell disease in children and adolescents: The relation of child and parent pain coping strategies to adjustment. *Journal of Pediatric Psychology, 16,* 643–663.

Gilger, J. W., Pennington, B. F., & DeFries, J. C. (1992). A twin study of the etiology of comorbidity: Attention-deficit hyperactivity disorder and dyslexia. *Journal of the American Academy of Child and Adolescent Psychiatry, 321,* 343–348.

Gill, M., Daly, G., Heron, S., Hawi, Z., & Fitzgerald, M. (1997). Confirmation of a dissociation between attention deficit hyperactivity disorder and a dopamine transporter polymorphism. *Biological Psychiatry, 2,* 311–313.

Gillberg, C. (1995). Endogenous opioids and opiate antagonists in autism: Brief review of empirical findings and implications for clinicians. *Developmental Medicine and Child Neurology, 37,* 239–245.

Gillberg, C., & Coleman, M. (1992). *The biology of the autistic syndromes* (2nd ed.). London: MacKeith.

Gillis, J., Gilger, J., Pennington, B., & DeFries, J. C. (1992). Attention deficit disorder in reading disabled twins: Evidence for a genetic etiology. *Journal of Abnormal Child Psychology, 20,* 303–315.

Ginsberg, S. (1996). *Family wisdom: The 2,000 most important things ever said about parenting, children, and family life.* New York: Columbia University Press.

Ginsburg, G., & Silverman, W. (1996). Phobic and anxiety disorders in Hispanic and Caucasian youth. *Journal of Anxiety Disorders, 10,* 517–528.

Ginsburg, G. S., Silverman, W. K., & Kurtines, W. K. (1995). Family involvement in treating children with phobic and anxiety disorders: A look ahead. *Clinical Psychology Review, 15,* 457–473.

Gittelman, R., & Eskinazi, B. (1983). Lead and hyperactivity revisited. *Archives of General Psychiatry, 40,* 827–833.

Gittelman, R., Mannuzza, S., Shenker, R., & Bonagura, N. (1985). Hyperactive boys almost grown up: I. Psychiatric status. *Archives of General Psychiatry, 42,* 937–947.

Gittelman-Klein, R. (1986). Questioning the clinical usefulness of projective psychological tests for children. *Developmental and Behavioral Pediatrics, 7,* 378–382.

Gladstone, T. R. G., & Kaslow, N. J. (1995). Depression and attributions in children and adolescents: A meta-analytic review. *Journal of Abnormal Child Psychology, 23,* 597–606.

Glicklich, L. B. (1951). An historical account of enuresis. *Pediatrics, 8,* 859–876.

Glow, P. H., & Glow, R. A. (1979). Hyperkinetic impulse disorder: A developmental defect of motivation. *Genetic Psychological Monographs, 100,* 159–231.

Goldberg, L. R. (1992). The development of markers for the big-five factor structure. *Psychological Assessment, 4,* 26–42.

Goldberg, S., Gotowiec, A., & Simmons, R. J. (1995). Infant-mother attachment and behavior problems in healthy and medically compromised preschoolers. *Development and Psychopathology, 7,* 267–282.

Goldblatt, P. B., Moore, M. E., & Stunkard, A. J. (1965). Social factors in obesity. *Journal of the American Medical Association, 192,* 1039–1044.

Goldentyer, T. (1994). *Gangs.* Austin, TX: Steck-Vaughn.

Goldfield, A., & Chrisler, J. C. (1995). Body stereotyping and stigmatization of obese persons by first graders. *Perceptual and Motor Skills, 81,* 909–910.

Goldstein, D. J., Wilson, M. G., Thompson, V. L., Potvin, J. H., Rampey, A. H., & the Fluoxetine Bulimia Nervosa Research Group. (1995). Long-term fluoxetine treatment of bulimia nervosa. *British Journal of Psychiatry, 166,* 660–666.

Gomez, R., & Sanson, A. V. (1994). Mother-child interactions and noncompliance in hyperactive boys with and without conduct problems. *Journal of Child Psychology and Psychiatry, 35,* 477–490.

Gonzalez, J. C., Routh, D. K., & Armstrong, F. D. (1993). Effects of maternal distraction versus reassurances on children's reactions to injections. *Journal of Pediatric Psychology, 18,* 593–604.

Goode, S., Rutter, M., & Howlin, P. (1994). *A twenty-year follow-up of children with autism.* Paper presented at the 13th biennial meeting of the ISSBD, Amsterdam, the Netherlands.

Goodman, K. (1986). *What's whole about whole language?* Portsmouth, NH: Heinemann.

Goodwin, F. K., & Jamison, K. R. (1990). *Manic-depressive illness.* New York: Oxford.

Goodyear, P., & Hynd, G. (1992). Attention-deficit disorder with (ADD/H) and without (ADD/WO) hyperactivity: Behavioral and neuropsychological differentiation. *Journal of Clinical Child Psychology, 21,* 273–305.

Goodyer, I. M., & Cooper, P. (1993). A community study of depression in adolescent girls: II. The clinical features of identified disorder. *British Journal of Psychiatry, 163,* 374–380.

Goodyer, I. M., Germany, E., Gowrusankur, J., & Altham, P. (1991). Social influences on the course of anxious and depressive disorders in school-age children. *British Journal of Psychiatry, 158,* 676–684.

Goodyer, I. M., Herbert, J., Tamplin, A., Secher, S. M., & Pearson, J. (1997). Short-term outcome of major depression: II. Life events, family dysfunction, and friendship difficulties as predictors of persistent disorder. *Journal of the American Academy of Child and Adolescent Psychiatry, 36,* 474–480.

Gordon, C. T., Frazier, J. A., McKenna, K., Giedd, J., Zametkin, A., Zahn, T., Hommer, D., Hong, W., Kaysen, D., Albus, K. E., & Rapoport, J. L. (1994). Childhood-onset schizophrenia: An NIMH study in progress. *Schizophrenia Bulletin, 20,* 697–712.

Gordon, C. T., Krasnewich, D., White, B., Lenane, M., & Rapoport, J. L. (1994). Translocation involving chromosomes 1 and 7 in a boy with childhood-onset schizophrenia. *Journal of Autism and Developmental Disorders, 24,* 537–545.

Gordon-Walker, J., Johnson, S., Manion, I., & Cloutier, P. (1996). Emotionally focused marital intervention for couples with chronically ill children. *Journal of Consulting and Clinical Psychology, 64,* 1029–1036.

Gorman-Smith, D., Tolan, H., Zelli, A., & Huesmann, L. R. (1996). The relation of family functioning to violence among inner-city minority youths. *Journal of Family Psychology, 10,* 115–129.

Gortmaker, S. L. (1985). Demography of chronic childhood diseases. In N. Hobbs & J. M. Perrin (Eds.), *Issues in the care of children with chronic illness: A sourcebook of problems, services, and policies* (pp. 135–154). San Francisco: Jossey-Bass.

Gortmaker, S. L., Dietz, W. H., Sobol, A. M., Wehler, C. A. (1987). Increasing pediatric obesity in the United States. *American Journal of Diseases of Children, 141,* 535–540.

Gortmaker, S. L., Perrin, J. N., Sobol, A. N., & Dietz, W. H. (1993). Social and economic consequences of overweight in adolescence and young adulthood. *The New England Journal of Medicine, 329,* 1008–1113.

Gortmaker, S. L., & Sappenfield, W. (1984). Chronic childhood disorders: Prevalence and impact. *Pediatric Clinics of North America, 31,* 3–18.

Gortmaker, S. L., Walker, D. K., Weitzman, M., & Sobol, A. M. (1990). Chronic conditions, socioeconomic risks and behavioral problems in children and adolescents. *Pediatrics, 85,* 267–276.

Gotlib, I. H., & Hammen, C. L. (1992). *Psychological aspects of depression: Toward a cognitive-interpersonal integration.* London: Wiley.

Gotlib, I. H., Lewinsohn, P. M., & Seeley. J. R. (1995). Symptoms versus a diagnosis of depression: Differences in psychosocial functioning. *Journal of Consulting and Clinical Psychology, 63,* 90–100.

Gotlib, I. H., Lewinsohn, P. M., Seeley, J. R., Rohde, P., & Redner, J. E. (1993). Negative cognitions and attributional style in depressed adolescents: An examination of stability and specificity. *Journal of Abnormal Psychology, 102,* 607–615.

Gottesman, I., & Goldsmith, H. (1994). Developmental psychopathology of antisocial behavior: Inserting genes into its ontogenesis and epigenesis. In C. A. Nelson (Ed.), *Threats to optimal development: Integrating biological, psychological, and social risk factors* (Vol. 27, pp. 69–104). Hillsdale, NJ: Erlbaum.

Gottfredson, D. C., Gottfredson, G. D., & Hybel, L. G. (1993). Managing adolescent behavior: A multi-year, multi-school study. *American Educational Research Journal, 30,* 179–215.

Gould, M. S., Fisher, P., Parides, M., Flory, M., & Shaffer, D.

(1996). Psychosocial risk factors of child and adolescent completed suicide. *Archives of General Psychiatry, 53,* 1155–1162.

Gowers, S., Norton, K., Halek, C., & Crisp, A. H. (1994). Outcome of outpatient psychotherapy in a random allocation treatment study of anorexia nervosa. *International Journal of Eating Disorders, 15,* 165–177.

Graber, J. A., Brooks-Gunn, J., Paikoff, R. L., & Warren, M. P. (1994). Prediction of eating problems: An 8-year study of adolescent girls. *Developmental Psychology, 30,* 823–834.

Graetz, B., & Schute, R. (1995). Assessment of peer relationships in children with asthma. *Journal of Pediatric Psychology, 20,* 205–216.

Graham, P., & Rutter, M. (1973). Psychiatric disorders in the young adolescent: A follow-up study. *Proceedings of the Royal Society of Medicine, 66,* 1226–1229.

Graham, S., Hudley, C., & Williams, E. (1992). Attributional and emotional determinants of aggression among African-American and Latino young adolescents. *Developmental Psychology, 28,* 731–740.

Graham, S., MacArthur, C., Schwartz, S., & Voth, T. (1992). Improving LD student's compositions using a strategy involving product and process goal-setting. *Exceptional Children, 58,* 322–334.

Grattan, L. M., & Eslinger, P. J. (1991). Frontal lobe damage in children and adults: A comparative review. *Developmental Neuropsychology, 7,* 283–326.

Gray, J. A. (1982). *The neuropsychology of anxiety: An inquiry into the functions of the septo-hippocampal system.* New York: Oxford University Press.

Gray, J. A. (1985). Issues in the neuropsychology of anxiety. In A. H. Tuma & J. Dmaser (Eds.), *Anxiety and the anxiety disorders* (pp. 5–25). Hillsdale, NJ: Erlbaum.

Gray, J. A. (1987). *The psychology of fear and stress* (2nd ed.). New York: Cambridge University Press.

Graziano, A. M., & Mooney, K. C. (1984). *Children and behavior therapy.* New York: Aldine.

Green, W. H., Campbell, M., & David, R. (1984). Psychosocial dwarfism: A critical review of the evidence. *Journal of the American Academy of Child Psychiatry, 23,* 39–48.

Greenberg, H. S., Kazak, A., & Meadows, A. T. (1989). Psychologic functioning in 8- to 18-year-old cancer survivors and their parents. *Journal of Pediatrics, 114,* 488–493.

Greenberg, M. T., DeKlyen, M., Speltz, M. L., & Endriga, M. C. (1997). The role of attachment processes in externalizing psychopathology in young children. In L. Atkinson & K. J. Zucker (Eds.), *Attachment and psychopathology* (pp. 196–222). New York: Guilford Press.

Greenberg, M. T., Speltz, M. L., & DeKlyen, M. (1993). The role of attachment in the early development of disruptive behavior problems. *Development and Psychopathology, 5,* 191–213.

Greenberg, M. T., Speltz, M. L., DeKlyen, M., & Endriga, M. C. (1991). Attachment security in preschoolers with and without externalizing behavior problems: A replication. *Development and Psychopathology, 3,* 413–430.

Greene, R. W., Biederman, J., Faraone, S. V., Ouellette, C. A., Courtney, P., & Griffin, S. M. (1996). Toward a new psychometric definition of social disability in children with attention-deficit hyperactivity disorder. *Journal of the American Academy of Child and Adolescent Psychiatry, 35,* 571–578.

Greene, R. W., Biederman, J., Faraone, S. V., Sienna, M., & Garcia-Jetton, J. (1997). Adolescent outcome of boys with attention-deficit/hyperactivity disorder and social disability: Results from a 4-year longitudinal follow-up study. *Journal of Consulting and Clinical Psychology, 65,* 758–767.

Greenspan, S. I. (1981). *The clinical interview of the child.* New York: McGraw-Hill.

Greenspan, S. I., & Wieder, S. (1994). Diagnostic classification of mental health and developmental disorders of infancy and early childhood. *Zero to Three, 14,* 34–41.

Greey, M. (1995, November). Special families, special needs: The rigours and rewards of raising children with disabilities. *Today's Parent,* 96–106.

Gresham, F. M., & Macmillan, D. L. (1997a). Autistic recovery? An analysis and critique of the empirical evidence. *Behavioral Disorders, 22,* 185–201.

Gresham, F. M., & Macmillan, D. L. (1997b). Denial and defensiveness in the place of fact and reason: Rejoinder to Smith and Lovaas. *Behavioral Disorders, 22,* 219–230.

Grinspoon, L., & Singer, S. B. (1973). Amphetamines in the treatment of hyperkinetic children. *Harvard Educational Review, 43,* 515–555.

Grisso, T., Baldwin, E., Blanck, P. D., Rotheram-Borus, M. J., Schooler, N. R., & Thompson, T. (1991). Standards in research: APA's mechanism for monitoring the challenges. *American Psychologist, 46,* 758–766.

Grogan, D., & Bane, V. (1995, September 1). In touch at last. *People,* pp. 42–44.

Gross, M. D. (1995). Origin of stimulant use for treatment of Attention Deficit Disorder. *American Journal of Psychiatry, 152,* 298–299.

Gross-Tsur, V., Shalev, R. S., & Amir, N. (1991). Attention deficit disorder: Association with familial-genetic factors. *Pediatric Neurology, 7,* 258–261.

Grych, J. H., & Fincham, F. D. (1993). Children's appraisals of marital conflict: Initial investigations of the cognitive-contextual framework. *Child Development, 64,* 215–230.

Guerra, N. G., Huesmann, L. R., Tolan, P. H., Van-Acker, R., & Eron, L. D. (1995). Stressful events and individual beliefs as correlates of economic disadvantage and aggression among urban children. *Journal of Consulting and Clinical Psychology, 63,* 518–528.

Guerra, N. G., Tolan, P. H., Huesmann, L. R., Van Acker, R., & Eron, L. D. (1995). Stressful events and individual beliefs as correlates of economic disadvantage and aggression among urban children. *Journal of Consulting and Clinical Psychology, 63,* 518–528.

Guralnick, M. J., Connor, R. T., Hammond, M., Gottman, J. M., & Kinnish, K. (1995). Immediate effects of mainstreamed settings on the social integration of preschool children. *American Journal of Mental Retardation, 100,* 359–377.

Guralnick, M. J., Connor, R. T., Hammond, M. A., Gottman, J. M., & Kinnish, K. (1996). The peer relations of preschool children with communication disorders. *Child Development, 67,* 471–489.

Gurley, D., Cohen, P., Pine, D. S., & Brook, J. (1996). Discriminating depression and anxiety in youth: A role for diagnostic criteria. *Journal of Affective Disorders, 39,* 191–200.

Gurman, A. S., & Kniskern, D. P. (Eds.). (1991). *Handbook of family therapy* (Vol. 2). New York: Brunner/Mazel.

Guskin, S. L., Bartel, N. R., & MacMillan, D. L. (1975). Perspective of the labeled child. In N. Hobbs (Ed.), *Issues in the classification of children* (Vol. 2, pp. 185–212). San Francisco: Jossey-Bass.

Gzowski, P. (1993, April). Gzowski's Canada: Extraordinary guests. *Canadian Living*, p. 91.

Habler, F. (1992). The hyperkinetic child: A historical overview. *Acta Paedopsychiatrica, 55*, 147–149.

Hadwin, J., Frost, S., French, C. C., & Richards, A. (1997). Cognitive processing and trait anxiety in typically developing children: Evidence for an interpretation bias. *Journal of Abnormal Psychology, 106*, 486–490.

Haenlein, M., & Caul, W. F. (1987). Attention deficit disorder with hyperactivity: A specific hypothesis of reward dysfunction. *Journal of the American Academy of Child and Adolescent Psychiatry, 26*, 356–362.

Hagberg, B. (1995). Clinical delineation of Rett Syndrome variants. *Neuropediatrics, 26*, 62.

Hagberg, B., Hagberg, G., Lewerth, A., & Lindberg, U. (1981). Mild mental retardation in Swedish school children: II. Etiological and pathogenetic aspects. *Acta Paediatrica Scandinavica, 70*, 445–452.

Hagerty, B. K. (1984). Psychiatric–mental health assessment. St. Louis, MO: Mosby.

Hallahan, D. P., Kauffman, J., & Lloyd, J. (1996). *Introduction to learning disabilities*. Needham Heights, MA: Allyn & Bacon.

Hallowell, E. M., & Ratey, J. J. (1994). *Answers to distraction*. New York: Pantheon Books.

Halmi, K. A. (1985). Classification of the eating disorders. *Journal of Psychiatric Research, 19*, 113–119.

Halperin, J. M., Matier, K., Bedi, G., Sharma, V., & Newcorn, J. H. (1992). Specificity of inattention, impulsivity, and hyperactivity to the diagnosis of attention-deficit hyperactivity disorder. *Journal of the American Academy of Child and Adolescent Psychiatry, 31*, 190–196.

Halperin, J. M., & McKay, K. E. (1998). Psychological testing for child and adolescent psychiatrists: A review of the past 10 years. *Journal of the American Academy of Child and Adolescent Psychiatry, 37*, 575–584.

Halpern, A. S., Lehmann, J. P., Irvin, L. K., & Heiry, T. J. (1982). *Contemporary assessment for mentally retarded adolescents and adults*. Baltimore: University Park Press.

Hamalainen, M., & Pulkkinen, L. (1996). Problem behavior as a precursor of male criminality. *Development and Psychopathology, 8*, 443–455.

Hammen, C. (1991). *Depression runs in families: The social context of risk and resilience in children of depressed mothers*. New York: Springer-Verlag.

Hammen, C. (1992). Cognitive, life stress, and interpersonal approaches to a developmental psychopathology model of depression. *Development and Psychopathology, 4*, 191–208.

Hammen, C., Burge, D., Burney, E., & Adrian, C. (1990). Longitudinal study of diagnoses in children of women with unipolar and bipolar affective disorder. *Archives of General Psychiatry, 47*, 1112–1117.

Hammen, C., & Compas, B. E. (1994). Unmasking unmasked depression in children and adolescents: The problem of comorbidity. *Clinical Psychology Review, 14*, 585–603.

Hammen, C., & Rudolph, K. D. (1996). Childhood depression. In E. J. Mash & R. A. Barkley (Eds.), *Child psychopathology* (pp. 153–195). New York: Guilford Press.

Hammill, D. D. (1993). A brief look at the learning disabilities movement in the United States. *Journal of Learning Disabilities, 26*, 295–310.

Hancock, L. (1996, February 19). Why do schools flunk biology? *Newsweek*, pp. 58–59.

Hancock, L. (1996, March 18). Mother's little helper. *Newsweek*, pp. 51–56.

Handen, B. L., Breaux, A. M., Janosky, J., McAuliffe, S., Feldman, S., & Gosling, A. (1992). Effects and noneffects of methylphenidate in children with mental retardation and ADHD. *Journal of the American Academy of Child and Adolescent Psychiatry, 31*, 455–461.

Handen, B. L., McAuliffe, S., Janosky, J., Feldman, H., & Breaux, A. M. (1994). Classroom behavior and children with mental retardation: Comparison of children with and without ADHD. *Journal of Abnormal Child Psychology, 22*, 267–280.

Hankin, B. L., Abramson, L. Y., Moffitt, T. E., Silva, P. A., McGee, R., & Andell, K. E. (1998). Development of depression from preadolescence to young adulthood: Emerging gender differences in a 10-year longitudinal study. *Journal of Abnormal Psychology, 107*, 128–140.

Hanna, G. (1995). Demographic and clinical features of obsessive-compulsive disorder in children and adolescents. *Journal of the American Academy of Child and Adolescent Psychiatry, 34*, 19–27.

Hannaway, P. (1978). Failure to thrive: A study of 100 infants and children. *Clinical Pediatrics, 9*, 69–99.

Hansen, D. E., & Vandenberg, B. (1997). Neuropsychological features and differential diagnosis of sleep apnea syndrome in children. *Journal of Clinical Child Psychology, 26*, 304–310.

Hansen, D. J., Warner-Rogers, J. E., & Hecht, D. B. (1998). Implementing and evaluating an individualized behavioral intervention program for maltreating families. In J. R. Lutzker (Ed.), *Handbook of child abuse research and treatment* (pp. 133–158). New York: Plenum.

Hanson, C. L., Henggeler, S. W., & Burghen, G. A. (1987). Social competence and parental support as mediators of the link between stress and metabolic control in adolescents with insulin-dependent diabetes mellitus. *Journal of Consulting and Clinical Psychology, 55*, 529–533.

Hanson, C. L., Henggeler, S. W., Harris, M. A., Burghen, G. A., & Moore, M. (1989). Family system variables and the health status of adolescents with insulin-dependent diabetes mellitus. *Health Psychology, 8*, 239–253.

Happe, F. G. E. (1994a). Current psychological theories of autism: The "theory of mind" account and rival theories. *Journal of Child Psychology and Psychiatry, 35*, 215–230.

Happe, F. G. E. (1994b). Wechsler IQ profile and theory of mind in autism: A research note. *Journal of Child Psychology and Psychiatry, 35*, 1461–1471.

Happe, F. G. E. (1995a). The role of age and verbal ability in the theory of mind task performance of subjects with autism. *Child Development, 66*, 843–855.

Happe, F. G. E. (1995b, March). *Wechsler IQ profile and theory of mind in autism*. Paper presented at the biennial meeting of the Society for Research in Child Development, Indianapolis, IN.

Happe, F. G. E., & Frith, U. (1996). The neuropsychology of autism. *Brain, 119*, 1377–1400.

Harbeck-Weber, C., & Peterson, L. (1996). Health-related disorders. In E. J. Mash & R. A. Barkley (Eds.), *Child psychopathology* (pp. 572–601). New York: Guilford Press.

Hare, R. D. (1993). *Without conscience: The disturbing world of the psychopaths among us*. New York: Pocketbooks.

Hare, R. D., Hart, S. D., & Harpur, T. J. (1991). Psychopathy and the DSM-IV criteria for antisocial personality disorder.

Journal of Abnormal Psychology, 100, 391–398.

Haring, T. G., & Breen, C. G. (1992). A peer-mediated social network intervention to enhance the social integration of persons with moderate and severe disabilities. *Journal of Applied Behavior Analysis, 25*(2), 319–333.

Harlow, H. F., & Harlow, M. K. (1962). Social deprivation in monkeys. *Scientific American, 207,* 136–146.

Harrington, D., Dubowitz, H., Black, M. M., & Binder, A. (1995). Maternal substance use and neglectful parenting: Relations with children's development. *Journal of Clinical Child Psychology, 24,* 258–263.

Harrington, R. C. (1993). *Depressive disorder in childhood and adolescence.* Chichester, England: Wiley.

Harrington, R. C., Fudge, H., Rutter, M., Bredenkamp, D., Groothues, C., & Pridham, J. (1993). Child and adult depression: A test of continuities with data from a family study. *British Journal of Psychiatry, 162,* 627–633.

Harrington, R. C., Fudge, H., Rutter, M., Pickles, A., & Hill, J. (1990). Adult outcomes of childhood and adolescent depression: Psychiatric status. *Archives of General Psychiatry, 47,* 465–473.

Harrington, R. C., Rutter, M., & Fombonne, E. (1996). Developmental pathways in depression: Multiple meanings, antecedents, and endpoints. *Development and Psychopathology, 8,* 601–616.

Harrington, R. C., & Vostanis, P. (1995). Longitudinal perspectives and affective disorder in children and adolescents. In I. M. Goodyer (Ed.), *The depressed child and adolescent: Developmental and clinical perspectives* (pp. 311–334). London: Cambridge University Press.

Harris, K. R., Wong, B. L., & Keogh, B. K. (Eds.). (1985). Cognitive-behavior modification with children: A critical review of the state of the art [Special issue]. *Journal of Abnormal Child Psychology, 3,* 329–476.

Hart, E. L., Lahey, B. B., Loeber, R., Applegate, B., Frick, P. J. (1996). Developmental change in attention-deficit hyperactivity disorder in boys: A four-year longitudinal study. *Journal of Abnormal Child Psychology, 23,* 729–749.

Hart, S. (1996, January 29). How the brain processes speech. *Time,* p. 37.

Hartman, C. R., & Burgess, A. W. (1989). Sexual abuse of children: Causes and consequences. In D. Cicchetti & V. Carlson, (Eds.), *Child Maltreatment: Theory and research on the causes and consequences of child abuse and neglect* (pp. 95–128). Cambridge, England: Cambridge University Press.

Hartmann, T. (1993). *Attention deficit disorder: A different perception.* Lancaster, PA : Underwood-Miller.

Hartung, C. M., & Widiger, T. A. (1998). Gender differences in the diagnosis of mental disorders. Conclusions and controversies of DSM-IV. *Psychological Bulletin, 123,* 260–278.

Hartup, W. W. (1996). The company they keep: Friendships and their developmental significance. *Child Development, 67,* 1–13.

Haskett, M. E., & Kistner, J. A. (1991). Social interactions and peer perceptions of young physically abused children. *Child Development, 62,* 979–990.

Hatch, M. L., Friedman, S., & Paradis, C. M. (1996). Behavioral treatment of obsessive-compulsive disorder in African Americans. *Cognitive and Behavioral Practice, 3,* 303–315.

Hauri, P. (1982). *The sleep disorders.* Kalamazoo, MI: Upjohn.

Hauser, P., Soler, R., Brucker-Davis, F., & Weintraub, B. D. (1997). Thyroid hormones correlate with symptoms of hyperactivity but not inattention in attention deficit hyper-activity disorder. *Psychoneuroendocrinology, 22,* 107–114.

Hauser, P., Zametkin, A. J., Martinez, P., Vitiello, B., Matochik, J. A., Mixsen, A. J., & Weintraub, B. D. (1993). Attention-deficit hyperactivity disorder in people with generalized resistance to thyroid syndrome. *New England Journal of Medicine, 328,* 997–1001.

Haviland, M. G., Sonne, J. L., & Woods, L. R. (1995). Beyond posttraumatic stress disorder: Object relations and reality testing disturbances in physically and sexually abused adolescents. *Journal of the American Academy of Child and Adolescent Psychiatry, 34,* 1054–1059.

Hawton, K. (1986). *Suicide and attempted suicide among children and adolescents.* Newbury Park, CA: Sage.

Hay, P. J., & Hall, A. (1991). The prevalence of eating disorders in recently admitted psychiatric inpatients. *British Journal of Psychiatry, 159,* 562–565.

Hayman, L. L., Meininger, J. C., Coates, P. M., & Gallagher, P. R. (1995). Nongenetic influences of obesity on risk factors for cardiovascular disease during two phases of development. *Nursing Research, 44,* 277–283.

Haynes, C. F., Cutler, C., Gray, J., & Kempe, R. S. (1984). Hospitalized rates of nonorganic failure to thrive: The scope of the problem and short-term lay health visitor intervention. *Child Abuse and Neglect, 8,* 229–242.

Haynes, R. B. (1976). Strategies for improving compliance: A methodologic analysis and review. In D. L. Sackett and R. B. Haynes (Eds.), *Compliance with therapeutic regimens* (pp. 69–82). Baltimore: Johns Hopkins University Press.

Hayward, C., Killen, J. D., Hammer, L. D., Litt, I. F., Wilson, D. M., Simmonds, B., & Taylor, C. B. (1992). Pubertal stage and panic attack history in sixth- and seventh-grade girls. *American Journal of Psychiatry, 149,* 1239–1243.

Hayward, C., Killen, J. D., Wilson, D. M., & Hammer, L. D. (1997). Psychiatric risk associated with early puberty in adolescent girls. *Journal of the American Academy of Child and Adolescent Psychiatry, 36,* 255–262.

Hazzard, A. (1993). Trauma-related beliefs as mediators of sexual abuse impact in adult women survivors: A pilot study. *Journal of Child Sexual Abuse, 2,* 55–69.

Hazzard, A., Celano, M., Gould, J., Lawry, S., & Webb, C. (1995). Predicting symptomatology and self-blame among child sex abuse victims. *Child Abuse and Neglect, 19,* 707–714.

Health and Welfare Canada. (1988). *The epidemiology of mental retardation* (Cat. No. H39-113/1987E). Ottawa: Supply and Services Canada.

Healy, W., & Bronner, A. F. (1926). *Delinquents and criminals, their making and unmaking: Studies in two American cities* (Judge Baker Foundation Pub. No. 3). New York: Macmillan.

Heatherton, T. F., Mahamedi, F., Striepe, M., Field, A. E., & Keel, P. (1997). A 10-year longitudinal study of body weight, dieting, and eating disorder symptoms. *Journal of Abnormal Psychology, 106,* 117–125.

Heatherton, T. F., Nichols, P., Mahamedi, F., & Keel, P. K. (1995). Body weight, dieting, and eating disorder symptoms among college students 1982 to 1992. *American Journal of Psychiatry, 152,* 1623–1629.

Heatherton, T. F., & Polivy, J. (1992). Chronic dieting and eating disorders: A spiral model. In J. H. Crowther, D. L. Tennenbaum, S. E. Hobfall, & M. A. P. Stephens (Eds.), *The etiology of bulimia nervosa: The individual and familial context* (pp. 133–155). Washington, DC: Hemisphere Publishing.

Hechtman, L. (1994). Genetic and neurobiological aspects of attention deficit hyperactivity disorder: A review. *Journal of Psychiatric Neurosciences, 19,* 193–201.

Hedley, M. (1994). The presentation of gendered conflict in popular movies: Affective stereotypes, cultural sentiments, and men's motivation. *Sex Roles, 31,* 721–740.

Heffernan, K. (1996). Eating disorders and weight concern among lesbians. *International Journal of Eating Disorders, 19,* 127–138.

Heller, T. (1954). About dementia infantalis. *Journal of Nervous and Mental Disease, 119,* 610–616.

Hendren, R. L., Hodde-Vargas, M. S., Vargas, L. A., Orrison, W. W., & Dell, L. (1991). Magnetic resonance imaging of severely disturbed children: A preliminary study. *Journal of the American Academy of Child and Adolescent Psychiatry, 30,* 466–470.

Hendrickson, L. (1996). *Phenomenal talent: The autistic kind.* © Copyright 1996 by Lyndall Hendrickson. (http://www.nexus.edu.au/teachstud/gat/hendric1.htm). Last revised April 17, 1996.

Henggeler, S. W. (1991, April). *Treating conduct problems in children and adolescents: An overview of the multisystemic approach with guidelines for intervention design and implementation.* Division of Children, Adolescents and Their Families, South Carolina Department of Mental Health, Charleston, SC.

Henggeler, S. W. (1992). *Family preservation using multisystemic treatment: A cost-savings strategy for reducing recidivism and institutionalization of serious juvenile offenders.* Department of Psychiatry and Behavioral Sciences, Medical University of South Carolina, Charleston, SC.

Henggeler, S. W. (1996). Treatment of violent juvenile offenders—We have the knowledge: Comment on Gorman-Smith et al. (1996). *Journal of Family Psychology, 10,* 137–141.

Henggeler, S. W., & Borduin, C. M. (1990). *Family therapy and beyond: A multisystemic approach to treating the behavior problems of children and adolescents.* Pacific Grove, CA: Brooks/Cole.

Henggeler, S. W., Melton, G. B., & Smith, L. A. (1992). Family preservation using multisystemic therapy: An effective alternative to incarcerating serious juvenile offenders. *Journal of Consulting and Clinical Psychology, 60,* 953–961.

Henggeler, S. W., & Santos, A. B. (Eds.). (1997). *Innovative approaches for difficult-to-treat populations.* Washington, DC: American Psychiatric Press.

Henggeler, S. W., Schoenwald, S. K., Borduin, C. M., Rowland, M. D., & Cunningham, P. B. (1998). *Multisystemic treatment of antisocial behavior in children and adolescents.* New York: Guilford Press.

Henggeler, S. W., Schoenwald, S. K., & Pickrel, S. G. (1995). Multisystemic therapy: Bridging the gap between university- and community-based treatment. *Journal of Consulting and Clinical Psychology, 63,* 709–717.

Henin, A., & Kendall, P. C. (1997). Obsessive-compulsive disorder in childhood and adolescence. *Advances in Clinical Child Psychology, 19,* 75–131.

Hennessy, K. D., Rabideau, G. J., Cicchetti, D., & Cummings, E. M. (1994). Responses of physically abused children to different forms of interadult anger. *Child Development, 65,* 815–828.

Henry, B., Caspi, A., Moffitt, T. E., & Silva, P. A. (1996). Temperamental and familial predictors of violent and nonviolent criminal convictions: Age 3 to age 18. *Developmental Psychology, 32,* 614–623.

Henry, M. (1996, April 2). *What to do before the diagnostician arrives* [On-line]. Available: http://pie.org/TM/E23783736 35. Orton Dyslexia Society.

Herbert, M. (1991). *Clinical child psychology: Social learning, development and behavior.* Chichester, England: Wiley.

Herman, J. L. (1992). *Trauma and recovery: The aftermath of violence—from domestic abuse to political terror.* New York: Basic Books.

Herman-Stahl, M., & Petersen, A. C. (1996). The protective role of coping and social resources for depressive symptoms among young adolescents. *Journal of Youth and Adolescence, 25,* 733–753.

Herrenkohl, R. C., Herrenkohl, E. C., & Egolf, B. P. (1983). Circumstances surrounding the occurrence of child maltreatment. *Journal of Consulting and Clinical Psychology, 51,* 424–431.

Herrnstein, R. J., & Murray, C. (1994). *The bell curve: Intelligence and class structure in American life.* New York: Free Press.

Herzberger, S. D., Potts, D. A., & Dillon, M. (1981). Abusive and nonabusive parental treatment from the child's perspective. *Journal of Consulting and Clinical Psychology, 49,* 81–90.

Herzog, D. B., Keller, M. B., Sacks, N. R., Yeh, C. J., & Lavori, P. W. (1992). Psychiatric comorbidity in treatment seeking anorexics and bulimics. *Journal of the American Academy of Child and Adolescent Psychiatry, 31,* 810–818.

Herzog, D. B., & Rathbun, J. M. (1982). Childhood depression: Developmental considerations. *American Journal of Diseases of Children, 136,* 115–120.

Hetherington, E. M., Bridges, M., & Insabella, G. M. (1998). What matters? What does not? Five perspectives on the association between marital transitions and children's adjustment. *American Psychologist, 53,* 167–184.

Hetherington, E. M., Reiss, D., & Plomin, R. (Eds.). (1994). *Separate social worlds of siblings: The impact of nonshared environment on development.* Hillsdale, NJ: Erlbaum.

Hewitt, P. L., & Flett, G. L. (1993). Dimensions of perfectionism, daily stress, and depression: A test of the specific vulnerability hypothesis. *Journal of Abnormal Psychology, 102,* 58–65.

Hibbs, E. D., & Jensen, P. S. (Eds.). (1996). *Psychosocial treatments for child and adolescent disorders: Empirically based strategies for clinical practice.* Washington, DC: American Psychological Association.

Hillson, J. M. C., & Kuiper, N. A. (1994). A stress and coping model of child maltreatment. *Clinical Psychology Review, 14,* 261–285.

Hilsman, R., & Garber, J. (1995). A test of the cognitive diathesis-stress model of depression in children: Academic stressors, attributional style, perceived competence, and control. *Journal of Personality and Social Psychology, 69,* 370–380.

Hinden, B. R., Compas, B. E., Howell, D. C., Achenbach, T. M. (1997). Covariation of the anxious-depressed syndrome during adolescence: Separating fact from artifact. *Journal of Consulting and Clinical Psychology, 65,* 6–14.

Hinshaw, S. P. (1987). On the distinction between attentional deficits/hyperactivity and conduct problems/aggression in child psychopathology. *Psychological Bulletin, 101,* 443–463.

Hinshaw, S. P. (1992a). Externalizing behavior problems and academic underachievement in childhood and adolescence: Causal relationships and underlying mechanisms. *Psycho-

logical Bulletin, 111, 127–155.

Hinshaw, S. P. (1992b). Interventions for social competence and social skill. In G. Weiss (Ed.), *Child and adolescent psychiatric clinics of North America* (Vol. 1, 2, October, 539–552). Philadelphia: Saunders.

Hinshaw, S. P. (1994a). *Attention deficits and hyperactivity in children.* Thousand Oaks, CA: Sage.

Hinshaw, S. P. (1994b). Conduct disorder in childhood: Conceptualization, diagnosis, comorbidity, and risk factor for antisocial functioning in adulthood. In D. C. Fowles, P. Sutker, & S. H. Goodman (Eds.), *Progress in experimental personality and psychopathology research* (pp. 3–44). New York: Springer.

Hinshaw, S. P., & Anderson, C. A. (1996). Conduct and oppositional defiant disorders. In E. J. Mash & R. A. Barkley (Eds.), *Child psychopathology* (pp. 113–149). New York: Guilford Press.

Hinshaw, S. P., Herbsman, C., Melnick, S., Nigg, J., & Simmel, C. (1993, February). *Psychological and familial processes in ADHD: Continuous or discontinuous with those in normal comparison children?* Paper presented at the Society for Research in Child and Adolescent Psychopathology, Santa Fe, NM.

Hinshaw, S. P., Lahey, B. B., & Hart, E. L. (1993). Issues of taxonomy and comorbidity in the development of conduct disorder. *Development and Psychopathology, 5,* 31–49.

Hirschi, T., & Gottfredson, M. (1983). Age and the explanation of crime. *American Journal of Sociology, 89,* 552–583.

Hirshfeld, D. R., Biederman, J., Brody, L., & Faraone, S. V. (1997). Associations between expressed emotion and child behavioral inhibition and psychopathology: A pilot study. *Journal of the American Academy of Child and Adolescent Psychiatry, 36,* 205–213.

Hirshfeld, D. R., Biederman, J., & Rosenbaum, J. F. (1997). Expressed emotion toward children with behavioral inhibition: Associations with maternal anxiety disorder. *Journal of the American Academy of Child and Adolescent Psychiatry, 36,* 910–919.

Hirshfeld, D. R., Rosenbaum, J. F., Biederman, J., Bolduc, E. A., Faraone, S. V., Snidman, N., Reznick, J. S., & Kagan, J. (1992). Stable behavioral inhibition and its association with anxiety disorder. *Journal of the American Academy of Child and Adolescent Psychiatry, 31,* 103–111.

Hoagwood, K., Jensen, P. S., & Fisher, C. B. (Eds.). (1996). *Ethical issues in mental health research with children and adolescents.* Hillsdale, NJ: Erlbaum.

Hoagwood, K., Jensen, P. S., Petti, T., & Burns, B. J. (1996). Outcomes of mental health care for children and adolescents: I. A comprehensive conceptual model. *Journal of the American Academy of Child and Adolescent Psychiatry, 35,* 1055–1063.

Hobson, R. P. (1993). *Autism and the development of mind.* Hillsdale, NJ: Erlbaum.

Hodapp, R. M., & Dykens, E. M. (1996). Mental retardation. In E. J. Mash & R. A. Barkley (Eds.), *Child psychopathology* (pp. 362–369). New York: Guilford Press.

Hodapp, R. M., & Zigler, E. (1995). Past, present, and future issues in the developmental approach to mental retardation and developmental disabilities. In D. Cicchetti & D. J. Cohen (Eds.), *Developmental psychopathology: Vol 2. Risk, disorder, and adaption* (pp. 299–331). New York: Wiley.

Hoek, H. W. (1993). Review of the epidemiological studies of eating disorders. *International Review of Psychiatry, 5,* 61–74.

Hoek, H. W., Bartelds, A. I. M., Bosveld, J. J. F., van der Graaf, Y., Limpens, V. E. L., Maiwald, M., & Spaaij, C. J. K. (1995). Impact of urbanization on detection rates of eating disorders. *American Journal of Psychiatry, 152,* 1271–1278.

Hoffman, L., & Halmi, K. A. (1993). Psychopharmacology in the treatment of anorexia nervosa and bulimia nervosa. *Psychiatric Clinics of North America, 16,* 767–778.

Hoffmann, H. (1845). *Struwwelpeter.* Blackie: London and Glasgow.

Hoffman-Plotkin, D., & Twentyman, C. T. (1984). A multimodal assessment of behavioral and cognitive deficits in abused and neglected preschoolers. *Child Development, 55,* 794–802.

Hoge, R. D., Andrews, D. A., & Leschied, A. W. (1996). The investigation of risk and protective factors in a sample of youthful offenders. *Journal of Child Psychology and Psychiatry, 37,* 419–424.

Holden, E. W., Chmielewski, D., Nelson, C. C., & Kager, V. A. (1997). Controlling for general and disease-specific effects in child and family adjustment to chronic childhood illness. *Journal of Pediatric Psychology, 22,* 15–27.

Holmes, F. B. (1936). An experimental investigation of a method of overcoming children's fears. *Child Development, 7,* 6–30.

Hook, E. B. (1982). Epidemiology of Down syndrome. In S. M. Pueschel & J. E. Rynders (Eds.), *Down syndrome: Advances in biomedicine and the behavioral sciences* (pp. 11–88). Cambridge, England: Ware Press.

Hooper, S. R., Montgomery, J., Swartz, C., Reed, M., Sandler, A., Levine, M., Watson, T., & Wasileski, T. (1994). Measurement of written language. In G. R. Lyon (Ed.), *Frames of reference for the assessment of learning disabilities: New views on measurement issues* (pp. 375–418). Baltimore: Paul H. Brookes.

Hoover, D. W., & Milich, R. (1994). Effects of sugar ingestion expectancies on mother-child interactions. *Journal of Abnormal Child Psychology, 22,* 501–514.

Hops, H. (1995). Age- and gender-specific effects of parental depression: A commentary. *Developmental Psychology, 31,* 428–431.

Hops, H., Davis, B., & Longoria, N. (1995). Methodological issues in direct observation: Illustrations with the Living in Familial Environments (LIFE) coding system. *Journal of Clinical Child Psychology, 24,* 193–203.

Hops, H., Lewinsohn, P. M., Andrews, J. A., & Roberts, R. E. (1990). Psychosocial correlates of depressive symptomatology among high school students. *Journal of Clinical Child Psychology, 19,* 211–220.

Hopwood, N. J., & Becker, D. J. (1979). Psychosocial dwarfism: Detection, evaluation and management. *Child Abuse and Neglect, 3,* 439–447.

Horesh, N., Apter, A., Ishal, J., Danziger, Y., Miculincer, M., Stein, D., Lepkifker, E., & Minouni, M. (1996). Abnormal psychosocial situations and eating disorders in adolescence. *Journal of the American Academy of Child and Adolescent Psychiatry, 35,* 921–927.

Horne, J. A. (1993). Human sleep loss and behavior implications for the prefrontal cortex and psychiatric disorder. *British Journal of Psychiatry, 162,* 413–419.

Hotopf, M., & Bolton, P. (1995). A case of autism associated with partial tetrasomy 15. *Journal of Autism and Developmental Disorders, 25,* 41–49.

Houts, A. C., Berman, J. S., & Abramson, H. (1994). Effectiveness of psychological and pharmacological treatments for nocturnal enuresis. *Journal of Consulting and Clinical Psychology, 62,* 737–745.

Howard, B., & Kendall, P. C. (1996a). *Cognitive-behavioral family therapy for anxious children: Therapist manual.* Ardmore, PA: Workbook Publishing.

Howard, B. L., & Kendall, P. C. (1996b). Cognitive-behavioral family therapy for anxiety-disordered children: A multiple-baseline evaluation. *Cognitive Therapy and Research, 20,* 423–443.

Howlin, P., & Rutter, M. (1987). *Treatment of autistic children.* New York: Wiley.

Hsu, L. K. G. (1990). *Eating disorders.* New York: Guilford Press.

Hsu, L. K. G., Chesler, B. E., & Santhouse, R. (1990). Bulimia nervosa in eleven sets of twins: A clinical report. *International Journal of Eating Disorders, 9,* 275–282.

Hsu, L. K. G., Crisp, A. H., & Challender, J. S. (1992). Recovery in anorexia nervosa: The patient's perspective. *International Journal of Eating Disorders, 11,* 341–350.

Hudson, J. I., Pope, H. G., Jonas, J. M., & Yurgelun-Todd, D. (1983). Family history study of anorexia nervosa and bulimia. *British Journal of Psychiatry, 142,* 133–138.

Hudson, S. M., & Ward, T. (1997). Intimacy, loneliness, and attachment style in sexual offenders. *Journal of Interpersonal Violence, 12,* 323–329.

Huesmann, L. R., Eron, L. D., Berkowitz, L., & Chaffee, S. (1992). The effects of television violence on aggression: A reply to a skeptic. In P. Suedfeld & P. E. Tetlock (Eds.), *Psychology and social policy* (pp. 191–200). New York: Hemisphere Publishing.

Huesmann, L. R., Eron, L. D., Lefkowitz, M. M., & Walder, L. O. (1984). Stability of aggression over time and generations. *Developmental Psychology, 20,* 1120–1134.

Hughes, J. N., Cavell, T. A., & Grossman, P. B. (1997). A positive view of self: Risk or protection for aggressive children? *Development and Psychopathology, 9,* 75–94.

Humphrey, L. L. (1988). Relationships within subtypes of anorexics, bulimics, and normal families. *Journal of the American Academy of Child and Adolescent Psychiatry, 27,* 544–551.

Humphries, T., Kinsbourne, M., & Swanson, J. (1978). Stimulant effects on cooperation and social interaction between hyperactive children and their mothers. *Journal of Child Psychology and Psychiatry, 19,* 12–22.

Hurlbert, R. T., Happe, F., & Frith, U. (1994). Sampling the form of inner experience in three adults with Asperger syndrome. *Psychological Medicine, 24,* 385–395.

Huston, A. C., & Alvarez, M. M. (1990). The socialization context of gender role development in early adolescence. In R. Montemayor, G. R. Adams, & T. P. Gullota (Eds.), *Advances in adolescent development: Vol. 2. From childhood to adolescence: A transitional period?* (pp. 156–182). Newbury Park, CA: Sage.

Hynd, G. W., Hern, K. L., Novey, E. S., Eliopulos, D., Marshall, R., Gonzalez, J. J., & Voeller, K. K. (1993). Attention-deficit hyperactivity disorder and asymmetry of the caudate nucleus. *Journal of Child Neurology, 8,* 339–347.

Hynd, G. W., Marshall, R., & Gonzalez, J. (1991). Learning disabilities and presumed central nervous system dysfunction. *Learning Disability Quarterly, 14,* 283–296.

Hynd, G. W., & Semrud-Clikeman, M. (1989). Dyslexia and brain morphology. *Psychological Bulletin, 106,* 447–482.

Hynd, G. W., Semrud-Clikeman, M., Lorys, A. R., Novey, E. S., & Eliopulos, D. (1990). Brain morphology in developmental dyslexia and attention deficit disorder/hyperactivity. *Archives of Neurology, 47,* 919–926.

Hynd, G. W., Semrud-Clikeman, M., Lorys, A. R., Novey, E. S., Eliopulos, D., & Lyytinen, H. (1991). Corpus callosum morphology in attention deficit-hyperactivity disorder: Morphometric analysis of MRI. *Journal of Learning Disabilities, 24,* 141–146.

Ialongo, N., Edelsohn, G., Werthamer-Larsson, L., Crockett, L., & Kellam, S. (1995). The significance of self-reported anxious symptoms in first grade children: Prediction to anxious symptoms and adaptive functioning in fifth grade. *Journal of Child Psychology and Psychiatry, 36,* 427–437.

Ialongo, N., Edelsohn, G., Werthamer-Larsson, L., Crockett, L., & Kellam, S. (1994). The significance of self-reported anxious symptoms in first grade children. *Journal of Abnormal Child Psychology, 22,* 441–455.

Illick, J. E. (1974). Childrearing in seventeenth century England and America. In L. deMause (Ed.), *The history of childhood.* New York: Psychohistory Press.

Innocenti, G. M. (1982). Development of interhemispheric cortical connections. *Neurosciences Research Program Bulletin, 20*(4), 532–540.

Institute of Medicine. (1989). *Research on children and adolescents with mental, behavioral and developmental disorders.* Washington, DC: National Academy Press.

Israel, A. C., Guilem, C. A., Baker, J. E., & Silverman, W. K. (1994). An evaluation of enhanced self-regulation training in the treatment of childhood obesity. *Journal of Pediatric Psychology, 19,* 737–749.

Issacs, M. R., & Benjamin, M. P. (1991). *Towards a culturally competent system of care: Programs which utilize culturally competent principles.* Washington, DC: Georgetown University, Child Development Center.

Jacob, T., Krahn, G. L., & Leonard, K. (1991). Parent-child interactions in families with alcoholic fathers. *Journal of Consulting and Clinical Psychology, 59,* 176–181.

Jacobson, J. W. (1982). Problem behavior and psychiatric impairment within a developmentally disabled population: I. Behavior frequency. *Applied Research in Mental Retardation, 3,* 121–139.

Jacobson, J. W., & Mulick, J. A. (1992). A new definition of mental retardation or a new definition of practice? *Psychology in Mental Retardation and Developmental Disabilities, 18,* 9–14.

Jacobson, J. W., Mulick, J. A., & Schwartz, A. A. (1995). A history of facilitated communication: Science, pseudoscience, and antiscience. *American Psychologist, 50,* 750–765.

Jacobvitz, D., & Sroufe, L. A. (1987). The early caregiver-child relationship and attention-deficit disorder with hyperactivity in kindergarten: A prospective study. *Child Development, 58,* 1496–1504.

Jacobvitz, D., & Sroufe, L. A., Stewart, M., & Leffert, N. (1990). Treatment of attention and hyperactivity problems in children with sympathomimetic drugs: A comprehensive review. *Journal of the American Academy of Child and Adolescent Psychiatry, 29,* 677–688.

Jaffe, P., Lemon, N., Sandler, J., & Wolfe, D. (1996). *Working together to end domestic violence.* Tampa, FL: Mancorp.

Jaffe, P., Wolfe, D. A., & Wilson, S. (1990). *Children of*

battered women. Thousand Oaks, CA: Sage.

Jamison, K. R. (1997, January). Manic-depressive illness and creativity. *Scientific American* (Special Issue), 7(1), 44–49.

Jansen, A., Broekmate, J., & Heymans, M. (1992). Cue-exposure vs. self-control in the treatment of binge eating: A pilot study. *Behavior Therapy, 30,* 235–241.

Jay, S. M., & Elliott, C. H. (1990). A stress inoculation program for parents whose children are undergoing painful medical procedures. *Journal of Consulting and Clinical Psychology, 58,* 799–804.

Jaycox, L. H., Reivich, K. J., Gillham, J., & Seligman, M. E. P. (1994). Prevention of depressive symptoms in school children. *Behaviour Research and Therapy, 32,* 801–816.

Jayson, D., Wood, A., Kroll, L., Fraser, J., & Harrington, R. (1998). Which depressed patients respond to cognitive-behavioral treatment? *Journal of the American Academy of Child and Adolescent Psychiatry, 37,* 35–39.

Jensen, A. R. (1969). How much can we boost IQ and scholastic achievement? *Harvard Educational Review, 39,* 1–23.

Jensen, P. S., & Hoagwood, K. (1997). The book of names: DSM-IV in context. *Development and Psychopathology, 9,* 231–249.

Jensen, P. S., Hoagwood, K., & Petti, T. (1996). Outcomes of mental health care for children and adolescents: II. Literature review and application of a comprehensive model. *Journal of the American Academy of Child and Adolescent Psychiatry, 35,* 1064–1077.

Jensen, P. S., Koretz, D., Locke, B. Z., Schneider, S., Radke-Yarrow, M., Richters, J. E., & Rumsey, J. M. (1993). Child and adolescent psychopathology research: Problems and prospects for the 1990s. *Journal of Abnormal Child Psychology, 21,* 551–580.

Jensen, P. S., Martin, B. A., & Cantwell, D. P. (1997). Comorbidity in ADHD: Implications for research, practice, and DSM-IV. *Journal of the American Academy of Child and Adolescent Psychiatry, 36,* 1065–1079.

Jessor, R. (1991). Risk behavior in adolescence: A psychosocial framework for understanding and action. *Journal of Adolescent Health, 12,* 597–605.

Jimerson, D. C., Lesem, M. D., Kaye, W. H., & Brewerton, T. D. (1992). Low serotonin and dopamine metabolite concentrations in cerebrospinal fluid from bulimic patients with frequent binge episodes. *Archives of General Psychiatry, 49,* 132–139.

Johnson, C., & Conners, M. E. (1987). Demographic and clinical characteristics. In E. Johnson & M. E. Conners (Eds.), *The etiology and treatment of bulimia nervosa: A biophysical perspective* (pp. 31–60). New York: Basic Books.

Johnson, M. H., Siddons, F., Frith, U., & Morton, J. (1992). Can autism be predicted on the basis of infant screening tests? *Developmental Medicine and Child Neurology, 34,* 316–320.

Johnson, S. B. (1988). Diabetes mellitus in childhood. In D. K. Routh (Ed.), *Handbook of pediatric psychology* (pp. 9–31). New York: Guilford Press.

Johnson, S. M., & Lobitz, G. K. (1974). Parental manipulation of child behavior in home observations. *Journal of Applied Behavior Analysis, 7,* 23–32.

Johnson, W. G., Tsoh, J. Y., & Vanrado, P. J. (1996). Eating disorders: Efficacy of pharmacological and psychological interventions. *Clinical Psychology Review, 16,* 457–478.

Johnston, C. (1996). Addressing parent cognitions in interventions with families of disruptive children. In K. S. Dobson & K. D. Craig (Eds.), *Advances in cognitive-behavioral therapy* (pp. 193–209). Thousand Oaks, CA: Sage.

Johnston, C., & Freeman, W. (1998). Parent training interventions for sibling conflict. J. Briesmeister & C. E. Schaefer (Eds.), *Handbook of parent training: Parents as co-therapists for children's behavior problems* (2nd ed., pp. 153–176). New York: Wiley.

Johnston, C., & Pelham, W. E. (1985). Peer relationships in ADHD and normal children: A developmental analysis of peer and teacher ratings. *Journal of Abnormal Child Psychology, 13,* 89–100.

Johnston, H., & Fruehling, J. J. (1994). Pharmacotherapy for depression in children and adolescents. In W. M. Reynolds & H. F. Johnston (Eds.), *Handbook of depression in children and adolescents* (pp. 365–397). New York: Plenum.

Joiner, T. E., Heatherton, T. F., Rudd, M. D., & Schmidt, N. B. (1997). Perfectionism, perceived weight status, and bulimic symptoms: Two studies testing a diathesis-stress model. *Journal of Abnormal Psychology, 106,* 145–153.

Joiner, T. E., & Wagner, K. D. (1995). Attribution style and depression in children and adolescents: A meta-analytic review. *Clinical Psychology Review, 15,* 777–798.

Joiner, T. E., Jr., Catanzaro, S. J., & Laurent, J. (1996). Tripartite structure of positive and negative affect, depression, and anxiety in child and adolescent psychiatric inpatients. *Journal of Abnormal Psychology, 105,* 401–409.

Jolliffe, T., & Baron-Cohen, S. (1997). Are people with autism and Asperger syndrome faster than normal on the Embedded Figures Test? *Journal of Child Psychology and Psychiatry, 38,* 527–534.

Jones, D. J., Fox, M. M., Babigian, H. M., & Hutton, H. E. (1980). Epidemiology of anorexia nervosa in Monroe County, New York: 1960–1979. *Psychosomatic Medicine, 42,* 551–558.

Jones, M. C. (1924a). A laboratory study of fear: The case of Peter. *Journal of Genetic Psychology, 31,* 308–315.

Jones, M. C. (1924b). The elimination of children's fears. *Journal of Experimental Psychology, 1,* 383–390.

Jones, N. A., Field, T., Fox, N. A., Lundy, B., & Davalo, M. (1997). EEG activation in 1-month-old infants of depressed mothers. *Development and Psychopathology, 9,* 491–505.

Jordan, A. E., & Cole, D. A. (1996). Relation of depressive symptoms to the structure of self-knowledge in childhood. *Journal of Abnormal Psychology, 105,* 530–540.

Jumper, S. (1995). A meta-analysis of the relationship of child sexual abuse to adult psychological adjustment. *Child Abuse and Neglect, 19,* 715–728.

Jung, C. G. (1939). The integration of the personality. New York: Farrar & Rinehart.

Kachur, S. P., Potter, L. B., James, S. P., & Powell, K. E. (1995). *Suicide in the United States, 1980–1992* (Violence Survey Summary Series, No. 1). Atlanta: Centers for Disease Control and Prevention, National Center for Injury Prevention and Control.

Kagan, J. (1983). Stress and coping in early development. In N. Garmezy & M. Rutter (Eds.), *Stress, coping, and development in children* (pp. 191–216). New York: McGraw-Hill.

Kagan, J. (1997). Temperament and the reactions to unfamiliarity. *Child Development, 68,* 139–143.

Kagan, J., Rossman, B. L., Day, D., Albert, J., & Philips, W. (1964). *Psychological Monographs, 78*(Whole No. 578).

Kagan, J., Snidman, N., & Arcus, D. M. (1992). Initial reactions to unfamiliarity. *Current Directions in Psychological Science, 1,* 171–174.

Kagan, J., Snidman, N., Arcus, D. M., & Reznick, J. S. (1994). *Galen's prophecy: Temperament in human nature.* New York: Basic Books.

Kahkonen, M., Alitalo, T., Airaksinen, E., Matilamen, R., Laumiala, K., Auno, S., & Leisti, J. (1987). Prevalence of Fragile X syndrome in four birth cohorts of children of school age. *Human Genetics, 30,* 234–238.

Kales, A., & Kales, J. D. (1974). Sleep disorders: Recent findings in the diagnosis and treatment of disturbed sleep. *New England Journal of Medicine, 290,* 487.

Kales, J. D., Soldatos, C. R., & Kales, A. (1980). Childhood sleep disorders. *Current Pediatric Therapy, 9,* 28–30.

Kallman, F. J., & Roth, B. (1956). Genetic aspects of preadolescent schizophrenia. *American Journal of Psychiatry, 112,* 599–606.

Kamphaus, R. W. (1993). *Clinical assessment of children's intelligence.* Needham Heights, MA: Allyn & Bacon.

Kamphaus, R. W., & Frick, P. J. (1996). *Clinical assessment of child and adolescent personality and behavior.* Needham Heights, MA: Allyn & Bacon.

Kamphaus, R. W., Slotkin, J., & DeVincentis, C. (1990). In C. R. Reynolds & R. W. Kamphaus (Eds.), *Handbook of psychological and educational assessment of children: Intelligence and achievement* (pp. 552–568). New York: Guilford Press.

Kanbayashi, Y., Nakata, Y., Fujii, K., Kita, M., & Wada, K. (1994). ADHD-related behavior among non-referred children: Parent's ratings of DSM-III-R symptoms. *Child Psychiatry and Human Development, 25,* 13–29.

Kanner, L. (1943). Autistic disturbances of affective contact. *Nervous Child, 2,* 217–250.

Kanner, L. (1944). Early infantile autism. *Journal of Pediatrics, 25,* 211–217.

Kanner, L. (1946). Irrelevant and metaphorical language in early infantile autism. *American Journal of Psychiatry, 103,* 242–246.

Kanner, L. (1962). Emotionally disturbed children: A historical review. *Child Development, 33,* 97–102.

Kanner, L. (1964). *A history of the care and study of the mentally retarded.* Springfield, IL: Charles C Thomas.

Kanner, L. (1973). *Childhood psychosis: Initial studies and new insights.* Washington, DC: V. H. Winston.

Kaplan, A. S., & Woodside, D. B. (1987). Biological aspects of anorexia nervosa and bulimia nervosa. *Journal of Consulting and Clinical Psychology, 55,* 645–653.

Kaplan, H. I., & Sadock, B. J. (1991). *Synopsis of psychiatry* (6th ed.). Baltimore: Williams & Wilkins.

Kaplan, S. J., Pelcovitz, D., Salzinger, S., Mandel, F., & Weiner, M. (1997). Adolescent physical abuse and suicide attempts. *Journal of the American Academy of Child and Adolescent Psychiatry, 36,* 799–808.

Karier, C. J. (1986). *Scientists of the mind: Intellectual founders of modern psychology.* Urbana: University of Illinois Press.

Kasen, S., Cohen, P., Brook, J. S., & Hartmark, C. (1996). A multiple-risk interaction model: Effects of temperament and divorce on psychiatric disorders in children. *Journal of Abnormal Child Psychology, 24,* 121–150.

Kashani, J. H., Allan, W. D., Dahlmeier, J. M., Rezvani, M., & Reid, J. C. (1995). An examination of family functioning utilizing the circumplex model in psychiatrically hospitalized children with depression. *Journal of Affective Disorders, 35,* 65–73.

Kashani, J. H., & Carlson, G. A. (1987). Seriously depressed preschoolers. *American Journal of Psychiatry, 144,* 348–350.

Kashani, J. H., & Orvaschel, H. (1990). A community study of anxiety in children and adolescents. *American Journal of Psychiatry, 147,* 313–318.

Kaslow, N. J., Brown, R. T., & Mee, L. L. (1994). Cognitive and behavioral correlates of childhood depression: A developmental perspective. In W. M. Reynolds & H. F. Johnston (Eds.), *Handbook of depression in children and adolescents* (pp. 97–122). New York: Plenum.

Kaslow, N. J., & Racusin, G. R. (1988). Assessment and treatment of depressed children and their families. *Family Therapy Today, 3,* 39–59.

Kaslow, N. J., & Thompson, M. P. (1998). Applying the criteria for empirically supported treatments to studies of psychosocial interactions for child and adolescent depression. *Journal of Clinical Child Psychology, 27,* 146–155.

Kaufman, A. S., & Kaufman, N. L. (1983). *Administration and scoring manual for the Kaufman Assessment Battery for Children.* Circle Pines, MN: American Guidance Service.

Kaufman, J. L. (1991). Depressive disorders in maltreated children. *American Journal of Child and Adolescent Psychiatry, 30,* 257–265.

Kaufman, J. L., & Zigler, E. (1989). The intergenerational transmission of child abuse. In D. Cicchetti & V. Carlson (Eds.), *Child maltreatment: Theory and research on the causes and consequences of child abuse and neglect* (pp. 129–150). New York: Cambridge University Press.

Kaufman, J. M. (1989). *Characteristics of children's behavior disorders.* (4th ed.). Columbus, OH: Charles E. Merrill.

Kaufman, M., Agard, J. A., & Semmel, M. E. (1985). *Mainstreaming: Learners and their environment.* Cambridge, MA: Brookline Books.

Kavale, K. A., & Forness, S. R. (1983). Hyperactivity and diet treatment: A meta-analysis of the Feingold hypothesis. *Journal of Learning Disabilities, 16,* 324–330.

Kavale, K. A., & Forness, S. R. (1996). Social skill deficits and learning disabilities: A meta-analysis. *Journal of Learning Disabilities, 29(3),* 226–237.

Kavanagh, K., & Hops, H. (1994). Good girls? Bad boys? Gender and development as contexts for diagnosis and treatment. In T. H. Ollendick & R. J. Prinz (Eds.), *Advances in clinical child psychology* (Vol. 16, pp. 45–79). New York: Plenum.

Kaye, W. H., & Weltzin, T. E. (1991). Neurochemistry of bulimia nervosa. *Journal of Clinical Psychiatry, 52,* 617–622.

Kazak, A. E., Barakat, L. P., Meeske, K., Christakis, D., Meadows, D., Casey, R., Penati, B., & Stuber, M. (1997). Posttraumatic stress, family functioning, and social support in survivors of childhood leukemia and their mothers and fathers. *Journal of Consulting and Clinical Psychology, 65,* 120–129.

Kazak, A. E., Christakis, D., Alderfer, M., & Coiro, M. J. (1994). Young adolescent cancer survivors and their parents: Adjustment, learning problems, and gender. *Journal of Family Psychology, 8,* 74–84.

Kazak, A. E., Penati, B., Boyer, B. A., Himelstein, B., Brophy, P., Waibel, M. K., Blackall, G. F., Daller, R., & Johnson, K. (1996). A randomized controlled perspective outcome study of a psychological and pharmacological intervention protocol for procedural distress in pediatric leukemia. *Journal of*

Pediatric Psychology, 21, 615–631.

Kazdin, A. E. (1981). Drawing valid inferences from case studies. *Journal of Consulting and Clinical Psychology, 49,* 183–192.

Kazdin, A. E. (1982). *Single-case research designs: Methods for clinical and applied settings.* New York: Oxford University Press.

Kazdin, A. E. (1988). *Child psychotherapy: Developing and identifying effective treatments.* New York: Pergamon Press.

Kazdin, A. E. (1989). Developmental psychopathology: Current research, issues, and directions. *American Psychologist, 44,* 180–187.

Kazdin, A. E. (1990). Evaluation of the Automatic Thoughts Questionnaire: Negative cognitive processes and depression among children. *Psychological Assessment, 2,* 73–79.

Kazdin, A. E. (1992). Overt and covert antisocial behavior: Child and family characteristics among psychiatric inpatient children. *Journal of Child and Family Studies, 1,* 3–20.

Kazdin, A. E. (1993a). Adolescent mental health: Prevention and treatment programs. *American Psychologist, 48,* 127–141.

Kazdin, A. E. (1993b). Psychotherapy for children and adolescents: Current progress and future. *American Psychologist, 48,* 644–657.

Kazdin, A. E. (1993c). Treatment of conduct disorder: Progress and directions in psychotherapy research. *Development and Psychopathology, 5,* 277–310.

Kazdin, A. E. (1995). *Conduct disorders in childhood and adolescence* (2nd ed.). Thousand Oaks, CA: Sage.

Kazdin, A. E. (1996a). Combined and multimodal treatments in child and adolescent psychotherapy: Issues, challenges, and research directions. *Clinical Psychology: Science and Practice, 3,* 69–100.

Kazdin, A. E. (1996b). Developing effective treatments for children and adolescents. In E. D. Hibbs & P. S. Jensen (Eds.), *Psychosocial treatments for child and adolescent disorders: Empirically based strategies for clinical practice* (pp. 9–18). Washington, DC: American Psychological Association.

Kazdin, A. E. (1996c). Problem solving and parent management training in treating aggressive and antisocial behavior. In E. D. Hibbs & P. S. Jensen (Eds.), *Psychosocial treatments for child and adolescent disorders: Empirically based strategies for clinical practice* (pp. 377–408). Washington, DC: American Psychological Association.

Kazdin, A. E. (1997a). A model for developing effective treatments: Progression and interplay of theory, research, and practice. *Journal of Clinical Child Psychology, 26,* 114–129.

Kazdin, A. E. (1997b). Parent management training: Evidence, outcomes, and issues. *Journal of the American Academy of Child and Adolescent Psychiatry, 36,* 1349–1365.

Kazdin, A. E. (1998). *Research design in clinical psychology* (3rd ed.). Needham Heights, MA: Allyn & Bacon.

Kazdin, A. E., Bass, D., Ayers, W. A., & Rodgers, A. (1990). Empirical and clinical focus of child and adolescent psychotherapy research. *Journal of Consulting and Clinical Psychology, 62,* 100–110.

Kazdin, A. E., French, N. H., Unis, A. S., Esveldt-Dawson, K., & Sherick, R. B. (1983). Hopelessness, depression, and suicidal intent among psychiatrically disturbed inpatient children. *Journal of Consulting and Clinical Psychology, 51,* 504–510.

Kazdin, A. E., & Johnson, B. (1994). Advances in psycho-therapy for children and adolescents: Interrelations of adjustment, development, and intervention. *Journal of School Psychology, 32,* 217–246.

Kazdin, A. E., & Kagan, J. (1994). Models of dysfunction in developmental psychopathology. *Clinical Psychology: Science and Practice, 1,* 35–52.

Kazdin, A. E., & Marciano, P. L. (1998). Child and adolescent depression. In E. J. Mash & R. A. Barkley (Eds.), *Treatment of childhood disorders* (2nd ed., pp. 211–248). New York: Guilford Press.

Kazdin, A. E., Siegel, T. C., & Bass, D. (1990). Drawing upon clinical practice to inform research on child and adolescent psychotherapy. *Professional Psychology: Research and Practice, 21,* 189–190.

Kazdin, A. E., Siegel, T. C., & Bass, D. (1992). Cognitive problem-solving skills training and parent management training in the treatment of antisocial children. *Journal of Consulting and Clinical Psychology, 60,* 733–747.

Kazdin, A. E., & Weisz, J. R. (1998). Identifying and developing empirically supported child and adolescent treatments. *Journal of Consulting and Clinical Psychology, 66,* 19–36.

Kearney, C. A. (1993). Depression and school refusal behavior: A review with comments on classification and treatment. *Journal of School Psychology, 31,* 267–279.

Kearney, C. A. (1995). School refusal behavior. In A. R. Eisen, C. A. Kearney, & C. A. Schaefer, (Eds.), *Clinical handbook of anxiety disorders in children and adolescents* (pp. 19–52). Northvale, NJ: Jason Aronson.

Kearney, C. A., Albano, A. M., Eisen, A. R., Allan, W. D., & Barlow, D. A. (1997). The phenomenology of panic disorder in youngsters: An empirical study of a clinical sample. *Journal of Anxiety Disorders, 11,* 49–62.

Kearney, C. A., & Allan, W. D. (1995). Panic disorder with or without agoraphobia. In A. R. Eisen, C. A. Kearney, & C. A. Schaefer (Eds.), *Clinical handbook of anxiety disorders in children and adolescents* (pp. 251–281). Northvale, NJ: Jason Aronson.

Kearney, C. A., & Silverman, W. K. (1993). Measuring the function of school refusal behavior: The School Refusal Assessment Scale. *Journal of Clinical Child Psychology, 22,* 85–96.

Kearney, C. A., & Silverman, W. K. (1995). Family environment of youngsters with school refusal behavior: A synopsis with implications for assessment and treatment. *American Journal of Family Therapy, 23,* 59–72.

Kearney, C. A., & Silverman, W. K. (1996). The evolution and reconciliation of taxonomic strategies for school refusal behavior. *Clinical Psychology: Science and Practice, 3,* 339–354.

Keenan, K., & Shaw, D. (1997). Developmental and social influences on young girls' early problem behavior. *Psychological Bulletin, 121,* 95–113.

Keller, M., Lavori, P., Wunder, J., Beardslee, W., Schwartz, C., & Roth, J. (1992). Chronic course of anxiety disorders in children and adolescents. *Journal of the American Academy of Child and Adolescent Psychiatry, 31,* 595–599.

Keltner, D., Moffitt, T. E., & Stouthamer-Loeber, M. (1995). Facial expressions of emotion and psychopathology in adolescent boys. *Journal of Abnormal Psychology, 104,* 644–652.

Kempe, C. H., Silverman, F. N., Steele, B. F., Droegenmueller, W., & Silver, H. K. (1962). The battered child syndrome. *Journal of the American Medical Association, 181,* 17–24.

Kemper, T. L., & Bauman, M. L. (1993). The contribution of

neuropathologic studies to the understanding of autism. *Neurologic Clinics, 11,* 175–187.

Kendall, P. C. (1988). *Stop and think workbook* (2nd ed.). Ardmore, PA: Workbook Publishing.

Kendall, P. C. (Ed.). (1991a). *Child and adolescent therapy: Cognitive-behavioral procedures.* New York: Guilford Press.

Kendall, P. C. (1991b). Guiding theory for therapy with children and adolescents. In P. C. Kendall (Ed.), *Child and adolescent therapy: Cognitive-behavioral procedures* (pp. 3–22). New York: Guilford Press.

Kendall, P. C. (1992). Childhood coping: Avoiding a lifetime of anxiety. *Behaviour Change, 9,* 229–237.

Kendall, P. C. (1993). Cognitive-behavioral therapies with youth: Guiding theory, current status, and emerging developments. *Journal of Consulting and Clinical Psychology, 61,* 235–247.

Kendall, P. C. (1994). Treating anxiety disorders in children: Results of a randomized clinical trial. *Journal of Consulting and Clinical Psychology, 62,* 100–110.

Kendall, P. C., & Brady, E. (1995). Comorbidity in the anxiety disorders of childhood. In K. Craig & K. Dobson (Eds.), *Anxiety and depression in adults and children.* Newbury Park, CA: Sage.

Kendall, P. C., & Flannery-Schroeder, E. (in press). Methodological issues in treatment research for anxiety disorders in youth. *Journal of Abnormal Psychology.*

Kendall, P. C., Flannery-Schroeder, E., Panichelli-Mindel, S. M., Southam-Gerow, M., Henin, A., & Warman, M. (1997). Therapy for youths with anxiety disorders: A second randomized clinical trial. *Journal of Consulting and Clinical Psychology, 65,* 366–380.

Kendall, P. C., Howard, B. L., & Epps, J. (1988). The anxious child: Cognitive-behavioral treatment strategies. *Behavior Modification, 12,* 281–310.

Kendall, P. C., & MacDonald, J. P. (1993). Cognition in the psychopathology of youth and implications for treatment. In K. S. Dobson & P. C. Kendall (Eds.), *Psychopathology and cognition* (pp. 387–427). San Diego: Academic Press.

Kendall, P. C., Panichelli-Mindel, S. M., Sugarman, A., & Callahan, S. A. (1997). Exposure to child anxiety: Theory, research, and practice. *Clinical Psychology: Science and Practice, 4,* 29–39.

Kendall, P. C., & Southam-Gerow, M. A. (1996). Long-term follow-up of a cognitive-behavioral therapy for anxiety-disordered youth. *Journal of Consulting and Clinical Psychology, 64,* 724–730.

Kendall, P. C., & Treadwell, K. H. (1996). Cognitive-behavioral treatment for childhood anxiety disorders. Psychosocial treatments for child and adolescent disorders: In E. D. Hibbs & P. S. Jensen (Eds.), *Empirically-based strategies for clinical practice* (pp. 23–41). Washington, DC: American Psychological Association.

Kendall, P. C., & Warman, M. J. (1996). Anxiety disorders in youth: Diagnostic consistency across DSM-III-R and DSM-IV. *Journal of Anxiety Disorders, 10,* 452–463.

Kendall-Tackett, K. A., Williams, L. M., & Finkelhor, D. (1993). The impact of sexual abuse on children: A review and synthesis of recent empirical studies. *Psychological Bulletin, 113,* 164–180.

Kendler, K. S. (1995). Genetic epidemiology in psychiatry: Taking both genes and environment seriously. *Archives of General Psychiatry, 52,* 895–899.

Kendler, K. S., MacLean, C., Neale, M., Kessler, R., Heath, A.,

& Eaves, L. (1991). The genetic epidemiology of bulimia nervosa. *American Journal of Psychiatry, 148,* 1627–1637.

Kendler, K. S., Neale, M. C., Kessler, R. C., Heath, A. C., & Eaves, L. J. (1992a). Generalized anxiety disorder in women: A population-based twin study. *Archives of General Psychiatry, 49,* 267–272.

Kendler, K. S., Neale, M. C., Kessler, R. C., Heath, A. C., & Eaves, L. J. (1992b). The genetic epidemiology of phobias in women: The interrelationship of agoraphobia, social phobia, situational phobia, and simple phobia. *Archives of General Psychiatry, 49,* 273–281.

Kennedy, P., Terdal, L., & Fusetti, L. (1993). *The hyperactive child book.* New York: St. Martin's Press.

Kessler, J. W. (1980). History of minimal brain dysfunctions. In H. E. Rie & E. D. Rie (Eds.), *Handbook of minimal brain dysfunctions: A critical review* (pp. 18–51). New York: Wiley-Interscience.

Kessler, R. C., Sonnega, A., Bromet, E., Hughes, M., & Nelson, C. B. (1996). Posttraumatic stress disorder in the National Comorbidity Survey. *Archives of General Psychiatry, 52,* 1048–1060.

Kevles, B. H., & Kevles, D. J. (1997, October). Scapegoat biology. *Discover,* pp. 58–62.

Killen, J. D., Taylor, C. B., Hayward, C., Haydel, K. F., Wilson, D. M., Hammer, L., Kraemer, H., Blair-Greiner, A., & Strachowski, D. (1996). Weight concerns influence the development of eating disorders: A 4-year prospective study. *Journal of Consulting and Clinical Psychology, 64,* 936–940.

King, B. H., DeAntonio, C., McCracken, J. T., Forness, S. R., & Ackerland, V. (1994). Psychiatric consultation in severe and profound mental retardation. *American Journal of Psychiatry, 151,* 1802–1808.

King, C. A. (1997). Suicidal behavior in adolescence. In R. W. Maris, M. M. Silverman, S. S. Canetto (Eds.), *Review of suicidology, 1997* (pp. 61–95). New York: Guilford Press.

King, D. F., & Goodman, K. S. (1990). Whole language: Cherishing learners and their language. *Language, Speech, and Hearing Services in Schools, 21,* 221–227.

King, N. J., & Ollendick, T. H. (1997). Treatment of childhood phobias. *Journal of Child Psychology and Psychiatry, 38,* 389–400.

King, N. J., Ollendick, T. H., & Gullone, E. (1991a). Negative affectivity in children and adolescents: Relations between anxiety and depression. *Clinical Psychology Review, 11,* 441–459.

King, N. J., Ollendick, T. H., & Gullone, E. (1991b). Test anxiety in children and adolescents. *Australian Psychologist, 26,* 25–32.

King, N. J., Ollendick, T. H., & Mattis, S. G. (1994). Panic in children and adolescents: Normative and clinical studies. *Australian Psychologist, 29,* 89–93.

Kirk, S . A., & Hutchins, H. (1994, June 20). Is bad writing a mental disorder? *New York Times,* pp. A11, A17.

Klein, D. N., Lewinsohn, P. M., & Seeley, J. R. (1997). Psychosocial characteristics of adolescents with a past history of dysthymic disorder: Comparison with adolescents with past histories of major depressive and non-affective disorders, and never mentally ill controls. *Journal of Affective Disorders, 42,* 127–135.

Klein, R. G., & Last, C. G. (1989). *Anxiety disorders in children.* Newbury Park, CA: Sage.

Klein, R. G., & Mannuzza, S. (1991). Long-term outcome of hyperactive children: A review. *Journal of the American*

Academy of Child and Adolescent Psychiatry, 30, 383–387.

Klin, A. (1991). Young autistic children's listening preferences in regard to speech: A possible characterization of the symptom of social withdrawal. *Journal of Autism and Developmental Disorders, 12,* 29–42.

Klinger, L. G., & Dawson, G. (1995). A fresh look at categorization abilities in persons with autism. In E. Schopler and G. B. Mesibov (Eds.), *Learning and cognition in autism* (pp. 119–136). New York: Plenum.

Klinger, L. G., & Dawson, G. (1996). Autistic disorder. In E. J. Mash & R. A. Barkley (Eds.), *Child psychopathology* (pp. 311–339). New York: Guilford Press.

Klorman, R., Salzman, L. F., & Borgstedt, A. D. (1988). Brain event-related potentials in evaluation of cognitive deficits in attention deficit disorder and outcome of stimulant therapy. In L. Bloomingdale (Ed.), *Attention deficit disorder* (Vol. 3, pp. 49–80). New York: Pergamon Press.

Kloth, S. A. M., & Janssen, P. (1995). Communicative behavior of mothers of stuttering and nonstuttering high-risk children prior to the onset of stuttering. *Journal of Fluency Disorders, 20,* 365–377.

Knoff, H. M. (1990). Evaluation of projective drawings. In C. R. Reynolds & R. W. Kamphaus (Eds.), *Handbook of psychological and educational assessment of children: Vol. 2. Personality, behavior, and context* (pp. 89–146). New York: Guilford Press.

Knox, L. S., Albano, A. M., & Barlow, D. H. (1991, January). *Treatment of OCD in children: Exposure and response prevention—A companion manual to the parent training manual* (rev. September 1993). Unpublished manual, University of Louisville, Department of Psychology.

Knox, L. S., Albano, A. M., & Barlow, D. H. (1996). Parental involvement in the treatment of childhood compulsive disorder: A multiple-baseline examination incorporating parents. *Behavior Therapy, 27,* 93–115.

Kochanska, G., & DeVet, K. (1994). Maternal reports of conscience development and temperament in young children. *Child Development 65,* 852–868.

Koegel, L. K., & Koegel, R. L. (1996). The child with autism as an active communicative partner: Child-initiated strategies for improving communication and reducing behavior problems. In E. D. Hibbs & P. S. Jensen (Eds.), *Psychosocial treatments for child and adolescent disorders: Empirically based strategies for clinical practice* (pp. 553–572). Washington, DC: American Psychological Association.

Kolb, B. (1992). Brain development, plasticity, and behavior. *American Psychologist, 44,* 1203–1212.

Kolko, D. J. (1987). Depression. In M. Hersen & V. B. Van Hasselt (Eds.), *Behavior therapy with children and adolescents: A clinical approach* (pp. 137–182). New York: Wiley-Interscience.

Kolko, D. J. (1992). Characteristics of child victims of physical violence: Research findings and clinical implications. *Journal of Interpersonal Violence, 7,* 244–276.

Kolko, D. J. (1996). Individual cognitive behavioral treatment and family therapy for physically abused children and their offending parents: A comparison of clinical outcomes. *Child Maltreatment, 1,* 322–342.

Kolvin, L., Miller, F. J., Fleeting, M., & Kolvin, P. A. (1988). Risk/protective factors for offending with particular reference to deprivation. In M. Rutter (Ed.), *Studies of psychosocial risk: The power of longitudinal data* (pp. 77–95). New York: Cambridge University Press.

Koplowicz, S., & Barkley, R. A. (1995). *Sense of time in*

children with attention deficit hyperactivity disorder and normal children. Unpublished manuscript, University of Massachusetts Medical Center, Worcester, MA.

Kopp, C. B. (1992). Emotional distress and control in young children. In N. Eisenberg & R. A. Fabes (Eds.), *Emotion and its regulation in early development* (pp. 41–56). San Francisco: Jossey-Bass.

Korbin, J. (1994). Sociocultural factors in child maltreatment. In G. B. Melton & F. D. Barry (Eds.), *Protecting children from abuse and neglect: Foundations for a new national strategy* (pp. 182–223). New York: Guilford Press.

Kortlander, E., Kendall, P. C., & Panichelli-Mindel, S. M. (1997). Maternal expectations and attributions about coping in anxious children. *Journal of Anxiety Disorders, 11,* 297–315.

Kovacs, M. (1987). Diagnosis of depressive disorders in children: An interim appraisal of the pertinent DSM-III categories. In G. L. Tischler (Ed.), *Diagnosis and classification in psychiatry: A critical appraisal of DSM-III* (pp. 369–383). New York: Cambridge University Press.

Kovacs, M. (1991). *The children's depression inventory* (CDI). North Tonawanda, NY: Multi-Health Systems.

Kovacs, M. (1996). Presentation and course of major depressive disorder during childhood and later years of the life span. *Journal of the American Academy of Child and Adolescent Psychiatry, 35,* 705–715.

Kovacs, M. (1997). Depressive disorders in childhood: An impressionistic landscape. *Journal of Child Psychology and Psychiatry, 38,* 287–298.

Kovacs, M., Akiskal, H. S., Gatsonis, C., & Parrone, P. L. (1994). Childhood-onset dysthymic disorder: Clinical features and prospective naturalistic outcome. *Archives of General Psychiatry, 51,* 365–374.

Kovacs, M., & Devlin, B. (1998). Internalizing disorders in childhood. *Journal of Child Psychology and Psychiatry, 39,* 47–63.

Kovacs, M., & Gatsonis, C. (1994). Secular trends in age at onset of major depressive disorder in a clinical sample of children. *Journal of Psychiatric Research, 28,* 319–329.

Kovacs, M., & Goldston, D. (1991). Cognitive and social cognitive development of depressed children and adolescents. *Journal of the American Academy of Child and Adolescent Psychiatry, 30,* 388–392.

Kovacs, M., Goldston, D., & Gatsonis, C. (1993). Suicidal behaviors and childhood-onset depressive disorders: A longitudinal investigation. *Journal of the American Academy of Child and Adolescent Psychiatry, 32,* 8–20.

Kovacs, M., Iyengar, S., Goldston, D., Stewart, J., Obrosky, D. S., & Marsh, J. (1990). Psychological functioning of children with insulin-dependent diabetes mellitus: A longitudinal study. *Journal of Pediatric Psychology, 15,* 619–632.

Kovacs, M., Obrosky, D. S., Gatsonis, C., & Richards, C. (1997). First-episode major depressive and dysthymic disorder in childhood: Clinical and sociodemographic factors in recovery. *Journal of the American Academy of Child and Adolescent Psychiatry, 36,* 777–784.

Kovacs, M., Paulauskas, S., Gatsonis, C., & Richards, C. (1988). Depressive disorders in childhood: A longitudinal study of comorbidity with and risk for conduct disorders. *Journal of Affective Disorders, 15,* 205–217.

Koverola, C., Pound, J., Herger, A., & Lytle, C. (1993). Relationship of child sexual abuse to depression. *Child Abuse and Neglect, 17,* 393–400.

Kraemer, G. W. (1992). A psychobiological theory of attachment. *Behavioral and Brain Sciences, 15,* 493–541.

Krasner, L. (1991). History of behavior modification. In A. S. Bellack, M. Hersen, & A. E. Kazdin (Eds.), *International handbook of behavior modification and therapy* (2nd ed., pp. 3–25). New York: Plenum.

Kratochwill, T. R., & Morris, R. J. (Eds.). (1993). *Handbook of psychotherapy with children and adolescents.* Des Moines, IA: Allyn & Bacon.

Kratzer, L., & Hodgins, S. (1997). Adult outcomes of child conduct problems: A cohort study. *Journal of Abnormal Child Psychology, 25,* 65–81.

Kraus, N., McGee, T. J., Carrell, T. D., Zecker, S. G., Nicol, T. G., & Koch, D. B. (1996, August 16). Auditory neurophysiologic responses and discrimination deficits in children with learning problems. *Science, 273,* 971–973.

Krauss, M. W. (1993). Child-related and parenting stress: Similarities and differences between mothers and fathers of children with disabilities. *American Journal on Mental Retardation, 97,* 393–404.

Kroll, L., Harrington, R., Jayson, D., Fraser, J., & Gowers, S. (1996). Pilot study of continuation cognitive-behavioral therapy for major depression in adolescent psychiatric patients. *Journal of the American Academy of Child and Adolescent Psychiatry, 35,* 1156–1161.

Krueger, R. F., Schmutte, P., Caspi, A., Moffitt, T. E., Campbell, K., & Silva, P. A. (1994). Personality traits are linked to crime among males and females: Evidence from a birth cohort. *Journal of Abnormal Psychology, 103,* 328–338.

Kuhl, P. (1995, May). *Speech perception, memory, and cognition: Implications for automatic speech recognition systems.* Paper presented at the annual meeting of the American Speech Association, Washington, DC.

Kuhlmann, F. (1940). One hundred years of special care and training. *American Journal of Mental Deficiency, 45,* 8–24.

Kurtz, P. D., Gaudin, J. M., Jr., Wodarski, J. S., & Howing, P. T. (1993). Maltreatment and the school-aged child: School performance consequences. *Child Abuse and Neglect, 17,* 581–589.

Kutcher, S. (1997). The pharmacotherapy of adolescent depression. *Journal of Child Psychology and Psychiatry, 38,* 755–767.

Kutcher, S., Reiter, S., & Gardner, D. (1995). Pharmacotherapy: Approaches and applications. In J. March (Ed.), *Anxiety disorders in children and adolescents* (pp. 341–395). New York: Guilford Press.

Lacey, E. P. (1990). Broadening the perspective of pica: Literature review. *Public Health Reports, 105,* 29–35.

Lacey, J. H. (1992). The treatment demand for bulimia: A catchment area report of referral rates and demography. *Psychiatric Bulletin, 16,* 203–205.

Lacharité, C., Boutet, M., & Proulx, R. (1995). Intellectual disability and psychopathology: Developmental perspective. *Canada's Mental Health, 43,* 2–8.

La Greca, A. M. (1990). Social consequences of pediatric conditions: Fertile area for future investigation and intervention. *Journal of Pediatric Psychology, 15,* 285–307.

La Greca, A. M., Silverman, W. K., Vernberg, E. M., & Prinstein, M. J. (1996). Symptoms of posttraumatic stress in children after Hurricane Andrew: A prospective study. *Journal of Consulting and Clinical Psychology, 64,* 712–723.

La Greca, A. M., Swales, T., Klemp, S., Madigan, S., & Skyler, J. (1995). Adolescents with diabetes: Gender differences in psychosocial functioning and glycemic control. *Children's Health Care, 24,* 61–78.

Lahey, B. B., Applegate, B., McBurnett, K., Biederman, J., Greenhill, L., Hynd, G. W., Barkley, R. A., Newcorn, J., Jensen, P., & Richters, J. (1994). DSM-IV field trials for attention deficit hyperactivity disorder in children and adolescents. *American Journal of Psychiatry, 151,* 1673–1685.

Lahey, B. B., & Carlson, C. L. (1992). Validity of the diagnostic category of attention deficit disorder without hyperactivity: A review of the literature. In S. E. Shaywitz & B. A. Shaywitz (Eds.), *Attention deficit disorder comes of age: Toward the twenty-first century* (pp. 119–144). Austin, TX: Pro-ed.

Lahey, B. B., Hart, E. L., Pliszka, S., Applegate, B., & McBurnett, K. (1993). Neurophysiological correlates of conduct disorder: A rationale and review of current research. *Journal of Clinical Child Psychology, 22,* 141–153.

Lahey, B. B., Hartdagen, S. E., Frick, P. J., McBurnett, K., Connor, R., & Hynd, G. W. (1988). Conduct disorder: Parsing the confounded relationship between parental divorce and antisocial personality. *Journal of Abnormal Psychology, 97,* 334–337.

Lahey, B. B., Loeber, R., Hart, E. L., Frick, P. J., Applegate, B., Zhang, Q., Green, S. M., & Russo, M. F. (1995). Four-year longitudinal study of conduct disorder in boys: Patterns and predictors of persistence. *Journal of Abnormal Psychology, 104,* 83–93.

Lahey, B. B., Loeber, R., Quay, H. C., Frick, P. J., & Grimm, S. (1992). Oppositional defiant and conduct disorders: Issues to be resolved for DSM-IV. *Journal of the American Academy of Child and Adolescent Psychiatry, 31,* 539–546.

Lahey, B. B., Pelham, W. E., Schaughency, E. A., Atkins, M. S., Murphy, H. A., Hynd, G. W., Russo, M., Hartdagen, S., & Lorys-Vernon, A. (1988). Dimensions and types of attention deficit disorder with hyperactivity in children: A factor and cluster analytic approach. *Journal of the American Academy of Child and Adolescent Psychiatry, 27,* 330–335.

Lahey, B. B., Piacentini, J. C., McBurnett, K., Stone, P., Hartdagen, S., & Hynd, G. (1988). Psychopathology and antisocial behavior in the parents of children with conduct disorder and hyperactivity. *Journal of the American Academy of Child and Adolescent Psychiatry, 27,* 163–170.

LaHoste, G. J., Swanson, J. M., Wigal, S. B., Glabe, C., Wigal, T., King, N., & Kennedy, J. L. (1996). Dopamine D4 receptor gene polymorphism is associated with attention deficit hyperactivity disorder. *Molecular Psychiatry, 1,* 121–124.

Lam, R. W., Goldner, E. M., & Grewal, A. (1996). Seasonality of symptoms in anorexia and bulimia nervosa. *International Journal of Eating Disorders, 19,* 35–44.

Lambert, M. C., & Weisz, J. R. (1992). Jamaican and American adult perspectives on child psychopathology: Further exploration of the threshold model. *Journal of Consulting and Clinical Psychology, 60,* 146–149

Lambert, N. M., Sandoval, J., & Sassone, D. (1978). Prevalence of hyperactivity in elementary school children as a function of social system definers. *American Journal of Orthopsychiatry, 48,* 446–463.

Landau, S., & Milich, R. (1988). Social communication patterns of attention-deficit-disordered boys. *Journal of Abnormal Child Psychology, 16,* 69–81.

Lang, A. R., Pelham, W. E., Johnston, C., & Gelernter, S. (1989). Levels of adult alcohol consumption induced by interactions with child confederates exhibiting normal versus externalizing behaviors. *Journal of Abnormal Psychology, 98,* 294–299.

Larrance, D. T., & Twentyman, C. T. (1983). Maternal attributions and child abuse. *Journal of Abnormal Psychology, 92,* 449–457.

Larson, R. W., Raffaelli, M., Richards, M. H., Ham, M., & Jewell, L. (1990). Ecology of depression in late childhood and early adolescence: A profile of daily states and activities. *Journal of Abnormal Psychology, 99,* 92–102.

Lask, B., & Bryant-Waugh, R. (1992). Early-onset anorexia nervosa and related eating disorders. *Journal of Child Psychology and Psychiatry, 33,* 281–300.

Last, C. G. (1988). Separation anxiety. In M. Hersen & C. G. Last (Eds.), *Child behavior therapy casebook* (pp. 11–17). New York: Plenum.

Last, C. G. (1991). Somatic complaints in anxiety disordered children. *Journal of Anxiety Disorders, 5,* 125–138.

Last, C. G., Francis, G., Hersen, M., Kazdin, A. E., & Strauss, C. C. (1987). Separation anxiety and school phobia: A comparison using DSM-III criteria. *American Journal of Psychiatry, 144,* 653–657.

Last, C. G., Hersen, M., Kazdin, A. E., Finkelstein, R., & Strauss, C. C. (1987). Comparison of DSM-III separation anxiety and overanxious disorders: Demographic characteristics and patterns of comorbidity. *Journal of the American Academy of Child and Adolescent Psychiatry, 26,* 527–531.

Last, C. G., & Perrin, S. (1993). Anxiety disorders in African-American and white children. *Journal of Abnormal Child Psychology, 21,* 153–164.

Last, C. G., Perrin, S., Hersen, M., & Kazdin, A. E. (1992). DSM-III-R anxiety disorders in children: Sociodemographic and clinical characteristics. *Journal of the American Academy of Child and Adolescent Psychiatry, 31,* 1070–1076.

Last, C. G., Perrin, S., Hersen, M., & Kazdin, A. E. (1996). A prospective study of childhood anxiety disorders. *Journal of the American Academy of Child and Adolescent Psychiatry, 35,* 1502–1510.

Last, C. G., & Strauss, C. C. (1989a). Obsessive-compulsive disorder in childhood. *Journal of Anxiety Disorders, 3,* 295–302.

Last, C. G., & Strauss, C. C. (1989b). Panic disorder in children and adolescents. *Journal of Anxiety Disorders, 3,* 87–95.

Latham, P., & Latham, R. (1992). *ADD and the law.* Washington, DC: JKL Communications.

Laufer, M., Denhoff, E., & Solomons, G. (1957). Hyperkinetic impulse disorder in children's behavior problems. *Psychosomatic Medicine, 19,* 38–49.

Laughlin, C. (1995). Kevin needed time, not medication. *Learning,* pp. 56, 58.

Lavigne, J. V., & Faier-Routman, J. (1992). Psychological adjustment to pediatric physical disorders: A meta-analytic review. *Journal of Pediatrics, 17,* 133–158.

Lavigne, J. V., & Faier-Routman, J. (1993). Correlates of psychological adjustment to pediatric physical disorders: A meta-analytic review and comparison with existing models. *Journal of Developmental and Behavioral Pediatrics, 14,* 117–123.

Layton, L. (1994). Who's that girl? A case study of Madonna. In C. E. Franz & A. J. Stewart (Eds.), *Women creating lives: Identities, resilience, and resistance* (pp. 143–156). Boulder, CO: Westview Press.

Lease, C. A., & Ollendick, T. H. (1993). Development and psychopathology. In A. S. Bellack & M. Hersen (Eds.),

Psychopathology in adulthood (pp. 89–103). New York: Allyn & Bacon.

Le Couteur, A., Bailey, A., Goode, S., Pickles, A., Robertson, S., Gottesman, I., & Rutter, M. (1996). A broader phenotype of autism: The clinical spectrum in twins. *Journal of Child Psychology and Psychiatry, 37,* 785–801.

Leffert, J. S., & Siperstein, G. N. (1996). Assessment of social-cognitive processes in children with mental retardation. *American Journal of Mental Retardation, 100,* 441–455.

Le Grange, D., Eisler, I., Dare, C., & Russell, G. F. M. (1992). Evaluation of family therapy in anorexia nervosa: A pilot study. *International Journal of Eating Disorders, 12,* 347–357.

Leitenberg, H., Rosen, J. C., Gross, J., Nudelman, S., & Vara, L. S. (1988). Exposure plus response prevention treatment of bulimia nervosa: A controlled evaluation. *Journal of Consulting and Clinical Psychology, 56,* 535–541.

Leitenberg, H., Rosen, J. C., Wolf, J., Vara, L. S., Detzer, M. J., & Srebnik, D. (1994). Comparison of cognitive-behavior therapy and desipramine in the treatment of bulimia nervosa. *Behaviour Research and Therapy, 32,* 37–45.

Leland, J. (1995, December 11). Violence, reel to real. *Newsweek,* pp. 46–48.

Lendon, C. L., Ashall, F., & Goate, A. M. (1997). Exploring the etiology of Alzheimer's disease using molecular genetics. *Journal of the American Medical Association, 277,* 825–831.

Leonard, H. L., & Dow, S. (1995). Selective mutism. In J. S. March (Ed.), *Anxiety disorders in children and adolescents* (pp. 235–250). New York: Guilford Press.

Lerer, R. J., Lerer, M. P., & Artner, J. (1977). The effects of methylphenidate on the handwriting of children with minimal brain dysfunction. *Journal of Pediatrics, 91,* 127–132.

Lesch, K, P., Bengel, D., Heils, A., Sabol, S. Z., Greenberg, B. D., Petri, S., Benjamin, J., Muller, C. R., Hamer, D. H., & Murphy, D. L. (1996). Association of anxiety-related traits with a polymorphism in the serotonin transporter gene regulatory region. *Science, 274,* 1527–1531.

Lesem, M. D., George, D. T., Kaye, W. H., Goldstein, D. S., & Jimerson, D. C. (1989). State-related changes in norepinephrine regulation in anorexia nervosa. *Biological Psychiatry, 25,* 509–512.

Lesser, S. T. (1972). Psychoanalysis with children. In B. B. Wolman (Ed.), *Manual of child psychopathology* (pp. 847–864). New York: McGraw-Hill.

Leutwyler, K. (1997, January). Depression's double standard. *Scientific American,* 53–54.

Levine, K. (1995, October). Childhood depression. *Parents,* 42–45.

Levine, M., & Levine, A. (1992). *Helping children: A social history.* New York: Oxford University Press.

Levine, M. D. (1982). Encopresis: Its potentiation, evaluation, and treatment. *Pediatric Clinics of North America, 29,* 315–330.

Levine, M. L., & Smolak, L. (1992). Toward a model of the developmental psychopathology of eating disorders: The example of early adolescence. In J. H. Crowther, D. L. Tennenbaum, S. E. Hobfall, & M. A. P. Stephens (Eds.), *The etiology of bulimia nervosa: The individual and familial context* (pp. 59–80). Washington, DC: Hemisphere Publishing.

Levitt, E. E., & French, J. (1992). Projective testing of children. In C. E. Walker & M. C. Roberts (Eds.), *Handbook of clinical child psychology* (2nd ed., pp. 149–162). New York: Wiley.

Levitt, P. (1995). Experimental approaches that reveal principles of cerebral cortical development. In M. S. Gazzaniga (Ed.), *The cognitive neurosciences* (pp. 147–163). Cambridge, MA: MIT Press.

Levy, F., & Hay, D. (1992, February). *ADHD in twins and their siblings.* Paper presented at the Society for Research in Child and Adolescent Psychopathology, Sarasota, FL.

Lewin, K. (1951). Problems of research in social psychology. In D. Cartwright (Ed.), *Field theory in social science: Selected theoretical papers of Kurt Lewin.* New York: Harper & Row.

Lewin, L. M., Hops, H., Davis, B., & Dishion, T. J. (1993). Multimethod comparison of similarity in school adjustment of siblings and unrelated children. *Developmental Psychology, 29,* 963–969.

Lewinsohn, P. M. (1974). A behavioral approach to depression. In R. Friedman & M. Katz (Eds.), *The psychology of depression: Contemporary theory and research* (pp. 157–185). Washington, DC: Winston-Wiley.

Lewinsohn, P. M., Clarke, G. N., Hops, H., & Andrews, J. (1990). Cognitive-behavioral group treatment of depression in adolescents. *Behavior Therapy, 21,* 384–401.

Lewinsohn, P. M., Clarke, G. N., & Rohde, P. (1994). Psychological approaches to the treatment of depression in adolescents. In W. M. Reynolds & H. F. Johnston (Eds.), *Handbook of depression in children and adolescents* (pp. 309–344). New York: Plenum.

Lewinsohn, P. M., Clarke, G. N., Rohde, P., Hops, H., & Seeley, J. R. (1996). A course in coping: A cognitive-behavioral approach to the treatment of adolescent depression. In E. D. Hibbs & P. Jensen (Eds.), *Psychosocial treatments for child and adolescent disorders: Empirically based strategies for clinical practice* (pp. 109–135). Washington, DC: American Psychological Association.

Lewinsohn, P. M., Clarke, G. N., Seeley, J. R., & Rohde, P. (1994). Major depression in community adolescents: Age at onset, episode duration, and time to recurrence. *Journal of the American Academy of Child and Adolescent Psychiatry, 33,* 809–818.

Lewinsohn, P. M., Gotlib, I. H., Lewinsohn, M., Seeley, J. R., & Allen, N. B. (1998). Gender differences in anxiety disorders and anxiety symptoms in adolescents. *Journal of Abnormal Psychology, 107,* 109–117.

Lewinsohn, P. M., Gotlib, I. H., & Seeley, J. R. (1997). Depression-related psychosocial variables: Are they specific to depression in adolescents? *Journal of Abnormal Psychology, 106,* 365–375.

Lewinsohn, P. M., Hops, H., Roberts, R. E., Seeley, J. R., & Andrews, J. A. (1993). Adolescent psychopathology: I. Prevalence and incidence of depression and other DSM-III-R disorders in high school students. *Journal of Abnormal Psychology, 102,* 133–144.

Lewinsohn, P. M., Klein, D., & Seeley, J. R. (1995). Bipolar disorders in a community sample of older adolescents: Prevalence, phenomenology, comorbidity, and course. *Journal of the American Academy of Child and Adolescent Psychiatry, 34,* 454–463.

Lewinsohn, P. M., Roberts, R. E., Seeley, J. R., Rohde, P., Gotlib, I. H., & Hops, H. (1994). Adolescent psychopathology: II. Psychosocial risk factors for depression. *Journal of Abnormal Psychology, 103,* 302–315.

Lewinsohn, P. M., Rohde, P., & Seeley, J. R. (1993). Psychoso-

cial characteristics of adolescents with a history of suicide attempts. *Journal of the American Academy of Child and Adolescent Psychiatry, 32,* 60–68.

Lewinsohn, P. M., Rohde, P., Seeley, J. R., & Fischer, S. (1993). Age-cohort changes in the lifetime occurrence of depression and other mental disorders. *Journal of Abnormal Psychology, 102,* 110–120.

Lewinsohn, P. M., Rohde, P., Seeley, J. R., & Hops, H. (1991). The comorbidity of unipolar depression: Part 1. Major depression with dysthymia. *Journal of Abnormal Psychology, 100,* 205–213.

Lewinsohn, P. M., Seeley, J. R., Hibbard, J. H., Rohde, P., & Sack, W. H. (1996). Cross-sectional and prospective relationships between physical morbidity and depression in older adolescents. *Journal of the American Academy of Child and Adolescent Psychiatry, 35,* 1120–1129.

Lewis, B. A. (1990). Familial phonological disorders: Four pedigrees. *Journal of Speech and Hearing Disorders, 55,* 160–170.

Lewis, D. O., Pincus, J. H., & Glaser, G. H. (1979). Violent juvenile delinquents: Psychiatric, neurological, psychological, and abuse factors. *Journal of the American Academy of Child Psychiatry, 18,* 307–319.

Lewis, D. O., Yeager, C. A., Cobham-Portorreal, C. S., Klein, N., Showalter, B. A., & Anthony, A. (1991). A follow-up of female delinquents: Maternal contributions to the perpetuation of deviance. *Journal of the American Academy of Child and Adolescent Psychiatry, 30,* 197–201.

Lewis, M. (1990). Models of developmental psychopathology. In M. Lewis & S. M. Miller (Eds.), *Handbook of developmental psychopathology* (pp. 15–27). New York: Plenum.

Lewis, M. H., Aman, M. G., Gadow, K. D., Schroeder, S. R., & Thompson, T. (1996). Psychopharmacology. In J. W. Jacobson & J. A. Mulick (Eds.), *Manual of diagnosis and professional practice in mental retardation* (pp. 323–340). Washington, DC: American Psychological Association.

Liberman, I. Y., & Shankweiler, D. (1991). Phonology and beginning reading: A tutorial. In L. Rieben & C. A. Perfetti (Eds.), *Learning to read: Basic research and its implications* (pp. 46–73). Hillsdale, NJ: Erlbaum.

Lincoln, A., Courchesne, E., Allen, M., Hanson, E., & Ene, M. (1998). Neurobiology of Asperger Syndrome: Seven case studies and quantitative magnetic resonance imaging findings. In E. Schopler, G. B. Mesibov, & L. J. Kunce (Eds.), *Asperger syndrome or high-functioning autism?* (pp. 145–163). New York: Plenum.

Lincoln, A. J., Courchesne, E., Mascarello, J., Yeung-Courchesne, E., & Schreibman, L. (1996). *Autism and the Fragile X Syndrome: No demonstrable relationship found between FMR1 (CGG) n expansions and autism.* Unpublished manuscript, Autism and Brain Development Research Laboratory, Children's Hospital Research Center, La Jolla, CA.

Lipsey, M. W. (1995). What do we learn from 400 research studies on the effectiveness of treatment with juvenile delinquents? In J. McGuire (Ed.), *What works: Reducing reoffending: Guidelines from research and practice* (pp. 63–78). Chichester, England: Wiley.

Lisak, D. (1994). The psychological impact of sexual abuse: Content analysis of interviews with male survivors. *Journal of Traumatic Stress, 7,* 525–548.

Lisak, D., Hopper, J., & Song, P. (1996). Factors in the cycle of violence: Gender rigidity and emotional constriction. *Journal of Traumatic Stress, 9,* 721–743.

Lloyd, J. W., Hallahan, D. P., Kauffman, J. M., & Keller, C. E. (1991). Academic problems. In T. R. Kratochwill & R. J. Morris (Eds.), *The practice of child therapy* (2nd ed., pp. 145–173). Toronto: Pergamon Press.

Locke, J. L., & Mather, P. L. (1989). Genetic factors in the ontogeny of spoken language: Evidence from monozygotic and dizygotic twins. *Journal of Child Language, 16,* 553.

Loeber, R. (1990). Development and risk factors of juvenile antisocial behavior and delinquency. *Clinical Psychology Review, 10,* 1–42.

Loeber, R. (1991). Questions and advances in the study of developmental pathways. In D. Cicchetti & S. L. Toth (Eds.), *Rochester symposium on developmental psychopathology: Vol. 3. Models and integrations.* (pp. 97–116). Rochester, NY: University of Rochester Press.

Loeber, R., Green, S. M., Lahey, B. B., Christ, M. A. G., & Frick, P. J. (1992). Developmental sequences in the age of onset of disruptive child behaviors. *Journal of Child and Family Studies, 1,* 21–41.

Loeber, R., & Keenan, K. (1994). Interaction between conduct disorder and its comorbid conditions: Effects of age and gender. *Clinical Psychology Review, 14,* 497–523.

Loeber, R., Lahey, B. B., & Thomas, C. (1991). Diagnostic conundrum of oppositional defiant disorder and conduct disorder. *Journal of Abnormal Psychology, 100,* 379–390.

Loeber, R., Stouthamer-Loeber, M., & Green, S. M. (1991). Age at onset of problem behaviour in boys, and later disruptive and delinquent behaviours. *Criminal Behaviour and Mental Health, 1,* 229–246.

Logan, G. D. (1994). On the ability to inhibit thought and action: A users' guide to the stop signal paradigm. In D. Dagenbach & T. H. Carr (Eds.), *Inhibitory processes in attention, memory, and language* (pp. 189–239). San Diego: Academic Press.

Lombroso, P. J., Pauls, D. L., & Leckman, J. F. (1994). Genetic mechanisms in childhood psychiatric disorders. *Journal of the American Academy of Child and Adolescent Psychiatry, 33,* 921–938.

Lonigan, C. J., Carey, M. P., & Finch, A. J. (1994). Anxiety and depression in children and adolescents: Negative affectivity and the utility of self-reports. *Journal of Consulting and Clinical Psychology, 62,* 1000–1008.

Lonigan, C. J., & Elbert, J. C. (Eds.). (1998). Empirically supported psychosocial interventions for children [Special issue]. *Journal of Clinical Child Psychology, 27*(Whole No. 2).

Lonigan, C. J., & Fischel, J. E. (1992). The role of otitis media in the development of expressive language disorder. *Developmental Psychology, 28,* 430–440.

Lotter, V. (1978). Follow-up studies. In M. Rutter & E. Schopler (Eds.), *Autism: A reappraisal of concepts and treatment* (pp. 475–495). New York: Plenum.

Lou, H. C., Henriksen, L., Bruhn, P., Borner, H., & Nielson, J. B. (1989). Striatal dysfunction in attention deficit and hyperkinetic disorder. *Archives of Neurology, 46,* 48–52.

Loveland, K. A., Tunali-Kotoski, B., Pearson, D. A., Brelsford, K. A., Ortegon, J., & Chen, R. (1994). Imitation and expression of facial affect in autism. *Development and Psychopathology, 6,* 433–444.

Lowe, M. R. (1993). The effects of dieting on eating behavior: A three-factor model. *Psychological Bulletin, 114,* 100–121.

Lucas, A. R., Beard, C. M., O'Fallon, W. M., & Kurland, L. T. (1991). Fifty-year trends in the incidence of anorexia nervosa in Rochester, Minnesota: A population-based study. *American Journal of Psychiatry, 148,* 917–922.

Luckasson, R., Coulter, D. L., Polloway, E. A., Reiss, S., Schalock, R. L., Snell, M. E., Spitalnik, D. M., & Stark, J. A. (1992). *Mental retardation: Definition, classification, and systems of supports* (9th ed.). Washington, DC: American Association on Mental Retardation.

Lung, C. T., & Daro, D. (1996). *Current trends in child abuse reporting and fatalities: The results of the 1995 annual fifty state survey.* Chicago: National Committee to Prevent Child Abuse.

Luria, A. (1961). *The role of speech in the regulation of normal and abnormal behavior.* New York: Liveright.

Luthar, S. S. (1993). Annotation: Methodological and conceptual issues in research on childhood resilience. *Journal of Child Psychology and Psychiatry, 34,* 441–453.

Lutzker, J. R., Bigelow, K. M., Doctor, R. M., Gershater, R. M., & Greene, B. F. (1998). An ecobehavioral model for the prevention and treatment of child abuse and neglect. In J. R. Lutzker (Ed.), *Handbook of child abuse research and treatment* (pp. 239–266). New York: Plenum.

Lutzker, J. R., & Rice, J. M. (1987). Using recidivism data to evaluate Project 12-Ways: An ecobehavioral approach to the treatment and prevention of child abuse and neglect. *Journal of Family Violence, 2,* 283–290.

Lynam, D., Moffitt, T. E., & Stouthamer-Loeber, M. (1993). Explaining the relation between IQ and delinquency: Race, class, test motivation, school failure, or self-control. *Journal of Abnormal Psychology, 102,* 187–196.

Lynam, D. R. (1996). Early identification of chronic offenders: Who is the fledgling psychopath? *Psychological Bulletin, 120,* 209–234.

Lyon, G. R. (1996). Learning disabilities. In E. J. Mash & R. A. Barkley (Eds.), *Child psychopathology* (pp. 390–435). New York: Guilford Press.

Lyon, G. R. (in press). Foundations of neuroanatomy and neuropsychology. In G. R. Lyon & J. Rumsey (Eds.), *Neuroimaging: A window to the neurological foundations of learning and behavior.* Baltimore: Paul H. Brookes.

Lyon, G. R., & Cutting, L. (1998). Treatment of learning disabilities. In E. J. Mash & L. C. Terdal (Eds.), *Treatment of childhood disorders* (2nd ed.). New York: Guilford Press.

Lyons-Ruth, K. (1995). Broadening our conceptual frameworks: Can we introduce relational strategies and implicit representational systems to the study of psychopathology? *Developmental Psychology, 31,* 432–436.

Lyons-Ruth, K., Alpern, L., & Repacholi, B. (1993). Disorganized infant attachment classification and maternal psychosocial problems as predictors of hostile-aggressive behavior in the preschool classroom. *Child Development, 64,* 572–585.

Lyons-Ruth, K., Zeanah, C. H., & Benoit, D. (1996). Disorder and risk for disorder during infancy and toddlerhood. In E. J. Mash & R. A. Barkley (Eds.), *Child psychopathology* (pp. 457–491). New York: Guilford Press.

Lytton, H. (1990). Child and parent effects in boys' conduct disorder: A reinterpretation. *Developmental Psychology, 26,* 683–697.

MacArthur, C. A., Haynes, J. A., Malouf, D. B., & Harris, K. R. (1990). Computer assisted instruction with learning disabled students: Achievement, engagement, and other factors that influence achievement. *Journal of Educational Computing Research, 6,* 311–328.

Maccoby, E. E. (1986). Social groupings in childhood: Their

relationship to prosocial and antisocial behavior in boys and girls. In D. Olweus, J. Block, & M. Radke-Yarrow (Eds.), *Development of antisocial and prosocial behavior* (pp. 263–284). Orlando, FL: Academic Press.

Maccoby, E. E., & Martin, J. A. (1983). Socialization in the context of the family: Parent-child interaction. In P. H. Mussen (Ed.), *Handbook of child psychology* (4th ed.): *Vol. IV. Socialization, personality, and social development* (pp. 1–101). New York: Wiley.

Macdonald, H., Rutter, M., Howlin, P., Rios, P., Le Couteur, A., Evered, C., & Folstein, S. (1989). Recognition and expression of emotional cues by autistic and normal adults. *Journal of Child Psychology and Psychiatry, 30,* 865–877.

MacDonald, L. (1986). Ethical standards for therapeutic programs in human services: An evaluation model. *The Behavior Therapist, 9,* 213–215.

MacGillivray, M. H. (1987). Disorders of growth and development. In P. Felig, J. D. Baxter, A. C. Broadus, & L. A. Frohman (Eds.), *Endocrinology and metabolism* (2nd ed., pp. 1581–1628). New York: McGraw-Hill.

Mackillop, W. J., Zhang-Salomons, J., Groome, P. A., Paszat, L., & Holowaty, E. (1997). Socioeconomic status and cancer survival in Ontario. *Journal of Clinical Oncology, 15,* 1680–1689.

MacLean, R. E. G. (1960). Imipramine hydrochloride (Tofranil) and enuresis. *American Journal of Psychiatry, 117,* 551.

MacLean, W. E., Jr., Perrin, J. M., Gortmaker, S., & Pierre, C. B. (1992). Psychological adjustment of children with asthma: Effects of illness severity and recent stressful life events. *Journal of Pediatric Psychology, 17,* 159–172.

MacMillan, D. L., Gresham, F. M., & Siperstein, G. N. (1993). Conceptual and psychometric concerns about the 1992 AAMR definition of mental retardation. *American Journal on Mental Retardation, 98,* 325–335.

MacMillan, D. L., & Keough, B. (1971). Normal and retarded children's expectancy for failure. *Developmental Psychology, 4,* 343–348.

MacMillan, H. L., Fleming, J. E., Trocme, N., Boyle, M. H., Wong, M., Racine, Y. A., Beardslee, W. R., & Offord, D. R. (1997). Prevalence of child physical and sexual abuse in the community: Results from the Ontario Health Supplement. *Journal of the American Medical Association, 278,* 131–135.

Magnusson, D. (1988). Aggressiveness, hyperactivity, and autonomic activity/reactivity in the development of social maladjustment. In D. Magnusson (Ed.), *Paths through life: Individual development from an interactionary perspective: A longitudinal study* (Vol. 1, pp. 153–175). Hillsdale, NJ: Erlbaum.

Main, M., & George, C. (1985). Responses of abused and disadvantaged toddlers to distress in agemates: A study in the daycare setting. *Developmental Psychology, 21,* 407–412.

Main, M., & Goldwyn, R. (1984). Predicting rejecting of her infant from mother's representation of her own experience: Implications for the abused-abusing intergenerational cycle. *Child Abuse and Neglect, 8,* 203–217.

Main, M., & Hesse, E. (1990). Parents' unresolved traumatic experiences are related to infant disorganized attachment status: Is frightened and/or frightening parental behavior the linking mechanism? In E. M. Greenberg, D. Cicchetti, & E. M. Cummings (Eds.), *Attachment in the preschool years* (pp. 161–182). Chicago: University of Chicago Press.

Main, M., & Solomon, J. (1990). Procedures for identifying infants as disorganized/disoriented during the Ainsworth Strange Situation. In M. Greenberg, D. Cicchetti, & E. M. Cummings (Eds.), *Attachment in the preschool years* (pp. 121–160). Chicago: University of Chicago Press.

Makari, G. J. (1993). Educated insane: A nineteenth-century psychiatric paradigm. *Journal of the History of the Behavioral Sciences, 29,* 8–21.

Malamuth, N. M., Sockloskie, R. J., Koss, M. P., & Tanaka, J. S. (1991). Characteristics of aggressors against women: Testing a model using a national sample of college students. *Journal of Consulting and Clinical Psychology, 59,* 670–681.

Malchiodi, C. A. (1998). *Understanding children's drawings.* New York: Guilford Press.

Malinosky-Rummell, R., & Hansen, D. J. (1993). Long-term consequences of childhood physical abuse. *Psychological Bulletin, 114,* 68–79.

Malone, M. A., & Swanson, J. M. (1993). Effects of methylphenidate on impulsive responding in children with attention deficit hyperactivity disorder. *Journal of Child Neurology, 8,* 157–163.

Maloney, M., & Kranz, R. (1991). *Straight talk about eating disorders.* New York: Facts on File.

Manassis, K., & Bradley, S. (1994). The development of childhood anxiety disorders: Toward an integrated model. *Journal of Applied Developmental Psychology, 15,* 345–366.

Manassis, K., Bradley, S., Goldberg, S., Hood, J., & Swinson, R. P. (1994). Attachment in mothers with anxiety disorders and their children. *Journal of the American and Adolescent Psychiatry, 33,* 1106–1113.

Mancini, C., van Ameringen, M., Szatmari, P., Fugere, C., & Boyle, M. (1996). A high-risk pilot study of the children of adults with social phobia. *Journal of the American Academy of Child and Adolescent Psychiatry, 35,* 1511–1517.

Mannuzza, S., & Klein, R. (1992). Predictors of outcome of children with attention-deficit hyperactivity disorder. In G. Weiss (Ed.), *Child and adolescent psychiatric clinics of North America: Attention-deficit hyperactivity disorder* (pp. 567–578). Philadelphia: Saunders.

Mans, L., Cicchetti, D., & Sroufe, L. A. (1978). Mirror reactions of Down's syndrome infants and toddlers: Cognitive underpinnings of self-recognition. *Child Development, 49,* 1247–1250.

March, J. S. (Ed.). (1995a). *Anxiety disorders in children and adolescents.* New York: Guilford Press.

March, J. S. (1995b). Cognitive-behavioral psychotherapy for children and adolescents with OCD: A review and recommendations for treatment. *Journal of the American Academy of Child and Adolescent Psychiatry, 34,* 7–18.

March, J. S., & Mulle, K. (1996). Banishing OCD: Cognitive-behavioral psychotherapy for obsessive-compulsive disorders. In E. D. Hibbs & P. S. Jensen (Eds.), *Psychosocial treatments for child and adolescent disorders: Empirically-based strategies for clinical practice* (pp. 83–102). Washington, DC: American Psychological Association.

March, J. S., & Mulle, K. (1998). *OCD in children and adolescents: A cognitive-behavioral treatment manual.* New York: Guilford Press.

March, J. S., Parker, J. D. A., Sullivan, K., Stallings, P., & Conners, C. K. (1997). The Multidimensional Anxiety Scale for Children (MASC): Factor structure, reliability, and validity. *Journal of the American Academy of Child and Adolescent Psychiatry, 36,* 554–565.

Marchi, M., & Cohen, P. (1990). Early childhood eating behaviors and adolescent eating disorders. *Journal of the*

American Academy of Child and Adolescent Psychiatry, 29, 112–117.

Marciano, P. L., & Kazdin, A. E. (1994). Self-esteem, depression, hopelessness, and suicidal intent among psychiatrically disturbed inpatient adolescents. *Journal of Clinical Child Psychology, 23,* 151–160.

Mariani, M. A., & Barkley, R. A. (1997). Neuropsychological and academic functioning in preschool boys with attention deficit hyperactivity disorder. *Developmental Neuropsychology, 13,* 111–129.

Marshall, W. L. (1993). The role of attachment, intimacy, and loneliness in the etiology and maintenance of sexual offending. *Sexual and Marital Therapy, 8,* 109–121.

Marten, P. A., Albano, A. M., & Holt, C. S. (1991, January). *Cognitive-behavioral group treatment of adolescent social phobia with parent participation.* Unpublished manuscript, University of Louisville, Department of Psychology, Louisville, KY.

Martin, J. F. (1995, Fall/Winter). Life with Karl. *Entourage,* p. 10.

Mash, E. J. (1991). Measurement of parent-child interaction in studies of child maltreatment. In R. Starr, Jr., & D. Wolfe (Eds.), *The effects of child abuse and neglect: Research issues* (pp. 203–256). New York: Guilford Press.

Mash, E. J. (1998). Treatment of child and family disturbance: A behavioral-systems perspective. In E. J. Mash & R. A. Barkley (Eds.), *Treatment of childhood disorders* (2nd ed., pp. 3–54). New York: Guilford Press.

Mash, E. J., & Barkley, R. A. (Eds.). (1998). *Treatment of childhood disorders* (2nd ed.). New York: Guilford Press.

Mash, E. J., & Dozois, J. A. (1996). Child psychopathology: A developmental-systems perspective. In E. J. Mash & R. A. Barkley (Eds.), *Child psychopathology* (pp. 3–62). New York: Guilford Press.

Mash, E. J., & Johnston, C. (1982). A comparison of mother-child interactions of younger and older hyperactive and normal children. *Child Development, 53,* 1371–1381.

Mash, E. J., & Johnston, C. (1983). Parental perceptions of child behavior problems, parenting self-esteem and mothers' reported stress in younger and older hyperactive and normal children. *Journal of Consulting and Clinical Psychology, 51,* 86–99.

Mash, E. J., & Johnston, C. (1990). Determinants of parenting stress: Illustrations from families of hyperactive children and families of physically abused children. *Journal of Clinical Child Psychology, 19,* 313–328.

Mash, E. J., & Johnston, C. (1996). Family relational problems. In V. E. Caballo, J. A. Carrobles, & G. Buela-Casal (Eds.), *Handbook of psychopathology and psychiatric disorders* (pp. 589–621). Madrid: Siglo XXI.

Mash, E. J., Johnston, C., & Kovitz, K. (1983). A comparison of the mother-child interactions of physically abused and non-abused children during play and task situations. *Journal of Clinical Child Psychology, 12,* 337–346.

Mash, E. J., & Terdal, L. G. (1997a). Assessment of child and family disturbance: A behavioral-systems approach. In E. J. Mash & L. G. Terdal (Eds.), *Assessment of childhood disorders* (3rd ed., pp. 3–68). New York: Guilford Press.

Mash, E. J., & Terdal, L. G. (Eds.). (1997b). *Assessment of childhood disorders* (3rd ed.). New York: Guilford Press.

Mash, E. J., & Wolfe, D. A. (1991). Methodological issues in research on physical child abuse. *Criminal Justice and Behavior, 18,* 8–29.

Mason, D. A., & Frick, Paul J. (1994). The heritability of antisocial behavior: A meta-analysis of twin and adoption studies. *Journal of Psychopathology and Behavioral Assessment, 16,* 301–323.

Masten, A. S., & Coatsworth, J. D. (1998). The development of competence in favorable and unfavorable environments: Lessons from research on successful children. *American Psychologist, 53,* 205–220.

Mather, N. (1992). Whole language reading instruction for students with learning disabilities: Caught in the crossfire. *Learning Disabilities Research and Practice, 7,* 87–95.

Matson, J. L., & Coe, D. A. (1991). Mentally retarded children. In T. R. Kratochwill & R. J. Morris (Eds.), *The practice of child therapy* (2nd ed. pp. 298–327). Toronto: Pergamon Press.

Matson, J. L., & Frame, C. L. (1986). *Psychopathology among mentally retarded children and adolescents.* Newbury Park, CA: Sage.

Matson, J. L., & Hammer, D. (1996). Assessment of social functioning. In J. W. Jacobson & J. A. Mulick (Eds.), *Manual of diagnosis and professional practice in mental retardation* (pp. 157–163). Washington, DC: American Psychological Association.

Mattis, S. G., & Ollendick, T. H. (1997a). Children's cognitive responses to the somatic symptoms of panic. *Journal of Abnormal Child Psychology, 25,* 47–57.

Mattis, S. G., & Ollendick, T. H. (1997b). Panic in children and adolescents: A developmental analysis. *Advances in Clinical Child Psychology, 19,* 27–74.

Maughan, B., Gray, G., & Rutter, M. (1985). Reading retardation and antisocial behavior: A follow-up into employment. *Journal of Child Psychology and Psychiatry, 26,* 741–758.

Maughan, B., & Hagell, A. (1996). Poor readers in adulthood: Psychosocial functioning. *Development and Psychopathology, 8,* 457–476.

Maughan, B., Pickles, A., Hagell, A., Rutter, M., & Yule, W. (1996). Reading problems and antisocial behavior: Developmental trends in comorbidity. *Journal of Child Psychology and Psychiatry, 37,* 405–418.

Maurice, C. (1993a, June). Rescuing my daughter. *McCall's,* pp. 75, 76, 78, 84, 156.

Maurice, C. (1993b). *Let me hear your voice: A family's triumph over autism.* New York: Fawcett Columbine.

Maxfield, M. G., & Widom, C. S. (1996). The cycle of violence: Revisited 6 years later. *Archives of Pediatric and Adolescent Medicine, 150,* 390–395.

Maxwell, S. E., & Delaney, H. D. (1990). *Designing experiments and analyzing data: A model comparison perspective.* Belmont, CA: Wadsworth.

Mayes, S. D., Humphrey, F. J., Handford, H. A., & Mitchell, J. F. (1988). Rumination disorder: Differential diagnosis. *Journal of the American Academy of Child and Adolescent Psychiatry, 27,* 300–302.

McAlpine, C., & Singh, N. N. (1986). Pica in institutionalized mentally retarded persons. *Journal of Mental Deficiency Research, 30,* 171–178.

McArthur, D. S., & Roberts, G. E. (1982). *Roberts Apperception Test for children.* Los Angeles: Western Psychological Services.

McBurnett, K. (1992). Psychobiological approaches to personality and their application to child psychopathology. In B. B. Lahey & A. E. Kazdin (Eds.), *Advances in clinical child psychology* (Vol. 14, pp. 107–164). New York: Plenum.

McBurnett, K., & Lahey, B. B. (1994). Neuropsychological and neuroendocrine correlates of conduct disorder and antisocial behavior in children and adolescents. In D. C. Fowles, P. Sutker, & S. H. Goodman (Eds.), *Progress in experimental personality and psychopathology research* (pp. 199–231). New York: Springer.

McBurnett, K., Lahey, B. B., Frick, P. J., Risch, C., Loeber, R., Hart, E. L., Christ, M. A. G., & Hanson, K. S. (1991). Anxiety, inhibition, and conduct disorders in children, II: Relation to salivary cortisol. *Journal of the American Academy of Child and Adolescent Psychiatry, 30,* 192–196.

McCabe, M. A. (1996). Involving children and adolescents in medical decision making: Developmental and clinical considerations. *Journal of Pediatric Psychology, 21,* 505–516.

McCall, R. B. (1977). Childhood IQs as predictors of adult educational and occupational status. *Science, 197,* 482–483.

McCauley, E., Myers, K., Mitchell, J., Calderon, R., Scholoredt, K., & Treder, R. (1993). Depression in young people: Initial presentation and clinical course. *Journal of the American Academy of Child and Adolescent Psychiatry, 32,* 714–722.

McClaren, J., & Bryson, S. E. (1987). Review of recent epidemiological studies of mental retardation: Prevalence, associated disorders, and etiology. *American Journal of Mental Retardation, 92,* 243–254.

McClellan, J., McCurry, C., Ronnei, M., Adams, J., Eisner, A., & Storck, M. (1996). Age of onset of sexual abuse: Relationship to sexually inappropriate behaviors. *Journal of the American Academy of Child and Adolescent Psychiatry, 35,* 1375–1383.

McCloskey, L., Figueredo, A., & Koss, M. (1995). The effects of systematic family violence on children's mental health. *Child Development, 66,* 1239–1261.

McClung, H. J., Boyne, L. J., Linsheid, T., Heitlinger, L. A., Murray, R. D., Fyda, J., & Li, B. U. K. (1993). Is combination therapy for encopresis nutritionally safe? *Pediatrics, 91,* 591–594.

McCormick, M. C., Gortmaker, S. L., & Sobol, A. M. (1990). Very low birth weight children: Behavior problems and school difficulties in a national sample. *Journal of Pediatrics, 117,* 687–693.

McCracken, J. T. (1991). A two-part model of stimulant action on attention-deficit hyperactivity disorder in children. *Journal of Neuropsychiatry, 3,* 201–209.

McDermott, P. A. (1993). National standardization of uniform multisituational measures of child and adolescent behavior pathology. *Psychological Assessment, 5,* 413–424.

McDermott, P. A. (1996). A nationwide study of developmental and gender prevalence for psychopathology in childhood and adolescence. *Journal of Abnormal Child Psychology, 24,* 53–66.

McDermott, P. A., & Weiss, R. V. (1995). A normative typology of healthy, subclinical, and clinical behavior styles among American children and adolescents. *Psychological Assessment, 7,* 162–170.

McDougle, C. J., Holmes, J. P., Bronson, M. R., Anderson, G. M., Volkmar, F. R., Price, L. H., & Cohen, D. J. (1997). Risperidone treatment of children and adolescents with pervasive developmental disorders: A prospective open-label study. *Journal of the American Academy of Child and Adolescent Psychiatry, 36,* 685–693.

McEachin, J. J., Smith, T., & Lovaas, O. I. (1993). Long-term outcome for children with autism who received early intensive behavioral treatment. *American Journal on Mental Retardation, 97,* 359–372.

McEvoy, M. A., Shores, R. E., Wehlby, J. H., Johnson, S. M., & Fox, J. J. (1990). Special education teachers' implementation of procedures to promote social interaction among children in integrated settings. *Education and Training in Mental Retardation, 25,* 267–276.

McGee, R., & Feehan, M. (1991). Are girls with problems of inattention underrecognized? *Journal of Psychopathology and Behavioral Assessment, 13,* 187–198.

McGee, R., Feehan, M., Williams, S., & Anderson, J. (1992). DSM-III disorders from age 11 to age 15 years. *Journal of the American Academy of Child and Adolescent Psychiatry, 31,* 50–59.

McGee, R., Stanton, W. R., & Sears, M. R. (1993). Allergic disorders and attention deficit disorder in children. *Journal of Abnormal Child Psychology, 21,* 79–88.

McGee, R., Williams, S., Bradshaw, J., Chapel, J. L., Rubins, A., & Silva, P. A. (1986). The relationship between specific reading retardation, general reading backwardness, and behavioral problems in a large sample of Dunedin boys: A longitudinal study from five to eleven years. *Journal of Child Psychology and Psychiatry, 27,* 597–610.

McGee, R. A., Wolfe, D. A., & Wilson, S. K. (1997). Multiple maltreatment experiences and adolescent behavior problems: Adolescents' perspectives. *Development and Psychopathology, 9,* 131–149.

McGrath, P. A. (1993). Psychological aspects of pain perception. In N. L. Schechter, C. B. Berde, & M. Yaster (Eds.), *Pain in infants, children and adolescents* (pp. 39–63). Baltimore: Williams & Wilkins.

McGrath, P. J., & McAlpine, L. (1993). Psychologic perspectives on pediatric pain. *Journal of Pediatrics, 122,* 52–58.

McGrew, K. & Bruininks, R. H. (1989). The factor structure of adaptive behavior. *School Psychology Review, 18,* 64–81.

McGue, M. (1997). The democracy of genes. *Nature, 388,* 417–418.

McGue, M., Bouchard, T. J., Jr., Iacono, W. G., & Lykken, D. T. (1993). Behavioral genetics of cognitive ability: A lifespan perspective. In R. Plomin & G. E. McClearn (Eds.), *Nature, nurture and psychology* (pp. 59–76). Washington, DC: American Psychological Association.

McKeough, A., Yates, T., & Marini, A. (1994). Intentional reasoning: A developmental study of behaviorally aggressive and normal boys. *Development and Psychopathology, 6,* 285–304.

McKnew, D. H., Jr., Cytryn, L., & Yahraes, H. (1983). *Why isn't Johnny crying? Coping with depression in children.* New York: Norton.

McLean, M. M. (1995). It's a blackboard jungle out there: The impact of media and film on the public's perceptions of violence in schools. *English Journal, 84*(2), 19–21.

McLean, W. E. (1993). Overview. In J. L. Matson & P. R. Barrett (Eds.), *Psychopathology in the Mentally Retarded* (2nd ed., pp. 1–16). Needham Heights, MA: Allyn & Bacon.

McLeer, S. V., Callaghan, M., Henry, D., & Wallen, J. (1994). Psychiatric disorders in sexually abused children. *Journal of the American Academy of Child and Adolescent Psychiatry, 33,* 313–319.

McLoyd, V. C. (1998). Socioeconomic disadvantage and child development. *American Psychologist, 53,* 185–204.

McMahon, R. J., & Estes, A. M. (1997). Conduct problems. In E. J. Mash & L. G. Terdal (Eds.), *Assessment of childhood disorders* (3rd ed., pp. 130–193). New York: Guilford Press.

McMahon, R. J., & Wells, K. C. (1989). Conduct disorders. In

E. J. Mash & R. A. Barkley (Eds.), *Treatment of childhood disorders* (pp. 73–132). New York: Guilford Press.

McMahon, R. J., & Wells, K. C. (1998). Conduct problems. In E. J. Mash & R. A. Barkley (Eds.), *Treatment of childhood disorders* (2nd ed.). New York: Guilford Press.

McNeil, T. F. (1988). Obstetric factors and perinatal injuries. In M. T. Tsuang & J. C. Simpson (Eds.), *Handbook of schizophrenia: Vol. 3. Nosology, epidemiology and genetics* (pp. 319–344). New York: Elsevier.

Mednick, S. A., Machon, R. A., Huttunen, M. O., & Bonett, D. (1988). Adult schizophrenia following prenatal exposure to an influenza epidemic. *Archives of General Psychiatry, 45,* 189–192.

Medvescek, C. R. (1997, April). Special kids. *Parents,* pp. 67–70.

Meichenbaum, D. (1977). *Cognitive-behavior modification: An integrative approach.* New York: Plenum.

Meichenbaum, D., & Goodman, J. (1971). Training impulsive children to talk to themselves: A means of developing self-control. *Journal of Abnormal Psychology, 77,* 115–126.

Meichenbaum, D., & Turk, D. (1987). *Facilitating treatment adherence: A practitioner's guidebook.* New York: Plenum.

Melnick, S. M., & Hinshaw, S. P. (1996). What they want and what they get: The social goals of boys with ADHD and comparison boys. *Journal of Abnormal Child Psychology, 24,* 169–185.

Melton, G. B. (1990). Child protection: Making a bad situation worse? *Contemporary Psychology, 35,* 213–214.

Melton, G. B., & Ehrenreich, N. S. (1992). Ethical and legal issues in mental health services for children. In C. E. Walker & M. C. Roberts (Eds.), *Handbook of clinical child psychology* (2nd ed., pp. 1035–1055). New York: Wiley.

Merzenich, M. M., Jenkins, W. M., Johnston, P., Schreiner, C., Miller, S. L., & Tallal, P. (1996). Temporal processing deficits of language-learning impaired children ameliorated by training. *Science, 271,* 77–81.

Messer, S. C., & Gross, A. M. (1995). Childhood depression and family interaction: A naturalistic observation study. *Journal of Clinical Child Psychology, 24,* 77–88.

Messick, S. (1983). Assessment of children. In W. Kessen (Ed.), *Handbook of child psychology* (4th ed.): *Vol. 1. History, theory, and methods* (pp. 477–526). New York: Wiley.

Meyer, G. J., Finn, S. E., Eyde, L. D., Kay, G. G., Kubiszn, T. W., Moreland, K. L., Eisman, E. J., & Dies, R. R. (1998, June). *Benefits and costs of psychological assessment in healthcare delivery: Report of the Board of Professional Affairs psychological assessment work group, Part 1.* American Psychological Association, Washington, DC.

Miedzian, M. (1995). Learning to be violent. In E. Peled, P. G. Jaffe, & J. L. Edelson (Eds.), *Ending the cycle of violence: Community responses to children of battered women* (pp. 10–24). Thousand Oaks, CA: Sage.

Milberger, S., Biederman, J., Faraone, S. V., Chen, L., & Jones, J. (1996). Is maternal smoking during pregnancy a risk factor for attention deficit hyperactivity disorder in children? *American Journal of Psychiatry, 153,* 1138–1142.

Milberger, S., Biederman, J., Faraone, S. V., Chen, L., & Jones, J. (1997). ADHD is associated with early initiation of cigarette smoking in children and adolescents. *Journal of the American Academy of Child and Adolescent Psychiatry, 36,* 37–44.

Miles, M. B., & Huberman, A. M. (1994). *Qualitative data analysis: An expanded sourcebook* (2nd ed.). Thousand Oaks, CA: Sage.

Milich, R., & Kramer, J. (1984). Reflections on impulsivity: An empirical investigation of impulsivity as a construct. In K. Gadow & I. Bialer (Eds.), *Advances in learning and behavioral disabilities* (Vol. 3, pp. 57–94). Greenwich, CT: JAI Press.

Milich, R., & Landau, S. (1982). Socialization and peer relationships in hyperactive children. In K. D. Gadow & J. Bialer (Eds.), *Advances in learning and behavioral disabilities* (Vol. 1, pp. 283–339). Greenwich, CT: JAI Press.

Milich, R., & Landau, S. (1989). The role of social status variables in differentiating subgroups of hyperactive children. In L. M. Bloomingdale & J. M. Swanson (Eds.), *Attention deficit disorder* (Vol. 4, pp. 1–16). Oxford, England: Pergamon Press.

Milich, R., & Lorch, E. P. (1994). Television viewing methodology to understand cognitive processing of ADHD children. In T. H. Ollendick & R. J. Prinz (Eds.), *Advances in Clinical Child Psychology* (Vol. 16, pp. 177–202). New York: Plenum.

Milich, R., & Okazaki, M. (1991). An examination of learned helplessness among attention-deficit hyperactivity disordered boys. *Journal of Abnormal Child Psychology, 19,* 607–623.

Milich, R., Wolraich, M. C., & Lindgren, S. (1986). Sugar and hyperactivity: A critical review of empirical findings. *Clinical Psychology Review, 6,* 493–513.

Miller, G. E., & Prinz, R. J. (1990). Enhancement of social learning family interventions for childhood conduct disorder. *Psychological Bulletin, 108,* 291–307.

Miller, J. B. (1976). *Toward a new psychology of women.* Boston: Beacon Press.

Miller, S. L., & Tallal, P. (1995). A behavioral neuroscience approach to developmental language disorders: Evidence for a rapid temporal processing deficit. In D. Cicchetti & D. J. Cohen (Eds.), *Developmental Psychopathology: Vol. 2. Risk, disorder, and adaptation* (pp. 274–298). New York: Wiley.

Miller, S. L., & Watson, B. C. (1992). The relationships between communication attitude, anxiety, and depression in stutterers and nonstutterers. *Journal of Speech and Hearing Research, 35,* 789–798.

Millstein, S. G., Petersen, A. C., & Nightingale, E. O. (1993). Adolescent health promotion: Rationale, goals, and objectives. In S. G. Millstein, A. C. Petersen, & E. O. Nightingale (Eds.), *Promoting the health of adolescents: New directions for the twenty-first century* (pp. 3–10). New York: Oxford University Press.

Milner, J. S. (1993). Social information processing and physical child abuse. *Clinical Psychology Review, 13,* 275–294.

Milner, J. S., & Dopke, C. (1997). Child physical abuse: Review of offender characteristics. In D. A. Wolfe, R. J. McMahon, & R. Dev Peters (Eds.), *Child abuse: New directions in prevention and treatment across the lifespan* (pp. 25–52). Thousand Oaks, CA: Sage.

Minshew, N. J. (1996). Brain mechanisms in autism: Functional and structural abnormalities. *Journal of Autism and Developmental Disorders, 26,* 205–209.

Minshew, N. J., & Dombrowski, S. M. (1994). In vivo neuroanatomy of autism: Neuroimaging studies. In M. L. Bauman & T. L. Kemper (Eds.), *Neurobiology of autism* (pp. 66–85). Baltimore: Johns Hopkins University Press.

Minuchin, S., Rosman, B. L., & Baker, L. (1978). *Psychosomatic families: Anorexia nervosa in context.* Cambridge, MA: Harvard University Press.

Mischel, W. (1986). *Introduction to personality* (4th ed.). New York: Holt, Rinehart & Winston.

Mitchell, J., McCauley, E., Burke, P. M., & Moss, S. J. (1988). Phenomenology of depression in children and adolescents. *Journal of the American Academy of Child and Adolescent Psychiatry, 27,* 12–20.

Moats, L. C., & Lyon, G. R. (1993). Learning disabilities in the United States: Advocacy, science, and the future of the field. *Journal of Learning Disabilities, 26,* 282–294.

Moffatt, M. E. K., Kato, C., & Pless, I. B. (1987). Improvements in self-concept after treatment of nocturnal enuresis: A randomized clinical trial. *The Journal of Pediatrics, 110,* 647–652.

Moffitt, T. E. (1990). Juvenile delinquency and attention deficit disorder in boys' developmental trajectories from age 3 to age 15. *Child Development, 61,* 893–910.

Moffitt, T. E. (1993a). Adolescence-limited and life-course-persistent antisocial behavior: A developmental taxonomy. *Psychological Review, 100,* 674–701.

Moffitt, T. E. (1993b). The neuropsychology of conduct disorder. *Development and Psychopathology, 5,* 135–151.

Moffitt, T. E., Caspi, A., Belsky, J., & Silva, P. A. (1992). Childhood experience and the onset of menarche: A test of a sociobiological model. *Child Development, 63,* 47–58.

Moffitt, T. E., Caspi, A., Dickson, N., Silva, P., & Stanton, W. (1996). Childhood-onset versus adolescent-onset antisocial conduct problems in males: Natural history from ages 3 to 18 years. *Development and Psychopathology, 8,* 399–424.

Moffitt, T. E., & Lynam, D. (1994). The neuropsychology of conduct disorder and delinquency: Implications for understanding antisocial behavior. In D. C. Fowles, P. Sutker, & S. H. Goodman (Eds.), *Progress in experimental personality and psychopathology research* (pp. 233–262). New York: Springer.

Moffitt, T. E., Lynam, D., & Silva, P. A. (1994). Neuropsychological tests predict persistent male delinquency. *Criminology, 32,* 101–124.

Moffitt, T. E., & Silva, P. A. (1988). IQ and delinquency: A direct test of the differential detection hypothesis. *Journal of Abnormal Psychology, 97,* 330–333.

Montague, C. T., Farooqi, I. S., Whitehead, J. P., Soos, M. A., Rau, H., Wareham, N. J., Sewter, C. P., Digby, J. E., Mohammed, S. N., Hurst, J. A., Cheetham, C. H., Earley, A. R., Barnett, A. H., Prins, J. B., & O'Rahilly, S. (1997). Congential leptin deficiency is associated with severe early-onset obesity in humans. *Nature, 387,* 903–907.

Mooney, K. C., & Harrison, A. J. (1987). A content analysis of child psychological evaluations. *Journal of Child and Adolescent Psychotherapy, 4,* 275–282.

Moore, L. A., & Hughes, J. N. (1988). Impulsive and hyperactive children. In J. N. Hughes (Ed.), *Cognitive behavior therapy with children in schools* (pp. 127–159). Toronto: Pergamon Press.

Moreau, D., Mufson, L., Weissman, M. M., & Klerman, G. L. (1991). Interpersonal psychotherapy for adolescent depression: Description of modification and preliminary application. *Journal of the American Academy of Child and Adolescent Psychiatry, 30,* 642–651.

Moreau, D., Weissman, M. M., & Warner, V. (1989). Panic disorder in children at high risk for depression. *American Journal of Psychiatry, 146,* 1059–1060.

Morelli, G. A., Rogoff, B., Oppenheim, D., & Goldsmith, D. (1992). Cultural variations in infants' sleeping arrangements: Questions of independence. *Developmental Psychology, 28,* 604–613.

Moreno, A. B., & Thelen, M. H. (1995). Eating behavior in junior high school females. *Adolescence, 30,* 171–174.

Morgan, W. P. (1896). A case of congenital word-blindness. *British Medical Journal, 2,* 1543–1544.

Morris, R. J. (1978). Treating mentally retarded children: A prescriptive approach. In A. P. Goldstein (Ed.), *Prescriptions for child mental health and education* (pp. 88–174). Elmsford, NY: Pergamon Press.

Morris, R. J., & Kratochwill, T. R. (Eds.). (1998). *The practice of child therapy* (3rd ed.). Needham Heights, MA: Allyn & Bacon.

Morton, J., & Frith, U. (1995). Causal modeling: A structural approach to developmental psychopathology. In D. Cicchetti & D. J. Cohen (Eds.), *Developmental psychopathology: Vol. 1. Theory and methods* (pp. 357–390). New York: Wiley-Interscience.

Moser, H. W. (1992). Prevention of mental retardation (genetics). In L. Rowitz (Ed.), *Mental retardation in the year 2000.* New York: Springer-Verlag.

Moser, H. W., Ramey, C. T., & Leonard, C. O. (1990). Mental retardation. In A. E. H. Emery & D. L. Rimion (Eds.), *Principles and practice of medical genetics* (2nd ed., pp. 495–511). Edinburgh, Scotland: Churchill-Livingstone.

Mowrer, O. H. (1947). On the dual nature of learning: A reinterpretation of "conditioning" and "problem solving." *Harvard Educational Review, 17,* 102–148.

Mowrer, O. H. (1950). *Learning theory and the personality dynamics.* New York: Arnold Press.

Mowrer, O. H., & Mowrer, W. M. (1938). Enuresis: A method for its study and treatment. *American Journal of Orthopsychiatry, 8,* 436–459.

Mrazek, P. J., & Haggerty, R. J. (Eds.). (1994). *Reducing risks for mental disorders: Frontiers for preventive intervention.* Washington, DC: National Academy Press.

Mueller, C., Field, T., Yando, R., Harding, J., Gonzalez, K. P., Lasko, G., & Bendell, D. (1995). Under-eating and over-eating concerns among adolescents. *Journal of Child Psychology and Psychiatry, 36,* 1019–1025.

Mufson, L., Moreau, D., & Weissman, M. M. (1996). Focus on relationships: Interpersonal psychotherapy for adolescent depression. In E. D. Hibbs & P. S. Jensen (Eds.), *Psychosocial treatments for child and adolescent disorders: Empirically based strategies for clinical practice* (pp. 137–155). Washington, DC: American Psychological Association.

Mufson, L., Moreau, D., Weissman, M. M., & Klerman, G. L. (1993). *Interpersonal psychotherapy for depressed adolescents.* New York: Guilford Press.

Mufson, L., Moreau, D., Weissman, M. M., Wickramaratne, P., Martin, J., & Samoilov, A. (1994). Modification of interpersonal psychotherapy with depressed adolescents (IPT-A): Phase I and II studies. *Journal of the American Academy of Child and Adolescent Psychiatry, 33,* 695–705.

Mulhern, R. K., Carpentieri, S., Shema, S., Stone, P., & Fairclough, D. (1993). Factors associated with social and behavioral problems among children recently diagnosed with brain tumor. *Journal of Pediatric Psychology, 18,* 339–350.

Mulick, J. A., Jacobson, J. W., & Kobe, F. H. (1993). Anguished silence and helping hands: Autism and facilitated communication. *Skeptical Inquirer, 17,* 270–280.

Mulick, J. A., Schroeder, S. R., & Rojahn, J. (1980). Chronic ruminative vomiting: A comparison of four treatment procedures. *Journal of Autism and Developmental Disorders, 10,* 203–213.

Mullen, P. E., Martin, J. L., Anderson, J. C., Romans, S. E., & Herbison, G. P. (1996). The long-term impact of the physical, emotional, and sexual abuse of children: A community study. *Child Abuse and Neglect, 20,* 7–21.

Murphy, C. C., Yeargin-Allsopp, M., Decoufle, P., & Drews, C. D. (1995). The administrative prevalence of mental retardation in 10-year-old children in metropolitan Atlanta, 1985 through 1987. *American Journal of Public Health, 85,* 319–322.

Murphy, D. A., Pelham, W. W., & Lang, A. R. (1992). Aggression in boys with attention deficit hyperactivity disorder: Methylphenidate effects on naturally occurring observed aggression, response to provocation, and social information processing. *Journal of Abnormal Child Psychology, 20,* 451–465.

Murphy, L. B. (1992). Sympathetic behavior in very young children. *Zero to Three, 12*(4), 1–5.

Murphy, T. R. (1986). "Woeful childe of parents rage": Suicide of children and adolescents in early modern England, 1507–1710. *The Sixteenth Century Journal, 17,* 259–270.

Murray, I. (1993). Looking back: Reminiscences from childhood and adolescence. In G. Weiss & L. T. Hechtman, *Hyperactive children grown up: ADHD in children, adolescents, and adults* (2nd ed., pp. 301–325). New York: Guilford Press.

Nada-Raja, S., Langley, J. D., McGee, R., Williams, S. M., Begg, D. J., & Reeder, A. I. (1997). Inattentive and hyperactive behaviors and driving offences in adolescence. *Journal of the American Academy of Child and Adolescent Psychiatry, 36,* 515–522.

Nader, K., Pynoos, R., Fairbanks, L., & Frederick, C. (1990). Children's PTSD reactions one year after a sniper attack at their school. *American Journal of Psychiatry, 147,* 1526–1530.

Narayan, M., Srinath, S., Anderson, G. M., & Meundi, D. B. (1993). Cerebrospinal fluid levels of homovanillic acid and 5-hydroxyindoleacetic acid in autism. *Biological Psychiatry, 33,* 630–635.

National Childhood Cancer Foundation. (1997). *Facts about childhood cancer* [On-line]. Available: http://www.nccf.org/nccf/facts.htm#ped.

National Commission on Children. (1991). *Beyond rhetoric: A new American agenda for children and families.* (Final report of the National Commission on Children). Washington, DC: U.S. Government Printing Office.

National Institute of Justice. (1996). *Victim costs and consequences: A new look.* Washington, DC: Author.

National Institute of Mental Health. (1994a). *Attention deficit hyperactivity disorder: Decade of the brain.* (NIMH Publication No. 94–3572). Washington, DC: Author.

National Institute of Mental Health. (1994b). *Eating disorders.* (DHHS Publication No. NIMH 94–3477). Washington, DC: U.S. Government Printing Office.

National Institute of Mental Health. (1996). *Learning Disabilities* [On-line]. Available: http://www.nimh.nih.gov/publicat/learndis.htm.

National Joint Committee on Learning Disabilities. (1988, April). [Letter from NJCLD to member organizations]. Austin, TX: NJCLD. Cited in Lyon, 1996, p. 397.

National Research Council. (1993). *Understanding child abuse and neglect.* Washington, DC: National Academy Press.

Nay, W. R. (1979). *Multimethod clinical assessment.* New York: Gardner Press.

Neal, A. M., & Turner, S. M. (1991). Anxiety disorders research with African Americans: Current status. *Psychological Bulletin, 109,* 400–410.

Neal-Barnett, A. M., & Smith, J. M., Sr. (1996). African American children and behavior therapy: Considering the Afrocentric approach. *Cognitive and Behavioral Practice, 3,* 351–369.

Needleman, H. L., Reiss, J. A., Tobin, M. J., Biesecker, G. E., & Greenhouse, J. B. (1996). Bone lead levels and delinquent behavior. *Journal of the American Medical Association, 275*(5), 363–369.

Neisser, U., Boodoo, G., Bouchard T. J., Jr., Boykin, A. W., Brody, N., Ceci, S. J., Halpern, D. F., Loehlin, J. C., Perloff, R., Sternberg, R. J., & Urbina, S. (1996). Intelligence: Knowns and unknowns. *American Psychologist, 51*(2), 77–101.

Nelles, W. B., & Barlow, D. H. (1988). Do children panic? *Clinical Psychology Review, 8,* 359–372.

Nelson, C. A., & Bloom, F. E. (1997). Child development and neuroscience. *Child Development, 68,* 970–987.

Nelson, K. B. (1991). Prenatal and perinatal factors in the etiology of autism. *Pediatrics, 87,* 761–766.

Nemeth, M. (1994, April 4). Altered states. *Maclean's,* pp. 48–49.

Newacheck, P. W., Budetti, P. P., & Halfon, N. (1986). Trend in activity-limiting chronic conditions among children. *American Journal of Public Health, 76,* 178–184.

Newborg, J., Stock, J. R., Wnek, L., Guidubaldi, J., & Svinicki, J. (1984). *Battelle Developmental Inventory.* Allen, TX: DLM Teaching Resources.

Newman, D. L., Moffitt, T. E., Caspi, A., Magdol, L., Silva, P. A., & Stanton, W. R. (1996). Psychiatric disorder in a birth cohort of young adults: Prevalence, comorbidity, clinical significance, and new case incidence from ages 11 to 21. *Journal of Consulting and Clinical Psychology, 64,* 552–562.

Newsom, C. M. (1998). Autistic disorder. In E. J. Mash & R. A. Barkley (Eds.), *Treatment of childhood disorders* (2nd ed., pp. 416–467). New York: Guilford Press.

Newsweek. (1993, August 2). Girls will be girls. *122*(5), p. 44.

Newsweek. 1996, May 13.

New York Times. (1946, April 14).

New York Times Service. (1996, February 8).

Nezu, C. M., Nezu, A. M., & Gill-Weiss, M. J. (1992). *Psychopathology in persons with mental retardation: Clinical guidelines for assessment and treatment.* Champaign, IL: Research Press.

Nichols, M. (1995, January 30). Schizophrenia: Hidden torment. *Maclean's,* pp. 70–74.

Nichols, P. L., & Chen, T. C. (1981). *Minimal brain dysfunction: A prospective study.* Hillsdale, NJ: Erlbaum.

Nisbett, R. E. (1972). Hunger, obesity, and the ventromedial hypothalamus. *Psychological Review, 79,* 433–453.

Noam, G. G., Chandler, M., & LaLonde, C. (1995). Clinical-developmental psychology: Constructivism and social cognition in the study of psychological dysfunctions. In D. Cicchetti & D. J. Cohen (Eds.), *Developmental psychopathology: Vol. 1. Theory and methods* (pp. 424–464). New York: Wiley.

Nolan T., Debelle, G., Oberklaid, F., & Coffey, C. (1991). Randomized trial of laxatives in treatment of childhood encopresis. *The Lancet, 338,* 523–527.

Nolen-Hoeksema, S., & Girgus, J. S. (1994). The emergence of gender differences in depression during adolescence. *Psychological Bulletin, 115,* 424–443.

Nolen-Hoeksema, S., Girgus, J. S., & Seligman, M. E. P. (1986). Learned helplessness in children: A longitudinal study of depression, achievement, and explanatory style. *Journal of Personality and Social Psychology, 51,* 435–442.

Nolen-Hoeksema, S., Girgus, J. S., & Seligman, M. E. P. (1992). Predictors and consequences of childhood depressive symptoms: A 5-year longitudinal study. *Journal of Abnormal Psychology, 101,* 405–422.

Noll, R. B., Bukowski, W. B., Rogosch, F. A., LeRoy, S., & Kulkarni, R. (1990). Social interactions between children with cancer and their peers: Teacher ratings. *Journal of Pediatric Psychology, 15,* 43–56.

Noll, R. B., LeRoy, S., Bukowski, W. M., Rogosch, F. A., & Kulkarni, R. (1991). Peer relationships and adjustment in children with cancer. *Journal of Pediatric Psychology, 16,* 307–326.

Norcross, J. C., Karg, R. S., & Prochaska, J. O. (1997). Clinical psychologists in the 1990s: II. *The Clinical Psychologist, 50*(3), 4-11.

Norgaard, J. P., Pederson, E. B., & Djurhuus, J. C. (1985). Diurnal antidiuretic hormone levels in enuretics. *Journal of Urology, 134,* 1029–1031.

Northam, E., Anderson, P., Adler, R., Werther, G., & Warne, G. (1996). Psychosocial and family functioning in children with insulin-dependent diabetes at diagnosis and one year later. *Journal of Pediatric Psychology, 21,* 699–717.

Nottelman, E. D., & Jensen, P. S. (1995). Comorbidity of disorders in children and adolescents: Developmental perspectives. In T. H. Ollendick & R. J. Prinz (Eds.), *Advances in clinical child psychology* (Vol. 17, pp. 109–155). New York: Plenum.

Noyes, R., Woodman, C., Garvey, M. J., Cook, B. L., Suelzer, M., Clancy, J., & Anderson, D. J. (1992). Generalized anxiety disorder vs. panic disorder: Distinguishing characteristics and patterns of comorbidity. *Journal of Nervous and Mental Disease, 180,* 369–379.

O'Brien, B. S., & Frick, P. J. (1996). Reward dominance: Associations with anxiety, conduct problems, and psychopathy in children. *Journal of Abnormal Child Psychology, 24,* 223–240.

O'Conner, T. G., McGuire, S., Reiss, D., Hetherington, E. M., & Plomin, R. (1998). Co-occurrence of depressive symptoms and antisocial behavior in adolescence: A common genetic liability. *Journal of Abnormal Psychology, 107,* 27–37.

O'Connor, M., Foch, T., Sherry, T., & Plomin, R. (1980). A twin study of specific behavioral problems of socialization as viewed by parents. *Journal of Abnormal Child Psychology, 8,* 189–199.

Offer, D., & Ostrov, E. (1981). *The adolescent: A psychological self-portrait.* New York: Basic Books.

Offord, D. R. (1995). Child psychiatric epidemiology: Current status and future prospects. *Canadian Journal of Psychiatry, 40,* 284–288.

Offord, D. R., Alder, R. J., & Boyle, M. H. (1986). Prevalence and sociodemographic correlates of conduct disorder. *American Journal of Social Psychiatry, 4,* 272–278.

Offord, D. R., Boyle, M. H., Fleming, J. E., Munroe Blum, H., & Rae-Grant, N. I. (1989). The Ontario Child Health Study: Summary of selected results. *Canadian Journal of Psychiatry, 34,* 483–491.

Offord, D. R., Boyle, M. H., Racine, Y. A., Fleming, J. E., Cadman, D. T., Blum, H. M., Byrne, C., Links, P. S., Lipman, E. L., MacMillan, H. L., Grant, N. I. R., Sanford, M. N., Szatmari, P., Thomas, H., & Woodward, C. A. (1992). Outcome, prognosis, and risk in a longitudinal follow-up study. *Journal of the American Academy of Child and Adolescent Psychiatry, 31,* 916–923.

Offord, D. R., Boyle, M. H., Szatmari, P., Rae-Grant, N. I., Links, P. S., Cadman, D. T., Byles, J. A., Crawford, J. W., Blum, H. M., Byrne, C., Thomas, H., & Woodward, C. A. (1987). Ontario Child Health Study: II. Six-month prevalence of disorder and rates of service utilization. *Archives of General Psychiatry, 44,* 832–836.

Offord, D. R., Kraemer, H. C., Kazdin, A. E., Jensen, P. S., & Harrington, R. (1998). Lowering the burden of suffering from child psychiatric disorder: Trade-offs among clinical, targeted, and universal interventions. *Journal of the American Academy of Child and Adolescent Psychiatry, 37,* 686–694.

Ojemann, G. A. (1991). Cortical organization of language. *Neuroscience, 11,* 2281–2287.

Olds, D., Eckenrode, J., Henderson, C. R., Kitzman, H., Powers, J., Cole, R., Sidora, K., Morris, P., & Pettit, L. M. (1997). Long-term effects of home visitation on maternal life course and child abuse and neglect: Fifteen-year follow-up of a randomized trial. *Journal of the American Medical Association, 278*(8), 637–643.

Olds, D., Henderson, C. R., & Kitzman, H. (1994). Does prenatal and infancy nurse home visitation have enduring effects on qualities of parental caregiving and child health at 25 to 50 months of life? *Pediatrics, 93,* 89–98.

O'Leary, K. D., Malone, J., & Tyree, A. (1994). Physical aggression in early marriage: Prerelationship and relationship effects. *Journal of Consulting and Clinical Psychology, 62,* 594–602.

O'Leary, K. D., Vivian, D., & Nisi, A. (1985). Hyperactivity in Italy. *Journal of Abnormal Child Psychology, 13,* 485–500.

Ollendick, T. H., & King, N. J. (1994a). Diagnosis, assessment, and treatment of internalizing problems in children: The role of longitudinal data. *Journal of Consulting and Clinical Psychology, 62,* 918–927.

Ollendick, T. H., & King, N. J. (1994b). Fears and their level of interference in adolescents. *Behaviour Research and Therapy, 32,* 635–638.

Ollendick, T. H., King, N. J., & Yule, W. (Eds.). (1994). *International handbook of phobic and anxiety disorders in children and adolescents.* New York: Plenum.

Ollendick, T. H., Lease, C. A., & Cooper, C. (1993). Separation anxiety in young adults: A preliminary examination. *Journal of Anxiety Disorders, 7,* 293–305.

Ollendick, T. H., Mattis, S. G., & King, N. J. (1994). Panic in children and adolescents: A review. *Journal of Child Psychology and Psychiatry, 35,* 113–134.

Ollendick, T. H., Yang, B., Dong, Q., Xia, Y., & Lin, L. (1995). Perceptions of fear in older children and adolescents: The role of gender and friendship status. *Journal of Abnormal Child Psychology, 23,* 439–452.

Ollendick, T. H., Yang, B., King, N, J., Dong, Q., & Akande, A. (1996). Fears in American, Australian, Chinese, and Nigerian children and adolescents: A cross-cultural study. *Journal of Child Psychology and Psychiatry, 37,* 213–220.

Olshan, A. F., Baird, P. A., & Teschke, K. (1989). Paternal occupational exposure and the risk of Down's syndrome.

American Journal of Human Genetics, 44, 646–651.

Olson, R. A., Mullins, L. L., Gillman, J. B., & Chaney, J. M. (1994). *The sourcebook of pediatric psychology.* Boston: Allyn & Bacon.

Olson, R. K., Foresberg, H., Wise, B., & Rack, J. (1994). Measurement of word recognition, orthographic, and phonological skills. In G. R. Lyon (Ed.), *Frames of reference for the assessment of learning disabilities: New views on measurement issues* (pp. 243–278). Baltimore: Paul H. Brookes.

Olweus, D. (1979). Stability of aggressive reaction patterns in males: A review. *Psychological Bulletin, 86,* 852–875.

Olweus, D. (1987). Testosterone adrenaline: Aggressive antisocial behavior in normal adolescent males. In S. A. Mednick, T. E. Moffitt, & S. A. Stack (Eds.), *The causes of crime: New biological approaches* (pp. 263–283). New York: Cambridge University Press.

Olweus, D. (1995). Bullying or peer abuse at school: Facts and intervention. *Current Directions in Psychological Science, 4,* 196–200.

Orton Dyslexic Society. (1996, January 16). [On-line]. Available: http://www.pie.org/ods.

Osborne, R. B., Hatcher, J. W., & Richtsmeier, A. J. (1989). The role of social modeling in unexplained pediatric pain. *Journal of Pediatric Psychology, 14,* 43–61.

Osofsky, J. D. (1996). When the helper is hurting: Burnout and countertransference issues in treatment of children exposed to violence. *Zero to Three, 16*(1), 35–38.

Osofsky, J. D. (1998). On the outside: Interventions with infants and families at risk. *Infant Mental Health Journal, 19,* 101–108.

Oster, G. D., & Montgomery, S. S. (1995). *Helping your depressed teenager: A guide for parents and caregivers.* New York: Wiley.

Osterling, J. & Dawson, G. (1994). Early recognition of children with autism: A study of first birthday home videotapes. *Journal of Autism and Developmental Disorders, 24,* 247–257.

Overton, W. F., & Horowitz, H. A. (1991). Developmental psychopathology: Integrations and differentiations. In D. Cicchetti & S. L. Toth (Eds.), *Models and integrations: Rochester symposium on developmental psychopathology* (Vol. 3, pp. 1–42). Rochester, NY: University of Rochester Press.

Owen, B. (1993, May 18). Kids in the dumps. *Winnipeg Free Press,* p. C1.

Owens, R. G., & Slade, P. D. (1987). Running and anorexia nervosa: An empirical study. *International Journal of Eating Disorders, 6,* 771–775.

Ozols, E. J., & Rourke, B. P. (1985). Dimensions of social sensitivity in two types of learning disabled children. In B. P. Rourke (Ed.), *Neuropsychology of learning disabilities: Essentials of subtype analysis* (pp. 281–301). New York: Guilford Press.

Ozonoff, S. (1994). Executive functions in autism. In E. Schopler & G. Mesibov (Eds.), *Learning and cognition in autism* (pp. 199–219). New York: Plenum.

Ozonoff, S., & McEvoy, R. (1994). A longitudinal study of executive function and theory of mind development in autism. *Development and Psychopathology, 6,* 415–431.

Ozonoff, S., & Miller, J. N. (1995). Teaching theory of mind: A new approach to social skills training for individuals with autism. *Journal of Autism and Developmental Disorders, 25,* 415–433.

Ozonoff, S., Pennington, B. F., & Rogers, S. J. (1991). Executive function deficits in high-functioning autistic individuals: Relationship to theory of mind. *Journal of Child Psychology and Psychiatry, 32,* 1081–1105.

Papp, L. A., & Gorman, J. M. (1995). Respiratory neurobiology of panic. In G. M. Asnis & H. Meir van Praag (Eds.), *Panic disorder: Clinical, biological, and treatment aspects* (pp. 255–275). New York: Wiley.

Parke, R. D., & Slaby, R. C. (1983). The development of aggression. In P. H. Mussen (Series Ed.) & E. M. Hetherington (Volume Ed.), *Handbook of child psychology: Vol. 4. Socialization, personality, and social development* (pp. 547–641). New York: Wiley.

Parry-Jones, W. L., & Parry-Jones, B. (1994). Implications of historical evidence for the classification of eating disorders: A dimension overlooked in DSM-III-R and ICD-10. *British Journal of Psychiatry, 165,* 287–292.

Pate, J. E., Pumariega, A. J., Hester, C., & Garner, D. M. (1992). Cross-cultural patterns in eating disorders: A review. *Journal of the American Academy of Child and Adolescent Psychiatry, 31,* 802–809.

Paternite, C. E., Loney, J., & Roberts, M. A. (1996). A preliminary validation of subtypes of DSM-IV Attention-Deficit/Hyperactivity Disorder. *Journal of Attention Disorders, 1,* 70–86.

Patterson, G. R. (1975). *Families: Applications of social learning to family life* (rev. ed.). Champaign, IL: Research Press.

Patterson, G. R. (1982). *Coercive family process.* Eugene, OR: Castalia.

Patterson, G. R. (1984). Siblings: Fellow travelers in coercive family processes. In R. J. Blanchard & D. C. Blanchard (Eds.), *Advances in the study of aggression* (Vol. 1, pp. 173–215). Orlando, FL: Academic Press.

Patterson, G. R. (1993). Orderly change in a stable world: The antisocial trait as a chimera. *Journal of Consulting and Clinical Psychology, 61,* 911–919.

Patterson, G. R. (1996). Some characteristics of a developmental theory for early-onset delinquency. In M. F. Lenzenweger & J. J. Haugaard (Eds.), *Frontiers of developmental psychopathology* (pp. 81–124). New York: Oxford University Press.

Patterson, G. R., & Cobb, J. A. (1973). Stimulus control for classes of noxious behaviors. In J. Knutson (Ed.), *The control of aggression: Implications from basic research* (pp. 145–199). Chicago: Aldine.

Patterson, G. R., & Dishion, T. J. (1985). Contributions of families and peers to delinquency. *Criminology, 23,* 63–79.

Patterson, G. R., Forgatch, M. S., Yoerger, K. L., & Stoolmiller, M. (in press). Variables that initiate and maintain an early-onset trajectory for juvenile offending. *Development and Psychopathology.*

Patterson, G. R., Reid, J. B., & Dishion, T. J. (1992). *Antisocial boys.* Eugene, OR: Castalia.

Patton, M. Q. (1990). *Qualitative evaluation and research methods* (2nd ed.). Beverly Hills, CA: Sage.

Pauls, D. L. (1991). Genetic factors in the expression of attention-deficit hyperactivity disorder. *Journal of Child and Adolescent Psychopharmacology, 1,* 353–360.

Pearce, J. W., & Pezzot-Pearce, T. D. (1997). *Psychotherapy of abused and neglected children.* New York: Guilford Press.

Pelcovitz, D., Kaplan, S., Goldenberg, B., Mandel, F., Lehane, J., & Guarrera, J. (1994). Post-traumatic stress disorder in physically abused adolescents. *Journal of the American*

Academy of Child and Adolescent Psychiatry, 33, 305–312.

Pelham, W. E. (1993). Pharmacotherapy for children with attention-deficit hyperactivity disorder. *School Psychology Review, 22,* 199–227.

Pelham, W. E., & Bender, M. E. (1982). Peer relationships in hyperative children: Description and treatment. In K. D. Gadow & I. Bialer (Eds.), *Advances in learning and behavioral disabilities* (Vol. 1, pp. 365–436). Greenwich, CT: JAI Press.

Pelham, W. E., Greiner, A. R., Gnagy, E. M., Hoza, B., Martin, L., Sams, S. E., & Wilson, T. (1996). Intensive treatment for ADHD: A model summer treatment program. In M. Roberts & A. LaGreca (Eds.), *Model programs in child and family mental health* (pp. 193–213). Mahwah, NJ: Erlbaum.

Pelham, W. E., & Hoza, B. (1996). Intensive treatment: Summer treatment program for children with ADHD. In E. D. Hibbs & P. S. Jensen (Eds.), *Psychosocial treatment research of child and adolescent disorders: Empirically based strategies for clinical practice* (pp. 311–340). Washington, DC: American Psychological Association.

Pelham, W. E., Hoza, B., Kipp, H. L., & Gnagy, E. M. (1997). Effects of methylphenidate and expectancy of ADHD children's performance, self-evaluations, persistence, and attributions on a cognitive task. *Experimental and Clinical Psychopharmacology, 5,* 3–13.

Pelham, W. E., & Lang, A. R. (1993). Parental alcohol consumption and deviant child behavior: Laboratory studies of reciprocal effects. *Clinical Psychology Review, 13,* 763–784.

Pelham, W. E., Lang, A. R., Atkeson, B., Murphy, D. A., Gnagy, E. M., Greiner, A. R., Vodde-Hamilton, M., & Greenslade, K. E. (1997). Effects of deviant child behavior on parental distress and alcohol consumption in laboratory interactions. *Journal of Abnormal Child Psychology, 25,* 413–424.

Pelham, W. E., Milich, R., & Walker, J. L. (1987). Effects of continuous and partial reinforcement and methylphenidate on learning in children with attention deficit disorder. *Journal of Abnormal Psychology, 93,* 319–325.

Pelham, W. E., Murphy, D. A., Vannatta, K., Milich, R., Licht, B. G., Gnagy, E. M., Greenslade, K. E., Greiner, A. R., & Vodde-Hamilton, M. (1992). Methylphenidate and attributions in boys with attention-deficit hyperactivity disorder. *Journal of Consulting and Clinical Psychology, 60,* 282–292.

Pelton, L. H. (1994). The role of material factors in child abuse and neglect. In G. B. Melton and F. D. Barry (Eds.), *Protecting children from abuse and neglect: Foundations for a new national strategy* (pp. 131–181). New York: Guilford Press.

Pendergrast, M., Taylor, E., Rapoport, J. L., Bartko, J., Donnelly, M., Zametkin, A., Ahearn, M. B., Dunn, G., & Wieselberg, H. M. (1988). The diagnosis of childhood hyperactivity: A U.S.-U.K. cross-national study of DSM-III and ICD-9. *Journal of Child Psychology and Psychiatry, 29,* 289–300.

Pennington, B. F., Gilger, J., Pauls, D., Smith, S. A., Smith, S. D., & DeFries, J. C. (1991). Evidence for major gene transmission for developmental dyslexia. *Journal of the American Medical Association, 266,* 1527–1534.

Pennington, B. F., Groisser, D., & Welsh, M. C. (1993). Contrasting cognitive deficits in attention deficit hyperactivity disorder versus reading disability. *Developmental Psy-*

chology, 29, 511–523.

Pennington, B. F., & Ozonoff, S. (1991). A neuroscientific perspective on continuity and discontinuity in developmental psychopathology. In D. Cicchetti & S. L. Toth (Eds.), *Rochester symposium on developmental psychopathology: Vol. 3. Models and integrations* (pp. 117–159). New York: University of Rochester Press.

Pennington, B. F., & Ozonoff, S. (1996). Executive functions and developmental psychopathology. *Journal of Child Psychology and Psychiatry, 37,* 51–87.

Perez, C., & Widom, C. (1994). Childhood victimization and long-term intellectual and academic outcomes. *Child Abuse and Neglect, 18,* 617–633.

Perfetti, C. A. (1985). *Reading ability.* New York: Oxford University Press.

Perrin, E. C., Ayoub, C. C., & Willett, J. B. (1993). In the eyes of the beholder: Family and maternal influences on perceptions of adjustment of children with a chronic illness. *Journal of Developmental and Behavioral Pediatrics, 14,* 94–105.

Perrin, S., & Last, C. G. (1997). Worrisome thoughts in children clinically referred for anxiety disorder. *Journal of Clinical Child Psychology, 26,* 181–189.

Petersen, A. C., Compas, B., Brooks-Gunn, J., Stemmler, M., Ey, S., & Grant, K. E. (1993). Depression in adolescence. *American Psychologist, 48,* 155–168.

Petersen, A. C., Sarigiani, P. A., & Kennedy, R. E. (1991). Adolescent depression: Why more girls? *Journal of Youth and Adolescence, 20,* 247–271.

Peterson, L., & Brown, D. (1994). Integrating child injury and abuse-neglect research: Common histories, etiologies, and solutions. *Psychological Bulletin, 116,* 293–315.

Peterson, L., Harbeck, D., Farmer, J., & Zink, M. (1991). Developmental contributions to the assessment of children's pain: Conceptual and methodological implications. In J. P. Bush & S. W. Harkins (Eds.), *Children in pain: Clinical and research issues from a developmental perspective* (pp. 33–58). New York: Springer-Verlag.

Peterson, L., Mullins, L. L., & Ridley-Johnson, R. (1985). Childhood depression: Peer reactions to depression and life stress. *Journal of Abnormal Child Psychology, 13,* 597–609.

Pfeffer, C. R. (1985). Self-destructive behavior in children and adolescents. *Psychiatric Clinics of North America, 8,* 215–226.

Pfeffer, C. R. (1986). *The suicidal child.* New York: Guilford Press.

Pfeffer, C. R., Martins, P., Mann, J., Sunkenberg, M., Ice, A., Damore J. P., Jr., Gallo, C., Karpenos, I., & Jiang, H. (1997). Child survivors of suicide: Psychosocial characteristics. *Journal of the American Academy of Child and Adolescent Psychiatry, 36,* 65–74.

Pfiffner, L. J., & Barkley, R. A. (1990). Educational placement and classroom management. In R. A. Barkley, *Attention deficit hyperactivity disorder: A handbook for diagnosis and treatment* (pp. 498–539). New York: Guilford Press.

Phares, V., & Compas, B. (1992). The role of fathers in child and adolescent psychopathology: Make room for daddy. *Psychological Bulletin, 111,* 387–412.

Philips, I. (1979). Childhood depression: The mirror of experience, interpersonal interactions, and depressive phenomena. In A. French & I. Berlin (Eds.), *Depression in children and adolescents* (pp. 69–86). New York: Human Sciences Press.

Phillips, W., Gomez, J. C., Baron-Cohen, S., Laa, V., & Riviere A. (1995). Treating people as objects, agents, or "subjects":

How young children with and without autism make requests. *Journal of Child Psychology and Psychiatry, 36,* 1383–1398.

Piacentini, J. (1997). *Cognitive-behavioral treatment of OCD in children and adolescents.* Unpublished manuscript, UCLA, Los Angeles, Childhood OCD and Related Disorders Program.

Piacentini, J., & Graae, F. (1997). Childhood OCD. In E. Hollander & D. Stein (Eds.), *Obsessive-compulsive disorders: Diagnosis, etiology, treatment* (pp. 23–46). New York: Marcel Dekker.

Piacentini, J., & Jacobs, C. (1997). *Individual behavioral treatment for children and adolescents with obsessive-compulsive disorder: Preliminary treatment manual outline.* Unpublished manuscript, UCLA, Los Angeles, Childhood OCD and Related Disorders Program.

Piacentini, J., Jacobs, C., & Maidment, K. (1997). *Behavioral family treatment for families of children and adolescents with obsessive-compulsive disorder: Preliminary treatment manual outline.* Unpublished manuscript, UCLA, Los Angeles, Childhood OCD and Related Disorders Program.

Pianta, R., Egeland, B., & Erickson, M. (1989). The antecedents of maltreatment: Results of the mother-child interaction research project. In D. Cicchetti & V. Carlson (Eds.), *Child maltreatment: Theory and research on the causes and consequences of child abuse and neglect* (pp. 203–253). New York: Cambridge University Press.

Pike, K. M., & Rodin, J. (1991). Mothers, daughters, and disordered eating. *Journal of Abnormal Psychology, 100,* 198–204.

Pine, D. S., Cohen, P., & Brook, J. (1997). Emotional problems during youth as predictors of stature during early adulthood: Results from a prospective epidemiologic study. *Pediatrics, 99,* 499–500.

Pine, D. S., Wasserman, G. A., Coplan, J., Fried, J. A., Huang, Y.-Y., Kassir, S., Greenhill, L., Shaffer, D., & Parsons, B. (1996). Platelet serotonin 2A (5-HT$_{2A}$) receptor characteristics and parenting factors for boys at risk for delinquency: A preliminary report. *American Journal of Psychiatry, 153,* 538–544.

Piven, J., Harper, J., Palmer, P., & Arndt, S. (1996). Course of behavioral change in autism: A retrospective study of high-IQ adolescents and adults. *Journal of the American Academy of Child and Adolescent Psychiatry, 35,* 523–529.

Piven, J., Nehme, E., Simon, J., Barta, P., Pearlson, G., & Folstein, S. E. (1992). Magnetic resonance imaging in autism: Measurement of the cerebellum, pons, and fourth ventricle. *Biological Psychiatry, 31,* 491–504.

Piven, J., Simon, J., Chase, G. A., Wzorek, M., Landa, R., Gayle, J., & Folstein, S. (1993). The etiology of autism: Pre-, peri- and neonatal factors. *Journal of the American Academy of Child and Adolescent Psychiatry, 32,* 1256–1263.

Piven, J., Wzorek, M., Landa, R., Lainhart, J., Bolton, P., Chase, G. A., & Folseten, S. (1994). Personality characteristics of the parents of autistic individuals. *Psychological Medicine, 24,* 783–795.

Pless, I. B., & Perrin, J. M. (1985). Issues common to a variety of illnesses. In N. Hobbs & J. M. Perrin (Eds.), *Child health and the community* (pp. 78–94). New York: Wiley.

Pless, I. B., & Pinkerton, P. (1975). *Chronic childhood disorders: Promoting patterns of adjustment.* Chicago: Year-Book Medical Publishers.

Pless, I. B., Taylor, H. G., & Arsenault, L. (1995). The relationship between vigilance deficits and traffic injuries involving children. *Pediatrics, 95,* 219–224.

Pliszka, S. R. (1989). Effect of anxiety on cognition, behavior, and stimulant response in ADHD. *Journal of the American Academy of Child and Adolescent Psychiatry, 28,* 882–887.

Pliszka, S. R. (1992). Comorbidity of attention-deficit hyperactivity disorder and overanxious disorder. *Journal of the American Academy of Child and Adolescent Psychiatry, 31,* 197–203.

Pliszka, S. R., McCracken, J. T., & Maas, J. W. (1996). Catecholamines in attention-deficit hyperactivity disorder: Current perspectives. *Journal of the American Academy of Child and Adolescent Psychiatry, 35,* 264–272.

Plomin, R. (1989). Environment and genes: Determinants of behavior. *American Psychologist, 44,* 105–111.

Plomin, R. (1994). Genetic research and identification of environmental influences. *Journal of Child Psychology and Psychiatry, 35,* 817–835.

Plomin, R. (1995). Genetics and children's experiences in the family. *Journal of Child Psychology and Psychiatry, 36,* 33–38.

Plomin, R., & Neiderhiser, J. M. (1991). Quantitative genetics, molecular genetics, and intelligence. *Intelligence, 15,* 369–387.

Plomin, R., Nitz, K., & Rowe, D. C. (1990). Behavior genetics and aggressive behavior in childhood. In M. Lewis & S. Miller (Eds.), *Handbook of developmental psychopathology* (pp. 119–133). New York: Plenum.

Polaino-Lorente, A., & Domenech, E. (1993). Prevalence of childhood depression: Results of the first study in Spain. *Journal of Child Psychology and Psychiatry, 34,* 1007–1017.

Polansky, N. A., Gaudin, J. M., & Kilpatrick, A. C. (1992). Family radicals. *Children and Youth Services Review, 14,* 19–26.

Polivy, J., & Herman, C. P. (1993). Etiology of binge eating: Psychological mechanisms. In C. G. Fairburn & G. T. Wilson (Eds.), *Binge eating: Nature, assessment, and treatment* (pp. 173–205). New York: Guilford Press.

Pollak, S. D., Cicchetti, D., Klorman, R., & Brumaghim, J. T. (1997). Cognitive brain event-related potentials and emotion processing in maltreated children. *Child Development, 68,* 773–787.

Pollock, L. (1987). *A lasting relationship: Parents and children over three centuries.* Hanover: University of New Hampshire Press.

Polloway, E. A., Schewel, R., & Patton, J. R. (1992). Learning disabilities in adulthood: Personal perspectives. *Journal of Learning Disabilities, 25,* 520–522.

Pope, H. G., Mangweth, B., Negrao, A. B., Hudson, J. I., & Cordas, T. A. (1994). Childhood sexual abuse and bulimia nervosa: A comparison of American, Austrian, and Brazilian women. *American Journal of Psychiatry, 151,* 732–737.

Popper, C. W. (1993). Psychopharmacologic treatment of anxiety disorders in adolescents and children. *Journal of Clinical Psychiatry, 54,* 52–63.

Porrino, L. J., Rapoport, J. L., Behar, D., Sceery, W., Ismond, D. R., & Bunney, W. E., Jr. (1983). A naturalistic assessment of the motor activity of hyperactive boys. *Archives of General Psychiatry, 40,* 681–687.

Poskitt, E. M. E. (1980). Obese from infancy: A re-evaluation. *Topics in Pediatrics, 1,* 81–89.

Post, R. M. (1992). Transduction of psychosocial stress into the neurobiology of recurrent affective disorder. *American Journal of Psychiatry, 149,* 999–1010.

Post, R. M., Weiss, S. B., Leverich, G. S., George, M. S., Frye, M., & Ketter, T. A. (1996). Developmental psychobiology of cyclic affective illness: Implications for early intervention. *Development and Psychopathology, 8,* 273–305.

Powell, C. (1917). *English domestic relations, 1487–1653: A study of matrimony and family life in theory and practice as revealed by the literature, law, and history of the period.* New York: Russell & Russell.

Powers, S., Blount, R., Bachanas, P., Cotter, M., & Swan, S. (1993). Helping preschool leukemia patients and parents cope during injections. *Journal of Pediatric Psychology, 18,* 681–695.

Poznanski, E. O. (1979). Childhood depression: A psychodynamic approach to the etiology of depression in children. In A. French & I. Berlin (Eds.), *Depression in children and adolescents* (pp. 46–68). New York: Human Sciences Press.

Poznanski, E. O., & Mokros, H. B. (1994). Phenomenology and epidemiology of mood disorders in children and adolescents. In W. M. Reynolds & H. F. Johnston (Eds.), *Handbook of depression in children and adolescents* (pp. 19–39). New York: Plenum.

Price-Bonham, S., & Addison, S. (1978). Families and mentally retarded children: Emphasis on the father. *The Family Coordinator, 27,* 221–230.

Prince, J. B., Wilens, T. E., Biederman, J., Spencer, T. J., et al. (1996). Clonidine for sleep disturbances associated with attention-deficit hyperactivity disorder: A systematic chart review of 62 cases. *Journal of the American Academy of Child and Adolescent Psychiatry, 35,* 599–605.

Pring, L., Hermelin, B., & Heavey, L. (1995). Savants, segments, art and autism. *Journal of Child Psychology and Psychiatry, 36,* 1065–1076.

Prino, C. T., & Peyrot, M. (1994). The effect of child physical abuse and neglect on aggressive, withdrawn, and prosocial behavior. *Child Abuse and Neglect, 18,* 871–884.

Prinz, R. J., & Miller, G. E. (1996). Parental engagement in interventions for children at risk for conduct disorder. In R. Dev Peters, & R. J. McMahon (Eds.), *Preventing childhood disorders, substance abuse, and delinquency* (Vol. 3, pp. 161–183). Thousand Oaks, CA: Sage.

Pritchard, J. C. (1837). *A treatise on insanity and other disorders affecting the mind.* Philadelphia: Haswell, Barrington, & Haswell.

Prizant, B. (1996). Communication, language, social, and emotional development. *Journal of Autism and Developmental Disorders, 26,* 173–178.

Prizant, B., & Wetherby, A. (1989). Enhancing language and communication in autism: From theory to practice. In G. Dawson (Ed.), *Autism: Nature, diagnosis, and treatment* (pp. 282–309). New York: Guilford Press.

Puig-Antich, J., Lukens, E., Davies, M., Goetz, D., Brennan-Quattrock, J., & Todak, G. (1985). Psychosocial functioning in prepubertal major depressive disorders: II. Interpersonal relationships after sustained recovery from affective episode. *Archives of General Psychiatry, 42,* 511–517.

Putnam, F. W., & Trickett, P. K. (1993). Child sexual abuse: A model of chronic trauma. *Psychiatry, 56,* 82–95.

Pyle, R. L., Mitchell, J. E., Eckert, E. D., Hatsukami, D., Pomeroy, C., & Zimmerman, R. (1990). Maintenance treatment and 6-month outcome for bulimic patients who respond to initial treatment. *American Journal of Psychiatry, 147,* 871–875.

Pynoos, R. S., Frederick, C., Nader, K., Arroyo, W., Steinberg, A., Eth, S., Nunez, F., & Fairbanks, L. (1987). Life threat and posttraumatic stress in school-age children. *Archives of General Psychiatry, 44,* 1057–1063.

Quay, H. C. (1988). The behavioral reward and inhibition systems in childhood behavior disorders. In L. M. Bloomingdale (Ed.), *Attention deficit disorder* (Vol. 3, pp. 176–186). Oxford, England: Pergamon Press.

Quay, H. C. (1993). The psychobiology of undersocialized aggressive conduct disorder: A theoretical perspective. *Development and Psychopathology, 5,* 165–180.

Quay, H. C. (1997). Inhibition and attention deficit hyperactivity disorder. *Journal of Abnormal Child Psychology, 25,* 7–13.

Quay, H. C., & Werry, J. S. (Eds.). (1986). *Psychopathological disorders of childhood* (3rd ed.). New York: Wiley.

Rabin, A. I. (1986). Concerning projective techniques. In A. I. Rabin (Ed.), *Projective techniques for adolescents and children* (pp. 3–13). New York: Springer.

Racusin, G. R., & Kaslow, N. J. (1991). Assessment and treatment of childhood depression. In P. A. Keller & S. R. Heyman (Eds.), *Innovations in clinical practice: A sourcebook* (Vol. 10, pp. 223–243). Sarasota, FL: Professional Resource Exchange.

Radbill, S. X. (1968). A history of child abuse and infanticide. In R. E. Helfer & C. H. Kempe (Eds.), *The battered child* (pp. 3–17). Chicago: University of Chicago Press.

Radke-Yarrow, M., & Brown, E. (1993). Resilience and vulnerability in children of multiple-risk families. *Development and Psychopathology, 5,* 581–592.

Radke-Yarrow, M., & Zahn-Waxler, C. (1990). Research on children of affectively ill parents: Some considerations for theory and research on normal development. *Development and Psychopathology, 2,* 349–366.

Raine, A. (1993). *The psychopathology of crime: Criminal behavior as a clinical disorder.* San Diego: Academic Press.

Raine, A., Venables, P., & Williams, P. H. (1996). Better autonomic conditioning and faster electrodermal half-recovery time at age 15 years as possible protective factors against crime at age 29 years. *Developmental Psychology, 32,* 624–630.

Rains, P. M., Kitsuse, J. I., Duster, T., & Friedson, E. (1975). The labeling approach to deviance. In N. Hobbs (Ed.), *Issues in the classification of children* (Vol. 1, pp. 88–100). San Francisco: Jossey-Bass.

Ramey, C. T., Mulvihill, B. A., & Ramey, S. L. (1996). Prevention: Social and educational factors and early intervention. In J. W. Jacobson & J. A. Mulick (Eds.), *Manual of diagnosis and professional practice in mental retardation* (pp. 215–227). Washington, DC: American Psychological Association.

Ramey, C. T., & Ramey, S. L. (1992). Effective early intervention. *Mental Retardation, 6,* 337–345.

Randall, S. (1993, April 4). What makes Sammy run. *Alta Vista Magazine,* pp. 7–15.

Rao, J. M. (1990). A population-based study of mild mental handicap in children: Preliminary analysis of obstetric associations. *Journal of Mental Deficiency Research, 34,* 59–65.

Rapee, R. M. (1997). Potential role of childrearing practices in the development of anxiety and depression. *Clinical Psychology Review, 17,* 47–67.

Rapee, R. M., Craske, M., & Barlow, D. H. (1996). Psycho-education. In C. G. Lindemann (Ed.), *Handbook of the treatment of the anxiety disorders* (2nd ed., pp. 311–322). Northvale, NJ: Jason Aronson.

Rapoport, J. L. (1989). *The boy who couldn't stop washing: The experience & treatment of obsessive-compulsive disorder*. New York: Signet.

Rapoport, J. L., Quinn, P. O., & Lamprecht, F. (1974). Minor physical anomalies and plasma-beta-hydroxylase activity in hyperactive boys. *American Journal of Psychiatry, 131,* 386–390.

Rappaport, L. (1993). The treatment of nocturnal enuresis: Where are we now? *Pediatrics, 92,* 465–466.

Rapport, M. D., & Kelly, K. L. (1993). Psychostimulant effects on learning and cognitive function. In J. L. Matson (Ed.), *Handbook of hyperactivity in children* (pp. 97–135). Boston, MA: Allyn & Bacon.

Rapport, M. D., Murphy, H. A., & Bailey, J. S. (1982). Ritalin vs. response cost in the control of hyperactive children: A within-subject comparison. *Journal of Applied Behavior Analysis, 15,* 205–216.

Rasmussen, S., & Eisen, J. L. (1992). The epidemiology of differential diagnosis of obsessive-compulsive disorder. *Journal of Clinical Psychiatry, 53,* 4–10.

Rast, J., Johnston, J. M., Drum, C., & Conrin, J. (1981). The relation of food quantity to rumination behavior. *Journal of Applied Behavior Analysis, 14,* 121–130.

Rastam, M. (1992). Anorexia nervosa in 51 Swedish adolescents: Premorbid problems and comorbidity. *Journal of the American Academy of Child and Adolescent Psychiatry, 31,* 819–828.

Raynham, H., Gibbons, R., Flint, J., & Higgs, D. (1996). The genetic basis for mental retardation. *Quarterly Journal of Medicine, 89,* 169–175.

Reed, E. W., & Reed, S. G. (1965). *Mental retardation: A family study*. Philadelphia: Saunders.

Rees, J. R. (1939). Sexual difficulties in childhood. In R. G. Gordon (Ed.), *A survey of child psychiatry* (pp. 246–256). New York: Oxford University Press.

Rehm, L. P., & Carter, A. S. (1990). Cognitive components of depression. In M. Lewis & S. M. Miller (Eds.), *Handbook of developmental psychopathology* (pp. 341–351). New York: Plenum.

Rehm, L. P., & Sharp, R. N. (1996). Strategies for childhood depression. In M. A. Reineke, F. M. Dattilio, & A. Freeman (Eds.), *Cognitive therapy with children and adolescents: A casebook for clinical practice* (pp. 103–123). New York: Guilford Press.

Reid, A. H., & Ballanger, B. R. (1995). Behaviour symptoms among severely and profoundly mentally retarded patients: A 16-18 year follow-up study. *British Journal of Psychiatry, 167,* 452.

Reid, J. B., Patterson, G. R., Baldwin, D. V., & Dishion, T. J. (1988). Observations in the assessment of childhood disorders. In M. Rutter, A. H. Tuma, & I. Lann (Eds.), *Assessment and diagnosis in child psychopathology* (pp. 156–195). New York: Guilford Press.

Reid, J. B., Taplin, P., & Lorber, R. (1981). A social interactional approach to the treatment of abusive families. In R. B. Stuart (Ed.), *Violent behavior: Social learning approaches to prediction, management, and treatment* (pp. 83–101). New York: Brunner/Mazel.

Reinecke, M. A., Ryan, N. E., & DuBois, D. L. (1998). Cognitive-behavioral therapy of depression and depressive symptoms during adolescence: A review and meta-analysis. *Journal of the American Academy of Child and Adolescent*

Psychiatry, 37, 34–36.

Reinking, D., & Bridwell-Bowles, L. (1991). Computers in reading and writing. In R. Barr, M. L. Kamil, P. B. Mosenthal, & P. D. Pearson (Eds.), *Handbook of reading research* (Vol. 2). Mahwah, NJ: Erlbaum.

Reitan, R. M., & Wolfson, D. (1992). *Neuropsychological evaluation of older children*. Tucson, AZ: Neuropsychology Press.

Remschmidt, H. E., Schulz, E., Martin, M., Warnke, A., & Trott, G. (1994). Childhood-onset schizophrenia: History of the concept and recent studies. *Schizophrenia Bulletin, 20,* 727–746.

Rende, R., & Plomin, R. (1995). Nature, nurture, and the development of psychopathology. In D. Cicchetti & D. J. Cohen (Eds.), *Developmental psychopathology: Vol. 1. Theory and methods* (pp. 291–314). New York: Wiley.

Renick, M. J., & Harter, S. (1989). Impact of social comparisons on the developing self-perceptions of learning-disabled students. *Journal of Educational Psychology, 81,* 631–638.

Renouf, A. G., & Harter, S. (1990). Low self-worth and anger as components of the depressive experience in young adolescents. *Development and Psychopathology, 2,* 293–310.

Renouf, A. G., & Kovacs, M. (1995). Dysthymic disorder during childhood and adolescence. In J. H. Kocsis & D. N. Klein (Eds.), *Diagnosis and treatment of chronic depression* (pp. 20–40). New York: Guilford Press.

Reschly, D. J., & Jipson, F. J. (1976). Ethnicity, geographic locale, age, sex, and urban-rural residence as variables in the prevalence of mild retardation. *American Journal of Mental Deficiency, 81,* 154–161.

Resnick, M. D., Harris, L. J., & Blum, R. W. (1993). The impact of caring and connectedness on adolescent health and well-being. *Journal of Paediatrics and Child Health, 29*(Suppl. 1), 3–9.

Rey, J. M., Bashir, M. R., Schwarz, M., Richards, I. N., Plapp, J. M., & Stewart, G. W. (1988). Oppositional disorder: Fact or fiction? *Journal of the American Academy of Child and Adolescent Psychiatry, 27,* 157–162.

Rey, J. M., & Walter, G. (1997). Half a century of ECT use in young people. *American Journal of Psychiatry, 154,* 595–602.

Reynolds, C. R., & Kamphaus, R. W. (Eds.). (1990a). *Handbook of psychological and educational assessment of children: Intelligence and achievement*. New York: Guilford Press.

Reynolds, C. R., & Kamphaus, R. W. (Eds.). (1990b). *Handbook of psychological and educational assessment of children: Personality, behavior, and context*. New York: Guilford Press.

Reynolds, C. R., & Kamphaus, R. W. (1992). *Behavior Assessment System for Children (BASC)*. Circle Pines, MN: American Guidance Services.

Reynolds, M. C. (1962). A framework for considering some issues in special education. *Exceptional Children, 28,* 367–370.

Reynolds, W. M. (1993). Self-report methodology. In T. H. Ollendick & M. Hersen (Eds.), *Handbook of child and adolescent assessment* (pp. 98–123). Needham Heights, MA: Allyn & Bacon.

Reynolds, W. M., & Johnston, H. F. (Eds.). (1994a). *Handbook of depression in children and adolescents*. New York: Plenum.

Reynolds, W. M, & Johnston, H. F. (1994b). The nature and study of depression in children and adolescents. In W. M.

Reynolds & H. F. Johnston (Eds.), *Handbook of depression in children and adolescents* (pp. 3–17). New York: Plenum.

Reynolds, W. M., & Mazza, J. J. (1994). Suicide and suicidal behaviors in children and adolescents. In W. M. Reynolds & H. F. Johnston (Eds.), *Handbook of depression in children and adolescents* (pp. 535–580). New York: Plenum.

Richardson, S. A., Katz, M., & Koller H. (1986). Sex differences in number of children administratively classified as mildly mentally retarded: An epidemiological review. *American Journal of Mental Deficiency, 91,* 250–256.

Richters, J. E. (1993). Community violence and children's development: Toward a research agenda for the 1990's. *Psychiatry, 56,* 3–6.

Richters, J. E., Arnold, L. E., Jensen, P. S., Abikoff, H., Conners, C. K., Greenhill, L. L., Hechtman, L., Hinshaw, S. P., Pelham, W. E., Swanson, J. M. (1995). NIMH collaborative multisite multimodal treatment study of children with ADHD: I. Background and rationale. *Journal of the American Academy of Child and Adolescent Psychiatry, 34,* 987–1000.

Richters, J. E., & Cicchetti, D. (1993). Mark Twain meets DSM-III-R: Conduct disorder, development, and the concept of harmful dysfunction. *Development and Psychopathology, 5,* 5–29.

Richters, J. E., & Martinez, P. E. (1993). Violent communities, family choices, and children's chances: An algorithm for improving the odds. *Development and Psychopathology, 5,* 609–627.

Rie, H. E. (1971). Historical perspective of concepts of child psychopathology. In H. E. Rie (Ed.), *Perspectives in child psychopathology* (pp. 3–50). Chicago: Aldine-Atherton.

Rie, H. E. (1980). Definitional problems. In H. E. Rie & E. D. Rie (Eds.), *Handbook of minimal brain dysfunctions: A critical review* (pp. 3–17). New York: Wiley-Interscience.

Rimland, B. (1964). *Infantile autism: The syndrome and its implications for a neural theory of behavior.* New York: Appleton-Century-Crofts.

Ritvo, E. R., Freeman, B. J., Scheibel, A. B., Duong, T., Robinson, H., Guthrie, D., & Ritvo, A. (1986). Lower purkinje cell counts in the cerebella of four autistic subjects: Initial findings of the UCLA-NSAC autopsy research report. *American Journal of Psychiatry, 143,* 862–866.

Roberts, C., Pratt, C., & Leach, D. (1991). Classroom and playground interaction of students with and without disabilities. *Exceptional Children, 57,* 212–224.

Roberts, M. A. (1990). A behavioral observation method for differentiating hyperactive and aggressive boys. *Journal of Abnormal Child Psychology, 18,* 131–142.

Roberts, M. C., & Hurley, L. K. (1997). *Managing managed care.* New York: Plenum.

Roberts, R. E., Chen, R., & Roberts, C. R. (1997). Ethnocultural differences in prevalence of adolescent suicidal behaviors. *Suicide and Life-Threatening Behavior, 27,* 208–217.

Roberts, R. E., & Gotlib, I. H. (1997). Temporal variability in global self-esteem and specific self-evaluation as prospective predictors of emotional distress: Specificity in predictors and outcomes. *Journal of Abnormal Psychology, 106,* 521–529.

Roberts, R. E., Roberts, C. R., & Chen, Y. R. (1997). Ethnocultural differences in prevalence of adolescent depression. *American Journal of Community Psychology, 25,* 95–110.

Robin, A. L., Siegel, P. T., Koepke, T., Moye, A. W., & Tice, S. (1994). Family therapy versus individual therapy for adolescent females with anorexia nervosa. *Journal of Develop-*

mental and Behavioral Pediatrics, 15, 111–116.

Robin, A. L., Siegel, P. T., & Moye, A. (1995). Family versus individual therapy for anorexia: Impact on family conflict. Topical section: Treatment and therapeutic processes. *International Journal of Eating Disorders, 17,* 313–322.

Robins, L. N. (1966). *Deviant children grown up: A sociological and psychiatric study of sociopathic personality.* Baltimore: Williams & Wilkins.

Robins, L. N. (1978). Aetiological implications in studies of childhood histories relating to antisocial personality. In R. D. Hare & D. Schalling (Eds.), *Psychopathic behaviour: Approaches to research* (pp. 255–271). Chichester, England: Wiley.

Robins, L. N. (1986). The consequences of conduct disorder in girls. In D. Olweus, J. Block, & M. Radke-Yarrow (Eds.), *The development of antisocial and prosocial behavior: Research, theories, and issues* (pp. 385–414). Orlando, FL: Academic Press.

Robins, L. N. (1991). Conduct disorder. *Journal of Child Psychology and Psychiatry, 32,* 193–212.

Robins, L. N., & McEvoy, L. (1990). Conduct problems as predictors of substance abuse. In L. N. Robins & M. Rutter (Eds.), *Straight and devious pathways from childhood to adulthood* (pp. 182–204). Cambridge, England: Cambridge University Press.

Robins, L. N., & Rutter, M. (1990). *Straight and devious pathways from childhood to adulthood.* Cambridge, England: Cambridge University Press.

Robinson, N. S., Garber, J., & Hilsman, R. (1995). Cognitions and stress: Direct and moderating effects on depressive versus externalizing symptoms during the junior high school transition. *Journal of Abnormal Psychology, 104,* 453–463.

Rochlin, G. (1959). The loss complex. *Journal of the American Psychoanalytic Association, 7,* 299–316.

Rodriguez, N., Ryan, S., Vande Kemp, H., & Foy, D. (1997). Posttraumatic stress disorder in adult female survivors of childhood sexual abuse: A comparison study. *Journal of Consulting and Clinical Psychology, 65,* 53–59.

Rogers, S. J. (1998). Empirically supported comprehensive treatments for young children with autism. *Journal of Clinical Child Psychology, 27,* 168–179.

Rogers, S. J., Ozonoff, S., & Maslin-Cole, C. (1993). Developmental aspects of attachment behavior in young children with pervasive developmental disorders. *Journal of the American Academy of Child and Adolescent Psychiatry, 32,* 1274–1282.

Rohde, P., Lewinsohn, P., & Seeley, J. (1991). Comorbidity of unipolar depression: II. Comorbidity with other mental disorders in adolescents and adults. *Journal of Abnormal Psychology, 100,* 214–222.

Rohde, P., Lewinsohn, P., & Seeley, J. (1994). Are adolescents changed by an episode of major depression? *Journal of the American Academy of Child and Adolescent Psychiatry, 33,* 1289–1298.

Rojahn, J., & Tassé, M. J. (1996). Psychopathology in mental retardation. In J. W. Jacobson & J. A. Mulick (Eds.), *Manual of diagnosis and professional practice in mental retardation* (pp. 147–156). Washington, DC: American Psychological Association.

Rorty, M., Yager, J., & Rossotto, E. (1994). Childhood sexual, physical, and psychological abuse and their relationship to comorbid psychopathology in bulimia nervosa. *International Journal of Eating Disorders, 16,* 317–334.

Rosen, J. C., & Leitenberg, H. (1985). Exposure plus response prevention treatment of bulimia. In D. M. Garner & P. E. Garfinkel (Eds.), *Handbook of treatment for eating disorders* (pp. 193–209). New York: Guilford Press.

Rosen, J. C., Leitenberg, H., Fisher, C., & Khazam, C. (1986). Binge-eating episodes in bulimia nervosa: The amount and type of food consumed. *International Journal of Eating Disorders, 5,* 255–257.

Rosenbaum, J. F., Biederman, J., Bolduc, E. A., Hirshfeld, D. R., Faraone, S. V., & Kagan, J. (1992). Comorbidity of parental anxiety disorders as risk for childhood-onset anxiety in inhibited children. *American Journal of Psychiatry, 149,* 475–481.

Rosenbaum, J. F., Biederman, J., Hirshfeld, D. R., Bolduc, E. A., & Chaloff, J. (1991a). Behavioral inhibition in children: A possible precursor to panic disorder or social phobia. *Journal of Clinical Psychiatry, 52*(Suppl. 5), 5–9.

Rosenbaum, J. F., Biederman, J., Hirshfeld, D. R., Bolduc, E. A., Faraone, S. V., Kagan, J., Snidman, N., & Reznick, J. S. (1991b). Further evidence of an association between behavioral inhibition and anxiety disorders: Results from a family study of children from a non-clinical sample. *Journal of Psychiatric Research, 25,* 49–65.

Rosenblatt, B. (1971). Historical perspectives of treatment modes. In H. E. Rie (Ed.), *Perspectives in child psychopathology* (pp. 51–84). Chicago: Aldine-Atherton.

Rosenshine, B., & Stevens, R. (1986). Teaching functions. In M. C. Wittrock (Ed.), *Handbook of research on teaching* (3rd ed., pp. 376–391). New York: Macmillan.

Rosenstein, D. S., & Horowitz, H. A. (1996). Adolescent attachment and psychopathology. *Journal of Consulting and Clinical Psychology, 64,* 244–253.

Rosenthal, D. (1970). *Genetic theory and abnormal behavior.* New York: McGraw-Hill.

Rosenthal-Malek, A. L., & Yoshida, R. K. (1994). The effects of metacognitive strategy training on the acquisition and generalization of social skills. *Education and Training in Mental Retardation and Developmental Disabilities, 29*(3), 213–221.

Ross, D. M., & Ross, S. A. (1982). *Hyperactivity: Current issues, research, and theory* (2nd ed). New York: Wiley.

Ross, D. M., & Ross, S. A. (1984). Childhood pain: The school-aged child's viewpoint. *Pain, 20,* 179–191.

Ross, D. P., Shillington, E. R., & Lockhead, C. (1994). *The Canadian fact book on poverty—1994.* Ottawa: Canadian Council on Social Development.

Ross, R. T., Begab, M. J., Dondis, E. H., (1985). *Lives of the retarded: A forty-year follow-up study.* Stanford, CA: Stanford University Press.

Rothbart, M. K., & Mauro, J. A. (1990). Questionnaire measures of infant temperament. In W. J. Fagen & J. Colombo (Eds.), *Individual differences in infancy: Reliability, stability, and prediction* (pp. 411–429). Hillsdale, NJ: Erlbaum.

Rothbart, M. K., Posner, M. I., & Hershey, K. L. (1995). Temperament, attention, and developmental psychopathology. In D. Cicchetti & D. J. Cohen (Eds.), *Developmental psychopathology: Vol. 1. Theory and methods* (pp. 315–340). New York: Wiley.

Rothbaum, B. O., Hodges, L. F., Kooper, R., Opdyke, D., Williford, J., & North, M. M. (1995). Virtual reality graded exposure in the treatment of acrophobia: A case report. *Behavior Therapy, 26,* 547–554.

Rothbaum, F., & Weisz, J. R. (1994). Parental caregiving and child externalizing behavior in nonclinical samples: A meta-analysis. *Psychological Bulletin, 116,* 55–74.

Rourke, B. P. (Ed.). (1985). *Neuropsychology of learning disabilities: Essentials of subtype analysis.* New York: Guilford Press.

Rourke, B. P. (1987). Syndrome of nonverbal learning disabilities: The final common pathway of white-matter disease/dysfunction. *Clinical Neuropsychologist, 1,* 209–234.

Rourke, B. P. (1988). The syndrome of nonverbal learning disabilities: Developmental manifestations in neurological disease, disorder, and dysfunction. *Clinical Neuropsychologist, 2,* 293–330.

Rourke, B. P. (1989). *Nonverbal learning disabilities: The syndrome and the model.* New York: Guilford Press.

Rourke, B. P. (1993). Arithmetic disabilities, specific and otherwise: A neuropsychological perspective. *Journal of Learning Disabilities, 26,* 214–226.

Rourke, B. P., & Del Dotto, J. E. (1994). *Learning disabilities: A neuropsychological perspective.* Thousand Oaks, CA: Sage.

Rourke, B. P., Fiske, J., & Strang, J. (1986). *Neuropsychological assessment of children.* New York: Guilford Press.

Routh, D. K. (1990). Taxonomy in developmental psychopathology: Consider the source. In M. Lewis & S. M. Miller (Eds.), *Handbook of developmental psychopathology* (pp. 53–62). New York: Plenum.

Routh, D. K., & Ernst, A. R. (1984). Somatization disorder in relatives of children and adolescents with functional abdominal pain. *Journal of Pediatric Psychology, 9,* 427–437.

Routh, D. K., & Sanfilippo, M. D. (1991). Helping children cope with painful medical procedures. In J. P. Bush & S. W. Harkins (Eds.), *Children in pain: Clinical and research issues from a developmental perspective* (pp. 397–424). New York: Springer-Verlag.

Rowan, A. B., Foy, D. W., Rodriguez, N., & Ryan, S. (1994). Posttraumatic stress disorder in a clinical sample of adults sexually abused as children. *Child Abuse and Neglect, 18,* 51–61.

Rowe, D. C. (1994). *The limits of family influence: Genes, experience, and behavior.* New York: Guilford Press.

Rubin, K. H., Coplan, R. J., Fox, N. A., & Calkins, S. D. (1995). Emotionality, emotion regulation, and preschoolers' social adaptation. *Development and Psychopathology, 7,* 49–62.

Rubin, K. H., & Stewart, S. L. (1996). Social withdrawal. In E. J. Mash & R. A. Barkley (Eds.), *Child psychopathology* (pp. 277–307). New York: Guilford Press.

Rudolph, K. D., Dennig, M. D., & Weisz, J. R. (1995). Determinants and consequences of children's coping in the medical setting: Conceptualization, review, and critique. *Psychological Bulletin, 118,* 328–357.

Ruma, P. R., Burke, R. V., & Thompson, R. W. (1996). Group parent training: Is it effective for children of all ages? *Behavior Therapy, 27,* 159–169.

Russell, A. T. (1994). The clinical presentation of childhood-onset schizophrenia. *Schizophrenia Bulletin, 20,* 631–646.

Russell, A. T., Bott, L., & Sammons, C. (1989). The phenomenology of schizophrenia occurring in childhood. *Journal of the American Academy of Child and Adolescent Psychiatry, 28,* 399–407.

Russell, D. E. H. (1986). *The Secret Trauma.* New York: Basic Books.

Rutter, M. (1970). Autistic children: Infancy to adulthood. *Seminars in Psychiatry, 2,* 435–450.

Rutter, M. (1972). Childhood schizophrenia reconsidered.

Journal of Autism and Childhood Schizophrenia, 2, 315–337.

Rutter, M. (1979). Protective factors in children's responses to stress and disadvantage. In M. W. Kent and J. E. Rolf (Eds.), *Primary prevention of psychopathology: Social competence in children* (Vol. 3, pp. 49–74). Hanover, NH: University Press of New England.

Rutter, M. (1981). The city and the child. *American Journal of Orthopsychiatry, 51,* 610–625.

Rutter, M. (1987). Psychosocial resilience and protective mechanisms. *American Journal of Orthopsychiatry, 57,* 316–331.

Rutter, M. (1989a). Isle of Wight revisited: Twenty-five years of child psychiatric epidemiology. *Journal of the American Academy of Child and Adolescent Psychiatry, 28,* 633.

Rutter, M. (1989b). Pathways from childhood to adult life. *Journal of Child Psychology and Psychiatry, 30,* 23–51.

Rutter, M. (1991a). Autism: Pathways from syndrome definition to pathogenesis. *Comprehensive Mental Health Care, 1,* 5–26.

Rutter, M. (1991b). Nature, nurture and psychopathology: A new look at an old topic. *Development and Psychopathology, 3,* 125–136.

Rutter, M., Bailey, A., Bolton, P., & Le Couteur, A. (1994). Autism: Syndrome definition and possible genetic mechanisms. In R. Plomin & G. E. McClearn (Eds.), *Nature, nurture, and psychology* (pp. 269–284). Washington, DC: APA Books.

Rutter, M., Bolton, P., Harrington, R., Le Couteur, A., Macdonald, H., & Simonoff, E. (1990). Genetic factors in child psychiatric disorders—I. A review of research strategies. *Journal of Child Psychology and Psychiatry, 31,* 3–37.

Rutter, M., & Garmezy, N. (1983). Developmental psychopathology. In P. H. Mussen (Ed.), *Handbook of child psychology* (4th ed.): Vol. IV. *Socialization, personality, and social development* (pp. 775–911). New York: Wiley.

Rutter, M., & Giller, H. (1983). *Juvenile delinquency: Trends and perspectives.* New York: Penguin.

Rutter, M., & Rutter, M. (1993). *Developing minds: Challenge and continuity across the life span.* New York: Basic Books.

Rutter, M., & Smith, D. J. (Eds.). (1995). *Psychosocial disorders in young people: Time trends and their causes.* Chichester, England: Wiley.

Rutter, M., Tizard, J., & Whitmore, K. (1970). *Education, health, and behavior.* London: Longmans, Green.

Rutter, M., Tizard, J., Yule, W., Graham, P., & Whitmore, K. (1976). Research report: Isle of Wight studies, 1964–1974. *Psychological Medicine, 6,* 313–332.

Rutter, M., Yule, B., Quinton, D., Rowlands, O., Yule, W., & Berger, M. (1974). Attainment and adjustment in two geographical areas: III—Some factors accounting for area differences. *British Journal of Psychiatry, 125,* 520–533.

Rutter, M., & Yule, W. (1970). Reading retardation and antisocial behaviour: The nature of the association. In M. Rutter, J. Tizard, & K. Whitmore (Eds.), *Education, health, and behaviour* (pp. 240–255). London: Longmans.

Ryan, C. M., & Morrow, L. A. (1986). Self-esteem in diabetic adolescents: Relationship between age at onset and gender. *Journal of Consulting and Clinical Psychology, 54,* 730–731.

Ryan, N. D., Dahl, R. E., Birmaher, B., Williamson, D. E., Iyengar, S., Nelson, B., Puig-Antich, J., & Perel, J. M. (1994). Stimulatory tests of growth hormone secretion in prepubertal major depression: Depressed versus normal children. *Journal of the American Academy of Child and Adolescent Psychiatry, 33,* 824–833.

Ryan, N. D., Puig-Antich, J., Ambrosini, P., Rabinovich, H., Robinson, D., Nelson, B., Iyengar, S., & Twomey, J. (1987). The clinical picture of major depression in children and adolescents. *Archives of General Psychiatry, 44,* 854–861.

Rydell, A. M., Dahl, M., & Sundelin, C. (1995). Characteristics of school children who are choosy eaters. *Journal of Genetic Psychology, 156,* 217–229.

Sabaratnam, M., Laver, S., Butler, L., & Pembrey, M. (1994). Fragile X syndrome in North-East Essex: Towards systematic screening: Clinical selection. *Journal of Intellectual Disability Research, 38,* 27–35.

Safer, D. J., & Allen, R. P. (1976). *Hyperactive children: Diagnosis and management.* Baltimore: University Park Press.

Safer, D. J., Zito, J. M., & Fine, E. M. (1996). Increased methylphenidate usage for attention deficit disorder in the 1990s. *Pediatrics, 98,* 1084–1088.

Saigh, P. A. (1991). The development of posttraumatic stress disorder following four different types of traumatization. *Behaviour Research and Therapy, 29,* 213–216.

Sajwaj, T., Libet, J., & Agras, S. (1974). Lemon juice therapy: The control of life-threatening rumination in a six-month-old infant. *Journal of Applied Behavior Analysis, 7,* 557–563.

Sallee, R., & Greenawald, J. (1995). Neurobiology. In J. S. March (Ed.), *Anxiety disorders in children and adolescents* (pp. 3–34). New York: Guilford Press.

Salzinger, S., Kaplan, S., Pelcovitz, D., Samit, C., & Kreiger, R. (1984). Parent and teacher assessment of children's behavior in child maltreating families. *Journal of the American Academy of Child Psychiatry, 23,* 458–464.

Sameroff, A. J. (1993). Models of development and developmental risk. In C. H. Zeanah, Jr. (Ed.), *Handbook of infant mental health.* (pp. 3–13). New York: Guilford Press.

Sameroff, A. J. (1995). General systems theories and developmental psychopathology. In D. Cicchetti & D. J. Cohen (Eds.), *Developmental psychopathology: Vol. 1. Theory and methods* (pp. 659–695). New York: Wiley.

Sampson, R. J. (1992). Family management and child development: Insights from social disorganization theory. In J. McCord (Ed.), *Advances in criminological theory: Facts, frameworks, and forecasts* (Vol. 3, pp. 63–91). New Brunswick, NJ: Transaction.

Sampson, R. J., & Groves, W. B. (1989). Community structure and crime: Testing social-disorganization theory. *American Journal of Sociology, 94,* 774–802.

Sampson, R. J., & Laub, J. H. (1994). Urban poverty and the family context of delinquency: A new look at structure and process in a classic study. *Child Development, 65,* 523–540.

Sampson, R. J., & Lauritsen, K. (1994). Violent victimization and offending: Individual-, situational-, and community-level risk factors. In A. J. Reiss, Jr., & J. Roth (Eds.), *Understanding and preventing violence, Vol. 3: Social influences* (pp. 1–114). Washington, DC: National Academy Press.

Sampson, R. J., Raudenbush, S. W., & Earls, F. (1997). Neighborhoods and violent crime: A multilevel study of collective efficacy. *Science, 277,* 918–924.

Sanders, M. R., & Dadds, M. R. (1992). Children's and parents' cognitions about family interaction: An evaluation of video-mediated recall and thought listing procedures in the assessment of conduct-disordered children. *Journal of Clinical Child Psychology, 21*, 371–379.

Sanders, M. R., & Dadds, M. R. (1993). *Behavioral family intervention*. Needham Heights, MA: Allyn & Bacon.

Sandler, A., & Robinson, R. (1981). Public attitudes and community acceptance of mentally retarded persons: A review. *Education and Training of the Mentally Retarded, 16*, 97–103.

Sandoval, J., & Irvin, M. G. (1990). Legal and ethical issues in the assessment of children. In C. R. Reynolds & R. W. Kamphaus (Eds.), *Handbook of psychological and educational assessment of children: Intelligence and achievement* (pp. 86–104). New York: Guilford Press.

Sapolsky, R. (1997, October). A gene for nothing. *Discover*, pp. 40–46.

Sas, L., Hurley, P., Hatch, A., Malla, S., & Dick, T. (1993). *Three years after the verdict: A longitudinal study of the social and psychological adjustment of child witnesses referred to the child witness project* (FVDS No. 4887-06-91-026). Health and Welfare Canada, Family Violence Prevention Division.

Sattler, J. M. (1988). *Assessment of children* (3rd ed.). San Diego, CA: Jerome M. Sattler.

Sattler, J. M. (1992). *Assessment of children: Revised and updated third edition*. San Diego, CA: Jerome M. Sattler.

Sattler, J. M. (1998). *Clinical and forensic interviewing of children and families: Guidelines for the mental health, education, pediatric, and child maltreatment fields*. San Diego, CA: Jerome M. Sattler.

Sattler, J. M., & Mash, E. J. (1998). Introduction to clinical assessment interviewing. In J. M. Sattler, *Clinical and forensic interviewing of children and families: Guidelines for the mental health, education, pediatric, and child maltreatment fields* (pp. 2–44). San Diego, CA: Jerome M. Sattler.

Scarr, S. (1992). Developmental theories for the 1990's: Development and individual differences. *Child Development, 63*, 1–19.

Scarr, S. (1998). American child care today. *American Psychologist, 53*, 95–108.

Scerbo, A. S., & Kolko, D. (1995). Child physical abuse and aggression: Preliminary findings on the role of internalizing problems. *Journal of the American Academy of Child and Adolescent Psychiatry, 34*, 1060–1066.

Schachar, R. (1986). Hyperkinetic syndrome: Historical development of the concept. In E. A. Taylor (Ed.), *The overactive child* (pp. 19–40). London: MacKeith.

Schachar, R., & Tannock, R. (1995). Test of four hypotheses for the comorbidity of attention-deficit hyperactivity disorder and conduct disorder. *Journal of the American Academy of Child and Adolescent Psychiatry, 34*, 639–648.

Schachar, R., Tannock, R., & Logan, G. (1993). Inhibitory control, impulsiveness, and attention deficit hyperactivity disorder. *Clinical Psychology Review, 13*, 721–740.

Schachtel, D. (1988). Effects of adult and peer social initiations on the social behavior of withdrawn, maltreated preschool children. *Journal of Consulting and Clinical Psychology, 56*, 34–39.

Schaefer, C. E. (1979). *Childhood encopresis and enuresis*. New York: Van Nostrand Reinhold.

Scharfman, M. A. (1978). Psychoanalytic treatment. In B. B. Wolman, J. Egan, & A. O. Ross (Eds.), *Handbook of treatment of mental disorders in childhood and adolescence* (pp. 47–69). Englewood Cliffs, NJ: Prentice Hall.

Schiff, M., & Lewontin, R. (1986). *Education and class: The irrelevance of IQ genetic studies*. Oxford, England: Clarendon.

Schlundt, D. G., & Johnson, W. G. (1990). *Eating disorders: assessment and treatment*. London: Allyn & Bacon.

Schmich, M. (1997, June 1). *Chicago Tribune*.

Schneider-Rosen, K., Braunwald, K., Carlson, V., & Cicchetti, D. (1985). Current perspectives in attachment theory: Illustration from the study of maltreated infants. *Monographs of the Society for Research in Child Development, 50*(Serial No. 209), 194–210.

Schopler, E., Mesibov, G. B., & Kunce, L. J. (Eds.). (1998). *Asperger syndrome or high-functioning autism?* New York: Plenum.

Schreibman, L., & Koegel, R. L. (1996). Fostering self-management: Parent-delivered pivotal response training for children with autistic disorder. In E. D. Hibbs & P. S. Jensen (Eds.), *Psychosocial treatments for child and adolescent disorders: Empirically based strategies for clinical practice* (pp. 525–552). Washington, DC: American Psychological Association.

Schreier, H. A., & Libow, J. A. (1993). *Hurting for love: Munchausen by proxy syndrome*. New York: Guilford Press.

Schroeder, C. S., & Gordon, B. N. (1991). *Assessment and treatment of childhood problems: A clinician's guide*. New York: Guilford Press.

Schteingart, J. S., Molnar, J., Klein, T. P., Lowe, C. B., & Hartmann, A. H. (1995). Homelessness and child functioning in the context of risk and protective factors moderating child outcomes. *Journal of Clinical Child Psychology, 24*, 320–331.

Schwebel, A. I., & Fine, M. A. (1994). *Understanding and helping families: A cognitive-behavioral approach*. Hillsdale, NJ: Erlbaum.

Scott, S. (1990). Mental retardation. In A. E. H. Emery & D. H. Rimoin (Eds.), *Principles and practice of medical genetics* (2nd ed.) (pp. 1639–1673). Edinburgh: Churchill-Livingstone.

Scotti, J. R., Morris, T. L., McNeil, C. B., & Hawkins, R. P. (1996). DSM-IV and disorders of childhood and adolescence: Can structural criteria be functional? *Journal of Consulting and Clinical Psychology, 64*, 1177–1191.

Sedlak, A. J., & Broadhurst, D. D. (1996, September). *Third national incidence study of child abuse and neglect: Final report*. Washington, DC: U.S. Department of Health and Human Services.

Seguin, J. R., Pihl, R. O., Harden, P. W., Tremblay, R. E., & Boulerice, B. (1995). Cognitive and neuropsychological characteristics of physically aggressive boys. *Journal of Abnormal Psychology, 104*, 614–624.

Seidel, W. T., & Joschko, M. (1990). Evidence of difficulties in sustained attention in children with ADHD. *Journal of Abnormal Child Psychology, 18*, 217–229.

Seidman, L. J., Biederman, J., Faraone, S. V., & Weber, W. (1997). A pilot study of neuropsychological function in girls with ADHD. *Journal of the American Academy of Child and Adolescent Psychiatry, 36*, 366–373.

Selfe, L. (1983). *Normal and anomalous representational drawing ability in children*. London: Academic Press.

Seligman, L. D., & Ollendick, T. H. (1998). Comorbidity of anxiety and depression in children and adolescents: An integrative review. *Clinical Child and Family Psychology Review, 1*, 125.

Seligman, M., Peterson, C., Kaslow, N., Tanenbaum, R., Alloy, L., & Abramson, L. (1984). Attributional style and depressive symptoms among children. *Journal of Abnormal Psychology, 93,* 235–238.

Seligman, M. E. P. (1971). Phobias and preparedness. *Behavior Therapy, 2,* 307–320.

Seligman, M. E. P. (1975). *Helplessness: On depression, development, and death.* San Francisco: W. H. Freeman.

Selman, R. L., Beardslee, W., Schultz, L. H., Krupa, M., & Podorefsky, D. (1986). Assessing adolescent interpersonal negotiation strategies: Toward the integration of structural and functional models. *Developmental Psychology, 22,* 450–459.

Selman, R. L., Schultz, L. H., Nakkula, M., Barr, D., Watts, C., & Richmond, J. B. (1992). Friendship and fighting: A developmental approach to the study of risk and prevention of violence. *Development and Psychopathology, 4,* 529–558.

Selvini Palazzoli, M. P. (1974). *Self-starvation.* London: Chaucer.

Semenak, S. (1996, November 21). Coping with autism is a full-time job. *Montreal Gazette,* pp. A1, A15.

Semrud-Clikeman, M., Biederman, J., Sprich-Buckminster, S., Lehman, B. K., Faraone, S. V., & Norman, D. (1992). Comorbidity between ADHD and learning disability: A review and report in a clinically referred sample. *Journal of the American Academy of Child and Adolescent Psychiatry, 31,* 439–448.

Semrud-Clikeman, M., Filipek, P. A., Biederman, J., Steingard, R., Kennedy, D., Renshaw, P., & Bekken, K. (1994). Attention-deficit hyperactivity disorder: Magnetic resonance imaging morphometric analysis of the corpus callosum. *Journal of the American Academy of Child and Adolescent Psychiatry, 33,* 875–882.

Serbin, L. A., Moskowitz, D. S., Schwartzman, A. E., & Ledingham, J. E. (1991). Aggressive, withdrawn, and aggressive/withdrawn children in adolescence. In D. J. Pepler & K. H. Rubin (Eds.), *The development and treatment of childhood aggression* (pp. 55–70). Hillsdale, NJ: Erlbaum.

Sergeant, J., & Sholten, C. A. (1985). On resource strategy limitations in hyperactivity: Cognitive impulsivity reconsidered. *Journal of Child Psychology and Psychiatry, 26,* 97–109.

Serketich, W. J., & Dumas, J. E. (1996). The effectiveness of behavioral parent training to modify antisocial behavior in children: A meta-analysis. *Behavior Therapy, 27,* 171–186.

Seroczynski, A. D., Cole, D. A., & Maxwell, S. E. (1997). Cumulative and compensatory effects of competence and incompetence on depressive symptoms in children. *Journal of Abnormal Psychology, 106,* 586–597.

Sexton, J. (1996, September 5). For dead child's family, long history of troubles. *New York Times,* p. B3.

Shadish, W. R., Matt, G. E., Navarro, A. M., Siegle, G., Crits-Christoph, P., Hazelrigg, M. D., Jorm, A. F., Lyons, L. C., Nietzel, M. T., Prout, H. T., Robinson, L., Smith, M. L., Svartberg, M., & Weiss, B. (1997). Evidence that therapy works in clinically representative conditions. *Journal of Consulting and Clinical Psychology, 65,* 355–365.

Shaffer, D., Fisher P., Dulcan, M. K., Davies, M., Piacentini, J., Schwab-Stone, M. E., Lahey, B. B., Bourdon, K., Jensen, P. S., Bird, H. R., Canino, G., & Regier, D. A. (1996). The NIMH Diagnostic Interview Schedule for Children Version 2.3 (DISC–2.3): Description, acceptability, prevalence rates, and performance in the MECA study. *Journal of the American Academy of Child and Adolescent Psychiatry, 35,* 865–877.

Shaffer, D., Fisher, P., & Lucas, C. (Eds.). (1997). *NIMH-DISC-IV.* Ruane Center.

Shaffer, D., Garland, A., Gould, M., Fisher, P. & Trautman, P. (1988). Preventing teenage suicide: A critical review. *Journal of the American Academy of Child and Adolescent Psychiatry, 27,* 675–687.

Shaffer, D., Gould, M., Fisher, P., Trautman, P., Moreau, D., Kleinman, M., & Flory, M. (1996). Psychiatric diagnosis in child and adolescent suicide. *Archives of General Psychiatry, 53,* 339–348.

Shaffer, D., Gould, M., & Hicks, R. C. (1994). Worsening suicide rate in black teenagers. *American Journal of Psychiatry, 151,* 1810–1812.

Shaffi, N., Carrigan, S., Whittinghill, J. R., & Derrick, A. (1985). Psychological autopsy of completed suicide of children and adolescents. *American Journal of Psychiatry, 142,* 1061–1064.

Shankweiler, D., & Liberman, I. Y. (Eds.). (1989). *Phonology and reading disability: Solving the reading puzzle.* Ann Arbor: University of Michigan Press.

Shapiro, L. R., Crawford, P. B., & Clark, M. J. (1984). Obesity prognosis: A longitudinal study of children from age six months to nine years. *American Journal of Public Health, 74,* 968–972.

Shapiro, S., Newcomb, M., & Loeb, T. B. (1997). Fear of fat, disregulated-restrained eating, and body esteem: Prevalence and gender differences among eight- to ten-year-old children. *Journal of Clinical Child Psychology, 26,* 358–365.

Shaw, D. S., & Bell, R. Q. (1993). Developmental theories of parental contributors to antisocial behavior. *Journal of Abnormal Child Psychology, 21,* 493–518.

Shaw, D. S., & Vondra, J. I. (1994). Chronic family adversity and early child behavior problems: A longitudinal study of low income families. *Journal of Child Psychology and Psychiatry, 35,* 1109–1122.

Shaywitz, B. A., & Shaywitz, S. E. (1994). Measuring and analyzing change. In G. R. Lyon (Ed.), *Frames of reference for the assessment of learning disabilities: New views on measurement issues* (pp. 29–58). Baltimore: Paul H. Brookes.

Shaywitz, B. A., Shaywitz, S. E., Byrne, T., Cohen, D. J., & Rothman, S. (1983). Attention deficit disorder: Quantitative analysis of CT. *Neurology, 33,* 1500–1503.

Shaywitz, S. E., Cohen, D. J., & Shaywitz, B. A. (1978). The biochemical basis of minimal brain dysfunction. *Journal of Pediatrics, 92,* 179–187.

Shaywitz, S. E., Escobar, M. D., Shaywitz, B. A., Fletcher, J. M., & Makuch, R. (1992). Evidence that dyslexia may represent the lower tail of a normal distribution of reading ability. *The New England Journal of Medicine, 326*(3), 145–150.

Shaywitz, S. E., Fletcher, J. E., & Shaywitz, B. A. (1994). Issues in the definition and classification of attention deficit disorder. *Topics in Language Disorders, 14,* 1–25.

Shaywitz, S. E., Shaywitz, B. A., Fletcher, J. M., & Escobar, M. D. (1990). Prevalence of reading disability in boys and girls: Results of the Connecticut longitudinal study. *Journal of the American Medical Association, 264,* 998–1002.

Shearer, D. E., & Loftin, C. R. (1984). The Portage Project: Teaching parents to teach their preschool children in the home. In R. F. Dangel & R. A. Pollster (Eds.), *Parent Training: Foundations of research and practice* (pp. 93–126). New York: Guilford Press.

Sheeber, L., Hops, H., Alpert, A., Davis, B., & Andrews, J. (1997). Family support and conflict: Prospective relations to adolescent depression. *Journal of Abnormal Child Psychology, 25,* 333–344.

Sheeran, T., Marvin, R. S., & Pianta, R. C. (1997). Mothers' resolution of their child's diagnosis and self-reported measures of parent stress, marital relations, and social support. *Journal of Pediatric Psychology, 22,* 197–212.

Shelley-Tremblay, J. F., & Rosen, L. A. (1996). Attention deficit hyperactivity disorder: An evolutionary perspective. *Journal of Genetic Psychology, 157,* 443–453.

Shelton, T. L., & Barkley, R. A. (1994). Critical issues in the assessment of attention deficit disorders in children. *Topics in Language Disorders, 14,* 26–41.

Sherman, D. K., Iacono, W. G., & McGue, M. K. (1997). Attention-deficit hyperactivity disorder dimensions: A twin study of inattention and impulsivity-hyperactivity. *Journal of the American Academy of Child and Adolescent Psychiatry, 36,* 745–753.

Sherman, D. K., McGue, M. K., & Iacono, W. G. (1997). Twin concordance for attention-deficit hyperactivity disorder: A comparison of teachers' and mothers' reports. *American Journal of Psychiatry, 154,* 532–535.

Sherman, J. B., Liao, Y. C., Alexander, M., Kim, M., & Kim, B. D. (1995). Family factors related to obesity in Mexican-American and Anglo preschool children. *Family and Community Health, 18*(2), 28–36.

Shirk, S., & Harter, S. (1996). Treatment of low self-esteem. In M. A. Reineke, F. M. Dattilio, & A. Freeman (Eds.), *Cognitive therapy with children and adolescents: A casebook for clinical practice* (pp. 175–198). New York: Guilford Press.

Sholevar, G. P., & Sholevar, E. H. (1995). Overview. In G. P. Sholevar (Ed.), *Conduct disorders in children and adolescents* (pp. 3–26). Washington, DC: American Psychiatric Press.

Shugar, G., & Krueger, S. (1995). Aggressive family communication, weight gain, and improved eating attitudes during systemic family therapy for anorexia nervosa. *International Journal of Eating Disorders, 17,* 23–31.

Shure, M. B. (1992). *I can problem solve (ICPS): An interpersonal cognitive problem solving program.* Champaign, IL: Research Press.

Sidman, M. (1960). Tactics of scientific research: *Evaluating experimental data in psychology.* New York: Basic Books.

Siegel, J. M., Nienhuis, R., Fahringer, H. M., Paul, R., Shiromani, P., Dement, W. C., Mignot, E., & Chiu, C. (1991). Neuronal activity in narcolepsy: Identification of cataplexy-related cells in the medial medulla. *Science, 252,* 1315–1318.

Siegel, L. J., Smith, K. E., & Wood, T. A. (1991). Children medically at risk. In T. R. Kratochwill & R. J. Harris (Eds.), *The practice of child therapy* (2nd ed., pp. 328–363). Toronto: Pergamon Press.

Sigman, M. (1995). Behavioral research in childhood autism. In M. Lenzenweger & J. Haugaard (Eds.), *Frontiers of developmental psychopathology* (pp. 190–206). New York: Springer-Verlag.

Sigman, M., & Mundy, P. (1989). Social attachments in autistic children. *Journal of the American Academy of Child and Adolescent Psychiatry, 28,* 74–81.

Silver, H., & Finkelstein, M. (1967). Deprivation dwarfism. *Journal of Pediatrics, 70*(3), 371–324.

Silverman, I. W., & Ragusa, D. M. (1992). Child and maternal correlates of impulse control in 24-month-old children. *Genetic, Social, and General Psychology Monographs, 116,* 435–473.

Silverman, J. A. (1997). Anorexia nervosa: Historical perspective on treatment. In D. M. Garner and P. E. Garfinkel (Eds.), *Handbook of treatment for eating disorders* (2nd ed., pp. 3–10). New York: Guilford Press.

Silverman, W. K., & Ginsburg, C. S. (1995). Specific phobia and generalized anxiety disorder. In J. S. March (Ed.), *Anxiety disorders in children and adolescents* (pp. 151–180). New York: Guilford Press.

Silverman, W. K., & Kurtines, W. M. (1996a). *Anxiety and phobic disorders: A pragmatic approach.* New York: Plenum.

Silverman, W. K., & Kurtines, W. M. (1996b). Transfer of control: A psychosocial intervention model for internalizing disorders in youth. In E. D. Hibbs & P. S. Jensen (Eds.), *Psychosocial treatments for child and adolescent disorders: Empirically based strategies for clinical practice* (pp. 63–81). Washington, DC: American Psychological Association.

Silverman, W. K., La Greca, A. M., & Wasserstein, S. (1995). What do children worry about? Worries and their relation to anxiety. *Child Development, 66,* 671–686.

Silverman, W. K., & Nelles, W. B (1989). An examination of the stability of mothers' ratings of child fearfulness. *Journal of Anxiety Disorders, 3,* 1–5.

Silverstein, B., Caceres, J., Perdue, L., & Cimarolli, V. (1995). Gender differences in depressive symptomatology: The role played by "anxious somatic depression" associated with gender-related achievement concerns. *Sex Roles, 33,* 621–636.

Silverstein, J. (1994). Diabetes: Medical issues. In R. A. Olson, L. L. Mullins, J. B. Gillman, & J. M. Chaney (Eds.), *The sourcebook of pediatric psychology* (pp. 111–117). Boston: Allyn & Bacon.

Silverthorn, P., Frick, P. J., Kuper, K., & Ott, J. (1996). Attention deficit hyperactivity disorder and sex: A test of two etiological models to explain the male predominance. *Journal of Clinical Child Psychology, 25,* 52–59.

Simonoff, E., Bolton, P., & Rutter, M. (1996). Mental retardation: Genetic findings, clinical implications and research agenda. *Journal of Child Psychology and Psychiatry, 37,* 259–280.

Simonoff, E., Pickles, A., Meyer, J. M., Silberg, J. L., Maes, H. H., Loeber, R., Rutter, M., Hewitt, J. K., & Eaves, L. J. (1997). The Virginia Twin Study of adolescent behavioral development: Influences of age, sex, and impairment on rates of disorder. *Archives of General Psychiatry, 54,* 801–808.

Sines, J. O. (1985). Review of the Roberts Apperception Test for children. In J. V. Mitchell (Ed.), *The Ninth Mental Measurements Yearbook* (Vol. II, pp. 1289–1291). Lincoln: University of Nebraska Press.

Singer, G. H. S., & Irvin, L. (1990). Supporting families of persons with severe disabilities: Emerging findings, practices, and questions. In L. H. Meyer, C. A. Peck, & L. Brown (Eds.), *Critical issues in the lives of people with severe disabilities* (pp. 271–312). Baltimore, MD: Paul H. Brookes.

Singer, M. I., Hussey, D. L., & Strom, K. J. (1992). Grooming the victim: An analysis of a perpetrator's seduction letter. *Child Abuse and Neglect, 16,* 877–886.

Singer, W. (1993). Synchronization of cortical activity and its putative role in information processing and learning. *Annual Review of Physiology, 55,* 349–374.

Siperstein, G. N., & Leffert, J. S. (1997). Comparison of socially accepted and rejected children with mental retardation. *American Journal on Mental Retardation, 101*(4), 339–351.

Siqueland, L., Kendall, P. C., & Steinberg, L. (1996). Perceived family environment and observed family interaction styles. *Journal of Clinical Child Psychology, 25,* 225–237.

Sites, P. (1967). *Lee Harvey Oswald and the American dream.* New York: Pageant Press.

Skogan, W. G. (1990). *Disorder and decline.* New York: Free Press.

Slavin, L. A., & Rainer, K. (1990). Gender differences in emotional support and depressive symptoms among adolescents: A prospective analysis. *American Journal of Community Psychology, 18,* 407–421.

Sloper, P., & Turner, S. (1996). Progress in social-independent functioning of young people with Down's syndrome. *Journal of Intellectual Disability Research, 40,* 39–48.

Smart, D., Sanson, A., & Prior, M. (1996). Connections between reading disability and behavior problems: Testing temporal and causal hypotheses. *Journal of Abnormal Child Psychology, 24,* 363–383.

Smith, C., & Lapp, L. (1991). Increases in the number of REMS and REM density in humans following an intensive learning period. *Sleep, 14,* 325–330.

Smith, D. W., & Saunders, B. E. (1995). Personality characteristics of father/perpetrators and nonoffending mothers in incest families: Individual and dyadic analyses. *Child Abuse and Neglect, 19,* 607–617.

Smith, I. M., & Bryson, S. E. (1994). Imitation and action in autism: A critical review. *Psychological Bulletin, 116,* 259–273.

Smith, T., Eikeseth, S., Klevstrand, M., & Lovaas, O. I. (1997). Intensive behavioral treatment for preschoolers with severe mental retardation and pervasive developmental disorder. *American Journal on Mental Retardation, 102,* 238–249.

Smith, T., & Lovaas, O. I. (1997). The UCLA Young Autism Project: A reply to Gresham and Macmillan. *Behavioral Disorders, 22,* 202–218.

Smith, T., & Lovaas, O. I. (1998). Intensive early behavioral intervention with autism: The UCLA Young Autism Project. *Infants and Young Children, 10,* 67–78.

Snyder, J. (1991). Discipline as a mediator of the impact of maternal stress and mood on child conduct problems. *Development and Psychopathology, 3,* 263–276.

Society for Research in Child Development. (1996). Ethical standards for research with children. In *SRCD: Directory of members* (pp. 337–339). Ann Arbor, MI: Author.

Solin, S. (1995a, November). Dying to be thin. *Seventeen,* pp. 124–129.

Solin, S. (1995b, April 1). I did not want to live. *Seventeen,* pp. 154–156, 176.

Sommers-Flanagan, J., & Sommers-Flanagan, R. (1996). Efficacy of antidepressant medication with depressed youth: What psychologists should know. *Professional Psychology: Research and Practice, 27,* 145–153.

Sondheimer, D. L., Schoenwald, S. K., & Rowland, M. D. (1994). Alternatives to the hospitalization of youth with a serious emotional disturbance. *Journal of Clinical Child Psychology, 23,* 7–12.

Sonuga-Barke, E. J., Lamparelli, M., Stevenson, J., Thompson, M., & Henry, A. (1994). Behaviour problems and preschool intellectual attainment: The associations of hyperactivity and conduct problems. *Journal of Child Psychology and Psychiatry, 35,* 949–960.

Spaccarelli, S. (1994). Stress, appraisal, and coping in child sexual abuse: A theoretical and empirical review. *Psychological Bulletin, 116,* 340–362.

Spaccarelli, S., & Fuchs, C. (1997). Variability in symptom expression among sexually abused girls: Developing multivariate models. *Journal of Clinical Child Psychology, 26,* 24–35.

Spanos, N. P., Cross, P. A., Dickson, K., & DuBreuil, S. C. (1993). Close encounters: An examination of UFO experiences. *Journal of Abnormal Psychology, 102,* 624–632.

Spector, M. (1997, January 7). *Jailed coach feels "betrayed" by revelations of sex abuse.* London Free Press, pp. D1, D3.

Speier, P. L., Sherak, D. L., Hirsch, S., & Cantwell, D. P. (1995). Depression in children and adolescents. In E. E. Beckham & W. R. Leber (Eds.), *Handbook of depression* (2nd ed., pp. 467–493). New York: Guilford Press.

Speltz, M. L., Greenberg, M. T., & DeKlyen, M. (1990). Attachment in preschoolers with disruptive behavior: A comparison of clinic-referred and nonproblem children. *Development and Psychopathology, 2,* 31–46.

Spence, S. H., & Dadds, M. R. (1996). Preventing childhood anxiety disorders. *Behaviour Change, 13,* 241–249.

Spinetta, J. J., & Rigler, D. (1972). The child abusing parent: A psychological review. *Psychological Bulletin, 77,* 296–304.

Spirito, A., Stark, L. J., & Tyc, V. L. (1994). Stressors and coping strategies described during hospitalization by chronically ill children. *Journal of Clinical Child Psychology, 23,* 314–322.

Spitz, H. H. (1996). Comment on Donnellan's review of Shane's (1994) "Facilitated communication: The clinical and social phenomenon." *American Journal on Mental Retardation, 101,* 96–100.

Spitz, R. (1945). Hospitalism: An inquiry into the genesis of psychiatric conditions in early childhood. *Psychoanalytic Study of the Child, 1,* 53–74.

Spitz, R. A., & Wolf, M. (1946). Anaclitic depression: An enquiry into the genesis of psychiatric conditions in early childhood: II. *Psychoanalytic Study of the Child, 2,* 342–363.

Spock, B. (1995). Baby and child care. London: The Bodley Head.

Spoont, M. R. (1993). Modulatory role of serotonin in neural information processing: Implications for human psychopathology. *Psychological Bulletin, 112*(2), 330–350.

Sprague-McRae, J. M., Lamb, W., & Homer, D. (1993). Encopresis: A study of treatment alternatives and historical and behavioral characteristics. *Nurse Practitioner, 18,* 52–53; 56–63.

Springs, F. E., & Friedrich, W. N. (1992). Health risk behaviors and medical sequelae of childhood sexual abuse. *Mayo Clinic Proceedings, 67,* 1–6.

Sroufe, L. A. (1989). Pathways to adaptation and maladaptation: Psychopathology as developmental deviation. In D. Cicchetti (Ed.), *Rochester Symposium on Developmental Psychopathology: Vol. I. The emergence of a discipline* (pp. 13–40). Hillsdale, NJ: Erlbaum.

Sroufe, L. A., & Fleeson, J. (1986). Attachment and the construction of relationships. In W. Hartup & Z. Rubin (Eds.), *Relationships and development* (pp. 51–76). Hillsdale, NJ: Erlbaum.

Sroufe, L. A., & Jacobvitz, D. (1989). Diverging pathways, developmental transformations, multiple etiologies and the problem of continuity in development. *Human Development, 32,* 196–203.

Sroufe, L. A., & Rutter, M. (1984). The domain of developmental psychopathology. *Child Development, 55,* 17–29.

Stahl, S. A., McKenna, M. C., & Pagnucco, J. R. (1994). The effects of whole language instruction: An update and a reappraisal. *Educational Psychologist, 29,* 175–185.

Stanger, C., Achenbach, T. M., & Verhulst, F. C. (1994). Accelerating longitudinal research on child psychopathology: A practical example. *Psychological Assessment, 6,* 102–107.

Stanger, C., Achenbach, T. M., & Verhulst, F. C. (1997). Accelerated longitudinal comparisons of aggressive versus delinquent syndromes. *Development and Psychopathology, 9,* 43–58.

Stanovitch, K. E. (1994). Romance and reality. *The Reading Teacher, 47,* 280–291.

Stanovitch, K. E., & Siegel, L. S. (1994). Phenotypic performance profile of children with reading disabilities: A regression-based test of the phonological-core variable-difference model. *Journal of Educational Psychology, 86,* 24–53.

Stark, K. D., & Kendall, P. C. (1996). *Treating depressed children: Therapist manual for "Taking ACTION."* Ardmore, PA: Workbook Publishing.

Stark, K. D., Humphrey, L. L., Laurent, J., Livingston, R., & Christopher, J. (1993). Cognitive, behavioral, and family factors in the differentiation of depressive and anxiety disorders during childhood. *Journal of Consulting and Clinical Psychology, 5,* 878–886.

Stark, K. D., Kendall, P. C., McCarthy, M., Stafford, M., Barron, R., & Thomeer, M. (1996). *Taking ACTION: A workbook for overcoming depression.* Ardmore, PA: Workbook Publishing.

Stark, K. D., Rouse, L. W., & Livingston, R. (1991). Treatment of depression during childhood and adolescence: Cognitive-behavioral procedures for the individual and family. In P. C. Kendall (Ed.), *Child and adolescent therapy: Cognitive-behavioral procedures* (pp. 165–206). New York: Guilford Press.

Stark, K. D., Schmidt, K. L., & Joiner, T. E., Jr. (1996). Cognitive triad: Relationship to depressive symptoms, parents' cognitive triad, and perceived parental messages. *Journal of Abnormal Child Psychology, 24,* 615–631.

Stark, K. D., Swearer, S., Kurowski, C., Sommer, D., & Bowen, B. (1996). Targeting the child and the family: A holistic approach to treating child and adolescent depressive disorders. In E. D. Hibbs & P. S. Jensen (Eds.), *Psychosocial treatments for child and adolescent disorders: Empirically based strategies for clinical practice* (pp. 207–238). Washington, DC: American Psychological Association.

Statistics Canada. (1997). *People in low income.* Cat. No. 13-207-XPB. Ottawa, ON: Author. Available: http://www.statcan.ca/english/pgdb/people/families/famil41.htm.

Steege, M. W., Wacker, D. P., Cigrand, K. C., Berg, W. K., Novak, C. G., Reimers, T. M., Sasso, G. M., & DeRaad, A. (1990). Use of negative reinforcement in the treatment of self-injurious behavior. *Journal of Applied Behavior Analysis, 23,* 459–467.

Stein, M. A., Szumoski, E., Blondis, T. A., & Roizen, N. J. (1995). Adaptive skills dysfunction in ADD and ADHD children. *Journal of Child Psychology and Psychiatry, 36,* 663–670.

Steiner-Adair, C. (1990). The body politic: Normal female adolescent development and the development of eating disorders. In C. Gilligan, N. P. Lyons, & T. J. Hammer (Eds.), *Making connections: The relational worlds of adolescent girls at Emma Willard School* (pp. 162–182). Cambridge, MA: Harvard University Press.

Steinhauer, P. D. (1996). *Model for the prevention of delinquency.* Ottawa: National Crime Prevention Council.

Steinhauer, P. D. (1998). Developing resiliency in children from disadvantaged populations. In *Canadian health action: Building on the legacy: Vol. 1. Children and youth* (pp. 47–102). Sainte-Foy, Quebec: Editions Multimondes.

Steinhauer, P. D., Santa-Barbara, J., & Skinner, H. (1984). The process model of family functioning. *The Canadian Journal of Psychiatry, 29,* 77–88.

Steinhausen, H. C. (1997). Annotation: Outcome of anorexia nervosa in the younger patient. *Journal of Child Psychology and Psychiatry and Allied Disciplines, 38,* 271–276.

Steinhausen, H. C., & Reitzle, M. (1996). The validity of mixed disorders of conduct and emotions in children and adolescents: A research note. *Journal of Child Psychiatry and Psychology, 37,* 339–343.

Steinhausen, H. C., Willms, J., & Spohr, H. (1994). Correlates of psychopathology and intelligence in children with Fetal Alcohol Syndrome. *Journal of Child Psychology and Psychiatry, 35,* 323–331.

Sternberg, E. M., & Gold, P. W. (1997). The mind body interaction in disease. *Scientific American,* pp. 8–15.

Stevenson, J. (1992). Evidence for a genetic etiology in hyperactivity in children. *Behavior Genetics, 22,* 337–343.

Stevenson, J., Pennington, B. F., Gilger, J. W., DeFries, J. C., & Gilies, J. J. (1993). Hyperactivity and spelling disorders: Testing for shared genetic aetiology. *The Journal of Child Psychology and Psychiatry, 34,* 1137–1152.

Stewart, J. T., Myers, W. C., Burket, R. C., & Lyles, W. B. (1990). A review of the psychopharmacology of aggression in children and adolescents. *Journal of the American Academy of Child and Adolescent Psychiatry, 29,* 269–277.

Stewart, M. A., Thach, B. T., & Friedin, M. R. (1970). Accidental poisoning and the hyperactive child syndrome. *Diseases of the Nervous System, 31,* 403–407.

Still, G. F. (1902). Some abnormal psychical conditions in children. *Lancet, 1,* 1008–1012, 1077–1082, 1163–1168.

Stoleru, S., Nottelmann, E. D., & Ronsaville, D. (1997). Sleep problems in children of affectively ill mothers. *Journal of Child Psychology and Psychiatry, 38,* 831–841.

Stone, W. L., Ousley, O. Y., & Littleford, C. D. (1997). Motor imitation in young children with autism: What's the object? *Journal of Abnormal Child Psychology, 25,* 475–485.

Strain, P. S., Kohler, F. W., & Goldstein, H. (1996). Learning experiences . . . An alternative program: Peer-mediated interventions for young children with autism. In E. D. Hibbs & P. S. Jensen (Eds.), *Psychosocial treatments for child and adolescent disorders: Empirically based strategies for clinical practice* (pp. 573–587). Washington, DC: American Psychological Association.

Strandburg, R. J., Marsh, J. T., Brown, W. S., Asarnow, R. F., & Guthrie, D. (1994). Information processing deficits across childhood- and adult-onset schizophrenia: ERP correlates. *Schizophrenia Bulletin, 20,* 685–696.

Straus, M. A., & Donnelly, D. A. (1994). *Beating the devil out of them: Corporal punishment in American families.* New York: Lexington Books.

Straus, M. A., & Gelles, R. J. (1986). Societal change and change in family violence from 1975 to 1985 as revealed by two national surveys. *Journal of Marriage and the Family, 48,* 465–479.

Straus, M. A., & Gelles, R. J. (Eds.). (1990). *Physical violence in American families.* New Brunswick, N.J: Transaction Books.

Straus, M. A., Gelles, R. J., & Steinmetz, S. K. (1980). *Behind closed doors: Violence in the American family.* New York: Anchor Press.

Strauss, A. A., & Lehtinen, L. E. (1947). *Psychopathology and education of the brain-injured child.* New York: Grune & Stratton.

Strauss, A. A., & Werner, H. (1943). Comparative psychopathology of the brain-injured child and the traumatic brain-injured adult. *American Journal of Psychiatry, 19,* 835–838.

Strauss, C. C., Frame, C., & Forehand, R. (1987). Psychosocial impairment associated with anxiety in children. *Journal of Clinical Child Psychology, 16,* 235–239.

Strauss, C. C., Lahey, B. B., Frick, P., Frame, C. L, & Hynd, G. W. (1988). Peer social status of children with anxiety disorders. *Journal of Consulting and Clinical Psychology, 56,* 137–141.

Strauss, C. C., & Last, C. G. (1993). Social and simple phobias in children. *Journal of Anxiety Disorders, 7,* 141–152.

Strauss, C. C., Last, C. G., Hersen, M., & Kazdin, A. E. (1988). Association between anxiety and depression in children and adolescents with anxiety disorders. *Journal of Abnormal Child Psychology, 16,* 57–68.

Strauss, C. C., Lease, C. A., Kazdin, A. E., Dulcan, M. J., & Last, C. G. (1989). Multimethod assessment of the social competence of children with anxiety disorders. *Journal of Clinical Child Psychology, 18,* 184–189.

Strauss, C. C., Lease, C. A., Last, C. G., & Francis, G. (1988). Overanxious disorder: An examination of developmental differences. *Journal of Abnormal Child Psychology, 16,* 433–443.

Streissguth, A. P., Aase, J. M., Clarren, S. K., Randels, S. P., LaDue, R. A., & Smith, D. F. (1991). Fetal Alcohol Syndrome in adolescents and adults. *Journal of the American Medical Association, 265,* 1961–1967.

Streissguth, A. P., Martin, D. C., Barr, H. M., Sandman, B. M., Kirchner, G. L., & Darby, B. L. (1984). Intrauterine alcohol and nicotine exposure: Attention and reaction time in 4-year-old children. *Developmental Psychology, 20,* 533–541.

Striegel-Moore, R. H. (1993). Etiology of binge eating: A developmental perspective. In C. G. Fairburn & G. T. Wilson (Eds.), *Binge eating: Nature, assessment and treatment* (pp. 144–172). New York: Guilford Press.

Striegel-Moore, R. H., Schreiber, G. B., Pike, K. M., Wilfley, D. E., & Rodin, J. (1995). Drive for thinness in black and white preadolescent girls. *International Journal of Eating Disorders, 18,* 59–69.

Striegel-Moore, R. H., Silberstein, L. R., & Rodin, J. (1986). Toward an understanding of risk factors for bulimia. *American Psychologist, 41,* 246–263.

Strober, M. (1991). Disorders of the self in anorexia nervosa: An organismic-developmental paradigm. In C. Johnson (Ed.), *Psychodynamic treatment of anorexia nervosa and bulimia* (pp. 354–373). New York: Guilford Press.

Strober, M., & Humphrey, L. L. (1987). Familial contributions to the etiology and course of anorexia nervosa and bulimia. *International Journal of Eating Disorders, 5,* 654–659.

Strober, M., Lampert, C., Morrell, W., Burroughs, J., & Jacobs, C. (1990). A controlled family study of anorexia nervosa: Evidence of familial aggregation and lack of shared transmission with affective disorders. *International Journal of Eating Disorders, 9,* 239–253.

Strober, M., Lampert, C., Schmidt, S., & Morrell, W. (1993). The course of major depressive disorder in adolescents: Recovery and risk of manic switching in a 24-month prospective, naturalistic follow-up of psychotic and nonpsychotic subtypes. *Journal of the American Academy of Child and Adolescent Psychiatry, 32,* 34–42.

Strober, M., Schmidt-Lackner, S., Freeman, R., Bower, S., Lampert, C., & DeAntonio, M. (1995). Recovery and relapse in adolescents with bipolar affective illness: A five-year naturalistic, prospective follow-up. *Journal of the American Academy of Child and Adolescent Psychiatry, 34,* 724–731.

Stroh Becvar, D., & Becvar, R. J. (1988). *Family therapy: A systemic integration.* Needham Heights, MA: Allyn & Bacon.

Strosahl, K. D. (1994). Entering the new frontier of managed mental health care: Gold mines and land mines. *Cognitive and Behavioral Practice, 1,* 5–23.

Stuber, M., Christakis, D., Houskamp, B., & Kazak, A. (1996). Post trauma symptoms in childhood leukemia survivors and their parents. *Psychosomatics, 37,* 254–261.

Stunkard, A. J., & Burt, V. (1967). Obesity and body image: II. Age of onset in the body image. *American Journal of Psychiatry, 123,* 1443–1447.

Stunkard, A. J., D'Aquill, E., Fox, S., & Filion, B. D. (1972). Influence of social class on obesity and thinness in children. *Journal of the American Medical Association, 221,* 579–584.

Stuss, D. T., Gow, C. A., & Hetherington, C. R. (1992). "No longer Gage": Frontal lobe dysfunction and emotional changes. *Journal of Consulting and Clinical Psychology, 60,* 349–359.

Sullivan, P. F. (1995). Mortality in anorexia nervosa. *American Journal of Psychiatry, 152,* 1073–1074.

Sutker, P. B. (1994). Psychopathy: Traditional and clinical antisocial concepts. In D. C. Fowles, P. Sutker, & S. H. Goodman (Eds.), *Progress in experimental personality and psychopathology research* (pp. 73–120). New York: Springer.

Sutton, A. (1995). The new gene technology and the difference between getting rid of illness and altering people. *European Journal of Genetics and Society, 1,* 12–19.

Suzuki, D. (1994, October 6). *The nature of things with David Suzuki: Easy targets.* Ottawa: Canadian Broadcasting Corporation.

Swackhamer, K. (1993). Believer. *Journal of the American Medical Association, 270,* 312.

Swanson, J. M., McBurnett, K., Christian, D. L., & Wigal, T. (1995). Stimulant medications and the treatment of children with ADHD. In T. H. Ollendick & R. J. Prinz (Eds.), *Advances in clinical child psychology* (Vol. 17, pp. 265–322). New York: Plenum.

Swedo, S. E., & Leonard, H. L. (1992). Trichotillomania: An obsessive-compulsive spectrum disorder? *Psychiatric Clinics of North America, 15,* 777–790.

Swedo, S. E., Leonard, H. L., Mittleman, B. B., Allen, A. J., Rapoport, J. L., Dow, S. P., Kanter, M. E., Chapman, F., & Zabriskie, J. (1997). Identification of children with pediatric autoimmune neuropsychiatric disorders associated with streptococcal infections by a marker associated with rheumatic fever. *American Journal of Psychiatry, 154,* 110–112.

Swedo, S. E., Pleeter, J. D., Richter, D. M., Hoffman, C. L., Allen, A. J., Hamburger, M. A., Turner, M. D., Yamada, B. A., & Rosenthal, N. W. (1995). Rates of seasonal affective disorder in children and adolescents. *American Journal of Psychiatry, 152,* 1016–1019.

Swedo, S. E., & Rapoport, J. L. (1991). The neurobiology of obsessive-compulsive disorder in childhood. In M. A. Jenike & M. Asberg (Eds.), *Understanding obsessive-compulsive disorder (OCD)* (pp. 28–39). Bern, Switzerland: Hogrefe Publishers.

Swedo, S. E., Rapoport, J. L., Leonard, H., Lenane, M., & Cheslow, D. (1989). Obsessive-compulsive disorder in children and adolescents: Clinical phenomenology of 70 consecutive cases. *Archives of General Psychiatry, 46,* 335–341.

Swensen, C. H. (1968). Empirical evaluations of human figure drawings: 1957–1966. *Psychological Bulletin, 70,* 20–44.

Szasz, T. S. (1970). *The manufacture of madness.* New York: Dell.

Szatmari, P. (1992). The epidemiology of attention-deficit hyperactivity disorders. In G. Weiss (Ed.), *Child and adolescent psychiatric clinics of North America: Attention-deficit hyperactivity disorder* (pp. 361–372). Philadelphia: Saunders.

Szatmari, P., Boyle, M. H., & Offord, D. R. (1993). Familial aggregation of emotional and behavioral problems of childhood in the general population. *American Journal of Psychiatry, 150,* 1398–1403.

Szatmari, P., Offord, D. R., & Boyle, M. H. (1989). Correlates, associated impairments, and patterns of service utilization of children with attention deficit disorders: Findings from the Ontario Child Health Study. *Journal of Child Psychology and Psychiatry, 30,* 205–217.

Tager-Flusberg, H. (1993). What language reveals about the understanding of minds in children with autism. In S. Baron-Cohen, H. Tager-Flusberg, & D. J. Cohen (Eds.), *Understanding other minds: Perspectives from autism* (pp. 138–157). Oxford, England: Oxford University Press.

Tager-Flusberg, H. (1996). Brief report: Current theory and research on language and communication in autism. *Journal of Autism and Developmental Disorders, 26,* 169–172.

Takanishi, R. (1993). The opportunities for adolescence: Research, interventions, and policy. *American Psychologist, 48,* 85–87.

Tallal, P., Miller, S. L., Bedi, G., Byma, G., Wang, X., Nagarajan, S. S., Schreiner, C., Jenkins, W. M., Merzenich, M. M. (1996). Language comprehension in language-learning impaired children improved with acoustically modified speech. *Science, 271,* 81–84.

Tallal, P., Ross, R., & Curtiss, S. (1989a). Familial aggregation in specific language impairment. *Journal of Speech and Hearing Disorders, 54,* 167–173.

Tallal, P., Ross, R., & Curtiss, S. (1989b). Unexpected sex ratios in families of language/learning-impaired children. *Neuropsychologia, 27,* 987.

Tallal, P., Townsend, J., Curtiss, S., & Wulfeck, B. (1991). Phenotypic profiles of language impaired children based on genetic/family history. *Brain and Language, 41,* 81–95.

Tallmadge, J., & Barkley, R. A. (1983). The interactions of hyperactive and normal boys with their mothers and fathers. *Journal of Abnormal Child Psychology, 11,* 565–579.

Tannert, C. (1996, February/March). Star power: Starbright World enlivens the pediatric-healthcare experience. *Video,* pp. 33–37.

Tannock, R. (1998). Attention deficit hyperactivity disorder: Advances in cognitive, neurobiological, and genetic research. *Journal of Child Psychology and Psychiatry, 39,* 65–99.

Tannock, R. (in press). Attention deficit disorders with anxiety disorders. In T. E. Brown (Ed.), *Subtypes of attention deficit disorders in children, adolescents, and adults.* Washington, DC: American Psychiatric Press.

Tannock, R., Fine, J., Heintz, T., & Schachar, R. J. (1995). A linguistic approach detects stimulant effects in two children with attention-deficit hyperactivity disorder. *Journal of Child and Adolescent Psychopharmacology, 5,* 177–189.

Tannock, R., Purvis, K., & Schachar, R. (1993). Narrative abilities in children with attention deficit hyperactivity disorder and normal peers. *Journal of Abnormal Child Psychology, 21,* 103–117.

Tappan, P. W. (1949). *Juvenile delinquency.* New York: McGraw-Hill.

Tapscott, M., Frick, P. J., Wootton, J., & Kruh, I. (1996). The intergenerational link to antisocial behavior: Effects of paternal contact. *Journal of Child and Family Studies, 5,* 229–240.

Tarter, R. E., Hegedus, A. E., Winsten, N. E., & Alterman, A. I. (1984). Neuropsychological, personality, and familial characteristics of physically abused delinquents. *Journal of the American Academy of Child Psychiatry, 23,* 668–674.

Tarver-Behring, S., Barkley, R. A., & Karlsson, J. (1985). The mother-child interactions of hyperactive boys and their normal siblings. *American Journal of Orthopsychiatry, 55,* 202–209.

Tate, D. C., Reppucci, N. D., & Mulvey, E. P. (1995). Violent juvenile delinquents: Treatment effectiveness and implications for action. *American Psychologist, 50,* 777–781.

Taub, D. E., & Blinde, E. M. (1994). Disordered eating and weight control among adolescent female athletes and performance squad members. *Journal of Adolescent Research, 9,* 483–497.

Taylor, A. R., Asher, S. R., & Williams, G. A. (1987). The social adaptation of mainstreamed mildly retarded children. *Child Development, 58,* 1321–1334.

Taylor, E. (1995). Dysfunctions of attention. In D. Cicchetti & D. J. Cohen (Eds.), *Developmental psychopathology: Risk disorder, and adaptation* (Vol. 2, pp. 243–273). New York: Wiley-Interscience.

Taylor, H. G. (1988). Learning disabilities. In E. J. Mash & L. G. Terdal (Eds.), *Behavioral assessment of childhood disorders* (2nd ed., pp. 402–450). New York: Guilford Press.

Taylor, H. G. (1989). Learning disabilities. In E. J. Mash & R. A. Barkley (Eds.), *Treatment of childhood disorders* (pp. 347–380). New York: Guilford Press.

Taylor, H. G., & Fletcher, J. M. (1983). Biological foundations of specific developmental disorders: Methods, findings, and future directions. *Journal of Clinical Child Psychology, 12,* 46–65.

Taylor, H. G., & Fletcher, J. M. (1990). Neuropsychological assessment of children. In G. Foldstein & M. Hersen (Eds.), *Handbook of psychological assessment* (2nd ed., pp. 228–255). New York: Pergamon Press.

Tellegen, A., Lykken, D. T., Bouchard, T. J., Wilcox, K. J., Segal, N. L., & Rich, N. S. (1988). Personality similarity in twins reared apart and together. *Journal of Personality and Social Psychology, 54,* 1031–1039.

Terman, L. M. (1921). A symposium: Intelligence and its measurement. *Journal of Educational Psychology, 12,* 127–133.

Terr, L. C. (1983). Chowchilla revisited: The effects of psychic trauma four years after a school-bus kidnapping. *American Journal of Psychiatry, 140,* 1543–1550.

Terr, L. C. (1991). Childhood traumas: An outline and overview. *American Journal of Psychiatry, 148,* 10–20.

Thatcher, R. W. (1994). Psychopathology of early frontal lobe damage: Dependence on cycles of development. *Development and Psychopathology, 6,* 565–596.

Thatcher, R. W., Lyon, G. R., Rumsey, J., & Krasnegor, N. (Eds.). (1996). *Developmental neuroimaging: Mapping the development of brain and behavior.* San Diego, CA: Academic Press.

Thomas, A., & Chess, S. (1977). *Temperament and development.* New York: Brunner/Mazel.

Thompson, J. K., Coovert, M. D., Richards, K. J., Johnson, S., & Cattarin, J. (1995). Development of body image, eating disturbance, and general psychological functioning in female adolescents: Covariance structure modeling and longitudinal investigations. *International Journal of Eating Disorders, 18,* 221–236.

Thompson, R. A. (1994a). Emotion regulation: A theme in search of definition. *Monographs of the Society for Research in Child Development, 59*(2–3), 25–52.

Thompson, R. A. (1994b). Social support and the prevention of child maltreatment. In G. B. Melton and F. D. Barry (Eds.), *Protecting children from abuse and neglect: Foundations for a new national strategy* (pp. 40–130). New York: Guilford Press.

Thompson, R. J., Jr., Gil, K. M., Burbach, D. J., Keith, B. R., & Kinney, T. R. (1993). Role of child and maternal processes in the psychological adjustment of children with sickle cell disease. *Journal of Consulting and Clinical Psychology, 61,* 468–474.

Thompson, R. J., Jr., & Gustafson, K. E. (1996). *Adaptation to chronic childhood illness.* Washington, DC: American Psychological Association.

Thompson, R. J., Jr., Gustafson, K. E., George, L. K., & Spock, A. (1994). Change over a 12-month period in the psychological adjustment of children and adolescents with cystic fibrosis. *Journal of Pediatric Psychology, 19,* 189–203.

Thompson, S., & Rey, J. M. (1994). Functional enuresis: Is desmopressin the answer? *Journal of the American Academy of Child and Adolescent Psychiatry, 34,* 266–271.

Thorndike, R. L., Hagen, E. P., & Sattler, J. P. (1986). Guide for administering and scoring the Stanford-Binet Intelligence Scale (4th. ed.). Chicago: Riverside Publishing.

Time (1996, January 15). p. 22.

Timmerman, M. G., Wells, L. A., & Chen, S. (1990). Bulimia nervosa and associated alcohol abuse among secondary school students. *Journal of the American Academy of Child and Adolescent Psychiatry, 29,* 118–122.

Tingelstad, J. B. (1991). The cardiotoxicity of the tricyclics. *Journal of the American Academy of Child and Adolescent Psychiatry, 30,* 845–846.

Toch, T. (1993, November 8). Violence in schools. *U.S. News & World Report,* pp. 31–36.

Tolan, P. H., & Guerra, N. (1994, July). *What works in reducing adolescent violence: An empirical review of the field.* Boulder, CO: Center for the Study and Prevention of Violence.

Tolan, P. H., Guerra, N. G., & Kendall, P. C. (1995). A developmental-ecological perspective on antisocial behavior in children and adolescents: Toward a unified risk and intervention framework. *Journal of Consulting and Clinical Psychology, 63,* 579–584.

Tolan, P. H., & Loeber, R. (1993). Antisocial behavior. In P. H. Tolan & B. J. Cohler (Eds.), *Handbook of clinical research and practice with adolescents* (pp. 307–331). New York: Wiley.

Tolan, P. H., & Thomas, P. (1995). The implications of age of onset for delinquency risk: II. Longitudinal evidence. *Journal of Abnormal Child Psychology, 23,* 157–181.

Toth, S., Manly, J. T., & Cicchetti, D. (1992). Child maltreatment and vulnerability to depression. *Development and Psychopathology, 4,* 97–112.

Toth, S. L., & Cicchetti, D. (1996). Patterns of relatedness, depressive symptomatology, and perceived competence in maltreated children. *Journal of Consulting and Clinical Psychology, 64,* 32–41.

Treadwell, K. H., Flannery-Schroeder, E. C., & Kendall, P. C. (1994). Ethnicity and gender in a sample of clinic-referred anxious children: Adaptive functioning, diagnostic status, and treatment outcome. *Journal of Anxiety Disorders, 9,* 373–384.

Treadwell, K. H., & Kendall, P. C. (1996). Self-talk in youth with anxiety disorders: States of mind, content specificity, and treatment outcome. *Journal of Consulting and Clinical Psychology, 64,* 941–950.

Tremblay, R., Pihl, R. O., Vitaro, F., & Dobkin, P. L. (1994). Predicting early onset of male antisocial behaviour from preschool behaviour. *Archives of General Psychiatry, 51,* 732–739.

Trickett, P. K., Aber, J. L., Carlson, V., & Cicchetti, D. (1991). The relationship of soioeconomic status to the etiology and development sequelae of physical child abuse. *Developmental Psychology, 27,* 148–158.

Trickett, P. K., McBride-Chang, C., & Putnam, F. W. (1994). The classroom performance and behavior of sexually abused females. *Development and Psychopathology, 6,* 183–194.

Trimble, B. K., & Baird, P. A. (1978). Maternal Age and Down Syndrome: Age specific incidence rates by single year intervals. *Journal of Medical Genetics, 2,* 1.

Trocmé, N., McPhee, D., Tam, K. K. & Hay, T. (1994). *Ontario incidence study of reported child abuse and neglect.* Toronto: The Institute for the Prevention of Child Abuse, 25 Spadina Ave., Toronto, Ont. M5R 2S9.

Troiano, R. P., Kuczmarski, R. J., Johnson, C. L., Flegal, K. M., & Campbell, S. M. (1995). Overweight prevalence and trends for children and adolescents: The National Health and Nutrition Examination Surveys, 1963 to 1991. *Archives of Pediatrics and Adolescent Medicine, 149,* 1085–1091.

Trommer, B. L., Hoeppner, J. B., Rosenberg, R. S., Armstrong, K. J., & Rothstein, J. A. (1988). Sleep disturbances in children with attention deficit disorder. *Annals of Neurology, 24,* 325.

Trowbridge, F. L. (1984). Prevalence of growth stunting and obesity: Pediatric nutritional surveillance system. *Morbidity and Mortality Weekly Report, 32,* 23–76.

Tubman, J. G., Windle, M., & Windle, R. C. (1996). The onset and cross-temporal patterning of sexual intercourse in middle adolescence: Prospective relations with behavioral and emotional problems. *Child Development, 67,* 327–343.

Turner, B. G., Beidel, D. C., Hughes, S., & Turner, M. W. (1993). Test anxiety in African American school children. *School Psychology Quarterly, 8,* 140–152.

Turner, J. E., & Cole, D. A. (1994). Developmental differences in cognitive diatheses for child depression. *Journal of Abnormal Child Psychology, 22,* 15–32.

Turner, S. M., Beidel, D. C., & Wolff, P. L. (1996). Is behavioral inhibition related to the anxiety disorders? *Clinical Psychology Review, 16,* 157–172.

Twain, M. (1994). *Life on the Mississippi.* New York: Modern Library. (Original work published 1883)

Uhde, T. W. (1994). Anxiety and growth disturbance: Is there a connection? A review of biological studies in social phobia. *Journal of Clinical Psychiatry, 55*(Suppl. 6), 17–27.

Ullmann, L. P., & Krasner, L. (Eds.). (1965). *Case studies in behavior modification.* New York: Holt, Rinehart & Winston.

UN General Assembly. (1989, November). *Adoption of a convention on the rights of the child.* (UN Doc. A/Res/44/25). New York: Author.

U.S. Advisory Board on Child Abuse and Neglect. (1990). *Child abuse and neglect: Critical first steps in response to a national emergency.* Washington, DC: U.S. Government Printing Office.

U.S. Department of Education. (1989). *To assure the free appropriate public education of all handicapped children: Eleventh report to Congress on the implementation of the Education of the Handicapped Act.* Washington, DC: Author.

U.S. Department of Health and Human Services. (1996). *1995 National Household Survey on Drug Abuse (NHSDA).* Rockville, MD: Substance Abuse and Mental Health Services Administration.

U.S. Department of Health and Human Services. (1997). *Preliminary Results from the 1996 National Household Survey on Drug Abuse (NHSDA).* Rockville, MD: Substance Abuse and Mental Health Services Administration.

U.S. Department of Health and Human Services. (1991). *Healthy people 2000.* Washington, DC: U.S. Government Printing Office.

U.S. News & World Report. (November 8, 1993). Violence in schools. pp. 31–36.

Valentine, J., Rossi, E., O'Leary, P., Parry, T. S., Kurinczuk, J. J., & Sly, P. (1997). Thyroid function in a population of children with attention deficit hyperactivity disorder. *Journal of Paediatric Child Health, 33,* 117–120.

van den Oord, E. J. C. G., Boomsma, D. I., & Verhulst, F. C. (1994). A study of problem behaviors in 10- to 15-year-old biologically related and unrelated international adoptees. *Behavior Genetics, 24,* 193–205.

Vanderberg, S. A., Weekes, J. R., & Millson, W. A. (1995). Early substance abuse and its impact on adult offender alcohol and drug problems. *Forum on Corrections Research, 7*(1), 14–16.

Vandereycken, W. (1994). Emergence of bulimia nervosa as a separate diagnostic entity: Review of the literature from 1960–1979. *International Journal of Eating Disorders, 16,* 105–116.

Vandereycken, W., & Van Deth, R. (1996). *From fasting saints to anorexic girls: The history of self-starvation.* New York: New York University Press.

Van der Kolk, B. A., & Fisler, R. E. (1994). Childhood abuse and neglect and loss of self-regulation. *Bulletin of the Menninger Clinic, 58,* 145–168.

Van der Kolk, B. A., Perry, C., & Herman, J. L. (1991). Childhood origins of self-destructive behavior. *American Journal of Psychiatry, 148,* 1665–1671.

van der Meere, J. J. (1996). The role of attention. In S. T. Sandberg (Ed.), *Monographs in child and adolescent psychiatry: Hyperactivity disorders of childhood* (pp. 109–146). Cambridge, NY: Cambridge University Press.

van der Meere, J. J., van Baal, M., & Sergeant, J. (1989). The additive factor method: A differential diagnostic tool in hyperactivity and learning disability. *Journal of Abnormal Child Psychology, 17,* 409–422.

Van Houten, R., Axelrod, S., Bailey, J. S., Favell, J. E., Foxx, R. M., Iwata, B. A., & Lovaas, I. (1988). The right to effective behavioral treatment. *The Behavior Analyst, 11,* 111–114.

Vasey, M. W. (1993). Development and cognition in childhood anxiety: The example of worry. In T. H. Ollendick & R. Prinz (Eds.), *Advances in clinical child psychology* (Vol. 15, pp. 1–39). New York: Plenum.

Vasey, M. W. (1995). Social anxiety disorders. In A. R. Eisen, C. A. Kearney, & C. A. Schaefer (Eds.), *Clinical handbook of anxiety disorders in children and adolescents* (pp. 131–168). Northvale, NJ: Jason Aronson.

Vasey, M. W., Crnic, K. A., & Carter, W. G. (1994). Worry in childhood: A developmental perspective. *Cognitive Therapy and Research, 18,* 529–549.

Vasey, M. W., & Daleiden, E. L. (1994). Worry in children. In G. C. L. Davey & F. Tallis (Eds.), *Worrying: Perspectives on theory, assessment and treatment* (pp. 185–207). Chichester, England: Wiley.

Vasey, M. W., El-Hag, N., & Daleiden, E. L. (1996). Anxiety and the processing of emotionally threatening stimuli: Distinctive patterns of selective attention among high- and low-test anxious children. *Child Development, 67,* 1173–1185.

Vaughn, B. E., Contreras, J., & Seifer, R. (1994). Short-term longitudinal study of maternal ratings of temperament in samples of children with Down Syndrome and children who are developing normally. *American Journal on Mental Retardation, 98,* 607–618.

Vaughn, S. R., & Bos, C. S. (1991). *Strategies for teaching students with learning and behavior problems.* Needham Heights, MA: Allyn & Bacon, Simon & Schuster Education Group.

Velez, C. N., Johnson, J., & Cohen, P. (1989). A longitudinal analysis of selected risk factors for childhood psychopathology. *Journal of the American Academy of Child and Adolescent Psychiatry, 28,* 861–864.

Verhulst, F. C., Akkerhuis, G. W., & Altaus, M. (1985). Mental health in Dutch children: 1. A cross-cultural comparison. *Acta Psychiatrica Scandinavica, 72*(Suppl. 323).

Verhulst, F. C., & Koot, H. M. (1991). Longitudinal research in child and adolescent psychiatry. *Journal of the American Academy of Child and Adolescent Psychiatry, 30,* 361–368.

Vernon, P. (1979). *Intelligence: Heredity and environment.* San Francisco: W. H. Freeman.

Vernon-Feagans, L., Manlove, E. E., & Volling, B. L. (1996). Otitis media and the social behavior of day-care-attending children. *Child Development, 67,* 1528–1539.

Vitiello, B., & Jensen, P. S. (1997). Medication development and testing in children and adolescents: Current problems, future directions. *Archives of General Psychiatry, 54,* 871–876. New York: Columbia University, Division of Child Psychiatry, Ruane Center for Early Diagnosis.

Voeller, K. S. (1991). What can neurological models of attention, intention, and arousal tell us about attention-deficit hyperactivity disorder? *Journal of Neuropsychiatry,* 3, 209–216.

Voeller, K. S. (1996). Developmental neurobiological aspects of autism. *Journal of Autism and Developmental Disorders,* 26, 189–193.

Volkmar, F. R., Burack, J. A., & Cohen, D. J. (1990). Deviance and developmental approaches in the study of autism. In R. M. Hodapp, J. A. Burack, & E. Zigler (Eds.), *Issues in the developmental approach to mental retardation* (pp. 246–271). New York: Cambridge University Press.

Volkmar, F. R. Klin, A. (1998). Asperger syndrome and nonverbal learning disabilities. In E. Schopler, G. B. Mesibov, & L. J. Kunce (Eds.), *Asperger syndrome or high-functioning autism?* (pp. 107–121). New York: Plenum.

Volkmar, F. R., Klin, A., Schultz, R., Bronen, R., Marans, W. D., Sparrow, S., & Cohen, D. J. (1996). Grand rounds: Asperger's syndrome. *Journal of the American Academy of Child and Adolescent Psychiatry,* 35, 118–123.

Volkow, N. D., Wang, G., Fowler, J. S., Logan, J., Angrist, B., Hitzemann, R., Lieberman, J., & Pappas, N. (1997). Effects of methylphenidate on regional brain glucose metabolism in humans: Relationship to dopamine D_2 receptors. *American Journal of Psychiatry,* 154, 50–55.

Vyas, D., & Chandra, R. K. (1984). Functional implications of iron deficiency. In A. Stekel (Ed.), *Iron nutrition in infancy and childhood* (pp. 45–59). New York: Raven.

Vygotsky, L. (1962). *Thought and language.* Cambridge, MA: MIT Press. (Original work published 1934)

Wacker, D. P., Peck, S., Derby, K. M., Berg, W., & Harding, J. (1996). Developing long-term reciprocal interactions between parents and their young children with problematic behavior. In L. K. Koegel, R. L. Koegel, & G. Dunlap (Eds.), *Positive behavioral support: Including people with difficult behavior in the community* (pp. 51–80). Baltimore: Paul H. Brookes.

Wagner, B. M., & Reiss, D. (1995). Family systems and developmental psychopathology: Courtship, marriage, or divorce? In D. Cicchetti & D. J. Cohen (Eds.), *Developmental psychopathology: Vol. 1. Theory and methods* (pp. 696–730). New York: Wiley.

Wakefield, J. C. (1992). The concept of mental disorder: On the boundary between biological facts and social values. *American Psychologist,* 47, 373–388.

Waldman, I. D., & Lilienfeld, S. O. (1995). Diagnosis and classification. In M. Hersen & R. T. Ammerman (Eds.), *Advanced abnormal child psychology* (pp. 21–36). Hillsdale, NJ: Erlbaum.

Waldman, I. D., Lilienfeld, S. O., & Lahey, B. B. (1995). Toward construct validity in the childhood disruptive behavior disorders. In T. H. Ollendick & R. J. Prinz (Eds.), *Advances in clinical child psychology* (Vol. 17, pp. 323–363). New York: Plenum.

Waldrop, M. F., Bell, R. Q., McLaughlin, B, & Halverson, C. F. (1978). Newborn minor physical anomalies predict short attention span, peer aggression, and impulsivity at age 3. *Science,* 199, 563–565.

Walker, C. E., Kenning, M., & Faust-Campanile, J. (1989). Enuresis and encopresis. In E. J. Mash & R. A. Barkley (Eds.), *Treatment of childhood disorders* (pp. 423–448). New York: Guilford Press.

Walker, C. E., & Roberts, M. C. (Eds.). (1992). *Handbook of clinical child psychology* (2nd ed.). New York: Wiley.

Walker, E., & Lewine, R. J. (1990). Prediction of adult-onset schizophrenia from childhood home movies of the patients. *American Journal of Psychiatry,* 147, 1052–1056.

Walker, J. L., Lahey, B. B., Hynd, G. W., & Frame, C. L. (1987). Comparison of specific patterns of antisocial behavior in children with conduct disorder with or without coexisting hyperactivity. *Journal of Consulting and Clinical Psychology,* 55, 910–913.

Walker, J. L., Lahey, B. B., Russo, M. F., Frick, P. J., Christ, M. A. G., McBurnett, K., Loeber, R., Stouthamer-Loeber, M., & Green, S. M. (1991). Anxiety, inhibition, and conduct disorder in children: I. Relation to social impairment. *Journal of the American Academy of Child and Adolescent Psychiatry,* 30, 187–191.

Walker, L. S., Garber, J., & Greene, J. W. (1994). Somatic complaints in pediatric patients: A prospective study of the role of negative life events, child social and academic competence, and parental somatic symptoms. *Journal of Consulting and Clinical Psychology,* 62, 1213–1221.

Walker, L. S., Garber, J., Van Slyke, D. A., & Greene, J. W. (1995). Long-term health outcomes in patients with recurrent abdominal pain. *Journal of Pediatric Psychology,* 20, 233–245.

Wallander, J. L., & Thompson, R. J., Jr. (1995). Psychosocial adjustment of children with chronic physical conditions. In M. C. Roberts (Ed.), *Handbook of pediatric psychology* (pp. 124–141). New York: Guilford Press.

Wallander, J. L., Varni, J. W., Babani, L., Banis, H. T., & Wilcox, K. T. (1988). Children with chronic physical disorders: Maternal reports of their psychological adjustment. *Journal of Pediatric Psychology,* 13, 197–212.

Wallander, J. L., Varni, J. W., Babani, L., Banis, H. T., & Wilcox, K. T. (1989). Family resources as resistance factors for psychological maladjustment in chronically ill and handicapped children. *Journal of Pediatric Psychology,* 14, 157–173.

Wallerstein, N. (1992). Powerlessness, empowerment, and health: Implications for health promotion programs. *American Journal of Health Promotion,* 6, 197–205.

Wallis, C. (1994, July 18). Life in overdrive. *Time,* pp. 42–50.

Walter, G., & Rey, J. M. (1997). An epidemiological study of the use of ECT in adolescents. *Journal of the American Academy of Child and Adolescent Psychiatry,* 36, 809–815.

Walters, A. S., Barrett, R. P., Knapp. L. G., & Borden, M. C. (1995). Suicidal behavior in children and adolescents with mental retardation. *Research in Developmental Disabilities,* 16, 85–96.

Wang, M. C., Walberg, H. J., & Reynolds, M. C. (1992). A scenario for better—not separate—special education. *Educational Leadership,* 44, 26–31.

Wang, S., Mason, J., Southwick, S., Johnson, D., Lubin, H., & Charney, D. (1995). Relationships between thyroid hormones and symptoms in combat-related posttraumatic stress disorder. *Psychosomatic Medicine,* 57, 398–402.

Warner, V., Mufson, L., & Weissman, M. M. (1995). Offspring at high and low risk for depression and anxiety: Mechanisms of psychiatric disorder. *Journal of the American Academy of Child and Adolescent Psychiatry,* 34, 786–797.

Wasserman, G A., Shilansky, M., & Hahn, H. (1986). A matter of degree: Maternal interaction with infants of varying levels of retardation. *Child Study Journal,* 16, 241–253.

Waters, E., & Sroufe, L. A. (1983). Social competence as a developmental construct. *Developmental Review,* 3, 79–97.

Watkins, C. E., Campbell, V. L., Nieberding, R., & Hallmark, R. (1995). Contemporary practice of psychological assessment by clinical psychologists. *Professional Psychology: Research and Practice, 26,* 54–60.

Watson, D., Clark, L. A., & Carey, G. (1988). Positive and negative affectivity and their relation to anxiety and depressive disorders. *Journal of Abnormal Psychology, 97,* 346–353.

Watson, J. B. (1925). *Behaviorism.* New York: People's Institute Publishing.

Watson, J. B., & Rayner, R. R. (1920). Conditioned emotional reactions. *Journal of Experimental Psychology, 3,* 1–14.

Watson, R. R (1996, August). I am the mother of a behaviorist's sons. *Parent's Magazine, 50.* (Original article published August 1930)

Weaver, T., & Clum, G. (1993). Early family environments and traumatic experiences associated with borderline personal disorder. *Journal of Consulting and Clinical Psychology, 61,* 1068–1075.

Weber, J. (1936). An approach to the problem of fear in children. *Journal of Mental Science, 82,* 136–147.

Webster-Stratton, C. (1994). Advancing videotape parent training: A comparison study. *Journal of Consulting and Clinical Psychology, 62,* 583–593.

Webster-Stratton, C. (1995). Early intervention with videotape modeling: Programs for families of children with oppositional defiant disorder or conduct disorder. In E. D. Hibbs & P. S. Jensen (Eds.), *Psychosocial treatments for child and adolescent disorders: Empirically based strategies for clinical practice* (pp. 435–474). Washington, DC: American Psychological Association.

Webster-Stratton, C. (1996). Early-onset conduct problems: Does gender make a difference? *Journal of Consulting and Clinical Psychology, 64,* 540–551.

Webster-Stratton, C., & Herbert, M. (1994). *Troubled families—problem children: Working with parents: A collaborative process.* New York: Wiley.

Wechsler, D. (1974). *Manual for the Wechsler Intelligence Scale for Children—Revised (WISC-R).* New York: Psychological Corporation.

Wechsler, D. (1989). *Wechsler Preschool and Primary Scale of Intelligence.* San Antonio: Psychological Corporation.

Wechsler, D. (1991). *Manual for the Wechsler Intelligence Scale for Children—Third edition (WISC-III).* New York: Psychological Corporation.

Weeks, S. J., & Hobson, R. P. (1987). The salience of facial expression for autistic children. *Journal of Child Psychology and Psychiatry, 28,* 137–152.

Weigle, D. S. (1990). Human obesity: Exploding the myths. *The Western Journal of Medicine, 153,* 421–429.

Weinberg, N. Z., Rahdert, E., Colliver, J. D., & Glantz, M. D. (1998). Adolescent substance abuse: A review of the past 10 years. *Journal of the American Academy of Child and Adolescent Psychiatry, 37,* 252–261.

Weinberger, D. R. (1987). Implications of normal brain development for the pathogenesis of schizophrenia. *Archives of General Psychiatry, 44,* 660–669.

Weiner, I. B. (1986). Assessing children and adolescents with the Rorschach. In H. M. Knoff (Ed.), *The assessment of child and adolescent personality* (pp. 141–172). New York: Guilford Press.

Weiss, B., Weisz, J. R., & Bromfield, R. (1986). Performance of retarded and nonretarded persons on information-processing tasks: Further tests of the similar structure hypothesis. *Psychological Bulletin, 100,* 157–175.

Weiss, G., & Hechtman, L. T. (1993). *Hyperactive children grown up: ADHD in children, adolescents, and adults* (2nd ed.). New York: Guilford Press.

Weiss, L. (1992). *Attention deficit disorder in adults.* Dallas, TX: Taylor Publishing Company.

Weissman, M. M., Gammon, G., John, K., Merikangas, K., Warner, V., Prusoof, B, & Sholmskas, D. (1987). Children of depressed parents. *Archives of General Psychiatry, 44,* 847–853.

Weissman, M. M., Warner, V., Wickramaratne, P., Moreau, D., & Olfson, M. (1997). Offspring of depressed parents: 10 years later. *Archives of General Psychiatry, 54,* 932–940.

Weissman, M. M., Warner, V., Wickramaratne, P., & Prusoff, B. A. (1988). Early-onset major depression in parents and their children. *Journal of Affective Disorders, 15,* 269–277.

Weisz, J. (1982). Learned helplessness and the retarded child. In E. Zigler & D. Balla (Eds.), *Mental retardation: The developmental-difference controversy* (pp. 27–40). Hillsdale, NJ: Erlbaum.

Weisz, J. R. (1990). Cultural-familial retardation: A developmental perspective on cognitive performance and "helpless" behavior. In R. M. Hodapp, J. A. Burack, & E. Zigler (Eds.), *Issues in the developmental approach to mental retardation* (pp. 137–168). New York: Cambridge University Press.

Weisz, J. R. (1997). *Primary and secondary control enhancement training (PASCET) program.* Unpublished therapist's manual. University of California, Los Angeles, Department of Psychology.

Weisz, J. R. (1998). Empirically supported treatments for children and adolescents: Efficacy, problems, and prospects. In K. S. Dobson & K. D. Craig (Eds.), *Empirically supported therapies: Best practice in professional psychology* (pp. 66–92). Newbury Park, CA: Sage.

Weisz, J. R., Chayasit, W., Weiss, B., Eastman, K. L., & Jackson, E. W. (1995). A multimethod study of problem behavior among Thai and American children in school: Teacher reports versus direct observations. *Child Development, 66,* 402–415.

Weisz, J. R., Donenberg, G. R., Han, S. S., & Weiss, B. (1995). Bridging the gap between laboratory and clinic in child and adolescent psychotherapy. *Journal of Consulting and Clinical Psychology, 63,* 688–701.

Weisz, J. R., & Suwanlert, S. (1989). Over- and undercontrolled referral problems among children and adolescents from Thailand and the United States: The wat and wai of cultural differences. *Journal of Consulting and Clinical Psychology, 55,* 719–726.

Weisz, J. R., Thurber, C. A., Sweeney, L., Proffitt, V. D., & LeGagnoux, G. L. (1997). Brief treatment of mild-to-moderate child depression using primary and secondary control enhancement training. *Journal of Consulting and Clinical Psychology, 65,* 703–707.

Weisz, J. R., & Weiss, B. (1991). Studying the "referability" of child clinical problems. *Journal of Consulting and Clinical Psychology, 59,* 266–273.

Weisz, J. R., & Weiss, B. (1993). *Effects of psychotherapy with children and adolescents.* Newbury Park, CA: Sage.

Weisz, J. R., Weiss, B., Alicke, M. D., & Klotz, M. L. (1987). Effectiveness of psychotherapy with children and adolescents: A meta-analysis for clinicians. *Journal of Consulting and Clinical Psychology, 55,* 542–549.

Weisz, J. R., Yeates, K., & Zigler, E. (1982). Piagetian evidence and the developmental-difference controversy. In E. Zigler & D. Balla (Eds.), *Mental retardation: The developmental-difference controversy* (pp. 213–276). Hillsdale, NJ: Erlbaum.

Weithorn, L. A., & McCabe, M. A. (1988). Emerging ethical and legal issues in pediatric psychology. In D. K. Routh (Ed.), *Handbook of pediatric psychology* (pp. 567–606). New York: Guilford Press.

Wekerle, C., & Wolfe, D. A. (1996). Child maltreatment. In E. J. Mash & R. A. Barkley (Eds.), *Child psychopathology* (pp. 492–537). New York: Guilford Press.

Weller, R. A., Weller, E. B., Fristad, M. A., & Bowes, J. M. (1991). Depression in recently bereaved prepubertal children. *American Journal of Psychiatry, 148,* 1536–1540.

Welner, Z., Welner, A., Stewart, M., Palkes, H., & Wish, E. (1977). A controlled study of siblings of hyperactive children. *Journal of Nervous and Mental Disease, 165,* 110–117.

Welsh, M. C., & Pennington, B. F. (1988). Assessing frontal lobe functioning in children: Views from developmental psychology. *Developmental Neuropsychology, 4,* 199–230.

Werner, E. E. (1993). Risk and resilience in individuals with learning disabilities: Lessons learned from the Kauai Longitudinal Study. *Learning Disabilities Research and Practice, 8,* 28–34.

Werner, E. E. (1995). Resilience in development. *Current Directions in Psychological Science, 4,* 81–85.

Werner, E. E., & Smith, R. S. (1992). *Overcoming the odds: High risk children from birth to adulthood.* Ithaca, NY: Cornell University Press.

Werry, J. S. (1992). Child and adolescent (early onset) schizophrenia: A review in light of DSM-III-R. *Journal of Autism and Developmental Disorders, 22,* 601–624.

Wesch, D., & Lutzker, J. R. (1991). A comprehensive 5-year evaluation of Project 12-Ways: An ecobehavioral program for treating and preventing child abuse and neglect. *Journal of Family Violence, 6,* 17–35.

West, M. O., & Prinz, R. J. (1987). *Psychological Bulletin, 102*(2), 204–218.

Whalen, C. K., & Henker, B. (1985). The social worlds of hyperactive (ADHD) children. *Clinical Psychology Review, 5,* 447–478.

Whalen, C. K., & Henker, B. (1992). The social profile of attention-deficit hyperactivity disorder: Five fundamental facets. In G. Weiss (Ed.), *Child and adolescent psychiatric clinics of North America: Attention-deficit hyperactivity disorder* (pp. 395–410). Philadelphia: Saunders.

Whalen, C. K., Henker, B., & Dotemoto, S. (1980). Methylphenidate and hyperactivity: Effects on teacher behaviors. *Science, 208,* 1280–1282.

Whelan, J. P., & Houts, A. C. (1990). Effects of a waking schedule on primary enuretic children treated with full-spectrum home training. *Health Psychology, 9,* 164–176.

White, J. L., Moffitt, T. E., Caspi, A., Bartusch, D. J., Needles, D. J., Stouthamer-Loeber, M. (1994). Measuring impulsivity and examining its relationship to delinquency. *Journal of Abnormal Psychology, 103,* 192–205.

White, J. L., Moffitt, T. E., Earls, F., Robins, L., & Silva, P. (1990). How early can we tell? Predictors of childhood conduct disorder and adolescent delinquency. *Criminology, 28,* 507–528.

White, W. A. T. (1988). A meta-analysis of the effects of direct instruction in special education. *Education and Treatment of Children, 11,* 364–374.

Whitehurst, G. J., Fischel, J. E., Arnold, D. S., & Lonigan, C. J. (1992). Evaluating outcomes with children with expressive language delay. In S. F. Warren & J. Reichle (Eds.), *Causes and effects in communication and language intervention* (pp. 277–313). Baltimore: Paul H. Brookes.

Whitehurst, G. J., Fischel, J. E., Lonigan, C. J., Valdez-Manchaca, M. C., Debarsyhe, B. D., & Caulfield, M. B. (1988). Verbal interaction in families of normal and expressive-language-delayed children. *Developmental Psychology, 24,* 690–699.

Whitman, T. L., Scherzinger, M. F., & Sommer, K. S. (1991). Cognitive instruction and mental retardation. In P. C. Kendall (Ed.), *Child and adolescent therapy: Cognitive-behavioral procedures* (pp. 276–315). New York: Guilford Press.

Whitmore, E. A. W., Kramer, J. R., & Knutson, J. F. (1993). The association between punitive childhood experiences and hyperactivity. *Child Abuse and Neglect, 17,* 357–366.

Widiger, T. A. (1993). The DSM-III-R categorical personality disorder diagnoses: A critique and an alternative. *Psychological Inquiry, 4,* 75–90.

Widom, C. S. (1989a). Does violence beget violence? A critical examination of the literature. *Psychological Bulletin, 106,* 3–28.

Widom, C. S. (1989b). The cycle of violence. *Science, 244,* 160–165.

Widom, C. S. (1996, May/June). Childhood sexual abuse and its criminal consequences. *Society,* pp. 47–53.

Wilens, T. E., Biederman, J., Mick, E., Faraone, S. V., & Spencer, T. (1997). Attention deficit hyperactivity disorder (ADHD) is associated with early onset substance use disorders. *Journal of Nervous and Mental Disease, 185,* 475–482.

Wilkinson, G. S. (1993). *Wide Range Achievement Test 3.* Wilmington, DE: Jastak Associates.

Willerman, L. (1973). Activity level and hyperactivity in twins. *Child Development, 44,* 1411–1415.

Williams, D. (1992). *Nobody nowhere: The extraordinary autobiography of an autistic.* New York: Times Books.

Williams, L. M. (1994). Recall of childhood trauma: A prospective study of women's memories of childhood sexual abuse. *Journal of Consulting and Clinical Psychology, 62,* 1167–1176.

Williams, L. M., & Finkelhor, D. (1990). The characteristics of incestuous fathers: A review of recent studies. In W. L. Marshall, D. R. Laws, & H. E. Barbaree (Eds.), *Handbook of sexual assault: Issues, theories, and treatment of the offender* (pp. 231–256). New York: Plenum.

Williams, S., & McGee, R. (1994). Reading attainment and juvenile delinquency. *Journal of Child Psychology and Psychiatry, 35,* 441–459.

Williamson, D. E., Dahl, R. E., Birmaher, B., Goetz, R. R., & Ryan, N. D. (1995). Stressful life events and EEG sleep in depressed and normal control adolescents. *Biological Psychiatry, 37,* 859–865.

Willis, T. J., & Lovaas, I. (1977). A behavioral approach to treating hyperactive children: The parent's role. In J. B. Milichap (Ed.), *Learning disabilities and related disorders* (pp. 119–140). Chicago: Yearbook Medical Publications.

Wilson, G. T. (1991). The addiction model of eating disorders: A critical analysis. *Advances in Behavior Research and Therapy, 13,* 27–72.

Wilson, G. T. (1993). Relationship of dieting and voluntary weight loss to psychological functioning and binge eating. *Annals of Internal Medicine, 119,* 727–730.

Wilson, G. T. (1995). Behavior therapy. In R. J. Corsini & D. Wedding (Eds.), *Current Psychotherapies* (5th ed.) (pp.

197–228). Itasca, IL: F. E. Peacock.

Wilson, G. T., Eldredge, K. L., Smith, D., & Niles, B. (1991). Cognitive-behavioral treatment with and without response prevention for bulimia. *Behaviour Research and Therapy, 29,* 575–583.

Wilson, G. T., Heffernan, K., & Black, C. M. D. (1996). Eating disorders. In E. J. Mash & R. A. Barkley (Eds.), *Child psychopathology* (pp. 541–571). New York: Guilford Press.

Wing, L. (1980). Childhood autism and social class: A question of selection? *British Journal of Psychiatry, 137,* 410–417.

Wing, L. (1981). Asperger's syndrome: A clinical account. *Psychological Medicine, 11,* 115–129.

Wing, L. (1993). The definition and prevalence of autism: A review. *European Child and Adolescent Psychiatry, 2,* 61–74.

Wing, L., & Gould, J. (1979). Severe impairments of social interaction and associated abnormalities in children: Epidemiology and classification. *Journal of Autism and Developmental Disorders, 9,* 11–29.

Wirt, R. D., Lachar, D., Klinedinst, J. K., & Seat, P. S. (1990). *Personality Inventory for Children—1990 edition.* Los Angeles: Western Psychological Services.

Wiseman, C. V., Gray, J. J., Mosimann, J. E., & Ahrens, A. H. (1992). Cultural expectations of thinness: An update. *International Journal of Eating Disorders, 11,* 85–90.

Wittig, R., Zorick, F., Roehrs, T., Sicklesteel, J., & Roth, T. (1983). Narcolepsy in a 7-year-old child. *Journal of Pediatrics, 102,* 725–727.

Wolfe, D. A. (1985). Child abusive parents: An empirical review and analysis. *Psychological Bulletin, 97,* 462–482.

Wolfe, D. A. (1991). *Preventing physical and emotional abuse of children.* New York: Guilford Press.

Wolfe, D. A. (1999). *Child abuse: Implications for child development and psychopathology.* Thousand Oaks, CA: Sage.

Wolfe, D. A., & Jaffe, P. (1991). Child abuse and family violence as determinants of child psychopathology. *Canadian Journal of Behavioral Science, 23,* 282–299.

Wolfe, D. A., Jaffe, P., Wilson, S., & Zak, L. (1985). Children of battered women: The relation of child behavior to family violence and maternal stress. *Journal of Consulting and Clinical Psychology, 53,* 657–664.

Wolfe, D. A., & McGee, R. (1994). Dimensions of child maltreatment and their relationship to adolescent adjustment. *Development and Psychopathology, 6,* 165–181.

Wolfe, D. A., & Mosk, M. D. (1983). Behavioral comparisons of children from abusive and distressed families. *Journal of Consulting and Clinical Psychology, 51,* 702–708.

Wolfe, D. A., & Sandler, J. (1981). Training abusive parents in effective child management. *Behavior Modification, 5,* 320–335.

Wolfe, D. A., Sandler, J., & Kaufman, K. (1981). A competency-based parent training program for child abusers. *Journal of Consulting and Clinical Psychology, 49,* 633–640.

Wolfe, D. A., Sas, L., & Wekerle, C. (1994). Factors associated with the development of posttraumatic stress disorder among child victims of sexual abuse. *Child Abuse and Neglect, 18,* 37–50.

Wolfe, D. A., St. Lawrence, J. S., Graves, K., Brehony, K., Bradlyn, A. S., & Kelly, J. A. (1982). Intensive behavioral parent training for a child abusive mother. *Behavior Therapy, 13,* 438–451.

Wolfe, D. A., & St. Pierre, J. (1989). Child abuse and neglect.

In T. H. Ollendick & M. Hersen (Eds.), *Handbook of child psychopathology* (2nd ed., pp. 377–398). New York: Plenum.

Wolfe, D. A., & Wekerle, C. (1993). Treatment strategies for child physical abuse and neglect: A critical progress report. *Clinical Psychology Review, 13,* 473–500.

Wolfe, D. A., Wekerle, C., Reitzel-Jaffe, D., & Lefebvre, L. (1998). Factors associated with abusive relationships among maltreated and nonmaltreated youth. *Development and Psychopathology, 10,* 61–85.

Wolfe, D. A., Wekerle, C., & Scott, K. (1997). *Alternatives to violence: Empowering youth to develop healthy relationships.* Thousand Oaks, CA: Sage.

Wolfe, V. V., & Finch, A. J. (1987). Negative affectivity in children: A multitrait-multimethod investigation. *Journal of Consulting and Clinical Psychology, 55,* 245–250.

Wolfe, V. V., Gentile, C., & Wolfe, D. A. (1989). The impact of sexual abuse on children: A PTSD formulation. *Behavior Therapy, 20,* 215–228.

Wolfe, V. V., & Wolfe, D. A. (1988). Sexual abuse of children. In E. J. Mash & L. G. Terdal (Eds.), *Behavioral assessment of childhood disorders* (2nd ed., pp. 670–714). New York: Guilford Press.

Wolk, S. I., & Weissman, M. M. (1996). Suicidal behavior in depressed children grown up: Preliminary results of a longitudinal study. *Psychiatric Annals, 26,* 331–335.

Wonderlich, S. (1992). Relationship of family and personality factors in bulimia. In J. H. Crowther, D. L. Tennenbaum, S. E. Hobfall, & M. A. P. Stephens (Eds.), *The etiology of bulimia nervosa: The individual and familial context* (pp. 103–126). Washington, DC: Hemisphere Publishing.

Wong, B. Y. L. (1992). On cognitive process-based instruction. *Journal of Learning Disabilities, 25,* 150–152, 172.

Wong, B. Y. L., Harris, K. R., & Graham, S. (1991). Academic applications of cognitive-behavioral programs with learning disabled students. In P. C. Kendall (Ed.), *Child and adolescent therapy: Cognitive-behavioral procedures.* New York: Guilford Press.

Wood, A. (1993). Pharmacotherapy of bulimia nervosa: Experience with fluoxetine. (1993). *International Clinical Psychopharmacology, 8*(4), 295–299.

Wood, A., Harrington, R., & Moore, A. (1996). Controlled trial of a brief cognitive-behavioural intervention in adolescent patients with depressive disorders. *Journal of Child Psychology and Psychiatry, 37,* 737–746.

Wood, F. B., & Felton, R. H. (1994). Separate linguistic and attentional factors in the development of reading. *Topics in Language Disorders, 14,* 42–57.

Wood, F. B., Felton, R. H., Flowers, L., & Naylor, C. (1991). Neurobehavioral definition of dyslexia. In D. D. Duane & D. B. Gray (Eds.), *The reading brain: The biological basis of dyslexia* (pp. 1–26). Parkton, MD: York Press.

Woodhouse, W., Bailey, A., Rutter, M., Bolton, P., Baird, G., & Le Couteur, A. (1996). Head circumference in autism and other pervasive developmental disorders. *Journal of Child Psychology and Psychiatry, 37,* 665–671.

Woolston, J. L. (1989). Eating disorders in infancy and early childhood. In B. J. Blinder, B. F. Chaitin, & R. Goldstein (Eds.), *The eating disorders* (pp. 275–285). New York: Spectrum Medical.

Woolston, J. L. (1991). *Eating and growth disorders in infants and children.* Newbury Park, CA: Sage.

Woolston, J. L., & Forsyth, B. (1989). Obesity of infancy and early childhood: A diagnostic schema. In B. B. Lahey &

A. E. Kazdin (Eds.), *Advances in clinical child psychology* (Vol. 12, pp. 179–192). New York: Plenum.

Wootton, J. M., Frick, P. J., Shelton, K. K., & Silverthorn, P. (1997). Ineffective parenting and childhood conduct problems: The moderating role of callous-unemotional traits. *Journal of Consulting and Clinical Psychology, 65,* 292–300.

World Health Organization (1997, March). *Child abuse and neglect.* [On-line]. Available: http://www.who.ch/programmes/inf/facts/fact150.html.

Wright, K. (1997, October). Babies, bonds, and brains. *Discover, pp.* 74–78.

Wurtele, S. K. (1990). Teaching personal safety skills to four-year-old children: A behavioral approach. *Behavior Therapy, 21,* 25–32

Wyatt, G. E., & Newcomb, M. (1990). Internal and external mediators of women's sexual abuse in childhood. *Journal of Consulting and Clinical Psychology, 58,* 758–767.

Wysocki, T. (1993). Associations among teen-parent relationships, metabolic control, and adjustment to diabetes in adolescents. *Journal of Pediatric Psychology, 18,* 441–452.

Yairi, E., & Ambrose, N. (1992). Onset of stuttering in preschool children: Selected factors. *Journal of Speech and Hearing Research, 35,* 782–788.

Yates, A. (1989). Current perspectives on the eating disorders: I. History, psychological, and biological aspects. *Journal of Child and Adolescent Psychiatry, 28,* 813–828.

Yates, A., Leehey, K., & Shisslak, C. M. (1983). Running: An analogue of anorexia? *New England Journal of Medicine, 308,* 251–255.

Yoder, P. J., & Feagans, L. (1988). Mothers' attributions of communication to prelinguistic behavior of developmentally delayed and mentally retarded infants. *American Journal on Mental Retardation, 93,* 36–43.

Yoritomo-Tashi. (1916). *Timidity: How to overcome it.* (M. W. Artois, Trans.). New York: Funk & Wagnalls.

Yule, W. (1994). Posttraumatic stress disorder. In T. H. Ollendick, N. J. King, & W. Yule (Eds.), *International handbook of phobic and anxiety disorders in children and adolescents: Issues in clinical child psychology* (pp. 223–240). New York: Plenum.

Zahn-Waxler, C. (1993). Warriors and worriers: Gender and psychopathology. *Development and Psychopathology, 5,* 79–89.

Zahn-Waxler, C., Cole, P. M., Welsh, J. D., & Fox, N. A. (1995). Psychophysiological correlates of empathy and prosocial behaviors in preschool children with behavior problems. *Development and Psychopathology, 7,* 27–48.

Zametkin, A. J., Ernst, M., & Silver, R. (1998). Laboratory and diagnostic testing in child and adolescent psychiatry: A review of the past 10 years. *Journal of the American Academy of Child and Adolescent Psychiatry, 37,* 464–472.

Zametkin, A. J., Liebenauer, L. L., Fitzgerald, G. A., King, A. C., Minkunas, D. V., Herscovitz, P., Yamada, E. M., & Cohen, R. M. (1993). Brain metabolism in teenagers with attention-deficit hyperactivity disorder. *Archives of General Psychiatry, 50,* 333–340.

Zametkin, A. J., Nordahl, T. E., Gross, M., King, A. C., Semple, W. E., Rumsey, J., Hamburger, S., & Cohen, R. M. (1990). Cerebral glucose metabolism in adults with hyperactivity of childhood onset. *New England Journal of Medicine, 323,* 1361–1366.

Zametkin, A. J., & Rapoport, J. L. (1987). Neurobiology of attention deficit disorder with hyperactivity: Where have we come in 50 years? *Journal of the American Academy of Child and Adolescent Psychiatry, 26,* 676–686.

Zelizer, V. A. (1994). *Pricing the priceless child: The changing social value of children.* Princeton: Princeton University Press.

Zentall, S. S. (1985). A context for hyperactivity. In K. Gadow & I. Bialer (Eds.), *Advances in learning and behavioral disabilities* (Vol. 4, pp. 273–343). Greenwich, CT: JAI Press.

Zero to Three/National Center for Clinical Infant Programs (1994). *Diagnostic classification of mental health and developmental disorders of infancy and early childhood* (DC: 0-3). Washington, DC: Author.

Zigler, E. (1967). Familial mental retardation: A continuing dilemma. *Science, 155,* 292–298.

Zigler, E., & Hodapp, R. (1986). *Understanding mental retardation.* New York: Cambridge University Press.

Zigler, E., Taussig, C., & Black, K. (1992). Early childhood intervention: A promising preventative for juvenile delinquency. *American Psychologist, 47,* 997–1006.

Zilbovicius, M., Garreau, B., Samson, Y., Remy, P., Barthelemy, C., Syrota, A., & Lelord, G. (1995). Delayed maturation of the frontal cortex in childhood autism. *American Journal of Psychiatry, 152,* 248–252.

Zimmerman, M. A., & Arunkumar, R. (1994). Resiliency research: Implications for schools and policy. *Social Policy Report, 8*(4), 1–17.

Zoccolillo, M. (1992). Co-occurrence of conduct disorder and its adult outcomes with depressive and anxiety disorders: A review. *Journal of the American Academy of Child and Adolescent Psychiatry, 31,* 547–556.

Zoccolillo, M. (1993). Gender and the development of conduct disorder. *Development and Psychopathology, 5,* 65-78.

Zoccolillo, M., Pickles, A., Quinton, D., & Rutter, M. (1992). The outcome of conduct disorder: Implications for defining adult personality disorder and conduct disorder. *Psychological Medicine, 22,* 971–986.

Zoccolillo, M., & Rogers, K. (1991). Characteristics and outcome of hospitalized adolescent girls with conduct disorder. *Journal of the American Academy of Child and Adolescent Psychiatry, 30,* 973–981.

Zoccolillo, M., & Rogers, K. (1992). Characteristics and outcome of hospitalized adolescent girls with conduct disorder: Erratum, *Journal of the American Academy of Child and Adolescent Psychiatry, 31,* 561.

Zoglin, R. (1996, February 19). Chips ahoy. *Time, pp.* 46–49.

Zubieta, J. K., & Alessi, N. E. (1993). Is there a role of serotonin in the disruptive behavior disorders? A literature review. *Journal of Child and Adolescent Psychopharmacology, 3,* 11–35.

Zuckerman, B., Stevenson, J., & Bailey, V. (1987). Sleep problems in early childhood: Predictive factors and behavioral correlates. *Pediatrics, 80,* 664–671.

Subject Index

[Note: Numerals followed by *f* refer to figures and illustrations; numerals followed by *t* refer to tables; numerals followed by *b* refer to boxed information.]

ABA *See* Applied behavior analysis
Abnormal behavior
  case study, 3
  child
    assessment, 16–17
    causes, 16
    describing, 4–11
    diagnosis, 16–17
    primary considerations, 6
    study methods, 70
    treatment, 16–17
  use of term, 5
Abnormal child psychology
  background, 1–26
  features, 3–4
  research strategies, 58–96
  terminology, 3–4
Abnormal development
  assumptions, underlying, 34–38
  case study, 28–29
  continuities and discontinuities, 36–38
  multiple, interactive causes, 34
  multiply determined, 34
  quantitative and qualitative, 37
  theories and causes of, 28–56
Abnormality
  in individuals, 5
  or relationships, 5
Abuse, incidence of, 534–535
Abused children, sexual and nonsexual
    comparison, 544f
Academic achievement, 266–267
Accelerated longitudinal design, 89–90
Active contributors, 35
Acts, violent *vs.* nonviolent, 193
Acute lymphoblastic leukemia (ALL), 480
Acute stress disorder, 266
Adaptation
  failure of, 31, 528
  resiliency and, 441b
Adaptive functioning, 340
ADD. *See* Attention deficit disorder/
    conduct disorder
ADH. *See* Antidiuretic hormone
ADHD. *See* Attention–deficit/hyperactivity
    disorder

Adipose tissue, 496
Adjustment disorder, 475
Adolescence
  disorders distinguished from adult, 4
  female development, 495f
  growth, 496–497
Adoption, 212–213
Adrenal glands, 44
Adrenalin, 44
Advertising, fear and sex in, 25b
Affective disorder, 284
Age, 100–101
  considerations, 13–14
Aggregation studies, familial, 42
Aggression, 191
  instrumental *vs.* hostile, 192
Aging effects, 89
Agoraphobia, 262
Agreement, interrater, 70
Ainsworth Strange Situation, 77f
ALL. *See* Acute lymphoblastic leukemia
American Psychiatric Association (APA),
    5, 127
Amplifier hypothesis, 220
Amygdala, 44
Anaclitic depression, 289
Analysis, problem-solving, 102
Angelman syndrome, 360
Anhedonia, 285
Anomalies, minor physical, 171
Anonymity, 93, 95
Anorexia nervosa, 491, 506–508
  biological dimension, 513
  causes, 513–515
  course, 512
  cross-cultural considerations, 511
  danger signals, 508
  development, 511–512
  diagnostic criteria, 507t
  etiology and course, 521
  family influences, 516–517
  genetic factors, 513–514
  neurobiological factors, 514–515
  outcome, 512f
  pharmacological treatment, 520
  prevalence, 511
  psychological dimension, 517–520
  psychosocial treatment, 520–521
  restricting type, 508
  sex-role identification, 515
  social dimension, 515–517

Anorexia nervosa *(continued)*
  sociocultural factors, 515–516
  treatments, 520–521
Antecedents, 110f
Antidiuretic hormone (ADH), 471
Antisocial behavior, 185–188
  across life span, 209f
  causal influences and outcomes of
    early-onset, 224t
  destructive-nondestructive, 190–101
  developmental pathways, 206–208
  ecological framework, 212f
  normal development and, 187–188
  ordering of forms, 207f
  overt-covert, 190–101
  parent-reported frequencies, 189f
  patterns of, 206
  types, 191–194
Antisocial personality disorder (APD), 194,
    197–198
Anxiety, 29, 204, 268–269
  anatomy of, 240
  defined, 235
  dimensions of, 240
  experience of, 234–235
  expressions of, 240
  vs. fear and panic, 237
  free-floating, 246
  general, 240
  normal, 239
  separation, 240
  social, 105
  symptoms of, 236t
  temperament and, 271–273
Anxiety disorders, 158–159, 233–283
  accompanying disorders, 268–269
  associated characteristics, 266–269
  attentional biases, 267
  behavior therapy, 278–270
  cognitive-behavioral therapy, 279
  cognitive disturbances, 266–268
  cognitive errors and biases,
    267–268
  culture, 269–270
  developmental pathway, 275, 276t
  ethnicity, 269–270
  facing it, 277b
  family
    influences, 274–275
    interventions, 280
    risk, 273

Anxiety disorders *(continued)*
gender, 269–270
genetic risk, 273
main features, 241b
medications, 279–280
neurobiological factors, 273–274
neurotransmitter system, 274
overview, 240–241
physical symptoms, 268
primary treatments, 278–280
social deficits, 268
theories, 270–271
treatment, 275–282
overview, 277–278
Anxious/depressed syndrome, 293t
APA. *See* American Psychiatric Association
APD. *See* Antisocial personality disorder
Apiphobia, 250
Applied behavior analysis (ABA), 49
Appraisal, 52
Apprehensive expectation, 246
Approaches, classical, 124
Apraxia, 394
Arachnophobia, 248
Arousal
level, deficits in, 164–165
parasomnias, 466–467
Asperger's disorder, 393
Assent, 93
Assessment
ABCs of, 110
approach to neuropsychological, 123f
areas of evaluation, 104t
behavioral, 109–111
role-play, 139f
clinical. *See* Clinical issues, assessment
purposes of, 101–104
value of methods, 70f
Attachment, 51–52
Bowlby's theory of, 270
and psychopathology, 53t
theories, 217–219
Attentional capacity, 147
Attention deficit disorder (ADD)/conduct disorder (CD), 83
Attention-deficit/hyperactivity disorder (ADHD), 13, 58–59, 143–183, 203–204
academic functioning, 153–154
accompanying disorders and symptoms, 157–159
in adolescence, 163
in adulthood, 163–164
associated characteristics, 152–157
causes of, 166–173
cognitive deficits, 153
combined (ADHD-C), 152
concerns of children and adolescents with, 180b
controversial treatments, 182
core characteristics, 146–151
deficits, 164–166
defined, 160
defining features, 146
description, 143–145
developmental course, 161–162
diagnostic criteria, 147t
differential diagnosis, 152
DSM-IV criteria, 152
educational intervention, 178–179

Attention-deficit/hyperactivity disorder (ADHD) *(continued)*
in elementary school, 162–163
environmental toxins, 172
ethnicity, 161
family
influences, 172–173
problems, 156
gender, 160–161
genetic contributions, 167–168
girls with, 161f
health-related problems, 155
historical background, 145–146
impact on relationships, 59–60
important questions, 150–151
in infancy, 162
intellectual deficits, 153
intensive interventions, 180–182
interpersonal difficulties, 155–156
interventions, 179–180
key treatment considerations, 173–174
language impairments, 154–155
learning disabilities, 154
medical and physical characteristics, 155
medication, 174–175
effects, 181f
myths about stimulant medication, 176b
neurobiological factors, 168–171
neurochemical findings, 171
neurophysiological findings, 171
outcome, 161–162
peer problems, 156–157
predominantly hyperactive-impulsive, 152
predominantly inattentive type, 151–152
preschoolers with, 162
prevalence, 160
regions of brain implicated in, 170f
risk taking, 155
speech impairments, 154–155
subtypes, 151–152
summer treatment program, 181b
symptoms first described, 145f
task and situational factors, 159–160
theories, 164–166, 165b
treatments, 173–183, 174t
controversy, 175–177
Attitude, changes in, 287
Attributions, 52
internal, stable, and global, 307
Attrition, 79
Autism, 372–411
accompanying disorders, 392
affective disorder in relatives, 391
associated characteristics, 384–394
with average intelligence, 376–377
behavior
reducing disruptive, 405
repetitive, 383–384
brain abnormalities, 399–400
causes, 396–401
classroom
placements, 409t
transition, 408
cognitive deficits, 386–390
communication impairments, 379–383
core characteristics, 378–384
course, 395–396
curriculum content, 407
defining features, 374–378
description, 373–374

Autism *(continued)*
diagnosis
criteria, 375t
differential, 392
as disorder of brain development, 401
early intervention, 407
early infantile, 373
extreme aloneness, 373
face-to-face communication, 403f
family
involvement, 408
member characteristics, 391–394
risk, 397
training and counseling, 409–411
findings
neurophysiological, 400–401
neuropsychological, 398, 398t
fragile-X, 396–397
general deficits, 389
genetic contributions, 396–398
historical background, 372–373
incidental training, 405
initial stages, 405
intellectual deficits and strengths, 384–385
intensive intervention, 408
IQ changes, 409t
with mental retardation, 375–376
link, 384t
neurobiological factors, 398–401
onset, 394–395
outcome, 395–396
perceptual impairments, 385–386
pervasive developmental disorders, 392
physical characteristics, 390–391
predictability, 408
pregnancy and birth problems, 396
prevalence, 394
problem behaviors, 408
readiness skills, 405
repetitive interests, 383–384
routines, 408
savants, 385
sensory, 385–386
similar deficits in relatives, 391
social impairments, 378–384
specific deficits, 386–389
spectrum of, 374–378
speculations, 397–398
stress in home, 391–392
subtypes, 392
symptoms, 392
teaching child 405–408
training
and counseling family, 409–411
trial, 405
treatment, 401–411
for high-functioning children, 403
for low-functioning children, 403
overview, 403–411
program, 402b
UCLA project, 410b
Aveyron, wild boy of, 22b, 338
Avoidant disorder, 241

Barbie, life-size, comparison to normal human counterparts, 516f
BAS. *See* Behavioral activation system
BASC-SRP. *See* Behavior, Assessment System for Children—Self-Report of Personality

Battered child syndrome, 533
Beck Depression Inventory (BDI), 74
    cognitive model, 307–308
Beers, Clifford, 23
Behavior, 49–51, 110f
    adaptive, 339–341
    analysis, 110
    assessment, adaptive content areas, 341t
    Assessment System for Children—
        Self-Report of Personality
        (BASC-SRP), 122
    child. See Child behavior
    compensatory, 509
    depressive, 287
    externalizing pattern, 190
    individual, 85–87
    multiply determined, 31
    patterns of, 37
    repetitive, 239–240
    sexually opportunistic and predatory, 554
    steps of aggressive children, 216t
    therapy, 26
    undercontrolled, 190
Behavioral conditions and issues
    activation system (BAS), 214
    assessment, 109–111
    definitions, 115t
    disorders, 19
    family systems therapy (BFST), 521
    genetics, 42
    impulsivity, 149
    influences, 29–30
    inhibition, 29
        deficits in, 165–166
    inhibition system (BIS), 213
Behaviorism, 24–25
Bell curve, 343
BFST. See Behavioral conditions and issues,
        family systems therapy
Bidirectional influence, 217
Binet, Alfred, 115
Binge, 509
Biological influences, 15f, 29
Biological perspectives, 39–45
Bipolar disorder (BP), 286, 316–322
    associated characteristics, 321–322
    causes, 322
    comorbidity, 320
    course, 320–321
    criteria for episodes, 317t
    differential diagnosis, 320
    ethnicity, 321
    gender, 321
    incidence and age of onset, 319f
    onset, 320–321
    outcome, 320–321
    prevalence, 319–320
    subtypes, 318t
    treatment, 333–334
BIS. See Behavioral conditions and issues,
        inhibition system
Block Design, 384
    subtest, 389, 390f
Blood flow, regional images, 400f
Borderline personality disorder, 127
Boundaries, establishing, 5–6
BP. See Bipolar disorder
Brain
    abnormalities, as cause of ADHD,
        169–171
    activity, left-hemisphere, 444f

Brain (continued)
    development of, 39
    function, structure, 42–44, 74
    lobes, 44
    structure, 42–44
Breathing-related sleep disorder,
        464–465
Broca's area, 444
Bulimia nervosa, 491, 508–511
    causes, 513–515
    compensatory behaviors of
        full-syndrome, 510f
    course, 512
        etiology and, 521–522
    cross-cultural considerations, 511
    development, 511–512
    diagnostic criteria, 509t
    dimensions
        biological, 513
        psychological, 517–520
        social, 515–517
    factors, 513–515
    family influences, 516–517
    pharmacological treatment, 520
    prevalence, 511
    sex-role identification, 515
    treatments, 520–521
        psychosocial, 520–521
Bullies, 193b

Callous-unemotional interpersonal
        style, 198
Cancer
    in childhood, 479–483
    development and course, 480–481
Care
    categories of, 528–529
    models, continuing, 134
Caretaking behaviors, omissions and
        commissions, 551
Case formulation
    idiographic, 99
    nomothetic, 99
Cataplexy, 464
Categories, 124–126
    classification systems, 124
Causation, transactional process, 37b
Causes, original, 68
CBCL. See Child Behavior Checklist
CBT. See Cognitive behavior, therapy
CD. See Conduct disorders
CDI. See Children's Depression
        Inventory
Cerebellar hypoplasia, 399
Cerebellum, 43
Cerebral cortex, lobes, 44f
Changes
    patterns of, 13
    typical and atypical, 32–33
Checklist for Autism in Toddlers
        (CHAT), 395
Checklists, 111–113
Child
    abuse of, 524–561
        integrated model, 553f
    behavior of, integrative approach,
        38–39
    environment and, 35t
    data base for, 216
    disorders, distinguishing from adult, 4
    functioning, 133

Child Behavior Checklist (CBCL),
        67b, 111
    profile, 112f
Childhood disorders
    disintegrative, 394
    questions about, 65–66
    treatment of, 130–140
Childhood-onset schizophrenia (COS),
        411–418
Child psychology
    breakthroughs, 20–26
    historical views, 20–26
Child psychopathology, 3
    abuse, 18
    common occurrence, 17
    costly outcomes, 18
    dimensions of, 125t
    neglect, 18
    new pressures, 17–18
    ongoing difficulties, 17
    priorities, 18
    resources, 18
    social changes, 17–18
Child-rearing, perspectives on,
        526–529
Children
    characteristics of victimized, 535
    with disabilities, 135b
    referred and nonreferred, 101t
    seriously injured, 535
    rights for disabled, 135b
Children's Depression Inventory (CDI),
        111–112
Chronic childhood illness, 474–488
    accompanied by disability, 480
    characteristics, 484
    estimated prevalence, 478t
    family
        effect on, 481–483
        empowerment, 486
        functioning, 485
    intervention, 486
    models
        biopsychosocial, 483–485
        transactional stress and coping,
            483f
    parental adaptation, 485
    psychiatric disorders and, 481f
    representative, 477–488
    school performance, 482–483
    social adjustment, 482–483
Chronotherapy, 468
Cingulate gyrus, 44
Circadian rhythm sleep disorder, 465
Classification, 124–130
    cutpoints in, 126f
    diagnostic, 129–130
Clinical issues, 98–123
    assessment, 99–100
        multimethod approach, 103
        strategies, 104
    interviews, 104–109
        initial, 105
Co-articulated sounds, 424
Coaxial tomography (CT), 75
Code-emphasis approach, 450
Coercion theory, 217
Cognition, 49–51, 50. See also Cognitive
        issues
    impairments in, 199–200
    structures and content, 50–51

Cognitive behavior
self-control training, 179
therapy (CBT), 26
in eating disorders, 520
treatments, combined for specific
disorders, 280–282
Cognitive issues
deficits, 199–200
distortions, 215
functions, 123
model of impairments, 166f
impulsivity, 149
influences, 29–30
processes, 153
restructuring, 281
triad, negative, 308
Cohort effects, 89
Communication
deviance, 416
disorders, 422, 425–431
acquired type, 427
developmental type, 427
early, 380b
facilitation, 62–63
Community social disorganization, 222f
Comorbidities, 13, 79
Comparisons, known-group, 82
Compensatory behavior, 509
Competency, 7, 52, 134
self-perceived personal, 303–304
Compulsions, 255
Concurrent validity, 71
Conditioning, classical, 49–50
Conduct disorders (CD), 13, 157–158,
194, 195–197
compared with ODD, 196–197, 198t
diagnostic criteria, 197t
gender differences, 205–206
Conduct problems, 185–231
accompanying disorders, 203–204
associated characteristics, 199–204
causal influences, 224
causes of, 209–224
cost, 187
course, 208–209
defining features, 194–198
description, 185–188
terms, 190
developmental pathways, 207–208
dimensions, 192f
early temperament, 211
factors
biological, 211–213
cultural, 223–224
ethnic, 223–224
family, 216–220
neurological, 213–215
social-cognitive, 215–220
societal, 220–223
general progression, 206–207
genetic influences, 211–213
direct, 213
growth over life span, 210f
outcomes, 208–209
perspectives, 188–194
preventive interventions, 229–230
significance, 187
symptoms, 203–204
treatment, 224–230
Confidentiality, 93, 99
Configuration, of symptoms, 12

Consent, informed, 93
Consequences, 110f
Construct validity, 71
Context, 31
in diagnosis, 128
social and cultural, 55–56
Continuity, 37, 38f
patterns of, 13
Continuous performance test (CPT), 148
assessing sustained attention and
impulsivity, 148b
Control enhancement training, 329–331
Convergent validity, 71
Co-occurrences, 13
Coping
management, 487
responses, 330f
strategies, 487
Corpus callosum, 169
Correlation
coefficient, 80
questions about risk and protective
factors, 66–68
COS. See Childhood-onset schizophrenia
Coupling, 461
CPT. See Continuous performance test
Cretins, 337
Criterion-related validity, 71
CT. See Coaxial tomography
Culture, 100–101
considerations, 14–15
Cycle-of-violence hypothesis, 543
Cyclothymic disorder, 317

Data
collection methods comparison, 72t
qualitative, 91
DD. See Dysthymic disorder
Decision-making process, 99–100
Defecation dynamics, 474
Deficits, 51
Delinquency, 190
Delusions, 372
Demographic parameters, 483
Depression, 159, 204, 268–269, 286–292
anatomy of, 290–292
causes, 310–316, 315–316
clinical range, 125
cognitive factors, 314
description, 286–288
developmental framework, 315f
diathesis-stress models, 309
at different developmental periods,
289–290
emotion regulation, 314–315
family
influences, 312–313
risk, 310
genetic risk, 310
historical background, 288–289
in institutionalized infants, 290f
interventions, 329–332
medications, 332–333
mood disturbances and behavioral
symptoms of, 291–292t
neurobiological influences, 311–312
physical changes in, 287
prevention, 333
rates by gender and age, 297f
stressful life events, 313–314
suicide and, 322–327

Depression (continued)
as symptom, 290–292
as syndrome, 290–292
theories, 306–310
attachment, 306–307
behavioral, 307
biological/neurobiological, 309
cognitive, 307–309
interpersonal, 309
overview, 310
psychodynamic, 306
self-control theory, 309
socioenvironmental, 309–310
therapy
drug, 332f
interpersonal, 331
treatment, 327–333, 328t
in young people, 289
Depressive disorders, 285–286
associated characteristics, 301–306
cognitive disturbances, 302–303
difficulties
interpersonal, 304–306
peer, 304–305
family relationships, 305–306
functioning
academic, 302
intellectual, 301–302
social withdrawal, 304–305
Depressive ruminative style, 302
Designs
A-B-A-B, 85
accelerated longitudinal, 89–90, 90f, 91f
between-group comparison, 87
catch-up prospective, 83
cohort, 83
cross-sectional, 88
of developmental change, 87–90
longitudinal, 88–89
multiple-baseline, 85–87, 86f
quasi-experimental, 82
real-time prospective, 83
retrospective, 82
reversal, 85f
single-case, 87
experimental, 85–87
Desmopressin, 472
Despair, 306
Detachment, 306–307
Development, 100–101
considerations, 31
course, 15–16
vs. difference controversy, 351
disorders, 19
dyscalculia, 436
family history and, 106–107
organization of, 32
overview, 33f
process in children, 33
tasks, 7, 7t
tests, 116
Dexamethasone suppression test
(DST), 311
Dextroamphetamine, 174
Diabetes mellitus, 478–479
Diagnosis, 12, 101–102, 124–130
Diagnostic and Statistical Manual
(DSM), 127
axes of, 127–129
categories applicable to children, 19t
criticisms of, 129

Diagnostic classification:0-3 (DC:0-3), 129–130
Diencephalon, 43–44
Dieting, 495
Digit Span, 384
Dimensions, 124–126
Direct aggression, 192
Direct instruction, 450
  with behavioral methods, 451b
  thinking operations script, 452b
Disability, 5
  children with, 135
Disaster, helping children after, 267b
Discontinuity, 37, 38f
Discriminant validity, 71
Disorders
  chronic, 15
  episodic, 15
  disruptive behavior, 194
  onset
    acute, 15
    insidious, 16
  psychological. *See* Psychological disorders
  time-limited, 15
  types of, 19
  use of term, 5
Dissociation, 546
Distortions, 51, 52
Distractibility, 147
Distress, 5
Diversification, 206
Dizygotic (DZ), 42, 397
Dopamine receptor gene (DRD4), 168
Double depression, 300
Down syndrome, 352f, 353, 359, 363
  rates by maternal age, 360f
DRD4. *See* Dopamine receptor gene
Dry-bed training, 472
DSM. *See* Diagnostic and Statistical Manual
DSM-IV. *See* Diagnostic and Statistical Manual-IV
DST. *See* Dexamethasone suppression test
Duplication, 41
Dynamic interaction, 35
Dysfunction, 6
Dyslexia, 422
Dysphoria, 285
Dyssomnias, 461, 462, 463t
Dysthymic disorder (DD), 286, 298–301
  comorbidity, 300
  course, 300–301
  diagnostic criteria, 299t
  onset, 300–301
  outcome, 300–301
  prevalence, 300
DZ. *See* Dizygotic twins

Eating
  attitudes, early 493–494
  behaviors
    early, 493–494
    troublesome, 494f
  biochemistry of, 497
  disorders, 491–522
    in adolescence, 505–511
    determinants, 519f
    in infancy and early childhood, 497–505

Eating (*continued*)
  habits
    developmental continuum, 493f
    early, 493–494
  pathology, developmental risk factors, 493
  patterns
    in adolescence, 494–495
    biological regulators, 496
    development of, 492–497
    normal, 492
Echolalia, 382
ECT. *See* Electroconvulsive therapy
Educational neglect, 531
Education for All Handicapped Children Act, 135
Ego-oriented individual therapy (EOIT), 521
Electroconvulsive therapy (ECT), 138
Electroencephalogram, 74–75
  asymmetrical pattern, 74
Electrophysiological measures, 74
Elimination disorders, 469–474
  course, 470–471
  prevalence, 470–471
Embedded figures, 390f
  test, 389
Embedded in task, 148
Emotional issues
  abuse, 533
  cues, 47
  disorders, 19
  dysregulation, 48
  executive control, 123
  influences, 30, 46–47
  neglect, 531–532
  processes, 153
  reactivity, 47–48
  regulation, 47–48, 314–315, 539
Encoding, 52
Encopresis, 473–474, 473t
Endocrine system, 44–45
Enuresis, 469–473
Environment
  child and, passive and active roles, 35t
  models, ecological, 52–54, 54f
EOIT. *See* Ego–oriented individual therapy
Epidemiological studies, 12
Epinephrine, 44
Equifinality, 9f
ERP. *See* Evoked response potential; Exposure, plus response prevention
ERPs. *See* Event-related potentials
Escape-conditioning sequence, 218b
Esquirol, Etienne, 126
Ethical issues, 93–96
  standards for research with children, 94–95b
Etiology, 16
Eugenics, 338–339
Euphoria, 285
Evaluation, 102, 103–104
Event-related potentials (ERPs), 75
Evoked response potential (ERP), 169
Evolution, of infant/care-giver attachment, 51–52
Evolutionary degeneracy theory, 338
Executive control, 461
Executive function(ing), 153, 166, 389
  training, 368
Exosystem, 53

Expectable environment, 527
Expectancies, 52
Experience, role of, 40
Experiments
  natural, 82
  true, 80
Exposure, 282
  plus response prevention (ERP), 522
Expressive language disorder, 425–430
  causes, 428–430
  course, 427
  diagnostic criteria, 426t
  treatment, 427
Externalizing dimensions, 191f
Extreme autistic aloneness, 373
Extrinsic dyssomnias, 461

Face validity, 71
Facilitated communication (FC), 62b
Failure to thrive, 501
False belief, 388
False negatives, 126
Family
  context, 527–528
  counseling, 179
  disharmony in, 528
  disturbances, 201–202, 219
  functioning, 133
  healthy, 527–528
  history and development, 106–107, 106b
  influences, 30
  Kallikaks, 338b
  peer context and, 54–55
  and social influences, 52–56
  stress in, 220, 528
  structure, 219–220
  systems, 55
  transitions, 219–220
  values, antisocial, 220
FAS. *See* Fetal alcohol syndrome
Fat spurt, 494
FC. *See* Facilitated communication
FEAR plan, 280
Fears, 29, 237
  hierarchy of, 278b
  infant reactivity, 272b
  normal, 238
  objects of, by age, 238t
  study of, 25b
  subclinical, 240
Feeding disorders, 491
  diagnostic criteria, 500t
  in infancy and early childhood, 497–505
Fetal alcohol syndrome (FAS), 171, 361, 362f
Fight/flight response, 235
  behavioral system, 236–237
  cognitive system, 236–237
  physical system, 235–236
Findings
  clarifying correlational, 82
  inconclusive, 61
  specificity of, 87
Flooding, 278
fMRI. *See* Functional magnetic resonance imaging
Fool, 337
Forebrain, 44
Fort Bragg Project, 140
Fragile-X syndrome, 359, 361f
Frequency, of problem, 12

Frontostriatal circuitry, 169
Full-spectrum home training, 472
Functional analysis, 110f
  of behavior, 110
Functional magnetic resonance imaging
  (FMRI), 75
Functional segregation, 444
Functions, neuropsychological assessments
  of, 123

GAF. *See* Global Assessment of Functioning
Gastroesophageal reflex (GER), 499
Gender, 100–101
  considerations, 13–14
General intellectual functioning, 340
Generalized anxiety disorder (GAD), 233,
  246–248
  comorbidity, 247–248
  developmental course, 248
  diagnostic criteria, 247t
  model for, 248
    integrative, 24f
  onset, 248
  outcome, 248
  prevalence, 247–248
  treatment, 280
Generalized resistance to thyroid hormone
  (GRTH), 168
Genes, nature of, 41–42
Genetic(s)
  behavioral, 42
  contributions, 40–42
Genotype, 42, 358
GER. *See* Gastroesophageal reflex
Gestures
  expressive, 381f
  instrumental, 381f
GH. *See* Growth hormone
Global Assessment of Functioning
  (GAF), 128
Goodness-of-fit, 172
  concept, 36f
Graduated guidance, 367
Graphemes, 434
Group
  comparison, 87
  control, 87
  experimental, 87
Growth hormone (GH), 496
  inhibiting factor, 497
  releasing factor, 497
GRTH. *See* Generalized resistance to
  thyroid hormone

Hallucinations, 372
Health
  chronic problems in children, 5
  concerns, variations in expression,
    476–477
  issues, children's and adolescents, 1–3
  -related disorders, 455–490
    historical developments, 456–457
  -related problems, 202–203
Heritability, 358
Hindbrain, 43
Hippocampus, 44
Hospitalization, children coping with,
  486–488
Hostile aggression, 192
HPA. *See* Hypothalamic pituitary–adrenal
Human figure drawings, 120–122, 121f

Hyperactivity, 144, 149–150
  -impulsivity, 148–149
Hyperglycemia, 479
Hypersomnia, 462–463
Hypervigilant, 539
Hypnagogic hallucinations, 464
Hypoglycemia, 479
Hypothalamic pituitary-adrenal (HPA)
  axis, 45b
Hypotheses
  testable, 65
  testing, 99, 103
Hypothyroidism, 337

ICD. *See* International Classification of
  Diseases
IDDM. *See* Insulin–dependent diabetes
  mellitus
IEP. *See* Individualized Education Program
Illness parameters, 483–484
Impairment, in functioning, 6–7
Impulsivity, 144, 149
Inattention, 144, 146–148
Inborn errors of metabolism, 361
Incidence rates, 65
Inclusion movement, 450
Index offenses, 190
Indirect aggression, 192
Individual counseling, 179–180
Individualized Education Program
  (IEP), 135b
Individuals with Disabilities Act, 135
Influences
  early biological, 22–23
  early psychological, 23–24
Information
  normative, 101
  processing
    biases, 307
    disturbances, 551
    social, 51
  strategies, 487
Informed consent, 93
Insanity, masturbatory, 23b
Insecure-disorganized attachment, 539
Instrumental aggression, 192
Insulin-dependent diabetes mellitus
  (IDDM), 478–479
Intelligence, 266–267
  defining and measuring, 339–341
  deviation IQ, 340
  differences, 350f
  perspectives on, 337–343
  quotient (IQ), 340
    controversy, 341–343
  tests
    Flynn effect, 342
    pros and cons, 342t
    scores, 342–343
    unfairness in, 343
Intensity, of problem, 12
Interdependence, child and environment,
  34–36
Internalization, 166
International Classification of Diseases
  (ICD), 126
Interpersonal difficulties, with peers,
  200–201
Interventions, 131–132
  questions about, 69–70
  spectrum, 132f

Interviews, 72–73
  child-friendly approach, 105
  semistructured, 108, 109t
  structured diagnostic schedule, 73b
  structured parental format, 73t
Inversions, 435
In vivo exposure, 279
IQ. *See* Intelligence quotient
Irritability, 285
Islets of ability, 385
Issues
  ethical, 93–96
  pragmatic, 93–96
Itard, Jean-Marie, 21

Joint social attention, 378

Kauffman Assessment Battery for
  Children, 340

Labels, diagnostic, 130
Language
  development, 423–425
  disorders, 423–425
  functions, areas of brain involved in, 428f
  inconsistency, 380
  pragmatic use, 382f
  processes, 153
LCP. *See* Life–course–persistent
Lead, childhood exposure to and behavior
  from, 215b
Learning disabled, 423
Learning disorders, 19, 422, 431–453
  adult outcomes, 440–441
  behavior
    problems, 440f, 447f
    strategies, 451
    systems model, 448f
  causes, 441–448
  class, 438
  clinical description, 433–434
  cognitive-behavioral interventions, 451
  computer-assisted learning for, 452–453
  course, 437–438
  cultural, 438
  development, 438–439
    pathways, 447f
  diagnostic criteria, 434t
  factors
    constitutional, 442
    genetic, 442
    neurobiological, 442
    psychological, 446–448
  gender variations, 438
  instructional methods, 450–451
  language-based, 442–445
  nonverbal patterns, 445
  prevalence, 437–438
  prevention, 448–453
  psychological adjustment, 439–440
  reading, 434–435
    program, 453b
  regular education initiative, 450
  social adjustment, 439–440
  social factors, 446
  treatment, 448–453
Learning problems, 200
  disabilities
    defined, 421–422
    description, 420–422
    historical background, 422–423

Learning problems (continued)
helplessness, 307
impairments in, 199–200
nonverbal, 420, 445–446
Least restrictive environment (LRE), 135b
Leptin, 504
Life-course-persistent (LCP) path, 207
Lifetime prevalence, 65
Limbic system, 44
Locke, John, 21
Loss, 41
LRE. See Least restrictive environment
Lymphoblasts, 480

MA. See Mental age
Macroparadigm, 31
Magnetic resonance imaging (MRI), 75
Mainstreaming, 427
Maintenance, 131
Major depressive disorder (MDD), 129,
        286, 292–298
comorbidity, 295–296
course, 296–297
differential diagnosis, 294
ethnicity, 297–298
gender, 297–298
onset, 296–297
outcome, 296–297
prevalence, 294–295
treatment, 328
Major depressive episode, 294t
Maltreated children. See also Maltreatment
    of children
adaptation, 537–538
adjustment
    school, 541–543
    sexual, 546–547
adult characteristics, 550–551
adult outcomes, 543–548
affect disturbances, 545
behavior, antisocial and criminal, 547
early attachment, 539–540
emerging view of self and others,
        540–541
long-term criminal consequences, 548b
mental health, 544
mood disturbances, 545
neglect, 549–556
peer problems, 541–543
post-traumatic stress-related problems,
        545–546
resilience, 537–538
toddlers, responses to distress of
        peers, 542f
Maltreatment of children, 526. See also
    Maltreated children
affect regulation, 539–540
causes, 548–557
child influences, 551–552
context, 533–536
cross-cultural comparisons, 536
description, 529–533
development
    consequences, 538–543
    course, 536–537
family
    and perpetrator characteristics,
        535–536
    influences, 551–552
implications, 547–548
incidence of, 534f

Maltreatment of children (continued)
increasing rate, 535
integrated model of maladaptive pattern,
        552–554
perspectives on, 526–529
physical abuse, 549–556
prevalence, 533–536
prevention, 557–561
psychopathology, 536–537,
        543–548
treatment, 557–561
Mania, 285, 316
MAOA. See Monoamine oxidase A
Marginalization, 56
Massachusetts' Stubborn Child Act (1654),
        20–21, 527
Masturbatory insanity, 23b
Matching Familiar Figures Test (MFFT),
        149, 150b
Mathematics
    computation errors, 436f
    disorder, 435–436
    pills, 175b
MBD. See Minimal brain dysfunction
        (MBD)
MDD. See Major Depressive Disorder
Measurement
    characteristics of, 71
    methods of, 71–78
    value of methods, 70f
Media influences, 221–223
Mediator variable, 68
Medical condition, psychological factor
        affecting, 476t
Medical procedures, 488b
    children coping with, 486–488
Medulla, 43
Megacolon, 474
Mental age (MA), 340
Mental health
    children's, magnitude of, 1
    problems, 19
    significance in children, 17–20
Mental Hygiene Movement
        (19th century), 23
Mentalization, 387
Mental retardation, 337–371
    Axis II disorder, 355
    behavior
        problems, 355–356
        social, 353–355
        treatments, 366–367
    causes, 349t, 356–363
    chromosome abnormalities, 359
    clinical description, 344–346
    cognitive-behavioral therapy,
        367–368
    development
        course, 350–356
        disabilities, 353
        progress, 352
    diagnostic criteria, 345t
    early intervention, 365–366
    education, 363–364
        classifications, 348–349
    emotional problems, 355–356
    environmental, 358–359
    factors
        constitutional, 359
        protective, 364f
        risk, 364f

Mental retardation (continued)
family
    members with, 357f
    -oriented strategies, 368–370
features, 343–349
functioning, levels of, 346–349
genetic, 359
heritability, 358–359
impairment, degrees of, 346–348
language, 353–355
motivation, 351–352
needed supports, 348t
neurobiological influences, 361–363
outcomes, 350–356
peers, 354b
perspectives on, 337–343
prenatal education, 364–365
prevalence, 349t, 349–350
prevention, 363–364
problems, 354b
profound, 347–348
vs. psychiatric disorder, 21–22
psychological dimensions, 362–363
related disabilities, 352–353
relationship with organic brain damage
        and learning problems, 423
screening, 364–365
single-gene conditions, 361
social and sports events, 366f
social dimensions, 362–363
supportive services, 348
treatment, 363–370
two-group approach, 357
Mental status examination, 107b, 107–108
Mesosystem, 53
Metacognition, 153
    training, 368
Metastrategical training, 368
Methylphenidate, 174
MFFT. See Matching Familiar Figures Test
Microsystem, 53
Midbrain, 43
Minimal brain damage, 145
Minimal brain dysfunction (MBD), 145
Minitheories, 65
Minnesota Multiphasic Personality
        Inventory–Adolescent (MMPI-A), 122
Mixed receptive-expressive language
        disorder, 426
MMPI-A. See Minnesota Multiphasic
        Personality Inventory–Adolescent
Modeling, 367
Models
    biological disease, 23
    chronic care, 134
    continuing care, 134
    dental care, 134
    organic disease, 22
Monoamine oxidase A (MAOA), 213
Monosomy, 41
Monozygotic (MZ), 42
    twins, 397
Mood, 287
    disorders, 284–336, 285–286
        main features, 286b
        treatment, 327–334
    episodes, 285
    state
        future-oriented, 237
        present-oriented, 237
Moral guidance, 22

Moral imbecile, 339
Morbidity, 475
Moron, 339
Mothering, 289
Motivation, deficits in, 164
Motor activity, 151f
  control, 166
  functions, 123
  overactivity, 149
  processes, 153
MRI. *See* Magnetic resonance imaging
MST. *See* Multisystemic treatment
Multifinality, 8, 9f
Multiple dimensions, 34
Multiple intelligence, 421–422, 422b
Multiple problems, case study of, 98
Multisystemic intervention, principles and
    treatment strategies, 228–229b
Multisystemic treatment (MST), 227–228
Munchausen by proxy, 550b
MZ. *See* Monozygotic

Narcolepsy, 463–464
Negative affectivity, 269
Neglect, 524–561, 549–556, 558–560
  incidence of, 534–535
Neighborhood
  disorder in, 221
  influences, 221
Neural plasticity, 39–40
Neurobiological perspectives, 39
Neurobiology, 42–45
Neurochemical findings, 400–401
Neuroimaging research methods, 74–75
Neuroleptics, 229
Neurological profiles, associated behavior
    patterns and, 214f
Neuropsychological testing, 122–123
Neurotic paradox, 235
Neurotransmitters, 41, 45
  major, 46t
  roles in psychopathology, 46t
New York Society for Prevention of
    Cruelty to Children (1874), 524
Nightmares, 465, 466
  compared to sleep terrors, 467t
Nocturnal panic, 268
Nondisjunction, 359
Nonrapid eye movement (NREM), 458
Norm group, 115
Nosologies, 24
NREM. *See* Nonrapid eye movement

OAD. *See* Overanxious disorder
Obesity, 502–505
  childhood-onset, 503
  prevalence, 503–504
  treatment, 504–505
Observations
  behavioral, 113–115
  code design system, 77
  methods of, 75–78
  naturalistic, 75
  structured, 76
Obsessions, 255
Obsessive-compulsive disorder (OCD),
    233, 255–260, 274
  comorbidity, 259
  developmental course, 259–260
  diagnostic criteria, 256t
  onset, 259–260

Obsessive-compulsive disorder (OCD)
    (continued)
  outcome, 259–260
  prevalence, 259
  treatment, 280–281
Obstructive sleep apnea syndrome
    (OSAS), 464
OCD. *See* Obsessive–compulsive disorder
ODD. *See* Oppositional defiant disorder
Operant speech training, 407
Oppositional defiant disorder (ODD),
    157–158, 194, 195
  compared with CD, 196–197, 198b
  diagnostic criteria, 195t
Oppositional disorder, 76
Optimal stimulation theory, 164–165
Organic disease model, 22
OSAS. *See* Obstructive sleep apnea
    syndrome
Outcomes, 102–103, 133
  questions about, 69
Overanxious disorder (OAD), 241

PANDAS. *See* Pediatric autoimmune neu-
    ropsychiatric disorders and associated
    disorders
Panic, 237
  attacks, 233, 260–261
    diagnostic criteria, 260t
  disorder (PD), 261–262, 262b, 274
  somatic, 240
Paradigm, biological disease model, 23
Parasomnias, 461–462, 465–466, 466t
Parental criminality, 220
Parental psychopathology, 220
Parentectomy, 506
Parent(s)
  management training (PMT), 177,
    225–226
    common features, 226t
  recording, 113f
  values and, 133t
Participation, voluntary, 93
PASCET. *See* Primary and Secondary
    Control Enhancement Training
Pathways, developmental, 7–8, 9f
PD. *See* Panic disorder
PDD-NOS. *See* Pervasive developmental
    disorder not otherwise specified
PDDs. *See* Pervasive developmental
    disorders
Pediatric autoimmune neuropsychiatric
    disorders and associated disorders
    (PANDAS), 274
Pediatric coping strategies scale, 488b
Pedophilia, 554
Peers
  context, family and, 54–55
  setting, specialized or mainstream, 427b
Perceptual functions, 123
Period effects, 89
Perseverative speech, 382
Personality
  Big 5 factors, 122
  disorders, 127
  Inventory for Children (PIC), 122
  self-report scale definitions, 122t
  testing, 122
Perspective, interdisciplinary, 16
Pervasive developmental disorder not oth-
    erwise specified (PDD-NOS), 394

Pervasive developmental disorders
    (PDDs), 372
Pessimistic outlook, 303
PET. *See* Positron emission tomography
Phase treatment, advance and delay, 468
Phenotype, 42, 358
Phenylketonuria (PKU), 361
Phobia
  school, 240
  simple, 241
  social, 240, 251–255, 252t
  specific, 248–251, 250t
Phonemes, 420, 423, 434
Phonology, 424
  awareness, 424–425
  disorder of, 426
Physical issues
  abuse, 530, 549–556, 558–560
  aggression, 191
  condition, psychological factors
      affecting, 475
  disorders
    psychophysiological, 456
    psychosomatic, 456
  health, problems related to, 19
  neglect, 531
PIC. *See* Personality Inventory for Children
Pica, 497–499
  causes, 498
  development, 497–498
  diagnostic, 498t
  prevalence, 497–498
  treatment, 498–499
Pituitary gland, 44
PKU. *See* Phenylketonuria
Plasticity, neural, 39–40
PMT. *See* Parent(s), management training
Pons, 43
Positive affectivity, 269
Positron emission tomography (PET), 75
Posttraumatic stress disorder (PTSD),
    263–266
Prader-Willi syndrome, 360
Pragmatics, 382
  issues, 93–96
Predatory violence, 193
Predictive validity, 71
Preservation of sameness, 373
Prevalence, 12
  of conduct problems, 204–205
  rates, 65
Prevention, 131
Primary and Secondary Control Enhance-
    ment Training (PASCET), 329
Proactive aggression, 192
Proband, 42
Problems
  parent-rated, 101t
  self-reported internalizing, 69f
Problem-solving skills training (PSST)
  cognitive, 226–227
  primary elements of cognitive, 227b
  steps and self-statements of cognitive,
    227b
Procedures, nonharmful, 95
Profile, 111
Prognosis, 102–103
Prolongation, 166
Pronoun reversals, 382
Protective factors, 67
  and risk factor correlates, 66–68

Protest, 306
Protodeclarative gestures, 380
Protodyssomnia, 462–463
PSST. *See* Problem–solving skills training
Psychiatric disorders
  vs. mental retardation, 21–22
  prevalence by age and sex, 14f
Psychoanalytic theory, 24
Psychogenic theory, 373
Psychological disorders
  clinical description, 12–13
  describing, 11–17
Psychological perspectives, 45–52
Psychopathic behavior, 194
Psychopathology
  attachment and, 53t
  developmental, 3
    framework, 31–32
    microparadigm, 32f
  violence, 193
Psychopathy, screening device for, 198t
Psychophysiological research methods,
  74–75
Psychosocial dwarfism, 502
Psychotic disorders, 411
PTSD. *See* Posttraumatic stress disorder
Purging, 509
Purkinje cells, 399, 399f

Qualitative research, negotiation
  process, 92b
Quantiphrenia, 61
Questionnaires, 73–74

Random assignment, 82
Random selection, 79
Rapid eye movement (REM), 458
  parasomnias, 466
Rating scales, 111–113
Reactions, predicting children's, 266f
Reactive aggression, 192
Reactivity, 76
Reading disorder, 434–435
Reciprocal influence, 217
Reconstitution, 166
Recordings, by parents, 114
Refusal behavior, 244–245
Regimen adherence, 479
Regular education initiative (REI), 450
Regulated breathing, 431
Regulation training, 368
REI. *See* Regular education initiative
Rejection, by peer group, 89f
Relational disorders, 548
Relationship
  influences, 30
  violence, 193
Reliability, 70–71
  test-retest, 70
REM. *See* Rapid eye movement
Reporting methods, 72–74
Representational models, 540
Research
  analogue, 83, 84f
  case study, 83–85
  common questions, 65–70
  cross-sectional, 87
  designs, 83–85
  epidemiological, 65–66
    cross-cultural, 67b
  ethical standards for, 94–95b

Research (*continued*)
  general approaches, 80–83
  hypotheses for, 64–65
  ideas, 64–70
  identifying sample, 78–80
  longitudinal, 87
  nonexperimental *vs.* experimental,
    80–82
  process, 63f, 63–70
  prospective *vs.* retrospective, 82
  qualitative, 90–93, 92t
  questions, 64–70
  scientific approach, 60–61
  strategies, 58–96
  studies, planning and implementing,
    59–60
  theory and, 64–65
Residential care, 369
Resiliency, 8–11, 10b
  adaptation and, 441b
  characteristics of, 11f
  protective triad of resources, 9–10
Resilient peer treatment (RPT), 560
Response
  -contingent positive reinforcement, 307
  -cost procedures, 178
  prevention, 278
Retardation
  familial, 351
  organic, 351
Rett's disorder, 393–394
Reversals, 435
Reward dominance, 213
Risk, 8–11
  factors and protective factor correlates,
    66–68
Rituals, normal, 239–240
Roberts Apperception Test for Children
  (RATC), 120
Role-play simulation, 114
Rorschach inkblot test, 120
Routines, age of onset, 240t
RPT. *See* Resilient peer treatment
Rumination disorder, 499–500, 499t

SAD. *See* Separation anxiety disorder
Samples, research, 79
Sampling, biased, 89
Schizophrenia, 372
  causes, 413–416
  childhood-onset (COS), 411–418
  comorbidities, 413
  defining features, 412–413
  factors
    biological, 414–415
    environmental, 415–416
  prevalence, 413
  symptoms
    psychotic, 413, 414b
    related, 413
  treatment, 416–417
Schizotypal personality disorder
  (SPD), 416
School
  influences, 221
  problems, 200
  reluctance, 244–245
Screening test, domains assessed by, 116t
Secure readiness to learn, 543
Selective attention, 146–147
Selective mutism, 254–255

Selective serotonin reuptake inhibitors
  (SSRIs), 138
Self-esteem, 303–304
  deficits, 200
Self-injurious behavior (SIB), 86, 356, 392
Self-perceived personal competence,
  303–304
Self-regulation, 52, 166
  deficits in, 165
Self-report, 72–74
Self-stimulation, 383, 384f
Sensitivity, periods of, 32
Sensory dominance, 385
Separation, 77f
  anxiety, 233
Separation anxiety disorder (SAD),
  241–244, 242t
Septum, 44
SES. *See* Socioeconomic status
Severity, of problem, 12
Sexual abuse, 532, 554–556, 560–561
  adult characteristics, 554–555
  child-rearing practices and, 556–557
  cultural dimensions, 556
  delayed disclosure, 555
  family
    and situational influences, 555–556
    privacy, 556–557
  poverty and, 556
  social dimensions, 556
  social isolation, 556
  treatment, 560
Shaping, 367
Showing gesture, 380
SIB. *See* Self–injurious behavior
Sign language training, 407
Similar sequence hypothesis, 351
Similar structure hypothesis, 351
Situational violence, 193
Skepticism, 61
Skill building, 281
Sleep
  attacks, 463–464
  cultural influences, 459–460
  cycles, 459f
  disorders, 457–469
    features, 461–467
    treatment, 467–469
  maturational pattern changes, 459
  normal stages, 458–459
  paralysis, 464
  regulatory function, 460–461
  situational influences, 459–460
  terrors, 466–467
    compared to nightmares, 467t
Sleepwalking, 466–467
Slowing and stability hypothesis, 352
Social anxiety, 233
Social cognition
  deficits, 201
  terms and concepts, 52t
Socialization practices, 15f
Social learning, 50
Social phobia
  cognitive-behavioral group treatment,
    281–282
  treatment, 280
Social referencing, 539
Social situation, children in, 379b
Social skills, 281
  training, 179, 367

Socioeconomic status (SES), 13
  survival rates and, 478
Solutions, multiple, 138–139
Somatoform disorders, 475
SPD. *See* Schizotypal personality
  disorder
Specificity, of findings, 87
Speech
  brain processing, 443f
  comprehension, 444
  production, 444
Splinter skills, 385
SSRIs. *See* Selective serotonin reuptake
  inhibitors
Standardization, 70–71
Standford-Binet-IV, 340
  distribution of IQs, 340f
Statistical power, 79
Status offenses, 190
Stimulant medications, 174
Stimulus overselectivity, 386
Stop Task, 149, 151b
Strategical training, 368
Stress management, 487
Studies
  correlational, 80
  prospective longitudinal, 83
Stuttering, 430–431, 431t
Subject selection biases, 78
Subtype, 151
Suicide, 322–327
  associated depressive disorder and,
    325b
  comorbidity, 325–326
  course, 326
  estimated rate in children, 326f
  ethnicity, 326–327
  gender, 326
  ideation in potential, 324
  onset, 326
  outcome, 326
  potential scale for child, 323t
  prevalence, 325–326
  risk factors, 327
Summer Treatment Program, 180–182
Support, 22
  groups, 179
Survival rates, socioeconomic status
    and, 478
Sustained attention, 147–148
Symptom, 290
Syndrome, 290
Systematic desensitization, 278
Systems, evolution of current, 126–130

Target behaviors, 109, 115t
Teenagers, crime-prone, 188f
Temperament, 48–49, 122
  difficult, 162, 206
  early, 271f

Testing
  anxiety toward, 245–246
  educational, 116–119
  empirical, 65
  intelligence, 116–119
  neuropsychological, 122–123
  personality, 122
  projective, 119–122
  psychological, 115–119
T4. *See* Thyroid, hormone
Theoretical foundations, 33–39
Theories. *See also* specific theory.
  levels of, 64–65
  psychoanalytic, 24
  research and, 64–65
  role of, 30–33
Theory of mind (ToM), 387–390
  Sally-Anne test, 388b
Therapies, 131
  behavior, 26
  cognitive-behavioral, 26
  discrepancy between research and
    clinical, 140
Thinking
  depressive, 287
  steps in aggressive children, 216t
Thyroid
  gland, 44
  hormone (T4), 497
Timing, 444
ToM. *See* Theory of mind
Tourette's disorder, 159
Trait confluence, 201
Transaction, 35
Transient frontal hypoperfusion, 400f
Translocation, 41
Transpositions, 435
Traumatic sexualization, 546
Treatment, 131
  applications, evolving, 26
  behavioral, 136–137
  biological, 138
  of childhood disorders, 130–140
  client-centered, 137
  cognitive, 137
  cognitive-behavioral, 137
  combined, 138
  conventional model, 134
  delivery models, 133–134
  effectiveness, 139–140
  ethical considerations, 134–136
  family, 137
  general approaches, 136–139
  goals, 133
  legal considerations, 134–136
  options, 132
  planning, 102, 103–104
  psychodynamic, 136
  special considerations, 132–136
  validity, 110

Trichotillomania, 259
Trisomy, 41
Truancy, 5–6
True positives, 126
Tuberous sclerosis, 397
Twins, 42
  studies, 212–213

Uncoupling, 461
Unexpected discrepancy, 422
United Nations Convention on the
    Rights of Children (1989), 21
United States Advisory Board on
    Child Abuse and Neglect
    (1990), 525
Urine-alarm treatment, 472
Use-dependent, 39

Validity, 70–71
  assessing, 71
  external, 78
  internal, 78
Values, 52
  parenting and, 133t
Variables, 68
  correlated, 66
  dependent, 80
  independent, 80
  mediating, 69f
  moderating and mediating,
    68–69
Verbal expression
  aggression, 191
  deficits, 199–200
Victimizations, 527, 533–534
Victor of Aveyron, 22b, 338
Violence, types of, 193
Virtual support groups, 487b
Vulnerability-stress model, 413

Watson, John, 24–25
Weapons signs, 222f
Wechsler Intelligence Scale for
    Children (WISC-III),
    117–119, 118–119b,
    340, 384
  subscales, 117t
Wernicke's area, 444
Whole language methods, 450
Wide Range-Achievement Test
    (WRAT-3), 119
WISC-III. *See* Wechsler Intelligence Scale
    for Children
Working memory, 166
Worries, normal, 239
WRAT-3. *See* Wide Range–Achievement
    Test
Writing disorder, 436–437

Zemmiphobia, 250

Name Index

Abel, C. B., 554
Aber, J. L., 530, 539, 543, 556
Abikoff, H. B., 138, 160, 457
Abrahamian, R. P., 473
Abrams, E. Z., 92
Abramson, L. Y., 307, 470
Achenbach, T. M., 1, 4, 12, 13, 22, 23, 24,
    32, 33, 38, 56, 64, 65, 66, 90, 100,
    101, 102, 110, 111, 112, 125, 127,
    187, 189, 190, 195, 206, 224,
    238, 239, 293, 297, 338, 340, 439,
    457, 484
Ackerland, V., 355
Ackerman, B. P., 30
Adams, M. J., 435
Addison, S., 363
Adelman, H. S., 124, 131, 134
Adler, T., 373, 479
Adrian, C., 312
Agard, J. A., 354
Ageton, S. S., 219
Agras, W. S., 500, 520, 522
Ahrens, A. H., 516
Ainsworth, M. D. S., 53, 76, 353, 531
Akande, A., 270
Akiskal, H. S., 296, 320
Akkerhuis, G. W., 13
Alaghband-Rad, J., 415
Albano, A. M., 138, 233, 243, 244, 245,
    246, 247, 248, 249, 250, 253, 254,
    259, 260, 262, 263, 268, 269,
    271, 278, 280, 281, 282
Alder, R. J., 205
Alderfer, M., 485
Alegria, M., 172
Alessandri, S., 538, 541
Alessi, N. E., 215
Alexander, K. L., 446
Alicke, M. D., 139
Allan, J. S., 260
Allan, M. J., 312
Allan, W. D., 262, 263
Allen, B., 279
Allen, J. P., 155, 219, 395, 539
Allen, N. B., 269, 273
Allgood-Merten, B., 304
Alloy, L. B., 307
Alpern, L., 219
Alpert, A., 312
Alpert, J., 546
Altaus, 13

Alterman, A., 547
Altham, P., 297
Altmann, E. O., 305
Alvarez, M. M., 298
Aman, M. G., 364
Amaya-Jackson, L., 265
Ambrose, N., 430
Ambrosini, P. J., 332
Amir, N., 154
Ammerman, R. T., 20
Anastasi, A., 120
Anastopoulos, A. D., 59, 153, 155, 156, 175
Anders, T. F., 457, 459, 460, 461, 462,
    463, 464, 465, 467, 468
Anderson, C. A., 149, 156, 173
Anderson, E. 217, 224
Anderson, G. M., 401
Anderson, I. M., 514
Anderson, J. C., 13, 37, 188, 190, 200,
    205, 211, 214, 216
Anderson, J. L., 547
Anderson, K. E., 188, 190, 200, 205, 211,
    214, 216
Anderson, P., 479
Anderson, W. F., 349, 359
Andrea, H., 249
Andres, M., 201
Andrews, D. A., 233
Andrews, D. W., 204, 206
Andrews, G., 430
Andrews, J. A. 233, 273, 295, 312, 333
Angold, A., 1, 2, 21, 24, 65, 66, 195,
    269, 297
Annin, P., 186
Antonak, R. F., 369
Appareddy, V., 457
Applegate, B., 152, 161
Apter, A., 517
Arbisi, P., 46
Arcus, D. M., 271, 272
Ardelt, M., 220
Aries, P., 20
Arin, D. M., 394
Armbruster, P., 226
Armstrong, D. D., 394, 400
Armstrong, F. D., 488
Armstrong, K. J., 155
Arndt, S., 396
Arnold, D. S., 429
Arnold, L. E., 138, 161, 180
Arsenault, L., 155

Arslanian, S., 479
Artiles, A. J., 349
Artner, J., 174
Arunkumar, R., 8, 10
Asarnow, J. R., 301, 312, 327, 412, 413,
    414, 415, 416
Asarnow, R. F., 412, 413, 414, 415,
    416, 417
Asdigian, N., 557
Ashall, F., 353
Asher, S. R., 354
Asperger, H., 373, 393
Atkins, M. S., 534
Attie, I., 492, 493, 494, 501, 505, 506,
    515, 517
Attwood, A., 379
August, G. J., 179
Augustyn, M., 265
Avison, W. R., 298
Axline, V. M., 137
Ayers, W. A., 139
Aylward, E., 352
Ayoub, C. C., 484
Azar, S. T., 551, 557, 558, 559
Azrin, N. H., 472

Babani, L., 481, 485
Babigian, H. M., 511
Bachanas, P., 488
Baer, R. A., 179
Bailey, A., 390, 391, 396, 397, 398,
    399, 400
Bailey, D. 178
Bailey, J. S., 178, 363, 368
Bailey, V., 463
Baine, S., 487
Baird, P. A., 349, 359
Baker, B. L., 154, 368, 369
Baker, J. E., 505, 516
Baker, L., 154, 505, 516
Baker, S. C., 392
Bakken, L., 494
Bakwin, H., 471
Baldwin, D. V., 77
Baldwin, W. K., 450
Ball, E. W., 449
Ballanger, B. R., 356
Bandura, A., 50
Banez, G. A., 482
Banis, H. T., 481, 485
Bank, L., 226

Barakat, L. P., 485
Baran, S. A., 521
Barber, M. A., 164
Barkley, R. A., 73, 78, 79, 81, 136, 146, 149, 150, 152, 154, 155, 156, 157, 160, 161, 162, 163, 164, 165, 166, 168, 169, 170, 171, 172, 173, 174, 175, 178, 179, 182, 446
Barlow, D. A., 233, 234, 235, 237, 239, 243, 245, 249, 260, 261, 262, 268, 269, 271, 274, 277, 280, 281, 346
Barlow, D. H., 43, 44, 70, 85, 107, 346, 430, 463
Barnard, M. V., 332
Barnett, D., 133, 307, 539
Baron-Cohen, S., 376, 377, 378, 385, 387, 388, 389, 395, 401
Barr, C. E., 416
Barrett, P. M., 275, 280, 356
Barrios, B. A., 236, 238, 239, 240
Bartel, N. R., 130
Barth, C., 398
Bartley, M., 2
Bass, D., 136, 139, 227
Bates, J. E., 88, 193, 211, 217, 220, 226, 438, 541
Bauermeister, J. J., 172
Baum, A., 41
Bauman, L. J., 400, 486
Bauman, M. L., 394, 398, 399
Baumeister, J. J., 200
Baumeister, R. F., 172
Baumgardner, T. L., 169
Bayley, N. K., 116, 211
Bazyk, S., 486
Beardslee, W. R., 215, 310, 313, 333
Beautrais, A. L., 326, 327
Beck, A. T., 50, 51, 307, 329
Becker, D., 479, 502, 560
Becvar, R. J., 137
Bedi, G., 150
Beeghly, M., 354, 457, 540
Beeler, T., 449
Befera, M., 161
Begab, M. J., 341
Begley, S., 342
Beglin, S. J., 511
Behr, S. K., 368
Beidel, D. C., 239, 245, 246, 273, 275
Beitchman, J. H., 154, 165, 440
Bell, A. 498
Bell, K. E. 498
Bell, M. A., 39
Bell, R. Q., 171, 211, 219
Bellack, A. S., 71, 95, 109
Bell-Dolan, D. J., 239, 253, 267, 268, 312
Belsky, J., 206, 549
Bem, D. J., 205
Bemporad, J. R., 306, 309, 374, 381
Benasich, A. A., 439, 445
Bender, M. E., 156
Bengston, B., 546
Benjamin, J., 168, 365
Bennett, D. S., 211, 481
Benoit, D., 460, 497, 501
Berendt, I., 471
Berg, W. K., 90
Berger, M., 47
Beriama, A., 534
Berk, L. E., 165
Berkowitz, L., 222

Berliner, L., 560, 561
Berman, A. L., 322, 323, 324, 325, 327
Berman, J. S., 139, 470
Bernheimer, C., 341
Bernstein, G. A., 251, 263, 269, 275, 279
Besalel-Azrin, V., 472
Bettelheim, B., 17, 373
Beumont, P., 510
Bhatia, M. S., 161
Bianchi, M. D., 332
Bickett, A. D., 560
Bickett, L. R., 157, 202
Bickham, N. L.,90, 140
Biederman, J., 152, 155, 157, 159, 161, 167, 171, 196, 220, 272, 275, 332
Bierman, K. L., 230
Biesecker, G. E., 215
Bigbee, M. A., 101, 192
Bigelow, K. M., 559
Biglan, A., 203
Bijur, P. E., 155
Biklen, D., 62
Binder, A., 551
Binet, A., 339
Birch, H. G., 349
Bird, H. R., 13, 172
Birmaher, B., 240, 289, 294, 295, 296, 297, 300, 306, 311, 312, 314, 328, 333
Bishop, D. V. M., 392, 429
Bjorklund, D. F., 146
Bjorkqvist, K., 206
Blacher, J. B., 369
Blachman, B. A., 424, 435, 449
Black, B., 255
Black, K., 230
Black, M. M., 551
Black, R. S., 449
Blader, J. C., 457, 462
Blanck, P. D., 95
Blane, D., 2
Blasco, P., 363
Blatt, B., 340
Blehar, M. C., 53, 76, 353
Bleuler, E., 372
Blinde, E. M., 519
Block, J. H., 203, 220
Blondis, T. A., 163
Blood, G. W., 431
Bloom, F. E., 39, 41, 75
Bloomquist, M. L., 179
Blount, R. L., 488
Blum, H. M., 2, 13
Blum, K., 213
Blum, N. J., 467, 468
Blum-Hoffman, E., 359
Boden, J. M., 200
Boergers, J., 306
Boetsch, E. A., 439, 440, 446
Bogdan, R., 337, 345, 355
Bohra, N., 161
Bolduc-Murphy, E. A., 272
Boll, T. J., 123
Bollard, J., 472
Bolton, P., 341, 376, 377, 385, 396, 397
Bonagura, N., 163
Bonett, D., 416
Bootzin, R. R., 455, 458, 462, 467, 468
Borchardt, C. M., 251
Borden, M. C., 356
Borduin, C. M., 227

Borgstedt, A. D., 169
Borkovec, T. M., 248
Borman-Spurrell, E., 219
Borner, H., 169
Bornstein, M. H., 32
Borowitz, S., 473
Borstelmann, L. J., 20
Boruch, R., 534
Bos, C. S., 368
Bott, L., 413
Bouchard, T. J., 358
Boucher, C., 460
Boucher, J., 378
Boulerice, B., 199
Bowen, B., 331
Bowes, J. M., 314
Bowlby, J. A., 30, 51, 65, 270, 306
Bowler, P. J., 338
Bowring, M. A., 316, 318
Boyle, 13, 42, 151, 205, 233, 273, 480
Braafladt, N., 314
Bradbury, T. N., 541
Bradley, S., 275
Bradlyn, A. S., 559
Brady, E., 268
Brandenburg, N. A., 17
Brathwaite, J., 543
Braunwald, K., 539
Braverman, E. R., 213
Brazelton, T. B., 36
Breakfield, X. O., 213
Breaux, A. M., 356
Breen, C. G., 367
Bremner, R., 369
Brent, D. A., 314, 325, 327, 328
Breslau, N., 102, 482
Bretherton, T. D., 47, 52, 539
Brewerton, T. D., 495
Bridge, J., 327
Bridge, M., 67
Bridwell-Bowles, L., 452
Brier, N., 448
Briere, J., 546, 547
Bristol, M. M., 411
Broadhurst, D. D., 18, 524, 530, 531, 532, 533, 534, 535, 536
Brody, L., 275
Broekmate, J., 522
Bromet, E., 265
Bromfield, R., 130
Bronfenbrenner, U., 20, 52, 54
Bronner, A. F., 211, 225
Brook, J. S., 203, 219, 248, 268, 295
Brooks-Gunn, J., 10, 17, 55, 349, 350, 446, 492, 493, 494, 501, 505, 506, 515, 517
Brophy, P., 332
Brown, D., 18, 446
Brown, E., 538
Brown, F. R., 352
Brown, J. A., 239
Brown, R. T., 171, 302
Brown, S., 202, 211
Brown, W. S. 415
Browne, A., 532, 541, 545, 546, 554
Browne, K., 543
Brownell, K. D., 491, 495, 515, 516
Bruch, H., 518
Bruck, M., 439, 441
Brucker-Davis, F., 168
Bruhn, P., 169

Bruininks, T. J., 341
Brumaghim, J. T., 540
Brumberg, J. J., 506
Brunner, H. G., 213
Bryant-Waugh, R., 511
Bryson, S. E., 358, 378, 389, 390, 394, 396
Budd, K. S., 501
Bugental, D. B., 267
Bukowski, W. B., 482
Burack, J. A., 355, 358
Burbach, D. J., 483
Burge, D., 312
Burgess, A. W., 556
Burgess, R. L., 540, 545
Burghen, G. A., 479
Burke, J. D., 546
Burke, K. C., 45, 546
Burke, L., 45, 546
Burke, P. M., 293
Burket, R. C., 229
Burley, S. K., 504
Burney, E., 312
Burns, B. J., 139, 269
Burroughs, J., 513
Burt, V., 503
Bush, M., 353, 539
Butler, M. G., 358, 360
Butow, P., 510
Butterfield, E. C., 368
Buysse, V., 368
Byrne, T., 169

Caceres, J., 298
Cadman, D. T., 480, 481, 483
Cadoret, R. J., 213
Cairns, B. D., 201
Cairns, R. B., 201
Calkins, S. D., 39, 47
Callaghan, M., 545
Camargo, C. A., 511
Campbell, F. A., 366
Campbell, K., 208
Campbell, M., 229
Campbell, R. V., 560
Campbell, S. B., 162, 173
Campbell, S. M., 503
Campbell, V. L., 120
Campione, J. C., 368
Canino, G., 172
Cannon, T. D., 416
Cantwell, D. P., 154, 171, 289, 290,
    297, 392.
Capaldi, D. M., 190, 203, 219, 221
Caplan, R., 413
Capps, L., 273, 378
Capron, C., 358
Cardinal, D. N., 62
Cardon, L. R., 442
Carey, G., 42
Carey, M. P., 269
Carey, W. B., 467, 468
Carlat, D. J., 511
Carlson, C. L., 152, 159, 161
Carlson, E. A., 32, 33, 40, 51, 53
Carlson, G. A., 288, 293, 294, 316, 318,
    320, 321, 327, 334
Carlson, V., 539, 556
Carnine, D., 451
Carosella, N., 415
Carpentieri, S., 482
Carr, E. G., 378, 392

Carroll, B. J., 311
Carskadon, M. A., 459, 464
Carter, A. S., 309
Carter, W. G., 309
Casanova, M. F., 415
Casey, B. J., 169
Casey, R. J., 139, 445, 446
Caspi, A., 187, 199, 205, 206, 207, 209,
    211, 213, 216, 220, 221, 222, 272
Cass, L. K., 127
Cassidy, J., 46, 47, 48
Castellanos, F. X., 169
Castelloe, P., 392
Catanzaro, S. J., 269
Cattarin, J. A., 504
Cattell, R. B., 23
Catts, W., 424
Caul, W. F., 164
Caulfield, M. B., 427
Cavell, T. A., 74
Cecalupo, A., 475
Celano, M., 541
Chaffee, S., 222
Challender, J. S., 521
Chaloff, J., 272
Chambers, M. J., 455, 458, 462, 467, 468
Chandler, L. A., 120
Chandler, M., 50
Chandola, C. A., 171
Chandra, R. K., 498
Chaney, J. M., 456
Chansky, T. E., 268
Chapman, J. W., 439
Charman, T., 392
Chase, G. A., 399
Chaudry, A., 55
Chayaisit, W., 161
Chazan, R., 219
Chen, R., 298
Chen, S., 518
Chen, W. J., 171
Chen, X., 14
Chen, Y. R., 326
Chesler, B. E., 514
Cheslow, D., 255
Chesney-Lind, M., 205
Chess, S., 35, 48, 145, 172
Chethik, M., 121, 131, 136
Chiariello, M. A., 312, 305
Chilcoat, H. D., 102
Childress, A. C., 495
Chisum, H., 399
Chmielewski, D., 484
Chorpita, B. F., 233, 239, 245, 247,
    268, 269
Christ, M. A. G., 196
Christakis, D., 482, 485
Christen, H. J., 394
Christian, D. L., 174
Christian, R. E., 198
Christopher, J., 302
Ciaranello, R. D., 45
Cicchetti, D., 5, 7, 8, 9, 30, 32, 33, 39, 47,
    65, 87, 190, 194, 306, 307, 314, 315,
    353, 354, 457, 527, 528, 530, 537,
    539, 540, 541, 542, 543, 545,
    547, 556, 557
Cimarolli, V., 298
Cipani, E., 348
Clark, D. C., 504
Clark, K. A., 315, 320

Clark, L. A., 269
Clark, M. J., 503
Clark, R. W., 424
Clarke, G. N., 295, 296, 331, 333
Clementz, B. A., 126
Cloutier, P., 482
Clum, G., 546
Cluss, P. A., 479
Coates, D. L., 365, 504
Coatsworth, J. D., 7, 11
Cobb, J. A., 551
Coe, D. A., 367
Coffey, C., 474
Cohen, D. J., 355, 365, 492, 493, 494, 498
Cohen, E., 295
Cohen, J., 65, 79, 248, 268
Cohen, J. A., 561
Cohen, M. A., 187, 203, 219, 223
Cohen, P., 2, 8, 187, 203, 219, 223,
    248, 268
Cohen, R. M., 169, 171
Coie, J. D., 230
Coiro, M. J., 485
Colapinto, J., 186
Colder, C. R., 275
Cole, D. A., 268, 301, 302, 304, 314
Cole, G., 400
Cole, P. M., 14
Cole, R., 528
Coleman, M., 397, 398
Coles, C., 171
Collacott, R. A., 352
Collica, T. J., 239
Collings, S., 512
Collins, P., 46
Colliver, J. D., 203
Comings, B. G., 159, 168, 213
Comings, D. E., 159, 168, 213
Compas, B. E., 54, 289, 297, 309, 482,
    484, 520, 522
Cone, J. D., 77
Conger, R. D., 16, 220, 314
Conners, C. K., 13, 56, 66, 101, 172, 187,
    240, 439
Connolly, J., 327
Connor, R. T., 354, 427
Conners, C. K., 518
Conners, M. E., 518
Conover, N. C., 108
Conrin, J., 499
Contreras, J., 353
Cook, E. H., 168, 401
Coolahan, K. C., 560
Cooley, W. C., 365
Cooper, C., 244
Cooper, P., 285, 305
Cooper, S. A., 352
Coovert, M. D., 504
Copeland, D. R., 483
Copeland, P. M., 514
Coplan, R. J., 47
Corcoran, M. E., 55
Cornwell, J., 486
Cortez, V. L., 267
Cosentino, C. E., 546
Costello, A. J., 108
Costello, E. J., 1, 2, 12, 21, 24, 65, 66, 195,
    223, 269, 297
Costigan, C. L., 368
Cote, G., 243
Cotter, M., 488

Courchesne, E., 397, 399
Courtney, P., 160
Cousens, P., 483
Cousins, J. H., 503
Cowan, C. P., 55
Cowan, P. A., 55
Cowen, P. J., 514
Cowie, V. A., 400
Cox, D. J., 473, 474
Coyne, J. C., 306, 309, 312
Craighead, L. W., 520
Cramer, B. G., 36
Craske, M. G., 268
Crawford, J. W., 483
Crawford, P. B. 503
Crick, N. R., 51, 100, 101, 192, 201, 206,
    215, 216
Crijnen, A. A. M., 67
Crimmins, D. B., 559
Crisp, A. H., 518, 521
Crittenden, P. M., 531, 539, 542, 551
Crnic, K. A., 239
Crockett, L. J., 267, 494
Crosby, L., 201, 203, 512
Cross, P. A., 464
Crossland, C. L., 354
Cuffe, S. P., 155
Cull, J. G., 213
Cullinan, D., 354, 356
Cummings, E. M., 528
Cunningham, C. E., 156, 227, 369
Curry, J. F., 268
Curtiss, J., 420, 424, 429
Cutler, C., 501
Cutting, L., 449, 450, 451, 453
Cytryn, L., 288, 311

Dadds, M. R., 76, 77, 131, 275, 277, 280
Dahl, R. E., 311, 457, 458, 459, 460,
    461, 463, 464, 492
Dahlmeier, J. M., 312
Dahlquist, L. M., 487, 488
Daleiden, E. L., 239, 267
Damasio, A., 442
Damasio, H., 442
Danford, D. E., 498
Danforth, J. S., 81, 174
Daniels, M., 358
D'Aquill, E., 503
Dare, C., 520, 521
Daro, D., 556
Dauber, S. L., 446
Davidson, C. E., 219
Davidson, R. J., 40
Davidson, S., 294, 311
Davis, B., 77, 312
Davis, N., 486, 488
Davis, S., 202, 486, 560
Dawson, G., 29, 311, 378, 382, 383, 386,
    387, 389, 392, 395, 398, 401, 402,
    407, 408, 409
Dean, R. S., 123
Dean, R. R., 45
DeAntonio, C., 355
Deater-Deckard, K., 216, 217, 226
Debelle, G., 474
DeBellis, M., 45, 546
Deblinger, E., 561
Decoufle, P., 349
DeFries, J. C., 42, 154, 168, 438, 442

deGrouchy, J., 359
DeJong, P. J., 249
DeKlyen, M., 219
DeKraai, M. B., 134
Delamater, A., 479
Delaney, H. D., 34
Del Dotto, J. E., 445, 451
De Lisi, L. E., 415
Dell, L., 415
Denhoff, E., 145
Denicola, J., 559
DeNil, L., 431
Dennig, M. D., 487
Denzin, N. K., 92
Depue, R. A., 46
Deren, D. M., 299
Derryberry, D., 39
Desmond, A., 262
DeSpelder, L. A., 327
Despert, J. L., 257
Deutsch, C. K., 42
DeVet, K., 198
DeVincentis, C., 119
Devlin, B., 288, 358, 364
Dickson, N., 187, 464
Diekstra, R. F. W., 543, 544
Dietz, W. H., 503, 504
DeLalla, D. L., 539
DiLalla, L. F., 212, 213, 273
DiLella, A., 361
Dillon, K. M., 62, 63, 541
Dishion, T. J., 65, 77, 201, 202, 203, 206,
    204, 208, 212, 214, 219, 225, 226
Djurhuus, J. C., 471
Dobash, R. E., 556
Dobash, R. P., 556
Dobkin, P. L., 2
Dobson, K. S., 50
Doctor, R. M., 559
Dodge, K. A., 51, 88, 89, 192, 193, 201,
    215, 216, 217, 220, 226, 227, 541,
    542
Dolan, B., 511
Doleys, D. M., 457
Dombrowski, S. M., 399
Domenech, E., 300
Dondis, E. H., 341
Donenberg, G. R., 70, 139
Dong, Q., 238, 270
Donnellan, A. M., 379
Donnelly, D. A., 547
Donohue, B., 20
Doris, J., 543
Dotemoto, S., 156
Douglas, V. I., 146, 148, 165
Dowling, C. G., 322, 455
Downey, G., 306, 312
Down, J. L. H., 338
Dozois, D. J. A., 24, 31, 310
Drash, A., 479
Drews, C. D., 349
Drezner, K., 333
Droegemueller, W., 533
Drotar, D., 485, 486, 501, 552
Drum, C., 499
DuBois, D. L., 331
Dubowitz, H., 551
DuBreuil, S. C., 464
Duffy, A., 294
Dujovne, V. F., 332
Dulcan, M. J., 108

Dulcan, M. K., 159
Dumas, J. E., 226
Duncan, G. J., 10, 17, 55
Duncan, P. M, 337, 349
Dunlap, K., 26
Dunst, C. J., 486
DuPaul, G. J., 59, 110, 131, 155, 156, 162,
    165, 169, 175, 178, 179
Durand, D. M., 43, 44, 70, 346, 463
Durand, V. M., 249, 274
Durlak, J. A., 139
Duster, T., 130
Duyme, M., 358
Dykens, E. M., 340, 346, 348, 349, 352,
    353, 355, 357, 358, 362, 365
Dzuiba-Leatherman, J., 526, 527, 533, 557

Earls, F., 211, 221
Easterbrooks, M. A., 219
Eastman, K. L., 161
Eastwood, D., 396
Eaves, L. J., 273
Ebstein, R. P., 168
Eckenrode, J., 543
Eckert, E. D., 512
Eckert, T. L., 179
Edelbrock, C. S., 32, 108, 154, 156, 163,
    168, 212, 224
Edelson, G., 267, 552
Eden, G. F., 444
Egeland, B., 219, 290, 353, 531, 538
Egolf, B. P., 469, 552
Eiben, L. A., 459, 461, 462, 463, 464, 465,
    467, 468
Eiberg, H., 471
Eikeseth, S., 409
Eiraldi, R. B., 152
Eisen, A. R., 234
Eisen, J. L., 247, 262, 273, 278
Eisenmajer, R., 393
Eisikovits, Z. C., 552
Eisler, I., 520, 521
Elbert, J. C., 131
Elder, G. H., 16, 205, 220
Eldredge, K. L., 522
El-Hag, N., 267
Elia, J., 332
Eliopulos, D., 169
Ellinwood, C. G., 137
Elliott, C. H., 488
Elliott, D. S., 203, 219, 223
Elliott, M., 554, 555
Ember, C. R., 223
Ember, M., 223
Emde, R., 46
Eme, R. F., 205, 213
Emery, G., 2, 329
Emslie, G. J., 309, 311, 333
Endriga, M. C., 219
Engelmann, S., 451, 452
Engler, L. B., 247
Entwistle, D. R., 446
Epps, J., 51
Epstein, L. H., 505, 517
Epstein, M. H., 356, 479
Epstein, R., 506
Erhardt, D., 157
Erickson, M. F., 219, 290, 353, 497,
    531, 543
Erkanli, A., 269, 297
Ernst, A. R., 475, 477

Ernst, M. R., 75, 171
Eron, L. D., 220, 222
Ervin, R. A., 110
Escobar, M. D., 427, 437
Eskinazi, B., 172
Eslinger, P. J., 153, 169
Estes, A. M., 185
Esveldt-Dawson, K., 303
Evans, D. W., 239, 240
Evans, I. M., 132, 346, 353
Ewing, L. J., 173, 208
Exner, J. E., 120
Ey, S., 309
Eyberg, S. M., 225

Faier-Routman, J., 481, 482
Fairbanks, J. M., 265
Fairbanks, L., 279
Fairburn, C. G., 492, 511, 514, 517, 521, 522
Fairclough, D., 482
Falco, R., 451
Famularo, R., 265
Fantuzzo, J. W., 534, 559, 560
Faraone, S. V., 155, 157, 159, 161, 167, 168, 171, 196, 220, 275
Farber, E., 538
Farmer, E. M. Z., 269, 477
Farrell, A. D., 68
Farrington, D. P., 89, 188, 200, 203, 208, 211, 220
Fauber, R. L., 24, 136, 138
Faust, J., 555
Faust-Campanile, J., 15
Fava, M., 514
Favaro, A., 504
Feagans, L., 87
Feehan, M., 160, 205
Fein, D., 398
Feldman, C. M., 547
Feldman, H., 356
Feldman, M., 324
Feldman, R. S., 542
Feldman, S., 356
Felton, R. H., 154, 427, 429, 453
Fenton, T., 265
Ferber, T., 458
Fergusson, D. M., 172, 195, 203, 310, 470
Fernald, C. D., 130
Ferretti, R. P., 368
Fichman, L., 302
Fiedler, C., 369
Field, A. E., 512
Field, T. M., 74, 311
Fielding, D. M., 457
Fiese, B. H., 90
Figueredo, A., 532
Filipek, P. A., 169
Fillion, B. D., 503
Finch, A. J., 203, 269
Finch, S. J., 227
Fincham, F. D., 216, 541
Fine, E. M., 155, 175
Fine, M. A., 137
Fine, S., 329
Fingerhut, L. A., 185
Finkelhor, D., 18, 525, 526, 527, 532, 533, 535, 536, 541, 543, 545, 546, 549, 554, 555, 557, 560
Finkelstein, R., 273, 502
Finney, J. W., 101

Fischel, J. E., 427, 429
Fischer, M., 154, 156
Fischer, S., 289
Fish, B., 416
Fisher, M., 73, 93, 155, 163, 509
Fisher, P., 326
Fiske, J., 123
Fisler, R. E., 45, 540
Flannery-Schroeder, E. C., 269, 280
Fleeson, J., 539
Fleeting, M., 220
Flegal, K. M., 503
Fleming, J. E., 13, 233, 437, 439, 449
Fleming, J. F., 295
Fletcher, J. M., 123, 483
Fletcher, K. E., 155, 156, 265
Fletcher, P. C., 388
Flett, G. L., 518
Flicek, M., 157
Flint, J., 349, 360
Flisher, A. J., 544
Flory, M., 326
Flowers, L., 429
Floyd, F. J., 368, 369
Flynn, J., 342
Foch, T., 168
Foley, C., 457
Fombonne, E., 295
Fonagy, P., 24
Foorman, B. R., 449, 450
Forehand, R. L., 131, 133, 225, 226, 268
Foresberg, H., 435
Foreyt, J. P., 503, 504, 511, 520
Forgatch, M. S., 221
Forness, S. R., 172, 355, 440
Foster, S. L., 137, 202
Foster, T., 77
Fowler, A. F., 439
Fox, J. J., 367
Fox, L. W., 311, 320
Fox, M. M., 503, 511
Fox, N. A., 14, 39, 40, 41, 47, 74
Fox, S., 528
Foxx, R. M., 472
Foy, D. W., 545
Frame, C. L., 204, 268, 356
Francis, C., 243, 247, 251
Francis, D. H., 439, 449
Francis, D. J., 439, 449
Francis, G., 42
Francis, P. J., 449
Frank, Y., 169
Fraser, B. G., 328
Fraser, J., 332
Fraser, W. I., 400
Frazer, D. R., 198
Frazier, J. A., 413, 415
Frederick, C., 265
Freedman, J. L., 222
Freeman, R., 202
French, A. P., 268
French, J. L., 115, 120
French, N. H., 303
French, S. A., 519
French, V., 20
Freud, S., 24, 270
Frey, K., 29, 311
Frick, P. J., 71, 73, 111, 122, 160, 161, 190, 192, 196, 198, 200, 204, 212, 213, 214, 216, 217, 220
Friedin, M. R., 155

Friedman, A. G., 480, 483
Friedman, H. S., 155
Friedman, J., 504
Friedman, R. M., 17
Friedman, S., 269
Friedrich, W., 546
Friedson, E., 130
Friman, P. C., 101
Fristad, M. A., 314
Frith, C., 379, 385, 387, 388, 389, 390, 393, 395, 398, 401, 441, 444, 445
Frith, U., 379, 385, 387, 388, 389, 390, 393, 395, 398, 401, 441 444, 445
Fritsch, S., 475
Fritz, G. K., 475
Fritz, J., 539
Frost, R., 424
Frost, S., 268
Fruehling, J. J., 332
Fuchs, C., 545
Fudge, H., 289
Fugere, C., 273
Fuhrman, T., 139
Fujii, K., 161
Fulker, D. W., 442
Fulkerson, J. A., 519
Fultz, S. A., 499
Fusetti, L., 143, 155
Fuster, J. M., 166, 169

Gabel, S., 2
Gabowski, T. J., 442
Gadow, K. D., 138, 222, 223, 228, 356, 364
Gagnon, M., 431
Gaines, R., 546, 551
Galaburda, A. M., 442
Gallagher, P. R., 504
Ganiban, J., 307, 539
Garbarino, J., 533
Garber, J., 37, 124, 301, 302, 303, 309, 312, 314, 315, 475, 477
Garcia-Jetton, J., 155
Gardner, D., 279
Gardner, H., 422
Garfinkel, P. E., 493, 510, 511, 516, 517, 518
Garland, A., 326
Garmezy, N., 2, 9, 10, 34, 528
Garn, S. M., 504
Garnefski, N., 543, 544
Garner, D. M., 492, 493, 495, 496, 511, 516, 519, 520, 522
Garrison, W. T., 457, 476
Gastonis, C., 204, 289, 296, 323
Gaub, M., 152, 161
Gaudin, J. M., 543, 556
Ge, X., 16, 220, 314
Gelb, S. A., 338, 339
Gelernter, S., 83
Geller, V., 316, 317, 318, 319, 320, 321, 334
Gelles, R. J., 525, 527, 535, 552, 557
Gena, A., 406
Gentile, C., 546
George, D. T., 542
George, L. K., 483
George, M. S., 298
Gerber, A., 24
Germany, E., 297
Gershater, R. M., 559

Gersten, R. M., 451
Geschwind, A. F., 442
Gettys, L., 130
Giaconia, R. M., 306
Gibbons, R., 349
Gibson, D., 352
Giedd, J. N., 169, 415
Gil, K. M., 483, 485
Gilbert, M., 397
Gilger, J. W., 42, 154, 168
Gill, M., 168
Gillberg, C., 395, 398, 401
Giller, H., 217
Gillis, J. J., 42
Gillman, J. B., 456
Gill-Weiss, M. J., 355
Ginsburg, C. S., 269, 280
Ginsburg, G. S., 246
Girgus, J. S., 297, 302, 303
Gittelman, R., 163, 172
Gittelman-Klein, R., 120
Gjerde, R. F., 220
Gladstone, T. R. G., 303
Glantz, M. D., 203
Glaser, G. H., 547
Glicklich, L. B., 469
Glow, P. H., 164
Glow, R. A., 164
Gnagy, E. M., 176
Goate, A. M., 353
Goddard, H., 338, 340
Goetz, R. R., 311
Goins, C., 559, 560
Goldberg, L. R., 122, 275
Goldberg, S., 481, 482
Goldblatt, P. B., 503
Goldentyer, T., 208
Goldfield, A., 503
Golding, J., 155
Goldner, E. M., 518
Goldsmith, D., 460
Goldsmith, H., 212, 213
Goldstein, C. E., 312
Goldstein, D. S., 520
Goldstein, D. J., 520
Goldstein, H., 416
Goldstein, M. J., 312, 407
Goldston, D., 301, 302, 305, 323
Goldwyn, R., 542
Gomez, R., 160, 378
Gonzalez, J. C., 442, 488
Gonzalez, N. M., 229
Goode, S., 385
Goodman, J. F., 92
Goodman, K., 165, 450
Goodwin, F. K., 318
Goodyear, P., 152
Goodyer, I. M., 285, 297, 305, 312, 313
Gordon, B. N., 132
Gordon, C. T., 99, 415, 473
Gordon-Walker, J., 482
Gorman, J. M., 274
Gorman-Smith, D., 193
Gortmaker, S. L., 2, 477, 478, 481, 483, 484, 503
Gotlib, I. H., 269, 295, 296, 301, 303, 304, 305, 309
Gotowiec, A., 481
Gottesman, I. J., 212, 213
Gottfredson, D. C., 209
Gottfredson, G. D., 221

Gottfredson, M. 221
Gottman, J. M., 354, 427
Gould, J., 541
Gould, M. S., 326
Gow, C. A., 311
Gowers, S., 328, 521
Gowrusankur, J., 297
Graae, F., 3, 138, 256, 259, 273, 274, 279, 280
Graber, J. A., 494
Graetz, B., 482
Graham, J. M., 355, 365
Graham, P. 216
Graham, S., 216, 451, 452
Grant, K. E., 309
Grant, R., 13
Grattan, L. M., 169
Gray, J. A., 123, 166, 200, 213, 501, 516
Graziano, A. M., 472
Green, A. H., 502
Green, P. A., 439
Green, S. M., 196, 203
Green, W. H., 551
Greenawald, J., 273, 274
Greenberg, H. S., 219, 481
Greenberg, M. T., 230
Greene, B. F., 560
Greene, J. W., 475, 477
Greene, R. W., 155
Greenhill, L. L., 332
Greenhouse, J. B., 215
Greenspan, S. I., 105, 129
Greer, M., 352
Greey, M., 474
Gresham, F. M., 345, 409
Grewal, A., 518
Grimm, S., 196
Grisso, T., 93, 95
Grodzinsky, G., 165, 169
Groisser, D., 446
Groome, P. A., 478
Gross, A. M., 306, 312
Gross, J., 522
Gross, M. D., 175
Grossman, P. B., 74
Gross-Tsur, V., 154
Grove, W., 512
Groves, W. B., 221
Grunberg, N. E., 41
Grych, J. H., 216, 541
Guerra, N. G., 56, 193, 194, 224, 230
Guevremont, D. C., 59, 155, 156, 178
Guidubaldi, J., 116
Guilem, C. A., 505
Gullone, E., 245, 269
Guralnick, M. J., 354, 368, 427
Gurley, D., 268, 295
Gurman, A. S., 131, 137
Guskin, 130
Gustafson, K. E., 475, 478, 479, 480, 481, 482, 483, 484, 487
Guthrie, D., 312, 415
Guttman, E., 533, 552
Gzowski, P., 385

Haaga, D. A., 520
Haas, E., 201
Haenlein, M., 164
Hagberg, B., 358, 394
Hagberg, G., 358, 394
Hagell, A., 200, 441

Hagen, E. P., 117
Hagerty, B. K., 323
Hagino, O., 475
Hahn, H., 87
Haldwin, J., 268
Hale, R. L., 115
Halek, C., 521
Hall, A., 492
Hall, G. S., 339
Hall, R., 559, 560
Hallahan, D. P., 450
Hallmark, R., 120
Hallowell, E. M., 180
Halmi, K. A., 498, 512, 520
Halperin, J. M., 116, 150
Halpern, D. F., 341
Halpern, L., 459
Halverson, C. F., 171
Ham, M., 306
Hamalainen, M., 208
Hamburger, S. D., 415
Hamilton, E. B., 312
Hammen, C. L., 289, 292, 293, 296, 298, 305, 306, 307, 309, 310, 311, 312, 314, 315, 316
Hammer, L. D., 261, 367
Hammill, D. D., 422, 423, 450
Hammond, M. A., 354, 427
Hammond-Laurence, K., 239
Han, S. S., 70, 139
Hancock, L., 174, 175, 424
Handen, B. L., 356
Hanefeld, F., 394
Hankin, B. L., 297
Hanna, G. L., 171, 259
Hansen, D. E., 464, 465
Hansen, D. J., 540, 543, 559
Hanson, C. L., 479
Happe, F. G. E., 384, 385, 388, 389, 390, 393, 398, 401
Harbeck, D., 477
Harbeck-Weber, C., 456, 470, 473, 474, 475, 477, 479
Harden, P. W., 199
Hare, R. D., 194
Haring, T. G., 367
Harlow, H., 51
Harnish, J. D., 193
Harper, J., 475
Harper, L. V., 396
Harpur, T. J., 194
Harrington, D., 551
Harrington, K., 134, 289, 295, 296, 297, 310, 328, 331, 332
Harrington, R. C., 81
Harris, K. R., 137, 451, 452
Harris, L. J., 2
Harris, M. A., 479
Hart, E. I., 161, 162, 163
Hart, S. D., 194, 199, 203
Harter, S., 304, 439, 446
Hartman, C. R., 540, 545
Hartmann, A. H., 236, 238
Hartmann, D. P., 55, 239, 240
Hartmann, T., 164
Hartmark, C., 219
Hartung, C. M., 100
Hartup, W. W., 201
Haskett, M. E., 542
Haslum, M., 155
Hatch, M. L., 269

Hatcher, J. W., 477
Hauri, P., 459
Hauser, P., 168
Hauser, S. T., 219
Haviland, M. G., 546
Hawkins, R. P., 110
Hawkins, W., 333
Hawton, K., 326
Hay, D., 168
Hay, P. J., 492
Hay, T., 511, 536
Hayman, L. L., 504
Haynes, C. F., 501
Haynes, J. A., 452
Haynes, R. B., 479
Hayward, C., 261
Hazzard, A., 541
Heath, A. C., 273
Heatherton, T. F., 495, 512, 513, 516, 518
Heavey, L., 385
Hechtman, L. T., 154, 155, 163, 164,
    167, 175
Hedeker, D., 518
Heffernan, K., 515
Hegedus, A. E., 547
Heimberg, R. G., 245
Heintz, T., 155
Heller, M. R., 45
Heller, T., 394
Heming, G., 55
Henderson, A. S., 273
Henderson, C. R., 365
Hendren, R. L., 415
Henggeler, S. W., 202, 224, 225, 227,
    228–229, 479
Henin, A., 255
Henker, B., 156, 157, 273
Hennessy, K. D., 528, 539
Henriksen, L., 169
Henry, A., 153
Henry, B., 272
Henry, D., 545, 561
Henry, M., 199, 211, 219, 435
Herbert, J., 305
Herbert, M., 132, 185, 200
Herbison, G. P., 547
Herbsman, C., 163
Herman, 493, 515, 539, 545, 546
Herman, J. L., 536
Herman-Stahl, H., 295
Hermelin, B., 379, 385
Hernstein, R. J., 343
Herrenkohl, B. C., 552
Herrenkohl, E. C., 469, 552
Herrenkohl, R. C., 469
Herscovitch, P., 298
Hersen, M., 20, 42, 71, 85, 109, 243, 244,
    247, 273
Hershey, K. L., 48
Herzberger, S. D., 541
Herzog, D. B., 289, 291, 292, 514, 518
Hesse, E., 539
Hessl, D., 29, 311
Hester, C., 511
Hetherington, C. R., 311
Hetherington, E. M., 54, 67, 204
Hewitt, P. L., 518
Heymans, M., 522
Hibbard, J. H., 297
Hibbs, E. D., 131
Hichwa, R. D., 442

Hicks, R. C., 326
Higgs, D., 349
Hill, J., 289
Hill, N. L., 171, 198
Hillson, J. M. C., 551
Hilsman, R., 303, 312, 314
Hinden, B. R., 297
Hinshaw, S. P., 145, 146, 148, 149, 157,
    163, 164, 167, 171, 173, 179, 188,
    190, 194, 196, 199, 200, 203,
    204, 205, 211, 214, 216, 224,
    446, 448
Hirsch, S., 297
Hirschi, T., 209
Hirshfeld, D. R., 272, 275
Hoagwood, K., 93, 129, 133, 139
Hobson, R. P., 379
Hodapp, R. M., 340, 346, 348, 349, 351,
    352, 353, 355, 356, 357, 358, 362
Hodde-Vargas, M. S., 415
Hodgins, S., 202
Hoek, H. W., 511
Hoeppner, J. B., 155
Hoffman, L., 520
Hoffman, H. G., 144
Hoffman-Plotkin, D., 542
Holden, E. W., 484
Hollister, A., 455
Holmes, F. B., 26
Holowaty, E., 478
Holt, C. S., 138, 254, 281
Holttum, J., 463
Hommer, D., 473
Hood, J., 154, 165, 275
Hook, E. G., 360
Hook, J., 440
Hooper, S. R., 437
Hoover, D. W., 60, 172
Hope, R. A., 521
Hopper, J., 555
Hops, H., 13, 14, 77, 100, 202, 204,
    233, 295, 296, 297, 300, 304, 312,
    331, 333
Hopwood, N. J., 502
Horesh, N., 517
Horne, J. A., 461
Horobin, G., 349
Horowitz, H. A., 64, 219
Horwood, L. J., 172, 195, 203, 310, 470
Hotaling, G. T., 525
Hotopf, M., 397
Houskamp, B., 482
Houts, A. C., 470, 471, 472
Howard, B. L., 51, 133, 280
Howell, C. T., 13, 56, 66, 101, 110, 187,
    439, 484
Howell, D. C., 297
Howes, C., 101, 192
Howie, P., 430
Howing, P. T., 543
Howlin, P., 385, 411
Hoza, B., 176, 180
Hsu, L. K. G., 508, 511, 512, 513, 514,
    515, 521
Hu, S., 248
Hua, J., 459
Huberman, A. M., 92
Hubert, A. M., 498
Hudley, C., 216
Hudson, J. I., 513, 517
Hudson, S. M., 555

Huesmann, L. R., 193, 220, 222
Hughes, J. N., 51, 74
Hughes, M., 245, 265
Huizinga, D., 203, 219
Humphrey, F. J., 513, 517
Humphrey, L. L., 302
Humphries, T., 82, 172
Hunt, H., 352
Hurlbert, R. T., 385, 393
Hurley, L. K., 132
Hussey, D. L., 554
Huston, A. C., 298
Hutchins, H., 195
Hutton, H. E., 511
Huttunen, M. O., 416
Huxsahl, J., 546
Hybel, L. G., 221
Hynd, G. W., 152, 169, 204, 442

Iacono, W. G., 126, 168, 358
Ialongo, N., 267
Illick, J. E., 21
Illsley, R., 349
Inglis, A., 165
Innocenti, G. M., 39
Insabella, G. M., 67
Inz, J., 248
Irvin, L. K., 368
Irvin, M. G., 134
Ishal, J., 517
Israel, A. C., 505
Issacs, M. R., 365
Itard, J. M., 21
Izard, C. E., 30

Jackson, E. W., 161
Jackson, Y. K., 212, 217
Jacob, T., 87
Jacobs, C., 281, 513
Jacobsen, L., 346
Jacobson, J. W., 62, 355, 401
Jacobvitz, D., 8, 172, 175
Jaffe, P., 526, 532, 543, 552, 556
James, N. M., 323
Jamison, K. R., 316, 318
Janosky, J., 356
Jansen, A., 522
Janssen, P., 430
Jarrell, M. P., 495
Jaworski, T., 546
Jay, S. M., 488
Jaycox, L. H., 333
Jayson, D., 328, 332
Jensen, P. S., 18, 93, 129, 131, 133, 134,
    139, 158, 203, 204
Jewell, L., 306
Jimerson, D. C., 514
Jipson, F. J., 349
Jobes, D. A., 322, 323, 324, 325, 327
Johnson, B., 2, 327
Johnson, C., 518
Johnson, J., 223
Johnson, M. H., 367, 395
Johnson, S. B. 479, 482
Johnson, S. M., 76, 115
Johnson, W. G., 503, 504, 514, 520,
    521, 522
Johnston, B. A., 288
Johnston, C., 83, 102, 130, 156, 157, 162,
    172, 202, 226
Johnston, H. F., 289, 332

Johnston, J. M., 499
Joiner, T. E., 269, 303, 309, 518
Jolliffe, T., 389
Jonas, J. M., 513
Jones, D. J., 511
Jones, J., 171
Jones, M. C., 25
Jones, N. A., 74
Jones, R., 521
Jordan, A. E., 304
Joschko, M., 148
Joyce, P. R., 326
Jumper, S., 547

Kachur, S. P., 323, 326
Kagan, J., 34, 68, 125, 271, 272, 273, 538
Kager, V. A., 484
Kahkonen, M., 359
Kalas, R., 108
Kales, A., 459, 466
Kales, J., 459
Kales, J. D., 466
Kallman, F. J., 415, 416
Kamphaus, R. W., 71, 73, 111, 116, 117, 119, 122
Kanbayashi, Y., 161
Kanner, L., 20, 337, 338, 339, 373, 382, 390, 395, 396
Kaplan, A. S., 513
Kaplan, F., 340
Kaplan, H. I., 39
Kaplan, S. J., 543, 545
Karg, R. S., 132
Karlsson, J., 156
Kasen, S., 219
Kashani, J. H., 233, 293, 294, 312
Kaslow, N. J., 302, 303, 305, 307, 309, 312, 313
Kastner, J., 369
Kastner, S., 369
Kato, C., 471
Kaufman, A. S., 117
Kaufman, J. L., 545, 547, 559
Kaufman, J. M., 450, 451
Kaufman, M. 328, 354
Kaufman, N. L., 117
Kavale, K. A., 440
Kavanagh, K. A., 13, 100, 205, 225
Kavanaugh, L., 213
Kaye, W. H., 514, 521
Kazak, A. E., 481, 482, 485, 488
Kazdin, A. E., 3, 24, 26, 34, 42, 60, 61, 64, 65, 68, 69, 78, 80, 84, 85, 125, 131, 132, 133, 134, 136, 138, 139, 140, 177, 186, 187, 195, 205, 208, 224, 225, 226, 227, 243, 244, 247, 273, 302, 303, 311, 315, 328, 331, 332
Kearney, C. A., 234, 245, 260, 262, 263, 302
Keefe, F. J., 520
Keel, P. K., 512, 516
Keenan, K., 100, 159, 161, 203, 205, 220
Keith, B. R., 483
Kellam, S., 267
Keller, C. E., 451
Keller, J., 310
Keller, J. A., 518
Keller, M. B., 233, 243, 247
Kelly, K. L., 175, 559
Kelsey, J. E., 45

Keltner, D., 198
Kemp, D. C., 378, 545
Kempe, C. H., 501
Kempe, R. S., 533
Kemper, T. L., 394, 398, 399
Kendall, P. C., 29–30, 50, 51, 131, 133, 136, 137, 138, 230, 241, 255, 268, 269, 274, 275, 277, 279, 280, 329
Kendall-Tackett, K. A., 532, 538, 547
Kendler, K. S., 273, 310, 514
Kennard, B. D., 309
Kennedy, D. H., 143
Kennedy, J. L., 155
Kennedy, P., 143
Kennedy, R. E., 304
Kenning, M., 15
Kenny, M. C., 555
Keogh, B. K., 137
Keough, B., 341, 351
Kerbeshian, J., 413
Kern, R. A., 364
Kessler, J. W., 145
Kessler, R. C., 265, 273
Ketter, T. A., 298
Keyes, S., 203
Khazam, C., 509
Kilcoyne, J., 554
Killen, J. D., 261, 492, 494
Kilpatrick, A. C., 556
King, B. H., 355
King, C. A., 327
King, D. F., 450
King, M., 512
King, N. J., 545
King, R. A., 233, 234, 238, 245, 260, 263, 269, 270, 277
King, S., 487
Kinney, T. R., 483, 485
Kinnish, K., 354, 427
Kinsbourne, M., 42, 82, 172
Kinscherff, R., 265
Kipp, H. L., 176
Kirk, S. A., 195
Kistner, J. A., 542
Kita, M., 161
Kitsuse, J. I., 130
Kitzman, H., 365
Klebanov, P. K., 17, 349
Klein, B. H., 355
Klein, C. A., 327
Klein, D. F., 450
Klein, M., 512
Klein, N. J., 545
Klein, R. A., 233, 234, 238, 245, 260, 263, 269, 270, 277
Klein, S., 487
Kleinman, J. C., 185, 415
Klemp, S., 484
Klerman, G. L., 331
Klevstrand, M., 409
Klin, A., 378, 393
Klinedinst, J. K., 122
Klinger, L. G., 378, 383, 386, 389, 392, 398
Klorman, R., 169, 540
Kloth, S. A. M., 430
Klotz, M. L., 139
Knapp, L. G., 356
Kniskern, D. P., 131, 137
Knoff, H. M., 120
Knox, L. S., 260, 280, 281
Knutson, J. F., 552

Kobe, F. H., 62
Kochanska, G., 198
Koegel, L. K., 404, 407
Koegel, R. L., 407
Koestner, R., 302
Kohler, F. W., 407
Kolb, B., 311
Kolko, D. J., 98, 106, 108, 114, 115, 138–139, 541, 545, 559, 560
Kolvin, P. A., 220
Koot, H. M., 82
Koplewicz, H. S., 160, 457
Koplowicz, S., 163
Kopp, C. B., 314
Korbin, J., 528
Kortlander, E., 275
Koss, M. P., 532, 547
Kotchick, B. A., 133, 226
Kovacs, M., 111, 204, 288, 289, 293, 296, 297, 299, 300, 301, 302, 305, 306, 310, 313, 314, 315, 316, 318, 323, 324, 325, 326, 328, 333, 481
Koverola, C., 545
Kovitz, K., 102
Kowatch, R. A., 309
Kraemer, H. C., 134
Kraemer, G. W., 51
Krahn, G. L., 87
Kramer, J. R., 149, 552
Krantz, P. J., 406
Krasnegor, N., 75
Krasner, L., 136
Krasnewich, D., 415
Kratochwill, K. R., 136
Kratzer, L., 202
Kraus, N., 439, 441, 445
Krauss, M. W., 363
Kroll, L., 328, 332
Krueger, S., 521
Kruh, I., 220
Krupa, M., 215
Kuczmarski, R. J., 503
Kuhl, P., 423
Kuhlmann, F., 338
Kuiper, N. A., 551
Kulkarni, R., 482
Kunce, L. J., 393
Kuper, K., 160
Kurowski, C., 331
Kurtines, W., 278, 280
Kurtz, P. D., 543, 556
Kutcher, S., 279, 332
Kwasnik, D., 155, 175
Kyle, K. E., 131

Lacey, E. P., 498
Lacey, J. H., 492
Lacharité, C., 364
Ladouceur, R., 431
LaGreca, A. M., 239, 265, 266, 482, 484
Lahey, B. B., 56, 66, 146, 149, 152, 161, 191, 194, 195, 196, 199, 203, 204, 214, 215, 220, 224, 268
LaHoste, G. J., 168
Laird, M., 543
Lam, R. W., 518
LaMarche, J. A., 123
Lamb, W., 473
Lambert, M. C., 14, 15
Lambert, N. M., 160

Lamparelli, M., 153, 199
Lampman, C., 139
Lamprecht, F., 171
Landau, S., 156
Landry, R., 389
Lang, A. R., 83, 156, 174
Langenbeck, U., 359
Lapey, K., 157
Lapp, L., 459
Larranee, D. T., 551
Larson, R. W., 306, 315
Larzelere, R., 101
Lask, B., 511
Last, C. G., 42, 238, 239, 242, 243, 244, 247, 248, 251, 254, 255, 262, 263, 269, 273
Latham, P., 178
Latham, R., 178
Laub, J. H., 221
Laufer, M., 145
Laumann-Billings, L., 2
Laurent, J., 269, 302
Lauritsen, K., 220
Laver, S., 358
Lavigne, J. V., 481, 482
Lavori, P. W., 310, 518
Lawry, S., 541
Layton, L., 10
Lazar, J. W., 169
Leach, C., 354
Lease, D. A., 244, 247
Leckman, J. F., 41, 239
Le Couteur, A., 396, 397
Ledingham, J. E., 205
Lefebvre, L., 40, 547
Leffert, J. S., 175, 354
Lefkowitz, M. M., 220, 222
LeGagnoux, G. L., 329
LeGrange, D., 521
Lehtinen, L. E., 145
Leitenberg, H., 509, 520, 522
Leland, J., 222
Lemon, N., 526
Lenane, M. C., 255, 415
Lendon, C. L., 353
Leon, A., 46
Leon, G. R., 519
Leonard, C. O., 358
Leonard, H. L., 255, 279
Leonard, K., 87
Lerer, M. P., 174
Lerer, R. J., 174
LeRoy, S., 482
Lesch, K. P., 273
Lesem, M. D., 514
Lesser, S. T., 136
Leutwyler, K., 298
Leventhal, B. L., 401
Leventhal, J. M., 486
Levine, 312, 332, 469
Levine, A., 23, 24
Levine, K., 469
Levine, M. D., 23, 24
Levine, M. L., 494, 495
Levitt, E. E., 120
Levitt, P., 461
Levy, D. L., 168
Levy, F., 168
Levy, S. E., 446
Lewerth, A., 358
Lewin, L. N., 202

Lewine, R. J., 416
Lewinsohn, M. 233, 269
Lewinsohn, P. M., 204, 233, 269, 289, 295, 296, 297, 300, 301, 302, 303, 304, 307, 312, 314, 319, 325, 327, 329, 331, 333
Lewis, B. A., 442
Lewis, D. O., 538, 541, 547
Lewis, I. A., 525
Lewis, M. H., 31, 35, 364
Lewis, V., 378
Lewontin, R., 358
Lewy, A., 392
Li, Z. Y., 14
Liberman, I. Y., 424, 435
Libet, J., 500
Libow, J. A., 550
Lilienfeld, S. O., 124, 195
Lin, L., 238
Lincoln, A. J., 393, 397
Lincoln, Y. S., 92
Lindberg, U., 358
Lindgren, S., 172
Ling, W., 473
Linney, J. A., 485
Lipsey, M. W., 224
Lisak, D., 541, 555
Littleford, C. D., 378
Livingston, R., 51, 302
LLoyd, J. W., 203, 450, 451
Lobitz, G. K., 76, 115
Lochhead, C., 2
Lochman, J. E., 275
Locke, J. L., 429
Loeb, T. B., 494
Loeber, R., 8, 31, 158, 161, 191, 193, 195, 196, 200, 203, 206, 207, 297
Loftin, C. R., 369
Logan, J., 146, 151, 166
Lombroso, P. J., 41, 42
Loney, J., 152
Long, N., 24, 138
Lonigan, C. J., 131, 269, 429
Lorber, R., 552
Lorch, E. P., 146, 148
Lorenz, F. O., 16, 220, 314
Lorys, A. R., 169
Lotter, V., 396
Lou, H. C., 169
Lovaas, O. I., 172, 408, 409
Loveland, K. A., 379
Lovett, M., 415
Lowe, C. B., 55
Lowe, M. R., 504
Luby, J., 316, 317, 318, 319, 320, 321, 334
Lucas, C., 73
Luciana, M., 46
Luckasson, R., 348
Lung, C. T., 556
Luria, A., 165
Luthar, S. S., 10
Lutzker, J. R., 559, 560
Lykken, D. T., 358
Lyles, W. B., 229
Lynam, D. R., 128, 198, 199, 206, 208, 215
Lynch, M., 527, 537, 539, 540, 541, 542, 543, 547
Lynskey, M. T., 172, 310

Lyon, G. R., 75, 423, 424, 425, 429, 435, 436, 437, 438, 439, 440, 442, 445, 446, 449, 450, 451, 453
Lyons-Ruth, K., 130, 219, 460, 497, 500, 501
Lytle, C., 545
Lytton, H., 217

MacArthur, C. A., 452
Maccoby, E. E., 30, 48, 206, 527
MacDonald, H., 51, 211
MacDonald, J. P., 29–30, 51
MacDonald, L. B., 134
MacDonald, R., 379
MacGillivray, M. H., 496
Machon, R. A., 416
Mackillop, W. J., 478
MacLean, R. E. G., 472
MacLean, W. E., 483
MacMillan, D. L., 130, 345, 349, 351
Macmillan, H. L., 409, 535
Madigan, S., 484
Maffei, M., 504
Magnusson, D., 214
Mahamedi, F., 512, 516
Maher, M. C., 153
Main, M., 539, 542
Makari, G. J., 17
Malamuth, N. M., 547
Malchiodi, C. A., 121
Malik, S. C., 161
Malinosky-Rummell, R., 540, 543
Malone, M. A., 149, 547
Maloney, M., 519
Malouf, D. B., 452
Manassis, K., 275
Mancini, C., 273
Mandel, F., 545
Mangweth, B., 517
Manion, I. G., 294, 482
Manlove, E. E., 429
Manly, J. T., 545
Mannarino, A. P., 561
Mannuzza, S., 158, 163, 164
Mans, L., 354
March, C. L., 173, 208
March, J. S. 234, 240, 265, 281
Marchi, M., 492, 493, 494, 498, 512
Marciano, P. L., 303, 311, 315, 328, 331, 332
Marcus, M. D., 522, 534
Mariani, M. A., 154, 162
Marini, A., 88
Marlowe, J. H., 226
Marsh, W. L., 415
Marshall, W. L., 442, 554, 555
Marten, P. A., 138, 254, 281, 282
Martin, J. A., 30, 48, 413
Martin, J. F., 363
Martin, J. L., 527, 547
Martin, J. M., 301
Martin, N. G., 430
Martinez, P. E., 190
Marvin, R. S., 482
Mascarello, J., 397
Mash, E. J., 24, 31, 71, 72, 76, 99, 102, 104, 109, 111, 115, 124, 125, 127, 129, 130, 131, 132, 136, 156, 162, 172, 547
Maslin-Cole, C., 378
Masten, A. S., 7, 11

Mather, P. L., 429
Matier, K., 150
Matson, J. L., 356, 367
Mattis, S. G., 260, 261, 262, 263
Maughan, B., 200, 441
Maurice, C., 372, 408
Mauro, J. A., 48
Mawhood, L., 392
Mawrer, O. H., 26
Mawrer, W. M., 26
Maxfield, M. G., 548
Maxwell, S. E., 34, 304
Mayes, S. D., 499
Mazza, J. J., 323
McAlpine, C., 498
McAlpine, D. D., 298
McAlpine, L., 476
McArthur, D. S., 120
McAuliffe, S., 356
McBride-Chang, C. K., 543
McBurnett, K., 166, 174, 198, 204, 213,
    214, 215
McCabe, M. A., 134
McCall, R. B., 342
McCauley, E., 293, 296
McClannahan, L. E., 406
McClaren, J., 358
McClellan, J., 546
McCloskey, L., 532
McClough, J. F., 518
McClung, H. J., 474
McConaughy, S. H., 110, 484
McCormick, M. C., 2
McCracken, J. T., 171, 174, 355
McCullough, E. L., 155
McCurley, J., 505
McCurry, C., 546
McDermott, P. A., 17, 111, 205
McDougle, C. J., 405
McEachin, J. J., 408
McEvoy, M. A., 194, 367, 390
McGavin, J. K., 520
McGee, R. A., 13, 37, 68, 69, 160, 172,
    200, 205, 211, 543
McGee, R. O., 272
McGrath, P. A., 476
McGrath, P. J., 477
McGrew, K., 341
McGue, M. K., 168, 358, 359
McGuffin, P., 171
McGuire, S., 204
McKay, K. E., 116
McKenna, M. C., 450
McKeough, A., 88
McKnew, D. H., 288, 302, 311
McLaughlin, B., 171
McLean, W. E., 355
McLeer, S. V., 545, 561
McLoyd, V. C., 2, 55
McMahon, R. J., 131, 185, 225, 226
McMurray, M. B., 162, 175
McNeil, T. F., 110
McPhee, D., 536
McQuiston, S., 457, 476
Meadows, A. T., 481
Mednick, S. A., 416
Medvescek, C. R., 482
Mee, L. L., 302
Meichenbaum, D., 137, 165, 176,
    479, 487
Meininger, J. C., 504

Melnick, S. M., 157, 163
Melton, G. B., 134, 202, 538
Melville-Thomas, G., 171
Menard, s., 203
Merzenich, M. M., 429
Mesibov, G. B., 393
Messer, I., 130
Messer, S. C., 306, 312
Messick, S., 71
Metalsky, G. I., 307
Meundi, D. B., 401
Meyer, L. H., 99, 132
Meyer-Bahlburg, H. F., 546
Mick, E., 155
Mikhail, C., 511
Milberger, S., 167, 171
Miles, M. B., 92
Milich, R., 60, 146, 148, 149, 156, 157,
    159, 164, 172, 202
Millard, W., 337
Miller, F. J., 187, 220, 226
Miller, G. E., 187, 220, 226
Miller, J. B., 515
Miller, J. M., 55
Miller, J. N., 406
Miller, N. B., 55
Miller, P. P., 243
Miller, T. R., 226
Millstein, S. G., 18, 56, 486
Milner, J. S., 551
Minde, K. K., 460
Mineka, S., 315
Minshew, N. J., 399, 400, 401
Minuchin, S., 516, 521
Mischel, W., 153
Mitchell, J., 293, 303, 304, 305, 323
Moats, L. C., 438
Moffatt, M. E. K., 471
Moffitt, T. E., 187, 194, 198, 199, 201,
    204, 206, 207, 208, 209, 211, 213,
    215, 216, 221, 222, 272
Mohr, J., 471
Mokros, H. B., 294
Molnar, J., 55
Montague, C. T., 504
Montgomery, S. S., 287, 327
Mooney, K. C., 116, 120, 472
Moore, A., 331
Moore, J., 262
Morre, L. A., 51
Moore, M., 479
Moore, R. E., 503
Moreau, D., 310, 331
Morelli, W., 460
Moreno, A. B., 495
Morgan, W. P., 442
Morrell, W., 297, 513
Morris, R. J., 110, 367
Morris, T. L., 136
Morris-Yates, A., 430
Morrow, L. A., 484
Morton, J., 387, 395
Moser, H. W., 356, 358
Mosimann, J. E., 516
Mosk, M. D., 66
Moskowitz, D. S., 205
Moss, S. J., 293
Mowrer, W. M., 235, 270
Mowrer, O. H., 471
Mowrer, W. M., 471
Moye, A. W., 521

Mueller, C., 515
Mufson, L., 310, 331
Mulder, R. T., 326
Mulhern, R. K., 480, 482, 483
Mulick, J. A., 62, 346, 401, 500
Mulle, K., 281
Mullen, P. E., 547
Mullins, L. L., 305, 456
Mulvey, E. P., 225
Mulvihill, B. A., 366
Mundy, P., 378
Munroe, H., 13
Murdoch, D., 308
Muris, P., 249
Murphy, C. C., 349, 352, 353, 368
Murphy, D. A., 92
Murphy, H. A., 155, 174, 178
Murphy, K. R., 155, 174, 178
Murphy, L. B., 92, 268
Murphy, T. R., 333
Murray, C., 343
Murray, I., 154, 162, 180, 343
Myers, W. C., 228

Nada-Raja, S., 155
Nader, K., 265
Nakata, Y., 161
Napolitano, M. A., 516
Narayan, M., 401
Nawrocki, T., 311
Nay, W. R., 106
Naylor, C., 429, 545
Neal, A. M., 269
Neal, J. W., 400
Neale, M. C., 273
Needleman, H. L., 215
Needleman, L. D., 520, 522
Negrao, A. B., 517
Neiderhiser, J. M., 358
Neisser, U., 341, 343, 358
Nelen, M., 213
Nelles, W. B., 239, 260
Nelson, C. A., 39, 41, 75
Nelson, C. B., 265
Nelson, C. C. 484
Nelson, K. B., 396
Nelson, W. M., 227
Nemeth, M., 389
Nettelbeck, T., 472
Newborg, J., 116
Newcomb, M., 494, 541
Newcorn, J. H., 150, 159
Newman, D. L., 14
Newsom, C. M., 395, 402, 403, 404, 407,
    409, 411
Nezu, C. M., 152, 355
Nichols, A. M., 411
Nichols, P. L., 171, 411, 416, 516
Nieberding, R., 120
Nielson, J. B., 169
Niemela, P., 206
Nietzel, M. T., 179
Nigam, V. R., 161
Nigg, J., 163
Nightingale, E. O., 18, 486
Niles, B., 522
Nisbett, R. E., 503
Nisi, A., 161
Nitz, K., 213
Noam, G. G., 50
Nolan, T., 474

Nolen-Hoeksema, S., 297, 302, 303
Noll, R. B., 482
Norcross, J. C., 132
Norgaard, J. P., 471
Northam, E., 479
Norton, K., 521
Nottelman, E. D., 203, 204, 312
Novey, E. S., 169
Noyes, R., 273
Nudelman, S., 522

Oberklaid, F., 474
O'Brien, B. S., 198, 213, 214, 560
Obrosky, D. S., 296
O'Connor, M. E., 521
O'Connor, T. G., 168, 204
Offer, D., 494
Offord, D. R., 13, 17, 42, 134, 151, 204,
    205, 233, 295, 480
Ojemann, G. A., 443
Okazaki, M., 159
Olds, D., 365, 557
O'Leary, K. D., 547
O'Leary, P., 161
Olfson, M., 310
Ollendick, T. H., 233, 234, 238, 244,
    245, 260, 261, 262, 263, 269, 270,
    277, 292
Olshan, A. F., 359
Olson, R. A., 456
Olson, R. D., 438,
Olson, R. K., 435, 545
Olweus, D., 13, 37, 188, 193, 215, 216
Oppenheim, D., 460
Orrison, W. W., 415
Orvaschel, H., 233, 305, 312
Osborn, C. A., 554
Osborne, P., 364
Osborne, R. B., 477
Osofsky, J. D., 116
Oster, G. D., 287, 327
Osterling, J., 311, 395, 402, 407, 408, 409
Ostrander, R., 179
Ostrov, E., 494
Ott, E. S., 227
Ott, J., 160
Ousley, O. Y., 378
Overton, W. F., 64
Owen, B., 284, 296
Owens, R. G., 519
Ozols, E. J., 440
Ozonoff, S., 46, 153, 214, 378, 389,
    390, 406

Paikoff, R. L., 494
Palazzoli, S., 516
Palkes, H., 167
Palmer, P., 396
Panagiotides, H., 311, 392
Panichelli-Mindel, S. M., 268, 275
Papp, L. A., 274
Paradis, C. M., 269
Parekh, P. I., 298
Parides, M., 326
Parke, R. D., 192
Parker, J. D. A., 240
Parrone, P. L., 296
Parry-Jones, B., 498, 506
Parry-Jones, W. L., 498, 506
Pate, J. E., 511
Paternitre, C. E., 152

Paterson, M., 440
Patterson, G. R., 65, 77, 190, 199, 201,
    202, 206, 210, 211, 216, 217, 218,
    219, 220, 221, 225, 226, 551
Patton, M. Q., 91
Paulauskas, S., 204
Pauls, D. L., 41, 167, 239
Pearce, J. W., 121
Pearson, J., 305
Pederson, E. D., 471
Peeke, L., 268
Pelcovitz, D., 543, 545, 546
Pelham, W. E., 83, 84, 458
Pelham, W. W., 156, 157, 160, 164, 174,
    176, 177, 180, 181, 182
Pelton, L. H., 535
Pembrey, M., 358
Pendergrast, M., 161
Pennington, B. F., 42, 46, 153, 154, 168,
    214, 389, 438, 439, 442, 446
Perdue, S., 298
Perez, C., 543
Perfetti, C. A., 435, 452
Perrin, E. C. 484, 486
Perrin, J. M., 486
Perrin, J. N., 503
Perrin, S., 239, 243, 244, 269, 484
Perry, C. L., 545
Perwien, A. R., 251
Peters, K. G., 146
Peters, T. J., 171
Petersen, A. C., 18, 486
Petersen, I., 295, 298, 304
Peterson, L., 18, 154, 305, 312, 456, 470,
    473, 474, 475, 477, 479, 494
Petti, T., 133, 139
Pettit, G. S., 88, 193, 217, 226
Pettit, L. M., 541
Peveler, R. C., 521
Peyrot, M., 542
Pezzot-Pearce, T. D., 121
Pfeffer, C. R., 314, 323
Pfiffner, L. J., 178, 179
Phares, V., 54
Philips, I., 313
Phillips, W., 378, 390
Piacentini, J., 3, 138, 220, 256, 258, 259,
    273, 274, 278, 279, 280, 281
Pianta, R. C., 290, 482, 531
Pickard, E. M., 445
Pickens, J., 311
Pickles, A., 200, 204, 289
Pickrel, S. G., 224
Pierce, E. W., 173, 208
Pihl, R. O., 2, 199
Pike, K. M., 516, 517
Pincus, J. H., 547
Pine, D. S., 215, 268, 295
Pinkerton, P., 475
Piven, J., 391, 396, 399
Platzman, K., 171
Pless, I. B., 155, 471, 475, 486
Pliszka, S. R., 159, 174
Plomin, R., 40, 41, 42, 54, 168, 204, 212,
    213, 310, 358, 442
Podell, D. M., 369
Poderefsky, D., 215
Polaino-Lorente, A., 300
Polansky, N. A., 556
Polivy, J., 493, 495, 515
Pollak, S. D., 540

Pollock, L., 457
Polloway, E. A., 441
Pomeroy, J. C., 138
Pope, H. G., 517
Porrino, L. J., 150
Poskitt, E. M. E., 503
Posner, M. I., 48
Post, R. M., 297, 298
Potter, L. B., 323
Potts, D. A., 541
Potts, M. K., 165
Poulin, F., 201
Poulson, C. L., 406
Pound, J., 545
Powell, C., 527
Powell, K. E., 323
Power, E., 551
Power, T. J., 152
Powers, B., 301
Powers, L. E., 368
Powers, S. W., 488
Poznanski, E. O., 294, 306
Pratt, C., 354
Price-Bonham, S., 363
Prince, J. B., 155
Pring, L., 385
Prino, C. T., 542
Prinstein, M. J., 265
Prinz, R. J., 55, 226
Prior, M., 446
Pritchard, J. C., 21
Prizant, B., 381, 382
Prochaska, J. O., 132
Proffitt, V. D., 329
Pulkkinen, L., 208
Pumariega, A. J., 155, 511
Purvis, K., 154
Putnam, F. W., 45, 543, 546
Pynoos, R. S., 265

Quay, H. C., 13, 56, 66, 101, 146, 150,
    166, 187, 196, 213, 214, 288, 439
Quillian, W., 473
Quinn, P. O., 171
Quinton, D., 204

Rabideau, G. J., 528
Rabin, A. I., 120
Rabinovich, H., 332
Rack, J., 435
Radbill, S. X., 20, 526
Radke-Yarrow, M., 313, 538
Raffaelli, M., 306
Ragusa, D. M., 172
Rahdert, E., 203
Raine, A., 212, 213, 214, 215
Rainer, K., 312
Rains, P. M., 130
Ramey, C. T., 342, 366
Ramey, S. L., 342, 366
Rapee, R. M., 237, 275, 280
Rapoff, M. A., 332
Rapoport, J. L., 171, 255, 415
Rappaport, L., 472
Rapport, M. D., 175, 178
Raskin, N. J., 137
Rasmussen, S., 273
Rast, J., 499, 500
Rastam, M., 518
Ratey, J. J., 180
Rathbun, J. M., 289, 291, 292

Raudenbush, S. W., 221
Rayner, R. R., 25, 270
Raynham, H., 349
Reaven, N. M., 312
Redner, J. E., 303
Reed, E. W., 39, 357
Reedm, S. G., 39, 357
Rees, J. R., 23
Rehder, H., 359
Rehm, L. P., 309
Reid, A. H., 356
Reid, J. B., 65, 77, 226, 552
Reid, J. C., 312
Reinecke, M. A., 331
Reinking, D. R., 452
Reiss, D., 54, 55
Reiss, J. A., 204, 215
Reitan, R. M., 123
Reiter, S., 279
Reitzel-Jaffe, D., 40, 547
Reitzle, M., 204
Remschmidt, H. E., 413
Rende, R., 40, 41, 42, 168, 212
Renick, M. J., 439, 446
Renouf, A. G., 300, 301, 304
Repacholi, B., 219
Reppucci, N. D., 225
Reschly, D. J., 349
Resnick, M. D., 2
Rey, J. M., 195, 328, 472
Reynolds, C. R., 113, 116, 119, 122
Reynolds, M. C., 450
Reynolds, W. M., 288, 289, 323
Reznick, J. S., 271, 273
Rezvani, M., 312
Rice, J. M., 560
Richards, A., 268
Richards, I. N., 204
Richards, K. J., 504
Richards, M. H., 296, 306
Richardson, S. A., 349
Richters, J. E., 5, 7, 32, 180, 190, 194
Richtsmeier, A. J., 477
Ridge, B., 211
Ridgeway, D., 539
Ridley-Johnson, R. R., 305
Rie, H. E., 20, 21, 23, 126, 145
Rigler, D., 549
Ritvo, A., 399
Ritvo, E. R., 399
Roberts, C., 354
Roberts, C. R., 302, 304
Roberts, G. E., 120, 132, 136
Roberts, J. E., 289, 295, 298
Roberts, M. A. 152
Roberts, M. C., 488
Roberts, R. E., 204, 233, 302, 304
Robertson, E. B., 220, 369
Robin, A. L., 137, 202, 521
Robins, L. N., 194, 203, 204, 208, 211
Robinson, N. S., 303
Robling, M. R., 171
Rochlin, Q., 288
Rochon, J., 154, 440
Rodgers, A., 139
Rodin, J., 495, 515, 516, 517
Rodin, K., 358
Rodriguez, N., 545
Rogers, K., 204, 209
Rogers, S. J., 378, 389, 409
Rogoff, B., 460

Rogosch, F. A., 482, 537, 557
Rohde, P., 289, 295, 296, 297, 303, 325, 331, 333
Roizen, N. J., 163
Rojahn, J., 355, 499, 500
Romans, S. E., 547
Romig, C., 494
Romney, D. M., 217
Ronsaville, D., 312
Ropers, H. H., 213
Rorty, M., 517
Rosen, J. C., 509, 522
Rosenbaum, J. F., 272, 275, 487
Rosenberg, R. S., 155
Rosenblatt, B., 136
Rosenshine, B., 451
Rosenstein, D. S., 219
Rosenthal, D., 415
Rosenthal-Malek, A. L., 368
Rosman, B. L., 516
Ross, D., 145
Ross, D. M., 476, 477, 487
Ross, D. P. 2, 161
Ross, R. 429
Ross, R. T., 341
Ross, S. A., 145
Rossman, S. B., 187
Rossotto, E., 517
Ross, S., 145
Ross, S. A., 476, 477, 487
Roth, G., 415, 416
Rothbart, M. K., 48
Rothbaum, B. O., 278
Rotheram-Borus, M. J., 95
Rothman, S., 169
Rothstein, J. A., 155
Rourke, B. P., 123, 436, 439, 440, 445, 451
Rouse, L. W., 51
Routh, D. K., 127, 475, 477, 488
Rowan, A. B., 545, 546
Rowe, D. C., 213, 358
Rowe, E., 543
Rowe, M. K., 268
Rowland, M. D., 225, 227
Rubin, K. H., 14, 47, 254, 272
Rubio-Stipec, M., 172
Rudd, M. D., 518
Rudolph, K. D., 292, 293, 298, 305, 306, 310, 311, 314, 315, 316, 487
Ruma, P. R., 226
Rumsey, J. M., 75
Runtz, M., 546
Runyon, M. K., 555
Rush, A. J., 329
Rush, B., 21
Russell, A. T., 196, 413, 414
Russell, D. E. H., 547
Russell, G. F. M., 521, 528
Rutter, M. 10, 11, 31, 32, 34, 37, 200, 204, 211, 217, 220, 221, 223, 289, 290, 295, 341, 343, 355, 358, 373, 385, 390, 392, 396, 411, 446, 483
Ryan, C. M., 484
Ryan, N. D., 275
Ryan, N. E., 311, 324, 328, 331, 332
Ryan, S., 545
Rydell, A. M., 492

Sabaratnam, M., 358
Sabornie, E. J., 354

Sack, W. H., 297
Sacks, N. R., 310, 518
Sadeh, A., 457
Sadock, B. J., 39
Safer, D. J., 155, 175
Saigh, P. A., 265
St. Lawrence, J. S., 559
St. Pierre, J., 501
Sajwaj, T., 500
Sales, B. D., 134
Sallee, R., 273, 274
Salt, P., 333
Salzinger, S., 543, 545
Salzman, L. F., 169
Sameroff, A. J., 35, 40, 55
Samit, C., 543
Sampson, R. J., 220, 221
Sanders, M. R., 76, 77, 131
Sandgrund, A., 551
Sandler, A., 369
Sandler, J, 526, 559
Sandoval, J., 134, 160
Sanfilippo, M. D., 488
Sanson, A., 160, 446
Santhouse, R., 514
Santonastaso, P., 504
Santos, A. B., 225
Sapolsky, R., 41
Sarigiani, P. A., 304
Sas, L., 526, 541, 555, 556
Sassone, D., 160
Sattler, J. M. 72, 326, 341, 342, 358, 424
Sattler, J. P., 101, 104, 105, 108, 109, 116, 117, 119
Saunders, B. E., 555
Scarr, S., 527
Scerbo, A. S., 541
Schachar, R. J., 145, 146, 151, 154, 155, 158, 166
Schachtel, D., 560
Schaefer, C. E., 234, 473
Scharfman, M. A., 136
Schiff, M., 358
Schlundt, D. G., 514, 521
Schmich, M., 239
Schmidt, K. L., 297, 309
Schmidt, N. B., 518
Schneider-Rosen, K., 539
Schoenwald, S. K., 224, 225, 227
Schooler, N. R., 95
Schopler, E., 393
Schreibman, L., 397, 404
Schreier, H. A., 550
Schroeder, C. S., 99, 132
Schroeder, S. R., 364, 473, 500
Schteingart, J. S., 55
Schultz, L. H., 215
Schulz, E., 413
Schute, R., 482
Schwaiger, U., 514
Schwartz, A. A., 62, 401
Schwartz, S., 452
Schwartzman, A. E., 205
Schwebel, A. I., 137
Scott, K., 547
Scott, S., 41, 124, 129
Scotti, J. R., 110
Sears, M. R., 172
Seat, P. S., 122
Secher, S. M., 305
Secord-Gilbert, M., 369

Sedlak, A. J., 18, 524, 530, 531, 532, 533, 534, 535, 536
Seeley, J., 289, 295, 296, 297, 301, 303, 319, 325, 331
Seeley, J. R., 233, 269, 533
Seguin, J. R., 199
Seidel, W. T., 148
Seiden, J. A., 169
Seidman, L. J., 161
Seifer, R., 353
Sela-Amir, M., 552
Selfe, L., 121, 386
Seligman, L. D., 292, 302, 303, 307
Seligman, M. E. P., 50, 250
Selman, R. L., 215
Semenak, S., 392
Semmel, M. E., 354
Semrud-Clikeman, M., 154, 169, 170, 442
Sena, R., 273
Serafica, F. C., 87
Serbin, L. A., 205
Sergeant, J., 148
Serketich, W. J., 226
Seroczynski, A. D., 304, 308
Sexton, J., 524
Shadish, W. R., 140
Shaffer, D., 38, 54, 73, 108, 325, 326
Shalev, R. S., 154
Shanahan, M., 16
Shankweiler, D., 424, 435
Shanley, N., 301
Shannon, F. T., 470
Shapiro, L. R., 503
Shapiro, S., 494
Sharma, V., 150
Sharp, R. N., 309
Shaw, B. F., 329
Shaw, D. S., 100, 205, 211, 219, 221
Shaywitz, B. A., 169, 171, 424, 427, 437, 439
Shaywitz, S. E., 169, 171, 424, 427, 437, 438, 439
Shearer, D. E., 369
Sheeber, L., 312, 333
Sheeran, T., 482
Shelden, R. G., 205
Shelton, K. K., 217
Shelton, T. L., 59, 155, 156, 446
Shenker, R., 163
Sherak, D. L., 297
Sherick, R. B., 303
Sherman, G. F., 442
Sherman, D. K., 168
Sherman, J. B., 504, 505
Sherry, T., 168
Sholevar, E. H., 188
Sholevar, G. P., 188
Sholten, C. A., 148
Shores, R. E., 367
Shugar, G., 521
Shure, M. B., 227
Siddons, F., 395
Sidman, M., 65
Siegel, J. M., 464
Siegel, L. J., 456, 481, 486
Siegel, L. S., 156, 439
Siegel, P. T., 521
Siegel, T., 136, 227
Sienna, M., 155
Sigman, M., 273, 378, 387
Silberstein, L. R., 515

Silva, P., 13, 187, 199, 205, 206, 208, 211, 229, 272
Silva, R. R., 187, 199, 205, 206, 208, 211, 229
Silver, H. L., 502, 533
Silver, S. E., 17, 75
Silverman, F. N., 533
Silverman, I. W., 172
Silverman, J. A., 518
Silverman, W. K., 239, 245, 246, 265, 269, 278, 280, 505
Silverstein, B., 298
Silverstein, J., 479
Silverthorn, P., 160, 161, 217
Simeonsson, R., 363
Simmel, C., 149, 163
Simmons, R. J., 481
Simonoff, E., 289, 295, 296, 298, 341, 342, 358, 359, 360, 365
Simons, R. L., 220, 314
Simon, T., 339
Sines, J. O., 120
Singer, G. H. S., 368
Singer, J. E., 41
Singer, M. I., 554
Singer, W., 461
Siperstein, G. N., 345, 354
Siqueland, L., 274
Sites, P., 5
Skogan, W. G., 221
Skyler, J., 484
Slaby, R. C., 192
Slade, P. D., 519
Slavin, L. A., 312
Sloper, P., 363
Slotkin, J., 119
Smallish, L., 154, 156, 163
Smart, D., 446
Smith, A., 378
Smith, C., 522
Smith, D., 2
Smith, D. J., 202, 223
Smith, D. W., 525, 555
Smith, G. D., 10
Smith, I. M., 396, 408, 409
Smith, J. M., 133
Smith, K. E., 456, 459
Smith, L. A., 202, 223
Smith, R. S., 11
Smith, S. A., 438
Smith, S. D., 438
Smith, T., 396, 408, 409
Smolak, L., 494, 495
Snidman, N., 271, 272
Snyder, J., 220
Sobol, A. M., 2, 481, 503
Sockloskie, R. J., 547
Soldatos, C. R., 466
Soler, R., 168
Solin, S., 285, 305, 507
Solomon, J., 539
Solomons, G., 145
Sommer, D., 331
Sommers-Flanagan, J., 332
Sommers-Flanagan, R., 332
Sondheimer, D. L., 225
Song, P., 555
Sonne, J. L., 546
Sonnega, A., 265
Sonuga-Barke, E. J., 153, 199
Southam-Gerow, M. A., 280

Spaccarelli, S., 545, 549
Spanos, N. P., 464
Spector, M., 555
Speier, P. L., 297
Speltz, M. L., 219
Spence, S. H., 277
Spencer, T. J., 155
Spinetta, J. J., 549
Spisto, M. A., 153
Spitz, H. H., 401
Spitz, R. A., 26, 289
Spock, B., 457, 483
Spohr, H., 362
Spracklen, K. M., 201
Sprague-McRae, J. M., 473, 474
Sprich, S., 159
Springs, F. E., 546
Sroufe, L. A., 8, 31, 32, 33, 40, 51, 53, 172, 175, 219, 353, 354, 528, 539
Stahl, S. A., 450
Stallings, P., 240
Stanger, C., 90, 91
Stanovich, K. E., 435, 439, 450
Stanton, W. R., 172, 187
Stark, K. D., 51, 302, 309, 328, 329, 331
Steege, M. W., 85, 86
Steele, B. F., 533
Steele, M., 24
Stein, D. M., 501
Stein, M. A., 163, 498
Steinberg, L., 274
Steiner-Adair, C., 494, 515
Steinhauer, P. D., 2, 10, 56
Steinhausen, H. C., 204, 362, 512
Steinmetz, S. K., 552
Steissguth, A. P., 171
Stevens, M., 483
Stevens, R., 451
Stevenson, D., 153, 154, 168, 199
Stevenson, H., 463
Stewart, A. J., 155
Stewart, G. W., 228
Stewart, J. T., 228
Stewart, M. 155, 167, 175, 213
Stewart, S. L., 254, 272, 273
Still, G. F., 145
Stock, J. R., 116
Stoddard, H. H., 339
Stokes, T. F., 81, 174
Stoleru, S., 312
Stone, P., 482
Stone, W. L., 378
Stoolmiller, M., 203, 221
Stouthamer-Loeber, M., 198, 199, 203
Strain, P. S., 406
Strandburg, R. J., 415
Strang, J., 123
Straus, M. A., 423, 525, 527, 534, 547, 552, 557
Strauss, A. A., 145
Strauss, C. C., 239, 243, 247, 248, 251, 254, 256, 262, 263, 268, 273
Streissguth, A. P., 362
Strickland, A. L., 327
Striegel-Moore, R. H., 516
Striepe, M., 512
Strober, M., 297, 321, 322, 513, 518
Stroh-Becvar, D., 137
Strom, K. J., 554
Strosahl, K. D., 139
Stuber, M., 482

Stunkard, A. J., 503
Stuss, D. T., 311
Sullivan, K., 240
Sullivan, P. F., 512
Sundelin, C., 492
Sutker, P. B., 194, 211
Sutphen, J., 473
Sutton, A., 365
Suwanlert, S., 15
Svinicki, J., 116
Swackhamer, K., 373, 401
Swales, T., 484
Swan, S., 488
Swanson, J. M., 82, 149, 172, 174
Swedo, S. E., 255, 274, 279
Sweeney, L., 329
Swensen, C. H., 120
Szasz, T. S., 23
Szatmari, P., 42, 151, 155, 160, 161, 273, 480
Szumowski, E., 163, 173, 208

Tager-Flusberg, H., 380, 382, 383
Takanishi, R., 56
Tallal, P., 420, 424, 429, 440, 442, 453
Tallmadge, J., 156
Tam, K. K., 536
Tamplin, A., 305
Tanaka, J., 547
Tangel, D. M., 449
Tannert, C., 487
Tannock, R., 75, 146, 149, 151, 154, 155, 158, 159, 166, 167, 168
Taplin, P., 552
Tappan, P. W., 187
Tapscott, M., 220
Target, M., 24
Tarter, R. E., 547
Tarver-Behring, S., 156
Tassé, M. J., 355
Tate, D. C., 225
Taub, D. E., 519
Taussig, C., 230
Taylor, A. R., 354, 355
Taylor, C. B., 345
Taylor, E., 337
Taylor H. G., 146, 148, 155, 158, 448
Taylor, S. J., 337
Teasdale, J. D., 307
Tellegen, A., 212
Terdal, L. G., 71, 99, 109, 111, 124, 125, 127, 129, 143, 155
Terman, L. M., 340
Terr, L. C., 265
Teschke, K., 359
Thach, B. T., 155
Thatcher, R. W., 39, 40, 75
Thelan, M. H., 495
Thienes-Hontos, P., 472
Thisted, R. A., 332
Thomas, A. 35, 48
Thomas, C. B., 127
Thomas, H., 172
Thomas, P., 191, 193, 195
Thompson, J. K., 504
Thompson, L., 153, 168
Thompson, L. A., 199, 212, 226,
Thompson, M., 504
Thompson, M. P., 315
Thompson, R. A., 153, 168

Thompson, R. J., 480, 481, 482, 483, 484, 485, 487
Thompson, R. W., 504
Thompson, S., 483
Thorndike, R. L., 117
Thurber, C. A., 329
Timmerman, M. G., 518
Tingelstad, J. B., 332
Tizard, J., 290, 355, 483
Tobin, M. J., 215
Toch, T., 185
Tolan, H., 224, 230
Tolan, P. H., 193, 194
Tompson, M., 312, 416
Toth, S. L., 306, 307, 315, 353, 539, 545
Touyz, S., 510
Townsend, J., 399, 420
Tracey, S. A., 239
Tranel, D., 442
Trautman, P., 326
Treadwell, K. H., 268, 269, 279, 280
Tremblay, R. E., 2, 199
Trent, S. C., 349
Trickett, P. K., 45, 543, 546, 556
Trimble, B. K., 359
Trivette, C. M., 486
Trocmé, N., 536
Troiano, R. P., 503
Trommer, B. L., 155
Trott, G., 413
Troughton, E., 213
Trowbridge, F. L., 500
Trubnick, L., 463
Truglio, R., 268, 301
Tsoh, J. Y., 520
Tsuang, M. T., 159, 161, 220
Tubman, J. G., 203
Tucker, D., 33, 39
Tumuluru, R., 364
Turk, D., 479, 487
Turleau, C., 359
Turner, B. G., 245, 246, 269
Turner, J. E., 314
Turner, M. D., 273, 275
Turner, M. W. 245, 246, 269
Turner, S., 363
Turner, S. M., 245, 246, 269
Twentyman, C. T., 542, 551
Twigg, D. A., 554
Tyler, L., 198
Tyree, A., 547

Uhde, T. W., 255
Ullmann, L. P., 136
Ungerer, J. A., 483
Unis, A. S., 303
Urbina, S., 120

Valente, E., 217
Valentine, J., 168
Valoski, A. M., 505
van Ameringen, M., 273
Vandenberg, B., 464, 465
Vandereycken, W., 491, 492
Van der Kolk, B. A., 45, 540, 545
van der Meere, J. J., 148
Van Deth, 491, R., 492
Van Houten, R., 367
Van Nguyen, T., 220
Van Oost, B. A., 213
Vanrado, P. J., 520

Van Slyke, D. A., 475
Vara, L. S., 522
Vargas, L. A., 415
Varni, J. W., 481, 485
Vasey, M. W., 239, 254, 267
Vaughn, B. E., 353
Vaughnn, S. R., 368
Velez, C. N., 2, 223
Venables, P., 215
Verhulst, F. C., 13, 82, 90
Vernberg, E. M., 265
Vernon-Feagans, L., 429
Vietze, P. M., 365
Vitaro, F., 2
Vitiello, B., 93
Vivian, D., 161
Voeller, K. K. S., 148, 401
Volkmar, F. R., 355, 393
Volkow, N. D., 174
Volling, B. L., 429
Vondra, J. I., 221
Vostanis, P., 297
Voth, T., 452
Vyas, D., 498
Vygotsky, L., 165

Wada, K., 161
Wadden, T. A., 491
Wagner, B. M., 55
Wagner, K. D., 303, 309
Wainwright, J., 389
Wakefield, J. C., 6
Walberg, H. J., 450
Walder, L. O., 220, 222
Waldman, I. D., 124, 195
Waldrop, M. F., 171
Walker, C. E., 15, 416
Walker, D. K. 475, 477
Walker, J. L. 136, 164, 204
Walker, L. S., 481
Wall, S. 53, 76
Wallander, J. L., 481, 484, 485
Wallen, J., 545
Wallerstein, N., 486
Wallis, C., 144, 164
Walter, G., 328
Walters, A. S., 356, 510
Wang, M. C., 450
Wang, S., 546
Ward, T., 555
Warman, M. J., 241
Warne, G., 479
Warner, V., 310
Warner-Rogers, J. E., 559
Warnke, A., 413
Warren, M. P., 494
Wasserman, G. A., 87
Wasserstein, S., 239
Waterhouse, L., 398
Waters, E., 53, 76, 353
Watkins, C. E., 120
Watson, D., 269, 270, 315
Watson, J. B., 269, 270, 315
Watson, R. R. 25
Watson, T., 431
Weaver, T., 546
Webb, C., 541
Weber, J., 26
Weber, W., 161
Webster-Stratton, C. 185, 200, 205, 206, 230

Wechsler, D., 117
Weeks, S. J., 379
Wehlby, J. H., 367
Wehler, C. A., 503
Weigle, D. S. 503, 505
Weinberg, N. Z., 203
Weinberg, S. L., 546
Weinberg, W. A., 309
Weinberger, D. R., 415
Weiner, I. B., 120
Weiner, M., 545
Weinrott, M. R., 226
Weintraub, B. D., 168
Weiss, A. D., 560
Weiss, B., 17, 70, 131, 139, 140, 187, 351, 352
Weiss, G, 154
Weiss, L., 154
Weiss, R. V., 1, 155, 161, 163, 164, 175
Weiss, S. B., 301
Weissman, M. M., 290, 310, 312, 313, 324, 331
Weisz, J. R., 1, 14, 15, 69, 70, 130, 131, 139, 140, 161, 187, 329, 351, 352, 487
Weithorn, L. A., 134
Weitzman, M., 481
Wekerle, C., 18, 40, 532, 538, 541, 547, 548, 554, 558, 560
Welch, S. L., 511
Weller, E. B., 314
Weller, R. A., 314
Wells, K. C., 138, 225, 226, 275
Wells, L. A., 518
Welner, A., 167
Welner, Z., 167
Welsh, J. D., 14, 528
Welsh, M. C., 153, 164, 446
Weltzin, T. E., 514, 521
Werner, E. E., 10, 11, 14, 423
Werner, H., 440, 441
Werry, J. S., 288, 411
Werthamer-Larsson, L., 267
Werther, G., 479
Wesch, D., 560
Wessler, A. E., 267
West, M. O., 55
Wetherby, A., 382
Whalen, C. K., 156, 157
Wheelock, I., 313
Whelan, J. R., 472
White, J. L., 149, 211
White, K. S., 68
White, W. A. T., 415, 451
Whiteman, M., 203
Whitman, T. L., 368

Whitmore, E. A. W., 552
Whitmore, K., 290, 355, 483
Wickramaratne, P. M., 310
Widiger, T. A., 100, 127
Widom, C. S., 538, 543, 547, 548
Wieder, S., 129
Wiess, L., 163
Wigal, S. B., 174
Wigal, T., 174
Wilcox, K. T., 481, 485
Wilens, T. E., 155
Wilfley, D. E., 516
Willerman, L., 42
Willett, J. B., 484
Williams, D. A., 383
Williams, E., 200, 205, 215, 216
Williams, G. A., 354
Williams, L. M., 520, 532, 541, 549
Williams, P. H. 200, 205, 215, 216
Williams, S. 13, 37, 485
Williamson, D. E., 311, 328
Willis, T. J., 172
Willms, J., 362
Wilson, A., 324
Wilson, D. M., 495
Wilson, G. T., 49, 261
Wilson, M. B., 512, 513, 514, 515, 522
Wilson, S., 532, 552
Wilson, S. K., 68
Windle, M., 203
Windle, R. C., 203
Wing, L., 384, 391, 393, 394
Wing, R. R., 505
Winikates, D., 449
Winsten, N. E., 547
Wirt, R. D., 122
Wise, B., 435
Wiseman, C. V., 516
Wish, E., 167
Wisniewski, L., 517
Wittig, R., 464
Wnek, L., 116
Wodarski, J. S., 543
Wolf, M., 289
Wolfe, D. A., 18, 40, 66, 68, 114, 501, 526, 527, 528, 532, 538, 541, 543, 546, 547, 548, 549, 550, 551, 552, 553, 554, 557, 558, 559, 560, 561
Wolfe, V. V., 269, 546
Wolff, R. L., 273
Wolfson, D., 123
Wolk, S. I., 324
Wolraich, M. C., 172
Wonderlich, S., 517
Wong, B. Y. L., 137, 437, 451
Woo, S. L. C., 361

Wood, A., 331, 332
Wood, F. B., 154, 427, 429, 446
Wood, L. R., 520
Wood, T. A. 456
Woodhouse, W., 391
Woods, A., 546
Woods, L. R., 520
Woodside, D. B., 513
Woodworth, G., 213
Wooley, S. C., 496
Woolston, J. L., 497, 499, 500, 502, 503, 504, 505, 510
Wootton, J. M., 198, 217, 220
Wray, L., 559
Wright, E. J., 333
Wulfeck, B., 420
Wurtele, S. K., 561
Wyatt, G. E., 541
Wysocki, T., 485

Yager, J., 517
Yairi, E., 430
Yang, B., 238, 270
Yates, A., 511
Yates, T. 88
Yates, W. R., 213
Yeargin-Allsopp, M., 349
Yeh, C. J., 518
Yeung-Courchesne, E., 397
Yoder, P. J., 87
Yoerger, K. L., 221
Yoshida, R. K., 368
Youngblade, L. M., 556
Yule, W., 200, 234, 265, 355, 360, 446
Yurgelun-Todd, D., 513

Zahn-Waxler, C., 14, 100, 206, 313, 528, 539
Zak, L., 532
Zametkin, A. J., 75, 165, 171
Zarate, R., 243
Zeanah, C. H., 460, 497, 501
Zelizer, V. A., 20
Zelli, A., 193
Zeman, J., 314
Zentall, S. S., 165
Zhang-Salomons, J., 478
Zigler, E., 230, 351, 356, 358, 547
Zilbovicius, M., 400
Zimmerman, M. A., 8, 10
Zink, M., 477
Zito, J. M., 175
Zoccolillo, M., 204, 205, 206, 209
Zoglin, R., 222
Zorick, F., 464
Zubieta, J. K., 215
Zuckerman, B., 463
Zuroff, D. C., 302

Credits

Chapter 1: **3:** Case based on a case from "Childhood OCD," by J. Piacentini and F. Graae, 1997. In E. Hollander & D. Stein (Eds.) *Obessive-Compulsive Disorders: Diagnosis, Etiology, Treatment*, pp. 23–46. Marcel Dekker, Inc. **4:** Cartoon 1.1 *Calvin and Hobbes* © Watterson. Reprinted with permission of Universal Press Syndicate. All rights reserved. **5:** Excerpt from *Lee Harvey Oswald and the American Dream* by P. Sites, p. 73. Copyright © 1967 Pageant Press. **7:** Table 1.1 from "The Development of Competence in Favorable and Unfavorable Environments: Lessons from Research on Successful Children," by A. S. Masten and J. D. Coatsworth, 1998, *American Psychologist, 53,* 205–220. Copyright © 1998 by the American Psychological Association. Reprinted by permission of the author. **8:** Case based on "Resiliency Research: Implications for Schools and Policy," by M. A. Zimmerman and R. Arunkumar, 1994, *Social Policy Report, Vol. 8(4),* 1–17. Society for Reseach in Child Development. **10:** Box 1.1 from "Who's That Girl? A Case Study of Madonna," by L. Layton, 1994. In C. E. Franz & A. J. Stewart (Eds.), *Women Creating Lives: Identities, Resilence, and Resistance,* 143–156. Westview Press. **11:** Figure 1.2 based on "The Development of Competence in Favorable and Unfavorable Environments: Lessons from Research on Successful Children," by A. S. Masten and J. D. Coatsworth, 1998, *American Psychologist, 53,* 205–220. **14:** Figure 1.3 adapted from "Ontario Child Health Study: II. Six-Month Prevalence of Disorder and Rates of Service Utilization," by D. R. Offord, M. H. Boyle, P. Szatmari, N. I. Rae-Grant, P. S. Links, D. T. Cadman, J. A. Byles, J. W. Crawford, H. M. Blum, C. Byrne, H. Thomas & C. A. Woodward, 1989, *Archives of General Psychiatry, 44,* 832–836. Copyright © 1989 by the American Medical Association. Adapted by permission. **16:** Cartoon 1.2 by permission of Dave Coverly and Creators Syndicate. **19:** Table 1.2 based on *Diagnostic and Statistical Manual of Mental Disorders,* Fourth Edition, 1994 by the American Psychiatric Association. **22:** Box 1.2 from *A History of the Care and Study of the Mentally Retarded,* by L. Kanner, 1964, p. 15. Courtesy of Charles C. Thomas, Publisher, Springfield, Illinois. **25:** Box 1.4 based on *Scientists of the Mind: Intellectual Founders of Modern Psychology* by Clarence J. Karier, 1986. University of Illinois Press.

Chapter 2: **32:** Figure 2.1 based on "Conceptualization of Developmental Psychopathogy," by T. M. Achenbach, 1990. In M. Lewis & S. M. Miller (Eds.), *Handbook of Developmental Psychopathy,* (3–14). Plenum Publishing Group. **33:** Figure 2.2 based on *Developmental Psychopathology, 2nd Ed.,* by T. M. Achenbach, 1982. John Wiley & Sons. **37:** Figure 2.B1 from "General Systems Theories and Developmental Psychopathology," by A. J. Sameroff, 1995. In D. Cicchetti & D. J. Cohen (Eds.), *Developmental Psychopathology, Volume 1: Theory and Methods,* pp. 659–695. Copyright © 1995 by John Wiley & Sons. Reprinted by permission of John Wiley & Sons, Inc. **38:** Figure 2.4 based on "Social Psychology from a Social-Developmental Perspective," by D. R. Shaffer, 1977. In C. Hendrick (Ed.), *Perspectives on Social Psychology.* Lawrence Erlbaum Associates, Inc. **41:** Cartoon 2.1 *Calvin and Hobbes* © Watterson. Reprinted with permission of Universal Press Syndicate. All rights reserved. **43:** Figure 2.5 from *Abnormal Psychology* by David H. Barlow and V. Mark Durand, 1995, p. 49. Copyright © 1995 by Brooks/Cole Publishing Company. **44:** Figure 2.6 from *Abnormal Psychology* by David H. Barlow and V. Mark Durand, 1995, p. 51. Copyright © 1995 by Brooks/Cole Publishing Company. **53:** Table 2.4 based on "Contributions of Attachment Theory to Developmental Psychopathology," by E. A. Carlson & L. A. Sroufe, 1995, pp. 581–617. In D. Cicchetti & D. J. Cohen (Eds.), *Developmental Psychopathology, Vol. 1, Theory and Methods.* John Wiley & Sons, Inc. **54:** Figure 2.7 adapted from *Developmental Psychology: Childhood and Adolescence, 4th ed.,* by David R. Shaffer, 1996, p. 59, based on U. Bronfenbrenner, 1979. Brooks/Cole Publishing Company.

Chapter 3: **62:** Excerpt from "Facilitated Communication, Austism, and Ouija," by K. M. Dillon, 1993, *Skeptical Inquirer, 17,* 281–287. **67:** Box 3.2 adapted from "Comparisons of Problems Reported by Parents of Children in 12 Cultures: Total Problems, Externalizing, and Internalizing," by A. A. M. Crijnen, T. M. Achenbach & F. C. Verhulst, 1997, *Journal of the American Academy of Child & Adolescent Psychiatry, 36,* 1269–1277. Adapted by permission. **67:** Figure 3.B2 adapted from "Comparisons of Problems Reported by Parents of Children in 12 Cultures: Total Problems, Externalizing, and Internalizing," by A. A. M. Crijnen, T. M. Achenbach & F. C. Verhulst, 1997, *Journal of the American Academy of Child & Adolescent Psychiatry, 36,* 1269–1277. Copyright © 1997 by the Journal of the American Academy of Child & Adolescent Psychiatry. Adapted by permission. **69:** Figure 3.2 from "Multiple Maltreatment Experiences and Adolescent Behavior Problems: Adolescents' Perspective," by R. A. McGee, D. A. Wolfe & S. K. Wilson, 1997, *Development and Psychopathology, 9,* 131–149. Copyright © 1997 by Cambridge University Press. Reprinted by the permission of Cambridge University Press. **70:** Figure 3.4 from *Abnormal Psychology* by David H. Barlow and V. Mark Durand, 1995, p. 80. Copyright © 1995 by Brooks/Cole Publishing Company. **73:** Table 3.2 adapted from *Attention Deficit Hyperactivity Disorder: A Handbook for Diagnosis and Treatment,* by R. A. Barkley, 1990,

with *Children and Adolescents: A Clinical Approach*, pp. 163–164. Copyright © 1987 by John Wiley & Sons, Inc. Reprinted by permission of John Wiley & Sons, Inc. **139:** Figure 4.9 from "Depression," by D. J. Kolko, 1987. In M. Hersen and V. B. Van Hasselt (Eds.), *Behavior Therapy with Children and Adolescents: A Clinical Approach,* p. 164. Copyright © 1987 by John Wiley & Sons, Inc. Reprinted by permission of John Wiley & Sons, Inc.

Chapter 5: 143: Case Copyright © 1993 by Patricia Kennedy, Leif Terdal and Lydia Fusetti. From *The Hyperactive Child Book*, by Patricia Kennedy, Leif Terdal and Lydia Fusetti, [pp. 8–9] Reprinted by permission. of St. Martin's Press, Incorporated. **144:** Poem from *Struwwelpeter,* by Heinrich Hoffmann, 1845, pp. 18–19. Translation © 1972 by Blackie & Son Ltd. Reprinted by permission of Blackie & Son, Ltd., Glascow. **144:** Case adapted from *Time,* July 18, 1994, p. 43. **145:** Case adapted from *Hyperactivity: Current Issues, Research and Theory,* by D. M. Ross and S. A. Ross, 1982, p. v. John Wiley & Sons. **146:** Case from *Attention Deficit Hyperactivity Disorder: Decade of the Brain,* 1994. National Institute of mental Health (NIH Publication No. 94-3572). **147:** Table 5.1 reprinted with permission from *Diagnostic and Statistical Manual of Mental Disorders, Fourth Edition.* Copyright © 1994 by the American Psychiatric Association. **148:** Case from *Attention Deficit Hyperactivity Disorder: Decade of the Brain,* 1994. National Institute of mental Health (NIH Publication No. 94-3572). **150:** Box 5.2 from *Psychological Monographs 78,* Whole No. 578, by J. Kagan, B. L. Rossman, D. Day, J. Albert, W. Philips, 1964. Copyright © 1964. Reprinted by permission of the author. **151:** Box 5.3 from "Inhibitory Control, Impulsiveness, and Attention Deficit Hyperactivity Disorder," by R. J. Schachar, R. Tannock & G. Logan, 1993, *Clinical Psychology Review, 13,* 721–740. Copyright © 1993 by Elsevier Science, Ltd. **153:** Excerpt adapted from "On the Interface of Cognition and Personality: Beyond the Person-Situation Debate," by W. Mischel, 1979, *American Psychologist, 34,* 740–754. **153:** Excerpt from "Looking Back: Reminiscences from Childhood and Adolescence," by I. Murray, 1993, pp 301–325. In. G. Weiss and L. T. Hechtman (Eds.), *Hyperactive Children Grown Up: ADHD in Children, Adolescents and Adults* (2nd ed.) Copyright © 1993 Guilford Publications. Reprinted by permission. **155:** Excerpt Copyright © 1993 by Patricia Kennedy, Leif Terdal and Lydia Fusetti. From *The Hyperactive Child Book,* by Patricia Kennedy, Leif Terdal and Lydia Fusetti, [p. 80] Reprinted by permission of St. Martin's Press, Incorporated. **156:** Excerpt from "Looking Back: Reminiscences from Childhood and Adolescence," by I. Murray, 1993, pp 301–325. In G. Weiss and L. T. Hechtman (Eds.), *Hyperactive Children Grown Up: ADHD in Children,*

Adolescents and Adults (2nd ed.) Copyright © 1993 Guilford Publications. Reprinted by permission. **157:** Excerpt from a chapter by R. A. Barkley and L. J. Pfiffner in *Taking Charge of ADHD: The Complete, Authorized Guide for Parents,* by R. A. Barkley, 1995, p. 180. Copyright © 1995 by Guilford Publications. **158:** Cartoon 5.1 Cartoon: Edward Koren © 1988 from *The New Yorker Collection.* All rights reserved. **158:** Excerpt from "Attention Deficit Disorders with Anxiety Disorders," by R. Tannock (in press). In T. E. Brown (Ed.), *Subtypes of Attention Deficit Disorders in Children, Adolescents, and Adults.* Copyright © [in press] American Psychiatric Association. **162:** Excerpt from a chapter by R. A. Barkley and L. J. Pfiffner in *Taking Charge of ADHD: The Complete, Authorized Guide for Parents,* by R. A. Barkley, 1995, p. 208. Copyright © 1995 by Guilford Publications. **162:** Excerpt from a chapter by R. A. Barkley and L. J. Pfiffner in *Taking Charge of ADHD: The Complete, Authorized Guide for Parents,* by R. A. Barkley, 1995, p. 208. Copyright © 1995 by Guilford Publications. Reprinted by permission. **163:** Excerpt from *Attention Deficit Disorder in Adults,* by L. Weiss, 1992, p. 5. Copyright © 1992 by Taylor Publishing Company. **163:** Excerpt from *Attention Deficit Disorder in Adults,* by L. Weiss, 1992, p. 11–12. Copyright © 1992 by Taylor Publishing Company. **164:** Box 5.4 "Hail to the Hyperacitve Hunter," from *Time,* July 18, 1994, p. 43. Copyright © 1994 Time, Inc. Reprinted by permission. **165:** Excerpt from "Training Impulsive Children to Talk to Themselves: A Means of Developing Self-Control," by D. Meichenbaum and J. Goodman, 1971, *Journal of Abnormal Psychology, 77,* 115–126. **166:** Figure 5.2 from "ADHD, Self-Regulation, and Time: Towards a More Comprehensive Theory of ADHD," by R. A. Barkley, 1998, *Journal of Developmental and Behavioral Pediatrics.* Copyright © 1997 by Williams & Wilkins. Reprinted by permission. **167:** Cartoon 5.2 *For Better or For Worse* © Lynn Johnston Prod., Inc. Reprinted with permission of United Media. All rights reserved. **170:** Figure 5.3 adapted from an illustration by Carol Donner in "Understanding Parkinson's Disease," by M. B. Youdim and P. Riederer, 1997, *Scientific American, 276 (1),* 52–59. Copyright © 1997 by Scientific American. All rights reserved. Reprinted by permission of the publisher and illustrator. **173:** Case from *Attention Deficit Hyperactivity Disorder: Decade of the Brain,* 1994. National Institute of mental Health (NIH Publication No. 94-3572). **173:** Case adapted from *Attention Deficit Hyperactivity Disorder: Decade of the Brain,* 1994. National Institute of mental Health (NIH Publication No. 94-3572). **175:** Box 5.6 adapted from "Origin of Stimulant Use for Treatment of Attention Deficit Disorder," by M. D. Gross, 1995, *American Journal of Psychiatry, 152,* 298–299. Copyright © 1995 by American

Psychiatric Association. **176:** Box 5.7 from *Attention Deficit Hyperactivity Disorder: Decade of the Brain,* 1994. National Institute of mental Health (NIH Publication No. 94-3572). **177:** List from *Taking Charge of ADHD: The Complete, Authoritative Guide for Parents,* by R. A. Barkley, 1995, p. 136. Copyright © 1995 by Guilford Publications. Reprinted by permission. **178:** Case from a chapter by R. A. Barkley and L. J. Pfiffner in *Taking Charge of ADHD: The Complete, Authorized Guide for Parents,* by R. A. Barkley, 1995, p. 209. Copyright © 1995 by Guilford Publications. Reprinted by permission. **179:** Case from "Looking Back: Reminiscences from Childhood and Adolescence," by I. Murray, 1993, pp 301–325. In. G. Weiss and L. T. Hechtman (Eds.), *Hyperactive Children Grown Up: ADHD in Children, Adolescents and Adults* (2nd ed.) Copyright © 1993 Guilford Publications. Reprinted by permission. **180:** Box 5.8 adapted from *Driven to Distraction,* by E. M. Hallowell and J. J. Ratey, 1994, pp. 53–71 Pantheon Books, a division of Random House. **181:** Box 5.9 from "Intensive Treatment for ADHD: A Model Summer Treatment Program," by W. E. Pelham, Jr., A. R. Greiner, E. M. Gnagy, B. Hoza, L. Martin, S. E. Sams, & T. Wilson, 1996, pp. 193–213. In M. Roberts and A. LaGreca (Eds.), *Model Programs in Child and Family Mental Health.* Copyright © 1996 by Lawrence Erlbaum Associates, Inc. Reprinted by permission. **181:** Figure 5.4 from "Intensive Treatment for ADHD: A Model Summer Treatment Program," by W. E. Pelham, Jr., A. R. Greiner, E. M. Gnagy, B. Hoza, L. Martin, S. E. Sams, & T. Wilson, 1996, pp. 193–213. In M. Roberts and A. LaGreca (Eds.), *Model Programs in Child and Family Mental Health.* Copyright © 1996 by Lawrence Erlbaum Associates, Inc. Reprinted by permission. **182:** List from "Intensive Treatment for ADHD: A Model Program Summer Treatment Program," by W. E. Pelham, Jr., A. R. Greiner, E. M. Gnagy, B. Hoza, L. Martin, S. E. Sams, & T. Wilson, 1996, pp. 193–213. In M. Roberts & A. LaGreca (Eds.) *Model Programs in Child and Family Mental Health.* Copyright © 1996 by Lawrence Erlbaum Associates. Reprinted by permission. **182:** Excerpt from a chapter by R. A. Barkley and L. J. Pfiffner in *Taking Charge of ADHD: The Complete, Authorized Guide for Parents,* by R. A. Barkley, 1995, p. 211. Copyright © 1995 by Guilford Publications. Reprinted by permission.

Chapter 6: 185: Excerpt adapted from *Troubled Families—Problem Children: Working with Parents: A Collaborative Process,* by C. Webster-Stratton and M. Herbert, 1994, pp. 44–45. Copyright © 1994 by John Wiley & Sons, Ltd. Reprinted by permission of John Wiley & Sons, Ltd. **185:** Excerpt from "Superpredators Arrive: Should We Cage the New Breed of Vicious Kids?," by Peter Annin, 1996,

of *Conflict Resolution, 38,* 639–640. **224:** Table 6.6 adapted from "Conduct and Oppositional Defiant Disorders," by S. P. Hinshaw and C. A. Anderson, 1996, pp. 113–149. In In E. J. Mash and R. A. Barkley (Eds.), *Child Psychopathology.* Copyright © Guilford Publications. Reprinted by permission. **226:** Table 6.7 adapted from *Conduct Disorders in Childhood and Adolescence,* by A. E. Kazdin, pp. 83–84. Copyright © 1995 by Sage Publications. Adapted by permission. **227:** Box 6.5 adapted from "Problem Solving and Parent Management Training in Treating Aggressive and Antisocial Behavior," by A. E. Kazdin, 1996, pp. 377–408 (383). In E. D. Hibbs & P. S. Jensen (Eds.), *Psychosocial Treatments for Child and Adolescent Disorders: Empirically Based Strategies for Clinical Practice.* Copyright © 1996 by the American Psychological Association. Reprinted by permission of the author. **227:** Table 6.8 adapted from *Conduct Disorders in Childhood and Adolescence,* by A. E. Kazdin, pp. 81–82. Copyright © 1995 by Sage Publications. Adapted by permission. **228:** Box 6.6 adapted from *Treating Conduct Problems in Children and Adolescents: An Overview of the Multisystemic Approach with Guidelines for Intervention Design and Implementation,* by S. W. Henggeler, 1991, Division of Children, Adolescents and Their Families, South Carolina Department of Mental Health, Charleston, SC. Reprinted by permission of the author.

Chapter 7: 236: Table 7.1 adapted from "Fears and Anxieties," by B. A. Barrios and D. P. Hartmann, 1997, p. 235. In E. J. Mash and L. G. Terdal (Eds.), *Assessment of Childhood Disorders,* 3rd ed. Copyright © 1997 by Guilford Publications. Reprinted by permission. **238:** Table 7.2 adapted from *Anxiety Disorders in Children,* by R.G. Klein and C. G. Last, 1989, pp. 100–101. Copyright © by Sage Publications. Reprinted by permission. **239:** Excerpt from column by Mary Schmich, June 1, 1997, *Chicago Tribune.* © Copyrighted Chicago Tribune Company. All rights reserved. Used with permission. **240:** Table 7.3 from "Ritual, Habit, and Perfectionism: The Prevalence and Development of Compulsive-Like Behavior in Normal Young Children," by D. W.. Evans, J. F. Leckman, A. Carter, J. S. Reznick, D. Henshaw, R. A. King, D. Pauls, 1997, *Child Development, 68,* 58–68. Copyright © 1997 by The Society for Research in Child Development. Reprinted by permission. **240:** List adapted from "Screen for Child Anxiety Related Emotional Disorders (SCARED): Scale Construction and Psychometric Characteristics," by B. Birmaher, K. Suneeta, D. Brent, M. Cully, L. Balach, J. Kaufman, S. M. Neer, 1997, *Journal of the American Academy of Child and Adolescent Psychiatry, 36,* 545–553. Copyright © 1997 by Williams & Wilkins. Adapted by permission. **241:** Box 7.1 based on *Diagnostic and Statistical Manual of Mental Disorders, Fourth Edition.* Copyright © 1994 by the American Psychiatric Association. **241:** Case adapted from "Separation Anxiety," by C. G. Last, 1988, pp. 11–17. In M. Hersen and C. G. Last (Eds.), *Child Behavior Therapy Casebook.* Copyright © 1988 by Plenum Publishing Group. Reprinted by permission. **242:** Table 7.4 reprinted with permission from *Diagnostic and Statistical Manual of Mental Disorders, Fourth Edition.* Copyright © 1994 by the American Psychiatric Association. **244:** Case adapted from "School Refusal Behavior," by C. A. Kearney, 1995, p. 35. In A. R. Eisen, C. A. Kearney & C. A. Schaefer (Eds.), *Clincial Handbook of Anxiety Disorders in Children and Adolescents.* Copyright © 1995 by Jason Aronson, Inc. **247:** Table 7.5 reprinted with permission from *Diagnostic and Statistical Manual of Mental Disorders, Fourth Edition.* Copyright © 1994 by the American Psychiatric Association. **249:** Figure 7.1 from *Abnormal Psychology,* by D. H. Barlow and V. Mark Durand, 1995, p. 164. Brooks/Cole Publishing Company. **250:** Table 7.6 reprinted with permission from *Diagnostic and Statistical Manual of Mental Disorders, Fourth Edition.* Copyright © 1994 by the American Psychiatric Association. **250:** List reprinted with permission from *Diagnostic and Statistical Manual of Mental Disorders, Fourth Edition.* Copyright © 1994 by the American Psychiatric Association. **251:** Excerpt from *Timidity: How to Overcome It,* by Yoritomo-Tashi, translated by M. W. Artois, 1916. Funk & Wagnalls Company. **252:** Table 7.7 reprinted with permission from *Diagnostic and Statistical Manual of Mental Disorders, Fourth Edition.* Copyright © 1994 by the American Psychiatric Association. **253:** Cartoon 7.2 *The Far Side* © 1993 Farworks, Inc. Used by Universal Press Syndicate. All rights reserved. **253:** Excerpt from *Timidity: How to Overcome It,* by Yoritomo-Tashi, translated by M. W. Artois, 1916. Funk & Wagnalls Company. **254:** Excerpt adapted from "Therapist's Manual: Cognitive-Behavioral Group Treatment of Adolescent Social Phobias," by A. M. Albano, P. A. Marten, & C. S. Holt, 1991, p. 18, unpublished manual. Department of Psychology, University of Louisville, KY. Reprinted by permission. **254:** Case adapted from "Selective Mutism," by H. L. Leonard and S. Dow, 1995, pp. 246–47. In J. S. March (Ed.), *Anxiety Disorders in Children and Adolescents.* Copyright © 1995 by Guilford Publications. **255:** Excerpt adapted from *The Boy Who Couldn't Stop Washing: The Experience & Treatment of Obsessive Compulsive Disorder,* 1989, p. 73. Signet, an imprint of Penguin USA. **256:** Table 7.8 reprinted with permission from *Diagnostic and Statistical Manual of Mental Disorders, Fourth Edition.* Copyright © 1994 by the American Psychiatric Association. **260:** Table 7.9 reprinted with permission from *Diagnostic and Statistical Manual of Mental Disorders, Fourth Edition.* Copyright © 1994 by the American Psychiatric Association. **262:** Box 7.2 from *Darwin,* by A. Desmond and J. Moore. Copyright © 1991 by Viking, an imprint of Penguin USA. **263:** Excerpt adapted from "Behavioral Assessment and Treatment of PTSD in Prepubertal Children: Attention to Developmental Factors and Innovative Strategies in the Case Study of a Family, " by A. M. Albano, P. P. Miller, R. Zarate, G. Cote, D. H. Barlow, 1997, pp. 245–262, *Cognitive and Behavioral Practice, Vol. 2,* Copyright © 1997 by the Association for Advancement of Behavior Therapy. Reprinted by permission. **264:** Table 7.10 reprinted with permission from *Diagnostic and Statistical Manual of Mental Disorders, Fourth Edition.* Copyright © 1994 by the American Psychiatric Association. **266:** Figure 7.2 from "Symptoms of Posttraumatic Stress in Children After Hurricane Andrew: A Propsective Study," by A. M. La Greca, W. K. Silverman, E. M. Vernberg & M. J. Prinstein, 1996, *Journal of Consulting and Clinical Psychology, 64,* 712–723. Copyright © 1996 American Psychological Association. Reprinted by permission of the author. **267:** Box 7.3 adapted from *Facts For Families #36: Helping Children After a Disaster,* 1995, American Academy of Child and Adolescent Psychiatry. Adapted by permission. **271:** Excerpt from "Temperament and the Reactions to Unfamiliarity," by J. Kagan, 1997, *Child Development, 68,* 139–143. Copyright © 1997 by The Society for Research in Child Development. Adapted by permission. **272:** Box 7.4 adapted from "Temperament and the Reactions to Unfamiliarity," by J. Kagan, 1997, *Child Development, 68,* 139–143. Copyright © 1997 by The Society for Research in Child Development. Adapted by permission. **277:** Box 7.5 reprinted courtesy of *Sports Illustrated,* June 30, 1997, pp 24–25. Copyright © 1997, Time, Inc. "Lovestruck" by Richard Hoffer. All rights reserved. **278:** Box 7.6 adapted from "An Update on the Treatment of OCD in Children and Adolescents," by J. Piacentini, 1997, *Masters in Psychiatry,* pp. 9–12. Copyright © 1997 by Cliggot Communications. Adapted by permission. **278:** Excerpt adapted from "Obsessive-Compulsive Disorder," p. 302. In A. R. Eisen, C. A. Kearney & C. A. Schaefer (Eds.), *Clincial Handbook of Anxiety Disorders in Children and Adolescents.* Copyright © 1995 by Jason Aronson, Inc. **279:** Cartoon 7.3 *The Far Side.* Copyright © 1986 Farworks, Inc. Used by Universal Press Syndicate. All rights reserved. **281:** Excerpt adapted from "Therapist's Manual: Cognitive-Behavioral Group Treatment of Adolescent Social Phobias," by A. M. Albano, P. A. Marten, & C. S. Holt, 1991, p. 15, unpublished manual. Department of Psychology, University of Louisville, KY. Reprinted by permission. **282:** Excerpt adapted from "Therapist's Manual: Cognitive-Behavioral Group Treatment of Adolescent Social Phobias, " by A. M. Albano, P. A. Marten, & C. S.

C. M. Newsom, 1998 In E. J. Mash and R. A. Barkley (Eds.), *Treatment of Childhood Disorders, 2nd ed.* Copyright © 1998 Guilford Publications. Reprinted by permission. **411:** Excerpt from "Schizophrenia: Hidden Torment," by M. Nichols, *Macleans,* January 30, 1995, p. 73. Copyright © 1995 by Maclean's. Reprinted by permission. **412:** Case from "Childhood-Onset Schizophrenia," by J. R. Asarnow and R. F. Asarnow, 1996. In E. J. Mash and R. A. Barkley (Eds.), *Child Psychopathology,* p. 340. Copyright © 1996 by Guilford Publications, Inc. **412:** List reprinted with permission from *Diagnostic and Statistical Manual of Mental Disorders, Fourth Edition.* Copyright © 1994 by the American Psychiatric Association. **414:** Box 10.6 adapted from "The Clinical Presentation of Childhood-Onset Schizophrenia," by A. T. Russell, 1994, *Schizophrenia Bulletin, 20,* 631–646. Adapted by permission of the author. **415:** List based on "Cognitive/Neurospyschological Studies of Children with a Schizophrenic Disorder," by R. F. Asarnow, J. Asamen, E. Granholdm, T. Sherman, J. Watkins & M. Williams, 1994, *Schizophrenic Bulletin, 20,* 647–670. **416:** Excerpt from "Schizophrenia: Hidden Torment," by M. Nichols, *Macleans,* January 30, 1995, p. 73. Copyright © 1995 by Maclean's. Reprinted by permission.

Chapter 11: 426: Table 11.1 reprinted with permission from *Diagnostic and Statistical Manual of Mental Disorders, Fourth Edition.* Copyright © 1994 by the American Psychiatric Association. **428:** Figure 11.1a Illustration of brain and text Copyright © 1996 *Time,* Inc. Reprinted by permission of Time, Inc. [Canadian edition 7/5/95, U.S. edition 1/31/96] Copyright © Time 1996. **431:** Table 11.2 reprinted with permission from *Diagnostic and Statistical Manual of Mental Disorders, Fourth Edition.* Copyright © 1994 by the American Psychiatric Association. **434:** Table 11.3 adapted with permission from *Diagnostic and Statistical Manual of Mental Disorders, Fourth Edition.* Copyright © 1994 by the American Psychiatric Association. **436:** Figure 11.2 from "Learning Disabilities," by H. G. Taylor, 1988, p. 422. In E. J. Mash and L. G. Terdal (Eds.) *Behavioral Assessment of Childhood Disorders, 2nd ed.* Copyright © 1988 The Guilford Press. Reprinted by permission. **440:** Figure 11.4 Data from "Language, Learning, and Behavorial Disturbances in Childhood: A Longitudinal Perspective," by A. A. Benasich, S. Curtiss & P. Tallal, 1993, *Journal of American Academy of Child and Adolescent Psychiatry, 32,* 585–594. **441:** Excerpt from "Learning Disabilities in Adulthood," by E. A. Polloway, R. Schewel, J. R. Patton, 1992, *Journal of Learning Disabilities, 25,* 520–522. **441:** Box 11.3 based on "Risk and Resilience in Individuals with Learning Disabilities: Lessons Learned from the Kauai Longitudindal Study," by E. E. Werner, 1993, *Learning Disabilities Re-* search *and Practice, 8,* 28–34. **443:** Figure 11.5 "How the Brain Processes Speech" Copyright © 1996 *Time,* Inc. Reprinted by permission. **444:** Figure 11.6 from "A Biological Marker for Dyslexia," by C. Frith and U. Frith, 1996, *Nature, 382,* p. 19. Copyright © 1996 by Macmillan Publishers, Ltd. Reproduced by permission of the publisher and author. **448:** Figure 11.8 from "Learning Disabilities," by H. G. Taylor, 1989. In E. J. Mash & L. G. Terdal, 1989, *Treatment of Childhood Disorders,* pp. 347–380. Copyright © 1989 by Guilford Publications. Reprinted by permission. **451:** Box 11.4 from "Treatment of Learning Disabilities," by G. R. Lyons and L. Cutting, 1998. In E. J. Mash and L. C. Terdal (Eds.), *Treatment of Childhood Disorders.* Copyright © 1998 Guilford Publications. Reprinted by permission. **452:** Box 11.5 from *Thinking Basics: Corrective Reading,* by S. Englemann, P. Haddox, S. Hanner & J. Osborn, 1978, p. 121. Copyright © 1978 Science Research Associates, Inc. Reprinted by permission of McGraw-Hill Companies. **453:** Box 11.6 from "Effects of Instruction on the Docoding Skills of Chldren with Phonological-Processing Problems," by R. H. Felton, 1993, *Journal of Learning Disabilities, 26,* 583–589. Copyright © 1993 PRO-ED. Reprinted by permission.

Chapter 12: 455: Excerpt "An Epidemic of Sneezing and Wheezing" by C. G. Dowling and A. Hollister, *Life Magazine,* May 1997, p. 79. Copyright © Time Inc.. Reprinted by permission. **455:** Excerpt adapted from "Childhood Sleep Disorders," by R. R. Bootzin and M. J. Chambers, 1990, p. 218–219. In A. M. Gross and R. S. Drabman, *Handbook of Clinical Behavioral Pediatrics.* Copyright © 1990 Plenum Publishing Group. **459:** Figure 12.1 adapted from "Sleep Disorders: Recent Findings in the Diagnosis and Treatment of Disturbed Sleep," by A. Kales and J. D. Kales, 1974, *New England Journal of Medicine, 290,* p. 487. Copyright © 1974 by the Massachusetts Medical Society. Reprinted by permission. **462:** Cartoon 12.1 *The Buckets* reprinted by permission of United Feature Syndicate, Inc. **463:** Excerpt based on "Narcolepsy in a 7-Year-Old Child," by R. Wittig, F. Zorick, T. Roehrs, J. Sicklesteel, and T. Roth, 1983, Journal of Pediatrics, 102, 725–727. CV Mosby Company. **467:** Table 12.3 from "Sleep Problems Among Infants and Young Children," by N. J. Blum and W. B. Carey, 1996, *Pediatrics in Review, 17,* 87–93. Copyright © 1996 American Academy of Pediatrics. Reprinted by permission. **468:** Case adapted from "Childhood Sleep Disorders," by R. R. Bootzin and M. K. Chambers, 1990, p. 218–219. In A. M. Gross and R. S. Drabman, *Handbook of Clinical Behavioral Pediatrics.* Copyright © 1990 Plenum Publishing Group. **470:** Table 12.4 reprinted with permission from *Diagnostic and Statistical Manual of Mental Disorders, Fourth Edition.* Copyright © 1994 by the American Psychiatric Asso-

ciation. **473:** Table 12.5 reprinted with permission from *Diagnostic and Statistical Manual of Mental Disorders, Fourth Edition.* Copyright © 1994 by the American Psychiatric Association. **474:** Excerpt from "Special Families, Special Needs: The Rigours and Rewards of Raising Children with Disabilities," by M. Greey, 1995, *Today's Parent,* November 1995, p. 97. Copyright © Today's Parent. Reprinted by permission. **476:** Table 12.6 reprinted with permission from *Diagnostic and Statistical Manual of Mental Disorders, Fourth Edition.* Copyright © 1994 by the American Psychiatric Association. **476:** Excerpt [pp 476–477] from "Childhood Pain: The School-Aged Child's Viewpoint," by D. M. Ross and S. A. Ross, 1984, *Pain, 20,* 179–191. **481:** Figure 12.2 Data from "Chronic Illness, Disability, and Mental and Social Well-Being: Findings of the Ontario Child Health Study," by D. Cadman, M. Boyle, P. Szatmari, & D. R. Offord, 1987, *Pediatrics, 79,* 805–813. **483:** Figure 12.3 adapted from "Change Over a 12-Month Period in the Psychological Adjustment of Children and Adolescents with Cystic Fibrosis," by R. J. Thompson, Jr., K. E. Gustafson, L. K. George, & A. Spock, 1994, *Journal of Pediactric Psychology, 19,* pp.189–203. Copyright © 1994 by the American Psychological Association. Reprinted by permission of the author. **487:** Box 12.1 from "Star Power: Starbright World Enlivens the Pediatric-Healthcare Experience," by C. Tannert, 1996, *Video,* Feb/Mar. pp. 33, 35. Copyright © 1996 by Hachette Filipacchi Magazines. Reprinted by permission. **487:** Excerpt from "Childhood Pain: The School-Aged Child's Viewpoint," by D. M. Ross and S. A. Ross, 1984, *Pain, 20,* 179–191. **488:** Box 12.2 adapted from "Helping Children Cope with Painful Medical Procedures," by D. K. Routh and M. E. Sanfilippo, 1991, pp. 402–403. In J. P. Bush and W. W. Harkins (Eds.), *Children in Pain: Clinical and Research Issues from a Developmental Perspective.* Copyright © 1991 by Springer-Verlag, New York. Adapted by permission.

Chapter 13: 494: Figure 13.2 Data from "Early Childhood Eating Behaviors and Adolescent Eating Disorders,", by M. Marchi and P. Cohen, 1990, *Journal of the American Academy of Child and Adolescent Psychiatry, 29,* 112–117. **495:** Box 13.1 based on "Eating Disorders," by G. T. Wilson, K. Hefferman, and C. M. D. Black, 1996. In E. J. Mash and R. A. Barclay (Eds.), *Child Psychopathology,* pp. 558–559. Guilford Press. **498:** Table 13.1 reprinted with permission from *Diagnostic and Statistical Manual of Mental Disorders, Fourth Edition.* Copyright © 1994 by the American Psychiatric Association. **499:** Table 13.2 reprinted with permission from *Diagnostic and Statistical Manual of Mental Disorders, Fourth Edition.* Copyright © 1994 by the American Psychiatric Association. **500:** Table 13.3 reprinted with permission from *Diagnostic and Statistical Manual of Mental Disorders, Fourth Edition.* Copyright © 1994 by the American Psychiatric Association. **502:** Case from "Obesity," by J. P. Foreyt and J. H. Cousins, 1987, pp. 502–503. In M. Hersen and V. B. Van Hasselt (Eds.) *Behavior Therapy with Children and Adolescents.* Copyright © 1987 by John Wiley & Sons, Inc. Reprinted by permission of John Wiley & Sons, Inc. **506:** Case from "Dying to be Thin," by S. Solin, 1995, *Seventeen,* November, pp 124–129. Copyright © Primedia Corp. Reprinted by permission. **507:** Table 13.4 reprinted with permission from *Diagnostic and Statistical Manual of Mental Disorders, Fourth Edition.* Copyright © 1994 by the American Psychiatric Association. **509:** Table 13.5 reprinted with permission from *Diagnostic and Statistical Manual of Mental Disorders, Fourth Edition.* Copyright © 1994 by the American Psychiatric Association. **510:** Figure 13.3 Data from "Bulimia Nervosa in a Canadian Community Sample: Prevalence and Comparison of Subgroups," by P. E. Garfinkel, E. Lin, P. Goergin, C. Spegg, D. S. Goldbloom, S. Kennedy, A. S. Kaplan, D. B. Woodside, 1995, *American Journal of Psychiatry, 152,* 1052–1058. **512:** Figure 13.4 Data from "Annotation: Outcome of Anorexia Nervosa in the Younger Patient," by H. C. Steinhausen, 1997, *Journal of Child Psychology and Psychiatry, 38,* 271–276. **513:** Cartoon 13.1 *Cathy* © Cathy Guisewite. Reprinted with permission of Universal Press Syndicate. All rights reserved. **519:** Box 13.2 from "Dying to Win," by Alison Bell, 1996, *Teen,* March, p. 34. Copyright © Petersen Publishing Co. Reprinted by permission. **519:** Figure 13.6 from "Pathogenesis of Anorexia Nervosa," by D. M. Garner, 1993, *Lancet, 341,* 1631–1635. Copyright © 1993 by Lancet. Reprinted by permission.

Chapter 14: 524: Excerpt from "For Dead Child's Family, Long History of Troubles," by Joe Sexton. *The New York Times,* September 5, 1996, p. B6. Copyright © 1996 by *The New York Times.* Reprinted by permission. **528:** List from *Preventing Physical and Emotional Abuse of Children,* by David A. Wolfe, 1991, p. 13. Copyright © The Guilford Press. Reprinted by permission. **533:** Excerpt Transcribed quote from "The Trouble with Evan," for the television program *The Fifth Estate,* executive producer, David Studer for the Canadian Broadcasting Corporation, originally aired on March 25, 1994. **542:** Excerpt from "Predicting Rejecting of Her Infant from Mother's Representation of Her Own Experience: Implications for the Abused-Abusing Interngenerational Cycle," by M. Main and R. Goldwyn, 1984, *Child Abuse and Neglect, 8,* 203–217. **542:** Excerpt from "Responses of Abused and Disadvantaged Toddlers to Distress in Agemates: A Study in the Daycare Setting," by M. Main and C. George, 1985, *Develop-*

mental Psychology, 21, 407–412. **542:** Figure 14.2 from "Responses of Abused and Disadvantaged Toddlers to Distress in Agemates: A Study in the Daycare Setting," by M. Main and C. George, 1985, *Developmental Psychology, 21,* 407–412. Copyright © 1985 by the American Psychological Association. Reprinted by permission of the author. **544:** Figure 14.3 from "Child Sexual Abuse and Emotional and Behavioral Problems in Adolescence: Gender Differences," by N. Garnefski and R. F. W. Diekstra, 1997, *Journal of the American Academy of Child and Adolescent Psychiatry, 36,* 323–329. Copyright © 1997 by American Academy of Child and Adolescent Psychiatry. Reprinted by permission of Williams & Wilkins **545:** Excerpt Transcribed from *The Nature of Things with David Suzuki,* executive producer, Michael Alder for the Canadian Broadcasting Corporation, originally aired on 10/6/94. **545:** Excerpt Transcribed from *The Nature of Things with David Suzuki,* executive producer, Michael Alder for the Canadian Broadcasting Corporation, originally aired on 10/6/94. **550:** Box 14.2 from Herbert Schreier and Judith A. Libow, *Hurting for Love.* Guilford Publications.

Photo Credits

Chapter 1: 2: © Bob Dammerich/Stock, Boston. **10:** © Steven Rubin. **15 (left):** Author's collection. **15 (right):** Author's collection. **18:** © Donna Binder/Impact Visuals. **21:** *Harper's Weekly,* March 1, 1884. **22:** From "An Historical Account of the Discovery and Education of A SAVAGE MAN or of the First Developments, Physical and Moral, of the YOUNG SAVAGE Caught in the Woods near Aveyron in the Year 1798." Reproduced by permission of the Houghton Library, Harvard University.

Chapter 2: 35: Digital Stock Corporation. **47:** Author's collection. **55:** PhotoDisc, Inc.

Chapter 3: 60: PhotoDisc, Inc. **75:** From Figure 2 from "Child Development and Neuroscience," by C. A. Nelson and F. E. Bloom, 1997, *Child Development, 68,* 970–987. Photo courtesy of Charles A. Nelson. **77:** Courtesy of Dr. Margaret McKim, University of Saskatchewan with permission of the participants. **78:** © Cary Wolinski/Stock, Boston. **89:** PhotoDisc, Inc.

Chapter 5: 144 (bottom): From "The Goulstonian Lectures on Some Abnormal Physical Conditions in Children," *The Lancet,* April 19, 1902, p. xx. **151 (right):** © Jose Azel/Aurora. **151 (left):** Courtesy of Phyl Prout. **154:** © Elizabeth Crews. **161:** © Jose Azel/Aurora. **170:** From "Attention-Deficit Hyperactivity Disorder: Magnetic Resonance Imaging Morphometric Analysis of the Corpus Callosum," by M. Semrud-Clikeman, P. A. Filipek, J. Biederman, R. Steingard, D. Kennedy, P. Renshaw, & K. Bekken, 1994, *Journal of the American*

Academy of Child and Adolescent Psychiatry, 33, 875–882. Photograph courtesy of Margaret Semrud-Clikeman. **182:** Courtesy of William E Pelham, Ph.D., Professor of Psychology and Director of Clinical Training, SUNY, Buffalo.

Chapter 6: 186: © Eli Reed/Magnum Photos. **191 (right):** © Elizabeth Crews. **191 (left):** © Elizabeth Crews. **205:** © Jim Tynan/Impact Visuals. **222:** © Bonnie Ericson.

Chapter 7: 238: © J. Barndt/The Picture Cube. **257:** © Michael DelSol. **261:** © Chris Collins/The Stock Market. **271:** © Elizabeth Crews. **277:** Manny Millan/Sports Illustrated.

Chapter 8: 288: © Elizabeth Crews. **290:** From the film "Grief" by Renee Spitz, Archives of the History of American Psychology—University of Akron, Ohio. **298:** Courtesy of Dr. Mark S. George, Functional Neuroimaging Division, Medical University of South Carolina. **325:** © Hugo Dixon/Capitol Pictures/Retna Ltd., NYC.

Chapter 9: 352: © Sievking/Petit Format/Photo Researchers, Inc. **361:** Christine J. Harrison. **362:** K. L. Jones/LLR Research. **366:** © Julie O'Neil/The Picture Cube.

Chapter 10: 375: MGM/Shooting Star. **379:** © 1991 *Behavior Disorders of Childhood,* produced by Alvin H. Perlmutter, Inc., in association with Toby Levine Communications. Reproduced by permission. **380:** © 1991 *Behavior Disorders of Childhood,* produced by Alvin H. Perlmutter, Inc., in association with Toby Levine Communications. Reproduced by permission. (To order the video program, *Behavior Disorders of Childhood,* or the series, *The World of Abnormal Psychology,* call 1-800-LEARNER.) **384:** From *Behavioral Treatment of Autistic Children,* © 1988 by Edward L. Anderson (producer) of studies conducted by Dr. O. Ivar Lovaas. Reprinted by permission of Focus International. **399:** From "Lower Purkinje Cell Counts in the Cerebella of Four Autistic Subjects: Initial Findings of the UCLA/NSAC Autopsy Research Report," by E. R. Ritvo, B. J. Freeman, A. B. Scheibel, T. Duong, H. Robinson, D. Guthrie, & A. Ritvo, 1986, *American Journal of Psychiatry, 143,* 862–866 (p. 864). **400:** From "Delayed Maturation of the Frontal Cortex in Childhood Autism," by M. Zilbovicius, B. Garreau, Y. Samson, P. Remy, C. Barthelemy, A. Syrota, & G. LeLord, 1995, *American Journal of Psychiatry, 152,* 248–252. Copyright © American Psychiatric Association. Reprinted by permission. **402:** From *Behavioral Treatment of Autistic Children,* © 1988 by Edward L. Anderson (producer) of studies conducted by Dr. O. Ivar Lovaas. Reprinted by permission of Focus International. **402:** From *Behavioral Treatment of Autistic Children,* © 1988 by Edward L.